NEW TESTAMENT EPISTLES

JAMES
1,2,3 JOHN

A CRITICAL AND EXEGETICAL COMMENTARY

_____ *by* _____

GARETH L. REESE

HEAD OF NEW TESTAMENT DEPARTMENT
CENTRAL CHRISTIAN COLLEGE OF THE BIBLE
MOBERLY, MISSOURI

Scripture Exposition Books, LLC
803 McKINSEY PLACE
MOBERLY, MISSOURI
65270

The information in this book is intended for classroom and pulpit use by Bible students and teachers. Therefore readers who wish to produce any of the comments or special studies in the form of free handouts to students or listeners, or in sermon outlines as they are being preached, are encouraged to do so with no need to seek prior permission. We ask that you simply include a line giving credit to the source you have copied.

ACKNOWLEDGMENT

The Scripture quotations contained herein, unless otherwise noted, are from the New American Standard Bible, copyrighted 1960, 1962, 1063, 1968, 1971, 1972, 1975, 1977, by the Lockman Foundation. Used by permission.

ISBN: 097-176-526X

Dedication

This book is dedicated to the second
of two sons God has given
to Kathleen and me, and whom we
named after David's special friend.
We call him Jon, and it seems appropriate
to recognize him in this commentary on a
book written by another John.

JONATHAN ANDREW REESE

TABLE OF CONTENTS

The commentary on each New Testament epistle included in this book has its own separate pagination.

THE EPISTLE OF JAMES

FIRST JOHN

SECOND JOHN

THIRD JOHN

INDEXES

Commentary On

James

PREFACE

My indebtedness to many others in the development of the comments on James is evident from the footnotes and bibliography.

This commentator's interest in James was first whetted by R.C. Foster in a class on James taught at The Cincinnati Bible Seminary in the early 1950's. Mr. Foster himself had studied under J.H. Ropes, and often interacted with and reacted not only to what Ropes had taught in class but what also appeared in print in his volume on James in the *International Critical Commentary*. A class on James was one of the first courses this commentator taught when beginning his lifetime of teaching at Central Christian College of the Bible. The questions asked by thoughtful students only proved to stimulate more interest in this brief letter.

Through the years students have asked "What's a good commentary on James?" Sometimes they were seeking help with understanding the meaning of the verses. Sometimes they were looking for lesson or sermon helps. It was difficult to give a very satisfactory recommendation since there were not many who were doing any detailed work in the epistle, and many available commentaries were written more on a popular level than an in-depth scholarly level. The past quarter century has seen a new interest in James as redaction critics and social science critics try to reconstruct what first century Christianity was like. The working thesis of these recent writers is that James may be one of our earliest witnesses to that period of time, so a prodigious amount of labor has been expended trying to distill from his brief notes some kind of picture of what life was like both in his world and in his church.

However, many of the scholarly works leave much to be desired. One reason is that the recent works show little interest in the message of James. Another reason is that many of them treat James as a pseudonymous work, put together by some editor or redactor who used a cut-and-paste method to assemble these bits and pieces that make up our present "letter." If this is true, it attacks the very reason books were included in our New Testament canon, namely their inspiration. Contemporary scholarship seems more interested in demonstrating that the letter can be forced to fit into whatever method of interpretation the scholar is currently interested in, be it tradition-criticism, redaction criticism, social science criticism, literary criticism, or rhetorical criticism. One comes away from such tomes feeling spiritually hungry for some word from God.

This commentator is aware his previous commentaries have been dismissed by some contemporary teachers as being "dated" because they have followed a conservative viewpoint theologically. But this commentator does not subscribe to the viewpoint that a work is scholarly only if it parrots the latest darling Bible-study methodology of those who might be labeled "higher critics." A horse, working hard on a hot summer day, could sweat until the sides of the animal were covered with a white lather. However, the lather did not provide nourishment for man or beast. A number of the products of current scholarship, in this commentator's opinion, are "lather." They do show a prodigious amount of work, but the "blather" provides little nourishment for the hungry soul. It is precisely because there are so few conservative Bible studies being published that this commentator is writing the books he is. In his mind, it is one way to contend earnestly for the faith once for all delivered to the saints.

Without apology for starting with a conservative foundation, it is this commentator's hope to demonstrate that James is much more than "a right strawy epistle". Rather, it highlights and emphasizes some of the great spiritual principles our Lord and Savior taught, ethical principles by which He expected His followers to live, and by which they will be judged.

Synopsis of the Introductory Studies

The introductory studies stretch over a number of pages. The arguments over the book of James are detailed and intricate and interwoven, sometimes almost labyrinthine. To keep us from losing our way, perhaps it would be beneficial to keep in mind a brief synopsis of the framework we will be proposing.

Author – James, the Lord's brother, an apostle and long-time leader of the Christian church at Jerusalem.

Destination – The traditional view is that the letter is addressed to Christians who were ethnically Jewish and who were living all over the Roman world.

Date – Conservative Bible students have vigorously defended two possible dates for the writing of the letter. Some have opted for a date shortly before the Jerusalem Conference (which was held in AD 51). Others have advocated a date shortly before James' death which occurred in AD 62. This commentator is going to propose a date in the early or mid-50's AD, just after the Jerusalem Conference.

Purpose – To encourage his readers to live an ethical and morally productive Christian life, in total harmony with what Jesus taught. We offer the hypothesis that this letter is James' answer to the misuse of his name and example made by the Judaizers who troubled the churches just before and just after the Jerusalem Conference (Acts 15, Galatians 2).

Now the way is open for a careful study of the evidence to see if these hypotheses can be tested and verified. When the study of introductory matters is concluded and we begin a study of the text proper, the important thing to keep in mind is that James' message is a Word from the Lord, and the commands he writes to his readers must be obeyed. After all, when we all come to the final judgment, our eternal destiny will be determined by how consistently our lives have reflected our Lord's expectations as revealed in His Word.

THE EPISTLE OF JAMES

INTRODUCTORY STUDIES

HISTORICAL ALLUSIONS

We use the historical-grammatical method of interpreting Scripture. "Grammatical" means we pay attention to the Greek grammar and the meanings of the words. "Historical" means we try to determine the historical situation to which and out of which the work was written. It is in pursuit of this latter information that a study of the "historical allusions" in the letter becomes important.

The usual place to look for historical allusions is in the opening and closing sentences of first century letters, but in the case of James we must look throughout the letter for hints.

Title

Our New Testament books now have titles affixed to them. The titles were not on the autograph copies but were added later by church men. At first the title may have been no more than one word in the genitive case, *IAKOBOU*, "of James."[1] As time passed, the titles tended to get longer. Soon it read "Epistle of James," then "Catholic Epistle of James," and even "Catholic Epistle of the Apostle James." Eventually there was a heading "Catholic Epistles" for the letters of James, Peter, John, and Jude, with a subheading "of James," or whoever the writers of the other letters were.

James 1:1 – In this verse we see the typical way a first century letter began, giving a signature, the address, and greetings. Hundreds of papyrus letters have been uncovered from the sands of Egypt that bear a similar epistolary opening. The *author* signs his name "James" and briefly identifies which "James" is writing, i.e., it is one who is a bondservant of God and the Lord Jesus Christ. In other words, he has a special position of authority and leadership, and he is a Christian. The letter is *addressed* "to the twelve tribes who are dispersed abroad." As the marginal note shows, there is some question whether or not to capitalize the word "Dispersion." With a capital "D" the word becomes the technical term used to describe where the Jewish people were living since the Babylonian Captivity,

---

[1] In those manuscripts that carried the one word title "of James," most likely the word *epistolē* ("letter") was understood before "of James," though Windisch (*Die katholischen Briefe* in HNT [Tubingen: Mohr, 1951], p.3) offered the suggestion the implied word was *didachē* ("teaching").

at which time they had been carried away and driven away from the land of Israel.[2]   Since James also addresses his readers as "my brethren," the combination of "brethren" and "Dispersion" would suggest the readers are "completed Jews," that is, Jewish Christians living all over the Mediterranean world.   If we choose lower case "d," then it is supposed that the letter is addressed to Christian believers of whatever ethnic background who are away from their heavenly homeland.   The "twelve tribes" are spiritual Israel, the Israel of God (Galatians 6:16).[3]   The *greeting* was the typical Hellenistic way to greet the readers to whom a letter was addressed.

Questions immediately come to mind.   Who is this James that he needs no more identification than is given here, yet the readers will know who wrote the letter?   Why should this James feel a responsibility for these "dispersed" brethren?   What possible date for the letter might be implied in this first verse?   Concerning the date for the writing of the letter, the fact that James talks about the Lord Jesus Christ requires a post-AD 30 date. The fact that the readers are believers who have been scattered implies a date after AD 34 when the church was scattered by the persecution that arose with the martyrdom of Stephen (Acts 8:1-4).   As early as AD 37, James, the brother of the Lord, was an apostle of Jesus and a leader at the Jerusalem church (Galatians 1:19).   An apostle would have worldwide responsibility for the growth and welfare of believers.   Some of his scattered readers may at one time have been part of the congregation to which he ministered in Jerusalem.   Were the scattered Christians no longer in contact with the apostles (who stayed behind at Jerusalem, Acts 8:2), so James responds to the need to instruct them and exhort them? Other factors also influence the possible dates for the letter.   Until about AD 40 or 41, when the first gentile, Cornelius, became a convert to Christianity, all the believers would have been ethnically Jewish.   Until about AD 45 when Paul made some missionary journeys to Gentile communities, the majority of converts were Jewish.   If we date the writing of James before AD 45, we must capitalize the "D" and speak of "Dispersion," for Jewish Christians made up the bulk of the converts at this early date.

James 1:2ff tells us the readers are experiencing "trials," adversity, privations, hardships, perhaps poverty and hunger.   Their lives are threatened by a daily struggle with a variety of external circumstances, every one of which could become a source of temptation (James 1:13ff) that would threaten their faith.   Is it possible this is a picture of how hard life was for years for people who are refugees?   Acts 8:1 tells us that as they fled the city after the death of Stephen, some of the scattered Jerusalem church members went to Judea and Samaria.   Acts 11:19 tells us others went as far as Phoenicia, Cyprus, and Syrian Antioch. In those places most of them would have to start all over again to build their homes, businesses, and lives.   James 1:12 is another implication that the readers are Christians who "love the Lord," and that faithfulness in face of whatever "trials" they meet will result in a "crown of life" when this life is over.

---

[2] James writes "twelve tribes".   The idea that there have been "Ten Lost Tribes" ever since the Captivities, and that these lost tribes are comprised of the Anglo-Saxon peoples (the theory is sometimes called "British Israelism") is a fiction not supported by the Bible.   See also "our twelve tribes" in Acts 26:7.

[3] Compare also 1 Peter 1:1 and Matthew 19:28.

James 1:18 reminds the readers of how they became Christians. They were "brought forth by the word of truth," and they were "the firstfruits" of a huge harvest of souls for Christ. "Firstfruits" fits the idea the readers are ethnically Jewish, since the gospel went to the Jews first (Romans 1:6; 2:9,10). "His creatures" reminds us that Christians are a "new creation" (Galatians 6:15).

James 1:22 -- James is anxious that his readers prove to be doers of the Word, not just hearers only. If we identify the "Word" with the Gospel, the "word of truth" that 1:18 spoke about being involved in their conversion, and the "perfect law of liberty" that 1:25 calls attention to, then we may imply the readers are being tempted to abandon the Gospel. We will offer the hypothesis that James reflects the struggle the church faced when the Pharisaic Judaizers began invading the congregations and drawing away disciples after them (Acts 15, Galatians 2). To embrace what the Judaizers taught would result in being entangled in a yoke of bondage (Galatians 2:4; Acts 15:10; Galatians 5:1), with all their liberty gone![4]

James 1:27 -- Have the readers, themselves facing hardship, been neglecting those who are less fortunate, namely, the widows and orphans?

James 2:1 is a solid statement that the readers are Christians, adherents of the "faith" Jesus taught. As such, they must be exceedingly careful lest they show special favoritism to rich people[5] who may visit the weekly assembly of believers. "Assembly" is *sunagogē* ("synagogue") in the Greek. This is not the usual word for the Christian assembly, which was *ekklēsia*. Does the use of "synagogue" reflect the common language of Jewish people for their religious assembly, even after they became Christians?[6] Does the use of the word "synagogue" imply the Christians are still meeting in the synagogues, not as yet having separated from the unbelieving Jews?[7] "Glorious Lord" or "Lord of glory" is certainly a reflection of the risen Christ who appeared in a glorified body after His resurrection from the dead, and who now sits enthroned in glory at the right hand of the Majesty on high.

---

[4] As we attempt to prove our hypothesis about the time and purpose of James, we shall look for similar arguments and language used by Paul to refute the Judaizers (both at the Jerusalem Conference and in his anti-Judaizer letters, Romans and Galatians), with which we may compare what James writes.

[5] Were the "rich" unconverted visitors whom the brethren were trying to impress, or were they church members who were being shown favoritism? Are the "rich" of 2:2 a different group than the "rich" of 1:10?

[6] Later, Christians will use the Greek term *ekklēsia* for the assembly. In fact, James himself uses "church" in 5:14, and his use of both terms seems to treat them as equivalent, meaning "a Christian congregation."

[7] Paul left the synagogues he first preached in when the Jewish leadership opposed him, making assembly with them no longer convenient or possible. What was usual or customary in communities where preachers like Paul have not yet been ostracized?

James 2:6 has the rich oppressing and dragging Christians into court. Is this one of the "trials" that 1:2 referred to?

James 2:7 -- "Do they not blaspheme the fair name by which you are called?" Are the rich blaspheming the name of Christ or the name Christian? If it is the name "Christian," that requires a date for James later than AD 44. We recall that the disciples were first called Christians at Antioch (Acts 11:26) during Paul's and Barnabas' year-long ministry in that town, a ministry dated about AD 42 or 43.[8] Is the name "Christ," so that blasphemy of Christ reflects what the Judaizers were doing as they tried to win converts away from the churches?

James 2:8-12 call attention to the "royal law" and "the law." Passages from Leviticus and Exodus or Deuteronomy are quoted. Is James appealing to the Law of Moses as a basis of his instruction to his Christian readers? Is James appealing to something Jesus taught (note the margin reads "law of your King")? Verse 12 again speaks of the "law of liberty." Has the Gospel superseded the Law of Moses as the rule of faith and practice for Christians?

James 2:14-26 again emphasizes the imperative of ministering to the poor and needy. Such ministry is an inherent part of the "faith." This is something any Christian can do, whether he himself is rich or poor. It is in this paragraph that we have James' famous statement about "faith and works" with the example of Abraham used to make the point perfectly clear that living "faith" automatically assumes the corresponding works of faith. "Faith" without works is not a living faith, it is dead! Bible students immediately recall what Paul wrote about faith and works (in Romans and Galatians). "Was James written after Paul wrote Romans and Galatians?" they ask, "or before?"[9] They ask, "Do Paul and James say the same thing?" or "Do Paul and James contradict?"[10] Are Paul and James dealing with the same issue (i.e., the teachings of the Judaizers) and are they using the same Scriptural arguments (e.g., both quote Genesis 15:6) to refute those church destroyers?

---

[8] The ministry in Antioch (Acts 11) was before Herod Agrippa I died (as recorded in Acts 12) in AD 44.

[9] The date we assign for the writing of Romans is AD 57, and for Galatians is AD 58. See the commentator's New Testament Survey Notes for an outline presentation of the reasons for these dates. See his commentary on Romans for detailed notes on the dating of Romans. We date Galatians late because Galatians 4:13 indicates Paul has visited Galatia at least twice before he wrote his letter to them. The second visit would have occurred during Paul's second missionary journey (AD 51-54). We date Romans, Galatians, and both letters to the Corinthians from Paul's third missionary journey (AD 54-58).

[10] Do Paul and James use "faith" and "works" and "justify" with the same meanings? "Faith" in James is more than mental assent (the demons "belief" is mental assent, and that's valueless); for James, it is a faith that shows itself in "works." "Faith" to Paul in Romans is faithfulness to what God has said, an "obedient faith," a "walking in the steps of Abraham's faith." Paul says "works of law" (i.e., man-made religious rules like the Pharisees/Judaizers demanded of people) do not justify. Paul also says that at the final judgment what a man has "done" (whether or not he has faithfully done what God has commanded) will be one of the key issues investigated (Romans 2:6-11). James would certainly agree when he speaks of being judged by the law of liberty (James 2:12). This issue is of such importance that a detailed study of it will appear later in these Introductory Studies.

James 3:1ff contain a prohibition about becoming teachers. Just why did James try to discourage his readers from seeking to be teachers? Is the reason to be found in the fact that all of us have difficulty controlling what we permit to come out of our mouths? Was there some connection between a desire to be "teachers" and the general attempt to spread Judaizing dogma? And why does James call attention to the fact that some ideas the teacher teaches may come from the Devil himself (verse 6)? When James says "we shall incur stricter judgment" he is including himself as a "teacher" in the church.

James 3:13ff speak of jealousy, strife, disorder, and every evil thing. Is this a glance at the evil effects the Judaizers were producing among the congregations they invaded? Do verses 17 and 18 say that what the Judaizers are teaching is not wisdom from above, nor does it produce "righteousness" (right relationships with God and man)?

James 4:1ff speaks about being careful when it comes to choosing one's friends. Is James saying one should be very cautious about choosing to develop friendships with the Judaizers? To be a friend of the world automatically makes you at war with God. God is a jealous lover who will share his beloved with no rival.

James 4:10-17 is a call to submit to the lordship of Jesus Christ. Is this another bold repudiation of the Judaizers who bristled at the idea Jesus might be Lord or Christ? However, a man does not have to speak publicly against Jesus. One can just as surely repudiate the lordship of Jesus by failing to take His will into account when we plan our future activities. Such planning, unconscious of Jesus' will, is sin.

James 5:1-11 call for patience and endurance when facing injustice. Someone rich has been systematically oppressing the poor among James' Christian readers. Who are these rich oppressors? And who is the "righteous one" who was put to death (verse 6)? Several verses in this paragraph promise a coming of the Lord very soon. What coming? Did James mistakenly believe the Second Coming was imminent? If he believed that and wrote it, what does this say about his possible inspiration? Or is this one of the places in the New Testament where the sending of the Roman armies to destroy unbelieving Jerusalem (AD 70) is spoken of as something King Jesus (the "Lord of Hosts," verse 4) did as He providentially moves history from His throne on high?[11] Are commentators who treat these verses as a reference to the Second Coming mistaken? The illustration about the "early and late rains" clearly suggests the writer (and perhaps the readers) is familiar with the Palestinian climate and the whole eastern coast of the Mediterranean.

James 5:12, with its warning against evasive distinctions in oaths, reminds us of a similar warning made by Jesus (Matthew 5:34-37). In fact a number of verses in James remind us of Jesus' instructions about how He expected His followers to live their everyday lives. How did James come to such intimate knowledge of all these sayings of Jesus?

---

[11] If the "coming of Jesus" that resulted in the destruction of Jerusalem is the thing promised as being near, this would call for a late date for the writing of James.

James 5:13-18 deal with prayer. Included are instructions to people who are sick in bed about summoning the elders of the church for prayer. As the elders pray, they will anoint the sick with oil. Is this a reflection of a Jewish practice still being done by the Jewish Christians to whom James writes? Does James, who often did things according to the Jewish way he grew up (Acts 21:18ff), anywhere else in his letter reflect some of the Jewish practices which he had perfect liberty in Christ to continue to do, but which we would not be obligated to do? The reference to "elders" and "church" give us a picture of life in the various places where the readers of this letter lived. There were "congregations" of believers, and each was shepherded by "elders."

James 5:19-20 closes with the sad warning that there was a danger some of the readers would stray from the truth. Does this picture what a person had to do who embraced what the Judaizers were teaching? James also encourages his readers to make a valiant attempt to try to bring the wanderers to repentance, knowing that if they did so, they would save a soul from death and cover a multitude of sins. Is there a glance at Judaism, where the blood of bulls and goats never could take away sins? Is this James' final warning against what the Judaizers were trying to do?

James does not include the customary epistolary ending. The letter ends abruptly, with no benediction. Was the abrupt ending deliberate? Have the last verses of the letter been lost? Did something happen to the author so that he was unable to finish the letter?

Several notable items emerged during our review of possible historical allusions.

(1) *There are similarities of language* between this epistle and the speech and letter of James recorded in Acts 15.[12] The classic epistolary form *chairein* ("greeting") is used in both James 1:1 and Acts 15:23, and elsewhere only at Acts 23:26. "The honorable name by which you are called" (James 2:7) reminds us of Acts 15:17. The exhortation to the "brethren" (*adelphoi*) to hear is found in both James 2:5 and Acts 15:13. Further parallels are found in such individual words as *episkepteusthe* (James 1:27, Acts 15:14); *epistrepsein* (James 5:19,20, Acts 15:19); *tērein* (James 1:27, Acts 15:29); and *agapētos* (James 1:16,19, 2:5, Acts 15:25).[13]

(2) *The Greek in this epistle is "good Greek."* The Greek has been pronounced by Moulton and Howard as among the best found in the New Testament.[14] Some have wondered if a

---

[12] This argument assumes that the speech of James records the exact words James spoke. The modern suggestion that Luke simply composed the speeches and put them in the mouths of the characters he is writing about is hardly an acceptable view.

[13] Not all scholars are ready to admit any evidential value to these similarities. Tasker (*The General Epistle of James* in TNTC [Grand Rapids: Eerdmans, 1957], p.26) has cautioned against placing too much weight on these resemblances, because resemblances between James' speech (Acts 15) and other New Testament books could be cited where similarity of authorship is not even being discussed. Nevertheless, the easiest explanation of the parallels is that the words come from the same James.

[14] J. H. Moulton and W. F. Howard, *A Grammar of New Testament Greek* (1929), V.2, p.27. See more on this matter of "excellent Greek" in the section below on "style."

person who grew up in Galilee, as the brother of the Lord did, could have had such a command of the Greek. However, it must be remembered that Galilee was bilingual, and the region on the east side of the lake called Decapolis was comprised of ten Greek cities. It would have been within the power of any Galilean to gain a knowledge of Greek. Further, the leader of the church at Jerusalem, which had numerous Hellenistic Jews in it, would be obliged to learn Greek if he were going to communicate with his church members. If he didn't have a facility to use Greek from his days in Galilee, he certainly could have acquired it in his days in Jerusalem.

(3) *The number of imperative verbs.* In the 108 verses there are over 50 imperative verbs.[15] James writes as though he were conscious he had a right to be recognized as one who could speak authoritatively to his readers. An apostle is one who could so speak as they give divine directives to men. From James it becomes evident that Christianity is one of the few religions in the world that makes ethical demands upon its members.

(4) *A number of allusions to the teachings of Jesus.* A number of writers have produced a chart showing there is scarcely a thought in the epistle which cannot be traced to Christ's personal teaching.[16] A typical chart compares what James writes with what Jesus said in His Sermon on the Mount:

Compare: James 1:2 with Matthew 5:10-12
James 1:4 with Matthew 5:48
James 1:5, 5:15 with Matthew 7:7-12
James 1:9 with Matthew 5:3
James 1:20 with Matthew 5:22
James 2:13 with Matthew 6:14,15, 5:7
James 2:14 with Matthew 7:21-23
James 3:17,18 with Matthew 5:9
James 4:4 with Matthew 6:24
James 4:10 with Matthew 5:3,4
James 4:11 with Matthew 7:1-5
James 5:2 with Matthew 6:19
James 5:10 with Matthew 5:12
James 5:12 with Matthew 5:33-37

One begins to wonder whether James has seen a copy of Matthew's Gospel,[17] or whether

---

[15] The number varies depending on which Greek text is being used to count the number of imperatives. Some count 60. Some count 59. Some count 54.

[16] Writers who believe the synoptic writers made use of the hypothetical source "Q" are not enamored with this comparison between James and the teaching of Jesus because they hold that we cannot know how much of "Q" derives from Jesus and how much is the result of editing. It is amazing (and exasperating to folk who wish to be believers] how current synoptic studies tend to obfuscate more than the gospels!

[17] The possibility James has seen a copy of Matthew's Gospel is discussed in the comments on James 5:12.

both James and Matthew were in Jesus' audience the day He delivered the Sermon,[18] or whether James is producing reminiscences of oral teaching which he heard since his conversion.[19]   The apostle Paul, who (like Jerusalem James) was not one of Jesus' original apostles, received his knowledge about Jesus' ministry by direct revelation (Galatians 1:12).   What is to keep us from supposing something similar occurred in James' case?

(5) *Indications the readers were Christians* are found in 1:1 and 2:1.   In addition there are features that make sense only if the readers are followers of Jesus, namely the striking number of parallels between the commands James writes and the teachings of Jesus, and the appeals to the lordship of Jesus Christ.

(6) *The writer had an intimate knowledge* of the circumstances and behavioral characteristics of his readers.   The readers have been scattered (1:1) and face difficult times that can even become temptations.   In those places where they have settled, there are congregations (2:2) each having its own elders (5:14).   It is imperative they put into daily practice what their Lord and Savior taught.   Their public assemblies together are open to visitors (2:2-3) and this indicates they have not been forced into a ghetto nor have they created a closed community as a defense mechanism.   The Christians, for the most part, are poor, and are suffering injustice at the hands of their wealthy neighbors (2:6,7; 5:1-6).   Poor though they may be, they still have means to relieve the needs of those less fortunate (1:27; 2:15,16).   Typical tensions that arise when folk are struggling to make ends meet are anger (1:19-20), jealousy (4:1-2), slander and criticism (4:11-12).   Calls to demon-strate their "faith" by appropriate actions, and warnings about "straying from the way of truth," show something threatens to lure the readers away from following Jesus Christ.   Those who have begun to stray need to be encouraged to repent or they will perish.

(7) *There are quotations and allusions to the Old Testament Scriptures.*   Direct quotations number five (1:11, 2:8, 11,23, 4:6) – three from the Pentateuch, one from Isaiah, and one from Proverbs.[20]   All three divisions of the Old Testament canon are represented.   Indirect allusions are numerable (e.g., 1:10; 2:21,23,25; 3:9; 4:6; 5:2,11,17,18).[21]   When

---

[18] While Matthew was certainly present, we do not know if the Lord's brother was present on the Mount.   Not only are there parallels to what is found in Matthew, but some writers have found parallels in James to what is recorded about Jesus by Mark and Luke.   For example, there is a parallel to James 5:17 in Luke 4:2ff (the reference to the three and one-half years of rainlessness in Elijah's time).   Who is to say that James did not hear our Lord speak these words when they were spoken in the synagogue at Nazareth?

[19] Oral traditions certainly preceded the writing of the Gospel accounts.   These were carefully monitored for accuracy by "ministers of the Word" (Luke 1:2).   We flatly reject the idea that Matthew's Gospel is a composite of Mark and another source (Q), and that Mark redacted the material he was adapting into his "Gospel."   If we must go through Mark and Q (yes, and even different alleged recensions of Q) to get to Matthew, it is of little value to note any supposed similarities between Jesus and James.

[20] Most of the quotations of Old Testament books are taken from the text of the LXX, though there are places where James substitutes a word of his own choosing for the word actually found in the LXX. The citation of Proverbs 3:34 at James 4:6 differs markedly from the LXX.

[21] Mayor (*The Epistle of James* [Grand Rapids: Zondervan, 1954 reprint, p.lxix ff) finds parallels from Genesis, Exodus, Leviticus, Numbers, Deuteronomy, Joshua, 1 Kings, Job, Psalms, Proverbs, Ecclesiastes, Isaiah, Jeremiah, Ezekiel, Daniel and seven Minor Prophets.

the writer wants an illustration for prayer and patience he turns to Old Testament characters. When he approaches ethical problems, there are times his denunciations and warnings sound just like the Old Testament prophets (and no wonder, if he is a "bondservant of God," 1:1).

(8) While James is very practical with numerous calls to consistent, everyday Christian living, *there also is a solid doctrinal basis* for what James writes. The theology found in James is in complete harmony with Apostolic truth everywhere recorded in the New Testament Scriptures. There is a doctrine of God,[22] a doctrine of sin,[23] a doctrine of salvation,[24] a solid Christology that emphasizes the teachings of Jesus, His lordship,[25] and even makes allusion to His resurrection,[26] a doctrine concerning the Law and the Gospel,[27] and even incidental allusions to church polity and congregational life.

AUTHORSHIP AND ATTESTATION

While there is little that the writer tells us directly of himself in the historical allusions, there are few writings from this same period in which the historical allusions (in such a short letter) tell any more about the author than is found in the epistle of James. He calls himself "James, bondservant of God and of the Lord Jesus Christ" and he addresses "the twelve tribes who are dispersed." To these he speaks with authority.

---

[22] God is generous (1:5), holy (1:13), one in whom is no variation (1:17). He is the one and only God (2:19), the Father of His people and the prototype in whose likeness men were created (3:9). He is full of compassion and mercy (5:11). He hears men's prayers (1:5, 4:3). He judges men's behavior (1:27).

[23] All have sinned (3:2); all are tempted the same way (1:14,15); and sin results in death (1:15). Some individual expressions of sin include anger (1:20), disgusting and offensive conduct (1:21), blasphemy (2:7), discrimination (2:9-11), bitterness and lust (4:1-3), spiritual adultery and intimate ties with the evil world (4:4), pride (4:6), theft and oppression (5:4), and backsliding (5:19,20). Behind the evil in the world is the Devil (4:7) and his demons (2:19, 3:15).

[24] James speaks of regeneration (1:18), salvation of the soul (1:21), and justification (2:21-25). He promises the believer forgiveness of sins (5:15). He points out that saving faith is an obedient faith (2:14-26). There is a blessing from God to be had in rescuing wandering souls (5:19,20). Christians are heirs of the kingdom (2:5). The end time will feature a final judgment (2:12, 3:1). There will come a day when faithful Christians receive the crown of life (1:12).

[25] Jesus is called Lord numerous times in the letter. He exercises a providential control over His creation (4:15, 5:7-8). He is "Lord of Hosts" (5:4 NASB mg.). He now lives in glory and He is Judge (4:12). He is the One before whom humbling oneself is appropriate (4:10). The Lord is the one in whose name the sick are anointed and who will heal them (5:13-16).

[26] He is called "Lord of glory" at 2:1(KJV).

[27] The Law of Moses is alluded to (2:8-11), while the Gospel (the law of liberty) is the authority in these last days (1:25, 2:12, 5:3). The New Testament elsewhere (e.g., Hebrews 8-10) presents the temporary nature of the Law of Moses. James agrees with this presentation. He does not reassure his readers that the Law (the priceless possession of every Jew before Christ) is still a binding code of statutes. The Mosaic covenant has been abrogated in favor of the new covenant.

The name "James" (actually "Jacob" in the Hebrew and Greek) was a favorite with the Jews, since "Jacob" was the progenitor of the Jewish people.[1] This letter's writer is a "James" who is so well-known that no more identification is needed by the first readers of this epistle.

A cursory reading of the New Testament shows there are **several different persons named "James"**:

1) James, the son of Zebedee, one of the original 12 apostles

> He is the brother of the apostle John, their parents were Zebedee and Salome, and most think James was older than John since he is nearly always mentioned first. He was the first of Jesus' apostles to die, being put to death by Herod Agrippa I, about AD 44 (Acts 12:2). Likely the reason he is nowhere named in the fourth gospel is because John, the writer of that work, did not name himself or any of the characters who were related to him.

2) James, the son of Alphaeus, another of the original 12 apostles chosen by Jesus

> We read about this man in Matthew 10:3; Mark 3:18; Luke 6:15; and Acts 1:13. Several questions are raised: Was Alphaeus' wife named Mary? Where does it say so? Are "Alphaeus" and "Clopas" variations of the same name? Even though there is a superficial word resemblance, we can't rely on "Clopas" and "Alphaeus' being variations of the same name.

3) James, the Less

> This man's mother's name was Mary (Matthew 27:56; Luke 24:10), and he had a brother named Joses (Matthew 27:56). He apparently was given the description "the Less" (Mark 15:40) to distinguish him from the other men named James (i.e., the son of Zebedee and the son of Alphaeus). Whether it referred to his stature or his age, we have no way of knowing for certain.

4) James, the *father* of the apostle Jude

> This "Jude" is also called Thaddaeus and Lebbeus. He is carefully distinguished from "Iscariot" (Luke 6:16). The Greek at Acts 1:13 reads "Jude of James." This expression is rightly translated in the ASV, "Judas, the *son* of James." The KJV's "brother of" is in error.

5) James, the brother of the Lord

> He shares a family relationship to "the Lord" with Joses, Simon, and Judas, and with some unnamed sisters (Galatians 1:19; Matthew 13:55; Mark 6:3).

---

[1] "James" is the English form of the Hebrew name *Ya'aqov* (Jacob), which in Greek became *Iakōbos*, and in Latin *Jacobus*. The English spelling causes us to miss the Biblical history implied in the name.

6) James, leader of the Jerusalem church

After the apostle James (the son of Zebedee) was martyred (Acts 12:2), another James appears on the scene as leader of the Jerusalem church (Acts 12:17, 15:13, 21:18; 1 Corinthians 15:7; Galatians 2:9,12).

7) James, the brother of the author of the epistle called "Jude" (Jude 1:1)

8) James, a bondservant of God and the Lord Jesus Christ (James 1:1)

This list may reasonably be consolidated and reduced to four or five persons:
1) James, the son of Zebedee
2) James, the son of Alphaeus
3) James, the Less[2]
4) James, the father of Jude
5) James, the brother of the Lord[3]

Of these five persons, three have been singled out as the possible author of the epistle called "James." The arguments for and against each include:

1) James, Son of Zebedee

The subscription in Codex Corbeiensis (ff[1]), a 9th century manuscript, has in Latin *Explicit epistola Iacobi filii Zaebedei* ("epistle of James, a son of Zebedee").[4] Subscriptions in the Peshitto Syriac also ascribe the writing of this epistle to "the elder James" (i.e., the son of Zebedee). This James was one of the original twelve apostles of Jesus, and so would satisfy "bondservant" at James 1:1. Since he was martyred in AD 44 (Acts 12), if he were the author of our letter, it would settle several disputed matters. The destination would be to Jewish Christians (that's about all the converts we have at this early date), and this letter would be the earliest book of the New Testament to be written.

One thing that causes us to be hesitant about naming this man as the author of the letter is the address "to the twelve tribes who are scattered." We have some prob-

---

[2] Some allege that James the son of Alphaeus and James the Less are to be identified. As will be argued below, we are not convinced such an identification can be substantiated.

[3] Some attempt to identify James the Less and the brother of the Lord as being the same persons. Others, correctly in our view, identify the "brother of the Lord" and the "leader of the Jerusalem Church" as being the same man.

[4] This manuscript has a Spanish provenance. A series of Spanish writers from the seventh to the seventeenth centuries seem to have been led by national patriotism to claim the epistle was written by their patron saint, James, the son of Zebedee. The wording of the decision at the Council of Trent in AD 1564 that the letter was the work of "the apostle James" was deliberately vague in deference to the Spanish Catholics; it could be construed as the son of Zebedee or the brother of the Lord since both were "apostles."

lems finding Jewish Christians "scattered" (dispersed) before AD 40, to whom the son of Zebedee could have written before his death in AD 44. The preaching of the Gospel up to AD 34 (when Stephen was martyred) was confined mostly to within the limits of Judea and Samaria (Acts 8:2). The Jerusalem church was then scattered (Acts 8:2,4). By AD 40-42, some of the Christians who became refugees when Paul began the persecution that resulted in the death of Stephen went as far as Cyprus and Antioch (Acts 11:19). Is that enough of a "dispersion" to satisfy the address of this letter?

Few scholars have defended the proposition that this man was indeed the author of our epistle; most commentators reject the son of Zebedee as the "James" who wrote this epistle, arguing it is just too early in church history for this letter. Further, with the exception of the few references noted above, external evidence from Early Christian writers does not point to the son of Zebedee as the author.

2) James, the apostle, the son of Alphaeus

This view carefully distinguishes between "James, the son of Alphaeus" and "James, the Lord's brother" insisting these are not just two designations for the same person.[5]

Perhaps the 5th century copyists of the Peshitto Syriac who attributed the epistle to "James the apostle" had the son of Alphaeus in mind. (Copyists of the Syriac at a later age attributed the epistle to the son of Zebedee, for they state that the three Catholic Epistles admitted to that version – James, 1 Peter, and 1 John – are by the three apostles who witnessed the Transfiguration.[6])

Calvin thought that the James described in Galatians 2:9 as a "pillar of the church" was in fact the son of Alphaeus, but he hesitated to assign to him the authorship of the epistle. In the forward to his commentary he states that it is not for him to say whether this James (son of Alphaeus) or the ruler of the church in Jerusalem (the brother of the Lord) was the author of James.[7]

---

[5] In the fourth century, Jerome proposed that "the son of Alphaeus" and the "Lord's brother" were actually the same person. This has been the traditional view of the Roman Catholic Church since. However, Wikenhauser (Introduction to the New Testament [New York: Herder, 1958], p.480), a Catholic, notes that "the Protestants and a growing minority among modern Catholics distinguish the brother of the Lord from the son of Alphaeus" and concludes that the distinction is preferable. See notes below for more details on this matter.

[6] In A. Plummer's ("The General Epistles of St. James and St. Jude" in An Exposition of the Bible [Hartford, Conn.: S.S. Scranton, 1910], p.563) opinion this statement is a blundering misinterpretation of the earlier title, which assigned it to James, the apostle.

[7] John Calvin, Commentaries on the Epistles of Paul the Apostle on Galatians, Ephesians, Philippians and Colossians, translated by T.H.L. Parker (Grand Rapids: Eerdmans, 1972), p. 22.

J. Sidlow Baxter defends the son of Alphaeus as being the author of our epistle.[8]

If we assign this James as the author we are faced with several problems: (1) Why did some speak against including James in the canon if it were written by one of the original twelve apostles? (2) What date and destination shall we assign the letter? We have no evidence where the son of Alphaeus ministered. Nothing of special import is said of this James in the Gospels.

3) James, brother of Jesus

As early as AD 37 (Galatians 1:19), the brother of Jesus is styled an "apostle", thus satisfying the word "bondservant" of James 1:1. It is this man who is the "James of Jerusalem" so prominent in Acts 12:17, 15:13ff, 21:18.

This James is a Christian, but one who still holds many Jewish beliefs and social customs, as did the members of the congregation over which he presided (Acts 21:18ff). He was reputed as of equal authority ("one of the pillars") with Peter and John (Galatians 2:6ff).

What external testimony we have (see "Attestation" below) is in harmony with this identification.

If we opt for this man being our author, then the letter could be dated anywhere between AD 37 (Galatians 1:19) and his death in AD 62 (or AD 69).

Of these three men named "James," two appear with enough frequency in the pages of the New Testament and might, therefore, be well enough known to satisfy the criterion of needing to give no more identification than his name in order to be known by the first readers of this epistle – (1) James, the son of Zebedee, and (2) James, the brother of Jesus.

When all the options have been sorted and weighed, we have come to agree with the traditional view, that **James, the brother of the Lord, is the author of this letter**. This identification is supported by:

(1) The similarity of the language of the letter with that of James's speech and the circular letter of Acts 15.

(2) The consistency of the historical reports of the life and character of the Lord's brother with what is found in the epistle.

(3) The fact that no other James fits the situation as well as the Lord's brother.

(4) The fact that James, the Lord's brother, is uniformly mentioned "by his personal name alone (Galatians 2:9; Jude 1; Acts 12:17, 15:13, 21:18)" just as James 1:1 has it.[9]

---

[8] J. Sidlow Baxter, *Explore the Book* (Grand Rapids: Zondervan, 1962), 6:292-293.

[9] E.F. Harrison, *Introduction to the New Testament* (Grand Rapids: Eerdmans, 1971), p. 386.

Attempts to learn more about James' identity have raised at least **five difficult questions**.[10]

1. Jerusalem James is called the "brother of the Lord" (Galatians 1:19). *What does the word "brother" mean?*[11] *Adelphos* means "brother," literally "out of the same womb," but the word can also have a figurative meaning (James 1:2). There is a distinct Greek word for "cousin" (*anepsios*) which occurs at Colossians 4:10.[12] If some less-specific term for "relative" was needed, the word *suggenēs* was available (e.g., Luke 1:36, 38, 2:44). This word *suggenēs* is a word for "relative" without making the exact relationship clear. "No one, without a theological axe to grind, would ever have thought of trying to make *adelphos* mean 'cousin' instead of 'brother'."[13] The "brothers" of Jesus were named James, Joses ["Joseph" in some manuscripts], Simon, and Judas (Mark 6:3). If John 19:25 names four women, the parents of these "brothers" are Joseph and/or Mary.[14] Were they Joseph's chil-

---

[10] These pages following in which these questions are discussed may be skipped over without losing the general train of thought these introductory studies are dealing with. These questions have been debated for years, and there are no new arguments or evidence from archaeology which will help settle them once and for all. The reader who wishes to study the matters may return to these pages at a later date, if he or she wishes.

[11] We are immediately plunged into a study of what are called the Helvidian, Epiphanian, and Hieronymian views. This material was also introduced in the author's Commentary on Acts.

[12] The ancient tradition preserved by Hegesippus (c.AD 170) distinguishes James, the first leader of the church at Jerusalem, as the "brother of the Lord" and his successor, Symeon, as the "cousin of the Lord" (Eus. HE. II.xxiii.1). Could Hegesippus have written this way if James also were really a "cousin"?

[13] R.C. Foster quoted this comment by his teacher.

[14] If John 19:25 names four women, there is no way the "brothers" could be the children of Alphaeus/Clopas, as per the Hieronymian View. "Hieronymian" means "composed by Jerome." Jerome, during the years AD 382-385, while studying in Rome, wrote a reply to Helvidius in which (contrary to Helvidius' view) he affirmed the perpetual virginity of Mary. This view reduces the number of persons in the New Testament with the name of "James" to two apostles, the son of Zebedee and the son of Alphaeus. The "brothers" and "sisters" were identified as being "cousins" of Jesus, the children of His mother's sister, Mary the wife of Clopas (Alphaeus). Augustine adopted Jerome's view, and it generally held sway in the Roman Church (see *New Catholic Encyclopedia*, II, s.v. "brothers of Jesus"). Chrysostom and Theodoret held this view. Jerome's theory appears to have been wholly original with him. Both his own efforts and those of later Roman Catholic writers to find support for this theory in earlier ecclesiastical tradition must be deemed to have failed. The whole theory of the perpetual virginity of Mary, which Jerome's theory was invented to substantiate, arose from an attempt to adapt Christian doctrine to Greek philosophy. Further objections to Jerome's theory: (1) There is no New Testament or Classical Greek example of *adelphos* being used to denote "cousin." (2) Jerome's interpretation of John 19:25, which makes Mary of Clopas to be the sister of the virgin Mary, is unlikely. (3) Mary "of Clopas" is most naturally understood as referring to the **wife** of Clopas, and in that case (since the identification of the names Clopas and Alphaeus is not accepted) she cannot well have been the wife of Alphaeus. (4) The expression "James the less" (which title Jerome said was given so as to distinguish "the son of Alphaeus" from "the son of Zebedee") does not seem to be used of inferiority, but rather (note that it is positive, not comparative -- *ho mikros*) seems to refer to some personal characteristic, probably stature. (5) To hold Jerome's theory, one must make an unwarranted distinction between the James of Galatians 1:19 and the James of Galatians 2:9.

dren and so older than Jesus? This identification is called the Epiphanian View.[15] Arguments raised in support of it call attention to brothers' attempted interference with Jesus' conduct (Matthew 12:46, 13:54-56; Mark 3:21,31; 6:2,3; Luke 8:19-21) which to some people is supposed to imply that the brothers were older than He. If they were Joseph's children by a former wife, the brothers and sisters would be older than Jesus (who was Mary's first child). According to this view, in which the "brothers" of Jesus are actually "step brothers," the word *adelphos* must have the sense of "near relative."[16] Were they Mary's children, and so younger than Jesus? This identification is called the Helvidian View. Some have argued[17] that it must have been because the brothers were younger than Jesus that Jesus entrusted Mary to John's care (John 19:26,27). The word "firstborn" (Luke 2:7 and Textus Receptus of Matthew 1:25) has seemed to many to say

---

[15] The Epiphanian view (taught by Epiphanius, AD 380, bishop of Salamis on Cyprus) is sometimes called the "Agnatic theory" – i.e., that descent is traceable through male descent. Epiphanius held that the "brothers" of Jesus were the children of Joseph and his former wife, before he became engaged to and married to the virgin Mary. The earliest form of this theory seems to be found in the second-century apocryphal gospels (the *Protevangelium Jacobi* and the *Gospel of Peter*). In the former, at the time of his betrothal to Mary, Joseph is represented as a widower more than 80 years of age, with a number of children. Origen inclined to this view, although he admitted it had no backing other than the legendary apocryphal gospels and had only a dogmatic or sentimental basis. This theory had great appeal in the church during the time asceticism was being embraced since it safeguarded the virginity of Mary. The Greek orthodox and Eastern sects have generally taught this view. Many Protestants have also opted for the Epiphanian view, among them Luther and the English scholar Lightfoot (see his "Brethren of the Lord" in his commentary on Galatians, p. 247ff). Against this view: (1) No conclusive objection can be brought, other than the lack of any real evidence for it. It is not intrinsically improbable, nor contrary to anything in the New Testament that Joseph should have earlier been married, had a family, lost his wife, and then became engaged to Mary. (2) The apocryphal gospels, which are of doubtful authorship and are uninspired, are not a trustworthy source of information. (3) The Epiphanian view also has its roots in the dogmatic assumptions of Ascetic theology. (4) The Epiphanian view, if it is intended to demonstrate an ascetic lifestyle for Mary, does not agree with Matthew 1:25, "knew her not *until* she brought forth a son." (5) Nor does it agree with the use of *prōtotokos* ("firstborn") in Luke 2:7, which implies that Jesus was not the only child of his mother.

[16] The account given by Epiphanius and Theophylact is that Cleophas (a.k.a. Clopas and Alphaeus) and Joseph (the carpenter) were brothers. The former died without children. According to the Levitical law, Joseph married his brother's widow, and had children. James, being the firstborn, was called the son of Cleophas (Alphaeus). After she who had been Cleophas' wife died, Joseph was betrothed to and married Mary, the mother of Jesus. This view is quite improbable, and difficult to harmonize with Cleophas' wife still living and being present at the crucifixion of Jesus (Mark 15:40 and John 19:25).

[17] There are other possible reasons why Mary was entrusted to John's care. Joseph and Mary and their children were poor; John evidently was not. He could afford the responsibility of taking care of Mary. John was a believer in Jesus, while Jesus' brothers were not until after the Resurrection. Entrusting her to a believer was better than entrusting her to someone who might, or might not, become a believer.

Jesus was the oldest of Mary's children. (Cp. Exodus 13:2,12,15).[18] They would be "half brothers," *adelphos*, "out of the same womb." The natural interpretation of "brother" or "sister" is to take the words as meaning the children of Joseph and Mary, and thus half-brothers and half-sisters of Jesus.

2. *Are "James the son of Alphaeus" and "James the Lord's brother" the same person?*

a) First, a table of the 12 apostles will be a help as we try to answer this question.

	Matthew 10:2-4	Mark 3:16-19	Luke 6:14-16	Acts 1:13
1	Simon, called Peter	Simon, surnamed Peter	Simon, named Peter	Peter
2	Andrew, his brother	Andrew	Andrew, his brother	Andrew
3	James, son of Zebedee	James, son of Zebedee	James	James
4	John, his brother	John, brother of James	John	John
5	Philip	Philip	Philip	Philip
6	Bartholomew	Bartholomew	Bartholomew	Bartholomew
7	Matthew, the publican	Matthew	Matthew	Matthew
8	Thomas	Thomas	Thomas	Thomas
9	James, son of Alphaeus	James, son of Alphaeus	James, son of Alphaeus	James, son of Alphaeus
10	Simon, the Cananaean	Simon, the Cananaean	Simon, the Zealot	Simon, the Zealot
11	Thaddaeus	Thaddaeus	Judas of James	Judas of James
12	Judas	Judas Iscariot	Judas Iscariot	Judas Iscariot
	(who betrayed Him)	(who betrayed Him)	(became a traitor)	

b) Second, a listing of the women who watched the crucifixion of Jesus will help us arrive at an answer to this question.

Matt. 27:56		Mary Magdalene	Mary, mother of James & Joses	The mother of the sons of Zebedee
Mark 15:40		Mary Magdalene	Mary, mother of James the less, and Joses	And Salome
John 19:25	His mother	Mary Magdalene	Mary, the wife of Clopas	The sister of Jesus' mother

c) Matthew and Mark each name three women, whence it is thought that Salome (named by Mark) was the name of the mother of James and John ("the sons of Zebedee" as Matthew calls them).

d) But much of our problem lies with John 19:25, "But there were standing by the cross of Jesus his mother, and his mother's sister, Mary the wife of Clopas, and Mary Magdalene." Does John mention three or four women? If THREE, then Mary, the

---

[18] We admit that the description "firstborn" could be given to an only child. But had Jesus been an only child (Mary's first and last child), we would have expected *monogenēs* rather than *prōtotokos*, and we would have had no need for the other assertion "he knew her not until ..." (Matthew 1:25). "In the New Testament a negative followed by *eōs*, 'until,' always implies that the negatived action did, or will, take place after the point of time indicated by the particle (see for example Matthew 17:9, 18:34, Mark 9:1)." (A.H. McNeile, *Commentary on Matthew*, [London: Macmillan, 1915] at Matthew 1:25).

wife of Clopas, was Jesus' mother's sister. This would have two children named "Mary" in the same family. This would make James the Less and Joses to be COUSINS of Jesus. It is possible to read John 19:25 as though there were but three women there, namely, His mother, His mother's sister, and Mary Magdalene. If FOUR women are named, then Salome, the wife of Zebedee, was Jesus' mother's sister. This would make James and John, the sons of Zebedee, to be COUSINS of Jesus. In defense of this view it can be said: (i) John is giving two pairs of women, each pair coupled by "and." The first pair is kindred to Jesus, and the women are unnamed; it is paralleled by the other pair, who are not kindred, and whose names are given. (ii) It accords with John's custom to withhold the names of himself and all his kindred, so that in his Gospel he nowhere gives his own, his mother's or his brother's name, nor does he even give the name of our Lord's mother, who was his aunt. (iii) This family relationship would explain in part why Jesus, when dying, left the care of his mother to John. It was not an unnatural thing to impose such a burden upon a kinsman.

e) If John names FOUR women, then we have no Biblical basis for the idea that "James the son of Alphaeus" is to be identified with "James the Lord's brother."

3. *Can "James the son of Alphaeus" and "James the son of Clopas" be the same person?* Such an identification also requires us to say that "James the son of Alphaeus" must also have been known as "James the Less" (who was the son of Clopas). Is this identification possible? No. Who were the parents of James the Less? Not Joseph and Mary, but Clopas and Mary.[19] That being true, if it is James the Less who is called a "brother of Jesus" (as Paul describes him), the term "brother" must be used in a loose sense. Furthermore, there is no evidence that James the Less was ever one of Jesus' apostles, like "James the Son of Zebedee," and "James the son of Alphaeus" were. It is also apparent that "Alphaeus" and "Clopas" are not the same persons, since "Alphaeus" and "Clopas" [Cleophas] can hardly be two different ways of spelling the same man's name. As noted above, "Mary, the wife of Clopas" (who was the mother of James the Less and Joses) was at the cross when Jesus was crucified (Matthew 27:56, Mark 15:40, John 19:25). Only if "Clopas" could also be spelled "Cleophas" might an identification with "Alphaeus" be made. This is hardly possible.[20]

---

[19] The mother of "James the Less" is a woman named "Mary" (Matthew 27:56; Luke 24:10; Mark 15:40). He had a brother named "Joses" (Matthew 27:56). The father of "James the Less" is a man named "Clopas" (Matthew 27:56; Mark 15:40; John 19:25).

[20] McGarvey, *FourFold Gospel* (Cincinnati: Standard, nd), p.224, argued that "Clopas" and "Alphaeus" are two ways of spelling the same name. Ropes, "James" in the *International Critical Commentary* (Edinburgh: T&T Clark, 1916), p.58 argued that such an identification is "linguistically unsound." Robert Scott ("The General Epistle of James" in the *Bible Commentary* edited by F.C. Cook [New York: Scribners, 1904], p.108) shows how this is so. Summarizing what he wrote: "Cleophas" in the Textus Receptus of John 19:25 is a mistake, probably traceable to the Vulgate. The two names are, in fact, essentially distinct. If the name were *Klōpas*, that might be equal to the Aramaic *Halphai* (*Alphaios*). But the name is spelled *Kleopas*, which is a Greek name shortened from *Kleopatros*, as *Antipas* from *Antipatros*. *Kleo-* might become, by contraction, either *Klei-* or *Kleu-* (*Kleisthenēs* or *Kleudamos*), but not *Klō-*. In the Syriac Version we do not find both Alphaeus and Clopas represented by the Syriac *Chalpai*; but we do find Alphaeus rendered by *Chalpai*, while Clopas is represented as *Kleopha*.

This whole question has wider ramifications, since the Hieronymian view is dependent on identifying "Alphaeus" and "Cleophas" as being two ways of spelling the name. That's the only way the "sons of Alphaeus" (Clophas) could be Jesus' "cousins." The Hieronymian view seems to flounder on John 7:5, where Jesus' brothers are described as "not believing on Him." If that is true, how could any of them have been among the original 12 apostles?[21] If "Alphaeus" and "Clopas" are not the same people, then we have no way of knowing who Alphaeus' wife was, or whether he had any children other than a son named James.[22]

4. *Can "Jerusalem James" be identified with one of the original apostles of Jesus*, such as "James, the son of Alphaeus"? We have already shown that "James, the Lord's brother" and "James, the son of Alphaeus" are not the same person. In spite of this, arguments have been marshalled in favor of identifying the "son of Alphaeus" as being the same person as "the brother of the Lord". (a) If the two men are distinct, then one of them (James, the son of Alphaeus, one of the original 12 apostles) disappears altogether from the New Testament after Acts 1:13. It is asked, "Would we have James the apostle disappear, and another James (almost unintroduced as is Luke's custom in Acts) suddenly taking a prominent position in the church at Jerusalem?" Yet several of the apostles do disappear (e.g., Simon the Zealot, Bartholomew, and Thomas) and Acts 1:14 may be considered sufficient introduction for the second James (i.e., the Lord's brother), for at 1:14 Luke speaks of "His brethren." (b) If the two men are distinct, we have certainly two, and in all probability three, sets of brothers bearing the same names. We have James, Joseph, and Simon, the Lord's brothers. Then we have James, Joses, and Symeon, the sons of Clopas. And Alphaeus had a son named James. (Did he perhaps have other sons named Joseph and Simon?) Yet these names were in common use by many Jewish parents for their boys, so not much stress can be laid on this argument. (c) If the two men are one and the same, then there is little evidence in the Gospels that Mary, the mother of Jesus, gave birth to other children besides Jesus, which is a conclusion about Mary that is appealing to many. The fact that our Lord, on the cross, committed Mary to the care of the apostle John is then thought to support the conclusion that Mary did not have other children of her own. Yet there are several reasons to doubt that Mary was the mother of only Jesus: i) Jesus preferred to place His mother in the care of a believer rather than a non-believer; and His brothers were unbelievers until after His resurrection (John 7:5). ii) If John were a nephew of Jesus' mother (Mary and Salome were sisters), there is nothing unusual in Jesus' committing Mary to John's care. iii) If "the sons of Alphaeus" and the "brothers of the

---

[21] Defenders of the Hieronymian view have attempted to blunt the force of this argument from John 7:5. Some have tried to show that the word "belief" can have various shades of meaning, so it does not follow the brothers were total unbelievers. Others have tried to show that John 7:5 does not require all the brothers to be unbelievers. Still others have supposed there were several sets of "brothers" (cousins), and John 7:5 tells us only one set were unbelievers. The set who were believers could then be included among Jesus' original apostles.

[22] The apostle Matthew was also known as Levi. Levi's father was named Alphaeus (Mark 2:14). Whether or not it is the same Alphaeus who was the father of James, we have no way of ascertaining.

Lord" are the same group of people, then we must also defend the idea that *adelphos* can mean "cousin." As is shown above, this is hard to do. (d) The Epiphanian View (see page xv above) also treats the two men as one and the same. It is thought that the behavior of the brethren towards Jesus as they try to thwart His ministry and get Him out of the public spotlight (because they fear He has lost His senses) is that of elders towards a younger. But not necessarily. They came to assist His mother, if she needed help to persuade Jesus to give up His ministry and come home (Mark 3:21,31; Matthew 12:46). When all have grown to manhood (as Jesus and the brethren would have by the time Jesus is in His public ministry), a few years difference in age does not count for much. (e) Appeal has also been made to references in the apocryphal gospels to prove that the Lord's brother and the son of Alphaeus are the same person. A narrative contained in the *Gospel According to the Hebrews* (as quoted by Jerome),[23] represents James the Just, the Lord's brother, as present at the institution of the Lord's Supper. If true, he would be one of the Twelve (cf. Matthew 26:20). The superscription of the apocryphal gospel of James (*Protevangelium Jacobi*) assumes the same view, i.e., that James the Just was one of the original Twelve. However, the apocryphal gospels are hardly trustworthy sources of information.

To balance the account, it seems well to list again the arguments for insisting that "James the son of Alphaeus" and "James the brother of the Lord" are two distinct persons. (a) It enables us to give the term *adelphos*, "brother," its natural meaning. (b) The "Lord's brethren" are mentioned in the Gospels in connection with Mary the mother of Jesus, or with Joseph, His reputed father, never once with Mary of Clopas (the assumed wife of Alphaeus). It surely would have been otherwise if the latter Mary were the mother of "the brother of the Lord." (c) The attempted identification of "the son of Alphaeus" and "the "brother of the Lord" apparently began with Jerome in the 4th century AD; the identification was not heard of before Jerome's day. Jerome invented the theory of identification (see his *ad Matth.* xii), and it has been generally followed by Catholic scholars. It helps make the case for the "perpetual virginity" of Mary. There is no tradition in the Early Church Fathers in favor of the Epiphanian or Hieronymian theories. It was the opinion of Hegesippus, Eusebius, Gregory of Nyssa, the *Apostolic Constitutions*, and the majority of the church fathers that "the son of Alphaeus" and "the Lord's brother" were different persons.[24] The New Testament clearly shows a distinction between the "brethren" of the Lord, and the "Apostles (disciples)" of the Lord (John 2:12, 7:5; Mark 3:21,31). Moreover, early church traditions after the close of the apostolic age make James the Lord's brother one of the Seventy, but never one of the Twelve. If he were one of the Twelve, this would be hard to explain. The "brother of the Lord" could not have been one of the original apostles (as James the son of Alphaeus was), for the brothers of the Lord "did not believe on Him" (John 7:5).

---

[23] The apocryphal gospel exists only in such fragments as may be gleaned from Patristic writings.

[24] Samuel Davidson, *An Introduction to the New Testament* (London: Samuel Bagster, 1851), Vol.3, p. 303.

5. *How can "Jerusalem James" be called an "apostle"* in Galatians 1:19? If it could be shown that "Jerusalem James" and "James the son of Alphaeus" were the same persons, then he is called an "apostle" in Galatians 1 because he was one of the original Twelve. But since this identification cannot be made, then he must have become an "apostle" of Jesus at some time after Jesus' resurrection and ascension. Hieronymian-view defenders believe this is a hard doctrine to accept, yet Matthias, Barnabas and Paul became apostles of Jesus at a later time. Why not James, the brother of the Lord? James did see the risen Lord (1 Corinthians 15:7), thus meeting that qualification to be an apostle (Acts 1:22). He is identified as an apostle (Galatians 1) equal with the Twelve (Galatians 2).[25]

It is the studied conclusion of this commentator that "Jerusalem James," the "brother of the Lord" is not the same person as "James, the son of Alphaeus," and that "Jerusalem James" was not one of the original Twelve apostles whom Jesus chose. The attempt to identify "James, the son of Alphaeus" with "James the brother of the Lord" must be abandoned.

Our study of the authorship of this letter requires a careful look at the **External Evidence** for the authorship of the Epistle of James. External evidence comes in four kinds: allusions, quotations, annotated quotations, and canonical listings. Let us look at each.

1. *Allusions* (references or paraphrases that prove the book exists) and *Quotations* (the letter is quoted but the author is not named nor is the name of the book given).[26]

Clement of Rome (AD 96)
"Abraham called [God's] friend was found faithful in that he was obedient to the words

---

[25] We reject the view of some that Barnabas and James and some others called "apostles" were a sort of "sub-apostle" since they were not of the original Twelve. This is faulty church polity. No solid evidence has ever been presented that the apostolic college was limited to the Twelve and the Twelve only. (Remember, there are "apostles of Jesus" and "apostles of churches." Those called by Jesus are of equal authority and jurisdiction.) It is also a faulty interpretation of Galatians 1:19 to have Paul saying "I didn't see any other apostle [besides Peter], but I did see James." That James, too, is called an apostle is demanded by what follows in Galatians 2:6-9. In fact, Galatians 1:19 treats James, though not one of the original Twelve, as an apostle just as it speaks of Peter being an apostle of Jesus. There was a time that the inner three apostles were Peter, James (son of Zebedee) and John. After James' death (Acts 12), did the Lord's brother become one of the inner three, and thus a reputed pillar (Galatians 2)? We have rejected the argument of Davidson (*op. cit.*, p.309-311) that the James of Galatians 1 is the brother of the Lord, but is a different person from the James of Galatians 2, which Davidson proposes to be one of the original Twelve. Davidson insists that church tradition, which ascribes leadership at Jerusalem to "James the Lord's brother" is simply wrong, or at best, confused, obscure, and contradictory.

[26] The citations can be found in Mayor and Davidson. Not all the evidence adduced by these writers is admitted by other scholars. Ropes (ICC) has no reference to this type of evidence for authorship at all. Of course, those who adopt a second-century date for James must give some other explanation to the similarities between James and second-century early Christian literature (e.g., they all copied a common source, or the writer of "James" was acquainted with Clement and Hermas). So the evidence from these "allusions" must be carefully weighed.

of God ... Through faith and hospitality a son was given him in his old age; and by obedience he offered him a sacrifice to God." 1 Clement 10, cp. James 2:21,23.

"By faith and hospitality Rahab the harlot was saved." 1 Clement 12, cp. James 2:25 and Hebrews 11:31. There are also reminiscences of James 1:18 in 1 Clement 11, and of 4:1 in 1 Clement 46.

Clement's quotations of Proverbs 3:34 and 10:12 in chapter 30 and 49 agree closely with James' version of those passages, differing from both the Hebrew and LXX.

The Epistle of Barnabas (AD 130)
Mayor has noted what appear to be allusions to James 1:8,18,21, 2:6,7, 3:1, 5:5,9,12.[27]

Ignatius (d. AD 116)
Mayor suggests resemblances to James 1:4,5,16, 3:17.[28]

Polycarp (d. AD 155)
Mayor finds allusions to James 1:18,25,26, 3:2, 5:20.[29]

The Shepherd of Hermas (AD 150)

"For if you resist him (the Devil), he will flee from you with confusion." (Lib.ii. *Mandat.* xii.5). Cp. James 4:7. Note, there is some question whether Hermas alludes to James, since this saying was a current Jewish proverb, too.

For further parallels between Hermas and James, compare *Mand.* xii.6 with James 4:12; *Mand.* ix.1 with James 1:8; and *Vis.*iii.9 with James 5:4.[30]

Justin Martyr (d. c.AD 165)
Mayor lists allusions to James 1:18, 2:7,19, 5:12,16.[31]

---

[27] Mayor, *op. cit.*, p.liv, lv.

[28] *Ibid.*, p.lvii-lviii.

[29] *Ibid.*, p.lviii.

[30] Alfred Wikenhauser *(op. cit.,* p. 475) notes that on the basis of the evidence from Clement and Hermas, "many scholars infer that James was known and esteemed in Rome at an early date, but was later forgotten [since some have alleged it doesn't appear in the Muratorian Canon or the Old Latin Version]." "The allusions in Hermas are strong enough that both Moffatt and Laws use them to establish *a terminus ad quem* for the book of James at AD 90." (P.H. Davids, *Commentary on James*, NIGNTC [Grand Rapids: Eerdmans, 1982], p.8.)

[31] Mayor, *op. cit.*, p.lxii.

Irenaeus (d. AD 203)

"Abraham believed God, and it was counted to him for righteousness, and he was called the friend of God." (*Advers Haeres*. IV.xvi.2)   Cp. James 2:23.

Hippolytus (AD 220)

"Judgment will be without mercy to the one who shows no mercy" is a reflection of James 2:13.[32]

2. *Annotated quotations* (where the author is named).

Origen (d. AD 253) is the first to name James as the author of the letter we are studying.

"For though it be called faith, if it be without works it is dead, as we read in the epistle ascribed to James." (*Commentary on the Gospel of John*, at 19:6).   Cp. James 2:26.

"Ascribed" (*pheromenē*) likely reflects the fact that some in the third century questioned whether James was the author of the epistle, though Origen himself cited the epistle as being by James (especially in his works that exist only in Rufinus' Latin version).   (See *Ad Rom*. iv.1 and *Hom in Lev*. ii.4 and *Hom in Josh*. vii.1 and *In Psalm*. xxx.)

In Origen's *Commentary on Matthew* at 13:35, he discusses the four brothers of Jesus. Origen treated at some length the reputation and righteousness of James, whom Paul mentioned in Galatians 1:19, and then referred to Jude, who in the preface of his letter (Jude 1:1) referred to himself as the brother of James.   While it is not specifically stated, the whole discussion leaves the impression that Origen connected the epistle of James with the Lord's brother.

Jerome

"James, called the Lord's brother, surnamed Justus, wrote only one epistle, which is among the seven catholic ones; which too is said to have been published by another in his name, but gradually in process of time, it has obtained authority." (*Catal. Script. Eccles*. cap.2)

Jerome recognizes that in his time some spoke against the view that James was the author of the letter, i.e., it was *antilegomena* [see below].

Ephraem, the Syrian

He quotes James 4:9, prefacing the citation with "James, the Lord's brother says."

---

[32] E.C.S. Gibson, "James" in the *Pulpit Commentary* (Grand Rapids: Eerdmans, 1962), p.xii.

3. *Canonicity*

The epistle of James is quoted as "scripture" in *Two Letters Concerning Virginity* (1:11), a work for a while falsely attributed to Clement of Rome. This work was apparently written in Palestine or Syria in the first half of the third century.

When we come to the period of the guarding of the canon,[33] the epistle of James was treated as one of the "Antilegomena" (i.e., some folk in some places spoke against it being included in the New Testament canon).[34] It was rejected by some as late as the time of Eusebius (AD 325). Eusebius himself explained that some denied the book because few ancient writers had quoted from it (HE. 2.23 and 3.25 and 3.2).[35] Eusebius quotes 4:11 and 5:12,13,16, speaking of these verses as "scripture" and as written by "the holy apostle" (*Eccl. Theol.* ii.2, iii.2 and *Comm. in Psal.*). It was not questioned because any fault was found with its doctrine, but merely because it had not been widely used in the church in earlier years. The lack of use can be attributed to: (a) Its general address (sent to no specific person or church); (b) Its non-theological nature (it is full of commands to practical living, but little of a doctrinal nature); and/or (c) The perplexity over the identity of the persons called "James" in the apostolic period (as the debate about the "brethren of Jesus" raged). The Muratorian Canon omits James, but it also makes no mention of Hebrews or the letters of Peter and the text of the manuscript is corrupt (or at best doubtful), so that little weight can be attached to any evidence from this source. Some of our extant copies of the Old Latin Version contain James, but how early it was translated into Latin is debated. There is some question whether Tertullian, who used the Old Latin Version, has any allusions to James. There are some resemblances to James in his writings, but they are quite insufficient to prove he was acquainted with the book. The Peshitto Syriac ver-

---

[33] The period we call "the Guarding of the Canon" is not the first time New Testament books were accepted or rejected as being canonical. Apostolic writings were accepted as soon as they were received. It is only when heretical books (with apostles' names forged) appeared that the whole question of "canon" had to be re-examined. The later church, only with care and deliberation, continued to accept the books that earlier had won approval as canonical.

[34] Other books included in Eusebius' "Antilegomena" were the Epistles of Jude, 2 Peter, 2 & 3 John. When the period of the "guarding of the books" was at its zenith, the decision to include books in the canon was not made mechanically or without consideration of doubts and difficulties. There was no central authority to impose the decision, but rather independent churches and scholars arrived at pretty much the same conclusion. Once it was pronounced (e.g., at the Council of Laodicea, AD 364) it was unanimously accepted in both East and West because it was universally recognized as being the correct decision. So, when different scholars would question the decision reached, the burden of proof falls to those who would question or reject the decision then made. It is not the books that ought, on demand, again and again to be placed on trial, but the pleas of those who would once more call their genuineness or authenticity into question.

[35] In HE. II.23 he wrote, "These accounts are given respecting James, who is said to have written the first of the Catholic Epistles; but it is to be observed that it is considered spurious [by some]. Not many, indeed, of the ancients have mentioned it, nor yet that called the Epistle of Jude, which is also one of the seven called Catholic Epistles. Nevertheless, we know that these with the rest are publicly used in most of the churches." In Book III.25, Eusebius ranks James as among the "antilegomena," "which are nevertheless well known and recognized by most."

sion[36] (which was a revision of the Old Syriac and was completed about AD 425) included James in the canon of sacred books. If the original readers of James were chiefly in Syria and regions adjacent, they would be in the best situation to know the truth about the subject.

As the period of the guarding of the canon came to a close, Eusebius and Jerome (c. AD 400) placed their stamp of approval on the book. Then the Council of Carthage (AD 397) also recognized its canonicity.[37]

The Greek fathers of the fourth century all quote James as canonical, and are supported by their contemporary Latin fathers. "Athanasius of Alexandria, the author of the *Synopsis Sacrae Scripturae*, Cyril of Jerusalem, Gregory of Nazianzum, Epiphanius, Philastrius, Chrysostom, etc. all received James as canonical."[38] At the time when the canon was being guarded, the churches in the east showed less hesitation about continuing to include James than did those in the west.

Some Reformation leaders mistrusted James, some on account of internal evidence, and some (e.g. Luther, Erasmus) because they thought James contradicted Paul's writings (on justification by faith). When Luther wrote his opinion that our epistle was "not the writing of any apostle" he was starting from the erroneous supposition that "James" the writer was to be identified as being the "son of Zebedee," which Luther denied strenuously. James was one of four books that Luther relegated to his appendix – Hebrews, James, Jude, and Revelation. However, the Lutheran church has not followed Luther's lead. They have restored these books to the "canon." Moreover, the passage in Luther's German New Testament (AD 1522) containing the statement about "an epistle of straw" was never reproduced in any later edition and is now omitted from the preface of his translation that is made available to today's church.

German rationalists attacked the authenticity of the epistle of James, alleging a post-apostolic date for its writing. Modern criticism arose with DeWette in his *Einleitung*, 1826. Allegations were advanced that James shows an acquaintance with Old Testament

---

[36] What commentators before 1900 called the "Old Syriac Version" is now called "Peshitto Syriac Version." It is now known there was an older Syriac version, dated about the close the second century, or AD 190-200), of which only 2 manuscripts survive. This older version is now designated "Old Syriac." The Peshitto canon contained all the New Testament books except 2 Peter, 2 & 3 John, Jude and Revelation. About AD 508 a new translation was made, called the Philoxenian Syriac, of which very little has come down to us. The manuscripts that are known to us contain only the books not found in the Peshitto.

[37] The doubts which Eusebius recorded were even in his own time ceasing to exist. Athanasius, writing a very short time afterwards (AD 367), in his thirty-ninth festal letter, makes no distinction between acknowledged and disputed books, and uses the order of books common even now to the Eastern Church, placing all seven of the Catholic Epistles immediately between Acts and the Epistles of Paul, thus showing they are of equal authority,. Cyril of Jerusalem (AD 349) did the same (Lect., IV.x.36).

[38] Davidson, *op. cit.*, p. 338.

apocryphal writings [Wisdom and Ecclesiasticus] which were not alluded to in Christian writings until after the apostolic fathers, and if the writer of James were so acquainted, it could not be the brother of the Lord who wrote it. Further allegations were advanced that the writer of James 5:12 was acquainted with the post-apostolic *Gospel According to the Hebrews*.

Modern critical scholars who treat James as a pseudonymous writing thereby impugn its right to a place in the New Testament canon.

Theories of Pseudonymity[39]

Origen, Eusebius, and Jerome noted that because at the time (2nd and 3rd centuries) many heretical books were being written pseudonymously, there were some in the church who were suspicious that James was possibly pseudonymous. Carefully observe that they do not say that as early as the first century there were those who thought it pseudonymous.[40] Nor is there any heretical or Gnostic doctrine taught in the letter that would make James anything like the works that actually were pseudonymous.

A majority of modern scholars favor a post-apostolic date for our letter and pseudonymity for authorship. What follows are three examples which are typical of how modern writers are treating James.

> Barclay marvels that in James there are only two incidental references to Jesus, and none at all to His resurrection or to Jesus as the Messiah. No mention is made directly, or by implication, of Christ's sufferings or death. Add to this the good Greek and "it is next door to impossible to think of James actually penning this letter."[41]

> Dibelius wrote, "It is comprehensible that a Christian at the end of the first century who wished to impress a practical Christianity upon the church would choose

---

[39] Pseudonymity says the name signed to many of our Bible books was not the real author's name. Whoever collected the materials in their present form assigned the name of some famous (or even obscure) Bible person as being the author.

[40] Some appeal to 2 Thessalonians 2:2 for evidence that even during the time of the apostles there were those who were forging apostles' names to documents they wanted circulated. There is no way to show whether or not the documents alleged to be by Paul which were being circulated at Thessalonica were even signed. 2 Thessalonians 3:17ff might indicate they were not.

[41] William Barclay, *Letters of James and Peter* in Daily Study Bible (Philadelphia: Westminster, 1960), p.38,39. The answer to Barclay's assertions is based upon the purpose of the book. James is not presenting the Gospel. He is appealing to Jesus' teaching as the reason for careful living. He assumes their common roots in the Christian religion and emphasizes man's obligation. Further, there may be a reference to the resurrection of Jesus in "Lord of Glory" (James 2:1). Finally, how can Barclay claim there is no reference to Jesus as the Messiah when James constantly uses the title "Christ" of Him?

James as his patron since he was called 'the righteous'."[42] Dibelius is essentially accusing a Christian of lying. And without evidence,[43] Dibelius also insists that pseudonymity was practiced by the church in the late first century!

Others set forth[44] the hypothesis that the Biblical form of James actually evolved in two distinct stages of composition. James the Just was responsible for most of the books' raw materials, which he delivered first as sermons and which were then preserved by the Jewish Christian Diaspora (James 1:1, Acts 8:4, 11:19). These precious memories of James were then edited and written by another, likely after James' death, under the pressures of the educational mission of an expanding church. The editor who produced the Biblical form of James may have done so without any religious agenda of his own; he simply wanted to preserve the most enduring "sayings of James" for a future readership.[45]

Proponents of the idea that James is a pseudonymous work have problems finding a reason for making this forgery. Would not a writer composing a "fictitious" work have taken more pains to identify the "James" who supposedly was the writer? A separate extant spurious letter with "James" forged on it as a signature reads, "James, bishop of Jerusalem, to Quadratus."[46] And would not a second century writer composing this "fictitious" work have avoided the appearance of contradicting Paul's doctrine of justification by faith? There is no sufficient motive for a forgery, for the epistle of James is singularly lacking in doctrinal statements. By contrast, most second-century and later forgeries were done in defense of Gnosticism.[47] The abundance and naturalness of the verbal parallels in James to the teaching of Jesus (see pg. vii) do not suggest the work of some second century forger. A decisive argument against pseudonymity is the lack of detail about the writer's personality or activities. Critics who insist on the pseudonymity

---

[42] Martin Dibelius, *Fresh Approach to the New Testament and Early Christian Literature* (Westwood, Conn: Greenwood Press, 1979), p. 230.

[43] It will not do to quote second century authors to the effect that Mark was the "interpreter" of Peter, as though this were evidence of pseudepigraphy. Mark "translated" [into Latin?] what Peter was preaching. He did not publish books after forging the name "Peter" on them.

[44] See Davids, *op. cit.,* p.12-13.

[45] Redaction criticism is struggling here since, according to redaction critics, most redactors did have a specific theological, sociological, or literary intention in mind, as well as a specific *sitz im lebem* in some second-century church setting. All this is conveniently discarded by those attempting to use the redaction criticism method on the epistle of James.

[46] Theodore Zahn, *Introduction to the New Testament* (Chicago: Kregel, 1953), Vol. 1, p.148.

[47] Proponents of pseudepigraphy may reject calling such a production a "forgery." Nevertheless, there is a moral issue involved that should be recognized. See D. Guthrie, Appendix C, "Epistolary Pseudepigraphy" in Vol.2 of *New Testament Introduction* (Chicago: InterVarsity, 1961), p.282ff.

of the Catholic Epistles cannot have it both ways when they attempt to prove the forged authorship of the letters of James and Peter, for they elsewhere reject the Petrine authorship on the basis that the forger spent too much time trying to prove he was Peter. How strange that James is rejected because it has too little in the way of personal details!

The result of 19th, 20th, and 21st century higher critical handling of James is that the critics and their followers tend to regard James as an inferior product compared to some of the other books included in our Bibles. This is a sad and unwarranted conclusion.

THE LIFE OF JAMES

What do we know about the life of "Jerusalem James" from the pages of the New Testament and from early Christian literature?

1. He was a half-brother of Jesus. The two had the same mother, but not the same father (Matthew 13:55; Mark 6:3).

2. He was probably among those who sought an interview with Jesus somewhere in Galilee (Matthew 12:46).

3. He probably also went with Jesus to Capernaum (John 2:12).

4. He probably later joined in the attempt to persuade Jesus to go to Judea for the Feast of Tabernacles (John 7:3).

5. He himself went up to the Feast of Tabernacles, about 6 months before the crucifixion, but he was an unbeliever at the time (John 7:5,10).

6. After the crucifixion of Jesus, he apparently remained with his mother in Jerusalem.

7. We are told that after the resurrection, Jesus appeared to James also[1] (1 Corinthians 15:7). We suppose this post-resurrection appearance not only convinced him about who Jesus really was, but also served [when he told it] to convince the other brothers.

---

[1] Jerome (c. AD 345-419), *Lives*, ch.2, alluded to an apocryphal Gospel (*The Gospel According to the Hebrews*, fragments of which are quoted in various patristic writings), which contained an account of the risen Christ's appearance to James. The apocryphal gospel has several questionable claims in it. It claims that this was the first appearance of the risen Lord after his resurrection (which contradicts Mark 16:9) and that James had vowed to eat no bread from the time of the Last Supper until he had seen the risen Lord (which apparently contradicts the statement that only the Twelve were present with Jesus at the Last Supper, Matthew 26:20).

Also notice how Paul records this appearance. First he speaks of the appearance to James, and then He appeared to all the apostles. It seems that James was not one of the apostles at the time of the post-resurrection appearances.

8. He is next seen among the Lord's brethren, waiting for the coming of the day of Pentecost, which became the birthday of the church (Acts 1:14).

9. About AD 37, James was in Jerusalem and had a visit with Paul. Paul has just fled from Damascus, after a three-year visit to Arabia (Galatians 1:18,19; Acts 9:26).

James was regarded as an apostle (Galatians 1:19), though he was not one of the original Twelve.

Tradition says that James was appointed to his position of leadership at Jerusalem by the Lord Himself, and that the original apostles agreed with the choice. Eusebius wrote, "... there was James the Lord's brother, who is mentioned as having been appointed first bishop of the church at Jerusalem by the Savior himself." (HE ii.23)

Clement of Alexandria (as preserved by Eusebius, HE.ii.1) says this: "Peter and James and John, after the ascension of our Savior, did not contend for the honor, but chose James the Just as bishop of Jerusalem."[2]

10. By AD 44, James was a recognized leader in the church at Jerusalem (Acts 12:17).

11. In AD 51, James apparently presided at the Jerusalem Conference (Acts 15:13, 19 and cp. Galatians 2:1,9,10).

James may have worded the letter which was sent to the churches of Antioch, Syria, Cilicia, and Galatia (Acts 16:4) following the Conference.

12. After the conference, some Jews, professing to be Christians, came to Antioch of Syria in the interests of a Judaistic (Pharisaic) life-style, representing themselves as coming "from James" (Galatians 2:12).

This, however, does not mean that James sent them or even that he approved of their mission.

---

[2] Because Galatians calls James an "apostle" while Acts 15 ascribes to him no specific office (yet does show he held a commanding position in the local church), Guthrie thinks it was an anachronism to call him "bishop" of Jerusalem (something Jerome did, *De vir.* ill.2). This view may be modified by the fact that apostles did have "overseer" type duties and authority over all the churches.

13. The only other time James is mentioned in the New Testament is in connection with Paul's visit to Jerusalem at the close of his third missionary journey (AD 58). Paul presented the offering for the poor at Jerusalem to James (Acts 21:18-25). James, at this time, is still sympathetic to Jewish Christians exercising their Christian liberty and embracing certain Jewish practices (kosher food, vows and their corresponding sacrifices, etc.)

14. Concerning the death of James, two accounts have been preserved.

   a. Josephus, writing about AD 93, gives one of them.

   > Caesar, having learned of the death of Festus, sent Albinus as governor of Judea ... The younger Ananus, who followed the sect of the Sadducees who are very harsh in judging offenders ... having succeeded to the high-priesthood ... supposing that he had favorable opportunity in consequence of the death of Festus, Albinus being still on the way [to Judea], assembled the Sanhedrin, and brought before it James (the brother of him who is called Christ), and some others, and having charged them with being transgressors of the Law, delivered them over to be stoned. But those of the city who seemed moderate and most accurate in observing the Law were greatly offended at this, and secretly sent to the king [Herod Agrippa II] entreating him to order Ananus to act in such a way no more, saying that he had not acted legally even before this. And some of them went to meet Albinus on his journey from Alexandria, and inform him that Ananus had no authority to assemble a Sanhedrin without his permission ... For this reason King Agrippa took away the high-priesthood from him after he had been in office three months, and conferred it upon Joshua the son of Damnaeus.[3]

   If Josephus is correct, James was killed about AD 62.

   b. Hegesippus wrote in his *Memoirs*, AD 174-189 (they are preserved by Eusebius, HE. ii.23)

   > To the government of the church [at Jerusalem] in conjunction with the apostles succeeded the Lord's brother, James -- he whom all from the time of the Lord to our own day call the Just, for many have been named James ... There was a disturbance among the Jews and the Scribes and the Pharisees, saying that there was a danger that all the people would look to Jesus as the Christ. They came together therefore and said to James, "We pray thee restrain the people, for they have gone astray in regard to Jesus, thinking Him to be the Christ. We pray thee to persuade all that have come to the Passover about Jesus. For we all listen to thee ... Take thy stand

---

[3] Ant. XX.9.1.   Ralph Martin, "James" in *Word Biblical Commentary* (Waco, TX : Word, 1988). p.lxii, calls this passage from Josephus "the clearest and most historically reliable report" of James' fate.   Emil Schurer, *The History of the Jewish People in the Time of Christ* (Edinburgh: T&T Clark, 1890-91), Vol.1.ii, p.186ff) attempted to prove this passage in Josephus was an interpolation, but its genuineness has been defended by Mayor (p.lviii, note 2), Lightfoot (*Galatians*, p.366, note 2), and by Ropes (p.64).

therefore on the pinnacle of the temple, that up there thou mayest be well seen, and thy words heard by all the people, and persuade them not to go astray about Jesus ...."

Then the aforementioned Scribes and Pharisees set James on the pinnacle of the temple, and cried to him, "O thou just one to whom we are all bound to listen, since the people are going astray after Jesus who was crucified, tell us what is the door of Jesus." And he answered with a loud voice, "Why do you ask me concerning Jesus the Son of man? He is both seated in Heaven on the right hand of Power, and will come on the clouds of heaven." And when many were convinced and gave glory at the witness of James, and cried, "Hosanna to the Son of David," the same Scribes and Pharisees said to each other, "We have done ill in bringing forward such a testimony to Jesus, but let us go up and cast him down that they may fear to believe in him." And they cried out, saying, "Ho, Ho! Even the Just has gone astray," and they fulfilled that which is written in Isaiah, "Let us take away the just, for he is not for our purpose: wherefore they shall eat the fruits of their deeds."

And they went up and the cast down James the Just, and said to one another, "Let us stone James the Just." And they began to stone him, since he was not killed by the fall; but he turned round and knelt down saying, "O Lord God my Father, I beseech thee, forgive them, for they know not what they do." While they were thus stoning him one of the priests of the sons of Rechab, of whom Jeremiah the prophet testifies, cried out, "Stop! What do ye? The Just is praying for you." And one of them who was a fuller smote the head of the Just one with his club. And so he bore his witness. And they buried him on the spot, and his pillar still remains by the side of the temple [with this inscription], "He hath been a true witness both to Jews and Greeks that Jesus is the Christ." And immediately Vespasian commenced the siege.

Some of Hegesippus' details border on the fabulous. We should probably agree with Hort and Lightfoot that Hegesippus is reflecting an Ebionite romantic glorification of James, rather than a Biblical view.[4] In Hegesippus, James is called "the Just" because of his reverence for "the Law." To a Jew the word implied not merely being impartial and upright, but also having a studied and even scrupulous reverence for everything prescribed by the Law – the Sabbath, the synagogue worship, the feasts and fasts, purification, tithes, the moral and ceremonial ordinances. Since few of his details stand careful scrutiny, perhaps his statement that the siege immediately followed the death of James is in error, too. However, if his dating of James' death (just before Vespasian began the siege of Jeru-

---

[4] Lightfoot, *Galatians*, p.367. Hort, *The Epistle of James* (Minneapolis: Klock & Klock, 1980 reprint), p.xxii. Ebionites were an early Jewish-Christian sect who rejected the Pauline epistles and regarded James as their patron, falsely supposing he was in opposition to Paul. Hegesippus' account portrays James as a strict legalist (a Pharisee of the Pharisees, a Nazarite held in high repute by all the Jews). It also has him entering the Holy Place of the temple (that's improbable!) and has Jews setting him up as a witness against Christians. While the Ebionites would like to have pictured James in this way, it is not how he is portrayed in the pages of the New Testament.

salem) at the hand of unbelieving Jews is correct, we could date James' death as late as AD 68.[5]

DATE OF WRITING

Clearly, the date we might assign for the writing of this letter is closely connected with the question of authorship. Those who embrace the view that the epistle is pseudepigraphic (i.e., published under a forged name) will likely assign a late date for the letter. If an "apostle James" is the author, whether he be the son of Alphaeus or the brother of the Lord, the letter likely will be assigned a date in the middle of the first century.

Two extreme views have been proposed, both reflecting a denial of the traditional view of authorship.

1. Some have advocated a PRE-CHRISTIAN (i.e., Jewish) AUTHORSHIP for our letter.[1]

Arguments for this view include the questionable allegation that the Christian ideas in the epistle are interpolated (i.e., the Christian ideas were added later by some editor/redactor), and that it is more reasonable to find antecedents for James' teaching in Jewish moral teaching than in the teaching of Jesus.[2]

It is true that the only references to "Christ" in the book are found in 1:1 and 2:1, but

---

[5] Martin thinks the way to harmonize Josephus and Hegesippus is to think of the latter as telescoping events that were separated by several years (from AD 62 to AD 67-68). He could do this telescoping if there were some cause and effect relationship between Ananus' execution of James and the resulting war against the unbelieving Jews by the Romans.

[1] Two such authors are L. Massebieau who wrote in France in 1895, and F. Spitta who wrote in Germany in 1896. In 1930, the Massebieau-Spitta theory was reworked and advanced by both Arnold Meyer (*Das Ratsel des Jacobus Briefes*), who tried to make a case that James is an adaptation for Christian purposes of the *Testament of the Twelve Patriarchs* [the author of both our epistle and the Testament was named "Jacobus"], and by Hans Windisch (*Die Katholischen Briefe*). R.V.G. Tasker, *The General Epistle of James*, TNTC (Grand Rapids: Eerdmans, 1957) (p.35) nicely summarizes the Meyer-Windisch hypothesis. The whole hypothesis has failed to gain much support from the scholars because it overlooks the basic Christian element in the Epistle.

[2] Davidson, *op. cit.*, p.327-328, wrote, "The author's standpoint is Jewish rather than Christian. The ideas are cast in a Jewish mould ... We see little more than the threshold of the new system. It is the teaching of a Christian Jew rather than of one who had reached a true apprehension of the essence of Christ's religion. The doctrinal development is imperfect. ... In warning his readers against transgression of the law by partiality to individuals, the author adduces Jewish rather than Christian motives (2:8-13)."

there is no evidence that 1:1 or 2:1 are interpolations.[3]   The context of both verses make it "awkward if not impossible" for those verses to be interpolations.   Further, the epistle says much of Jesus being "Lord" and this is certainly not a Jewish belief.   The Christian passages cited (James 1:1, 2:1,7, 5:6,8,14) are integral parts of the epistle, interwoven in its argument, and cannot be taken out.   The epistle contains absolutely no teaching which is distinctly Jewish, whereas it does contain much that is distinctively Christian.[4]   The idea that a Christian editor worked over and changed a Jewish document is farfetched and without tangible proof.

2. Some have advocated a POST-APOSTOLIC AUTHORSHIP for the epistle.

The supposition is that James was written AD 120-150 and was a pseudonymous letter[5] written by some Christian teacher in some half-Hellenistic city of Palestine (perhaps Caesarea)[6] or elsewhere in the Empire.

Several arguments are advanced to support this theory: (1) The similarities between James, 1 Clement, and Hermas are treated as evidence that "James" copied those late first and early second century works.   Therefore, "James" is to be dated after Hermas.[7]   (2) The "low moral and religious tone among the readers is implied by the language of the writer."   Evidences of this "low tone" are discovered in the implied worldliness, degeneracy (1:13, 2:14), and the taking of Christians before Roman courts (2:6).   We reply that it is not the Christians who are dragging others into court, and the sins mentioned hardly indicate a date for the letter since they were no more prevalent in AD 150 than at any other time.   (3) The Greek style is too good for James (the Galilean peasant).   Not

---

[3] It is said that 1:1 and 2:1 would read better if the name of Christ were omitted.   And it is true that there may be some examples of interpolation of the name of "Christ" or "Lord" in the New Testament (cited as evidence are Colossians 1:2; 2 Thessalonians 1:1; James 5:14).   However, in those cases there is manuscript evidence indicating their possible omission.   Not so in James.

[4] Werner G. Kummel (*Introduction to the New Testament*, Rev, ed. [Nashville: Abingdon, 1975], p.409) has pointed out that Spitta's hypothesis ignores "a series of features which are comprehensible only in view of a Christian origin" and refers to 1:18,21,25, 2:7, 5:8,12 as containing teaching which could not have had a non-Christian Jewish origin.

[5] In the matter of the identity of the writer of this epistle, the doubtful conjecture of pseudonymity has been discussed under the topic of "Authorship."

[6] Julicher and Harnack (Tubingen School) advanced this hypothesis.   In 1924 F.C. Burkitt (*Christian Beginnings*:   University of London Press) introduced this idea in an English language commentary.   His thesis is that a short Aramaic letter (written by James) was greatly expanded by whoever translated the Aramaic original.   F.W. Young (JBL, LXVII, 1948, p.339-348) suggested that the Rahab material in James and 1 Clement points to James as the borrower.   The strong points and weaknesses of this whole theory are detailed in Tasker, *op. cit.*, p.36-37.

[7] The more generally accepted view is that Clement is the one quoting James.   One author has written that Clement is a "born quoter, with little originative gift."   If Lightfoot and others are correct in seeing James alluded to in 1 Clement, then James must belong to the first century (before AD 96).

so![8] The negative critics try to build up a basis for saying that the author was of Greek instincts and origin in the literary field, rather than Hebrew. But there is a closer kinship to the Old Testament prophets, than to the Greek writers of AD 150. (4) Ropes argued that James is like a Greek Diatribe. (A diatribe is a short abusive discourse by a cynic or stoic philosopher.) While there are diatribe-like similarities in James (i.e., dialogue, habitual phrases, numerous imperatives, rhetorical questions, etc.), most all of the sixteen things Ropes points out are common to all writing, not just to James or to the Diatribes. In fact, Foster spent a good deal of time refuting his teacher's idea that James is nothing but a diatribe.[9] Foster pointed out: (a) There is a greater seriousness and restraint of tone in James. The Diatribes were more of a bitter laugh at the world. (b) James addresses his readers as a group ("brethren"); the diatribe preacher thought of his readers/ listeners as individuals. (c) Diatribes are full of oaths, picturesque but vulgar. James 5:12 speaks for itself in the opposite. (d) James does not discuss the usual themes of the stoic and cynic (i.e., the true nature of freedom, the paradox that death is life, the doctrine that sin is ignorance, and that evils are good). (5) It is claimed that James is so contradictory to Paul's treatment of "Faith and Works" that it must come much after Paul wrote. Certainly, it is claimed, James could not be contemporary with Paul. Such a claim is based on a misunderstanding of both men's writings.[10] (6) The evidence listed above under "External Evidence for Authorship" is interpreted to mean that the epistle of James came but slowly into general circulation and was late in winning acceptance into the canon precisely because it was of late origin. Conservative scholars reply that the allusions found in Clement and Hermas, etc. are evidence the work was not written in the early second century. Further, there is a plausible explanation to the doubts expressed as the canon was being guarded. After the church began to flourish among the Gentiles a letter addressed to Jewish Christians would appear to have little appeal to the church as a whole. In addition, a letter addressed to a specific congregation would be more likely to be kept and treasured, with copies made, collected and disseminated, than a letter such as James addressed to no specific Christian community. (7) If the writing is pseudonymous, the earliest we likely would date the letter is some years after James' death, and the quotation in Origen is the latest we could date the letter.

Conservative views note there is not any reference or allusion to any datable event in the epistle. While this makes dating difficult, still certain things help to suggest a possible time of writing. Many commentators write something similar to this: "The Jerusalem Conference (Acts 15, Galatians 2) held in AD 51 is not specifically alluded to in the letter.   Therefore, the date of writing was either before the Conference, or some

---

[8] A subsequent section in these Introductory Studies will take up in detail the matter of James' "good Greek."

[9] Davids, *op. cit.,* p.12, tells us, "In fact, some classical scholars now question whether a distinct literary form of diatribe ever existed."

[10] See below, the section about "Paul and James" in these Introductory Studies.

years after it, so that the question discussed at Jerusalem is not a problem when James writes." This rather common statement needs some careful examination.[11] Other matters taken into account as we try to date the letters include the earliest and latest possible dates. The *terminus a quo* is AD 34. This is the date of the first persecution and dispersion of Christians. James speaks as if his readers are being harassed. The *terminus ad quem* is the death of James. The date for this was AD 62.[12] Some have argued that the absence of any reference to the AD 70 fall of Jerusalem, which is important in any chronology affecting Jewish people, is a matter that must be taken into consideration when trying to arrive at a date for the letter.

Within these *termini*, two possible dates for the epistle have been proposed by those who accept the Lord's brother as the author of the letter – an early date or a late date.

1. EARLY DATE of AD 45-50.[13]

Arguments advanced to support this date: (1) Internal evidence points to an early date, it is claimed. (a) One alleged evidence of an early date for James is the fact that "no complicated church organization ("no mention of bishops or deacons"[14]) is reflected in the letter.[15] However, "elder" (James 5:14) is not the only church leader alluded to. We find leaders called "teachers" (James 3:1). Bishops and elders are the same office in the New Testament (Titus 1:5,7; Acts 20:17,28). Deacons came early in the Jerusalem church (Acts 6). What can be made of the failure to name "deacons" in James? Nothing substantive as far as the date of writing is concerned! In several of Paul's letters no mention is made of these officers, and no one therefore dates those letters early. (b) "Believers still met in the synagogue" (2:2), it is asserted. However, "synagogue" simply means "assembly." Paul met with people in the synagogues when trying to evangelize

---

[11] Indeed the words "Jerusalem Conference" or "Apostolic Decree" do not appear in James. This is an argument from silence. In fact, we may very well have in our letter numerous allusions to the general theme of that conference, namely, what are the criteria by which a holy life before God is judged? As James gives his "marks of a genuine Christian life," over and over again his presentation is the exact opposite of what the Pharisaic Judaizers insisted were important. Perhaps James should be read with the issues that led to the conference firmly in our minds.

[12] See the documentation in our earlier notes about the "Life of James" concerning Josephus' and Hegesippus' accounts of James' death.

[13] Thiessen, R.C. Foster, Gibson, Mayor, Plumptre, Alford, and Robertson have advocated an early date. Mayor's commentary on James has long been regarded as a classic, so his views have tended to be most influential.

[14] Implicit in this argument is the view that diocesan bishops did not appear till after the apostles have all died. Since James does not mention such "bishops," James must be a first-century work.

[15] It has also been urged that the reference to "elders of the church" (5:14) indicates the church is so young as to still be organized after the pattern of Jewish synagogues. This may be a flawed argument. At the close of the apostolic age, Christian congregations were still shepherded and overseen by elders, just as were the synagogues.

Jewish people, even up to the AD 60's. And in Egypt, Jews had better preachers than the Christians, so the Christians went to the synagogues to hear the Jewish preachers even in the second century AD. (2) The doctrinal character of the epistle is said to point to an early date. The question of the admission of the Gentiles into the church is not discussed, so the epistle must have been early, it is claimed. Yet this same point can also be used to prove that James was written late, since it might be posited that the problem of the admission of the Gentiles is not discussed in James because it had already been settled.

AD 45 has always seemed, to this commentator, to be too early for the writing of this epistle. We are hard pressed to explain the "Jewish Christian Dispersion" at such an early date. Proponents of this early date (such as R.C. Foster) have not given very satisfactory explanations for "manifold trials," etc.

2. LATE DATE of AD 60-62.[16]

Arguments advanced to support this date: (1) If James was written about 10 years after the Conference in Jerusalem, there would be no need to specifically mention the Conference, though the issues discussed and the Holy Spirit's prompted conclusion to the issues raised would still be of permanent validity for Jewish brethren. These James does reflect. (2) The subject matter of James is Christian living. You would expect the Gospels (and perhaps Acts) to be written before James, for these give instructions in "How to Become a Christian." (3) If James were written as early as AD 45, how many missionary journeys had Paul made? In fact, he is just beginning the first. So how could this letter be written to "the 12 tribes of the dispersion" (i.e., Christians the world over) if it were written so early? Since we do look to Paul as the one who carried the Gospel to the regions bordering the Mediterranean Sea, an early date for James likely requires that the epistle was written to areas where Christian converts had not yet been made. Of course, there were Jews present at Pentecost who became Christians, and by AD 45 there had been some missionary work (e.g., the Ethiopian treasurer, Cornelius, the Samaritans). (4) Co-incidences between James and other New Testament books have been pressed into the argument about date of writing. Among these similarities are coincidences between 1 Peter and James.[17] Which was first? Did James know Peter? Hardly, if James is written before AD 62, and Peter writes in AD 67. Did Peter know James? Possibly, since on any conservative dating for James, 1 Peter was written later. Also, there are co-incidences between James and Paul, especially Romans. Who wrote first? Did Paul know James? Possibly, if James were written before AD 58. Did James know Paul? Possibly, if James was written after AD 58. (5) Lewis A. Foster made this suggestion as he explained his thinking about the date of James:

If Paul wrote a letter to his beloved kinsmen (the Epistle to the Hebrews) in Palestine, then

---

[16] Lewis A. Foster, Barnes, Halley, Hort, Sanday (who encourages us to date the letter as late as it can be put in the life of James), and Tasker all opt for the late date.

[17] In three places, James and Peter both quote the same passages from the Old Testament.

it makes a beautiful picture to see James, the leader of the Jerusalem church, responding with a letter to his kinsmen in the West in answer to Paul's – showing the type of Christian living being preached in the East, and expected all over the Diaspora.[18]

A Proposed Date. The Conference at Jerusalem is dated AD 51. We propose dating James after the Jerusalem Conference.

- Such a date would allow us to take the address of James 1:1 at face value. It is possible to picture a widespread audience for the letter as Jewish Christians can (by this date) be found in a number of lands outside the Holy Land.

- Such a date would allow us to appeal to the stronger arguments used to corroborate both the early and late conservative dates.

- Such a date allows us to suppose that James did publicly answer the misuse of his name and example by the Judaizers (Galatians 2:12).

If James wrote a letter to his beloved kinsmen, the 12 tribes dispersed abroad, describing in that letter to them the kind of practical Christian living that adorned Christian doctrine, it makes a beautiful picture to then see Paul responding with a letter (i.e., the Epistle to the Hebrews) to his beloved kinsmen in the Holy Land, setting forth their need for faithfulness to the new covenant rather than allowing persecution and harassment to tempt them to defect back to Judaism.

One of the arguments often raised to show the error of the Judaizers was that if one were going to require circumcision, one had to keep the whole Law (Galatians 5:3). What is to keep us from thinking that James 2:10, "whosoever shall keep the whole law, and yet offend in one point, he is guilty of all," reflects the same post-Jerusalem Conference idea?

The anti-Judaizer passages in Romans and Galatians have some of the very same arguments found in James.[19] A mid-50's date for James, so that he deals with the same troubling issue for the church that Paul was, would provide an historical background that helps us explain the different emphases found in James' epistle. The Judaizers emphasized the traditions of the Pharisees as the condition of salvation. James and Paul both emphasize faithfulness to what God has revealed – whether, prior to the cross, it be faithfulness to the Law, or since the cross, faithfulness to the revelation has made through Jesus Christ.[20]

---

[18] Classroom lecture on New Testament Introduction by Lewis A. Foster at The Cincinnati Bible Seminary, 1954. Foster dates Hebrews in AD 63. Given James' apparent date of death in AD 62, Foster never did quite make clear how he could have James "responding" to Hebrews.

[19] Compare James 2:14-24 with Galatians 3:6,12 and Romans 3:19,29, 4:3.

[20] See below, the "Purpose of the Letter."

DESTINATION

The destination of *tois dōdeka phulais tais en tē diaspora* as given in James 1:1 is variously translated, with the variety attempting to convey to English readers the difficult decision that must be made by translators. The problem centers on the proper way to render *diaspora*. "To the 12 tribes dispersed abroad" is how the NASB has it. "To the 12 tribes of the Dispersion" is how the ASV translated it. What does "dispersed" (small "d") or "Dispersion" (capital "D") mean?

Diaspora or "Dispersion" is the technical name given to the Jews living outside the land of Israel and maintaining their religious faith while living among the Gentiles. This scattering of Jewish people throughout the inhabited world had resulted from two chief causes: forcible deportation and voluntary emigration. The Babylonians, Assyrians, Ptolemies, Seleucids, and Romans had all had a role to play in Jewish people becoming aliens away from their homeland.

Most contemporary scholars flatly reject what James itself says about its intended destination. A typical contemporary example is this:

> The address of James "to the twelve tribes in the Dispersion" (1:1) is impossibly wide for a real destination in geographical terms. [No other epistle takes so wide a range. 1 Peter, which comes nearest to it, does not extend beyond the small section of the "dispersion" that was to be found in the northern and central provinces of Asia Minor.] ... This epistle is not a letter sent from one place to another like the letters of Paul; rather the editor has adopted the letter form as a literary convention, to address the community to which he belonged.[1]

We see no plausible reason to reject what lies on the face of the letter. The writer addresses his letter to Jews (the regular meaning of "twelve tribes") who are living away from Palestine. About the only point to be discussed is whether he addresses all Jews or only those Jews who, like himself, have become followers of the Lord Jesus Christ. Three different interpretations have been given to "twelve tribes of the *diaspora*":

1. Jewish People Living Outside of Palestine

If "Dispersion" is taken literally, the reference is to Jewish people living in some part of the world other than the Holy Land (John 7:35).[2] "Twelve tribes" was a comprehensive designation for all the Jewish people. A brief review of Jewish history may prove helpful.

---

[1] Sophie Laws, "James, Epistle of," *Abingdon Bible Dictionary* (New York: Abingdon, 1992), V.3, p.623.

[2] Some social-science critics have attempted to demonstrate that in the first-century "Diaspora" had a metaphorical usage. It is asserted that references occur in Jewish literature from the period where the term diaspora is used of people living in the Holy Land, but who are cut off from social and religious support systems. Thus, some recent commentaries adopt the view that the letter is actually addressed to Jews living in the Holy Land. (It is certainly assuming too much to cite 1 Peter 1:1 and Isaiah 49:6 as examples of this metaphorical usage.)

At the death of Solomon, the Davidic kingdom was divided. The ten northern tribes were known as Israel, and the two southern tribes were known as Judah. As the years passed, the Jews were scattered (dispersed). In 722-21 BC, with the fall of the Northern Kingdom to Assyria, part of the Jewish dispersion took place. In 586 BC the two Southern tribes were captured by Babylon. All the leaders, political and social, were deported. Those who were left behind intermarried with the foreigners who were brought in. The Samaritans were the result of this intermarriage. At the close of the captivity (see Henry Halley's *Pocket Bible Handbook* on "Ezra") some from the tribes which had been deported returned to the Holy Land, and some did not. Pompey (63 BC) transported Jewish captives to the West, carrying hundreds of Jews to Rome. Thus, at the turn of the century, Jews recognized three great population centers of the Dispersion: Babylon, Syria, and Egypt. Rome was not far behind, nor were Asia Minor and North Africa.

It seems difficult to think of James as being addressed to the "Dispersion" in its technical sense. If this letter were sent to unconverted physical descendants of those who did not return, and to those scattered by later deportations, all of whom were unbelievers in Jesus, would it not say "Jesus is the long-promised Messiah. Accept Him!"? It seems apparent that the "twelve tribes of the dispersion" is not intended to be taken literally. It is not just "Jews" generally who are addressed, but as will be seen, the readers are also already believers in Jesus as the Messiah.

2. All Christians, whether ethnically Jew or Gentile, but who together comprise the "New Israel."

This second view of the words "twelve tribes" and "dispersion" is that they must be interpreted figuratively or symbolically. Such an understanding calls for a small "d" ("dispersion") or "scattered" as a translation for *diaspora*.

There is no doubt that at times "twelve tribes" has a figurative meaning. The Old Testament prophets used "twelve tribes" (or "tribes of Israel") to refer to a future, restored, spiritual Israel after the Messiah should come (Ezekiel 47:13,22; Isaiah 49:6; Zechariah 9:1). Paul contends that the "Israel of God" (Galatians 6:16) is a spiritual rather than an ethnic group. It is the "remnant" who belong to Christ that is "Israel" now that Christ has come (Romans 9-11). The Old Testament prophets looked forward to Gentiles being included in this "Israel of God" (1 Peter 2:10, Romans 9:25).

Diaspora can mean anyone away from home. Throughout the Scriptures, all Christians are considered as pilgrims, in a "dispersion" because they are away from their heavenly homeland (Galatians 3:7-9). This Christian pilgrimage is suggested in Hebrews 11:8-10 (when speaking of Abraham) and in 1 Peter 1:1 ("sojourners of the dispersion").[3]

---

[3] Whether "dispersion" means the same thing in both James 1:1 and 1 Peter 1:1 is difficult to decide. One could be taken literally, and one could be taken spiritually. The parallel between James 1:1 and 1 Peter 1:1 is not exact. Peter does not speak of "the twelve tribes" and, unlike James, Peter (in the Greek) uses "dispersion" without the article.

The geographical location where these readers are situated is not centered in any one locality. Commentators who opt for the late date of AD 60-62 for the writing of the letter are more likely to hold to the New Israel as being the destination of this letter, making this truly a "catholic epistle." James could be addressing the Christians all over the world, because an apostle has responsibility for all the churches (cp. 2 Corinthians 11:28).

3. Jewish Christians Living Outside of Palestine

Although 7% of the Roman Empire was ethnically Jewish, only a small subset of Jews lived in Palestine. Per Acts 2, the Jews present at Pentecost came from all over the world. Not only had their ancestors been scattered by forcible deportation, but years before Pentecost many Jews had voluntarily settled all over the world as traders, merchants, and in other jobs as opportunities arose. The commercial centers of Asia Minor, Alexandria, Antioch of Syria, Ephesus, Miletus, Pergamos, Cyprus, and Rhodes contained large numbers of Jews.[4] When the church began, the first converts were from among the Jewish people. When missions to foreign countries were undertaken, the first places visited were Jewish synagogues, and these furnished the first converts to Christianity in many cities and lands. There are intimations in James that the "dispersion" is limited; that it is not all the families of Israel, but is instead those among "Israel" who are Christians. Probably the reason the NASB has "who are dispersed" (small "d") is because the translators had decided this letter is addressed not just to Jews but to Jewish Christians.

Those who hold the readers were already **Christians** do so for the following reasons: (1) That they were Christian is seen from 2:1, "my brethren, as believers in our glorious Lord Jesus Christ." (2) That the readers were Christians is implied in the insistence of 5:7 that they need to be patient "because the Lord's coming is near." (3) If the readers were not Christians, we would expect instructions about how to become followers of Jesus Messiah. Such instructions are wholly lacking in our letter. (4) The readers are organized into "congregations" (churches) with elders. That is church (Christian) language. (5) The writer alludes to many of the teachings of Jesus as he authoritatively exhorts the readers how to live. An appeal to Jesus assumes a Christian sympathy on the part of the readers. (6) James would feel a responsibility for those who at a previous time were part of his congregation at Jerusalem, so attempts to instruct them about how to deal with the "trials" they are currently experiencing. (7) In addition, every Jewish feast would bring to Jerusalem representatives of the "dispersion" from "every nation under heaven." James likely would have come into contact with some of these. If some of these Jews were converted, as indeed were some on the first Pentecost after Jesus' resurrection, we can see James addressing his letter to include his newly converted brethren.

---

[4] In c. AD 40, Philo sent a letter to the Emperor Caius [Caligula] in Rome to get a revocation of the decree requiring Jews to pay divine homage to the Emperor's statue. He writes about Jews living in Jerusalem, Egypt, Phoenicia, Syria, Coele-syria, Pamphylia, Cilicia, Bithynia, Pontus, Asia Minor, Thessaly, Boetia, Macedonia, Aetolia, Attica, Argos, Corinth, Cyprus, Crete, Libya, etc. (*De Legat. ad Caium*, xxxvi.)

Those who hold the readers were not only Christians but were also **ethnically Jewish** do so for the following reasons: (1) That they were of Jewish descent is seen in the words "twelve tribes."[5] (2) Those Jewish Christians who were scattered by the persecution that erupted after the martyrdom of Stephen fled from Jerusalem to Judea and Samaria (Acts 8:2), and to Cyprus and Antioch of Syria (Acts 11:19). (3) The writer speaks of Abraham as "our father" (2:21) without any hint that this is to be understood in anything but the literal sense. By comparison, Paul speaks of Abraham as being the father of the faithful, but he specifically says "the father of all them who believe" (Romans 4:11). (4) The description of the meeting of the believers as being a "synagogue" (2:2) supports the idea the readers were Jewish, as does the use of the Hebrew title *kuriou sabaoth* ("Lord Almighty," "Lord of hosts", 5:4). In addition it could be affirmed that early Christian converts from Judaism did not cease to be Jewish in their life-styles and customs. (5) The writer assumes the readers are familiar with the lives of Abraham, Rahab, the prophets, Job, and Elijah. He assumes the readers are familiar with the Old Testament Scriptures. (6) There is use of "the Law" to enforce the commands against certain vices (2:9-11). Jewish people would be familiar with this authority.[6] (7) The language and illustrations (early and later rain, for instance) are Jewish.[7] (8) If the letter was written at the early date of AD 45-50, before the preaching of the Gospel to the Gentiles, the address must be to Christians who ethnically were Jewish.

The decision made about the date this letter was written will also influence the choice of destination. If a "Jewish Christian" destination for the letter is held, and the letter is held to be written early (i.e., AD 45-50), then you likely think the readers are living in Syria and other nearby neighboring states of Palestine.[8] If a "Jewish Christian" destination for the letter is held, but a date after the Jerusalem Conference is opted for, then you could have James addressing his letter to a larger portion of the Roman world, wherever Jews who have been converted in the first 30 years of the church's existence are now living. About the only viable explanation of "twelve tribes of the dispersion" is to have it addressed to Jewish Christians scattered over a wide region outside of Palestine, and have it written late enough that the gospel has reached these foreign lands.[9]

---

[5] Matthew 19:28 and Acts 26:7 also allude to "twelve tribes" so it cannot be said that the tribal divisions have long since disappeared (unless one is speaking of the actual division of the land into tribal inheritances). First-century Jewish folk could trace their ancestry to their respective tribes.

[6] This fact should be contrasted with the "royal law" to which he also appeals (2:8).

[7] Balanced against this is the fact that the epistle is written in very excellent Greek, and the fact that many of the illustrations are common Hellenistic ones.

[8] If the earlier date is adopted, the readers (converts to Christianity) would, of necessity, be living in a more restricted area outside of the Holy Land.

[9] At another place in these introductory studies we shall defend the idea that James was originally written in Greek (rather than Aramaic). That seems to D.E. Hiebert, *The Epistle of James* (Chicago: Moody, 1979), p.38, to be evidence the letter was originally addressed to readers living in the Greek, or Western, Dispersion.

PLACE OF WRITING

If we should be handed a letter to read, written in English, but which carried no postmark or return address, yet in it had references to sunshine, ocean breezes and beaches, citrus fruit, and hurricanes, we would naturally conclude that it was written by someone living in Florida. This would not be the only possible conclusion, but it would be the natural conclusion. If the letter talked of sunshine, citrus fruits, ocean breezes, mountain scenery, and earthquakes, we would conclude it likely came from California. If it talked of pea-soup fogs, brussels sprouts, and bombed-out buildings, we would probably think it originated from London, England, during World War II.

There are certain little indications of locale in the epistle of James. Combined with the evidence that the author was James, the brother of the Lord, who was connected with the Jerusalem church all his Christian life, these little indications of locale make convincing evidence that the letter was written in the land of Israel, perhaps Jerusalem. The scorching wind (1:11) suggests the terrible sirocco which sweeps up out of the desert. Springs that send up sweet water and springs that send up bitter water are common in Palestine (3:11). The three chief fruits of Palestine are mentioned – fig, olive, and vine (3:12). The early and latter rains, the former coming in October to make plowing and sowing possible and the latter coming in April to help assure a harvest, are plainly referred to (5:8).

If we accept the traditional view of authorship (i.e., James, brother of the Lord, with his life-long ministry in and around Jerusalem), we are limited to the conclusion the letter was written from Jerusalem.[1]

PURPOSE AND OCCASION OF THE LETTER

Almost every commentator, because of uncertainties about the letter's date and destination, has a different idea concerning the purpose James had in mind for writing. Here are some common examples:

1. James undertakes to meet the needs of his fellow Jewish Christians in the Dispersion. He wants each reader to become "a perfect man," writes one author.

---

[1] Those who reject James as the author offer numerous suggestions as to the place of authorship. One writer thinks it was written in Alexandria, another in Rome, and another in Antioch. These suggestions are the result of emphasizing those expressions in the letter that are alleged to reflect a Hellenistic rather than Palestinian milieu.

2. The author addresses any Christian into whose hands this letter may fall, and touches upon subjects of wide and general interest. Beneath the whole epistle plainly lie two pervading and strongly felt principles: (a) Against shams and pretense in the Christian life, and (b) the conviction that God and the world are incompatible as objects of man's allegiance. (R.C. Foster).

3. The object of the epistle is to console the readers in their adverse circumstances, to admonish and encourage them, and to censure the errors connected with their Christian lives. (Davidson)

4. The object of the epistle is evidently to exhort[1] these Jewish Christians to patience under the trials to which they were exposed. But while writing with this special object, James is not unmindful of the general needs of his readers, and takes occasion (a) to warn them against various sins and evil tendencies of which they stood in danger, and (b) to instruct them in various points of Christian morality. (Gibson).

5. Some writers detect what they think are "sermonic" themes, some finding portions of a dozen, some four or eight, different sermons.

6. On the supposition James was written early, the readers living in the "dispersion" were Jewish Christians, refugees from the persecution that began after Stephen's martyrdom. In such a situation the thrust of the letter might be how to handle the hardships of living when on the run, and when starting over in a new community.

7. Writers who have chosen a second-century date for the epistle suppose it has an anti-Gnostic purpose. Attempts have been made to identify certain Gnostic catch-words in the epistle.[2]

Having reached thoughtful decisions about authorship (James, the brother of the Lord) and destination (Jews who have become Christians, living outside of the Holy Land), and having wrestled with the possibilities for date of writing, we then examined likely situations into which this letter might fit. Consistent with the proposed date of AD 51 (i.e., after the Jerusalem Conference), the "dispersion" can be any Jewish Christian living

---

[1] A number of recent commentaries use the word "parenesis" to describe the purpose of James. The word comes from a Greek word that means "to exhort, to advise," and it is a favorite term of the literary critics. It was characteristic of parenesis to place together in loose organization a series of exhortations without any concern to develop one theme or line of thought that overarches the whole speech or writing.

[2] Gnosticism began as a Jewish heresy and later infiltrated the church. What is to keep us from supposing that the "catchwords" common to Gnosticism and James are from the Jewish background of each, rather than that James learned them from the Gnostics, or that the Gnostics culled them from James? Several commentators (Schammberger, Schoeps, Preisker) have seen James 3:13-18 (with its discussion of "wisdom that is earthly, devilish") as being a refutation of incipient Gnosticism.

outside the Holy land. This would include not only those refugees who fled from the persecution presided over by Saul (which resulted in the deaths of Stephen and others, Acts 6-8). It would also include Jewish Christians who are feeling the distress resulting from the push by the Pharisees to Judaize the church. There are evidences those false brethren went not only to Antioch, but also to Galatia and Achaia and perhaps even Rome.

This commentator has often wondered if James ever publicly answered the false use made by the Judaizers (i.e., Pharisees who pretended to become Christians, and who troubled the churches) of his name and example (Acts 15:1,24; Galatians 2:12). It would be Jewish Christians who would be most apt to be persuaded by the arguments of these false brethren. What about viewing this epistle as James' official response to that misuse of his public example? It would be addressed to those people most in danger of being misled by the Judaizers. Written after the Jerusalem Conference, it gives James' version of the Christian ethics that are really important in the Christian life, and without any mention of the things the false brethren emphasized!

LITERARY STYLE OF THE EPISTLE

What shall we call this writing? Is it an epistle, or a tract, or something else? James starts with an epistolary opening (i.e., signature, address, greeting), but there are no personal references or any farewell word. This is just the opposite of what we observe in Hebrews, where there is no epistolary opening, but we do have a typical epistolary ending for the work. There is no paragraph of thanksgiving as was customary in most first century letters and New Testament epistles. Sometimes James writes short, maxim-like sentences, which remind us of the book of Proverbs. At other times, as in James 2:5-10, he writes a long argument reminiscent of the long sentences in Paul. As a result, some identify James as part tract and part epistle. Others suggest that James originally was a sermon, edited into letter form at a later date. While we may not agree that it originally was sermonic in form, it does have all the characteristics of a work intended for public reading in the assembly of believers to whom it was addressed. Those who treat James as a second-century pseudonymous work tend to regard it as a moral treatise instead of a letter. We see no compelling reason to do other than identify this as an "epistle" from James.

Did James write in Greek or Aramaic? Not a few commentators opt for an Aramaic original, for a number of reasons. Aramaic was the language usually spoken by our Lord, they claim. Aramaic may have been the language used by Paul in his address to the mob at Jerusalem (Acts 21:40).[1] We are told by Papias that the Gospel of Matthew was originally written in *Hebraisti* (Aramaic?) and that, to begin with, everyone had to translate it as best he could. Papias also states that Mark acted as "interpreter" (translator) for Peter,

---

[1] *Hebraisti* may refer either to Hebrew or Aramaic. In the author's commentary on Acts it has been supposed Paul spoke pure Hebrew to the mob.

but this is capable of explanation without affirming Peter always spoke Aramaic.[2]   Jerome takes it for granted that the epistles of Peter were not originally written in Greek.   He bases his argument on the differences of readings in the various versions.   Some of the early church fathers suppose the epistle to the Hebrews was originally written in *Hebraisti* (Hebrew/Aramaic).   Also, a comparison of our present Greek text of James with several later versions shows some remarkable divergences.   These divergences are attributed by those arguing for an Aramaic original to the loss of meaning in translating from one language (Aramaic) to another (Greek).[3]

Arguments just as weighty can be advanced for a Greek original for James.   No ancient Aramaic manuscript of James has ever been found.   There are frequent examples of paronomasia (a play on similar sounding words[4]) that strongly argue against the Greek edition of James being a translation.   James uses many Greek expressions not easily retranslatable into a Semitic language.   The "Semitic idioms" acknowledged to be present in James may be explained by the author's knowledge of the LXX and his own ethnic background.[5]   The quality of the Greek in James rules out any theory that James might be a translation of an Aramaic original.   In fact, the author writes such good Greek that some try to use this as an argument against James (who they say was a Palestinian peasant) being the author.   Typical of the information used to call James "good Greek" is this paragraph:

> The author uses the Greek language with fluency and a certain sense of style.   Although not of the quality of classical literature, his writing shows grammatical ability and is virtually free of solecisms and colloquialisms.   He opens with "Greeting" using the infinitive *charein* as is usual in a Hellenistic letter (1:1, cf. 1 Macc. 10:18,25, 12:6, Acts 23:26); uses the rhetorical *age nun* (4:3, 5:1); and gives the correct oath form of the accusative of the thing sworn by (5:12), by contrast with Matthew's semitic idiom of *en* plus the dative.   He has a

---

[2] Peter and Mark were in Rome when Mark acted as his "translator."   What is to keep us from supposing Peter spoke Greek, and Mark translated it into Latin for his Roman audience?

[3] At the close of the 19th century, Wordsworth compared the epistle of James both in the Greek text available to him and in the Latin Codex Corbeiensis.   From this he was convinced that a different Greek text than our present one was behind the readings in Corbeiensis.   He offered the hypothesis that Corbeiensis reflected an Aramaic original.   Mayor has countered this hypothesis by showing that the variations in Corbeiensis can be explained by the usual principles of textual criticism without the need to postulate a theory of an Aramaic original.

[4] Often James links together clauses or sentences by a play on words.   See 1:1, 1:4, 1:12, 1:21, 5:16.

[5] Hebrew uses an infinitive absolute for emphasis.   For example, "Blessing I will bless" in the Hebrew means "I will surely bless you."   There are examples of this reduplication of the same word for emphasis in James, just as we would expect from someone who grew up in a Jewish home.   There are also places where James matches how the LXX translated certain Old Testament expressions.   "Thus he uses the compounds *prosopolempsia* and *prosopolempteo* (2:1,9, "partiality" and "to show partiality," derived from the LXX *prosopon lambanein*), and compound phrases like *poiein eleos* (2:13, "to show mercy"); *poietes logou* (1:22, "a doer of the word," cf. 4:11, *poietes nomou*, "a doer of the law"); *prosopon tes geneseos* (1:23, "natural face"); and *en pasais tais hodois autou* (1:8, "in all his ways," cf. 1:11).   Laws, *op. cit.*, p.627.

wide vocabulary, including some words not found elsewhere in the New Testament or LXX (e.g., "sea creature," *enalios*, 3:7; "daily," *ephemeros*, 2:15; "dejection," *katepheia*, 4:9). His style shows a fondness for alliteration, as in *peirasmois peripesete poikilois* (1:2, "you meet various trials") and *mikron melos estin kai megala auchei* (3:5, the tongue "is a little member and boasts great things"); and for the cadence of words with similar endings, as in *exelkomenas kai deleazamenos* (1:14, "lured and enticed") and *anemizomeno kai ripizomeno* (1:6, "driven and tossed by the wind" – the former word even may have been coined by James for this effect, as he may also have coined the evocative *chrysodaktylios*, "gold-ringed," 2:2). Alliteration and cadence are both found in James' admittedly imperfect hexameter: *pasa dosis agathe kai pan dorema teleion* (1:17, "every good endowment and every perfect gift"). This sensitivity to, and ability to make effective use of, the sound of the Greek language tells against any theory that the epistle has been translated from an Aramaic or Hebrew original.[6]

More can be said about the "good Greek." Greek is a participle loving language, and good Greek makes abundant use of participles. So does James. There is not a single instance of a genitive absolute, there are no optatives, and there is no accusative with an infinitive. There are 570 different vocabulary words used in the epistle. Of these about 70 (depending on which Greek text is being counted) do not occur elsewhere in the New Testament, and 25 of these do not occur in the LXX. Six words (*bruō, enalios, eupeithēs, euphēmos, thrēskos, katepheia*) are found in neither the New Testament nor the LXX. There are about twelve words that are rare, having their first known occurrence in James.

The current state of the evidence points to a Greek original for James, even when we assume it was written from Jerusalem. James is not the only Jerusalemite who was fluent in Greek. Since it had become available, the LXX was the version of choice, even in the temple services and synagogues.

TEXT

Modern Greek texts are critically reconstructed from evidence gathered from ancient Greek manuscripts, ancient versions, and patristic quotations.

A. Greek Manuscripts

1. *Papyrus manuscripts.* Among the papyri, fragmentary third century P[20] and P[23] and fifth century P[54] contain some verses of the epistle. P[20] contains James 2:19-3:9. P[23] contains James 1:10-18. The other papyrus manuscripts contain fewer verses. The sixth or seventh century papyrus P[74] has a substantial part of the whole epistle. The readings found in this manuscript are similar to those in Vaticanus and Alexandrinus.

---

[6] Laws, *ibid.*

2. *Uncial manuscripts*. The epistle is contained in Vaticanus, Sinaiticus, Alexandrinus, and Ephraemi, though Ephraemi is defective towards the close of the epistle, containing only 1:1 to 4:2. The majority of modern Greek texts of James tend to rely heavily on Vaticanus, which may be the oldest Greek manuscript of James still extant.[1] The epistle is also found in the later uncials Mosquensis of the ninth century; Angelicus [not to be confused with Codex Regius, of the Gospels] of the twelfth century; and Porphyrianus, a palimpsest of the ninth century in which James 2:12-21 are barely visible.

3. *Minuscule manuscripts*. Nearly 500 minuscules, most dating from the tenth to the eighteenth centuries, contain the letter, including 33 ("the queen of the cursives"[2]), an eighth or ninth century manuscript.

The Greek manuscripts display either the Alexandrian/Neutral text, or the Byzantine/Koine texts.[3] There is no manuscript extant which carries the Western text of James.

B. Versions

1. *Syriac*. The Peshitto (third century) and Philoxenian (fifth or sixth century) contain James.

2. *Egyptian Versions*. The Memphitic and Thebaic (second or third century) contain James.

3. *Latin Versions*. The New Testament was translated into Latin before AD 200. At this date, Tertullian in North Africa was using a Latin version that is now called the Old Latin. There are 30 or more manuscripts of the Old Latin, some being African and some being European Old Latin. All extant manuscripts are copies dating centuries later than the original translation into Latin. Some of them are witnesses that James was translated into the Old Latin. One of the best extant witnesses to James in the Old Latin is the ninth century Codex Corbeiensis, which is apparently an Italian recension of the Old Latin text.[4] Another example of an Old Latin manuscript of James are the readings extracted by Mai from the Speculum Pseudo-Augustini (wrongly ascribed to Augustine). Both of these manuscripts "testify to a common Greek text of which, ap-

---

[1] While a few words may differ in Sinaiticus, Alexandrinus, and Ephraemi, those uncial manuscripts tend to agree with the readings found in Vaticanus.

[2] The readings in Codex 33 generally agree with the text of James found in Codex Alexandrinus.

[3] The uncials from the ninth century and later, as well as the minuscules from the 10th century and later, became the textual basis for the Greek text of Erasmus and the Complutensian Polyglott. The Greek text of Erasmus eventually became the Textus Receptus, the Greek text that lies behind the KJV.

[4] Hort, *op. cit.*, p.109-111, has listed for us the "peculiarities of vocabulary in the Codex Corbeiensis of St. James." Mayor, *op. cit.*, p.3-27 reproduces the complete Latin text of Corbeiensis. The peculiar readings of this manuscript were the grist of many scholarly debates in the nineteenth century.

parently, a single translation [into Latin] was made."[5] The Greek text behind these Old Latin versions had close affinities to the text of Codex Vaticanus. A sixth century manuscript, Codex Bobiensis, also contains James. It, too, is classified as an Old Latin manuscript. The Old Latin was replaced with the translation made by Jerome known now as the Latin Vulgate. James is represented by numerous manuscripts from the Latin Vulgate. It is best preserved in Codex Amiantinus and Codex Fuldensis.

C. Today's Printed Texts

There is relative agreement among textual scholars concerning the text of James. It may be reconstructed with a high degree of accuracy from P^{74} and Codices Vaticanus, Sinaiticus, and Alexandrinus. Major textual variants are few.

PAUL AND JAMES

What is the relation of James 2:14-26 to the teaching of Paul in Romans and Galatians on "faith and works"? Answers to this question vary and often are mutually exclusive.

1. *James is deliberately contradicting the teaching of Paul* is one answer given since the time of F.C. Baur.

Based on Hegel's dialectic, Baur's theory proposed there were two antagonistic factions in the early church – a very pro-Jewish "Petrine" faction and a very anti-Jewish "Pauline" faction. Some books in our New Testament are Petrine, some are Pauline, and some present a mediating position (they were peacemakers). James is supposed to be one of the Petrine faction's books.

There are numerous items that make it difficult to accept the idea that "James is contradicting Paul." (a) In its original presentation, Baur's theory required acceptance of the view that the epistle of James was not genuine. For example, in two separate works (1853, 1860) Baur contended this epistle cannot be genuine, but must be the product of some unknown second century writer who is deliberately contradicting what Paul wrote. (b) The idea the writings are contradictory impinges on the doctrine of inspiration. To Baur and his followers, it may, perhaps, be a small thing that their doctrine is inconsistent with the belief that the teaching of James and Paul had, as its source, the inspiration of the Holy Spirit, who is the Spirit of truth.[1] (c) The idea that James and Paul were antagonists flies in the face of all the evidence that can be gleaned from the New Testament. It is not

---

[5] A.C. Barnett, "James, Letter of," in *Interpreter's Dictionary of the Bible* (Nashville: Abingdon, 1962), Vol.2, p.798.

[1] If consistency is the test for truth, then if the writers contradict, one or both is uninspired! If both writers are apostles, there is no way to argue that their writings contradict unless we are willing to admit the Holy Spirit could direct one apostle to write one thing and another to write the opposite.

at all probable that James, who supported Paul in the crisis at Jerusalem in AD 51 (Acts 15) and who had given Paul and Barnabas the right hand of fellowship (Galatians 2:9), should attack Paul's own teaching. If the letter of James was written early (AD 45), what need was there at this early date to write to Jewish Christians, and put them on their guard against the teaching of a man who has yet to make his first missionary journey? As late as the year AD 58, James still offered the "right hand of fellowship" to Paul (Acts 21:17-25), even after the Judaizing teachers had done their worst for years trying to destroy Paul's reputation with the folk at Jerusalem.

Instead of being contradictory, we shall show below that the two apostles are in harmonious agreement.

2. A second guess is that *James is correcting prevalent misunderstandings*, or anticipating probable misunderstandings, of what Paul wrote.

Readers at times did misunderstand what the apostles wrote. 2 Thessalonians 2 is intended to correct false conclusions drawn by the readers from 1 Thessalonians. Romans 6:1 apparently reflects a false conclusion drawn from Paul's teaching on grace. So if we were to suggest James is correcting a misunderstanding, there is nothing *ipso facto* against an assumption that Paul's writings could have been misunderstood.[2] But we believe we should be slow to accept this answer to the question of the relation of James' teachings to Paul's teachings.

There are three reasons for this hesitation. (a) In James, there is no trace of any such intention of correcting a misunderstood Paulinism, nor even of any anxiety on the subject. James 2 must be wrenched from its context to see it as an example of a correction of Paul. In its own context, the purpose of James 2:14-26 is to show the necessity of ministering to needy brothers and sisters in Christ, else one cannot claim to have a genuine Christian faith. Corresponding conduct is the only way to demonstrate that a man has the "faith" he claims he has. (b) For James to be correcting Paul requires a very late date for the writing of James' epistle. Whether James even knew what Paul wrote ("For we maintain that a man is justified by faith apart from works of the Law," Romans 3:28, or the parallel statement in Galatians 2:15,16) is open to question in the minds of most scholars.[3] (c) Had James been intending to give the true meaning of either of the passages from Paul, would he not have worded his correction so that all would recognize it, without doubt, as an allusion to what Paul wrote?

3. *James and Paul are not even dealing with the same subjects*, so how can they be said to contradict each other?

---

[2] As another, present-day example, we would in fact affirm that solifidism has flourished in the church since the Reformation precisely because Paul's "not of works" has been misunderstood or misinterpreted in order to defend the dogma that salvation is monergistic.

[3] If we date James as late as AD 58-60, it is possible he has seen a copy of Romans and/or Galatians. If James is written as early as AD 45, at this date neither of Paul's letters has yet been written.

It is true that James and Paul both use several significant terms – *pistis* ("faith"), *erga* ("works" or "deeds"), and *dikaiosunē* ("justification"). Efforts to show that Paul and James do not contradict each other have focused on each of these three words. (a) Perhaps their use of "justification" is dealing with two different subjects. Perhaps Paul speaks of man's justification before God, while James speaks of justification in the eyes of men. The former is certainly correct,[4] but where does the latter find proof in James 2:14-26? (b) Perhaps when Paul and James use "faith" they are not dealing with the same subject. (i) One variation of this theme has maintained that Paul deals with the "faith" that is the beginning of the Christian life (initial justification is by "faith only" say the defenders of this view), while James deals with "faith" much later in the Christian's life. Such a distinction is made by those who say, "We are saved by faith for a life of good works." What they mean is that (in their view) "deeds" or "works" have nothing to do with initial justification, but the works done by the Christian after he or she is saved are required to show that the faith is genuine. This subtle distinction ignores the fact that Romans 4 shows that Abraham was justified over and over again, a number of times throughout his walk with God. That being true, how can we say Paul deals with only initial justification? What Paul deals with when he says "faith" is "faithfulness" – i.e., the tenor of a man's life day in and day out over a long period of time. Is that not precisely how James uses "faith" that is alive? (ii) Another variation of this theme maintains that Paul speaks of true faith, while James speaks of a false or feigned or professed faith. Now if we remove a phrase or two from its context in James, such a definition of "faith" in James might be defended. In the theology of post-Luther medieval scholastics, when James speaks of "faith only" or a "dead faith," it is a *fides informis*, rudimentary and incomplete; whereas when Paul speaks of justifying "faith," it is a *fides formata*, developed and completed by love (Galatians 5:6). But on further study, is not James himself speaking of *fides formata* when he talks about faith being perfected (James 2:22)? Admittedly, in one or two verses out of the whole paragraph (2:14-26), James may be using "faith" in the sense of mere mental assent. But not in the whole paragraph! When it comes to the kind of faith which justifies, both quote Genesis 15:6 to prove their point, and this does not look like they are using different definitions for "faith." (c) Perhaps when Paul and James use "deeds" ("works"), they are not talking about the same subject. It has been held that when Paul speaks of "works" that are unable to justify, he is speaking of the "works of law," the traditions (i.e., the halakhic rules) of the elders on which the Pharisees laid stress. The "works" James emphasizes as "justifying" are deeds of ministry and benevolence to the poor, hungry, orphan, and widow. Of the three efforts to show Paul and James are not dealing with the same subject, this one

---

[4] Paul's views never did change on the matter of justification by faith. In his first recorded sermon, Paul taught justification by faith, not by works of Law (Acts 13:38-39). His doctrine in Romans and Galatians, written some years after his first recorded sermon at Antioch of Pisidia, does not reflect a different doctrine concerning faith and works than what he first preached. The "faith" which is the condition of justification in God's sight is "faithfulness to the revelation God has given." This consistency is exactly what we would expect if, as we affirm, his sermon was inspired, as are his letters.

is closest to the facts of the case.[5]   Those who, about the time of the Jerusalem Conference, used the name and example of James to give credence to their emphasis on Pharisaic rules ("works of law") as sufficient for man's acceptance with God, needed to be confronted with the truth that "the just shall live by faith" (faithfulness to God's rules, not to man-made rules).[6]   This, we believe, is exactly what James does when he himself over and over again emphasizes the very rules the Divine Christ taught while here on earth.   Faithfulness to God's rules – including practical demonstrations of love for one's brother – is the condition on which God justifies men.

4. *James writes without reference to, and probably without knowledge of, what Paul writes in his epistles.*

James may merely be following the course of his own argument without even thinking of, or even being aware of, Paul's teaching concerning the relation between faith and "works of law."   How much of Paul's teaching might be familiar to James depends on what they talked about when Paul visited Jerusalem, and it depends on the date assigned to this epistle, whether early or late.   At the opening of his epistle, James insists on the necessity of faith: "knowing that the testing of your faith produces endurance" (1:3); and "Let him ask in faith, without any doubting" (1:6).   He insists on the necessity of consistent practice, "Prove yourselves doers of the Word, and not hearers only" (1:22,25).   He calls attention to the "faith" of the readers in 2:1, and goes on to show how this must be accompanied by right practice.   The paragraph in James 2:14-26 follows along precisely the same lines.[7]   In other words, James' discussion of "faith and works" can be understood in its own context, with no need to appeal to Paul for a meaningful context.

5. In the debate about the relation of Paul and James, *why not appeal to their harmonious agreement?*

If our conclusions about date, destination, and purpose of writing are correct, then James and Paul are dealing with the same issue (i.e., Judaizers upsetting the faith of some)

---

[5] "Deeds" in James deal with the practical demonstrations that a man's faith in Jesus needs in order to be "perfected" (2:22).   "Deeds" in Paul sometimes refer to these very same evidences of "faithfulness." So if we are trying to see how Paul and James use "works" and we limit the investigation to two passages each in Romans and Galatians, we probably will conclude they use the terms with different meanings. However, "works of law" in Galatians and Romans are not such "deeds" or "works" that faith requires, but are the deeds and works that man-made religious rules require.   "Works of Law" must not be supposed to be the same as obeying what God's law requires.

[6] Habakkuk 2:4; Romans 1:17, 3:20,28; and Galatians 3:11.

[7] Alfred Plummer, *The General Epistles of St. James and St. Jude in An Exposition of the Bible* (Hartford, Conn. : S.S. Scranton Co., 1901), Vol.6, p.580.

and are using the same arguments to refute those trouble-makers.[8]

- "Faith working through love" (Paul, in Galatians 5:6) and "works" of benevolence to the needy (James, in James 2) both teach the same thing.

- Both Paul and James quote Genesis 15:6 and treat it exactly alike. In Paul, faithfulness to God's conditions of salvation is counted as righteousness. In James, faithfulness to what Christ has commanded is counted as righteousness. This is a harmonious presentation.

- The emphasis of James is not only in harmony with Paul, but is in harmony with the emphasis throughout the New Testament.

  It was the preaching of John the Baptist that men should bring forth fruits meet for repentance (Matthew 3:8, Luke 3:8), that, in fact, they prove the reality of their repentance by the excellence of their deeds. It was Jesus' preaching that men should so live that the world might see their good works and give glory to God (Matthew 5:16). Jesus insisted that it was by their fruits that men must be known, and that a faith which expressed itself in words could never take the place of a faith which expressed itself in the actual doing of the will of God (Matthew 7:15-21).

  Nor is this emphasis missing from Paul ... Few teachers have ever so stressed the ethical effect of Christianity as Paul does ... Paul repeatedly makes clear the importance he attaches to deeds. He speaks of God who will render to every man according to his deeds (Romans 2:6) ... Everyone must appear before the judgment seat of Christ and give an account of the deeds done in the body (2 Corinthians 5:10) ... No one can read the letters of Paul without seeing at once the importance he attaches to deeds as part of the Christian life.[9]

- What James calls the "royal law" Paul himself emphasizes in Romans 13:8-10, and uses the same argument as does James, quoting commands from the second table of the 10 Commandments. Here again is beautiful harmony.

- Compare Titus 3:8 with James 2:14ff. To Titus, Paul wrote, "Speak confidently ... so that those who have believed in God may be careful to engage in good deeds." James is saying the same thing, is he not?

- James declares more than once that the Gospel is the "law of liberty" (1:25; 2:12). Paul writes about Christian liberty (Galatians 5:1, etc.). Not only is there harmony in their presentation of liberty, but it may also be a sustainable thesis that both write on the topic precisely because the Judaizers have raised doubts and questions in the minds of the readers of both letters.

---

[8] Even if our conclusions about date and destination are incorrect, we would still affirm that apostles' writings, whether early or late in the apostolic age, will be consistent and harmonious.

[9] Barclay, *op. cit.*, p.84-85.

Once more we assert that perfect harmony is exactly what we would expect if both Paul and James are writing by inspiration. And harmony is indeed what we find between Paul and James.

CATHOLIC EPISTLES

Some English versions entitle the letters of James, Peter, John and Jude as "general" epistles. This is simply the equivalent of the older epithet "catholic." One word is Latin (*generalis*), the other word is Greek (*katholikos*).[1]

The meaning of the term "catholic" has been disputed. (1) Some treat it is synonymous with orthodox or canonical, supposing that the term reflects the dispute in the early church (as the canon was being guarded) when some people in some places spoke against the canonicity of these seven letters. Their defenders insisted they were "catholic," that is, canonical. However, that dispute was actually settled before we begin hearing the term "catholic epistles." From the sixth century on, we sometimes find these letters being called the "Canonical Epistles"[2] (2) Some think the letters are called "catholic" because they are addressed to both Jewish and Gentile Christians alike. This usage is doubtful since it is disputed whether or not all of them were originally addressed to Gentile Christians as well as Jewish. Further, Paul's letters were addressed to both Jewish and Gentile Christians and the term "catholic" was not applied to them. (3) Another suggestion is that the term "catholic" means that the letters embrace or teach the "whole truth." But it would be difficult to find many commentators who picture any of the seven letters as being a compendium of all Christian doctrine. (4) The best interpretation of the designation "catholic" is that each of the epistles in this group were originally "circular" letters, addressed to the church at large (i.e., the church universal), rather than to any one particular congregation (e.g., at Thessalonica, or Corinth, or Rome).[3]

The Collection of the Letters

After the close of the apostolic age, there were two collections of New Testament documents circulating. The books acknowledged by the church to be of binding authority

---

[1] Eusebius used "general" or "catholic" to describe the epistles known as James, Peter, John, and Jude. Clement of Alexandria referred to the letter sent out by the Council at Jerusalem (Acts 15:23ff) as being a "catholic epistle." Origen used the same terminology.

[2] About AD 550, Cassiodorus used such terminology in *De Justit. Divin. Litt.*," viii.

[3] This meaning is found in the preface to a commentary ascribed to Oecumenius (c. AD 600). He wrote, "These epistles are said to be catholic because they are encyclical ... [rather than being addressed to one nation or one city, or one church] ... this company of the Lord's disciples addressed their letters collectively to those who were believers."

were spoken of as "the Gospel" and "the Apostle" (much like the Jews spoke of "the Law and the Prophets"). When a third collection of Christian documents became widely known, another collective term was needed to distinguish it from the four Gospels and Paul's letters. One feature most of the seven epistles have is their lack of any address to a local church. Thus "catholic" or "general" or "universal" epistles became the collective term. In a prologue to these epistles, the Venerable Bede (c. AD 712) wrote, "Here begins the prologue to the seven Canonical Epistles" and it opens thus, "James, Peter, John, and Jude published seven epistles, to which ecclesiastical custom gives the name catholic, i.e., universal." The name is not strictly accurate; 2 and 3 John were apparently addressed to individuals, rather than being intended as encyclicals.

Scholars are still at work trying to decide the date when this third collection was made. Evidence of early collecting of the books is found in the Chester Beatty Papyri. Three codices, perhaps from late in the first century, are represented in the Chester Beatty Papyri: one containing the Gospels, one Paul's epistles, and one Revelation. The Catholic Epistles are not represented in this collection. Pamphilius collected his famous library at Caesarea in the third century. His collection included the seven Catholic Epistles, and we suppose he found the collection already existing, rather than making it for the first time himself. That the Catholic Epistles are included in Codices Vaticanus and Sinaiticus indicates the collection was known and accepted as early as AD 325. Eusebius' statement[4] shows the collection of seven Catholic Epistles was known in his time. Euthalius (c. AD 450) published an edition of the Catholic Epistles, in the production of which he collated "the accurate copies" in the library at Caesarea.

The Order of the Books in the Collections

The order of books in our New Testaments has been inherited from the Vulgate. Earlier in church history, it was the usual practice to place the Catholic Epistles immediately after Acts,[5] an arrangement that is quite ancient.[6] Many are bothered that the influence of Jerome and his Vulgate version universally disturbed this order for all the Western churches.[7] "The connection between these two portions (the Acts and the Catholic Epistles), commended by its intrinsic appropriateness, is preserved in a large proportion of Greek manuscripts of all ages, and corresponds to marked affinities of textu-

---

[4] See above under "External Evidence" for Eusebius' statement about the seven catholic epistles.

[5] Acts followed by the Catholic Epistles is the order of books in Codices Sinaiticus and Vaticanus. However, the overall order of books in these uncials is not uniform. In one manuscript, Acts and the Catholic Epistles follow the Pauline letters, while in another they precede the Pauline letters.

[6] One possible reason for combining Acts and the Catholic Epistles in one group is that these would fit nicely by themselves in a codex. In a similar way, Paul's letters fit nicely into another codex, and the four Gospels another. Such codices containing Acts along with the Catholic Epistles were known as praxapostoloi.

[7] Beginning with the Great Bible in AD 1539, English versions began to follow the order of books found in the Vulgate (i.e., the Catholic Epistles no longer follow Acts).

al history."[8] Acts followed by the Catholic Epistles is the order followed by Cyril of Jerusalem, Athanasius, John of Damascus, and the Council of Laodicea. It was the order of books in the Complutensian Polyglott, the first Greek Testament to be printed (though not the first published) after the invention of the printing press. It has been followed in the modern Greek texts edited by Tischendorf, Tregelles, and Westcott and Hort.

The order of the books within the collection of Catholic Epistles is not quite constant. Almost always James stands first.[9] The Syriac version has James, 1 Peter, and 1 John, in this order. (Some think the Syriac church was showing a special reverence for James of Jerusalem by their placement of the epistles.) In a very few places, Peter's letters stand first; we suppose this arrangement was preferred in the West where Peter's primacy was being defended.[10] In the East, priority was regularly given to James. One writer appended a note that James was placed first in his collection because James' epistle was more "catholic" than Peter's (which was addressed only to provinces in Asia Minor). Some have supposed Jerome got his "order" from Galatians 2:9, which speaks of James, Peter and John, "who were reputed to be pillars." Some have supposed that James, Peter, and John are so arranged because that is the chronological order in which they were written. (Jude does not fit this hypothesis.)

What If We Didn't Have This Collection of Catholic Epistles?

How enormous would be the loss if the Catholic Epistles had been excluded from the New Testament Canon. How we would miss James' emphasis on practical Christian living (expressed in greater detail than anywhere else); or Peter's careful criteria for identifying certain false teachers who were shortly to arise and agitate the church; or Jude's indication that by his time those false teachers had arrived on the scene of history; or John's refutation of incipient Gnosticism, the conflict between light and darkness, truth and falsehood, love and hate, God and the world, Christ and Antichrist, life and death.

But their presence or absence from our Bibles provides little ammunition on which to base an argument that the theology of the original Twelve Apostles differed from the theology of, say, Paul. We affirm it was not different! Baur's Petrine v. Pauline dichotomy has long since been abandoned. Even without the book of James, we would still know

---

[8] Plummer, *op. cit.*, p.558.

[9] C.L. Mitton (*The Epistle of James*, p.219) has suggested that the reason James is placed first among the non-Pauline epistles, even before those of Peter and John who were among the original apostles of Jesus, "can only be explained on the assumption that the author was regarded as the brother of the Lord, who later became the very influential head of the church at Jerusalem."

[10] In the listings given by Augustine, Rufinus, the Apostolic Constitutions, and the Council of Carthage, Peter is first, followed by the Johannine letters, then James and Jude. Another "canon," or list of books, found in Codex Claromontanus (from the 6th century AD) has the order of 1 and 2 Peter, James, 1,2,3 John, Jude.

about some Christians (Acts 21) who were very "Jewish" in their choices and how they exercised the liberty they had in Christ when it comes to lifestyles.

RELATION TO OTHER WRITINGS

Numerous writers have attempted to trace a connection between the epistle of James and certain other biblical and extra-biblical writings.[11] Similarities have been pointed out between James and Proverbs, James and the gospel of Matthew, James and the writings of Paul[12], James and 1 Peter,[13] James and Ecclesiasticus,[14] etc. Once similarities have been discovered, attempts are made to discern which writer influenced whom. Did James know Matthew, or did Matthew know James? Was James familiar with Paul's writings, or did Paul know James, etc.? In each of these cases, someone has argued for the priority of James, while another scholar has argued for the priority of the other writing. As a result, it can be said that it is difficult to argue from the similarities that there was any literary reliance at all. The similarities could just as well arise because two Bible writers (for ex-

---

[11] Ever since source criticism became a popular tool for studying Biblical documents, it has been widely held that the Bible writers made much use of materials already existing – be it the copying of some hymn, or "household instructions," or the adopting of ideas from the Greek mystery religions, etc. One oft-read statement is that the ethical statements found in the New Testament are simply copied from existing contemporary moral codes with some additional Christian interpretations imposed. Some writers have attempted to press James into service to help prove that it was a regular practice in the church to appropriate non-Christian codes and "baptize" them into the church. To make such a use of James is, we believe, part of a desperate attempt to defend a naturalistic view of the origins of the New Testament, in spite of the claims of the New Testament books themselves for their own inspiration. (James' use of "bondservant" at 1:1 is part of his claim for inspiration.)

[12] Samuel Davidson, op. cit., p.323-324, has a typical listing of examples of parallels – to Romans, 1 Corinthians, Galatians, etc. An example of the similarities between James and Romans, for example, can be seen by comparing James 1:3 with Romans 5:3; 1:22 with Romans 2:13; 4:1 with Romans 7:23.

[13] The parallelisms between James and Peter may be seen by comparing James 1:2 with 1 Peter 1:6-9; James 1:10 with 1 Peter 1:24; James 1:21 with 1 Peter 2:1; James 4:6,10 with 1 Peter 5:5; and James 5:20 with 1 Peter 4:8.

[14] Ecclesiasticus ("the wisdom of Jesus the son of Sirach"), though never included in the Hebrew canon, was included in the LXX version of the Bible. The book was written about 180 BC. The Latin name (Ecclesiasticus) was given to the book because it was one of the books allowed to be read in the church (Ecclesia) for edification, though not one of the books of the Canon which could be quoted in proof or disproof of doctrine. If James grew up being acquainted with this book (through his use of the LXX), it might account for some of the similarities. To see the similarities compare James 1:5 with Eccl. 20:18, 41:22; 1:8 with Eccl. 1:28, 2:12; 1:12 with Eccl. 1:11,16,18; 1:13 with Eccl. 15:11; 1:19 with Eccl. 5:11, 20:7; 1:23,24 with Eccl. 12:11; 1:25 with Eccl. 14:23, 21:23; 3:5 with Eccl. 28:10; 3:6 with Eccl. 38:19 [?]. Ecclesiasticus is found in Codices Vaticanus, Sinaiticus, and Alexandrinus. A. Plummer, op. cit., p.572ff, has a chapter dealing with the use of the Old Testament Apocrypha by the Jews of the Dispersion, and subsequently by some in the early church. While acknowledging the absence of inspiration in the original production of these books, he also calls attention to the value of the information found in some of those uninspired writings.

ample, the apostles James and Paul) are dealing with the same topic from the standpoint of what the Gospel of Christ requires.

We have already documented the similarity between what James writes and what Jesus said, especially as recorded in the Sermon on the Mount.[15]

One other area of affinity is that which has been pointed out between James and the book of Proverbs. Several similarities might be highlighted. (1) James has a pithy, pro-verbial style (1:8,22, 4:1). (2) There is a juxtaposition of good and evil (3:13-18). (3) James' use of the word "wisdom" has been called significant. (In James 1:5, "wisdom" is the understanding that enables a person to face manifold trials. In 3:13-17, "wisdom" is an attitude that determines how one lives.) In both Proverbs and James, wisdom has its source in God. (4) James is one of the few New Testament books to quote Proverbs (James 4:6 is a direct citation of Proverbs 3:34). (5) There are numerous concepts and expressions in James that remind us of Proverbs (cf. James 1:5 with Proverbs 2:6; 1:19 with Proverbs 29:20; 3:18 with Proverbs 11:30; 4:13-16 with Proverbs 27:1; 5:20 with Proverbs 10:12).

OUTLINE

Opinions have gone from one extreme to the other: that no particular outline is readily apparent within the epistle,[1] to James is "the most completely patterned book in the Bible."[2] In between these two extremes, many espouse various views about a composite authorship (where two or three or more hands have been detected[3]) for the book.

This commentator sees no reason to question the unity of the book, and from time to time in the comments we shall address the matter of the underlying unity or connection of thought from one paragraph to the next. Yet James has proven difficult to outline. This is confirmed by the great diversity of proposed outlines one finds in the commentaries. Outlines of this book have ranged from two points to twenty-five points. The outline offer-

---

[15] See *supra* under "Historical Allusions" for explanations of how James could have known what Jesus said in His Sermon.

[1] One author writes that James is like a string of beads; i.e., it is a series of loosely connected ideas. A. Julicher (*An Introduction to the New Testament* [New York: Putnam & Sons, 1904], p. 215) found no particular connection of thought in the letter. Tasker (*op. cit.*, p.9) talks about James being more like a "collection of sermon notes" than a polished sermon.

[2] A. Cadoux, *The Thought of St. James*, (London: J. Clarke, 1944), p.6. He found four major divisions, each containing four subdivisions.

[3] Oesterly (EGT, IV, 405) and Barclay (p.39) suggest the core of the epistle was the work of some "James" and that it was elaborated upon as time went on by commentary – much after the manner that, on a much larger scale, the comments on the words of Old Testament became the Mishna, the comments on these the Gemara, and finally the Talmud.

ed below is the result of observing how the letter naturally breaks up into blocks of material as James moves from one topic to another. We have attempted to assign suitable titles to each block of material.

The Marks of a Genuine Christian

THE EPISTLE OF JAMES

Signature, Address, and Greeting.   1:1

1:1 -- *James, a bond-servant of God and of the Lord Jesus Christ, to the twelve tribes who are dispersed abroad, greetings.*

James – The writer of this letter signs his name as "James."[1]   In the Introductory Studies, "James" was identified as the brother of the Lord, the one who, about a dozen or so years after Jesus' death and resurrection, became the leader of the church at Jerusalem (Acts 12:17, 15:13ff, 21:18).   While it is convenient for us to put the address and return address on the outside of the envelope in which we send a letter, in ancient times, when the writing material was a papyrus roll or sheet, it was customary to put the signature (in the nominative case) and address (in the dative case) at the very beginning.   Such a location made it unnecessary to unroll or unfold the whole letter before the important information about sender and destination could be determined.   Instead, the information was easily at hand.

A bond-servant of God and of the Lord Jesus Christ – Since many Jewish boys were named "James," these few words of self-identification helped the readers to know which man is the author of this letter.   He describes himself as a "bond-servant" and then names the Master whom he serves.   His master is Jesus, the long promised Messiah.   It is just possible that Jesus Christ is here called both "God and Lord."[2]   In the Greek, "bond-servant" stands at the end of the clause, putting emphasis on it.   It is a remarkable word, the common first-century word for "slave."   Because of forced servitude, "slave" can have a degrading connotation.   But when one belongs to and is a servant of Jesus Christ, there is nothing degrading about that.   A man is proud to belong, both body and soul, to Jesus Christ.   In this relational sense, of being submissive to a master, any Christian might be designated a "servant of Jesus Christ" (cp. 1 Corinthians 7:22 and 2 Timothy 2:24).   While many commentators on James treat this "bond-servant" description as throwing no light on James' identity or position, we are inclined to believe that James has in mind how this term

---

[1] If we are unfamiliar with name derivation, we will miss the fact that "James" in English represents "Jacob" in Hebrew, Greek, and Latin.   Our English Bibles, some twenty-five times, use "Jacob" to translate the word when the Old Testament patriarch is the person being spoken about.   "James" occurs when it is any of the New Testament characters who bore the name of the patriarch.

[2] Compare 2 Peter 1:1 and Titus 2:13.   This would be a strong affirmation of the deity of Jesus Messiah.   If two members of the Godhead are referred to (i.e., a servant of both God the Father and the Lord Jesus Christ, the Son) then the language about James being a servant of both affirms the equality of the Father and the Son.   Loyalty to Christ and to God would be equally binding.   It is not easy to understand how James can be a slave to two masters, and indeed, in the human realm, it was not possible for a person to be a slave to two different masters (Matthew 6:24).   "Lord" is a term that occurs over a dozen times in James.   Both here and at 2:1 it is Jesus who is called "Lord."   In the other occurrences of the term, it is not always clear whether the reference is to God the Father, or to Jesus Christ.

was often used in the Old Testament. God's Old Testament mouth-pieces, the prophets, were called "My servants."[3] James elsewhere (Galatians 1:19) is designated an "apostle" of Jesus Christ,[4] and we think that term, along with "bond-servant" here, gives James every right to speak for God, to speak authoritatively to the church, and to expect his Christian readers to give heed to what he has to say. It is enough identification that his readers knew which James was writing, and that he deserved a hearing.

To the twelve tribes who are dispersed abroad – "Twelve tribes"[5] likely identifies the readers as being able to trace their lineage back to one of the original patriarchs, and "who are dispersed" indicates they are living somewhere outside of the Palestinian holy land.[6] Several verses later, James will indicate that his readers are Christians, e.g., "believers in our glorious Lord Jesus Christ" (2:1). Perhaps some of the readers were at one time members of the congregation at Jerusalem but who now have fled to a safer place to avoid persecution such as arose about the time of the death of Stephen (Acts 8:1). Perhaps James, whose name and example were falsely appealed to by the Judaizers (Galatians 2:12, Acts 15:24), is herein setting the record straight among those Jewish Christians who otherwise might be the most likely to embrace the Pharisaic positions when the Judaizers came to town (Galatians 2:4). Whether as their former spiritual leader or in his role as apostle whose authority extends over the world-wide church, James is addressing this letter

---

[3] Compare notes on "bond-servant" at Romans 1:1 and 2 Peter 1:1.

[4] While James was not one of the original Twelve apostles chosen by Jesus, like Paul and Barnabas he apparently was chosen after Christ arose from the dead and appeared to him (1 Corinthians 15:7). Although James was present (Acts 1:14ff) when Matthias was chosen to fill the apostolic office from which Judas fell away, he was not one of the ones nominated for that post. His calling to be an apostle must have come at a later time in the church's history. He was treated as being equal with Peter and John, who were two of the original Twelve, in Galatians 2:6-9.

[5] The legend of "ten lost tribes of Israel" that has given rise to "British Israelism" (i.e., the idea that Old Testament prophecies about "Israel" are fulfilled in the Anglo-Saxon peoples, who are the ten lost tribes of Israel) is a fiction not substantiated by Scripture. This fantastic legend appears for the first time in the Apocryphal book of 2 Esdras (13:39-47). While it is true that many of the families of people carried captive to Assyria and Babylon never returned to the Holy Land, it is also true that many from each tribe did. They were not completely "lost." Paul can speak of "our twelve tribes" (Acts 26:7), and Jesus promised the apostles they would "judge [rule] the twelve tribes of Israel" (Matthew 19:28). The sealing of twelve thousand from each of twelve tribes (Revelation 7:5-8) also suggests that "ten" have not become lost, even though the twelve named in Revelation are not the usual twelve we typically think of when we recall the names of the twelve sons of Jacob.

[6] These conclusions have been discussed in detail in the Introductory Studies. "Diaspora" (here translated "dispersed") is a technical term used in the first century to denote those Jews who lived outside the Holy Land (cp. John 7:35). Perhaps the term came into use from the LXX at Deuteronomy 28:25, "There shall be a dispersion in all the kingdoms of the world." The term is also used in Judith 5:19 and 2 Maccabees 1:27. The ASV and the NASB margin offers "in the Dispersion" (with a capital "D") to indicate the translators' belief that this technical word should be interpreted quite literally.

to Jewish Christians wherever they may be living in the ancient world.[7]   He will seek to impress on their minds the things that are truly essential when one is a follower of Jesus Christ.   James doesn't need to address his letter to Christians living in the Holy Land because he can and does speak to them personally, since that is where he lives and ministers.

Greetings – *Charein* was the usual word of salutation in letters in the Greek world, as shown in hundreds of papyri that have been unearthed.[8]   The use of the infinitive is a condensed way of saying "I wish you joy!"   The epistolary opening of James, just fifteen words in the Greek, is among the shortest "signature, address, and greeting" found in any New Testament letter.[9]   While any first century writer might wish his readers joy, we think James has in mind the special, satisfying, lasting joy one finds as he serves and obeys Christ.

I. REMAIN FAITHFUL IN THE MIDST OF TRIALS AND TEMPTATIONS. 1:2-18

Summary: Verses 2-12 deal with trials that overtake the believer from without.

> James insists on a proper attitude toward trials (verses 2-4), urges that they resort to prayer for wisdom among their trials (verses 5-8), reminds those being tried that they must have a correct sense of values about the things of this life (verses 9-11), and finally indicates the glorious result of persevering under trial (verse 12).

Verses 13-18 deal with temptations to do evil.

> James deals with the source of the temptations which men experience (verses 13-14), portrays the sad results of yielding to temptation (verse 15), and adds a warning against being deceived into blaming God for the temptations (verses 16-18), for what God does in His world is only good and beneficent.

---

[7] Exactly how far and wide this letter eventually was delivered and read depends somewhat on the date assigned to it.   The Jewish communities and their synagogues furnished some of the best prospects for conversion to Christ.   The later in the first century we date the letter, the wider Christianity has spread.

[8] The same word of greeting is found in the letter sent from the Conference in Jerusalem over which James presided (Acts 15:23) and in the letter of Claudius Lysias to Felix (Acts 23:26).   It has also been found in the LXX for the Hebrew greeting "peace" at Isaiah 48:22, 57:21.   It is different from the usual Christian greeting found in Paul's letters ("grace and peace").   The same word (in the imperative) was translated "Hail" in the angel's greeting to Mary (Luke 1:28), in the mocking salutations of the soldiers to Jesus as He was on trial (Matthew 26:49, 27:29), and in Jesus' greeting to the women after His resurrection (Matthew 28:9).   In 2 John 10,11, the same word *charein* is rendered in colloquial English in the KJV as "bidding God speed" or "giving a greeting" (NASB).

[9] Of course Hebrews and 1 John have no epistolary opening, and there is some question about the length of the opening of 3 John.   The epistolary opening of 1 Thessalonians is also rather short.

1:2 -- *Consider it all joy, my brethren, when you encounter various trials;*

Consider it all joy – Following the brief epistolary opening, omitting the customary thanksgiving often found in first century letters, James enters at once into the theme of his letter. Some have called that theme, "Marks of the Genuine Christian Life." Others speak of ways to have the joy James has wished for in verse 1. Verses 2-18 unfold the first of these marks or ways to real and lasting joy: remaining faithful to Christ in the midst of trials and temptations. As we read the English, we miss the paronomasia which is evident in the Greek between "greetings" (*charein*) and "joy" (*charan*).[1] James can find reasons for joy even in circumstances and conditions that seem most adverse to it, and urges his readers to see those reasons for joy.[2] The expression "all joy" speaks of full and complete joy, nothing but joy, different forms of joy, in spite of initial outward appearances. James is not to be understood as meaning that these trials are joyful in themselves. He is not saying "enjoy them" in some masochistic sense. He means that they are beneficial in the wholesome effects they can produce, and in this are they to be rejoiced in. Each trial may have its corresponding element of joy.

My brethren – While "brothers" could be used of a blood relationship, in light of the word "faith" in verses 2 and 3, and in light of 2:1, we understand "brothers" to be used of the spiritual relationship James and the readers have with God the Father through the redemption that is in Christ Jesus. What James here says applies only to born-again Christians.

When you encounter various trials – As the context makes clear, when he speaks of "trials," James has principally in mind those external trials, such as poverty or persecution, which test our faith, loyalty, and obedience, and tempt us to abandon our trust in the Lord, and so cease to strive to please Him.[3] One might enumerate sickness, suffering, misfor-

---

[1] This carrying on of a word or thought from one sentence into the next (either by paronomasia or the repetition of the same word) is a characteristic of James. See "endurance" (1:3,4), "lacking" and "lacks" (1:4,5), "doubting" and "doubts" (1:6), "gives birth to" and "brings forth" (1:15), "anger" (1:19,20), "religion" (1:26,27), "stumble" (3:2), "fire" (3:5,6), etc.

[2] "Consider" is an aorist imperative and conveys a sense of urgency to their new way of thinking about the trials they are experiencing. Due deliberation is needed, mental evaluation is required, until they begin to "regard" or "think of" their trials in this light; namely, the same mental attitude toward trials which Jesus taught (Matthew 5:10-12; Luke 6:22,23).

[3] The word translated "trials" is *peirasmos*, a word that can mean either "test" (outward trials that require strengthening or purifying or proving in order to overcome them) or "temptation" (an inward entice-ment to sin). Each time we encounter the word, the context must indicate in which sense the word is used. The same double meaning is true for the cognate verb *peiradzo*. The KJV uses "temptation" in 1:2, and we think that causes readers to miss the actual thing being talked about in the early verses of chapter 1. In order to explain the use of *peirasmos* in the opening verses of this paragraph, Barclay chose to use "test" to translate it. He notes that a young bird is said to "test" (*peiradzein*) its wings. The Queen of Sheba was said to come to test (*peiradzein*) the wisdom of Solomon. God is pictured as testing (*peiradzein*) Abraham when He ordered Abraham to sacrifice Isaac (Genesis 22:1). When Israel came into the Promised Land, God did not remove the people who already lived there. Instead, He left them so that Israel might be tested (*peiradzein*) in the struggle against them (Judges 2:22; 3:1,4). So "trials" are "tests" intended to build spiritual strength in those who overcome them.

tune, persecution, hardships, and impoverishment as examples of such trials. The word translated "various" is *poikilois* which means "many colored, variegated, diversified." It is implied that the readers already were passing through a time of adversity, facing "trials of many kinds," or that they soon would (for he says "whenever" [*hotan*], not "if"). The word *peripiptō*, translated "encounter" in the NASB and "fall into" in the KJV, is the same word used of the man who "fell among thieves" (Luke 10:3). These trials were not self sought, they were not "run" into, rather, they "fall on" the readers. They are unlooked for, unsought, and unexpected occurrences of adverse circumstances. Moreover, the word "fall into" implies that this unforeseen misfortune is large enough to encircle and overwhelm someone.[4] James bids his readers to change their thinking.[5] "Consider it joy" when you fall into such trials. Every time they fall into one, look for the joy that comes when the test is passed with flying colors!

1:3 -- *Knowing that the testing of your faith produces endurance.*

Knowing – Verse 3 gives the reason why Christians can count trials as an occasion for rejoicing. They know[6] what the trials are capable of producing. They put the believer's faith to the test, and can leave the Christian stronger spiritually. James does not bid us to accept this doctrine of joy in trials based upon his own personal authority. Instead, he appeals to the readers own personal experience.

That the testing of your faith – What earlier was called a "trial" is here called a "testing" of a man's faith. The same valuable truth about trials being a test of faith is taught in 1 Peter 1:6,7. "Testing" translates *dokimion*, the word for the instrument or crucible or means by which silver was tested to determine if it was genuine (cp. Proverbs 27:21). Trials put the believer's faith[7] to the test to see if it will endure, to see if it is genuine. "Faith" in the Bible sometimes has reference to a body of doctrine, the sum of Christian truths. In this place, however, it more likely has reference to the response a man makes to the truth he has been taught, namely his faithfulness to that teaching. For James, there is no vital Christianity without faithfulness.

---

[4] Alfred Plummer, *op. cit.*, p.571.

[5] "Trials," contrary to what many Old Testament Jewish folk thought, are not a mark of God's disfavor. Jews were in error who thought it was a mark of God's favor when they were prosperous and otherwise blessed. Perhaps James' readers were thinking old Jewish thoughts when these trials came upon them.

[6] The participle "knowing" is present tense in the Greek. "You are constantly finding out and getting to know." It is continuous action, continuous awareness, continuous "knowing." *Ginōskontes* is the kind of knowledge that comes by experience. Each trial, successfully met, produces more knowledge.

[7] There is an article in the Greek before "faith," and as the context (1:1 and 2:1) makes clear, it can only mean their faith as Christians.

Produces endurance – "Produces" is a present tense verb, picturing the production of "endurance" as being a continuing process.   It takes more than one trial to produce "endurance."   *Hupomonē* is more than passive acceptance or resignation.[8]   It denotes the making of something good and positive out of what would otherwise be a catastrophe.[9]   Barclay has illustrated the word by saying "if life hands you a lemon, make lemonade!"   Paul wrote something similar in Romans 5:3, where he says that "afflictions produce endurance."[10] The effect of trials rightly borne is strength to bear still more and to conquer in still harder battles.   Trials do not automatically produce endurance.   They must be faced with a positive attitude ("count it all joy!") and an intentional effort must be made to turn what could have been devastating into something positive.

1:4 -- And let endurance have its perfect result, that you may be perfect and complete, lacking in nothing.

And let endurance have *its* perfect result – Verse 4 is tied to verse 3 by the repetition of "endurance" and highlights another thing trials can do besides test to see if faith is genuine. Endurance through trials can produce a "perfect[11] result."   "Let have" is a third person singular imperative verb in the Greek.   "Let" (which is the regular helper to translate third person imperatives) in English might sound like James is suggesting the readers "permit" something to happen, when in fact he is commanding them how to act.   "Endurance" has a job to do, and this result can only be reached if believers do not falter or give up when facing trials.   Endurance provides the atmosphere in which other virtues can grow.

That you may be perfect and complete, lacking in nothing – The development of endurance while under trial is not the final goal.   Rather, maturity of character is the goal. Such maturity is not so much the result of the number of trials one has to face, but is the result of the victorious way in which the trials are met.[12]   What we have called maturity of character is described by three participles in the original.   "Perfect" (*teleios*) means

---

[8] The choice in some English versions of "patience" as a translation at this place does not adequately convey the idea in the Greek word.

[9] Matthew 10:22 and 24:13 speak of "*endurance* unto the end."   It is a perseverance which does not falter under trials and suffering.

[10] There is an inspiring example of endurance to be observed in our Lord.   In Hebrews 12 we read, "Let us run with *endurance* the race set before us, fixing our eyes on Jesus the author and finisher of our faith, who for the joy set before Him endured the cross, despising the shame, and sat down at the right hand of the throne of God.   For consider Him who has *endured* such hostility by sinners against Himself, so that you may not grow weary and lose heart ... It is for discipline that you *endure*; God deals with you as sons; for what son is there whom his father does not discipline?"

[11] "Perfect" translates *teleion*, a word that means "complete, mature, full grown."

[12] The present tense verb points not just to a future ideal, but to a present progressive attainment.

"completely fit" or "mature" for the task in the world he has been sent to do.[13]   "Complete" translates *holoklēpos*, a word used to describe the lamb suitable for sacrifice to God; it was "without blemish, complete in all its parts."[14]   Used figuratively of the Christian, it suggests the person has no disfiguring or disqualifying blemishes of character.   "Lacking in nothing"[15] seems to express negatively what has been expressed positively in the previous two participles.   Perhaps it also suggests that in no area ("in nothing") of spiritual life or personality is there a failure to develop and reach the goal God has set forth.   The man or woman who turns trials into something positive, and does it consistently, will little by little find himself or herself living more victoriously, more and more becoming like Christ.[16]   What James here writes about the spiritual benefits that can accrue from trials withstood is similar to what both Paul (Romans 5:23-5) and Peter (1 Peter 1:5,6) also state in their books.   "The attitude James calls for [when facing manifold trials] is vastly superior to the natural human reaction of complaining and brooding in self-pity or the adoption of an attitude of stoic resignation and grim fortitude."[17]

1:5 -- *But if any of you lacks wisdom, let him ask of God, who gives to all men generously and without reproach, and it will be given to him.*

But if any of you lacks wisdom – *De* (translated "but") indicates there is some connection of thought between verse 5 and verses 2-4.[18]   The connection seems to be this: if any of James' readers, before endurance has finished its work, feels an inability to look at his trials as just indicated, let him turn to God in prayer for the needed wisdom.   To handle trials as just taught will require wisdom (verse 5a).   The follower of Christ can turn to the Heavenly Father in prayer and request the needed wisdom (verse 5b).   The readers are assured that

---

[13] Scripture apparently does not teach that believers may reach sinless perfection in this life, but they may grow towards spiritual maturity.   The contrast between childhood and "adulthood," or "maturity," is often alluded to in Scripture (1 Corinthians 13:10,11; 14:20; Ephesians 4:13).   Even Christ is said to have been made "perfect" (perfectly qualified) by the things he suffered (Hebrews 2:10).   The term "perfect" does not imply absolute perfection, as James 3:2 shows.   James uses the term five times (1:4 [twice],17,25, 3:2).   "Unfortunately, many believers succumb to spiritual infantile paralysis and remain in a state of childish backwardness in their spiritual life."   Hiebert, *op. cit.*, p.77

[14] Compare 1 Thessalonians 5:23, "may spirit and soul and body be preserved *complete*."   The word was used of the lame man who was healed (Acts 3:16).

[15] "The word is used of the defeat of an army, of the giving up of a struggle, of the failure to reach a standard that should have been reached."   Barclay, p.52.

[16] Many Christians lack some things, some lack many things.   How hard it is to find a well-rounded Christian, with all the graces in exactly the right proportion.   Most are too hard or too soft; too bitter or too sweet; just a little off color someplace.   One who has been through the fires of afflictions will have had many things brought home to him, and have had just the needed opportunity to make improvements.

[17] Hiebert, *op. cit.*, p.78.

[18] Another indication of some connection is the repetition of the prominent word ("lack") from the preceding clause.

the requested wisdom will be granted if the faithfulness of life needed for effective prayer is present in their lives (verses 5c-8). When Christians fall into manifold trials, they need not feel guilty if they recognize they need help to be wise enough to use aright the difficult experiences of this life. At some time or other, every one of us will have to turn to God in prayer in order to know how to meet this or that trial so that we can be spiritually victorious. In this epistle, James has much to say about wisdom (see also James 3:13-17), yet an exact explanation of what "wisdom" is does not come easily.[19] Someone has remembered that "the fear of God is the beginning of wisdom" (Proverbs 9:10), and surely a proper reverence for and recognition of accountability to God for one's decisions and actions will help a man sort out his options when he is in the midst of trials. Another has let the context help explain what "wisdom" means, describing it as the ability in the midst of trials to recall that trials can have a God-given benefit, and to recognize what is needed for the right conduct of a man's life so that he continues to be pleasing to God.

Let him ask of God – If the Christian cannot count it all joy, or cannot see how to "endure," or does not understand how this circumstance can contribute to being "perfect and complete," then he or she lacks wisdom. That's the time to go to God in prayer, not just once, but repeatedly (the verb is present tense, continuous action).[20] Again, "let him" does not just grant permission; it is a command (a third-person singular imperative).

Who gives to all men generously and without reproach – That God will grant the request for wisdom in response to prayer is a deduction from His nature, for one of His greatest characteristics is "giving."[21] He loves to do it! He does it continually.[22] "Generously" (*haplōs*) says either that God gives with a simple motive[23] (to further the welfare of His children), or that there is no selfishness on His part. There are no parsimonious calculations on His part before He gives, and there is nothing stinted nor held back in His

---

[19] Not a few writers immediately appeal to passages in the Biblical books of Proverbs or Ecclesiastes, while others turn to the non-canonical books named the Wisdom of Solomon and Ecclesiasticus. However, the wisdom James would have Christians pray for is not exactly the same kind of wisdom one reads about in Proverbs (1:2-4, 2:10-15, 4:5-9).

[20] This is the first of many references to prayer in the epistle of James. Here, James is suggesting prayer for help in times of trial. In 4:3, he speaks of unanswered prayers, because the one praying is asking for selfish purposes. In 5:13-15, it is prayer in time of physical trouble. In 5:16, it is prayer for one another. In 5:17,18, it is prayer about material things, as Elijah prayed for rain.

[21] Two other ways of explaining the verse have been proposed: (1) One is to emphasize "all men" and then to emphasize that God is no respecter of persons. Christians who ask for wisdom come in all kinds, from Jewish, Greek, and barbarian backgrounds, high or low, rich or poor. God doesn't take one's ethnicity or social position into account when He answers prayers. (2) Another alternative explanation is that God gives to all who ask. The context is talking about asking for wisdom. It is to be had for the asking, but will not be given unless Christians ask.

[22] The participle is present tense, indicating continuous action.

[23] The same root word is translated "single" in Matthew 6:22 and Luke 11:34.

giving. "Without reproach" says He doesn't find fault with our asking; He doesn't scold his children for asking, or berate them for their deficiency.[24] If you ask men for favors, they may be granted, but the granting may come with plenty of advice and complaint. "If you hadn't wasted my earlier gifts, you would not need to ask for this favor." "Why are you asking me for this help? I can hardly afford it." "You are always coming at the wrong time." Humans, when giving, sometimes mention their former acts of kindness, or tell the recipient not to expect another gift in the future. They may remind the recipient of the pitiful little gift they have received. But God never acts like this. He doesn't spoil the gift or humiliate the recipient by bitter speeches.[25] He doesn't rub it in that you have had to ask. You can come to Him any time, day or night, just as often as you like. He doesn't act harshly towards His children. He does not coldly turn them away. He meets us with a spirit of entire kindness and with promptness in granting requests for wisdom.[26]

And it will be given to him – These words remind us of Jesus' words in the Sermon on the Mount (Matthew 7:7-11), "Ask and it shall be given to you." The promise is definite and sure. God has wisdom to give, wants to give it, and will give it for the asking. But we must ask. This promise in regard to a prayer for wisdom is absolute. We may be sure that if it be asked in a proper manner (verses 6-8), it will be granted to us. And how may we expect that He will bestow wisdom on us? (1) Through the Word, as He enables us to see clearly the meaning of the sacred Text, and to understand the directions which He has given there to guide us. (2) By the influences of the Holy Spirit, suggesting to our minds the way which we should go, inclining us to do that which is prudent and wise. (3) By the events of providence making plain to us the path of duty and removing the obstructions that might be in our path.

1:6 -- *But let him ask in faith without any doubting, for the one who doubts is like the surf of the sea driven and tossed by the wind.*

But let him ask in faith without any doubting – The promises of verse 5 are absolutely null and void if our asking is not accompanied by "faith." Perhaps James is reflecting what Mark 11:24 records from the lips of Jesus, "Therefore I say unto you, all things for which you pray and ask, believe that you have received them, and they shall be granted you." If this is what James is saying, then "doubting" is a halting between belief and unbelief.[27] It is a disquiet in the soul which prevents a man who is being tried from lean-

---

[24] Sometimes, it is true, God does "upbraid" or "reproach" people. Jesus "upbraided His disciples for their unbelief and hardness of hearts" (Mark 16:14). God does rebuke sins. But when it comes to giving to believers, He permanently abstains from "upbraiding" (a present tense participle).

[25] Folk who have supposed James draws on Ecclesiasticus find an example here in the description of "the gift of a fool" (Eccl. 20:15 and 41:23) "who gives little and upbraids much."

[26] Of course, we cannot expect God to give anything that is not in harmony with His will.

[27] If we render the middle voice participle as "without doubting" then as the person asks God for wisdom, he at one moment thinks in his heart, "Yes, God will give it" and then at another moment he thinks, "No, I'm not confident He will."

ing on God. Or, perhaps, James is saying that consistent Christian living ("faithfulness") is a condition of answered prayer. In this case we would translate the last part of the phrase "without any wavering."[28] In this commentator's opinion, the second option is the better one. It would give prominence to "faithfulness" here in chapter 1 just as it is emphasized in chapter 2:14-26. It would allow us to translate *diakrinomenos*[29] in such a way that the illustrations which follow fit beautifully. It pictures a man who is undecided and so his behavior is sometimes faithful to God, and sometimes not. "Let him ask" translates a present imperative verb. James is setting forth a command that reflects a standing demand on God's part before He answers prayers.

For the one who doubts is like the surf of the sea driven and tossed by the wind – "For" indicates James is explaining what he means by "wavering." The versions differ on how to translate *kludōni*; some use "wave"; some use "surf."[30] "Driven" translates *anemidzomenō* and "tossed" translates *hripidzomenō*. James evidently was a keen observer of nature.[31] Very probably, during his boyhood, he and the Master had stood on the shores of Galilee and saw those tempestuous winds ("tossed" pictures sudden gusts and squalls) whip up the sea. He saw as the waves were first driven this way, and then that, as the wind blew first from one direction, then another. He saw how they washed up on the beach, only to roll back into the sea. He notices that the waves respond to forces from without. The water has no inner stability to stand against the outer forces. How like[32] the Christian who is not consistent in his living![33]

---

[28] The present tense denotes a "habitual wavering."

[29] *Diakrinomenos* is used of the "wondering" the disciples did as they gazed at the withered fig tree (Matthew 21:21). It is used of Abraham who "didn't waver in unbelief" (Romans 4:20).

[30] Hiebert says the word here does not refer to an individual wave [*kuma*] but to one long ridge of water after another being swept along by the wind. ("Surf's up!" they say in California and Hawaii, or "the angry billows roll" is how one song words the figure.) Most commentaries use a figure of speech to describe folk who are inconsistent. Some speak about a ship drifting on the waves; one moment you are in the depths of a trough between waves, and the next you are lifted high on top of a wave. Mayor calls attention to a cork floating on the wave, now carried towards the shore, now away from it, the opposite of those who have "hope as an anchor of the soul, sure and steadfast ..." (Hebrews 6:19). Others recall Ephesians 4:14 which describes how some are "carried about by every wind of doctrine."

[31] If James has not observed nature, he could have been familiar with the description of a storm in Proverbs 23:34, and the comparison of the wicked to the "troubled sea" in Isaiah 57:20. And James has other illustrations drawn from nature (see 1:10,11; 1:17,18,26; 3:3-5,7,11,12; 5:7,17,18).

[32] The Greek word for "is like" is *eoiken*, a perfect tense form but having the force of a present tense.

[33] It is easy to "doubt" when trials and afflictions assail. When everything goes wrong, it is easy to say, "Where is the Lord? Why does He not answer and deliver?" Likewise it is easy to "waver" when trials beset on every hand. Allegiance wavers between God and Satan, between the church and the world, between righteousness and wickedness. Where will you find this man? It depends on which way the wind is blowing. It depends upon whether he is with other Christian men, or with men of the world.

1:7 -- For let not that man expect that he will receive anything from the Lord.

For -- "For" likely introduces a further reason why a man must be "faithful" (verse 6) if he expects the Lord to answer his prayer for wisdom.

Let not that man expect that he will receive anything from the Lord – "That man" is somewhat derogatory. "Let him not expect" is a present imperative with *mē*, which prohibits the continuance of an action already going on.[34] Folk who habitually live an inconsistent life are to stop entertaining any thought they will receive a positive answer to their prayer.[35] There is some question whether "the Lord" is used in the Old Testament sense of God the Father or in the New Testament sense for Jesus Christ.[36] In the light of the context (verse 5), it might be well to understand this as referring to God the Father.

1:8 -- **being** *a double-minded man, unstable in all his ways.*

Being **a double-minded man** – The italics show there is no verb in the Greek here in verse 8. Some versions supply "is," making it read "he is a double-minded man ...." The NASB translators put the two descriptive words in apposition with "that man" in verse 7. If verse 8 is thus tied to verse 7, it gives reasons why "that man"[37] receives nothing from the Lord. The word *dipsuchos*, not found in any Greek literature before James, and used in the New Testament only here and at James 4:8, was perhaps coined by James. It literally means "two-souled" and in 1 Clement Lot's wife is given as an illustration of someone who is "two-souled." She had one for the earth, and another for heaven; she wished to secure both worlds. She will not give up earth, and she is loath to let heaven go.

---

[34] The verb *oiesthō* (used also at John 21:25 and Philippians 1:17) denotes "a subjective judgment which has feeling rather than thought for its ground." Thayer, *Lexicon*, p.276.

[35] Scriptures indicate other reasons why Christians' prayers are not answered. "You ask and receive not, because you ask amiss, that you may consume it upon your lusts" (James 4:23). "If I regard iniquity in my heart, the Lord will not hear me" (Psalms 66:18). Perhaps we have some idols in our heart. If so, the Lord will not hear (Ezra 14:3). Do we have a fierce temper? "I will therefore that men pray everywhere, lifting up holy hands, without wrath and doubting" (1 Timothy 2:8). Maybe we have an unforgiving spirit towards others. If so, we should not expect the Lord to show a forgiving spirit towards us (Matthew 6:14,15). Perhaps husbands do not show proper honor to their wives, and so their prayers are hindered (1 Peter 3:7). Perhaps we have not been persevering in prayer (Luke 18:1).

[36] In the LXX, the word "Lord" was often used to translate the Hebrew 4-letter sacred name (YHWH). Perhaps James is using the term without any thought of distinction between the Divine Persons. In the New Testament Jesus also, no less than the Father, is thought of as giving or not giving answers to prayer (cp. John 14:14). See also James 5:7,14,15, where prayers are addressed to Jesus.

[37] In verse 8, James uses *anēr* (male, husband) whereas in verse 7 he used *anthrōpos* ("humans" in general). This substitution of terms leads us to believe verse 8 is not limited to "males" only. Women who have professed Christ can also be inconsistent.

Unstable in all his ways – It is not just in his prayer life. His instability marks "all he does."[38] Hort suggests that "unstable" pictures the two-souled man as being drunk and staggering from side to side along the road, and getting nowhere. Once more James has vividly pictured the fact that inconsistent Christian living and character will cost the person any opportunity to "receive anything from the Lord" in answer to his prayers.

1:9 -- *But let the brother of humble circumstances glory in his high position;*

But – There is a *de* in the beginning of this verse, and this conjunction serves to connect this sentence to what has been our topic ("various trials") since verse 2.[39] Verse 12 will explicitly refer to "persevering under trial," so it seems best to treat verses 9-11 as being related to the same subject.[40] This sentence says these "trials" may affect rich and poor alike as they experience a sudden change of external circumstances.

Let the brother of humble circumstances – "Brother" seems to show that James is referring to Christian believers.[41] James describes the "circumstances" (i.e., the amount of money, food, and clothing necessary for living in this world[42]) as "humble." The word he uses is *tapeinos*, which means "lowly" or "poor" or "weak" or "insignificant." The readers who have been "dispersed" and who, perhaps, are refugees fleeing from persecution will by their flight be reduced to meager living and subjected to numerous physical hardships. What will be the believers' response to these trying circumstances?

Glory in his high position – One is inclined to think of the Christian's heavenly birthright

---

[38] Examples of inconsistency would include these: He may talk nicely in the Sunday School class, but he also talks as nicely around the pool table or the card game the rest of the week. He thinks the church is good, but so is the lodge and the tavern. He may say grace at the table, and then swear at the shop or in the field. If you have a revival meeting at church, he will be there every service, but you won't see him after that. He may want to teach a Bible School class, but you cannot depend on him being there over half the time. And often when he comes, he is not very well prepared to teach the class. "Woe to fearful hearts and faint hands, and the sinner who goes two ways" (Ecclesiasticus 2:12).

[39] Lenski is more than likely correct when he notes that *de* here is not to be taken as adversative but as a common transitional particle. If so, we would translate it "and."

[40] Some commentaries, such as *Expositor's Greek Testament*, treat verses 9-11 as an entirely new subject. Plummer suggests the train of thought lies in the words of Jesus that love of mammon is one of the most common sources of "double-mindedness" (Matthew 6:24), both in the rich and the poor.

[41] About AD 41 or 42, the disciples were first given the name "Christian." It would be a while before the term comes into common use. Before that it was common to speak of "brothers" and "sisters" in Christ, reflecting a common brotherhood with Christ, and a common spiritual sonship under the One Father in heaven.

[42] We should probably avoid the interpretation that would make *ho tapeinos* refer to "poor in spirit" (cp. Matthew 5:3) or "humble in heart" (Matthew 11:29). Instead, take the words literally.

when he reads "high position."[43]   One calls to mind what Paul wrote in 1 Corinthians 7:22, "He that was called in the Lord, being a slave, is the Lord's freeman; likewise, he that was called being free, is Christ's bond-servant."   Rather than be fixated on a few more dollars, or other fleeting riches of this world, the Christian should concentrate on his glorious new status in God's family.   "Glory" (*kauchasthō*) stands first in the verse for emphasis and is a present imperative form; this is to be the characteristic response adopted by the believer. "The word denotes a strong personal reaction, a feeling of pride or exultation in the condition [i.e., the "high position"] mentioned."[44]   Such an attitude is a good safeguard against succumbing to despondency when trials reduce one to poverty.

1:10 -- and *let the rich man* **glory** *in his humiliation, because like flowering grass he will pass away.*

And *let* **the rich man** – Is the "rich man" a Christian believer or an unsaved man of the world?[45]   The decision made about this question will affect our comments on the next phrase.[46]   Since James has addressed his letter to Christians, it seems natural to treat the "rich man" here addressed as being one of those Christians.[47]   There were rich men who were members of the church, though not many (1 Corinthians 1:26).   We think of Joseph of Arimathea, Nicodemus, Zacchaeus, James and John (sons of Zebedee).   See also 1 Timothy 6:17-19.   The words of verse 10 are a continuation of the sentence begun in verse 9.   *Plousios*, "rich," denotes "one who does not need to work for a living."[48]

Glory **in his humiliation** – The italics indicates we must supply a verb for this sentence. The most natural verb to supply is it is "let him glory,"   the same imperative verb used in

---

[43] Barnes (*op. cit.*, p.21) understands the poor man has suddenly, due to a change in circumstances, become financially wealthy. We think it better to understand "high position" as denoting one's exalted spiritual position when he or she is a Christian. Hattie Buell caught the idea in the lyrics, "A tent or a cottage, why should I care? They're building a palace for me over there.   Tho' exiled from home, yet, still I may sing: All glory to God, I'm a child of the King!"

[44] Hiebert, *op. cit.*, p.89.

[45] Are non-Christians, whether rich or not, alluded to anywhere else in the epistle?   How about at 2:6-8 and 5:1-6? Dibelius, Easton, and Plummer are three commentators who have insisted the "rich" are unsaved people. Would non-Christians have an opportunity to hear James' appeal to them?   Christians would hear James' epistle read out loud in the Sunday assemblies for worship.

[46] No interpretation of this passage has yet been suggested which is entirely free from difficulty.

[47] Some would insist that just as the Greek would supply the verb "glory" from verse 9, so the Greek would naturally supply "brother" in this verse, since it was used in verse 9 in a parallel sentence.

[48] Arndt, Wm., and Gingrich, F. Wilbur, *A Greek-English Lexicon of the New Testament* (Chicago: University of Chicago Press, 1952), p.679.

the previous verse.[49]   In this seeming parallel to verse 9, is "humiliation" to be treated the same way "high position" was, as some kind of spiritual quality?   Or is "humiliation" here a similar idea to what was expressed in "humble circumstances" in verse 9, namely, the loss of earthly possessions?   Both of these options have been defended by some writer or another.   (a) If we take it literally, as a loss of earthly possessions, the rich man is pictured as having lost most or all his earthly possessions as he has suffered persecution for his faith, and fled as a refugee in order to save his life.[50]   He can rejoice ("glory") because the trial which brought poverty[51] was a test of the reality of his religion.   He can "glory" because he has come to see that real wealth lies in the things that abide because they are eternal. (b) Those who take the word figuratively, and opt for "humiliation" being some kind of spiritual quality, write on this fashion: "Humiliation" is the humbling experience of suffering persecution for Christ's sake.   The rich man has an opportunity to experience firsthand what Jesus meant when he said, "Rejoice and be exceeding glad when you are persecuted for righteousness' sake."   The very same trial that gives the poor man an opportunity to develop his sense of spiritual values also gives the rich man an opportunity to do the same.   The rich man is taught that he has no more of a lease on life here on earth, i.e., his life is no more permanent, than a "wild flower," just like the last clause of verse 10 goes on to explain.[52]   When we comment on "humiliation," should we not think of some loss that corresponds to the analogy of grass withering under a scorching wind?

Because like flowering grass he will pass away – "Because" shows James is now giving a reason for the attitude just commanded.   Note, it is the rich man himself, not his wealth,

[49] Some have suggested we make this read, "Let the brother of humble circumstance glory in that he is exalted" and then "let the rich (be humbled) in that he is made low [humiliated]."   However, this does not seem to fit the context.

[50] Goodspeed translated it "to rejoice at being reduced in circumstances."   C.L. Mitton (*The Epistle of James* [Grand Rapids: Eerdmans, 1966], p.39) suggested that the experience of humiliation was social; the rich man who has become a Christian is now ostracized by his former rich friends, being treated as a social outcast.

[51] This interpretation has been rejected by some because it tends to ignore the parallelism between verses 9 and 10.   "High position" in verse 9 is something spiritual.   "Humiliation" (under this interpretation) is something physical.

[52] Either of these two options seem preferable to some other explanations that have been suggested. (1) Humiliation refers to the humiliation and shame in the Day of Judgment the rich man faces.   (A reference to the final judgment does not connect easily to the present "trials" which still seem to govern the context.)   (2) Shall we think of the humiliation one must embrace as he repents?   (3) A. Plummer ("The General Epistles of St. James and St. Jude," in *An Exposition of the Bible* [Hartford, Conn: Scranton, 1903], Vol.6, p.576) thinks James speaks here with severe irony: "Let the brother of low degree glory in his high estate; and the rich man – what is he to glory in? – let him glory in the only thing upon which he can count with certainty, viz., his being brought low; because as the flower of the grass he shall pass away." (4) H. Alford (*The Greek Testament* [London: Rivingtons, 1871], Vol.4, p.278), to avoid any note of irony, suggests that an indicative rather than imperative verb be supplied, "he glories in his humiliation."   It is difficult to follow the train of thought if we adopt Alford's suggestion.   Nor does the Greek grammar support a mood other than the imperative found in verse 9.

that is said to "pass away" and "fade away in the midst of his pursuits" (verse 11). The subject of the third person singular verb "pass away" is not "riches" (plural) but "the *one who is rich.*" The same is true for the verb in the last part of verse 11. This is another of James' illustrations drawn from nature. "Flowering" (*anthos*) does not speak only of what we call the bloom or blossom or "flowers" that bloom from buds. It speaks of "green" versus the "brown" of wilted flowers and dried up grass. "Grass" (*chortou*) is a comprehensive term for herbage. The same word here translated "grass" is translated "lilies" (Matthew 6:28), "grass" (Matthew 6:30), and "grain" (Matthew 13:26). As verse 11 shows, the wild flowers of the Holy Land, which grow abundantly and brilliant among the grass, soon lose their petals when the hot wind hits. The green stalks of grass and grain soon wilt and turn to brown. Perhaps James had in mind Isaiah 40:6 ("all flesh is like grass") when he compares the rich man with flowering grass that soon passes.[53] The rich man is to rejoice if he loses all his wealth if that loss serves as a reminder that he too shall soon pass away. It will help both the poor man and the rich man to focus on spiritual values as they face the "manifold trials." Prayer for wisdom will help (verse 5); living a consistent Christian life will help (verse 6-8); so will having right priorities (verses 9-10).

1:11 -- *For the sun rises with a scorching wind, and withers the grass; and its flower falls off, and the beauty of its appearance is destroyed; so too the rich man in the midst of his pursuits will fade away.*

For the sun rises with a scorching wind – "For" introduces an explanation of what was just said in verse 10, "like flowering grass he will pass away." The brief duration of the grass and flowers in the Holy Land was a standard metaphor for the short-lived nature of human life (Psalms 90:5-6, 102:11, 103:15; Isaiah 51:12).[54] There is some question whether *ho kausōn* is the burning heat one experiences daily under the summer sun,[55] or whether there is reference to the furnace-like blast of hot wind called "Sirocco" that blows in off the Arabian desert in the early morning on some days (as in Luke 12:55).[56]

And withers the grass – In the Holy Land, after the early rains, the grass and trees green up with a luxuriant growth, but the grass is green only for a very short time. At the feeding

---

[53] The LXX of Isaiah 40:7 is followed almost verbatim. Peter quotes the passage from Isaiah at 1 Peter 1:24.

[54] The KJV reads "the sun is no sooner risen ... but it is withered." However, there are no words in the Greek that answer to "no sooner."

[55] The word *kausōn* in some passages simply means "heat" (Genesis 31:40; Daniel 3:6-7; Isaiah 25:5; Matthew 20:12).

[56] This southeast wind is referred to at Job 27:21; Hosea 13:15; Jonah 4:8; Ezekiel 17:10 and 19:12. In late May 1970, the author experienced one of these siroccos while visiting the Sea of Galilee. In mid-morning it was already 120 degrees; the heat boiled up off the grass into your face. It felt just like the blast of hot air one gets when opening the door of an oven. Green things wilted before the day was over.

of the 5000, John records that there "was much grass in the place" (John 6:10), and the people were commanded to sit upon the "green grass" (Mark 6:39). This note is a specific indication of the time of year when the miracle took place. As soon as the rains cease and the summer heat begins to pervade, the vegetation withers and turns brown. When a sirocco comes, the withering process is speeded considerably. Jesus one day spoke about the grass which today is, and tomorrow is cast into the oven (Matthew 6:30). It can be used for fuel to heat the oven "tomorrow" because it has withered and become dry that quickly.

And its flower falls off – The plant wilts, and the petals are pictured as falling to the ground. *Anthos* is the beautiful colored flower that grows out of buds on the end of the stems or stalks of plants.

And the beauty of its appearance is destroyed – Literally, "the gracefulness of its face." *Euprepeia* occurs only here in the New Testament. It denotes the flower's outward attractive appearance.[57] The heat is the thing that destroyed the pleasant appearance of the flower.

So too the rich man in the midst of his pursuits will fade away – "So" picks up the rapid succession of events pictured in the four verbs "rises, withers, falls, destroyed" and applies them to the rich man. The "rich man" is identical with the expression in verse 10. The Greek verb *maranthēsetai* ("will fade away") occurs only here in the New Testament;[58] it is a future passive and might be translated "will be blighted." An adjective derived from the same root is found in "the unfading crown" (1 Peter 5:4), and in the "inheritance that doesn't fade away" (1 Peter 1:4). The contrast between the temporary nature of earthly riches and the permanent character of heavenly riches is brought vividly to mind. Rich men die just as certainly as poor men. In the parable of Luke 16, the rich man died. In Luke 12 the rich farmer said to himself, "Soul, you have many goods laid up for many years ..." but God said, "This *very* night your soul is required of you!" "Pursuits" literally reads "in his journeyings," as in Luke 13:22.[59] Perhaps James had in mind the business trips rich men went on, or perhaps he has in mind pleasure trips that can cost more than the average working man can afford. "It is while he is engaged on one of his business journeys, mentioned again in James 4:13, that the rich man is struck down by what seems to be an ill-wind of fate."[60] Unexpectedly, in the midst of a busy life, death comes.

---

[57] The expression "the beauty of its face" reveals that James had "something of the same appreciation of the loveliness of God's creation which we find in the words of Jesus, who said that the simple beauty of the wild flowers exceeded that of the splendour of Solomon's court." (Mitton, *op. cit.*, p.42).

[58] The verb is found in the Wisdom of Solomon 2:8, and because of the similarity some source critics have supposed James has this passage in mind when he writes verse 11.

[59] A manuscript variation here has "in his gettings," but "goings" is the better attested reading.

[60] Tasker, *op. cit.*, p. 44.

1:12 -- *Blessed is a man who perseveres under trial; for once he has been approved, he will receive the crown of life, which* **the Lord** *has promised to those who love Him.*

Blessed is a man who perseveres under trial – James continues his discussion[61] of how Christians are to face up to the "various trials"[62] they encounter (verse 2), showing the need for perseverance, and how perseverance results in blessing (the crown of life). Those trials can be counted as "joy" only when they are victoriously endured. "Blessed is a man"[63] reminds us of the language of the Old Testament (Psalms 1:1, 32:2, 34:8, 84:12; Proverbs 8:34; Isaiah 56:2), and *makarios* ("blessed") is the same word that begins the Beatitudes.[64] This beatitude has no verb in the Greek. It may be a prayer, or it may be an exclamation, "Oh, the blessing!" It carries the idea of being "spiritually prosperous." James tells us that Christians who are meeting trials and "enduring" (see notes on verse 3) are not miserable as the world would judge them to be. He also drives home the point that the mere experience of trials and afflictions will not win the promised crown. Unless the trials are withstood and endured in the right spirit, there will be no crown.

For once he has been approved – James here gives the reason he can say, "Oh, the blessing!" "Approved" means "he has passed the test." We've had a form of this same word at verse 3 where it was translated "testing." The same adjective is applied in Romans 14:18 and 16:10 to one who has been tested and approved.[65] The term "describes the enviable state of the man who does not give up when confronted with trying circumstances but remains strong in faith and devotion to God."[66] "Become approved" (*dokimos genomenos*) pictures a process before the state of approval is finally reached. Is it God

---

[61] The NASB starts a new paragraph with verse 12. We might start the new paragraph, instead, with verse 13. Verse 12 is related to the preceding verses by the repetition of terminology ("trials," verse 2; "testing," verse 3) and by the fact that "perseveres" in verse 12 picks up the idea of "endurance" introduced in verses 3 and 4.

[62] We have had this word at verse 2, where we learned it can mean either "testing" or "temptation." At this place, some would translate *peirasmov* as "temptation," making this verse a promise that temptation successfully resisted results in a crown of life. However, it is not easy to see how *hupomonē* ("endures," compare notes at verses 2 and 3) is to be explained if the topic is "temptation." If "temptation" were the topic, "resistance" would be a better term than "endurance."

[63] James uses the word for "man" or "male" just as he did in verse 8, with no thought of restricting the beatitude to males only.

[64] "Happy is the man whom God corrects," Job 5:17. Even in secular Greek the word described "the transcendent happiness of a life beyond care, labour and death" (TDNT, 4:362). In Biblical usage it speaks of "the distinctive religious joy" which is one of the benefits of salvation (TDNT, 4:367)." (Donald Burdick, "James" in *Expositor's Bible Commentary* [Grand Rapids: Zondervan, 1981] Vol.12, p.171)

[65] The word was used to describe the testing of precious metals and coins to determine if they were genuine.

[66] Burdick, *ibid.*

who decides when a man has "passed the test"? Romans 5:4 speaks of a similar "proven character" which results in "hope that will not be disappointed." Perhaps this approval results in joy in this life. It certainly results in joy in the next.

He will receive the crown of life – Here we are told there is joy hereafter. "He will receive" indicates the anticipated reward is still future. "Crowns" (*stephanos*[67]), "garlands" made of branches or flowers woven in a circle, were rewards for winning a contest, or ornaments worn on occasions of joy (feasts, weddings, celebrations). The genitive is probably descriptive; that is, the "crown" consists of "life," the eternal life of bliss to be enjoyed by the redeemed. "Life" itself is the crown.[68] The "crown of life" is a gift that expresses the approval of God who gives it.

Which *the Lord* has promised to those who love Him – The italics indicate the Greek reads "He promised" with no noun being expressed in the Greek. Here again[69] there is a question whether "Lord" is to be taken in its New Testament sense (speaking of Jesus Christ) or in its Old Testament sense (speaking of God the Father). Jesus did make such promises as James here alludes to (Mark 9:41; John 14:21,23; Revelation 2:7[70]). The Old Testament Scriptures also have God making and carrying out such promises (Psalm 103:4; Deuteronomy 30:15-20; Zechariah 6:14 (LXX); cp. Romans 2:7). "Promised" indicates that the "life" being talked about is not just the "life" given to the believer at the time of his salvation (John 3:16,36; 5:24). "Those who love Him" is the usual designation or description of the redeemed people of God.[71] Not everyone receives a crown of life – only those "who love Him, keep His commandments, and serve Him faithfully whatever the cost may be."[72] The trials are to be met in a spirit of loving trust in the God who sends them or allows them.

---

[67] Another word, *diadēma*, translated "crown," is the royal crown, a fillet made of gold, often with inlaid jewels.

[68] The article with "life" (*tēs zōēs*) points to the well-known life, eternal life, life that is really living. Two different Greek words are translated life, *bios* and *zōē*. The former speaks of life in its *manifestations*, i.e., those things (food, clothing, shelter) that make up a man's earthly existence. The latter is used for life in its *principle*, spiritual and immortal life. (Geo. R. Berry, *New Testament Synonyms* [Chicago: Wilcox & Follett, 1948], p. 19).

[69] Compare notes on "Lord" in verse 7.

[70] Because the exact words about "a crown of life to all who love Him" are not found in the four Gospels, some have supposed James refers to some saying of Jesus (like Acts 20:35) which is not recorded in the Gospels, but which had been handed down by oral tradition.

[71] See Exodus 20:6; Psalms 97:10, 145:20; Romans 8:28; 1 Corinthians 2:9; 2 Timothy 4:8; 1 Peter 1:7-8. Why identify Christians as "those who love Him" rather than "those who serve Him" or "those who obey Him," or some other description? Perhaps the ideas of loving Him and obeying him are not mutually exclusive. "If you love Me, you will keep My commandments," Jesus said (John 14:15).

[72] Tasker, *op. cit.*, p.45.

1:13 -- *Let no one say when he is tempted, "I am being tempted by God"; for God cannot be tempted by evil, and He Himself does not tempt anyone.*

Let no one say when he is tempted – As we begin this verse we are plunged immediately into the question of an outline for the book. Is this a new subject ("temptations") or a continuation of the previous subject ("trials")? Because the word *peirazomenos* can have the same double meaning as *peirasmos* (see verse 2), it can be translated either "when he is tried" or "when he is tempted." We are inclined to treat verse 13ff as a continuation of the topic begun in verse 2, namely, how to victoriously endure trials. So we would translate it, "Let no one say when he is being tried ...." In the second half of verse 13, James then warns his readers not to let their on-going trials be confused with or actually become a source of temptation. The present tense "when he is tried" pictures the trials as continuing. James gives his readers a command ("Let no one say" is in the imperative mood), and the form of the command is the one that prohibits the continuance of an action already going on. Some of his readers were already making such claims, they were already mistaking trials for temptations, and they were to stop doing so!

"I am being tempted by God" – James quotes the actual words men were using as they blamed God for their temptations.[73] Trials (outward adverse circumstances) can indeed become temptations (inner enticements to sin).[74] Beginning here, and continuing for several verses, James more deeply explores the topic of "temptations."[75] It is common for folk to attempt to blame God when they succumb to temptation,[76] to view the temptations as having come "from God."[77] As one contemplates the trials he is experiencing, it often leads to a deeper inquiry as to the cause and nature and potential spiritual danger of the trials. If one is not careful, this will be his thinking: God has permitted the trials; as a result of the trials I was tempted to sin, and I failed to stay true to God. Since He permitted

---

[73] The Greek phrase begins with a *hoti*. Someone has said that *hoti* "is Greek for quotation marks."

[74] The right inner reaction to trials is "endurance." If this inner reaction is absent, the trials can become an occasion for sin. We are certainly more susceptible to the Devil's suggestions when our inner reaction to trials is wrong in the first place.

[75] Some have argued that whereas a noun form was used in verse 2ff for "trials," when the topic becomes "temptation" (here in verse 13b-18) James begins to use a verb form. Further indicators that the topic is now "temptation" is the use of the words "evil" (verse 13), "lust" (verse 14), and "sin" (verse 15).

[76] As far back as Adam, this has occurred. Adam tried to put the blame for his fall on God. He said, "The woman whom you gave me ...." The hardest words to cross human lips are, "I have sinned." Instead, we try to rationalize, or make excuses, or blame others.

[77] The better attested Greek text reads *apo theou* ("from God") rather than *hupo theou* ("by God"). The preposition *apo* suggests the thought of remote source, whereas *hupo* denotes direct agency. 'God may not do the actual tempting, but He is behind the situation which results in the temptation,' is what folk were quoted as saying.

the trials, He must be the one responsible for the temptations to which those trials led.[78]

For God cannot be tempted by evil – With "for" James begins to give a series of reasons for the command just given. This series of reasons extends through verse 18. As he directs his readers to right thinking about temptations, he identifies the source of temptation (verses 13,14), pictures the result of yielding to temptation (verse 15), and adds a warning against being deceived (verse 16). We might have expected James to state immediately "God does not tempt men to do evil." Instead, before saying God does not tempt men, he writes, "God cannot be tempted[79] by evil." How shall we understand that? The hidden thought may well be, "Before God could tempt anyone, He would have to have evil thoughts. Before He could have any evil thoughts, the Devil would have to tempt Him. This whole process is an absolute impossibility, for God just cannot think any evil thoughts."[80] Our belief in God's own character, His perfect purity and holiness, makes it impossible for us to suppose that it is from Him that our temptations proceed. In the stainless purity of His character lies one argument why no one should ever accuse God of tempting man to sin.

And He Himself does not tempt anyone – A second thing that should keep men from ever thinking God is the source of temptation is the fact that God simply does not personally tempt anyone! That's an eternal truth men would do well to keep in mind![81] Instead of

---

[78] One wonders if the reason behind the reader's attempt to blame God isn't the result of old Pharisaic theology. Remember, we have pictured James writing this epistle to counteract the emphases of the Pharisees who tried to infiltrate the churches in order to Judaize them. Popular Pharisaism taught a doctrine of divine predestination (Josephus, *Ant.* XVIII.1.3; *Wars* II.8.14), and such a doctrine was likely to develop into a fatalism where God is blamed for the temptation and sin in the world. James counters by saying, "That's not right!" It has also been observed that the writer of Ecclesiasticus gave the same warning to his readers, "Say not thou, It is through the Lord that I fell away ... Say not thou, It is he that caused me to err" (Eccl. 15:11,12).

[79] "Cannot be tempted" translates a verbal adjective *apeirastos*, a word not found elsewhere either in Scripture or in classical Greek. James Moffatt (*The General Epistles, James, Peter, and Judas* [London: Hodder and Stoughton, 1947], p.18) suggested the word was coined by James. Like its root, which can have two meanings, the verbal adjective can mean "untried" or "untempted." God may "try" or "test" men, but He does not "tempt" them. God "tries" men because such testings are necessary to develop the desired moral maturity (verse 4), but there is no evil intent in God's mind, nor any attempt on His part to solicit them to do evil.

[80] There is absolutely nothing in the nature of God that responds to evil, so He is untemptable. He cannot be seduced or tempted into evil thoughts or actions.

[81] Some have supposed that this flat assertion in James contradicts Matthew 4:1 or Matthew 6:13. Matthew 4:1 has Jesus led by the Holy Spirit into the wilderness to be tempted by the Devil. It was not God or the Holy Spirit who tempted Jesus; it was the devil. The model prayer has this petition, "Do not permit us to be tempted, but deliver us from the Evil One." Again, God is not the one doing the tempting. In fact, He can put limits on the devil so that he cannot tempt us as he otherwise might. If God did not permit men to be tempted, He would have to take away our free moral agency. "The general teaching of the Bible as a whole on this subject would seem to be that, while God allows men to be tried, as Abraham's faith and Job's sincerity were tried, such trials may be used by the evil one, designated Satan or the devil, as temptations to do evil." (Tasker, *op. cit.*, p.45) Scripture sometimes speaks of God's blinding men's hearts and giving them up to vile passions (see Romans 1:24,26), but Scripture does not assign to Him the beginning of this blindness. Instead, these are God's judicial responses to man's previous sin.

God doing evil (tempting any one), 1 Corinthians 10:12-13 promise the Christian that God does good by limiting how much the Devil is able to tempt, and by planting in our minds thoughts about the way of escape from each individual temptation the Devil is allowed to stir up.[82] The next verse gives us the true source of the temptations we struggle with.

1:14 -- *But each one is tempted when he is carried away and enticed by his own lust.*

But – In contrast with an attitude that blames God for temptation (verse 13), James here sets forth the right understanding of the source of temptation.

Each one is tempted ... by his own lust – The word order in Greek puts "by his own lust" alongside "each man is tempted." "Is tempted" is present tense, suggesting that being tempted is a repeated experience in each human being's life. If we did not have the following participles which suggest the Devil's activity in stirring up men's desires, we could probably agree with all those commentaries that find here in James 1:14 a proof text for the doctrine of hereditary total depravity.[83] Because James does not specifically implicate the Devil by name in this whole temptation process, some have asserted that James' doctrine of temptation contradicts what the New Testament elsewhere teaches.[84] *Epithumia* is "desire," and the desire, depending on the context, can be either good or bad.[85] The context here requires us to take it in the bad sense, i.e., a desire for forbidden things, a passionate craving for what God has forbidden. "Lust" (in its broader meaning, if it is not

---

[82] When a Christian sins, our wills have not been overpowered, leaving us helpless. Instead, we have simply refused to exercise our moral choice. This is exactly the position of James that it is man's own fault when he fails to resist the Devil's temptations.

[83] Typical are the comments of J. Nieboer (*The Practical Epistle of James* [Erie, Pa: Our Daily Walk, 1950], p.70), "Every man has a corrupt nature that he has received from Adam" and Tasker (*op. cit.*, p.46), "This verse, in fact, so far from being opposed to the doctrine of original sin, substantiates it," and Burdick (p.172), "The source of temptation lies within man himself ... It is by man's own sinful nature that 'he is dragged away and enticed'." See the author's commentary on Romans for a careful discussion and refutation of the doctrine of hereditary total depravity. See also the author's presentation at the Forum on Calvinism, titled "Total Hereditary Depravity – The Big Lie," sponsored by the Christian Restoration Association, October 22-23, 1998.

[84] Ropes held that the significance of James' failure to explain the origin of sin as due to the Devil is that he had outgrown that "old Jewish idea." "It is highly significant that James' mind naturally turns for the true explanation of temptation not to the Jewish thought of Satan (cf. the explanation of the origin of sin in the Book of Enoch 69:4ff), or of the 'evil root', but to a psychological analysis, strongly influenced by Greek conceptions of human nature" (Ropes, *op. cit.*, p.155,156). In reply, would we say that Paul didn't believe in the Devil because he makes no mention of him when he writes in Roman about the war between the flesh and spirit? No, for we find frequent reference to the Devil elsewhere in Paul's writings. Likewise in James, we elsewhere find reference to the demons and to the Devil (2:9, 4:7).

[85] Your appetite for something to eat is *epithumia*. Gold "fever" would be *epithumia*. A desire for more knowledge of God's Word would be *epithumia*. A desire for safety is *epithumia*. The word occurs in a good sense at Luke 22:15; Philippians 1:23; and 1 Thessalonians 2:17.

limited to desire for illicit sensual gratification) is a good choice of words. "His own" denotes that the desires that influence men vary from person to person.

When he is carried away and enticed – "Carried away" and "enticed"[86] are present passive participles agreeing with "each one." Thus, it might be translated to read, "Each one, while being carried away and enticed, is tempted by his own desires."[87] Who or what is the agent acting in these passive participles? Is it the man's own desires[88] or is the Devil the unnamed agent? The "carrying away" and "enticement" are aimed at the man's desires, and the desires then cry out to be satisfied. This cry is what is here described as "being tempted." The Devil's temptations would have no power if there were no answering response in us. If we controlled our desires, if we checked the wrong suggestions the Devil plants in our minds, the Devil would be powerless and helpless in his attempts to ruin men. Rather than blaming God for our sins, James is emphasizing man's personal responsibility for sinning.

1:15 -- ***Then when lust has conceived, it gives birth to sin, and when sin is accomplished, it brings forth death.***

Then when lust has conceived – In order to show that our sins are not to be traced to God, James changes from the language of hunting and fishing to the language of the conception and birth of a child. First, temptation comes and desire is triggered (verse 14). Then conception occurs, i.e., the desire receives the assent of the will. If when an impulse to evil comes, we straightway squelch it, we have not sinned. While we cannot avoid all the Devil's enticements, we do not have to nurture and embrace them.[89]

---

[86] The Greek words are used to refer to the way animals are caught by hunters or fishermen. The first one is used of animals taken by hook or noose, as the fish or crocodile (Herod. II.70). The second one is used of beasts or birds which are attracted by bait to get into the trap or net. The game is lured from its path and drawn off towards something attractive, only to discover there is a deadly hook in it, or a snare that captures them.

[87] Eve is a good illustration of how the Devil works. She was first moved away from her secure trust in God by the words of the tempter. Then she was attracted to the fruit itself. In other words, she was "drawn away" and "enticed." Then her desires took over, tempting her to depart from what she knew to be the will of God.

[88] Shall we read that "his own desire" is the source of both being "drawn away" and "enticed"? If so, must we not say that Christians, even *after* being born again and having the old slavery to sin broken when they were immersed, *still* have an evil nature that is able to war against the inner man without any outside provocation by the Tempter? Is the evil nature hereditary, or is it the result of the Christian's continual yielding to temptations, so that he becomes a slave of sin again (Romans 6:12ff)?

[89] Jesus was tempted, but He was without sin. So, it is not sin just to be tempted. Luther said, "You cannot keep the birds from flying over your head, but you can keep them from building a nest in your hair." We do not have to provide a guest room in our minds for evil thoughts. When Jesus spoke about "looking on a woman" (Matthew 5:28), He used a present tense verb; hence it pictures continued action, continued looking. We do not have to give the temptation a continuing welcome until what was suggested to our desires actually conceives and gives birth to sin.

It gives birth to sin – Sin is pictured as being the child and offspring of evil desire. Each lust gives birth to its own kind of sin. Perhaps we must be careful not to press the details of the illustration too far. We must not suppose that "lust" is permitted just as long as we don't do the act that lust suggests. The lust (*epithumia*) can be as wrong as the act. Paul wrote, "I would not have known that desire (*epithumia*) was sin if the Law had not said, You shall not desire!" (Romans 7:7). Jesus said, "You have read in the Law, You shall not commit adultery. But I say to you, that every one who looks on a woman to lust for her has committed adultery with her already in his heart" (Matthew 5:27,28). "Just as a child is alive before the actual moment of birth, so sin does not begin to be sinful only when it is manifest in a specific, visible action."[90]

And when sin is accomplished, it brings forth death – Sin has a way of growing. Like a baby develops until it is "full grown," so sin (unless its life and growth are terminated by repentance) grows till it is ready to produce offspring. When it is "full grown,"[91] it "gives birth to death."[92]   James is writing to Christians, and his presentation of sin is very similar to Paul's presentation in Romans 6. In Romans, Paul explains that when a person is immersed into Christ he is freed from his old slavery to sin (6:3,4,17).[93]   Now, as a Christian, he is free to choose which master he will serve. He may serve obedience, which will result in righteousness. Or he may serve sin, which will result in death (6:16). Habitual service to righteousness will result in sanctification (6:19). Habitual service to sin results in death (Romans 6:21,23). So James says that habitual sinning[94] will result in "death" for the Christian. "Death" likely includes both spiritual death and eventually punishment in Hell,[95]   the exact antithesis to the blessed state alluded to as "the crown of

---

[90] Tasker, *op. cit.*, p.47.

[91] Mayor (*op. cit.*, p.53) suggested that sin becomes "full grown when it has become a fixed habit determining the character of the man."

[92] The verb translated "brings forth" (*apokueō*) is different from the verb "gives birth to" (*tiktō*) used earlier in this verse. "Brings forth" (*apokueō*) is used of the new birth at James 1:18, so the suggestion of E.G. Punchard ("The General Epistle of James" in *Ellicott's Commentary on the Whole Bible* [Grand Rapids: Zondervan, 1954], p.55) that this verb denotes "some monstrous deformity" is probably not correct. More likely is the note in Moulton and Milligan (*The Vocabulary of the Greek Testament* [London: Hodder & Stoughton, 1963], p.65) that the words are synonyms, and that *apo* pictures "coming forth from the womb." This passage that pictures the conception and birth of lust and sin in James lies behind the marvelous allegory of Sin and Death in Milton's *Paradise Lost* (Book II.745-814).

[93] When a man commits his first sin, his spirit dies and he becomes what the Bible calls "a slave to sin." This whole fatal situation is reversed when a man becomes a Christian. His spirit is alive (John 3:6); he can walk in newness of life (Romans 6:4); and he is freed from the old slavery (Romans 6:7,17-18).

[94] It is not one isolated sin that results in "death" for the Christian, but an accumulation of sins. James' theology agrees with Romans 2:8 ,which speaks of the lost as being folk who have habitually not obeyed the truth, but have habitually obeyed unrighteousness.

[95] Anyone who indulges in a sinful thought or a corrupt desire should remind himself that it may end in death – death both temporal and eternal. This reflection should check any evil thought or desire at its beginning.

life" (verse 12).   The great value of these verses in James is that they urge on us a personal responsibility to resist temptation, rather than blaming God for the temptation.

1:16 -- *Do not be deceived, my beloved brethren.*

Do not be deceived – The prohibition (*mē* and the present imperative) demands the cessation of an action already going on.   It is difficult to decide whether to take verse 16 with the preceding or the following verses.[96]   If we choose the preceding, which of the topics does James have in mind?   Perhaps they have been deceived concerning God being the author of sin (verse 13).   Perhaps they have allowed the Devil to "carry away and entice" them (verse 14) too long.   If we choose the following, then the topic is "Stop being deceived into thinking God gives anything but good and perfect gifts!"

My beloved brethren – Because the truth about God being presented is so important, James reminds his readers that he writes what he does because he loves them dearly, because they are brothers in Christ.

1:17 -- *Every good thing bestowed and every perfect gift is from above, coming down from the Father of lights, with whom there is no variation, or shifting shadow.*

Every good thing bestowed and every perfect gift is from above – God's character as a giving God was introduced in verse 5.   This verse and the next are evidently intended as further proof that this giving God is not the source of temptation to do evil (verse 12).   God who gives only good gifts could not be the source of temptation to do evil.   "God's gifts are marked by kindness and helpfulness, not destructiveness."[97]   The KJV reads "every good gift and every perfect gift,"[98] hiding the fact that two different Greek words are used by James: "thing bestowed" translates *dosis*, while "gift" translates *dōrēma*. The first word denotes the act of giving, while the second puts emphasis on the gift itself.   God's act of giving is described as "good" (*agathē*), a word which denotes "good in general, good in itself and its effects, profitable."[99]   Every gift is described as "perfect" (*teleion*), a word already explained in notes at verse 4.   It means "complete, mature, full-grown."   God's

---

[96] In Paul's writings, "Do not be deceived" often serves as a pointed introduction for the significant statement which follows (1 Corinthians 6:9, 15:33; Galatians 6:7).

[97] Burdick, *op. cit.*, p.173.

[98] The cadence of the KJV wording reflects the fact the Greek text has the cadence of a hexameter. Because of this hexameter, some think James has quoted a poem or an early Christian hymn.   Others think James himself was the original author of this line.   (A similar meter is found in the direct quotations in 1 Corinthians 15:33; Titus 1:12; and in the Greek of Hebrews 12:13 and Revelation 19:12.)

[99] Berry, *op. cit.*, p.1.

gifts are entire; there is nothing lacking to complete them.[100]   "From above" is a way of speaking about heaven where God the Father lives.   God in heaven above[101] showers His gifts from on high, from above.

Coming down from the Father of lights – The beneficial gifts are pictured by the present participle as continually coming down.   The reason why the gifts from above were perfect is because they come from the Father of lights.   The same One who created the "lights" is the One who gives the gifts.   They all, alike, are nothing but beneficial.   As the next clause shows, the plural "lights" certainly includes the heavenly bodies (i.e., sun, moon, and stars) set in the firmament of heaven (Genesis 1:14,15; Psalm 135:7), but it may include more.[102] "Father" probably has "a twofold significance, pointing on the one hand to the creation of the lights and on the other to God's continuing sovereignty over them."[103]

With whom there is no variation – The first part of the verse has shown that God's gifts are nothing but good.   The remainder of the verse says this is invariably true.   The Greek words *ouk eni* indicate there is absolutely no place, no possibility[104] of any such change as might be described as "variation."   "Variation" translates *parallagē*, which is the root of our scientific term "parallax," a word used to describe the change of position, real or apparent, of the stars, the moon, and the sun.   James seems to say that the sun, moon, and

---

[100] When commentators attempt to identify what the gifts are that are perfect, that have no element of incompleteness, they point to the greater gifts of righteousness and peace and joy, the gift of the Holy Spirit, the gift of His one and only Son which is the crowning gift of all.

[101] "From above" is the same as saying "from heaven."   See James 3:15,17; John 3:31, 19:11.

[102] The Word of God is a light.   Prophecy is a light shining in a dark place.   The Gospel is a light shining throughout the world.   The heavenly city is a place of light, illumined by the glory of God.   Jewish people with the Law to guide them thought of themselves as a light to those who were in darkness (Romans 2:19).   The Urim and Thummim, the "lights" and "perfections" which symbolized God's gifts of wisdom in its highest forms (Exodus 28:30; Leviticus 8:8; Deuteronomy 33:8) might be included.   Jesus is the light of the world, and whoever follows Him does not walk in darkness (John 8:12).   Christians are described as "children of light" (Ephesians 5:8).   God, "who is light, and in whom is no darkness at all" (1 John 1:5) is the Father of them all (Psalm 36:9).

[103] Burdick, *op. cit.*   Notice, also, as their Creator and Sustainer, God is not to be identified with the "lights."   Pantheism is not a true presentation of our cosmos.

[104] This view holds that *eni* is a strengthened form of *en*, which, used without a verb, with the negative *ouk* carries the force of "there is no place for, it is not possible."   See J.B. Lightfoot, *St. Paul's Epistle to the Galatians*, [Grand Rapids: Zondervan, 1957 reprint], p. 150, and H. Thayer, *A Greek-English Lexicon of the New Testament* [New York: American Book Co., 1889], p. 216.   Hiebert (*op. cit.*, p.113) expresses doubt about how far the idea of impossibility can be pressed, and urges that the NASB translation "there is" reflects the contemporary scholarly view that the expression conveys simply a negative fact.   What shall we say about "the openness of God" debate in light of this verse?

stars ("lights") may have their changes, but not so their Creator and their Father.[105] He does not change. When He gives, and that is regularly, His gifts are always good! There is no change or variation from His established course or pattern.

Or shifting shadow – This translates the reading *hē tropēs aposkiasma*.[106] It appears to refer to the varying measure of light seen on the earth from the sun, "now the full light of high noon, now the dimness of twilight, and at night no light at all."[107] "The heavenly luminaries, which He created, are symbols of His holiness, but they are imperfect. In their revolutions they are sometimes overshadowed. The moon is not always at the full; the sun is sometimes eclipsed. In Him there is no change, no loss of light, no encroachment of shadow."[108] This statement by James is very striking. One would think that James knew that day and night are caused by the turning of the earth on its axis. History gives Copernicus the credit for discovering this truth in AD 1520. The fact that James uses this expression as he does is an incidental proof that he wrote by the inspiration of the Spirit of God. Another reading, *parallagē ē* [or *hē*] *tropēs aposkiasmatos*, found in Codex Vaticanus, the first hand of Sinaiticus, and in P[23], a fourth century papyrus fragment found at Oxyrhynchus in 1914, would be translated "variation due to a shadow of turning."[109] It apparently is intended to give one example of the "variation" just alluded to, namely, the long or short shadow cast on the earth as the sun appears high or low in the

---

[105] "The design here is clearly to contrast God with the sun in a certain respect. As the source of light there is a strong resemblance. But in the sun there are certain changes. It does not shine on all parts of the earth at the same time. It does not shine in the same manner all the year. It rises and sets. It crosses the equator, and seems to go far to the south, and sends its rays obliquely on the earth. Then it ascends to the north, recrossing the equator, and sends its rays obliquely on the southern regions. By its revolutions it produces the changes of the seasons, and makes a constant variety on the earth in the productions of different climes. In this respect, God is NOT like the sun. With Him there is no variableness, not even the appearance of turning. He is the same at all seasons of the year, and in all ages. There is no change in His character, His mode of being, His purposes and plans. What He was millions of ages before the worlds were made, He is now. What He is now He will be countless millions of ages hence. We may be sure that whatever changes there may be in human affairs; whatever reverses we may undergo; whatever oceans we may cross, or whatever mountains we may climb, or in whatever worlds we may hereafter take up our abode, GOD IS THE SAME." A. Barnes, *Notes on the New Testament, Explanatory and Practical – James, Peter, John, and Jude.* Edited by Robert Frew (Grand Rapids: Baker, 1951), p.28

[106] This reading is found in the third hand of Sinaiticus, in Alexandrinus and Ephraemi, numerous minuscules, and several versions. It is characterized as "the least unsatisfactory reading" among the numerous ones found at this place. (B.M. Metzger, *A Textual Commentary on the Greek New Testament,* [London: United Bible Society, 1971], p.679-80.)

[107] Ropes, *op. cit.*, p.161.

[108] Alfred Plummer, *op. cit.*, p.579. Because one cognate of the word "shadow" refers to the shadow seen on the face of a sundial, some writers have attempted to use the slowly moving shadow to illustrate the truth that there is no such change or movement in God.

[109] This is the reading adopted by Goodspeed, RSV mg, NEB, NIV.

heavens.[110]   James' portrayal of God's character (e.g., verses 13 and 17) is an important topic in this letter.

1:18 -- ***In the exercise of His will He brought us forth by the word of truth, so that we might be, as it were, the firstfruits among His creatures.***

In the exercise of His will He brought us forth by the word of truth – James is still giving reasons for denying that God is the author of temptation (verse 13).   His argument here is that God acts constructively, rather than destructively (as would be the case if He were the author of temptation).   His "lights" which pervade the universe are not the chief proofs of His goodness.   That God is good all the time is best seen in His provision for the salvation of lost mankind.   Salvation is made available because of an "exercise of His will."[111]   What is set forth is that God does not deliberately and directly tempt man to sin.   Rather, he willingly and deliberately provides a way of salvation.[112]   "Brought us forth" is the same verb used of the process of sin that ends in death (verse 15).   That being true, we suppose the salvation of men is a process which ends in life, rather than death.[113]   Purposely, James shows that God does not "bring forth sin and death."   Instead, what He does is good and beneficial; He "brings us forth" into life.   "By the word of truth" shows that the "birth" referred to here must be spiritual rather than natural.[114]   "By the word of truth" should guard us from interpreting this passage as Calvinism has tended to interpret

---

[110] *Tropē* is a word used for the solstice (compare the English "tropic"), and *aposkiazō* means "to cast a shadow."   The word *tropē* is used in the LXX of Job 38:33 and Deuteronomy 33:14 of the apparent motion of the stars and planets in the heavens.   *Aposkiasma* is used of the shadow effect produced on the earth when the sun is eclipsed by the moon.

[111] The participle "willingly" agrees with the subject of the verb "He brought us forth," and the construction seems to be similar to one found in Colossians 2:18 which reads "let no one willing ...," and seems to mean "let no one by the exercise of his will defraud you ...."   "Will" (*boulētheis*) suggests a "choice resulting from deliberation" as compared to "will" (*thelēma*) which proceeds from inclination (Thayer, *op. cit.*, p.286).   (Exactly the opposite definitions of the synonyms is given in Cremer's Lexicon.   Understand that this differing opinion concerning the distinction between *boulē* and *thelō* hides a Calvinistic hair-splitting theological agenda concerning predestination, involving what God wills, and what God is only said to wish.   When He wills it, it has to happen; when He only wishes it, it may or may not happen.)

[112] We understand that since Christ was a lamb slain since the foundation of the world that God willed and planned for salvation before He ever created man.

[113] James may not specifically mention repentance, confession and immersion, but it is implied in this allusion to the new birth.   God, giving mankind a good gift, provided them with the Word of truth, in which the "how to be born again" process is clearly explained so that we may be adopted as sons into God's family.   The Spirit works through the Word of truth leading us to belief and the desire to be immersed into Christ.   The same Spirit then helps the new Christian to live the Christian life.

[114] Hort interprets "us" in this verse as mankind in general, and refers the "bringing forth" to man's original creation with a supremacy over His other creatures.   Since in the beginning God simply spoke, and it was so, Hort thinks "word of truth" in James has reference to God's spoken creative word.   "Brought us forth" is a figure that suits the new birth, but hardly the creation.

it, as though man is wholly passive in salvation, while God rather miraculously does it all.[115]   That "word of truth"[116] means "the Gospel" is evident from parallel passages (1 Peter 1:23,25; Ephesians 1:13, 5:26; Colossians 1:5), where we are told that men are made His sons when they hear and respond to the gospel of salvation (i.e., the Word of truth). Men become believers in Christ through the word of the apostles (John 17:20).   Our Lord made the "word which is truth" the instrument by which sanctification or consecration of His followers would occur (John 17:17-19).

So that we might be as it were the firstfruits among His creatures – If we have judged the destination of this letter correctly as being to Jewish Christians, then "we" who are "firstfruits" are James and his contemporaries, the first generations of believers who came from ethnic Jewish stock.   Indeed, a few decades later, Revelation treats the converts from the twelve tribes of Israel as being "the firstfruits unto God and to the Lamb" (Revelation 14:4).   "Firstfruits" means "more to come."[117]   As Christian missionaries continue to go into all the world, not only from among ethnic Jewish people, but also from among gentile peoples, converts (new "creatures"[118]) will continue to be "brought forth."   It was part of the way God willed to do things that the Gospel went to the Jews first, then to the Greeks. The Jewish converts were to be a kind of "firstfruits."

When we sum up all the known facts, there is only one conclusion about God's nature at which we can justly arrive: that is, as far as it is known to us, His nature is utterly opposed to evil.

---

[115] "Of his own will" in Calvinism is explained in this fashion: No other consideration (save His own will) influences Him in this matter of who shall be "brought forth."   Predestination of certain individuals to salvation is said to be the result of God's will in action.

[116] "Word of truth" can be either a message that consists of truth, or a message which proclaims the truth.   The reference in "Word" is not to the personal Word, Jesus Christ (as in John 1:1-14).

[117] The meaning of the term can be traced back to a Jewish ritual (Exodus 34:22, Leviticus 23:10, Deuteronomy 26:2).   During the feast of Passover, a sheaf of barley, just recently harvested, is waved before the Lord in thanksgiving – thanksgiving for the rest of the harvest to be reaped just as soon as they returned home from the Passover celebration.   That first sheaf, "firstfruits," was evidence of more to come. Using the same figure of speech, the risen Christ is called "the firstfruits of them that sleep" (1 Corinthians 15:20), and the household of Stephanas is designated as "the firstfruits of Achaia" (1 Corinthians 16:15).

[118] "Creation" (*ktisma*), which denotes something that is the product of creative activity (*ktisis* is the form used at Galatians 6:15 to speak of Christians being a "new creation"), is thought by some to be an unusual way of speaking of Christians as being God's "new creation."   Because the term is commonly used of God's material creation, some commentators suppose there is a reference to Christians being the "firstfruits" of the coming transformation of the whole creation (Romans 8:19-22, Revelation 21:1). Creation, which was subjected to futility when Adam sinned, will one day be set free from its slavery to corruption into the glorious freedom of the sons of God.

II. WELCOMES AND PRACTICES WHAT THE WORD OF TRUTH TEACHES. 1:19-27

Summary: A second mark of a genuine Christian life, and a second way to ensure the experience of real joy, is how one responds to the word of truth.

The function of the word of truth is given under the figures of a seed (verse 21), a mirror (verse 23), and the law of liberty (verse 25).   For a listener to this truth to experience real joy there must be a proper attitude toward the Word (verses 19,20), a careful and wholesome lifestyle (verse 21), and a ready obedience to what the Word requires (verses 22-27).

1:19 -- This *you know, my beloved brethren.   But let every one be quick to hear, slow to speak* and *slow to anger.*

This **you know** – In the KJV, this verse begins "wherefore ... let every man be ...," because a few manuscripts have *hōste* as the first word in the verse.   A majority of manuscripts read *iste*, a form which can be either indicative ("you do know this", i.e., act upon your knowledge) or imperative ("know this!").   Most of those who decide it should be treated as an imperative make the first part of verse 19 to be an exclamation point to close the previous paragraph (i.e., God tempts no man and God gives good gifts, the best of which is that He brought us forth by the word of truth.   Know this!   Never forget it!).[1]   A few treat it as an introduction to what follows.   In that case, "Take note of this!" calls for the reader's attention as James launches into his presentation of a readiness to listen to the Word of God.

My beloved brethren – Just as he did in verse 16, so here at verse 19 James expresses his love for his fellow Christian brothers.

But let everyone be quick to hear – In verse 18 James called attention to the "word of truth."   In verses 21,22 he will write about the "implanted word" and "doers of the word." In this context "quick to hear" evidently means "quick to hear the Word of God."   Once one has responded positively to the "word of truth" (verse 18), he has a continuing responsibility to quickly and readily listen when God speaks through His New Testament apostles and prophets.   The readers of this letter would hear not only traveling missionaries and local teachers (Acts 13:1),   but could "hear" as apostolic books are read

---

[1] That we should translate it as imperative is supported by the "but" that introduces the last half of the verse.   You readers must never forget the reality of what has just been said, "but" don't stop there.   You must allow the word of truth to continue to function in your lives.

out loud in the public worship services.[2]   "Let everyone be quick" is an imperative, and the present tense makes this "quick to hear" a continuing duty for Christians.

Slow to speak – Perhaps James has in view the disobedience and obstinance of many of his countrymen (cp. Romans 10:21), especially the Judaizers who were quick to speak against the gospel.   It hardly means that Christians are to "be slow to speak to others about Christ."[3]   Someone who continually talks has a difficult time hearing what anyone else is saying.   (Remember how the Jewish leaders at Antioch of Pisidia contradicted what Paul and Barnabas were saying even while the preachers were trying to preach, Acts 13:45.) "Slow to speak" is a call for restraint upon hasty and ill-considered reactions to what has just been heard.

And **slow to anger** – There are times when foolish souls become angry when they hear the calls to repentance and duty in the word of God.   One essential condition of listening when God speaks through His word is to control one's distracting thoughts of resentment or anger at what is being spoken.   (Remember how the Jews at Jerusalem angrily responded to Paul's presentation of the Gospel from the steps up to the tower of Antonia, Acts 22:22,23.) Such anger precludes the message from having any chance of being welcomed or embraced by the listeners.   Slow to speak and quick to hear are harder than ever when men are roused to anger.[4]

1:20 -- *for the anger of man does not achieve the righteousness of God.*

For the anger of man – "For," which connects this verse with verse 19, shows that verse 20 is intended to give a reason for the command about being "slow to anger."   "Man" (*andros*) does not mean this warning about anger is limited to men (males) only (cp. 1:8,12), but it perhaps does picture an assembly in which the men were likely to actively respond in one way or another to what was preached or read in the assembly.

Does not achieve the righteousness of God – Anger towards the word of God is not an

[2] The earlier the date we assign to the writing of James, the less of the New Testament there is that would be in written form.   An early date for James necessarily implies the "hearing" of oral instruction in the Christian faith.

[3] Writers who treat James as being a series of rather disconnected proverbs will write at length at this place about how ancient wise men have recognized the value of being "slow to speak."   "Men have two ears, and but one tongue, that they should hear more than they speak."   "I have had occasion to regret what I have spoken in haste, but never that I was silent."   Some even point to passages in Proverbs or Ecclesiastes or Ecclesiasticus as being similar "wise sayings."

[4] The word translated "anger" is *orgē*, a word which denotes more than momentary anger.   It denotes a strong and persistent feeling of indignation and active anger, a settled habit of anger.   *Thumos*, another word translated "anger," denotes the momentary, impulsive, passionate outburst of anger that can just as quickly subside.   (See Geo. R. Berry, *A Greek-English Lexicon to the New Testament* [Chicago: Wilcox and Follett, 1948], p.47)

atmosphere in which "the righteousness of God"[5] can be produced or can flourish.[6] "Righteousness" might speak of righteous living (i.e., a right relationships with one's fellow man), or it might speak of God's way of saving man, or it might speak of a right relationship with God.[7]   The negative particle with the present tense verb indicates that not at any time does continuing anger towards the Word of God produce righteousness.   The on-going anger does not help produce in our own lives the right conduct that God requires,[8] and it does not help us win others to Jesus Christ.[9]

1:21 -- *Therefore putting aside all filthiness and all that remains of wickedness, in humility receive the word implanted, which is able to save your souls.*

Therefore – Not only must one be quick to hear in order to be ready to give reception to the word of truth.   Verse 21 will indicate a second preparation needed – namely, careful and wholesome Christian living.   James is still describing the kind of person who is most apt to be teachable when he or she hears the Word.

Putting aside all filthiness – The word picture in the verb "putting aside" is that of stripping off dirty clothes, or scraping off dirt from the body.[10]   What is involved in putting off unchristian characteristics or deeds is repentance and self-control when tempted.   The word *hruparia* ("filthiness") occurs nowhere else in the New Testament.[11]   *Hrupos*, a word somewhat akin to it, is used of the wax in the ear.   (I.e., 'Get the wax out of your ears, so you are able to hear God speaking to you through His Word.')   Here, the word is apparently applied to evil conduct that is considered disgusting or offensive, including the "anger" of the previous verses.   These get in the way of hearing the Word.   The Lord said, "Out of

---

[5] "Of God" likely means that God demands or requires such righteousness

[6] The manuscripts give two different forms for the verb translated "achieve" or "worketh" (KJV).   One means "to bring to completeness" and the other means "to do or practice."   One pictures a growth in "righteousness"; the other simply pictures a practice of right conduct.

[7] "Righteousness of God" is a phrase that is found in Paul's writings (Romans 1:17, 10:3; 2 Corinthians 5:21; Philippians 3:9).   James and Paul, both apostles of Jesus, are in perfect agreement on this doctrinal and practical matter.

[8] What God requires is that a man "do justly" (Micah 6:8), and anger will prevent the fulfillment of this requirement.

[9] Again, we wonder if there is a side glance at the Judaizers whose behavior resulted in the Jerusalem Conference (Acts 15).   Their anger at the gospel (word of God) made no contribution to the righteousness of God, either before the Conference or after it.

[10] The same verb is used at 2 Peter 2:1,2, and Hebrews 12:1.   The plural participle here is dependent on the plural imperative ("receive") and suggests that each person must strip off the "old clothes" if he or she is to be ready to receive the Word.

[11] A cognate adjective is found in its literal sense in James 2:2.   A noun from the same root is found at 1 Peter 3:21 and in the LXX of Proverbs 30:12.

the heart of men proceed evil thoughts, adulteries, fornications, murders, thefts, covetousness, wickedness, deceit, lasciviousness, an evil eye, blasphemy, pride, foolishness; all these evil things come from within, and defile the man" (Mark 7:21-23). Perhaps this is the kind of "filthiness" James has in view.

And *all* that remains of wickedness – "Wickedness" translates *kakias*, "evil." There is more involved than simply "malice."[12] It is a generic word for "sin." The Greek word used here (*perisseian*) can mean "surplus," so the KJV "superfluity of ..." might be accurate. However, we doubt that only a surplus, or the "extra" amount, of wickedness must be laid aside; the verse is not permitting a "moderate" degree of wickedness. Instead, *perisseian* likely has the same sense as *perisseuma*, "remainder." What James teaches is that any "hang-over" of old sinful habits from pre-conversion days is to be laid aside.[13] As long as a man cherishes some of his old sins, he will have a hard time hearing the Word of truth.

In humility receive the word implanted – *Prautēs*, the word translated "humility," has no precise English equivalent. Some versions offer "meekness."[14] The word speaks of one who has his feelings and emotions and impulses under control. We might offer the word "teachable" or "tractable." The right approach to the Word of truth is that one is willing to hear, be taught, and be directed in whatever way God points. "Implanted" suggests the word picture of seed being sown.[15] We are reminded of Jesus' Parable of the Sower, where the "seed" is the Word and the soil is the "heart," and where the soil's fertility is "an honest and good heart" (Matthew 13:23), i.e., a heart free of prejudice and bitterness. When the Word of God falls into good soil, it is welcomed; it takes root, and soon the soil produces beautiful Christian virtues that are elsewhere called the "fruit of the spirit" (Galatians 5:22). The word "implanted" implies the readers are Christians who already

---

[12] The word used in the KJV, "naughtiness," had a different connotation in the 1600's than it does today. Then, as its use in Latimer and Shakespeare shows, it was equivalent to "sin" or "wickedness." Now it has lost its evil connotation and is applied almost exclusively to the faults of children.

[13] Those who teach that everyone inherits a sinful nature from Adam are likely to find in this verse evidence that the old sinful nature still lurks in the life of the immersed believer, and must still be struggled against on a daily basis. Concerning "all filthiness and overflowing wickedness," Calvin wrote that "these are the innate evils of our nature, and that ... we are never wholly cleansed from them in this life, but that they are continually sprouting up ...." The picture Paul gives in Romans 6:12ff is much better than any doctrine of total hereditary depravity. That Scripture teaches that after a person becomes a Christian, the Devil still tries some of the old temptations that used to work, just to see if they still are enticing to us.

[14] We should avoid any idea of spineless weakness. Instead, we are speaking of a strong man who so controls himself that he can deliberately be docile and submissive rather than haughty and bullheaded.

[15] The translation "engrafted" suggests a different word picture than "implanted." "Grafting" (where a shoot is grafted into a budhead, and produces fruit of its own, whatever may be the original character of the budhead onto which it was grafted) and "planting" are two different ways of encouraging the process of growth.

possessed Gospel truth. James is not calling for initial acceptance of the Gospel message, but for a full and hearty welcome of the truth by those who already are Christians. He is speaking of Christians growing in spiritual understanding and lifestyle.

Which is able to save your souls – As a result of the growth in Christian character which is helped by the Word of truth, a man's full and final salvation is made certain. The Word of God is living and active and powerful, but it does not work in a man by compulsion or like a charm. The cooperation of the man is required, or there will be no growth and no salvation. Man, it seems, is composed of body, soul, and spirit.[16] All three parts are affected by the salvation God has provided. However, in this place, "soul" apparently stands for the whole person (as in Acts 27:37). James' statement here about how the Word of God operates is the same doctrine as Paul taught the Ephesian elders when he commended them "to God, and to the Word of His grace, which is able to build you up, and give you an inheritance among all them who are sanctified" (Acts 20:32).

1:22 -- But prove yourselves doers of the word, and not merely hearers who delude themselves.

But prove yourselves doers of the word – The conjunction *de* here is likely continuative; it could be translated "and." James wishes to say something further on the subject than simply "receive" the implanted word (verse 21). By "the word" is meant what was just called "the implanted word" and "the word of truth" (1:18,21), and what will shortly be called "the perfect law, the law of liberty" (1:25). James is referring to Gospel truth, to New Testament presentations of the will of God, whether in spoken (i.e., the primary medium at the time when James wrote) or written form.[17] Within the phrase "prove yourselves doers" both the verb itself (*ginesthe*) and the tense (present imperative) are remarkable. It could best be rendered "become doers of the Word." True Christian practice is a thing of growth; it is a process, and a process which has already begun and which is continually going on.[18] The "implanted word" doesn't produce growth automatically. We must constantly put into practice what we are taught. "Continue to be doers of the Word!" The Restoration Movement emphasis on "speaking where the Scriptures speak" is bound up with what James here writes. "Do what the Word says!" is the idea behind New Testament Christianity and all James writes.

---

[16] See notes at 1 Thessalonians 5:23, and the Special Study on the new birth at the close of Acts 2 in the author's commentary on Acts. Man shares the physical make-up of his body with animals. The soul animates the body of man, just as it animates the body of an animal. In humans, God intended the spirit to give directions to the soul which in turn animates the body. When a man commits his first sin, the spirit "dies" and ceases to function as God intended. Man is left a physical or soulical being. When the new birth occurs, what is reborn is the "spirit" (John 3:6).

[17] James says "be doers of the word," not "be doers of men's traditions." Is there a side glance at the man-made rules the Judaizers were championing?

[18] We may compare "become wise as serpents and as harmless as doves" (Matthew 10:16); "become ready" (Matthew 24:44); "become not faithless but believing" (John 10:27). "Become doers" is considerably more expressive than "Be doers." (A. Plummer, *op. cit.*, p. 580)

And not merely hearers – Obey the Gospel, don't merely listen to it![19] "Hearers" naturally suggests hearing the public reading of Scriptures and the public preaching of New Testament preachers. Just like the public reading of Scripture had been a vital part of the weekly synagogue service (Acts 15:21), so public reading of the Gospels and Apostles became a vital part of early Christian worship meetings. "We are indeed to be hearers, for nothing takes the place of regular listening to God's word; but we are not to be hearers only."[20] On the principle of available light, the responsibility of those who hear is greater than that of those who have never heard.

Who delude themselves – A man is only cheating himself when he listens with much attention to the reading of the Word and then does not act. Originally the word *paralogizomenoi* meant to mislead with fallacious reasoning. Somehow, by false reasoning, or bad logic, the person who listens persuades himself that it is perfectly sufficient simply to attend the public assembly and to hear the Word, as though that is all it takes to remain a Christian in good standing. We know such reasoning is bad since Jesus Himself pronounced His benediction on those who both "hear the word and habitually keep it" (Luke 11:28).

1:23 -- *For if any one is a hearer of the word and not a doer, he is like a man who looks at his natural face in a mirror;*

If anyone is a hearer of the word, and not a doer – James is still emphasizing the wisdom of being a doer, rather than just a hearer only. Verses 23 and 24 give an illustration of a man who deceives himself.

He is like a man who looks at – James writes *eoiken andri*, and the word "man" usually excludes women, and sometimes boys also. James does not say "like a person" (*anthrōpoi*), which would have included both sexes and all ages. A somewhat quaint explanation is that "men," as a rule, give only a passing look at themselves in the mirror, whereas it is a feminine practice to give more prolonged attention to how they look. But this suggested explanation may not withstand the word used for "beholding" (*katanoein*), which means "to fix one's mind on" or "consider attentively."[21] (It is the word for "consider the ravens" and "consider the lilies" in Luke 12:24,27.) Moreover, the Greeks

---

[19] Why do so many think that all they have to do to get to heaven is just go to church and listen to a sermon once a week. In 2 Thessalonians 1:8 we read of the vengeance of God upon those who do not obey the Gospel. Likewise, in His Sermon on the Mount, Jesus spoke of the wise and foolish builders (Matthew 7:24-27). The wise builder not only heard Jesus' sayings, but habitually put them into practice! The foolish builder merely heard the words, but habitually did nothing he was taught to do. Even in Old Testament times, God expected men to be "doers" of the Law, and not just hearers, if they expected to be justified (Romans 2:13).

[20] Tasker, *op. cit.*, p.52. A "hearer only" is one who doesn't follow instructions. An old maxim says, "If all else fails, follow instructions!" The way to real joy in the Christian life is to follow the instructions one finds in the Word of God.

[21] TDNT, 4:975.

sometimes did what we ourselves frequently do in speaking of the human race; they employed the masculine noun as representative of both (cp. Luke 11:31,32). This use of "man" in the sense of human being is common in James (1:8,12,20,23, 2:2, 3:2).[22]

His natural face – *To prosōpon tēs geneseōs* is literally "the face of his birth," i.e., the face or appearance which we have in virtue of our natural birth.[23]   When it comes to application to spiritual things, why not think of the "face of our new birth" (verse 18)? After we become Christians, there are still areas of behavior and character that need sanctifying. As we look into the mirror of the Word of God, we see ourselves as we are. Where there is something unlovely, sinful, unattractive, the revelation of what is seen in the mirror is meant to lead the person to change.

In a mirror – This word (*esoptrō*) is better translated "mirror" as in the ASV, NASB, rather than "glass." The mirrors of the ancients were of polished silver, copper, or tin.[24] They would give a good reflection, though not as perfect as modern glass mirrors. The Word of God provides each "looker" with a measure of self-knowledge so that we can see ourselves just as God sees us.

1:24 -- for once he has looked at himself and gone away, he has immediately forgotten what kind of person he was.

For *once* he has looked at himself and gone away – James uses a subtle variation of past tense verbs (aorist tense, perfect tense, aorist tense) in his comparison of a man looking into a mirror and looking into the Word of God. It apparently was his style (see verse 11) to use past tense verbs to give a lively simplicity to his narration. In verse 24 James references a common behavior we all likely have done at one time or another. We contemplate[25] ourselves in a mirror, see the smudges and mussed hair and wrinkled garments, and walk away from the mirror, sufficiently satisfied with how we look to ourselves that we make no attempt to make any changes for the better.

He has immediately forgotten what kind of person he was – This is the key point of the comparison between looking into a mirror and looking into God's Word – namely, not do-

---

[22] Plummer, *op. cit.*, p. 581.

[23] Hort suggests that James is saying we get a temporary glimpse of our face as it would have been if sin had not come in to "deface" it. Mayor treats the figure differently. He thinks the contrast is between the "face that belongs to this transitory life" and the "reflection as seen in the Word of the character that is needed for eternity."

[24] "Glass mirrors were not available until late Roman times." Harold D. Koos, "Mirror," in *Wycliffe Bible Encyclopedia*, 2:1139. Glass mirrors such as we are accustomed to, coated with quicksilver, were invented in the 13th century AD.

[25] The verb translated "looked" here is the same verb used in verse 23. The verb does not describe a hasty or superficial glance as some have suggested.

ing anything about what was seen. Rather quickly, the awareness of what he saw vanishes from the mind. So it is when many people come to the mirror of the soul, i.e., to God's Word. They get a good look at the state of their soul, at whether or not there are any spiritual disfigurements, spots, or blemishes. How easy it is to leave the assembly where the Word was read or preached and do nothing about what we've heard. An hour or two after the sermon they cannot tell you the theme or the main points. Such forgetfulness will not be an acceptable excuse before the Lord (verse 25). It is doubtful any will be excused even if they are able to say, "Yes, I did notice there were some sins of commission and some sins of omission as I heard the Scriptures being read, but I forgot what I heard before I got around to doing something about what I saw."

1:25 -- *But one who looks intently at the perfect law, the* law *of liberty, and abides by it, not having become a forgetful hearer but an effectual doer, this man shall be blessed in what he does.*

But – In contrast to the person who sees himself in God's Word but does nothing about it (verses 23-24), this verse describes one who both listens and does something about it.

One who looks intently at the perfect law, the *law* of liberty – The "perfect law of liberty" is a mirror for the soul, just like the metal mirror is for the natural face. The verb translated "looks intently at" is *parakuptō*, the same verb used of Peter and John and Mary Magdalene looking into the empty tomb on resurrection morning (John 20:5,11). It is the word used of the angels who stoop down to look into our salvation (1 Peter 1:12). Here in James it pictures a man zealously searching the Scripture to hear its message.[26] James' use of "law" here needs special attention. His use of "law" hardly makes this a reference to the Mosaic Law; Christians have been released from that tutor now that faith in Christ has come (Galatians 3:23-25). In another place, having stated that he was no longer under the Law of Moses, Paul indicates he is under the law of Christ (1 Corinthians 9:20,21). It is very likely James is calling the truth of the Gospel the "perfect law,[27] the law of liberty."[28] There is "liberty" because in Christ a man is set free from the old slavery to sin (Romans 6:7ff). Having become obedient from the heart to that form of doctrine to which he was

---

[26] It is doubtful there is any contrast in the manner of looking between the man who does not remember what he sees (verse 24) and the man who does (verse 25), even though Peter uses two different verbs. The lexicons give "attentive scrutiny" as a meaning for both verbs.

[27] There will be a similar use of the word "law" at James 2:8,12. The earlier expressions "implanted word" (verse 21) and "word" (verse 22) make it clear James is speaking of the Word we call the Gospel. By calling it a "law" James intends his readers to understand that the inspired message Christians live by is an authoritative body of truth.

[28] Some have objected that the expression "law of liberty" is an oxymoron. They may think laws are made to restrict liberty; that liberty is composed of freedom from law; that liberty is license to do as one pleases. But what kind of liberty would we have if all laws were suddenly suspended, and all restraining officers and all courts were suddenly abolished? It would be anarchy. We would hardly dare leave our homes after dark, or even in the daylight. But in submission to the laws taught by Christ there is genuine freedom.

committed, he is free to choose which master he will serve from here on (preferably obedience rather than sin, Romans 6:16). This is exactly the situation needed by any of James' readers who would make the changes indicated by his or her intent looking into the mirror of God's Word. The "law of liberty" is the Christian gospel which sets us free. There is liberty in Christ, for if Christ shall make you free, you shall be free indeed (John 8:32-36). If we are correct in dating James after the Jerusalem Conference, perhaps the expression "law of liberty" is a pointed, vivid contrast to the "yoke of bondage" (Acts 15:10) which the Judaizers with their Pharisaic rules were trying to impose on men, thus taking away the freedom men have in Christ. In a similar way, Galatians (an anti-Judaizer document) speaks of the freedom we have in Christ, and warns about being entangled again in a yoke of bondage (Galatians 5:1). James likely calls the Gospel "perfect" or "complete" in contrast with the Law of Moses, which was never intended by God to be anything but temporary, and was valid only till Christ (the One to whom it pointed) came.[29]

And abides by it – This expression apparently speaks of looking into the perfect law of liberty not once, but often and long.[30] It would speak not only of hearing the Word, but meditating on it.

Not having become a forgetful hearer – This contrasts with what was written in verse 24. This hearer is characterized not by forgetfulness[31] of what he hears, but he keeps them in mind, preparatory to acting on what he has heard.

But an effectual doer – As the marginal notes indicates, the Greek reads "a doer of work." This hearer actively practices what is attentively heard. Habitual action is the prominent idea. Earlier James wrote of being "doers of the word" (verse 22). Now he writes "doer of work." A "doer that acts" in harmony with what the "word" teaches cannot fail to find joy in what he does.[32]

This man shall be blessed in what he does – "This man" (*houtos*) indicates this man and

---

[29] Perhaps, too, "perfect" says the same thing that Jude 3 says: the Gospel is God's final revelation. He has spoken in the Son (Hebrews 1:1,2), and it is His last message to mankind.

[30] In the Greek, the participles "looking into" and "abiding in" are connected by "and" and are governed by one article. This precludes us from treating "looking into" as being a cursory look, a quick glance.

[31] The construction, literally "becoming not a hearer of forgetfulness," is the same as "steward of injustice" for the "unjust steward" (Luke 16:8, 18:6). The genitive "of forgetfulness" is the characteristic attribute being used instead of the adjective. "Forgetfulness" (*epilēsmonēs*) occurs nowhere else in the New Testament, but does occur in Ecclesiasticus 11:27.

[32] In this century there is a keen interest in the Scriptures. As new versions proliferate they are grabbed up. Commentaries, expositions, introductions, helps of all kinds – e.g., exegetical, homiletical, historical, textual, CDs for the computer – suitable for the learned and beginner. Great care must be exercised lest we are more eager to know all about God's Word than we are to learn from it His will respecting ourselves, that we may put it into practice!

no one else! Some readers recall Psalm 1:2, "Blessed is the man whose delight is in the law of the Lord; and who meditates on the Law day and night." Others recall the words of Jesus, "If you know these things, blessed are you if you habitually do them" (John 13:17).[33] Doing God's work in accordance to His Word brings blessings.[34] The Lord wants more than isolated acts of obedience; he wants disciples whose lives are characterized by obedience. We should note there was no corresponding promise in the verse about the forgetful hearer. Are we to think that James means to imply the forgetful hearers are liable to lose his or her eternal reward because they have not habitually done what the Lord has told them to do?

1:26 -- *If any one thinks himself to be religious, and yet does not bridle his tongue but deceives his* own *heart, this man's religion is worthless.*

If any one thinks himself to be religious – There is no connecting word in this or many of the following verses. Are verses 26 and 27 connected with what precedes, or do they begin a new topic? These comments will treat them as connected to what precedes, as examples of the changes for the better a man should make when he sees himself in the mirror of God's Word.[35] Without such changes there will be no real joy, for he would be a hearer and not a doer. The KJV reads "seems to be religious among you"[36] – i.e., to himself and to others. He looks just like other people in the assembly of believers: he will be at many of the church services and his name will be on the church roll. But his talk gives him away as an imposter. *Dokei* means "seems in his own estimation." NASB has the person himself thinking he is "religious." "Religious" (*thrēskos*) occurs only here in the New Testament, and a cognate term occurs only four times in Scripture (James 1:26,27; Acts 26:5, where it describes the ceremonial worship of the Pharisee; and Colossians 2:18, where it has a bad connotation as it describes the worship of angels). Josephus used the term to describe the public and ceremonial worship conducted in the Temple at Jerusalem. Obviously, "religious" is not talking about being zealous for Buddha or Mohammed. James is dealing with a man's relation to Jesus Christ, and his topic is Christian life and practice.   The Greek word speaks of religious observances and

---

[33] See notes on verse 12 for the meaning of "blessed."

[34] We are reminded of the Beatitudes. Notice, the Beatitudes do not pronounce a blessing because of what one believes; but rather because of what one does or is. In his commentary, Plumptre has observed that it is as though, by use of the words "doing" and "blessed," James has brought together the beginning and ending of the Sermon on the Mount.

[35] A case could just as well be made that these two verses go with what follows, that a new topic of emphasis begins here, namely, examples of behavior that can negate "religion" – a topic that stretches through 2:13.

[36] The text behind the KJV is slightly different from the text behind the NASB.

the zealous performance of religious duties, the outward rituals of religion.[37]   The word here (and its cognate at the close of the verse) seem to describe a scrupulous attention to the details of formal worship.[38]

And yet does not bridle his tongue – James likens the human tongue to a horse that needs bridling.   A bit and bridle are used to direct the horse and hold it in check.[39]   Christians need to hold their tongue in check.[40]   If a man fails to control his speech in the ordinary relationships of life, at other times than when at worship (being "religious"), if a man prays at the Lord's Table on Sunday yet curses and tells filthy stories the rest of the week, he gives evidence that he is not the Christian he pretends to be.   Exactly in what way he fails to control his speech – whether it be cutting criticism, or foul language, or unclean speech, or by other ways – is not specified.   A man's religious acts ought to make a difference in the way he lives, just like hearing the truth ought to be reflected in a changed lifestyle (verse 22).   Control of the tongue "is a particularly excellent test of genuine religion."[41]

But deceives his *own* heart – James repeats what he said in verse 22 about hearers (and not doers) who delude themselves, though the word used here (*apataō*) is the more common one for "deceive."   A man may convince himself by his "ritual" on Sunday that he is a Christian, but if habitually (the present tense indicates habitual action) there are sins remaining in his life like lying, swearing, filthy conversation, he is deceiving his own heart about his standing with God.   "Heart" refers to the man's thoughts.

This man's religion is worthless – *Thrēskeia*, used again at end of verse, pictures the outward expression of religion in ritual and liturgy and ceremony.   His attendance at the assembly, his participation in the different "acts of worship," are all to no avail.   *Mataios* means "useless, purposeless, aimless."[42]   His "religion" fails in its essential purpose.   It

---

[37] It is not easy to find an exact equivalent in English.   "Religious" in its modern sense is too wide; its old pre-Reformation connotation of one who belonged to a monastic order is too narrow.   Devout, pious, reverent, worshipper, and ritualist, have all been suggested.   In modern liturgy, the person being described would be very careful to perform the right actions, speak the right words, wear the right robes for the specific occasion.

[38] One wonders if in the back of James' mind is the recent heated controversy with the Pharisees who were scrupulous in their outward performance of religious acts.   Is James helping his readers to distinguish between what the Pharisees claimed was acceptable religion and what Jesus Christ would adjudge as being acceptable religion?

[39] The compound verb *chalinagōgeō* means to guide and hold in check with a bridle (*chalinos*).

[40] James uses the same figure in 3:2,3.

[41] Robert Johnstone, *Lectures Exegetical and Practical on the Epistle of James* (Grand Rapids: Baker, 1954), p. 159-60.

[42] *Mataios* and *kenos* are synonyms.   The latter means "empty" and refers to contents.   The former means "aimless" or "purposeless" and refers to the results.   Berry, *Lexicon*, p.55.

leaves his inner life unchanged.[43]   Jesus said, "By your words you are justified, and by your words you are condemned" (Matthew 12:37).   That text is a guide for self-examination rather than casting a stone at our neighbor.

1:27 -- *This is pure and undefiled religion in the sight of our God and Father, to visit orphans and widows in their distress,* and *to keep oneself unstained by the world.*

This is pure and undefiled religion – What James is saying is, "The finest ritual and the finest liturgy you can offer to God is practical service to needy brethren and purity in one's own personal life."   "Pure" deals with the inner effects of the Gospel.   In the area of ethics, "pure" deals with that which is free from moral corruption.   "Undefiled" deals with the outward effects of the gospel.   Does James here reflect again on Pharisaic Judaizer's emphases dealing with what is ceremonially pure and what is defiled?[44]   It is not whether one has his hands washed when he eats, nor is it what he eats (the old distinctions between clean and unclean foods have been abolished in Christ, Mark 7:17-23), nor into what building he enters (John 18:28) that defiles, but it is failure to meet the needs the poor and the orphans that defiles a person.   In his commentary, Barclay notes that for James real religion "did not lie in elaborate vestments, or in a noble liturgy, or in magnificent music, or in a carefully wrought service."   James does not give a complete and comprehensive definition of "religion" in these verses, but does show that genuine religion is a life-changing experience.

In the sight of *our* God and Father – There seems to be a contrast to how we appear in the eyes of our fellow men.   A man who is meticulous in his "ceremonial observances" might appear good before the eyes of man.   But the Judge whose verdict really matters is "our God and Father,"[45] and He has different standards for what constitutes "pure and undefiled religion" than men do.   The kind of "religion" God accepts is the kind that results in a positive change in a man's lifestyle.   Acceptable religion is that which is in harmony with the Divine standard.   (Remember the sacrifices of Cain and Abel, and the kind which was acceptable and the kind which was not.)

To visit orphans and widows in their distress – This is the second of the three specific areas where looking into the mirror of God's Word should make a difference in the lives of Christians.   Pure and undefiled religion will express itself in love to others.   "Visit" translates *episkeptomai,*   the very same word Jesus used when he spoke of "visiting" His

---

[43] In the LXX this same word "vain" is used of pagan idols and idol worship.   That religion did not change a person's inner nature for the better.   Just going through the motions of the Christian religion is not much of an improvement on idolatry!

[44] The word *amiantos* is commonly used in the LXX to denote that which is polluted or ceremonially unclean (see Leviticus 5:3, 11:23).

[45] Hiebert has written (*op. cit.*, p.111), "As 'God,' He is omnipotent and sovereign and will authoritatively deal with our religious practices.   But He is also our 'Father,' not merely an impartial Judge but also a loving Father who has the interest of His children at heart."   These two characteristics should encourage worshippers to evaluate all our religious practices in light of how they look to Him.

sick and needy and imprisoned and hungry brethren (Matthew 25:36,43).[46] To "visit" the fatherless[47] (i.e., orphans) and widows means more than just to stop in for a cheery visit. One translation put it, "Pure religion and undefiled is to *look after* the orphans and widows." Another has it, "*to give aid to* the orphans and widows." The "visitor" has as his or her aim the caring for and supplying of the needs of those visited. The lot of orphans and widows was often very bitter in Bible times; in the KJV it is called "affliction," in the NASB it is called "distress".[48] In many parts of the world, their situation has not improved significantly. Therefore, there is a crying need for Christians to be concerned and involved. "Visiting" includes helping them; if necessary, feeding them, clothing them, paying their rent, etc. It is ministering to their needs. Individuals and congregations can have a well-planned ministry to widows and widowers.[49] Individuals and congregations can have a vital involvement in ministry to the orphans.[50] Paul spoke of the faith that saves as being a "faith that expresses itself through love" (Galatians 5:6).[51]

---

[46] "Brethren." our brothers in Christ, are the chief object of our benevolent actions, but not the sole object. "Do good to all men, but especially those of the household of faith" (Galatians 6:10).

[47] Those who have been deprived of their parents, either through death or abandonment.

[48] Grief, loneliness, unscrupulous exploitation, homelessness, and cruelty were some of the common circumstances first-century orphans faced. If left with no financial means, and if there were no close relatives on whom a widow could depend, since there were few careers or jobs open to women, the widow was especially helpless in the ancient world. 1 Timothy 5 gives instructions to local congregations about caring for those who are widows indeed, and what recourse widows who had living relatives were to follow, in order that their dire situations might be eased.

[49] How wonderful the behavior of those congregations who have cared for the needs of the widows after their husbands have died.

[50] There are children's homes in most of the states where our churches are found. Why not encourage each family in the local church to be financially involved with the local children's home. Perhaps a good beginning goal would be a gift each year worth two or three weeks' wages. This would be one part of each person's Christian stewardship. After all, it is not really our money; we just manage it for God, Whose money it really is. Eventually, He is going to require that an accounting be made of how we've managed His riches. We and our congregation will want to reply well when He asks us if we visited the orphans and widows.

[51] This commentator is convinced that there is not enough of the practical in our religion. Too long we've sat in a pew with a hymnbook, listened to the sermon with our Bibles open, and then gone home and forgotten what we've sung and heard. While Catholics built the hospitals, Baptists ran rescue missions, the Salvation Army help the poor, and the Methodists took care of the temperance part, many of the rest of us did precious little in the area of ministry to the needy. Pure religion, religion that will get us to heaven, includes the visiting of the fatherless and the poor and the widows and the sick and the imprisoned. As far as doctrine is concerned, the churches of the Restoration Movement are likely as close to the pattern given in the New Testament as any religious group. But when it comes to the humanities, for years we were about as far from the Christ-approved plan of social work as any group. Without easing up on our insistence on right doctrine, let us give a greater emphasis to right living! Let there be involvement on an individual basis where brethren are in need, as well as cooperative participation in children's homes, rest homes for the aged, disaster relief, and medical missions.

***And* to keep oneself unstained by the world** – Along with a practice of personal ministry to the needy, there must also be a continual striving after personal holiness.[52]   This is a third example of how looking into the mirror of God's word should result in changed lives, holy lives.   "Unstained" is *aspilos*, a synonym similar to "undefiled" in the previous clause.   The "world" speaks of all those circumstances that tempt to sin, those selfish actions that characterize unsaved humanity, out of which Christians have been called and into which Christians are in danger of sinking back.[53]   Compare James 4:4.   Just as Paul did (1 Timothy 5:22), James also stresses each believer's personal responsibility to "keep one's self pure."[54]   The lambs that were acceptable for use as sacrifices in Old Testament times had to be without blemish.   The Christian who would offer his body to God as a living sacrifice must also be holy and unspotted (Romans 12:1).

---

[52] There is no connecting "and" in the Greek.   The way the exhortation is worded makes the duty of personal purity all the more prominent.

[53] Again there may be a side glance at the Pharisees' standards.   To them "defilement" came from touching a cup or garment that was ceremonially unclean, whereas the real defilement to be guarded against was contact with the "world" that could result in spiritual decline.

[54] Some scholars have pointed out that Philo has a teaching similar to what we read in James.   Philo speaks of those who practice "a ritual religion" (he uses the same Greek word James does) "instead of holiness" (Philo, p.173).

III. AVOIDS PARTIALITY AS HE LOVES HIS NEIGHBOR. 2:1-13

Summary: A third mark of a genuine Christian life, and a third way to ensure the experience of real joy, is to love your neighbor as yourself. But be certain to avoid any partiality or personal favoritism, especially toward wealthy persons during public worship, as you deal with those whom you are loving.

This avoidance of personal favoritism towards the rich is so serious that James gives five reasons to scrupulously guard against it: (1) Favoritism of certain humans is inconsistent with the Lord Jesus Christ being the object of our "glory." (2) Favoritism is indicative you are wavering and have evil motives. (3) Favoritism of the rich is exactly opposite of God's choice of the poor to be rich in faith. (4) Favoritism is sin because it transgresses what God has taught in His "royal law." (5) Favoritism will make it very difficult to receive a favorable verdict in the final judgment.

2:1 -- *My brethren, do not hold your faith in our glorious Lord Jesus Christ with* **an attitude of** *personal favoritism.*

My brethren – Verse 1 seems to begin a distinct paragraph[1] setting forth another way to test whether or not one's faith is genuine, or a different area where right or wrong attitudes can affect the joy James prays his readers may enjoy (James 1:1). The readers and James were brethren – perhaps as physical descendants of Abraham, or more likely because not only were they all "Jewish" but they were also "Jews who had become Christians" and thus were brothers in Christ. He will shortly speak of "faith in our ... Lord Jesus Christ." Both James and the readers acknowledged Jesus as their Messiah and Lord.

Do not hold your faith – James begins this section with a prohibition.[2] Do not try to mix "faith in Jesus" with an "attitude of personal favoritism"! The Greek construction prohibits the continuance of a practice already going on. "Stop showing favoritism!" is what

---

[1] The topic of chapter 2 is not completely disjointed from what James wrote in chapter 1. He closed that chapter by telling what pure religion is. In addition to what is said in 1:27, one might add avoidance of partiality as another staple of pure religion. The similar thoughts that tie the paragraphs together are religious worship and the treatment of the poor.

[2] The Greek might be translated as a question, "Do you hold?" but then the negative particle would imply a negative answer. It is difficult to see how James could be saying "No, you aren't partial" and then write what he does in the following verses. This being the case, it is better to treat the imperative with the negative particle that James wrote as a prohibition.

James calls for.   His tone is almost indignant as he calls them to cease showing partiality. "Hold your faith" is a way of describing the practice of the Christian religion.[3]

In our glorious Lord Jesus Christ – In "Lord Jesus Christ" we have the deity of Jesus the Messiah emphasized.[4]   "Faith in our … Lord Jesus Christ" emphasizes the fact that He is the object of faith to Christians.   The possessive pronoun "our" is how James identifies himself with his readers.[5]   Both he and they acknowledge they owe to Jesus their entire devotion and obedience.   Where the NASB reads "glorious Lord" the ASV had "*the Lord* of glory," with the italics indicating the two words "the Lord" do not appear in the Greek. The Greek reads "our Lord Jesus Christ of glory" ("of glory" being in the genitive case). In fact, seven words in a row are in the genitive case, thus making various connections between the words possible.   The words "of glory" could be connected with "faith" as though James had in mind "faith in the (future) glory" or "the glorious faith," or "faith in the glory of our Lord Jesus Christ."   Another possibility is to connect "of glory" with "Jesus Christ."   Accepting this second option, (1) some have interpreted it as being a genitive of origin.   Jesus came from "glory" (heaven) when He came to earth in His incarnate state.   If folk are going to look on a person's "wealth" as a criterion for paying respect,[6] then no one is richer than Jesus!   Why pay undue respect to wealthy humans, when one has the "wealthy Christ" to respect?   (2) Some treat it as a genitive of quality or characteristic, which results in the NASB translation "glorious Lord."   This emphasis on quality might call attention to the vast contrast between Jesus and the wealthy visitors.[7] Or it might be a reference to where Jesus is now: He is "in glory" seated at the right hand of the Majesty on high.   (3) Some put it simply in apposition to "Jesus Christ" and find a

---

[3] "Pure and undefiled religion" (James 1:27) was another way of describing the practice of the Christian religion.   In the Scriptures, "faith" sometimes stands for a body of doctrine (as Jude 1:3) and sometimes for a man's personal response to that doctrine.   Such personal responses sometimes are merely mental assent to a truth (James 2:19) that results in no corresponding change for the better in lifestyle.   But sometimes the personal response denoted by "faith" is synonymous with "faithfulness," a lifetime of careful obedience to the truth that makes up the body of doctrine.   When one's response to God's truth includes knowledge, assent, confidence, and obedience, we call that "saving faith," i.e., the kind of faith God looks for as a condition on which He will "justify" penitent sinners.

[4] Just as in 1:1, where Jesus is called "Lord" (i.e., an Old Testament word that means Jehovah) and where God and Lord Jesus are placed side by side as equal, this passage, too, points to Jesus' deity.

[5] He does not say "my Lord," or "my brother, Jesus Christ."   The Lordship of Jesus was not acknowledged by James alone, but also by the readers of this epistle.

[6] The Greek word "glory" is often used with the connotation of "esteem."

[7] One of the things that most reflects Jesus' "glory" is His willingness to empty Himself and take on the form of a servant.   His poverty and humiliation brilliantly demonstrate His real "glory."   This interpretation was first suggested by Bengel, and then adopted by Mayor and Hort.   Those writers thought the same truth was unfolded in passages such as Luke 2:14 and 2:32.   A slightly different way of expressing the implied contrast in the use of the word "glory" is to make it a contrast between Jesus and the readers who were showing partiality.   Showing partiality is one thing in Jesus' behavior that even his enemies could find no trace (Luke 2:21; Mark 12:14; Matthew 22:16).

reference to His deity (as in John 1:14-18, 17:5; 1 Corinthians 2:8; and Hebrews 1:3).[8] James uses this striking phrase, which expresses the majesty and power of Jesus whichever way we explain "glory," to suggest how shallow is the greatness of those wealthy persons to whom these readers were paying undue respect.   Why cheapen your faith in Christ by bowing down to transitory worldly wealth?

With *an attitude of* personal favoritism – In the Greek this phrase stands in an emphatic position immediately after the negative early in the sentence.   In addition the word is plural in the Greek, suggesting all the varied forms in which this evil tendency can show itself. Were James' readers affected by how things were in their pre-Christian days when, in spite of partiality being specifically forbidden in the Mosaic Law (Deuteronomy 1:17), showing respect of persons was a great and faulty habit?   The Pharisees especially loved the praise of men.   A rich man was always highly honored.   The Jews loved to have the chief seats at the feasts and in the synagogues.   Whatever the reason behind their present behavior, James tells his readers to stop it!   Given that we find it so often and consistently condemned in the New Testament, it is evidently common for men to have a problem with the temptation to show undue favoritism or unfair partiality.[9]   This prohibition of personal favoritism does not in any way cancel the fact that we are to show "honor to whom honor" is due (Romans 13:7).   In the Christian assembly, honor is to be paid to spiritual worth rather than worldly standing.

2:2 -- *For if a man comes into your assembly with a gold ring and dressed in fine clothes, and there also comes in a poor man in dirty clothes,*

For – James gives a specific example of the kind of faulty respect of persons he is prohibiting.   Two non-Christian visitors are pictured as entering the place where the congregation is meeting.[10]   Both ought to be welcomed as equals, for either might be won to Christ.   But the two visitors, one wealthy and the other poor, are not treated as equals when the Christians act towards them out of an attitude of respect of persons.

If a man comes into your assembly   –   "If there comes into your *synagogue*" is how the

---

[8] The same phrase "of glory" is applied to the Father at Ephesians 1:17 and to the Holy Spirit at 1 Peter 4:14.   "If the author of this epistle is James the Lord's brother, as we hold, this title is really his confession of faith concerning the true identity of Jesus Christ. ... In New Testament usage, the noun 'glory' denotes the 'divine and heavenly radiance' manifesting God's visible presence" (Hiebert, *op. cit.*, p. 149).

[9] The lesson Peter learned from the vision of the sheet with the clean and unclean animals on it was that God is no respecter of persons (Acts 10:34).   When Paul tells the standards that God will apply in the final judgment, he specifically calls attention to the fact that God is no respecter of persons (Romans 2:11). Paul over and over again calls attention to this truth (e.g., Ephesians 6:9; Colossians 3:25).

[10] Visitors were welcome at the assemblies of Christians, as is clear from 1 Corinthians 14:23-25.

Greek reads.[11]   This is the only place in the New Testament where the Jewish word is used for a Christian congregation.[12]   As noted in the Introductory Studies, the use of this particular word here is one of the reasons some have assigned an early date to the writing of James, and is a reason others have supposed the original audience was composed of Jewish people who were still meeting in the synagogue.   However, James also uses the word "church" to refer to the assembly of believers (James 5:14).   Perhaps for a while Christian converts did continue to use the Jewish meeting place (as in Acts 18:4-7) until opposition from unbelievers made that option no longer expedient.[13]   Or perhaps the word "synagogue" was naturally used by the converts from Judaism to designate their assembly until it was superseded by *ekklēsia*, a word more commonly used by Gentile converts and which would be more expressive.[14]   There is no need to suppose that James would have had to visit the various assemblies where his readers gathered to be aware of how rich and poor were treated.   Just recall how unspiritual people regularly act.

A man ... with a gold ring and dressed in fine clothes – The RSV employs the plural "gold rings" to express the nuance of *chrusodaktulios*, "a gold-fingered man."   There were enough gold rings on the fingers that the fingers were "covered with gold."   To wear a gold ring was a mark of special wealth in those days.   Only a rich man could afford such a ring, and only the very rich could afford a plurality of such rings.   The more ostentatious rich people wore rings on every finger except the middle one, and wore more than one on each finger.   Wealthy Jews often copied the Romans, and this is one area where the copy-

---

[11] A "synagogue" can be either the place where they met (Luke 7:5) or the company of folk assembled (Acts 6:9).   See the word used at Matthew 4:23 and Acts 17:1.   Here the word may refer to the place of meeting since verse 3 speaks of an assigned place to sit.

[12] In Revelation 2:9 and 3:9 we find the expression "synagogue of Satan" and in Acts 13:43 it is used of the Jewish assembly for worship.

[13] What must be assumed, under this scenario, is that the Christians were meeting at a different time than the unconverted Jews (James calls it "your synagogue").   If the Christians were meeting with the Jews, and the Jews (think of the duties of the ruler of the synagogue) were in charge of the synagogue, the Christians would have no control over how guests were seated.   However, James' language indicates the Christians are responsible for the ill-treatment of the poor and the unfair preferential treatment of the wealthy.

[14] The use of the word "the synagogue" has caused no little difficulty, and the commentators have advanced various hypotheses to explain it.   Some have argued that 2:2 contradicts 1:1 on the supposition that the article (*tēn sunagōgēn humōn*) indicates but the one synagogue used by the whole audience of readers, whereas 1:1 spoke of a more scattered audience.   Others have supposed the word "synagogue" has reference to judicial courts which were often held in synagogues, as reflected in such phrases as "beaten in every synagogue" (Matthew 10:17; Acts 22:19, 26:11).   James would then be saying, "Don't give a verdict in favor of the rich, just because he is rich."   However, to find reference here to a Jewish judicial process would destroy the contrast between "pure religion" and worldly respect of persons in the public assembly of Christians.   Still others, reflecting a later polity back onto the narrative, suppose that James has in mind a "convention" or "meeting" in which church business is conducted.   James then would be faulting the practice of giving the rich preacher the big pulpit and the poor preacher the little, backwoods mission station.

ing was slavish, just to make an impression on those less fortunate.[15] "In fine clothes" translates *en esthēti lampra*, "elegant, luxurious, shining (Acts 10:30), bright (Revelation 15:6), clear (Revelation 22:1)." *Lampra* (in an adverbial form) is the word used at Luke 16:19 of the "fine linen" worn by the rich man who fared "sumptuously" every day. It is the same word used at Luke 23:11 where we are told that Herod's people arrayed Jesus in "gorgeous apparel" and sent him back to Pilate. It denotes the type of cloth only the very rich could afford, and anyone who appeared in public in such garments was immediately recognized as being well off financially. Some have argued from this verse that it is wrong for Christians to wear any rings or luxurious garments,[16] but that is drawing an unintended conclusion. Judah had a signet ring (Genesis 38:18,25), and Pharaoh, as a token that Joseph had been promoted to honor, gave Joseph his ring. The broken hearted father in the parable gave the returning son a ring for his finger (Luke 15:22). Even the verses that prohibit Christian women from depending on jewelry or clothing to attract their husbands do not forbid all jewelry. We do not advocate that a Christian has liberty to ornament himself like a Christmas tree, but the Scriptures do not forbid all jewelry or fine raiment. It does say it is wrong to especially favor the man who does so dress.

And there also comes in a poor man in dirty clothes – We suppose that both the gold-fingered man and the poor man are visitors who are not Christians.[17] The repetition of "comes in" seems to picture this man's entrance at a different time than the rich man made his entrance. His dress at once made it evident he was a poor man. "Dirty clothes" translates *hrupara esthēti*.[18] *Hrupara* means "filthy, foul, sordid, shabby, squalid." The

---

[15] Roman satirists had much to say about the ostentatious dandies of their time. Juvenal (Sat. I.28.30) describes one rich man who, though born as an Egyptian slave, now appears with Tyrian robes on his shoulders and golden rings, light or heavy, according to the season, on his fingers. Martial (XI.60) tells of one who wore six rings on every finger, day and night, and even when he bathed. Barclay (p.75) tells how there was a shop in the capital city from which Roman people rented rings to wear when, on occasion, they wished to give an impression of special wealth. "We adorn our fingers with rings," said Seneca, "and we distribute gems over every joint."

[16] Clement of Alexandria, 100 years after James wrote, felt it necessary to urge Christians to wear only one ring, and he granted this permission because such a ring was needed for purposes of sealing (Paidogogos 3.11.) The Apostolic Constitutions 1.3, from the fourth century, warned Christians against fine clothing and rings since these were all signs of lasciviousness.

[17] This comment may have to be modified depending on how "rich in faith" (verse 5) is explained.

[18] "Clothes" (*esthēs*) is rendered by three different words in KJV (apparel, raiment, clothing) where only one word is used in the Greek. In the "Preface to the Authorized Version" printed in the KJV, the translators of 1611 use (misuse?) this very passage to defend their lack of precision in such matters, and avow that in many cases precision was deliberately sacrificed to variety and to a wish to honor as many English words as possible by giving them a place in the Bible! "In the passage before us the repetition of one and the same word for "clothing" is possibly not accidental. The repetition accentuates the fact that such a thing as clothing is allowed to be the measure of a man's heart. The rich man is neither the better nor the worse for his fine clothes, the poor man neither the better nor the worse for his shabby clothes. The error lies in supposing that such distinctions have anything to do with religion, or ought to be recognized in public worship ...." (Plummer, *op. cit.*, p.584, 585).

shabbily dressed man doesn't smell nice,[19] and he certainly is not attractive to the eyes (if one looks only at his dress). It is obvious from his dress that he is a poverty stricken (*ptōchos*) "beggar" and doesn't have much by way of prestige to offer his hosts.

2:3 -- *And you pay special attention to the one who is wearing fine clothes, and say, "You sit here in a good place," and you say to the poor man, "You stand over there, or sit down by my footstool",*

And you pay special attention to the one who is wearing fine clothes – The Greek *epiblepsēte* means "to look with favor on, to look on with special admiration." The rich man is shown special attention, he is given improper preferential treatment, simply because it is obvious from his dress that he is rich.[20]

And say, "You sit here in a good place" – "And you say" is plural in the Greek, and represents the whole congregation as agreeing with the sentiment expressed by the one of their number who actually speaks to the rich man. The English paraphrases the Greek which runs literally "You (with emphasis on "you") sit here honorably."[21] In Jewish synagogues, the most coveted seats were those at the end of the room. Thus, when seated, the whole audience could see the honored person, and the honored person himself was facing Jerusalem, while at the same time sitting very near the ark of the covenant (i.e., the chest containing the scrolls of Old Testament Scriptures). We don't know whether the meeting places used at first by the Christian congregations followed the same seating arrangement, or whether the Table of the Lord (1 Corinthians 10:21) was located in the place where the Ark of the Covenant stood in a Jewish floor plan. In a contemporary setting, the honored visitor would be given a place on the platform near the pulpit, where he would be conspicuous. They were treating this visitor with fawning respect on the first appearance merely from the indications that he was a rich man, without knowing anything about his character or his spiritual condition. Picture the vivid scene that James brings before us. A room is filled with Christians. The door opens, and immediately there is a commotion in the room. Everyone looks and whispers to his neighbor, "Look who just came in. He is one of the richest men in the city. Look at those gold rings on his fingers, and what excellent clothing he wears!" One of the leading men quickly arises from his seat, greets the guest, and welcomes him most heartily. "Come with me! You are doing

---

[19] The same word was used in the LXX at Zechariah 3:3,4 where mention is made of the high priest's "filthy (covered with dirt and manure) garments" which was indicative of the calamitous state of the Temple and God's people in Zechariah's time.

[20] The Greek words "fine clothing" (literally, "the clothing, the bright", where the restrictive attributive position of "bright" emphasizes that word) show the congregation was awed by the luxuriousness of the clothing.

[21] The exact force of the adverb *kalōs* is not certain. In the papyri it sometimes has the sense of "please," an expression of courtesy. Moulton and Milligan, *Vocabulary of the Greek Testament*, p. 319.

us such a favor. Sit here in this fine seat!" He then leads the guest up front, and seats him in one of the seats facing the audience.[22]

And you say to the poor man, "You stand over there, or sit down by my footstool" – The door of the meeting house opens a second time, and another stranger enters. This time it is one of the common people, certainly, by the looks of his clothes, from the poorer class. There is no excitement, no stir, no one arises to greet him cordially. Some Christian, perhaps one of the elders or deacons,[23] gives him a curt (almost contemptuous) alternative.[24] Again the plural "you say" pictures the whole congregation acquiescing with the sentiment expressed by the speaker, an attitude that reveals indifference concerning the visitor's comfort or feelings. "You can stand over there (anywhere out of the sight of the other worshippers, and in an undesirable spot far from sight and hearing), or, if you prefer a seat, you can sit here on the floor beside my footstool."[25] Because of the visitor's obvious lack of worldly goods, the church members do not even have the civility to offer him a seat. Thus, the rich man is highly honored while the poor man is despised, and in it all, the Lord is greatly displeased! Barclay tries to help us get a feel for the social problems faced by members of the early church.

> The Church was the only place in the ancient world where social distinctions did
> not exist [at least they weren't supposed to]. There must have been a certain ini-

---

[22] There is little evidence at this early date that congregational seating arrangements had a special place for the clergy to sit and a special place for the common people (laity) to sit. Nor does 1 Corinthians 14:16 ("the place of the unlearned") refer to such a segregated seating arrangement. Plumptre thinks there is an application of what James writes to many present-day seating arrangements. "What is to be urged in excuse for the special pews in churches and chapels, hired and appropriated, furnished luxuriously, and secured by bolt and lock? If in the high places sit the men and women in goodly raiment still, while the poorly clad and those from a lower social scale are crowded into side benches and corners, or beneficently told to stand and wait till room be found somewhere beneath the daintier feet – how can modern congregations escape from the condemnation with which James is about to charge his readers?" (E.H. Plumptre, "The General Epistle of St. James," *The Cambridge Bible for Schools and Colleges*, edited by J.J.S. Perowne [Cambridge: University Press, 1915], p. 254-255).

[23] While we are not convinced the suggestion should be adopted, we note that Allen Cabaniss ("A Note on Jacob's Homily," *Evangelical Quarterly* 47:4 [October-December 1975], p.219-222) has outlined the epistle of James according to different groupings of people he supposes are addressed. He thinks 2:1-26 are addressed to the deacons, so that the one speaking to the visitors is one of the deacons. At a time much later than James, the fourth-century *Apostolic Constitutions* has the bishop putting the deacons in charge of seating the people, and instructing that if the service were already in progress, the bishop should not interrupt the service to direct any late-arriving rich visitor to "an upper place" (*Apos. Constit.*, 2.57-58).

[24] As the critical apparatus of our Greek Testament shows, the exact words that James has being spoken to the poor visitor are uncertain. The way the KJV reads, the visitor is given two choices "stand there, or sit here" with the place where he might sit being closer to the speaker than the place where he was shown he might stand. Our newer English versions represent what was most likely how James worded it.

[25] The Greek says "under my footstool." The contrast between the "usher" who is sitting comfortably with a footstool for his feet and the beggar who must sit on the floor (a position that quickly becomes uncomfortable) vividly heightens the discrimination being shown.

tial awkwardness when a master found himself sitting next to his slave, or when a master arrived at a service in which his slave was actually the leader, and he, the master, might end up serving the emblems of the Lord's Supper to his slave. Further, in its early days the Church was made up of predominantly poor and humble people ["not many mighty, not many noble, are called"]. So when one of the rich, the mighty, or noble, visited or became converted, there must have been a very real temptation to make a fuss over him ... How difficult it is to downplay earthly distinctions, to ignore rank and place and prestige, even when men are meeting in the presence of the Lord Jesus Christ who is the King of glory. Yet this is precisely what early church members were expected to do. And so are we, if we understand this paragraph of James' instructions aright.[26]

2:4 -- *Have you not made distinctions among yourselves, and become judges with evil motives?*

Have you not made distinctions among yourselves – Here in verse 4 we have further reasons given why the kind of favoritism just illustrated is wrong.[27] The question (with the negative particle *ou*[28]) expects an affirmative answer. James expects his readers to agree with his assessment of the behavior. The meaning of James' question is variously given in the commentaries, because of the different possible meanings for *diekrithēte*. (1) As it did in 1:6, here it can mean "you are wavering, vacillating, halting between two opinions, doubting."[29] James would be asserting that when they pay special honor to the rich while dishonoring the poor, they were doing so because they were torn between two standards – the standards of the world and the standards of God. "Among yourselves" would mean "in your own minds." They couldn't make up their minds which they were going to abide by. They were double-minded in this matter, trying to make the best of both worlds. 'By your worldly behavior, you are showing lack of faith in Christ and His teaching.'[30] (2) It could mean, "You are guilty of discrimination, the very favoritism that God has everywhere condemned." Giving the rich man a good place, and the poor man a bad one, is discrimination. You have followed a pattern of behavior which is totally con-

---

[26] Barclay, *op. cit.*, p.76, paraphrased and edited. Again, let it be remembered that Christianity does not forbid proper respect to rank, to office, to age, or to distinguished talents and services. We must give honor to whom honor is due. But it is discrimination to honor someone only because he is wealthy, or to despise another only because he is poor. After reading James' criticism of respect of persons, we must be careful lest we go to the other extreme, namely, despising the rich simply because they are rich. It is not a sin to be rich. There are many rich men who are very Christ-like and very generous in the distribution of the wealth which God has entrusted to them to manage for Him.

[27] In the Greek, verse 4 is the conclusion of the long conditional sentence begun in verse 2.

[28] Codex Vaticanus omits the word "not." In that manuscript the sentence becomes an affirmation instead of a question, "You are doubting," "You are discriminating."

[29] This is the way the word is regularly used elsewhere in the New Testament. See Matthew 21:21; Mark 11:23; Acts 10:20; Romans 4:20 and 14:23.

[30] Faith in Christ's words concerning the deceitfulness of riches may be in James' mind.

trary to what God has taught.   "Among yourselves" would mean "in your congregation." Have they not already acknowledged the abolition of class distinctions (James 1:9-11)?

And become judges with evil motives? – The reason behind their discrimination is terribly wrong.   They are judges,[31] acting as they do to honor one and dishonor another, because their thoughts or motives are evil![32]   Again the question is worded in such a way as to imply an affirmative answer.[33]   When the readers examine their own thoughts and motives[34] they will arrive at the same conclusion James has.[35]   The adjective "evil" (*ponēros*) is the synonym that means not just evil in itself, but something that tends to encourage others to be evil, too.[36]   Such partial behavior is the result of a character quality that is vicious, injurious, and destructive.

2:5 -- *Listen, my beloved brethren: did not God choose the poor of this world* to be *rich in faith and heirs of the kingdom which He promised to those who love Him?*

Listen, my beloved brethren – Verses 5-11 advance two more arguments against the practice of improper preferential treatment of the rich and poor.   The imperative "Listen!" calls attention to the importance of these arguments.   "My beloved brethren" indicates that James is speaking in an affectionate manner as he appeals to their hearts.   He is motivated by love as he writes seeking their welfare.

Did not God choose the poor of this world – In verses 5-7, in his first argument, James points out that their favoritism towards the rich is inconsistent with both God's choice of the poor and with the hostile actions of the rich towards the readers themselves.   As far

---

[31] In the Greek the words "distinctions" and "judges" are based on the same root.

[32] The construction is similar to "hearer of forgetfulness (forgetful hearer)" and "doer of work (effectual doer)" in James 1:25.   It is similar to the English phrase "a man of bad temper" or "men of evil habits," and is analogous to "unjust judge" (judge of injustice) at Luke 18:6.   The "evil thinking" is thus highlighted or emphasized.   This is what characterizes their behavior.   Their own thoughts were evil.

[33] We have two verbs connected by "and" in this verse, and the negative particle attached to the first verb naturally goes with the second also.

[34] The KJV, "are become judges of evil thoughts" might be interpreted to mean they were judging the evil thoughts of others.   The ASV's "with evil thoughts" better reflects the idea in the Greek.

[35] The word for "motives" (*dialogismos*) is one which in itself suggests evil, even without any epithet (such as "evil" which James here includes).   It is the word used for the "reasonings" of the Pharisees when they taxed our Lord with blasphemy for forgiving sins (Luke 5:22, cp. 24:38).   Paul uses it for those who are "vain in their reasonings" (Romans 1:21; 1 Corinthians 3:20), and couples it with "murmurings" (Philippians 2:14).   These men, who even while engaged in the public worship of God set themselves up as judges to honor the rich and condemn the poor, were not holding the faith of Jesus Christ, but were full of evil doubts, questionings, and distrust.   (Plummer, *op. cit.*, p.585)

[36] Berry, *Synonyms*, p. 126.

as God's behavior is concerned, He has chosen to bestow special honor upon the poor rather than the wealthy.[37]   James is giving an argument why his readers should not show preferential treatment to the rich just because they are rich.   If God chose the poor and James' readers choose the rich, then James' readers are at cross-purposes with God (as the contrast in verse 6a clearly states).   The "poor of this world" may be "poor in the things of the world" or "poor in the world's estimation of them."   God, James tells us, made a choice, a selection, that out of the people living in this world, He would show a special interest in the poor.[38]   Barclay has called attention to some of the passages where God's choice of the poor is taught.

> "God," said Abraham Lincoln, "must love the common people because He made so many of them."   Christianity has always had a special message for the poor. In Jesus' first sermon in the Synagogue at Nazareth His claim was "He has anointed me to preach the gospel to the poor" (Luke 4:18).   Jesus' answer to John's puzzled inquiries, as to whether or not He was God's Chosen One, culminated in the claim, "the poor have the gospel preached to them" (Matthew 11:5).   The first of the Beatitudes was a Beatitude of promise, "Blessed are ye poor, for yours is the Kingdom of God" (Luke 6:20).[39]

To be **rich in faith** – This phrase indicates how those who are poor financially can be exalted in this present life.[40]   Though they are poor in the world's goods, they are spiritually rich because of their faith.   "Faith" denotes people's response to the gospel, the faith that comes by hearing the Word of God and the obedience of faith that is an integral part of that response.   It is much more desirable to be "rich in faith" than to be "rich in the things of this world."   (Remember what God told the wealthy Laodiceans who supposed they needed nothing, Revelation 3:17-18.)   The man who finds favor with God is the man who is abounding in faith, and that favor is worth more than all the gold of Ophir.

---

[37] The negative particle in this question implies an affirmative answer.   Yes, God did so choose the poor.   Of course, there is no contradiction between God "choosing the poor" (as James puts it) and "God is no respecter of persons" (as Peter words it, Acts 10:34).

[38] When was the choice made?   Was it part of how God, before He ever created, chose to do things as He formed His eternal purpose?   Romans 8:28 speaks of this eternal plan.   Ephesians 1:4 tells how we were chosen in Christ before the foundation of the world.   Or was the choice to focus on the poor made when Jesus came into the world?

[39] Barclay, *op. cit.*, p. 77.   Burdick calls attention to 1 Corinthians 1:26-28, and suggests some reasons why poor people are God's chosen.   From the rich young ruler we learn the lesson, "how difficult it is for a rich man to enter the Kingdom" (Mark 10:23-25).   A second reason is found in 1 Corinthians 1:29, where we are told that God selects those who have nothing or are nothing in themselves "so that no one may boast before God."

[40] The careful reader has noted the words "to be" in italics.   One might suppose the ones God has chosen are already rich in faith before they are chosen.   The translators added "to be" because they suppose "rich in faith" is (in technical terms) a secondary predicate (with the infinitive "to be" understood). He does not say that all poor people are automatically "rich in faith," nor does he imply that all rich people are automatically excluded from the ranks of those who can be rich in faith.

And heirs of the kingdom – This phrase indicates how God will, in the future, exalt the poor who become believers. An "heir" is a person who is appointed to receive an inheritance. The "kingdom" is here thought of as still future, as is shown by the word "promised" which begins the next clause.[41] Here we think of the beatitude spoken by Jesus, "Blessed are the poor in spirit, for theirs is the kingdom of Heaven" (Matthew 5:3; Luke 6:20). "Kingdom" in this passage seems to speak of the sum of all the blessings of salvation in the eternal state.[42]

Which He promised to those who love Him? – Man's promises are often valueless, because many such promises are not kept; the man is unable to, or never intended to, fulfill what he promised. But God's promises are "yes" and "amen" (2 Corinthians 1:20). We can absolutely trust the promises of God. He keeps His word! "God is not a man, that He should lie; nor a son of man, that He should [change his mind]: Has He said, and will He not do it? Or has He spoken, and will He not make it good?" (Numbers 23:19). God has promised a kingdom to those who habitually love Him.[43] It is as good as ours! Let it be recalled that Jesus identified this behavior that God expects when He said, "If you love me, you will keep My commandments" (John 14:15).[44] It is God's good pleasure to give the kingdom to such as these (Luke 12:32).

2:6 -- *But you have dishonored the poor man. Is it not the rich who oppress you and personally drag you into court?*

But you have dishonored the poor man – "But you" (*humeis de*) emphasizes a contrast to God's choice of the poor (verse 5), and there is great emphasis on "you." With Haman-like impiety you would disgrace "the man whom the King delights to honor." 'God chose the poor, but you readers dishonor the poor.' How inconsistent! "Dishonored" points to the outward act ("sit here on the floor!") that expressed their contempt. The poor could become rich in faith, but the readers' worldly attitude caused them to miss the opportunity

---

[41] Some have hesitated to interpret this verse as referring to the future kingdom. Romans 14:17 says that what is important in the kingdom of God (now, in this life) is not whether one gets what he wants to eat or drink, but whether he acts in such a way as to promote righteousness, peace, and joy in the lives of others. In other words, the "kingdom" emphasizes the ethical aspects of a man's life. That, it is affirmed, is exactly the point James makes at this place. James is emphasizing the fact that partiality towards the rich (just because they are rich) and dishonoring the poor (just because they are poor) is unethical. That action is not up to kingdom standards.

[42] In some passages, there is a relationship between the church militant and the Kingdom of God/Heaven (as Matthew 16:18,19). In other passages, "kingdom" has reference to what is styled the church triumphant (as in Acts 14:22 and Matthew 25:34,46).

[43] This "habitual love" (the Greek participle is present tense) is the condition God looks for, and upon which He has promised folk they will participate in the "kingdom."

[44] There are other promises in the Bible to those who love Him. A "crown of life," James 1:12. The "showing of mercy unto thousands of them that love me and keep my commandments," Exodus 20:6. "I love them that love me," Proverbs 8:17. "Eye hath not seen, nor ear heard, neither have entered into the heart of man the things which God hath prepared for them that love him," 1 Corinthians 2:9.

to evangelize. The poor could be heirs of the kingdom, but the readers preferred the man with earthly possessions. The poor man should have been specially favored if the Christians had exhibited Christ-likeness, rather than being Pharisee-like.[45] Jesus always sought out the poor and needy and helped them. The Christians should have thought, "Here comes a poor man into the meeting. God is specially interested in him. He has a tough time out in the world; let us be kind to him. Let us have compassion on him like Christ always had. Perhaps we can lead him to Christ."

Is it not the rich who oppress you – James asks three questions of his readers in order to show them their behavior towards the rich borders on the irrational. All three questions expect a "yes" answer. So James, in effect, says, "You are showing honor to the very ones who are your most violent oppressors." The word *katadunasteuō* ("exploit, oppress") denotes brutal and tyrannical deprivation of another's rights.[46] Today we speak of civil and human rights violations. It is likely the Jewish rich (e.g., religious leaders, Sadducees) who are oppressing the church members.[47] In James 5:1-6 it is apparently the wealthy, unbelieving Jews who are principally in the writer's mind and he gives one example of oppression: the refusal to pay the laborer his wage, or a refusal to pay fair wages. In the years AD 35-65, the rich Sadducees were among the worst oppressors of the poorer Jews, and were especially bitter against those who had become followers of "the Way" and who therefore were deemed to be renegades from the faith of their forefathers. That the rich often found it in their interests to oppress the Christians in the early days of the Church can be seen from Acts 4:1-3, where the rich Sadducees are said to have "laid hands on" Peter and John; and from Acts 13:50, where at Pisidian Antioch the Jews and devout women led the persecution against Paul and Barnabas. Jews at Thessalonica were attacking the church in the early AD 50s (Acts 17:5ff; 1 Thessalonians 2:14-16, 3:3). As regards the relations between rich and poor, James is a picture of how things were prior to AD 70.

> The destruction of Jerusalem introduced so complete a change into the situation of Judaism and of Christianity that it is easy to distinguish a writing subsequent to the catastrophe in AD 70 from a writing contemporary with the third Temple. In the years before the revolt of AD 66, which put an end to the reign of the Sadducees, women bought the priesthood for their husbands from Herod Agrippa II, and went to see them officiate, over carpets spread from their own door to the Temple; when wealthy priests were too fastidious to kill the victims for sacrifice without first putting on silk gloves; when their kitchens were furnished with every appliance for luxurious living, and their tables with every delicacy; and when, supported by the Romans, to whom they truckled, they made war upon the poor

---

[45] The word "Pharisee" means "separated." They did indeed separate themselves, especially from the poor and the unlearned and the unclean.

[46] In the LXX the term is frequently used of the exploitation of the poor and needy (Jeremiah 7:6; Ezekiel 22:29; Amos 4:1; Zechariah 7:10).

[47] It is hardly the Christian rich who are oppressors. If it were, would not James have some words calling for their repentance, and a different behavior on their parts?

priests who were supported by the people.   Like Hophni and Phinehas, they sent out their servants to collect what they claimed as offerings, and if payment was refused the servants took what they claimed by force.   Facts like these help us to understand the strong language used by James, and the still sterner words at the beginning of chapter 5.   In such a state of society the mere possession of wealth certainly established no claims upon the reverence of a Christian congregation; and the fawning upon rich people, degrading and unchristian at all times, would seem to James to be specially perilous and distressing then.[48]

And personally drag you into court? – This is a second question intended to remind the readers of just how the rich behaved with hostility toward them.   They were by their own hands, forcibly and violently,[49] dragging poor persons into court.   While enduring such negative and oppressive behavior from the rich as a class, why did they persist in showing favoritism to the rich who happened to visit the Christian assemblies?   The rich were the Christians' persecutors,[50] not their friends.   The "judgment seats" or "tribunals" (the Greek is plural) before which the wealthy Jews were dragging their poorer brethren may be either heathen or Jewish courts.   Acts has examples of Jews, in the years prior to AD 63, initiating courtroom action before Roman government officials.[51]   More likely, James' reference is to Jewish courts which were customarily held in the synagogues.

> The Roman government allowed the Jews very considerable powers of juris-diction over their own people, not only in purely ecclesiastical matters, but in civil matters as well.   The Mosaic Law penetrated into almost all the relations of life, and where it was concerned it was intolerable to a Jew to be tried by heathen law.   Consequently the Romans found that their control over the Jews was more secure, and less provocative of rebellion, when the Jews were permitted to retain a large measure of self-government.   This applied not only to Palestine, but to all places in which there were large settlements of Jews.   Even in the New Testament we find ample evidence of this.   The high priest grants Saul "letters to Damascus, unto the synagogues" to arrest all who had become converts to "the Way" (Acts 9:2).   Before Herod Agrippa II, Paul declares that, in his fury against converts to Christianity, he "persecuted them even unto foreign cities" (Acts 26:11).   Most,

---

[48] Plummer, *op. cit.*, p.586-87.

[49] *Helkō* sometimes means no more than "draw" or "attract," but other times, such as here, it describes forcibly dragging a person (e.g. Acts 16:19, 21:30).   "Personally" is an attempt to translate the third person personal pronoun *autoi*, "they themselves," i.e., "they" (emphatic) – the very rich to whom you propose to pay special respect.   Mayor thought it means "with their own hands."

[50] The persecution may have been religious, or it may have been civil action which arose from the ordinary working of social forces in an oriental community, having to do with wages, debts, rents, and the like.   The rich were using the courts to exploit the poor, perhaps by making use of unjust laws, or perhaps by taking advantage of judges who sided with the rich against the poor.

[51] That the dragging before the judgment seats refers to bringing Christians before Roman magistrates, in a time of Roman governmental persecution of Christians, would be hard to demonstrate. It is beyond what this verse says to imply evidence from it that James should be given a late date (e.g., during the time of Domitian or Trajan).

if not all, of the five occasions on which he himself "received of the Jews forty stripes save one" (2 Corinthians 11:24) must have been during his travels outside Palestine. The proconsul Gallio told the Jews of Corinth, not only that they might, but that they must, take their charges against Paul, for breaking a Jewish law, to a Jewish tribunal; and when they ostentatiously beat Sosthenes before his own tribunal, for some Jewish offense, he abstained from interfering. It is likely enough that provincial governors, partly from policy, partly from indifference, allowed Jewish officials to exercise more power than they legally possessed; but they possessed quite enough to enable them to handle severely those who contravened the letter or the traditional interpretation of the Mosaic Law.[52]

2:7 -- *Do they not blaspheme the fair name by which you have been called?*

Do they not blaspheme the fair name by which you have been called? – This is the third question by which James tries to show his readers that the rich Jews had no claim to the special treatment the Christians were lavishing on them. In fact, such favoritism was reprehensible; it not only involved flattering the very men who oppressed them (verse 6), but the favoritism also showed reverence to those who were blaspheming Jesus.[53] The pronoun "they" again is emphatic. "Is it not they (indeed it is!) who blaspheme?"[54] The word *kalon* – rendered "fair" (NASB) or "worthy" (KJV) – is difficult to adequately translate. It is the same word translated "good" when we speak of the "Good Shepherd" (John 10:11). It suggests what is beautiful, noble, good, and attractive, and it highlights the disgracefulness of the blasphemy. Commentators are divided over whether the name James has in mind is "Jesus" or "Christian." (1) In this commentator's opinion, "Christian" is the less likely of the two options. About AD 41 or 42 (an earlier date than any suggest for the writing of James) "the disciples were called Christians" for the first time at Antioch (Acts 11:26). It certainly is an honorable name, having been given to the believers by Paul and Barnabas who were speaking by inspiration.[55] If we were to choose this option we would likely have to translate *blasphēmeō* as "revile." (2) "Jesus" is the better choice for

---

[52] Plummer, *op. cit.*, p. 586.

[53] This passage certainly throws light on our discussion earlier about whether or not the "rich" visitors were Christians. Their behavior, as depicted by the questions asked by James in verses 6,7, tends toward the conclusion they were not Christians, but were unbelievers, and likely Jewish unbelievers. If the blasphemers were Christians, this verse would not read "which was called on you" (literal Greek) but instead might be expected to read "which was called on them."

[54] The verb has two meanings: "reviling" when a man is the object, and "blasphemy" when it is directed towards God. The word means to "rail against" by injurious speech; "to ridicule, insult," especially irreverent allusion to God and sacred things.

[55] See this explanation of the present active infinitive which means "divinely called" in the author's commentary on Acts, *in loc.* That the name was divinely given would match what James says about the name "being called upon you."

"name."[56]   To translate *blasphēmeō* as "blaspheme" (a word used of speaking against God) implies we have accepted the view that Jesus is God.   The last clause, "By which you have been called," literally means "which was called upon you" (*to epiklēthen eph' humas*).   The reference is likely to the name of Jesus Christ which was invoked upon them at their baptism.[57]   The unbelieving Pharisees certainly blasphemed Jesus.   The rich, following the example of the Jewish religious leaders, were speaking evil of the very Jesus into whose name James' readers had been baptized.[58]   The rich were showing bitter religious hostility towards Jesus.   How incongruous for Christ's followers to show partiality to such people.

2:8 -- *If, however, you are fulfilling the royal law, according to the Scripture, "YOU SHALL LOVE YOUR NEIGHBOR AS YOURSELF," you are doing well.*

However – Having shown how foolish or senseless the partiality being shown to the rich oppressors was, James now (verses 8-11) turns to Scripture to show that such partiality is condemned therein.   There is an adversative particle (*mentoi*) in the Greek which ties this verse with what has just been written.[59]   Nothing James has written to disparage showing favorable treatment to rich people is to be thought of as being at variance with the great law of love.   We must read verses 8 and 9 together to see the contrast James is making.   He says, "You do well if you are fulfilling the law of love (verse 8); you are sinning if you are just showing unfair partiality (verse 9)."

---

[56] Jews might well blaspheme the name of "Jesus" but they would hardly revile the name "Messiah" or "Christ."   Jesus was referred to among Christians as "the Name" (Acts 5:41, 15:14; 3 John 7).

[57] Something like "you are being baptized in the name of Jesus" or "you are being baptized into the name of ... the Son ..." apparently was spoken as the penitent believer was being immersed.   Barclay calls attention to the fact that the word James uses for "called" is the word which is used for a wife taking her husband's name in marriage, or for a child being given the same name as (called after) his father or some illustrious ancestor (cp. Genesis 48:16).   The same expression is found in the LXX of those who are called by God's name (Deuteronomy 28:10; 2 Chronicles 7:14; Jeremiah 14:9, 15:16; Amos 9:12).   If in the Old Testament a man was dedicated to God by calling God's name over him, then in the New Testament a man is dedicated to Christ by calling His name over him.

[58] The text "cursed is everyone who hangs on a tree" was a favorite one with the Jews as they tried to refute Christianity, and James would know it well (cp. Galatians 3:13).   Jews treated as "accursed" anyone who was crucified (hung on a tree).   Justin Martyr explained the passage on this fashion: "It is not as if God were cursing the crucified one, but rather that God foretold that which would be done by all of you (Jews) and those like you" (*Dial c. Trypho*, xcvi).   In Justin's time it had become the practice in the synagogues to curse all those who had become Christians (i.e., followers of Christ).   All this tends to show that what James was describing was literal blasphemy by word of mouth, and not the virtual blasphemy which is involved in conduct that dishonors Christ.   (Plummer, *op. cit.*, p.587)

[59] Some have supposed James is anticipating an excuse the brethren might give for their treatment of the rich.   "We are just fulfilling the law about loving our neighbor," they might say.   James replies, "If that is true, well and good; but if you are actually showing partiality, that's transgression of God's law."   Hort thinks such an interpretation put on the adversative particle is way beyond what James is contemplating as he writes.   Alford (*op. cit.*, p.294) held that James is not replying to "a fancied objection on the part of others, but is guarding his own argument from misconstruction."   What he has said about the rich is true, but they must not assume he is suggesting they exclude them from their assemblies.

If ... you are fulfilling the royal law, according to the Scripture – When James appeals to "Scripture" he could have the Gospel of Matthew (22:37-40) in mind,[60] or he could be appealing to the book of Leviticus (19:18). "You shall love your neighbor as yourself" is called "the royal law" or the "law of our King." It may be called "kingly" because King Jesus spoke it. It may be called "royal" because this is the "king of all laws" since it governs all our relationships with our fellow men.[61] It may be called "royal" because it is a law fit for kings (remember Christians are kings and priests, Revelation 1:6).[62] God has revealed this royal law very clearly in the Scripture. "Are fulfilling" is a present tense verb, indicating habitual action, habitually putting into practice what this law commanded.

"YOU SHALL LOVE YOUR NEIGHBOR AS YOURSELF" – The singular verb "you" indicates this is a duty obligatory on each individual follower of Jesus. What is "love"? *Agapaō* denotes a love that is intelligent and purposeful, something deliberately willed and done. It has been defined as doing what is spiritually best for the other person. The Christian love is a practical love. It is not sentimental, gushing all over its objects. It is a practical love that serves the needs of others, especially the spiritual ones. Who is your "neighbor"? He may be rich or poor (not just the rich only), religious or irreligious, of the same race, or a different race. The neighbor is not limited in practice to fellow Jews. Jesus insisted that anyone who needs our help in any way is to be regarded as "neighbor" (Luke 10:29-37). How much are we to love our neighbors? "As we love ourselves." It is natural to seek to make things work to our own advantage. At the same time, we are to seek the welfare of others equally with our own welfare.

You are doing well – This is the conclusion of the "if" clause with which the verse began. Some have suggested that James' way of wording this conclusion is an understatement when it is remembered that the observance of this "royal law" was stated by Jesus to be an essential part of the condition of eternal life (Luke 10:27,28). There is a contrast between *kalōs*, "well, right, nobly," in this verse and "committing sin" (verse 9). "The right course of action is to show favor to everyone, whether he is rich or poor. Love overlooks such superficial distinctions as wealth and quality of clothing."[63] "A life of service thus motivated will surely receive the 'well done' of the Lord at the judgment seat."[64]

---

[60] We date the writing of Matthew about AD 45 (for the Aramaic version) or AD 50 (for the Greek version). If James is written late, as we have proposed, he could be citing the words of Jesus as recorded in Matthew, and be calling Matthew "Scripture." Modern critics of the New Testament do not like to think of New Testament books being called "Scripture" till the second century AD, but this flies in the face of 2 Peter 3:16 (written by Peter before his death in AD 68) which calls Paul's collected writings "Scripture."

[61] So Ropes, Mayor, Tasker, Ross, and Lenski explain it.

[62] Hardly does it mean a law which binds even earthly kings or makes kings of those who observe it.

[63] Burdick, *op. cit.*, p. 179.

[64] Hiebert, *op. cit.*, p. 164.

2:9 -- *But if you show partiality, you are committing sin* and *are convicted by the law as transgressors.*

But if you show partiality – *Prosōpolēmpteite* is the verb form of the same root used in 2:1 for "personal favoritism."   "But" marks verse 9 as a sharp contrast to the commendation ("you are doing well") just given in verse 8.

You are committing sin – The original is more emphatic, "It is sin you are working."   The conduct called "respect of persons" or "partiality" is specifically forbidden by the "law" God has revealed.   It is forbidden by the "royal law," and it is expressly forbidden in the very Old Testament passage where "You shall love your neighbor" is recorded.   In Leviticus 19:18 we read "You shall love your neighbor."   Just three verses earlier (19:15) God clearly indicated examples of violations that are contrary to this rule on which all the law and prophets hang.   He said, "You shall do no injustice in judgment; you shall not be partial to the poor nor defer to the great, but you are to judge your neighbor fairly."   Showing favoritism is not just an insignificant breach of manners or social etiquette; it is sin!

***And* are convicted by the law as transgressors** – "Being convicted by the law" is a parti-cipial phrase in the Greek.   It tells why James says their behavior is "sin."[65]   "Sin is transgression of the law" (1 John 3:4).[66]   These respecters of persons have been transgressing what Jesus has specifically forbidden.[67]   That's sin!   "Convicted"[68] pictures a person being tried in court for a definite crime and found guilty.   Every time respect of persons is shown a sin is committed.   It is a clear case of disobedience to a known law.

2:10 -- *For whoever keeps the whole law and yet stumbles in one* point, *he has become guilty of all.*

---

[65] *Hamartanō*, used earlier in this verse, is the synonym for "sin" that means "to miss the mark."   The word used here, *parabainō*, means deliberately "to cross over the line."   God has clearly drawn a line between what is sin and what is not, and the person showing respect of persons is crossing the line into sin.

[66] 1 John 3:4 is a verse worth memorizing.   Concerning what God calls "sin," other verses worth memorizing are 1 John 5:17, "All unrighteousness is sin"; Proverbs 21:4, "A high look, a proud heart, and the plowing [prosperity?] of the wicked, is sin"; and James 4:17, "To one who knows the right thing to do, and does not do it, to him it is sin."

[67] In the Greek it reads "the law" (the article of previous reference) and looks back to the "royal law" spoken about in verse 8.

[68] The word used in the KJV, "convinced," has changed somewhat in meaning since 1611.   It now commonly refers to the impression made on a man's mind by showing him the truth of a thing which before was doubted.   In 1611 it meant that a person was found to be guilty in a court room.

For – By beginning this sentence with "for," James indicates he is going to explain why he can say what he just did in verse 9 about being "convicted by the law as being transgressors."

Whoever keeps the whole law and yet stumbles in one *point* – Dozens of laws may be on the books, but whoever breaks one of the laws is guilty, however diligently he may keep all the rest.   One may not pick and choose which laws to keep and which ones to ignore, and at the same time suppose he is "keeping" the whole law.   In order to "keep the law" or "fulfill the law" (verse 8), we must keep it all around, independently of our own likes or dislikes.[69]   "One point" could be any command or prohibition in the law, but what James has in mind, in this context, is the law against respect of persons.[70]   "Stumble" (*ptaiō*) is a synonym for "sinning" and gives no indication of the degree of seriousness.[71]

He has become guilty of all – The law is like a chain: each precept is a link.   To break one link is to ruin the whole chain.   James is not saying the person has broken all the laws. What James is maintaining is that no one can claim to be an observer of the Law when there is any portion of it which he willfully ignores or disobeys.   What James writes is a simple principle everywhere recognized.   A man who has stolen a car is held to be a violator of the law, no matter if he wore his seat belt when driving, or if he drove it all the time within the speed limits, and stopped at all the stop signs, and observed the no parking zones.   The thief cannot plead his obedience to the law in all these other respects as a reason why he should not be punished for his theft.   No man is going to be able to plead before God that he has kept all His law "except" this one point, and expect to be justified.

2:11 -- *For He who said, "DO NOT COMMIT ADULTERY," also said, "DO NOT COMMIT MURDER." Now if you do not commit adultery, but do commit murder, you have become a transgressor of the law.*

For – "For" shows that this verse is an explanatory illustration of what was just said in verse 10.

---

[69] Is there a glance at Pharisaism, which emphasized their traditions and ignored the Law.   That is the context of similar language in Romans and Galatians to the language James uses here.   Is this another subtle evidence that the epistle of James is his public response to the efforts the Pharisees made to force all Jews to keep their particular set of rules?   Some understand that James is combating an opinion which was then very common, that obedience in some things made amends for their neglect and disobedience in other things.   One Rabbi said, "Everyone has his merits and his sins: He whose merits are equal to his sins, he is the righteous man; he whose sins are greater than his merits, he is the wicked man."   Some of the Rabbis actually taught that obedience to certain laws, e.g., about phylacteries and fringes, was as good as obedience to the whole.

[70] No one should suppose from this that men in general keep all the commands but one.   James 3:2 says "we all stumble in many ways."

[71] Some have supposed that by the use of "stumble" James has in mind an insignificant offense.   The Bible may recognize degrees of sin (1 John 5:16), as well as degrees of punishment, but James' use of "stumble" should not be pressed to prove either.

He who said, "DO NOT COMMIT ADULTERY," also said, "DO NOT COMMIT MURDER." – James quotes two of the Ten Commandments as he builds his illustration of the fact that a violation of any one point is an infraction of the Law, and makes one a transgressor. Every part of the Law was given by God. James words both prohibitions with *mē* and an aorist subjunctive, a construction which implies "Don't even begin to ...!" Not even a single act of adultery or murder is condoned. The same God who said, "Do not commit adultery!" also said, "Do not commit murder!"[72] He has also said both "Love your neighbor!" and "Have no respect of persons!" Every part of the Law is given by God, and one part is as obligatory as the other. The individual commands equally express the will of Him who gave the commands.

Now if you do not commit adultery, but do commit murder, you have become a transgressor of the law – All a person has to do to become a "lawbreaker" is break one law. One could reverse the commands in the illustration, and still the breaker becomes a transgressor. If only one commandment is broken, the will of the Lawmaker has been flouted. Perhaps James' readers were carefully resisting many temptations, but giving in to the temptation to favoritism. Since God has commanded on this matter, the showing of favoritism was far from insignificant. It is transgression. It is deliberate disobedience to the expressed will of God. It is folly to assume that if most commands are kept, a few may be violated with impunity.

2:12 -- *So speak and so act, as those who are to be judged by* the *law of liberty.*

So speak and so act – In this verse James gives a command that summarizes all he has been saying since 2:1 on the subject of respect of persons. "So" (*outōs*) is emphatic and is repeated before each verb, and focuses attention on what he is about to say concerning the coming judgment. James would have his readers behave in light of the fact they are "going to be judged." Both "speak" and "act" are present tense imperatives, calling for

---

[72] Some scholars have been bothered by the fact that the order here seems to be inverted, with the seventh commandment mentioned before the sixth. (In fact, the same inverted order is seen at Matthew 5:21-27; Luke 18:20; and Romans 13:9; though not at Matthew 19:18 and Mark 10:19). While James could cite any two commands he wanted to, and in whatever order he wished to, as he makes his illustration, if there is any "reason" behind the order in most of the New Testament citations of these two, that reason may be found in the order of the commands as given in the LXX of Exodus 20 (which in most of the LXX manuscripts has "you shall not commit adultery" in verse 13, and "you shall not commit murder" in verse 15). Looking for some more subtle reason, scholars have offered: (1) adultery is a more heinous sin than murder; (2) James deliberately puts "murder" last to show that dishonoring the poor was a violation of the law just as much as were the bad thoughts that Jesus said were as wrong as the act of murder. As for the former, both adultery (Leviticus 20:10) and murder (Genesis 9:6) were punishable by death. Can we say one is worse than the other?

Some say the two tables of the Law (duties to God, and duties to man) each have five commands (since duty to parents was classified in the Greek and Roman worlds as being part of "Godliness" rather than justice). Thus the same writers are able to say that the two commandments chosen by James "head the second table." Catholics and Protestants have a different order in their listings of the Ten Commandments, apparently because of the different orders found in the ancient versions. It is of some interest that Philo (*De Decal.* XII.24) makes a direct comment on the order that has adultery before murder, but that is certainly not proof that James copied Philo, as some have proposed.

continuous action.   "Love for one's neighbor" can be shown in both speech and action, and both are to be done regularly.

As those who are to be judged – Since James is writing to believers, this is but one of numerous verses in the New Testament which indicate that Christians are going to be judged in the Final Judgment.[73]   "Judged" conveys the picture of standing before the judge who will assess each individual person's character and conduct.

By the law of liberty – Scriptures everywhere suggest that in the Final Judgment men's lives will be compared to the Word of God they had.[74]   People who lived under the Law of Moses will find their lives compared to the Law (Romans 2:12).   Christians will not be judged by the Law of Moses, but by the "law of liberty" (see James 1:25[75]) and in particular, when it comes to partiality, by the "royal law" (James 2:8).   The "books" will be opened, and men will be judged out of the books according to their deeds (Revelation 20:12). Christ's own message will be the standard of judgment for those who have heard it (John 12:48).   We can expect to give an account if we break any of the various statutes found in the law of Christ.

2:13 -- *For judgment* will be *merciless to one who has shown no mercy; mercy triumphs over judgment.*

For – Verse 13 seems intended as a reason for the appeal just made in verse 12.   The final judgment will be an awesome time for any soul, but especially for those who have shown no mercy to their fellows in this life.

Judgment *will be* merciless to one who has shown no mercy – We suppose James singles out "one who has shown no mercy" because he has the poor man of verse 2 in mind, who

---

[73] The doctrine of some (perhaps influenced by a desire to "protect" the dogma of "unconditional eternal security") that Christians will not face a probatory judgment, but only receive their respective rewards "at the judgment seat of Christ," is not compatible with the numerous passages that have Christians being "judged" for the "deeds done in the body whether good or bad." Scriptures seem to present one general judgment (in distinction to certain contemporary eschatological theories that have numerous judgments at the close of the age).   Christians are present at the "Great White Throne" judgment, as indicated by the "sea" giving up the dead which are in it (the sea of glass on which the souls of the redeemed were standing, Revelation 6:9 and 15:2), and as indicated by the implication that some were found written in the book of life (Revelation 20:15).   Passages that may be profitably studied concerning Christians at the judgment are Matthew 16:27, 25:31-46; Hebrews 13:17; 1 Corinthians 3:12-15, 4:5; James 3:1; Colossians 3:25; 2 Corinthians 5:10; Romans 14:12 (where both strong and weak Christian brothers will give an account of their behavior towards the other).

[74] A favorable comparison will result in the Judge saying, "Well done, good and faithful servant!"   An unfavorable comparison will result in, "I'm sorry.   You'll have to go!"

[75] "Liberty" does not mean that each person is free to do as he or she pleases, because we are "free" from having to obey any of God's holy commandments.   See notes at 1:25 on the meaning of "liberty" in the phrase "law of liberty."

had been treated mercilessly when he came to visit the Christian assembly. How will it be in the judgment[76] for those who showed no mercy? Respect of persons involves a breach of the law of mercy, and it has as its consequence unmerciful treatment by the Judge of the universe. There are many passages in the Word, and examples too, that tell us that those who show no mercy in this life will receive none in the judgment. In Luke 16, in the story of the rich man and Lazarus, we see what happened to the rich man who showed no mercy to the poor beggar. Judges 1:4-7 tells about Adoni-bezek, a great warrior who conquered seventy kings. He cut off their thumbs and big toes and made them eat under the table like dogs. When Israel captured him, they cut off his thumbs and toes. He had shown no mercy and received none. The wicked servant, who would not forgive a small debt after he had been forgiven a huge one, found that the mercy originally shown to him was rescinded. He was thrown into prison because he was merciless (Matthew 18:23-34). We say, "Good, he got what he deserved!" Jesus Himself said, "Blessed are the merciful, for they shall obtain mercy" (Matthew 5:7). In the Model Prayer, Jesus taught us to pray, "Forgive us our debts, as we have forgiven our debtors" (Matthew 6:12). Jesus goes on to say, "If you forgive men their transgressions, your heavenly Father will also forgive you. But if you do not forgive men, then your Father will not forgive your transgressions." So, anyone familiar with Jesus' "royal law," "the law of liberty," knows about the need for showing mercy.

Mercy triumphs over judgment – The word *katakauchatai* ("triumphs") is variously translated. It can mean "boast [against], to lift up the head, to exult, to rejoice."[77] As a result comments offered on this phrase vary. One has translated it, "Mercy applauds such judgment." Another thinks that the merciful man will be able to lift up his head with joy as he stands at the judgment seat of Christ. The one whose present life is marked with mercy will have nothing to fear in the judgment. The NASB translators supposed it means that the mercy God shows them triumphs over His judgment. As He judges each man's case, God's attributes of mercy and justice seem to come in conflict, but mercy prevails. John Chrysostom preached it with exceeding beauty:

> Mercy is dear to God, and intercedes for the sinner, and breaks his chains, and dissipates the darkness, and quenches the fire of hell, and destroys the worm, and rescues from the gnashing of teeth. To her the gates of heaven are opened. She is the queen of virtues, and makes men like to God, for it is written "Be ye merciful as your Father also is merciful" (Luke 6:36). She has silver wings like the dove, and feathers of gold, and soars aloft, and is clothed with divine glory, and stands by the throne of God; when we are in danger of being condemned she rises up and pleads for us, and covers us with her defence, and enfolds us in her wings. God loves mercy more than sacrifice (Matthew 9:13).[78]

---

[76] The Greek reads "the judgment," "the" being the article of previous reference.

[77] At Romans 11:18 and James 3:14 in the NASB the verb is rendered "be arrogant towards."

[78] "Homilies on Hebrews," *Nicene and Post-Nicene Fathers*, edited by Philip Schaff (Peabody, MA: Hendrikson, 2004), Vol.14, p.513. James Moffatt tended to sit in judgment of the wording of many of our Bible books. He supposed certain passages have come to be wrongly arranged in our English versions (see his treatment of John 14-17, for example). He thinks James 4:11, 12 should be inserted after James

IV. HAS A LIVING FAITH. 2:14-26

Summary: A fourth mark of a genuine faith, and a fourth way to experience real joy, is to practice your faith.   A dead faith is barren and produces no satisfaction; a living faith is anything but barren and unsatisfying.[1]

We have titled this paragraph "a living faith", having taken our cue from the times James insists that a faith without works is "dead," "useless," "barren," and "alone."[2]   The passage divides into several sections: the point being developed (verse 14); illustrations about how a dead, barren faith is useless (verse 15-19); an appeal for agreement with what James writes (verse 20); some illustrations from Scripture about the value of a living faith (verses 21-23); and a concluding summary about the uselessness of a dead faith (verses 24-26).

2:14 -- *What use is it, my brethren, if a man says he has faith, but he has no works?   Can that faith save him?*

What use is it, my brethren – James introduces the point he now develops with two questions, the second of which is a partial answer to the first.   A "dead faith" is of no use or profit when it comes to salvation.   Verse 20 will give a second answer to the first question.   A "dead faith" is barren; that is, there are no good works such as benevolence to needy brethren.   The readers are being challenged to think carefully concerning this matter of "faith."

2:13 because "at some early period the passage was misplaced."   Moffatt's claim that "its proper and original position" is after 2:13 is completely without textual support since there is no manuscript that has 4:11,12 after 2:13.

[1] The paragraph which we are now beginning to study has been a battlefield.   It has clashed with many a theologian's cherished beliefs; at times, James itself has been rejected rather than the cherished doctrines of men with which James clashes.   In the Introductory Studies we documented Luther's struggle with James.   Modern students who are immersed in Calvinism, with its doctrine that faith alone is the condition of salvation, have also struggled to explain away what James has here written.   How much better to jettison the "faith only" doctrine than to jettison James!

[2] We have thought long and hard about this paragraph title.   Some titles suggested by others (e.g., "faith and works") tend to perpetuate the idea that saving faith is something quantitatively different from "obedient faith."   That will not work, for the same book (Romans) that deals with "justification by faith" also emphasizes more than once the "obedience of faith."   In this author's commentary on Acts, it has been documented that saving faith is made up of four things: knowledge, assent, confidence, and obedience.   We have even noted (by comparing translations at Matthew 23:23) that *pistis* can be rendered either by "faith" or by "faithfulness."   Now "faithfulness" is a matter of continued action, a matter of habitually putting one's faith into action.   We cannot leave out the "obedience" part and still have a living faith.   We wanted a title for this paragraph of James that would not automatically appear to be contradictory to "faithfulness."

If a man says he has faith, but he has no works? – "Faith" is this verse, as the context shows, is mental assent to what God has revealed, but it is a "belief" unaccompanied by those corresponding actions that would indicate the faith is living.[3]   Who might the "man" be (whom James later calls a "foolish man" in verse 20) who has a truncated idea of what "faith" is?[4]   Have Jewish believers brought into their church some old Jewish ideas?   Is the "man" who tells others what he believes an unconverted Jewish religious leader?[5]   For the time being, let us suppose the "foolish man" could be any one of us.   How easy it is to fool ourselves concerning our obedience to what the Lord has commanded.   "Has no works" is a present tense verb, indicating a continuing absence of "works."   This is not the first time James has dealt with an idea that the foolish man holds.   Just as James earlier (1:19-27) drove home the same truth that hearing must be accompanied by doing, now he drives home the point that faith must be accompanied by works.   The plural "works" points to the numerous individual deeds that might have been done.   What are the "works" that are absent?   Benevolence, in the nearer context; obedience to God's commands, in Abraham's case; a changed lifestyle, in Rahab's case.[6]

---

[3] Luther's definition of faith in the introduction to his commentary on Romans made it impossible for him to accept what James here says about "faith," for James uses the word in a way that Luther's definition could not possibly embrace.   Just as it is difficult to find a term expressive of "living faith" or "saving faith," so commentators have struggled to find a term to designate what James calls "faith without works."   Some write about an "inoperative faith."   Some speak of "faith by itself."   Some speak of "personal faith."   One writes of "spurious faith."   Others talk about "private convictions."   In our comments on chapter 2, we shall use "dead faith" or "barren faith" or "faith alone" (which are all terms we find in James 2) to designate the mental assent which James says is not sufficient to result in salvation.

[4] There is probably no need to read the question with an emphasis on "says," as though the man is continually saying (claiming) he has faith when he really has none.   If that were the case, it would be needless to ask, "Can his faith save him?"   James no more casts doubt on the truth of the foolish man's statement of what he believes than he casts doubt on what the demons' believe (verse 19).   James' point in both cases is that "saving faith" or "living faith" is more than simply mental assent ("faith alone").

[5] Watch out for ramifications of each of these options.   The first might indicate the Christian was initially obedient to the gospel, but now is living a life devoid of good works.   What was initially a living faith has become a dead faith, and the person's salvation is in doubt.   The second might be an attempt to wean the readers away from any awe or deference to the erroneous theology of the rich who were oppressing them.   We've noted earlier (see comments on verse 10) that Jewish thinking held that obedience to some things more than made up for absence of obedience in others.   Is there any evidence Jews taught that right doctrine was all that mattered?   See notes below on verse 19.   See also Titus 1:16, "they profess to know God, but in deeds they deny Him, being detestable and disobedient, and worthless for any good deed."

[6] The "works" are emphatically not, as some have tried to maintain, simply ceremonial or ascetic. When Paul wrote (Romans 3:20,28; Galatians 2:16; Ephesians 2:8) "by works of law shall no man be justified," the works he was rejecting were man-made religious rules such as the traditions of the elders. He was saying that first-century pharisaic Judaism was not the way of salvation.   He was in agreement with Jesus who said that emphasis on the traditions of the elders (i.e., works of law) led to transgression of the Law of Moses (Matthew 15:3ff).   Faithfulness to what God has commanded, not to man-made religious rules, is the condition on which God justifies sinners.

Can that faith save him? – The question is so worded in the Greek (the negative particle is *mē*) that it expects a negative answer.   Such a faith cannot save!   There is an article before "faith" in the Greek, likely the article of previous reference, namely, a "faith" without "works."[7]   How shall we understand the word "save"?   Perhaps the idea in this verse is connected to 2:12,13 where the behavior of this life is assessed at the final judgment.   Or, perhaps, since there was no connecting link in the Greek between verses 14 and 13, James is speaking (here in verse 14) in broader terms than simply the final judgment.   The Scriptures everywhere teach "justification by faith" – i.e., that God justifies (forgives, treats as saved) those in whom He sees "faith" (a living faith, an obedient faith, faithfulness).[8]   "Faith alone" never did meet the condition upon which God reckons justification, whether it be initial justification or continuing justification.[9]   When James talks about the absolute necessity of a living faith, he is echoing the teaching of Jesus recorded in Matthew 7:21-27

2:15 -- *If a brother or sister is without clothing and in need of daily food,*

If a brother or sister is without clothing – Verses 15 and 16 vividly illustrate what James meant when he wrote "has no works" in verse 14.   Nothing is done to help the needy.   It is a Christian man or woman ("brother or sister") whom the "foolish man" sees in need, and the "foolish man" is pictured as doing nothing to alleviate the need.[10]   "Without cloth-

---

[7] If the article is left untranslated, we have "Can faith save him?"   That translation could be misleading, as though "faith" generally is slighted.

[8] Paul, in Romans 3:20 through 4:25, shows that Abraham was justified more than once in his life. From time to time, as it were, God checked up on how Abraham was doing.   When God saw continued faithfulness, God continued to reckon him as "righteous."   By parity of reasoning, if somewhere along the way faithfulness had been lacking on Abraham's part, he no longer would have been reckoned as righteous.   The Bible teaches the security of the believer (see 1 Peter 1:5; Colossians 1:23), but the Bible does not hold out any promise of continuing security for the person who quits believing, who quits being faithful to what God has revealed.

[9] Since the Reformation, commentators have struggled to harmonize James ("works are a necessary condition to salvation") with what Paul was interpreted as saying ("no works are a necessary condition for salvation").   Different hypotheses are offered in an attempt to solve the resulting difficulty.   (1) One suggests that James is dealing with justification before men as being by works, whereas justification before God is by faith.   This is a faulty definition of saving faith.   (2) It is often stated that Paul speaks of initial justification, whereas James speaks of final salvation.   The "works" James talks about, they say, are the works that come *after* a man is converted.   We are not convinced that this dichotomy is helpful when it comes to understanding what the Bible says about "faith" in those places where "faith is reckoned as righteousness."   It is an obedient faith (a living faith) that is so reckoned, whether initially, or continuing on through a man's days of probation here on earth.

[10] Whether the needy person is male or female has no bearing on whether or not they are to be helped. That they are "Christian brethren" does have a bearing, according to Galatians 6:10.   As noted earlier in our study of James (1:19, 2:1), the terms "brother" and "sister" were used to denote spiritual relationships in the early church.

ing" translates *gumnoi*, a word that means to be without an outer garment.[11] To be "ill-clad" or "poorly clothed" is to be without sufficient clothing to counteract the elements. It is a case of desperate need, for not only does the person suffer in the daytime, he or she is without sufficient covering while asleep, since the outer garment often served as a blanket. James' illustration reminds us of Jesus' teaching about ministering to "the least of these my brethren" who were without clothing or hungry or sick or in prison (Matthew 25:31-46). Why might a Christian brother or sister be "without clothing"? Are they refugees, who have lost all they owned as they fled for their lives? Are they oppressed by the wealthy? Have their wages been withheld? Have they been from among the poorer class since the day they became Christians?[12]

And in need of daily food – Much of the population of the ancient world had only "bread for today." There was no means of refrigeration for perishables so that one might have on hand several days' supply of food. Others would be unable to purchase any produce at the markets because no one hired them, or because their wages were withheld. Why might Christians be without daily food? Is it because they are "scattered" refugees? Is it a time of worldwide famine (like one predicted by Agabus, Acts 11:28-30)? Not every reader was destitute of clothing and food, for it is implied the "foolish man" could have helped the needy man or woman he has seen. That implies the "foolish man" was not completely without resources.

2:16 -- *And one of you says to them, "Go in peace, be warmed and be filled," and yet you do not give them what is necessary for* their *body, what use is that?*

And one of you says to them, "Go in peace, be warmed and be filled" – James is still portraying how a "faith without works" behaves. Good wishes are not to be despised if the person speaking has nothing more to give. But here it is assumed that the person speaking had the means to do otherwise. It is a case of "dead, barren faith," not a case of inability to help. "Go in peace" was the standard Jewish benediction or farewell, but in this case ought to have been preceded by a provision of needed food and clothing for the poor brother or sister.[13] *Thermainesthe kai chortazesthe*, "be warmed and be filled," may be either middle or passive in voice.[14] If taken as middle, the poor person is admonished "to get yourself some warm clothes and something to eat!" Pious good advice! If taken as passive, the speaker is telling the unfortunate person that someone else will have to feed

---

[11] A person wearing only the undergarment was described as "naked" in the ancient world. See 1 Samuel 19:24; John 21:7.

[12] *Huparchōsin*, translated "is," suggests a state they have been in for a while.

[13] Jesus used the same word of "farewell" (Luke 7:50, 8:48) but only after he had met the needs of the person seeking help.

[14] The words match the order of the previous verse, "without clothing" and "in need of food." The speaker is well aware of the poor brother's needs.

and clothe him, since he himself has no intention of doing so.[15]

And yet you do not give them what is necessary for *their* body – "You" is plural in this clause, whereas it was singular in the previous clause.   James pictures the whole congregation as being responsible for the callous remarks even though only one gave utterance to them.   As was true in James 2:2, perhaps we should picture the poor person who is being callously dismissed as having visited the public assembly.   The pretended concern for the welfare of the poor brother or sister is a worthless bit of play acting.   "Things needful for the body," in this context, are identified as clothing and food.

What use is that? – This is the same question with which verse 14 began.   What good are nice words with no action?   What do they help?   They do not help the poor fellow uncovered outside and unfilled inside.   Nor is there any profit to him who might have helped.   Matthew 25:45 indicates that those who thus help Christ (by ministering to His "least" brothers) shall be honored.   James also indicates that "profit" will be forfeited by failure to do good works.   Such empty words neither help the poor, nor the potential giver, nor the cause of Christ.   In fact, such action would be a hindrance, rather than help.

2:17 -- *Even so faith, if it has no works, is dead,* being *by itself.*

Even so – Here James drives home the truth he has just illustrated.   In fact, for emphasis, he will state three times (verses 17, 20, 26) that mental assent ("faith being by itself") is not the "faith" that saves.

Faith, if it has no works, is dead, *being* by itself – The "faith" about which James is speaking, and to which he objects, is what he calls "faith by itself" or "faith with no deeds" (NASB 1960).   In the illustration just finished, it was the awareness of a desperate situation minus any effort at providing a practical remedy.   As we scarcely call a corpse a man, so faith by itself is hardly worthy of the name faith.

2:18 -- *But some one may* well *say, "You have faith, and I have works; show me your faith without the works, and I will show you my faith by my works."*

But some one may *well* say – James is continuing to develop his argument in support of the point just made in verse 17.   However it is not easy to determine the thread of the argument.   Because there were no punctuation marks or quotation marks in ancient manuscripts, commentators have offered various scenarios in an attempt to unfold what James wrote.   Tasker summarizes the problems as follows: (1) Who is the "one" speaking the words "you have faith ..."?   Is it someone sympathetic with what James writes, or someone objecting to what James has written about faith alone?   (2) Where does does the quotation beginning with "you have faith" end?   Does it end after just one clause,

---

[15] We have treated the two verbs as imperatives.   The verbs could also be indicative, but neither verb carries the idea that the unfortunate person is already properly clothed and fed before this benediction is pronounced.   Both the preceding verse and the clause which follows indicate that is not the case.

or with the second clause, or does it include all the rest of the verse?   (3) To whom do the emphatic personal pronouns refer in the clause "you have faith, and I have works"?[16]

(1) Who is speaking?   This expression "someone may well say" elsewhere (e.g., 1 Corinthians 15:35; Romans 9:19; 11:19) introduces an objection to the previous argument.   It is most naturally understood in this fashion here in James, as introducing the remarks of an objector.[17]   We picture the objector being one of the "faith alone" readers whom James is attempting to correct as he writes.   James is anticipating his or her response when the letter is read out loud in the assembly.

(2) How far does the quotation extend?   Only as far as the first statement, "You have faith"?[18]   Or to the middle of the verse, "you have faith and I have deeds"?   Or do the words extend through verse 19?   Or to the end of verse 18?[19]   Tasker and others, including the RSV, NIV, TEV, are convinced that the words of the objector end in the middle of the verse, "You have faith and I have works."   The remainder of verse 18 are the words of James' reply to the objector.   Our comments are based on the conclusion that this option is correct concerning where the quotation begins and ends.

(3) It is not easy to resolve the question of the identity of the persons referred to by the pronouns "You" and "I."   If an objector is speaking to James, he would hardly be saying to James, "You have faith" and of himself "I have works."   James didn't defend the "faith alone" position.   The objector was doing no works (or verses 14ff are pointless).   Should not the order, if an objector is speaking, have been, "You have works; I have faith"?[20]   Ropes tried to solve the difficulty by saying the pronouns do not refer to James and the objector, but are simply the equivalent of "one" and "another," and are a picturesque way of indicating two imaginary persons.[21]   The ob-

---

[16] The proposed solutions to these questions are covered in detail in Ropes, *op. cit.*, p. 211-214.

[17] It is difficult to explain the words if we assume the speaker is James himself, or an imaginary ally, either Christian or non-christian, who agrees with James.

[18] Westcott and Hort (*The New Testament in Original Greek* [New York: Macmillan, 1929], p.319), in the margin, offer the suggestion "Do you have faith?" as being the whole question asked by the objector, and he is speaking to James.   "You talk so highly of deeds.   What do you know about faith?"   This makes James' reply begin with the conjunction "and" ("and I have deeds").   This is difficult to explain, so the suggestion has not been adopted by many commentators.

[19] Mayor, Knox, Barclay, and others, including NASB, include the remainder of verse 18 inside the modern quotations marks.   Other interpreters have offered verses 19, 20, 23, and even 26, as the conclusion of the quotation by the objector.   It is rather certain that verse 20 is a challenge to the objector, rather than being part of what the objector says to James.   So somewhere in verse 18 or after verse 19 we must put the closing quotation marks.

[20] Indeed, this inversion is found in the Old Latin manuscript Corbiensis (ff[1]), but no other manuscripts invert them.

[21] Barclay (*op. cit.*, p.90) has the objector as saying, "Faith is a fine thing; and works are fine things.   They are both perfectly real and genuine manifestations of real religion.   But the one man does not necessarily possess both.   One man will have faith and another will have works ... It is the objector's view that you can have either faith or works, that faith and works are alternative expressions of the Christian religion.   But James will have none of that."

jector is asserting that faith and works are not necessarily related.[22]   In his view it is possible for one person to have faith by itself, and for another to have a living faith, and who is to say which is better?[23]   To this James responds strongly.

"Show me your faith without the works"[24] – This apparently is the beginning of James' response to the objector, and this response runs through verse 19.   The claim that it is possible to have either faith or works and that either is equally valid cannot be demonstrated from experience or Scripture.   James challenges the objector to demonstrate his personal convictions so James or anyone else can see what they are.   Without "works" the objector cannot do it.   He can tell folk what he believes, but he cannot demonstrate it.   A belief cherished in the heart cannot be demonstrated apart from action.

"And I will show you my faith by my works" – James declares, "I have no difficulty demonstrating what my convictions are.   My actions show my beliefs."   James is willing and able to give the very kind of demonstration that he has challenged the objector to provide.[25]

2:19 -- *You believe that God is one.   You do well; the demons also believe, and shudder.*

You believe that God is one – This verse and the next are evidently addressed to the objector (verse 18a) who has said faith alone and works are equally valid in God's sight.[26]   Rather than an appeal any further to his own experience (verse 18c), James now appeals to Scripture to show that "faith alone" and a "living faith" are not of equal value in God's sight.   He proves one by the fact the demons exhibit faith alone.   He proves the other by appealing to the examples of Abraham and Rahab, both of whom exhibited a living faith.

---

[22] It probably is a misuse of 1 Corinthians 12:10 to insist that "faith" among the diversity of gifts listed in that passage is proof one could have the gift of faith, and another the gift of good works.   Faith in that Corinthians passage and faith here in James are two different uses of the word "faith."

[23] This view is represented in the NEB, "Here is one who claims to have faith and another who points to his deeds."   It has proven difficult for some to accept this view that James is using two emphatic pronouns when there were actual Greek idioms to express "one" and "another."

[24] A manuscript variation here, "by your works," is unintelligible.   It destroys the whole point of the antithesis.

[25] Note what this verse does to some contemporary maxims.   One of those maxims is, "It doesn't matter what you believe just so long as you live it."   That belittles faith.   A person can disbelieve 3/4 of the Bible, but that doesn't matter.   The works ("living it") spoken of are not works that spring from a new life in Christ, but are more apt to be fleshly works.   Another maxim is, "I'm a Christian, but I just can't ... (go calling, etc.)"   Show me your faith!   Give me some works so I can see you have faith.

[26] Some instead have it addressed once more to the faith-only readers whom James is trying to correct in this section.

In "that God is one"[27] there apparently is an allusion to the Shema, the Jewish creed, "Hear, O Israel, the Lord our God is one" (Deuteronomy 6:4-6).[28]

You do well – The objector's doctrinal content concerning God was correct, as far as it went.[29]

The demons also believe, and shudder – The doctrinal content of the faith of the demons is absolutely correct, but it is useless because it does not bring a positive change in conduct. Instead it results in a feeling of terror. In Scripture, the demons are frequently spoken of as plural in number.[30] They are represented as evil spirits, subject to Satan, under his control, and engaged with him in carrying out his diabolical plans to thwart all God is attempting to do in His world.[31] "Believe" is mental assent to the doctrine that "God is one." "There are no atheists or skeptics among the demons." They once lived in heaven, before they sinned and were cast out (Revelation 12:7-9), and they were well-acquainted with omnipotent deity. The demons shuddered in terror particularly when they faced the incarnate Christ. They know they are doomed to perish ultimately at the hands of omnipotent deity, and they worried that when they confronted Jesus that their time had come. "What have we to do with You, Son of God?", they cried. "Have You come here to torment us before the time?" (Matthew 8:29; Mark 1:24, 5:7). The word rendered

---

[27] The Greek manuscripts at this place have several different readings. Some, like the Textus Receptus, have "there is one God." Others read as the NASB, "that God is one."

[28] There is some difference of opinion here whether this first clause in verse 19 is a statement or a question. Westcott and Hort took the first part as a question. So do the Greek texts of Nestle and the United Bible Society. They treated "you do well" as a touch of irony, as if James were saying, "Fine! That puts you on the same basis of the demons if you go no further than merely believe."

[29] Whether the objector held a Jewish or a Christian view of "God is one" is not easy to decide. If he held a Jewish view, he would be rejecting Jesus as being the Son of God. Because their view of God was monistic (i.e., only one person in the Godhead), first century Jewish religious leaders denied that Jesus was deity. Jesus tried to help a Jewish audience to understand the real meaning of the Shema (Matthew 22:41ff). "Jehovah, our Elohim, is the only Jehovah" does not teach but one person in the Godhead. The Hebrew word translated "only" does not mean "single, solitary" but speaks of "unity." "Jehovah" (YHWH) speaks of self-existent deity. Elohim is plural, and, in Scripture, three beings (Father, Son, and Holy Spirit) are called "Jehovah." There can be one member of the Godhead in heaven, and another (Jesus) just like Him on earth at the same time. While Jesus was on earth, the demons certainly recognized who He was.

[30] The KJV translation "the devils believe ..." is misleading. There is only one devil (*ho diabolos* or *ho satan*) but there are many demons (*ta daimonia*).

[31] Elsewhere the New Testament speaks of demons being kept in chains of darkness awaiting the great day of judgment (Jude 6). In light of this, some have wondered how the demons were active during Jesus' ministry, and in our current world (Ephesians 6:12ff; Revelation 9:1-11). Were only some demons imprisoned, while others are free to act at Satan's behest? Does "imprisoned" merely mean "limited in what they can do to the redeemed"? Bible students should be cautious when they hear statements like "this reference to demons reflects the first-century understanding of the existence of demons." What is implied is that modern scholars know better than to believe in the existence of demons. Was Jesus, too, mistaken, for He certainly believed in them? Hardly! The exploding interest in the occult beginning late in the 20th century certainly testifies to the tragic reality of the demonic world.

"tremble" or "shudder" is *phrissein*, and expresses physical horror, especially as it affects the hair (stands up).[32]   It occurs nowhere else in the New Testament, but is used in the LXX at Job 4:15, "Then a spirit passed before my face; the hair of my flesh stood up."   It is a stronger word than either "fear" or "tremble."[33]   The demon's response to their belief shows that it is a strong conviction.   The present tense pictures this terror as a characteristic or repeated reaction whenever they face the reality of the eternal God.   Saving faith, living faith, is more than a mere intellectual acceptance of a theological truth.   Living faith is made up of four parts: knowledge, assent, confidence and obedience.   Mere intellectual assent does not result in peace with God.

2:20 -- *But are you willing to recognize, you foolish fellow, that faith without works is useless?*

But are you willing to recognize – By this question (*theleis gnōnai*), James introduces a further argument in support of the point being made since verse 17.   There is a shift from an argument from reason (verse 19) to an argument from Scripture to support the truth that living faith (the opposite of faith without works) is what matters to God.   James' language is stronger than "Do you want more evidence?"   The wording of the question implies that the objector's refusal to acknowledge what James writes does not result from lack of proper information but is a deliberate act of the will.   The only way he will correct (recognize or acknowledge) his erroneous views is by another deliberate act of the will.

You foolish fellow – The Greek reads "O foolish man."   One doesn't often find the Greek interjection "O," a word that can be spoken with different tones of voice, each of which has a different meaning.   In some contexts it is an exclamation of admiration; in others, as here, it is a word of rebuke or censure.   By using the word *kenos* ("empty, vain") James rather bluntly accuses the opponent of being an "empty man."[34]   It might mean "empty of understanding."   Your argument doesn't make sense!   There are other ways the "faith only" man is "empty."   He is empty headed if he thinks a dead faith is of any profit.   He is empty handed if he has no good works to benefit his needy neighbor.   He is empty hearted if he has no love for his fellow man.[35]   "The 'foolish fellow' addressed is anyone who is so devoid of spiritual understanding that he or she does not see that faith which never results in works is merely a sham."[36]

---

[32] Think of the bristles standing up on an animal's neck when in danger or at bay, e.g., a porcupine or a cat.

[33] If demons, who are great exponents of "faith only", are terrified thinking about the judgment that awaits them, should not men who are "faith only" also be terrified because of their sins of omission and rejection of Christ?

[34] Used to describe men, the term is not found elsewhere in the New Testament.   It is found at Judges 9:4 in the LXX.

[35] These ideas of the different ways a person can be "empty" are adapted from Plummer, p.593.

[36] Tasker, *op. cit.*, p.67.

That faith without works is useless? – "Faith" here is *hē pistis*. The definite article is an article of previous reference, namely "mental assent." "Works" likewise has an article, pointing to "the works" (as in verses 15,16) by which a living faith demonstrates itself (verse 18). "Useless" here is *argē*; perhaps James intended a play on words with *ergon*[37] ("works" which are "dead"). *Argē* means "unproductive, barren".[38] When we recall the shame that it was in the Jewish world for a woman to be barren of children, we begin to catch the flavor of what James writes about faith alone. It produces no children; it produces no fruit; it accomplishes nothing. Folk ought to be ashamed of a barren faith! Recall the parable of Jesus, where the landowner came for several years expecting to find fruit and found none. "Why cumbereth it the ground? Cut it down and cast it into the fire!" was his verdict (Luke 13:7). God has been waiting a long time for some fruit in some of us.

2:21 -- *Was not Abraham our father justified by works, when he offered up Isaac his son on the altar?*

Was not Abraham our father justified by works – James appeals to two Old Testament examples, Abraham (verses 20-23) and Rahab (verse 25), as incontrovertible evidence for his position that living faith and not faith alone is the correct Christian idea of what faith is. In contrast to the barren faith which makes a man's spiritual condition no better than that of demons, James highlights two conspicuous instances of living and fruitful faith. The way James words this question in the Greek shows that he expects a "yes" answer from his readers. The designation of Abraham as "our father" agrees with the conclusion reached earlier that the readers of James' letter were Jewish Christians.[39] It also implies that his spiritual children are expected to exhibit the same kind of living faith. If they do not, if they have only a "dead faith", they should not rightly claim to be his "children." "Justified" means that God[40] reckoned Abraham as "righteous," as being in a saving relationship with God.[41] The same expression "justified by works" is also used of Rahab

---

[37] The manuscript variation at this place (some read "dead" rather than "barren") probably resulted from scribes who altered this verse to "dead" so that it matches verses 17 and 26. One papyrus manuscript reads "empty," a scribal change likely influenced by the use of the word "empty" ("foolish").

[38] The adjective was used of money that was yielding no interest, or of a field lying fallow. It is the same word used at Matthew 12:36 where Jesus affirmed that every "idle" word will have to be accounted for in the final judgment. James' readers ought not suppose "idle" faith will be any less a subject of judgment on that day.

[39] It is also true that "our father" is used with reference to all Christians, even those of Gentile descent (Galatians 3:7-9), of whom Abraham is father because of their adoption into the spiritual family of God (Romans 4:11).

[40] Who the agent was who did the justifying is not specified in this verse, but it is made plain in verse 23. It is God who reckons Abraham as "righteous."

[41] "Righteousness" is imputed, not infused. It is a forensic term, picturing a judge passing sentence on the person in the dock, and the sentence pronounced on the sinner is "not guilty" because the Judge sees the person's "faith" (not sinless perfection, but faithfulness).

in verse 25.[42] One of the "works," i.e., one of the "deeds"[43] which Abraham did as he consistently obeyed what God required, is described in the following phrase, "when he offered up Isaac on the altar."[44]

When he offered up Isaac his son on the altar? – This familiar event of Abraham's obedience to God's command is recorded in Genesis 22:1-14. Verses 22 and 23 are James' explanation of the significance of what Abraham did. His sacrifice of Isaac[45] is a vivid example of living faith. It can in no way be harmonized with "faith alone."[46] "His son" reminds us of the seeming contradiction between Isaac being the promised seed and the command to kill him. Hebrews 11:17-19 tells us Abraham resolved the problem in his own mind by thinking God would raise Isaac from the dead.

2:22 -- *You see that faith was working with his works, and as a result of the works, faith was perfected;*

You see that – This may be either an indicative ("it is so plain you cannot but see it") or an interrogative ("Is it clear? Do you see it?"). James is calling the Scriptural evidence to the objector's attention.

Faith was working with his works – *Sunergeō* ("works with") suggests cooperation.

---

[42] All the Old Testament saints and all the New Testament saints who have ever been "justified" have met this same condition of having a living faith.

[43] "Deeds" is plural. There were many times that Abraham's faith was manifested in action. Hebrews 11:8 speaks of the faith shown by Abraham's departure for an unknown country. Hebrews 11:9 speaks of his residence in Canaan. Romans 4:17ff refers to the belief of God's promise of a son. James 2:21 and Hebrews 11:17ff refer to the sacrifice of Isaac. Those events cover over a quarter of a century. Abraham's faith was a living, vital principle all through his life, manifested by his daily actions.

[44] The close correspondence in phraseology between James 2:20 and Romans 4:2 ("If Abraham were justified by works, he has something to boast about; but not before God") has caused some to suppose there is a flat contradiction between James and Paul. It has led some to affirm that James is correcting or modifying Paul; it has led others to affirm that Paul is correcting or modifying James. The proper view, in our opinion, is that the "works" Paul rejects as valid and saving actions are "works of Law" (as just defined in Romans 3:20,28), namely, the man-made Jewish halakhic rules sometimes identified as "the traditions of the elders." James' emphasis is on doing what God has said, on living faithfully according to God's rule. This is why James, over and over again, references the very rules the Divine Christ taught while here on earth.

[45] In Abraham's mind he fully intended to slay the boy, and he would have, had not his intent been stayed by the angel (Genesis 22:11ff).

[46] Suppose Abraham had stayed in Beersheba instead of going to the land of Moriah to make the sacrifice. The record is clear, that had he stayed in Beersheba (even though he had "faith"), he would not have been justified in God's sight.

"Faith"[47] and "works" together (not "faith only"), as equal and inseparable partners, contributed to the blessed results.[48] The plural "deeds" and the imperfect tense, "was working," suggest that the offering of Isaac was but one instance of such co-operation of faith and action in Abraham's life. All along in his walk with God faith and action were working together.

And as a result of the deeds, faith was perfected – In the case of Abraham, it was not by one of these things alone (not by faith alone, not by works alone, as the objector argued in verse 18), but both together, in tandem, that resulted in his "justification." As a result of the deeds faith was "completed, finished, brought to its goal" (*eteleiōthe*).[49] By the works the mental assent was turned into something productive.[50] Without these works "faith" was incomplete, barren (verse 20), dead (verse 17). The "goal" ultimately was that Abraham should continue to be in an intimate relationship with God (as verse 23 will explain).

2:23 -- *And the Scripture was fulfilled which says, "AND ABRAHAM BELIEVED GOD, AND IT WAS RECKONED TO HIM AS RIGHTEOUSNESS," and he was called the friend of God.*

And the Scripture was fulfilled – The word "Scripture" (literally, "the writings") is a technical term used to refer to the sacred writings that make up our Bibles.[51] Jewish people, reserving the term for the Old Testament canonical writings, used the term as though there were no other "writings" in existence that were of any real importance. James is about to quote (Genesis 15:6) a statement made by God to Abraham thirty or more

---

[47] The Greek reads "the faith," i.e., Abraham's faith. James simply assumes his readers understand that Abraham did what he did because he was determined to be faithful to God (just as Hebrews 11:17 says, and just as Genesis 15:6 said).

[48] Modern "faith-only" proponents are forced to flatly deny what James here has written. Burdick (*op. cit.*, p.184) is a typical example. "... [T]his may sound as if Abraham's justification resulted from a mixture of faith and works, each being equally efficacious. If this is what James meant, he is in conflict with Paul, who insists that faith is the only means of justification. However, it is not necessary to take James' statement in this way. Other New Testament passages show plainly that a person is justified by faith alone." Contrary to what Burdick has written, in Paul, the "faith" that saves (i.e., that is the condition of justification) is an obedient faith, not just a mental assent. That is exactly the same position James is teaching as he cites the Old Testament examples of Abraham and Rahab.

[49] When James says his faith was "made perfect," it is not implied that previously Abraham's faith was weak, or somehow defective. On the occasion of the sacrifice of Isaac ("perfected" is an aorist tense, pointing to a single act), if there had been no "action" his faith would have been incomplete.

[50] The language of James indicates that "mental assent" existed before the "action" occurred which "completed" it and made it "justifying faith."

[51] Peter indicates that Paul's writings were also to be classified as "Scripture" (2 Peter 3:16), and Paul shows that Luke's Gospel is also "Scripture" (1 Timothy 5:18).

years before the sacrifice of Isaac (narrated in Genesis 22).[52] "Justification by faith" is something that happened more than one time in Abraham's life.[53] "Fulfilled" is a word usually applied to the later fulfillment of a prophetic utterance. James treats what happened at Genesis 15:6 as an anticipation of what was later to occur again.

Which says, "AND ABRAHAM BELIEVED GOD, AND IT WAS RECKONED TO HIM AS RIGHTEOUSNESS" – James quotes Genesis 15:6, a passage that belongs to that period of time in Abraham's life before the births of Ishmael and Isaac when the childless Abraham was fretted about who would be his heir. God made him a promise, and Abraham went right on faithfully doing what God required of him. The Hebrew word for "believed" (*aman*[54]) is an unusual form and speaks of a continuing faithfulness as being the thing which God saw and reckoned as righteousness. In the Hebrew of Genesis 15:6, "reckoned" is active in voice, "God counted it to him as righteousness."[55] As James and Paul (Romans 4:3) quote the passage, it is an exact quotation of the LXX which has the passive voice ("it was reckoned"). Abraham was not sinless perfect, but God saw Abra-

---

[52] The rabbis said that Genesis 15 was 50 years before the sacrifice of Isaac. See Mayor, *op. cit.*, p.100.

[53] Footnote #43 on "works" in verse 21 above noted several occasions on which Abraham was "reckoned righteous." Abraham was faithful to God long before God even called him from Ur of the Chaldees. Genesis 15:6 was not the first time in his life he was justified. Romans 4:5 also asserts that "justification" is something that occurs over and over in the life of the person who walks with God, following in the steps of Abraham's faith. This truth from Romans 4:5 tends to throw into serious question the comments of some who try to say Abraham was justified once in his life, and that was long before the sacrifice of Isaac. This one-time justification is by "faith only" [which they claim Paul taught] and "works" – such as Abraham's in the case of Isaac –simply verify that the faith by which they were justified is still a living thing.

The faith that saves excludes man-made rules such as the halakhic traditions of the Pharisees, but it never excludes the actions (such as repentance, confession, immersion, benevolence) which God has indicated He requires of those who would be His children. A large share of the folk who could roughly be categorized as "faith only" actually require a potential convert to repent. As soon as you require repentance (something other than "faith" by their definition of terms), which is something a man does (not something God does to him), by parity of reasoning immersion can no longer be excluded from being a part of the "faith that saves." In the cases of conversion recorded in Acts, repentance is not mentioned in all cases. "Is it implied?" "Yes," you say. Well, immersion is mentioned in all cases of conversion. By what laws of reasoning is it excluded from being a part of what one must do to be saved, when repentance is not excluded?

[54] The Hebrew word means "to be firm, to be faithful, to remain steadfast." Abraham was not the first man who ever believed in God, but he was the first of whom the Old Testament Scriptures specifically say that he believed in God. Indeed, the very first time the word "believe" occurs in the Bible it is in Genesis 15:6.

[55] *Logizomai* means "to count, to calculate, to think," and in the bookkeeping world it means to credit one's account with the equivalent to something else just mentioned. In the courtroom the word speaks of what the judge is "thinking" or "takes into account" as he passes sentence.

ham's faithfulness and continued to voice His approval of Abraham.[56]

And he was called the friend of God – Though these words are not part of Genesis 15:6, James tells us that Abraham was called "friend of God." The way he words it ("he was called"), James seems to be saying that this honorable title is also found in Scripture. Perhaps there is a reference to 2 Chronicles 20:7 or Isaiah 41:8 where some versions read "friend" of God while others have "my beloved."[57] Perhaps this was a current way among Abraham's descendants of speaking of their notable forefather.[58] In early Christian literature this title was frequently applied to Abraham.[59] In the upper room just before His crucifixion, Jesus told the eleven disciples they were his "friends" (John 15:15), and that this close relationship included the privilege of their being told what God's great plan was that Jesus was working out in history. If Abraham is not specifically called "friend" in the Old Testament, he was often described as such, for God talked with him as a man talks with a friend (Genesis 18:17). It was his living faith over decades of time that led to Abraham's intimacy with God, and this intimacy resulted in his being called "the friend of God." Likewise, Jesus said, "You are my friends, if you do [habitually] what I command you" (John 15:14).

2:24 -- *You see that a man is justified by works, and not by faith alone.*

You see – James now addresses his readers and invites them to acknowledge the obvious lesson that can be learned from Genesis 15 and 22. The Greek verb may be indicative, imperative, or interrogative. Perhaps James is appealing to their will ("see it!"), or perhaps he is asking if they have gotten over their "foolishness" (verse 20). The only possible conclusion that can be drawn from the case of Abraham just cited is that living faith is what God requires.

A man is justified by works, and not by faith alone – What was true in Abraham's case is now broadened and made general ("a man," any man). Before God justifies ("reckons a man as righteous," verse 23), He looks for a living faith rather than barren faith (a mental

---

[56] God can do such a thing, namely pronounce the guilty as "innocent," because one day on a hill outside of Jerusalem the Son of God went to Calvary to set a world of sinners free. If there were no atoning death, there would be no forgiveness possible even for those who are faithful.

[57] In both these places the Vulgate has *amicus* ("friend") and some copies of the LXX and Symmachus have "friend" at one or the other of these two passages. However, most critically reconstructed texts of the LXX read "beloved" at both places.

[58] The Arabs still call Abraham *El-Khalil Allah* or simply *El-Khalil* ("the friend"). Hebron, the town identified with Abraham, has become *El-Khalil*.

[59] E.g., 1 Clement 1.10. Whether Clement derived the name from James or from first-century usage among Jewish people, we do not know. The distinctive title "friend" first appears in Philo's citation of Genesis 18:1 (*De Resipisc. Noe*, c.11), which suggests it was a current phrase among Jewish people.

assent with no corresponding actions), or what is here designated as "faith alone."[60]   This is a formal and conclusive reply to the question asked in verse 14 where it was asked, "Can that faith save him?"   No, "faith alone" can not save!

2:25 -- *And in the same way was not Rahab the harlot also justified by works, when she received the messengers and sent them out by another way?*

And in the same way – James here begins his second argument from Scripture (see verses 20 and 21) to show that "faith without deeds is useless."   "In the same way" underlines the fact this second illustration teaches the same truth the first illustration did.

Was not Rahab the harlot also justified by works – See Joshua 2 for the story of Rahab. She believed the Jews to be God's people.   She believed that God and his people were about to conquer the city of Jericho.   She heard and accepted the report of the miracles in Egypt and the Red Sea.   James' question, as it is worded in the Greek, expects an affirmative answer.   Yes, she was so justified!   Many writers try to soften the reference by suggesting some other sense for *hē pornē* ("harlot") besides the literal one.   "Cook," "landlady," "idolater," "inn-keeper,"[61] have all been offered, but the literal sense is probably the correct one.   She was a prostitute before she repented and was justified.[62]   The choice by James of Rahab as one of his two Scriptural examples might be surprising.   You would expect Abraham, the father of the faithful, to be cited.   But you might not expect Rahab, a Gentile with an outrageous past, to be cited.   We suppose this latter example is picked to show that all people are justified the same way, by a living faith.[63]   These two examples cover the whole wide range of possibilities, from initial justification (Rahab) to continuing

---

[60] Proponents of "faith only" as the condition of initial justification try desperately to reconcile James to that dogma.   A typical example is Nieboer's (p.222): "Paul speaks of works that precede salvation when he says a man is not justified by works.   James is thinking of works that follow salvation, that are a consequence of it."   Instead of trying to say Paul deals with justification while James deals with the life of sanctification that begins from the moment a man is justified, why not recognize that "not by faith alone" in James and "faith" (in "justified by faith") in Paul are equal expressions of the same truth?   (Why not recognize from the Dead Sea Scroll 4QMMT that the expression "works of Law," which Paul in Romans and Galatians says will not save, refer to man-made religious rules, rather than God's rules?)   If one wishes to be justified, according to Paul it requires an obedient faith; according to James it requires a living faith (a faith that works).   Instead of emphasizing Romans 3:20,28 as though James contradicted Paul, why not appeal to Galatians 5:6 as showing the two apostles as being in perfect agreement?

[61] Josephus, *Ant.* V.1.2, makes Rahab the keeper of an inn.

[62] Hebrews 11:31 tells us that, because she was determined to be faithful to her new-found relationship with God, she received the spies in peace and did not perish with those of her neighbors who did not believe.   The same thing is recorded in Joshua 6:25.

[63] In 1 Clement 1:12 we have a mention of Rahab, with the additional explanation of the "scarlet thread" (Joshua 2:18) as being typical of the blood of Christ, by which those of all nations, even the harlots and the unrighteous, obtain salvation.   James does not specifically speak of Rahab's "faith."   He simply assumes the readers are aware of it, for they certainly knew how she acknowledged the supremacy of the God of Israel (Joshua 2:11).   The whole context here in James which speaks of "by works (deeds)" is talking of "faith that is perfected by those works (deeds)."

justification later in life (Abraham).   Rahab had heard of the miraculous deliverance of Israel from Egypt and of the great power God exerted against the Amorite kings on the other side of the Jordan River.   Accordingly, she believed no earthly power could resist God.   She was going to side with the God of Israel.   Without her act of getting involved in protecting the spies whom Joshua had sent, her faith would not have saved her from death in the destruction of Jericho.   It is implied in Hebrews 11:31 and elsewhere that she kept on believing.   The one-time harlot came to have a part in the family line from which the Messiah was born (Matthew 1:5).[64]   When he says Rahab was "justified," "James does not give approval of Rahab's former life; it is her living faith, seen against the background of her previous immorality, he commends."[65]

When she received the messengers and sent them out by another way? – Two of the "works" which showed her faith was not barren was her involvement with the spies who came to spy out the land; she "received" them, and "sent them out."   James speaks not of "young men" as does Joshua 6:23, nor of "spies" as does Hebrews 11:31, but of "messengers."   Perhaps they were "messengers" in the sense that they brought God's message (an unwelcome message to the unbelieving inhabitants of Jericho) to Rahab.[66]   She not only welcomed the spies into her own house, she hid them.   The king of Jericho heard that the two spies had entered into Rahab's house.   It wasn't long until soldiers were knocking at the door.   What to do now?   She hid the spies on the roof of the house among some bundles of flax.   She then went downstairs and sent the soldiers off on a "wild-goose chase."   Said she, "They left about the time the gate of the city was shut for the night.   Pursue after them!   Perhaps you can catch them."   After the soldiers were gone, she hurriedly sent the spies away safely.[67]   One wall of her home was part of the wall of the city, so she opened a window on the outer side, tied a scarlet cord and let them slide down it.   She also tells them not to go directly back to Joshua's camp, but to go to the mountains and hide there for three days, until the soldiers who were on the "wild-goose chase" had returned.[68]

---

[64] Perhaps Salmon, her husband, was one of the spies she harbored.   The Talmud mentions a quite untrustworthy tradition that Rahab married Joshua and became the ancestress of eight persons who were both priests and prophets.   For documentation see Hermann L. Strack and Paul Billerbeck, "Das Evangelium Nach Matthaus Erlautert Aus Talmud Und Midrach," in *Kommentar Zum Neuen Testament Aus Talmud Und Midrach* (Munich: Beck'she, 1926), pp.20-23.

[65] Burdick, *op. cit.*, p.185.

[66] Some commentators wonder whether James' readers have had similar opportunities to welcome and send out preachers who have been sent by Jesus Christ.   If so, this would be another opportunity for "living faith" to result in joy for the sender.   Remember, our title for this paragraph reminds us that living faith can produce the joy that James wishes for his readers.

[67] The Greek literally says "hastened" or "thrust them out."   It shows her fear (for their safety, or for her own?) and haste.

[68] Rahab practiced deception when she told the soldiers the spies had left.   Yet we are clearly told she was justified by her deeds.   Some have wondered how these two apparently contradictory things can both be true, especially when there are no liars in heaven.   Some have tried to excuse what Rahab did by saying the standards for telling the truth were not as strict in Old Testament times as they are since Jesus has come.   A more satisfactory explanation, given by Lloyd Pelfrey, the chancellor of Central Christian

2:26 -- *For just as the body without* the *spirit is dead, so also faith without works is dead.*

For – One final argument by James to show that faith alone is useless is drawn from an analogy to the human body.[69]

Just as the body without *the* spirit is dead – A body without the spirit is nothing but a dead body, a corpse. *Pneuma* is "spirit," though the margin of some versions has "breath" at this place. Scripture seems to present the components that make up a man as being body, soul, and spirit (e.g., 1 Thessalonians 5:23). Sometimes physical death is said to result from the soul leaving the body (as in Stephen's case, Acts 7:60, and in 1 Kings 17:22). In other places, as here, physical death is said to result from the spirit leaving the body.[70]

So also faith without works is dead – Some writers have expressed mild surprise at the comparison James makes here. Our first thought might be that works ought to be compared to the body, and faith to the spirit as the vivifying principle. That might be true if he were comparing a living faith to the spirit, but James is dealing with faith only (e.g., an intellectual assent to a dogma or series of dogmas), and that kind of "faith" is not a vivifying principle. What James does say in his comparison is this: If there are no acts springing from faith, that faith is no more alive than a "body without spirit."[71] James does not disparage the importance of correct doctrine, but if such views are simply held as a personal conviction which has no bearing on how the holder of the views lives, then that "faith is barren, being alone."

College of the Bible, is that there is a difference between lying and deception in wartime. He defines lying as a deliberate falsehood told to bring evil on someone else. Deception is something done in the interests of self-preservation. Joshua practiced deception and ambushed the defenders of Ai. Samuel was told by God to say he was going to sacrifice if anyone asked him about his trip to anoint David as the new king (1 Samuel 16:2); Samuel did sacrifice, but that was not the whole truth about his trip. In Jeremiah 38:24ff, Zedekiah suggested to Jeremiah what to say if anyone asked what he and the king talked about. Jeremiah spoke about presenting a petition to the king, but that was only a part of what Jeremiah told the king. In John 7:8, in response to a taunt from those who did not believe on Jesus, and wanted Him to go publicly to Jerusalem and do something spectacular to prove He really was the Messiah, Jesus said he was not going to Jerusalem for the feast. It was true that he did not make a dramatic public trip to Jerusalem, but He did go (John 7:10ff). Perhaps the lesson can be drawn from these illustrations that when one is dealing with another who is opposing what God is trying to do in His world, we do not have to help the opposer accomplish his intended goals. On two occasions early in Acts, the apostles state that when God and man are on opposite sides, we must obey God rather than men.

[69] Codex Vaticanus and a few versions omit the conjunction "for," but the evidence for keeping it seems conclusive. Most of the critical texts include it, though Westcott and Hort have it in the margin rather than in the text.

[70] Perhaps James is using popular language to describe man. He could have made the same point if he had spoken about "body and soul." It would be improper to use James' language as proof that James rejects or contradicts the doctrine of trichotomy. It likewise would be unwarranted from this one passage to affirm that James held the doctrine of dichotomy.

[71] The first clause in this verse opens with "just as." The second clause opens with "so also." In both clauses, when the second member is missing, the only verdict possible is "dead."

V. PRACTICES SELF-CONTROL.   3:1-12

Summary: There are several areas where a Christian needs to practice self-control. He may control whether or not he teaches.   He may specially work on controlling his tongue, for if he gets that under control, it is likely he has other areas of his life under control.

3:1 -- *Let not many* **of you** *become teachers, my brethren, knowing that as such we shall incur a stricter judgment.*

My brethren – As James begins this new mark of the genuine Christian life, he writes affectionately as one Christian to another (see notes at 1:2 and 2:1 on "my brethren"). James again acknowledges his readers as fellow-members of God's family.   There is a sense in which this new topic is somewhat related to the foregoing.   Twice James has already alluded to sins of the tongue (1:19, 1:25).   The change from the topic of a dead and living faith to the topic of self-control is not so abrupt and arbitrary as it might appear at first sight.   Idle faith that produces no good works is not so different from a faith that produces no self-control.   Neither person is practicing what they teach or preach.

Let not many *of you* **become teachers** – The Greek construction (*mē* with a present imperative) prohibits the continuance of an action already going on.   "Stop being teachers!"   It is not easy to decide whether James is speaking of the office of teacher[1] or of a function any Christian on occasion could undertake.[2]   In the Jewish synagogues, as indicated in Luke 4:16ff and Acts 13:14-16, anyone who was so inclined might request permission or accept an invitation from the synagogue leaders to be the "preacher" who expounded the day's readings from the Law and the Prophets.   1 Corinthians 14:26,31 seems to indicate that a similar practice prevailed in the congregational meetings of the early church.   While at the same time admitting that such teachers are necessary to the life of the church, James is warning his brethren to practice self-control when invitations come to speak to the public assembly.   If one were to teach out of pride, simply desiring recognition and adulation (like certain Jewish teachers wanting to be called "rabbi"), or if

---

[1] Verses that may refer to the temporary office of teacher in the early church are Acts 13:1 (where they are ranked with prophets), 1 Corinthians 12:28 (where they are ranked up near apostles and prophets), and perhaps Ephesians 4:11.   In a moment, when he writes "we shall receive stricter judgment," James will include himself among the "teachers" whom he cautions folk about becoming.

[2] Hebrews 5:12 is a passage that seems to refer to occasional opportunities to teach either in the public assembly or one-on-one privately.   The KJV reads "be not many masters" (why the KJV sometimes used "teacher" and sometimes "master" to translate the same Greek word, save for the sake of euphony, is difficult to understand).   It was not unusual in former times to refer to school teachers as "school masters."   James is not warning his readers against becoming "teachers" in the public realm (though what he says about the teachers' lives and words are certainly true in that forum).   He is, we believe, dealing with the realm of church life and the teaching of Christian doctrines and lifestyles.

his lifestyle is inconsistent (e.g., the days go by, with no attempt to control his tongue, regularly permitting both blessing and cursing to come from his mouth), there is something blameworthy in that person's "volunteering" to be a teacher in the Christian assembly.[3] Perhaps as James warns about the perils and responsibilities of teaching, he has in his mind's eye the Judaizing Pharisees who were confident that their knowledge of God and the Law made them competent to become "a guide for the blind, a light to them that are in darkness, a corrector of the foolish, a teacher of babes, because they had in the Law the form of knowledge and of the truth" (Romans 2:17ff). 1 Timothy 1:7 reflects a situation where certain folk wanted to be "teachers of the Law" even though they didn't "understand either what they are saying or the matters about which they make confident assertions." In spite of an overblown confidence and assumed superiority, when they taught the "traditions of the elders" and emphasized "works of Law," they were leaving their students in darkness rather than pointing them to the light. When they failed to practice the very things they preached, they became liable to the penalty Jesus warned about when He promised He would condemn those who preach but don't practice (Matthew 23:3).

Knowing that as such we shall incur a stricter judgment – This clause gives the reason for the prohibition just stated. The present tense participle ("knowing") indicates something prospective teachers are to keep in mind constantly. James changes from "you" ("be not many of you teachers") to "we." With sober recognition and persuasiveness he includes himself in the judgment.[4] The KJV/ASV read "greater condemnation." The Greek word *krima* denotes the verdict pronounced by a judge.[5] The term itself is a neutral one; the verdict may be favorable or adverse, so the context must decide. In this place both translators and commentators are divided as to the import of the language, though most are agreed it is God's judgment, not man's, that James has in view.[6] The future tense *lēmpsometha* ("we shall receive") looks forward to the time when we all shall stand before

---

[3] As we have suggested the possible background behind James' warning, we have deliberately avoided several explanations we find with some regularity in the commentaries. (1) Some religious groups think any leader needs a special miraculous call to the ministry. Working from this presupposition, some writers have suggested "the condemnation James here writes is pointed to those who appointed themselves as teachers. No man has the right to take the honor of priesthood unto himself, 'but he that was called of God, as was Aaron' (Hebrews 5:4)." This commentator doubts that James is protesting against "teaching" without a "miraculous call from God." God calls men to minister though the Word. He calls through the personal invitation of other leaders (as 2 Timothy 2:2 implies). When Hebrews 5:4 speaks of the Old Testament priesthood, it is a misuse of the passage to apply it to church leaders. See the author's commentary on Hebrews *in loc.* (2) Some have supposed James wants heretical teachers removed from office. (3) Some suppose he wants his brethren to make sure false teachers have no platform from which to promulgate their views.

[4] In this sentence, James does something like John did in 1 John 2:1. John broke the logical flow of the sentence in a similar manner, rather than seem not to include himself, "If any one sins, we have an Advocate ...." John was as much in need of the Advocate as others. So here also, James, as being a teacher, shares in the heavier judgment/condemnation of teachers. Plummer, *op. cit.*, p.596.

[5] *Krisis* is the word for the act of judging before the verdict is reached.

[6] "It was the conviction that the word is not neutral, but condemnatory, which produced the rendering

the judgment seat of Christ to answer for the deeds done in the body (2 Corinthians 5:10). Some think a condemnatory sentence at the final judgment is the thing James talks about.[7] On the basis of available light,[8] teachers will receive greater punishment than the students at the final judgment since their knowledge is greater than that of the students. Some think "judgment" is not a condemnatory verdict but rather a determination that "rewards" are to be forfeited, though not salvation itself (as 1 Corinthians 3:12-15 depict). Teachers have a greater responsibility, for their words and actions leave an indelible impression for good or evil upon receptive and immature minds. Those who lead impressionable students astray will be required to answer for it in the judgment. Teachers who continually, by virtue of their task, pass moral and intellectual judgments on others as they point out to others the way in which they should live, will receive a stricter judgment than their students if those teachers have failed to walk in the right way themselves. Teachers who are severely critical of others will find Jesus severely critical of them, and one of the things He will focus on is the matter of self-control.

3:2 -- *For we all stumble in many ways. If any one does not stumble in what he says, he is a perfect man, able to bridle the whole body as well.*

For we all stumble in many ways – Here is one reason for the "stricter judgment" that verse 1 warned about. "Stumble" (*ptaiō*, "to stumble, to trip, to fall, to err, to fail in duty") is not used here as though we are causing others to stumble (as in Matthew 24:10; Mark 9:42; Romans 14:13,21; and 1 Corinthians 8:13). Rather, it speaks of the sins we ourselves commit (as in Matthew 18:8,9; 1 Peter 2:8; 2 Peter 1:10; and James 2:10) when we are disobedient to the Word of Christ.[9] James could have written "we all sin." His use of "stumble" suggests that many of our moral lapses occur as the result of a slip up when we are off our guard, when we are not diligent in practicing self-control.[10] "We all" (the strong form of the adjective *apantes* is used, rather than simply *pantes*) is placed last

---

('ye' rather than 'we') in the Vulgate, 'knowing that ye receive greater condemnation' (*scientes quoniam majus judicium sumitis*), it being thought that James ought not be included in such a judgment." Plummer, *op. cit.*, p.596.

[7] Advocates of "once saved, always saved" are most vocal that "judgment" is the proper meaning here, for otherwise (if we read "condemnation") James would be suggesting that he (an apostle of Jesus Christ) too could yet be condemned if he fails to practice self-control.

[8] The greater our knowledge, and the more responsible our position, the greater our accountability. "For unto whomsoever much is given, of him shall much be required" (Luke 12:48 KJV). To teach others, when we don't attempt to control our tongues, and when we do not attempt to practice what we preach, will make our judgment more severe.

[9] It is a present tense verb, and suggests such experiences of stumbling occur repeatedly in our daily lives.

[10] The word picture is of walking along and tripping over some obstacle because we were not carefully paying attention to what we were doing. Lenski writes that "stumble" does not necessarily suggest a fatal fall, but it does denote an arrest of progress in our daily walk, and that recovery is needed before we can continue along the road we are travelling.

for emphasis. "Many ways" is probably to be taken as an adjective, calling attention to numerous sins of omission and commission. James declares the universality of sin, even among Christians. Teachers are no exception, not even James himself.[11] Every one of us sins,[12] and each will have to answer in the judgment for his or her own sins. But those of us who become teachers will receive a stricter judgment than our students, for our obligations to live up to the commands of Christ which we teach and know and profess and urge upon others are far greater.[13] James goes on to speak about one particular way we all stumble, namely, "stumbling in word." When Paul is giving scriptural proof that "all have sinned," he makes the following composite quotation from the Psalms: "Their throat is an open grave, with their tongues they keep deceiving; the poison of asps is under their lips; whose mouth is full of cursing and bitterness" (Romans 3:13,14). James would heartily agree.

If any one does not stumble in what he says, he is a perfect man – Improper words, boastful words, bitter words, cursing words, false words, critical words, come out of our mouths at the very time our self-control is relaxed.[14] The tongue, the very organ the teacher uses most, is the area where we most frequently fall. However, by using "any one," James indicates he is not thinking merely of the teacher. It is not just the teacher who needs to practice self-control. Every one of us, any one of us, whatever our sphere of life, will find the tongue the hardest member of our bodies to get under control. By "perfect" (*teleios*) James means one who has attained full spiritual and moral development, the kind of person before described as "perfect and complete, lacking in nothing" (James 1:4).[15] "Does not stumble" is a present tense verb in the Greek, picturing continuous action. It does not say the person "never stumbles" or "never sins," but rather that he so controls his life that sin is not a habitual or customary action. The "perfect man" is not

---

[11] Lenski calls what James writes "James' great confession of sin" in his own life. "By making this honest confession, James establishes his right to be heard," says Hiebert, *op. cit.*, p.207.

[12] Some Bible students think "perfectionism" is attainable in this lifetime. James here admits he still sins, just as do his Christian brethren. A life of holiness, or perfection, is a goal we reach for, but it is likely not fully attained till we are in glory where the devil can no longer offer us temptations to do other than the Lord expects us to do. In harmony with what James teaches, John says to his Christian readers, "If we say that we have no sin, we are deceiving ourselves, and the truth is not in us" (1 John 1:8). "There is not a just man on the earth who habitually does good and who sins not" (Ecclesiastes 7:20).

[13] Perhaps one reason the epistle of James is neglected is because we do not want to hear the truth about ourselves that we read in this and the following verses. Perhaps we teachers need to turn to this third chapter often, and meditate on what it says, and make sure we are working on our self-control so our lives conform to Christ's expectations.

[14] "In word" ("in what he says") is not confined to teaching, but has reference to speech in general.

[15] In the Jewish religious world there were two sorts of persons: (1) the *asketai* (from *askeō*), "beginners," folk who were in training, receiving instruction, diligently learning how to practice what the Jewish religion required; and (2) the *teleios*, "fullgrown," those who had attained somewhat, and had made progress in the matters learned.

sinless perfect, but he does practice self-control so that he is not habitually sinning. He sins less and less as time goes by and his self-control is sharpened.[16] James is not advocating that men should plunge themselves into prolonged periods of silence in order to reach perfection. He is teaching the absolute imperative of practicing self-control over what we think (2 Corinthians 10:5 KJV, "bringing into captivity every thought to the obedience of Christ"), for "out of the abundance of the heart [mind] the mouth speaks" (Matthew 12:34). Jesus also emphasized that "from within, out of the heart" proceed both evil actions and evil words (Mark 7:21-23).

Able to bridle the whole body as well – In this phrase, James himself explains how he uses the term "perfect." James says a man is "perfect" if he is able to keep the other members of his body in subjection. The word rendered "bridle" (*chalinagōgeō*) means "to lead or guide with a bridle" or with a "bit." James will fully unfold the connection between a "bridle" and "self-control" in the verses following. When we are babes in Christ, self-control will not be as full and complete as it is after we have grown spiritually and matured in our Christian walk.[17] The last area where we become "mature" (perfect) in our practice of self-control is control over the tongue, over the words that come out of our mouths.[18] It is the hardest of all members of our body to control.[19] When we get to the place we consistently control the tongue, it follows that we have learned to control the other members of our bodies, too: the hands, feet, brain, heart, eyes, ears, etc.[20]

3:3 -- Now if we put bits into the horses' mouths so that they may obey us, we direct their entire body as well.

---

[16] One writer has noted that the tongue reveals health or sickness. The doctor looks at the tongue to help him judge the patient's health. A Christian's tongue is also a guide to his spiritual health. Often, whether a person is a Christian or not, whether one is carnal or not, can be determined by listening to a person talk.

[17] Non-Christians will find practicing self-control to be a thing almost impossible (Romans 6:8-12). And it takes more than just being initiated into the Christian life to be able consistently to control the tongue. Such self-control is something that results from a long line of practice by one who has the help of the indwelling Holy Spirit to live the Christian life.

[18] Christ, who was the world's only sinless man, practiced perfect self-control over his tongue. Nothing but gracious words proceeded out of His mouth (Luke 4:22). When He was under great provocation, "He opened not his mouth" (Isaiah 53:7). "Neither was guile found in His mouth" (1 Peter 2:22 KJV). His is the example His followers set as their goal to emulate.

[19] We think Grotius was incorrect to interpret "body" in this passage to refer to the church. Though there are passages where the local congregation is compared to a human body (e.g., 1 Corinthians 12:20; Ephesians 4:12), we think the context here in James is of self-control, rather than controlling the church by our "speech" as we teach.

[20] We are not saying that the tongue governs the body. It is the soul of man that animates and governs his body. (God intended that man's spirit give directions to the soul. When a man commits his first sin, his spirit "dies" and is unable to give proper directions. When a man is born again, it is his spirit that is reborn [John 3:6].) If there are evil passions and evil words, it is evidence something is wrong with the directions the soul is receiving.

Now if – In the KJV, verse 3 begins with "behold" because the Greek text behind that translation reads *ide* or *idou*, whereas the text behind the NASB reads *ei de*. James does from time to time write "behold" (see *idou* at 3:4,5, 5:4, etc., a Semitic expression to introduce a vivid illustration), but he nowhere else used *ide* (another form of the verb "behold"). Textual scholars suppose James wrote *ei de*, then some copyist accidentally left out a letter so it became *ide*, which later copyists attempted to correct by writing *idou*. The wording of the verse as found in the Nestle-Aland and UBS texts must be interpreted. Some make it a long "if" clause with the conclusion understood (i.e., "if we ... control their whole body [then much more can we control our whole body if we can control our tongue]"), or we can treat "we control their whole body" as the conclusion to the "if' clause as our NASB translators have done.

We put bits into the horses' mouths so that they may obey us – In verse 3 James seems to be illustrating the truth he just wrote in verse 2. The sense of what James wrote seems to be this: If we can control the whole body of living animals when we control their mouths, then how much more is it true that if we humans can control the mouth we can control the whole body. The word translated "bits" (*chalinous*) is the noun form from the same root as "bridle" (*chalinagōgeō*) in verse 2. In some places *chalinos* is used of the "bridle" proper including the "reins"; in others it is used of the "bit"; and in some places it is used of the "bridle and bit" together. It is just the metal bit attached to the bridle that goes into the horse's mouth. The verb "put" (*ballomen*) has a mild force; it does not imply violence to get the bit into the animal's mouth. The present tense indicates that putting bits into horses' mouths is a regular practice with which James and his readers ("we," "us") were familiar.

We direct their entire body as well – Some bits have curbs (a "u" shaped bend in the middle of the bit). These curbs are designed to hurt the horse's tongue when he resists the driver's pull on the reins. Just a little tug on the reins, and even the spirited animal obeys. Once the wild animal is broken, a simple metal bit is all that is needed. The horse soon learns to stop, turn right or turn left, back up, stand still, walk slowly or run, depending on no more than just a light touch on the reins. If you can control the mouth you obviously have control of the whole animal.

3:4 -- *Behold, the ships also, though they are so great and are driven by strong winds, are still directed by a very small rudder, wherever the inclination of the pilot desires.*

Behold, the ships also – James continues illustrating the point made in verse 2, that one who can control a little member like the tongue can control the whole body. Ships are a stronger illustration of James' point than horses. Horses can be taught obedience, and they eventually use their great strength to co-operate with their rider. But a ship is devoid of life. It offers a dead resistance. Nevertheless it can be controlled.

Though they are so great and are driven by strong winds – An ocean-going ship is a large object. The grain ships that ran between Egypt and Rome were 180' long, 45' wide at the beam, and 43' from the deck to the bottom of the hold. In addition to its cargo of grain, the ship Paul was on which was bound for Rome had room for 276 passengers (Acts

27:37). It seems unmanageable by its vastness. It is driven by great storms, with howling winds[21] sometimes producing waves 50 or 60 feet high. Yet the person who has control of the small rudder is in control of the ship itself.

Are still directed by a very small rudder – Small oar-shaped or blade-shaped pieces of wood fastened to the end of a long piece of timber (a tiller) which was attached to a sort of oarlock and trailed alongside the stern of the ships served as ancient rudders.[22] Compared to the size of the ship, the rudder was "very small" (the Greek *elachistou* is the superlative form of *mikros*, thus heightening the contrast in size). Yet how necessary the rudder is. If something goes wrong with it, the ship surely is in danger. It may drift to destruction. It will never be able to make it to port.

Wherever the inclination of the pilot desires – The "pilot" or "helmsman" is the one who controls the rudder. With pressure on the tiller, pushing it to one side or the other, or simply holding it steady, he can control the direction the ship moves. The "inclination" (impulse) is either the movement by which the rudder is turned, or the pilot's guiding will that leads to the movement of the rudder.[23] If the one who has control of the rudder has control of the whole ship, how much more likely is it that the one who has control of his tongue has control of his whole body?

3:5 -- *So also the tongue is a small part of the body, and yet it boasts of great things. Behold, how great a forest is set aflame by such a small fire!*

So also the tongue is a small part of the body – In comparison to the size of the whole human body, the human tongue is small, like the horse's mouth is small in comparison to the body, and like the rudder is small in comparison to the size of the ship. "So also" begins James' application of the two preceding verses. The point of the illustrations in verses 3-4 has been that control of a little bit and a little rudder can achieve big results. In

---

[21] The expression "strong (rough) winds" (*sklerōn anemōn*) is peculiar, "rough" meaning hard or harsh, especially to the touch, and hence of what is intractable or disagreeable in other ways (1 Samuel 25:3; Matthew 25:24; John 6:60; Acts 26:14; Jude 15). Perhaps in only one other passage in Greek literature previous to this epistle is it used as an epithet of wind (in Proverbs 27:16, a passage in which the LXX differs widely from the Hebrew and from our versions). James, who appears fond of the wisdom books in Scripture, may have derived this expression from Proverbs. Plummer, *op. cit.*, p.597

[22] The KJV reads "helm," a word that used to refer to the rudder of the ship, but has changed meaning so that it is now generally applied to the whole steering apparatus. Some ancient ships had two of these oar-like rudders, one affixed to each side of the stern (Acts 27:40).

[23] One writer, treating the passage as though it is not self-control, but an outside person who ultimately directs a person's life, asks, "Who is the steersman who has his hand on the rudder of your life? If it is the devil, your ship is bound for the rocks of eternal punishment. Let each one of us allow the Lord Jesus to keep his hand on our wheel, that He may govern our whole life, and bring us safely into the haven of rest." We may, with a certain imagination, follow the example of Bede, and turn the verse into an allegory. Bede made the sea to mean human life; the winds were temptations; and so on. But we should also beware lest we suppose anything of the kind was in the mind of James (adapted from Plummer, *ibid.*).

the same way, control of the little tongue has far-reaching consequences.   Such control is needed to curb the harm the tongue can do if it is not kept under control.

And yet it boasts of great things – James writes "boasts great things" rather than "does great things" as he makes a transition to a new thought.   "Boast" can be taken either in a positive sense,[24] or in a negative one.[25]   Positively, the tongue can accomplish great things for good.   History is full of illustrations of the power of great oratory to sway multitudes to noble action.   It has been used to alter the destinies of nations.   The tongue can speak the matchless truths of the Gospel of Christ, and offer to men the great invitation, which if embraced will change their eternal destinies.   On the other hand, the tongue can utter empty boasts.   Men have been known to boast of what they did in the past, what they are doing now, and what they are going to do in the future, and none of what is said is true.[26] Not only are men's words at times defiant of the living God, the words pouring forth from a man's mouth can cause great harm.   No wonder James is emphasizing the imperative need to control the tongue.

Behold, how great a forest is set aflame by such a small fire! – As in verse 4, "behold" serves to introduce a fresh illustration.[27]   The following verses seem to indicate the topic is the harm and havoc that can be done by the tongue.   There is a play on words in the Greek that is difficult to reproduce in English translation.   The literal rendering of the Greek is "what a fire kindles what a wood."   Our translators have translated the same word *hēlicon* (which calls attention to the size of a thing) by the words "great" and "small." Evidently the idea is "how small a fire" and "how large a wood."   The word *hulē* ("wood, forest") can mean either "wood" such a firewood, fuel, a stack of timber, or "wood" such as a grove of trees, a forest,[28] the brush and timber that cover a mountainside.   We are familiar both with how much damage to a house or factory can start with a little fire,[29] and how many acres of forest can be consumed by the fire that began as a small campfire, but which soon got out of control because it was carelessly left unattended.   Fire can be a good

---

[24] Some Greek manuscripts read two separate words, the adjective *megala* ("great things") and the verb *auchei* ("boast").

[25] Some manuscripts read it as one word, the compound verb *megalauchei* ("arrogant boasting").

[26] Pharaoh boasted against God.   "Who is the Lord, that I should obey His voice and let Israel go?" But Pharaoh wasn't as great as he thought he was.   Nebuchadnezzar boasted, "If you do not worship [the idol], you shall be cast the same hour into the midst of the burning fiery furnace.   And who is God that He shall deliver you?" (Daniel 3:15).   That was the wrong thing to say, for it was a challenge to the Almighty.

[27] Some have proposed that when we divide the chapter into verses, a new verse should begin at this place.

[28] As long ago as when the Bible was translated into Latin, the word "forest" was used here whereas James wrote "wood."

[29] They say the great Chicago fire in 1871, which burned down about 1/3 of the city, was started by a cow kicking over a lantern.   17,450 buildings were destroyed, 250 people perished, and 100,000 were made homeless.

servant, but it is a bad master.   Kept under control, it cooks our food, warms our homes, and fuels our generators.   But lose control over it, and it begins to do untold damage.   So it is with the tongue.

3:6 -- *And the tongue is a fire, the* very *world of iniquity; the tongue is set among our members as that which defiles the entire body, and sets on fire the course of* our *life, and is set on fire by hell.*

And the tongue is a fire – While there are several decisions to be made as we try to understand and explain this verse,[30] its general thrust is clear.   What James does is first identify the tongue as being like a fire, and then he describes some of its devastating effects. A little fire and a little word alike can start a terrible conflagration.   Fire hurts; burns are painful.   Likewise, some have been mortally wounded by a few unkind words.   Fire spreads as long as there is material to burn.   Likewise, as long as there are ears willing to listen, words of the tongue will pass from one to another, whether the words be good or bad.   Fire destroys anything combustible in its path.   Likewise, an evil tongue has destroyed many a home and many a work for God.   The tongue is more incendiary than any little flame ever was.

The *very* **world of iniquity** – One of the initial decisions to be made when translating this verse concerns punctuation.   The punctuation adopted in the KJV makes an awkward sentence and necessitates the insertion of the word "so" to begin the clause immediately following this one.   Not a few commentators think we should put a period after "fire," and treat the words "a world of iniquity" as being the object of the verb in the following clause.[31] When this is done it reads "The tongue is a world of iniquity among our members."[32]   The meaning of "world of iniquity" has been much discussed, and this leads to the making of further decisions.   "Iniquity" is *adikias*, a word that reeks of "injustice."   "World" represents *kosmos*, a word that has eight different meanings according to Thayer's lexicon.[33]   "World" is sometimes used to denote one of the largest units of measure which

---

[30] Different ways of punctuating the verse are possible.   There have been alterations of the text, and the critical apparatus shows a number of variants.

[31] The ASV ("And the tongue is a fire.   The world of iniquity among our members is the tongue, which defileth the whole body ....") is an example of this way of explaining what James wrote.

[32] Other ways of translating and punctuating the verse may be studied by comparing the various English versions.   Another possible suggestion (with a stop after "fire") is to render it "The tongue, that very world of iniquity, is a fire."   The NASB is an example of this option.

[33] Thayer (*op. cit.*, p. 356,357) lists this passage in James under meaning number 8.   This usage of "world" apparently does not occur in classical Greek; so to illustrate its usage in James, attention is called to Proverbs 17:6 in the LXX, where the Greek differs from the Hebrew text.   What is remarkable about the passage in Proverbs (in the LXX) is that "world" occurs right after a mention of sins of speech: "An evil man listens to the tongue of the wicked; but a righteous man gives no heed to false lips.   The faithful man has the whole world of wealth, but the faithless not even a penny."

the human mind can conceive ("universe" being a larger measure[34]). There are possibilities for sin with the tongue that would fill the world.[35]

> Think of the foul stories and impure jests and innuendoes; think of the oaths and curses that befoul the souls of those who utter them while they lead the hearers into sin. They create an atmosphere in which men sin with a light heart, because the grossest sins are made to look not only attractive and easy, but amusing. The captious word, that makes everything a subject of blame; the discontented word, that would show that the speaker is always being ill-treated; the biting word, that is meant to inflict pain; the sullen word, that throws a gloom over all who hear it; the provoking word, that seeks to stir up strife – all these are but a few examples of the "world of evil."[36]

Still others pick the meaning "a world characterized by iniquity" as being possibly what James had in mind. In other words, all the evil characteristics of a fallen world, its covetousness, its idolatry, its blasphemy, its lust, its rapacious greed, find expression through the tongue.[37] "There are few sins people commit in which the tongue is not involved."[38]

The tongue is set among our members as that which defiles the entire body – The uncontrolled tongue not only is destructive of others, it defiles the very man who doesn't control his tongue. The word for "is set" is *kathistatai* (not *esti* or *huparchei*). Its literal meaning is "constitutes itself" or "makes itself" (as it is rightly translated in James 4:4).[39] Mayor says *kathistēmi* implies a sort of adaptation or development as contrasted with the natural or original state.[40] The tongue was not created by God to be a permanent source of all kinds of evil. Like the rest of creation, it was made "very good," "the best member we have." It is because of an undisciplined and uncontrolled use that it becomes "a world of iniquity" and defiles (present participle, continuous action) the entire body. Jesus said that it is not what goes into a man, but what comes out of him, out of his heart, and out of his mouth, that defiles the man (Mark 7:20).

---

[34] The Vulgate renders this passage *universatias iniquitatis*, "a universe of iniquity."

[35] Who can measure the evils which an uncontrolled tongue causes? Who can measure the evils which arise from scandal, slander, profaneness, perjury, falsehood, blasphemy, obscenity, and false teaching? Who can gauge the amount of broils, and contentions, and strifes, and wars, and suspicions, and enmities, and alienations among friends and neighbors, which the tongue produces. If all men were unable to speak, what a portion of the sins of the world would soon cease. If men controlled the tongue, the number of sins would certainly diminish.

[36] Plummer, *op. cit.*, p.601.

[37] Tasker, *op. cit.*, p. 76.

[38] Burdick, *op. cit.*, p.187.

[39] This treats the verb as a middle voice, rather than a passive voice form.

[40] Mayor, *op. cit.*, p.111.

And sets on fire the course of *our* life – Decisions must be made here concerning both translation and the resultant meaning.[41]   The general meaning of *ton trochon tēs geneseōs* is evident, but we cannot be sure what image James had in his mind when he wrote these words.   Both nouns can have several meanings.[42]   The ASV reads "wheel of nature." Another offers "the orb of creation."   Some writers speak of the "wheel of life" that starts rolling at birth and continues on till death (an individual wheel of nature).   Some writers speak of the daily round of activities that reoccur time after time in men's lives.   Some writers speak of successive generations (one cycle of humans after another).[43]

And is set on fire by hell – How did the fire spread by the tongue begin?   How does the tongue, created for other purposes, acquire this destructive and deadly ability?   James leaves no doubt: it is inspired by the evil one.[44]   The old serpent, the Devil, is constantly setting the tongue on fire (present tense).   Sins that men commit are traced back beyond the evil desires to the one who stirred up the evil desires (cp. James 1:14,15).   Satan will use our tongue, and all of our members, for his evil purposes if we relax our self-control and let him.

3:7 -- *For every species of beasts and birds, of reptiles and creatures of the sea, is tamed, and has been tamed by the human race.*

For – A verse which begins with "for" can do one of two things: it can give a reason for something just said, or it can be a further explanation of something just said.   Perhaps the

---

[41] Beginning with the previous clause, "defiling the body," the remainder of the verse has no finite verb, but consists of three participles, all in apposition to the statement that the tongue is a world of iniquity. The first participle has an article, the last two do not.   All three may be governed by the one article, or the first participle (having the article) may be in apposition, and the last two explain what James means by "defiling the body."

[42] "Nature" or "life" (NASB) are two possible ideas in *genesis*.   The primary sense of the word is "birth" and seems to refer to a man's life from his birth onwards.   We had this same word at James 1:23 ("the face of his existence").   *Trochos* (depending on the position of its accent) can mean "wheel" (something that revolves on the same axis) or "cycle" (human life rolls onward).   The early Latin translators offered *rotam nativitatis nostrae.*

[43] Either of these options seems more plausible than some we have read.   (1) Some have thought James was alluding to the doctrine of reincarnation, the transmigration of souls.   Indeed, the Orphic worshipers (snake worshipers) and the Pythagoreans taught the transmigration of souls to new bodies after death, and applied the term *trochos* (wheel) to the supposed unending round of death and rebirth. But this makes the passage pure nonsense, and is contrary to James' faith (Christianity does not teach reincarnation, e.g., Hebrews 9:27).   (2) Clarke thought James had reference to the circulation of the blood in the body.   Angry or irritating language has an astonishing influence on the circulation of the blood.

[44] Just as "heaven" can be used to refer to God, so "hell" is used to refer to the devil.   "Hell" translates *gehenna* (Gehenna), the Greek form of the Hebrew *ge-hinnom,* literally "the valley of Hinnom," the garbage dump outside the south-southwest wall of Jerusalem, where the refuse and garbage were tossed to rot and burn.   The valley became a figure of speech to describe "Hell," as the place where the refuse of society is to be sent after the final judgment (Matthew 5:22, 18:9; Revelation 20:14,15).   The continual burning of rubbish became an apt figure for eternal punishment.

connection is with "the tongue being set on fire by the devil" (verse 6). That's the reason why men find it so difficult by themselves to tame and control the tongue, as compared with taming and controlling creatures in the animal kingdom. Perhaps there is a connection with the whole destructive picture (verses 5 and 6) of what the tongue can do. It is destructive precisely because men have found it difficult to tame.

Every species of beasts and birds, of reptiles and creatures of the sea, is tamed, and has been tamed by the human race – A fourfold division of the animal kingdom such as James gives here is not unfamiliar to us.[45] "Every species" or "all kinds" means some from each kind, though not all of any one type. "Beasts" (*thērion*) has a wider and narrower meaning. Wider, it may include bees, fishes, and worms. Narrower, it refers to domestic quadrupeds (elephants, lions, tigers, hyenas, cows, horses, sheep, dogs, and others). "Birds" (*peteinōn*) such as the eagle, parakeet, canary, hen, goose, duck, pigeon, martin, and hawk have been made subject to the will of man. "Reptiles" (*hereptōn*) has a wider sense referring to animals that walk on all fours (such as crocodiles and lizards), but which are commonly characterized as "reptiles"; and it has a narrower sense referring to what we call "snakes."[46] "Creatures of the sea" (*enaliōn*) include such marine creatures as the seal, shark, dolphin, and fish.[47] To "tame" means to control, and to render the animal useful and beneficial to mankind.[48] The combination of present and perfect tenses ("tamed and has been tamed") recalls the fact that when God first created man, He gave "dominion over the fish of the sea, over the fowl of the air, and over every living thing that moves upon the earth" (Genesis 1:28[49]) to man. Man has carried out that dominion mandate ever since.[50] "Human race" is the NASB suggestion for translating *tē phusei tē anthrōpinē* ("human kind"[51]). Various members of the animal kingdom have been tamed and put into service for mankind. However, because of the devil's activities, men find it more difficult to tame the tongue and put it into similar service.

---

[45] Compare Acts 10:12 for a slightly different threefold division. See also 1 Kings 4:33 and Genesis 1:26.

[46] Most of us have seen snake handlers at the zoo or circus. We are also likely acquainted with the snake charmers of India with their musical reeds and performing puff adders.

[47] Barclay (*op. cit.*, p.104) tells us that "the Roman world knew of tame fish in the fish ponds which were in the open central hall or *atrium* of a Roman house."

[48] The word is used at Mark 5:4 of the Gadarene demoniac who could not be controlled.

[49] The same promise was repeated to Noah after he came out of the Ark (Genesis 9:2).

[50] The dominion given to man was in some measure lost when Adam sinned (Psalm 8:6-8). Now it takes an effort on man's part to keep animal life in subjection. In fact, Christ's death and resurrection had as part of its agenda the winning back of man's lost dominion (see Hebrews 2:5-10).

[51] *Phusis* is the same word translated "species" in the first part of this verse. We might represent what James wrote if we translated "every nature [of the animal kingdom] is subject to control by the human nature."

3:8 -- *But no one can tame the tongue;* it is *a restless evil* and *full of deadly poison.*

But no one can tame the tongue – Or more correctly, "But no one is able to tame the tongue of men."[52]   Animals may be tamed by someone else (verse 7), but controlling the tongue is not something we can expect others to do for us.   With the Holy Spirit's help, it is something each person himself or herself must do.   What James writes does not mean that the tongue can *never* be brought under control.[53]   If this were to be taken absolutely, how could the Psalmist (34:13) have said, "Keep your tongue from evil and your lips from speaking deceit"?   Or how could the Psalmist have vowed not to sin with his tongue (Psalm. 17:3, 39:1)?   James is hardly to be thought of as saying no one can tame his own tongue.   Such a pessimistic view would be in conflict with the whole point of this passage, in which James emphasizes the need to exercise self-control.   This verse may say that the tongue will not be controlled 100% of the time even by the "perfect" man (cp. James 3:2). Lion and tiger tamers never relax their care and watchfulness of their big trained "pets." Like some animals that have been broken must be watched carefully, so the tongue must be watched carefully.   If care and watchfulness are laid aside, the evil words will burst out again and the results will be calamitous.

It is **a restless evil** – The italics indicate there is no verb in the Greek.   Because "full of" in the following phrase hardly can modify "tongue," our translators have treated both these phrases as being predicate nominatives after supplying the verb "is".   The KJV reading "an unruly evil" follows the reading *akatascheton* ("unrestrainable, ungovernable") of the later Greek manuscripts.   As previously explained, James is hardly saying that the tongue can *never* be brought under control.   The translation "restless evil" follows the better attested reading *akatastaton* ("disorderly, inconsistent, chaotic, restless").   Again, think of the animal that has been tamed, checked and penned, and which restlessly paces back and forth looking for an opportunity to break away from the tamer.   Given the least opportunity it will revert to its wild nature.   Likewise the tongue cannot be trusted to stay submissively in its proper place.   Constant vigilance is needed.

Full of deadly poison –James may be echoing the words of Psalm 140:3.   It is not only venomous serpents whose sting produces death in the victim.   There are bottles or con-

---

[52] The Pelagians attempted to punctuate this as a question, "But can anyone tame the tongue?" However, with the use of *oudeis* for "no one," this punctuation can hardly be defended.   The Pelagians may have had a theological reason for attempting to make this a question, for thereby they avoided a proof-text for universal sinfulness.

[53] We must be careful how we word our comments of explanation.   Those who believe in total hereditary depravity think they find in these verses about the tongue a ready source of corroborative evidence.   They write about the "evil propensity" of the tongue; they write about its "evil nature."   Is this the proper language for someone who has become a Christian?   Even if there is an inherited sinful nature, did not folk become new creatures when they were immersed into Christ?   It is hardly a Biblical doctrine to teach that the old sinful nature (if there is such a thing) must be struggled with the entire Christian life, or that there is a second work of grace needed by the Christian before he or she can overcome the sinful nature.

tainers full of poison.   How careful we are with such containers.   We put labels on them, and are careful to keep them out of the reach of children.   Even with these precautions some get it by mistake and are poisoned.   Uncontrolled speech is as deadly as any poison. Little ones are caused to stumble, lifetime friendships have been broken, reputations ruined, lives destroyed, souls damned.

3:9 -- *With it we bless* our *Lord and Father; and with it we curse men, who have been made in the likeness of God*

With it we bless *our* Lord and Father – In verses 9-12 we have the inconsistency and restlessness of the tongue (verse 8) illustrated.   A man can praise the Lord one minute, and the next he can curse his fellow man.   There is in each of us, and likely more than we wish to admit, a moral inconsistency with regard to how we use our tongues.   "With it" indicates that the tongue is only the instrument we use to express our thoughts.   "We" speaks of Christians, the people James calls "my brethren" in the next verse.   "Lord and Father"[54] may be treated as two names referencing the same person (i.e., "Lord, even the Father") or as referring to two different members of the Godhead.   "Father" refers to the first member of the Godhead.   Because of Jesus' incarnation, He is called the Father of the Lord Jesus Christ.   Because Christians are adopted into God's family, God is called the Father of all believers.[55]   Perhaps "Father" even anticipates the second half of verse 9, with its reference to "the divine likeness" which the men He has created bear.   In the LXX, "Lord" (*kurios*) was regularly used to translate the four-letter sacred name YHWH ("Yahweh," or "Jehovah").   In the New Testament, this title usually is applied to Jesus, though it is sometimes also applied to the Father.   We think the phrase is best viewed as referencing two different members of the Godhead, that James is here treating Jesus and the Father as equal deity; both are equally the objects of the Christian's "blessing."   "Blessing" (*eulogeō*) means to speak well of the Lord and of the Father.   It means to express our gratitude to them.[56]   This is a wonderful and noble way to employ the human tongue! Such "blessing" probably does not just occur spontaneously.   It is the result of self-controlled thought and action.   (Cursing comes out of the Christian's mouth when self-control is relaxed.)   "Bless the Lord, O my soul, and all that is within me bless His holy

---

[54] There is a manuscript variation at this place. As a result, the KJV reads "God, even the Father" while the NASB following a different manuscript tradition has "Lord and Father." KJV advocates think the reading in the more ancient manuscripts, "Lord and Father," is strange and have tried to make a case for favoring the Received Text with the argument that it more strongly upholds the deity of Jesus than do the readings in the Alexandrian text. Yet a case could also be made here in James that this better attested reading ("Lord and Father") exalts Jesus more than the KJV reading does. Certainly the Alexandrian text of John 1:18 is a stronger witness to Jesus' deity than the Textus Receptus.

[55] As a Father, He loves us, cares for us, watches over us night and day. He supplies us with the necessities of life, and is ever on the lookout for our good.

[56] It was customary for Jewish people, whenever they uttered the name of God, to add "Blessed be He." Perhaps James' readers from Jewish backgrounds were still so expressing their delight in the Lord whenever they spoke His name.

name" (Psalm 103:1-2). The Word commends such blessing always, and James is not belittling it here.[57] "Blessing" certainly ought to come out of the mouth. What James is doing is pointing out that both blessing and cursing ought not be allowed out of the same mouth.

And with it we curse men – "With it" again treats the tongue as but an instrument used to express the thoughts and feelings of the heart. The cursing that is condemned is the cursing which is uttered with an unbridled tongue under the violence of passion and bitterness and hatred of men.[58] It often occurs just after a person has lost his temper. There is a cursing that was permissible in Old Testament times,[59] and a cursing that is permissible for Christians.[60] When the tongue is not controlled, we find ourselves improperly "cursing whom the Lord has not cursed, and defying whom the Lord has not defied" (Numbers 23:8).[61] "Bless" and "curse" are present tense verbs indicating the action is not just isolated instances, but can occur often.[62]

Who have been made in the likeness of God – The addition of this phrase indicates that cursing men amounts, in effect, to cursing God Himself. "Praising God and cursing men

---

[57] Various scriptures could be recalled to show the appropriateness of "praising the Lord with the tongue." Psalm 147:1, "Praise ye the Lord: for it is good to sing praises unto our God; for it is pleasant and praise is becoming." Hebrews 13:15, "Through [Jesus] then, let us continually offer up a sacrifice of praise to God, that is, the fruit of lips that give thanks to His name." Psalm 105:6, "Let everything that has breath praise the Lord." Barclay reminds us that three times a day the devout Jew repeated the "Shemoneh Esreh" – the 18 prayers or Eulogies, everyone of which begins with "Blessed be Thou, O God."

[58] "Cursing" speaks not so much of what we call "profanity" but of calling down a curse from God on others because of ill-will towards them.

[59] The Old Testament required the Israelite to curse on Mount Ebal and bless on Mount Gerazim. The fact that cursing was forbidden in special cases (as against parents, Exodus 21:17; the king, Exodus 22:28; the deaf, Leviticus 19:14) seems to indicate that it was not generally condemned under the old covenant. Cursing is referred to without implying blame in Proverbs 11:26, 24:24, 26:23, 30:10; Ecclesiastes 7:21, 10:20. Compare also the curse of Canaan by Noah (Genesis 9:25), that of Simeon and Levi by their father (Genesis 49:7), of the builder of Jericho by Joshua (Joshua 6;26), Abimelech by Jotham (Judges 9:20,57), Meroz by Deborah (Judges 5:23), the children of Elisha (2 Kings 2:24), and the apostate Jews by Nehemiah (Nehemiah 13:25). There are many imprecations in the Psalms.

[60] In the New Testament we have an example of cursing in the "Anathemas" pronounced by Paul in 1 Corinthians 16:22 and Galatians 1:8. Do we not find an example of "cursing men" in the denunciation of the Pharisees by Jesus (Matthew 23)? Or in Peter's words to Elymas the sorcerer (Acts 13:10)? These stern utterances had their source in love; not, as human curses commonly have, in hate.

[61] In an attempt to warn Christians to control their tongues and refrain from uttering curses, Plummer pointedly asks, "Is it quite certain that the supposed evil is something which God abhors: that those whom we would denounce are responsible for it; that denunciation of them will do any good; that this is the proper time for such denunciation; that we are the proper persons to utter it?"

[62] When James writes "we curse," is he confessing that he, too, at times, misuses his tongue? Compare notes at 3:2.

is tantamount to praising and cursing the same person."[63]   "Made in the likeness of God" reminds us of Genesis 1:26,27, "Let Us make man in our image, according to Our likeness."[64]   "Have been made" is a perfect tense verb, signifying past completed action with present continuing results; men have been and still are in God's "likeness" or "image." The "likeness of God" and the "image of God" still remains in men generations after the fall of Adam.   After the flood (Genesis 9:6), while men are now permitted to kill animals, they are prohibited from killing men because men are "in the image of God."   Here in James 3:9, men are prohibited from cursing other men because they are in "the likeness of God."   If man did not still retain the image and likeness of God, there would be no sin either in killing or cursing him.   It may just cause men to hesitate to curse men if they remember that in actuality they are cursing the One who made the man.

3:10 -- *From the same mouth come* both *blessing and cursing.   My brethren, these things ought not to be this way.*

From the same mouth come *both* blessing and cursing – This half of verse 10 summarizes what was said in verse 9.   Summarizing from time to time is a telling method of argument which James continually uses.   The emphasis is on "the same mouth."   As before, "cursing" is not to be equated with what we call profanity.   Rather, James has in mind those words that express bitter feelings towards one's fellowman.[65]

My brethren, these things ought not to be this way – "My brothers"[66] highlights the fact that James has in mind Christians whose tongues are inconsistent.   If both blessing and cursing come forth from the same mouth, there is a gross inconsistency.   How strange that the being who is lord and master of the animal creation should be unable, or unwilling, to govern himself.   "How strange that man's chief mark of superiority over the brutes should be the power of speech, and that he should use this power in such a way as to make it the instrument of his own degradation, until he becomes lower than the brutes!"[67]   Of course,

---

[63] Burdick, *op. cit.*, p. 188.

[64] James is quoting the second phrase "after our likeness" (*Demuth* in Hebrew, or *homoiōsis* in Greek), not the first phrase "in our image" (*kat' eikona*).   Tasker's comment (*op. cit.*, p.78) is not quite right.   He wrote, "In fallen man the image of God has become marred because of sin; and this is perhaps why James says here 'made after the likeness of God' rather than 'made in the image of God'."   However, both Genesis 1:26 and James 3:9 have *homoiōsin* ("likeness").   See the Special Study on "The Image and Likeness of God" following comments on James 3:12.

[65] R.J. Knowling (*The Epistle of James* [London: Methuen, 1904], p.81) offers as illustrations of such "cursing" the "tones of bitter contempt against the Gentiles of Cornelius' house who were recently converted" (Acts 11:2,3), and the spirit expressed by the Judaizers (Acts 15:1) who refused to think for a moment that the Gentiles of Antioch who had become Christians were within the pale of salvation.   James had personally heard both these examples of "cursing."

[66] The term is used throughout this letter to address Christian believers (see 1:2,16,19,14;   3:1, etc.).

[67] Plummer, *op. cit.*, p.600.

James is not to be thought of as saying it is OK if only cursing comes out.[68] What he is driving home is that it is one of the Christian's plainest duties to see to it that the tongue does not issue words of unwarranted cursing, but rather only words that bless God and express love and kindness and edification to men. The words James uses translated "ought not" are *ou chrē*, "it is not fitting" or "it is contrary to natural circumstances."[69] This "ought not" arises not so much from a written or spoken divine revelation about the difference between right and wrong. Rather, it arises from the fact that it is incongruous with the way God has created things in His world. Praise loses its noble character if it comes out of the same opening as words of cursing.

3:11 -- *Does a fountain send out from the same opening* both *fresh and bitter* water?

Does a fountain send out from the same opening *both* fresh and bitter *water*? – The question in the Greek expects a negative answer. To illustrate what he means by "these things ought not to be" (verse 10) or "it is not fitting" (KJV), James draws some lessons from God's creation.[70] Travelers who walked or rode beasts through the land of Israel knew about the springs where life-giving water (*gluku*, "sweet, fresh") was to be found, and also about those springs which were to be avoided because the water was brackish or sulfurous or laden with salt (*pikron*, "bitter, salt").[71] "Send out" is literally "spurt," being a poetic form describing water pouring out as if it were under pressure. "Fountain" is literally "hole, opening, fissure;" such are prevalent on the eastern slopes of the mountain ridges that run across the land of Judea.[72] The ones that are sweet are always sweet and refreshing, and the ones that are bitter are always bitter. Sometimes the two different kinds of springs are very close together, but no one spring runs alternately sometimes sweet and sometimes bitter. When one observes how God has created "openings" and what flows out of them, it should quickly become rather obvious that sweet and bitter (i.e., words

---

[68] In one sense there is little difference between words of "cursing" and the "words" which Paul writes against when he objects to those who are "speaking things they ought not" (1 Timothy 5:13) and "teaching things which they ought not" (Titus 1:11).

[69] See Thayer, *Lexicon*, p. 126, where the difference between the Greek synonyms for "it is necessary" (*dei* v. *chrē*) are explained. The former suggests a necessity or constraint which arises from divine appointment; the latter signifies a necessity resulting from time and circumstances.

[70] Jesus drew lessons about marriage from the way God created man and woman (Matthew 19:1ff). Paul drew lessons from God's creation as he identifies idolatry as sin (Romans 1:19ff). In Old Testament times, David called attention to the lessons to be learned from God's creation (Psalm 19:1). James follows in this tradition.

[71] There is no word for "water" in the original, though it is implied. The result is that the two adjectives "sweet" and "bitter" are set in sharper contrast.

[72] Bible students are acquainted with Endor, Engedi, Enrogel, Enhakkore, Aenon, Enshemish, Enhaddah, Enrimmon, Enmishpat, and the hot springs of Callihroe (which are bitter and salty), among others.

of blessing and cursing) should not come out of the same opening.   That's not what God intended when He made the "opening."

3:12 -- *Can a fig tree, my brethren, produce olives, or a vine produce figs?   Neither* can *salt water produce fresh.*

Can a fig tree, my brethren, produce olives, or a vine produce figs? – Two more illustrations from nature should help the "brethren" to see how inconsistent it is to utter both blessings and cursings from the same mouth.   These kinds of trees and plants abounded in the Holy Land.   Jesus used a similar figure in the Sermon on the Mount (Matthew 7:15-20).   The trees and vines God has created are not inconsistent in the fruit they produce. Why then should man think it is acceptable when his mouth (and heart, for "for the mouth speaks out of that which fills the heart," Matthew 12:33-35) produces inconsistent speech.[73]

Neither *can* salt water produce fresh – The reading of this clause is very confused in the Greek manuscripts.   The Textus Receptus reads *houtōs oudemia pēgē halukon gluku poiēsai hudōr*, "Thus, not even one fountain is able to produce [both] salt water and fresh." If we accept this reading, then James is driving home the point he has just made in the preceding illustrations.[74]   The text in the Nestle-Aland and UBS editions is *oute halukon gluku poiēsai hudōr*.   In this reading there is no verb in this half of the verse, so we supply *dunatai* ("can" or "is able") from the first half of the verse.   In addition we must treat one of the adjectives, either "salt" or "fresh," as the subject of the understood verb.   The adjective "salty" occurs only here in the New Testament; however, in the LXX, *halukon* is used for the Dead Sea, i.e., the Salty Sea (Numbers 34:3,12; Deuteronomy 3:17; Joshua 15:2,5).   Perhaps we should translate it, "Neither is the Salt Sea able to produce fresh water."[75]   The NIV offers "Can a salt spring produce fresh water?"   While "spring" is commonly supposed to be a suitable noun to supply for the adjective,[76] this translation ("salt spring") does not let the English reader know that the Greek in verse 12 is different

---

[73] You can rightly tell what a man is by listening to him speak.   James is arguing that we Christian brethren ought to make our words harmonize with our principles and character.

[74] Perhaps James is saying that it is impossible for genuine worship (blessing) to proceed from a heart which, because little or no self-control is exercised, continually vents itself in curses against other men. The Pharisees, for example, professed to be godly.   How they could pray, and they were the teachers. Yet they could rob widow's houses and reject and revile the Christ.   The Lord will not accept the worship from a double-tongued man, and he may become a stumbling block in the way of the unsaved.

[75] The implication of this way of reading James is that what you get from the uncontrolled tongue is more salt water than sweet.

[76] At times, the Greek simply has an adjective and we must supply the noun.   Any noun that agrees in number and gender may be supplied, as long as the resultant idea makes sense in the context.

from the Greek in verse 11.[77]   But at this place, the NIV does convey more meaning than the NASB; the NASB seems to have one kind of water producing another kind of water, an idea totally unexpected in a context where James has been talking about springs and trees and vines and what they produce.

In the inanimate world which God has created, save where sin has warped and defiled things, everything continues consistently to function as God made it. A careful and thoughtful look at God's creation should warn man there is something radically out of harmony with God's will in an inconsistent life ("double-minded" of James 1:8) or an inconsistent tongue.

With the ending of verse 12, James has finished his presentation of self-control, having emphasized that control of the tongue is the most difficult part of the body to keep in subjection because of the constant care and watchfulness that is needed. James' readers are left with the sobering awareness this is an area on which each of us Christians must keep working.

---

[77] The English reader would have no way of knowing that the word for "salt" in verse 12 is not the same word translated "bitter" or "salt" in verse 11, nor would the reader of the NIV be aware that there is no word for "spring" in verse 12.

Special Study #1

THE "IMAGE" AND "LIKENESS" OF GOD

MAN IN THE IMAGE OF GOD IN THE OLD TESTAMENT

Passages of special interest are Genesis 1:26,27, Genesis 5:1-3, and Genesis 9:6.

At Genesis 1:26,27 we read, "Then God said, Let us make man in Our image, according to Our likeness; and let them rule over the fish of the sea and over the birds of the sky and over the cattle and over all the earth, and over every creeping thing that creeps on the earth. And God created man in His own image, in the image of God He created him; male and female He created them." Following is an explanation of the key terms:

GOD, *'elohim* (plural), is speaking.

LET US MAKE translates the plural form *na'aseh*. It is a different word than has been used for "create" (*bara*) earlier in the Genesis account. The members of the Godhead are conferring and deliberately planning and purposing what They would do.

MAN, *'adam*, seems to designate a species of creatures, just as in verse 24 *chayyah* ("beast") marks the wild beasts that live in general a solitary life, and *behemah* ("cattle"), domestic or gregarious animals, and *remes* ("creeping thing"), all kinds of reptiles and worms. As verse 27 indicates, "Adam" includes both the male and female of the species.

IMAGE is *tselem* in the Hebrew, *eikōn* in the Greek. *Tselem* is the shadow of a figure, the shadow-outline, a copy, reproduction, duplicate. *Tselem* denotes the visible form of an external object. *Eikōn* denotes similarity in looks, like the head of the emperor on a coin (Matthew 22:20; Mark 12:16; Luke 20:24). The coin is not of the same material as the emperor, but the shape of the head is the same. *Eikōn* presupposes an original form from which there is derivation. Apart from the "image of God" passages, the word "image" occurs 12 times in the Old Testament. 10 times it refers to a physical representation of something – i.e., golden images of mice and tumors (1 Samuel 6:5,11); images of Baal (2 Kings 11:18); pictures of Babylonians painted on the walls (Ezekiel 23:14).[1] In Romans 1:23 fallen man exchanged the glory of the incorruptible God for "an image (*eikōn*) in the form of (*homoiōma*) corruptible man ...", and then "image in the form of" is used of idols made in the form of birds, animals, and reptiles. Again it appears that *eikōn* refers to a "figure" or a "shape."

---

[1] "Image" could be translated "perfect reflection." Sitting beside a quiet pool of water, with trees on the bank, one can see the reflection of trees in the pool. The outline in the water is the same as that of the tree standing against the sky, but the leaves and limbs of the tree are in no way identical to their reflection. That "image" in the water is *tselem* or *eikōn*.

LIKENESS is *demuth* in the Hebrew, *homoiōsis* in the Greek. *Demuth* means a copy, an imitation, resemblance, similarity. It is used at 2 Chronicles 4:3 for the "shape" ("figures" NASB) of the oxen which supported the laver in Solomon's temple. It is used of the "likeness" of a sound at Isaiah 13:4. It is used in Ezekiel 8:2 where one with the "appearance" ("likeness" NASB) of a man caught Ezekiel away. A similar usage is found in Daniel 10:16,18. It is used at 2 Kings 16:10 of the plans or copy or model of an altar Ahaz saw in Damascus and sent to Uriah the priest so that he might design one just like it. The word is used in Isaiah 40:18,25, and Psalm 50:21 where God chides men for attempting to make an image of Him, saying there is no one "comparable" to Him. The Greek word *homoiōsis* denotes "the same kind," or "like" (but not "equal"), "of like disposition," of holding possessions "in common," or "similar" in shape (from geometry). While there is no connotation of derivation, *homoiōsis* denotes likeness, just as one egg resembles another, or there may be similarity between two men who are in no way related. Its usage elsewhere in Scripture helps us to grasp its meaning. In the creation, each species was to bring forth "after its kind." Jesus, when incarnate, was in the "likeness of the flesh of sin" (Romans 8:3 NASB mg.). In all points He was made "like" (*homoiōthēnai*) his brethren (Hebrews 2:14-17). Paul uses the root word to say that since we humans are the offspring of God, God is not like the animal figures pagans set up as images (Acts 17: 28ff). At Revelation 1:13 (NASB mg.), one "like the Son of Man" was seen among the candlesticks. At Matthew 22:39 we find the word means "of equal value" ("a second [commandment] is just like it"). The word occurs at Galatians 5:21 ("and things like these") to designate works of flesh similar to those already specifically named.

Perhaps no distinction or different connotation should be sought between the words *tselem* and *demuth*. Luther and Calvin both found virtually no distinction between the two words. In Genesis 1:26, which is God's resolution to create, both words are used. But in verse 27, the actual act of creation, only *tselem* is used, not *demuth*. The two words are so intertwined that nothing is lost by the omission of *demuth*. Also, the LXX translates *demuth* at Genesis 5:1 not by the usual *homoiōsis* but by *eikōn*, the Greek counterpart for Hebrew *tselem*.[2] Trench argues that *eikōn* and *homoiōma* may be used as equivalents, (and cites Plato, *Phaedr*. 250b as proof) the words being used interchangeably to identify earthly copies and resemblances of heavenly bodies.[3] A ninth-century BC statue of an ancient king at Tell Fekheriye has both *tselem* and *demuth* in an Aramaic inscription explaining what the statue represents.[4] Their application to the physical form of the statue indicates that the physical human form is a critical aspect of the function of image. It was apparently not till the Arian controversy became a heated issue that careful distinction between the two words began to be made.

---

[2] W.H. Schmidt quoted by Victor P. Hamilton in "*dama/demuth*" in TWOT, 1:192.

[3] Richard C. Trench, *Synonyms of the New Testament* (Grand Rapids: Eerdmans, 1996), p.49-52.

[4] Millard, A.R., and Bordreuil, P., "A Statue from Syria with Assyrian and Aramaic Inscriptions," BA 45/3, p.135-41.

The image and likeness of God (Genesis 1) are how man was made, and this was prior to the Fall. Though Adam and Eve sinned (Genesis 3), and man has "fallen," Scripture indicates that men still bear the image and likeness of God. Neither Genesis 9:6 nor James 3:9 would have any meaning if the image/likeness had been lost in the Fall. In Genesis 5:1-3, when Adam fathers Seth, we are told that the "image" was passed on to Seth. The image is passed on to each succeeding generation, for 1 Corinthians 15:49 speaks of men generations removed from Adam and Seth as bearing the image (*eikona*) of the earthly (Adam). After the flood (Genesis 9:6), when murder is prohibited, it is because men are still in the image of God. Both *eikōn* and *homoiōsis* are claimed for man in the New Testament: *Eikōn* at 1 Corinthians 11:7 ("man is the image ... of God"); *homoiōsis* at James 3:9. Nevertheless, something happened to man and to creation when Adam sinned. The creation was subjected to futility (Romans 8:20). Death entered the world when Adam sinned, and all of Adam's physical descendants were subjected to physical death (Romans 5:12ff). When men sin, their share in "the glory of God" is diminished (Romans 3:23). Hebrews 2:5-11 (quoting Psalm 8) shows that the dominion granted to man (Genesis 1:26) has been lost, but that in Christ it is being regained for fallen man.

Genesis directly asserts that "mankind" (*adam*, man and woman, not just man alone[5]) resembles God in some important ways, but the difficulty is that Genesis gives no indication of exactly wherein the likeness and image between God and mankind (*adam*) consists, save for the function of exercising dominion. As a result, theologians have never been able to agree concerning precisely wherein that resemblance lies. The nature of the likeness has been conceived as physical, personal, or functional; all can easily fall within the semantic range of the terms involved. Yet care must especially be exercised here, for in the Hebrew mind man is not treated as being so many separate parts (say a body and a soul and a spirit), but rather as a total personality, so that the whole man (body on the outside, and soul/spirit on the inside) is somehow in the image and likeness of God.

NEW TESTAMENT REFERENCES TO THE IMAGE OF GOD

New Testament references to image and likeness of God need careful attention, especially since some of them have been used to show that Christians do not yet have the image or likeness of God, but after being born again must keep growing until they finally achieve the goal of being "transformed into the divine image."

Ephesians 4:21-24 -- "You ... have been taught (verse 21) that ... you lay aside your old self (verse 22) ... corrupted in accordance with the lusts of deceit, and that you are being

---

[5] The statement of Genesis 1:27 must be balanced with 1 Corinthians 11:7, where Paul explains that a man must not cover his head because he is the image of God, whereas a woman ought to cover hers because she is the glory of the man. This does not contradict what is written in Genesis, because it is through the man that the woman shares in God's image, given that she was created out of him.

renewed in the spirit of your mind (verse 23), and put on the new self, which in *the likeness of* God has been created in righteousness and holiness of the truth (verse 24)."

Several things need to be emphasized:

1) The old self is corrupt, not because of what Adam did, but because of what men themselves have done (men are "dead through their own trespasses and sins," Ephesians 2:1 ASV).   Verse 22 says that when men indulge in the lusts springing from deceit, that brings corruption to the old self.   "Corrupted" is a present participle, picturing a corruption that is a process that goes on, a condition that progresses to worse and worse.

2) "Renewed" (being renewed, an infinitive) is somehow related to "lay aside" (the main verb) the old man.   The infinitives "lay aside" and " renewed" are dependent on "you were taught" (verse 21).   "You were taught that you lay aside ... and you are (being) renewed ..." is how the Greek reads.

3) It is the "spirit of (the) mind" that is habitually being renewed (a present tense infinitive depicting continuing action).   The verb *ananoeō* occurs only here in the New Testament.[6]   "Spirit of your mind" (Greek) is an unusual expression which has generated much discussion.[7]   Paul is highlighting the continual challenge a believer has to bring his or her thoughts more into line with God's revealed will, parallel to Romans 12:2 where the mind is said to be renewed and thus behavior is transformed.   Perhaps "spirit" here has reference to "attitude."[8]   The renewal takes place in the "spirit" (dative

---

[6] Does the *ana-* in *ananeousthai* imply restoration to a former state?   In classical Greek the word does mean "to restore" and the object of the verb denotes what was the original state that is brought into existence again.   However, there are many compound verbs with *ana-* that express nothing more than change.   For a typical list, see Salmond, *Expositor's Greek Testament*, 3:342.   If a former state is restored, was it the state which man had after creation before Adam sinned, or is it the state the man himself had before he committed his own first sin?

[7] The view defended by Ellicott, that this phrase is a name for the Holy Spirit, is probably not to be accepted.   According to this view, Paul is writing about the indwelling "Spirit" prompting men's "minds" concerning how to think and behave.   While that may be a true doctrine, we are not convinced this Ephesians 4 passage teaches it.   The Greek does not say "Be renewed by the Spirit in your mind," but rather "of your mind."   While the Holy Spirit may be designated as "of Christ" or "of God," hardly is the divine Spirit to be pictured as belonging to a human being or to part of a human being.

[8] Each time we come to the word *pneuma* ("spirit") we must decide whether it speaks of the Holy Spirit, the human spirit, or an "attitude."   Sometimes in Scripture "spirit" has reference to the human spirit, one of the constituent parts of man (e.g., body, soul, spirit).   There are times (such as 1 Corinthians 14:14) when "mind" and "spirit" are distinguished.   A case can be made that "spirit" in this passage is the human spirit, rather than an "attitude."   It should be remembered that it is man's "spirit" that dies when the man commits his first sin, and it is the "spirit" that is born again (John 3:6) when he becomes a Christian.   When a man has become a Christian, the "spirit is alive because of righteousness" (Romans 8:10).   In the unregenerate, when the spirit is dead or enslaved (Romans 7), we see the "mind" pronouncing approval of what God has required in the law, but unable to make the man resist the motions of sin.   Once the old slavery to sin has been broken at baptism (Romans 6), the new man is able to practice self-control.   The "spirit" can give directions to the man's soul, and the soul then animates the body in harmony with what the "mind" approves.

of reference) which controls the mind (subjective genitive). In Titus 3:5 it is the Holy Spirit who is the agent doing the renewing. The present tense infinitive and the passive voice suggest the continuous nature of the renewal and that it takes place as believers allow themselves to be renewed in their thinking. 2 Corinthians 4:16 speaks of a "day by day" or "every day" repeated renewal (*anakainountai*) of the inner man.

4) Both infinitives, "lay aside" (verse 22) and "put on" (verse 24), are aorist tense and seem to point to a single act in the past, to the time when the Ephesians became Christians.

5) "In *the likeness of* God" (verse 24) is literally 'according to God' (*kata theon*). The "new self" ("new man" ASV)," put on when the readers became Christians, is what is described as being "according to God." Can it be said that "new man" or "new self" is somehow synonymous either with "image" of God or "likeness" of God? One should be hesitant to arrive at such a conclusion.[9] Since neither the word "image" nor "likeness" actually occurs in the Greek here in Ephesians 4:24, it would be reading into the text to affirm it says the "image" or "likeness" that was (allegedly) lost when man sinned is what is restored in Christ.

6) "Created" (verse 24), *ktisthenta*, is an accusative singular aorist passive participle, agreeing with "new self." It does not say that "righteousness" and "holiness" are the things being created. The "new self" was created at one time in the past, and we would suppose the act of creating took place at the new birth.

7) "In righteousness and holiness of the truth" (verse 24), *en dikaiosunē kai hosiotēti tēs alētheias*, are two areas wherein the new man is "new" or is being "renewed." The idea contained in our Greek text is this: "Righteousness and holiness" "come from the truth."[10] This reading balances what Paul wrote earlier. The evil desires which characterized the old person sprang from deceit (verse 22). The virtues which characterize the new person come from "the truth." This "truth" has been disclosed in the Gospel preached by Jesus and His apostles. The usual distinction between the nouns is that "holiness" has reference to God, and "righteousness" to men. The synonym translated "holiness" means "in harmony with the divine constitution of

---

[9] Admittedly, there are times when *kata* expresses "likeness" (2 Kings 11:10; Hebrews 8:8; Galatians 4:28; 1 Peter 1:15, 4:6), but it should not be automatically assumed that is the meaning here in Ephesians. Whether "according to the image of the One who created" at Colossians 3:10 expresses the same idea as Ephesians 4:24 will be discussed in notes below. "According to God" can also mean "according to what pleases God" or "according to *the will of* God" (Romans 8:27; 2 Corinthians 7:9,10, 11:17).

[10] The KJV reads "righteousness and true holiness" and is doubly wrong, says Abbott ("Epistle to the Ephesians," in ICC, p.138), in connecting the genitive (of truth) with the latter substantive only, and in treating the genitive adjectivally. If we were going to treat the genitive adjectivally, Chrysostom would be closer to being correct when he applied "truth" to both nouns. He spoke of "true righteousness" and "true holiness." It should also be observed that there is a manuscript variation at this place. Instead of the genitive *tēs alētheias*, some manuscripts read the dative case, *kai alpstheia*. This dative reading would tend to support the Westminster standards interpretation that the image of God consists in "righteousness and holiness and knowledge."

the universe." It speaks of "right relationships to God." In this context, "righteousness" likely speaks of right relationships with men. The two terms together are a summary of human virtue, and picture the thoughts that fill the renewed mind, and which in turn transforms the behavior. Righteousness and holiness are characteristics of God (LXX of Psalm 144:17 and Deuteronomy 32:4 and Revelation 16:5). New creatures who reflect God's image likewise demonstrate such qualities.[11]

Colossians 3:9-11 -- "Stop lying (mg.) to one another, since you laid aside the old self with its *evil* practices, and have put on the new self who is being renewed to a full knowledge according to the image of the One who created him – *a renewal* in which there is no *distinction between* Greek or Jew ...."

Several things need to be emphasized:

1) The context is this: 3:5-9a name some sins the sinner used to commit which are to be put away, or put to death, now that he has become a Christian. 3:9b-11 give the reason why they are to be put away. The fact they have become new creatures in Christ requires such abandoning of old sins.

2) "Laid aside" (verse 9) and "put on" (verse 10) are aorist participles, referring to one time in the past. Colossians 2:11ff shows it was at the time of baptism the old man was stripped off, and the new man put on.[12] We should translate the participles truly as participles[13] which describe the past event. The readers have already put off the old nature and put on the new; that is the basis for the call to abandon the old ways and embrace the new.

3) "Old self" ("old man," mg.) is used consistently by Paul to denote what belonged to life prior to faith in Christ (1 Corinthians 5:7-8). The "old man" is not just the former manner of existence "in Adam." The "old self" is one who has personally committed his first sin, whose spirit has died (because of his own trespasses and sins), and who is now a slave of the devil. That whole way of life had been abandoned when folk were immersed into Christ. "The Christian has had a radical, life-changing experience in which he has put off the old self with its practices (i.e., habits or characteristic actions) and has put on the new self."[14]

---

[11] Instead of speaking of the image or likeness of God being absent in the unregenerate, perhaps we should say that ideas of "righteousness" and "holiness" are what are missing.

[12] Baptism was said in effect to be the stripping off, not of any insignificant scrap of bodily tissue, as the old circumcision was, but of the whole "body of flesh," the old nature in its entirety. (Simpson and Bruce, "Ephesians" in NICNT, p.272).

[13] When the passage can be easily translated treating the participles as dependent on the verb "stop lying," there is no reason to try to treat them as having an imperative sense, as though the "laid aside" and "put on" are something the Christian has yet to do.

[14] Curtice Vaughn, "Colossians" in EBC, p.213.

4) "New self" – All the Greek has is the adjective "new," so we must supply the noun.   The one to be supplied from the previous verse is *anthrōpos*, "man" or "self."

5) "Renewed" (*anakainoumenou*) is a present participle, setting forth another side to this newness.   The new self is constantly being renewed (*kainos*); it is in the process of being renewed.   The same verb form here translated "renewed" is used at 2 Corinthians 4:16, "our inner man is being renewed day by day."   The participle is passive in form. Who is the agent who does this "renewing"?   Is it the Holy Spirit, as 2 Corinthians 3:18 and Titus 3:5 may suggest?   Or is it the Christian himself, who stops making provisions to fulfill the lusts of the flesh (Romans 13:14)?

6) "To a true knowledge" (*eis epignōsin*) means that "knowledge" is either the goal of the renewing (*epignōsin* is the object of *eis*) or the sphere (NIV) in which this process of renewal occurs.[15]   It is not the "image of God" that is constantly renewed,[16] but it is the new man's "knowledge" which is being constantly renewed.   For Christians, the Word of God is the source of knowledge (2 Timothy 3:16,17; 1 Peter 2:2).   "Knowledge" was at the heart of man's first failure (Genesis 2:17, 3:5,7).   If Christians embrace the "knowledge" available in Christ, they have all the information they need to live holy and acceptable lives.   It is failure to act in accordance with their knowledge of God that gets men into trouble, and is rather how the "old man" lives.

7) "According to the image of the One who created him" has been given many and diverse interpretations. Who is "him"?   The "new man" of verse 10 or "Adam" ("mankind") of Genesis 1:26-28?   The best choice is that the "him" is the new man about whom Paul is writing. Who is the "One who created"?   If the "One who created him" is speaking of God the Father, there is clearly an allusion to the "image of God" in Genesis 1:26-28.[17]   If "Christ" is the "One" Paul has in mind as creator of the new man, then Christ (who is the image of the invisible God, Colossians 1:15; 2 Corinthians 4:4) serves as the model or archetype for the new man.   If "Christ" is the "One" Paul has in mind, then we likely will say there is no allusion to Genesis 1:26-28.[18]   "According to" here

---

[15] It is likely that in *epignōsin* ("true knowledge," or "full knowledge") there is a polemic against incipient Gnostic ideas that are influencing the Colossian readers.   One learns such "full knowledge" from Christian doctrine, not through Gnostic ideas and practices.

[16] If the image was never lost (see Genesis 5:1-3 and 9:6), then "renewal" can have little to do with the "image" being restored.

[17] O'Brien ("Colossians" in WBC, p.191) argues that in numerous passages in the New Testament, God the Father is the subject of the verb "create."

[18] More will be said in the next section about 2 Corinthians 3:18 and Romans 8:29, where believers in this life are growing into the image of Christ and finally (in their resurrection bodies) are to be conformed to His image.

likely means "in harmony with."   But just what is it which is said to be in harmony with the "image of the One who created"?   Likely it is the "renewal" which is in harmony with the image.   If so, the passage says that the Christian's continual, daily renewal in full knowledge makes him what the Creator intended him to be.   It is an integral and necessary part of putting on the new man.   Instead of the divine image being a future goal, it is something we are realizing every day.

8) "In which there is no distinction between Greek and Jew ...."   In the condition where men are "new men," the old distinctions and barriers that divided people from one another – racial, religious, cultural, and social – are abolished.   A person can be a "new man" whether he be Greek or Jew, circumcised or uncircumcised, barbarian, Scythian, bond or free.   When men are in Christ they have a new status, they are "God's elect, holy and beloved" (verse 12 ASV).[19]

JESUS CHRIST IN THE IMAGE OF GOD

The pre-incarnate Jesus was the "exact representation of His nature" (Hebrews 1:3). He "exists" (the Greek is a present participle) in the "form" (*morphē*) of God (Philippians 2:6).   Paul tells us in Colossians 1:15 that Christ is "the image of the invisible God." Jesus, as the "image" of God, was both in external shape and inwardly in that image. "Image" was not restricted to His body, nor to His inner essence.

The incarnate Jesus Himself bore the "image" of God since He was "the son of Adam, the son of God" (Luke 3:38).   In this "human" form He gives help to the seed of Abraham (Hebrews 2:16).   Jesus' earthly body was just like the bodies of other humans (Romans 8:3; Hebrews 2:14,17), who were in the "image of God" (Genesis 1:26,27).

When Jesus Christ is spoken of as the image of God, the idea is that He is the visible representation of God.   "He who has seen me has seen the Father" (John 12:45, 14:9).   In 2 Corinthians 4:4, Paul indicates that Christ's glory is an expression of the divine glory. The light of the knowledge of the glory of God is seen in the face of Jesus Christ (2 Corinthians 4:6).

"Image" is also used of Christ's resurrection body, a body which Christians, too, one day will share.   Men will one day bear the image of the heavenly (1 Corinthians 15:49). The glorified body men receive will be just like the glorified body Jesus now has.

- God's plan, made back in eternity before He created, was that believers might be conformed to the image of Christ.   "For whom He foreknew, He also predes-

---

[19] All the terms in verses 11 and 12 reflect the situation in Colossae which Paul is addressing. Someone (Jewish Gnostics) was making Jewish distinctions important.   Paul says, in effect, such emphasis is a threat to the church and is to be rejected.   Terms that used to be applied to physical Israel are here applied to those who are in Christ.

tined to become conformed to the image of His Son, that He might be the first-born among many brethren" (Romans 8:29).   At the Second Coming of Christ, when men are glorified, they will finally and completely bear the image Christ now bears.

- "As we have borne the image of the earthly, we shall also bear the image of the heavenly" (1 Corinthians 15:49).   This, too, speaks of the resurrection body. Here "image of the earthy" clearly refers to our bodily form, our humanity which we have inherited from Adam.

- "For our citizenship is in heaven, from which also we eagerly wait for a Savior, the Lord Jesus Christ; who will transform the body of our humble state into conformity with the body of His glory, by the exertion of the power that He has even to subject all things unto Himself" (Philippians 3:20,21).   We shall have a glorified body just like the one Jesus now has.

- "When He shall appear we shall be like Him" (1 John 3:2).

Without the concept of man in the image of God, the idea of adoption as God's children (Romans 8:23) would be difficult to understand.

Now that we have studied the pertinent Scriptures, we should be able to rightly critique the dogmas the theologians have advanced as they have tried to explain the "image" and "likeness" of God.

IMAGO DEI -- Battlefield for Theologians

Theologians and scholars have debated the meaning and relationship between the words "image" and "likeness."   Interpretations have swung between two extremes: that the body is all that bears the image and likeness of God, to the soul alone bearing the image and likeness of God.   Among the explanations offered[20] are these:

(1) Jewish Biblical writers thought of the "image" as being physical, bodily.   The belief that men are made in the material likeness of God is taught both in Biblical and post-Biblical Jewish literature.[21]

Intertestamental Jewish speculation held that God's image gave the human soul the ability to distinguish between good and evil.   As time went on, the rabbis argued,

---

[20] Some of the information following is adapted from Harris, Archer, and Waltke, *TWOT*, p.438.

[21] W.E. Oesterly, "James" in *EGT*, 4:454.

this ability diminished, and so the image was corrupted.[22]

Judaism in the Second Temple period and later shows surprisingly little interest in the concept of the image of God (cf. Wis. 2:23; Sir 17:3). *Genesis Rabbah* 8:10,11 reports that when the Lord created Adam the angels thought he was divine and would have worshipped him had not the Lord caused him to fall asleep, thus revealing his mortality. Moreover, humans are like the angels in that they stand upright, speak, understand and see peripherally. On the other hand, humans are like the animals in that they eat and drink, procreate, excrete and die. Clearly the "image and likeness" of God here includes both resemblance to the divine as well as a functional role.[23]

(2) Little agreement is found among Early Church Fathers who tried to explain the image and likeness of God.

Some Fathers were of the opinion that *tselem* and *demuth* are synonyms.[24]

Some early Fathers were of the opinion that "image" and "likeness" were expressive of separate and distinct ideas.[25] For some, "image" referred to the body, which by reason of its beauty, intelligent aspect, and erect stature was an adumbration of God. "Likeness" referred to the soul, or the intellectual and moral nature.[26] It is likely one sees in the Fathers the inroads of Greek philosophy in this distinction. For others, as Philo had done, "image" was locatable in man's soul (or mind or spirit), not in his body.[27]

For many, the view was that *Imago Dei* was something distinctive of man unfallen. When Adam sinned, the image was lost. In the loss of the image by sin lay man's need for redemption. "What we lost in Adam, to wit, the divine image and simili-

---

[22] G.L. Bray, "Image of God," *New Dictionary of Biblical Theology* (Downers Grove: InterVarsity, 2000), p.575.

[23] E.H. Merrill, "Image of God" in *Dictionary of the Old Testament: Pentateuch* (Downers Grove: InterVarsity, 2003), p.444.

[24] Athanasius (*Gent.* 34; *Inc.* 13), Didymus the Blind (*Trin.* 2:12), Cyril of Alexandria (*Dogm.* 3).

[25] See Irenaeus (*Adv. Haer.* 5.16.2) who maintained "image" has reference to a bodily likeness to God. See also Clement of Alexandria (Prot. 12), Origen (*Princ.* 3.6.1; Cels. 4.30), and Cyril of Jerusalem (*Catech.* 14.10).

[26] If all there is to man is an "image" and a "likeness" to God (i.e., body and soul), then the Bible must teach dichotomy. This extrapolation then requires a long discussion defending the view that "soul" and "spirit" somehow denote only a functional difference, rather than being a difference of entity. Buswell has several paragraphs (p.238-240) where he defends dichotomy and rejects the trichotomy of Delitzsch (*A System of Biblical Psychology*).

[27] Clement of Alexandria (*Strom.* 2.19); Tatian (*Orat.* 12;15), Athanasius (*Gent.* 34); Chrysostom (*Hom. in Gen.* 8:3-4).

tude, we receive again in Christ Jesus" (Irenaeus). For others, this seemed too sweeping (e.g., Epiphanius of Salamis [Jerome, chap. 89] argued against Origen and his followers that Adam had never lost the image), so it was modified.

Clement of Alexandria, and Origen taught that "image" was something given to men at creation, which is common to all, and which remains after the Fall (Genesis 9:6), whereas "likeness" is something *for* which man was created, that he should strive after it in order to attain it. The striving might involve personal ethical conflict, or it might be accomplished through the influence of grace. "Likeness" was something that by a gradual process can become like the archetypal image.[28]

Some identified the image with man's free will to do good or evil,[29] while others reckoned man's dominion over irrational creatures as an aspect or a corollary of the image.[30] Some argued that both image and likeness had to do only with physical resemblance to God's body.[31]

The words "image" and "likeness" played a key role in the Arian controversy, as the eternality of Jesus was debated. Arius taught that Jesus was a created being, and that only the Father was eternal. Those who opposed Arius insisted the term "image" should not be applied to the pre-incarnate Christ, since the word implies derivation. Jesus was not a created being, they insisted, so no idea of derivation can be embraced. "Likeness" is a proper term to apply to Jesus, since he is "just like" the Father in his Divine essence.

Gregory Nyssa, while dealing with controversies raging in his own day, devoted a treatise to the question of the relation between "image" and "likeness." He argued for a real distinction between the two. He reckoned *tselem* (image) as the more static and *demuth* (likeness) the more dynamic aspects of the same reality.

---

[28] Colossians 3:10 improperly has been used to prove there is a growth into the "image" of God. See *supra*. There is little trace in Genesis of any idea of a likeness that needs to be grown into. The reference is rather to what God originally made men to be, not to what they may grow to be under His fatherly nurture. (F.J.A. Hort, *The Epistle of James*, p.78.)

[29] Irenaeus (*Haer.* 4.4.3; 4.38.4), Tertullian (*Marc.* 2.6), Basil the Great (*Quod Deus non est auctor malorum* 6).

[30] Eusebius (D.E.4.6), Gregory of Nyssa (*Hom. opif.*4), Chrysostom (*Stat.* 7.3).

[31] This was the view of the Audaeans according to Theodoret (*Eccl. Hist.* 4.19). They held the view that man is physically the image of God, who also has a shape or form or "body." This treats seriously the connotation of "image" and also treats seriously the "image" of Christ which will inhere in the resurrection body.

(3) Because the Godhead was viewed as a trinity, some tried to find "three parts" to the "image of God."

> For Augustine, the "image" was located in man's soul. "We must find in the soul of man the image of the Creator ...."[32] Augustine then developed a number of theories about the supposed threefold nature of the human soul. In one of these, he identified the *vestigia* ('foot prints' or 'traces' or 'marks') of the trinity in man's memory, intelligence, and will. According to Augustine, "image" had reference to the *cognitio veritatis* (knowledge of the truth); "likeness" to *amor virtutis* (love of moral excellence).

> Such a view is attractive in its trinitarian foundation and in its consistency with the Biblical assumption that the image was not utterly destroyed by the Fall. A weakness lies in the idea the image is located in the soul which is "in (i.e., inside, within) man," whereas Genesis suggests that man *as such* is the divine image.

> When Greek philosophy (i.e., that matter is evil and spirit is good) began to make inroads into theological beliefs, and men began to embrace the idea of hereditary total depravity, the idea that the image of God is located either in body or in soul began to be a problem. How can men be born evil, or with a bent toward sinning, and still have the image and likeness of God? Theologians therefore said the image was either lost or badly defaced.

Since somehow the "image of God" has been passed on to succeeding generations, Buswell[33] at this point introduces a study on the origin of the soul: pre-existence, traducianism, or creationism.

- He tells how Jerome was a creationist (i.e., when a baby is conceived, a new soul is created for that person). Hodge argued for creationism, thinking it more in harmony with the doctrine of the sinless humanity of the incarnate Christ.
- Augustine hesitated between traducianism (i.e., the soul is "conceived" just like the body is conceived) and creationism, not being able to prove either from Scripture. He wrote a letter to Jerome asking questions about Jerome's view, which Jerome never answered. Augustine inclined towards traducian theory because of his view of inherited sin. How can the soul contract sin from Adam and not itself be contracted from Adam?
- The doctrine of inherited original sin seems to demand traducianism. Buswell, adopting the traducian theory, argues the virgin birth is how Jesus was kept from inheriting a sinful nature.[34]

---

[32] *De Trinitate* 14:4.

[33] J.O. Buswell, *A Systematic Theology of the Christian Religion*, p.248.

[34] It begins to become almost mind-boggling to see how many issues are lurking in the background of this discussion about the image and likeness of God.

(4) The Eastern Church tended to think of the image as that which distinguishes man from other created beings. The Greek Christian Fathers defined it as something metaphysical rather than ethical.

> The Eastern Church surely took a wrong turn in the road when it interpreted the two Hebrew words as referring to different parts of man's being (e.g., his body and his spirit, or the substance and the form.)

> Is it not a fact that "image of God" and "likeness of God" characterize the whole man, not just a part?

(5) Western Catholicism has tended to maintain that "image" refers to man's structural likeness to God, which has survived the Fall, and that "likeness" refers to man's moral image with which he was supernaturally endowed but which was marred or destroyed by the Fall.

> *Similitudo Dei* means the "likeness of God" and is, according to some Roman Catholic teaching, to be distinguished from the "image of God" (*Imago Dei*) which Adam also possessed before the Fall. The *Similitudo Dei* refers to those supernatural graces Adam possessed and which were obliterated when he sinned, while the "image of God" refers to his natural endowments of reason and free will that remained intact even after the Fall.[35]

> The Roman Catholic view that "likeness" was marred or obliterated seems contradicted by James 3:9, where we are told the likeness (*homoiōsis*) still remains. (Remember, James uses a perfect tense verb in this verse.[36])

(6) Views about the image and likeness of God differed among the Reformers.

> Some insisted that the image of God designates man's "original righteousness" that was lost in the Fall. (Note, though, Roman Catholics and Protestants have a different definition of "original righteousness.") According to the Reformers, Adam's "original righteousness" included the harmony of understanding, will, and affections that enabled him to obey the divine Law both inwardly and externally.

> Luther argued that man lost the image of God in everything but name only, and this involved the loss of freedom of the will. In general, Lutheran tradition has emphasized the loss of the image of God. The Lutheran Confessions understand the "image of God" in the sense that man is capable of receiving the knowledge of God.

---

[35] Hugo Vict. *De Sacram.* I.i, p.6. c.ii;   Peter Lomb. *Sent.* I.ii., dist.16.D;   Bellarmine, *De Grat. Prim. Hominis*, v.5.

[36] See notes in the commentary *in loc.*

Calvin regarded the image of God as a kind of integrity possessed by Adam whereby the passions were governed by the reason and his nature was a harmoniously ordered whole. This integrity was not annihilated or effaced by the Fall, but was "so corrupted that whatever remains is but a horrible deformity." In general, Reformed tradition has regarded it as corrupted but not lost.

Following the Reformation, some began to suggest that "image of God" and man's "dominion" are somehow related.

- Socinianism and Arminianism defined the image as man's dominion over the animal creation.

- The Westminster Shorter Catechism suggests "image of God" has to do with man being created to exercise dominion over creation as God's Vice-regent under the Divine Providence. Defenders of this view have argued that this relationship between image and dominion is stated in Genesis 1:28 and reasserted at Genesis 8:15-9:17, especially 9:1,2. Not only so, but Psalm 8 is a reflection on Genesis 1. While "image" is not specifically referred to in Psalm 8, the Psalm does emphasize the Psalmist's recognition of man's lost dominion (which was lost at the Fall). Hebrews 2:5ff shows that, on this side of Calvary, man still does not exercise this dominion now, but that in Christ it is being restored. Christ has been crowned with glory and honor, and Christians soon will join Him in that dominion. Luke 19:13ff pictures redeemed men, after the King returns, ruling over cities, their lost dominion restored.

Following the Reformation, some began to use certain New Testament passages to explain what the image of God is. Adam Clarke gives a typical Protestant explanation. Among the points he makes are these:

- According to the authors of the Westminster standards, what the "image of God" consists in is based upon a combination of Ephesians 4:22-25 and Colossians 3:9,10, from which the words "righteousness, true holiness, and knowledge" are highlighted.

- With these two passages should be coupled several Scriptures, including Romans 8:29, 2 Corinthians 3:18, which teach that the regenerate are being made to conform to the image of Christ, who already is said to be "the image of the invisible God" (Colossians 1:15; 2 Corinthians 4:4).

- Hence, man (when first made in the image of God) was *wise* in his *mind*, *holy* in his *heart*, and *righteous* in his *actions*.

(7) Higher Criticism since the 1940's has insisted the more important of the two words is "image."

> According to the assured conclusions of higher criticism, the more important word is "image" and to avoid the implication that man is a precise copy of God, albeit in miniature, the less specific and more abstract *demuth* was added. *Demuth* then defines and limits the meaning of *tselem*.[37]

> Barr's view is that the priestly writer of the three "image of God" passages in Genesis was strongly influenced by Second Isaiah (especially the latter's view that God could not be legitimately compared with anyone or anything on earth).[38] The priestly writer could not ignore the traditional view of man as being unique among the creatures in his similarity to God. So the priestly writer used terms that could call attention to the similarity without specifying the nature of the similarity more than was absolutely necessary. Barr attempts to justify his view by showing that no other terms in the semantic range of *tselem* were suitable for showing this similarity. Objectionable is not only Barr's alleged late date for Genesis, but the same arguments used to disqualify other terms could be used to disqualify *tselem* also. (The traditional view that *tselem* calls to mind corporeal similarity is something the priestly writer wished to avoid in Barr's theory.)

(8) Form Criticism has gone searching for the original "forms" which the Bible writers have changed and adapted as they wrote about the "image and likeness of God." The critics have not been able to agree.

> Some form critics have insisted that in Genesis the key word is *demuth* and that *tselem* is intended by the redactor to correct a wrong idea he found in his source. Form-Criticism supposes the [alleged] priestly author of Genesis 1-9 got his ideas from Mesopotamian religion. *Demuth* is related to the Hebrew for "blood" (*dam*). In Mesopotamian tradition the gods created man from divine blood (so men would work and the gods could rest). According to form critics, Genesis is a conscious rejection of and a polemic against pagan teaching. *Tselem* shows that the similarity to which *demuth* refers, viz., man's corporeal appearance, has nothing to do with the blood that flows in his veins.[39]

> The comparative religions school has argued that Paul's view of the image is dependent on ideas found in Hellenic mystery religions. Reitzenstein affirmed (*Die hellenistischen Mysterienreligionen*, p.7ff) that Paul's teaching on the image is indebted to the private mystery cults in Egypt, Phrygia, and Persia, particularly those

---

[37] J. Barr, "The Image of God in the Book of Genesis," BJRL 51:11-26.

[38] "Priestly writer" and "Second Isaiah" are Barr's terms, and the concepts are not this author's views.

[39] J.M. Miller, "In the 'Image' and 'Likeness' of God," JBL 91:289-304.

of Isis, Attis and Cybele, and Mithra, with their goal of salvation secured through personal union with the god or goddess. But A.A. Kennedy has argued convincingly in *St. Paul. and the Mystery Religions* that the basic New Testament ideas are forged against the background of Hebrew theology rather than of the Hellenistic cults.[40]

(9) More recently, as neo-orthodox theologians have struggled to explain the "image of God," attention has focused on the *societal nature* of the image of God. In neo-orthodox circles, the "image of God" has been a lively issue.

Love for God and neighbor is the material image of God in man, say the neo-orthodox writers. Man as sinner does not love God or his neighbor, therefore he has lost the material image. But he is still God's creature and therefore still responsible before God; he retains the formal image; sin cannot negate the formal image. When man becomes a Christian, he now loves God and his neighbor, so the material image is restored. Brunner insisted it is necessary to make the distinction between the material and formal image of God.

The doctrine of the image of God has been used as a basis upon which to insist that mankind can have a purely natural knowledge of God without benefit of special revelation. Barth and Brunner debated this matter early in the 20th century.

Barth has proposed at least two interpretations of the image, and Brunner three. They have proposed new ones because the old ones were full of difficulties. So are the latest versions.

For Brunner, enough of the material image (natural knowledge of God) remains in fallen man that it constitutes a "point of contact" between God and man.

Thus Brunner argued that the divine "us" and "our" of Genesis 1:26 is reflected in man as the "them" of Genesis 1:27. The image of God is not the possession of the isolated individual but of man-in-community expressing his "existence-for-love" by actual "existence-in-love."[41]

Barth rejected this view and claimed that the "image of God" was an "eschatological" concept, and in no sense the basis for declaring that man has a natural (innate) knowledge of God.

Barth developed the idea of "image" in characteristically Christocentric fashion: the image of God is reflected in man-and-woman created as the sign of the hope

---

[40] Carl F.H. Henry, "Image of God" in *Evangelical Dictionary of Theology*, p.545.

[41] *Dogmatics*, 2:64.

of the coming Son of Man who is Himself the image of God. (To suggest that man *in himself* could be the image of God would be to establish in man the "point of contact" which Barth so strenuously rejected.)

Barth's Christocentrism ultimately undermines the historicity of the creation narrative and the significance of the flow of redemptive history.

Existential philosophy behind neo-orthodoxy has tended to reject the historicity of the Genesis account. Adam is a sort of religious "every man." It didn't really happen the way the writer of Genesis depicts it. The image is not a state, but a relationship.

(10) Social science critics have made their attempt at explaining "image."

No longer does man "resemble" God in any way, but simply represents him. Man does not "have" the image of God, but man "images" God.

The word "likeness," rather than diminishing the word "image," actually amplifies it and specifies its meaning. Man is not just an image but a likeness-image. He is not simply representative but representational. Man is the visible, corporeal representation of the invisible, bodiless God. *Demuth* guarantees that man is an adequate and faithful representative of God on earth.[42] Ancient kings set up statues [images] of themselves in the far-off conquered lands to remind the people they had a ruler over them. Supposedly, the image represented the king's authority over the conquered peoples. Likewise, Man is the "statue" God set up when He created.

This view requires we take the *beth* before *tselem* as being equal to *kaph* before *demuth*. If so, we could translate the first clause to say God created man "*as* his image" (as his representative) rather than "*in* his image." This is very doubtful (though in 5:3 both the terms and the prepositions are reversed). To translate the *beth* "as" requires that the *beth* be what could be called a "*beth essentiae*" (or *beth* of identity). This identification is crucial to the argument. (An argument based on the reversal at 5:3 would require taking the *kaph* as a "*kaph essentiae*" yet that is a sense never found elsewhere in Hebrew literature. *Kaph* is hardly the preposition to signify function rather than similitude.)

Who is to say the statues were anything other than memorials to the kings and their mighty deeds -- and are not at all representations of their royal authority?

PERSISTENT QUESTIONS

Perhaps it is true that no subject has exercised the devout speculation of the greatest

---

[42] D.J.A. Clines, "The Image of God in Man," *Tyndale Bull*. 19:53-103.

theologians with as little tangible result as this question, "Wherein does the Image of God in us consist?"

As we study the Scriptures and the history of the debate, we discover several points for which final answers are hard to come by.

1) *What is the nature of the image and likeness that Genesis speaks about?*

We must think in terms of the whole man as we look for "image" and "likeness." Not only do we take into account the shape or form of man's body, but also the fact that the shape/form is animated by soul and directed by spirit. In this, man is like God, who also has a shape, which can be animated, and can behave in harmony with what is thought or willed. He thinks, plans, creates, speaks, loves, exercises dominion, etc. So can man.

It is difficult to avoid the conclusion that "image of God" has some reference to the form or shape man has. The idea is that God who is spirit has a shape; man has a shape or form that is similar, alike, but not an exact or precise copy. In Ezekiel 1:26-28, God is described in appearance like (*demuth*) a human in form. The anthropomorphic language of the Old Testament seems to point in this direction. God's bodily shape and man's bodily shape are essentially alike.

2) *What shall we call what was lost in the Fall?*

Image? Likeness? Dominion? Holiness and righteousness based on true knowledge? Spiritual death? Creation subjected to vanity? Man dies physically? Habitual communion with God?

Several negative things happened to man at the Fall. Perhaps Adam died spiritually. He surely began to die physically. Dominion was lost. Creation was adversely affected. Communion with God was broken, for God no longer walked and talked with Adam in the cool of the evening.

Did any of these negative things mar or deface or erase either the image or the likeness of God? Apparently not.

3) *What is restored or recreated when man is saved?*

Hardly the image or likeness, for even unsaved men still have these. Each man's "spirit" that died when he sinned is again alive because of righteousness. He can now be exhorted to practice self-control (Romans 6:121ff). He is warned that the wages of continual, habitual sin will be death (Romans 6:23). The redeemed man's "spirit" is fixed now. He gets his glorified body at the resurrection, and then man will bear the image of Christ.

4) *What does constant "renewal" do for the new man?*

> With his thinking in harmony with the truth of the Gospel, and his spirit alive and empowered by the indwelling Holy Spirit, the "new man" is able to function as God intended man to function, in right relationship with God and his fellow man. His reborn "spirit" continues to live, and the day will come when he will experience the adoption as a "son of God" as Romans 8:23 promises.

BIBLIOGRAPHY

J. Barr, "The Image of God in the Book of Genesis -- A Study in Terminology," BJRL 51 (1968), p.11-26.

D. Cairns, *The Image of God in Man.*   London: Collins, 1973.

D.J. Clines, "The Image of God in Man," Tyndale Bulletin 19 (1968), p.53-103.

F. Delitzsch, *A System of Biblical Psychology.*   Grand Rapids: Baker, 1966 reprint.

J. Laidlaw, "Image" in *Hastings Dictionary of the Bible.*   New York: Scribners, 1909. Vol. 2, p.452-453.

J.G. Machen, *The Christian View of Man.*   London: Banner of Truth Trust, 1965 reprint.

J.M. Miller, "The 'Image' and 'Likeness' of God," JBL 91 (1972), p.289ff.

J. Orr, *God's Image in Man and Its Defacement in the Light of Modern Denials.*   Grand   Rapids: Eerdmans, 1948.

VI. DEMONSTRATES WISDOM FROM ABOVE. 3:13-18

Summary: Another of the marks of a genuine Christian is the wisdom demonstrated in his or her life.   This wisdom is from above, not the wisdom that is earthly, sensual, demonic.

3:13 -- *Who among you is wise and understanding?   Let him show by his good behavior his deeds in the gentleness of wisdom.*

Who among you is wise and understanding? – "Who among you" seems to point to a group that is somehow to be distinguished from those addressed in 3:1ff.   (Compare this description to the numerous times James used "we" earlier in chapter 3.)   Therefore, as we have offered an outline for James, we have treated verses 13-18 as a new point.   Yet it is not at all certain that there is a change of subjects beginning here at verse 13.

- Is James addressing all Christians, and is it possible the topic of self-control is still the underlying connecting current?   If so, then James' point is that just as all Christians (not just teachers) need to exercise control over what comes out of their mouths, so they also need to carefully monitor which wisdom guides and directs their behavior.

- Is it possible there is a connection between "teachers" (verse 1) and those here identified as "wise and understanding" (titles often used to identify teachers)?   If so, is James affirming that teachers must constantly be concerned not only about the words that are allowed to come out of their mouths, but they must be doubly sure they are guided by the wisdom from God, rather than the wisdom of the world?

As was noted in the Introductory Studies for this letter, one of the felt problems with interpreting James is our lack of precise knowledge concerning the exact historical circumstances to which it was originally addressed.   This inability to identify the particular historical situation in turn makes the use of the preferred historical-grammatical method of interpretation difficult.   We have proposed dating James shortly after the Jerusalem Conference (Acts 15, Galatians 2).   The events which led to that Conference were the upsetting and divisive actions of some "false brethren," identified as Pharisees (Acts 15:5) who pretended to become Christians (Galatians 2:4), and who, then, infiltrated the churches in order to try to control them from the inside.[1]   When those false brethren first came to Antioch and began agitating the new converts from among the Gentiles, claiming these new Christians now had to keep the Pharisaic Halakhic traditions in order to be saved, they

---

[1] As the Old Testament dispensation drew to a close, the Pharisees had tried to impose their traditions on all the Jewish people.   Some listened.   However, the Pharisees failed to stop the influence of Jesus while He was on earth.   In fact, Jesus several times publicly repudiated the traditions of the elders.   After Pentecost (Acts 2), the Pharisees found they could no more control the church from the outside than they could control Jesus.   So they came up with the diabolical way of trying to get on the inside and bring the Christians "into bondage" (Galatians 2:4).

apparently falsely claimed they had instructions from the leaders at Jerusalem (i.e., James, Peter and John, Galatians 2:9) to do so (Acts 15:24). Those Pharisees cast a large shadow and many folk in the churches were impressed by their arguments, so much so that what the apostles Paul and Barnabas taught came to be doubted.

We are suggesting that James wrote when he did and what he did in order to set the record straight and blunt the Judaizers' influence – to deliberately show that, far from having instructions from the leaders at Jerusalem, the Judaizers completely misrepresented what was genuinely important to the very essence of New Testament Christianity. The "false brethren" (from Jerusalem) whose intrigue and surreptitious actions triggered the Jerusalem Conference had no sanction from the apostles at Jerusalem (Acts 15:24). Their claim to "have instructions from Jerusalem" may have been a deliberate misrepresentation of the case just to gain entrance into the churches outside of Judea. Perhaps we may also infer from their appeal to James and the other "pillars" (Galatians 2:9) that James is influential enough in the homeland that what he says has some influence among them. We suggest, then, as we begin this last paragraph of chapter 3, that James is addressing these words to those "false brethren" who are trying to capitalize on his influence, and part of James' purpose in writing was to win the Judaizers away from their ill-chosen path. This is the view we shall present in these notes.[2]

In this view of things, "wise" (*sophos*) would be treated as a technical term for "teacher,"[3] and so would "understanding." The word translated "understanding" (*epistēmōn*) occurs only here in the New Testament, but it is used in Classical Greek for a skilled or experienced or scientific person as opposed to one who has no special knowledge or training.[4] James' question does not imply that no one is wise or understanding; rather it appeals to each person's conscience to examine what wisdom they actually live by.

Let him show by his good behavior his deeds – The "wisdom" by which a man lives will be seen in the man's behavior.[5] "Good" is *kalēs*, which implies that the behavior is attrac-

---

[2] The idea that "wisdom from above" is much to be preferred to the "wisdom of the world" should be, of course, a matter of concern for more than just the Judaizers. The basic principles from which James attempts to appeal to the Judaizers are principles all Christians must be concerned about, too.

[3] Compare Matthew 11:25 and Luke 10:21 for Jewish teachers, and Matthew 23:34 for Christian teachers. Especially we would call attention to "wise" in 1 Corinthians 1:20, where it is used for Jewish teachers. It will be recalled that Group Two of Paul's letters (Romans, 1 and 2 Corinthians, and Galatians) are all "soteriological" in nature, each expressing certain anti-Judaizer sentiments, just as we are proposing James does in this letter. In comparison, some commentators, instead of recognizing this technical sense for "wise", have tried to give the word "a practical sense, i.e., one who in action is governed by piety and integrity" (Thayer, *Lexicon*, p.582). But *sophos* ("wise") is not quite synonymous with *sophia* ("wisdom"), that intellectual endowment for which Christians are to pray (James 1:5,6).

[4] *Epistēmōn*, from *epistamai*, expresses the knowledge obtained by proximity to the thing being known (cf. our "understand," Germ. *verstehen*); and then expresses knowledge viewed as the result of prolonged practice or careful attention and study, in opposition to the process of learning on the one hand and to the uncertain knowledge of a dilettante on the other. (Thayer, *op. cit.*, p. 118).

[5] James could have simply said, "Let him show his wisdom by his conduct." Instead he words it in an especially strong way.

tive, that is, it is obvious to others that it is "lovely" or "noble" or "beautiful." *Anastrophē* ("behavior") was translated "conversation" in the Vulgate and KJV. "Conversation" once was a word that covered a man's whole walk in life, his going out and his coming in, his behavior or conduct. It has changed meaning and now is used only of "speaking." Modern translations offer "manner of life" or "living" or "behavior" in an attempt to catch the meaning of the Greek word. "Deeds" is the same word emphasized in chapter 2 when James was telling us that faith without "works" is dead. Some of the specific "deeds" James has in mind by which "wisdom" is demonstrated will be identified in the verses following.[6] We have been finding pointed rebukes of the Judaizers all through this epistle. Is there a rebuke here of the Judaizers' behavior? They were contemptuous of all who were not of the stock of Israel, and were prone to self-assertion.

In the gentleness of wisdom – The first characteristic of the "good life" which James emphasizes is "gentleness" or "meekness" – a meekness consistent with true wisdom, or that comes from wisdom.[7] James lays great stress on meekness (see 1:21 and 3:17). As explained earlier, "meekness" might be defined as submission to God and gentleness towards man. It exhibits itself in a special way when giving and receiving instruction, or in administering and accepting rebuke. The meek person is serene in the full confidence that truth and right will prevail, even if that should involve our being proved to be in the wrong. True meekness is mild, calm, patient, self-restraining and teachable.[8] At the same time it should be remembered that Paul appealed to the "meekness of Christ" when he wanted to assert his authority in no uncertain terms and vindicate his behavior as a Christian teacher and missionary (2 Corinthians 10:1).

3:14 -- *But if you have bitter jealousy and selfish ambition in your heart, do not be arrogant and* so *lie against the truth.*

But – Scripture everywhere teaches that men must constantly choose between the right and the wrong. This choice even extends to the realm of wisdom. There are two kinds of wisdom which men may cherish and demonstrate in their lives. Verses 14-16 describe the wrong kind of wisdom and its results. Verses 17-18 describe Godly wisdom and its results. In a few brief sentences, James helps his readers to identify the two, and as he describes how each kind of wisdom behaves, he is pointing his readers towards the obviously better of the two choices.

---

[6] The NIV breaks the last part of verse 13 into two clauses: "Let him show it by his good life, by deeds done in the humility that comes from wisdom."

[7] "Wisdom" here is *sophia*, the wisdom for which Christians are to pray, and which God grants to them (James 1:6,7).

[8] As noted before, Jesus was "meek and lowly in heart" (Matthew 11:29). Jesus was ever patient and calm and gentle when it concerned Himself. But when it concerned the cause of the Father, He was not so calm and gentle. He was not a bit easy on the money changers in the temple (John 2:14-17). He was not easy going when dealing with the Scribes and Pharisees, who made a great profession of godliness, yet proved by their actions that their hearts were far from God (Matthew 23:31-36).

If you have bitter jealousy and selfish ambition in your heart – James writes in such a way that he causes each reader[9] to look into his own heart to see whether or not it is free from these two evils. If they are not free, they are being guided by the wrong kind of wisdom. "Bitter jealousy" could also be translated "bitter envy." *Zēlos* is a neutral word. It can be either a good thing or a bad thing that is desired, depending on the motive which inspires it. There is an "envy" that makes a man copy that which is noble and great and good.[10] There is that "envy" which makes a man do evil and ignoble acts.[11] To make it quite plain that it is a bad kind of envy he has in mind, James adds the adjective "bitter" which recalls what he has just written in verse 11 about a fountain that spouts forth "salt water."[12] Zealots for a cause, such as the Pharisees were, and who are bitter will argue, contest, and fight for their ideas of the truth, and will manifest a spirit of enmity and hatred towards those who dare to differ with them. *Eritheia* is translated both as "strife" and as "selfish ambition."[13] Originally the word did not carry a negative connotation, for it denoted a person who worked for "hire" (Isaiah 38:12) in order to earn money for living. Then it came to denote any work that is done simply and solely for what can be got out of it. It then came to be used for partisans hired by political leaders (where both the leaders and followers were pursuing office by unfair means because they were looking out only for themselves).[14] Then it came to denote "party spirit, selfish ambition, intrigue, rivalry, factious, plotting by any means to gain its own end." It pictures a struggle to be on top, to be the pre-eminent one. If we recall how the Judaizers acted, we might picture James as "speaking particularly of bitter religious animosity; a hatred of error (or what is supposed to be such), manifesting itself, not in loving attempts to win over those who are at fault, but in bitter thoughts, and words, and party plots and intrigue."[15] "In your heart" goes with both nouns. "Bitter jealousy" and a willingness to 'use unworthy and divisive means' are both motives in the mind (evil inner attitudes) that in turn trigger actions. James warns his readers that bitter zeal and selfish ambition are the exact opposites of the motives that should guide a Christian's behavior.

---

[9] We would explain "you" in this verse the same way it was explained in verse 13.

[10] Some familiar passages where "zeal" is attributed to God or to Jesus are Isaiah 59:17 and John 2:7. Paul tells us he works hard at his ministry to the Gentiles so that he may provoke the Jews to jealousy and thus lead them to Christ (Romans 11:13,14).

[11] Romans 10:2 speaks of a "zeal not according to knowledge." Such zeal was obvious when the High Priest and Sadducees arrested the apostles (Acts 5:17), or when Saul persecuted the church (Philippians 3:6). It is listed as one of the works of the flesh in Galatians 5:20.

[12] In verse 11 the word "bitter" was used literally. Here in verse 13 it is used figuratively to denote a bitter or harsh attitude.

[13] It was rendered as "contention" in the Vulgate, a translation that has influenced subsequent English translators.

[14] See Romans 2:8, Philippians 1:16, 2:3. As Hort says, by derivation the word refers to "the vice of a leader of a party created for his own pride; it is partly ambition and partly rivalry." See also Arndt-Gingrich, *Lexicon,* page 309.

[15] Plummer, *op. cit.,* p. 603.

Do not be arrogant and *so* lie against the truth – It is a very common sin for men[16] following the wisdom from below (verse 15) to be proud of their accursed zeal and ambition. *Katakauchasthe* ('boasting, exulting over') is something that a man does in his thoughts. He secretly "gloats over another on the ground of some assumed superiority."[17] It is a feeling of delight because one point of advantage has been thought to be gained over an opponent in a dispute.[18] The present imperative with *mē* prohibits the continuance of an action already going on among James' readers. At first, we might wonder when and where James' readers were displaying this attitude in their daily actions, until we contemplate our own behavior and see how easily it can become part of our lifestyle. After calling for an end to arrogance, James adds another warning, "And stop lying against the truth" (the present imperative with *mē*[19] again prohibiting the continuance of an action already going on).[20] "Against the truth" probably is to be taken only with the second verb. In so doing we avoid the accusation that this is mere tautology. Is "the truth" (as it was in 1:18) a reference to the Gospel, and is it the Judaizers and their followers who are to stop lying against the truth?[21] Or, is "the truth" a reference to the way of truth in which James'

---

[16] It is not only those who are teachers who find themselves being arrogant, puffed up in spirit. Perhaps it is true that there are few who are in such constant spiritual peril as the teacher and preacher. Whether this be true or not, the man in the pew needs to hear this warning as much as the teacher.

[17] Hiebert, *op. cit.*, p. 230.

[18] In James 2:13 the same compound verb was used of the triumph of mercy over strict justice in the future judgment.

[19] The one negative *mē* should be taken with both verbs.

[20] Some of our modern versions have added italicized words to the text, supposing they would help their readers to better grasp what they believe James was writing. The NIV adds "about it" ("do not boast *about it* or deny the truth"). Those added words give the verse this thrust, "Do not boast about your bitter zeal and selfish ambition." Have James' readers been priding themselves in their partisan defense of the truth, a defense that was to their own advantage and advancement? (So Burdick, op. cit., p.190). The NASB translators treated the two prohibitions as having a cause and effect sequence when they supplied the word "so." If we add "so," we have added an idea that may not have been in James' mind. Hort explains, "The mere possession of truth is no security for true utterance of it: all utterance is so coloured by the moral and spiritual state of the speaker that truth issues as falsehood from his lips in proportion as he himself is not in a right state: the correct language which he utters may carry a message of falsehood and evil in virtue of the bitterness and self-seeking which accompanies his speaking." (Hort, *The Epistle of James*, p.83.)

[21] We have proposed to identify the teachers of verse 13ff as being Judaizers, i.e., Pharisees who just pretended to become Christians but had not really become converts. Contrary to our suggestion, there are those commentators who suppose James has Christian teachers in view, just as he did in 3:1ff. It is rather common to find this second group of interpreters struggling to reconcile what is here written by James about teachers whose motives are bad with the attitude expressed by Paul on the occasion when he could rejoice that Christ was proclaimed even by those who had strife and envy in their hearts (Philippians 1:15-18). (One attempt to harmonize explains: In James, it is the congregation of believers that is harmed by the bad motives of the teachers; in Philippians, it is Paul himself whom the preachers of Christ hope to harm. Paul is willing to suffer if the church be helped, but James will not sit quietly by if the church were hurt!) As we suggest, one advantage to identifying the "wise and understanding" as being

readers should be habitually walking? It is a flat denial of Christian principles to exhibit bitter zeal and ambitious strife. By bad actions resulting from wrong motives, we present a message that is diametrically opposite to what Christ teaches. James has already indicated (verse 13) that wisdom from above is best packaged with a life of good works and gentleness.[22]

3:15 -- *This wisdom is not that which comes down from above, but is earthly, natural, demonic.*

This wisdom is not that which comes down from above – "From above" is a way of saying "God-given." "This wisdom" which James is describing in verses 14-16, which is accompanied by bitter zeal, selfish ambition, boasting, and lying against the truth, and which lacks gentleness, is not God inspired, nor is it the kind one would receive who prays to God for wisdom (1:5). "A wisdom which exhibits such a thoroughly unchristian disposition is of no heavenly origin."[23] Just as James identifies two different kinds of wisdom, Paul likewise made a clear distinction between the same two kinds of wisdom, "the wisdom of the world" (1 Corinthians 1:20, 2:5,6) and "the wisdom from God" (1 Corinthians 1:24, 2:7).

But is earthly, natural, demonic – In these three words, describing the nature, sphere, and origin of the wisdom men boast about, we have a descending climax which indicates a "mounting sense of distance and alienation from God."[24] "Earthly" suggests those who exhibit such wisdom as verse 14 describes are governed by worldly motives and use worldly methods to accomplish worldly purposes. It is suited to earthly minds; it is employed about earthly things; it is working for an earthly purpose; its methods are worldly; it measures success in worldly terms. Its mind is set on earthly things (Philippians 3:19). "Natural" is the NASB translation for *psuchikos*, a word for which it is difficult to find a satisfactory English equivalent.[25] 'Fleshly,' 'carnal,' 'animal,' 'soulical,'

Jewish teachers is that we are not forced to find some way to harmonize passages which seem to teach opposite views on motives.

[22] As history has rolled along through the ages, there have been many occasions when the truth of the message was denied because of the bitterness and partisanship of the messenger. Some zealous proponents of the Restoration Plea have driven would-be listeners and seekers away by their harsh rhetoric. Let James be a warning to us all!

[23] Plummer, *op. cit.*, p.603.

[24] Harold S. Songer, "James" in *The Broadman Bible Commentary* (Nashville: Broadman, 1972), Vol.12, p.125.

[25] The word does not occur in the LXX, but is found six times in the New Testament – 4 times in 1 Corinthians (2:14; 15:44,46), once in Jude 19, and here in James.

and even 'psychical' are attempts offered in other verses and versions.[26] It describes the wisdom of the world as being something 'pertaining to the life of the soul.' The "natural" or "sensual" man is the man who is ruled by his animal passions, and is far below the "spiritual" man who is ruled by the highest portion of his nature, which (in the case of the Christian) also has the help and guidance of the indwelling Holy Spirit.[27] "The wrong kind of wisdom is no different from an animal kind of thing; it is the kind of wisdom that makes an animal snap and snarl with no other thought than that of prey or personal survival."[28] "Demonic" is a better translation of *daimoniōdēs* than was "devilish" in some of our older English versions.[29] This is the lowest stage. What starts out as merely "earthly" becomes "natural" and then, even worse, comes under the influence of the demons.[30] Paul spoke of the demons as being "deceitful spirits" and as teaching their hellish doctrines to men ("doctrines of demons", 1 Timothy 4:1).[31] When a man allows himself to be motivated by the wrong kind of wisdom, he slowly descends to where his ideas and actions are inspired by the demons. "Just as there is a faith which a man may share with demons (James 2:19), and a tongue which is set on fire by hell (3:6), so there is a wisdom which is demoniacal in its source and its activity."[32] We do not teach that demons can tempt men, but when men invite their attention and help, the demons will do all they can to corrupt the harmony and the very life of the body of Christ.

3:16 -- *For where jealousy and selfish ambition exist, there is disorder and every evil thing.*

---

[26] When dichotomy is taught, and man's nature is divided into body and soul, or flesh and spirit, everyone understands that the body and flesh indicate the lower and material part, and the soul or spirit the higher and immaterial part. To treat "natural" here in James as though it somehow has a higher connotation leaves us confused. When trichotomy is taught, with its body, soul, and spirit, it is understood that soul (*psuchē*, the root of *psuchikos* here in James 3:15) is distinguished not only from flesh, but from spirit, and that "soul" represents a part of our nature which is more closely connected with the body and flesh than with spirit. The "bodies" of men and animals are made of the dust of the ground. The "soul" is the thing that animates the body of both animals and men. God intended that in man the "spirit" give directions to the soul, which in turn would animate the body. When a man commits his first sin, the "spirit" dies and ceases to function as God intended. The New Birth brings the "spirit" part back to life (John 3:6).

[27] Often in Scripture, the "natural" man is the unsaved man, while the carnal man is the Christian who walks according to the flesh rather than according to the spirit. Compare what Paul wrote in 1 Corinthians 2:14,15, and what Jude 19 says.

[28] Barclay, *op. cit.*, p.109.

[29] There is only one devil, but there is a great host of fallen angels who do his bidding.

[30] We were introduced to demons (fallen angels) at James 2:19.

[31] We call attention to Paul's language to illustrate how the demons work. Paul was warning against incipient Gnosticism when he wrote 1 Timothy. There is no evidence that James has this particular heresy in mind when he writes of wisdom that is "demonic." Gnosticism is not the only system inspired by Hell.

[32] Plummer, *op. cit.*, p.603.

For where jealousy and selfish ambition exist – With the word "for," James introduces his substantiation for his strong condemnation of wisdom that is "earthly, natural, demonic" (verse 15). Again he writes "jealousy and selfish ambition," exactly the same words used in verse 14, thus showing that verses 14-16 are tied together.

There is disorder and every evil thing – Here James finishes his presentation of the wisdom of this world by showing where it leads. "Disorder" translates *akatastasia*, "confusion, tumult, uproar, internal disorder, anarchy, instability."[33] Where there is confusion "the whole mental outlook is thrown into disorder, the understanding is darkened, and this spiritual instability is reflected in the instability of human society."[34] Such disruption of the harmony that Christianity produces was certainly the fruit of the work of the Judaizers. We read in Proverbs 6:16, "There are six things which the Lord hates, yes, seven which are an abomination to Him," and the seventh thing listed is the "one who spreads strife among brothers." If the "wisdom" a man teaches results in "disorder," we may be sure the wisdom is not from above, for "God is not a God of confusion, but of peace" (1 Corinthians 14:33). *Pan phaulon pragma* may be translated "every vile deed" or "every evil work" or "every evil thing."[35] We can see several dismal catalogues of evil deeds in 2 Corinthians 12:20 and Galatians 5:19. The wisdom from above tends to reduce the amount of evil in the world; the wisdom from below does just the opposite – it encourages sinful behavior which never produces any real benefit.[36]

3:17 -- *But the wisdom from above is first pure, then peaceable, gentle, reasonable, full of mercy and good fruits, unwavering, without hypocrisy.*

But the wisdom from above – "But" calls attention to the vivid contrast there is between the motives and effects that mark the wisdom of the world and those that characterize the wisdom that comes from God.[37] True wisdom is one of those good and perfect gifts that

---

[33] Luke uses this word to refer to political revolts and revolutionary movements (Luke 21:9). In James 1:8, James used this word to describe how the double-minded man behaved. In James 3:8 it was used to describe some of the results of the uncontrolled tongue.

[34] Tasker, *op. cit.*, p.81.

[35] *Phaulon* is a synonym for evil. It emphasizes not some aspect of its "active or passive malignity" but rather its "good-for-nothingness, the impossibility of any true benefit ever coming from it." Trench, *op. cit.*, p.317.

[36] There are men and women and organizations who resolve that their ideas must be forced on others. They are determined to have their way in the churches. They will either run things, or ruin things. They try to get various people on their side. They will make secret visits and call secret meetings. They will use all kinds of subterfuge and intrigue. They will flatter those who agree with them, but condemn and even revile those who dare to disagree. They will tell all manner of falsehood and spread vicious rumors in an attempt to squelch those who "won't cooperate." Such people and organizations have caused great confusion in the churches, and have even caused splits in the Restoration Movement.

[37] The adverb *anōthen* is a Jewish way of saying something comes from God.

comes down from the Father of Lights (James 1:5,17). In these last two verses of this chapter we have eight characteristics of heavenly wisdom identified. If we are correct when we suggest James has Judaizers in view in this paragraph (3:13-18), then here are some criteria by which they or any other would-be teacher can evaluate their activities in order to see whether they are in harmony with what God would want them to do.

Is first pure – "Pure" is *hagnos*, "undefiled," "pure" or "clean" (in both a moral and ceremonial sense).[38] In 1 John 3:3 this term is used to describe the character of Christ, who is the pattern for all believers. A person who is motivated by God's wisdom is free from any faults such as "bitter zeal" and "strife." Not only is he pure in motive, he is pure in thought and habit.[39] This inner quality stands "first" in importance. It is the basic attitude out of which all the following characteristics spring.

Then peaceable – "Then" tells us the remaining seven characteristics flow out of "purity." Because of the purity inherent in God's wisdom, the person who is guided by it produces the following characteristics which James names. The root of *eirēnikos*[40] ("peaceable") is *eirēnē*. *Eirēnē* means "peace," and when used of men its basic meaning is 'right relationships between man and man' and 'right relationships between man and God.' Motivated by God's pure wisdom, the Christian's behavior promotes right relationships.[41] Contradiction does not ruffle it, hostility does not provoke it to retaliate, because its motives are thoroughly disinterested and pure. It is interested only in bringing men closer to God and closer to one another.[42]

Gentle – It is difficult to find an English equivalent for *epieikēs*. 'Mild, inoffensive, clement' have been offered. So have 'sweet reasonableness' and 'considerate' (in the demands it makes on others). The term conveys the thought of respect for the feelings of

---

[38] Berry, *Synonyms*, p.117.

[39] Some writers, giving a peculiar interpretation to "pure," have found in this verse a justification of the ascetic lifestyle. They suppose James is saying the wise and understanding Christian must first free himself or herself from the society of all whom he believes to be in error, and then, but not till then, will he be peaceable and gentle. However, on the contrary, neither James nor Paul nor Jesus ever encouraged an ascetic lifestyle.

[40] *-ikos* when added to noun stems make adjectives that denote relation, fitness, or ability.

[41] We recall the Sermon on the Mount, where Jesus said, "Blessed are the peacemakers ..." (Matthew 5:9). Blessed is the man who leads another to peace with God.

[42] This passage does not prohibit a Christian from "contending earnestly for the faith" (Jude 3). James is condemning the attempt to establish one's own opinion in defiance of the truth, lying against the Scriptures. He is not condemning contending for the faith. A pure heart will never relinquish its hold on God's truth (right doctrine) for the sake of peace. Such a price for peace is too high.

others.   It is a God-like characteristic that God's children also reproduce.[43]   Such a person "knows when to make allowances ... when not to stand on his rights ... how to temper justice with mercy ... when not to apply the strict letter of the law."[44]   Gentleness is the opposite to severity of practices, rigor of censures, and insobriety in disputes.   It is never sarcastic, or biting, or filled with harsh criticism.

Reasonable – *Eupeithēs* can mean "ready to obey" or "willing to yield."   If we take the former meaning,[45] wisdom from above is ever ready to obey whatever God says.   It is submissive to superiors.   If we take the latter meaning, wisdom from above is ever willing to listen to reason and appeal rather than being stubborn and inflexible.[46]   It is willing to yield to reasonable requests.   A teacher motivated by heavenly wisdom is not obstinate in one view of things, but will candidly receive the suggestions of others.   Of course, this has no reference to yielding to things which are wrong in themselves.

Full of mercy and good fruits – "Full of" modifies both "mercy" and "good fruits." Heavenly wisdom is characterized by an abundant measure of both these next two characteristics.   "Mercy is more than a feeling of pity; it is an attitude of compassion towards those in distress that leads to practical help to relieve the distress."[47]   Barclay has called attention to the fact that "mercy" acquired a new meaning in Christian thought. "The Greeks defined *eleos* as pity for the man who is suffering unjustly ... In Christian thought *eleos* means mercy for the man who is in trouble, even if the trouble is his own fault."[48]   He explains that this change is a reflection of God's pity for man.   God's pity (Psalm 86:5; 100:5; 103:8; Ephesians 2:4) goes out to men whether those men are suffering unjustly or whether they suffer as the result of their own sins.   The wisdom from above never leads a man to convince himself he has no responsibility to another because "It is his own fault; he brought it on himself."   Instead, the wisdom from above is "eager to take the initiative in doing all the good in its power to those whom it can reach or influence."[49]

---

[43] In the LXX, "gentle" is often used of God's disposition toward men.   He has every right to be stern and punitive toward men in their sin, but during the time He is offering them opportunity to repent, He is gentle and kind and exercises love's leniency.   The day will come when He will be stern and punitive toward those who have refused to repent.

[44] Barclay, *op. cit.*, p.112.   Jesus pictured (Matthew 18:24-30) how people behave when they lack this characteristic as he told the story of the servant who had much forgiven but who then acted with harsh unreasonableness towards one who owed him a small amount.

[45] The term is often found in a context of military discipline.

[46] The RSV has "open to reason" as a suggested meaning.

[47] Hiebert, *op. cit.*, p.235.

[48] Barclay, *op. cit.*, p.113.

[49] Plummer, *op. cit.*, p.606.   "God desires and approves the practice of mercy in human relations (Isaiah 58:6; Hosea 6:6; Micah 6:8; Matthew 23:23; Luke 10:37)."   Hiebert, *op. cit.*, p.235.

Standing in direct opposition to "every vile deed" (verse 16), "good fruits" speak of practical help to those in need. James has emphasized that "pure religion" visits the fatherless and widows in their affliction (1:27), and he has already indicated he has no sympathy for a faith which does not clothe the naked and feed the hungry (2:15). Now he has indicated that if one merely feels an emotion of pity but holds himself or herself mercilessly aloof from brethren or neighbors who are in need, such a one cannot claim to be motivated by heavenly wisdom!

Unwavering – The absence of two negative characteristics completes the picture of heavenly wisdom. The term *adiakritos* has perplexed translators who try to find an equivalent English word.[50] One suggestion is 'without discrimination.' James has already condemned discrimination in 2:1-4. True wisdom does not show partiality to the rich and contempt for the poor. Another suggestion is 'without suspicion.' True wisdom does not suspiciously inquire concerning other men's faults. Another suggestion is 'without wrangling.' True wisdom is an enemy to brawling disputes. Another suggestion is 'undivided' or 'single-minded.' True wisdom has certain convictions, based on God's revelation through Jesus Christ, which will not change.

Without hypocrisy – This is the last of the qualities which James gives as characteristics of heavenly wisdom. In the Greek, there is a similarity of sound between the last two terms (*adiakritos* and *anupokritos*) which cannot be preserved in English. We generally think of a "hypocrite" as one who professes to be a Christian but who lives like the devil. Wisdom from above never leads a person to just play a part, or to pose as holy when indeed he or she is not. Such play-acting is deception in order to gain its own ends. Heavenly wisdom is unselfish and does not pretend to be what it is not. A teacher, especially, dare not play the hypocrite, either in his addresses to God or in his actions toward men.

3:18 -- *And the seed whose fruit is righteousness is sown in peace by those who make peace.*

And the seed whose fruit is righteousness – The Greek reads simply "the fruit of righteousness is sown." But since one sows seed rather than the fruit that grows from the seed, the NASB has added some words that seem implicit in James' compressed sentence. Christian teachers are pictured as broadcasting seed. What is that seed? Perhaps the seed is the heavenly wisdom James has been characterizing. One is reminded of Jesus' parable where "the seed is the Word" (Luke 8:11) and of Peter's statement explaining that men are born again of an imperishable seed, that is the Word of God (1 Peter 1:23). The "righteousness" which is pictured as being "fruit,"[51] which is hidden in the seed, may be

---

[50] This word occurs nowhere else in the Old or New Testament, though its cognate word occurs twice in James 1:6 ("without doubting").

[51] The NASB treats the genitive as an objective genitive. Some have treated "fruit of righteousness" as a genitive of origin, that is, the fruit which righteousness produces. These commentators then speak of the fruit as being perhaps holiness or sanctification or the rewards which righteous conduct produces, not the least of which is peace. It has even been suggested that James is echoing the teaching of Isaiah 32:17, "And the work of righteousness shall be peace; and the effect of righteousness [shall be] quietness and assurance for ever."

either right relationships with men or right relationships with God because He has justified us. Eternal life would ultimately be in the picture since "whom He called He justified, and whom He justified, He also glorified" (Romans 8:30).

Is sown in peace – The present tense "is sown" marks a customary practice. "In peace" which stands before the verb in the Greek, stresses the circumstances needed if a crop is to be produced. We've already learned (verse 17) that "peace" speaks of right relationships between man and man, "a state in which men are in uninterrupted friendship and fellowship with one another."[52] The soil in which the seeds will grow and produce the fruit of righteousness is one where right relationships are encouraged (just as the wisdom from above does). Judaizers, following the wisdom of the world, fostering bitter jealousy and selfish ambition (verse 14), have a soil which will produce only weeds and thistles. There will certainly be no "fruit of righteousness." James has already written (1:20) that God's righteousness is not achieved by the anger of men.

By those who make peace – "Teachers" are those who are broadcasting the seed.[53] They are "peacemakers,"[54] for they are working to bring about right relationships between man and God, and between man and man.[55] The "seed of the kingdom" is sown by men of peace who thoughtfully and with self-control exhibit the characteristics of heavenly wisdom (verse 17). In peaceful scenes in the assembly on the Lord's Day, and by noiseless and unobtrusive laborers going from house to house, the seed is scattered over the world. The wisdom that is from above will prove winsome to sinners who will respond to the Gospel and be reconciled to God, and saints will have peace in their hearts and peace with one another. Righteousness produces some delicious fruit!

---

[52] Barclay, *op. cit.*, p.114. The farmer sows his seed in peace. The fields are not sown amidst the tumults of a mob, or the excitement of a battle. Nothing is more peaceful, quiet, calm, and composed, than the farmer as he walks with measured tread over his fields, scattering his seed.

[53] The dative case in the Greek should probably be rendered "by those who make peace," though "for those who make peace" is also possible. Perhaps James deliberately left out any preposition so readers would pause to consider both meanings. The seed whose fruit is righteousness is not only sown by peacemakers, but they also enjoy the results of their work.

[54] What James writes recalls one of Jesus' beatitudes, "Blessed are the peacemakers, for they shall be called sons of God" (Matthew 5:9).

[55] No official status (i.e., one must be an "ordained clergyman") is required before one may engage in the activity of being a peacemaker. Acts 8:4 indicates ordinary Christians, as they fled Saul's persecution, went everywhere preaching the Word.

VII. CHOOSES FRIENDSHIPS CAREFULLY.   4:1-9

Summary: Men's behavior can be turbulent and destructive when they choose to be friends with the world, when they choose to live by rules other than those the Lord Jesus has set forth. A man cannot be both a friend of the world and a friend of God, so James warns his readers what will happen if they continue to choose to make friends of the world. He gives a call to repentance and also gives his readers specific directions for behavior by which they can show they wish to be friends with God.

4:1 -- *What is the source of quarrels and conflicts among you? Is not the source your pleasures that wage war in your members?*

What is the source – As chapter 3 came to a close, James contrasted the wisdom which is from above with that which is earthly and demonic. Following the wisdom from God, man will find his ultimate good in what can best be described as "peace," whereas the contrasting wisdom promotes jealousy and selfish ambition which in turn result in confusion and every vile deed (3:16). James is now asking his readers whether they are going to demonstrate they know how to live in harmony with the wisdom from above by submitting to God and thus showing they have renounced any friendship with the world, or whether they are going to continue to gratify their own desires for the pleasures of this world and thus clearly showing themselves to be enemies of God. He tries to help them make this momentous decision by first calling attention to some serious negative consequences of choosing friendship with the world (verses 1-5), and then by giving several admonitions they will need to heed if they are going to be God's friends (verses 6-9). In this way James urges his readers to choose their friendships carefully. The mark of a genuine Christian is that he deliberately chooses and nurtures friendship with God!

Of quarrels and conflicts among you? – Quarrels and conflicts are two of the negative consequences of choosing to live like the world's wisdom prompts men to live. Some of the older translations offer "wars and fightings" for *polemoi* and *machai*, but the two words, in this context, are probably not to be taken literally.[1] "The plurals indicate that the reference is not to an isolated event but to a chronic condition."[2] Writing "among you," we think James does not have in mind international warfare between civil governments or even civil war within one country, but has in mind private quarrels, lawsuits, social rivalries, factions, and even religious controversies and sectarianism such as the Judaizers

---

[1] Clement of Rome seems to have this passage in mind when he wrote (c. AD 96) to the church at Corinth, "Wherefore are the strifes and wraths, and factions and divisions, and war among you?" (1 Cl. xlvi).

[2] Hiebert, *op. cit.*, p.242.

were stirring up wherever they went.[3] "Among you" seems to indicate that wherever this circular letter was read, the hearers in the churches needed such rebuke and admonition.[4]

Is not the source your pleasures that wage war in your members? – James here answers the question he asked in the first part of the verse. The Greek shows he expects his readers to agree with his answer. *Hedonōn* (compare "hedonism," the philosophy which views pleasure as the chief goal in life) was translated "lusts" in the KJV, but "pleasures" (i.e., satisfied desires) is the common meaning of the word.[5] In Luke 8:14 it is the "pleasures of this life" coupled with "cares and riches" which choke out the seed of the Word and prevent it from taking root in the human heart. The pleasures/desires are described by James as "waging war in [their] members."[6] The present participle *strateuomenōn* pictures the continuous battle going on. "Members" suggests there is no part of the human frame which at one time or another has not become a battleground. "The desires of various sorts of pleasures are like soldiers in the devil's army, posted and picketed all over us, in the hope of winning our members, and so ourselves, back to his allegiance, which we have renounced in our baptism."[7] Peter says of such fleshly lusts (1 Peter 2:11) that they "war against the soul." Fightings and conflicts soon follow when we make worldly pleasure the great end in life. When everyone is trying to please themselves, rather than God, trouble naturally follows. Scripture gives several examples in of people getting into trouble when they seek to serve pleasure rather than God. Herod got into trouble because of the love of pleasure (Mark 6:14-29); Judas Iscariot, because of the love of money (Mark 14:10,11);

---

[3] When it comes time to explain chapter 4, the commentator is greatly hindered by our lack of knowledge of the specific historical situation to which this letter is addressed. As a result, most commentators offer comments that are general in nature, and not a few readers wonder whether or not the actual point James was making has been uncovered by us. We don't know what the specific disputes and contentions were, for it is not indicated. But we can all identify with the rancorous, greedy, and worldly spirit in which such disputes are conducted, and James' condemnation of such a spirit is something we all need to hear.

[4] In the Introductory Studies, we have studied the pros and cons this verse suggests concerning the destination of this letter, whether a specific community, or whether it is an encyclical.

[5] The ordinary Greek word for "desire" or "lust" is *epithumia*, the verb form of which occurs in James 4:2. "Pleasure" comes from the satisfaction of desire, and sometimes the desire results from the anticipation of the pleasure to be experienced. While serving the Lord can result in sublime "pleasure," the context here refers to the "pleasure" that springs from the satisfaction of evil desires. In fact it has been observed that the term "pleasure" is rare in the New Testament, and always used with a bad connotation.

[6] It should be carefully noted that James does not say the lusts reside in their bodies. This is no proof text for inherited depravity. But different pleasures satisfy different members of our bodies (our eyes, hands, etc.). As a result the desires that lead to sin are devilishly excited first in this bodily member, then in that, with the intent that the man will listen to the desires and seek the illicit pleasure. (The Bible does not speak of two natures still living in the Christian – e.g., the old sinful nature v. the new nature received at baptism. Romans 7:14ff is how things were in the life of Paul the Jew. It was not his flesh that was the cause of temptations, but was instead the devil stirring up sinful desires in his flesh. Compare notes at James 1:13-15.)

[7] Bishop Moberly, quoted in Punchard, *op. cit.*, p.274.

Hezekiah, because of the love of display (2 Kings 20:12-18); Adoni Bezek, because of the love of power (Judges 1:5-7); Diotrephes, because of the love of pre-eminence (3 John 9,10). A man can become a slave to lusts and pleasures; and when he does, malice and envy and hatred enter his life (Titus 3:3). One of the marks of genuine Christianity is choosing to please God rather than to please oneself.[8]

4:2 -- *You lust and do not have;* so *you commit murder. And you are envious and cannot obtain;* so *you fight and quarrel. You do not have because you do not ask.*

You lust and do not have – Scholars for years have debated the proper punctuation for this verse, and whether "you commit murder" is to be understood literally or not.

- The KJV represents one way the verse has been punctuated: "Ye lust, and have not: ye kill, and desire to have, and cannot obtain: ye fight and war ...." Yet this punctuation results in a sort of an anticlimax. "You lust, you KILL, you desire." "Desire" seems miscast next to "kill." Several methods were suggested to remove this anticlimax. Some try to weaken the force of "kill" (i.e., everyone who hates his brother is a murderer, 1 John 3:15). Some try to strengthen the force of "you desire to have" (i.e., "you become zealots," bloody assassins and revolutionaries). Some supposed "kill and desire" form a hendiadys[9] meaning "you murderously envy." Some supposed the anti-climax was deliberate because "James wanted to bring out the illogical consequences of the life devoted to pleasure."[10]
- The NASB represents the other way the verse has been punctuated. It is treated as three short, sharp, telling sentences, with the first two being parallel like couplets in Hebrew poetry. The NASB translators have twice supplied "so" to help readers see the flow of thought. Our comments will follow the lead of the NASB.

Just as verse 1 gave some, verse 2 gives more concrete examples of the sad and harmful effects of "pleasure seeking." "Lust" translates *epithumeite*, and denotes the longing, the urge, the craving for the object thought to bring pleasure.[11] The present tense verb pictures a repeated situation, and "have not" (a thought mentioned twice in this verse) indi-

---

[8] In the *Phaedo* of Plato (66,67) there is an excellent passage which presents some striking parallels with the words of James. (Barclay quotes this, and similar expressions from Philo, Lucian, and Cicero.) The conclusion to which Plato arrives is that of a philosopher who leaves God out of the picture. The conclusion to which James arrives is one that exhorts his readers to cast themselves off, not from the body, but from friendship with the world. Put God into the picture! Resist the evil one. Make use of the grace which God gives. Humble yourselves, repent, and strengthen your friendship with God. That's how to master selfish pleasures and the temptations/lusts which feed off those desires for pleasure.

[9] A hendiadys is the expression of a thought by two nouns coupled by "and" or two verbs coupled by "and" rather than using a noun and an adjective, or a verb and an adverb.

[10] H. Maynard Smith, *The Epistle of St. James*. Lectures (Oxford: Blackwell, 1914), p. 219.

[11] See notes on the noun form of this verb at James 1:14. "Cravings" may be good or bad, depending on the context. Here the context calls for an evil connotation. In the LXX of Exodus 20:17 and at Romans 7:7, *ouk epithuméseis* is the way the tenth commandment ("you shall not covet") is written. The origin and growth of any evil act is traced here in chapter 4 in somewhat the same way as in 1:14.

cates the desires are regularly left unsatisfied. Those desires can become so strong and insistent that folk will commit crimes to get satisfaction for their desires.

So you commit murder – The meaning of this short sentence is that "unsatisfied desire leads to murder."[12] With the murdered person out of the way, perhaps now the pleasure can be satisfied. We do not see James as describing the condition of any special community (a particular local town known for its violence, for instance), but as describing the result of choosing pleasure (friendship with the world) instead of friendship with God. We see this shocking picture of behavior as being just as true for any Christian as it is for any unbeliever.[13] James is clearly depicting what can happen and does happen in any person's life when men choose the pleasures and friendship with the world. What happened when Ahab desired Naboth's vineyard (1 Kings 21) is not the only time covetousness has led to a tragic end. The history of humanity from the days of Cain to the present time are filled with examples of how people misbehave when God's revealed will is disregarded while at the same time they live to satisfy this or that pleasure.

And you are envious and cannot obtain – "Envy" (*zēloute*) is another attitude or passion that is common when the person living for pleasure finds his seeking blocked and frustrated. The word means to "covet" or "hotly desire to possess" what presently belongs to someone else.[14] The word rendered "envious" describes a thing which love never does: "Love envies not" (1 Corinthians 13:4). The Greek verb tense for "cannot obtain" pictures a repeated inability to actually possess what they so ardently desire. They "cannot obtain" by any fair and honest means, not by purchase or negotiation. This frustrated desire leads to broken relationships and eventually to bloody conquest.[15]

So you fight and quarrel – The idea in this short sentence is that "unsatisfied desire leads to violence" in order to take from their present owner what you wish. "Fight" and "quarrel" are the same words, in reverse order, used in verse 1. He does not mean that the desires war within a man; he means that they set men warring against each other. Obedi-

---

[12] Because "covet" seemed so tame after "kill," Erasmus offered a conjectural emendation of the text, offering "you envy" (*phthoneite*) rather than "you murder" (*phoneuete*). The two words are not very similar, yet Codex Vaticanus, at 1 Peter 2:1, confuses the cognate nouns and reads "murders" for "envyings." Here in James, Tyndale and Calvin accepted Erasmus' emendation, as did the translators of the KJV ("ye desire to have"). Not a single manuscript, version, or Early Church Father can be quoted to defend this conjectural emendation of the text. According to the manuscript evidence, James wrote "murder."

[13] Because "fight and war" was taken figuratively in verse 1, not a few think we should take "kill" figuratively (a hyperbole for "hatred") here in verse 2. They point to Matthew 5:21-22 to show that hatred is equal to murder. James' readers are Christians (James 2:1), but have we really removed the difficulty if we say that James' Christian readers could be guilty of one sin ("hatred") but not of the other ("murder")?

[14] See the comments on the noun form of this word at James 3:14,16.

[15] "There was, perhaps, a grim truth in the picture which James draws. It was after the deed was done that the murderers began to quarrel over the division of the spoil, and found themselves as unsatisfied as before, still not able to obtain that on which they had set their hearts, and so plunging into fresh quarrels, ending as they began, in bloodshed." Plumptre, *op. cit.*, p.89.

ence to God's will draws men together, for it is God's will that men should love and serve one another. Obedience to the craving for pleasure drives men apart, for pleasure drives men to rivalry, shameless selfish competition, and violent deeds to obtain the thing desired.

You do not have because you do not ask – "You do not have" returns to the matter of unsatisfied desire, and points out another aspect of the futility of pleasure as the supreme goal in life. "You do not ask" refers to prayers, of asking something of God through prayer.[16] This short, crisp sentence[17] seems to say that prayer has not much place in the life of the person who is a friend of the world. Not only do such people kill and fight and quarrel, they do not pray much. They do not even think to ask the One who could actually give real pleasure by helping them to control their improper desires, and by giving gifts and opportunities for service that completely satisfy. Even when worldly wisdom momentarily gets the thing that it thinks will give pleasure, that pleasure is short-lived and proves disappointing. Not so when God satisfies a man's thirst. The water He gives leaves men never to thirst again (John 4:13,14). Answered prayer is the way to full contentment and solid joy (Philippians 4:6). By aiming at worldly pleasure, men cut themselves off from the only sure source of true and lasting satisfaction.

4:3 -- *You ask and do not receive, because you ask with wrong motives, so that you may spend* it *on your pleasures.*

You ask and do not receive – In verse 2 James has observed that the friend of the world doesn't spend much time praying. Now in this verse, he indicates that when such folk do pray, they often do so with the wrong motives. As a result, God does not grant what they have asked. "You ask" is a reference to prayer to God, just as it was in verse 2. James is writing to Christians and reminds them how easy it is to offer selfish prayers. A desire to be a friend of the world can invade a man's prayer life and render it ineffective.

Because you ask with wrong motives – As the marginal note ('wickedly') shows, the Greek word here is *kakōs*, 'badly' or, as the remainder of the verse explains, 'with selfish purpose' of securing pleasure, rather than serving God. The 'asking amiss' consists not in asking for temporal things, but in seeking them for the wrong purpose, merely to satisfy selfish pleasure. The right purpose for asking would be to enable us to serve God and His people better. It has been observed that James mentions several hindrances to effective prayer: (1) in 1:5-7, it was double-mindedness; (2) in this place, the request was selfish; (3) in 4:8, uncleanness of life will keep the Lord from answering; and (4) in 5:16, the lack

---

[16] The Greek verb is a present tense, middle voice. It pictures repeated failure to ask, and the middle voice implies an asking that involved something for their own benefit. (Scholars have noted that the verb "ask" occurs three times in verses 2 and 3, in the middle voice the first and third times, and in the active voice the second time. Ropes, *op. cit.*, p.259, is probably correct when he says there "is no difference in meaning ... between the active and middle.")

[17] In the KJV, this part of the verse begins with "yet." The better manuscripts omit the word, and this helps us see they should be taken as a separate clause.

of fervency or sincerity is likewise a hindrance. The promises of God are that prayers of the righteous and the penitent will be heard and answered (Psalm 34:15-17, 145:18; Proverbs 10:24; Song of Solomon 6:8; Luke 18:9-14; 1 Peter 3:10-12; 1 John 5:14).

So that you may spend *it* **on your pleasures** – "Pleasures" is the same word as in verse 1, and stands emphatically forward in this clause. On their own pleasures is where they intended to use what they asked of God. "Spend" is exemplified in the behavior of the Prodigal Son who "spent" (same Greek verb) his substance in riotous living (Luke 15:14). It is possible to ask God for good things for a bad reason. The reason why the requests are not granted is not in the things prayed for. The reason stems from the purpose for which the things are desired – i.e., are they desired for pleasure or for the service of God.[18] James is likely reflecting Jesus' own teaching in the Sermon on the Mount. Make the service of God and righteousness your supreme goal, and God will fulfill the desires you express to Him in prayer (Matthew 6:31-34, 7:7-11). A lack of temporal necessities can be a hindrance to good service, and then it is right to ask God to relieve them. But in all such things the rule laid down by Jesus is the proper one: "Seek first the kingdom of God and His righteousness, and all these things [food, shelter, clothing] shall be added to you." James is reflecting what his Master taught; he is not prohibiting his readers from asking God for temporal blessings, whether for ourselves or for others. James plainly implies that when a person has temporal needs, he or she should go to God in prayer. But he must go with a right purpose and in a right spirit. In chapter 5, James specifically teaches his readers to pray for the recovery of the sick. Elsewhere, John prayed that Gaius "in all respects ... may prosper and be in good health, just as your soul prospers" (3 John 2).

4:4 -- *You adulteresses, do you not know that friendship with the world is hostility toward God? Therefore whoever wishes to be a friend of the world makes himself an enemy of God.*

You adulteresses – Many of the descriptive terms in the context ("wars," "fightings," "murder") have been given a figurative meaning, rather than literal. James has been condemning greed and worldly pleasures in general, so we suppose this feminine form[19] is to be given a figurative meaning also, namely, "spiritual unfaithfulness." Jewish folk were accustomed to such a figurative use to describe spiritual adultery in the Old Testament Scriptures,[20] where Israel was called the adulteress wife of God. Jesus used similar lan-

---

[18] Plummer, *op. cit.*, p.610, has written, "Prayer for temporal blessings that is offered in a grasping spirit is like a bandit praying for the success of his raids." Barclay (*op. cit.*, p.118) observes that it is not possible for God to grant requests that are essentially selfish, "for to answer them would be to do nothing other than to provide the man with ways of sinning."

[19] The KJV reads "ye adulterers and adulteresses" (i.e., both a masculine and a feminine form). The better supported text has only the feminine form. Plummer (*op. cit.*, p.610) suggests that the interpolation of the masculine form was made by those who supposed the term of reproach was to be understood literally, and who therefore thought it inexplicable that James should rebuke only female offenders.

[20] Hosea 1:2; Psalm 73:27; Isaiah 50:1, 54:5; Jeremiah 3:20, 9:2, 31:32.

guage to describe the Jews in His audience, "an evil and adulterous generation craves for a sign" (Matthew 12:39, 16:4; Mark 8:38).   Since the church is the bride of Christ, she too can be charged with spiritual adultery.   In fact, each individual soul can be guilty of spiritual unfaithfulness.   Christians who prefer to satisfy their "pleasures" (James 4:1-3) are guilty of breaking their marriage promise to God by loving the world more than Him.[21] In God's estimation, worldly-minded Christians are adulteresses!   They are deliberately breaking the intimate, loving relationship they had with God, and giving the love due Him to some thing they cherish above or instead of Him.   We suppose James uses this blunt and shocking word to jar and awaken his readers to their true spiritual condition.

Do you not know that friendship with the world is hostility toward God? – The question is so worded that it is implied that the readers certainly should know this truth. They should have known it from Jesus' own teaching, since we have a distinct echo of the Sermon on the Mount (Matthew 6:24) and Jesus' teaching in Perea (Luke 16:13).   He Himself made it plain that divided allegiance is impossible, for He said, "No man can serve two masters."   "Friendship" (*philia*) denotes intimate affection.[22]   As we learned in comments on James 1:27, "world" (*kosmos*) is a word that has multiple connotations. Here it refers not so much to the physical globe we live on,[23] or even to all the people who live on that globe.[24]   It refers rather to the set of people and ideas who are alienated from God and who are not part of the people of God.   This world has the devil for its ruler (John 14:30); its ideas and motives and desires are derived from below (James 3:15); and these are passing away (1 John 2:17).   Demas forsook the Christian ministry and Paul because he loved this present world (2 Timothy 4:10).   The expression "friendship with the world" points out the true nature of the pleasure-seeking activity James has been condemning.   If we seek to find our joys and pleasures apart from the church and God's people and God's

---

[21] 2 Corinthians 11:1-2; Ephesians 5:22-23; and Revelation 19:7 seem to say that Christians are but engaged to Christ.   Nevertheless, "engagement" was considered a much more binding pledge in Bible times.   (Compare Joseph and Mary, where the breaking of the engagement required a bill of divorcement, Matthew 1:19.)   The Christian who turns from Christ to follow the pleasures of the world is like an engaged woman who leaves her husband-to-be to follow other lovers.

[22] The noun is derived from a word meaning "to kiss (as an expression of affection)" or "to love."

[23] "There is no sin in a passionate love of the ordered beauty and harmony of the universe, as exhibited either in this planet or in the countless bodies which populate the immensity of space; no sin in devoting the energies of a lifetime to finding out all that can be known about the laws and conditions of nature in all its complex manifestations.   Science is no forbidden ground to God's servants, for all truth is God's truth, and to learn it is a revelation of Himself.   If only it be studied as His creature, it may be admired and loved without any disloyalty to Him."   Plummer, *op. cit.*, p.611.

[24] John tells us (we cannot tell for certain if the words are his, or Christ's) that "God loved the world" (John 3:16).   John also warns us not to love the world (1 John 2:13).   It is obvious that "world" has two different meanings in these two Johannine passages.   James has already explained that the truly religious man keeps himself unspotted from the world (James 1:27).

expressed will, then we are "friends of the world."[25]   To be a "friend of the world" is to be on good terms with the persons and forces and things that are openly hostile to God.   It is to adopt this present world's set of values instead of choosing according to divine standards. "Hostility" (*echthra*) denotes an attitude of personal hostility, and God is the object of that hostility.[26]   God and the world are at war.   If we make friends with the world (and we do that by selfishness and love of pleasure and self-gratification), we have thereby chosen sides.   This is a fact; James says it is true, whether we think so or not.   Unless the friendship with the world is renounced, the eternal destiny of these enemies of God will be Hell (Romans 6:19-23).

Therefore whoever wishes to be a friend of the world makes himself an enemy of God – This is not merely simple repetition of what James has already written.   James' readers are now shown that their own free choice is a very important element in this whole matter. They are free to choose between friendship with the world and friendship with God. *Boulēthē* ("wishes") emphasizes the truth that this choice is something each individual Christian does deliberately.[27]   Both Moses and Jesus called for such a deliberate choice. Moses' words were, "And now, Israel, what does the Lord your God require from you, but to fear the Lord your God, to walk in all His ways, and love Him, and to serve the Lord your God with all your heart and with all your soul, and to keep the Lord's commandments, and His statutes, which I am commanding you today for your good?" (Deuteronomy 10:12,13; cp. 16:5 and 30:6).   Jesus said that to "love the Lord your God with all your heart, and with all your soul, and with all your mind" was the great commandment in the Law (Matthew 22:36,37).   "Makes himself" (*kathistatai*) is the same verb used in James 3:6.   It asserts that by making a decision to be a friend of the world, each individual "constitutes himself" or takes his stand as an enemy of God.[28]   Neutrality is impossible.

4:5 -- *Or do you think that the Scripture speaks to no purpose: "He jealously desires the spirit which He has made to dwell in us"*?

Or – Lest someone objects, thinking "I'm not really being hostile to God," James seems to be showing why this is an absolutely truthful presentation of the situation.   Verses 5 and 6 are filled with a series of difficult phrases.[29]   Here are some of the issues to be decided:

---

[25] Greek students have noted that this genitive construction could be construed either as an objective or a subjective genitive.   If subjective, the idea would be "the friendship the world has for us."   Since the whole context is speaking of our desires and pleasures, we think it correct to treat it as an objective genitive, denoting "our friendship for the world."

[26] The Greek *tou theou* is genitive and should be treated as an objective genitive.

[27] The word implies "purpose, intention, design."

[28] "Enemy" is the same root that was translated "hostility" earlier in this verse.

[29] Some say they are the most difficult in James; some say they are the most difficult in the whole New Testament.

(1) How shall we punctuate this verse?   Shall we make it two questions, as did the ASV? Shall we make it one long question, as does the NASB?[30]

(2) Are two Scriptures quoted, or only one?

(3) If verse 5 is a Scripture quotation, where is it to be found?

(4) Who or what is it that "jealously desires" or "longs" – is it God, the Holy Spirit, or our human spirit?

(5) What is it that is desired or longed for?

(6) What is the connection between verse 5 and the preceding verses?

(7) How shall we understand the sequence of thought as verse 6 begins with an appeal to God's greater grace?

Do you think that the Scripture speaks to no purpose – There are two alternatives: either friendship with the world is enmity with God, or else the Scripture speaks without meaning.[31]   As was explained in comments at James 2:23, the expression "the Scripture" is usually used to introduce a quotation from the Old Testament, though Peter uses it to identify Paul's writings (2 Peter 3:15-16), and Paul calls Luke's Gospel "Scripture" (1 Timothy 5:18).   While a portion of verse 6 is found in the Old Testament canonical books, the sentence that follows here in verse 5 does not occur in the Old Testament.[32]   Our options are these: either the words of verse 5 are not a quotation at all,[33] or they are from some book no longer extant,[34] or they are a montage of several Old Testament passages.[35] Before we go looking for some passage to which James refers, we must settle several other questions, including the difficulties encountered in translating the last sentence in verse 5.

---

[30] The NIV offers another option.   It treats all of verse 5 and the first part of verse 6 as one long question.   It then treats the last half of verse 6 as the answer to the question.

[31] Hiebert (*op. cit.*, p.252) suggests that the question probes the reader's personal attitude toward the authoritative message of Scripture.

[32] Failing to find anything like verse 5 in the Scriptures, some commentators have tried to make a case for the closing sentence of verse 4 being the "Scripture" James has in mind.   For this explanation to be valid, the passage must be punctuated as it is in the ASV with a question mark in the middle of verse 5. Though the words "the Scripture speaks" usually introduce a quotation which follows, these words may refer to something already said (e.g., Romans 2:24; Matthew 26:24; Mark 9:13).   Note also that in the Greek the words "the Scriptures" do not come first in the order, and this is often a sign that they refer to what precedes.   Further, the word "or" which the KJV translators ignored, points back to what precedes. Under this proposed interpretation, there are two possibilities for the meaning and source of the closing sentence of verse 4:   (1) Some suppose the words point to a specific passage (either in the Old or New Testaments) where the fact of spiritual adultery is mentioned (perhaps Jeremiah 3:14 or Hosea 2:19).   (2) Others suggest this phrase ("the Scripture speaks") points to the general attitude everywhere expressed in the Scriptures, that friendship with the world is enmity with God.   There is no one passage which says precisely that, but there are several passages that teach such an idea (see Matthew 6:24; 1 John 2:15).

[33] The NIV is a representative of the view that the actual Old Testament quotation is found in the second half of verse 6, and verses 5-6a are introductory or parenthetical to the quotation.

[34] It is difficult to show that any books once regarded as canonical have, through the centuries, become lost.

[35] We discard at once those suggestions that find verse 5 to be a quotation from some apocryphal or pseudepigraphical writing (such as *Eldad and Modad*).   Those two collections were not "Scripture."

But anticipating the conclusion to which we shall arrive, when all the scholarly discussion about this verse has been weighed,[36] we agree with the way the verse is translated in the text of the NASB: we shall opt for those words being a montage of several Old Testament passages.

"He jealously desires the spirit which He has made to dwell in us"? – The NASB margin offers another possible translation, "The Spirit which He has made to dwell in us jealously desires us."[37] The Greek reads, *pros phthonon epipothei to pneuma ho katōkisen en hēmin*,[38] and raises a number of disputed issues.

(a) The prepositional phrase *pros phthonon* is capable of several explanations. It may be taken with the verb "say" that precedes,[39] or it may be taken with the verb that follows.[40] *Pros* can also mean "against"[41] or "toward" or "with reference to."[42] The idea seems to be that the "desire" expressed in the verb soon tends toward jealousy.[43]

(b) *To pneuma* can either be nominative (the subject of the sentence) or accusative (the ob-

---

[36] We shall quote only the most telling arguments for each view studied, and point to references where those who are interested may do further research. Exhaustive notes, with references, are in Alford and Hiebert.

[37] Translators so rendering the Greek suppose the meaning is that the indwelling Holy Spirit, imparted to us by God when we are immersed, yearns enviously for our total loyalty and devotion to God. Some appeal to Galatians 5:17 as being a similar statement of the Spirit's opposition to the desires of the flesh. (This commentator is not convinced "spirit" should be capitalized either here in James or in Galatians 5.)

[38] The KJV, which reads "The spirit that dwelleth in us ...," represents a different Greek text, one that has an aorist active form of *katoikeō* ("dwell") rather than the better attested aorist active form of *katoikizō* ("cause to dwell").

[39] Some try to give the prepositional phrase the force of an adverb ("enviously"), but we already have the adverb *kenōs* ("without purpose", "vainly") modifying the verb "say." Others would translate it "with reference to envy." Thus the first half of the verse reads, "Do you think the Scripture speaks to no purpose with reference to [God's] envy?"

[40] Commentators have largely come to a consensus that the prepositional phrase should be taken with the verb *epipothei* "(to desire, to long for") that follows.

[41] *Pros* can mean "against," but only when paired with verbs that imply hostility. *Pros* can never mean "against" when paired with a word which implies strong affection like *epipothei*. If James meant "against," the proper preposition would be *para*.

[42] "With reference to" would better be expressed by *peri* than *pros*.

[43] The fact that "envy" can be evil, and that such evil envy is elsewhere in the New Testament condemned, makes its use here somewhat startling. The powerful human emotions of envy and jealousy can hardly be distinguished. Perhaps James simply treats the Greek word for "envy" (giving it a good sense) in the same way Paul treated the word for "jealousy" (which commonly has a bad connotation, but also can have a good one, as in 2 Corinthians 11:2 or Galatians 4:17,18). BAG (p.718) indicates this prepositional phrase was a Greek adverbial idiom meaning "jealously." Ropes (*op. cit.*, p.262-63), citing examples from Classical Greek, opts for the word "begrudgingly" as describing a spirit which absolutely refuses to share something with another. God is unwilling to share man's affections; He wants all of His creatures' affections!

ject of the verb),[44] and it can refer either to the Holy Spirit or to the human spirit.[45]

(c) The verb *epipothei* means "yearn, yearn over, long for, to desire earnestly, to love, to have affection for."[46] It expresses the mighty and affectionate longing of God's love, if we understand the passage aright.[47]

(d) "In us" can be either "us believers" or "us human beings." We teach that human beings are tripartite: body, soul, and spirit.[48] The spirit gives directions to the soul which in turn animates the body. God watches what each man's spirit prompts (whether it be 'satisfy your selfish pleasures,' or 'habitually surrender to God's will'), and when the spirit prompts to spiritual infidelity, God very quickly burns with jealousy. He doesn't like it when affection due to Him is bestowed on another. How do we know? The Bible[49] tells us so! God is a jealous God, and Divine love is a jealous love; it brooks no rival.[50]

(e) Concerning God "making this spirit to dwell in us," see Genesis 2:7; Isaiah 42:5; Ecclesiastes 12:7; Numbers 16:22, 27:16; Zechariah 12:1; and Hebrews 12:9.

---

[44] These options are well illustrated in the two readings offered in the text and margin of the NASB. If we take *to pneuma* as nominative, we must supply an "us" in order to have an object for the verb "desires."

[45] Commentators have tried every possible option.   One that seems farfetched is the rendering that says "He (God) desires the (Holy) Spirit who dwells in us."   While the indwelling of the Spirit is a Biblical doctrine, it is hard to understand in what sense God would long for or desire the Spirit.

[46] Those translations which attempt to give the verb a bad sense ("lusts") fly in the face of evidence elsewhere in the New Testament.   In every one of the passages where the verb appears (Romans 1:11; 2 Corinthians 5:2, 9:14; Philippians 1:8, 2:26; 1 Thessalonians 3:10; 2 Timothy 1:4; 1 Peter 2:2), it is used in a good sense.   The same is true for nouns and adjectives formed off the same root (Romans 15:23; 2 Corinthians 7:7,11; Philippians 4:1).   We therefore reject any interpretation of this sentence (e.g., "the spirit [corrupted by the Fall] lusts to envy") that requires giving a bad sense to the verb.   We also question the NIV which translates the verb "tends" ("the spirit tends toward jealousy").   The verb means "yearns for" or "longs for"; "tends" is not an equivalent idea.

[47] The Greek word for "yearning" or "longing" is found in the LXX of Deuteronomy 32:11, and is followed in verses 13-19 by an account of the manner in which God's love so shown had been turned to jealousy and anger by the sins of Israel.

[48] See notes at James 2:26.

[49] The truth James is summarizing can be found in Genesis 6:3-5, 8:21; Numbers 11:29; Deuteronomy 5:9, 32:21; Psalm 36:17, 83:1ff; Proverbs 21:10; Song of Solomon 8:6; Isaiah 63:8-16; and Zechariah 1:14, 8:2, as well as in other passages already cited in these comments.   BAG (p.165) points out that "the Scripture" at times has reference to "the Scripture as a whole" rather than just a single passage.   They call attention to John 7:38,42; Acts 8:32; Romans 4:3, 9:17, 10:11; and Galatians 4:30 as instances of the collective use of the singular "the Scripture."

[50] According to Ephesians 1:4, God created mankind because He wanted someone who would love Him.   He will not tolerate His creatures trying to love Him and someone or something else at the same time.

When all the disputed matters have been decided, the conclusion to which we have come is this: the NASB translators have handled this verse correctly.[51]   Verse 5 gives scriptural authority for what was stated in verse 4 about the incompatibility of friendship with the world and friendship with God.   The root idea of James' sentence is identical with that of the jealousy of God over Israel as His bride (Jeremiah 3:1-11; Ezekiel 16; Hosea 2:3). Those who have been addressed as "adulteresses" in verse 43 are forgetting this.   All that they can read about the love and jealousy of God was to them idle talk.

4:6 -- *But He gives a greater grace.   Therefore it says,* "GOD IS OPPOSED TO THE PROUD, BUT GIVES GRACE TO THE HUMBLE."

But He gives a greater grace – The sequence of thought seems to be this: God makes rigorous requirements of devotion, but He gives gracious help in order that men may be able to render the undivided allegiance which He expects.   God expects us to keep absolutely true to Him, and He gives strength to resist as the temptations to be unfaithful increase (1 Corinthians 10:13).   When humble Christians occasionally waver in their devotion, God in His love does not abandon them.   Where sin abounds, grace more than abounds (Romans 5:20).   In "greater grace"[52] there may even here be a reference to the help the indwelling Holy Spirit gives to believers, so they may live the Christian life in unswerving love and devotion to their Maker and Redeemer.   If believers want something that truly satisfies human desires, let them remember Jesus' promise: "Truly, I say to you, there is no one who has left house or brothers or sisters or mother or father or children or farms, for My sake and for the gospel's sake, but that he shall receive a hundred times as much now in the present age, houses and brothers and sisters and mothers and children and farms, along with persecutions; and in the world to come, eternal life" (Mark 10:29,30). The more we surrender, and the more we love Him, the more He bestows.

Therefore it says – The point of the passage about to be quoted is that it contains proof of what James has been saying, both about hostility and grace.   What James is promising can be read in God's word.[53]   A man is either for God, or is against Him.   God does not deal with His enemies like He deals with His friends.

GOD IS OPPOSED TO THE PROUD, BUT GIVES GRACE TO THE HUMBLE –

---

[51] The subject of the verb is "He" (God), and the object of the verb is "the spirit."   The sentence is to be treated as a statement rather than a question (note the question mark is outside the quotation marks in the NASB).

[52] "Greater" is a comparative adjective, but the point of the comparison is not actually stated in James. Our comments have suggested several possibilities, and even treated the comparative as though it might mean "more and more" or "abundant" grace.

[53] The verb is a third person singular form.   It can either be "it says" (as the ASV/NASB have it) or "He says" (as the KJV has it).   Because the Scriptures are God's inspired word, they are often characterized as "God speaking."

This quotation comes from Proverbs 3:34,[54] and is quoted also in 1 Peter 5:5.[55] The "proud" (*huperēphanois*) would be those who have deliberately chosen to be a friend of the world, who have deliberately turned away from their Creator, who despise and scorn God's promises and program. They get no gracious help from God. In fact, God "resists" or "ranges Himself against" them.[56] The "humble" are those who recognize the value of friendship with God, of having an intimate relation with Him, and who are willing to walk in paths of righteousness just because they love Him and want to please Him.[57] These are the ones into whose lives God is delighted to graciously intervene.[58] He continually imparts His grace to those who exhibit a humble attitude. The greater His people's needs, the greater is God's supply of the needed grace.

4:7 -- *Submit therefore to God. Resist the devil and he will flee from you.*

Submit therefore to God – "Therefore" draws a logical lesson from Proverbs 3:34 just quoted. God resists the proud, therefore, submit to Him. God gives grace to the humble, therefore submit to Him. The imperative "submit" is an appeal to the will of the reader.[59] The idea in "submit" (*hupotagēte*) is "yield," to yield yourself to Him and what He has revealed is necessary for your welfare.[60] A readiness and willingness to submit to whatever God may impose is a characteristic of humility, and it is how friendship with Him

---

[54] The following words are an exact quotation of the LXX of Proverbs 3:34, with the exception that "God" is here substituted for "Lord" in the LXX.

[55] Clement of Rome also quotes it (c.30). It might be well if Bible students memorized and meditated on this verse that has been a law of life for centuries. By way of comment, Plummer wonders whether James may have been acquainted with the "Magnificat" (Luke 1:46-55). He thinks that perhaps James, the Lord's brother, had heard their mother recite it. The passage here in James is like an echo of some of Mary's words: "His mercy is upon generation after generation towards those who fear Him. He has done mighty deeds with His arm; He has scattered those who were proud in the thoughts of their heart. He has brought down rulers from their thrones, and exalted those who were humble. He has filled the hungry with good things; and sent away the rich empty handed."

[56] This is the meaning of the Greek word (*antitassetai*) translated "opposed." It is the word used of drawing up an army in battle array against an enemy.

[57] The humble man is the man who is utterly dependent on the Lord, and is content with what the Lord gives him. He is not covetous or envious. He is a man quick to confess his shortcomings and shows real repentance for any sins. A humble man will not fight and war for what he desires, but will wait on the Lord to give.

[58] Someone has observed that the devil doesn't pay his servants much: broken lives, sin and its consequences. What a contrast to what God gives!

[59] "Submit!" is the first of a series of aorist imperative verbs in verses 7-9. An aorist imperative calls for immediate response.

[60] Submission is not the same as obedience. Instead, the surrender of one's will is a prerequisite to obedience.

can be nurtured.   Verses 7-9 offer a practical exhortation to the choice of friendship with God (instead of pleasure and friendship with the world) as the chief end in life.   By doing all the things James commands in these verses is how a man goes about demonstrating a desire to be a friend of God.

Resist the devil and he will flee from you – This phrase allows us to better understand where the lust and envy came from that James wrote about earlier in this chapter.   James seems to imply that spiritual unfaithfulness to God is a result of the devil's influence.[61]   Those powerful desires and motives didn't just happen because folk were looking for a way to get satisfaction.   The one who sowed evil seed was the evil one.[62]   He springs right into action when he finds a soul interested in "pleasures."   "Resist" (from *anthistēmi*) is a military word meaning to "oppose, set in opposition, stand against."[63]   If a person wants to be hostile to someone (see verse 4), develop hostility toward the devil, not God, is James' advice.   James' readers may well recall the temptations of Jesus (Matthew 4:1-11), how He resisted the temptations offered by the devil, and how the devil departed for a season.[64]   "Do not give the devil an opportunity" (Ephesians 4:27).   On another occasion, when Jesus had fed the 5000, He anticipated the people would come and try to persuade Him to be their earthly king.   He resisted this temptation by withdrawing to the hills to be alone in prayer (John 6:15).   Another means of resisting is to make use of the shield of faithfulness to God (Ephesians 6:16; 1 Peter 5:8,9).   "He will flee from you" assures James' readers that successful resistance to the devil is possible.

4:8 -- *Draw near to God and He will draw near to you.   Cleanse your hands, you sinners; and purify your hearts, you doubleminded.*

---

[61] The Greek word translated "devil" (*diabolos*) means "slanderer, accuser," and reminds us that the devil is busy accusing the faithful day and night (Revelation 12:10).   In the LXX this Greek term was the one used almost uniformly to translate the Hebrew term *Satan*.

[62] The activities of the devil have been alluded to earlier in James, but this is the first time this evil being has been specifically identified.   This text is one of many which implies the personality of the devil; there is no plausible way the words of this verse could be given a figurative meaning and make any sense. If James did not learn about the personal devil from the Old Testament, he certainly could have learned it from the teachings of Jesus (see Mark 4:15; Luke 10:18, 14:11,16, 22:31; and "deliver us from the evil one," Matthew 6:13).   Paul showed no sympathy with the skepticism of the Sadducees (Acts 23:8).   He argued convincingly against them concerning the resurrection and the future life, and He gave full sanction to the belief in angels and spirits, both good and bad.   See the article on "Satan" by D.E. Hiebert in the *Zondervan Pictorial Encyclopedia of the Bible* (Grand Rapids: Zondervan, 1975), Vol.5, p. 282-286.

[63] It is implied that temptations are not irresistible.   At least in the case of the Christian, God does not allow the devil to tempt beyond what a man is capable of resisting (1 Corinthians 10:13).   If a person is going to resist the devil, he or she will have to quit deliberately surrendering to what they know to be evil.

[64] The same methods Jesus used to defeat what the devil was trying to do are methods we can use. Watch for the devil to plant the thought or stir up the desire, call to his attention what the Word of God says on the subject, and the devil has lost that encounter.   There is nothing left for him to do but withdraw, at least for the moment.

Draw near to God and He will draw near to you – The series of imperatives continues. Folk who draw near to God are not likely to be in places where they provoke the devil to tempt them. How then do we go about drawing near to God, to seek friendship with Him? Perhaps, as the whole paragraph suggests, by sanctification, constantly renouncing the way to satisfy one's "pleasures" which the devil suggests. Christians are to walk with God as Enoch walked (Genesis 5:24). In Hosea 12:6 and Psalm 119:169, earnest prayer is the way to draw near to God.[65] Submissive prayer is the very opposite of how friends of the world act ("do not ask," verse 2). The way to draw near is not only with "mouth" and "lips," but with hands and heart. Lip service, is in effect, to remain far from Him (Matthew 15:8; Isaiah 29:13).

This "drawing near to God" which James commands the Christian to do is actually a very special privilege. In Old Testament times, the right to approach God ("to draw near to God") was something only the priests could do (Exodus 19:22), and only at set times and to offer sacrifice on behalf of the people (Leviticus 10:3, 21:21-23; Ezekiel 44:13). In the Christian dispensation, the privilege is open to all believers; we can approach the throne of grace at any time. Nor need we come with hands full of sacrificial gifts. The blood of Jesus opens the way (Hebrews 4:14-16, 7:19). God responds favorably to those who draw near to Him.

Note the contrast between "he will draw near to you" and what was said in the last part of verse 7. When the devil is resisted, he flees. When the Christian draws near to God, God comes nearer.[66] Recall the father in the story of the Prodigal Son, who goes running to meet the returning son, and lavishes gifts on him (Luke 15). The effects of communion with God are unlimited. His power and protection come into action when the devil tries to tempt the Christian. The Christian will have peace of soul and calmness in life when the Lord spreads His tabernacle over him. The Christian will experience God's favor and blessing. The result is a satisfaction that is genuine and lasting.

Cleanse your hands, you sinners – An acceptable posture for prayer is to "lift up holy hands" while one is praying (1 Timothy 2:8). The way to assure that one's hands are holy is not just ceremonial cleansing, as God's Old Testament people were taught to do. (Hand washing was a ceremonial duty the priests observed before they were considered fit to perform their religious rituals, Exodus 30:19-21; Leviticus 16:4). By New Testament times, the Pharisees had extended the rules for the priests to the common man. They had a number of ceremonial purification rules which common men were expected to meticulously observe (Mark 7:3,4). People who ignored the rules of the Pharisees were

---

[65] The verb James uses for "draw near" is the same verb the LXX has at Hosea 12:6 and Psalm 119:169 which in our English Bibles is translated "wait on the Lord" or "come near the Lord." Both passages are dealing with prayer.

[66] The converse of this is also true, and it is a sobering fact to consider! Resist God, and He will depart from you. Attempt to get close to the devil and he will draw nigh to you. If we persist in hostility to God, he will judicially harden the heart, and eventually He will withdraw His gracious aid (God "gave them up," Romans 1:24,26,28).

Someone has suggested drawing near to God daily in three ways. Let the Lord speak to you every day by reading His word for 15 minutes. Speak to the Lord 15 minutes every day in prayer. Speak to someone about the Lord for 15 minutes every day.

classed as "sinners" (Luke 15:1) by the Pharisees.[67] James may well be saying to his readers, "What the Judaizers have been telling you does not make a man a 'sinner.' It is friendship with the world that actually makes a man a 'sinner' in the sight of God." For the Christian who has sinned, what will assure clean hands[68] is repentance and confession of his or her sins to God, in order that they may be covered and cleansed by the blood of Christ (1 John 1:7-9; Acts 8:22). Once forgiven, self-control must be practiced in order that evil deeds done by the hands may be done no more. James addresses his readers as "sinners" (*hamartōloi*), a sharp word intended to stab the conscience of each reader. Half-hearted Christians and those flirting with the pleasures of this world need to hear this assessment by an apostle of what their state really is. The word is very rare in secular Greek, and in the Old Testament it has the idea of "hardened sinner," "evil man."

Purify your hearts, you double-minded – The "double-minded" person (see 1:8) is the person who gladly supposes he or she can serve God and the world.[69] Their eager quest for pleasure (4:1) has resulted in sins of hand and heart, of thoughts and motives[70]. Just as the Psalmist (Psalms 24:4) and the Old Testament prophet included in "repentance" a change of mind and a change of action (Isaiah 55:7), so James calls not only for repentance in action but also for repentance for thoughts about friendship with the world.[71] The "heart" (motives and thoughts) is purified by quenching of unholy desires and by the cultivation of Godly thoughts and motives (Philippians 4:8). The verb translated "purify" is the same root as the adjective James used at 3:17, a "chastity" or "purity" of heart and life. Some suppose James uses it here with special contrast to the "adulteresses" in verse 4, though the meaning of the word is broad enough to cover what is implied in "double-minded" in this verse.[72] Paul called for bringing every thought into subjection to the will of Christ (2 Corinthians 10:5).

---

[67] The epithet "sinners" was used with disdain by the Pharisees to describe all who did not make any attempt to observe all the petty traditions of the elders.

[68] Actually, it is more than "hands" that need to be cleansed. "Cleanse your hands" is a command to James' readers to make all their conduct holy.

[69] Some have appealed to James 4:2,3, saying the "sinner" would be the man who asks not, and the "double-minded" is the man who asks amiss.

[70] See notes at James 1:26 and 3:14 for explanation of the Biblical "heart."

[71] Just as Jesus insisted on cleansing the inside of the cup (Matthew 23:26), so James insists a man should not rest satisfied with a mere external reformation, with only a cleansing of the hands. It does no good to wash the outside of the cup, if you do not cleanse the inside. God does not stand for impurity in the heart, however clean a man's hands may be.

[72] The word "purify" is often used in the Bible to refer to ceremonial cleansing (cp. John 11:55), but it is used by Peter to describe the purification of the soul which results from the initial obedience to the truth of the gospel (1 Peter 1:22; Acts 15:9), and also by John in 1 John 3:3 to remind Christians who have sinned that they have a need to constantly purify themselves. Such is James' insistence, too. For the rewards of a pure heart, see Matthew 5:8 and Hebrews 12:14.

4:9 -- *Be miserable and mourn and weep: let your laughter be turned into mourning, and your joy into gloom.*

Be miserable and mourn and weep – The imperatives here in verse 9 are all different ways of calling a man to repentance. "Make yourselves miserable" or "wretched" points to a feeling of misery[73] (cp. Romans 7:24, "O wretched man that I am."). A beautiful picture is found in the sinner who beats his breast while imploring God, "Be merciful to me, the sinner" (Luke 18:13). "Mourn" describes the general effect on the whole demeanor when repentance is genuine.[74] Jesus promised, "Blessed are they that mourn, for they shall be comforted" (Matthew 5:4; Luke 6:20-26). "Weep" describes the flowing of tears as the penitent's brokenheartedness over sin gives visible expression to itself.[75] Peter gave such an emotional expression of his feeling of shame over his denial of Jesus (Mark 14:72).

Let your laughter be turned into mourning – Folk who have no sense of the gravity and seriousness of sin tend to laugh at their sin. James commands that such a light and frivolous spirit where sin is concerned[76] must cease to be part of his readers' lifestyles. That will only happen when they understand their sins are a terrible affront to God, and when godly sorrow for sins leads them to repentance.[77] A synonym for repentance is to "turn" or "turn around" and go the other way.[78]

And your joy into gloom – Folk indulging in sin may claim, "It doesn't get any better than

---

[73] This verb *talaipōreō* does not refer to beating and flailing the body, as some monks did in the Middle Ages. James is not calling for ascetic practices, or for a voluntary abstinence from all comforts and luxuries. The verb is used of the feeling of dejection experienced by an army whose food has run out and who have no shelter from the stormy weather, and is therefore appropriate to describe how a sensitive Christian feels when sin rears its ugly head.

[74] "Mourn" (*pentheō*) expresses a passionate grief that cannot be hidden. It is behavior one sees at a funeral as folk grieve over what they feel they have lost. Such mourning over sins can be done without wearing any special clothing or other marks made on the body (i.e., literal "sackcloth and ashes"). The attempts of some to use this verse to justify the "mourner's bench" is also wresting it from its context.

[75] The verb *klauō* can be translated "wail," and is the word used of Jesus "weeping" over Jerusalem (Luke 19:41). It is the kind of cry torn from the heart when one laments the dead.

[76] Laughter that is a gift of God (Job 8:21; Psalm 126:2) is not prohibited. And there is a proper laughter that follows repentance (Luke 6:21). It is a flippant attitude toward sin that James condemns, just as Jesus pronounced woe on those whose laughter revealed an ignorance of their own true condition and standing before God (Luke 6:25).

[77] James is not advocating "mourning" as a religious exercise on certain, regular, stated occasions. Rather, anytime sin has been allowed to enter a man's life is an appropriate moment for repentance and mourning over the sin.

[78] The verb form used here (*metatrapētō*) occurs only here in the New Testament. The Textus Receptus has a form of the more familiar verb for "change" (*metastraphētō*).

this!" This is a false joy, a boisterous, lighthearted attitude towards sin. "Gloom" (*katēpheia*) is a downcast look. It is the word used of the publican in Luke 18:13. He was ashamed of his sin, and therefore refused to look up as he asked God for forgiveness (cp. Psalm 40:12; Ezra 9:6).[79] So James' readers are commanded in dramatic terms to repent because they have not been true to their pledge.

VIII. HUMBLY ACKNOWLEDGES THE LORDSHIP OF JESUS CHRIST. 4:10-17

> *Summary*: James calls for deliberate and thoughtful recognition of the Lordship of Jesus Christ. He gives two examples of the kind of wrong behavior which will cease if such lordship is acknowledged. One has to do with judging our brothers; the other has to do with how we make plans for the future.

4:10 -- *Humble yourselves in the presence of the Lord, and He will exalt you.*

Humble yourselves in the presence of the Lord – Unlike the paragraphing in many of our versions, we have chosen to begin a new paragraph and a new topic with this verse.[1] Some concrete examples of how a Christian goes about humbly acknowledging the lordship of Jesus follow the opening command. Since Jesus has risen and ascended and been enthroned at the right hand of the Father, He is Lord.[2] Unlike what the Pharisaic Judaizers did who repudiated Jesus as Lord, one of the marks of a genuine Christian is to acknowledge the lordship of Jesus Christ. That, we believe, is exactly what James is now urging on his readers. One does not have to go around saying "Anathema Jesus!" to be guilty of repudiating His lordship. It can just as surely be done in the subtle ways James is about to call attention to. To encourage them to humble themselves, he even reminds them that Jesus is watching what they do.[3] Perhaps the aorist passive *tapeinōthēte* has the

---

[79] Once more, let it be stated that James is not expressing the view that "mourning and gloom" are to be the constant characteristic behavior of the Christian. But mourning and repentance are proper behavior on those occasions when sin has marred a person's friendship with God.

[1] Verse 10 has been treated by some as the conclusion of the paragraph that began in 4:1, with the aorist imperative "humble yourself" included as another of the series of imperatives that began in verse 7. It can even be argued that verse 10 makes a promise to the people who will repent, just as blessings were promised in verse 6 and verse 8.

[2] God has demonstrated to the whole world that Jesus is both Lord and Messiah (Acts 2:32-36). Recall what James has already written about the Lord Jesus Christ at James 1:1 and 2:1.

[3] *Enōpion* can be translated "in the sight of" or "before (in the presence of)." If we prefer the latter translation, the picture is that of bowing down because we recognize that when we are in Jesus' presence, we are in the presence of ineffable majesty.

sense of a middle voice, and what James is asking for is voluntary submission, voluntary humility, voluntary acknowledgment of Jesus as Lord.[4]

And He will exalt you – Perhaps as James writes about humbling yourself and then being exalted, he is making another application of Proverbs 3:34 (verse 6). If so, then we have a statement of Jesus' deity, for verse 6 spoke of God, whereas this paragraph speaks of the Lord Jesus. Perhaps James here reproduces the teaching of Jesus Himself, who said, "Everyone who humbles himself shall be exalted" (Luke 14:11, 18:14; Matthew 23:12).[5] Philippians 2:5-11 tells how Jesus humbled Himself and was then highly exalted by God with this purpose in mind – that at the name of Jesus every knee should bow, and that every tongue should confess that Jesus Christ is Lord to the glory of the Father. Ultimately, the promise of being exalted includes the blessings of heaven, after He has healed the brokenhearted penitent and covered his sins and given him a new start in this life. He will wipe away your tears, remove your sadness of heart, fill you with joy, and clothe you with garments of salvation. Two things a man can do in everyday life that will demonstrate he acknowledges the lordship of Jesus are to stop speaking against his brother (verses 11-12), and stop being pretentious when making future plans (verses 13-17).

4:11 -- *Do not speak against one another, brethren. He who speaks against a brother, or judges his brother, speaks against the law, and judges the law; but if you judge the law, you are not a doer of the law, but a judge* of it.

Do not speak against one another, brethren – Here is one simple and practical test to determine whether or not a person recognizes and humbly submits to Jesus' lordship,[6] as verse 10 calls for. James is not addressing a new class of readers (cp. 2:1 and 3:1).[7] The Greek construction is the one that prohibits the continuance of an action already going on.

---

[4] Those who take it as passive will comment in this fashion: When a person becomes conscious that he is in the ineffable presence of the Lord, he will be humbled by the experience. The next thing one hears is a confession of sinfulness, just as Peter spoke, "Depart from me, for I am a sinful man, O Lord" (Luke 5:8); or just as Isaiah said, "Woe is me! I am undone because I am a man of unclean lips, and I dwell in the midst of a people of unclean lips: for mine eyes have seen the King, the Lord of Hosts" (Isaiah 6:5).

[5] In 1 Peter 5:5,6 there is an almost exact parallel to the language James uses. The same Old Testament passage is alluded to, and the same application is made, by both apostles.

[6] Moffatt in his *The New Testament: A New Translation*, moves verses 11 and 12 to a spot immediately following James 2:13, "to what [in his opinion] seems to have been its original place." This rearrangement of the text, typical of Moffatt, has no manuscript support, and results from a misunderstanding of the point James is making.

[7] Some have supposed the "brethren" here in verse 11 are not in any way to be identified with "you adulteresses" (verse 4), or "you sinners" (verse 8), or "you double-minded" (verse 8). Rather, they believe "brethren" indicates the coming rebuke is the result of unbrotherly conduct. Some are reminded of Moses' rebuke of the Israelites, "Sirs, you are brothers; why do you wrong one another?" (Acts 7:26).

"Stop speaking against one another!" The reciprocal construction "one another" indicates the practice of speaking against was not all one-sided. The defamed turned right around and spoke against their defamers. To backbite, to defame, to speak evil of a Christian brother[8] is straightforward evidence of disobedience to one of the rules laid down by the Lord. James perhaps alludes to what Jesus said in the Sermon on the Mount, "Do not judge lest you be judged *yourselves*" (Matthew 7:1, 1960 NASB).[9] Peter likewise condemns this sin (1 Peter 2:1).

> Faultfinding, the censorious temper, is utterly unchristian. It means that we have been paying an amount of attention to the conduct of others which would have been better bestowed upon our own. It means that we have been paying attention, not in order to help, but in order to criticize, and criticize unfavorably. It shows, moreover, that we have a very inadequate estimate of our own frailty and shortcomings. If we knew how worthy of blame we ourselves are, we should be much less ready to deal out blame to others.[10]

Rather than telling everyone else first about some fault we think we have seen, it would be more in line with Jesus' teaching to go to the brother first, and talk to him about the possible fault (Matthew 18:16-18).

He who speaks against a brother, or judges his brother – James seems to be saying that in the process of "speaking against"[11] a brother (a fellow Christian), the slanderer is in fact

---

[8] Usually *katalaleō* means to speak critical words about those who are absent, to talk another down. This evil of talking against others – against their actions, their motives, their manner of living, their families – is one of the most common things in the world. Some English versions read "do not slander," but "slander" means to make false charges or misrepresentations that damage a person's reputation. *Katalaleō* is a broader term covering any kind of speaking against. What is said may be true in its content, but the manner of presenting the information is harsh and unkind and perhaps hypocritical. See Kittel, who shows the point is not the falsity of what is said but rather the uncharitable way it is spoken (TDNT 4:4).

[9] Jesus' prohibition is not a prohibition of all judging. If it were, a mechanic could not fix our car because he dares not judge that anything is wrong with it. The doctor would not be able to make a diagnosis (judgment) that a man is sick. We cannot help but judge many things. The same chapter that says "Judge not!" also says "so then you will know them by their fruits" (Matthew 7:20). There are times when Christian duty calls us to judge. We cannot help but come to conclusions about certain things or people because of what we see or hear. Paul could pass judgment on the Judaizers (Galatians 1:6ff, 2:4, 5:4). The civil judge must decide on matters. The church elders must judge in certain matters. What Jesus prohibited was the passing of hypocritical, condemnatory judgments. If it is our lot to pass judgment on someone, let us be fair in our judgment. Give the condemned an opportunity to face his accuser and defend against the accusations before judgment is passed. Let us be sure we have the facts, not rumors. And be sure not to judge in matters of conscience or opinion (Romans 14-15).

[10] Plummer, *op. cit.*, p.616.

[11] The present participle indicates continuing action. The defamatory speech was characteristic or habitual.

passing judgment[12] on the brother, and at the same time showing rebellion and disobedience to the Lord.[13]

Speaks against the law, and judges the law – This is the first of two reasons why James condemns such "speaking against a brother." It is a breaking of the royal law (James 2:8), a transgression of the "law of liberty" (James 1:25, 2:12).[14] Unchristian judging of and talking down of a brother is not merely a transgression of the royal law; it is also a setting oneself above the law, as though that law were a mistake, or so defective as not to apply to the "superior" one doing the criticizing.

But if you judge the law, you are not a doer of the law, but a judge *of it* – By using "you" (second person singular), James confronts each of his readers individually. Whoever among them condemns a law assumes that he or she is in possession of some higher principle by which he sits in judgment of it, tests it, finds it wanting, and sets it aside. Well, James might ask, "What is that superior rule?" It turns out that it is the critic's own arrogance and self-confidence. When James states that such critics are not "doers of the law,"[15] there is a bad connotation, especially when we are reminded that only "doers of law" are justified (James 2:23ff; Romans 2:13). It is a denial of the lordship of Jesus to presume that any of us humans know better than He the principles by which men are to live.

4:12 -- *There is **only** one Lawgiver and Judge, the One who is able to save and to destroy; but who are you who judge your neighbor?*

---

[12] Again the present participle pictures continuous action.

[13] We do not discern a significant difference between the manuscript reading represented in the KJV ("and judges his brother") and the reading represented by the NASB "(or judges his brother").

[14] In comments earlier we identified the teaching of Jesus and the "law of liberty" and the "royal law" as being rather synonymous expressions designating the same body of truth. Though there is no definite article before "law" in the Greek, it is obvious that it is divine law that is in question, law laid down by the Lord Himself. It hardly refers to law in general for Kittel (*ibid.*) indicates that this evil was not stressed "in the ethical exhortations of the non-biblical world," and that "even the vice lists in the Stoics and Philo do not contain it." It also does not refer to the Law of Moses. Several commentators picture the one "speaking against the law" as emphasizing the truth that the Law of Moses was temporary and nailed to the cross, while James takes the position the Law is still binding on Christians. But this interpretation does not agree with the use of the word "law" elsewhere by James, nor with the usual meaning of "speak against" (which is malicious criticism), and would make James contradict the rest of the New Testament writers, who unanimously teach the temporary nature of the Law.

[15] The Greek *poiētēs nomou*, translated "doers of the law," could also be translated "makers of the law." In classical Greek, in fact, this is the phrase used for "lawgiver." However, we think "doer of the law" is the correct translation, for James uses a different expression for "lawgiver" in the next verse.

There is _only_ one Lawgiver and Judge[16] – Verse 12 is the second of two reasons why James condemns speaking against a brother. It is wrong because it requires sitting in judgment of the law, but it also wrong because one must presume to be Lawgiver and Judge,[17] and that is usurping the prerogatives of Jesus.[18] All this is the exact opposite of humble submission to His lordship. One who sits in judgment of His laws must presume to be a greater lawgiver than Jesus.[19] That's not right! Nor can any mere man carry out the sentence of salvation or destruction that ultimately attaches to the laws the Lord has made.

The One who is able to save and to destroy – James here has strikingly similar language to something Jesus said one day (Luke 12:4,5), "And I say unto you my friends, do not be afraid of those who kill the body, and after that have no more that they can do. But I will warn you whom to fear: Fear the One who after he has killed has authority to cast into hell; yes, I tell you, fear Him!" Both "save"[20] and "destroy"[21] refer to the final state. When Jesus pronounces judgment, He is able to carry it out. That shows He is the one all-

---

[16] Because the words "and Judge" are not found in the manuscripts behind the Textus Receptus, they are not found in the KJV either.

[17] The numeral "one" is the subject of the verb "is" rather than a numeral describing the predicate nominative "Lawgiver and Judge." There is emphasis on the uniqueness of this "One." "_Only_ one" does not suggest there are to be no human legislators who can make laws for society or no human judges who deal with infractions of civil law. James is affirming there is "only One" whose laws are of permanent significance and whose judgments are of eternal validity, "only One" who is Lord of life and death. Rather than ruling out civil law and judges, James is trying to rule out harsh, unkind, critical attitudes that continually search out and find fault with their brothers and then delights to broadcast these faults.

[18] Some commentators discuss whether the reference in "Lawgiver and Judge" is to God the Father or to Jesus Christ. Jesus is the one through whom God has spoken to this age (Hebrews 1:1-3), and Jesus is designated as the Judge who acts in the Father's interests.

[19] Plummer (_op. cit._, p.617) calls attention to the fact that usurpation of Divine prerogatives is an approach to sin that brought about the fall of the angels. It is a sin that by its very temper is diabolical, for is it not Satan's special delight to be the "accuser of the brethren" (Revelation 12:10)?

[20] Because of our sins, we deserve nothing but eternal punishment. Yet, because of the sacrifice for sins made at Calvary, Jesus is a Judge who can pardon. He can justify the one who is faithful to what has been revealed to men by their Creator. Perhaps there is also the idea that Jesus is able to save those brothers whom the critics have been condemning.

[21] Jesus is a Judge who can send a man to hell if that man refuses to humble himself and submit to the Lordship of Christ. Perhaps there is also included the idea that Jesus is able to condemn, and carry out the proposed punishment of the very man who has set himself up to judge others.

(A few have supposed that "destroy" is a word that teaches the annihilation of the wicked. However, when the use of _apollumi_ is studied, its occurrence at 2 Peter 3:6 indicates that the word does not necessarily either include or exclude the idea of annihilation. The present tense verb "burn" at John 15:6 and the description of torment and lack of rest forever at Revelation 14:11 cause this commentator to reject the doctrine of annihilation of the wicked.)

powerful Lawgiver and law enforcer. He can save those who habitually keep the law He has given; He can punish those who habitually violate His law.

But who are you who judge your neighbor?[22] – In the original, there is emphasis on the "you." "Who are *you*?"[23] Compared with the majesty and power and wisdom of the Lord Jesus, man is weak and frail and erring. Whatever possesses a man to think he can habitually judge and find fault[24] with his neighbor? In fact, both the judge and his neighbor must stand before the judgment seat of Christ. Will Christ find you, the judge, more righteous than the neighbor you are judging and talking down?

4:13 -- *Come now, you who say, "Today or tomorrow, we shall go to such and such a city, and spend a year there and engage in business and make a profit."*

Come now – Here comes a second simple test by which a person may ascertain whether or not he or she regularly acknowledges the lordship of Jesus. "Come now!" is a vigorous form of address that serves to attract attention.[25] The construction occurs nowhere else in the New Testament except here and at James 5:1, and it does occur in the LXX at Judges 19:6 and 2 Kings 4:24.

You who say – The participle is present tense in the Greek, and pictures habitual or continuous action. The fault can be spoken in our hearts (as we are making our plans), or spoken out loud (as we tell others about our plans). This test of our attitude about the lordship of Jesus deals with the habit of planning for the future with no thought of what the Lord Jesus might or will for them to do. "What would Jesus have me do?" never comes into the decision-making process.

"Today or tomorrow, we shall go to such and such a city, and spend a year there and engage in business and make a profit" – These statements vividly relate all the details they have planned.[26] "Today or tomorrow" is the exact day the fortune hunter will pull

---

[22] The proper reading here is "your neighbor" rather than "another" like the Textus Receptus reads. "Neighbor" calls to memory the law of love cited in James 2:8 as well as the memorable story of the Good Samaritan, which Jesus told to explain what the Lawgiver intended when He gave the law about "loving your neighbor as yourself."

[23] The NIV's "But you -- who are you?" tries to catch the force of the Greek construction.

[24] The participle is present tense in the original, suggesting continuing and repeated action.

[25] Originally it was an imperative singular, but over time it became an adverb that can be used when any number of persons is addressed. When used with an object, the verb *agō* usually means to "lead (by laying hold of)," "bear," "carry off," or "bring"; when used intransitively, it can mean "go" or "depart." "See here!" may be an English expression that captures the idea of the Greek idiom.

[26] The frequent conjunctions which separate the different items of the plan give us the picture of the steps of the whole plan being recited one by one, with complete confidence and satisfaction.

up stakes and move.[27] "We shall go" implies a fixed certainty in their plans. "Into this city here," they say, as if they were pointing out the exact city on a map. "We shall spend a year" fixes the exact time they planned to be living in the new place. "Make a profit" is the object of the journey, and of that profit they are confident, too! James' picture is very true to first-century life. Already in the first century AD, traders and businessmen were travelling to far away places where business could be conducted. New cities were being started, and often their founders looked for folk to occupy them, enticing them with offers of free land and citizenship. Roman peace and Roman roads helped facilitate such activities. The people migrating to such places included Christians.[28] Folk seeking a quick fortune can do some crazy and irrational and even illegal things.[29] The lure of quick riches is a powerful temptation, yielding to which can cause even Christians to temporarily forget their obligations to Jesus, their Lord. Recall that Jesus condemned such far-reaching plans for the future in the parable of the Rich Fool (Luke 12:16-21). The folk in Jesus' story and in James' mind are acting as if they could arrange their own lives, as if they were masters of their own destiny. Such an attitude is not compatible with the truth of the lordship of Jesus.

4:14 -- *Yet you do not know what your life will be like tomorrow. You are* just *a vapor that appears for a little while and then vanishes away.*

Yet you do not know what your life will be like tomorrow[30] – The marginal reading for "Yet you do not know" shows the Greek (*oitines ouk epistasthe*) literally means, 'since you are people of such a nature as not to know.' "What your life will be (like)" is *poia hē zōē humōn*, 'what sort the life of you [will be].'   What is its kind?   What is its nature?   We

---

[27] The manuscripts vary between "today or tomorrow" and "today and tomorrow." The latter reading pictures a two-day journey – today we set out and tomorrow we arrive.

[28] Remember Priscilla and Aquila. They lived at Rome and at Corinth (Acts 18:1,2), then at Ephesus (Acts 18:18), then back in Rome (Romans 16:3), and then back in Ephesus (2 Timothy 4:19). Certainly, Christians may travel on business as did this Christian couple, but care must be exercised that the Lord's will is considered before travel plans are finalized. Everywhere they went, Priscilla and Aquila were vitally involved in evangelism and church planting and other kingdom activities.

[29] Recall how folk have behaved when gold has been discovered, and there is a rush to stake out a claim, or to take advantage of those who have found riches on their claims.

[30] It is not easy to determine what the original text of James was at this place. The text we choose will affect the meaning we find in the verse. The issues that must be decided include:
- Do we include a neuter singular article before "tomorrow," or a plural article, or no article at all?
- Is there a "for" in the middle of the verse?
- How to punctuate the whole phrase? Shall we put a period or a question mark after "tomorrow" or should we read it as all one phrase?

The KJV presents one possible reading: "You know not what [singular article] shall be on the morrow. For what is your life? It is even a vapour ...." The NIV follows the same text the KJV does, and Metzger (*op. cit.*, p.684) argued it is supported by a wide variety of witnesses. Some object to the NASB reading since it has a built-in inconsistency: it implies we'll be alive tomorrow, but we do not know what the day will bring. Ropes (*op. cit.*, p.278) argues the point is not what the conditions of life will be tomorrow, but whether we will still be alive tomorrow. Whichever way we read it, the general idea is not in doubt.

human beings, whose lives are so full of changes and surprises, are not able to know or predict with certainty even what today will bring, let alone what tomorrow will bring. How foolish, then, to leave out of our plans what the Lord is doing in His world and in our lives. If James' readers were familiar with their Old Testament Scriptures, they likely would have known Proverbs 27:1, "Do not boast about tomorrow, for you do not know what a day may bring forth."

You are *just* a vapor that appears for a little while and then vanishes away[31] – "Vapor" might be the steam that comes from the spout of a teakettle, or the smoke that rises from a fire, or the mist that rises from a body of water, or the white breath exhaled on a cold day. Any one of these does not last long. "Appears" and "vanishes" are both present tense, denoting something that occurs regularly. If life is like a vapor, how foolish to assume we have another year or even day to live! All the profit-seeker's plans depended, of course, on the assumption they had at least a year longer to live. That may be assuming too much. Who can calculate how long a vapor will last? Who can build any solid hopes on the mist? Psalm 90:9-12 is a good commentary on this verse. Verse 9 tells us that "we finish our years with a sigh." How fleeting this makes it. Verse 10 reminds us "the days of our life, they contain seventy years; or if due to strength, eighty years, yet their pride is but labor and sorrow; for it is soon gone, and we fly away." Verse 11 calls attention to God's anger and wrath. Verse 12 gives a wise exhortation in view of all this, "So teach us to number our days, that we may present to Thee a heart of wisdom." There is no wisdom in leaving the Lord out of our plans for the future!

4:15 -- *Instead,* you ought *to say, "If the Lord wills, we shall live and also do this or that."*

Instead – Instead of saying something like verse 13 records the profit-seekers as saying, instead of simply assuming the future, instead of making plans with no thought of what the Lord in His providence may do to our work or lives, here is what our attitudes should be.

***You ought* to say, "If the Lord wills"** – There is no word for "ought" in the Greek, but the English rightly expresses the idea in the articular infinitive, a construction that expresses purpose. The person who is aware of the Lordship of Jesus Christ will take His wishes and His plans into account as thought is given to the future. Regularly, he says in his heart, and sometimes in spoken word, "If the Lord wills."[32] Jesus Christ is "Lord" (see James 1:1,7,12; 2:1). He is the One moving history to its goal (Hebrews 1:3). Jesus has

---

[31] Some manuscripts read "it is" (*esti*) or "it will be" (*estai*) rather than "you are" (*este*).

[32] The verb *thelēsē* is an aorist subjunctive after *ean*. It is one of the regular ways a conditional sentence was worded in ancient Greek. Though it is an aorist tense, the "willing" is pictured as being yet in the future, for outside the indicative, tense indicates only kind (not time) of action. By the very nature of the verb form, subjunctives and imperatives and optatives all refer to action in the future.

Theologians who use this verse as a proof text for fatalism, as though the Lord has already decided all events sometime in the past, are mistaken. Nor is this proof that the sovereignty of God rules out the existence of a man's free will. "If the Lord wills" leaves open the question of what His will may be in a specific situation. But whatever He decides, the believer accepts it, knowing the Lord has his ultimate good in mind.

a "will." There are things He wants to happen in His world, and those things Jesus wills are in complete harmony with what the Father wills (Romans 12:2). We use the term 'providence' to designate God's everyday care and preservation and government of His creation so that it accomplishes the purposes for which He made it. Since all authority in heaven and earth has been granted to Jesus, He is the One Who is in charge of the everyday providential ruling of God's world. The Lord's hand is guiding history, though there are times when it may not seem like it. The Lord's hand is on our daily lives. The world may talk about chance and luck, but the Christian knows it is not just chance and luck, but that the hand of the Lord is gently supporting and helping and disciplining, if need be.[33]

We are to take into account what the Lord wills as we make our plans, but how can we ascertain what the will of the Lord is? How can a man know the will of the Lord? Three things are taken into account: (1) the Word of God, (2) man's inner desire, and (3) the trend of circumstances (Acts 1:20-26). The Word of God of course rules out anything that is unlawful or ill-gotten. It also directs Jesus' followers to seek first the Kingdom of God, to make it their aim to so think and act that the Kingdom of God will be advanced. Men can see which way the Lord is pointing. They can see the trend of circumstances after they have spent time in prayer talking to God about the whole matter.

As a word of caution, readers of this verse must be careful lest we follow the letter of this instruction, while at the same time losing its spirit.[34] We need not pepper every spoken statement we make about some future event with phrases like "If the Lord wills," or "Please God," or make regular use of the initials "D.V." (*deo volente*, Latin for "if God wills) in all our correspondence.[35] It would be better not to use the words at all than to mouth them when they do not express the real thoughts of our hearts. The idea behind what James writes is that we speak these words because they represent what is really in our hearts, namely, that we remember that first and foremost we need to spend our time and energies for the Lord in a wise way. We must remember that we cannot escape His Lordship and we cannot live independently of the Lord's will.

"We shall live and also do this or that"[36] – Paul, as he made his future plans, gives us several instances when he recognizes that the Lord may overrule where he has planned to go. Concerning a possible trip to Corinth, Paul says he will come shortly "if the Lord wills" (1 Corinthians 4:19), and a possible long visit in Corinth after he arrives depends on

---

[33] Recall how Paul worded this same idea in his speech on Mars' Hill (Acts 17:24-28).

[34] As in much of the Sermon on the Mount, we have here "a principle given in the form of a rule. Rules are given that they may be observed literally. Principles are given that they may be applied intelligently and observed according to their spirit." (Plummer, *op. cit.*, p.619)

[35] See verses cited in the next paragraph. Paul at times used the phrase, and other times he did not use it. In both kinds of examples, whether he actually said it or not, we would affirm that he was aware that providence was at work in his life and that his plans were conditioned on what the Lord willed.

[36] There is a manuscript variation at this place. The Textus Receptus reads "If the Lord will, and we live, we will do this or that." The better manuscripts have both life and action to be something within the purview of the Lord's will.

whether or not "the Lord permits" (1 Corinthians 16:7).[37]   At a later date, Paul's hope to send Timothy to Philippi and his hope of visiting Philippi himself also rested squarely "in the Lord" (Philippians 2:19,24).   But he did not use the phrase mechanically.   He did not literally "say it" when he wrote Acts 19:21, Romans 15:28, or 1 Corinthians 16:5, 8. "Providence cannot be neglected and it cannot be defeated," Tasker reminds us.[38]   Only the ones who keep foremost in their minds what Jesus wants are those who can be said to recognize His Lordship.

4:16 -- *But as it is, you boast in your arrogance; all such boasting is evil.*

But as it is – Perhaps there is a contrast between what they ought to say (verse 15) and what they actually are saying.

You boast in your arrogance – "Boast" (*kauchasthe*) means to talk like a braggart.   "The verb *kauchaomai* followed by the preposition *en* ("in") occurs in sixteen other passages, and in every instance the prepositional phrase expresses the ground or reason for boasting."[39]   James is identifying the attitude behind the saying recorded in verse 13. "Arrogance" (i.e., confidence in one's own knowledge or cleverness) is an attempt to translate *alazoneia*, a noun that occurs nowhere else in the New Testament save at 1 John 2:16 ("the *pride* of life").   The word was defined by Aristotle as being the character of a man who lays claim to what will bring him credit when the claim is either altogether false or grossly exaggerated.[40]   Some translations offer "vainglory" (i.e., a feeling of bliss that has no basis, a pretense that is hollow).   The attitude the word describes is the opposite of humbling oneself in the presence of the Lord.

All such boasting is evil – Some boasting is legitimate (see James 1:9 or Philippians 3:3 or Galatians 6:14), but not when the thing being boasted about is an empty confidence that all future planning of our lives is in our own hands.   To leave the Lord out of the plan is bad enough.   But to boast of leaving Him out is sinful.   "Evil" translates *poneros*, the synonym for evil that carries the idea not only of being evil itself, but of trying to get others to do evil.   It is the word used when the devil is called "the evil one."   It reminds us that the devil, the Lord's opponent, is the real source of "vainglory," for it is one of his typical characteristics.

4:17 -- *Therefore, to one who knows the right thing to do, and does not do it, to him it is sin.*

Therefore – "Therefore" shows that verse 17 is intended to be a conclusion from what has

---

[37] Paul could also make plans contingent on God's will (Acts 18:21; Romans 1:10; Hebrews 6:3).

[38] Tasker, *op. cit.*, p.103.

[39] Burdick, *op. cit.*, p.198.

[40] *Eth. Nicom.* iv.13.

just been said. While some think this verse is a conclusion to all that has been said thus far in this letter,[41] we tend to agree with the idea that this verse is a conclusion of this paragraph about humbling oneself in the presence of the Lord (verse 12). James may also be offering an explanation of why he called their boasting evil (verse 16).

To one who knows *the* right thing to do – James' readers did know better than to speak against one another. They did know better than to presume to make plans without considering the will of the Lord. They did know what was "right" (*kalon* speaks of morally excellent, praiseworthy, winsome behavior). Men, of course, learn what God says is right from God's own special revelation of His will and expectations. James' readers could have learned some from the Old Testament, such as Micah 6:8, "What does the Lord require ... and to walk humbly with your God?" James' readers have learned it from the teachings of Jesus as handed on by those who heard Him. James' readers prided themselves on their knowledge (James 1:19); they were professed hearers of the Word of God (James 1:22,23). Knowledge brings responsibility. The moment we know the will of the Lord, we are responsible to do it. The better we know and the more we understand, the greater our responsibility.

And does not do it – Both participles ("knows" and "does") are present tense, indicating continuing knowledge and a habitual failure to do.[42] Theologians have been accustomed to call this failure to do right "sins of omission." They use the corresponding expression "sins of commission" for the doing of what God says is wrong and has therefore prohibited. The one verse (1 John 3:4) that defines sin can refer either to sins of commission ("Sin is the transgression of the Law," KJV) or to sins of omission ("Sin is lawlessness," NASB), or both. There is something deliberate about both sins of omission and sins of commission. Both are deliberate violations of known duty.

To him it is sin – *Hamartanō* means to "miss the mark." There is more to a Christian's duty than avoiding the wrong. They are expected also to do the right. "To leave undone what we ought to have done is sin, even when there is no outward act that men call crime or vice."[43] Jesus warned what would happen to those servants who knew their master's will and neglected to do it (Luke 12:47). In the parable of the talents, the man who buried his one talent was not condemned because he was guilty of using it for an evil purpose. He

---

[41] It certainly is a truism concerning all the positive things James has commanded. But if it is intended to be a summary of all that is said, why put the verse here rather than at the end of the epistle? Moffatt, because he could see no connection between verses 16 and 17, boldly moved verse 17 to a place immediately following 2:26.

[42] All of us, on occasion, fail to do what we know is right. While that is not as it should be, such occasional acts are not what James is castigating. James is dealing with deliberate, continuous, habitual failure to act.

[43] Punchard, *op. cit.*, p. 104.

was condemned because he omitted to do something productive. In the parable of the Good Samaritan, the priest and the Levite are portrayed as "bad guys" precisely because they deliberately avoided doing something good for the wounded Samaritan. In the parable of the rich man and Lazarus, the rich man failed to do something good for the beggar at his gates, and his sin of omission cost him dearly. In the Sheep and Goat Judgment (Matthew 25:31ff), those condemned committed sins of omission; they failed to minister to their needy brethren. Sins of omission, such as failing to humble oneself in the presence of the Lord, will cause a man to be condemned just as quickly as sins of commission.[44]

---

[44] In Roman Catholic moral theology, there is a doctrine called "Probabalism." This doctrine teaches that in those cases where there is doubt concerning whether a certain act is allowable or not, the less safe course may be followed (with no sin attaching to it), even when the balance of probability is against its being allowable, if only there are some grounds for supposing it is allowable. This doctrine has done mischief, for it allows folk with strong desires and passions to gratify them without scruple. If James' maxim here in verse 17 had been listened to, such a doctrine would never have taken root. Another useful Scriptural antidote to the doctrine of probabalism is Romans 14:23, "whatsoever is not from faith is sin."

IX. EXHIBITS ENDURANCE AND PATIENCE WHEN FACING INJUSTICE. 5:1-11

Summary: In a world where men are sinners, there will be much social injustice. How are Christians to respond when they themselves are the victims? In language reminiscent of the thunderings of Old Testament prophets, James pronounces a warning on the oppressors. He then counsels his brethren who are suffering injustice to exhibit patience and endurance, closing with a word of encouragement drawn from the example of Job.

5:1 -- *Come now, you rich, weep and howl for your miseries which are coming upon you.*

Come now, you rich – James uses the same call for attention to start this new section that he used at 4:13. This new section is composed of two parts. The first 6 verses contain a ringing denunciation of some wicked and oppressive rich people. Then, verses 7-11 set forth the expected response when Christians are being treated unjustly; this section is tied to the verses that detail the oppression by a "therefore".

The chief question in the first six verses is whether "the rich" who are denounced and warned by James were Christians or not. As he denounces the rich in these verses, James employs two word pictures reminiscent of how the Old Testament prophets warned their wicked contemporaries about judgment to come. Often, in the midst of sections addressed to God's people, those Old Testament prophets would suddenly burst forth with prophetic declarations of coming judgment on those who oppressed God's people.[1] "It would not surprise us to find language [with strains of righteous indignation] like James uses in Isaiah or Jeremiah."[2] That said, we still prefer the view that James has in mind unbelieving Jews as the oppressors of his Christian "brethren."[3] If our hypothesis concern-

---

[1] Isaiah 13-21,23; Ezekiel 25-32; Habakkuk 2:9.

[2] Plummer, *op. cit.*, p.622. The Old Testament prophets denounced social injustice in fiery terms. Isaiah 10:1-4; Amos 5:1-33, 8:4-10; Micah 2:1-5; Malachi 3:1-5.   Barclay (*op. cit.*, p.137-139) has a chapter on "The Social Passion of the Bible," in which he states that "there is no other book which condemns dishonest and selfish wealth with such searing passion as the Bible does." And Barclay wonders how anyone who is aware of the denunciation of social wrongs and the calls to right such wrongs ever came to regard the Christian religion as the "opiate of the people."

[3] Jesus pronounced similar woe on the oppressive rich. In the parable of the rich man and Lazarus, it is the Pharisees who are portrayed as being like the uncaring rich man who "fared sumptuously every day" while Lazarus was laid at his gate full of sores and desperately hungry. See also Jesus' warning recorded in Matthew 23:34. In James 1:10ff, the "rich" referred to certainly seem to have been Christians. However, in 2:2 the "rich" was a non-Christian visitor to the assembly (church), and in 2:6 the "rich" who exploited the Christians appear to be non-Christians (Sadducees?). If in this passage James addresses some prophetic warning to the non-Christian rich who are facing the wrath of God because of their ill-gotten and ill-spent gain, it would not be the first time they have been in his thoughts. The "rich" in 5:1 are likely not the same business people traveling in quest of riches addressed in 4:13ff, and they are clearly distinguished from the "brethren" [named three times] in 5:7-11.

ing the occasion and date of the writing of James is correct, we picture James as expressing what will happen to the Pharisees (the Judaizers) who have troubled the churches, and the Sadducees who oppressed the poor generally. James is responding to the Judaizers who have set forth some "marks" they say identify a man of God (viz., circumcision and keeping the Law of Moses). James is using them as a foil, saying the marks of a genuine Christian are quite different from the grasping, selfish, exploitive behavior of those men.

Weep and howl – In this language of prophetic denunciation, there may be an implied call to repentance,[4] and if so, there should be no delaying the repentance. Assuming their unrepentance, James vividly pictures what the rich will be doing shortly. "Weep" (*klaiō*) is used to describe audible weeping when tears of anguish are being shed, such as wailing for the dead (Luke 7:13,32; John 11:31-33). This sobbing and bitter weeping results from a feeling of being overwhelmed when they realize everything they valued is gone. "Howl" (*ololuzontes*) is onomatopoetic, imitating a cry or shriek or howl of anguish.[5] As the shriek is uttered it gives voice to the frantic terror of those who are suddenly aware they are facing the wrath of God (Isaiah 13:6, 14:31, 15:2,3, 16:7, 23:1, 65:14). The present participle "howl," following the verb "weep," pictures their sobs being repeatedly punctuated with shrieks of agony. James is not denouncing all rich men indiscriminately merely for being rich. As the following verses will show clearly, he denounces those who are guilty of getting their riches in an evil way, who hoard their riches while never trying to help the poor, and who waste their riches on selfish, wasteful luxuries and pleasures. While it is hard for rich men to enter the Kingdom of God (Matthew 20:23), rich men who are good stewards of what God has entrusted to them are nowhere denounced in Scripture.

For your miseries which are coming upon you – The punishment the oppressive rich will shortly experience will leave them "weeping and howling." It is likely James has in his immediate view the AD 70 destruction of Jerusalem which brought with it the disruption of the whole Jewish economy. During His earthly ministry, Jesus had warned this destruction was coming. When James writes, it is less than 20 years in the future. In true prophetic manner, James speaks of the miseries almost as if they were a present reality,

---

[4] Calvin and Reformed theologians generally fail to see in this passage a call to repentance, but only a denunciation of woe. In the sense, however, that all prophecy, whether evil or good, is conditional, there is room to believe that no irrevocable doom is being pronounced on the rich by James. Did not Jonah say "40 days and Nineveh shall be destroyed!" with the implied condition, "unless you repent." If the rich James is addressing are past any opportunity to repent, it is because they have hardened their hearts, and God in turn judicially hardened them. It is not a Biblical doctrine that some individuals are predestined to be lost no matter what they do.

[5] In classical Greek the word was used both of cries of jubilation as well as wails of grief or pain. In the LXX the word occurs only as an expression of violent grief or a howl of distress.

for come they will.[6]   God has spoken! The wealthy classes suffered terribly[7] after AD 70. Those Jews who were friendly to Rome and who hid behind Roman authority and influence as Rome oppressed their Jewish countrymen became the objects of the fanatical fury of the Zealots.   Though Rome's blow fell first and heaviest upon the Jews in Jerusalem and Judea, it was eventually felt by Jews throughout the Roman Empire (many of whom had come to Jerusalem for Passover and were caught in the siege that preceded the fall of the city).   And temporal punishment is not the end of the punishment of the wicked.   It can also be said that "miseries" ultimately includes a reference to hell's torments.

5:2 -- *Your riches have rotted and your garments have become moth-eaten.*

Your riches have rotted – Beginning with this verse, James lists four crimes the rich have committed and for which punishment is assuredly coming: hoarded wealth (verses 2-3), unpaid wages (verse 4), luxury and self-indulgence (verse 5), and condemnation and murder (verse 6).   As he charges the rich with hoarding their wealth, James seems to reference three different forms in which Eastern people could accumulate wealth. "Rotted" pictures something which grows rotten, moldy, and decayed.   Thus, "riches" likely refers to perishable products like grain and oil; such foodstuffs will spoil when stored and left unused over a period of time.[8]   The rich accumulated more than they needed for their own use.   Instead of distributing such wealth in order to do good to others, or employing the surplus in any useful way, they kept them until they rotted or spoiled.[9]

And your garments have become moth-eaten – Silk, linen and wool "garments" or "changes of clothing" in the East were a second form of wealth, and are often mentioned in the Bible side by side with silver and gold (e.g., Acts 20:33, "I coveted no man's silver, or gold, or apparel").[10]   They could be "used as a means of payment, given as presents, or handed down as heirlooms."[11]   Because they represented a very considerable portion of a

---

[6] The present participle seems to picture the miseries as already approaching and about to fall on them.

[7] The verb form for "miseries" was used at 4:9 to express all-out repentance.   Here it is the "misery" that will be felt when the unrepentant come upon devastating hard times.

[8] Jesus, in the Parable of the Rich Fool, speaks of vast quantities of grain being stored (Luke 12:16-20).

[9] A suitable provision for use in time to come is not forbidden.   But the reference here is to cases in which great quantities had been laid up and selfishly hoarded till they became useless, and this even when the poor were suffering and in need.

[10] See Matthew 22:11,12, where it is implied that the wedding clothes were provided for the king's guests.

[11] Tasker, *op. cit.*, p.110.   Barclay (*ibid.*) tells us "Joseph gave changes of garments to his brothers (Genesis 45:22).   It was for a garment that Achan brought disaster on the nation and death on himself and his family (Joshua 7:21).   It was changes of garments that Samson promised to anyone who would solve his riddle (Judges 14:12).   It was garments that Naaman brought as a gift to the prophet of Israel, and to obtain which garments Gehazi sinned (2 Kings 5:5,22).   See also Job 13:28."

man's possessions, the rich people James denounces have stored them away, left them unused, only to find that moths have preyed upon them and ruined them.[12]   What once represented great riches is now practically worthless.   This and the following verse call to mind the words of Jesus who counseled his followers to lay up treasures in heaven, "where moth and rust does not corrupt ..." (Matthew 6:19-20).

5:3 -- *Your gold and silver have rusted; and their rust will be a witness against you and will consume your flesh like fire.   It is in the last days that you have stored up your treasure!*

Your gold and silver have rusted – Precious metals were the third form of wealth in the ancient world.   The precious metals themselves do not corrode or become oxidized when exposed to the air, but the base alloy which was mixed with the precious metal to make coins does, and when it occurs we say the metal is "tarnished."[13]   In the ancient world, the gold and silver which anyone possessed was hidden in some secret place where its owner thought it would be safe.   There were no banks with safe-deposit vaults in which money might be secured; it was not common to invest money in the purchase of real estate; in some cities there were treasure rooms in idol's temples, but monies left there unused would as soon tarnish as if they were hidden in a hole in the ground.   When they have turned their wealth into gold or silver for easy storage, the rich may think they have something of more permanent value than grain or garments.   While that may be true as long as this world stands, the tarnish that builds up is proof the coins have not been used, but only hoarded.   The longer it lays idle, the more the tarnish builds up.   To hoard and allow valuable coins to tarnish when the monies could be used to benefit one's neighbor is sin.

And their rust will be a witness against you – It is possible the Greek (*humin*) should be translated "to you."   When the threatened judgment comes and the rich can look at their unused and now worthless riches,   the mold and moth   holes and tarnish[14] will convince

---

[12] Some treat the perfect tense verbs "rotted" and "moth-eaten" as being Hebrew prophetic perfects (i.e., something so sure to happen that it can be spoken of as already having actually happened), but we see no reason to treat them as predictions of the future.   At the time James writes, this is what the oppressive rich have already been doing.   Poor and needy people were hungry, while the rich people's hoarded food was going to waste.   Poorly clad people were cold while the clothing that might have benefited them becomes insect food.   "When such garments were stored in quantity in Oriental countries where there was a fairly high temperature during much of the year, damage by the larva of clothes moths was frequently extensive" (G.S. Candale, "Moth" in *The New Bible Dictionary* (Grand Rapids: Eerdmans, 1962), p. 850; and W.M. Whitwell, "Insects of the Bible, Moths and Butterflies," in the *Zondervan Pictorial Bible Dictionary* (Grand Rapids: Zondervan, 1963), p.377-38).

[13] *Katiōtai* literally means "to cause to rust, to be corroded with rust" and the compound verb implies "thoroughly or completely rusted."   Most of us have seen rusted iron and steel.   Silver and gold do not rust like that, but left in a damp place they will contract a dark color resembling rust in appearance.   When that occurs, technically we say that the gold is tarnished or the silver is corroded.

[14] In James 3:8 the word *ios* was translated "poison"; it can also refer to "rust" as in the LXX of Ezekiel 24:6,11.

them of their folly. If we translate it "against you" then the picture is that the rusted wealth will be produced as evidence (either here on earth, or in the judgment) to all observers that rich had not used their riches correctly, either in paying those to whom it was due, or in doing good to others. The rust on the unused treasures is a witness of the guilt and hard-heartedness of the rich.

And will consume your flesh like fire – *Phagetai* can be translated "eat" or "devour" (like a hungry animal), or it is understood metaphorically, "consume."[15] At this place, a choice must be made concerning punctuation. Shall we take "like fire" with what goes before, and put a period after "fire"? Some of our Bibles (including the NASB) do.[16] The "rust" is pictured as adding fuel to the fire of divine judgment. You and your wealth will perish together, James announces. Others (like Goodspeed) put a comma after "flesh," and start a new clause with the words "like fire," so that the rest of the verse reads "Since you have treasured up fire in the last days."[17] According to this interpretation of the verse, "rust ... will consume your flesh" is a graphic way of saying that their greed will result in their own destruction, as if the corrosion that ate away their riches will actually eat away their flesh. As earlier, we suppose there is an unspoken condition: this doom will fall on the earthly possessions and on the ungodly unless they repent. James' prophetic warning is a terror-inspiring picture of the disastrous results of treating money as the chief aim in life, while at the same time leaving God and His wishes out of the picture.

It is in the last days that you have stored up your treasure! – "You have laid up your treasure" is a single verb in the Greek (*ethēsaurisate*). "In the last days" (NASB) is a better translation of *en eschatais hēmerais* than "for the last days" (which is found in some older versions).[18] The questionable translation "for the last days" has led readers to several suspect interpretations: (1) Planning for financial security in one's old-age, i.e., for his or her last days on earth. The covetous men think they shall never have enough hoarded to sufficiently meet their needs in old age. (2) Somehow it has reference to the days immediately before the Second Coming of Christ, though how people might benefit

---

[15] The metaphorical use must not be pressed as though this verse taught the annihilation of the wicked. Some annihilationists have pictured the fires of hell burning till the body and soul are wholly "eaten up," i.e., there is nothing left. We think this view of eternal punishment does not satisfy all the verses that picture what that punishment will be like.

[16] Proponents of this view find it difficult to justify the translation the other punctuation requires, since *hos* (in *hos pur*) must be separated from "fire" and has to be translated "since" rather than "like" or "as." It also rather requires that "fire" would be the fires of Gehenna, which will be experienced "in the last days," i.e., after the Final Judgment. Jesus spoke about the "whole body" being cast into hell fire (Matthew 5:22, 5:29-30, 10:28).

[17] Defenders of this alternate punctuation give several reasons for adopting it: (a) the KJV/NASB reading is said to be colorless; (b) the phrase "last days" is difficult to interpret; (c) unless our text is defective, the verb "treasured up" is left without an object if we put a period after "fire." (Some Latin Vulgate manuscripts correct this deficiency by adding "anger" as the object of the verb.) The Westcott and Hort text adopts this punctuation.

[18] Other than this verse in some of our Bibles, this commentator knows of no example in Greek literature where the preposition *en* is translated "for."

by hoarding wealth for those days has proven difficult to explain. (3) It is an ironic reference to the Judgment Day, similar in thought to what Paul once wrote, "You are treasuring up wrath against the day of wrath and revelation of the righteous judgment of God" (Romans 2:5). Based on the preferred translation "in the last days," what James says is this: 'Here we are, living in the last days, and you are selfishly grasping for and hanging on to your temporal treasures. What folly!'

Because of the far-reaching ramifications resulting from interpretation of what James writes in verse 3 and following, we must pause to study in some detail what the expression "last days" means. Many contemporary Bible critics flatly assert the apostles and early church, in the first decades after Jesus' resurrection and ascension, expected His Second Coming to occur within their lifetimes. One of the key paragraphs of Scripture used to justify this conclusion is James 5:3,7,8,9. Other passages alleged to teach a soon return of Christ are 1 Peter 1:5; 1 Thessalonians 4:15; 1 Corinthians 15:51; 2 Timothy 3:1; 1 John 2:18; 2 Peter 1:19. The critics go on to affirm that this near universally-held expectation in the early church was mistaken, and it was not until nearly half a century after the church began that folk began to correct the mistake. As innocent as this theory may sound, we must insist there can be no mistake either in the teachings of Jesus or on the part of inspired writers. Freedom from error as they spoke by inspiration must be vindicated, or who will ever be able to ascertain the false gospel from the true? We have argued at Acts 2:39ff that when the apostles, after Pentecost, preached by inspiration, what they said was right. Sometimes it is true that they themselves had to search for the meaning; it took Peter ten years and a direct vision from God (Acts 10) before he finally understood the gospel really was for those afar off, just as he had preached it on Pentecost. Likewise, the apostle Paul wrote an early letter about the Second Advent. Because he was guided by inspiration, we affirm he expressed no erroneous opinion about the timing. Nevertheless, some of his hearers did not understand it aright, so 2 Thessalonians was written to correct some erroneous interpretations those readers made from 1 Thessalonians.

Perhaps a brief study of the Biblical expression "Day of the Lord" will help us understand how prophetic language was used. In the Old Testament, the prophets often spoke of God's temporal judgment on unfaithful Israel as being a "day of the Lord." Several temporal judgments occurred as the centuries passed. The time will come when the Final Judgment, the "great and terrible Day of the Lord," will occur. Every time we read about the "day of the Lord," we do not automatically see it as a reference to the final judgment. Perhaps the same use of prophetic language can be used to explain the passages that deal with the "kingdom of God" and those that deal with the "coming" of the Lord. There were temporal fulfillments, and there is yet to be one final fulfillment. In a similar way, we suppose, when we read the expression "last days" in the books of the Bible, sometimes it is the end of the Jewish age that is alluded to, sometimes it is the whole Christian age,[19] and sometimes it is the close of the Christian age that is in view. Care must be exercised lest each and every time one reads "last days" only the last idea is allowed

---

[19] New Testament writers constantly referred to the Christian, or Church, age, i.e., the time between the resurrection/ascension of Jesus and His Second Coming, as the "last days." (Acts 2:16,17; Hebrews 1:1-2.)

to come to mind.   In fact, we propose what when James says "it is in the last days ...," he has reference to the end of the Jewish economy caused by the AD 70 destruction of Jerusalem, and he is telling the rich that during the days of the siege and the fall of the city, their money would do them no good.[20]

5:4 -- *Behold, the pay of the laborers who mowed your fields,* and *which has been withheld by you, cries out* against you; *and the outcry of those who did the harvesting has reached the ears of the Lord of Sabaoth.*

Behold – Here in verse 4 we have a second reason why James condemns the rich.   It is the crime of unpaid wages.   "Behold" is an imperative, an impressive way of commanding men to "look" at what James now describes.

The pay of the laborers who mowed your fields, *and* which has been withheld by you – The rich obtained some of their wealth by defrauding the people who worked for them. "Laborers" refers to farmhands, day-laborers in general, as explained by the words "mowing" and "harvesting."   The word translated "fields" (*chōras*) is worth noting. "Fields" is not a good equivalent in English, for that word suggests to our minds too small a plot of ground.   *Chōra* means not a fenced subdivision, but extensive lands, a region (like the land of Galilee), a whole estate, under one ownership.[21]   Mowing and reaping of so many acres would require many laborers and multiple days to complete the tasks.   Some of the older versions read "kept back by fraud."[22]   Day-laborers lived in poverty, and if wages were withheld even for a day, he and his family would not eat.   Therefore, the employers of Old Testament times were expected to pay at the close of the work-day the wages of those who worked for them (Leviticus 19:13; Deuteronomy 24:14-15; Matthew 20:8).   These rich men whom James is rebuking, because of their selfish lust for riches, held back the pay for their workers.   And it may also be true that perhaps, for some petty

---

[20] Perhaps Luke 17:28-30 (which talks about a "day [on which] the Son of Man is revealed") refers to the destruction of Jerusalem in AD 70, and pictures the same feverish behavior James is here depicting among the rich.   We have outlined that "Sermon on the Time of the Coming of the Kingdom" (Luke 17:20-37) in this way: (1) The King is already present, and His earthly ministry is soon to be ended (verses 22-25), but His rule will continue till He again becomes visible at His Second Coming.   (2) Jesus explains that in the early days of His rule the city of Jerusalem would be destroyed (verses 26-32).   (3) Until that distant future time at the Second Coming, when one is taken and one is left, men must be careful to have their priorities set on spiritual things, or they will lose all (verses 33-37).   If that is a correct outline, then Jesus' words, "the day the Son of man is revealed" (verse 30) have reference to what happened when Jerusalem was destroyed.   Jesus, in the unseen world, because He is Lord of heaven and earth, is the One who providentially sent the Roman armies to destroy Jerusalem (cf. Matthew 22:7).   The destruction of the city was a "revelation" of the Son of Man, to let the world know who He is and what power He wields.

[21] In the Parable of the Rich Fool (Luke 12:16), the word implies extensive land holdings.

[22] The KJV translates *apesterēmonos*, which means "having been robbed or deprived of."   The Greek behind the NASB is *aphusterēmenos*, and simply means "having been withheld."

excuse or legal technicality, the rich men never paid part or all of it.[23] "By you" charges the landowners themselves with guilt in this matter.

Cries out *against you* – James' language reminds us of Exodus 2:23 ("their cry for help because of their bondage rose up to God") and Genesis 4:10 ("the voice of your brother's blood is crying to Me from the ground").   The hoarded riches are personified as continually crying out[24] from the store room wherein it was hoarded, that something should be done to punish those who oppressed the poor.

And the outcry of those who did the harvesting has reached the ears of the Lord of Sabaoth – "Harvesters" are those who cut and shocked the grain. At harvest time, when the new crop vastly increases the land owner's wealth, to withhold wages from such workers is despicable. Not only do the withheld wages figuratively cry out, the audible cries for help (*boaō*) spoken by the defrauded also are heard by the Lord. "Lord of Sabaoth" perhaps reflects Isaiah 5:9.[25] "Sabaoth" is a Hebrew word meaning "hosts, armies."[26] The defrauded may have no earthly protector, but they have the Lord of hosts. When James writes "Lord of Sabaoth," we cannot tell whether he has Jesus or the Father in mind.   In either case, the Lord has the power and resources to deal with the oppressors, and deal with them He will!   Those wealthy land owners may be high and rich in the world and able to contest with poor laborers and crush them; but can they contend with the Lord of hosts and prevail? No! We wonder whether in this place the "hosts" are none other than the armies of Rome, about to surround and crush the city of Jerusalem (AD 70).

---

[23] This verse was often used against slavery in years past.   The amount which the slave received for his or her labor was not what would have been a fair equivalent for the work done, or nearly equivalent to what a free man could be hired for.   Since the pay of the slave was so much less than his or her labor was fairly worth, the money saved became a dishonest source of gain for the master.

[24] The word is *krazō*, a loud cry, a scream.

[25] If James deliberately had that passage in mind, then the extensive fields also came into the employer's possession as a result of fraud and violence (Isaiah 5:8). The only other place in the New Testament where we find this designation "Lord of Sabaoth" is when Paul quotes language from Isaiah 1:9 at Romans 9:29. In both those Isaiah passages, the LXX retains the word in its Hebrew form. In most other places where the Hebrew word occurs, the LXX renders it by "Almighty" (*pantokratōr*), and this form appears at Revelation 1:8 where "Lord God Almighty" answers to "Lord God of Sabaoth." Since the designation does not occur in the Pentateuch or in Joshua, Judges, or Ruth, it is often suggested, since the expression occurs often in the prophetic books, that this name for God was first used in the School of the Prophets founded by Samuel.

[26] In some places the "host" of heaven, either the angels or the stars and planets, is in the writer's mind. In some places, "armies," either angelic (as in 2 Chronicles 18:18) or human (it is the armies of Israel in 1 Samuel 17:45), are in the writer's mind. "This is one of the most majestic of all the titles for Jehovah in the Old Testament, drawing attention, as it does, to His sovereign omnipotence" (Tasker, *op. cit.*, p.113). At least 23 times the name "Lord of Hosts" occurs in the little book of Malachi. In one passage (Malachi 3:1-5), the Lord is seated as judge on His throne; charges against the wicked are heard; the wrongdoers (such as those who oppress the hireling) are punished.

5:5 -- *You have lived luxuriously on the earth and led a life of wanton pleasure; you have fattened your hearts in a day of slaughter.*

You have lived luxuriously on the earth and led a life of wanton pleasure – Here begins the third reason why James condemns the rich. At the very time they were inflicting hardships on the poor, they were living in luxury and self-indulgence. The first of the words (*truphraō*) denotes ease and soft luxury.[27] The latter word (*spatalaō*) denotes the lavish, extravagant, wasteful expenditure by which the luxury related to the former word was maintained.[28] The rich were very careful that their employees got no more than they had to give them. To relieve the needy never entered their minds. But for themselves, having so much money, nothing was too good. Their homes were the best and luxuriously furnished. Their closets were full with garments. Their tables were laden with food. "On the earth" seems to say their desires and delights were limited to things of this world.[29]

You have fattened your hearts in a day of slaughter – Anyone who chooses the pathway of using their wealth selfishly has also chosen how their life will end. With the plenty their ill-gotten wealth provided, and with no restraint on their indulgence, the rich were fattening themselves.[30] Like stall-fed cattle, who live only to be slaughtered, the rich have a slaughter to face, too.[31] The particular "day" alluded to is not easily determined.

- It is possible that "day of slaughter" in this clause corresponds to "the last days" of verse 3. If so, and if our conclusions about the meaning of that verse are correct, James has the coming destruction of Jerusalem in view when he writes about a "day of slaughter."[32]

---

[27] One recalls Jesus' parabolic description of the rich man who "was clothed in purple and fine linen, and fared sumptuously every day" (Luke 16:19). Jesus also spoke about folk in royal palaces who "are clothed splendidly and live in luxury (*truphē*)" (Luke 7:25).

[28] The NASB choice of "wanton" to translate this second word tends to convey a sense which is not in the original. Our English word now has a connotation of lewd, lustful, lascivious. The Greek word has the idea of "squander."

[29] Some recall that in the Parable of the Rich Man and Lazarus, Abraham reminds the rich man that on earth he had good things, but now after his death, he was suffering (Luke 16:25).

[30] The text reads "they fattened their hearts." The "heart" here apparently refers to their desires for luxury and pleasure, and the rich are pictured as giving themselves everything their heart wanted.

[31] The KJV follows manuscripts which read "as in a day of slaughter." The NASB follows a more ancient text that omits the "as." There is no "the" in the Greek before "day of slaughter", but omitting the article was common before "day," "hour," or "fitting season." Thus it could be translated "the day of slaughter."

[32] Josephus tells us (*Wars*, V.x.2) it didn't matter whether the wealthy Jews caught in the city during the siege stayed or tried to flee. They were equally destroyed in either case. Starving Jews in the city would catch and put the wealthy to death on the pretext they were preparing to desert, but in reality this was done so that whatever the rich had might be plundered. Folk who were half-starved were left unmolested when they declared they had nothing. Those whose bodies showed no signs of privation were tortured to make them reveal the treasures which they were suspected of having concealed. If they did get away from the city, they were caught by the Romans, killed and their bodies cut open on the suspicion they had swallowed jewels in order to smuggle them out of town.

- God's judgments in history (e.g., days of carnage and bloodshed during war) are sometimes described in the Old Testament as a "sacrifice" (Jeremiah 46:10), or a "great slaughter" (Isaiah 34:6; Ezekiel 21:15; Jeremiah 12:3). The fatter the animal, the sooner the farmer leads it to the slaughter house. For the rich, the day has come!

- Some, following the KJV text that has the particle of comparison ("as"), have proposed we translate it "as in a festival," since the custom of the ancients on festival days was to feast on the animals that had been fattened and slaughtered. "Did any of those whom James here condemns remember his words when, a few years later, thousands of Jews of the Dispersion were once more gathered together at Jerusalem for the sacrifice of the Passover, and there became unwilling sacrifices to God's slow but sure vengeance?"[33] As Titus besieged the city, the temple floors ran with blood, and the flames burned the wooden roofs and interiors till all was utter desolation.

- An alternative interpretation finds "day of slaughter" contrasted with "on earth" found in the first part of this verse. The idea this view produces is that the reference is to the day of final judgment when the unrepentant rich will be sentenced to perdition.

5:6 -- *You have condemned and put to death the righteous* man; *he does not resist you.*

You have condemned and put to death the righteous *man* – Here begins the fourth reason why James condemns the rich. They have falsely accused and executed the righteous. In the Greek, the two verbs in this clause have no conjunction tying them together. Each verb pictures an independent activity against the righteous. In this context where ill-gotten and ill-used wealth is the burden of James' denunciation, we suppose the condemnation and the execution were carried out in the process of getting the wealth. "Condemnation" is a law-court term denoting a verdict against someone. James 2:6 has told how the rich dishonor and oppress the poor man, and drag him into court. This verse seems to say that the rich controlled the courts and influenced the judges to guarantee an adverse verdict against the righteous, and thus gain their assets. When a man's greed for more wealth gets out of hand, the greedy have been known to plot and arrange for the death of the person whose money or property they wished to acquire. In this, the rich have targeted "the righteous" as their most likely victim. In the Greek, "the righteous [one]"[34] is singular. Perhaps the rich targeted individual Christians rather than an entire group, perhaps supposing the individual would be less able to defend himself than

---

[33] Plummer, *op. cit.*, p.624. If we make this application, it would not be "Christians" who were slaughtered, for they fled the city before the final siege and slaughter began. That in turn might help determine who the "rich" are about whom James is writing in these opening verses of chapter 5.

[34] The Greek construction consists of an article and an adjective, but with no noun stated. When such constructions occur, we may add any noun that agrees in gender with the gender of the article and adjective, which in this instance is masculine. The adjective "righteous" is a New Testament term for "Christians." Perhaps the singular is a generic term, representative of a whole class.

than might be true of the entire group.[35]

He does not resist you – Two questions face us here: what is the antecedent of "he" and is this a statement or a question? If we read it as a statement, then the antecedent is "the righteous [one]."[36] Christians, having been taught by Jesus to submit patiently to acts of injustice and violence (Matthew 5:39), do not resist the attempts of the unscrupulous rich to exploit them. In other words, the rich have found easy victims among the Christians. If it is a question, it expects an affirmative answer. What does James mean if he is asking a question? If we take the "rich man" as the subject, then the question asks, "The rich man oppresses you, doesn't he?" "Why do you think it is so important to have wealth and be like the rich man? Are you going to oppress people like he does?" If we take "God" or "Lord of Sabaoth" as the subject, then this question to the rich says "God is opposing you, isn't He?" You'll find out on the judgment day that indeed He is! The cries of the oppressed have entered into the ears of the Lord (verse 4), and the Lord responds to those prayers.

5:7 -- *Be patient, therefore, brethren, until the coming of the Lord. Behold, the farmer waits for the precious produce of the soil, being patient about it, until it gets the early and late rains.*

Be patient, therefore, brethren – "Brethren" shows James is turning his attention away from the unbelieving rich back to the Jewish Christians to whom this epistle was addressed. "Therefore" shows there is a close relationship between verses 7-11 and verses 1-6. The oppression of the righteous poor described in 5:1-6 gives rise to this exhortation to patience and endurance (5:7-11). The righteous poor who have been cruelly oppressed by the rich are counted among these "brethren." Having announced that the rich oppressors would be suitably punished by God, James now offers his "brethren" consolation on two grounds:

---

[35] Commentators have not been able to agree on the identification of "the righteous one."

(1) Some have suggested that some famous Christian martyr, like Stephen, is in James' mind.

(2) Since James himself is known as "James the just [righteous]," some have supposed James is predicting his own death at the hands of rich Jews.

(3) That "the righteous one" who was condemned and put to death is none other than Jesus Christ has found advocates in all ages.

   (a) Peter's words in Acts 3:14,15 are alluded to as corroboration. So are Stephen's words in Acts 7:52. Others appeal to Acts 22:14 and 1 Peter 3:18. The present tense verb "He does not resist you" (James 5:6b) is interpreted to mean that since His ascension Christ has been longsuffering as He allows the wicked to go about their exploitation.

   (b) Objections to this interpretation include: (i) James is addressed to people living in the Dispersion. Can Jews scattered all over the Roman world, 20 or 30 years after Calvary, be charged with being personally involved in the condemnation and crucifixion of Jesus? (ii) The other charges against the rich in James 5 all deal with how they got and wasted their wealth. It seems to break the train of thought to suddenly allude to the crucifixion of Christ. (iii) The verb in the last part of verse 6 ("he does not resist you") is present tense, picturing something happening in the present. (iv) The whole context points to a generic evil, a class of sin, characteristic, like those of the previous verse, of the rich and powerful everywhere.

[36] In the previous footnote, we have seen how this phrase is interpreted by those who think "the righteous one" is Christ.

first, their sufferings are not going to last forever – on the contrary the Lord is about to step in and put an end to the rich men's opportunities to oppress; and second, the Lord rewards those who exhibit patience and endurance. In verses 7-11 two different root words occur: "patience" (*makrothumein* and *makrothumia*), which occurs four times in four verses, and "endurance" (*hupomenein* and *hupomenē*), which occurs twice in the last verse.[37] The difference between the two is that the first speaks of putting up with people,[38] while the latter is putting up with things.[39] The persecuted prophets in Old Testament times exhibited both qualities (patience and endurance); Job exhibited the latter quality (endurance). Christians will get to exhibit both as they develop Christlike character in response to the evil actions of the rich.

Until the coming of the Lord – The end of the longsuffering which James is asking of his readers will be found in "the coming of the Lord." Without doubt it is the Lord Jesus Christ who at His "coming" will remove the people with whom the readers are having to put up. The Greek word translated "coming" is *parousia*, a word the Greeks used to describe the official visit of a monarch to some city within his realm. On such state occasions the royal "presence" (for that is the literal meaning of the word) was such that none could fail to recognize the sovereign for what in fact he was.[40] *Parousia* was also used of the invasion of a country by an army. When Jesus arrives (in this case to deal with unbelieving Jerusalem), it is heaven invading earth. When Jesus "came" (in the sense the "king sent his armies to destroy those murderers") and Jerusalem was destroyed, the exploitation of poor Jewish Christians by rich unbelieving Jewish people would be over. Until then, James urges his brethren to be patient in their waiting and valiant in their endurance. It was only a short time; less than 20 years if our date for the writing of this letter by James is correct. When Jerusalem has fallen, Jesus will be seen to be Lord, and everyone also will know the Judaizers are wrong!

---

[37] The two words are frequently found together in the New Testament (e.g., 2 Corinthians 6:4-6; Colossians 1:11; 2 Timothy 3:10) and in early Christian literature.

[38] A good English equivalent is "longsuffering." It emphasizes the self-restraint which enables the sufferer to refrain from hasty retaliation. One of God's attributes is that He is "long-suffering" (Romans 2:4; 1 Peter 3:10), which means He is "slow to anger," of "great kindness," and does not speedily inflict upon transgressors the full punishment they deserve. But there does come a time when even His patience with sinners is exhausted. Ropes (*op. cit.*, p.293) observes that "longsuffering" is a word that does not occur often in secular Greek, perhaps because it is a virtue that does not flourish readily among natural men.

[39] As explained at James 1:3,4,12 where this word occurs, it does not describe passive endurance of affliction and disaster. Rather, it speaks of a heroic and gallant spirit which turns things that look bad into something positive. "If life hands you a lemon, make lemonade" is how Barclay illustrates "endurance."

[40] The word is often used in the New Testament for the Second Coming of Jesus (e.g., Matthew 24:27; 1 Thessalonians 4:15; 2 Thessalonians 2:1; 1 Corinthians 15:23). So not a few interpreters explain this passage – saying the early church expected a soon return of Jesus – an expectation in which it is now clearly evident they were mistaken. See this matter discussed in the footnotes on verse 3 above. In 2 Peter 1:16, the word is used of Jesus' first coming into the world (His incarnation). It also is used of the visits men like Paul and Titus made to various towns as they pursued their ministry for Christ.

Behold, the farmer waits for the precious produce of the soil – So important is this matter of patience and endurance that James uses several illustrations (the farmer, verses 7-9; the prophets, verse 10; and Job, verse 11) to emphasize his point. The tenant farmer or the landowner "waits" because there is always time between plowing and the harvest. The farmer's waiting is a watchful expectancy. He is looking forward to the "precious produce" because on it his life and welfare depend. Slowly the grain grows. It requires time for the crop to mature, and he does not become impatient or rush into the field and do something foolish in hopes of hurrying the process. It requires help from God, for the farmer cannot control the rain, the sun, the season, or the pests that may destroy the coming harvest. Nevertheless, he continues to watch and wait until in the regular course of events he has a harvest. There is something analogous between the farmer's waiting and the righteous man's waiting. In the Lord's fields, the present time is sowing and growing time. As the farmer waits for his crop, Christians too can afford to wait a little longer for His blessing of our labors with precious fruit. As in the case of the farmer, so it is with the Christian: the hope for the crop makes all earthly trials bearable.

Being patient about it, until it gets the early and late rains – There is a surprising diversity of readings at this place. The KJV reads "and has long patience for it," but there is no word for "long" in the better manuscripts. (Actually, after the seed was planted and began to sprout, the time between the first appearance of the blade and the harvest was about four months.) Some manuscripts have the farmer waiting on the "early and later rains," some have him waiting on the "early and later fruit," while the best manuscripts have no noun at all, the farmer is waiting on the "early and later [...]," and we must supply the noun. "Rain" is probably the best word to supply.[41] But wherein does the comparison between the oppressed Christian's "patience" and the farmer's "patience" lie? Is it in the waiting for God to intervene and provide His blessings like He provides the "rain" and the "precious produce"? Is it in not letting the uncertainties and difficulties that have to be faced destroy the "patience"? Is it to be found in the "self-restraint" and "self-control" that both need to survive? We should likely understand that James explains his own comparison in verse 8. The allusion to "early and late rains" is familiar to all who are acquainted with the Holy Land.[42] In the climate of the Holy Land there are two rainy seasons on which the harvest essentially depends (cp. Deuteronomy 11:14; Jeremiah 3:3, 5:24; Joel 2:23). The early rains (autumnal) usually commence in the latter half of Octo-

---

[41] In the LXX when the two adjectives "early and late" appear, the noun "rain" always appears.

[42] It is doubtful that we should seek some figurative meaning to the "early and late rains." Nevertheless, some 20th century Pentecostals have claimed that their movement is the latter rain of James 5:7 (KJV). They see the "early rain" as a picture of the Holy Spirit's miraculous work in the early church beginning on Pentecost (Acts 2). They then speak of modern Pentecostalism as being the "latter rain," another time of great revival just before the Second Coming of the Lord. The gifts of healing and tongues, they believe, are evidence of the Holy Spirit's latter rain. In the author's commentaries on Acts and 1 Corinthians, it has been shown that both Scripture and church history teach the cessation of the gifts. The "Latter Rain Movement" does not deny that the early rains ceased, just as cessationists affirm. What they do claim is that they have been restored. In this writer's opinion, however, such a claim flies in the face of those verses which suggest once the gifts have confirmed the Gospel message, there is no further use or need for the special spiritual gifts.

ber or the beginning of November. During the dry season (summer) from May to September, the ground is dry and hard and cannot be worked. If the early rains do not come, the farmers could not prepare the ground for planting. In autumn, the clouds come from the southwest and it will rain for two or three days at a time. Then the wind shifts round to the north or east, and several days of fine plowing weather follow. Then the wind shifts back to the southwest, and the cycle begins again, though perhaps when the second cycle of good weather comes, this is the time the seed will be planted. These early rains last through the months of November and December providing the moisture the crops will need during their early growth. The "late rains" usually come in March and April. This moisture helps the ears to fill and mature before the harvest. Even if the early rains were timely and adequate, if the late rains do not come, there is no crop. The farmer is anxious, hopeful, waiting on God to provide the needed blessing.

5:8 -- *You too be patient; strengthen your hearts, for the coming of the Lord is at hand.*

You too be patient – James here explains the point of his illustration about the patient farmer, and how such patience illustrates the kind of patience Christians must demonstrate. "You" is emphatic, and what James writes here is an imperative verb; this is a command.

Strengthen your hearts – Indeed, there are things a farmer can be fretful about: not enough rain, too much rain, insects, weeds. But he keeps waiting expectantly for God's help with those things over which he has no control. Likewise, the oppressed Christian can certainly look around and see a number of things that could cause him to lose faith and become fretful or angry, or even to nurture ideas of retaliation against his oppressors. Those are the moments he will have to "strengthen" his heart, to resolve to be patient. The LXX uses the word "strengthen" (*sterixate*) for the bolstering or holding up of Moses' hands (Exodus 17:12). James commands his brethren (again,the Greek is imperative) to "strengthen your hearts." There is solid support, there is help available to get through the hard times unmoved from their genuine Christian behavior. How does one "strengthen his heart"? Partially by reminding himself that "the coming of the Lord is at hand." The Lord will take care of the matter. The wicked will not always prosper. Till then, keep on being patient!

For the coming of the Lord is at hand – The "Lord" is Jesus, and "at hand" means the time is short until something occurs.[43] In this case, He is going to "come." We have been following the idea that James is promising his "brethren" that one source of their oppression (namely, rich and influential unbelieving Jews) will soon be ended by the destruction of Jerusalem.[44] In other words, James is promising his "brethren" that the particular difficul-

---

[43] Compare Matthew 3:2, "the kingdom of heaven is at hand." For the interpretation of this verse that has it declaring that Christ's Second Coming will occur rather quickly, see notes above on verse 3.

[44] Although it is not the point of the passage here in James, we do affirm there are times in our Bibles when the language "the coming of the Lord" refers not to the destruction of Jerusalem in AD 70, but to the yet-future return of Christ for judgment, when He will reward the righteous and assign the wicked to everlasting punishment.

ties that call for their "patience" will not last much longer. Jesus will soon come and take care of the oppressors.

5:9 -- *Do not complain, brethren, against one another, that you yourselves may not be judged; behold, the Judge is standing right at the door.*

Do not complain, brethren, against one another – This prohibition forbids the continuance of an action already going on. Not only are they to be patient and establish their hearts, but they are to stop complaining[45] against their fellow Christians. Most of us have experienced situations when men who are irritated and exasperated by trying persons or circumstances are likely to vent their discontent on someone who is in no way responsible for what is trying them. James is telling his readers to take special care lest they take turns blaming their brethren for their miseries, for after all, their brethren are not their oppressors. Rather, their Christian brethren are likely to be numbered among the oppressed themselves, and complaints against those who are already hurting when they are not guilty of doing what we complain about do nothing to help the hurting. "Complaining against a brother" is the exact opposite of "bearing one another's burdens and so fulfilling the law of Christ" (Galatians 6:2).[46]

That you yourselves may not be judged – What has already been carefully argued in James 4:11,12 is again called to the readers' attention. Grumbling against one another is a form of judging that requires a usurpation of the Divine prerogative to judge. James here repeats the exact words of the Greek in Matthew 7:1, thus reminding Christians that those who continue to complain against their brethren are in danger of being condemned to hell.

Behold, the Judge is standing right at the door – Before one can complain, he must assume the office of "judge." This is clearly wrong, for Jesus (not this or that Christian) is the Judge, and He is not off in some remote place where He can't hear or take note of what is happening. Compare this verse with that which is pictured in Revelation 3:20.[47] "He has the complete   knowledge needed to determine the true   measure of guilt in their

---

[45] The verb *stenazo* means "to sigh, to groan, to express impatience, to find fault, to complain." When the KJV translators chose "grudge not" to express the force of this word, the word "grudge" meant roughly what our word "grumble" means.   Christians may indeed groan (the same verb is used in the Greek) within themselves because of their individual sufferings (Romans 8:23), but we are not to groan or complain against one another.

[46] Burdick (*op. cit.*, p.202) offers a different thread of thought as he comments on this verse. He finds a second group of people towards whom Christians must be "patient." Not only are they to be patient toward outsiders who oppress them, but they are to be patient with insiders who irritate them. They are not to nurture unexpressed feelings of bitterness or give voice to smothered resentment with groans or sighs that are spoken almost under the breath.

[47] We do not see in the expression "right at the door" any implication that Jesus' Second Coming is so near that you might say His foot is on the doorstep, ready to enter at any time. The verse is not dealing with how soon He may be coming, but with His qualifications to judge Christians who grumble against one another.

feelings, thoughts, and reactions."[48]

5:10 -- *As an example, brethren, of suffering and patience, take the prophets who spoke in the name of the Lord.*

As an example, brethren, of suffering and patience – These words stand first in the Greek for emphasis. This is the second illustration of the importance of "patience," the topic introduced at 5:7. "Suffering" (*kakopathias*) is objective affliction, not the feeling that results from "ill treatment." "Patience" is the word for "putting up with people" that we have been studying since verse 7. James says the prophets experienced affliction or ill-treatment, and responded to it with longsuffering patience. "Example" (*hupodeigma*) is a pattern or model to be copied. The Greek reads "the suffering" and "the patience" – two different experiences are held up as an example for James' Christian brethren.

Take the prophets who spoke in the name of the Lord – By "prophets" James no doubt calls attention to the Old Testament prophets, such as Elijah, Jeremiah, and others, perhaps including John the Baptist. Those men of God had numerous occasions when they suffered bodily harm and had to exhibit patience toward their tormenters. Jesus one day used the Old Testament prophets as an example: "Blessed are you when men persecute you and say all manner of things against you falsely for my sake, for so they persecuted the prophets who were before you" (Matthew 5:11-12). The Old Testament biographical and autobiographical records of the prophets describe vividly their suffering and patience. For generations, Jewish people looked to Jeremiah for inspiration and courage. He was beaten, put in stocks, imprisoned in a dungeon, and thrown into a cistern by the very men he tried to lead to repentance and to safety from the doom that awaited them. In spite of this ill-treatment, he patiently persisted in his ministry. Hebrews11:36-38 gives a brief summary of the suffering of the prophets. "Others experienced cruel mockings and scourgings, yes, also chains and imprisonment. They were stoned, they were sawn in two, they were tempted, they were put to death with the sword; they went about in sheepskins in goatskins, being destitute, afflicted, ill-treated (men of whom the world was not worthy)." Elijah thundered, "the sons of Israel ... have killed Thy prophets with the sword" (1 Kings 19:10,14). As he defended himself before the Sanhedrin against charges of blasphemy, Stephen said, "Which one of the prophets did your fathers not persecute?" He answers his own question with these words, "They killed those who had previously announced the coming of the Righteous One" (Acts 7:52). These bad things happened because they "spoke in the name of the Lord." They had been sent by the Lord, to deliver the very words the Lord sent them to speak.[49] However, because they spoke in the name of the Lord, that did not save them from persecution. Rather it provoked it. The Jewish people to whom they preached would rather abuse and silence the prophets than repent. Those honored servants of God suffered much, and they endured it patiently. That's the

---

[48] Hiebert, *op. cit.*, p.301.

[49] Often in the pages of the Old Testament prophets we find the expression, "Thus saith the Lord God of hosts," or "The word that came to Jeremiah from the Lord," or "The word of God came expressly to Ezekiel," etc. Those men spake as they were moved by the Holy Spirit (2 Peter 1:21).

example James wants his readers to ponder.[50]   Folk living consistent Christian lives will face harassment and bullying and ostracism and false accusations and beatings from the wicked people of the world.[51]   They too will have to show marvelous restraint lest they retaliate in some ungodly manner.

5:11 -- *Behold, we count those blessed who endured. You have heard of the endurance of Job and have seen the outcome of the Lord's dealings, that the Lord is full of compassion and* is *merciful.*

Behold, we count them blessed who endured – This is how James drives home the point of his second illustration (5:10-11a) of the importance of patience.   "Behold" calls special attention to the endurance of the Prophets.   "We count them blessed" is the same root word used at James 1:12.   "Endured,"[52] also a word we had at James 1:12, was explained there and in notes at James 5:7 as "perseverance in difficult circumstances."   "Endurance" is regarded as an admirable quality in Scripture, for example in Daniel 12:12 ("Blessed is he who endures").   "We count them" says that both James and his readers are united in expressing their admiration, and the present tense verb says they do it regularly.   We speak of their patience and endurance with commendation.   They did what we would expect men of God to do, and their names are honored.   By parity of reasoning, the Christian who endures is likewise to be counted as "spiritually prosperous."   Or perhaps "blessed" looks forward to the reward which God bestows on those who have endured.

You have heard of the endurance of Job – James' third illustration is Job.   Where have James' readers "heard" about Job?   Perhaps Jewish people were familiar with the story of the endurance of Job by oral tradition, as history was recounted around the campfires.   Perhaps they were familiar with Job's story because they had regularly heard the Scriptures read during the synagogue services every Sabbath.[53]   By whichever means, every Jew was familiar with Job.[54]

---

[50] "Take" is an imperative verb, and suggests "hold this in your mind!"

[51] Instead of Christians asking, "Why should I be made to suffer for endeavoring to do good?" it would seem the better question would be, "Seeing what other servants of God have had to endure, why should I be spared?"

[52] The present tense "endure" found in the KJV and the Textus Receptus lacks the manuscript support that the past tense "endured" enjoys.

[53] The Law and the Prophets were read (Acts 13:15), but were the books of the Holy Writings also read in the synagogues?   "Heard" is the proper word for "oral instruction" or "oral tradition."

[54] Attention has been called to the fact that this is the only time Job is named in the whole New Testament.   (There is a verse taken from Job 5:19 quoted by Paul at 1 Corinthians 3:19.)   (In the Latin Vulgate edition of the Old Testament apocryphal book of Tobit, there is a remarkable insertion [at Tobit 2:12-15] that refers to Job.)   Most Bible students are convinced that Job was an actual historical character, rather than simply a mythological or fictional story-book figure.   Ezekiel 14:14-20, which names him along with Noah and Daniel, seems to treat all three figures as having actually lived in times past.   While affirming Job was an actual historical person, this does not say that all the questions about Job can be answered with confidence, questions such as: When did Job live?   Who wrote the book?   When was the book written?   Was the writing of the book inspired?

Briefly the account of Job's miseries are these: The Sabeans stole all his oxen and donkeys. The fire from God struck the barn that housed his sheep, and they were burned up. The Chaldeans came and stole all his camels. He went from a very rich man to one who had lost most of his wealth, and that almost overnight. Job's ten children were killed in a wind storm. Job's body was then afflicted with grievous sores. Job could not understand the purpose of the trials, nor could his three friends. It was commonly thought in the Old Testament times that prosperity resulted from right living, and trouble resulted from wickedness. But Job knew that his sufferings were not caused by his iniquity. He didn't know why he was suffering, but he knew it was not because of his sins. Job's replies show the faith that motivated his life. "Though He slay me, yet will I trust in Him" (Job 13:15). "I know that my redeemer lives, and at the last He will take His stand upon the earth. Even after my skin is flayed, yet without my flesh I shall see God; whom I myself shall behold, and whom my eyes shall see and not another" (Job 19:25-27). "He knows the way that I take: when He has tried me, I shall come forth as gold" (Job 23:10). "The Lord gave, and the Lord has taken away: blessed be the name of the Lord" (Job 1:21). Job endured because he had complete trust in his Maker, and faith in the outcome of the troubles. He seemed to anticipate that in the end all would turn out well.

We are so accustomed to using the proverbial formula ("the patience of Job") inherited from the KJV that we are slow to recognize that James actually wrote about "the endurance" of Job.[55] The NASB margin offers "steadfastness" as an alternate equivalent of *hupomonē*. That was the great virtue of Job, a virtue James wants his Christians readers to emulate. When we read the series of fearsome trials that Job faced without flinching, we agree with Hort who said, "No English word is quite strong enough to express the active courage and resolution here implied." We would not be surprised if there is an anti-Judaizer thrust here. James may be saying, "Don't let the oppressive tactics of the rich sway you from your determination to be faithful to Jesus Christ!"

And have seen the outcome of the Lord's dealings – It this context "the Lord" is clearly used in its Old Testament sense.[56] The older versions read simply, "have seen the end of the Lord." This short statement has received two different interpretations: (1) The end or outcome of the Lord's dealings with Job; or (2) how things went with the Lord Jesus (his death and resurrection), whose coming was alluded to in verse 7. The clause which closes this verse is difficult to explain if we opt for (2), so most Bible students opt for (1). The end of the Lord's dealing was the complete vindication of Job.

A well-supported reading has an imperative verb (*idete*) form here, "See!" instead of the indicative (*eidete*), "you have seen."   If we accept the imperative form, we have two

---

[55] It was not so much self-restraint ("patience") that Job exhibited under affliction, leading him to put up with his so-called comforters. In fact, in chapter 3, he showed indignation against his friends for their lack of faith in him. It was the determination to remain faithful to God, whatever lot might befall him, that James calls to the attention of his readers.

[56] "The Lord" (*ho kurios*) was the common LXX rendering of the name "Jehovah" (YHWH).

choices: either "You have heard of the endurance of Job: see also the end of the Lord's dealings!" or "You have heard of the endurance of Job and the end of the Lord's dealings: see that the Lord is compassionate ...!" The appearance of Jehovah (Job 38-42) to Job to end his trials was analogous to the coming of Christ to end the trials of James' persecuted and exploited readers. Job 42:12 may have been in James' mind, "And the Lord blessed the latter days of Job more than his beginning."

That the Lord is full of compassion and *is* merciful – This clause expresses partly the cause and partly the manner of "the outcome of the Lord's dealings." As men contemplate the close of the book of Job, if they look, they can see the compassion and mercy of the Lord in operation. The reason why Job had so good an end to his troubles was the Lord's "compassion." This adjective (*polusplagchnos*), of which the nearest English equivalent would be "large-hearted" or perhaps "tender-hearted," is not found in any other earlier writer and may have been coined by James. "Merciful" represents *oiktirmōn* (the poetic form of the more common *eleēmon*). This word also occurs at Luke 6:36 where Jesus uses it of God's mercy as the basis of an admonition for men to show mercy. Even when permitting trials and hardships to come, God is very merciful. This is something folk in the midst of their troubles are likely to forget. The Lord never permits trials heavier than we can bear. He is right there beside us as we endure through the trial. He has a beneficent purpose in all the trials He permits, and even in those disciplinary actions He Himself initiates. "The Lord is merciful and gracious, slow to anger, and abounding in lovingkindness" (Psalm 103:8). Job's prosperity was restored to him, and he was granted a fuller revelation of the unseen world than the statements of his faith already imply he had been granted. As God showed deep compassion in the case of Job, we have equal reason to suppose that He will in our own case. If we trust in God's care and providence, whatever our sufferings, the "end of the Lord" will be similar in our own case, as in Job's.

To sum up this mark of genuine Christian faith (5:7-11), James is urging his readers to respond with patience when they are oppressed by the rich, and to endure (turning the bad times and trying circumstances into something positive). Such a response on the part of Christians will bring the Lord's blessings.

X. HAS A REPUTATION FOR HONESTY AND INTEG-RITY OF SPEECH. 5:12

> *Summary*: James calls attention to a key emphasis of Jesus' teaching in His Sermon on the Mount. Jesus put special emphasis on honesty and integrity; no oaths are needed to persuade men that you intend to do what you have promised.

5:12 -- *But above all, my brethren, do not swear, either by heaven or by earth or with any other oath; but let your yes be yes, and your no, no; so that you may not fall under judgment.*

But above all, my brethren – We are treating verse 12 as another of the "Marks of a Genuine Christian Life."[1]   When James says "above all things" he wants his readers to put special emphasis on this matter.[2]   Other marks of a genuine Christian life are hardly to be neglected, but special attention is to be paid to this one. James has already had much to say about sins of the tongue (1:19,26, 3:1-12, 4:11,13. 5:9). One more very common form of sinful speaking needs to be addressed, because folk who habitually do it have a serious flaw in their Christian character.   "Duplicity is totally inconsistent with Christian honesty."[3]

Do not swear – The Greek forbids the continuance of an action already going on, "Stop swearing!"   The idea of "swearing" or "taking an oath" (*omnuō*) means to invoke the name of God to ensure the truthfulness of what one is saying. It is because Satan, the father of lies, has introduced falsehood into the world that oaths have come into use. The habit of swearing profusely and of using evasive distinctions in their oaths seems to be a relic from these Jewish-Christian's pre-Christian days. The problem needs working on, says James. This passage is almost identical with what Jesus said in His Sermon on the Mount (Matthew 5:33-37). How shall we explain this surprising similarity in wording? Either James was present when Jesus delivered that message, or what Jesus preached has been repeated by word of mouth and James has heard it, or the Gospel of Matthew is already in circulation and James has read it. We think the latter option is the most probable.[4] Whatever the words meant when Jesus first spoke them is what they mean when James repeats them.[5]

---

[1] Some commentators translate the conjunction *de* as "and", thus treating verse 12 as the conclusion of the previous paragraph about suffering unjustly. The connecting thought is this: when folk are suffering it is easy to say things you do not mean, to give voice to a wish that God would cause something bad to happen to the oppressor, or even make bargains with God in hopes He will remove the cause of suffering. If all James wrote were "Swear not at all!" we might agree with making such a connection. However, the rest of the verse is difficult to explain under this hypothesis. So we agree with the NASB and translate the conjunction "but" and begin a new paragraph here.

[2] Lenski *(op. cit.,* p.668) gives "above all" a temporal significance; he thinks James is saying, "Before you do anything else cease using oaths."   We are treating it as ranking things in order of their importance. (Arndt and Gingrich, *op. cit.,* p.708, put this verse under the topic of "precedence, rank, advantage".)

[3] Hiebert, *op. cit.,* p.308.

[4] We have suggested a date of about AD 52 for James. We date the writing (by Matthew) of the first Gospel in its Aramaic form about AD 45 and in its Greek form about AD 50. Papias (120 AD) said, "Matthew wrote his logia in Aramaic/Hebrew – and everyone translated as best he could" (Eusebius, H.E., III.39). The implication of Papias' statement is this: Matthew's Gospel was quickly made available in Greek, and folk no longer had to translate from the Aramaic as they once did.

[5] Are all oaths forbidden? Is "Stop swearing!" an absolute prohibition? This commentator believes it is a mistake to interpret either Jesus or James as laying down an absolute prohibition of all oaths. Views and opinions on this question have been divided during Church History. Pelagius took the position that all swearing was forbidden. Augustine contended that oaths were not unlawful, though he would have them avoided as much as possible. (See "Oath [NT and Christian]" in *Encyclopedia of Religion and Ethics,* 98: 434-436, and "Oath" in Mennonite Encyclopedias.)
   The reasons why all oaths are not forbidden are these: (1) All oath taking cannot be evil, for God Himself, on occasion, swore by Himself (Hebrews 6:17; Psalm 110:4). (2) The same Mosaic Law which included a commandment against swearing (taking the Lord's name in vain) also commanded the taking

The next phrase helps us understand what James is denouncing. This was an age when folk were accustomed to take an oath on most any occasion. Barclay calls attention to the problems with such a practice.

> The value of an oath depends to a large extent on the fact that it is very seldom necessary to take one. Its impressiveness lies in its exceptional character; and when oaths become commonplace, they cease to be respected as they ought to be. And for another thing, the practice of taking frequent oaths was nothing other than a proof of the prevalence of lying and cheating and falsehood and swindling. In an honest society no oath is needed; it is only when men cannot be trusted to tell the truth that they have to be put under oath.[6]

Either by heaven or by earth or with any other oath – This explains the kind of oaths James is forbidding.[7] These are Jewish oath formulas and "heaven" and "earth" were two such formulas specifically named by Jesus when He spoke against oaths and false vows (Matthew 5:34, 35). "With any other oath" means "any others (*allon*) of like kind." James is prohibiting the kind of oaths common among Jewish folk, self-serving oaths, intended to fool the person to whom the promise is being deceitfully made. Jewish people had devised cunning subtle and evasive distinctions in oaths – this or that formula determined how much binding force was intended when they were spoken. In an attempt to get people to believe what was being promised, folk who were not consistently honest resorted to an oath. If they took an oath while secretly not intending to keep it, they used substitutes for the divine, holy name. Matthew 5:33ff and 23:16ff list some of the common substitutes: heaven, the throne of God, the earth, Jerusalem, the temple, the altar,

---

of an oath in certain circumstances: "You shall swear by His name" (Deuteronomy 6:13, 10:20; Psalm 63:11; Isaiah 4:2, 12:16, 65:16), or "You shall swear, 'As the Lord lives'" (Jeremiah 4:2). (3) The commandment itself allowed for usage of oaths. It reads "Thou shalt not take the name of the Lord thy God in vain" (KJV). That implies there is a lawful use of God's name. (4) Jesus Himself answered when He was put under oath by Caiaphas (Matthew 26:63,64, "I put you under oath" [*exorkizō se*]), and He was not thereby sinning (i.e., disobeying a command of God) or being inconsistent with His own teaching. (5) Paul used modes of expression ("I call God to witness") which were essentially oaths (2 Corinthians 1:23, 11:31, 12:19; Romans 1:9; Galatians 1:20; Philippians 1:8). (6) The post-apostolic church would take an oath in court, but not if the oath committed them to idolatry. Christians would not swear by the "genius" or "numen" or "fortune" (*tuchē*) of the emperor, for that was the recognized formula for abjuring Christianity. Polycarp would not swear by the genius of Caesar, when to have done so would have resulted in his release [*Mart. Pol.* ix,x].

What oaths are condemned? Christ, in the Sermon on the Mount, and James (here), forbade the customary forms of swearing and oath taking practiced by the average Jew. They were guilty of frequent swearing, of swearing by expressions that avoided literally using God's sacred name (YHWH), and of never intending to keep most of the promises they made under oath. The Jews thought it alright to swear profusely, as long as they didn't use God's name (and thus break the commandment given through Moses). And then, since they had not used God's name, there was no real reason to keep the promises and the oaths they had made.

[6] Barclay, *op. cit.*, p.149.

[7] "Do not swear" is not about cursing (asking God to damn something or someone) or profanity (using God's name or Christ's name when it means nothing other than a way to give voice to exasperation or awe) or bad language (swearing in the modern sense of the term). While these are certainly not acceptable forms of speech for a Christian, they are not the topic of discussion here in James 5.

the gold in the temple, the offering on the altar, a person's head. In the opinion of their users, some of these substitutes created more binding oaths than others.[8] Jesus condemned this widely accepted practice as being nothing more than deceit, pure and simple. You are not really avoiding the use of the name of God by the substitution of such titles, Jesus taught. They could hardly be said to be interested in honesty and integrity of speech when they resorted to the use of such evasive distinctions. What also may be on James' mind is that when Jesus spoke Matthew 23:16-22, He was denouncing the Pharisees, the very people (Acts 15:5) who were the Judaizing sect which later caused such trouble for the churches, and which, we are proposing, James is deliberately answering as he writes.

But let your yes be yes, and your no, no – When Jesus forbad taking oaths, and when James does, in both cases the prohibition is followed by a plain command of what is to be done.[9] The present imperative ("let be," *ētō*) defines what the believer's unvarying speech behavior is to be. Among Christians there should be no untruthfulness, and therefore no need for oaths. The way to avoid swearing of the kind common among Jesus' and James' listeners is to be strictly truthful in ordinary speech. Be honest and have integrity of speech. Say what you mean, and mean what you say. If you say "yes," say it without reservations. If you say "no," say it without reservations. Let your life be of such consistency that your listeners know you mean it when you say "yes" or "no." Christians are not to be deceptive. They are to be honest and to deliberately work at their reputation for honesty.

> Cicero (first century BC) illustrated the kind of personal integrity James is saying is a mark of a genuine Christian life. He told the story of a man in the early days of the Athenian democracy. Called to give testimony in a trial, he was about to offer an oath when the jury protested that this was totally unnecessary for him. Cicero noted that was because "The Greeks did not want it to be thought that the credibility of a man of proven honesty was more strictly secured by a ritual observance than by the truthfulness of his character."[10]

So that you may not fall under judgment[11] – When God forbad meaningless oaths in the Third Commandment, it is stated "the Lord will not hold him guiltless that taketh His name

---

[8] In the Mishnah there is a whole tractate (*Shebuoth*) devoted to the subject of oaths. In the discussion of binding oaths, it is asserted that "oaths made 'by Shaddai' or 'by Sabaoth' or 'by the Merciful and gracious' or 'by Him that is long-suffering and of great kindness,' or any substituted name, they are liable," but "oaths made 'by heaven and earth' are exempt."

[9] Some manuscripts read, "But let your speech be yea, yea; nay, nay." This brings the passage into line verbally with Matthew 5:37.

[10] Cicero, *Pro Balbo* 5:12. Quoted by Bill Baker, *Preaching James* (St. Louis: Chalice Press, 2004), p.142.

[11] Erasmus and Tyndale accepted the reading, "lest you fall into hypocrisy," following those manuscripts which read *hupokrisin* as one word instead of two (*upo krisin*).

in vain" (KJV). It is doubtful if "judgment" or "condemnation" speaks of the false-swearer being found guilty by a human court of perjury. Rather it speaks of an adverse judgment by God when the great final judgment is held.

> There are few spheres of conduct in which the young Christian today needs to take the injunctions of the Epistle of James more to heart than in this matter of frivolous and indiscriminate oaths and the thoughtless mention of the divine name in general conversation. Not only is he guilty of violating the divine law on this subject, but his power of witnessing to others is rendered ineffective. For even those who do not recognize the existence of God are the first to notice the inconsistency and hypocrisy of those who profess to worship Him but who do not hesitate to use His name promiscuously. Moreover, the serious taking of oaths, when we are called to do so as witnesses in a court of law, must lose much of its dignity and solemnity if we are accustomed to use God's name freely and glibly.[12]

XI. PRAYS AND SINGS PRAISES. 5:13-18

Summary: James now gives instructions concerning prayer and praise: singing praise when things go well, and praying when things are not going well. Prayer is especially important in times of sickness (verses 14-15) especially when brothers have sinned against us (verse 16a). Using the example of Elijah, he then illustrates and asserts the tremendous effects that occur when righteous men pray (verses 16b-18).

5:13 -- *Is anyone among you suffering? Let him pray. Is anyone cheerful? Let him sing praises.*

Is anyone among you suffering? Let him pray – We are nearing the end of the "Marks of a Genuine Christian Life" to which James has been calling attention.[1] "Suffering" (*kakopathei*) is the same root word we met in verse 10 that summarized the troubles and

---

[12] Tasker, *op. cit.*, p. 125.

[1] We choose to treat these verses as a new paragraph. Not all agree. Some treat these verses as a continuation of the discussion of how to act under trials and suffering, or in joy and health that began with 5:1. Plummer ties this passage to verse 12 and suggests (using a faulty definition of "swear") that the proper way to give vent to strong feelings is not by taking oaths, but in worship (his explanation of what "prayer" and "praise" mean). But we treat these verses as a new paragraph because there is no conjunction or connecting particle in the Greek that ties this sentence to what has been written before. Also, after the indicatives and imperatives that characterized what went before, James' use of questions points to this being a new paragraph.

calamities that befell the Old Testament prophets. It speaks of "suffering ill" or "ill-treatment" or "adversity" of any kind – whether persecution, loss of property, oppression by the rich and powerful, or undeserved imprisonment. Indeed, in each of the communities to which James writes, there would be individual Christians who were being ill-treated. What is the proper way to express the strong feelings one has when such ill-treatment is experienced? "Let him pray" is not an option that may be chosen or not; rather, it is a command (a present tense imperative in the Greek). "Make it a practice to pray." "Pray continually, pray again and again!"[2] When they are hurting, Christians are not to indulge in self-pity, or to groan or complain against others, or to murmur against God. They are to pray for help and strength and wisdom, not just the removal of the trial. Pray that God's will be done in our lives. Prayer is the proper refuge in times like these. Long petitions, or many, cannot always be made. Short prayers, what Augustine called "Arrows of the Lord's deliverance shot out with a sudden quickness" are just as effective to bring help to the beleaguered Christian. Any Christian may go to God in prayer. None is so poor that he may not pray. No one is so disconsolate and forsaken that he may not find in God a friend. No one is so broken up but that God is able to bind up his spirit. Prayer is something that differentiates the Christian from the non-Christian. The Christian knows he has a standing invitation to draw near to God. He knows there is a new and living way into the presence of God made available by the shed blood of Christ. He knows he has an intercessor at the right hand of God. He knows the "eyes of the Lord are upon the righteous, and His ears attend to their prayers" (1 Peter 3:12).

Is anyone cheerful? Let him sing praises – Attempts to translate *euthumei* include "of good cheer, light hearted, joyful, pleasant, agreeable, in good spirits."[3] Cheerfulness is an emotion that is not dependent on prevailing conditions. A believer can be in good spirits, full of inner joy, whether things are going badly or going well. "Let him sing praises" likewise is not something optional; rather, it too is an imperative, a command and it calls for continuous action. "Sing again and again!" "Sing praises" is one word in the Greek (*psalletō*). The word originally meant "to pluck" (the way a stringed instrument was played), to make something vibrate (like the string on a bow), and so often means to sing with a harp, or to sing with instrumental accompaniment. This was the way Eastern people regularly sang the "Psalms." In fact *psallo* is the word from which our English word "psalm" is derived. However, a stringed instrument is not absolutely required to "sing praises," any more than one must use one of the 150 Biblical Psalms to provide the

---

[2] As they approach verses 13-18, not a few commentators make "prayer" the mark of a genuine Christian life. Some synonym for "prayer" occurs in each verse. In every circumstance of life, prayer is appropriate (verse 13). Prayer is vitally important in times of critical illness and when brethren have sinned against each other (verses 14-16a). James closes this topic with an illustration of how effective prayer can be (verses 16b-18).

[3] The verb occurs at Acts 27:22 where Paul makes an effort to cheer up his travelling companions before their shipwreck on the island of Malta.

lyrics for our praises.[4] *Psallo* is used in Romans 15:9 (quoting Psalm 18:49) of a general celebration of God's praises. It is used in Ephesians 5:19 where we read about "psalms, hymns, and spiritual songs, singing and making melody with your heart to the Lord." In 1 Corinthians 14:15 the word is used of "singing" in a congregational setting. Music is a very suitable way for the Christian to express joyous feelings. Christians may sing when only God is the audience, they may sing to other Christians, they may join with other Christians in a congregational expression of praise.[5] What James is asking for is that Christians remember to praise and thank God in the good times. Instead of indulging in riotous or boastful mirth, it is better to sing psalms, songs of praise to God for the good things that have resulted in the joyous feeling. "Praise" is the safeguard to keep one from forgetting God. Some seek the Lord when times are difficult, but forget Him in times of joy and prosperity. Christians will deliberately have to behave in a different way. When they are free from trouble they are to celebrate their thanksgiving to God by singing His praises. Virgil P. Brock has expressed the idea in the words of his song "A Prayer of Thanks":

> Start the day with a prayer, a prayer of thanks to God:
> Thank him for keeping you through the night,
> Thank Him for sending the morning light.
> Start the day with a prayer, a prayer of thanks to God.
>
> For our blessings, dear Lord, We bow in thanks to Thee;
> Thank Thee for giving us daily bread,
> Thank Thee for mercies around us spread;
> For our blessings, dear Lord, We bow in thanks to Thee.
>
> At the close of the day we bow in thanks to Thee;
> Thank Thee for wonderful saving power,
> Thank Thee for keeping us hour by hour;
> At the close of the day, We bow in thanks to Thee.[6]

---

[4] The KJV "Let him sing psalms" restricts the meaning too much. While many of the Psalms do express heart-felt thanks to God, and can be sung because they have been set to music, in this context, *psallo* must be not be restricted to the singing of the Psalms of David, but may have a wider reference to any words by which we give praise to God for what He has done in our lives.

[5] O.E. Payne published a book (*Instrumental Music is Scriptural*) giving numerous citations intended to prove that *psallo* always implies the use of an instrument, but folk in the acapella churches have exploded his thesis by producing classical examples where the instrument was not implied. In fact, in our Bibles, "Psalm" is the name given to 150 poems the words of which used to be sung to accompaniment, but in our Bibles we no longer have the notes or scores of music to aid or guide the instrumentalist. As the Bible neither commands the use of an instrument at all times, nor prohibits the use at any time, the use of such is left to the individual Christian to decide.

[6] "A Prayer of Thanks," copyrighted 1949 by the Rodeheaver Co., Winona Lake, Ind.

5:14 -- *Is anyone among you sick?   Let him call for the elders of the church, and let them pray over him, anointing him with oil in the name of the Lord;*

Is anyone among you sick? – "Among you" is used half-a-dozen times in chapters 3-5 to refer to the readers as a "group" or "congregation" in each place where they live. "Sick" (*asthenei*) literally means "no strength" and pictures the weakness and incapacitation that results from physical sickness.[7] Since Adam sinned, sickness and death have been the experience of every one of Adam's descendants. It is part of the "futility" to which the whole race was subjected by God (Romans 8:20) as part of the penalty for sin.[8] Not only is prayer appropriate when we are suffering ill-treatment (verse 13), it is very appropriate to pursue prayer when sickness invades our bodies.[9] The "sick" person is pictured as being bedfast, too ill and weak to go to the elders. At such times we may not think clearly and rationally, so the direction to call for the aid of others to lead our thoughts, and to aid us in our devotions, is very appropriate.

Let him call for the elders of the church – Since prayer is needed, James gives instructions how to go about it. "Let him call for the elders" is an imperative mood in the Greek. The sick person himself, or others at his request, is commanded to summon the elders of the church.[10] Several lines of thought are suggested by this brief mention of elders.

(1) There must have been a group of men in each congregation who were recognized as "elders."[11] As was true of the Jewish communities that chose leaders in the centuries

---

[7] Some have attempted to show *astheneō* means spiritual distress or spiritual weakness. Carl Armerding, "'Is Any Among You Afflicted?' A Study of James 5:13-20" in *Bib. Sac.* 95 (1938), p.195-201.

[8] Malnutrition has devastating effects on people's health. Many of James' readers were from the poorer classes, where famine and lack of money to purchase food would be felt first.

[9] We are treating "sickness" as another circumstance where prayer is needed, rather than as a particular example of "suffering" such as verse 13 talked about. If we could affirm that all cases of human sickness are caused by demons or by the devil, then we might lump sickness under the category of "suffering ill-treatment." But not all sickness can be so categorized (John 9:2-3).

[10] While visiting the sick is given as one of the expected tasks an elder will perform, it is here given as the duty of the sick to call for the elders. This commentator has heard of places where church members became perturbed because they have been sick and no one from church came to visit. If, when we are sick, we call the doctor (that is, we don't expect him to know when we are ill and just happen to drop in), then why expect our elders to know of our sickness if we don't tell them? Instead, if able, the patient can send a messenger to the elders, expressing the desire for a visit.

[11] In the language of the denominational world, James 5:14 makes a distinction between clergy and laity. In the present case, the sick person is not to send for just any members of the congregation, but for certain ones who hold a definite and apparently official position. Hebrews 13:17, 1 Timothy 3:1ff, 4:14, 5:17ff, and Titus 1:5-9 could also be used to corroborate the idea that "elder" is a function different from that held by the average member of the congregation.
     (The Restoration Movement has given the terms "clergy" and "laity" a particular definition when insisting there is no clergy-laity distinction in the New Testament, but that instead we all are brethren. We have (correctly) rejected the idea that only certain ordained "priests" or "bishops" (i.e., clergy) have sacerdotal powers invested in them by the laying on of hands. Sacerdotalism is a religious belief emphasizing the powers of priests as essential mediators between God and man. Christ is our one mediator, and all Christians are personally welcome to go to God in prayer. A special "clergy" class is not needed for this.)

before Jesus established His church,[12] the Christian congregations apparently chose their leaders from among the older and more mature members.[13]   The first mention of elders in the church at Jerusalem is just 14 years after Pentecost, when Paul and Barnabas make their famine visit to Jerusalem (Acts 11:30).   The Jerusalem Conference, AD 51, is the next mention of elders (Acts 15:6). If our proposed date for the writing of James (AD 52) is correct, then James 5 would be the third earliest reference[14] to elders, and it implies they are functioning all over the Diaspora wherever James' Christian readers happened to live.

(2) "Church" says that wherever James' readers are living, they are grouped into local congregations,[15] and these congregations have elders who lead, rule, teach, shepherd, oversee,[16] and serve the members of the congregation.

(3) James speaks of "elders" (plural) in complete harmony with the New Testament which consistently portrays a plurality of elders within each local congregation (Acts 14:23; Philippians 1:1; 1 Thessalonians 5:12).[17]

(4) Having been summoned, the elders come to the sick person's home, rather than the sick person being brought to a public healing service.

---

[12] Jewish "elders" ("the elders of Israel") are referred to in such passages as Exodus 24:1; Leviticus 4:15; Numbers 16:25; Deuteronomy 31:9; Judges 21:16; 2 Samuel 17:4; Ezra 10:15; and Matthew 26:3.

[13] *Presbuteros* ("elder") is a comparative term meaning "older" than some others. These leaders are called "elders" or "bishops" or "pastors" in the New Testament, but not "priests." Perhaps it was because of the anathemas thundered by the Council of Trent (see information in a subsequent footnote) that the Douay Version reads "priests" here at James 5:14 when the Latin Vulgate from which it was translated reads *presbyteros* and not *sacerdotes* (the usual Latin word for priests). The Greek word for priest (*hiereus*), while used of Jesus and the Jewish priests, is never found in the New Testament as a title for leaders in the church.

[14] Written about AD 51, 1 Thessalonians 5:12,13 likely refers to elders, but they are not actually named in that passage.

[15] In James 2:2, James called the assemblies of his Jewish Christian readers a "synagogue." When the church became filled with converts from among the Greeks, the Greek word *ekklēsia*, "church" or "congregation," came into widespread use to designate the regular assembly of believers. It called attention to the fact the believers had been "called out" of, or separated from, the world, and now they formed a distinct group. "Church" sometimes describes what theologians call "the church universal" (cp. Matthew 16:18; Ephesians 1:22, 3:10), but it more often denotes what we call a "local church" or a "local congregation" in a certain geographic location (cp. Acts 5:11; 1 Corinthians 4:17; Philippians 4:15).

[16] Perhaps among Jewish congregations, such leaders were called "elders," whereas among Gentile congregations the title "bishop" (overseer) came into use as a synonym for "elder" (Acts 20:20,27; Titus 1:5-7).

[17] It is commonly accepted that while the apostles of Jesus lived, congregations of Christians enjoyed local autonomy. There were no diocesan bishops who ruled all the congregations in a given area. That hierarchical form of church government is something that developed after the apostles were dead. J.W. Roberts (*A Commentary on the General Epistle of James* [Austin, TX : Sweet, 1963], p.165-66) has argued that J.B. Lightfoot's effort in his commentary on Philippians to show that the monarchical episcopate is a scriptural form of church government is flawed. Instead of developing while the apostles were still living, that form of government arose out of the desire to have a central authority to lead the church while the church was attempting to counteract the threat of Gnosticism.

(5) Some have tried to answer the question, "Why call for the elders?"   Did some of them have special miraculous gifts?[18]   Do they represent the whole church when they pray over the sick, so that each member was, as it were, praying for the sick person through their chosen leaders?   Because of their maturity, are they recognized to be men of prayer?   After all, sickness is a time when prayer is especially needed and appropriate.

And let them pray over him – The sick person is pictured as lying down.   We see the elders bending over the bedridden person while they offer their prayers (cp. Luke 4:39; Matthew 8:14).   Perhaps the elders reached over and touched the sick person as they prayed, but "over him" cannot be pressed to prove there was any such "laying on of hands."[19]   The elders do the praying, though the sick person certainly could make the prayer his and consent to what the elders asked of God by saying the "Amen."[20]

Anointing him with oil – "Anointing" is a participle dependent on the main verb "Let them pray over him."   In other words, prayer accompanied by anointing is the action the elders are expected to perform.   We cannot tell whether the picture James draws is that the anointing takes place before the elders prayed or while they were praying.[21]

This Scripture has occasioned much controversy.   What did the anointing consist of, what was its purpose, and what were its benefits?   Is this instruction a rule for all time in the church?

---

[18] Calvin taught that elders, in the age before the gifts ceased, possessed charismatic gifts.   A.B. Simpson (*The Gospel of Healing* [New York: Christian Alliance Publishing, 1915]) and A.J. Gordon (*The Ministry of Healing* [Harrisburg: Christian Publications, 1961]), both hold the elders had spiritual gifts and that the gifts are still available in the Church today.   What are we to conclude from the fact the elders were sent for, and not a charismatic healer, when at the time James writes spiritual gifts were still available and operative in the church?   Is James signaling a new course of action, or does James recognize that many of the communities to which he writes will not have had a visit by an apostle, and therefore be unlikely to have spiritual gifts available, since such gifts were received by the laying on of an apostle's hands?

[19] It is correct to take "over him" with the verb "to pray" rather than with the participle "to anoint."

[20] James recommends calling in the congregational leaders, not as anything new, nor as excluding other therapeutic methods.   Nor should we today exclude the help trained physicians can give.   After all, it can be said that Paul had a personal physician traveling with him on several of his missionary journeys, and Jesus recognized that physicians are treating sickness, when He said, "They that are whole have no need of a physician, but they that are sick" (Mark 2:17).

[21] The participle "anointing" is aorist tense, as is the verb "let them pray."   Thus it could be argued that the anointing precedes the praying (an aorist participle usually indicates action prior to the action of the main verb).   It could also be defended that the anointing and the praying are simultaneous since an aorist participle depending on an aorist tense verb may indicate action simultaneous with the action of the main verb.   Marshall's interlinear translation of the Greek has the anointing before the praying.

- The "oil" was likely olive oil (as *elaion* usually refers to in Scripture).[22] The word "anoint" (*aleipsantes*) originally meant to "rub" or "smear" or "daub," though it can also mean to "pour" the oil on the person (usually on the head, but it may be poured on other parts of the body).[23] We cannot tell for sure if the elders were to smear ointment or liquid on the sick, or were to pour liquid oil on the head of the one who was sick.

- What purpose did the oil serve? Because we are not told the purpose of the oil, and because it is not certain we have any Biblical examples to illustrate the practice in the church, commentators have been free to advance numerous guesses. Two of the guesses[24] found in our literature are: (1) Many suggest that the "oil" may have served a medicinal purpose. Prior to the discovery of modern pharmaceuticals and anti-biotics, olive oil was one of the most common medicines used by the ancients.[25] In those cases where oil helped promote the body's healing processes, its use was not to

[22] There are no instructions from James about any special preparation or consecration of the oil. There were three grades of olive oil, and nothing is said about any necessity to use only one grade. In time, it became the custom to drain some of the olive oil from the lamps used to light the meeting place of the church, and use it to anoint the sick. This was still the custom in the Greek church, noted one writer about a century ago. *Elaion* can speak of "oil" or "fat" or "grease" (like butter). If olive oil is boiled, it can be reduced to a paste or a salve form.

[23] Compare what Mary did for Jesus as she anointed Him beforehand for His burial (John 12:3). See also Luke 6:46 where Jesus noted that his host had not anointed His head. See also 1 Samuel 16:13 and Psalm 23:5.

[24] These two seem to be the best answers we have found to the question "What purpose was the oil intended to serve?" Other less-satisfying answers include: (1) Some have supposed that anointing with oil was a Christian religious act, and that the oil was symbolic. Perhaps it was symbolic of God's healing presence or His divine favor. Perhaps it was symbolic of the presence of the Holy Spirit. (While it was the Spirit who empowered the apostles to do miracles such as healing, and the Spirit who gave supernatural spiritual gifts to certain church members who could then heal [1 Corinthians 12:7,9], it appears to be reading too much into the "oil" to find the Holy Spirit here. James 5:15 says it was the Lord who raised up the sick person in answer to the prayer of faith.) A Franciscan priest, Robert Karris, "Some New Angles on James 5:13-20," *Review and Expositor* 97 (2000), p.207-219, has proposed the oil was symbolic of life, restoration to health, and eschatological gladness. There is no agreement among Bible students concerning what the oil may symbolize, even if the symbolic view is being defended. (2) Some (e.g., William Anderson, "Sacramental healing," *Christianity Today* 5:9 [January 30, 1961], p.8-9) have suggested the oil served a sacramental purpose; that is, it had to do with the forgiveness of sins. Baptism and the Lord's Supper have something to do with forgiveness (1 Peter 3:21 and 1 Corinthians 10:16), but the Scriptures nowhere say that oil does. One important objection to this view is that the Greek word used by James which has been translated "anoint" is *aleipsantes*. This is not the usual word for sacramental or ritualistic anointing, which was *chriō*. Trench (*Synonyms*, p.136-37) says that in Scripture *aleiphō* is the word used when it is "the mundane and profane" that is anointed; *chriō* is the "sacred and religious" term. However, Moulton and Milligan (*Vocabulary*, p.693) have shown that this distinction did not always hold in secular usage, and modern linguists are not happy with any "rigid distinction" such as Trench and others have made. Yet such a distinction between the words is still observed in modern Greek, where *aleiphō* means 'to daub' or 'to smear' while *chriō* means 'to anoint.'

[25] The *New American Bible* (an official Catholic version) has this study note at James 5:14: "... oil was used for medicinal purposes in the ancient world (see Isaiah 1:6; Luke 10:34)." Indeed, familiar examples of the medical use of oil include Isaiah 1:6 and the Samaritan who, as he helped the wounded traveler, poured oil and wine into his wounds (Luke 10:34). The use of the same oil and wine mixture as "medicine" was described in Greek writings (Dion Cass., LIII.29 and Strabo, XVI,p.780). Celsus recom-

be ruled out, even though Christians were to rely on prayer (verse 15) for healing.[26] (2) Many suppose that in some cases the oil served a practical purpose as well as being an aid to the sick person's desire to get well.[27] Folk who live in the dry climate of the Middle East were in the habit of anointing their hair and faces every day as a protection against the heat and dryness of the climate (compare our use sun-tan lotion). Olive oil or petroleum grease was commonly used, though the poor smeared on vegetable or animal fat. It was applied to exposed parts of the body, especially the face (Psalm 104:15). Jews did not anoint themselves when they were sick, or when they were fasting (Matthew 6:17) or mourning (2 Samuel 14:2; Daniel 10:3). The anointing with oil, then, was an indication that the sick man was to be no longer confined to his bed of sickness, but was getting ready to be up and out and about his work. Anticipation of getting well often helps hurry the body's healing processes.

- Critics of both these views have responded, "If the oil served either of these two purposes, medicinal or practical, why wait till the elders come? Why does not one of the sick man's friends or relatives apply the medicine? Why take medicine 'in the name of the Lord'?" Perhaps the fact the elders did the anointing in the name of the Lord showed this oil was intended to be "the oil of gladness" (Hebrews 1:9), not just an ordinary use of oil. It could even be supposed this "anointing with oil" by the elders was something that belonged to Jewish Christianity (remember, James exercised his Christian liberty, and during his whole life-time practiced certain Old Testament taboos and rituals, Acts 21:18ff). It could further be suggested that the practice of anointing, learned from Old Testament examples and practiced as a matter of liberty by the Jewish Christians, was then copied and continued by some churches into the second century.[28]

---

mended rubbing with oil in the case of fevers and other ailments (*De Medicina* II.1417; III.6.9,19,22; IV.2). Oil baths were used in hope of effecting a cure when Herod the Great was sick (Jos. *Ant.* XVII.6.5). *T. Shab.* 12.2 reads "A sick person may be rubbed on the Sabbath with a mixture of oil and wine." At the same time, it must be acknowledged that there were many ailments for which oil would be ineffective (e.g., broken bones, heart trouble, many infectious diseases). Gary Shogren ("Will God Heal Us -- A Re-examination of James 5:14-16a," *EQ* 61:2 [1989], p.99-108) has given 6 reasons to reject the idea that oil was a cure-all being used as "the best medical help available."

[26] Advocates of the idea the "oil" was "medicine" have not been able to explain how the elders might put the oil on the parts of the body that are usually not exposed, nor how they would anoint any part of a lady's anatomy save the head. The whole issue is further complicated for modern readers by the holistic health movement, the inner healing movement, the "Health and Wealth Gospel," and other faith-healers who flatly reject the use of any modern medical technology. The claim is made that if the patient has enough faith, God will make him or her well. An excellent critique of this whole idea is found in Bruce Barron's, *The Health and Wealth Gospel* (Downers Grove, IL: InterVarsity, 1987).

[27] This was R.C. Foster's explanation of the oil. Not a few suppose the Lord's use of saliva (Mark 7:33, 8:23) and clay made with spittle (John 9:6) were likewise to help the person believe that healing was possible.

[28] See *Clementine Recogn.* 1.44-45; Hippolytus, *Philos.* 9.15; Epiphanius, *Haer.* 19.1.6. Roberts (*op. cit.*, p.168) has well said, "It is impossible to say with certainty which of the uses of anointing oil James had in mind. In the context of their own time and practice, James' readers knew what he meant, but that context is not known to us today. We can only say which is more probable and what the application would be in any case."

In the name of the Lord – Not only have commentators struggled to explain what purpose the oil served, but they have struggled when trying to explain "in the name of the Lord."[29]

(1) At times this phrase means "because the Lord has commanded it." The "Lord" in whose name this was to be done is here, without doubt, the Lord Jesus. But where do we have any record He commanded that sick folk be anointed with oil?[30]

(2) Are the elders thus signifying they are acting in trustful dependence on Christ and His authority?

(3) Are the elders calling on Jesus to intervene and do something about the sick person's condition?

(4) Did the elders' emphasis "on the name of the Lord" make it clear that, if a healing was accomplished, it was the Lord's doing and not man's?[31]

(5) Some connect "in the name of the Lord" with the command to pray, so that the "prayer asked in the name of the Lord" means the elders ask the Father to grant their request only if it will benefit the Kingdom of Christ and be in harmony with Christ's will.

Whichever explanation of "in the name of the Lord" we adopt, it is evident that "anointing with oil," as the context shows, was done in anticipation of healing. Contrary to Roman Catholic dogma, neither this verse nor Mark 6:12 is a proof text for "extreme unction."[32]

---

[29] There is no reason to suppose that this phrase has any particular magical significance (comparable to the magical formulas used by strolling exorcists). At a later time, Gnostic heretics did use anointing with oil as a means of exorcism (see the *Acts of Thomas* 67, and Heinrich Schlier, "Aleipho" in TDNT, 1:230). Jewish people used anointing with oil in connection with exorcism (see Paul Billerbeck, *Die Briefe Des Neuen Testaments Und Die Offenbarung Johannis Erlautert Aus Talmud Und Midrasch*, p. 759; and the Midrash Rabba on Ecclesiastes). M.Dibelius, "James" in *Hermeneia – A Critical and Historical Commentary on the Bible* (Philadelphia: Fortress, 1976), citing no evidence whatever, asserts concerning James 5:14,15, "the whole procedure was an exorcism." John Wilkinson, *Health and Healing* (Edinburgh: Handsel Press, 1980), p.148, shows that physical, not demonic, affliction is intended by *astheneō*.

[30] Did Jesus command the use of any medium (oil, or spittle, or healing cloths) when He sent folk to heal? Perhaps He did so command the apostles during his Galilean ministry (Mark 6:13, though in this place it is difficult to decide whether anointing with oil and healing were two separate acts, or whether the oil produced the healing). But later, when Jesus gave the Great Commission, there was no mention of anointing oil or any other medium. He did promise "these signs would follow" (Mark 16:17), and He spoke about "laying hands on the sick," but there is no mention of oil. It cannot be assumed that the use of oil by the elders was a suitable substitute for the laying on of hands, though the "anointing" (if it means "rub" and not "pour") might have been the actual occasion when they did touch the patient.

[31] Some suppose we have an illustration of the meaning of James' instructions in Peter's healing of the lame man (Acts 3). Peter told a lame man, "In the name of Jesus – walk!" (I.e., "Jesus commands you to walk around!"). Later, Peter reiterated to the Sanhedrin that it was "by the name of Jesus Christ of Nazareth that this man stands before you whole" (Acts 4:10). But does this event in Acts 3 illustrate what James is asking the elders to do? Can "in the name of the Lord" without a corresponding imperative like "walk!" be a command ("Jesus Christ commands you to get well") spoken by the elders to the sick person?

[32] James 5:14 is the verse that has been used by the Roman Church to justify the practice of extreme unction. Thus, both Catholic and Protestant commentaries usually have extended comments at this place. We include these comments for the benefit of those unfamiliar with the practice and the theology behind it. Tasker (*op. cit.*, p.128) explains, "In that ceremony the priest anoints the eyes, ears, nostrils, hands and feet of a sick person considered to be *in extremis* in the belief that the application of such previously consecrated oil is an effective medium of forgiveness in the case of those who are no longer able to make conscious confession of sins and receive priestly absolution." The organs anointed are the ones employ-

5:15 -- *And the prayer offered in faith will restore the one who is sick, and the Lord will raise him up, and if he has committed sins, they will be forgiven him.*

And the prayer offered in faith – This verse (connected to verse 15 by "and") describes the results of the ministry of the elders to the sick person. That ministry, as verse 15 showed, was prayer accompanied by "anointing with oil." "The prayer" (with the article) points to the prayer the elders just offered. The prayer the elders offered over the sick person is here described as a "prayer of faith" (the Greek reads *hē euchē tēs pisteōs*). The phrase "the faith" in the genitive case seems to describe that prayer. The NASB treated it as a subjective genitive,[33] a prayer "motivated by faith." What is a "prayer of faith"? And faith on whose part (the elders', or the sick person's)?

---

ed during life in offending God. At each anointing, the priest pronounces these words, "May the Lord, by this holy anointing, and by His own most tender mercy, pardon thee whatever sin thou hast committed, by thy sight, hearing, ... etc." In the Douay version (for a long time the official Roman Catholic version of the Bible in English) there is this footnote on James 5:14: "See here a plain warrant of scripture for the Sacrament of Extreme Unction, that any controversy against its institution would be against the express words of the sacred text in the plainest terms." That assertion is hard to accept. The footnote was changed to read, "According to the teaching of the Council of Trent (Sess. 14.c.3) St. James promulgated here the Sacrament of Extreme Unction," when the Confraternity Edition was published in 1950. Except for the mention of "anointing with oil," James 5:14 does not even come close to speaking of the Roman practice of extreme unction. The sick person in James is pictured as getting well (5:15), not as (in the Roman practice) being so near death that recovery is considered almost or quite hopeless. There is hardly any relationship at all between the "elders" James writes about, and the "priest" the Roman church refers to. If there is any connection at all between James 5:14,15 and the Roman sacrament, it is this: the latter grew out of practices in the church based on this passage. For about eight centuries, the sick were anointed, not (save in the case of the Gnostic sect known as Heracleonites [Epiph. *Haer.* 36.2.4ff]) those who were about to die. Nor was it necessary for the anointing to be done by a priest, until, in AD 853, the function of anointing the sick was limited to the "priest." In the 13th century, the Schoolmen (Medieval theologians) included the anointing with oil as one of the seven sacraments. As the years passed, it became a rule that the sacred oil had to be prepared by the bishop. Then communion for the sick was added, and in the West that required a priest. The anointing with oil preceded the giving of communion – and thus we have the "last rites" (Extreme Unction, the "last oil") and the "Sacrament of the departing." The developed sacrament brought about a state of things quite inconsistent with the original starting point. The Scholastics made a major change. If bodily healing no longer followed the anointing with oil, it was because the anointing had become the sign and sacrament of a spiritual healing, and the special grace which it conveyed was adapted to the needs of the soul in its last struggles. The cardinals at the Council of Trent (AD 1545-1563) at first disputed, and then after their manner at last agreed, that extreme unction was instituted by Christ (*Sessio* xiv). After further debate they changed the word to "insinuated" by Christ, and then, they affirmed, it was James who published it (James 5). The council further ruled that priests must instruct their people that by this sacrament venial sins are remitted, the soul is freed from weaknesses contracted by sin, and filled with courage, hope, and joy. Canons III and IV anathematized those who think Jesus did not initiate this sacrament, or those who think it may be safely neglected. They also anathematized those who think that "priests" mentioned in James are any other than episcopally ordained priests. Since Vatican II the "Last Rites" have been known as the Anointing of the Sick. The Church in England at one time practiced extreme unction. But by the time the Prayer Book of 1552 was published, the idea of "unction" had disappeared, and has never been revived in the Church of England. Mormons still practice anointing of the sick with oil, believing it will effect healing. And in this, the Mormons are consistent, for they claim the miraculous spiritual gifts are extant in their church.

[33] The other option is to treat it as an objective genitive, that is, the prayer is a "prayer for faith." It seems doubtful the elders were praying the sick person would have enough faith to be healed. Faith is not a gift received in answer to prayer. The idea that a positive answer to such a prayer depends on sufficient degree of faith on the part of the patient is a difficult thesis to document in Scripture. It is cruel to lead a sick person to believe the reason he or she failed to recover is because his or her faith was faulty or deficient! It likewise seems doubtful the elders were praying that the sick person would begin to believe

(1) Some are confident the "faith" here is one of the spiritual gifts that enabled their recipients to work miracles. 1 Corinthians 12:9 does list "faith" as one of the miraculous gifts, and it differs from "gifts of healings" named in the same verse. In the early days of the church age when spiritual gifts still were available through the laying on of an apostles's hands, had the elders in the churches to which James writes been so gifted? We doubt it.[34]

(2) Is "faith" a reference to the body of doctrine known as the Christian faith? If so, James is saying that such prayers are effective if the one offering them is a Christian? Answered prayer for healing is not something promised to the non-Christian.[35]

(3) Does "the faith" mean that while the elders are praying there is "no latent doubt" about whether or not the Lord will heal? Is this an example of what is elsewhere called believing prayer? Jesus taught His disciples to pray with no latent doubt. "Everything you ask in prayer, believing, you shall receive" (Matthew 21:21-22).

(4) Is "faith" the conviction or confidence on the part of the elders that the Lord Jesus (in whose name the prayer was offered) can and will intervene?

"The faith" seems to be faith exercised by the elders as they prayed over the sick. While we do teach that instantaneous miracles have ceased, the Lord still does wonderful things in answer to prayer.[36] We do teach that what James asks sick people in his own time to do is still the thing for Jesus' followers to do when they are sick, even in this third millennium.

---

he would get well. If the sick had no hopes of getting better, why send for the elders in the first place? Not many commentators have been satisfied with where the attempt to treat "of faith" as an objective genitive leads them. It is doubtful, too, that the elders were praying for their own faith to be increased.

[34] Rendel Short, *The Bible and Modern Medicine* (Chicago: Moody, 1967), p.125, is an example of one who is of the opinion that "faith" in James 5:15 and in 1 Corinthians 12:9 are the same thing. This interpretation is weighted with many serious questions. When supernatural gifts ceased, was it still possible to pray a "prayer in faith" and expect the sick to be restored to health? When the supernatural gifts ceased, was there any reason to continue the practice of anointing with oil? Might it not be difficult to show that all the elders who might read James' letter had been in the presence of an apostle, to have hands laid on them? (Remember, James is written at about the same time the apostles were first scattered from Jerusalem, to go on their world missionary endeavors.) Acts 3:16 does seem to show that it was both the faith of Peter and John (a miraculous ability?) plus the faith of the lame man that resulted in that healing. Could this be an illustration of what the "prayer in faith" was that James writes about? We think not. Acts 3 is an apostolic miracle; James deals with answered prayer. The two should not be equated.

[35] This would be a rather pointed claim that Christian doctrine alone is valid, another point made by James as he repudiates the Judaizers' beliefs.

[36] This verse has caused "cessationists" to be hesitant in their affirmation that "miracles have ceased." By making a distinction between answered prayer and miracle, James 5:14-15 can be harmonized with the cessationist view, but there are enough questions remaining (which cannot be answered with absolute certainty) to cause the interpreter to be cautious in his affirmations. As we read this verse, we do not picture that James is describing an instantaneous miraculous healing as occurring every time elders prayed and anointed with oil. We do see it as providential healing as Jesus intervenes in His people's lives in answer to prayer.

Will restore the one who is sick – While assurance is given that the sick person will be restored, the future tense "will restore" leaves open the matter of how long the time interval may be between the prayer and the restoration. After the prayer, the sick person may "begin to get well" or they may get well all at once.[37] The Greek (*sōsei ton kamnonta*) could be translated "will save" as well as "will restore." *Sōzō* is the word used when Scripture speaks of being "saved" from sin (i.e., to save from a life of slavery to sin now, and to save from the guilt and penalty for sin both now and in the future). *Sōzō* can also mean "make well" when a person is sick.[38] Perhaps *sōzō* ("restore," "save") is used in a dual sense in this place, if we may treat the remainder of the verse as unfolding what is meant: "the Lord will raise him up" refers to physical restoration, and "sins will be forgiven" refers to being saved from sin. The word used for "sick" (*ton kamnonta*) is a present participle from a verb which means "to grow weary" with the secondary sense of 'grow weary by reason of sickness.'[39] Sick people often do not have much energy; it is easier to lie down in order to conserve what little energy they have, rather than to be up and around.

That James makes the promise of recovery without any restriction may at first sight appear to be surprising since Scripture elsewhere does put some restrictions on answered prayer. Even James has noted some, at James 1:6-8 and 4:3. All prayer is subject to the reservation, "Thy will be done." This promise of restoration can hardly be taken in an absolute or unconditional sense, for then sick people would never need to die. The apostles themselves had no indiscriminate power of healing. Philippians 2:27; 2 Timothy 4:20; and 2 Corinthians 12:7-9 are examples where the apostles did not heal.[40] How then are we to explain that James has no restrictions on his language of promise about healing? He leaves it to the common sense and the Christian submission of his readers to understand

---

[37] Future tense verbs can be punctiliar or linear, that is, the action described can be either a single act or continuous action.

[38] Passages where the verb deals with healing of the body are Matthew 9:22; Mark 5:23, 6:56; John 11:12; Acts 9:34.

[39] The verb is used at Revelation 2:3 (Textus Receptus) and at Hebrews 12:3. Roman Catholics interpret "save" to refer to "future salvation of the soul" and "sick" to mean "dying" as they try to use this passage as a proof text for extreme unction. In its aorist and perfect tense forms this verb was sometimes used by classical writers as a description of "the dead", but there is no example in Greek literature of the present participle conveying the meaning of "the dying." So that it is a stretch to suggest that the sufferer is *in extremis*. James views the elders ministering to one who is down in bed, but expected to live.

[40] Much current teaching in the contemporary church on the subject of "spiritual healing" rests on the false assumption that it is God's will that every Christian should enjoy perfect physical health at all times. There is nothing in the New Testament to justify this assumption, and in fact there is some evidence which points in the opposite direction. In addition to the verses just alluded to in the text (i.e., Paul's thorn in the flesh, and Trophimus being left at Miletus sick), attention should be given to Romans 8:23, which teaches that the suffering that is common to all of God's creatures applies to Christians. Even though Christians have the first-fruits of the Spirit, still they groan because of the suffering.

that elders have no power to cancel the sentence of physical death pronounced on the whole human race when Adam sinned. To pray that one should be exempt from this sentence would not be faith, but presumption.

And the Lord will raise him up – The verb "raise up" means "enable one to stand on his feet." It is the verb used when Jesus commanded the paralytic to "arise (stand up on your feet), take up your bed, and walk" (Mark 2:9). The sick person over whom the elders prayed will be able to get up from the sick bed.[41] "Lord" here is Jesus, the One in whose name the prayer was offered (verse 14). This makes it clear how the healing takes place. Jesus is Lord of heaven and earth. He providentially oversees people's lives. "In answer to the prayer, the Lord uses the medicine to cure the malady."[42]

And if he has committed sins, they will be forgiven him – This seems to be a further explanation of what is involved in "restoring/saving" the sick. Not only are physical needs met, but so are spiritual needs. Prayer for forgiveness is certainly one of the conditions of a Christian being forgiven (Acts 8:22). "And if" translates *kan* (a contraction of *kai ean*); the *kai* marks a connection between the sickness and committed sins, and the *ean* introduces a conditional statement. The conditional clause makes it clear that while not all physical sickness in a person's life is the result of personal sin, sickness *may* be the result of personal sin.[43] When the patient's own sins have occasioned the sickness, the sickness is a temporal punishment for sin.[44] Whenever sickness strikes the Christian, he or she should use the down time as an opportunity to do some serious self-examination. Is there unrepented-of sin embraced in the heart? Now is the time to repent![45] If it was sin that occasioned the sickness, the sin will be forgiven. These words assure the sick person that the situation is not hopeless.

---

[41] Gary Holloway, "James and Jude" in *The College Press NIV Commentary* (Joplin, MO.: College Press, 1996), p.127, suggests that "save" is intentionally ambiguous here: it might refer to physical healing, or it might have reference to future bodily resurrection. We are all aware of the fact that not every one is healed when we pray over them. So the ambiguous "save" means, "If the Lord God does not grant to them restored physical health, He does promise to raise them from the dead at the final resurrection."

[42] Burdick, *op. cit.*, p.204. Healing in answer to prayer is as much attributed to the risen Lord as was the miraculous healing of paralyzed Aeneas. We remember that Peter said to Aeneas, "Jesus Christ makes you whole" (Acts 9:34). The statement that "the Lord raises him" excludes "any magical operation of the oil with which the sick is to be anointed" (Heinrich Greeven, "Euchomai, Euche" in TDNT, 2:776).

[43] The plural "sins" indicates repeated occasions of sin (i.e., missing the mark of doing the known will of God). "Has committed" (*pepoiēkōs*) is a perfect tense verb, which indicates past completed action with present continuing results. Past sins have present results – the one who committed them is down in bed, sick, and is unforgiven.

[44] Though not all physical suffering is a punishment for the sins of the sufferer concerned, nevertheless, there are times men do suffer for their own sins (Mark 2:5-11; 1 Corinthians 11:30). We are convinced that such temporal punishments for sin were not confined to the apostolic age, but that they still occur in abundance. God sends temporal punishments for sin to warn us to turn away from the sin, lest we suffer a far worse condition, eternal punishment.

[45] Repentance is presupposed as a condition of forgiveness.

"Forgiven" (*aphiēmi*), the standard term in the New Testament for "forgiveness," pictures the sins as being "sent away" – like the scape goat was sent away (Leviticus 16:9,10), bearing the people's sins away so they are no longer held against them.[46]   When it here speaks of sins forgiven, we must not think of the unsaved having their sins thus forgiven simply by someone else praying for them.   This passage is not speaking of initial salvation of the unsaved.   It is speaking about a Christian sinning, confessing his sin, and having that sin forgiven.   It is the Lord who does the forgiving.[47]

5:16 -- *Therefore, confess your sins to one another, and pray for one another, so that you may be healed.   The effective prayer of a righteous man can accomplish much.*

Therefore – "Therefore" shows the very close connection between the last part of verse 15 and what James writes here in verse 16.[48]   Verse 15 has spoken of sickness, sin, and forgiveness when folk pray.   One of the inferences to be drawn is this: forgiveness implies confession of those sins, since confession is a condition of forgiveness (1 John 1:9).   Another inference that might be drawn is that the confession is somehow involved with the sin that resulted in the sickness, and the sick man confessed his sins to the elders for the purpose of their intercession.   Would not the sin, of necessity, have been confessed to the elders, before the prayer of faith could deal with it?   Perhaps we also infer a broader principle, that Christians generally are to practice the same duty of confession to each other.

Confess your sins to one another – It is difficult to know exactly what to make of this command to "confess to one another," which is inserted in the form of an inference from the preceding.   Let us state our conclusion before we look at the details.   We presume the sick confessed their sins to God, but there is someone else to whom confession needs be made.

---

[40] One wonders whether in the back of James' mind is the case of the healing of the paralytic (Mark 2:1-12).   Jesus' first statement to the sick man who had been let down into the room was "your sins are forgiven."   Then He went on to heal the person.   His discussion with the Jewish scribes on that occasion showed that the visible healing was proof Jesus also had the authority to forgive, which was something that could not be seen by the human eye.   Perhaps James is saying that if the sick person is healed, that is clear indication that any sins of the sufferer, which might have been responsible for this particular illness, were likewise forgiven.

[47] Somewhere around AD 400, the idea grew up from the practice taught in this passage that the priest (elder) had the power of absolution (Chrys. *De Sacerd*. III.6).   As a result, instead of "God forgives you," or "you are forgiven," now the priest says to the penitent, "I forgive you."   It is noteworthy to observe that the forgiveness of sins here promised by James is not dependent on the utterance of the quasi-judicial formula of the *Absolvo te* (that was, indeed, not used until the 13th century) by an individual priest, but on the prayer of the elders representing the church and the penitent sinner.   Only God can forgive sins! (Even when the apostles were told "If you forgive the sins of any, they have been forgiven" [John 20:33], the apostles were not the initiators of the forgiveness.   Rather, as the future perfect passive verb shows, they were simply publishing on earth what had already been done in heaven.)

[48] The KJV does not include a "therefore" in this verse, because the Greek text behind the KJV had none.   But manuscript evidence (Sinaiticus, A,B,K, Vulgate, Syriac, Coptic) supports its inclusion, as modern critical texts show.   *Oun* ("consequently, these things being so, accordingly, therefore") draws an inference from what was just said.

"To one another," says James.   The one who sinned needs to confess it to the brother who has been sinned against.   Before any such confession (either to God or to the offended) occurs, the person who committed will have repented, for confession presumes repentance.   Moreover, it is right that others who may have been cognizant of the sin should be equally aware of the repentance; the penitent may then have the benefit of their prayers also.   As long as the sinner attempts to hide his sin or his repentance, there will be no prayers offered.

Some key points must be taken into account as we attempt to understand what James is commanding:

(1) "Therefore" connects this command with the context about praying for the sick, and sins forgiven.   Likewise, "that you may be healed" indicates this confession to one another is in cases of sickness that need healing.

(2) "Confess" (*exomologeisthe*) is a compound verb meaning to 'say [something] openly' or 'forthrightly'; and it is a present imperative.   'Make it a practice to confess your sins to one another!'   When?   Regularly, when people are sick, and the sickness is the result of personal sin?[49]   Regularly, when people have sinned against God, whether they are sick or not?[50]   Regularly, every time people have sinned against their brothers?   "Confess" means 'to say the same thing,' that is, to say the same thing about sin that God says.   We recall the confession of the prodigal son, "I have sinned against heaven, and in your sight (against you), father" (Luke 15:18).   "Confession is a mark of repentance and a plea for forgiveness on the part of the sinner."[51]

(3) "Sins" (*tas hamartia*) is the same word used at verse 15.[52]   The word is used of 'offenses against your brethren' (Matthew 18:15); and also 'sins against God' (cp. Matthew 6:14,15).   The article "*the* sins" (translated "your sins" NASB) is likely an

---

[49] The verses about prayer for the sick are tied together with this one, and this one also speaks about "being healed."

[50] Emphasis on the present tense imperative "confess" would lead some to say Christians should not wait until they are sick before they confess their sins to one another.

[51] Simon Kistemaker, *Exposition of the Epistle of James and the Epistles of John* (Grand Rapids: Baker, 1986), p.178.

[52] Following a manuscript variation found in Erasmus (and the Textus Receptus), the KJV reads "faults" rather than "sins."   That word may have been intentionally introduced to prevent readers from assuming there is a close connection between verse 16 and what precedes it; or to make it clear that James is not advocating mutual confession by Christians to one another of *all* their sins; or to guard against abuses of public confession that had troubled the church in the years before the KJV was translated.   It seems clear that the translators of the Greek word *paraptōma*, which the Textus Receptus has here, treat it as having a less serious implication than *hamartia*.   Their rendering here and in Galatians 6:1 of *paraptōma* as "faults" is sufficient evidence of this.   Moulton and Milligan, *Vocabulary*, p.489, give examples from the papyri of the word meaning "slips" or "lapses" rather than willful sins.   They also caution that they do not propose to define the word in its New Testament occurrences from these examples in the papyri.   Even Trench (*Synonyms*, p.235) suggests at times *paraptōma* is sometimes "used of sins not of the deepest dye or the worst enormity."   Does this then say that when Christians confess to one another they can tell only about their peccadillos while hiding completely their real sins?   The KJV, while trying to prevent one misunderstanding, has produced another.

article of previous reference, the same sins talked about in verse 15. James calls for confession of specific sins, of the definite acts of which they are guilty.[53] The particular sin committed should be the thing confessed, rather than a general confession of all sins. "Wrongdoings which spoil the fellowship with one another and make it difficult, if not impossible, to worship together as the people of God, are the things confessed."[54] Perhaps James has another saying from Jesus' Sermon on the Mount in the back of his mind. "If therefore you are presenting your offering at the altar, and there remember that your brother has something against you [i.e., you have sinned against him], leave your offering there before the altar, and go your way. First be reconciled to your brother, and then come and present your offering" (Matthew 5:24).

(4) "To one another" ("one to another") is a key phrase within this verse.[55] The reciprocal pronoun (*allēlōn*) indicates a one-to-one confession: me to you, and you to me. It is not me to the whole church.[56] "Confess your sins not only to God but also to the persons who have been injured by your sins. Ask their forgiveness."[57] Have both parties committed sins? Is it the sinner who prays, and the injured party who prays? It does say, "Confess your sins to one another."[58]

(5) It is perhaps true that both Catholics and non-Catholics have misused this verse.

- Protestant misapplications include these: Public confession of sins was practiced in the 3rd and 4th centuries. Chrysostom preferred secret confession in opposition to the practice of confession before the congregation, before they were granted for-

---

[53] Care must be made to distinguish confession of sins (1 John 1:9, Mark 1:5) and confession of faith in who Jesus is (Matthew 10:32 and parallels, Romans 10:9; Philippians 2:11; 1 John 4:3). Both of these confessions are part of the conversion process. When we speak of confession of sins as part of the conversion process, perhaps that confession was made publicly (Matthew 3:6; Acts 19:18,19). However, James 5:16 is not dealing with something that is part of the initial conversion process. The people confessing to each other and praying for each other are the Christian brethren to whom James addresses this letter. They seem to do it one-on-one, and even the (implied) confession made to the elders visiting the sick room is a rather private thing.

[54] Joh. Ed. Huther, *Critical and Exegetical Handbook to the General Epistles of James, Peter, John, and Jude* (Winona Lake, IN: Alpha Publications, 1980 reprint), p.325.

[55] It is as this phrase is explained that the most doubt arises concerning the interpretation for the whole passage suggested above.

[56] Confession of *all* our sins to *all* the brethren, and *all* of them confessing *all* of their sins to us, seems not to be what James commands. Nor is confession of *all* our sins to *one* of our brethren what James commands. The mutual confession is not made member to elder, or elder to member, but member to member.

[57] Kistemaker, *op. cit.*, p.178.

[58] Is *allēlōn* a general word, not limited to sick offender and the offended? Is this a proof text for mutual confession even to brethren not sinned against? Not a few writers have so interpreted it. It is more than just sick people who need to confess sins. Well people need to do so, also, it is argued. "One another" is alleged to be a mutual activity where the members are equal, regarded as brethren. The present imperative "make it a habit of confessing your sins" and "to one another" suggest this is more than a sick person confessing to one who has been sinned against, it is affirmed. Does this passage say anything at all about healthy people confessing their sins to one another? Or between prayer partners, or to spiritual mentors? Perhaps it does, if we omit the inferential "therefore" as does the KJV.

giveness. What were called "penitentiary elders" came to be appointed to decide for penitents whether their sins must be confessed publicly to the congregation. Because public confessions could lead to abuses (e.g., bystanders who heard the confessions could use what they heard to blackmail the confessor), the practice of public confession fell into disuse. Wesley revived the practice of public confession in his "class meetings." Based on this passage alone and taken out of context, mutual confession of sins, prayer partners, and spiritual mentoring have come into vogue as the 21st century begins.

- Roman Catholics make this verse the Biblical basis of their confessional, where confession is made to a priest with a view to absolution of sin. Probably the real impetus to such auricular confession came from monasticism. Offenses against the rule of the order had to be confessed before the whole community. Other grave offenses were confessed in private to the abbot. The Catholic doctrine is that it is a duty to confess to a priest, at certain times, all our sins, secret and open, of which we have been guilty, for the priest has the power to declare on such confession that the sins are forgiven. The footnote in the Douay version reads, "That is, to the priest of the Church whom (verse 14) he had ordered to be called for and brought to the sick." The Council of Trent anathematizes all who deny that auricular confession is truly and properly a sacrament instituted by Christ Himself, and necessary for salvation (*jure divino*), or who say that the method of confessing secretly to the priest alone is alien to Christ's institution and of human invention. Barnes[59] has listed reasons why the passage from James cannot be used as the Catholics wish to use it. (i) The confession here enjoined is not to be made by a person in good health, that he may obtain forgiveness, but by a sick person, that he may be healed. (ii) A mutual confession is here enjoined: a priest would be as much bound to confess to the penitent as the penitent are to the priest. *Allelois* is quite fatal to this idea. No priest confesses back to the penitent on the other side of the confessional screen. Luther pointedly argued against the practice by saying he had never heard of a confessor named "one another". (iii) No mention is made of a priest at all, or even of a minister of religion, as the one to whom the confession is to be made. (iv) The confession referred to is for "faults" with reference to "one another," that is, where one has injured another. (Cp. Matthew 5:23-24.) Nothing is said of confessing faults to those whom we have not injured at all. (v) There is no mention here of absolution, either by a priest or any other person.[60] (vi) No priest or man whatever is empowered to say to another that he is forgiven. "Who can forgive sins but God only?" (Luke 5:21).

And pray for one another – "Pray" is present tense, a continuous action. Keep it up! The sinner prays for the one he has injured. The injured one prays for the sinner. The offender and offended pray for each other. They pray for the spiritual welfare of the other

---

[59] The following points are adapted from *Barnes Notes* on "James," p.95.

[60] James does say "if he has committed sins, they will be forgiven." However, this is not quite the same as "absolution" in the Roman Catholic practice. The primitive form of absolution, when confession was made to a priest, was precatory rather than declaratory: "May the Lord absolve you" (*Dominus absolvat*). By the 12th century, this had changed to "I absolve you" (*Absolvo te*). Plummer, *op. cit.*, p.638.

person. They commend each to the mercies of God. They do it continually. We picture the prayers dealing specifically with the sin and the harm received. The confession gives parameters to the prayers. Without such prayers, confession of sins may prove to be harmful rather than helpful. Such prayers sometimes are called "intercessory prayers." In fact, we will not soon quarrel with one for whom we pray constantly.

So that you may be healed – "So that" is *hopōs*. This states the purpose/result of the mutual prayers. As does the context and the "therefore" which begins verse 16, this seems to limit the counsel given about mutual confession and prayer to times when "healing" is needed. *Iathēte* is the regular word for "healing," whether of body (John 4:47) or spirit (Matthew 13:15, and probably Hebrews 12:13).[61] The word may be purposefully vague, to cover both sickness of the body and sickness of the soul, since both need healing.[62] "You" (plural) denotes the readers who stand in need of healing; the sinner and one sinned against both need "healing" (one of physical illness, the other of spiritual bitterness and feelings of animosity and estrangement resulting from being sinned against). When the offended and the offender pray for each other, a healing process takes place.

The effective prayer of a righteous man can accomplish much – Since verse 13, James has been urging prayer as one of the marks of a genuine Christian life. He has spoken of prayers when Christians are ill-treated (veres 13), prayers by the elders for the sick (verses 14-15), and prayers for one another (verse 16). Now, in an effort to encourage them to pray, he reminds his readers about the powerful things such prayers can accomplish.

Marshall's interlinear looks like this:

πολὺ	ἰσχύει	δέησις	δικαίου	ἐνεργουμένη
much (very)	is strong	a petition	of a righteous man	being made effective

Being able to see the words will aid our understanding as we comment upon them. *Energoumenē* ("being made effective") is a participle.[63] Translations of James 5:16b vary

---

[61] Commentators have emphasized one or both ideas as they explain this passage. Some understand the healing as being spiritual only; some take it of both spirit and body being healed; others take it of the body only. We wonder if many of the choices depend on the theology of the commentator, rather than on what James wrote. Since *astheneō* (5:14) can mean spiritually weak, and *kamnō* (5:15) can refer to weariness from spiritual battles, and *iaomai* (5:16) can speak of spiritual healing, it is not surprising to find Daniel Hayden, "Calling the Elders to Pray," *Bib Sac* 138 (1981) p.258-66, setting forth the thesis that James is giving instruction for dealing with persons who are discouraged or depressed, rather than dealing with physical sickness.

[62] Perhaps the "healing" should not be limited to bodily healing. Not a few would recall Isaiah 53:5 (and 1 Peter 2:24), "by whose stripes you were healed" and the reference to Isaiah 6:10 in Acts 28:27, John 12:40, Matthew 13:15, "and I should heal them" – and then give the word "heal" a wider significance than merely physical. Souls are healed, made well, too, when they are forgiven.

[63] Participles are verbal adjectives. They can modify nouns (they must agree with the noun they modify in gender, number, and case) or be used as adverbial modifiers. So in this passage, the participle could modify the noun "prayer" (e.g., "an energetic prayer of a righteous man is very powerful" or "a working prayer of a righteous man is very powerful"). It could modify the verb "is powerful" (e.g., "a prayer of a righteous man avails much (i.e., is very powerful) as it works").

because the Greek participle can be either in the middle or passive voice.[64] Not only so, but it is a compound word, formed from is a simple verb with a preposition prefixed. So debate has also centered on whether the preposition *en* ("in") simply intensifies the verb to which it is attached, or whether it literally means "working in." Decisions about these matters, and various combinations of the options, lead to an almost bewildering array of interpretations.[65] The illustration of what happened when Elijah prayed (verses 17,18) certainly unfolds the idea introduced in this last sentence of verse 16. When Elijah prayed, things happened! "Prayer" translates *deēsis*, not the same word for prayer (*euchē*) that James used in verse 15. *Deēsis* is a petition for a specific benefit. *Euchē* is a general word for prayers of any kind.[66] What the brethren were doing as they prayed for each other was offering specific petitions.

Who is it who is identified as "a righteous man"? Perhaps it is synonymous with "Christian," one who has been cleansed by the blood of the Lamb, a man who stands before God "justified." This would be another reminder that God doesn't hear the prayer of sinners. Perhaps "a righteous man" is one who shows his faith by his works (James 2:24, 5:6). James has been emphasizing practical Christian living, so perhaps "righteous" here refers to the person whose daily life is in harmony with Jesus' ethical teachings. Likely the singular is generic, the man is representative of a class. "Righteous" does not describe some kind of elite prayer warrior. All believers who have a relationship with God fit into this category of "righteous." A man doesn't have to be sinless perfect to be "righteous," but the tenor of his life must be right. Prayer offered by a forgiven believer gets results just as much as the prayer of the offended can get results.

---

[64] Evidence for either position is impressive, but on the basis of a number of New Testament examples (as in Matthew 14:2; Mark 6:14; 2 Corinthians 1:6; Galatians 5:6; Ephesians 2:2; Colossians 1:29; 1 Thessalonians 2:13), translators have come to favor the middle. (See K.W. Clark on "The Meaning of *energeo* and *katargeo* in the NT," JBL 54 (1935), p.93-101.) If we treat it as passive, it says prayer is mighty 'in what it is enabled to do.' If we treat it as middle, it says prayer is mighty 'in what it is able to do.'

[65] One thinks it is a "prayer in which the supplicant works for the accomplishment of his desire for which he has prayed." Another supposes it means "wrestling energetically with the Lord" as we pray. To arrive at this explanation, first we must suppose that the participle should be transliterated into "*energumeni*," a term synonymous with "demoniacs" found in Early Christian Literature. Just as those unhappy demon-possessed beings strove in their bondage, so, equally (and even infinitely more) should Christians wrestle with the Lord. Another opts for "inwrought," as though the Holy Spirit, helping us in our infirmities, with unutterable groanings, is intended. This interpretation appeals to Romans 8:26, where the Spirit Himself makes intercession, so that the prayer is more than the utterance of mere human feeling. (This is a misreflection of Romans 8, for in that passage there are no words, only groanings and sighs produced by the Spirit.) As far back as when the Bible was translated into Latin, there was no unanimity on the meaning of this passage. An Old Latin manuscript has *frequens* (repeated, frequent, constant), which is not a good choice for the Greek word. The Vulgate has *assidua*, (persistent). It was due to the Vulgate that Wycliffe translated "continual." Tyndale, and English translations following him, preferred "fervent." The KJV put the two ideas together, and reads "effective fervent prayer." Probably the KJV cannot be justified, since it is doubtful we are dealing with how earnest or fervent the prayer is. Would the prayer of a righteous man be indifferent or formal or listless or insincere?

[66] Berry, *Synonyms*, p.20. Trench, *Synonyms*, p. 179.

"Can accomplish much" (*polu ischuei*) means 'is of great power, is very strong, is able to do much.' Standing first in this clause in the Greek, these words are emphatic. The same expression is found in Acts 19:20 (KJV), "so mightly grew the word of the Lord and prevailed (*ischuen*)." It describes "power" that overcomes resistance; even sickness yields. In addition to the example of Elijah to illustrate the powerful things that happen when people pray, we could also appeal to the case of the importunate neighbor (Luke 11:5-8), the persistent widow (Luke 18:1-8), and the persevering Syrophoenician woman (Mark 7:24-30).

5:17 -- *Elijah was a man with a nature like ours, and he prayed earnestly that it might not rain; and it did not rain on the earth for three years and six months.*

Elijah was a man with a nature like ours – In verses 17 and 18, the Old Testament prophet Elijah is put forth as an illustrative proof that any human being who is righteous can offer a prayer that God will answer in a mighty way. We are sometimes apt to think that the heroes in the Bible were almost superhuman.[67] We think we could never rise to their level. Indeed, many of them were raised up to do a special work for their time. Yet for all that, they were still men! Elijah was no demigod, but rather was a man (*anthrōpos*, an 'ordinary human being') with a "nature (*homoiopathēs*) like ours"; he was subject to the same infirmities and weaknesses as other humans.[68] But look what happened when he prayed! Not only was the widow's son raised, but in answer to Elijah's prayers God brought a great famine on the land, and then because Elijah prayed again, God caused the famine to end. No righteous man should despair that nothing much will happen when he prays.

And he prayed earnestly that it might not rain – The Greek reads "he prayed a prayer," perhaps an attempt to reproduce the Hebrew language's way of giving emphasis. "Prayed

---

[67] First century people had their list of Bible heroes, including Abraham, Job, Moses, David and Elijah, several of whom have been named by James. One of the highest on the list was Elijah. Elijah was one of the earliest of the great prophets and so came to be a representative of the whole prophetic revelation, just as Moses was representative of the revelation embodied in the Law. The prophecy in Malachi 4:5 about Elijah being a forerunner of Messiah heightened Jewish interest in this famous person. (See this prophecy fulfilled in the Elijah-like John the Baptist, Mark 1:6 and 9:13.)

[68] The word translated "nature like ours" is the same root word used by Paul in Acts 14:15 (where the natives of Lystra mistakenly think Paul and Barnabas are gods in the likeness of men, to which Paul replies "we are also men of the same nature as you". The Greek word *homoiopathēs* literally means "suffering the same things," subject to the same feelings and experiences as are common to mankind. (The word "passions" [in the KJV's "like passions"] now has a meaning much more narrow than when that version was translated. It doesn't mean that Elijah was excitable or irritable, or driven by sexual desires.) "Like nature" reminds us that we find the prophet had ups and downs just like we humans do. "We find him alternating between the two extremes of buoyant confidence and of a self-distrust almost akin to despair" (Tasker, *op. cit.*, p.141). If God answered his prayers, why not ours?

earnestly" is a possible translation.[69]   In 1 Kings 17:1 Elijah announces the drought, but no mention is made of his praying for it.[70]   "As the Lord God of Israel liveth, before whom I stand, there shall not be dew or rain these three years, but according to my word."[71]   We should probably infer that Elijah offered his prayer before he made this announcement to Ahab.[72]   We also might infer that Elijah knew what to say to Ahab because God had revealed it to him in answer to his prayer.

And it did not rain on the earth for three years and six months – This was what resulted when Elijah prayed.   "The earth" is likely limited to the land ruled by Ahab and Jezebel plus some neighboring areas rather than speaking of the whole globe.   The famine was severe in Samaria (1 Kings 18:2), but the brook Cherith, which was likely outside of the area actually ruled by Ahab (1 Kings 17:3-7),[73] and Zarephath, which was not far from Tyre and Sidon on the Mediterranean coast, also suffered the effects of the drought (1 Kings 17:14).   How long did the drought last?   James says "three years and six months."   In Luke 4:25 the same length of time is assigned to the drought by Jesus as He spoke in the synagogue at Nazareth.   However, in 1 Kings 18:1, we read, "And it came to pass after

---

[69] Examples of an attempt to reproduce the Hebrew idiom (an infinitive absolute) are found at Luke 22:15 ("With desire I have desired" = "I have earnestly desired"), Genesis 2:17, 31:30; Jonah 1:10; John 3:29; Acts 5:28 ("charged with a charge" = "we gave strict orders").   It should not be deduced from this that only intense prayers are answered.   Instead of translating it "prayed earnestly," "prayed a prayer" might say 'that praying was precisely what he did.'   "Faced with his situation, Elijah specifically resorted to prayer."   Hiebert, *op. cit.*, p. 329

[70] Scholars have rushed in to make pronouncements concerning the likely source of James' information about Elijah's praying.   For example, Barclay says (*op. cit.*, p.156), "this is an excellent example of how Jewish rabbinic exegesis developed the meaning of Scripture."   Others refer to oral tradition as the source of James' information.   This commentator is not at all satisfied with the theory that James here merely relies upon tradition for his information.   With Baal worship being everywhere received, it is more than probable that this man of God prayed for a drought as a punishment upon the people.   After all, about the time of the end of the drought, he prayed for fire to come down on Mt. Carmel and prove once and for all whether Baal or Jehovah was God.   When we look for sources, why not appeal to a revelation made to James?

[71] "Before whom I stand" (1 Kings 17:1) has been said to be a reference to prayer since standing was the usual posture for prayer.   But Elijah is hardly praying at the same time he is making this announcement to Ahab.

[72] If God had already spoken through Elijah to Ahab before Elijah prayed, we would hardly say that the skies dried up because Elijah prayed.   Would we not say, instead, that the skies dried up because God had already told the Prophet they would?

[73] The exact location of Cherith is still debated, as is the meaning of the expression "before the Jordan" which describes its location, 1 Kings 17:3.   If Elijah is in Gilead as he speaks to Ahab "before the Jordan" would mean the "east" side of the Jordan.   If Elijah is in Samaria as he speaks, then "before the Jordan" means the "west" side of the Jordan.   Eusebius and Jerome located it to the east of Bethshean.   A medieval tradition has it on the east side of the Jordan, about 15 miles north of Jericho.   Since Gilead was Elijah's home, Ahab certainly would have searched for him there (1 Kings 18:10).   Modern tourists are shown a narrow, rock-walled chasm on the western shores of the Dead Sea where water flows down a Wady through the gorge into the sea.

many days, that the word of the Lord came to Elijah *in the third year*, saying, Go, show yourself to Ahab, and I will send rain upon the earth." Thus, it has been alleged, there is a discrepancy in the Bible concerning the length of the drought. We are not told from what point the third year (in 1 Kings) is dated. Many suppose the third year is reckoned from the time Elijah began to dwell at Zarephath (1 Kings 17:18). Before going to Zarephath, he had stayed at Cherith until the brook dried up, which would have occurred sometime after the failure of the rains to come. The length of his stay in Cherith is not mentioned by the writer of Kings, but add together that stay, plus his stay at Zarephath, and you would have a period roughly equal to the "three years and six months" we read in the New Testament.[74] Whatever the answer to the alleged discrepancy may be, it is evident that God sent a great famine to punish the people for their involvement in idolatry. And the famine was sent in answer to one man's prayer.

5:18 -- *And he prayed again, and the sky poured rain, and the earth produced its fruit.*

And he prayed again – We suppose this prayer for the rains to begin again, not recorded in the Old Testament,[75] was made before the contest with the prophets of Baal on Mt. Carmel. In fact, in that scene, Elijah arrives after God told him to "go, show yourself to Ahab, and I will send rain on the face of the earth" (1 Kings 18:1). After that contest was decided, Elijah announced to Ahab that there would be a heavy shower, the "sound of abundance of rain" (1 Kings 18:41, KJV), and then went to the top of the mountain and "crouched down on the earth and put his face between his knees" (1 Kings 18:42). This posture may well indicate he is praying, but we doubt it is the prayer for rain that James writes about.[76] We would hardly say "prayer changes things" if Elijah already knew the change was coming before he prayed. It is more likely that the directions to Elijah to go to Ahab and announce the end of the drought came to him in answer to his prayer for the rains to begin again.

And the sky poured rain – Elijah sent his servant to look into the west to see if storm clouds were coming up. Finally the servant came back and reported that "a cloud as small as a man's hand" was coming in off the Mediterranean. Elijah then runs to Moreh to escape the downpour. "The heaven was black with clouds and wind, and there was a great

---

[74] It is a slight variation of this explanation to say that the "third year" is counted from the first failure of the regular periodical rains after the preceding dry season. When Elijah then prays that the new rainy season not start, it had been six months since the last rainy season,. Three more years passed before another rainy season occurred. Either of these is to be preferred to those who seek symbolism in numbers. "Three and one half," they say, is half of the perfect number "seven" and so had become symbolic of the duration of times of calamity or distress (however long the calamity actually turned out to be).

[75] In fact, it is but one or two times we are told in the Old Testament that Elijah was a praying man (1 Kings 18:42 and 22:20-22).

[76] If God revealed to Elijah that He was going to send rain but did not reveal the exact time, the prayer of 1 Kings 18:42 could imply, "Let it begin now, Lord!"

rain" (1 Kings 18:45 KJV).   "Heaven" may be a reverential Jewish substitute for "God."

And the earth produced its fruit – The drought had led to a famine in the land. Now that the rains have returned, the crops will grow. All the parts of the harvest depended on one another, and all depended on God.[77] And God was moved by one man's prayer. One righteous man's prayers achieved tremendous results!

So concludes James' discussion of another mark of the genuine Christian life: he prays and sings praises. Before going to the last mark of a genuine Christian life that James covers, we must think carefully about what James has taught us about prayer. Prayer causes changes to be made in a man's outward circumstances as well as his inward spiritual condition. (1) That such changes can occur tells us something about God's providential control over His creation. It implies that God chooses to exercise a general rather than a meticulous providence over His creation, allowing space for us to operate and for God to be resourceful in working within it. It implies all details about the future are not settled; carving the details in stone would leave no room for changes in answer to prayer. God's sovereignty is not all-controlling so that everything is decided and programmed to the Nth degree. He apparently does not exercise exhaustive sovereignty (even to making the Devil do what he does).[78] (2) Can we say that answers to prayer suspend the laws of nature? They certainly seem to have when there were no seasonal rains for 3 years, and then the normal cycle of nature returned in answer to prayer.[79] Why did James pick Elijah for an illustration of his thesis about the power of prayer? Is there some similarity between praying for a change of weather and praying for recovery of the sick? Many sicknesses are part of the regularity of a fallen creaturely world, just as rain or the lack of it are part of that same regularity. As we pray, are we not asking God to intervene, at least temporarily, into that regularity He has ordained?   "A man who puts up a lightning rod

---

[77] The association of rain and the produce of fruit is found elsewhere in the Bible, for example, Acts 14:17 where Paul says, "He (God) did good, and gave us rain from heaven, and fruitful seasons."

[78] Classic theism (since the time Augustine baptized Greek philosophy into the church) says that God in His sovereignty and foreknowledge has minutely fixed and predestined the course of nature and even future history. Classic theism makes God the sovereign author of every crime and murder, and has Him holding people accountable for deeds He predestined them to do and they could not but do. Is God "open" to changing things when righteous men pray? No, say some (e.g., Plummer, *op. cit.*, p.639-40). If He were, what a chaos would result in our world. Each individual believer could pray for what is deemed best for this time and place, and the order of the world would be at the mercy everywhere of individual requests. Irregularity would take the place of the order we are familiar with in nature, and no man could possibly foretell what would be on the morrow. What we are doing when we pray is simply bringing our will into harmony with what God has already predetermined would happen. But in reply to Plummer's theism, we might ask: Are prayers for rain, or the end of rain, any more irregular than a prayer for wisdom (James 1:5)? Don't we expect God to give some wisdom we would not have had if we had not prayed? Believers are not praying that God will relinquish control over the forces of nature to mere man. We are praying that God will redirect those forces in such a way as to benefit His people and bring glory to His name.

[79] Folk who axiomatically hold to the absolute sovereignty of God do not want any changes in God's mind, or God's action, or God's world, as a result of prayer.

brings down the electric current when it otherwise might have remained above, or brings it down in one place rather than another; yet no one would say that man is interfering with the regularity of the course of nature."[80]   Is not God free to answer prayers for healing or rain without impinging on some fixed and meticulously ordained clock-work world?   (3) Some affirm it is missing the point of what James writes to suppose we can pray for rain like Elijah did.   They suppose that James is emphasizing spiritual showers and spiritual fruit rather than prayers for literal rain and literal food-producing crops.[81]   Instead of encouraging his readers to imitate Elijah and pray for rain, James' "main interest is to show that a righteous man praying effectively can delay or hasten the saving grace of God which is symbolized by rain."[82]   Another writer puts it like this: the result of prayer for the sick Christian is that the one who was formerly ill is now refreshed, much like the parched land that is revived by rain.   Fruit can again be brought forth in the healed person's life.   He or she can take a productive place in the congregation again.   James has already written about the "fruit of righteousness" (James 3:18).   (4) Answered prayer and miracles are not the same.   Answered prayer is providential, and answers to prayer are not to be thought of as miracles.   Miracles occurred but infrequently in Scripture, and then to credential the message or the messenger from God.[83]   Providence is God's everyday care and preservation and government over the things He has created so they accomplish the purposes for which He created them.   (5) This passage does not mean that God will grant *all* the requests of the righteous, for He did not give Elijah all he prayed for (1 Kings 19:4).[84]   But it is a call for confidence that the Lord to whom we pray will do mighty things in answer to prayer.

XII. ATTEMPTS TO RECLAIM THE STRAYING. 5:19-20

> *Summary:*   In a broad conclusion to the letter, James asks his readers to get involved in attempting to rescue any of their brethren who may start to stray away from the truth and into error (the error proclaimed by the Judaizers?).   We suppose these verses encapsulate the author's purpose for writing this letter.

---

[80] Plummer, *op. cit.*, p.640.

[81] Why they are hesitant to suppose we can talk God into changing the weather, but that we can talk Him into introducing spiritual changes, as though this neat dichotomy can protect His absolute unchangeableness and sovereignty and predestination, is difficult to understand.

[82] Bo Reicke, "The Epistles of James, Peter, and Jude" in *Anchor Bible* 37 [Garden City: Doubleday, 1964), p.61.

[83] In Elijah's day, the miracle of fire from heaven on Mt. Carmel was an answer to prayer from the prophet to credential his defense of Jehovah against Baal.

[84] James has earlier noted that some prayers are not answered (1:6-8 and 4:3), just as some prayers are answered (James 1:5).

5:19 -- *My brethren, if any among you strays from the truth, and one turns him back;*

My brethren – James prefaces his last appeal to his readers with an earnest and tender reminder of their "family" relationship resulting from the fact believers are adopted sons of God.   Both James and his readers are all part of the family of God.   This last exhortation is addressed to Christians.   It was in James 2:1 that James prefaced another important emphasis with the words "my brethren."

If any among you strays from the truth – "Among you" says the erring individual is a member of the local congregation in the place where the readers are living.   The indefinite pronoun ("any") marks this as something that could happen to any individual Christian. The "truth" here, as in 1:18 and 3:14, is the saving truth of the gospel of Jesus Christ, which the "brethren" who held "the faith in our glorious Lord Jesus" (2:1) had in common.   Verse 20 shows this truth is something that provides salvation for souls and a covering of a multitude of sins.   The Greek word for "stray" (*planaō*) was translated "deceived" at James 1:16.   The verb here may be either middle or passive.   If passive, the individual has been deceived and led astray by someone else (e.g., the Judaizers).[1]   If middle, the individual went off of his own will.   The word does not picture accidentally or unconsciously departing from the truth.   The brother has wandered from the word of truth that gave him spiritual birth (James 1:18).   The wanderer has gotten off the narrow way that leads to life; like the lost sheep in Jesus' story, a brother can wander away (Matthew 18:12-13; 1 Peter 2:25).   A person can stray from the truth either doctrinally or practically.[2]   Doctrinally, they may abandon the great doctrines of the Christian faith which they embraced at their conversion.   Practically, they may begin to ignore the great moral teachings (i.e., the marks of a genuine Christian life) which Jesus gave in His Sermon on the Mount and which have been reiterated by James in this letter.[3]   We have advocated the idea that James is responding to the Judaizer's use of his name and example as they went from town to town trying to recruit believers to their sect.   These verses form James' summary word against the Judaizers.[4]   When Christians embrace the Judaizer's doctrine and practice they have

---

[1] Such leading away is an act ultimately prompted by the devil, whoever the human tool may be who directs the Christian in the wrong way.   James has already identified certain misbehavior as the work of the devil (3:15, 4:7).

[2] The "if-clause" does not just picture a hypothetical case that never could happen.   It certainly speaks of the possibility that a Christian may "wander from the truth."   Care must be exercised at this place, for the doctrine of unconditional eternal security tends to influence the comments of many an expositor at this place.   One cannot wander from the truth unless he has already been in the truth.

[3] The expression "multitude of sins" in verse 20 seems to point to the "error of his way" as being more in the area of practice than in the area of doctrine.

[4] Throughout this epistle, largely due to a failure to reach agreement concerning the historical situation to which the letter is addressed, commentators have debated whether there is a thread of thought connecting one paragraph to the next.   That debate continues right up to these last two verses.   Some are confident these verses form an isolated unit.   Some attempt to find a connection with one of the thoughts (i.e., "sin" "confession to one another" or "healed") in the preceding section.   Some treat the exhortation concerning one who "strays from the truth" as being a summary of the leading ideas of the whole letter.   While treating the verses as one final mark of genuine Christian living, we see James' exhortation as a grand presentation of the danger inherent in the whole idea of embracing what the Judaizers wanted Christians to embrace.

been led away/have wandered away from the truth.

And one turns him back – Folk don't ordinarily let wandering sheep, or wandering children, go their own way and care for themselves. Likewise, we would not suppose that Christians would stand on the sidelines, refusing to get involved, when it is a brother who is straying. The brethren who are in peril are not to be left to themselves, allowed to go on travelling the wrong way, with no one to try to help them. "Turns him back" ultimately involves the repentance of the straying Christian.[5] The wanderer who is just beginning to stray may be won back. But if it is not done quickly, the wanderer may put himself beyond repentance (Hebrews 6:4ff). "Any one" (the indefinite pronoun *tis*) indicates that this opportunity and privilege was not confined to the elders. There are brothers and sisters in Christ who are aware of the peril the straying one is in, and it belongs to those same brothers or sisters to bring the wanderers back into the fold. How is the turning back, this restoration, brought about? James does not say specifically, but it will take personal contact with the wanderers to turn them back. The brother who intends to go to the one who is straying might start with a prayer for wisdom. The doctrinal aberrations learned from the Judaizers will have to be corrected by appealing to gospel truth. It will require teaching, warning, pleading, and admonishing as attention is called to the vital importance of exhibiting the marks of a genuine Christian life. A consistent Christian lifestyle, a good example, will help reinforce the attempts of the rescuer to convince and impress the one who is straying. In serious cases, it may even involve a personal and public confrontation like Paul did to Peter (Galatians 2:11ff) when Peter began to stray into Judaizing practices. In any of the congregations to whom James writes, the majority are staying true to Jesus. Members of the faithful majority in each congregation must have a sense of watchfulness and a clear feeling of responsibility for each individual.[6]

5:20 -- *Let him know that he who turns a sinner from the error of his way will save his soul from death, and will cover a multitude of sins.*

Let him know – There is a manuscript variation here, some having *ginōskete* (a plural form

---

[5] "Turn" (*epistrephō*) is the word used to signify repentance in a number of Scriptures (including Matthew 13:15; Lk 1:16-17; Acts 3:19, 11:21; 2 Corinthians 3:16; 1 Thessalonians 1:9). The same verb is used at Luke 22:32, where Jesus warns Peter that the devil is going to sift him like wheat, and he will wander, but "once you have turned again (i.e., repented), strengthen your brothers." The KJV's love of "be converted" as a way of translating this verb betrays a bias that in conversion man is wholly passive, and God is the active agent. While the Holy Spirit works through the Word to lead a person to repent, repentance is (in the final analysis) something the person himself or herself does. It is not done to them.

[6] Attention might be directed to some other passages which speak of the privilege and responsibility Christians have to win back their erring brothers, such as 1 Thessalonians 5:14; 2 Thessalonians 3:15; 2 Timothy 2:25; 1 John 5:16; and Jude 22-23.

which may be either indicative or imperative) and some have *ginōsketō* (a singular imperative form).[7]   The NASB translates the plural imperative and has the idea "all of you be assured!" James is letting his readers know how immense is the significance and how far reaching the consequences of rescuing the straying. There is something fatally wrong with us if we have no desire to attempt to bring the straying back into the fold.

That he who turns a sinner from the error of his way – The one who "strays from the truth" (verse 19) is designated here in verse 20 as a "sinner" (*hamartōlon*). What in verse 19 was called "straying from the truth" is here called "the error of his way" and the repetition of the "turns" expression highlights the crucial importance of such rescue work. "Error" is the noun form of the verb used in verse 19. "Sinner" (the same word used at James 4:8) indicates the wanderer has missed the mark of God's will for his life.   "Turns" speaks of repentance, just as it did in verse 19. The sinner is led to repentance. He quits his travelling on the wrong path. The singular "he who" indicates that "turning a sinner from the error of his way" is an activity that any Christian, however new or old in the faith, is able in some measure to perform. Few of us are qualified to deal with dogmatic, doctrinal errors, but all of us are qualified to deal with practical problems. It is one sinner at a time who is turned from his error. The task might seem overwhelming if we thought of multitudes of sinners who need help. But James speaks of one sinning brother at a time being turned from his error. Now the task does not seem so daunting. Such restoring work accomplishes two worthy results which James now identifies.

Will save his soul from death – This is the first of the two results which occur when wandering souls are rescued. The erring sinner will die physically, whether or not he repents, so physical death is hardly the "death" from which the erring can be saved. "Death" is likely the "second death" (condemnation in hell, Revelation 20:14), though before that ultimate penalty was incurred, there is a spiritual death that results from continued sin (Romans 6:16-23).[8]   The death he will be saved from is spiritual death in this life and the second death in the lake of fire. "Save" is used in the sense of "preserve from." Because Jesus has provided a sacrifice and a way of forgiveness, spiritual death can be averted and the second death avoided. Since the blood of bulls and goats never could take away sins (Hebrews 10:4), Christianity offers something to its followers that the Judaizers never could for their followers.   Whose soul ("his soul") is it that is saved from

---

[7] The singular form has better attestation in the manuscripts (Aleph, A,K,P, Vg) than the plural (found in B,69,1505,1568,2495, Syr.H).   It is supposed the plural form may have arisen when some scribe wanted to eliminate any question (necessarily present with the 3rd singular form) concerning who (the converter or the converted) was the subject of the verb.   The plural form adapts the person and number of the verb to the subject "brethren."

[8] In an earlier footnote (#16 on chapter 1), the difference between "body," "soul," and "spirit" was explained.   In this passage "soul" likely is used to designate the whole human person, rather than speaking simply of that which animates the body. A similar use of "soul" for the whole person might be at Acts 27:37, where Luke tells us there were "276 persons (souls)" on board the vessel that was wrecked in the storm.

death – the converter or the converted? Those manuscripts which read "his soul" settle the question.[9] The soul that is saved is the soul of the one who has turned from his straying

And will cover a multitude of sins[10] – This is the second of the two results which occur when wandering souls are rescued. "Cover" does not mean the sins are hidden or kept secret, but means "forgiven."[11] God is the One who forgives sins. Romans explains how God justifies the sinner so that his sins are covered by the blood of Christ (Romans 3:20-28). It is the penitent sinner, the believing sinner, the obedient sinner, who is counted as "just" in God's sight. As far as the Greek is concerned, it could be either the sins of the converter or the sins of the converted which are covered.[12] It is probably best to understand this as saying the sins of the repentant one are covered.[13] To have one's sins

---

[9] Codex Vaticanus reads "his." While most manuscripts have an *autou* after "way," Vaticanus and others have a second *autou* in the verse after the word "soul."

[10] A few manuscripts from the middle ages, and the Syr.H version, have an "Amen" at the close of the letter, but it is not genuine.

[11] The expression "cover sins" seems to have been familiar to the Jews. Peter makes use of it (1 Peter 4:8). Perhaps the source of the language is Proverbs 10:12 (though the LXX, perhaps because it followed a different Hebrew text, reads differently). Psalm 85:2 and 32:1 in the LXX also speak of "sins being covered." The latter passage, quoted at Romans 4:7, has "forgiven" and "covered" set in parallel expressions.

[12] Many commentators understand this phrase as hiding or covering the sins of the converter. They appeal to certain Jewish writers, and some references in Early Christian Literature, for the belief that one who converts or restores a sinner thereby secures a measure of forgiveness for himself. In Origen's Homilies (in Lev. ii.5) there is a remarkable passage concerning the things which brought remission of sins: 1) Baptism (Acts 2:38). 2) Martyrdom. 3) Almsgiving (Luke 11:41). 4) Forgiveness of others (Matthew 6:14). 5) Converting the sinner (James 5:20). 6) Love for the brother (Luke 7:47).
   Several objections have regularly been raised against this interpretation: 1) "No other Bible passage teaches such a doctrine," so it is doubtful this one does. Before it can be said "no other Bible passage," there are verses which have to be explained: (a) 1 Peter 4:8, "love covers a multitude of sins" apparently speaks of the eagerness of love not to expose or gloat over the sins of others. (b) Similar in meaning is Proverbs 10:12. (c) What about Matthew 6:14, "If you forgive men their trespasses, your heavenly Father will also forgive you"? While Matthew is not dealing with restoring the erring, is not the principle the same? God forgives in direct proportion to how much we forgive. (Is "forgive that you might be forgiven" in any way parallel with "convert, that you may be forgiven"?) (d) There are passages which speak of salvation to the one who warns his brothers of their danger (e.g., Ezekiel 3:18-21; 33:7-9; 1 Timothy 4:16). 2) This interpretation would form an anticlimax to the letter of James, since it puts the selfish motives of the converter above the need of the straying soul. 3) James 1:21 is said to be against the idea that soul-winning is a means of saving one's own soul. It is the implanted word which is operative in this process. 4) Some have called on 1 Corinthians 9:27 to refute the idea that it is the converter whose sins are covered. Corinthians says that a man may preach successfully to others, and yet himself be a castaway. It doesn't appear that Paul's preaching resulted in any of his sins being forgiven, or how could he have entertained the possibility that he could still be a castaway?

[13] A compromise view proposes the idea that James has in mind a blessing both for the sinner who is rescued and for his or her rescuer.

covered is one of God's greater blessings.   As Psalm 32:1 says, "Blessed is the man whose transgression is forgiven, whose sin is covered."   "Multitude of sins" is a reminder that sins pile up.   What was called "error of his way" earlier in the verse is now unfolded as involving a "multitude of sins."[14]   Think of how many sins a man can commit.   One sin a day is 365 sins a year; 3650 sins in 10 years!   And who is it who commits only one sin a day?   The person who strays from the truth will commit more sins in a day than the righteous man who is carefully guiding his steps in harmony with what His Master taught.

With these beautiful words the letter closes abruptly.   There is no formal epistolary close to the letter, no salutation, no doxology, no leave-taking of any kind.   It is a possible explanation that the conclusion to the letter has been lost (since papyrus was fragile).   But it is more probable that this abrupt ending was deliberate.[15]   We picture James as closing abruptly as he does so that these last words keep ringing in the ears and minds of his readers.   "A multitude of sins," "sinner," "the error of his way" is a fitting way to drive home to his readers that the Judaizer's religion is wrong.   Instead of embracing it, James says, in effect, "If you forget all else I have written, remember this! Keep away from sin yourselves, and rescue all you can who are beginning to stray away from Christianity into it!"

---

[14] James seems to be speaking more of lifestyle when he speaks of "straying from the truth" than he is of doctrinal error.

[15] John did something similar at the close of his first epistle (1 John 5:21).   John says, in effect, if you forget all else I have written, remember this, "Guard yourselves from idols!"

Special Study #2

IS ANYONE SICK?   WHAT SHOULD HE OR SHE DO?[1]

INTRODUCTION

Each one of us has health problems. As we get older the problems become more acute and life threatening. Oh, to feel well again! If we think someone we meet has some help to offer to overcome one of our problems, we listen.

Ever since Adam sinned and brought sickness and death into the world, people – every one of us – have been intensely interested in "getting well."

Healing occupies a prominent place in religious experience throughout the world. Often, the most important figure in the community is the one who can heal (or at least claim to heal). Think of the Indian medicine man, the shaman, medical people in the world of Islam. Even so, in our Christian circles, if someone comes along who can offer to sick people help to feel better or get well, he becomes an important figure. In the last half century, numerous folk have appeared in the churches who make well-advertised claims to miraculous healing. Since we who are hurting would dearly love to have some help to feel better, it certainly seems the path of wisdom to check what the Bible says about healing, lest we be fooled or deceived, and we stray away from the truth.

I.   HEALINGS IN THE NEW TESTAMENT

A. HEALINGS DURING JESUS' EARTHLY MINISTRY

During Jesus' earthly ministry, **healings were abundant**. At no other time in human history were so many people healed from such a multitude of sicknesses and diseases in so short a time as during Jesus' public ministry.

Jesus' miracles were done by the power of God. Several Scriptures make this fact very plain. At Matthew 12:28, Jesus says, "If I cast out demons by the Spirit of God ... then the kingdom of God has come upon you (come into your community)." So He has done it by the power of God, by the Spirit of God. At Luke 5:17 we read that during Jesus' Galilean ministry, "the power of the Lord was present for Him to perform healing."   Acts

---

[1] Originally entitled "What Do the Scriptures Say About How to Get Well When You Are Sick?" the contents of this special study were first prepared for and then presented at a weekend Bible study requested by the elders of the church at Milton, IA. (February 15, 2005).   They were recorded, transcribed, and lightly edited for publication here.

2:22 tells us Jesus wrought miracles by the power of God; God worked them through Him. Reminding his audience about Jesus' ministry, Peter says that "Jesus ... a man attested to you" – *how?* – "by miracles and wonders and signs which God performed through Him." So the Father was working through the Son as the Son did the miracles He did.   Jesus' miracles were done by the power of God.   According to Acts 10:38, "God anointed [Jesus] with the Holy Spirit and with power," and "He went about doing good, and healing all who were   oppressed by the devil, for God was with Him."

Jesus' miracles were done for a purpose, namely, to authenticate His Messianic claims.   We can see that in Scripture, too.   Matthew 11:2-19 (also Luke 7:18-23) is a good place to see the purpose of Jesus' miracles.   When John the Baptist was in prison, he sent to Jesus and said, "Are you the Coming One, or shall we look for someone else?" Jesus replied, "Go and report to John the things you see and hear."   He then enumerated what He had been doing: blind people getting their sight, lame people walking, lepers being cleansed, deaf people hearing; the dead being raised.   Those miracles credentialed that Jesus was the Messiah.

That was the purpose why Jesus performed the miracles.   If I'm the one being made well, I'm happy to be healed.   But Jesus wasn't healing just to make folk well.   He was healing so that we would see who He was.   Maybe what the messengers from John learned will help us to remember the purpose of Jesus' miracles.

B. HEALINGS BY THE APOSTLES OF JESUS

The twelve apostles chosen by Jesus, who received on-the-job training as they accompanied Him during His earthly ministry, from time to time also performed healings as they traveled from place to place representing Jesus.

The apostles were given temporary powers and sent on a preaching and healing mission, Matthew 10:1-15.

And on another occasion, the Seventy were sent on a similar mission, Luke 10:1-16.

On Pentecost (Acts 2), following the conclusion of Jesus' earthly ministry, the apostles were especially empowered for their church planting mission, just as Jesus had promised them they would be (Acts 1:4,5,8).   What had been temporary back earlier is now becoming more permanent.

A number of miracles were wrought through the apostles, as recorded in Acts (2:43, 3:6, 5:15, 9:30-43, 14:8-10, 19:11,12, 20:9-12, 28:8,9).

Indeed, some of the miracles the apostles did were **miracles of benefit** – sick and hurting people were benefited and helped.   But there were also **miracles of judgment**.   People were stricken with sickness, with blindness, with death, such as

Acts 5:1-11 (Ananias and Sapphira were stricken dead) and Acts 13:4-12 (Elymas the sorcerer was stricken blind, so he will learn to repent). We sometimes forget these miracles of judgment when we want to ask for power (to heal). Sometimes the power benefits, and sometimes the power results in judgment.

The miracles worked by the apostles were the **signs by which you recognized a man was an apostle**. Just like Jesus' miracles helped us to recognize He was the Messiah, so the miracles wrought by the apostles helped us to recognize they were apostles of Jesus. At 2 Corinthians 2:12, Paul reminded the Corinthian readers that "signs of a true apostle were performed among you"; i.e., 'you had better believe I [Paul] am an apostle of Jesus given the miraculous signs you have witnessed.'

C. HEALINGS BY PEOPLE OTHER THAN THE APOSTLES

In the New Testament church, when a healing was done by someone other than the apostles, healing was done in one of two ways. One of the ways healing was done was by exercising one of the "spiritual gifts." The second of the ways healing sometimes occurred was in answer to prayer. We'll first discuss "spiritual gifts."

1. Who was involved in the working of miracles after Pentecost?

We've already talked about the apostles, who were especially empowered (Acts 1:8; 1 Timothy 1:12; 1 Peter 1:3). Some miracles were done by them.

There were also certain Christians who were "spiritually gifted" in order to do miraculous things. Examples include Stephen (Acts 6:8) who spoke by inspiration, and Philip (Acts 8:6) who went down to Samaria and demonstrated miraculous abilities. There were others in the early church so gifted.[2]

Not every Christian was specially "gifted." To see this we might turn to 1 Corinthians 12:29,30 (ASV), "Do all speak in tongues? (No, is implied answer.) Do all work miracles? (No, is the implied answer.), etc." Why not? Because not everyone was spiritually gifted, and even those who were gifted did not receive all the gifts. 1 Corinthians 14:16 specifically talks about some church members who were ungifted. Or consider Simon, the ex-sorcerer, in Acts 8. After his conversion, Simon has seen Philip's miracles, but does not have such abilities himself. Simon says, "Here's some money. Show me how to do it." Peter replies to Simon, who was a Christian (see Acts 8:12; Simon had done the same thing to become a Christian the other folk at Samaria did to be-

---

[2] Luke, Mark, and Jude, whose writings are in the New Testament canon, are included because it is presumed they were close associates of an apostle, and therefore the possibility is strong they could have spiritual gifts. Each of these would have had the gift of inspiration.

come Christians), "You have no part or portion in this matter." He was ungifted[3] and wasn't going to get a miraculous spiritual gift. Some Christians were ungifted.

It is important to remember there are other folk who did miracles in Bible times, not just those Christians who were spiritually gifted. Per Acts 19:13ff, some Jewish renegades, the seven sons of Sceva, were "exorcists. " (They used an "oath" ["I adjure you by Jesus whom Paul preaches"] or a magical formula to cast out demons.) But these were recognized as being impostors. They were doing things by supernatural power, but it wasn't the Lord who was behind them. There were such things in the ancient world, as in our modern world, as lying wonders (see below). We include this paragraph just so we will have it impressed on our minds that not all miracles are from God, or wrought by the power of God.

2. "Spiritual Gifts" -- what are we talking about?

There are several listings of spiritual gifts in 1 Corinthians 12, and we ought to take a moment to read them. This should help us have a Biblical content in mind when we speak about "spiritual gifts." 1 Corinthians 12:1 reads, "Now concerning spiritual gifts ...." Verse 4 continues, "there are varieties of gifts ...." Verse 7 adds, "to each one is given a manifestation of the Spirit for the common good."

> 1 Corinthians 12:8-11 gives us one list of the kind of gifts Paul is writing about. As we read down through this list, we see that "gifts of healings" is one of the gifts (both words are plural in the Greek). *Opinion*: Each person with a gift of healing could heal one family of diseases, respiratory or circulatory or auditory or sight or digestive, etc.

> 1 Corinthians 12:28-30 has another listing of the gifts. When we compare this listing with the one read earlier, we observe there are more than "nine gifts of the Spirit." "Gifts of healings" occurs again in these verses.

These are the things we are talking about when we use the language "spiritual gifts." We sometimes call them "miraculous spiritual gifts."

3. "Spiritual Gifts" were temporary in the early church.

There are several reasons to believe the gifts were temporary. (a) The first reason has to do with how the "spiritual gifts" were received. Numerous passages show the gifts were received by the laying on of an apostle's hands. Look for "the laying on of hands" as the following passages are studied. In Acts 8:17 we read that Simon saw that the Spirit was given "by the laying on of an apostle's hands." In Acts 19:6 we read about some new Christians who had been followers of John the Baptist before their conversion to Christian-

---

[3] Having become a Christian, he would have had the indwelling gift of Holy Spirit (Acts 2:38), but he did not have spiritual gifts.

ity.   Verse 5 says they were baptized in the name of Jesus.   Verse 6 says Paul laid hands on them and the Holy Spirit came on them, and then they exhibited spiritual gifts (i.e., spoke in tongues and prophesied).   The new converts received their miraculous spiritual gifts by Paul the apostle laying hands on them.   Hebrews 2:3,4 says that folk who lived in Old Testament times were severely punished when they ignored the Law of Moses.   What is going to happen to us who ignore the gospel (with its many more wonderful privileges than the Jew had)?   "How shall we escape if we neglect so great a salvation?"   What makes it great?   It was first spoken by the Lord (when He was here on earth).   And then it was confirmed to us by the apostles of Jesus who heard Him.   How was it confirmed?   God was "bearing witness with them both by signs, and wonders, and miracles, and distributions ("gifts") of the Holy Spirit."   As the apostles distributed spiritual gifts, those miracles confirmed the Gospel message they were preaching.   According to Romans 1:11, Paul was anxious to come to Rome that he might impart to them "some spiritual gift."   No apostle had ever been to Rome (Romans 15:20); he would like to go do it.   According to 2 Timothy 1:6, Timothy had spiritual gifts by the laying on of the apostle's hands.   It is difficult to show from Scripture that miraculous spiritual gifts were received in any other way than by the laying on of an apostle's hands.

We are not quite done with this question of "How did you get a spiritual gift?"   We've highlighted the idea of laying on of hands by an apostle.   Now let's zero in on what we mean when we say "apostle" and the temporary nature of that office.   Remember, we are still working on the first reason for thinking the spiritual gifts were temporary.

"Apostle" (an apostle of Jesus) was **a temporary office/function** in the early church.   By "temporary" we mean that the job of apostle is not something that continues through the whole church age until the return of Jesus.   Several lines of thought indicate the temporary nature of the role: (i) The qualifications given to be an apostle when it was needful to fill Judas Iscariot's place (Acts 1:21-22).   The time is AD 30, just before Pentecost.   Two qualifications are given as requirements to take Judas' place as an apostle: have traveled with Jesus during His earthly ministry, and have witnessed one of Jesus' post-resurrection appearances.   Matthias was chosen.[4]   These two qualifications point to the temporary nature of the office.   (ii) James (son of Zebedee) was not replaced (Acts 12:2).   The time is AD 44, just before Herod Agrippa I dies.   James is the first of the apostles of Jesus to die (and the first to be martyred).[5]   That the vacancy was not filled when James the son of Zebedee died tends to confirm the idea that the office was temporary.   (iii) Apostles and prophets made up the foundation of the church (Ephesians 2:20).   This indicates the temporary nature of their jobs.   (iv) Paul was the "last" of the apostles of

---

[4] Matthias was an apostle of Jesus.   He was chosen by Jesus (just as were His other apostles), as the prayer shows.   "Lord [Jesus], show us which of the two you have chosen ... and the lot fell on Matthias."

[5] The "James" of Acts 15 is a different James.   The James in Acts 15 is the brother of the Lord, and he is called an apostle of Jesus in Galatians 1:19.   He was not chosen to fill the office left vacant by the death of the son of Zebedee.

Jesus (1 Corinthians 15:7,8).[6]   One reason for believing that spiritual gifts were temporary is related to how such gifts were received: by the laying on of an apostle's hands.   That is something that is no longer possible if the office of apostle was temporary.

     (b) A second reason for believing the spiritual gifts were temporary is that there are clear verses of Scripture that say so.   (i) Hebrews 2:2-4 tell us the gifts were to confirm the message.   The verb tense of "confirmed" (i.e., past tense) indicates that "confirmation" was over and done by the time Hebrews was written.   (ii) Mark 16:17-20 is an interesting passage we should spend a few moments with.   (α) Notice, verses 9-20 are in brackets in most Bibles, and a footnote explains there are some ancient manuscripts that do not contain these verses.   When it comes to making a harmony of the post-resurrection appearances of Jesus, I would be delighted if I did not have to try to include these verses in my harmony. If you have ever tried to harmonize the accounts of those appearances, you know it is not an easy task.   If we could leave Mark's record out of our harmony, it would be much easier to make the harmony.   But the evidence that these verses were originally part of Mark's Gospel is strong enough that I cannot just leave them out.   (β) The Christian churches like verses 15 and 16; they help us know how to become a Christian.   But what about the verses immediately following?   "These signs will accompany those who have believed: in My name they will cast out demons, they will speak with new tongues; they will pick up serpents, and if they drink any deadly poison, it shall not hurt them; they will lay hands on the sick, and they will recover."   Do verses 17 and 18 tell us what all Christians do? Mark's gospel was written ~AD 68, about the time Peter died.   (It is likely that Mark was Peter's translator, who wrote down what Peter preached).   Writing some 38 years after Pentecost, Mark closes his gospel with these words (verses 19,20), "So then, when the Lord had spoken to them, He was received up into heaven, and sat down at the right hand of God.   And they went out and preached everywhere, while the Lord worked with them, and confirmed the word by the signs that followed."   As was true in Hebrews 2, Mark uses past tense verbs.   The "confirmed" and "followed" were over and done by the time Mark wrote.   (iii) Compare 1 Peter 3:15 with Matthew 10:19.   It looks like there is a contradiction in our Bibles if spiritual gifts are permanent.   The passage in Peter says to "plan ahead of time what you will say when on trial for being a Christian."   ("Make a defense" is technical language dealing with the courtroom).   Matthew 10 says, "When you are on trial, do not plan ahead of time ...."   Matthew records what Jesus said before He died in AD 30.   To the first believers, He said "do not plan ahead of time what you shall say to defend yourselves when you are on trial."   But some 35 or so years later, Peter, by inspiration, says "plan ahead of time what you shall say when on trial ...."   How do we harmonize these passages if gifts are permanent?   But, if spiritual gifts were temporary, there is no contradiction.   If the special gifts are now gone, we must now plan what we shall say to the judge.   (iv) 1 Corinthians 13:8-13 tell us the "gifts" don't abide [last] as long as the graces called "faith, hope, and love" will last.   This passage indicates the spiritual gifts were temporary.   Remember that chapter 13 comes right between 12 and 14; the whole context is spiritual gifts.   When the "perfect" is come, the spiritual gifts will pass

---

[6] His calling was unusual or unique.   "As to one untimely born" ("an abortion") is the strong word in the Greek.

(verse 8).   Even if I don't know what "perfect" is, as I read the rest of chapter 13 I find out that the "gifts" (miraculous) don't last as long as the graces (faith, hope, and love). Faith, hope, and love, are going to last a lot longer than the miraculous spiritual gifts.   So, several Scriptures clearly show the spiritual gifts were intended to be but temporary.

(c) A third reason for believing the spiritual gifts were temporary is what can be learned about them from the history of the post-apostolic Early Church.   Early Christian literature shows the gifts ceased by the time the generation on whom apostles laid hands died out.[7]   About AD 200, after the first generation of believers (some of whom were spiritually gifted) had died off, something new (and called "spiritual gifts") began to be practiced in the churches.   They recognized these new things as being different from the miraculous spiritual gifts one reads about in the New Testament Scriptures, but nevertheless, they gave these new practices Scripture names.   'For tongues, for healing, for a number of these supposed miracles, although they are not like what was done in Bible times, we'll call them by Bible names,' was the thinking of the people doing them.[8]

(d) The fourth reason to teach that gifts were temporary is shown by their purpose. They were to confirm the message.   We are told this over and over again.   In Old Testament times, miracles were to confirm the message.   Study Deuteronomy 13:1 where the miracles were designated as being a "sign or a wonder" – a "sign" is a pledge or token that a man is speaking for God.   Remember Elijah and the prophets of Baal, with the ringing cry, "the God who answers by fire, He is God!"   Remember Naaman recognized the God of Elisha because of a miracle of healing.   He said, "Now I know there is a God in Israel" and I'm going to follow Him (2 Kings 5:15).   And multiple New Testament verses show that miracles were to confirm the message (Hebrews 2:2-4[9]; Mark 16:17-20; Acts 2:22). Verse after verse shows clearly that spiritual gifts were given to confirm the message.

Having studied the reasons for believing miraculous spiritual gifts were temporary in the early church, several ideas need to be emphasized so our thinking stays sharp: One, miracles are not needed today to authenticate the gospel message.   The faith has already been once-for-all delivered to the saints (Jude 3).[10]   Two, if someone today were to claim to work miracles like we read about in the Bible, should that someone not also claim to work them for the same purpose, namely, to authenticate the message?   But what new message do we have that needs authentication?   The faith was once for all delivered, long ago.   If we have no new message, what need is there for the confirmation?

---

[7] See this documented in the author's little booklet entitled *Do All Speak in Tongues?*

[8] If today you are practicing some of these things, are you doing like they did in the Bible, or are you doing the different things like they did in the 2nd century and just calling them Bible names?

[9] The Law of Moses was "confirmed" just as the Gospel is "confirmed."   (In the Greek, "unalterable" in Hebrews 2:2 is the same word as "confirmed" in Hebrews 2:3.)

[10] Jude was written about AD 75.

D. CONCLUSIONS THUS FAR:

We have taken time to study spiritual gifts in some depth. If we have understood the Scriptures aright, then today, if someone were to claim to heal, it is hardly likely he or she has a gift like the spiritual gifts one reads about in the New Testament, that were received by the laying on of an apostle's hands. Those gifts were temporary.

But someone may say, "If we affirm that spiritual gifts were temporary, aren't we guilty of trying to limit God"? No! Here is my response to that old defense: God, who knows all things and has all power, has limitless possibilities how He may work. Out of that limitless number, it has pleased Him to do things a certain way. Having chosen how He will do things, God has revealed to men how He does things. (I am so grateful He has told us which way He chooses to do what He does.) We are simply reflecting what He has revealed about Himself. If I affirm the gifts are temporary because that is the way God announced He would do it, I am not limiting God. He has chosen a way, and He told us about it. I'm simply reflecting what He has revealed about Himself.

Earlier in this study, we noted two ways in the early church that healing was done by people other than the apostles. One was the result of receiving miraculous spiritual gifts by the laying on of an apostle's hands (to transfer the gifts). We have explained what "spiritual gifts" were and the reasons for believing that they were temporary, lasting only till those on whom the apostles laid hands died. We are now ready to look at the second of the two ways healing was done: "It sometimes occurred in answer to prayer." To help us understand this topic, we must first define some terms.

II. MIRACLES, PROVIDENCE, AND ANSWERED PRAYER

A. *PROVIDENCE*

Providence has been defined as "The care, preservation, and government which God exercises over all things that He has created, so that those created things may accomplish the ends (purposes) for which they were created."

Do you remember Ben Franklin flying a kite in a thunderstorm? Franklin was a deist. Deists deny God exercises any providential control. To them, God simply wound up the universe like we would wind up a clock, and He then just went off somewhere, letting it run down, all the time uninterested in our world. That is not the Biblical view. My Bible pictures God with a hand on His creation. He cares for it. He preserves it. He is moving history to a goal.

Theologians are accustomed to talk about special providence and general providence. **Special Providence** is what God does for Christians; these are actions that He doesn't do for the average man. Typical verses that speak of such special providential actions include Romans 8:28, Philippians 1:27,28, and Matthew 6:33.

Romans 8:28 affirms that "God causes all things to work together for good to those who love God, to those who are called according to His purpose." God is providentially involved, working things out for the ultimate spiritual good of those who habitually love Him.

Philippians 1:27,28 read, "Conduct yourselves in a manner worthy of the gospel of Christ, so that whether I come and see you or remain absent," Paul writes, "I may hear of you that you are standing firm in one spirit, with one mind striving together for the faith of the gospel; in no way alarmed by your opponents. [When you are not alarmed, it] is a sign of destruction for them, but of salvation for you, and that too, [comes] from God." Paul is saying, "Your lack of fear is evidence of God's hand in your life."

Matthew 6:33 record Jesus words, "But seek first His kingdom and His righteousness: and all these things shall be added to you." What things? Food, shelter, clothing, in the context. Such provision is part of God's special providence for the Christian.

General Providence is language that denotes God's care over the life and activities of all men – believers and unbelievers alike. Such general providence is indicated in these passages:

Matthew 5:45 (KJV) – Jesus says concerning God, "He makes the rain to fall on the just and the unjust."

Acts 17:26 – In his Areopagus sermon, Paul declares, "He (God) made from [Adam] every nation of mankind to live on all the face of the earth, having determined their appointed times [i.e., when nations rise and fall] and the boundaries of their habitation [i.e., how far their boundaries spread]." That's general providence.

Hebrews 1:2,3 – This likely also talks about God's general providence. Just as Galatians 4:4 talks about the "fulness of time" so this passage in Hebrews says there was a proper time (as far as God's calendar is concerned) when the gospel should be preached ("in these last days"). The passage also says "[Jesus] upholds all things by the word of His power." He just speaks and moves things to their goal. When we read the verb "uphold," we ought not think of Jesus being like Atlas holding up the world. This word about "upholding" was used of Moses in the Old Testament as he was trying to get the children of Israel from Egypt to the Promised Land, and finding the task difficult and exasperating. On one occasion Moses said to God, "I can't bear (the same word translated "uphold" in Hebrews) this people." Moses was saying:

"I can't get them to go where You want them to go."   Jesus is the One who is moving history to its goal, getting it to go where God wants it to go.   He upholds all things, and all He has to do is speak, and it happens.   Jesus is as much involved in providence (He is "Lord") as the Father is.

Now we have the beginning of a concept of the "providence" of God.   The next word we need to define is "miracle."

B. *MIRACLE*

We often use the word "miracle" in a popular sense.   A few years ago, there was a TV advertisement for Xerox copiers.   The monk in the abbey is making copies very quickly on his new copy machine (not the old labor-intensive letter-by-letter copying by hand).   Watching the copies come streaming out, the Abbot exclaims "It's a miracle!"   Brother Dominic has just zoomed through 5 months of copying in 5 minutes.   Again, a popular song affirms belief in miracles because someone has "seen the lily push its way up through the stubborn sod."   Or again, "It's a miracle" when he walked away from the automobile wreck without a scratch.   None of these is a Biblical use of the word "miracle."   We use the word "miracle" in a popular way, but this popular meaning is not at all like what the Scriptures call "miracle."

Can we give a definition of "miracle" that will adequately describe and explain Biblical miracles?[11]   C.S. Lewis has offered a good definition of miracle.   Lewis wrote, "The divine art of miracle is not the art of suspending the pattern to which events conform, but the feeding of new events into the pattern."

Typically, events do conform to a pattern.   Hold a piece of chalk, let loose of it, and what happens?   Down it falls because of gravity.   Lewis says, "Miracle is not the suspension of the pattern, but feeding something new into the pattern."

For example, if you are God and want to have a virgin birth, what would you do?   You would induce pregnancy in a way that is not usual.   After the unusual beginning, then the usual pattern takes over, and in a few months, in the normal course of events, the virgin gives birth.   We've fed something new into the pattern.

---

[11] For further help to understand what is meant by "miracles," turn to the well-known Bible study help entitled *Halley's Bible Handbook*.   Several times Halley calls attention to the miracles in the Bible.   Two of the special articles are: "The Miracles of Jesus," two pages of summary information at Mark 5, and "Miracles in Acts," pages of information at the beginning of comments on Acts.

A rather standard definition for miracle is the one given in the *Westminster Dictionary of the Bible.* "In the Biblical sense miracles are events in the external world wrought by the immediate power of God and intended as a sign or attestation."

Note the ideas emphasized. "Wrought by the hand of God." "Intended as a sign or attestation."

They are possible because God sustains, controls, and guides all things, and is personal and omnipotent.

C. *THERE ARE DIFFERENCES BETWEEN "PROVIDENCE" AND "MIRACLE"*

In the Bible, "miracle" didn't happen every day. In fact, after Creation and after the Flood (both of which conform to the definition of miracle), there are only 3 or 4 short periods of time in all of Bible history when miracles were wrought.

One was the 40-year period of time at the Exodus and wilderness wanderings, ending about 1400 BC.

Another was the life and death struggle between Baal and Jehovah during the lives of Elijah and Elisha, about 750 BC.

Then there was the introduction of Christianity into the world through the ministry of Jesus and His apostles. That was a 40-or-so-year period of time, AD 26-70.

We don't find many miracles between these 3 or 4 short periods. There were a few in Daniel's time, etc. But as we try to understand "miracle" in the Biblical sense of the word, one thing to keep in mind is that miracles do not happen every day.

Further, Biblical miracles are called "signs" (e.g., 2 Corinthians 12:12; Acts 2:22) because the purpose of the miracle was to credential the message.

Now, what is the difference between "providence" and "miracle"? They are alike in one sense: both are done by the hand of God. But there are clear differences in their frequency and their purpose. Providence is **everyday**, it is God's every-day care, preservation, and government. Miracle is **not everyday**. Miracle doesn't happen very often throughout all of recorded Bible history. And the purpose of miracle is to credential the message; providence serves no such purpose.

D. *THE DEVIL CAN WORK "LYING WONDERS"*

Not every thing that looks like a miracle is actually done by the hand of God. Indeed, God has worked miracles, but the devil has the ability to imitate God's miracles. What the Devil does is done to draw people away from God. That is why the devil's marvelous deeds are called "lying wonders" (2 Thessalonians 2:9 KJV, or "false wonders" in the NASB). "Wonders" they are, but they do not credential God's Word. They are intended to get men to listen to the devil's word. Several passages of Scripture remind us of the devil's abilities.

> Matthew 7:22 (ASV) – Jesus pictures how it will be at the final judgment. Some will appeal a verdict of condemnation against them by saying, "Did we not ... by thy name cast out demons, and by thy name do many mighty works?" Jesus responds, "Depart from me, ye that work iniquity ... I never knew you." "Mighty works" (miracles) were done, but not by the power of God.

> Matthew 24:24 (ASV) – As Jesus tells the signs by which men may recognize the approaching destruction of Jerusalem (AD 70), He indicated that "false Christs and false prophets" would arise and "show great signs and wonders so as to lead astray, if possible, even the elect." Jesus warns His generation that "lying miracles" would be wrought, and their purpose was to "lead astray ... the elect." True to what He promised, in the years antedating the Roman destruction of Jerusalem, there were some amazing things that happened, but they were not done by the hand of God.

> 2 Thessalonians 2:9 (ASV) – As Paul tells what must happen before the Second Coming of Christ, he explains that the "man of sin" (whoever he is) will appear "according to the working of Satan" and will exhibit "all power and signs and lying wonders." The "signs" and "lying miracles" are wrought by the power of the Devil.

> Revelation 13:13,14 – The devil uses "great signs" to get men to worship the beast, rather than worship Christ. Revelation 19:20 calls the one doing the "great signs" a "false prophet," while 16:14 tells us the devil uses demons to perform the lying wonders.

It is important, after reading about lying wonders, to be on our guard against something that has happened in our lifetimes. Helen Schucman's book, *A Course In Miracles*, was spirit written.[12] It is devilish, demonic in origin. But it has been making the rounds of the churches in the last quarter century. Some denominations are using it for study purposes in Sunday School, and small group meetings! Do we ever think that demons will give us church people correct information?

---

[12] Spirit writing is done by deliberately entering into an altered state of consciousness, in order to appeal to the demons for information.

E. *THE DIFFERENCE BETWEEN GOD'S MIRACLES AND THE DEVIL'S LYING WONDERS*

God's miracles were instantaneous and "permanent" and credentialed the new message as being from God.

> Only one of Jesus' miracles was not instantaneous. You can read about it in Mark 8:22-25. Jesus put saliva on the blind man's eyes, touched him, and asked, "Do you see anything?" The blind man responded, "I see men as trees walking." Jesus touched him again, and immediately he could see everything clearly.

> We put "permanent" in quotation marks, because, for example, in the case of the raising of Lazarus, we presume he eventually died again and had to be buried a second time. But the verb regularly used of Jesus' physical miracles is a perfect tense verb (i.e., the tense indicates past completed action with present continuing results). They were healed, and they still are well. Their sight was restored, and they can still see. The healings were lasting, not temporary.

The devil's wonders are seldom instantaneous, are temporary in their effects, and often are accompanied by a feeling of "heat" as the "healer" touches the one being "helped."

> It is not uncommon for the modern "miracle" to last 3 or 4 weeks, and then the healed person suffers a relapse. ("You've lost your faith," the person will be told.) 77% of one "healer's" miracles are admitted to be but temporary.

> Every person I've talked to in the past 50 years who claims to have been healed at a healing meeting speaks of a feeling of heat when the "healer" touched them. Where do we read anything like this in the Scriptures?[13]

Since there are miracles from God and miracles ("lying wonders") from the devil, it behooves men to be very wary lest the devil's "counterfeits" accomplish their intended work. Modern miracles should not be credulously received as though all miracles must be from God. If we check the currency we receive to make sure the bills are not counterfeit, should we not check to make sure the "wonders" are genuinely from God, lest we lose something much more valuable than a few dollars? And there are tests by which we can determine if a "miracle" is genuine, that it comes from God):

1. They exhibit the character of God and teach truths concerning God.

2. They are in harmony with established truths of revealed religion (Deuteronomy 13:1-3). If a wonder is worked which contradicts the doctrines of the Bible, it is a "lying wonder" (Revelation 16:14).

---

[13] In two of Jesus' healings, "virtue" or "power" went out of Him (Mark 5:30; Luke 6:19). Is that the Biblical language for an "electric shock" or a feeling of "heat," or does it say that it sapped Jesus' energies to heal? The latter is this commentator's understanding of "virtue went out of Him." If a "healer" touches you and you get a feeling of shock or heat, it is this commentator's thesis that the healing is demonic.

3. There is an adequate occasion for them. God uses miracles for a great cause, for a religious purpose. They contribute to His redemptive purpose.

4. The validity of the miracle is established by the character and quality of the witnesses (not by the number of witnesses). Hearsay type of evidence should not be granted credence!

F. *SPECIAL PROVIDENCE IN MORE DETAIL*

We've talked about special providence earlier in this study. We need to broaden our understanding of this wonderful Biblical idea.

One area of special providence is the help God gives believers when they are tempted by the devil. "God ... will not allow you to be tempted beyond what you are able, but with the temptation will provide the way of escape ..." (1 Corinthians 10:12,13).

My illustration is the weigh-lifter. He lifts 50 lbs., 100 lbs., 150 lbs. Soon the weights are more than the person can snatch and press. Each of us can lift a different amount. In a similar fashion, God knows how much pressure, how much weight of temptation, each of us can lift.

And God then puts limits on how much the devil can tempt, on how powerful the temptations may be. He never permits the devil to overwhelm us. The devil can't force you to yield; the devil doesn't overpower you. God even suggests to our minds the way of escape from this temptation, so that we can avoid falling into sin.

Just before we are ready to commit the sin, it will pop to our minds, "You don't have to do it that way. There is another way, a better way." Then you have to decide which you are going to do. God has given "the way of escape" right at the moment we need it. And this is something He does every day; it is special providence. What a neat God!

Answered prayer is another example of special providence. In numerous passages, the Bible promises that God answers prayer.

Matthew 7:7-11 – "Ask ... seek ... knock," Jesus tells his listeners, and then He promises them that something will happen. God will answer.

James 5:15 (ASV) – "The prayer of faith shall save him that is sick." God responds to the prayer. (We'll come back to this verse.)

James 1:5 -- "If any of you lacks wisdom, let him ask of God ... and it will be given to him." God gives it. Answered prayer is special providence.

1 Peter 3:11,12 – "For the eyes of the Lord are upon the righteous, and His ears attend to their prayers." He is anxious to providentially get involved, if we but ask.

Matthew 6:11 – "Give us today the bread we need for today." Jesus promises providential provision, every day provision. "Do not permit us to be tempted, but deliver us from the evil one." God at times puts some limitations on the devil so he can't tempt me today.[14] That, too, is providence.

Since answered prayer is something God does every day, I would call that providence, rather than miracle. Although God does some amazing things in answer to prayer, we should not (in my opinion) call those amazing answers to prayer "miracle." We should call them examples of God's providence.

Mark was a High School senior who was working evenings and week-ends at McDonalds. One Friday evening he said to his parents, "Will you call them and tell them I'm not well enough to come in to work?" Before the evening was over, he was in critical shape. He was rushed to the hospital. X-rays revealed his heart was enlarged as big as a basketball (hindsight -- involved was a genetic birth defect). The parents called us to come to St. Louis. By the time we had arrived, Mark's kidneys had quit. When the kidneys quit, we are not going to live too much longer. They asked me to have a prayer. For what do you pray when someone's kidneys have quit? My prayer was, "God, What you do, do quickly." Soon, visiting hours over, and we headed for the parent's home. It is a 30 minute drive from hospital to his parents' home. When we arrived at the house and opened the door, the phone was ringing. "You had better come quickly," was the message. We hurriedly retraced our route, but Mark was gone before we got back to the Hospital. God in that case mercifully ended a life very quickly in answer to prayer.

Norris was diagnosed as having a very lethal and rapidly acting cancer. The family prayed that they might have one more Christmas together. The cancer went into remission, till after the holidays. God had answered prayer, gave the family several months of happy time together, but He did not reverse the penalty to the race that has resulted from Adam's sin.

God does some amazing things in answer to prayer. He is an amazing God! But I would affirm we should call such answers "providence." These answered prayers are something He does every day. He is not credentialing a message, so it is not "miracle." Rather, it is His providence.

---

[14] The Bible seems to teach that the devil has to ask permission from God before he can tempt the Christian. The devil is the accuser of the brethren, who accuses them before God day and night. As in Job's case, sometimes God gives the devil permission. But when that permission is granted, God says, "OK, devil – this far and no farther!" When we resist the devil, he flees – at least for the moment. After a while, he may come back and try again. Any time the devil finds some temptation that works for him, he'll keep trying it. Our resistance will grow, and our victories will become more common, if we practice resisting each time the devil tempts.

We have studied what the Scriptures tell us about miracles and about the providence of God.   Now we need to focus again on the specific question with which we began.

III. WHY DO PEOPLE GET SICK?   AND HOW DO WE HELP PEOPLE WHO ARE SICK?

We'd like to talk about it, and do it in a way that will honor our Lord.

A. *SCRIPTURES GIVE SEVERAL REASONS FOR SICKNESS.*

1. Some people get sick because of Adam's sin (Romans 8:19-23).

   There was a curse put on the race, so that folk die physically.   Dying is a process. As we are declining little by little, that's when we see sickness come in.

   If we are sick because it is part of the penalty to the race for Adam's sin, I'm not sure there's going to be healing in this life for that.

2. Some people get sick because of their own personal sins (1 Peter 3:15; Exodus 32:34).

   There are times when you and I have behaved unwisely, and have not only a hangover and headache, but more grievous ills than that.   We may be sick because we have worn ourselves out.

3. Some people get sick because of the sins of others (Exodus 20:5; Deuteronomy 5:9; 1 Peter 4:16).

   The bad things they do result in problems for us – environment, toxic, etc.

4. Some people got sick for the glory of God (John 9:3, 11:4).

   If we have one of these sicknesses, I doubt there is any healing that is going to occur until in God's own time he's ready to display that glory.

5. Some people get sick because whom the Lord loves He chastens (Hebrews 12:5).

   Sometimes you and I get sick because God sees there is some sin in our lives that He wants to call to our attention, sin that ought to be repented of.   Maybe when we are flat on our backs and can only look up, we'll seize the opportunity to do some repenting.   With the repenting, there may come healing of the sickness that was inflicted on us to get us to repent.

6. Some sickness is the result of spirit possession, witchcraft, or sorcery (Matthew 17:14ff).

Why are we sick?   It can be any one of these previous several reasons why we may be sick.

B. *SOME MISLEADING IDEAS FLOATING AROUND ABOUT SICKNESS & HEALTH.*

(1) One of the misleading ideas is found in a little book that has made the rounds entitled "JESUS WANTS YOU WELL!"   What can be read in the book is not the whole truth, for the book suggests that if you just get rid of the demons in your life, you will be well.   That's not the whole story.

In the Bible, we can read about men of God who did not enjoy good health, and their ill-health cannot be blamed on demonic involvement.   Paul had a thorn in the flesh (2 Corinthians 12:7ff).   He never got rid of it.   "A messenger from Satan (given) to buffet him," is the way he describes it.   Paul never did get well from that one.   "Trophimus I left at Miletus sick" (2 Timothy 4:20 ASV).   The apostle Paul, who can heal people right and left, didn't – or couldn't – heal Trophimus, and had to leave him behind.   Trophimus was too sick to travel.

(2) Another of the misleading ideas is the claim that there is "HEALING IN THE ATONEMENT."   That is, if we simply recognized this, we could be well, healed of our physical ailments.   This is a famous argument used by modern healers in an attempt to justify their healing ministry.[15]   Where do they get the idea?

Some appeal to Psalm 103:3 (ASV) – "Who forgives all your sins, who heals all your diseases" is often appealed to by folk who are claiming they have the ability to heal sick people.   However, this verse is more likely an example of Hebrew parallelism, in which the second line says the same thing the first line does, only in different words.   The first line of Psalm 103:3 talks about iniquities.   It means that "diseases," in the second line, is used in a figurative sense to stand for sin, rather than for physical sickness.

Some appeal to Isaiah 53:5 –In this famous Suffering Servant poem about Jesus, we are told that "By His stripes we are healed" (ASV).

Modern 'healers,' who insist there is redemption in the cross for all our illnesses in this life, are not telling the story the way it is when they quote Isaiah 53 as their proof text.   It will take two or three paragraphs to develop this point.

Romans 8:19-24 is important.   It says something to this effect -- 'even though [Christians] have the firstfruits of the Spirit (i.e., we've got the Holy Spirit, the indwelling gift), we still groan within ourselves (i.e., we hurt), yearning for our

---

[15] Our library is full of books claiming God has called men to be faith-healers today, who are to have great healing ministries.   Have you ever tried to find an example anywhere in the New Testament where anyone was called to have a "healing ministry"?   There are calls to church-planting ministry.   There are calls to preaching ministry.   There are calls to a missionary ministry.   But a healing ministry in Scripture? When folk in the church were sick, they didn't go to a healing revival or call for the 'faith healer.'   They were instructed to call for the elders of the church (James 5).

adoption, to wit, the redemption of our bodies.' Romans 8 says you can be a Christian, in good standing with the Holy Spirit, and still be hurting. That does not match the claim that "God wants you well!" in this life, or that there is "healing (in this life) in the atonement."

Matthew 8:14-17 has been wrongly used by healers of all generations, to justify their ministry. Read the passage. Peter's mother-in-law was sick; she didn't go to church (i.e., synagogue) that day. Instead, she was lying sick in bed with a "high fever" (Luke 4:38). When church was over, Jesus went to Peter's home and healed her. Jesus touched her and the fever left her; she arose and fixed dinner for all the guests who came home with Peter. When evening had come, some of the townspeople came bringing those who were sick, and Jesus healed them all. He cast out the demons with a word. Matthew tells us that all this was done in order that what was spoken of through Isaiah the prophet might be fulfilled, namely, "He Himself took our infirmities and carried away our diseases."

> Now, if I am a faith-healer, I will read that verse as a proof text that there is physical healing in the atonement. Verse 17 quotes Isaiah 53:5. "Isn't healing a fulfillment of Isaiah, just as much as Jesus going to the cross was a fulfillment?" the faith-healer will ask.[16]

> Look at Isaiah 53:5 again. Jesus' suffering was to take away sins. 1 Peter 2:24 interprets Isaiah 53 for us, and shows it is a reference to sins, not to healing.

What then is Matthew 8:17 saying? Jesus performed the miracles to show He was the long-promised Messiah. He was the one Isaiah promised was coming.

Christ did die for our body as well as our soul. But it is at the final resurrection that we will get our sickness-free bodies. While we are in this world we are liable to be sick. "Jesus Wants You Well" or "There is Healing in the Atonement" is not telling it as it is in the Bible.

C. *UNDERSTANDING JAMES 5:13ff.*

In the letters of both James and John, there are some difficult to understand verses; we must make the effort to discipline our minds if we are to attempt to master what the Word is saying to us. For example, 1 John 5:16 talks about the sin unto death and a sin not unto death, and we are to pray for one but not the other. What is that verse talking about? Bible students have found James 5:13-16 to be nearly as difficult. It reads like this:

---

[16] Just in passing, not every faith-healer treats Isaiah's "By His stripes we are healed" this way. K. Kuhlman argues that this Isaiah passage means that when Jesus was scourged (before He ever went to the cross), that's what provides healing.

Is any one among you suffering? Let him pray. Is any one cheerful? Let him sing praises. Is anyone among you sick? Let him call for the elders of the church, and let them pray over him, anointing him with oil in the name of the Lord; and the prayer offered in faith will restore the one who is sick, and the Lord will raise him up, and if he has committed sins, they will be forgiven him. Therefore, confess your sins to one another, and pray for one another, so that you may be healed. The effective prayer of a righteous man can accomplish much.

Briefly we need to explain each of the phrases.

"Is anyone among you sick?"

The picture is of one sick in bed – sick enough to be bedfast, and weak.

"Let him call for the elders of the church"

Call for the elders, the spiritual leaders of the congregation.   "Please come!"

"Let them pray over him"

We'll talk about the content of the prayer in a moment.

"Anointing him with oil in the name of the Lord"

Oil was the best medicine the ancients had. Compare the Parable of the Good Samaritan. When he helped the wounded traveler, he did what? He poured oil and wine onto the wounds. Some of us are old enough to remember using kerosene or coal oil for wounds on both man and animal. It helped the healing process.

In paraphrased form, James is basically saying, "Make sure the patient is taking his medicine, and then have a prayer. Both together will be useful toward the healing."

I'm not sure there is any miraculous thing in the oil since the Greek word for "oil" is the regular word for olive oil.

"The prayer offered in faith will *sōdzō* (Greek) the one who is sick."

The Greek word *sōdzō* (translated "restore" in the NASB) has five different meanings. In each passage where *sōdzō* occurs, we must determine which of the meanings is intended. Sometimes it is not easy to tell.

Each of the other times *sōdzō* is used in James, the meaning the context calls for is "save". James 1:21 ("save"), 2:14 ("save"), 4:12 ("save"), 5:20 ("save"). Perhaps it has a similar meaning in 5:15.

In James 5:15, it is possible that *sōdzō* should be translated "restore" – that we are talking about restoring the sick person to *spiritual* health.

It is possible that *sōdzō* should be translated "recover" – that we are talking about recovering bodily health, about recovering *physical* health.

John 11:12 – In Lazarus' case, "If he has fallen asleep, He will *recover*" say the disciples to Jesus. *Sōdzō* is the Greek word in John 11, too. It is used of folk who have been sick getting well, about physical/bodily health being recovered.

For the Catholic Church, this James 5 passage became the proof text for the practice of extreme unction (last rites for the dying) in the Middle Ages. As the practice has developed over the years, we also now have to have certain holy oil, specially prepared for use at a ceremony a day or so before Easter. Extreme unction involves anointing the sick with olive oil, giving them communion, and praying over them – their sins are now forgiven so that when they die and enter the next world they are without any unforgiven sin.[17]

Yet in the James 5 passage, it is the "prayer offered in faith" that is emphasized, not anointing with oil. What does "offered in faith" mean? James 1:6 talks about praying without doubting (without wavering) – i.e., the person who is praying has been consistent in his Christian living. James 1:8 talks about a double-minded man who is unstable in all his ways (i.e., not consistent in his living). "Offered in faith" may very well talk about a life-style. An inconsistent life-style on the part of the one who is praying will negate the prayer.

"The Lord will raise him up"

The word translated "raise" means to "stand up, stand on one's feet." It might speak of getting up out of bed (cp. Mark 2:9). It might speak of being raised from the dead at the second coming.

"If he has committed sins, they will be forgiven him"

Some sickness is the result of personal sins. Those sins need to be repented of if there is to be forgiveness from God.[18]

"Confess your sins to one another, and pray for one another, so that you may be healed."

Confession only happens after there has been repentance. The sick person and the offended person both pray for one another.

There are three future tense verbs in a row (will save/recover, will raise, will be forgiven). A future tense verb can describe one act in the future, or continuous/repeated action in the future. Maybe this passage is saying is the sick person will

---

[17] Because this passage speaks of folk getting well rather than dying, Catholics have had a hard time defending this text as a proof text for last rites. Since Vatican II, Catholics no longer use this passage for extreme unction. They now anoint the sick, but not the dying. They still have communion for the dying.

[18] Some sicknesses are stress related. Emotionally induced illnesses frequently have a reversible process. Removing the stress also helps remove the physical symptoms caused by that stress. Psalm 32:3-7 reveals the cause of David's physical distress and how it was removed.

slowly begin to get well (continuous action).   Maybe the passage is saying the sick person will get well in one moment (one act in the future).   You cannot tell from this future tense verb exactly what is being pictured or promised.

<u>"The effective prayer of a righteous man can accomplish much."</u>

The prayer of a righteous man avails much.   "Righteous" is not sinless perfect, but one whose life is consistently in harmony with God's revealed will.[19]

God hears the prayer.   The sins are forgiven.   The man who was sick because he sinned now has no reason to be sick longer, so he recovers.[20]

D. *WHAT TO DO WHEN YOU ARE SICK ENOUGH TO BE WEAK & BEDFAST.*

Call for the elders?   Yes.   Let them pray?   Yes.   Confess your sins and pray for each other?   Yes.   Expect a miracle?   Well, to answer that, let us once more remind ourselves about the power, the purpose, and the promise of healing we find in the ministry of Jesus.[21]

1.   **The power behind the healing** can be observed in John 9, as Jesus heals the man born blind.   There were many blind beggars in Jerusalem, and Jesus occasionally helped one.   The one who was healed in the temple that day told the religious leaders, "If this man were not from God, He could do nothing."   The power by which Jesus healed came from God.   Jesus did not perform miracles indiscriminately.   He did not heal everyone who needed healing (John 5:3-5; Matthew 11:5).

In Matthew 11, Jesus tells the messengers from John, "Go tell John what you see." Blind people see.   Deaf people hear.   There is no "the" in the Greek.   If the

---

[19] James' use of "righteous man" helps us to understand that he is not making a blanket promise. Elsewhere in Scripture there are other conditions to answered prayer. 1. Pray for the right reasons (James 4:1-3). 2. Pray with the right responses (1 John 3:22).   3. Pray for things in harmony with His will (1 John 5:14, 15).   4. Sometimes there is a need to be persistent in prayer (Luke 18:1).

[20] One person in the audience at this original presentation asked, "How do we know whether to respond to the call to the elders to come pray over the sick?   That is, how do we know ahead of time if the sickness is because of personal sin?"   That's a hard question.   In my early ministry, as I made hospital calls, I probably did not always do well.   The patient sometimes asked, "Preacher, why do you think I am sick?"   I used to launch right into all the theological reasons why people get sick, and often the patient would become quiet, or wanted to talk about something else.   I have learned that when the patient asks such a question, there is something they want to talk about and they are trying to find out if the preacher is willing to listen.   So now I respond, "Boy, I don't know why you are sick.   What do you think?"   Then the patient will speak about what they have been thinking about there on the sick-bed.   Sometimes they confess some sins I would never have dreamed were in their lives.   I must show no surprise in my facial expressions at what they are saying, or they will immediately stop.   They want forgiveness and prayer. So I listen to their confession.   Then we pray together.   The prayer zeroes in on the things confessed.

[21] Some of the following ideas are gleaned from a sermon preached by Richard A. Koffarnus at Central Christian College of the Bible on October 30, 2001.

Greek said, "*the* dead are raised," that means *all* the dead. But there is no "the" (even though in some of our Bibles there is a "the"). It wasn't all the blind whose sight was restored. It wasn't all the deaf whose hearing was restored. Not all were healed. Some blind people were healed, but not all. There were many, in fact, He didn't heal. He did not even perform signs on request (Matthew 12:38-40). John records this one, about the healing of the blind man, because it was so dramatic. The power for all healing, whether miraculous or providential, ultimately originates from God!

2. **The purpose of the healing** goes to the heart of the question, "Why doesn't God heal everyone?" Why do we have any occasions of divine healings recorded in the Scriptures at all? Mark 2:1-12 tells of the fellow who was let down through the roof. Especially verses 6 and 7 need our attention to help us answer the question, "Why did Jesus heal?" Verses 6 and 7 tell us the religious leaders who were there watching said, "Why is this man speaking this way? (Jesus had said something about the paralytic's sins being forgiven.) He is blaspheming; who can forgive sins but God alone?" And immediately, Jesus, perceiving in His spirit that they reasoning that way within themselves, said to them, "Why are you reasoning about these things within your hearts? Which is easier? To say to the paralytic, 'Your sins are forgiven;' or to say [to the paralytic], 'Arise, and take up your pallet and walk?' But in order that you may know that the Son of Man has authority on earth to forgive sins," He said to the paralytic, "I say to you, rise, take up your pallet and go home." Why did Jesus heal? What was the purpose? "That you may know that the Son of Man has power on earth to forgive sins." Whenever Jesus healed anyone in Scripture, it was to establish His identity as Messiah. That is why He healed, to prove His claims to deity. This is exactly the point He made to the messengers from John the Baptist (Matthew 11:5-6).

3. **The promise of healing.** John 11 is the record of the raising of Lazarus. Messengers were sent to Jesus telling Him of Lazarus' sickness. The messengers were sent back with this message, "This sickness is not unto death, but for the glory of God, and that the Son of God may be glorified by it" (John 11:4). Jesus then waited until Lazarus is dead before heading over to Bethany to raise him. When He arrives, the sisters say, "Lord, if you had just been here, my brother would not have died." Jesus responds (verse 21ff), "I [and it is an emphatic I ... 'I myself, and no one else') am the resurrection and the life ...." I am the One who causes it. I can do it in the future, and I can do it now. "Everyone who lives and believes in Me shall never die. Do you believe this?" Jesus is not just a healer – He is a raiser of the dead! That can mean rise to walk in newness of life, or that can be resurrection of the dead body (today, or one of these days). What a Savior we have who can do both of those for us!

CONCLUSION

A. A SUMMARY of the main points that have been emphasized.

1. Apostles of Jesus could miraculously heal, but the office of apostle was temporary. We don't expect anything like an apostle coming to heal us.

2. Certain believers received "spiritual gifts" by the laying on of an apostle's hands and they could heal, but those gifts, too, were temporary, and while they lasted were intended to credential the Gospel message.

3. God does some very wonderful things in answer to prayer, including (in some cases) physical healing. But those answered prayers are examples of His providence, not miracle.

4. God's answers to prayer are 'yes,' 'no,' and 'wait a while.'[22]   When we pray for healing, we may receive any one of the three possible answers – whatever turns out best for Him and for His glory.

B. WHERE IS GOD WHEN IT HURTS?   When you were young, were you ever promised something and then didn't get it? How disappointed you were! Do you know the agonizing despair that can be caused when we promise somebody "healing" and those promises are not fulfilled?   There is nothing quite so cruel as giving hope of healing if the Scriptures do not honestly and really provide that hope!

C. MEDICINE AND DOCTORS ARE OK!   Doctor Luke (Colossians 4:14) traveled and ministered with Paul. Remember the events on the island of Malta (Acts 28:7-10). Jesus indicated that those who were sick are the ones who need a physician (Matthew 9:13). Timothy was advised to take some "medicine" for his frequent ailments (1 Timothy 5:23). Doctors and medicine are OK.[23]

D. Some MISLEADING REPORTS of modern miracles have made the rounds.

Demythologizing Indonesia's Revival is a case in point. Mel Tari's book, *Like a Mighty Wind* made claims for modern miracles. Then George Peters, *Indonesian Revival*, showed the claims in Mel Tari's book were misleading if not downright false. Yet Tari's book has been used to justify modern claims to miracles, including healing. It was claimed to be written by the power of the Holy Spirit. Now it has been shown to be not quite right.

Such misleading reports continue today. Cases in point are the H. Bonneke meetings in South Africa, and Benny Hinn, who admits that he has fabricated some of the "wonders" he has told about.

E. Folk who wish for miracles today will sometimes ask cessationists, "IS THERE ANYTHING GOD CANNOT DO?"   Or they will ask, "Aren't you limiting God when you say you doubt that miracles (like the Bible describes) still occur?"

---

[22] Luke 18:1ff, where the persistent widow keeps asking, is an example of "wait a while."

[23] Consider also the "health aspects" of the Law of Moses: sanitation, sterilization, quarantine, hygiene, and diet. We are not under the Law of Moses any more, yet consider what God provided. There must be something valuable about doctors and medicine; they were OK, even in Old Testament times.

Let's thoughtfully analyze those questions. On the one hand, Jeremiah asserts of God, "Nothing is too difficult for Thee" (Jeremiah 32:17). So we might answer the question "Is there anything God cannot do" with a resounding, "No!"

Yet what about these verses?

> Titus 1:2 – God cannot lie.
> 2 Timothy 2:13 – He cannot deny Himself.
> Genesis 9:11 – God can't flood the earth again.
> James 1:13 – God cannot be tempted.

The issue involves God's nature and will and self-limitation, not just His power. Is there anything God cannot do? Can't He work a miracle of healing? Yet as importantly, how do the Scriptures explain how He has revealed Himself to be working?

F.   WHAT TO DO WHEN YOU GET SICK

Since Jesus said the sick call for physicians, we should not think it an evidence of lack of faith if we consult with doctors and specialists to get an accurate diagnosis. We may certainly follow the doctor's prescription, yet with the full realization that physical death is part of the penalty the whole human race pays because Adam sinned. Despite all the doctor does, each of us is still going to die one of these days.[24]

It would certainly be ideal if one clear Scripture said, "Any time you are sick, this is what you should do." But there is no such passage (not even James 5), so we must put several passages together to learn what to do when we are sick. When we do, here is what we learn:

1. Acknowledge that God is sovereign and rest in unshakable faith. God is in control, whether we are in sickness or in health (Deuteronomy 32:39).

2. Remind yourself of the Biblical reasons for sickness and the purposes God can accomplish through it.

3. It is extremely important to determine if a sickness is because of some continued sin in our lives. Is God using our illness as a chastisement? If we are sick because of sin in our lives, we ought to repent, for there will be no healing without repentance.

4. In faith, commit the entire matter to the Lord. Pray for His will to be done, seek His glory, and wait patiently for His response.

5. Seek professional medical attention. Never disregard nor ignore God's normal means to restored health through medical experts. Do not presume on God and wait too long

---

[24] I jokingly tell my doctor, "I'm going to be one of your success cases." He just smiles. The best doctors in the world bury more patients than they want to.

or ignore your doctor altogether.

6. It may be God's will that we fully recover.   Or it may not be God's will for us to fully recover.   Many of God's great servants were sick: Isaac, Jacob, Moses, Job, Daniel, Paul, Epaphroditus, Timothy.   And all eventually died.

7. Thank God for the circumstances in which He has placed you (Ephesians 5:20; 1 Thessalonians 5:18).   You are not thanking God that you are hurt.   Rather, you are thanking God that He is who He is, and that He can work all things for our ultimate good.

8. Ask God for the faith and patience to endure and the wisdom to understand why (James 1:2-5).   He has promised to give that wisdom, and He has promised that His grace will be sufficient (2 Corinthians 12:9).

9. Pray that your circumstances might be worked out for the glory of God (1 Corinthians 10:31).

10. When you are bedfast, call for the elders to visit and pray (James 5:13).   There is nothing wrong with asking God for healing.   He may say, "No."   But there is nothing wrong with asking.   Remember, Paul asked three times for healing (2 Corinthians 12:8).   His requests were denied.   Our requests may be denied, too.

11. Pray this prayer: *"Lord, if it will be to Your glory, heal suddenly.   If it will glorify You more, heal gradually.   If it will glorify You even more, may your servant remain sick for a while.   And if it will glorify Your name still more, take him to Yourself in Heaven."*   Ole Hallesby

---

HELPFUL READING SOURCES

Carrol M. Stegall, *The Modern Tongues and Healing Movement*

William Nolan, *Healing: A Doctor in Search of a Miracle*
   He tried for several years to find a genuine miracle among the "faith healers" prominent on TV.

Waymon Miller, *Modern Divine Healing*

Richard Mayhue, *Divine Healing Today*

Joni Eareckson's *Joni* and *A Step Further*
   Folk have said to her, "If you just had enough faith, God could heal you of your paralysis."   If you were confined to a wheel chair and struggling just to get food into your mouth because your arm won't work, how do you respond when someone says something like that to you?   Read in this book what Joni has to say about this whole matter of divine healing.

SELECTED BIBLIOGRAPHY FOR JAMES

Adamson, James B., *The Epistle of James*, in the New International Commentary on the New Testament series. Grand Rapids: Eerdmans, 1976.
> This volume replaces the more devotional work in the same series by A. Ross (1954). It includes a full Introduction, a rather literal translation, and detailed comments on the main issues. Adamson rejects the view the letter lacks cohesion, and vigorously argues that it has a theology and a Christology.

-----, *James: The Man and His Message*. Grand Rapids: Eerdmans, 1989.
> The ideas introduced in his 1976 work are further developed in this lengthy sequel. Adamson is a Presbyterian preacher, and this volume contains helpful homiletic material. Adamson argues that all the evidence – literary, social, didactic, and theological – indicates the letter of James comes from a nascent, pre-Pauline period in the early church, probably before AD 60 and even as early as AD 40.

Alford, Henry, *The General Epistle of James*, in Alford's Greek Testament. London: Rivingtons, 1871.
> Greek text. Variant readings cited by manuscript or ancient church father or ancient versions. Introductory studies. Verse-by-verse explanations.

Arndt, W.F. and Gingrich, F.W., *A Greek-English Lexicon of the New Testament*. Chicago: University of Chicago Press, 1978.

Baker, William R., and Thomas D. Ellsworth, *Preaching James*. St. Louis: Chalice Press, 2004.
> On each paragraph Baker writes a clear exposition of James with examples of how his message can be preached today. Ellsworth provides a sermon on the same paragraph with contemporary applications of the message of James.

Barclay, William, *The Letters of James and Peter,* in The Daily Study Bible series. Philadelphia: Westminster, 1958.
> Barclay holds that our book of James is the substance of a heavily-edited sermon preached by James, the Lord's brother, taken down by someone else and translated into Greek with a few additions. Barclay's own translation is printed at the beginning of each of the paragraphs into which the epistle is divided. Most valuable for its word studies and background material. This volume has fewer of the colorful anecdotes found in the other volumes in this series.

Barnes, Albert, *James, Peter, John, and Jude*, in Notes on the New Testament, Vol. X. Grand Rapids: Baker, 1953.
> These "notes" were written by Barnes during his 35-year ministry in a church in Philadelphia. The notes were prepared for the specific use by Sunday school teachers. Greek words were explained by quoting several different lexicons. He was specially gifted in making practical application of the truths taught in the Scriptures. In scattered places, his notes reflect three of the five points of Calvinism.

Barrett, Ethel, *Will the Real Phony Please Stand Up.* Glendale, CA: Regal Books, 1971.
James' letter (quoted from *The New Testament in Modern English* by J.B. Phillips) appears in this book along with comments intended for young people to help them take the letter of James seriously. Each of the twelve lessons ends with questions to help the reader apply the Christian principles emphasized.

Berry, George R., *New Testament Synonyms.* Chicago: Wilcox and Follett, 1948.
A knowledge of the connotation of synonyms is helpful to understanding the Greek text. Much material has been drawn from R.C. Trench, *Synonyms of the New Testament,* as well as from the New Testament Lexicons of Thayer and Cremer, as well as from the small ones by Green and Hickie.

Burdick, Donald W., *James,* in The Expositors Bible Commentary, Vol.12. Grand Rapids: Zondervan, 1981.
Provides an introduction, an outline, an exposition, and a bibliography. Notes on textual questions and special problems are correlated with the expository units. This whole twelve-volume set is now available on CD-Rom and can be installed on personal computers. Like most volumes in this series, the comments on James are what conservative evangelicals might expect.

Carr, Arthur, *The General Epistle of James,* in the Cambridge Greek Testament for Schools and Colleges series. Reprint. Cambridge: University Press, 1930.
Greek text. A scholarly interpretation of the original text by a conservative British scholar. Good introductory material. Adapted to the Greek student.

Chilton, Bruce, and Craig Evans, editors, *The Missions of James, Peter and Paul: Tensions in Early Christianity.* Leiden: Brill, 2005.
This is a collection of sixteen essays which were delivered at the "Consultation on James." The contributors accept the presuppositions of redaction criticism and of social-science criticism.

Davids, Peter H., *The Epistle of James,* in the New International Greek Testament Commentary series. Grand Rapids: Eerdmans, 1982.
Davids sees the epistle as a "two-stage" work, originating in the preaching of James the Just in the late 40s or early 50s, and later edited, either c. AD 55-65, or just possibly c. AD 75-85. The later editing accounts for the polished Greek, he claims. He sees Jewish traditions being used and modified in the letter. He argues that James does have a coherent structure, and does have a theology – of suffering, eschatology, poverty-piety, grace, law, faith, wisdom and prayer – as well as a Christology. Luther had criticized the lack of Christology in the letter, and Davids argues that *kurios* is James' "favorite term for Christ." The letter's abrupt changes of subject are the result of the editor putting together parts of James' sermons. Davids' hypothesis of a later editing is not followed through and he over-presses the evidence. Readers will need a working knowledge of Greek.

-----, *James,* in the Good News Commentary series. New York: Harper and Row, 1983.
This volume is a popular version of his NIGTC commentary. The 1983 edition is based on the Good News Bible, while the 1989 edition is based on the New International Version.

Dibelius, M., *James*, in the Hermeneia series.   Translated from the 11th German edition, rev. H. Greeven.   Philadelphia: Fortress Press, 1975.

> The comments in this volume are consistent with the theological liberalism displayed in most books in this series.   First published in 1921, Dibelius argued that James is pseudonoymous, and dates from AD 80-130.   He identifies its form as paraenesis, an imprecise term by which he intends a hortatory writing made up of loosely-related admonitions of general ethical content.   He does not find any coherent outline or continuity of thought.   Dibelius emphasizes the author's "*patriarchal-pietistic* ethic of the poor, his *pauperistic* animosity toward the rich, and his *apocalyptic* expectation of imminent punishment for the rich" (p.44 his italics).

Easton, Burton Scott and Poteat, Gordon, *The Epistle of James*, in The Interpreter's Bible, Vol. 12.   New York: Abingdon, 1957.

> The work of two noted liberal scholars, supporting the theory that the epistle is a purely Jewish writing which has been subjected to superficial Christian editing.   The author, Easton thinks, is not the Lord's brother.   Introduction and exegesis by Easton, exposition by Poteat.

Fickett, H.L., *James: Faith that Works*.   Glendale, CA: Regal Books, 1972.

> A verse-by-verse commentary with vivid illustrations of application.   From a series of sermons preached at First Baptist Church, Van Nuys, Calif.

Gaebelein, Frank E., *The Practical Epistle of James.   Studies in Applied Christianity.* Great Neck, NY: Doniger & Raughley, 1955.

> The substance of a series of popular lectures on James, neither exhaustive nor technical.   The author's aim is to apply the incisive ethical and spiritual teaching of James to our own times.

Gibson, E.C.S., *James*, in the Pulpit Commentary series.   Grand Rapids: Eerdmans, 1950.

> Introductory studies deal with author (James, the brother of the Lord), date ("the very earliest of the writings of the New Testament"), a discussion of the "brothers" of the Lord which explains the Epiphanian, Hieronymian, and Helvidian views, and the purpose for writing.   Verse-by-verse comments on each chapter are followed by homilies by various authors.

Gwinn, Ralph A., *The Epistle of James.   A Study Manual,* in the Shield Bible Study series. Grand Rapids: Baker, 1967.

> A concise interpretation of James based on the original Greek but adapted to the English reader.   A brief introduction simply indicates the critical problems.   A conservative guide for individual or group study of James.

Hartin, Patrick J., *James,* in the Sacra Pagina series.   Collegeville, MN: Liturgical Press, 2003.

> Starting from the hypothesis that our Bible books reflect three levels of material – what Jesus said and did, of which we know little; what the apostles said and did, of which we know little; and what the early church believed – much modern scholarship has focused on how James could be used to help fill in the gap in our knowledge of the crucial period between AD 60 and 135. The conclusion drawn is that Jewish Christianity, James himself, and his letter influenced both the Orthodox Church and Gnosticism.   Hartin believes that two relatively recent developments in New Testament studies can be applied with profit to this letter – sociological and anthropological methods, and examination of the alleged rhetorical style.   When these methods are used, one learns little of James' message.

Instead we read page upon page where it is debated which verse constitutes a *propositio*, where one divides the *rationis confirmatio* from the *exornatio*, etc. Hartin does not avoid issues where Catholic theology has found support in the text of James, though he treads gingerly at times.

Hiebert, D. Edmond, *The Epistle of James*. Chicago: Moody, 1979.

In the phrase-by-phrase comments, Greek words are transliterated, and Greek constructions are explained. In the introductory studies, Hiebert surveys the arguments for and against the traditional view of authorship (James, the Lord's brother). Concerning the outline of the book, "James sets forth a series of 6 basic tests whereby his readers are to test their own faith" (p.43). The date of writing is "just before the Jerusalem Conference" (p.41). An extensive bibliography is included.

Hort, F.J.A., *The Epistle of James*. London: Macmillan,1909. Reprinted Grand Rapids: Baker, 1980.

Greek text with commentary as far as James 4:7. Published posthumously, this volume was originally intended to be part of a commentary on the whole New Testament by that famous trio of Westcott, Lightfoot, and Hort. Hort tries to be sensitive to the epistle's Hebrew background. Hort accepts authorship by James the Lord's brother, and dates the epistle c. AD 50-60. He believed the epistle contains many hidden allusions to Jesus' sayings.

Hughes, R. Kent, *James*, in the Preaching the Word series. Wheaton, IL: Crossway, 1991

A series of 28 sermons on James.

Isaacs, Marie E., *Reading Hebrews and James: A Literary and Theological Commentary*, in Reading the New Testament series. Macon, GA: Smyth and Helwys, 2002.

The commentaries in this series aim at presenting current "cutting-edge research" in popular form. What this research asserts, Isaacs tells us, is that James is the work of an otherwise unknown teacher who lived in one of "those communities where being both Jewish and a follower of Jesus had yet to become regarded as incompatible" (p.173). The letter was written "at the turn of the first century" (p.176). James 2:14-26 is seen "as confronting a post-Pauline interpretation of the apostle's Law-free gospel." "It is clear that the Mosaic Law is not understood by James as antithetical to the Gospel" (p.196). No contribution by any scholar more recent than 1995 is included in the book.

Jacobsen, Henry, *The Good Life: Epistle of James*. Wheaton, IL: Scripture Press, 1973.

Intended for personal study and application of the letter of James, here are ten lessons based on James, with questions to be answered in writing as each reader slowly works through the lessons. Since spiritual growth is not merely a matter of merely knowing what is in the Bible, but depends on how well you obey what you know, there are "Think and Do" sections with each lesson.

Johnson, Luke Timothy, *The Letter of James*, in the Anchor Bible series. New York: Doubleday, 1995.

As always in the Anchor Bible series, this commentary abounds with bibliographical references, a great aid to further research. In the preface (p.ix), Johnson notes the changing character of the Anchor commentaries since Bo Reicke's *The Epistles of James, Peter, and Jude*, which launched the series in 1964, as justification for this commentary. One-fourth of his introductory studies tell us the history of the interpretation of James. He gives us this history so that Luther's defamation of James as anti-Pauline, which was followed in due course by the historical-critical school branding James as "early catholic," might be corrected. As he deals with the relationship between Paul and James, Johnson thinks there is no basis for thinking that James and Paul are "talking to each other" on the topic of faith and works. James, the Lord's brother is the author, and the date of writing is early (anywhere between AD 46 and 62). On occasion, Johnson interacts with contemporary writers of commentaries on James, such as Davids and Martin. Occasionally evangelical readers will disagree with Johnson's conclusions, but on the whole they will welcome this as a commentary to recommend to Bible students and scholars.

-----, *Brother of Jesus, Friend of God: Studies in the Letter of James*. Grand Rapids: Eerdmans, 2004.
> A series of essays written while Johnson was preparing his Anchor Bible commentary on *The Letter of James*. Johnson seeks to identify James, the Lord's brother, as the author of this letter, and to outline the place of James in early Christian history. Johnson makes a good case for recognizing that early traditions about Jesus are preserved in James.

Johnstone, Robert, *Lectures Exegetical and Practical on the Epistle of James*. 1871. Reprint. Grand Rapids: Baker, 1954.
> A new translation of the epistle (rather than simply using the KJV) with notes on the Greek text. The lectures give an interesting, full, and rewarding practical exposition.

King, Guy H., A *Belief That Behaves: An Expositional Study of the Epistle of James*. London: Marshall, Morgan & Scott, 1945.
> Devotional and expository studies of James. Abundant homiletical suggestions and practical applications.

Kent, Homer A., Jr., *Faith that Works: Studies in the Epistle of James*. Grand Rapids: Baker, 1986.
> A concise commentary divided into twelve chapters, with discussion questions after each chapter to make it useful for group study. The studies grew out of the writer's experience teaching James at the college level and preaching James in churches and Bible conferences.

Kistemaker, Simon J., *Exposition of the Epistle of James and the Epistles of John*, in the New Testament Commentary series. Grand Rapids: Baker, 1986.
> Written from a Reformed conservative position. Kistemaker believes that James originated in the sermons preached by the Lord's brother. He rejects Ropes' idea that the work is a diatribe, since, being a sacred text, it lacks the "bitter sarcasm, irony and name-calling" of that genre. Students with only limited Greek may find help in the grammatical notes.

Knowling, R.J., *The Epistle of St. James,* in the Westminster Commentaries series. London: Methuen, 1904.
> A valuable commentary by a conservative British scholar of the past century. Emphasizes the linguistic parallels to the epistle. Important introduction.

Lange, J.P., and Van Oosterzee, J.J., *The Epistle General of James,* in Lange's Commentary on *the Holy Scriptures.* Trans. from the German by J. Isidor Mombert in 1867. Reprint. Grand Rapids: Zondervan, n.d.

> A careful exegetical study of the epistle. It contains a mass of homiletical material, some of which (though originally written in the 1860's) is still of value today.

Laws, Sophie, *A Commentary on the Epistle of James*, in Harper's New Testament Commentaries series. San Francisco: Harper & Row, 1980.

> She believes James is pseudonymous, being written after the death of James the Lord's brother and before Hermas (c. AD 70-130). Her comments are strongly indebted to Dibelius. She sees James as taking issue with the apostle Paul and Pauline tradition.

Lenski, R.C.H., *The Interpretation of the Epistle to the Hebrews and of the Epistle of James.* Columbus, Ohio: Lutheran Book Concern, 1938.

> Lenski was a conservative Lutheran. His full and voluminous comments enable the English reader to get at the meaning of the Greek text. Important for exegetical study.

MacArthur, James, Jr., *James*, in the MacArthur New Testament Commentary series. Chicago: Moody, 1998.

> A detailed verse-by-verse, phrase-by-phrase exposition of James. James' purpose in writing this epistle, according to MacArthur, was "to challenge his readers to examine their faith to see if it was genuine saving faith" (p.5). So James presents a series of thirteen tests by which the genuineness of salvation can be determined (p.10). MacArthur gives a twist to James 2:14-16. He insists that James' statement that Abraham was "justified by works" does not contradict Paul's affirmation that justification is by faith, not works. "Justified" in James 2:21 speaks of "a person's standing before other men" (p.137) rather than their standing before God. He argues that *astheneo* in James 5:14,15, often translated "sick," actually means weak spiritually. Viewing James as being addressed to a congregation in which unbelievers were present, MacArthur takes James 4:7-10 as "one of the clearest calls to salvation in all of Scripture (p.201). One helpful feature of this commentary is the outlines of various passages, which would be helpful in preaching those texts.

Male, E. William, "Divine Healing According to James 5." *Grace Journal* I:2 (Fall 1960).

Manton, Thomas, *An Exposition of the Epistle of James.* London: Banner of Truth Trust, 1962.

> First published in 1693, these exhaustive studies highlight the special relevance of this epistle in the situations facing the church. In the seventeenth and early eighteenth centuries, this was considered the best commentary on James.

Martin, Ralph P., *James*, in the Word Biblical Commentary series. Waco, TX: Word, 1988.

> Martin believes in a "two-stage" composition of James, with the main content going back to James the Lord's brother. His most original contribution is to suggest a detailed *Sitz im Leben* for the work in the nationalistic controversies prior to the Jewish revolt (AD 66-70). He believes that James, a strong supporter of the poor and marginalized, opposed violent means to solving his nation's prob-

lems, and as a result was put to death in a patriotic reawakening under the High Priest Ananus II (Jos. *Ant*. XX.9.1). Thus he takes the references to wars, battles, and murder in 4:1ff literally, and links the cautions over oath-taking in 5:12 with the *sicarii*. Martin's volume, like the other volumes in this series, is rich with bibliographical references. Martin proposes the theory that the deposit of James' teaching was carried from Palestine to Antioch and adapted to meet the pastoral needs of some community in the Syrian province.

Mayor, Joseph B., *The Epistle of James*. London: Macmillan, 1892. Reprint of 3rd ed. Grand Rapids: Zondervan, 1954.
> Greek text. Valuable for its full grammar of James' Greek. The long introduction (260 pp.) is a treasury of information about the epistle. Tends to be liberal in places. In response to the then contemporary German scholarship, Mayor argued for the authenticity of the epistle as the work of James the Just. He favored an early date (c. AD 40-50) within James' lifetime. For those who can cope with quantities of untranslated Greek and Latin, this volume is an endless source of insight.

Mitton, C. Leslie, *The Epistle of James*. Grand Rapids: Eerdmans, 1966.
> A thorough, scholarly work by a British Methodist with a twofold aim: to expound the teaching of the epistle and to show that its teaching is an integral part of the total message of the New Testament. Critical problems are carefully dealt with and the Greek occasionally quoted in transliteration. Introductory problems are considered in an appendix.

Moffatt, James, *The General Epistles – James, Peter, and Judas,* in The Moffatt New Testament Commentary series. Reprint. London: Hodder & Stoughton, 1947.
> The English text used is Moffatt's own translation. The work of a noted liberal British scholar. The comments are rather slight.

Moo, Douglas J., *James*, in the Tyndale New Testament Commentary series. Grand Rapids: Eerdmans, 1985.
> A full and readable discussion of the English text. Moo believes that James was probably written by the Lord's brother in the late 40s, and addressed to Syrian or Palestinian Christians. Moo interacts with Davids, rejecting his theory of a later editing.

-----, *The Letter of James*, in the Pillar Commentary series. Grand Rapids: Eerdmans, 2000.
> While there is a significant similarity in a fair amount of the material published 15 years earlier in the Tyndale New Testament Commentary, there is a delightful addition, too. In the author's own words:
>
> "I remain convinced that the heart of the letter is a call to wholehearted commitment to Christ. James' call for consistent and uncompromising Christian living is much needed. Our churches are filled with believers who are only halfhearted in their faith, and, as a result, leave large areas of their lives virtually untouched by genuine Christian values. Nor am I immune to such problems. As I quite unexpectedly find myself in my 'middle age' years, I have discovered a tendency to back off in my fervor for the Lord and his work. My reimmersion in James has challenged me sharply at just this point. I pray that it might have the same effect on all readers of this commentary." (p.x)

Motyer, Alec, *The Message of James*, in The Bible Speaks Today series.   Downers Grove,
IL: Inter-Varsity Press, 1988.

> The aim of the series is threefold: to expound the Biblical text with accuracy, to relate it to
> contemporary life, and to be readable.   Therefore this volume is not a "commentary" which seeks to
> elucidate the text rather than apply it.   Motyer wonders if James wasn't originally a sermon.   "The
> 'letter' reads like sermon notes in which the preacher wrote down the main outline he wished to
> follow and the main points of material he wished to present, but waited for the inspiration of the
> moment to develop each point" (p.12).   In this way Motyer would explain the "abruptness with
> which James seems to swing from one topic to another."   Motyer interacts with current scholarly
> views that the author was some unknown author working at some point between AD 70 and AD 130.
> He comes down solidly for James, the Lord's brother, being the author.   At times Motyer offers a
> chiastic outline, as for example on James 2:14-26 (p.108).   The book highlights James' memorable
> theses, such as the link between trials and spiritual maturity, or faith, works, and Christian concern
> in a world of human need, or the church and healing.

Moyter, J.A., *The Tests of Faith*.   London: Inter-Varsity, 1970.

> A straightforward explanation of James by an Anglican evangelical scholar, it stresses the practical
> value of James for Christians today.   Motyer defends the idea that the address ("to the twelve tribes
> who are dispersed") is symbolic of the church as a whole in the world.

_____. *The Message of James*, in The Bible Speaks Today series.   Downers Grove, IL:
Inter-Varsity, 1985.

> This work is described as an "exposition" rather than exegesis, and provides helpful material for
> preachers.   He sees James, the Lord's brother, as the author.   He takes the opening address as
> indicative of James' belief in Jesus' full deity.   Motyer sees a clear plan to the letter.   He at times
> has strong applications (e.g., p.14 on Christian giving).   The work is intended to appeal to
> conservative evangelical readers.

Nieboer, James, *Practical Exposition of James*.   Erie, PA: Our Daily Walk Publishers,
1950.

> An intensely practical and reverent verse-by-verse treatment.   Abounds in keen observations and
> numerous illustrations.   It does not deal with critical problems; it is devotional in approach.   (The
> author chose this volume for the textbook in those early days when he first taught James at Central
> Christian College.)

Nystrom, David P., *James,* in The NIV Application Commentary series.   Grand Rapids:
Zondervan, 1997.

> Two approaches to the text are found in this volume: the original meaning is explained, and then
> the contemporary significance of the passage is given.   The volume contains many helpful points
> for preaching.   Useful illustrations include numerous anecdotes from Nystrom's own ministry.
> Nystrom adopts the same approach to introductory matters that Richardson and Davids did.   Clearly
> the concept of a Biblical commentary is undergoing a transition in American evangelicalism, with
> interest shifting away from the hard science of historical interpretation towards the process of
> contextualizing the Biblical message into the contemporary scene.

Oesterley, W.E., *The General Epistle of James*, in The Expositor's Greek Testament. Reprint. Grand Rapids: Eerdmans, 1967.
> Greek text. A scholarly introduction sets forth the critical problems; the author holds that the name of James is rightly attached to this document, but that in its present form it contains various additions and adaptations. The comments on the Greek text are of most value to the advanced student.

Plummer, Alfred, *The General Epistles of St. James and St. Jude,* in The Expositor's Bible series. Vol.6. London: Hodder and Stoughton, 1891. Reprint. Grand Rapids: Eerdmans, 1943.
> An important exposition of these two epistles by a noted British author of the past generation. Valuable for expository and homiletical purposes.

Plumptre, E.H., *The General Epistle of St. James,* in the Cambridge Bible for Schools and Colleges. Reprint. Cambridge: University Press, 1915.
> A concise, conservative commentary intended for the layman. Good discussion of introductory problems.

Punchard, E.H., *The Epistle of James*, in the Layman's Handy Commentary series, edited by Charles John Ellicott. Grand Rapids: Zondervan, 1957.
> The contents of this volume appear in a different format (complete in eight large double volumes) in *Ellicott's Commentary on the Whole Bible*. Ellicott's Commentaries rank as one of the outstanding standard commentaries on the Bible. A practical verse-by-verse explanation.

Reicke, Bo, *The Epistles of James, Peter, and Jude,* in The Anchor Bible series. Garden City, NY: Doubleday, 1964.
> A liberal introduction by the New Testament professor at the University of Basel. The comments are based on the author's own translation. Reicke rejects the traditional authorship and dates James around AD 90, during the reign of Domitian. The comments, reflecting the author's views concerning the occasion and purpose of James, are disappointingly brief. He sees James as a circular letter addressed to readers outside of Palestine (the rich man of 2:1-7 is taken to be an upper-class Roman).

Richardson, Kurt A., *James*, in the New American Commentary series. Nashville: Broadman, 1997.
> Richardson outlines the book under six points: (1) The Trial and Fulfillment of Faith (1:2-27); (2) All Works in Light of Judgment (2:1-26); (3) The Formidable Tongue (3:1-12); (4) Wisdom from Above and Below (3:13-4:10); (5) The Way of the Boastful (4:11-5:6); (6) Common Life before the Lord (5:7-20). Richardson thinks the commands in James 4:7-10 are addressed not to unbelievers but to believers to urge them to take those ten "steps of spiritual self-discipline" (p.183). Richardson believes the sick of James 5:13-18 are those who are physically ill, rather than being emotionally or spiritually weak. Richardson thinks the author was James, the Lord's brother, and that his work has the literary qualities of an epistle, a diatribe, and parenesis. He also believes the structure of the letter is not readily apparent. The basic outline offered by Davids is accepted without further discussion.

Roberts, J.W., *The Letter of James*, in the Living Word Commentary series. Abilene: ACU Press, 1963.

> This volume, too, was once used for the textbook on James at Central Christian College. James, the Lord's brother, is the author. A section detailing what we know of James' life is followed by consideration and refutation of modern objections to James as the author. The date of writing is "not long before the death of James" (p.22).

Robertson, A.T., *Studies in the Epistle of James*. Rev. ed. Nashville: Broadman, 1959.

> A practical study of James by a master of the Greek, this book was originally published in 1915 under the title *Practical and Social Aspects of Christianity*. This revision by Hebert F. Peacock has eliminated some of the more technical and dated material but retains the flavor and challenge of the original work. The contents of this volume grew out of lectures delivered at Northfield, Chautauqua, and Winona Lake.

-----, *Word Pictures in the New Testament*. Vol.6. Nashville: Broadman Press, 1933.

> Robertson accepts Mayor's arguments for an early date (c. AD 48) for the letter. He takes "twelve tribes which are dispersed" as literal, and comments "clearly James knew nothing of any 'lost' tribes, for the Jews of the dispersion were a blend of all the twelve tribes" (p.5). "The chief aim of the epistle is to strengthen the faith and loyalty of the Jewish Christians in the face of persecution from the rich and overbearing Jews who were defrauding and oppressing them. It is a picture of early Christian life in the midst of difficult social conditions" (p.6). Robertson transliterates the Greek words and explains the nuances of Greek verb tenses for the English reader.

Ropes, James Hardy, A *Critical and Exegetical Commentary on the Epistle of St. James*, in the International Critical Commentary series. Edinburgh: T&T Clark, 1916. Reprint 1978.

> Based on the Greek text, this commentary requires the reader to have a reasonable facility in Greek. Much valuable introductory material. Important commentary by an accomplished liberal scholar. Ropes makes use of classical parallels and rabbinic sources. He does not accept the traditional authorship (Ropes saw James as pseudonymous), and he dated the letter c. AD 75-100. He treated James as an example of a Greek diatribe. There is a useful discussion of the history of this epistle in the church.

Ross, Alexander, *The Epistles of James and John,* in The New International Commentary on the New Testament series. Grand Rapids: Eerdmans, 1954.

> A helpful, practical exposition by a noted, conservative, Scottish scholar. Follows in the Reformed tradition, including eschatology.

Simmons, Billy, A *Functioning Faith. Expositions on the Epistle of James*. Waco, TX: Word, 1967.

> A devotional and sermonic treatment of James, essentially producing the essence of the author's pulpit ministry in his Texas Baptist Church. Technical matters are not dealt with. Vivid applications of the message of James to our own day.

Smith, H. Maynard, *The Epistle of S. James. Lectures*. Oxford: Blackwell, 1914.

> A series of expository lectures on the epistle by a Church of England minister.

Stevenson, Herbert H., *James Speaks for Today*. Westwood, NJ: Revell, 1966.
> A lucid, popular-level sermonic study of the epistle of James with emphasis upon the relevance of the letter to our day. The author, an evangelical minister, brings the preaching of James into logical balance with the rest of the New Testament.

Strauss, Lehman, *James Your Brother*. New York: Loizeaux, 1956.
> A well-outlined, practical interpretation of the epistle with pointed illustrations and sermonic appeal by a conservative minister.

Tasker, R.V.G., *The General Epistle of James,* in the Tyndale New Testament Commentaries series. Grand Rapids: Eerdmans, 1957.
> A concise, readable, verse-by-verse commentary by a noted British scholar. Better than the author's other volumes in this series. Introductory data is carefully outlined, and the verse-by-verse exposition is practical and helpful.

Thayer, Joseph H., *A Greek-English Lexicon of the New Testament*. Chicago: American Book Company, 1889. Reprinted Edinburgh: T&T Clark, 1956.

Vaughan, Curtis, *James, A Study Guide*. Grand Rapids: Zondervan, 1969.
> A well-outlined expositional and devotional commentary by a distinguished Southern Baptist seminary professor. Vaughan frequently quotes various modern translations as an aid in presenting the precise force of the original for the lay reader. Has a three-page bibliography of commentaries and translations.

Wachob, Wesley H., *The Voice of Jesus in the Social Rhetoric of James*. Cambridge: Cambridge University Press, 2000.
> As we might expect from the title, this book is a socio-rhetorical study, drawing from a detailed reading of ancient rhetorical texts and contemporary scholarly studies flavored by sociology. Wachob identifies a number of the sayings by Jesus embedded in the epistle of James. Wachob's view is that "the Epistle of James is a deliberative discourse in the guise of a letter that uses sayings of Jesus to persuade an audience to think and act in ways that have significant social consequences"

Wessel, Walter W., "The Epistle of James" in the *Wycliffe Bible Commentary*, edited by Charles Pfeiffer and E.F. Harrison. Chicago: Moody, 1963.
> Wessel identifies the author as James, the Lord's brother, and dates the letter as early as AD 44, partly because he sees an eschatology in James that still expects an early return of the Lord, and partly because he has the letter addressed to Jewish Christians before Paul ever undertook his missionary journeys to the Gentiles. He thinks it impossible to outline James since "his short, abrupt paragraphs have been likened to a string of pearls – each is a separate entity in itself." (p.1430)

Wiersbe, Warren, *Be Mature: An Expository Study of the Epistle of James*. Wheaton, IL: Victor Books, 1981.
> Wiersbe believes God has given us a formula for growing to spiritual maturity in the epistle of James. This formula is unfolded in 13 sermons based on 13 different paragraphs in the letter.

Williams, R.R., *The Letters of John and James*, in the Cambridge Commentary on the New English Bible series.   Cambridge: Cambridge University Press, 1965.
> As Williams comments on these letters, he presents some perceptive comments on the strengths and weaknesses of the NEB.   He leans toward the idea that James is a pseudonymous writing, produced towards the end of the first century AD.   He finds no coherent structure, but sees James as a series of self-contained "sermonettes."

Winkler, Edwin T., *Commentary on the Epistle of James*, in An American Commentary on the New Testament.   1888.   Reprint.   Philadelphia: American Baptist Publication Society, nd.
> A concise exposition by a conservative Baptist of the last century.

Zodhiates, Spiro, *The Behavior of Belief.*   Formerly published as three volumes, *The Work of Faith, The Labor of Love, and* The *Patience of Hope.*   Grand Rapids: Eerdmans, 1959, 1960, 1970.
> A series of expository and devotional studies, at least one to a verse, setting forth in a practical and heartwarming manner the teaching of the epistle.   Working from an intimate knowledge of his native Greek, the General Secretary of the American Mission to Greeks gives a clear explanation of the original for the non-Greek reader.   Contains a full bibliography of the expository and sermonic literature on the epistle.   Has indexes of subjects, Scripture references, and English words with Greek equivalents.

INDEX TO JAMES

Roman numerals indicate pages in the Introductory Studies.   Arabic numbers are pages in the commentary section.

Commentary On

The Three Epistles of John

PREFACE

This commentator's interest in 1 John was first kindled by Owen Crouch. After having taught Greek at a Bible College in Illinois, Crouch became a preacher in northeastern Indiana. He was in demand, at camp and in the local churches, to teach a class on 1 John. He stirred this commentator's interest in studying Greek, for he showed how a careful recognition of Greek verb tenses helps us understand what John has written. The outline he offered for 1 John (a spiral outline similar to the one given by Law in his *Tests of Life: A Study of the First Epistle of John*) made sense to many of his students. Years later, Clint Gill, who had been one of Crouch's students in college and then his associate at Angola, Indiana, produced a commentary titled *Hereby We Know*, which reflected what Professor Crouch taught regularly as he covered 1 John.

Then there was a college class on the Johannine epistles under R.C. Foster. That stoked this commentator's interest further. When a new Bible college opened in Moberly, Missouri, it was now his turn to teach 1 John. Questions asked by sharp students resulted in deeper study of these brief but pointed letters. Certainly, no one can work his way through these epistles without having his faith and convictions more firmly grounded in the fundamentals of Christianity. "Jesus is the Christ, the Son of the Living God" becomes a confession that is understood to be loaded with truth and meaning.

The writer of 1 John claims to be an inspired messenger speaking on God's behalf. If we want to hear the Word of God, the same message that has been preached from the beginning of the church, then we need to read the epistles of John. As we shall point out in the Introductory Studies and in the comments from time to time, from John we may learn how knowledge of a few simple truths about God and Christ and Christianity can be a wonderful protection from error.

1 JOHN

INTRODUCTORY STUDIES

1 John differs from most of the letters included in our New Testament, and the differences make it difficult to pursue introductory studies in the way we are accustomed to doing. We usually begin with a careful study of each letter's internal evidence, looking for historical allusions, and from these learn all we can about author, date, destination, place, purpose and occasion of writing, etc. Then we go to external evidence for corroboration of what has been learned from internal evidence.[1]

1 John lacks the usual form of signature, address, greeting, and thanksgiving that we are accustomed to find in 1st century letters. It lacks the usual personal allusions, conclusion, or doxology with which we are familiar from the Pauline Epistles. Not only is this work unsigned, it has other unique features. "Among the books of the New Testament, 1 John is the only one that does not contain a single proper name (except our Lord's), or a single definite allusion, personal, historical, or geographical."[2]

Therefore, what we must do in the case of 1 John is to start with external evidence. We shall summarize the traditional views. Then, briefly, we shall study internal evidence to see if it appears to be in agreement with the traditional conclusions. We also will call attention to, and evaluate, certain contemporary reconstructions which flatly repudiate the traditional views.

TRADITIONAL VIEWS

Traditions that have existed uncontested from the second century till recently have connected Revelation, the Fourth Gospel, and 3 epistles with the apostle John,[3] have recog-

---

[1] These introductory studies, especially the historical allusions and the external evidence, are a distinctive feature of the author's commentaries; such studies are not typically found in most other contemporary commentaries. These studies are an extremely valuable tool, and are a vital part of the grammatical-historical method of interpretation.

[2] Robert Law, "John, The Epistles of" in *The International Standard Bible Encyclopedia*, edited by James Orr (Grand Rapids: Eerdmans, 1949 reprint), Vol.3, p.1711.

[3] Revelation does bear the signature of John. Though they do not bear John's signature, the Fourth Gospel and three Epistles in the New Testament collection of books have been, by an impressive tradition and by thematic summaries, connected with the apostle John. "The consensus of scholarly opinion throughout the centuries has held to a common authorship for the Fourth Gospel and the epistles of John. Tradition has connected the name of John the son of Zebedee with all these documents from the earliest times." (*Zondervan Pictorial Encyclopedia of the Bible*)

nized Ephesus as their place of publication, the churches of Asia Minor as their destination, and identified a philosophy or world view similar to that taught by Docetic or Cerinthian Gnostics as being the issue John is addressing or contesting, since it was troubling the churches, and threatened their fellowship with God, Christ, and each other. The traditional date assigned to the epistles is AD 85-90.

ASIA MINOR

Asia Minor was the name given in Bible times to the western part of the land called Turkey on our maps. The Roman province by this name included the Hellenistic countries of Mysia, Lydia, Caria, and a great part of Phrygia, plus the islands of Lesbos, Chios, Samos, Patmos, Cos, Mitylene.

Geography and Topography[4]

Along the western shore of Asia Minor, there were four river valleys whose sources were located in the higher central plateau that forms the main mass of Asia Minor. These valleys are separated by chains of mountains which, like fingers, extend westward from the main central plateau. From north to south, the four rivers are the Caicus with the city of Pergamos, the Hermus with the city of Smyrna near its mouth, the Cayster with Ephesus,[5] and the Meander with the city of Miletus near its mouth.

The valleys these rivers passed through were the main routes of travel from the ocean on the west to the interior of the province. Over the years, the Meander and Hermus rivers became the routes of choice, and Miletus and Ephesus vied for supremacy. In earlier times Miletus was the more important harbor. But the river slowly silted the harbor there.[6] Ephesus was ideally situated to serve as a port of entry for both these routes, and through

---

[4] The topographical information is taken from Wm. Ramsay, "Ephesus," in *Hastings Dictionary of the Bible* (New York: Scribners, 1908) Vol.1, p.721.

[5] According to Pliny the Elder, the Mediterranean Sea used to wash up to the very edge of the city of Ephesus. There was an island called Syria in the middle of the bay. But over the centuries silt filled the lowlands. In New Testament times, ships sailed up the Cayster River for about 3 miles in order to reach the harbor at Ephesus. Eventually the harbor silted up and the port closed, and other cities became the ports of entry for western Asia Minor. Good pictures and descriptions may be found in Smith's Bible Dictionary.

[6] Because of the lack of tides in the Mediterranean to scour out the detritus, the problem of sediment always plagued the harbors at the mouths of rivers.

the years powerful rulers chose to help Ephesus rise to become the "first and greatest metropolis of Asia."[7] Ephesus and the Cayster served as the port of entry for Sardis when that city served as the capital of Lydia about 550 BC. In Roman times, two great roads led eastward from Ephesus. One, the route through the "upper country" (Acts 19:1[8]), followed the Cayster around Mt. Gallesus, then led across the Tmolus Mountains through passes to Sardis and thence along the Hermus river toward Galatia (in the area of Pisidian Antioch) and then on towards the northeast. The other route left Ephesus by road in a southeasterly direction through the Magnesian gate, crossed the Messogis mountain range via a pass near Mt. Pactyas to Magnesia, thence it followed the Meander to Tralles, and then on up the valley to where the Lycus river flows into the Meander. At this juncture, travelers followed the Lycus by Laodicea towards Apamea and thence to Ladik and then across the Taurus Mountains through the Cilician Gates to Tarsus and on toward Syria or the Mesopotamian valley. This southern route has been the great road of history,[9] and was one of the chief avenues of commerce and travel, whence the communication was direct to Syrian Antioch and the Euphrates valley.

There were also coastal roads leading from Ephesus northward to Smyrna and southward to Miletus. So geography and politics led to Ephesus (rather than Miletus or Smyrna) becoming the port of entry for either of the roads into the interior, mainly because there was ready access by easy mountain passes to the Hermus and Meander valleys. The road across the mountains from Magnesia to Ephesus is a shorter way, by miles, to reach the sea than following the Meander River to Miletus. The route through the "upper country" via the Cayster and Hermus rivers leads over higher ground than the Meander route, and does not descend into the lower coastal valley till it comes nearer Ephesus; this makes it preferable in summer. Foot passengers to whom precipitous descents caused no difficulty would prefer that road to the longer but more level route by Apamea and Laodicea.

---

[7] This is the wording found on inscriptions from Ephesus. The worship of Diana, with the temple of Diana (Acts 19:27-35) located there, also helped the city to its leading position.

[8] Paul, journeying from Pisidian Antioch to Ephesus, took the Cayster route and traversed the higher-lying districts (Acts 19:1). The statement of Acts on this point is confirmed by Colossians 2:1, which shows that Paul had never visited Colossae or Laodicea (which were situated on the great highway up the Meander and Lycus). A traveler coming from the east along the Meander might take the road that branched north from the Lycus-Meander confluence. Shortly you would come to Philadelphia (on the banks of the Cogamus River). Follow this river to where it empties into the Hermus and you are at Sardis. From Sardis you could travel by way of Thyatira to Pergamos, or you could follow the Hermus to Smyrna. This route, too, would bypass the Lycus valley.

[9] Christianity came to Magnesia from Ephesus. Special missionary attention seems to have been devoted to the Meander-Lycus road, for one meets with congregations at Laodicea, Hierapolis, and Colossae. An important branch of this central route ran through Iconium through Pisidian Antioch and on to Apamea. Because this area was infested with bandits and robbers, Augustus built this branch road and located new military "colonies" along it (including one at Lystra) to try to protect travelers from the bandits.

History[10]

The cities of Asia Minor, including Adramyttium, Alexandria Troas, Pergamos, Smyrna, Ephesus, Miletus, Magnesia, Thyatira, Sardis, Philadelphia, Laodicea, Colossae, Hierapolis, etc., have witnessed some fascinating history. Outsiders often invaded, and many left a lasting mark. Numerous culture-changing and history-changing battles were fought in this part of the ancient world. The Hatti flourished ca. 2500-2000 BC. The Hittites supplanted them, and their empire in the central highlands of Anatolia reached its height ca. 1600-1200 BC. The Phrygian and Bithynian immigrants arrived from southeastern Europe about the end of the 2nd millennium BC. In about the 11th century BC, Greeks (Androclus, an Athenian) captured the city of Ephesus and Greek culture and civilization began to supplant Oriental civilization. Greek became the *lingua franca* instead of Asiatic. The kingdom of Phrygia was established in the 8th century BC. About 700 BC, Lydia replaced Phrygia as the leading power. Sardis was the capital city, and was the first city to mint coins of silver and gold. The last and most famous of the Lydian kings was Croesus (ca. 560-546 BC), whose name is still proverbial for wealth. He conquered the Greek cities on the west coast of Asia Minor. About 546 BC, Croesus of Lydia lost a war to Cyrus, king of Persia,[11] and all of the peninsula except Lycia came under the dominion of the Persian monarch. Sardis became the western metropolis of the new empire.

Over the centuries before the coming of Christ, Asiatic and Greek influences in the area waxed and waned. Eventually, about 500 BC, one Aristarchus was sent from Athens to Ephesus; from his time on, Greek influence continued to grow. Greek philosophy (Heraclitus and Thales), too, was influential in the area. The victory of the Greeks over Xerxes in 480 BC gave the Greek cities of Asia Minor some freedom, but Sparta yielded them back to Persia in 386 BC. Politically, the area remained under Persian domination until Alexander the Great defeated the Persians at Granicus and Issus in 334/333 BC. Alexander the Great established a seat of government at Ephesus. Lysimachus, who became ruler of the area after Alexander's death (323 BC), determined to impress upon the city a more Hellenic character. When Lysimachus was killed in battle in 281 BC, Ephesus came under the control of the Seleucids. However, the distance from Syria where the Seleucids had their capital permitted local rulers in western Asia Minor to regain ascendancy.

About 278 BC, Nicomedes I of Bithynia invited a Celtic army to help him gain and keep control of that area. These folk escaped his control and terrorized large areas of Asia

---

[10] C.J. Hemer's article "Asia Minor" in *The New International Standard Bible Encyclopedia,* edited by Geo. F. Bromiley (Grand Rapids: Eerdmans, 1976), Vol.1 p.322-329, is a concise source of information.

[11] Croesus, believing the fortress at Sardis to be unassailable, failed to keep watch (Herodotus i.84; cf. Revelation 3:3).

Minor for years, until they were finally restricted to an area in the central highlands that came to be called "Galatia" (the Greek word for "Gaul" or Celt). Gaulish speech still persisted there in the time of Jerome (AD 385).

The ancient city of Pergamos grew in power till about 241 BC, when Attalus I (after the victory over the invading Gauls) took the title of King and Soter ("savior"), and was the first ruler of the Attalid dynasty. This and other victories gave Attalus supremacy over a great portion of western Asia Minor. About this same time, Rome began to expand her control into Asia Minor. Alliances with Rome helped keep all the territory west of the Taurus Mountains in his domain, constituting the kingdom of Pergamum. After the defeat (190 BC) of Antiochus the Great, king of Syria,[12] by the Romans, the "Asia Minor" lands controlled by Antiochus, including Ephesus, were handed over by the conquerors to Eumenes, king of Pergamos, and became part of the kingdom of Pergamum. When Attalus III, the last king of Pergamum, died in 133 BC, he bequeathed his realm to the Roman senate and people, and after deliberating they decided to accept the bequest. They named the new province "Asia Minor." However, the Roman province was much smaller than the kingdom of Pergamum (for Pontus and Bithynia, Galatia, Lycia, Pamphylia and Cilicia became separate territories). For a time after it became a Roman Province, Pergamos was the capital of the province. However, after the time of Caesar Augustus, Ephesus became the administrative capital of the province. The change of the seat of government from Pergamos to Ephesus continued to take place during the reign of Claudius (AD 41-54), and was complete during the time of Hadrian (AD 125).

The policies and achievements of the Seleucids and Attalids had a great bearing on the political, religious, and social conditions of the land in New Testament times. Both dynasties were founders of great cities. The Seleucids peopled the area with cities called Antioch, Seleucia, Laodicea, and Apamea from their recurring dynastic names. They gave special privileges to the Jews in all these towns, and brought in thousands of Jewish families to settle in Lydia and Phrygia.[13] Thyatira and Philadelphia were Attalid frontier cities. The Attalids developed the resources of their land, both timber and metals. State religion was made an instrument of policy, exploiting the oriental tendency of ascribing divinity to their rulers. Pergamum became a focus of religious architecture, art, and culture. A strategic road extension from southeast of Laodicea on the Lycus gave them a south coast port at Attalia in Pamphylia.

---

[12] Only Rome had the military power to curb the ambition of Antiochus the Great. The Romans defeated Antiochus at the battle of Magnesia (Manisa, north of Smyrna) in 190 BC.

[13] Ramsay argues the Jews at Pergamos so embraced Greek culture that little distinction between them and non-Jews existed ("Pergamum," *Hastings Bible Dictionary*, Vol. 3, p.751). In the second century BC, 2000 Jewish families from Babylon and Mesopotamia were settled in Lydia and Phrygia by Antiochus III (Jos. *Ant.* XII.3.4). According to Josephus, there had been a Jewish community in Ephesus since Seleucid times (*Ant.* XIII.3.2, XIV.10.11-12). Acts 2:9 and 6:9 indicate there was a Jewish community in Asia early in the first Christian century. See also Acts 19:13-16.

Christianity in Asia Minor

Christianity was introduced to Asia Minor and Ephesus by the middle of the 1st century AD. When Luke became a part of Paul's evangelistic team during the second missionary journey, he was already famous for the gospel (2 Corinthians 8:18). We suppose he had been preaching in Asia Minor. At the close of the second missionary journey, Paul, accompanied by Aquila and Priscilla, came to Ephesus; when Paul journeyed on toward Jerusalem, Aquila and Priscilla remained behind. One of their converts was Apollos (Acts 18:24ff).

We can read about Paul's third missionary journey in Acts 19-21. For nearly 3 years (Acts 20:31) Paul devoted himself to the evangelization of Ephesus and the district of Asia Minor. For three months, he preached in the synagogue (19:8,10), then taught in the school of Tyrannus (19:9) and in private houses (20:20). Young preachers traveling with and studying under Paul evangelized outlying areas around Ephesus. "All Asia heard the word of God" (Acts 19:10). Trophimus and Tychicus were natives of Asia (Acts 20:4), with the latter probably (2 Timothy 4:12) and the former certainly (Acts 21:29) being natives of Ephesus. Epaphras (Colossians 1:7, 4:12-13), another young preacher, was responsible for planting the churches at Colossae, Hierapolis, and Laodicea. Philemon, owner of the slave Onesimus, was a Christian living in Colossae (Colossians 4:9). We are also introduced to Onesiphorus (2 Timothy 1:16-18) and his household (2 Timothy 4:19) who lived in Ephesus.

As the years passed, some well-known Christian leaders migrated to Asia Minor. Peter was one of these. His first epistle is addressed to the provinces of Pontus, Galatia, Cappadocia, Asia, and Bithynia (1 Peter 1:1). Perhaps so was his second epistle (2 Peter 3:1). These letters imply a ministry among the people to whom they are addressed. Another of the leaders who came to Asia was one named Philip. More likely this was Philip the apostle (Matthew 10:2) rather than Philip the evangelist (Acts 21:8). Polycrates (quoted by Eusebius, H.E.III.31) states that Philip, "one of the Twelve," lived as one of the "great lights of Asia," and is "buried at Hierapolis along with his two aged virgin daughters," and adds that another of his daughters was buried at Ephesus. The apocryphal *Journeyings of Philip the Apostle* (3rd cent.) also has Philip traveling through Lydia and Asia before settling at Hierapolis.[14] If John wrote his Gospel for the people of Asia Minor, Philip's residence in the province might explain why he is introduced by name on three occasions in the Gospel.[15] This of course reminds us that another well-known Christian leader came to settle in Ephesus: the apostle John. As we shall see in our study below of

---

[14] Because Philip the evangelist had 4 virgin daughters who prophesied, there is some confusion in early apocalyptic literature between Philip the apostle and Philip the evangelist. According to Acts, we find the evangelist in the land of Israel as late as AD 58 (Acts 21:8). Tradition has the evangelist settling in Tralles in Caria after AD 65. The notice in Polycrates may say that the apostle Philip married, had daughters, etc., some of whom were given in marriage (i.e., the one buried at Ephesus). It was not only the evangelist Philip who had virgin daughters. Clement of Alexandria (Eusebius, H.E. III.30) quotes Philip as one of the apostles who did not forbid marriage, as he "gave his daughters" in marriage.

[15] There is a Gnostic *Gospel of Philip* (with the apostle claimed as the author).

the life of John, he arrived in Ephesus after AD 70. He lived to a great age, until the time came when he was the sole survivor of the apostles who had been chosen by Jesus and who had personally witnessed His earthly ministry. People came from miles around to listen to John's first-hand telling about the ministry and message of Jesus. Two such folk, Polycarp and Papias, became some of the next-generation leaders of the church.

Something Ominous on the Horizon

As we have seen, wars that changed the political and cultural history of the world were fought in Asia Minor.[16] It is therefore not surprising that a spiritual battle whose outcome has eternal consequences began there.

There was an ominous note in Paul's address to the Ephesian elders. He warned, "From among your own selves men will arise, speaking perverse things, to draw away disciples after them" (Acts 20:30). Paul made this prediction in AD 58. By the early 60's, the prediction began to be fulfilled as perverse teachings began to arise in Asia Minor and Ephesus.

There was the issue now called the "Colossian Heresy." By the time Paul wrote the letter we call "Colossians" (AD 63), the heresy was already affecting the church at Colossae and other cities along the Lycus River, including Laodicea (Colossians 4:16). It was a strange and deadly mixture of Jewish doctrines, oriental mysticism, and Greek philosophy. Lightfoot[17] identifies the heretics of Colossae as holding doctrines similar to the Essenes who lived in the Holy Land. He notes that like the Colossian heresy, Essenism has certain affinities with Judaism and with elements that came later to be identified with Gnosticism. The heretical teaching at Colossae appeared under the garb of a "philosophy" (Colossians 2:8). There was an emphasis on ascetic practices (Colossians 2:16ff). The Colossians were in danger of doctrinal error respecting the Person of Christ (Colossians 2:3,4). Paul insisted that "principalities and powers are subject to Him" (Colossians 1:16, 2:10 KJV), apparently in contradiction to the idea that Jesus is just another angel. Against the heretics' erroneous ideas, Paul says Jesus is the image of the invisible God (Colossians 1:15), the perfect manifestation in human form of the Eternal Truth, the mystery of God (2:2) "in whom are hidden all the treasures of wisdom and knowledge" (2:3). The Christ of the

---

[16] The peninsula we call Turkey was on more than one occasion the battlefield of colliding cultures. The Trojan War, the Assyrian conflict with the Hittites (720 BC), the Persian War, the conflicts between Alexander the Great's successors, the defeat of the invading Gauls (278 BC) by the Attalids, the defeat of the Seleucids by the Romans, the defeat of Mithridates by the Roman army under Sulla (88 BC), and again by Pompey (65-62 BC). Mithridates VI the Great of Pontus (115-63 BC) emerged as Rome's most formidable and persistent antagonist. In 88 BC he briefly overran most of Asia Minor and was welcomed widely as a liberator. Nicomedes IV of Bithyinia bequeathed his kingdom to Rome in AD 74, and it became another province. Pompey finally overthrew Mithridates and established Rome's position in the East. He added much of Pontus to the province of Bithynia.

[17] See the special study on "The Colossian Heresy" in Lightfoot's *Commentary on Paul's Epistle to the Colossians* (Grand Rapids, MI : Zondervan, reprint of 1879 edition), p.73-113.

Colossians is not the aeon "christ" of later Gnosticism. Some belief similar to the later Valentinian usage of "pleroma" may be reflected in Colossians 1:19, 2:9 and Ephesians 1:23, 3:19, 4:13, where we are told that in Christ is found all the "fullness *(plērōma)* of the Godhead bodily."[18] To counteract these new teachings, Paul calls attention to the old-time gospel which they had heard from the beginning (Colossians 1:5-8). Paul was eager for the Christians to have "true knowledge" (Colossians 1:9, 2:2, 3:10), not the fraudulent "knowledge" offered by the heretics.

Ephesians, a companion letter to Colossians (carried by the same messengers, according to Colossians 4:7 and Ephesians 6:21), has many verses nearly alike to what we read in Colossians,[19] all attacking the same ideas that eventually developed into the Gnostic heresy. Among the ideas shown to be false is the idea that God is separated from the material world by generations of angels. The words aeons (*aiōnes*), pleroma (*plērōma*), and generations (*geneai*) – all words to which Gnosticism later gave special definitions – are found in Ephesians. There are possible allusions to Docetism in Ephesians 4:9, 5:21.

1 and 2 Timothy, written to Timothy while he served as evangelist in Ephesus in the mid-60's AD, trace problems that remind us of Gnosticism, e.g., "knowledge" falsely so-called (1 Timothy 6:20).

> The errorists attacked in the Pastoral Epistles profess a superior knowledge (Titus 1:16, 2 Timothy 3:7). Their profane and vain babblings (2 Timothy 2:16), old wives fables (1 Timothy 4:7), foolish questions and genealogies (Titus 3:9), denial of the resurrection of the body (2 Timothy 2:18), asceticism and deprecation of "everything created" (1 Timothy 4:3,4), and in other cases their antinomianism (2 Timothy 3:6, Titus 1:16) are all tokens of Gnosticism.[20]

Peter's epistles (late 60's) contain predictions of coming false teachers who would spout Gnostic ideas, and their arrival is documented in the epistle of Jude (AD 75). This took place in Asia Minor, the provinces of Pontus, Galatia, Cappadocia, Asia, and Bithynia, being addressed.

That brings us to the Johannine Writings (i.e., the Fourth Gospel, the Epistles, and Revelation), all of which, as we shall see, are full of anti-Gnostic warnings and repudiations of Gnostic doctrines. They picture false teachers, wandering from place to place as mis-

---

[18] The Gnostic doctrine was that the "fullness" of deity could flow out in no other way than in the emanations or aeons or angels, all of which are necessarily imperfect, the highest of them being more spiritual than the grade immediately below. Paul tells the Colossians, not through aeons, but through Christ is where one finds the fullness of deity flowing out to man.

[19] Out of 155 verses in Ephesians, 78 are found in Colossians in varying degrees of identity. See a list of these in Abbott, "Ephesians and Colossians" in the *International Critical Commentary* (Edinburgh: T. & T. Clark, 1956), p. xxiii.

[20] W.D. Niven, "Gnosticism," in Hasting's *Dictionary of the Apostolic Church* (Grand Rapids: Baker, 1973 reprint), Vol.1, p.456.

sionaries trying to spread their false ideas and win converts to their cause. What were believers to do when they heard messages from these missionaries that weren't quite what they had heard from John (or Paul, or Timothy, or Peter)? What Paul told the Colossians and what Peter said as he warned his readers are the same instructions we shall hear as we read 1 John.

LIFE OF JOHN, THE SON OF ZEBEDEE

1. Before Pentecost (AD 30)

A. *Family.* His parents were Zebedee and Salome (Mark 1:19,20; cp. Matthew 27:56 with Mark 15:40). His hometown was Bethsaida of Galilee (Mark 1:29, Luke 5:10). He was related to Jesus, since Jesus' mother Mary and John's mother Salome were sisters (cp. Matthew 27:56 and Mark 15:40 with John 19:25). Jesus and John were therefore cousins. The family of Zebedee was likely well-to-do. Zebedee carried on a fishing business with the aid of his sons and a number of hired day-laborers (Mark 1:20). This, of course, would require the possession of boats, fishing tackle, and a marketing arrangement. That James and John were called to follow Jesus at a time when they were busy mending their nets does not indicate that they were poor and not able to hire the work done. Further indication of the family's financial situation is indicated by the fact that Salome was one of the women who accompanied Jesus and the apostles on their preaching journeys and on the last journey to Jerusalem, using their own means to help defray the daily expenses needed to support such a large company of travelers (Mark 15:41; Luke 8:3). Salome is also mentioned among the women who purchased spices to embalm the body of Jesus after it was laid in the tomb (Mark 16:1; Luke 23:55-24:1). John was apparently younger than his brother James, for when the two are mentioned together, John's name is almost always mentioned last; it is typically listed as "James and John" (though "John and James" is found at Luke 8:51; Acts 1:13).

B. *A follower of John the Baptist.* When the Baptist appeared as the forerunner of the Messiah, preaching repentance, John became one of his disciples. John was present when the Baptist pointed to Jesus and exclaimed, "Behold, the Lamb of God ..." (John 1:29). John became one of Jesus' first full-time followers and accompanied Jesus during the early Perean and early Judean ministries. At the conclusion of Jesus' early Judean ministry, apparently John returned to the fishing business for a while (Luke 5:10), until Jesus formally called both him and James to follow Him (Matthew 4:21,22; Mark 1:19,20).

C. *"The Sons of Thunder" – Boanerges.* James and John were given this remarkable nickname (Mark 3:17); however, what it indicated we can only surmise. "Thunder" in the Hebrew idiom is "the voice of God." Perhaps by giving them this name, Jesus anticipates that both brothers will be mouthpieces for God before their lives were over. The sons of Zebedee appear to have given swift, startling, and vehement utterance to the Divine truth. There must have been something in the character of James the brother of John which made his cruel martyrdom by Herod Agrippa pleasing to the Jews (Acts 12:2,3)

– and it may have been his zeal, his intensity, his vehement utterance of the Divine truth. Or, perhaps, this nickname was given to the brothers because of a particular personality trait – quickness, intensity, fiery, enthusiastic. Scholars have called attention to several Biblical illustrations of this type of character: (a) Luke 9:54,55 – The Samaritans have refused to welcome Christ to their village, and the two brothers are roused to indignation. "Lord, do you want us to command fire to come down from heaven and consume them?" (b) Luke 9:49 – John says, "Master, we saw a certain one casting out demons in Your name; and we tried to hinder him because he does not follow [You] with us." (c) 2 John 10 and 3 John 9-11 – The same kind of burning indignation manifests itself against those who are disloyal to the Spirit and truth of Christ. (d) An example from early Christian literature is related by Eusebius (H.E. III.28). John was until the close of his earthly life a fiery and enthusiastic man. Once, having entered a bath house to wash, and ascertaining that Cerinthus (a Gnostic heretic) was inside, John leaped forth and exhorted all to leave, saying, "Let us flee, lest the bath fall in, as long as Cerinthus, that enemy of truth, is within."

D. *One of the inner-most circle of apostles (one of the favored three).* John was one of the three admitted to the death-chamber in the house of Jairus (Mark 5:37; Luke 8:51). He was one of the three taken up onto the Mount of Transfiguration (Matthew 17:1; Luke 9:28; Mark 9:2). At the institution of the Lord's Supper, he leaned upon Jesus' breast (John 13:23). The same three accompanied the Lord into the Garden of Gethsemane (Matthew 26:37). It was John and Peter who followed the recently arrested Christ into the high priest's palace (John 18:15,16,28).[21] As He hung on the cross, Jesus committed His mother into John's care and keeping (John 19:26-27).

E. *After Jesus' resurrection.* It is John and Peter who raced to the tomb (John 20:1-8). John saw the carefully arranged but empty grave clothes and believed Jesus had risen. John later identifies Jesus when seven of the apostles were fishing on Lake Galilee (John 21:7).

2. After Pentecost (AD 30)

A. *After Jesus' ascension.* John remained at Jerusalem with the other apostles. He is with the apostles at the time of the selection of Matthias (Acts 1:13ff). He is with Peter at the working of the first miracle (Acts 3:1). John accompanied Peter to Samaria (Acts 8:14). John was at the Jerusalem Conference in AD 51 (cp. Acts 15:4 with Galatians 2:9). At Revelation 1:9, we learn that the apostle John had been banished to the island of Patmos (assuming as true the traditional view that the author of Revelation is the apostle John).

---

[21] The family of Zebedee is apparently well known to the members of the high priest's household. It is John who gives us the name of the servant, Malchus, whose ear Peter cut off at the time of the arrest. John was also related to Elizabeth (the mother of John the Baptist), and that was a priestly family.

B. *The rest of his life.* For this, we must turn to tradition. As to when, and under what circumstances, John left Jerusalem, is entirely unknown. Perhaps he left shortly after the Jerusalem Conference. Perhaps he did not leave till the Christians fled the city (c. AD 68) just before it fell to the Romans. Traditions at this point are conflicting. Nicephorus relates that he left Jerusalem after the death of Mary (about AD 48). However, another account says that Mary accompanied John to Ephesus, where she died and was buried (Epiphanius, *Haer.* 78.11). Both traditions are historically uncertain. However, when Paul paid his last visit to Jerusalem (AD 58), it seems John was no longer there. James, the brother of the Lord, and "elders" are mentioned, but no apostles (Acts 21:18). But where John was – whether on a missionary journey or already living in Ephesus – we do not know. The traditions concerning the John's whereabouts share the general character of the materials from the period; that is, they are fragmentary and not always consistent or trustworthy. One very questionable tradition has John preaching to the Parthians (in the land we call Iran) after he left Jerusalem.[22] Another questionable tradition has John making a visit to Rome about the time Peter was martyred by Nero.[23] Once asceticism became popular in the church, there are some questionable traditions from the Leucian fragments about John being ascetic. One has him never marrying (celibacy was an example of asceticism). Another early writer, Epiphanius, has John being a rigorous ascetic. But if the story of the bath house is true, it would suggest he was not a rigorous ascetic.

---

[22] Documentation concerning this tradition will be given below. In flat opposition to this tradition about John going to Parthia, Eusebius (H.E. III.1.1) has Thomas going to Parthia, but John going to Asia, where after nearly of a quarter of a century of ministry he dies at Ephesus. A footnote in the *Ante-Nicene Fathers* says "the universal testimony of antiquity assigns John's later life to Ephesus."

[23] The story of John's visit to Rome rests upon the testimony of Tertullian (*Praescr. Haer.* xxxvi) and perhaps also on the testimony of Leucius. This visit allegedly was during Nero's reign. It has John thrown into boiling oil near the site of the Porta Latina and has him preserved unhurt. Two churches in Rome and a festival in the Calendar (May 6) perpetuate the tradition. (That a church building in Rome is named in honor of the apostle John is not evidence that he ever was in Rome. A church also is built in Rome in honor of John the Baptist. Was he ever in Rome?) Another story, that John was offered poison to drink, and that the drink became harmless in his hands, may have arisen in Rome. In paintings of the apostle John, he is often depicted holding a cup from which poison in the form of a viper is departing. Based on this weak tradition of a visit to Rome, some modern Preterist interpreters place John's exile to Patmos (and the writing of Revelation) during the late years of Nero's reign. The Preface to the Syriac Version reads, "The revelation which was given by God to the evangelist John on the island of Patmos, on which he was cast by NERO Caesar." (This preface flatly disagrees with Jerome. Jerome has John banished to Patmos during the reign of Domitian. See below.)

The Nero Redivivus myth, in some people's hands, has Nero returning to vex the church, and John returning to defend her. See Appendix B in Plummer's commentary on 1 John. This view requires an early date for Revelation, which is doubtful in view of Irenaeus' statements which have John banished to Patmos in Domitian's time. Plummer (p.27 of his introduction to 1 John), shares the view (growing in popularity in his day) that only on one hypothesis can one believe that the Fourth Gospel, 1 John, and Revelation were all by the same author; viz., that Revelation was written a good many years before the Gospel and the First Epistle. The writer of Revelation, it is asserted, has not yet learned to write Greek. The writer of the Gospel and Epistle writes Greek, not elegantly, but with ease and correctness.

J.A.T. Robinson, *Redating the New Testament* (Philadelphia: Westminster, 1976), has attempted to show that none of the New Testament books need be dated after AD 70. His writing does show that there is very little concrete evidence one way or the other for the dating of John's writings. This commentator is not ready to flatly reject Irenaeus' date (AD 96) for Revelation, and he thinks we must allow adequate time for the false teaching reflected in the Johannine Epistles to develop.

C. *His residence at Ephesus.* Nothing is better attested in early church history than the residence and work of the apostle John at Ephesus. This is not a questionable tradition. Justin Martyr (c. AD 150), probably within 50 years of John's death writes, "Among us also a certain man named John, one of the apostles of Christ, prophesied in a Revelation made to him, that the believers of our Christ shall spend a thousand years in Jerusalem." These words occur in the *Dialogue with Trypho* (lxxxi), which Eusebius tells us was held in Ephesus, so that "among us" naturally means at or near Ephesus. Irenaeus (a disciple of Polycarp, one of John's disciples), Clement of Alexandria, Apollonius, Polycrates, Origen, and Eusebius all affirm John's residence in Ephesus. Irenaeus, in his celebrated epistle to Florinus (a portion of which has been preserved in Eusebius, H.E, V.20.4,5), tells of how his teacher Polycarp, while living in Smyrna in Asia Minor, used to talk about his close interaction with the apostle John while the latter was still alive. That certainly harmonizes with John's residence in Asia Minor. Irenaeus (*Adv. Haer.* III.1.1) tells that John, the disciple of the Lord, who also leaned back on his breast (John 13:23), published a gospel during his residence at Ephesus. A few paragraphs later Irenaeus wrote, "The church in Ephesus founded by Paul, and having John continuing with them until the times of Trajan, is a truthful witness of the tradition of Apostles" (*Adv. Haer.* III.3.4). In still another place, Irenaeus says, "All the presbyters, who met John the disciple of the Lord in Asia, bear witness that John has handed on to them this tradition. For he continued with them until the times of Trajan," AD 98-117 (*Adv. Haer.* II.22.5). Polycrates, a bishop of Ephesus, in his Epistle to Victor (bishop of Rome, AD 190-200), tells us that the apostle John "lies asleep at Ephesus." Apollonius, sometimes said to be bishop of Ephesus, wrote a treatise against Montanism (c. AD 200), which Tertullian answered; and Eusebius tells us that Apollonius related the raising of a dead man to life by John at Ephesus (H.E. V.18.14). John probably did not arrive in Ephesus until after AD 67. Had John been at Ephesus while Paul was working there, or when Paul wrote letters to Timothy who was working there, it seems that some mention would have been made of him. Paul didn't build on another man's foundation (Romans 15:20); if John had been preaching in Ephesus before Paul arrived there, Paul would not have gone there.

D. *Were there two influential church leaders named "John" at Ephesus?* A few Bible scholars, studying the authorship of the "Johannine writings" in our New Testaments, have sometimes arrived at the conclusion there were two different men named "John" at Ephesus, one of whom (the apostle John) was responsible for some of the "Johannine writings" while the second man also named "John" wrote the others. The sole evidence for this is a statement made by Papias, quoted by Eusebius (H.E. III.39.3-4):

> Papias wrote, "But I shall not hesitate also to put down for you along with my interpretations whatsoever things I have at any time learned carefully from the elders and carefully remembered, guaranteeing their truth. For I do not, like the multitude, take pleasure in those that speak much, but in those that teach the truth; not in those that relate strange commandments, but in those that deliver the commandments given by the Lord to faith, and springing from truth itself. If then, any one came, who had been a follower of the *elders,* I questioned him in regard to the words of the *elders* – what Andrew or Peter SAID, or what WAS SAID by Philip, or Thomas, or by James, or by JOHN, or by Matthew, or by any other of the disciples

of the Lord, and what things Aristion and the presbyter JOHN, the disciple of the Lord SAY. For I do not think that what was gotten from the books would profit me as much as what came from the living and abiding voice." (Written c. AD 120).

Eusebius (writing AD 325[24]) then adds this comment,

> It is worth while to notice here that the name John is twice mentioned by him. The FIRST one he mentions in connection with Peter and James and Matthew and the rest of the Apostles, *clearly meaning the apostle*: but the *other John* he mentions after an interval, and places him among others outside the number of the Apostles, putting Aristion before him, and *he distinctly calls him a presbyter*. This shows that the statement of those is true, who say that THERE WERE TWO PERSONS IN ASIA that have the same name, and that there were two tombs in Ephesus, each of which, even to the present day, is called John's.

Is Eusebius correct in his interpretation? We think not. (1) Our English translation reads "elder John" and "presbyter John." Yet elder and presbyter both are translations of the *same* Greek word. If Papias refers to "elder John" twice in the same sentence, how does this show that they were different persons? The distinction Eusebius was making cannot be based on the idea that "elder" is different from "presbyter." (2) "John" is named twice by Papias. Why mention the same person twice in the same context? Perhaps it expresses timing. Those persons in the first list had been heard by Papias *in the distant past*, but all had been been dead for some time at the time he writes. With Aristion and John the case is different. If they were not still living at the time Papias speaks of them, then he is saying that *until only recently* he had been able personally to listen to them tell about Jesus. This may be why he changes from the past tense "he said" to the present tense "say." (3) "Two tombs" is a weak argument. Many people by the name of "John" would have lived and died by the time of Eusebius. And what led to two different tombs being pointed out as the place of John's burial? Was the original burial spot of the apostle John debated, and so traditions began naming two different spots – similar to what happened to the burial place of the virgin Mary at Jerusalem? (4) It appears that the title "elder" may have been given to the apostles. In 2 and 3 John, the author calls himself "the elder." May this not be similar to what Peter does, when in 1 Peter 5:1 he calls himself an "elder." We are not, at this point in our study, prepared to accept the idea that there were two Johns at Ephesus, and then try to assign this writing to one, and that writing to another. More will need to be written about this later as we study authorship in detail.

E. *Significant incidents at Ephesus.* Church tradition has preserved some events that happened while John was at Ephesus. One concerns his heroism in rescuing from robbers a youth who had been converted by him, and who had lapsed from his Christian walk (Eusebius, H.E. III.23). Another concerns his flight from the bathhouse in which

---

[24] How well could any of us speak with authority on what happened 300 years ago?

Cerinthus was (Irenaeus, *Adv. Haer.* III.3.28), a story Polycarp used to tell about John.[25] Another concerns the raising of a dead man by his hand at Ephesus (Eusebius, H.E. V.18.13). Another tells of his last sermon before he died, "Little children, love one another!" (Jerome, *Comm. ad. Gal.* VI.10).

3. On the Isle of Patmos[26]

John declares that he "was on the island of Patmos because of the word of God and the testimony of Jesus" (Revelation 1:9). There is also strong tradition to this effect. Irenaeus (quoted by Eusebius, H.E. V.8.6) said, "John beheld the vision, almost in our generation, towards the close of the reign of Domitian." Jerome (*De Viris Illust.* c.19) wrote, "In the fourteenth year [of his reign], Domitian, having instigated a second persecution after Nero, John, the apostle whom Jesus loved, was exiled to the island of Patmos, and wrote the Apocalypse." Eusebius (H.E. III.17 and III.18.1) wrote, "It is said that in [Domitian's] persecution, the apostle and evangelist John, who was still alive, was condemned to dwell on the island of Patmos in consequence of his testimony to the divine word." Hippolytus (*De Christo et Antichr.* c.36) says concerning John, "Who, on the isle of Patmos, saw the Apocalypse."

Tradition also has it, that after the death of the emperor who banished him, John returned to Ephesus. Clement of Alexandria wrote, "When after the death of the tyrant, John had returned to Ephesus from the isle of Patmos ..." (Eusebius, H.E. III.23.6). Eusebius affirms on "the basis of ancient Christian tradition" that when Nerva became emperor John returned to Ephesus from Patmos (Eusebius, H.E. III.20.11).

4. The Death of John

There is a tradition that John died early, killed by the Jews about the same time (i.e., AD 44) that his brother James was killed (Acts 12). It is also claimed that Mark 10:39 is a prediction that James and John were to die of martyrdom. Defenders of this early date for John's death also refer to tradition. Georgius Hamartolus (c.AD 850) wrote, "Papias, in the second logos, says that John the theologos and James his brother were killed by the Jews."[27] The DeBoor Fragment (a quotation of Codex Baroccianus) has the same note.

---

[25] Later versions of the story end with a sensational addition that when the apostle had gone out, the bath fell in ruins, and Cerinthus was killed.

[26] This arrangement of events in John's life – with his banishment to Patmos this late – reflects the studied choice of a late date (AD 96) for the writing of Revelation.

[27] Georgius Hamartolus is a 9th century document, resting on an 8th century fragment of a summary of the Chronicle of fifth-century Philip of Side. The fragment from Georgius tells that John lived till the time of Nerva, quotes a saying of Papias that he was killed by the Jews, and states that this was in fulfillment of the prophecy of Jesus (Mark 10:39; Matthew 20:23). Georgius then affirms that Origen also taught that John was martyred, but Origen's writings can be tested and it by no means bears out the meaning attached to it. Georgius does not say that James and John were slain at the same time, though that is what scholars attempt to interpret the fragment to mean.

It may be that both Georgius and the Codex Baroccianus writer copied the same source. Zahn asks, "If the tradition of John's dying at Ephesus (see below) is true, how did this alternate tradition get started?" Lightfoot has given a probable account of the origin of the blunder, by whomsoever made. Papias' work may have consisted of notes on the Gospels. It is likely that Papias, in commenting on Matthew 20:23, noted as a fulfillment of our Lord's words the fact that John had suffered banishment to Patmos, and James had been slain by the Jews (cp. Origen's *Commentary on Matt.*, tom. xvi.16). The statement then that we are discussing, which attributes to both James and John what Papias [Lightfoot believed] only said of James, may have assumed its form either through the dropping out of a line by a transcriber, or through the inaccuracy of a *memoriter* citation. One more bit of traditional evidence is cited. An ancient Syrian Calendar (5th century) places James' and John's death on the same day (December 27). This calendar also places the deaths of Peter and Paul on the same date in Rome. These coincidences would be extraordinary indeed, even if they took place in different years, and therefore this calendar's dates are suspicious. Finally, it is improbable that Acts would have been written without mentioning the death of John had his death occurred within the time frame covered by that history book. So the evidence that John died as early as AD 44 is weak.

There is a stronger (and earlier) tradition that John died late, toward the close of the 1st century and the opening of the 2nd. This same tradition indicates that John died at an advanced age; some writers suggest he was in his 90's, and others that he was as old as 120. Irenaeus specifies no particular age, but merely says that he lived till the time of Trajan, who reigned from AD 98-117 (*Haer.* II.22.5; III.1.1; III.3.4; III.23). According to Polycrates,[28] Origen,[29] and Eusebius,[30] John died at Ephesus, and their language leads us to infer that it was a natural death rather than a martyrdom. Chrysostom, however, assigns him the honor of martyrdom. Another says he did not die, but was translated.

Traditions concerning his burial differ. Leucius tells us, "On a Sunday after religious services, John went outside the city gates, accompanied by a few trusted disciples, ordered a deep grave dug, laid aside his outer garments which were to serve him as a bed, prayed once more, stepped down into the grave, greeted the brethren who were present, and gave up the ghost."[31] Another tradition says that he did not actually die, but only slept (John 21:22). His breathing was said to have moved the earth over his grave (Augustine, *Tract. cxxiv. in Johann.* xxi.19).

---

[28] Eusebius, H.E. V.24.3

[29] Eusebius, H.E. III.1.

[30] Eusebius, H.E. III.23.

[31] Leucius' *Acts of John* statement is summarized in Theo. Zahn, *Introduction to the New Testament* (Chicago: Kregel, 1953), Vol.3, p.193.

Introduction to 1 John, page xvi

HISTORICAL ALLUSIONS

We start our search for historical allusions by calling attention to the title that has been placed on the book. As we open our Bibles to the letters following 1 and 2 Peter, we find titles such as "The First Epistle of John," "The Second Epistle of John," "The Third Epistle of John." Such titles on our Bible books were added by men at the time churches began to make collections of the writings of the New Testament apostles and prophets. The names assigned to the books reflected the convictions of the churches into whose possession these letters had come. The oldest titles are the simplest. The title in the collection of catholic epistles in Codices Vaticanus and Alexandrinus is "Of John A." In Sinaiticus, the title reads "First Epistle of John." Codex Angelicus has "Catholic Epistle of the Holy Apostle John." Codex Porphyrianus reads "First Epistle of the Evangelist and Apostle John." Two things should be observed: without exception these titles attribute the letters to "John," and some say "the apostle John"; and, the older manuscripts speak of the work as being an "epistle" of John.

Next, consider 1 John 1:1-4. The first thing that catches our attention is the fact that there is no usual 1st century type of epistolary opening – no signature, no address, no greeting, no thanksgiving. Perhaps there is a ready explanation for this missing "epistolary opening." What form would an encyclical take? An encyclical was a letter intended for more than one congregation, delivered by messengers, and read in the public assembly. The absence of name, address, etc. would suit a work intended to be so delivered and read in the general assembly by an elder or by the messenger who carried the letter.

Though there is no epistolary opening and thus no signature, there are things to be learned about the author from what is written, both in these opening verses and later in the work. There are seven verbs in the first person plural ("we") in these opening verses, yet later in the composition, the author calls himself "I" (2:1,7,8,12-14,21,26; 5:13). The writer was a personal witness of the earthly ministry of Jesus the Christ (1:1-4; 4:14). The writer has preached the old-time gospel among the readers (1:1-3). He shows himself intimately acquainted with his readers' religious environment (2:19; 4:1), the dangers they faced (2:26; 3:7; 5:21), their attainments (2:12-14,21), their achievements (4:4), and their needs (3:19; 5:13).

In addition, though there is no address stated, there are things to be learned about the readers from what is written in the letter. According to verse 3, which might be called an address of sorts, this message is being sent to certain persons whom the author calls "you" (plural). Who are intended by the "you" (plural) in 1:3? And in 4:4-6,14? Members of one congregation, or several congregations? As we try to identify who is intended by "we" and by "you," what difference, if any, is there?

As we read through the rest of the verses in 1 John, there are a number of things that come to our attention, and there are a number of questions that are raised, as we seek for historical allusions:

1:1-4 – Calls attention to the fact that the historical Jesus was manifested in a tangible physical way: touch and sight and hearing all bore witness to His genuine humanity. Why was this an important topic?

1:5 – "God is light, and in Him there is no darkness at all." Is this not a strange way to begin?

1:6,8 – With the words "if we say," the writer seems to call attention to what others are saying. Why does he do that? Whom does he have in view? The writer emphasizes some expectations concerning Christian living: walking in the light (verse 7), and confessing our sins (verse 9). He speaks of commandments Jesus has given us to live by (2:3,4). We wonder, why such an emphasis?

2:4 – The writer exudes an unmistakable air of authority. He does not hesitate to call certain classes of people liars, deceivers, or antichrists. He supplies the tests by which anyone can be sorted into one or another of two categories, either for Christ or against Him. Pronouncements are made with authority (cf. 1:5; 2:1,2,8,17,23; 3:6,9; 4:18; 5:12). Positive commands are uttered (cf. 2:15,28; 4:1; 5:21). Who is it who presumes to make such dogmatic affirmations and to issue such commands? An apostle, speaking as Jesus' mouthpiece, could so order.

2:5,6 – How do we know we are saved? Habitually keeping Christ's command-ments is one test. Brotherly love is another test (3:19).

2:8 – "I am writing" suggests our text is a letter, or a written document of some kind. The places where the writer specifically says "I am writing to you" seem to identify this work is an epistle, rather than a treatise (a treatise is a literary composition presenting a subject in all its parts).

2:8 – Is the statement "The true light is already shining" a refutation of something the false teachers taught about "true light"?

2:12ff – Different age groups are mentioned. Were the false teachers using different arguments to try to deceive and persuade the different age groups? To insulate them from what the false teachers might try to do, John appeals to what each of them already knows, having learned it from the original apostles.

2:12ff – See the contrast between "I am writing" (verse 8,12,13b) and "I have written" (verse 13c,14). To what does "I have written" refer? To this letter, or some previous writing?

The writer can call his readers "little children" (2:1,12), indicating he stands in a position of authority over them, as well as being older than the readers. (Yet he can also call the readers his "brethren," 3:13).

2:17 – "The one who (habitually) does the will of God abides forever (heaven)."

2:18 – "The last hour" and "antichrist" is coming. Already many antichrists have arisen. Is this how the writer identifies the false teachers against whom he is warning his readers?

2:20 – How shall we read it? "You have an anointing from the Holy one, and you all know," or "you know all things" (NASB mg.)? How does verse 21 connect with the thought of verse 20?

2:21 – The writer wants his readers to distinguish between the truth they already had and a lie that was pushing for acceptance.

2:24 – The writer wants his readers' knowledge to be based on what they have "heard from the beginning." Is there some new speculative teaching making the rounds which is contrasted with the old gospel message they have heard from the beginning?

2:26 – The false teachers are trying to deceive John's readers.

2:27 – The readers are to abide in the teaching they had already received from the apostles, rather than listening to the deceiving words of the false teachers.

2:28 -- Jesus is coming back (the word translated "coming" is *parousia*). There will be a judgment when that occurs (see also 4:17).

2:29 – The person who habitually practices righteousness has been begotten/born again. There is no way for a person who is still dead in sin to practice self-control without a new birth. Were the false teachers calling what their teaching produced a "new birth"?

3:1 – We Christians already are children of God. Did this contradict something the false teachers claimed?

3:2 – What does the future hold for the Christian? We shall be like Jesus when He comes. (Not a return of a divine spark into the supreme light.) In the meantime, hope for the return of Christ leads to careful Christian living (3:3,4).

3:8 – The devil is the one who has sinned from the beginning. Does this contradict another idea of the false teachers? Did the false teachers hold that the God of creation, the God of the Old Testament, the God who is the Father of Jesus Christ, was the one who was the sinner?

3:8 – Jesus came to destroy the works of the devil. Does this contradict the false teachers' speculation about the good supreme being, Sophia, whom they acknowledged?

3:12 – Cain "was of the evil one, and slew his brother." Is this a polemic against views held by the false teachers?

3:14 – Love of Christian brethren is an important mark of the genuine Christian life. (See also 4:7ff.)

4:3 – An ancient variant reads, "everyone who separates Jesus from the Christ." Does this reflect Gnostic teaching that Jesus and the Christ were two separate beings?

4:6 – The writer claims "we are from God." He and the other apostles are not like the false teachers, whose inspiration is not from God. A man who does not listen to the apostles is motivated by the spirit of error.

4:9 – "God has sent His only begotten Son into the world." Is there anti-Gnostic doctrine here?

4:10 – God Who sent His Son is a loving God. Is this anti-Gnostic doctrine?

4:12 – No one has seen God at any time. Is there anti-Gnostic doctrine here?

4:14 – God sent His "Son to be the Savior of the world." Is this a direct assault on the Gnostic doctrine of auto-salvation?

4:15 – Christians are to habitually confess that Jesus is the Son of God.

5:3 – God's "commandments are not burdensome." Did the false teachers say they were?

5:7ff – Does the reference to the Spirit, the Father, and the Son contradict something the false teachers were saying?

5:11 – "God has given us eternal life." Is there anti-Gnostic doctrine here? Without the Son (like the Gnostics were) one does not have eternal life.

5:14 – The glorified Christ is involved in answering the prayers of the saints.

5:16 -- Was the "sin leading to death" something that some of the Gnostic defectors (2:19) have committed?

5:18 -- The glorified Christ is involved in the security of the believer. Gnostics who repudiate Jesus do not have such protection (5:19). They, and not the Christians, are under the power of the evil one.

The historical allusions also give us some rough parameters concerning the date of writing. The earthly ministry of Jesus has been concluded (1:1-4), He has died on Calvary (1:7), and He has ascended to Heaven, where He is an Advocate with the Father (2:1). This points to a date after AD 30. The traditional date assigned to the Fourth Gospel is about AD 80. As we shall document below, there are a number of phrases in 1 John that remind us of language we read in the Fourth Gospel. If it is reasonable to conclude that the Epistle was written after the Gospel, this would point to a date after AD 80 for the writing of the Epistle. If the false teachers are of the same persuasion as the false teachers introduced in the letters of Peter and Jude, this, too, points to a date in the last third of the 1st century for the writing of 1 John. The Johannine letters also do not reflect any threat of persecution. Christians were persecuted in the middle AD 60's by Nero, and then persecution of Christians subsided for a while. In AD 89, covering the last decade of his rule, Domitian commenced a persecution of Christianity. Does the absence of references to persecution within the epistles of John suggest a date of writing after Nero's persecutions ended (AD 68) and before the Domitianic persecutions got under way (AD 89)?

Two verses address the stated purpose for the writing of this letter. 1:3 indicates the writer is anxious that his readers continue to have fellowship with God, with His Son Jesus, and "with us" (i.e., the apostles of Jesus). They would continue in that fellowship by continuing to embrace the gospel they have heard from the beginning. 5:13 indicates the writer is anxious that his readers may continue to have the eternal life they already enjoy in Jesus, something that would be forfeited if the readers allow themselves to be converted to the beliefs of the false teachers. Nine times (2:3,5; 3:16,19,24; 4:2,6,13; 5:2) the writer says, "by this we know" ("hereby we know" KJV), and each time he sets out a criterion by which the readers may be assured that the faith they already hold is correct, whereas what the false teachers are preaching is a counterfeit and a sham.[1]

Several other observations, prompted by our search for historical allusions, are in order.

(1) John alludes to, and perhaps even quotes, certain slogans that capsulize the beliefs of the false teachers. A number of verses (cp. 1:6a, 8a, 10a; 2:4,6, 4:20) begin with, "If we say," or "he who says," and these certainly reflect views held by the false teachers.

(2) There was something radically wrong with the false teachers' doctrine about Jesus the Christ. They did not believe that Jesus was the Son of God (2:23). They did not believe that Jesus had come in the flesh (4:2,3; 2 John 7). When John affirms that Jesus came not only by water, but by water and blood (5:6), it would seem that this was denied by the false teachers.[2] The false teachers apparently denied the death of Jesus had any atoning significance (2:2). In direct reply to this, the writer affirms that

---

[1] Tests of genuine faith include a theological test (Jesus is the Christ, the incarnate Son of God, who perfectly reveals the Father); an ethical test (Christians have an obligation to live the righteous lives taught by Jesus; not sinless perfect, but certainly not living in habitual sin); a test that deals with inspiration (testing the spirits in order to distinguish between true and false inspiration); and a test regarding how carefully one listens to what the apostles taught from the beginning.

[2] As we shall show in due time, Cerinthus taught that the Christ descended upon Jesus *after* His baptism and departed from Him *before* His death. Likely what John is asserting, contrary to Cerinthian doctrine, is that "Jesus Christ," one person, passed *through* both baptism and death.

His death is a "propitiation" for our sins, that He appeared the first time to take away sins (3:5), and that He was Himself sinless (3:5).

(3) Individual verses from the Old Testament are not quoted in 1 John.[3]   Some Gnostics tended to repudiate the Old Testament.   Was John answering their mistaken ideas by arguing ad hominem at this point (proving his point without appealing to Old Testament Scriptures)?

(4) 1 John is full of abstractions (God is light; God is love).   What are we to make of the stark contrasts that fill the book – light and darkness, truth and untruth, love and hate, life and death, God and the world?   According to the record in the Fourth Gospel, Jesus Himself used many of these terms as He taught.   Have the Gnostics picked them up and poured a different meaning into them, so that John sets about to correct their slippery terminology?   Or might it be said that John is "contextualizing" his presentation of the gospel?   That is, John has not made up new terminology, but he may be using terms that a Greek audience, steeped in cosmic dualism, would understand – especially when he carefully defines how he is using those terms.

(5) One final observation is in order: Some verses are difficult to exegete.   For example, 2:29, 3:2,9,19, 5:6-8,16.

We are now in a position to propose some answers to the standard Introductory topics.   To do so, we shall draw upon what we have learned thus far, as well as introduce pertinent new materials where appropriate.

AUTHORSHIP AND ATTESTATION OF 1 JOHN

The consensus of scholarly opinion throughout the centuries has held to a common authorship for the Fourth Gospel and the epistles of John.[4]   Tradition has connected the name of the apostle John, the son of Zebedee, with all these documents from a very ancient date.   In the case of 1 John, the tradition for John's authorship goes as far back as Papias and Irenaeus;   in the case of 2 and 3 John, perhaps to Clement of Alexandria and Origen,

---

[3] While no verses are actually quoted, there are verses in 1 John that would be far less clear without a knowledge of the Old Testament.   "What we have heard" (1:1) might include the Old Testament Messianic prophecies.   "To forgive us our sins" (1:9) may reflect certain Psalms.   "His word is not in us" could include the Old Testament (1:10).   Cain slew his brother (3:12) certainly is an allusion to something recorded in Genesis 4:8.   Jesus was with the Father (1:2,3) is an Old Testament teaching.   The evil one (2:13) is one who has sinned from the beginning (3:8) reminds us of the devil's activities recorded in Genesis 3.   Antichrist is coming (2:18, 4:3) is something predicted in Daniel 7.   An anointing from the Holy One (2:20) may reflect certain prophecies from Joel (e.g., 2:28-32).   The Christ (2:22) is a well-known Old Testament title for "the Coming One" (cp. John 1:41).   That Jesus appeared in history (3:5) to destroy the works of the devil (3:8) recalls Genesis 3:15.   God has commanded us to believe in Jesus (3:23).   False prophets prompted by lying spirits (4:1ff) reminds us of certain false prophets in pre-Christian times.   God is greater than the devil who is in the world (4:4).   That God sent His Son to be a propitiation for sins (4:10) recalls the Suffering Servant poems of Isaiah.   The whole world lies in the power of the evil one (5:19).   Idolatry is to be avoided (5:21).   These are all ideas taught in the Old Testament.

[4] It is likely that Revelation, too, is by the same author, though this was not the unanimous opinion in the early church.   We shall deal with the authorship of 2 & 3 John (and incidentally also that of Revelation) in more detail in the introductions to 2 & 3 John later in this volume.

and certainly to Dionysius, the pupil of Origen.   It is only recently that the traditional view has been disputed by some scholars, with the connection to John being denied or assigned to another John (other than the son of Zebedee).   In fact, among contemporary writers one will find a variety of views defended: (1) All five books (the Gospel, the Epistles, and Revelation) were written by the apostle John.   (2) Three (Gospel, 1 John, Revelation) were by the apostle John; two (2 and 3 John) by the elder John.[5]   (3) Two (Gospel and 1 John) were by the apostle John; three (2 and 3 John, and Revelation) were written by the elder John.[6]   (4) None were written by the apostle; all were written by the elder John.   (5) None were written by the apostle; all were written by a Johannine school.[7]

Our study of the authorship of 1 John will show the probability that the traditional view regarding John the apostle's authorship is correct.   The study of authorship will pursue two lines of evidence: internal and external.

Internal Evidence of Authorship

From the study of historical allusions, the following bits of evidence are provided internally by the book of 1 John itself.

1.   The title (superscription) given in the ancient manuscripts (though not on the autograph itself) points to the apostle John as the author.
2.   The writing we call 1 John is not signed.
3.   The writer presents himself as an eyewitness of the ministry of Jesus Christ (1:1-4; 4:14).   There are limited options for identifying such a claimant.
4.   The writer seems to stand in the position of teacher, and his readers were those who had been taught (1:2,3).   The author indicates a measure of acquaintance with the circumstances of those to whom he writes.
5.   The writer claims Holy Spirit inspiration for his writing (2:20,27; 4:6,13; 5:7), and commensurate authority.   To be able to speak by Holy Spirit inspiration limits the writer to being either an apostle of Jesus or a New Testament prophet.
6.   There is practically a unanimity of opinion that the one who wrote the Fourth Gospel also wrote this epistle.   If both the Epistle and the Gospel are written by the same author, beyond all reasonable doubt, it is John the apostle.[8]   No other person has been

---

[5] This idea was defended by Jerome, and so might be designated as the Hieronymian View.   This view is thought by some of its defenders to account for the omission of 2 and 3 John from the canon of the Eastern Church till a late date.   In notes on the life of John we have discussed the evidence alleged to prove the existence of "Two Johns at Ephesus."

[6] This seems to be the view of the author of the Muratorian Canon.

[7] This is modern Redaction Criticism's view, according to which parts of the writings of the "school" reflected memories of what some John – whether apostle or elder – used to teach.   See the section on "Redaction Criticism" which follows later in these Introductory Studies.

[8] Two staunch defenders of the Johannine authorship of both the Gospel and First Epistle are A.E. Brooke, *Commentary on the Johannine Epistles*, ICC (Edinburgh, T & T Clark, 1912), p.i-xv, and John R.W. Stott, *The Epistles of John* in TNTC (Grand Rapids: Eerdmans, 1964).   Both give detailed reasoning

suggested who fits into the very complex position with even tolerable exactness.

External Evidence of Authorship

A. Allusions[9]

1. Ignatius (c. AD 110)

Ignatius has one or two possible allusions to 1 John, especially in his letter to the Ephesian church (VII.2). He speaks of the incarnation as "God having become in flesh," which could be a paraphrase of 1 John 4:2,3. (It also might come from John 1:14 or 2 John 7.) In his epistle to Smyrna (V) he also alludes to 1 John 4:2,3.

2. Polycarp (c. AD 115) has allusions to 1 John.[10]

"Everyone who confesses not that Jesus Christ is come in the flesh is an antichrist: and whosoever confesses not the witness of the cross is of the devil" (ad Philipp. VII). The likeness to 1 John 4:2,3 and 3:8 is remarkable. He goes on to urge a return to the message handed down from the beginning, which is a reminiscence of 1 John 2:22,24, and 2 John 7. In his letter to the Philippians (VIII) he alludes to 1 John 4:9.

We need to recall that the expression "antichrist" in the New Testament is unique to John's epistles, that it is not common in the literature of the sub-apostolic age, and that "confess" (2:19,23) and "witness" (4:14, 5:9,11) and "is of the devil" (3:8) are expressions very characteristic of John. All of this is strong argument that Polycarp was familiar with 1 John, though he does not name the author of his allusions.

---

for their conclusions. Other scholars have concluded that 1 John and the Gospel are by different authors. Moffatt (*Introduction to the Literature of New Testament* [Naperville, IL: Allenson, 1918], p.479-481) gave a list of 19th century writers who supported this view, as did he. In the 20th century, a challenge to the commonly held view was raised by H.J. Holtzmann and C.H. Dodd (*The Johannine Epistles*, pp. xlvii-lvi). Dodd's advocacy of the view has given it impetus in our time. Dodd raised three arguments against both books being by the same author: (1) The eschatology is more primitive in the gospel. (However, Dodd failed to find any attempted correction of the Gospel's wrong eschatology within 1 John. The critics are confident such correction occurred after the first generation of the church began to die.) (2) The interpretation of the death of Christ is more primitive in the Gospel. (It is called a "propitiation/expiation" in the epistle at 2:2, 4:10). (3) The doctrine of the Spirit in 1 John is not as elevated as in the Gospel. (Dodd claimed there is no reference to the Spirit's part in the new birth in 1 John).

[9] An "allusion" shows the writer who makes the allusion was acquainted with the work, though he does not "document" the source from which he quotes. Allusions, with a few exceptions, do not help establish authorship, but they do help establish the date of writing since the work quoted must antedate the writer quoting it.

[10] Polycarp died AD 155. This letter to the Philippians was written perhaps 30 or 40 years before his martyrdom.

3. Papias (c. AD 120) used 1 John.

Papias was bishop of Hierapolis, a town close to Ephesus, where John ministered for a quarter of a century. Eusebius relates that "[Papias] has used testimonies out of the first epistle of John" (H.E. III.39.16). This is the first specific reference to the existence of a Johannine Epistle. By balancing the name of John in this sentence with that of Peter, Eusebius evidently understood "John" to be the apostle John.[11]

4. Epistle of Barnabas (c. AD 130)

Some have found an allusion to 1 John 1:4 (about joy being made complete) in chapter 1 of the epistle of Barnabas. In addition, what is written in 1 John 5:9-11 about receiving the witness of God matches chapter 1 of Barnabas.

5. Shepherd of Hermas (c. AD 140)

"For they received the Spirit of Truth, and became habitations of the true Spirit" (*Com.* III) has been compared to 1 John 4:6, "Hereby we know the spirit of truth" (KJV) – because "the Spirit is the truth" (1 John 5:7). 1 John 5:15 may be alluded to in *Com.* IX, and 1 John 3:24, 5:14 may be alluded to in *Com.* X.

6. The Didache (c. AD 140) perhaps has allusions to 1 John.

In chapters X,XI, we find reminiscences of 1 John 2:5 and 4:12,18 in the language about love being completed or perfected, and we also find something reminiscent of "test the spirits" from 1 John 4:1. The Didache also speaks of "the world is passing away," which might be a reminiscence of 1 John 2:17 (though a very similar form appears in 1 Corinthians 7:31).

7. Carpocrates (the Gnostic) lived at the beginning of the 2nd century.

Carpocrates tried to pervert 1 John 5:19 ("the whole world lies in the power of the evil one") into a proof text for cosmological dualism. Origen complained about his misuse of 1 John (*in Genes.* cap.I).

8. Valentinus (c. AD 140) was a Gnostic writer.

Possible traces of 1 John in the *Gospel of Truth* are "the Father knows all things" (27:24; cf. 1 John 3:20), and "He came forth in flesh" (31:4ff, cf. 1 John 4:2).

---

[11] Irenaeus tells us that Papias "heard John [i.e., Papias was a disciple of John] and was a companion of Polycarp." If that is true, Papias is a 2nd century writer, one who personally knew John, and made use of 1 John. We can rely on the voice of witnesses who personally knew John. Eusebius, however (III.39.1, 2), has suggested that from Papias' own writings comes evidence he did not personally know the apostle John, and that Irenaeus is mistaken in his interpretation of what Papias wrote. See the discussion (*supra*) of "Two Johns in Ephesus."

9. Justin Martyr (AD 150)

Justin's statement that "we are called God's trueborn children, and so we are, if we keep his commandments" (*Dial. c. Trypho*. 123.9) looks very much like a reminiscence of 1 John 3:1 coupled with 2:3.

10. Epistle to Diognetus (a 2nd century work by an anonymous author).

Six of its chapters contain indisputable reminiscences of 1 John. Compare "how greatly will you love Him who so loved you first?" (*Diog*. X:3) with 1 John 4:19. Such phrases as "from the beginning," "God loved men," "so that we love him who first loved us" occur in *Diog*. VIII and IX. *Diog*. VI alludes to 1 John 4:4,5 (or John 17:11,14,16). Cap.X alludes to 1 John 4:9-11, and XII to 1 John 2:18-25; 4:4-6; and 5:6-12.

11. Epistle of the Churches of Vienne and Lyon (177 AD)

Contains an allusion to 1 John 3:16. Eusebius (H.E. V.1.10) quotes it as saying, "He showed this by the fullness of his love, being well pleased even to lay down his life in defense of the brethren."

These are some of the attestations to 1 John's early existence. Perhaps the number of allusions appears smaller than might have been expected, however: (1) The Johannine epistles were the last books of the New Testament to be written. Many of the other books had acquired a considerable circulation before these were in existence. (2) The comparative size of these letters is a factor. They are quite short, so we would not expect the number of allusions to be as many as from the longer books. (3) It is possible that much early Christian literature has perished, and with it, possibly, additional evidence respecting these epistles.

B. Annotated Quotations

1. Irenaeus (AD 180) – *This is the first direct, annotated quotation from 1 John*

Irenaeus frequently quotes 1 John. He identifies the author as the "disciple of the Lord" and the same person who wrote the Fourth Gospel. A typical example, as given in Eusebius (H.E. V.8.7) is, "John the disciple of the Lord testifies in his epistle ..." and then 1 John 3:18,19 is quoted. In Irenaeus *Adv. Haer*. (III.16.5) Irenaeus quotes 1 John 2:18-22, and ascribes the words, along with the Fourth Gospel, to the apostle John. He also quotes fully 1 John 4:1-3, 5:1 (*Adv.Haer*. III.18), and 2 John 7,8. Before settling in Lyons, Irenaeus was a native of the province of Asia, where John ministered for a quarter of a century.

2. Clement of Alexandria (AD 190)

Clement of Alexandria quotes passages from 1 John and names the apostle John as the author. For example, he quotes 1 John 5:16,17 (*Strom.* II.15.66), "John also in his larger epistle seems to show the difference of sins: 'If any man sees his brother sin a sin which is not unto death ....' "[12] In chapters 2-5 of *Stomateis* he quotes 1 John 1:6,7, 2:14,18,19, 3:3,18,19, 4:16,18, and 5:3,16,17, while in *Quis Dives Salvetur*? (chaps. 37 and 38) he quotes 1 John 3:15 and again 4:18. Other quotes of each of the five chapters of 1 John are found in *Strom.* III.4,5 [1 John 1:6ff]; III.5 [1 John 3:3]; IV.16 [1 John 3:18,19]. See also *Paedag.* III.11,12

3. Tertullian (AD 200)

Tertullian quotes 1 John 1:1 and attributes it to the apostle John. "Lastly, let us consider whom the apostle saw: 'That which we have seen,' says John, 'which we have heard, which we have seen with our eyes ...'" (*Adver Praxeam.* 15). More than fifty times, quotations of 1 John are found in Tertullian's writings (e.g., *Adv.Marc.* V.16.4 quotes 1 John 4:1ff: III.8 also), *Against Praxeas* (ch.28 quotes 1 John 1:7, 2:22, 4:1ff, 5:1), and *Scorp.* [Adv. Gnost.] 12. See also *de Praescript.* c.33, and *de Carne Christi*, c.24.

4. Origen (AD 210)

Speaking of the apostle John, after attributing the Gospel and the Revelation to the apostle, Origen says, "He has also left an epistle of a very few lines. Grant also a second and a third; for all do not allow these to be genuine. However, they do not both together make a hundred lines" (*Apud.* Euseb. H.E. vi.25). He continually cites the Epistle as John's (cf. *Ev. Jo.* tom. xiii.21, where he cites "God is light" from 1 John). Origen applied the epithet "catholic" to 1 John (*Comm. on Matt.* 17:19).[13] In an earlier note we have called attention to Origen's complaint against an abuse made of 1 John 5:19 by certain heretics.

5. Cyprian (AD 250)

In his *Epistle* 28,[14] he quotes 1 John 2:3,4, and attributes it to the apostle John. "And the apostle John, remembering the commandment, afterwards puts in his epistle, 'In this,' says he, 'we understand that we have known him, if we keep his commandments'." Elsewhere he quoted from 1:8, 2:6, and 2:15-17.

---

[12] Incidentally, this statement implies that Clement knew of at least two epistles by John.

[13] Origen's disciple Dionysius, bishop of Alexandria (d. AD 264), also speaks of 1 John as the Gospel writer John's "catholic epistle," perhaps in contrast to 2 and 3 John which are addressed to specified persons (H.E. VII.25.7,10; VII.25.11) Dionysius argues that while the Fourth Gospel and 1 John are by the apostle John, Revelation (on account of its very different style) cannot be by him (H.E.vii.25).

[14] In the collections of Cyprian's writings, some number the epistle as 25.

6. Eusebius (AD 325)

Eusebius ascribes 1 John to the apostle John (H.E. III.24,25). He writes that the authenticity of 1 John was never questioned in the early church.

7. Jerome (AD 385)

Writing of the apostle John, in his *Catalogue of Ecclesiastical Writers* (ch.9), Jerome says of him, "*Scripsit autem et unam epistolam, eujus exordium est, Quod fuit ab initio ... quae ab universis ecclesiasticis et eruditis viris probatur.*" In this there is a quotation of 1 John 1:1, "What was from the beginning ..." and Jerome tells us that 1 John received the sanction of all members of the church.[15]

8. During the fourth century, the Eastern churches, led by Cyril and Athanasius, came out strongly in favor of the apostolic authorship of all three epistles.

C. Canonical Listings

It is customary to find the epistles of James, Peter, John, and Jude bound together as a group, and placed between Acts and the Pauline Epistles in the codex manuscripts.[16] In the Eastern Church, this group of books was called "Catholic" or "General" (*katholikai*) epistles, a term which distinguished them from the Pauline epistles. In the Western Church, they were known as "Canonical" (*Canonicae*). It is likely the terms are used interchangeably.

1. The Muratorian Canon (AD 170)[17]

It is supposed that this list of New Testament books was written in Rome by a church-teacher for the purpose of instructing catechumens in the documents of the Christian faith which were received in his church. This list is preserved in a single incomplete Latin manuscript of the 7th or 8th century, discovered and published in 1740 by Cardinal L.A. Muratori (whence its designation). It now resides in the Ambrosian Library at Milan.

The manuscript introduces the Gospel of John (lines 26-34) with these words, "What wonder that John makes so many references to the Fourth Gospel in his Epistles, saying of himself, 'that which we have seen with our eyes, and have heard with our ears, and our hands have handled, that we have written'. For he thus pro-

---

[15] Jerome attributed the Gospel and 1 John to the apostle John; and ascribed 2 and 3 John to "John the elder." Through his influence all three epistles found a place in the Roman canonical list of AD 382.

[16] In some parts of the Eastern Church, not all seven epistles were included in the collection until perhaps the 4th century. Before this, the Syrian Church had only three, including 1 John.

[17] Scholars are divided as to whether the original manuscript from which this fragment is copied was composed at the end of the 2nd or at the end of the 4th century.

fesses himself not only the eye-witness, but also the hearer and the writer of all the wonders of the Lord in order."   1 John 1:1 is freely quoted and the whole quotation attests that the same John was the author of both the Gospel and epistle.[18]

2. Eusebius (AD 325)

This church historian placed 1 John among those canonical books of the New Testament which have been universally received *(homologoumena)* (H.E. III.25). He notes that 2 and 3 John were among the "disputed" *(antilegomena)*, because "they might be the work of the evangelist or of someone else with the same name" (H.E. III.24.17ff).

3. 1 John is found in the Peshitta Syriac (AD 425)

There was an earlier Syriac version, called the Old Syriac, made about AD 190-200 (i.e., about the same date as the original writing of the Muratorian canon). Only a few manuscripts of the Gospels survive in this Old Syriac version, though it is possible that the readings found in Ephraem's writings reflect this old version. In addition to the Gospels, the older Assyrian church also recognized the epistles of Paul and three catholic epistles (1 John, 1 Peter, and James) as being canonical, but we have no manuscript evidence of other than the Gospels in the Old Syriac.

The Peshitta version of the Syriac, now thought to be a revision of the Old Syriac, made about AD 425, has a "short canon," containing all the New Testament books our Bibles do, except for 2 Peter, 2 and 3 John, Jude and Revelation.

When all the quotations and canonical listings from the churches of East and West, of Syria, of Alexandria, of Africa, and of Gaul have been examined, **we have a consentient voice that 1 John is canonical and that 1 John was written by the apostle John.**[19]

---

[18] Later in the list (lines 68ff) two epistles "of the aforementioned John" are said to be included in *katholica*, which presumably means that they were accepted as canonical by the church in general.   The identity of these two is uncertain.   The compiler of the list may mean two in addition to the one already quoted (i.e., 2 and 3 John in addition to 1 John); he may mean 1 John together with one of the others, or if 2 and 3 John were taken together as one (which is not very probable), he may mean 1 John together with 2 and 3 John.   Most probably he means 1 and 2 John.   There is evidence that 3 John was rendered into Latin by another (and later?) translator than 1 and 2 John.   This being so, the Muratorian author, and the church whose New Testament canon he recorded, may well have known only 1 and 2 John.   This was the situation at the same time in Alexandria.   Clement of Alexandria (*Adumbrat.* IV,437; Misc. II.15.66) appears to have known 1 and 2 John only, whereas two generations later, in that same city, Origen and Dionysius knew 3 John as well.   (Adapted from Bruce, *The Epistles of John*, p.19.)

[19] Those who rejected the canonicity of 1 John include Cosmas Indicopleustes in the 6th century.   He affirms that none of the earlier Christian writers who have written about the canon makes any mention of the Catholic Epistles as canonical.   It is probable that the Alogoi mentioned by Epiphanius as rejecting the Gospel and Revelation, included the Epistles in this rejection.   (*Haer.* li.34).   Its rejection by Marcion is of little consequence.   He excluded from the canon all the writings of the apostle John since they did not suit his views.   One or two others argued for the omission of 1 John from the canon.   But that is all, so far as we know, till late in the 16th century, when a few men began to question the Johannine authorship.

REDACTION CRITICISM

Redaction Criticism's approach to the question of authorship is seriously flawed. Yet it is the approach that one reads in most any contemporary scholarly work, so it behooves us to become acquainted with the basic ideas being taught.

Basic Theory

Form Criticism and Redaction Criticism[1] have (its proponents believe) uncovered three levels of material in our New Testament books. The first level consists of what Jesus actually said and did, of which we know very little.[2] The second level is comprised of what the apostles of Jesus believed and taught. Again, we know very little of their beliefs, because this was the period when such beliefs were passed on by oral tradition. The great bulk of our books, instead, actually reflects the beliefs and practices and struggles of the early post-apostolic church. This, the third level of material, focuses on the "redactor" and his circumstances. Of course, as this scenario is being reconstructed, what the early church believed is two generations removed from Jesus, and in numerous aspects, according to the critics, differs materially from what both Jesus and the apostles actually taught.

---

[1] In the 20th century, two different methods of Bible study developed as men tried to make the Bible match current popular philosophy. About the time of WW I, from Hegel's Dialectic and Kierkegaard's Existentialism, came the theology known as "Neo-orthodoxy." Neo-orthodox thinkers (such as Rudolf Bultmann) developed a method of Bible study called Form Criticism. Form critics studied the Scriptures with the intention of ascertaining the original data behind the sayings, legends, miracle stories, etc., which the critics believed grew up around the stories as they were passed on orally over a period of time. According to form critics, the believing community, who told and preserved the stories, adapted and shaped the material into its present form. About the time of WW II, from Heidegger's Existentialism, came the theology known as "Neo-Liberalism." Neo-liberal thinkers (such as Gunther Bornkamm, Hans Conzlemann and Willi Marxen) developed a method of Bible study called Redaction Criticism. Redaction critics study how the stories, legends, etc., came to be pieced together, adapted, and unified into the documents we call Bible books. Each redactor ("editor" or "compiler") had his or her own theological agenda that allegedly contributed to and influenced the choice of materials that were ultimately included. Both methods are driven to identify the original life setting, or *Sitz im Leben*, as it is called, of the early church [i.e., not the life of Jesus, or the apostles' preaching] which called forth the form or the completed document. Under either method, what the written books actually say is no longer considered important. What is considered important is reconstructing the beliefs of the communities that produced the present documents.

[2] When the Form Critics have finished their work, Jesus virtually disappears. The Jesus Seminar has found little of Jesus' speeches and few of His miracles to have any historic authenticity to them. In the minds of the critics, the speeches and deeds attributed to Jesus in the Gospels are actually stories just made up as their tellers were trying to emphasize some point they thought important.

According to contemporary criticism, the signatures that appear in the text of some New Testament books, and the author's name that tradition has assigned to the unsigned books, are neither historically accurate nor technically correct, but may give us some clue as to which early leader was influential in the church or community or school that later produced the writings.

Attempts to Apply the Theory to Johannine Literature

As early as 1979, Raymond E. Brown[3] attempted to bring to general audiences what the scholars had been saying behind closed doors in the halls of academia. Today, following Brown's lead, when authorship of Johannine literature is discussed, it is commonplace for scholars to speak, not of "John," but of the "Johannine school," or "Johannine community," or the "Johannine circle," by which the teachings of John about Jesus were preserved and penned (Fourth Gospel) and where John's correspondence was preserved (1, 2, 3 John).[4]

In order to understand the Gospels and the letters, redaction critics attempt to reconstruct the social and theological history of this hypothetical community as best they can from the surviving literature.[5] To do this, study must be made concerning the order of writing, for conclusions concerning order will affect how the community's history is reconstructed.[6] Further, to do this reconstruction, the redaction critic must decide if all five "Johannine" letters came from same community, and perhaps the same man, or not. While there is as yet no agreement on this matter, a sort of consensus has emerged showing that all but Revelation stem from the same community and, for many, they share the same author.

Such a common compositional history argues that an early edition of the Fourth Gospel was followed by a theological crisis in the community. The crisis prompted a revision of the Gospel, and also prompted the writing of 1 John. This reconstructed history is supposed to explain the "obvious" redactional additions made by the "Johannine

---

[3] Raymond E. Brown, *The Community of the Beloved Disciple: The Life, Loves, and Hates of an Individual Church in New Testament Times* (New York: Paulist Press, 1979). Brown also produced the critically acclaimed commentary on *The Epistles of John* in the Anchor Bible Commentary (Garden City, NY: Doubleday, 1982), Vol.30.

[4] Observe that "Revelation" (which traditionally has been assigned to the apostle John) is studiously and deliberately ignored, probably because it doesn't fit the hypothesis.

[5] This "surviving literature" includes not only the Gospel and three epistles but also early church writings, apocryphal and pseudepigraphical materials, and even Gnostic (!) materials, as though somehow all of these forms are of equal value.

[6] Was the Gospel written first? Was 1 John written before the Gospel? Were 2 and 3 John written before or after? And what about Revelation? Is it even from the same school or circle?

circle" to the original document. These "obvious" additions include John 1:1-14 and all of chapter 21, plus the addition of "beloved disciple" as a description of the writer. This reconstructed history is also supposed to explain the parallels between the Gospel's prologue and that of 1 John, as well as parallels between 1 John and John 14-17 (often called Jesus' Farewell Discourse). Finally, the common compositional history theory has 2 and 3 John penned to address a subsequent local problem.[7] Once the reconstruction has been finished, the scholars assure us that the Letters and the Gospel provide important evidence of the character of John's churches. These documents tell us about the development of thought among John's followers: their passions, their wars, even their history.[8]

Some Intermediate Conclusions Reached by the Critics

While 2 and 3 John appear to come from the same pen, scholars have debated whether 1 John originates with the same author. The situation is sorely complicated by the reference in Eusebius (H.E. III.39.4) to the two John's at Ephesus, one called the "presbyter" and one called the "elder." The "elder" is thought to be different from the apostle John, who by then was universally assumed to stand behind the Gospel and 1 John. Furthermore, the critics also observe that Eusebius (H.E. III.24.17; III.25.2-3) puts 2 and 3 John among the disputed books of the canon, which the critics then connect to Eusebius' attribution of 2 and 3 John to the "elder" John. Some contemporary scholars have speculated the "elder" lived after the apostle died, and he is the author of 2 and 2 John.[9] In spite of these hesitations, Brown's overall conclusion has become the rather accepted conclusion. He wrote that "careful comparisons of style and content show striking similarities among all three writings and suggest that common authorship is not at all unlikely."[10]

A more compelling question is whether the same pen wrote the epistles and the Fourth Gospel. The Muratorian fragment attributes both the Gospel and several letters, one of which is clearly 1 John, to the same author, and this would tend to represent the majority opinion of the early church. As early as the 3rd century, Dionysius of Alexandria was making this claim based on similarities of content and style. Today, emphasis on the

---

[7] An easy introduction to this whole attempted reconstruction (G.M. Burge, "John, Letters of" in *Dictionary of the Later New Testament and Its Developments* edited by Ralph Martin and Peter Davids [Downers Grove, IL: InterVarsity, 1997], p.588ff) deals with the reconstructed History of John's Church, the Theological Struggle, John's Secondary Concerns, Authorship and Setting, and Epistolary Structure.

[8] Note they tell us about the churches, not about Jesus!

[9] I.H. Marshall (*The Epistles of John* in the New International Commentary on the New Testament [Grand Rapids: Eerdmans, 1978], p.42-48) has shown this does not necessarily have to be the case. Marshall also shows that even if two men named John did live in Ephesus at the same time, the attribution of epistolary authorship to the latter man is purely hypothetical.

[10] Brown, *Epistles*, p.14-35, 755-759. S. Smalley ("1,2,3 John," in *Word Biblical Commentary* [Waco, TX.: Word Books, 1984], Vol.51, p.xxii) writes in similar fashion, "The impressive amount of shared vocabulary between 1-2 John, coupled with the fact that there is little or no verbatim correspondence (such as a copier or forger might produce), supports common authorship for 1-2 John, hence for all three letters."

remarkable parallels between the Gospel and the letters, particularly 1 John, is common-place in New Testament studies. These parallels in style and content between the Gospel and 1 John are comparable to those found in Luke-Acts or even Colossians-Ephesians. This has led the vast majority of scholars to affirm common authorship for 1 John and the Gospel. Those who disagree point to the 1 John's absence of Old Testament quotations, its stress on future eschatology, its presentation of Jesus as paraclete (rather than the Spirit), its emphasis on Jesus' sacrificial death, and the promotion of ecclesiastical authority as differences versus the Gospel. For the most part these objections have not been decisive.

Redaction Critics propose several hypotheses about the "life situation" out of which John's writings came. Each of the early Christian leaders had his own peculiar beliefs, and a circle of converts who were fiercely loyal to their teacher. John's community of believers lived on the frontiers of Judaism. His church was heterogeneous: Jews who had moved into the Greek world lived alongside Greeks who knew little of the Old Testament.[11] Their common bond was a firm allegiance to Jesus, their Messiah, and John was their leader. Because John himself and his "Christian message" were rooted in Judaism, it was natural that this community would live in proximity to the synagogues of his city. In fact, it is here, in this relationship with the synagogue, that the Johannine community's "story" was forged. The Jewish synagogue was persecuting the church. Times were tough. Stories that had particular meaning for the struggling church are the ones that ended up in the church's archive and thus were included in the original edition of the Fourth Gospel. The blind man's expulsion from the synagogue mirrored what was happening to the Johannine circle (John 9). The sixty-four references to the "Jews" who were opponents of Jesus would strike a familiar cord with the Johannine circle. The importance of John the Baptist (cf. John 1:35-51, 3:22-36) would reflect a debate with followers of the Baptist in and around Ephesus, and were intended to encourage them to become followers of Jesus instead of John the Baptist. John's Gospel is filled with generous amounts of the teaching of Jesus. Such teaching warned of persecution and yet promised an intimacy with Christ which made such suffering immaterial. With its emphasis on the Holy Spirit, on the new birth, on "eating the flesh and drinking the blood," and on "drinking living water," the Fourth Gospel gave encouragement to Christians in John's circle who were prone to mystical experiences.

Assuming 1 John was written after the Gospel, Redaction Critics speculate that something serious happened after the [alleged] original edition of the Fourth Gospel began to circulate. The once-unified congregation began to tear apart. Folk who used to attend the public assembly of the Christians now separated themselves (1 John 2:19). The teachings of the "separatists" were causing doubt and confusion among the brethren. The "separatists" even based their doctrine on passages in the first edition of the fourth Gospel. Brown believes that at this point the Fourth Gospel went through a revision, with several passages added to preclude any further use by the "separatists." Not only was the Gospel

---

[11] This is an attempt to explain the lack of Old Testament quotations in 1 John.

revised, but supposedly John's letters were a response written in debate with those who were misinterpreting the Fourth Gospel.[12]

As they reconstruct the history, Redaction Critics propose the idea that the original Johannine community did not survive. 2 and 3 John give a glimpse into the sort of crises that gripped one congregation. The larger Johannine community divided, with strong leaders taking some of John's original circle into Gnosticism and Docetism,[13] while others from John's circle entered into communion with the churches (or circles, or communities) of Paul and the other apostles.

The Current Situation

In the last decade of the 20th century, scholars began to have serious doubts about Redaction Criticism. The prevailing philosophy was changing from existentialism to post-modernism, and so the old method of Bible study based on existentialism had to give way to something more "modern" and "acceptable."

It is not possible at present to identify any dominant theory or method of Bible interpretation on which scholars can agree. Some hold on to the older method, hoping that with a little tweaking it can be made to stand. Some have turned to an approach called "structuralism." Some have turned to "literary criticism," which in one or another of its forms is called "narrative criticism" or "reader-response criticism" or "rhetorical criticism." Still others have turned to any one of a number of approaches that fall under the heading of "social-science criticism." Tools invented by sociologists, anthropologists, and psychologists are applied to the books of the New Testament, with the result that our interest is directed not to the message, but to the social context or economic situation of the readers as implied in the writings we have.

In this commentator's opinion, **we should reject any method of interpretation based on current popular philosophy**. Whenever the current popular philosophy changes, some alternative method of interpretation must be produced to reflect what is now

---

[12] Some contemporary scholars treat 1 John as a cover letter for the new edition of the Gospel. Some treat it as an "epilogue" to make sure the Gospel is not misinterpreted.

[13] Evidence of this is drawn from the fact that the earliest commentaries on John (e.g., Heracleon) were written by Gnostics, a fact that shows the Fourth Gospel was embraced in these heretical circles. The Odes of Solomon (if they are Gnostic) likewise bear marks of Johannine influence. Even the Nag Hammadi Gnostic texts seem to describe a dualism that would fit the secessionists of John's church quite well. Concepts such as light and darkness, sinlessness, divine birth, the Spirit of Truth, and God's seed all appear in Nag Hammadi. Hippolytus (c.170-c.236) describes how Johannine language was used by his Gnostic opponents. Redaction critics suppose this may explain why the Orthodox Church (the "Great Church" as some label it) embraced the Fourth Gospel reluctantly. In fact, there is a surprising lack of interest in the Johannine writings among the leading 2nd century writers. Was that because the church's Gnostic opponents were using the Fourth Gospel or a form of it? Redaction critics suppose that it was the epistles of John – 1 John in particular – that redeemed the Fourth Gospel for the New Testament we possess today.

popular.[14] **How much better to rely on the time-proven method of interpretation called the "grammatical-historical method."**

WHO WERE THE "DECEIVERS"?

John does not give a specific name to the false teachers against whom he is writing. All we have are descriptions of the doctrines of the false teachers, and of the deleterious influence they were having on various congregations. However, a comparison of the contents of these letters with what is known from other New Testament books and from early church history gives a general answer as to their identification.

From a very early time these "deceivers" were given a name.   In one place Irenaeus, writing about Cerinthus, uses *gnōsis* ("knowledge") as a designation for this error.

> John, the disciple of the Lord, preaches this faith, and seeks, by the proclamation of the Gospel [i.e, the Gospel of John], to remove that error which by Cerinthus had been disseminated among men, and a long time previously by those termed Nicolaitans, who are an offset of that "knowledge" falsely so called, that he might confound them, and persuade them that there is but one God, who made all things by His Word; and not, as they allege, that the Creator was one, but the Father of the Lord another; and that the Son of the Creator was, forsooth, one, but the Christ from above another, who also continued impassible [i.e., unsuffering, not moved by human passions], descending upon Jesus, the Son of the Creator, and flew back again into His Pleroma; and that Monogenes was the beginning, but Logos was the true son of Monogenes; and that this creation to which we belong was not made by the primary God, but by some power lying far below Him, and shut off from communion with the things invisible and ineffable.[1]

In another place, the teaching of Cerinthus is thus summarized by Irenaeus:

> A certain Cerinthus in Asia taught that the world was not made by the primary God, but by a certain power which was widely separated and removed from that supreme power which is above them all, and did not know the God who is over all things. Jesus, he suggested, was not born of a virgin, for that seemed to him impossible, but was the son of Joseph and Mary, just like all the rest of men, but far beyond them in justice and prudence and wisdom.   After his baptism, the supreme Power Christ descended upon him in the form of a dove,   and then he proclaimed the unknown

---

[14] *The Jesus Crisis* (Robert L. Thomas and F. David Farnell, Chicago: Kregel, 1998) is a useful tool showing the inroads of historical criticism into Evangelical scholarship, and calls for evangelicals to abandon their love affair with the current methodology of Form and Redaction Criticism.

[1] *Against Heresies,* III.11.1).   "Knowledge" is *gnōsis*, the root word from which "Gnostic" comes.

Father and performed miracles.   But at the end Christ withdrew from Jesus, so that it was Jesus who suffered and rose again, while Christ remained impassible [i.e., unsuffering, not moved by human passions], since he was pure spirit [i.e., pneumatic].[2]

There is general agreement that certain Gnostic ideas and tendencies are in view as John writes against the "deceivers," but any attempt to identify one certain Gnostic group has not met with unqualified success.

By What Name Shall We Call Them?

We do need some term to refer to the deceivers against whom John contends.   John himself uses "antichrists" (2:18,22; 4:3), "liars" (2:4,22; 4:20), "deceivers" (2:26; 3:7), "children of the devil" (3:10), and "false prophets" (4:1).

It is improper to call them "Christians" (2:19), and even though for a while they did "attend church," John flatly says "they were not of us" (i.e., not Christians).[3]   The "deceivers" belonged to the evil one (2:14; 3:8,10).   They were of the world (4:5).   They had never risen to walk in newness of life (3:14,15), and by rejecting the Son of God as they did they did not have eternal life (5:12).   Thus "backslider" or "apostate" is not a proper term.

It seems that Paul called the same movement "philosophy and empty deception" (Colossians 2:8) and "arguments falsely called knowledge" (1 Timothy 6:20).   We'll follow Paul's example and use the term "Gnostics"[4] to designate the deceivers, but it is important to define the limits on how this term is being used within this commentary.   We are not speaking of the full blown 2nd century heresy.   Rather, the term is synonymous with "Gnostically inclined," or "incipient, beginning Gnosticism."   We will also call them false teachers, false prophets, heretics,[5] and separatists.

Some object to calling the false teachers "Gnostics."   One reason is that for years "Gnosticism" was a technical term with a specific meaning that excluded anything as early

---

[2] *Against Heresies*, I.26.1-2.   Hippolytus' summary of Cerinthus' teaching (*Refutation of All Heresies*, VII. 21) matches what we learn from Irenaeus.   1 John's emphasis that Christ Jesus came by water and blood (1 John 5:6) may be a polemic against this type of outlook.   The adoptionist doctrine is blatantly in error.

[3] 2 John 9 refers to church members, not to the deceivers.   The expressions "hates his brother" [3:15, 4:20] and "beholds his brother in need" [3:17] do not require us to affirm the deceivers were "Christian brethren."

[4] Some prefer to leave the underlying Greek word untranslated, and so speak of "Gnosis" when referring to the religious and philosophical tendencies that later became known as "Gnosticism."

[5] Technically, "heresy" may not be exactly the proper word.   "Heresy" is commonly used to designate a corrupt growth out of Christian truth, or a deflection from it.   That does not exactly fit the situation about which John writes.   The movement against which John writes seems to have first begun outside the church, then attempted to infiltrate it.   When their attempt failed, they disengaged from the church.

as the 1st century AD.[6]   Others object because they believe there was no such a thing as pre-Christian Gnosticism.[7]

But this commentator has concluded that ideas picked up from Eastern religions[8] and Greek philosophy,[9] ideas which became the major building blocks for the 2nd and 3rd century Gnostic doctrine or worldview, were already acceptable in the 1st century world among both Jews and Gentiles.   The records indicate that Gnostic ideas and tendencies in various stages of development were already extant during the time in which Christianity was born.   These ideas had already influenced Judaism[10]; they influenced Greek philosophy; they influenced the pagan religions of Greece and the East.[11]   As the last pre-Christian century closed, and the new Christian era dawned, men's views on religion and

---

[6] The term "Gnosticism" was first applied by 2nd and 3rd century Patristic writers to a large number of heretical teachers and sects then flourishing – such as Valentinus, Basilides, and others.   These heresies flourished and reached their zenith in the 2nd and 3rd centuries, and many persisted till the 7th century AD. Until recently, scholars attempted to limit the use of the name "Gnosticism" to these sects and teachers. By this limitation, "Gnostic" would not technically be a proper term to designate 1st century deceivers.

[7] Bultmann argued such a thing existed, and that many Christian doctrines were borrowed from pre-Christian Gnosticism.   Edwin Yamauchi (*Pre-Christian Gnosticism: A Survey of the Proposed Evidences* [Grand Rapids: Eerdmans, 1973]), in an attempt to refute Bultmann's idea that Christianity copied Gnostic sources, tried to show there was no pre-Christian Gnosticism.   Yamauchi was correct in his assumption that Christianity is a divinely revealed religion, not a religion copied from pagan sources, but he was evidently in error stating that there was no such thing as pre-Christian Gnosticism.

[8] From Eastern religion and philosophy came the key ideas of ethical dualism (i.e., an eternal struggle between good and evil, light versus darkness) and the speculations concerning emanations and lesser (planetary, hebdomad) deities as they grappled with the origin of the world and from whence comes evil. In addition certain mystical and magical ideas found in Eastern religions were embraced.

[9] Greek philosophy (Platonism) seems to be the source of the ideas that led to what has become known as cosmological dualism, the distinction and antagonism between spirit and matter.   Greek dualism saw a contrast between *phainomena* and *noumena*, between the world of sense-appearance and the realm of real being.   The lower was but a shadow of the higher; but still the lower was a copy of the higher.   At first, among the Greeks, the contrast was not, to any great extent, between the good and the evil, but between the real (on the one hand) and the empty, formless, unreal (on the other).   In Gnosticism we have the two kinds of dualism – both Eastern and Greek – combined.   Matter became evil and spirit good.   In the distinction between the real and unreal we have the terms used by the Docetics to explain Jesus Christ.

[10] Post-exilic Judaism was influenced both by Eastern religious ideas and by Greek philosophy and culture.   When the Jews began returning from the Babylonian Captivity in c. 538 BC, they brought with them certain Eastern religious ideas.   Inlaid in the tile of 1st century synagogue floors we see a surprising interest in the Persian deities found in the Zodiac.   The discovery of the Dead Sea Scrolls, beginning in 1947, opened up a new discussion of the origins of Gnosticism, for an ethical dualism was found not only in the Dead Sea Scrolls but also in Jewish apocalyptic literature written between the 1st century BC and the 1st century AD.   The words "know," "knowledge," and "mysteries" or "secrets" are used.   Some Jewish sects attempted to interpret their Jewish Scriptures in this new light.

[11] See the article on "Gnosticism" by G.W. MacRae in the *New Catholic Encyclopedia* (Washington, DC: Catholic University of America, 2002), Vol.6, p.254-261.   R.E.O. White ("Colossians" in the *Broadman Commentary* [Nashville: Broadman, 1971], v.11, p. 219) speaks of incipient Gnosticism as a religio-philosophical attitude rather than a well-defined system.   He speaks of a "climate of thought as widespread as evolutionary theory is today."

philosophy were oftentimes syncretistic, picking up one idea here, and another there. Many then tried to assimilate (and in some cases modified and adapted) into one world view all the "good ideas" from the various religions and philosophies current in the Hellenistic world. There is some evidence from Christian literature that the Gnostic system as we know it, with all the separate ideas now assembled together, began in Egypt, and from there spread over the Roman world. In any case, the record shows that Gnostic ideas and views were not first conceived inside the bosom of the church, only to spread over the world from there.[12] Rather, many of the basic ideas grew up outside of Christianity, and the Christian church was not very far advanced beyond its infancy when those contaminated and poisonous ideas began to be embraced by Christian people, to their sorrow. Consistent with its syncrestic practices, Gnosticism also borrowed language and images from Christianity, but the essence of the Christian message is ignored completely.

Over the years two other terms have come to be used to label or identify the "deception" we are dealing with. Those two terms are Docetism and Adoptionism. The term *Docetism* stems from the fact some Gnostic teachers claimed Jesus only "seemed" (Greek, *dokeō*, "to think," "to seem") to be human, and only seemed to suffer. Ignatius used the verb *dokeō* of the teaching of these "deceivers." The noun Docetists (*doketai*) was used first by Serapion, a leader in the Antioch church, AD 190-203. The term *Adoptionism* is used to identify ideas of Cerinthus and others about Jesus and the Christ being different, that the "Christ" temporarily "adopted" the body of Jesus.[13]

It will prove helpful to our study and understanding of the Johannine Epistles (and of the commentaries that have grown up around these writings) to spend a few more moments getting acquainted with Gnosticism.

Sources of Information about Gnosticism

There are multiple sources of information about the growth and spread of Gnostic ideas in the ancient world.

1) *1st century information can be gained from certain New Testament writings.*

Several of the New Testament writings have long been assumed to voice strong oppo-

---

[12] Instead of speaking of Jewish or Christian origins of Gnosticism (which seems to imply the heresy began in one of those circles), we should speak of the syncretism which led men, as they attempted to form their worldview, to pick and choose and assemble various ideas they found in Eastern religion, Greek philosophy, and in post-exilic Judaism. From Christianity were borrowed the ideas around which the Gnostic system finally crystallized and flourished. Importantly, from Christianity also came the historical truths with which Gnosticism could not be reconciled and which led to its demise.

[13] The denial that Jesus is God in the flesh by the Gnostics is a forerunner of modern Neo-orthodoxy with its Jesus of History v. the Christ of faith. The Gnostics, long ago, tried to separate Jesus, the Son of Man, from Christ, the Son of God. Perhaps if John's theology had been better known, the church would not have had to suffer through the ravages brought on by Neo-orthodoxy!

sition to Gnostic ideas or tendencies. 1 Timothy 6:20 (written c. AD 65) warns the readers in Asia Minor to avoid "knowledge falsely so called." Paul's letters to the Colossians and Ephesians, the letters of Peter and Jude, and the Johannine literature have all been explained as being refutations of incipient Gnosticism.[14]

> Nowhere is the tendency to Gnosticism more clearly or emphatically condemned than in 1 John ... "To know the depths" (Revelation 2:24). As time went on the Gnostics made greater and greater claims for themselves. A favorite claim was that they alone "knew the depths," and the Ophites in particular claimed this. According to John, the depths they knew were not of God, but were rather "the deep things of Satan," because their works were evil (Revelation 2:20-24).[15]

After the last of the books included in our New Testament canon was written, our information about the Gnostics comes from two sources: the refutations of Gnosticism by early Christian writers, and from recently discovered Gnostic works.

2) 2nd & 3rd century information is available from the Christian opponents of Gnosticism.

A roll call of the defenders of Christianity includes Ignatius in Asia Minor (AD 110),[16] Justin Martyr from Samaria (c.AD 150), Irenaeus of Lyons (c.AD 180), Clement of

---

[14] Some scholars believe that Gnostic ideas and tendencies began prior to their more pronounced 2nd century infiltration of and merger with Christianity. But these scholars have not been able to agree which New Testament books warn against such incipient Gnostic tendencies. Nor is there any agreement on whether or not any New Testament books may reflect the fact that by the close of the 1st century Gnosticism had already been accepted by some of the (Christian) people addressed. And while Greek philosophy was the cause of many of the troubles in the church at Corinth, we have not consented to accept H. Koester's views. H. Koester (*Introduction to the New Testament* [Philadelphia: Fortress, 1982]) assumes a Gnostic background for Corinthians because Paul spoke about "knowledge" and "wisdom" as well as the contrast between "physical" and "spiritual". Nor have we been able to agree with W. Schmithals who found Gnostics being refuted in Thessalonians and Galatians. Nor have we been convinced by Bultmann's attempts to identify the Gnostic sources alleged to be reflected in certain passages in Romans, such as the fall (Romans 8:20,21), baptism into the body of Christ (Romans 6:5), and the powers of this age (Romans 8:38,39).

[15] A.M. Renwick, "Gnosticism," in the *New International Standard Bible Encyclopedia* (Grand Rapids: Eerdmans, 1982), Vol.2, p.487-488.

[16] A typical example of what is found in these early writers is Ignatius, who commended his readers for not sharing certain Docetic Gnostic views that flourished in Asia Minor early in the 2nd century. He expresses gratitude that his readers were "... fully persuaded as touching our Lord that He is truly of the race of David according to the flesh, but Son of God by the divine will and power, truly born of a virgin and baptized by John that all righteousness might be fulfilled by Him, truly nailed up in the flesh for our sakes under Pontius Pilate and Herod the tetrarch ... For he suffered all these things for our sakes [that we might be saved]; and He suffered truly, as also He was raised Himself truly; not as certain unbelievers say, that He suffered in semblance .... For I know and believe that He was in the flesh even after the resurrection" (*Epistle of Ignatius to the Smyrneans*, ch.II-III). He also comments that these people "have no care for love, none for the widow, none for the orphan, none for the afflicted, none for the prisoner, none for the hungry or thirsty. They abstain from the Eucharist and prayer, because they allow not that the Eucharist is the flesh of our Savior Jesus Christ, which flesh suffered for our sins, and which the Father of His goodness raised up" (*To the Smyrneans*, VI.2). Other references in Ignatius are: *To the Trallians*, IX.10,

Alexandria (d. c.AD 215), Origen of Alexandria and Caesarea (c.AD 220), and Epiphanius of Salamis in Cyprus (d. AD 403).

Famous Gnostics identified in early Christian literature were located in Syria, Asia Minor, Alexandria, and Rome.

Syrian Gnosis. In the area of Samaria (ca. AD 180), Irenaeus and other early church fathers identified Simon the Sorcerer as the first Gnostic (i.e., the first one with Gnostic tendencies who also had some connection with Christianity). In Acts 8:9-25, Simon is described not by the term *Gnosis*, but as a "magician," whom his followers called "Great Power of God."[17]   Dositheus, founder of the sect of Dositheans, was said to have been the Gnostic teacher from whom Simon the Sorcerer learned. A writing full of Gnostic ideas called the *Great Exposition (Apophasis Megale)* was ascribed to Simon Magus by Hippolytus. In the form which Irenaeus knew Simon's Gnosticism, there were similarities to Christianity. Simon regarded himself as Father, Son, and Holy Spirit. His followers were saved by his grace, not by works of law (presumably an allusion to Ephesians 2:8-9). Simon's descent (sent as a savior from above) through several heavens is reminiscent of Gnosticism's idea of a good aeon coming to rescue the fallen aeon. Justin Martyr tells us that in Simon's system the fallen aeon was a female named Helena, also called "First Thought" *(Ennoia)* or the "Thought of God." Irenaeus reported a complete Gnostic system for the Simonians, which focused on the redemption of the "First Thought" (represented by Helena) from her captivity in the human material body. Simon seems to have influenced many to become his disciples through libertine behavior being condoned.[18]

Menander, from Samaria, who taught in Antioch of Syria, is named by Irenaeus as being one of Simon's pupils. Menander had a pupil, who also taught in Antioch, named Saturninus, who held a Docetic view of Christ. Saturninus flourished just after the turn of the century. Our knowledge of him, which comes from Hippolytus, has been summarized by Robert M. Grant.

---

and *To the Ephesians*, VII. According to Ignatius' *Letter to the Magnesians*, ch.IX-X, the group attacked by Ignatius also had strong Jewish beliefs and practices. Since such Jewish beliefs are not obvious in John's Epistles, some are hesitant to identify the false teachers in Ignatius with those in John. We shall show below that Gnostic ideas infiltrated Judaism before they did Christianity. Ignatius' writings can be studied in *The Ante-Nicene Fathers*, edited by A. Roberts and J. Donaldson (Grand Rapids: Eerdmans, 1953), Vol.1, p.87-89.

[17] Later Christian literature brings legendary tales about Simon, his school, and his opposition to the apostle Peter (Acts of Peter, the Pseudo-Clementines, and Epistula Apostolorum). We shall also learn in subsequent notes that some Gnostics did incorporate "magic arts" (cp. Acts 8:11) into their system. We just do not know whether Simon had Gnostic tendencies before he became a Christian, or whether it was after the event in Acts 8 that he embraced those ideas.

[18] One is reminded of Peter's false teachers who were "enticing (by sex) unstable souls" (2 Peter 2:14).

As is the case with most Gnostic systems, the supreme deity was completely unknown. Saturninus spoke of Christ rather than himself as the Savior (Aeon). The supreme power made spiritual beings who made the world. Those spiritual beings saw a "luminous image" which came from above, and they tried to copy it (an explanation of Genesis 1:26). Their attempt was only partially successful until a "spark of life" (a fallen aeon) came down to animate their product. This spark, present in good men, is the element which is saved. Redemption is produced by knowledge of what the good Aeon came to do. Christ (the good Aeon) came to destroy all the spiritual beings and men who are hostile to the supreme deity. Since ordinary human life, including marriage, procreation, and eating meat, is evil, he merely seemed to be a man (he may have been the luminous image which had appeared before [see John's "glory"]). As in the Simonian system, the Law was given by inferior spiritual beings; Saturninus added that the prophets were inspired by these inferior spiritual beings, and included among these inferior beings both Satan and the God of the Jews. Saturninus had no female principle, and he advocated extreme asceticism.[19]

Asian Gnosis. The Nicolaitans and Cerinthus were active in Asia Minor. Cerinthus taught that the divine Christ descended on the human Jesus at his baptism, and departed before the crucifixion.

Alexandrian Gnosis. Basilides, who emphasized dualism,[20] was active first in Alexandria, then in Asia Minor during the time of Hadrian (AD 117-138). He was a pupil of Menander. A distinctive feature of Basilides' own teaching is that the world is continuously evolved from a *pansperma,* from germinal "seed of the world" in which originally all things were potentially contained.

According to Irenaeus, Basilides taught an emanation of beings and angels from the "Unbegotten Father." Six spiritual powers formed the Pleroma (the "fulness" near God Himself): mind (*nous*) or Christ (*Christos*), word (*logos*), prudence (*phronesis*), wisdom (*sophia*), and power (*dunamis*). From the last of these six emanated 365 angelic beings (Aeons) in an unbroken, descending process, each creating a "heaven" as its habitat ... The lowest class of the powers was led by the demiurge God of the Jews called Abrasax (= 365) who created the physical world (*kosmos*) and men. To rescue men from the tyranny of this demiurge, the "Father" or "Unknown God" sent his Christ-Nous, who appeared in the divinely adopted hu-

---

[19] Robert M. Grant, "Gnosticism," in *Interpreter's Dictionary of the Bible* (Nashville: Abingdon, 1962), Vol.2, p. 405. The Syrian church father, Tatian, became a member of this Gnostic sect and exercised very great influence in the middle east, teaching the usual theory of Aeons and the Demiurge (Renwick, *op. cit.*, p.490).

[20] A comparison of what the early Christian writers say makes it clear that there was an earlier and a later form of Basilidean teaching. Clement of Alexandria and Hippolytus give the earlier form of the teaching, a form strongly pantheistic and Greek. Irenaeus gave an account of the Basilidean movement as it existed in Gaul fifty years later, when it had become dualistic (Renwick, *op. cit.*, p.490).

man being Jesus of Nazareth. Simon of Cyrene, not Jesus, was crucified, so that the Christ-Nous could escape and return to the Father without the knowledge of the evil powers. Only the soul, never the devalued physical human body, is the object of gnostic soteriology.[21]

Irenaeus reports that it was an Alexandrian contemporary of Basilides, Carpocrates, who with his son Epiphanes established the sect called simply "the Gnostics."[22] Among other things they were noted for their veneration of icons and the practice of magic.

Roman Gnosis. Marcion was active first in Pontus (northern Turkey) and then in Rome (AD 137-144). According to Irenaeus, Marcion came into contact with a Syrian-Gnostic teacher named Cerdo, and later joined Gnostic circles in Alexandria. Marcion taught his followers to distinguish between the God of the Old Testament (the harsh, evil creator) and the supreme deity of the New Testament who is completely unknown apart from his revelation in Jesus. The Old Testament prophets were inspired by the inferior Old Testament God, and even some of Jesus' apostles (not Paul) mistakenly held the view that the Old Testament Creator was a good God. To support his views, he produced a canon of Scripture that contained only one Gospel (Luke in a mutilated form) and ten epistles of Paul. He cut out of the Gospel of Luke everything that connected Christ with nature and history. Marcion rejected the other books because, in his view, they taught the wrong thing about the Old Testament God. He was a rigorous ascetic, refusing baptism to married persons and using water, not wine, in the Lord's Supper.

Valentinus taught there were a series of divine aeons. He moved from Alexandria to Rome about AD 140. No fewer than six separate accounts of this man's teachings are found in the church fathers. Perhaps we have two extant works written by Valentinus, the *Gospel of Truth* and the *Letter to Rheginus*.[23] According to Irenaeus, Valentinus taught a complicated system of emanations or aeons from the Supreme Being. The twelfth and lowest of these "aeons" was the female Sophia. Her instability led her to fall into the outer darkness, where she conceived spontaneously and brought forth a pre-mature infant who was the creator of the universe we know. This creator, called Ialdabaoth (a

---

[21] Kurt Rudolph, "Gnosticism" in the *Anchor Bible Dictionary* (New York: Doubleday, 1992), Vol.2, p.1037-1038. See Irenaeus, Against Heresies, I.24.4.

[22] Irenaeus, *Adv. Haer.* I.25.

[23] Both these works are included in the Nag Hammadi Library, about which more will be said below. The picture of Valentinus' teachings found in Irenaeus, and the picture found in these two extant works, differs. The *Gospel of Truth* presents Father, Son, and Holy Spirit as deity. It presents God Himself – not some Demiurge – as creator of the universe. We do not find several generations of Aeons; there is but one Son, the Father's beloved Son, who pre-existed as the Father's secret, His Word. Perhaps Irenaeus' picture of Valentinus' teachings comes from Valentinus' disciples and successors, who added the aeons (Bythos and Sige, Word and Life, Horus, Achamoth, etc.) to the earlier teaching of Valentinus himself (Renwick, *op. cit.*, p. 489-90). Perhaps Valentinus' teachings changed over the years.

parody of Yahweh Elohe Sabaoth?) in some systems,[24] regarded himself as the only god there was; he constantly struggled with his mother, Sophia, for control over mankind, since she had inserted a divine spark or spirit into man. In order to redeem both her and mankind, Jesus was sent down to collect the scattered spiritual seeds and to restore them to the "pleroma" (cf. Colossians 1:19, etc.) of spiritual being, the "aeons" above. Valentinus divided mankind into three classes: *hylics,* unbelievers immersed in nature and the flesh; *psychics*, common Christians who lived by faith; and *pneumatics*, or the spiritual Gnostics.

Valentinianism divided into two different schools, which they themselves called the "Anatolian" (Oriental, centered in Alexandria) and "Italian" (Western, centered in Rome). The difference between them centered on Christological issues. The "Italian School" is the one opposed by Irenaeus. Some of its influential leaders were Ptolemeus and Heracleon, whose commentary on the first eight chapters of John's Gospel is the earliest known commentary on that book.

3) *Still extant Gnostic writings are another source of information.*[25]

Texts written by Gnostics dated earlier than the 3rd century AD are few, and are mostly written in Coptic (a late form of Egyptian written mainly in Greek letters). Late in the 19th century, three Coptic Gnostic codices were published: the Askew Codex,[26] the Bruce Codex,[27] and the Berlin Codex.[28] In 1945, eleven Coptic codices and fragments of

---

[24] In the *Apocryphon of John*, there is a fuller description of the struggle between Ialdabaoth and Christ. Ialdabaoth made paradise and gave man a wife in order to chain him to the material world. Christ, however, persuaded man to eat from the tree of knowledge (*gnosis*). In the course of this struggle, Christ came again and gave his true teaching (the content of the myth) to his disciple, John – hence the title, the "secret doctrine" of John.

[25] The church fathers quoted abstracts from actual Gnostic texts. Irenaeus quotes from the *Book of Baruch*, by Justin the Gnostic (c. AD 150), a work now lost. Irenaeus also quotes from the *Apocryphon of John*, which is known to us from several Coptic versions. The *Apocryphon* denounces the Old Testament God for trying to hide the truth from humanity.

[26] The Askew Codex (*Codex Askewianus*) was acquired by the British Museum in 1785 and published in translation some 65 years later. Of the five works contained in it, the best known is the *Pistis Sophia*, named after a mythical figure in the Gnostic world of aeons. The work, in two books, purports to narrate conversations of the risen Jesus with His disciples, revealing esoteric knowledge of the world. The contents of this codex were composed probably in the 3rd century by members of one of the popular and somewhat decadent Gnostic sects (MacRae, *op. cit.*, p.257).

[27] The Bruce Codex (*Codex Brucianus*) was discovered in 1769 and first published in 1891. Included in it are the two *Books of Jeu* (cited in the *Pistis Sophia*), which unfold an immense system of magical names and symbols and which are intended to help the worshipper overcome evil in this world and make his way to heaven. Jeu is the primal man, prominent in Gnostic systems.

[28] The Berlin Codex (*Codex Beroliniensis* 8502), though discovered in 1896, was not published until 1955. It contains a *Gospel of Mary* (Magdalene), a *Sophia of Jesus Christ*, an *Acts of Peter*, and a copy of the *Apocryphon of John*, a work mentioned by Irenaeus in AD 180 as he described the Barbelo-Gnostics. The *Gospel of Mary* purports to reveal secrets which Jesus gave to Mary Magdalene alone and not to His male disciples.

two others were found by peasants near Nag Hammadi, on the Nile river about 370 miles south of Cairo, Egypt.[29] This "library" contains a variety of texts: non-Gnostic, non-Christian Gnostic, and Christian Gnostic.[30] The writings were apparently collected and used by Christian Gnostics in Egypt. The codices seem to have formed the library of a 4th century Sethian group, but include Hermetic[31] as well as Valentinian compositions. In all, 40 of the 51 tractates represented in the 13 codices are of Gnostic origin. The first tractate to be translated and published (1956) was the *Gospel of Truth* by Valentinus.[32] By 1977, the other tractates had been published, the most famous of which is probably *The Gospel of Thomas*.[33] There are numerous "Gospels" and "Acts" in the Pseudepigrapha that promote Gnostic ideas. One that has recently been published is the Coptic-Gnostic *Gospel of Judas*.[34] As these Gnostic texts become available, it becomes obvious that the representation of Gnosticism found in early Christian literature is basically correct.

4) *The writings of later Gnostics are also a source of information about the movement.*

Gnosticism flourished until the 7th century, and remnants of it still are visible here and there. However, for our purposes of understanding the background of New Testament writings, these later developments are not very reliable sources of information.

---

[29] James M. Robinson (ed.), *The Nag Hammadi Library in English* (Harper and Row, 1977), has made these writings accessible to English readers. The book is reviewed by Edward Yamauchi, *Christianity Today*, Oct. 6, 1978, p.36ff. Yamauchi divides the tractates into four broad categories: non-Christian, non-Gnostic; Christian, non-Gnostic; Christian, Gnostic; and non-Christian, Gnostic. He gives a brief introduction to each of the tractates he lists under each category. This article is a good introduction to what is contained in the library.

[30] Scholars have argued whether or not the Nag Hammadi texts are evidence that confirms the idea that Gnostic ideas existed in the world before the 2nd century AD. What is actually debated is two points: (1) whether any of the works (say the *Apocalypse of Adam*, or the *Paraphrase of Shem*) are actually non-Christian works, thus supporting Bultmann's thesis of a pre-Christian Gnosticism; and (2) whether any of the Coptic copies found represent a Greek text that antedates the merging of Christian and Gnostic ideas. Since the codices are Coptic copies of either Greek or Syriac originals, the time of the composition of the originals is earlier than the time when the copies were prepared. On the whole, the date of writing of the originals is given as the 2nd or 3rd centuries, with a few perhaps dating to the 1st century. A good argument can be made from the Nag Hammadi texts that the earlier scholarly hypothesis, that Gnosticism first was a Jewish heresy before it became a Christian heresy, can no longer be easily dismissed.

[31] "Hermetic" is the title given to writings from the 3rd or 4th century containing a jumble of Neoplatonism, theosophy, and other mystic-religious elements.

[32] In this account, Jesus' teachings liberate the soul from a flawed physical world.

[33] The *Gospel of Thomas*, written about AD 140 in Syria, contains 114 purported sayings of Jesus. In 1897 and 1904, Grenfell and Hunt had discovered papyri at Oxyrhynchus in Egypt which included non-canonical sayings or the so-called "Logia" of Jesus. We now know that these papyri came from copies of the Greek text of the *Gospel of Thomas*.

[34] See "The Judas Gospel," in *National Geographic* 209:5 (May 2006), p.78-95. The opening line of the text reads "The secret account of the revelation that Jesus spoke in conversation with Judas Iscariot."

With the current focus on Islam in the Middle East and around the world, it is noteworthy to see that Islam was affected by Gnosticism. The Christianity with which Mohammed was acquainted reflects a Docetic view of Christ. "They did not kill him and did not crucify him, but he was counterfeited for them"[35] (i.e., it was an effigy or simulacrum of Jesus that was fastened to the cross). Shi'ite Muslims still reflect certain ancient Gnostic views.[36]

The most extensive amount of Gnostic literature has been transmitted to us by the Mandaean communities in southern Iraq and southwestern Iran. The Mandaeans are surviving remnants of Gnosticism. The name Mandaean is a derivation of an Aramaic word meaning "knowledge." "The time and place of the origin of this religion are still matters of uncertainty and dispute. Mandaeism may safely be regarded as a late form of Gnostic religion, perhaps originating in the 5th century AD."[37] Their texts were perhaps written in the 7th century, but are known to us only through later (17th and 18th century copies) manuscripts. These Mandaean texts were used by the History-of-Religions scholars and Bultmann to reconstruct an alleged pre-Christian Gnosticism. It certainly is not clear that we are justified in attempting to illustrate the thought of 2nd century and earlier Gnostics by appealing to these Mandaean texts.

Characteristic Ideas in the Gnostic "Worldview"

There was no single unified system of Gnostic doctrine. But the philosophy called "gnosis" and the sects later roughly categorized as Gnostic shared certain ideas, to which each influential teacher added speculations of his own.[38] W.D. Niven has summarized the main features of Gnosticism.[39] The following paragraphs are adapted from that work.

1) Gnostics claimed special knowledge based on *special revelations*. Each Gnostic teacher or separate Gnostic group lived in the conviction that they possessed, because of special revelation, some secret or mysterious knowledge, in no way accessible to those outside their group. Once Gnosticism had tried to absorb Christian ideas into their religion, claims were made that the source of this special knowledge was Jesus, or one of His apostles, or at least one of their friends. Claims were made that many of the pseudepigraphical works were authored by one of the apostles or a close friend of Jesus or an apostle.

---

[35] *Qur'an* 4. 157.

[36] Rudolph, *op. cit.*, p.1039.

[37] MacRae, *op. cit.*, p.256.

[38] Irenaeus long ago complained that the Gnostic groups were inconsistent in their teachings (*Adv. Haer.* I.11.1). With "knowledge" based on multiple "revelations" from the father of lies, it is not surprising to find that we cannot identify an overall "creed" that covers all groups. The scheme that suited one group did not satisfy the next. Yet we do find certain basic ideas occurring again and again.

[39] Niven's article on "Gnosticism" is found in *Hasting's Dictionary of the Apostolic Church* (Grand Rapids: Baker, 1973 reprint), p. 453-455.

2) *Dualism* was the foundation principle of all Gnostic systems, and from it all else follows. As noted earlier, in the ancient world we meet two kinds of dualism. One was the ethical dualism of Eastern religion, the other was the dualism between the real and the unreal in Greek philosophy. In Gnosticism we have the two kinds of dualism combined. The real world of Greek philosophy and the Eastern world of light were put together, as were the phenomenal world of philosophy and the world of darkness taught by Eastern religion. Spirit and matter were separated, one being thought of as intrinsically good and the other being intrinsically evil. The real world of goodness and light came to be called the *Pleroma* ("fullness"); the phenomenal world of evil and darkness was called the *kenoma* ("emptiness"). Based on this idea that spirit is good and matter is evil, the Gnostic tried to explain his world.

3) *Cosmogony[40] and the Demiurge.* Gnostics sought an explanation for the problems of creation and the origin of evil. As the Gnostic surveyed the world of matter, he found traces of law and order ruling it. How did matter, in itself evil and lawless, come to be so orderly? Of course, the Supreme Being (conceived of as being an impersonal force) who is real and good could have nothing to do with an evil or material world. So the Gnostic postulated that from the Supreme Being there emanated a series of beings called "aeons,"[41] with each subsequent step in the genealogy[42] bringing a diminution of purity. Eventually the lowest aeon far down the family tree created a being called a Demiurge (master builder[43]) who, without the approval of the Supreme Being, was the creator of the material world. The character of this Demiurge was variously conceived by different Gnostic schools. Some, like Cerinthus, made him a being simply ignorant of the highest God. The tendency became strong, however, to make him hostile to God, an enemy of Light and Truth. Once Judaism and Gnostic ideas had merged, the God of the Old Testament was identified with this hostile Demiurge who was inferior to and infinitely remote from the Supreme Being. In final analysis, this elaborate speculation about emanations simply concealed the difficulties of the problem rather than solving them.

---

[40] "Cosmogony" is a better word than "cosmology," since the Gnostic's speculation took the form of mythological explanation for the origin of the universe, rather than a philosophical consideration of its composition.

[41] Some Gnostics spoke of 365 aeons, while a few schools spoke of seven. The origin of this latter number is clear. The seven are the seven astrological deities of Persio-Babylonian religion.

[42] Some New Testament writers refer to "endless genealogies" when they refer to the names, persons, and relationships invented by the Gnostics to explain all the intermediate emanations between God and man.

[43] "Demiurge" comes from the Greek *dēmiourgos*, literally a "public workman" (*dēmios* + *ergō*), "artisan," "builder." *Dēmiourgos* emphasizes the idea of *power*. A synonym; *technitēs*, emphasizes *wisdom*.

4) *Redemption and Salvation.* Christians and Gnostics agreed in finding both good and evil in this world, with the two in conflict. They differed entirely in their conception of the conflict. The Christian view, reflecting the Biblical account, is that into a world of perfect order and goodness a fallen angel brought confusion and evil. The common Gnostic view was that into a world of evil a good aeon brought a spark of life and goodness. In the Gnostic view, the lowly Demiurge set to work to create this world without the permission of the highest and therefore "unknown" god. In order to stop the monstrous process of physical (nonspiritual) creation started by the Demiurge, the highest God had only one choice: to initiate cunning counter-moves among human beings, who were the apex of the physical creation. So, without the knowledge or consent of the foolish Demiurge, the highest God (or one of his closest aeons) planted in man an otherworldly, divine substance variously called "spirit," "soul," or "spark." This enabled man (at least the part of man called the ideal Adam) to see reality and long to return to the Pleroma, the kingdom of light. This planting of a "spark" is what the Gnostic called "redemption." This "spark" is not something inherited; it is something that must be done for each man one at a time.[44] It occurs when the man has a vision of God as a result of an altered state of consciousness. Once initiated, this "redemption" imparts clear knowledge of the ideal world to be sought after, and prompts man to so strive. Just as "redemption" had to be redefined when Scripture and Gnosticism were combined, so "salvation" had to be given a different meaning. For the Gnostic, "salvation" is not a matter of deliverance from sin and guilt. Rather, "salvation" is the freeing of the spirit from matter (*hyle*), in particular, from the material human body. According to the Scriptures, Christ died for body as well as for soul, but Gnosticism had no place in its system for a new, glorified body.

From animistic religions came the idea that the soul at all points, before and after death, was opposed by hostile spirits. Thus, in the 2nd and 3rd centuries AD, a great part of Gnostic teaching consisted of instructions concerning how these enemies could be overcome. The methods used in Eastern religions to overcome the power of the evil spirits were now taught to Gnostic initiates. All sorts of magic rites, baptisms, stigmatizings, sealing, piercing the ears, holy foods and drinks, were enjoined. It was thought important also to learn the names of the spirits, and the words by which they could be mastered. Some systems taught a multitude of such "words of power." The Basilideans taught one master word, *caulacau.*[45]

5) *Christology.* When Christianity and Gnosticism merged, the good "aeon" who plants the divine "spark" was identified with Jesus. But dualism's distinction between spirit

---

[44] The Biblical idea of redemption as something accomplished for the whole human race in one definite historical moment on the cross of Calvary was an idea which Gnosticism never could assimilate into their system. The Christian idea of what the Savior did when He was "manifested" in history never could be made to match the Gnostic view that redemption was a myth, an allegory or figure, but not an historical event.

[45] Irenaeus, *Adv. Haer.* I.24.5.

(good) and matter (evil) required a denial of Jesus' true humanity. Some Gnostics taught a Docetic view, that Jesus was pure spirit and He only "seemed" to have a human body, and only "seemed" to suffer on the cross. Others taught an Adoptionistic view, that the "Aeon" Christ came on the human Jesus at His baptism and left before the crucifixion. Whichever way the "Aeon" made himself visible to men, he assumed the appearance of a man in order to reveal himself to the sensuous nature of man.

6) *Anthropology.* Man was regarded as a microcosm (a miniature representation of the universe) composed of three elements: a spirit (*pneuma*), a soul (*psuche*), and a material body (*hyle*). These three parts supposedly reflect the Supreme Being, the Demiurge, and matter. According to which ever element dominates in man, he falls into that particular category of existence. When Jewish and Christian ideas were assimilated into the system, it became customary to speak of three classes of mankind – merely material or carnal (*hulikoi*), psychic (*psuchukoi*), and spiritual (*pneumatikoi*). The heathen are hylic/*hulikoi*, swallowed up by the cares of life on this earth. Jews and non-Gnostic Christians were psychic/*psuchukoi*, aspiring by faith and obedience to join their God in eternal bliss. Only the Gnostics were truly spiritual/*pneumatikoi*, for only in them had the divine spark been rekindled. They alone are the true church, destined to rejoin the divine world to which they really belonged.

7) *Eschatology.* Gnostics alone were certain of the return of their spirits to the Kingdom of Light (the Pleroma). But some also taught a charitable destiny for the psychics, who might attain some measure of felicity. The psychics could look forward to an almost endless series of reincarnations, and perhaps during one of these stays on earth they would gain the "knowledge" needed to attain to the Kingdom of Light. Since the body was "matter" and therefore considered "evil," Gnostics denied any future resurrection of the body. Gnostics also believed that in time the Supreme Being would win the conflict and the world created by the Demiurge would be destroyed by fires springing from its own bosom. In the Gnostic view, the end (*telos*) of history was the ultimate dissolution of the cosmos that had been created by the foolish Demiurge, and the return of the human "sparks of light" to the Kingdom of Light.

8) *Gnostic Worship Practices.* Niven compares the two very opposite worship styles that developed among Gnostics as being comparable with puritanism and ritualism respectively. "The abhorrence of matter led some consistently to the utmost simplicity of worship. Some rejected all sacraments and other outward means of grace, and the Prodicans rejected even prayer (Epiphan. *Haer.* xxvi; Clem.Alex. *Strom.* i.15, vi.7). On the other hand, many groups, especially the Marcosians, went to the opposite extreme with a symbolic and mystic pomp in worship. With them sacraments were numerous, rites many and varied. Some of them (Bardesanes, Ophites, Valentinians) were distinguished as hymn-writers. The Simonians and Carpocratians first used images of Christ ..." (Niven, *op. cit.*, p.454).

9) *Gnostic ethics and morality.* According to early Church writers, Gnostic ethics took two different directions. Some (e.g., Nicolaitans, Ophites) taught unrestrained antino-

mianism. Since, in their view, the flesh can't harm the spirit, one is free to indulge the flesh to exhaustion.[46] These are sometimes identified as libertine Gnostics. Others, ascetic Gnostics (e.g., Saturninus, Tatian) abhorred evil matter, and so sought to avoid all contact with the flesh as far as possible. This led them to forbid marriage and indulgence in certain kinds of food.[47]

Final Thoughts Concerning the "Deceivers"

The first Gnostics were not heretical Jews or heretical Christians. For nearly a century now it has been known from a study of ancient history and literature that there was an environment of Gnostic ideas floating around the Mediterranean world before anyone ever tried to combine them with Judaism, or before these ideas became something against which Peter, Paul, and John found themselves compelled and inspired to write.[48] *We have found no compelling reason to abandon the traditional view that the deceivers about whom John was warning taught views similar to those later given the name Gnostics.* The more that comes to light as ancient Gnostic writings are discovered, the more the traditional view looks correct.

Our rather lengthy study of the origin and teachings of Gnosis and Gnosticism has provided us with an introduction to 1st century thought and likewise has given us a background which makes John's warnings more understandable. It also will give us a basis by which to judge the validity of claims made by certain contemporary scholars.

We are aware that certain modern scholars are not as inclined, as was Irenaeus,[49] to

---

[46] The libertine traits of some Gnostics are as yet attested only in early Christian literature. They have not been documented in any Gnostic writing so far discovered by the archaeologists. Irenaeus (*Adv. Haer.* I.6.2-3) told how they defended their practice: "As gold sunk in filth does not lose its beauty but preserves its own nature, the filth being unable to harm the gold, so they say of themselves that even if they be immersed in material deeds, nothing will injure them nor will they lose their spiritual essence. Therefore 'the most perfect' among them do unafraid all the forbidden things of which Scripture tells us that 'they who do such things will not inherit the kingdom of God'."

[47] Asceticism is documented in extant Gnostic writings.

[48] Paul and John did not copy. Instead, they are opposed to those pagan ideas!

[49] Various objections are raised to justify the hesitancy that contemporary writers express. Some are rather convinced there is no reflection in either the Fourth Gospel or 1 John of Cerinthus' distinctions between the Supreme Being and the Jehovah of the Old Testament. Others affirm there is no allusion to the series of divine emanations proceeding downward to the aeon who created the material universe. Others insist the false teachers warned about in 1 John taught things that have no known parallels to what Cerinthus taught: their claim to sinlessness [1:8-10]; their claim to visions and inspiration [2:4, 4:1-3]; their claim to fellowship with God [1:6]; their claim to life in the light [2:9].
But a careful, side-by-side study of the brief statements about Cerinthus' doctrine on the one hand and John's writings on the other shows that many of these various objections based on claimed distinctions are baseless. John's verses showing that Jehovah (the God of our Lord Jesus Christ) is not an evil being should not be ignored. Nor should the verses be ignored that insist Jesus created, and He created all things good! While we may not have a specific statement still extant from Cerinthus on "special revelations," such "revelations" were the source of the special knowledge claimed by the elite Gnostics.

identify "Gnosis" as taught by Cerinthus as being the specific problem John's Asiatic churches faced. We have quoted Irenaeus' description of "Gnosis" at length, if for no other reason than to allow readers to make their own decisions on this matter.

In this commentator's judgment, Irenaeus identified the heresy correctly. We are not ready to reject the picture of Gnosis and Gnostics painted by the Apologists as being the exaggerated statements and polemical rhetoric of biased heresiologists. Rather, we believe these Apologists, even while in the midst of condemning an evil, gave a clear and accurate statement of facts, and gave unedited quotation of what someone else had taught or said. None of the modern alternative identifications offered by contemporary writers provides as good a fit as "gnosis" for identifying and describing John's deceivers.

DATE OF WRITING

The traditional date assigned to John's epistles is AD 85-90, based largely on claims made about the epistles in early Christian literature. The actual evidence on which to make a decision for or against the traditional date is meager. About all that can be done is assess whether or not the traditional view is plausible. The historical allusions show 1 John is a Christian work, because the earthly ministry and death of Jesus are in the past. Decisions already made about authorship and the identity of the deceivers must be taken into account, and so must the scraps of evidence that can be gathered from the historical allusions. Finally, we must judge the truthfulness of the claims made in early Christian literature on which the traditional date rests.

It is this commentator's conclusion that the verses in 1 John which some use to posit an early date for its writing (i.e., before the AD 70 destruction of Jerusalem) are wrongly interpreted. Briefly, here are the arguments for an early, non-traditional, date of writing:

(1) The expression "it is the last hour" (2:18) is interpreted to mean the last hour of the duration of the Jewish state, and John's statement about "antichrist is coming" (2:18) is interpreted to be a reference to Nero, who is then affirmed to be the beast whose number is 666 (Revelation 13). "Many antichrists have arisen" (2:18) is taken to be similar to Jesus' prediction concerning the false teachers who were to arise before the destruction of Jerusalem (Matthew 24:24). The attempt to identify "last hour" as something occurring before AD 70 has a surprising and unacceptable side-effect. It causes commentators to have to explain as mistaken the reference to Jesus' Parousia (2:28) as being near.

(2) 2:13,14 – "You know Him who has been from the beginning" is interpreted to mean that the readers of this letter had personally witnessed Jesus' earthly ministry. If this were so, it almost requires a date of writing before AD 70. During the 40 years between AD 30 and AD 70, there must have been many living who had seen and conversed with Jesus during His ministry. In the years AD 85-90, there could not have been as many alive who had been blessed with such an opportunity. This explanation of 2:13,14 also produces an undesirable side-effect. It leads its proponents to suppose 1 John was addressed to Jewish

Christians living in the land of Israel,[1] which is contrary to the testimony of early Christian literature. This interpretation is likely a misapprehension of the real import of the words in 2:13,14. Perhaps 2:13,14 means that, contrary to the Gnostic doctrine of Jesus being an emanation, the Christian readers of this letter are acquainted with His eternality, having confessed that truth in preparation for being immersed into fellowship with Him.

(3) J.A.T. Robinson's reconstruction of how John's writings came to their present form is typical of Redaction Criticism's attempted reconstruction of the life situation.[2] Robinson has an alleged first edition of the Fourth Gospel written from Asia Minor about AD 50-55, dates the epistles about 60 or 65, and the final form of the Fourth Gospel in AD 65. Redaction Critics are interested in using bits and pieces from the Bible books to explore and possibly reconstruct the compositional history and social setting of the Johannine community, rather than searching for any message from God in the writings. Almost inevitably, the most fundamental reasons advanced today for rejecting apostolic authorship for the "Johannine writings," and then for assigning a date to the writings, do not rest on hard evidence but rather on imaginative scholarly reconstructions of the history and development of the Johannine "circle" or "community" or "school." Such reconstructions exercise controlling power over all other evidence, internal or external.[3]   Robinson has

---

[1] Some have appealed to the three witnesses on earth and the three in heaven (1 John 5:5-9, KJV) as they have tried to develop a case for the letter being addressed to Jewish Christians. At the proper time we shall point out that the reading found in the KJV is spurious, and that being so, it is an error to use it as proof that Jewish Christians in the Holy Land were the intended audience to whom this letter was addressed.

[2] J.A.T. Robinson, *Redating the New Testament* (Philadelphia: Westminster, 1976), p. 307.

[3] A common compositional history proposed by Redaction Critics argues that an early edition of the Fourth Gospel was followed by a theological crisis in the Johannine community. This crisis prompted a revision of the Gospel and the writing of 1 John. 2 and 3 John were penned later to address a subsequent local problem. A popular presentation of this contemporary scholarly speculative hypothesis can be found in the article on the "Letters of John" in the *Dictionary of the Later New Testament* edited by Martin and Davids (Downers Grove: InterVarsity, 1997).

Redaction critics also posit a Johannine community as the "author" of the "Johannine literature." Then they attempt to reconstruct the history of that Johannine community which was allegedly responsible for our writings. A common reconstruction seems to follow this path: In the years after Pentecost, the community was made up of a coterie John's followers who lived, taught, and ministered with a common theological heritage. They were responsible for the different layers and development of sources associated with the Gospel of John, as well as for certain redactional activity connected with that writing. This community began about the same time as the church in Antioch (AD 40). Persecution may have driven the leaders of the community from Jerusalem, and having fled Jerusalem, John may have gathered with some of the Samaritan converts along with some former followers of the Baptist. They probably located somewhere in southern Palestine, and continued their mission to the Jews. Sometime before AD 70 (Brown thinks closer to AD 80), perhaps as a result of increased hostility from the Jews (recall how many times the Fourth Gospel speaks in denunciatory tones about "the Jews"), the Johannine community migrated to Asia Minor and initiated what became a very successful mission to those Gentiles whose religious orientation was in the direction of "higher paganism." The need for a Gospel that would double as a missionary document to convince these potential converts became evident, and the Gospel of John was published by the Johannine community c. AD 75-80 to meet this challenge. Redaction critics claim John 20:31 expresses this very purpose for the Gospel. Heretical developments then plagued the community for about 10 years, and finally resulted in a secession of some members in order to found a rival community. 1 John was written by the Johannine community, or by a student of the Fourth Gospel, as a response to this crisis, c. AD 85-90. (Robert Kysar ["John, Epistles of," in *Anchor Bible Dictionary,*

the Fourth Gospel going through several editions and revisions, but not the epistles. For his reconstruction to be plausible, Robinson must have John in Ephesus as early as AD 50. As already documented from the life of John, this is something hard to accept. It is noteworthy that internal evidence is manipulated by the Redaction Critics to support their hypotheses, and external evidence that contradicts it is dismissed, either on the basis that the early church writer was mistaken, or else the generally accepted interpretation of the early Christian writer is attacked as being wrong.[4] Both are done so that the aimed-for reconstruction can proceed unhindered.

Tradition has John the apostle writing from Ephesus late in the 1st century AD. There is little within the letter itself that would cause us to question tradition's conclusions.

(1) Our study of the life of the apostle John has produced no compelling reason to reject the traditional view. We have noted the record of his long ministry in Ephesus and Asia Minor. Eusebius has John going to Asia about the time of the Jewish War, AD 68.[5] Polycarp's language, in his own letter to the Philippians, shows acquaintance with 1 John. Polycarp wrote immediately after Ignatius passed through on his way to martyrdom at Rome, somewhere between AD 110 and AD117. This would establish AD 110 as the latest possible date for the writing of 1 John. If John himself is the author, his date of death about the turn of the century would be the *terminus ad quem*. 3 John indicates that John is still able to travel and work. If he wrote these letters in the late AD 80's, he himself would have been aged 75-79, and so still able to travel and work as 3 John suggests.

(2) The study of the "deceivers" shows them to be of the same persuasion as the false teachers introduced in the letters of Peter and Jude, as well as some of Paul's letters. This helps corroborate a late 1st century date for the writing of 1 John since the epistle must be dated late enough to allow adequate time for the growth of the false teaching that is opposed in the letter. Paul foretold the Gnostic storm in his address to the Ephesian elders (Acts 20:29ff), and warned about it in his second epistle to Timothy, who was at the time working as the evangelist with the Ephesian church (2 Timothy 3:1, 4:3). This storm has broken over the church by the time John writes. The situation of John's churches as reflected in 1 John would suggest a date after the Colossians (AD 63) or the Pastorals (AD 65-67). Such

---

p.909], after arguing for an AD 90-95 date for the Gospel, assigns the dates of AD 100-105 for the Johannine epistles.) It was written to reassure those who had remained faithful, as 1 John 5:13 indicates. The letter is addressed to a single congregation, though it may have circulated throughout the geographical area where the Johannine churches had been established. The Johannine community eventually ceased to exist; the ominous statement about it being "the last hour" (2:18) for the community sadly came true. The Gnostically inclined supposedly were attracted to Gnostic movements akin to those which flowered in the 2nd century. The orthodox believers were absorbed into mainstream Christianity, and John's teaching was secured for the orthodox cause.

[4] Interaction with Robinson's presentations may require a restudy of assigned dates and of the historical accuracy of what is found in early Christian literature.

[5] Eus. HE. III.1.1.

teachers were still on the horizon, outside the church, as late as 2 Peter (AD 67). But when Jude wrote his letter (c. AD 75), the false teachers Peter predicted had arrived on the scene and were active. 1 John not only pictures the deceivers as present on the scene, but as having ceased to attend the regular church assemblies (1 John 2:19) as they once did. This tends to point to a date later than AD 75 for the writing of 1 John, for the false teachers Jude wrote about had not separated themselves from the brethren, but were still polluting the love feasts of the church (Jude 12).

(3) The absence of any reference to persecution being faced by John or his readers probably indicates a date after the persecution by Nero (AD 64-68), but before the time of the emperor Trajan (AD 98-117), and probably even prior to the last years of Domitian, who reigned until AD 96. The traditional date of AD 85-90 is within this interval between persecutions.

(4) All commentators acknowledge some kind of relationship between 1 John and the Gospel of John, and scholars have tried to use this relationship to help date the writing of the epistle.[6] B.F. Westcott set out the following list of notable parallels between the epistle and the Gospel of John.[7]

Epistle – Gospel	Epistle – Gospel
1:2,3 with 3:11	3:16 with 10:15
1:4 with 16:24	3:22 with 8:29
2:11 with 12:35	3:23 with 13:34
2:14 with 5:38	4:6 with 8:47
3:5 with 8:46	4:16 with 6:69
3:8 with 8:14	5:9 with 5:32
3:13 with 15:18	5:20 with 17:3
3:14 with 5:24	

The date we assign to the writing of 1 John must take into account this notable parallelism. The Gospel is regularly dated c. 80 or 85 AD, and early Christian literature has it written while John was living in Ephesus.[8] If any of the epistles were written after the Gospel, this would yield a date of 85 or 90 for the epistles.

---

[6] Care must be exercised here. We are not studying the age of the writings (did the Gospel come first, or the Epistle?) in order to somehow suggest one is a literary product derived from the other. We also are assuming that John's Gospel as we have it has not been reworked by one or more redactors so that it has a complex history of composition, but rather reflects what the apostle actually taught and wrote.

[7] B.F. Westcott, *The Epistles of St. John* (Grand Rapids: Eerdmans, 1952 reprint), p. xli-xliii.

[8] In our study of the life of John, we have seen that John didn't come to Ephesus before Paul's death. There is no evidence that John is at Ephesus at the same time of the writing of Paul's final epistles to Timothy, who was then preaching at Ephesus. If John wrote his Gospel at Ephesus after taking up residence there, it was unlikely it can be dated before AD 70. If John's Gospel is also anti-Gnostic, we must allow some time for that issue to get into the churches. Thus a date of AD 80 or 85 has traditionally been suggested. (Robinson, *Redating* [p.307], argues for several editions of the Fourth Gospel, and he desperately tries to get John to Asia as early as AD 50 in order to have the final form of the Gospel put in its present form about AD 65.)

Scholars have offered several views about the order in which the Gospel and epistle were written. (a) *Was the epistle written before the Gospel?* Based on vocabulary studies, some have the epistle written between Revelation and the Gospel. According to this scenario, Revelation was written before AD 70, the epistle in the late AD 80's, and the Gospel in the late 90's. Some have held the priority of the epistle on the grounds that writings of "momentary design, like letters, come naturally before writings of permanent design, like narratives or histories." Some have held the priority of the epistle on the grounds that it is a warning to a particular church, whereas the Gospel appears to be addressed to all Christendom. (b) *Was the epistle written at the same time as the Gospel,* serving as a cover letter or introduction for the Gospel, and sent out at the same time? Lightfoot thought it a cover letter or an epilogue intended to circulate with the Gospel so that no erroneous interpretations of it would be reached.[9] Yet Law argues that it is difficult to think of 1 John in this way, that 1 John stands as an independent work.[10] (c) *Was the epistle written after the Fourth Gospel?* While this has been the majority opinion through the years, variations of this view abound. One supposes the epistles were written in the reverse order that we have them, with Gospel written between 2 John and 1 John. 1 John is treated as a postscript to the Gospel, the Gospel having been written to explain how men might have eternal life (John 20:31) and the epistle written to give assurance they had it (1 John 5:13).[11] F.C. Baur held the epistle to be an imitation of the Gospel, but written by a different hand. Another supposes 1 John is a commentary on the Gospel. One rather contemporary view is that 1 John is a correction or clarification of the Fourth Gospel, aimed at those who were distorting its teachings.[12] However, scholarly attempts to produce an "earlier form" of the Gospel (one that preceded the redacted form we now have) from which the views of the heretics could have been drawn have so far not been successful.[13] If an ur-Gospel (an earlier form of the Gospel) cannot be reconstructed, it would follow that there is little reason to regard 1 John as a deliberate correction of such an "early form" lest unorthodox deductions be drawn from it. On the contrary, 1 John clearly respects the teaching of the Fourth Gospel in its present form as authoritative, and as being what was

---

[9] J.B. Lightfoot, *Biblical Essays* (New York, Macmillan, 1893), p. 194-98.

[10] R. Law, "John, Epistles of," in the *International Standard Bible Encyclopedia* (Grand Rapids: Eerdmans, 1929), Vol.3, p. 1717.

[11] This view rests on faulty exegesis of John 20:31. John is not about "how to get" eternal life, but how one may know he "continues to have" eternal life.

[12] Hippolytus (c.170-c.236) described how Johannine language was used by the Gnostics. Heracleon, a Gnostic, wrote one of the earliest commentaries on John's Gospel. Because allusions and quotations of the Fourth Gospel were few in the 2nd century, it is alleged that the orthodox church was reluctant to embrace the Fourth Gospel. Orthodox folk avoided the Gospel, the theory goes, because the church's Gnostic opponents were using the Fourth Gospel (or the early form of it). Scholars then hypothesize that it was the Epistles of John – 1 John in particular – that redeemed the Fourth Gospel for the New Testament we possess today.

[13] R. Brown, *The Epistles of John*, p.14-35, in a manner similar to Robinson, discusses the sequence of the Gospel and three epistles. In this present commentator's view, it has not proven to be a useful or fruitful pursuit to inquire into the redaction history of either the epistle or the Gospel, nor to try to assign the resulting various imaginary editions to a spot on the calendar.

"heard from the beginning." B.F. Westcott honestly stated that there is no definitive evidence to determine the relative dates of the epistle and the Fourth Gospel.[14] But he went on to say the epistle "presupposes in those for whom it was composed a familiar acquaintance with the characteristic truths which are preserved for us in the Gospel." On this basis he proposed that the Gospel was written and circulated before the Epistle.[15]

Although hard evidence is lacking, scholars have drawn certain deductions, and upon these have argued that the Gospel was written before the epistle.

- The epistle presupposes its readers' acquaintance with the substance of the Gospel, otherwise such expressions as "Word of Life" and "new commandment" would have been unintelligible. 1 John 1:1-4 is more understandable if one assumes acquaintance with the Gospel of John. 1 John 2:3-8 seems to presuppose the readers are familiar with the fuller exposition of these themes in the Gospel.

- How far the false teachers have influenced the readers is another deduction. When John's Gospel was written, he wanted them to "continue to believe" (John 20:31). It is implied the teachers of error are still where they can catch the ears of the readers of the Gospel. However, by the time 1 John is written, the teachers of error have left the church (1 John 2:19). Having 1 John written after the Gospel gives time for this change. At the same time, John insists (1 John 5:13) that eternal life continues to be available to those who continue to believe on the name of the Son of God.

- The verbs "I have written to you" (1 John 2:13,14) may be construed to be historical aorists referring to a former communication, namely, the Gospel.[16]

All things considered, we see no reason to deviate from the traditional dating of the letter. We will continue to date the letter AD 85-90.

PLACE OF WRITING

There is no direct evidence, either in 1 John or in early Christian literature, to show when and where 1 John was written. Most ancient tradition locates the writing of the Gospel at Ephesus.[17] If the Gospel and Epistle are both the work of the apostle John, and

---

[14] Westcott, *op. cit.*, p.xxxi.

[15] Those writers who hold to the priority of the Epistle say parallel ideas could have been learned from John's preaching rather than from his written Gospel.

[16] The other option is to treat them as epistolary aorists, referring to something written earlier in this very letter we call 1 John.

[17] Irenaeus, *Adv. Haer.* III.1, locates the writing of the Gospel at Ephesus. So does Jerome, *Prolog. to Matth.* vol.vii. p.5,6.

if they belong to the same period in John's life (which the discussion about date of writing affirms), it is reasonable to suppose the epistle as well as the Gospel was written at Ephesus. "In the absence of any other indication, it is natural to suppose it was written at Ephesus."[18]

DESTINATION

The traditional view is that the letter was addressed to Asia Minor. In form and content 1 John is a message sent to a group of Christians, intended to undergird their faith and reinforce their loyalty. What we cannot be sure of is whether it was sent to a single congregation or to several congregations in a given area.

The identification of Asia Minor as the likely destination is derived from several threads of thought. Tradition names the apostle John as the author, and he spent the last quarter century of his life in and around Ephesus and Asia Minor. If the epistle was written late in John's life, it is reasonable to suppose it was intended for readers among whom he had recently been ministering in Asia Minor. Internal allusions show the author has a personal relationship with his readers and is acquainted with the situation of the readers – their religious environment (2:19, 4:1), dangers (2:26, 3:7, 5:21), attainments (2:12-14, 21), achievements (4:4), and needs (3:19, 5:13). Such intimate knowledge of the readers argues for a destination close by where the author lives and writes. The author has fellowship with the readers and wants that fellowship to continue (1:3). If the teaching opposed in 1 John is linked with Cerinthus, this strengthens a case firmly based on the traditions that connect the author and readers with Asia Minor. The majority of readers to whom 1 John is sent were not recent converts, but had been Christians for some time (2:7,24, 3:11).

Was the letter intended to be read to one congregation or to several in the same general geographical area? To answer this question requires that the evidence be handled with care. (1) 1 John is often called one of the "catholic" epistles, a term that has come to carry the connotation of a "circular" or "general" letter intended for all the churches. But this current convention does not indicate it was originally an encyclical. How then did it come to be so called? Collections of writings included in ancient copies of the New Testament Scriptures were grouped under titles such as "Gospel" or "Epistles of Paul." The seven letters we know as James, Peter, John, and Jude belong to a group that occupied a position of their own in the canon, and also had a distinct title. This group was placed between Acts and the Pauline Epistles in most ancient codex manuscripts (with occasional exceptions, such as codex Sinaiticus). In the Eastern Church this collection was given the title *katholikai*, "general" or "catholic," while in the Western Church they came to be called *canonicae*, "canonical." Both titles seem intended to distinguish the letters as being "gen-

---

[18] Westcott, *op. cit.*, p.xxxii. Some recent redaction critics of the "Johannine Epistles" have been inclined to locate John's "community" somewhere in Palestine, and to affirm that both the Gospel and the Epistles were written there. Syria has been claimed as the place of authorship by Nauck (*Die Tradition und Charakter des ersten Johannesbriefes* [Tubingen: Mohr, 1957], p.165), but this depends very much upon his interpretation of 1 John 5:6ff, which has not won general acceptance. Other redaction critics see no reason to abandon the traditional view that the writings originated in Asia Minor.

uine and authoritative," and to distinguish them from the Pauline Epistles in the canon and from the spurious epistles that also were circulating but which were excluded from the canonical collection. (2) Certain verses have been pressed into action in an attempt to show 1 John was addressed to but one congregation. "They went out from us" (2:19) is interpreted to refer to a single congregation as the destination, namely, the congregation where the writer and readers worshiped together. However, there are other possible explanations for "they went out from us." Perhaps it says the Gnostic missionaries used to attend the same congregation where John still worships but no longer do so. Their departure should be carefully noted by the readers, for it has bearing on whether or not they ever were in fellowship with the original apostles of Jesus. 1:3 does not necessarily infer the addressees were part of but one congregation. Readers at a distance could continue to have fellowship with John, without attending the same assembly each Lord's Day. The directive to love one another (3:11) and to lay down their lives for one another (3:16) does not necessarily point to a single congregation as the destination. The directions about how to treat folk committing a sin to death (5:16) would be true in any congregation where folk listened to the false teachers. (3) John would hardly need to write a letter to the congregation with which he was accustomed to worship,[1] but a letter would be an appropriate way to communicate with numerous congregations over a wide area. Some have supposed the lack of a formal epistolary opening point to 1 John as being an encyclical intended for more than one congregation, being sent by messengers from church to church and being read in the general assembly of each.

Scholars have offered alternatives to the traditional view. (1) One ancient suggestion is that 1 John was addressed to Christians in Parthia, the land on the east side of the Euphrates River. Augustine, quoting 1 John 3:2, speaks of the passage as being John's "Epistle to the Parthians."[2] Scholars have shown great skepticism about the accuracy of this statement. Early Christian literature knows of no connection between the apostle John and the land of Parthia.[3] This designation *ad Parthos* appears to have been unknown to the Church of the East (a surprising fact if indeed the letter were first addressed to the East), and even to the Church of the West before Augustine's time. It has been sup-

---

[1] This comment anticipates a study yet to be made (see below, "Form of Writing?"). Some contemporary scholars have proposed the idea that 1 John was not a letter, but was a position paper intended for distribution among the members.

[2] The words in Latin are "...*quod dictum est a Joanne in epistola ad Parthos*" (*Quaest. Evang.* ii.39). This is the only certain occurrence of this designation in Augustine's works. Through the years, a few later writers picked up this curious note; so that it is found in the heading of some of the Benedictine editions of Augustine's Sermons on 1 John; in the *Indiculus Operum S. Augustini* of Possidius (a pupil of Augustine); in one or two Latin manuscripts; in the 5th century treatise against Varidamus the Arian by Vergilius Tapsensis (or Idacius Clarus?); and, if genuine, in Bede's *Prologus Super Septem Epistolas Canonicas*, where it is said that many ecclesiastical writers, and among them the great Athanasius, affirm this epistle to be "written to the Parthians." It is even found in a few modern Greek manuscripts of 2 John, though not 1 John ("John B to the Parthians," those manuscripts read.)

[3] According to the literature, Thomas was the apostle who evangelized Parthia. Plummer has written, "Whether the tradition that John once preached in Parthia grew out of the Latin superscription, or the latter produced the tradition, is uncertain." (Plummer, *op. cit.*, p. 32)

posed that this reading "to the Parthians" rests on some scribal mistake, but none of the conjectures thus far offered have satisfactorily explained the how this puzzling mistake began. Did some scribe read *pros parthenous* ("to the virgins," a title intended to express the pure condition of the churches) found in some MSS of 2 John, and not only mistake its meaning (writing instead *pros parthous*, "to the Parthians") but also accidentally transfer it to 1 John? Did Augustine himself make the first mistake? Did he misunderstand what was said by Clement of Alexandria in a fragment of Clement's *Adumbrations* on 2 John (Frag. 1011) about the second epistle being written *pros parthenous*, and transfer the title to the first epistle? Did some Latin scribe then compound the error by misinterpreting "virgins" and substituting "Parthians"? (2) Lightfoot tried to make a case for 1 John being addressed to Corinth.[4] 3 John is addressed to Gaius whom Lightfoot identifies as a member of the church at Corinth. Lightfoot then calls attention to 3 John 9 ("I wrote something to the church") and identifies this "writing" as being none other than 1 John. Before Lightfoot's hypothesis can be accepted two questions must be answered. (a) Has he properly identified the writing alluded to in 3 John 9? (b) Is the Gaius of Corinth (Acts 19:29, 1 Corinthians 1:14) the same as the Gaius of 3 John 1?[5] (3) Another idea is that 1 John is an encyclical written to Christians in the whole of the Roman Empire. John, in his old age and the last surviving apostle, would think of the worldwide church's needs. If Peter and Jude were written against Gnosticism a decade or so earlier, and those were addressed to a large geographical region (i.e., Pontus, Galatia, Cappadocia, Asia, and Bithynia), might it not be possible that the troublesome belief had spread and that John would therefore have to address his warning to a larger geographical territory than did Peter or Jude?[6] (4) Redaction critics tend to think of 1 John as addressed to the Johannine community rather than being a circular.[7] It is addressed to the congregation from which the false teachers had separated themselves, with the intent of keeping what was left of that community together. The writing (a collection of parts of homilies) was intended to reassure the "faithful" that the dissenters were guilty.

Though some were attractive for a time, none of the scholarly alternatives has commanded acceptance so as to displace the traditional view. **On the whole, there is no compelling reason to abandon the traditional view that the destination of 1 John was to the churches of Asia Minor.**

---

[4] See Davidson, *New Testament Introduction* (London: Bagster, 1848), V.3, p.466.

[5] If we opt for Corinth as the destination, there are other issues to be considered. If 1 John is written to Corinth, and if "Gnosis" is the problem, then are we to conclude that incipient Gnosticism was the problem that plagued the Corinthian church? In this commentator's Introduction to his commentary on 1 Corinthians, he has opted for Greek philosophy being the problem that led to the fight over preachers and a denial of the resurrection, but not the embodiment of that philosophy identified as gnosis.

[6] Some think the language of 1:3 points to a wider audience than Asia Minor. But in this commentator's judgment, the "to you" and "you also" in 1:3 do not suffice to establish a distinction between the Asiatic Christians ("we," 1:1,2) among whom John is writing, and those ("you") to whom this letter is directed.

[7] The community is located wherever the author/redactor was when he wrote, be it Syria, Palestine, Asia Minor, or wherever the composition history requires it to be located.

WHAT IS THE FORM OF THE WRITING?

Serious and thoughtful readers mentally treat what we read in the comic pages of our newspapers differently than the editorial pages. We recognize the difference between feature articles and news articles, between fiction books and history books. Certain principles guide our thinking after we mentally locate which type of work we are reading.

When we open our Bibles we need to be aware of the kind of literature we are reading. Is it history? Poetry? A parable? An illustration? A prophecy? A prayer? Is it sarcasm, or a heart-felt statement of truth? Is it a letter? Is it a sermon? Decisions made in answer to such questions affect how the Bible verses will be interpreted.

There are several key presuppositions that make a fundamental difference in how a reader interprets Scripture. One of the major issues is the interpreter's stance toward the inspiration and authority of the Scripture. Is it God's book, not just man's composition? Another important issue is the unity of Scripture. A third important issue is this very matter of deciding what kind of literature it is that we are reading. The modern term applied to the different kinds of literature is "genre" (literary form).

For several reasons, this commentator has been very cautious to venture into the dark swamp termed "genre criticism." First of all, the term has been made popular by humanism. The philosophy of humanism and the Scriptures have never had an amicable relationship. Humanism has said of the Bible, "Nothing supernatural here!" When a Bible book, such as Romans, has the "form" of a letter and yet the critics still go looking for some different "genre," we begin to be cautious, if not suspicious. And there is good reason to beware. Interest in genre criticism is a stepchild of Form and Redaction Criticism. Form Criticism went to seed trying to isolate which form was to be assigned to each paragraph of the Gospel accounts.[1] They even used the assigned form to determine whether or not the paragraph contained any real history or not. Genre criticism is part of a presupposition that seeks to discover the origin and composition history of each unit of Scripture, having already decided against its historicity. Form analysis has a tenuous nature and a subjectivity that make it difficult even for its defenders to agree upon. When Form and Redaction Criticism were applied to the Gospels, any message that might have been heard from God was lost in the frantic search for the form. After dissecting the Gospels, form critics tried to apply genre criticism to the other books of the New Testament, and again the message from God was pushed to the background as searches were made for the situation in the community that allegedly called forth this type of genre.

Genre criticism is basically incompatible with the grammatical-historical approach to Scripture this commentator champions. **The grammatical-historical method focuses our attention on the life situation of Jesus and His message from God to men,** rather

---

[1] For a useful introduction, see Craig L. Blomberg, "The Diversity of Literary Genres in the NT," in *New Testament Criticism and Interpretation*, ed. Black and Dockery, (Grand Rapids: Zondervan, 1991), p. 507-32.

than on the life situation of the early church. It allows us to hear the Word of the Lord, rather than the word of men.

As we surveyed 1 John looking for historical allusions, we observed that many of the features usually found in 1st century letters are absent from 1 John.[2] The absence of the usual epistolary form has led to efforts by literary critics to isolate the precise literary genre of 1 John, but the critics have not been able to agree on the form. (If determination of genre were such a straightforward matter, rather than being highly subjective, one would expect a greater measure of agreement on the "form" of 1 John.) Here are some samples of what the critics have decided concerning "form."

- One thinks of 1 John as a *treatise* (a writing that treats a particular subject in a methodical manner, and intended for wide distribution).
- Another thinks of it as a *libellus* (a little booklet or a pamphlet, easy to carry, written to be circulated).
- Another calls 1 John a *homiletical essay* (a sermon that was written down so it could be preserved and circulated to a wider audience).[3]
- Another calls 1 John a *manual of doctrine* (a tract, or broadside, aimed at a particular problem sweeping the church, and intended for reading by a Christian audience).
- In a similar vein, 1 John has been called a *manifesto* in that it is intended to make public a particular point of view. And the writer does assume a posture of authority with regard to the readers; he is confident what he writes is the truth.
- Another hypothesis which compares 1 John with 1 Timothy has led some to argue that a category like *pastoral epistle* is the best way to describe 1 John. (In such writings, the author demonstrates a deep concern for the readers and attempts to address their needs, emotional as well as moral and creedal.)[4]
- Though unlikely, Brown has suggested 1 John is a *commentary* on the Fourth Gospel.[5]

---

[2] It has no signature, address, word of greeting, or thanksgiving. It closes without benediction or doxology. We are so used to a "Grace be with you," that 5:21 sounds almost as if the writer's thoughts have been cut off. We expect more to be said, and it isn't! Though there is a tone of awareness on the writer's part about the situation of the readers, there are no personal allusions concerning the writer's own situation like we are accustomed to find in many 1st century letters. And some have called attention to what they affirm is the disconnected nature of the structure of writing, alleged to be unlike a letter.

[3] Robert Kyser (*op. cit.*, p.902) pictures the redactor of 1 John as having drawn together bits and pieces of several of John's sermons, delivered at different times and perhaps at different locations amidst the emerging crisis. These sermons were pulled together and published as an effort to make a more concerted response to the crisis, and to make the response more widely available.

[4] While the explanation may catch the thrust of 1 John, this "genre" title is a little fuzzy. Elders were the local congregation's "shepherds/pastors," whereas the apostles of Jesus had the responsibility of care of all the churches. They needed to make sure the sheep didn't stray or fall among wolves. We would expect such a tone in works written by an apostle and expected to be read in the congregational meetings.

[5] R. Brown, *Epistles,* p.90-92. Granted, we do observe that the opening of the Epistle reads very much like the prologue of the Fourth Gospel. And 1 John 5:13 reminds us of John 20:31. We have also commented on the relationship between the Fourth Gospel and 1 John as far as Christology is concerned. Both were written against the same deceivers. Brown goes farther. He even finds a two-part outline for 1 John similar to the two part outline usually given to the Gospel of John (see "Outline," below).

But if it were a "commentary," would it not have followed the text of the Gospel more closely and echoed it more explicitly?

If we must assign a "form" to 1 John, we will agree with the historic opinion and call 1 John an epistle or letter.[6]   From the earliest church times, the work is commonly called "the first *epistle* of John."   In the study of "Destination" we saw that ancient New Testament Scripture collections called 7 writings "epistles" (James, Peter, John, and Jude) – either catholic or canonical.   There are several features in 1 John which we regularly find in 1st century letters.   The readers are addressed 22 times with the plural "you." There are references to the readers' condition (2:1,7,13,18,20,23,24).   The writer frequently says "I write unto you" or "I wrote unto you" (1:4; 2:1,7,8,12,13,14, 21,26, 5:13).   The relationship suggested is one between writer and readers.   1 John does possess the character of the New Testament epistles in general, which is well described by William Ramsay:

> They spring from the heart of the writer and speak direct to the heart of the readers. They were often called forth by some special crisis in the history of the persons addressed, so that they rise out of the actual situation in which the writer conceives the readers to be placed; they express the writer's keen and living sympathy with and participation in the fortunes of the whole class addressed, and are not affected by any thought of a wider public ... On the other hand, the letters of this class express general principles of life and conduct, religion and ethics, applicable to a wider range of circumstances than those which called them forth; and they appeal as emphatically and intimately to all Christians in all time as they did to those addressed in the first instance.[7]

This present commentator's conclusions concerning the form of writing include:

- **1 John should be read as a "general epistle" intended to be passed among a number of congregations,** much as Galatians might have been intended for a number of Christian churches in the region of Galatia.
- Letters should be interpreted by: (1) **Noting the positive things taught,** e.g., concerning God, Christ, creation, man, sin, salvation, and eschatology.   (2) **Accepting what is clearly stated as being God's truth.**   (3) **Hearing the positive commands and clear prohibitions** in the New Testament Scriptures so that we understand what God expects our behavior to be.   (4) **Observing the errors corrected,** so that when we find similar errors in our contemporary world, we know the proper correction to keep us headed in the right direction.

---

[6] We are ignoring Deissmann's (*Bibelstudien*) attempted distinction between these two words. To him, an epistle was a formal composition, a didactic treatise, intended for a public audience; whereas a letter was a private *ad hoc* response to some crisis, and not intended for public audience.

[7] Wm. Ramsay, *Letters to the Seven Churches of Asia* (Grand Rapids: Baker, 1963 reprint), p.24.

TEXT

The texts of 1, 2, and 3 John are well-preserved, being attested in more than 80 Greek manuscripts.[1] As is typical for other New Testament writings, John's letters are included in three major groups of Greek manuscripts: Alexandrian, Byzantine and Mixed. The Latin versions contain a number of readings not attested in the Greek, frequently showing a tendency to add interpretive and explanatory glosses to the underlying Greek text.[2]

There are a number of passages where our modern critical texts differ from the Textus Receptus,[3] so that there is a corresponding difference between the NASB and KJV. Of these and for various reasons, a half-dozen are worthy of mention.[4]

1 John 1:4 contains the problem of whether "our joy" (NASB) or "your joy" (KJV) was what John wrote. The textual evidence is almost equally divided. USB gives "our" a "C" rating, which indicates a considerable degree of doubt whether "our" is the correct reading. That the writing of this letter may complete the writer's joy seems the more difficult reading which copyists might have attempted to resolve. The "your" may also reflect the influence of John 15:11 on copyists.

1 John 2:20 in the KJV reads "Ye know all things (*panta*)." That reading has the support of A,C, and the majority of Greek manuscripts. However, Sinaiticus and Vaticanus read "You all (*pantes*) know." UBS adopts *pantes* and gives it a "D" rating, indicating a high degree of doubt concerning the reading selected for the text. This textual variant makes a true difference in our understanding of the letter. The textual evidence itself is indecisive, so the issue must be determined on the basis of the sense of the context. Does the author intend to affirm as sufficient the knowledge the readers have, which would mark a flat rejection of Gnosticism's claims to have privy access to a knowledge the readers do not? Or does the author intend to declare that as a result of an anointing they need no further knowledge, such as the Gnostics offer? The latter seems more likely.

1 John 2:23 in the KJV has the second half of the verse printed in italics ("He that

---

[1] The text of the Johannine letters is well preserved, though the sheer number of manuscripts available is less than for other parts of the New Testament. When we recall that but two or three manuscripts of some ancient literary works are all that are still extant, and yet scholars are satisfied that from them they can reproduce a copy very similar to the original, the fact that more than four-score manuscripts of John's epistles are available helps give us confidence we have what John wrote. Westcott (*op. cit.*, p.xvii-ff) lists the Manuscripts and Versions (as of the close of the 19th century) that have 1 John.

[2] See Brooke, *op. cit.*, p. 197-223. It has been argued both that this fact renders the Latin witness of little value, and that the Latin witness hints at the existence of another Greek text which has not survived.

[3] *Word Biblical Commentary* has useful notes explaining the variations within the manuscripts at the beginning of each section of commentary.

[4] In the comments offered later for the verses, a decision is made which variant reading to accept, and an explanation is given concerning the resulting meaning.

acknowledgeth [confesses] the Son hath the Father also"). For some reason, that half verse was omitted from the Greek manuscripts on which this version was based. The translators followed the example of Stephanus, who on the sole authority of the Vulgate, had inserted the missing words into his edition of the Greek text. Not long after 1611, the reading was confirmed by Codex A. Soon, other manuscripts (Aleph,B,C,P) corroborated the reading, so the phrase is included without italics in the NASB.

1 John 3:14 in the modern critical Greek text has no object for the verb "love" in the phrase "He who does not love abides in death." In some manuscripts it does have an object (either "the brother" or "his brother"), and the KJV reads "his brother." The importance of this variation has to do with the author's concept of the community's love. UBS gives the reading without the object a "C" rating. Many prefer the shorter reading and argue that there was a tendency for copyists to add direct objects to verbs.

1 John 4:19 in the modern critical Greek text reads *agapōmen* ("we love" or "let us love" are possible translations) with no object for the verb "love." Some manuscripts read "we love God" and some read "we love Him." The KJV follows the majority text in reading "We love Him, because He first loved us." The critical text is given a "B" rating, indicating some degree of doubt concerning the true reading.

1 John 5:6-8 contains two significant variants. At verse 6, we find different forms. In some manuscripts "spirit" is substituted for "blood" after "this is the One who came by water and." In others "and spirit" is added after "by water and blood." In still others, we read "by spirit and blood." Perhaps the introduction of "spirit" was an effort to imitate John 3:5. The other variant concerns the three "heavenly witnesses" found in verse 7 in some Bibles, including the KJV and Douay.[5] There is not the slightest doubt that the words about the 3 heavenly witnesses in 1 John 5:7 are an interpolation. The fascinating story of how they came to be included in the Greek text that became the Textus Receptus is told in the comments at 1 John 5:7. The words occur in the Latin, but occur in only two late Greek manuscripts, and in each case the lack of articles betrays the Latin origin of the Greek text (i.e., someone has translated the Latin back into Greek).

At 1 John 5:18, the difference of one letter in the Greek (*heauton* versus *auton*) produces a striking difference in meaning. The KJV reads "He that is begotten of God keepeth himself," a reading which in 1611 had almost unqualified manuscript support and has since acquired the additional testimony of Sinaiticus. There can be little doubt, however, that the true reading is that of Vaticanus and the first hand of Alexandrinus, "He who was born of God keeps him" (i.e., Christ keeps the Christian).

The Greek of 1 John contains a 307 word vocabulary. Beginning Greek students profit from translating it, but very soon find the theology is profound.

---

[5] In 1897, Leo XIII, acting on the advice of a committee of cardinals, declared that no Roman Catholic might deny or even call in question the authenticity of this *comma Johanneum*, as 1 John 5:7 is titled. This decision reaffirmed the long held dogma that the Latin Vulgate is the official Bible of the Roman church. However, since 1927, Roman Catholic scholars have been free to use their own judgment when making translations of the Bible, or even critical Greek texts.

OUTLINE

Discovering a recognizable outline of thought in 1 John has proven to be a challenge to commentators. Many have tried, and the ways of outlining 1 John are almost as numerous as there are commentators.[1]

Some have pronounced 1 John to be *wholly without a plan*, and to consist simply of a number of reflections, counsels, maxims and aphorisms, loosely put together, without continuity or logical connection.[2] It is affirmed that the author did not present his themes one by one, developing his message and then drawing his conclusions; and that is what makes it almost impossible to outline the letter.

Others have gone to an opposite extreme and regarded 1 John as *a systematic composition*, following a deliberate plan, with a methodical arrangement of ideas in all its parts.[3] Proponents of this view, however, have not been able to agree on the details of the plan they claim to discern. Some find two main points in the letter,[4] some three,[5] some

---

[1] A readable overview of attempts to outline 1 John can be found in Barker, "1 John," in *Expositor's Bible Commentary* (Grand Rapids: Zondervan, 1981) Vol.12, p.298-99, and in Marshall, "The Epistles of John" in *The New International Commentary on the New Testament* (Grand Rapids: Eerdmans, 1978), p.22-27.

[2] Calvin, *Argumentum Epist. 1 Joh.* Marshall (*op. cit.*, p.26) opts for the view that all we have is a list of unconnected units, "governed by an association of ideas rather than by a logical plan."

[3] I.H. Marshall ("John, Epistles of," in *International Standard Bible Encyclopedia*, 1982, Vol.2, p.1093) calls attention to a chapter by J.S. Sibinga (in *Studies in John Presented to Professor Dr. J.N. Sevenster* [1970], pp. 194-208) in which, on the basis of an analysis of numbers of syllables, it is argued that the Epistle as we have it is a carefully balanced, rhetorical construction.

[4] The typical two-point outline identifies two great connected sections plus an introduction, conclusion. Both main sections, viz. 1:5-2:28, 2:29-5:3, set forth the same subject of fellowship with God the Father and the Lord Jesus Christ – the former having as its general theme that God is light, and the latter the proposition that God is righteous (Alford). Brown (*Epistles*) and Smalley (*op. cit.*) have become contemporary champions of a two-point outline. Smalley prefers to divide the epistle between 2:29 and 3:1, while Brown begins part one at 1:5 and part two at 3:11. Brown imposed a two part structure on the epistle that imitates the two-part structure of the Fourth Gospel (cf. The Book of Signs, John 1-12 v. The Book of Glory, John 13-21). Brown divided the letter between 3:10 and 3:11, giving two roughly proportionally-sized halves for the epistle. He also finds roughly parallel introductory statements for both halves at 1:5 and 3:11.

[5] The most famous threefold division belongs to Robert Law whose 1909 commentary argued that 1 John had three parts, each part offering three "tests of life," righteousness, love, and belief. The Gnostically-inclined failed to acknowledge the importance of righteous behavior, did not love fellow Christians, and denied belief in Jesus Christ, the Son of God. Law's system, reflected in Owen Crouch/Clint Gill (*Hereby We Know*), fails when one gets to the third point (1 John 4:7-5:13); the three themes common to the first two main points do not occur in the same order. (This present commentator remembers the delight he felt as he listened to Crouch's presentation of the first two main points. That delight faded as Crouch tried to work through the last point, because it didn't fit the outline he had so confidently presented.) Proponents of a three-part outline (Westcott, Dodd, Brooke, Schnackenburg, and Haas) have difficulty identifying where to make the breaks. Breaks at 1 John 2:17 or 2:27/28/29, at 3:22/24, and at 4:1 or 4:6 or 4:12/13, plus an introduction and a conclusion, are presented and defended. Three-part proponents also cannot agree on what title to give the main points they have discovered.

four,[6] some five,[7] and some eight.

Another suggestion is that the letter is arranged according to a *topical plan*. The proposition is advanced that the best internal evidence as to any organization of thought in the mind of the author of 1 John is found in connection with the ideas about God that he advanced; (1) God is light (1:5); (2) God is life (2:5); (3) God is love (4:8). The subject discussed in connection with each idea is hortatory in nature: (1) walk in the light, (2) live God's life, (3) dwell in love.[8]

Having found the letter difficult to outline following some linear arrangement, a number of commentators have opted for what might be called a *spiral* development.[9] Characteristic of the spiral is that its thought moves forward in a circular fashion, with the same ideas constantly recurring for new consideration and further development. The problem is that in 1 John, though some ideas are picked up and developed further, the ideas do not recur in the same order as they would in a true spiral.

It should not be surprising to find that some contemporary scholars have attempted to produce a logical outline by *rearranging the verses* we find in our Bibles until an acceptable outline is achieved. The supposition is that some redactor has clumsily revised an earlier document into the form we now have, and this is the reason we have trouble discovering any outline. The belief is that we are simply correcting the redactor's mistake when we rearrange the verses so they can be outlined.

Newer attempts to find a *chiastic arrangement* (i.e., a careful literary structure) are beginning to appear. However, such attempts thus far have not been very successful.

There is a certain measure of agreement in these different attempts to discern the outline of the letter. There are main ideas and within these main ideas a certain order and succession of thoughts. The ideas are not systematically carried with neat logical connections. The writing has the freedom that is proper to a letter, the unstudied character that belongs to a series of thoughts that come to mind as one writes.

---

[6] The four divisions encompass 1:5-2:11; 2:12-28; 2:29-3:22; and 3:23-5:17. Respectively, the four parts deal with the danger of moral indifference, the love of the world, the necessity of a life of brotherly love, and faith as the foundation of the Christian life.

[7] Main divisions are affirmed to include 1:5-2:11; 2:12-27; 2:28-3:24a; 3:24b-4:21; and 5:1-21.

[8] H.L. Drumwright, Jr., "John, Epistles of" in *Zondervan Pictorial Encyclopedia of the Bible* (Grand Rapids: Zondervan, 1975), Vol. 3, p.649.

[9] Brooke and Dodd are two recent writers who have opted for a spiral pattern of thought as they have tried to analyze the letter's structure.

Perhaps one major difficulty behind many of the attempts to outline 1 John is a flawed exegesis at certain key places in the letter. Once an erroneous decision has been made on one verse or clause, it shortly compounds into a multitude of further problems and apparently disconnected thoughts, and suddenly, no outline is possible. However, various commentators have achieved a good grasp of the different sections of 1 John. We have tried to make use of such insights to propose an outline.

Working through the verses, certain ideas stand out. These ideas are used to form the framework of our outline. In the commentary that follows, as we begin each new paragraph, we'll offer a *Summary Statement* of the key ideas in that paragraph which have captured our attention.

Since John indicates his interest is "fellowship" (1:3), we have taken that as our key idea.

Preface: The Divine Provision for Fellowship. 1:1-4

I. Fellowship's Conditions. 1:5 - 2:11
    A. Conformity to a Standard. 1:5-7
    B. Consciousness of and Confession of Sin. 1:8-2:2
    C. Copying the Example of Christ. 2:3-6
    D. Compassion for Our Brothers. 2:7-11

II. Cautions About Dangers that Can Ruin Fellowship. 2:12-27
    A. John's Threefold Statement of Assurance About Their Standing with God and Christ. 2:12-14
    B. Warning Against Worldliness. 2:15-17
    C. Warning Against Antichrists. 2:18-27

III. Fellowship's Distinctive Rewards and Blessings. 2:28-3:24a
    A. Hope for the Future. 2:28-3:3
    B. The Practice of Righteousness Increases. 3:4-9
    C. Brotherly Love and Benevolence. 3:10-18
    D. Answered Prayer. 3:19-24a

IV. Fellowship's Encouragements. 3:24b-5:17
    A. The Inspiration of the Holy Spirit. 3:24b-4:6
    B. Encouragement to Love One Another Because of God's Love. 4:7-12
    C. Encouragement Because of the Apostles' Testimony. 4:13-16a
    D. Encouragement Because of Loss of Fear. 4:16b-21
    E. Encouragement Because of the Victory Won Through Faithfulness. 5:1-4
    F. Encouragement Because of God's Testimony Concerning Eternal Life. 5:5-12
    G. Encouragement Because of Opportunities to Pray for the Erring. 5:13-17

V. Fellowship's Confidences.   5:18-20
    A. The Christian is Confident of the Lord's Protection.   5:18
    B. The Christian is Confident He Belongs to God.   5:19
    C. The Christian is Confident that the Son of God Has Come.   5:20

Conclusion: Final Plea.   5:21

VALUE OF 1 JOHN

1 John raises issues of permanent interest and importance for Christian faith and practice.   Attention is drawn to these issues and emphases from time to time in footnotes, as well as in the text.   Let's introduce some of the permanent benefits of a study of 1 John.

The New Testament is Our Rule of Faith and Practice

John lays down one of the paramount criterion for distinguishing between genuine and spurious faith – that Christians are expected to conform their beliefs and practices to the apostolic teaching about Jesus Christ and given by Jesus Christ, and must preserve it, undiminished and uncorrupted.   1 John thus leads to one of the guiding principles of the Restoration Movement: to be apostolic the church must be controlled by the New Testament Scriptures.   The New Testament is our rule of faith and practice.   The reason for this appeal to the words of the apostles is readily apparent.   The apostles had an anointing.   They spoke by inspiration of the Holy Spirit.   Their message is pure, holy truth (2:27, 4:6).   Christians are to "abide in it" (2:27)!   There is an imperative need to receive the witness of God as given through Jesus and His apostles (5:9).

Deity of Jesus

We have not followed cunningly devised myths when we embrace the doctrine of the powerful coming of our Lord Jesus into the world to save sinners.   The facts about His manifestation and His ministry on earth have been empirically verified (1:1-3; 5:6-8).   It is not possible to be soft on the deity of Jesus and still be a Christian (4:15; 5:12).   Men who have heard the Gospel are expected to believe in the name of God's Son Jesus (3:23). A man cannot deny the Son and at the same time have a living relationship with God the Father (2:23).   The Neo-orthodox distinction between the "Jesus of history" and the "Christ of faith" is a flawed distinction (2:22; 5:6-8).   God sent Jesus the Christ to be the propitiation for our sins (4:10), to be the Savior of the world (4:14).   Confession of Jesus as the Son of God is a prerequisite to being in fellowship with God (4:15).

Denying all God has said about His beloved Son, opponents of Christ (anti-Christs) are going abroad up and down the land.   They are "deceivers."   They are liars when they say a man can believe in God while at the same time denying the deity of His Son Jesus.

Thoughts Concerning Fellowship

The English word "fellowship" (which to many means little more than spending time together at a potluck meal, or in a class meeting) is a word that has been robbed of its real meaning, namely, joint participation in a common cause. Jesus came into the world to make it possible for God and men to have a common ground of meeting and to share a deep and mutual relationship with each other.

One thrust that sounds over and over again in 1 John is that no fellowship with God, or with Jesus, or with Jesus' followers, is possible if the deity of Jesus is denied. No fellowship is possible if habitual loose living is involved and tolerated. Continuing fellowship with the apostles and with God is contingent on beliefs and actions in harmony with the original apostolic message (1:3,4).

What we read in 1 John about fellowship is in perfect harmony with what we read in Acts 15 about fellowship. In that chapter, the "right hand of fellowship" is extended to brethren who are in doctrinal agreement about who is eligible to be saved – Gentiles as well as Jews – without demanding Pharisaic legalism of the new converts. In 1 John fellowship does not require the man-made Gnostic rules. In both cases, man-made rules are what destroy any possibility of fellowship.

2 Corinthians 6:14ff asks "what portion hath a believer with an unbeliever?" (ASV) "What harmony is there be between Christ and Belial?" (NIV) What does a believer have in common with an unbeliever?" (Goodspeed) "What fellowship has light with darkness?" No idolatry can be permitted if fellowship is to continue. To be in fellowship with each other, both parties must be "walking in the light" (1:7).

Fellowship with God and Christ is exclusive. It excludes all except those who have been begotten of God and who are committed to obedience to His Son's commands and example. It excludes all except those who confess Jesus as the Christ, the incarnate Son of God, and who depend on Him for forgiveness and for overcoming the evil one. It excluded the false teachers about whom John warns, and those who might become their followers. This is why John provides tests by which false teachers can be identified, and by which faithful followers of Christ can be identified. Those who actually are the children of God are the ones who may continue to enjoy fellowship.

Walking in the Steps of the Savior

Another note struck over and over again in 1 John is the imperative of habitually keeping His commandments (2:3; 3:24; 5:2). Righteousness is something to be continually practiced (3:7). Christians are to practice the truth, and habitually walk in the light (1:7), rather than habitually walking in darkness (1:6).[1] Christians are to walk as Jesus walked (2:6). They are to stop sinning (2:1). They are to love their brothers (3:10ff), and they have an obligation to lay down their lives for their brothers (3:16). Anticipation of the return of Jesus, and of the new bodies we shall receive, and of the final judgment, and of the unhampered access the redeemed will have to the Father, should lead Christians to constantly be purifying themselves (3:3).

Redaction Criticism is a Flawed Method

Redaction Criticism's major premise of three levels of material in our New Testament[2] books is totally out of harmony with 1:3. Writing nearly half a century after Calvary, John says the message he writes is the same message which the apostles have been "continually proclaiming." There has been a single, unified message from the apostles since day one ("what was from the beginning ... we proclaim unto you"). "Let that abide in you which you heard from the beginning" is John's plea (2:24).

It is noteworthy that Redaction Critics have little to offer in the way of permanent value to the epistle. Instead, we find that commentators who have adopted this flawed method are critical and dismissive of the methods and doctrines set forth in 1 John as being acceptable today.[3] Indeed!

Pluralism

The idea, that there were numerous Christian "faiths" all jockeying and competing for acceptance in the 1st century, with our New Testament books being written by the eventual winner, is hardly consistent with the thrust of 1 John or Jude 3 (which speaks of "the faith," not many faiths, being delivered to the saints).

---

[1] Care must be exercised here lest when we read about "the light" we immediately think of our own religious party's interpretation of the New Covenant Scriptures as being "the light." To "walk in the light," as John describes it, is hardly the same as living up to the man-made religious rules that distinguish one contemporary denominational party from another. W. Carl Ketcherside was on the right track when he lamented about the dozens of factions among the brethren with whom he identified himself. "Each [segment] thinks that it alone is in the light and all of the others are in darkness. Since 'fellowship with one another' is conditioned upon 'walking in the light,' and since the light is the legalistic code of the faction [that is the party's special emphasis], fellowship is regarded as ordained of God to be limited to fellow-partisans." ("The Fallacy of Orthodoxy," quoted by Clint Gill, *Hereby We Know* [Joplin, MO: College Press, 1966], p.181.)

[2] See the explanation of Redaction Criticism given above in these Introductory Notes, pages 29-34.

[3] "The defense and polemical stance of the authors of 1,2,3 John do not exemplify the best response to diversity – indeed, one would hope that there are more creative possibilities" wrote Robert Kysar (*op. cit.,* p. 911). Is Kysar affirming the apostle John (or whomever he believes wrote the letters) was led to make a mistake as he tried to deal with the arising crisis among his readers?

Instead of studying 1 John in order to learn the composition history behind the writing, or to understand the emerging church at the end of the 1st century,[4] as many contemporary authors at content to do, this commentator insists 1 John should be studied to hear the message embodied in the faith once for all delivered to the saints (Jude 3).

How to Deal with Groups Leaving Church

According to 1 John 2:19, a large number of folk who used to frequent the public assembly of the church had quit attending. Whatever the issue that causes folk to leave (and in 1 John it was not a praiseworthy issue, but rank unbelief in Jesus the Christ), such times are traumatic for those who continue to attend, and an array of emotions arise. Families can become divided. Folk who have been faithful for years can get discouraged and begin to drop out. At such times, the true believers need assurance they are walking in the truth. They need simple tests they can apply every day, lest they too become deceived. They need instructions concerning their prayer life – yes, pray for those sinning not unto death, but not necessarily for those sinning unto death (5:16). Brethren who are beginning to waver need tender love and affection ("brotherly love"), and some special attention.

New Age Gnostic Ideas Counteracted

The New Age Movement's revival of Gnostic ideas is just as wrong-headed as was Gnosis in the 1st century. Altered states of consciousness, messages from spirits, and visions as the source of personal religious views are just as false now as they were then. That God is an impersonal force is just as wrong now as it was then. That Eastern Religions have anything of eternal value to contribute to men's relationship with God is just as devilish now as it was then. That we all can become "Christs" simply by tapping into a reservoir of secret knowledge, available only to the privileged elite, is just as arrogant now as it was then. That the death of Jesus on Calvary had nothing to do with man's redemption from sin is a soul-damning falsehood now just as it was then.

The revived interest in the Gnostic movement – as though its writings were of equal value with Apostolic writings – is a wrong notion. 1 John will help us understand such documents as the *Gospel of Thomas* and the *Gospel of Judas*. The idea that the *Gospel of Thomas* is a valid "Fifth Gospel" is an abominable affirmation. That the *Gospel of Judas* is as legitimate a presentation of what happened when Judas betrayed Jesus as one finds in the differing account in the canonical Gospels, is blasphemy.

---

[4] The idea that 1 John tells us 'the church found it necessary to begin to draw clear lines between what constituted an authentic Christian faith and what needed to be deemed an aberration of that faith,' is a misleading way to word it. So is the sentence that says 'The church thought it important to develop an orthodoxy in the light of which claims of truth could be evaluated.' The "church" did this? Who is the Lord? Has He said anything? Is not John simply delivering a message from the Lord when he directs the church to "test the spirits"?

A Firm but Loving Way to Counteract Religious Error

1 John teaches the followers of Jesus to be discriminating in what they believe. They are to "test the spirits" (4:1ff), for there are such a things as "false prophets" in the world. Christians are expected to compare teachings to the Word of God (the message delivered by the apostles) with religious ideas currently being taught. Check the spirits, because not every spirit is of God.

From John we learn to be firm but loving in our handling of religious error. His example offers some guidelines for us. He doesn't name names, but he does name erroneous beliefs and practices. 'He who says .... is in error, because ...' is the way he words it. Over and over again, he drives home what is the correct belief and what is the correct practice.

How to Know We Are Saved

Numerous times, using *ginōskō* (i.e., a knowledge that comes by experience), John says "Hereby we know" (KJV). Anyone who has been begotten of God can apply these tests to his or her own life, and "know by experience" whether or not he or she is saved. How comforting! How encouraging!

In anticipation of these matters of permanent value, we turn to comments on the text John wrote, listening for the Word of God.

THE FIRST EPISTLE OF JOHN[1]

PREFACE: THE DIVINE PROVISION FOR FELLOWSHIP. 1:1-4

Summary: The fellowship of the churches to whom John is writing was threatened by a new brand of religious teaching, a teaching generally acknowledged to be closely related to what later came to be called "Gnosticism." Because he wants the churches' fellowship to continue, John writes this succinct letter to guide the readers' thinking and behavior. He begins (verses 1-2) by calling attention to how God's Son, Jesus Christ, has made such fellowship possible. He became incarnate; He revealed the Father; He commissioned messengers to proclaim the Good News. We might summarize these two verses under the title "The Person." Verses 3-4 could be titled "The Purpose," for they tell the reason why John is writing. He is eager that their fellowship continue. Fellowship is contingent on a whole-hearted embracing of the message just as Jesus and the apostles taught it.

It is helpful to have John's Gospel in mind as one reads 1 John, for many of the expressions in the epistle are explained by their counterparts in the Gospel. Stott calls attention to the similarity between the Preface of 1 John and the Prologue of the Gospel.

> Both open with a reference to the beginning; both speak of the Logos in connection with the Father and with life; both declare that the Eternal entered history; both add that the divine manifestation was seen by men; both mention testimony resulting from what men saw; both speak of Christ as the Father's Son; both describe the result of responding to Christ in terms of a new relationship with God.[2]

1:1 -- *What was from the beginning, what we have heard, what we have seen with our eyes, what we beheld and our hands handled, concerning the Word of Life –*

What – Verses 1-4 form a single, long, involved sentence in the Greek.[3] There are

---

[1] See Introductory Studies concerning how titles came to be added to the Bible books.

[2] John R.W. Stott, The Epistles of John in The Tyndale New Testament Commentaries (Grand Rapids: Eerdmans, 1964), p.66,67.

[3] Modern translations sometimes break the one sentence in the original into two or three shorter sentences. They do so by repeating the main verb so each of the new, shorter sentences is a complete thought.

places where rules of syntax are broken, and one place where the syntax is ambiguous.[4] By common usage we have grown accustomed to expecting a certain normal word order in sentences – namely, subject, verb, and object.[5]   We do not have to read very far in 1 John to see that such is not what we have here.   We do not come to the main verb until we read "we proclaim to you" in verse 3.   The content of what was proclaimed is expressed by the four relative clauses with which verse 1 begins.   John begins this long sentence by writing four relative clauses, each beginning with the neuter pronoun *ho* ("what" or "that which").   Since he is talking about Jesus (as the context makes plain), we might have expected the masculine pronoun, *hos*, "He who."   Perhaps John employed the neuter here in verse 1 just as he does in verse 3 because he wanted to emphasize the content of what is proclaimed.   Perhaps John employed the neuter[6] ("that which ... which" or "what") because it was "the most comprehensive expression to cover the attributes, words and works"[7] of the incarnate life of the Son of God.   We presume John wrote this way deliberately, to cause us to pause and contemplate what he writes.   It is difficult in translation and exposition to express all the ideas John packs into this sentence, for while 1 John is simple Greek, it is profound theology and Christology.

Was from the beginning – As they read this phrase in 1 John, many readers familiar with their Bibles naturally recall both Genesis 1:1 and John 1:1, which point to the time of Creation.   Others will recall that the same expression was used to denote the beginning of Jesus' earthly life and ministry.[8]   So the commentaries debate what John's emphasis here likely is.   Dodd interprets it as the beginning of the gospel.[9]   If so, John is declaring that

---

[4] The view that has generally come to be adopted is that the sentence begins in verse 1, only to be broken off by a parenthetical verse 2 inserted to explain verse 1.   The sentence is resumed again in verse 3 (some words being repeated from verse 1 for the sake of perspicuity) and finally the broken sentence is completed in verse 4.

[5] Because in Greek the function of words (subject or object or verb) is determined by spelling, not word order (as it is in English), Greek allows its users to emphasize certain ideas by putting them first or last in sentences.   The spelling of the Greek word tells you it is the subject, verb, or object, wherever it occurs in the sentence.

[6] John frequently uses the neuter to express a collective whole or a comprehensive idea.   See John 1:11, 4:22, 6:37, 17:2.   Grammar here is not straightforward.   "What" is a neuter relative pronoun.   The antecedent it refers to ("Word [of Life]") is masculine in gender.   Does this suggest that there are things about the "Word" that cannot be clearly described in human language?

[7] Alfred Plummer, *Commentary on the Epistles of St. John* in the Cambridge Greek Testament for Schools and Colleges (Cambridge: Cambridge University Press, 1894), p.72. Plummer also has the exposition of the epistles of John in the *Pulpit Commentary*.

[8] See John 6:64 and 16:4.   Perhaps at 1 John 2:7 the expression speaks of the beginning of the preaching of the gospel.   Usually when the phrase refers to the beginning of the gospel preaching, we are told in the context that such is the meaning (cp. 1 John 2:24, 3:11).

[9] C.H. Dodd, *Commentary on the Johannine Epistles* in the Moffatt New Testament Commentary (London: Hodder & Stoughton, 1946), p.5. Calling attention to the different prepositions used, some writers think "from the beginning" in 1 John 1:1 has a different meaning than did "in the beginning" of John 1:1.

what he now writes in this letter is no innovation or afterthought or change from what was preached as gospel from day one of this dispensation. Implied is the idea that any Gnostic idea that recently had been embraced is a new and unusual form of doctrine. But in light of what John writes in verse 2, it is difficult to limit "beginning" to the beginning of the gospel. Brooke has asserted that "the parallels in Genesis and the prologue of the Gospel [of John] exclude the possibility of a reference *merely* to the beginning of the Christian dispensation."[10] Accordingly, by using the imperfect tense verb "was"[11] (the tense implying continuous action in the past), John declares that the Son of God was eternally pre-existent, not an aeon or emanation of recent origin such as the Gnostics claimed. Not only was He eternally pre-existent, He has existed and been active ever since. John is claiming that his and the other apostles' public explanation about Jesus is something that was true of Jesus even before the work of creation (Genesis 1:1) began. This assertion is anti-Gnostic. If Jesus eternally existed before creation ever began, He cannot be an aeon like the Gnostics attempt to explain Him. Furthermore, if Jesus was "from the beginning," then the doctrine like that which Cerinthus taught, that the divine Christ came on Jesus at His baptism and left before His crucifixion, is patently wrong!

What we have heard – In the first four verses, "we" must refer to the apostles of Christ, of whom John was the last surviving representative.[12] The participles (seen, heard, handled) the writer uses show he claims to be one of a group of persons who were personal eyewitnesses of Jesus' earthly ministry.[13] One of the stated qualifications to be an apostle

---

[10] A.E. Brooke, *Commentary on the Johannine Epistles* in the International Critical Commentary (Edinburg: T & T Clarke, 1912), p.2. The same Greek phrase is used in the LXX for "Art Thou not *from everlasting,* O Lord my God? (Habakkuk 1:12). The expression is equivalent to "from all eternity."

[11] The imperfect tense verb is *hēn*, not *egeneto* (which would mean "came into existence" or "was made"). *Hēn* has the connotation of "being" or "existence," and shows that before His manifestation, Jesus always existed with the Father. The difference between "to be" (*hēn*) and "come to be" or "become" (*egeneto*) which is used at 1 John 2:18, must be carefully noted. "Christ was from all eternity; antichrists have arisen, have come into existence in time." (Plummer, *ibid.*)

[12] This explanation of "we" in the first four verses should not be interpreted to mean that every time we find the word "we" in the rest of the epistle, the reference is to the apostles, rather than to Christians in general. See 4:13,14 where the context indicates the reference is broader than just the apostles. Though this writing is not signed, the identity of the writer would have been known to the readers.

[13] Lightfoot's suggestion that John here associates himself with the elders of Ephesus, whom he believes were the men who certified the authenticity of the Fourth Gospel (John 21:24), is doubtful because it treats the claims to be an "eyewitness" too loosely. Brooke (*op. cit.*, p.3) replies to the passages sometimes quoted from Tacitus (*Agricola*) and Augustine (Ep.88.8) in an attempt to explain the "we" as including the writer and the readers. This whole topic is of interest to those scholars who insist that, as the New Testament books were produced, redaction has occurred, and our Bible books represent the beliefs, not of the first-generation eyewitnesses, but of a third generation of followers. By the third genera- tion, it would not be possible to claim all were personal witnesses of the actual earthly ministry of Jesus. So attempts must be made to explain that "eyewitness" should not be taken literally. One writer suggests the "we" is a pseudonymous device by which the actual writer claims to have personally known John who was an eyewitness. One writer talks of the church's common experience of salvation in Jesus as the object of their testimony. Another supposes the third generation could speak of themselves as sharing an experience only the first generation actually had. (Like the fan watching the game says "We won!" when he only was a spectator, not an actual participant. What is meant is "the team I support won.") Or every Jew of later generations, while observing Passover, regarded themselves as if personally involved in the

is that one must have witnessed the earthly ministry of Jesus and been present for at least one of His post-resurrection appearances (Acts 1:22). This eyewitness is apparently writing to persons who have not themselves been eyewitnesses to Jesus' earthly ministry (see "to you" in verses 2 and 3). "Heard" reminds us of the words of Jesus, with special reference to His discourses as recorded in Matthew, Luke, and John. Its place, first in the sentence, may show that John regarded the *words* of Christ with special reverence. It makes us feel how the apostle would have shrunk from inventing language for Jesus, and putting words and speeches into His mouth (like the Gnostics did, e.g., the "sayings" in the *Gospel of Thomas*). This verb is in the perfect tense in the Greek, signifying past completed action with present continuing results. What John and the other apostles "heard" Jesus speak many times as they traveled with Him was still ringing in their ears. What they "heard" remains with them, vividly, so that they can make it known to others who have not themselves had the same opportunities and privileges.[14] John was with the Savior through the whole of His earthly ministry, and he has recorded more of what the Savior said than any of the other Gospel writers.

What we have seen with our eyes – John does not use "see" (*horaō*) in a figurative sense. Rather, it is the expression of a literal, historic fact. "With our eyes" (not other men's eyes) emphasizes a personal experience the writer and other apostles experienced. With their physical eyes (not the eyes of their minds, or just in their imagination) they saw Him. This verb, too, is in the perfect tense. The impression made by what John saw as he looked at Jesus the Son of God is still vivid in his mind.

What we beheld – The verb *theaomai* ("beheld") denotes steady contemplation, attentive viewing, deliberate and intentional looking in order to investigate.[15] It is an aorist tense verb, and may point to a specific occasion, such as Jesus' transfiguration.[16] John refers to

---

Exodus from Egypt (Amos 2:10ff; Joshua 24:7, etc.) None of these watered-down presentations of subjective faith would ever have answered the equally subjective arguments of the Gnostic heretics. Since neither would be based on historical facts and evidence, both would be arguing from the same epistemo-logical basis. There is no way to harmonize Redaction criticism's ideas with what John here writes! If we accept John's witness, Redaction Criticism's conclusions and methods must be abandoned.

[14] If all we had were the verb "heard," Socinus might have been right to interpret the passage as referring only to *doctrine*, as he and his followers did, as they attempted to deny the deity of Jesus and the doctrine of the trinity. See also footnote 21 for additional comments on the teaching of Socinus.

[15] The verb *theaomai* is applied by the angel to those who were witnessing Jesus' ascension into heaven (Acts 1:11, "watched").

[16] "The transfiguration is not mentioned in John's Gospel. Perhaps it is pointed to here and in John 1:14. It is also referred to by another of the three who witnessed it, in a tone which implies that it was a well-known part of Christian teaching and preaching (2 Peter 1:16-18)." W. Alexander, *The First Epistle General of John* in the Bible Commentary edited by F. C. Cook (New York: Charles Scribners, 1904), p.303.

"seeing" in some form[17] four times in the first three verses. This is what qualifies John and the apostles to be witnesses. They can tell what they saw!

And our hands handled – "Handled" (*psēlaphaō*), the climax of these four relative clauses in verse 1, means more than to "touch." It has the idea of "examine closely," to "handle with a view to investigation."[18] That John and the others used their "hands" to examine Jesus indicates that "handling" was not just a mental process, and also that He was not, like the Gnostics claimed, just a phantom or apparition. "And [what] our hands have handled" likely has an anti-Docetic emphasis. No Docetic Christ could have been "handled," touched, examined since the words require something real and tangible to touch. "Touching" the historical Jesus is something one can only have done personally; there is no way this language can be explained as somehow having second-hand knowledge of the Christian message. The writer claims to be a personal eyewitness who "handled" the human body in which Jesus lived.[19] The Jesus the apostles proclaimed was both eternal ("from the beginning") and historical and perfectly human (he was heard, seen, and touched by the apostles). "Heard, seen, beheld, handled" – by putting these relative clauses first, John emphasizes the idea that certain people can testify concerning the "Word of Life" precisely because they had personal experience of the Son of God, Jesus Christ. Their testimony concerning Him was based on verifiable historical facts, not on speculations or fabricated fables as was the testimony of the Gnostics.[20]

Concerning the Word of Life – Each of the four relative clauses with which verse 1 began say something important about *peri* ("concerning") the "Word of Life."[21] *Peri* takes the

---

[17] John uses two different verbs for "sight." *Horaō* three times, *theaomai* once. "If *blepō* is to 'look' and *horaō* is to 'see,' *theaomai* is to 'behold' intelligently, so as to grasp the meaning and significance of that which comes within our vision." (Brooke, *op. cit.*, p.4) The same verb *theaomai* is used at John 1:14, "the Word became flesh and dwelt among us, and we beheld His glory."

[18] The word is used in the LXX of blind Isaac "feeling" the hands of Jacob (Genesis 27:22). It is used (Luke 24:39) when Jesus invites Thomas to "handle Me [with a view to investigation] and see ...."

[19] "The writer here expresses himself as a member of the group of eyewitnesses of the ministry of Jesus, and his claim must be a genuine one; had it been false, his readers would have known not to believe him, and his message would have carried no force." I.H. Marshall, *The Epistles of John* in the New International Commentary on the New Testament (Grand Rapids: Eerdmans, 1978), p.107.

[20] Tertullian, as he wrestled with the Gnostics, was very fond of insisting on the fact the Lord was "handled" (*Adv. Parax.* xv; *De Anima* xvii; *De Pat.* iii; cp. *Ad Uxorem* iv). See also Ignatius (*Smyrn.* lii).

[21] "Word" is capitalized in the NASB because the translators thought John was referring to Jesus, the personal Logos, rather than to a "word," i.e., "doctrine." We agree. C. Haas, in *A Translator's Handbook on the Letters of John* (New York: United Bible Societies, 1972, p.29), gives 3 reasons why we should take the term as a reference to Jesus rather than to the gospel: (1) The verses under discussion have similarities with John 1:1 and 1:4. (2) One expects the direct object of "to touch" to be a reference to a person or a thing, not to an event-word like "message." (3) If "word" had been used in the sense of "message" one would expect it to be construed as the direct object of the verb "to proclaim" and not with the preposition rendered "concerning." Alexander (p.422) words it another way: If John is writing about something other than Jesus Himself, then peculiar meanings must be assigned to most of the expressions John uses in his preface. (It should be noted that Socinus and the Unitarians insist the reference is not to

genitive case, and both "Word" and "life" are in the genitive case in the Greek. Scholars struggle to explain the import of this double genitive. We find a double genitive in John 2:21 ("the temple which is his body") and in John 11:13 ("that taking of rest which is sleep"). On that analogy, we should render this clause "concerning the Word which is also the Life." It is the pre-existent and incarnate Jesus who is here called "Word" (*logos*), just as He was called "Word" in John 1:1. Everything said about the *logos* at John 1:1 would be true here. He was with God and He was God! He created all things. The *logos* became flesh and we beheld His glory, glory as of the only begotten of the Father (John 1:14). No man has seen God at any time, but the only begotten God (Jesus), who is now in the bosom of the Father (since His return to Heaven), has explained Him (John 1:18). It is the pre-existent and incarnate Jesus who is also called "Life" (*zōē*).[22] Everything that is said about Jesus creating life and being the life of man in John 1:3,4 would be in John's mind here. Of the two terms used for Jesus in this clause, "Life" is the more important, as is shown by verse 2, and by the fact that "life" is one of the main topics of this letter (see 2:25; 3:14; 5:11,12,20), whereas "Word" is not used again.[23]

1:2 -- *And the life was manifested, and we have seen and bear witness and proclaim to you the eternal life, which was with the Father and was manifested to us --*

And the life was manifested – Plummer thinks the "and" is John's characteristic use of the simple conjunction. Note the dashes at the end of verse 1 and verse 2 in the NASB. Those dashes tell us that verse 2 is a sort of parenthetical explanation of how it came to be that John and the apostles could personally see, hear, and examine the pre-existent "Word of life." "The life" picks up one of the words used in verse 1 to refer to Jesus. "The life" is the Lord Himself who is the Life (John 14:6). "Manifest" (*phaneroō*) is one of John's

---

Jesus, but to the "message concerning life" which Jesus and His apostles preached. Adopting this position, they can then hold their low view of Christ, for these verses would now say nothing about His pre-existence or deity or eternal Being. What Gnostic would not have welcomed such a way of explaining 1 John 1:1-3? It is obvious that such a denial of the eternality and deity of Jesus is a wrong-headed approach to explaining what John has here written.)

[22] The term *zōē* ("life") conveys a different idea than does *psuchē*, the breath of life, the personal life, the soul that animates the body. *Bios* (1 John 2:16) is another word for "life," and it denotes life's *manifestations*, the manner of life, the basic essentials what sustain everyday physical life (livelihood, property). In the Johannine literature, *zōē* is something which man does not possess by nature, but which God gives to those who believe in Christ (John 3:16). It is not an abstraction, but a reality, and is equated with Christ Himself (1 John 1:2, John 11:25, 14:6, Colossians 3:4).

[23] Just why John chose to use "Logos" and "Logos of life" in the introduction to his writings, we do not know. Perhaps "Logos of life" was an expression used by the Gnostics, though there is no corroboration of this suggestion in the Gnostic literature extant. Perhaps John intends the unexpected expression to trigger our theological meditation on exactly Who Jesus is. If we get our Christology right, we will not be susceptible to Gnostic influences.

favorite words, found frequently in the Gospel and this epistle, and twice in Revelation.[24] The verb is used of Jesus' incarnation (1 John 3:5; John 1:31), of Jesus' post-resurrection appearances (John 21.1,14), and of His "appearance" at His coming Parousia (1 John 2:28; Colossians 3:4; 1 Peter 5:4). In the New Testament *ephanerōthē* is used of something someone else does for the observer's benefit. "Revealed, made manifest, made visible" is not a subjective sensation; it is something done by someone else outside the observer which the observer then is able to see and experience. John used the aorist tense of the verb "manifested," indicating that Jesus' earthly ministry, His appearance in history, is over when John writes.[25]

And we have seen – This is a succinct way of summarizing all that was said in verse 1. Because Jesus was made visible, because He came in the flesh (1 John 4:2), one result was that John and the other apostles could personally experience all they have claimed they did (John 1:14).

And bear witness and proclaim to you – John uses two present tense verbs to describe what the apostles went about doing after they had "seen," after they had spent three intimate and instructive years with the incarnate Jesus. One thing they did was to "bear witness," a courtroom word meaning to testify or affirm something one has seen or heard or experienced.[26] Peter made a similar claim for the apostles when he spoke, "This Jesus did God raise up, whereof we are all witnesses" (Acts 2:32 ASV). A true witness does not speak of what he or she has gathered second-hand from others, but of what he or she has personally seen and heard.[27] "Proclaim" (*apaggellō*) is an authoritative presentation because one was commissioned to tell it. Jesus Himself gave the Great Commission to those who had personally traveled with Him during His earthly ministry. John here affirms the apostles did as they were commanded to do. They went everywhere preaching the Good News concerning the "Word who is life." Perhaps this claim by John to possess the necessary credentials to tell about Jesus exactly as it is includes a sideways glance at the uncredentialled Gnostics. The "you" to whom the apostles witnessed and proclaimed were readers and hearers who had not seen Jesus in the flesh as John and the apostles had seen Him.

The eternal life   –   This clause (*tēn zōēn tēn aiōnion*, where both terms have an article)

---

[24] "Words and phrases which connect the Epistle with the Gospel, and either of these with the Apocalypse, should be carefully noted." Plummer, *op. cit.*, p.74.

[25] Compare the language (past tense verbs used) and thought in 1 Timothy 3:16.

[26] "Bear witness" (*martureō*) is another of John's favorite words. It occurs frequently in the Gospel, this epistle, and in Revelation.

[27] See the Introductory Studies, where we called attention to the bearing of this term ("bear witness") on the authorship of 1 John.

expresses another truth about Jesus ("the life") who became incarnate.[28]   He is an "eternal" Being.[29]   Two notions are emphasized: He is "life" and He is "eternal."   Standing after the noun, the adjective "eternal" has the strongest emphasis of which Greek is capable.   In popular language "eternal" is used to denote duration.   Actually, it would be better to think of *aiōnion* as denoting a spiritual quality of life, a quality superior to anything in the present age.   In the strongest way he can word it, John says that Jesus was no Gnostic emanation greatly inferior to the "spiritual" God who began the series of emanations.   He Himself had a "spiritual quality of life."

Which was with the Father – The relative "which" is not the simple relative (*hē*), but the "qualitative" relative (*hētis*).[30]   It was One who possessed the spiritual *quality* just highlighted Who was "with the Father."   "Was with the Father" is exactly parallel to "was with God" at John 1:1.[31]   Jesus is the One who taught us to think of God as being like a father.   When He prayed, He called God "Father" (Matthew 6:9; Mark 14:36).   He spoke of Him as "My Father" (Luke 2:49).[32]   We suppose this is one of the wonderful truths John "heard" from Jesus' own lips (verse 1).   The use of this descriptive expression describing what God is like may well be a reminder to John's readers that the Gnostic presentation of God was in error.

And was manifested to us – This is the second time in this verse that this verb has been used.   No man could have seen the One who was eternally with the Father unless that One had taken the initiative deliberately to make Himself visible to men's eyes.   Man can know about God only what God has been pleased to reveal about Himself.[33]

---

[28] It wasn't "eternal life" (an abstract idea) that John and the apostles saw, but the eternal Christ who is life that John saw and witnessed.

[29] "Eternal" here is an attribute of Christ.   It is also an attribute of God the Father (Romans 16:26; Isaiah 26:4 and 40:28 in LXX).

[30] English doesn't have a word to adequately translate the qualitative relative.   "Which is of such a quality" would catch the idea.   (The distinction between *hos* and *hostis*, which disappears altogether in late Greek, can still, as a rule, be traced in the New Testament.)

[31] "Was" (as in verse 1) indicates continuous action in the past.   The eternal pre-existence of the "Life" who is Jesus again is here affirmed and is another anti-Gnostic thrust.   "With" translates *pros*, which means "face to face with" or "at home with."   (Cp. its use in 1 Corinthians 16:7; 1 Thessalonians 3:4; and Philemon 13.)   It is not just fellowship (*meta*) with God, or accompanying (*sun*) God wherever He goes, but relationship (*pros*, "face to face") with Him.   There is a distinction of persons in the eternal Godhead, and there is a closeness between the persons in the Godhead.

[32] Westcott, *op. cit.*, p.27ff, has a long and excellent "additional note" on "the Fatherhood of God."

[33] The stress on Jesus being historically "manifest" is directed against the Gnostics who were troubling the churches to whom John writes.   The Gnostics flatly denied about Jesus what John powerfully affirms. Jesus was not a created being, but eternally pre-existent with God.   The God whom He was with is the "Supreme Being" the Gnostics talked about; John allows no distinction between the Eternal and the Jehovah of the Old Testament whom Gnostics said was a lesser being.   The eternally pre-existent Jesus

*1:3 -- **What we have seen and heard we proclaim to you also, that you also may have fellowship with us; and indeed our fellowship is with the Father, and with His Son Jesus Christ.***

What we have seen and heard we proclaim to you also – The parenthetical explanation of verse 2 has been completed, and now the sentence begun in verse 1 is resumed. To show the thought of verse 1 is being resumed, two verbs from verse 1 are repeated, but in reverse order.[34] Using the verbs "seen and heard," John again claims to have been a personal observer of what was "manifested." Repeating the verb "proclaim" (the same verb used in verse 2), John affirms that his presentation is the authoritative one, the one divinely commissioned by the Lord Himself. "Proclaim" is a present tense verb, denoting continuing action in the present: We are proclaiming it right now! What he writes about Jesus is no new message, but a continuation of what apostles have always preached and written.[35] "You also" expresses the idea that what John is telling his present readers is the exact same message he regularly shares with others.[36] Whether "you also" implies that John is here addressing a circle of readers (perhaps in Asia Minor), different from those among whom he began his Apostolic work (i.e., in the Holy Land), is debated by scholars.[37]

That you also may have fellowship with us – With a *hina* ("that") clause, John explains the purpose why he continues to proclaim what he has seen and heard. It is so that mutual fellowship may continue. "May have," a present tense subjunctive, means "continue to have."[38] Verse 3 is not giving the conditions for entry into fellowship; rather, it prescribes

---

is the very One who, in the incarnation, became perfectly human. It is impossible to distinguish between Jesus and the Christ. Neo-orthodox theologians, with their distinction between the Jesus of history and the Christ of faith need to hear what John here says! The New Age mystic who tends to become preoccupied with his subjective religious experience, supposing he too can be a "christ", needs a reminder about the danger of neglecting God's objective self-revelation in Jesus Christ.

[34] Whether the reverse order was deliberate, intended to convey some slight change of meaning, or simply a matter of style, is difficult to determine. In fact, scholars have struggled to explain the minute differences that characterize not only this epistle but the Johannine writings in general.

[35] Some writers (e.g., Plummer, Barnes, and Alexander) think verse 3 is a reference to John's Gospel, the ideas of which are summarized in verses 1-3 and which John assumes the readers have in hand. These writers then think verse 4 is a reference to this present letter.

[36] How many times John wrote "also" (*kai*) in this sentence is debated. Some manuscripts (including Sinaiticus) have *kai* before "proclaim" – "we also proclaim to you." Most omit the *kai* before "proclaim." Some manuscripts read *kai humin* ("you also"); others omit the *kai* before *humin*. Some manuscripts read *hina kai* ("in order that you also"); others read *hina* and omit the *kai*. Of course, the presence or absence of the *kai* makes a difference in the explanations offered for the different phrases. Our comments follow the Greek text translated in the NASB.

[37] Theodore Zahn, *Introduction to the New Testament* (Grand Rapids: Kregel, 1953), Vol.3, p.358, and Brooke, *op. cit.*, p.7.

[38] John is rather fond of using the verb "to have" with nouns to intensify the meaning of the verb (he uses it with 'sin,' 'hope,' 'life,' 'necessity,' 'freedom of speech'). In some of these expressions the idea is 'to have and enjoy' or 'to have and make use of,' while in others it means 'to have and be controlled by,' or 'to have and be responsible for.'

what is necessary if fellowship already enjoyed is to continue.   "You also" indicates that the intended benefit was not only for those who had personally seen Jesus during His earthly ministry; it was for those also who had not seen.   The English word "fellowship" today has a different meaning than the New Testament idea of *koinōnia* ("fellowship"). Our word speaks of companionship or social comradery.[39]   The Greek word speaks of "joint participation in a common cause."   In Hellenistic Greek it denoted "partners in a business," or "joint-owners of a piece of property," or "shareholders in a common enterprise."[40]   There are two sides to Biblical "fellowship."   There is the participation together in a common cause, and there is the common enjoyment of what they do together. "With us" means "us apostles."   If the Gnostics succeed in leading the readers astray, the fellowship will be broken, for the apostles have not embraced the Gnostic message.[41]

And indeed our fellowship is with the Father – If any should question why fellowship with the apostles is to be so desired, John goes on to explain.   There is more than simply partnership with the apostles.   This "fellowship" also includes the Father and the Son as partners.   There is a double conjunction in the Greek, *kai ... de*, a construction that suggests something emphatic.   The NASB tries to catch this by rendering *de* "indeed." This is what "fellowship with us" really means.   "Our" (in "our fellowship") translates the possessive pronoun *hēmeteros*, an emphatic form that implies a contrast.   Yes, there is a "fellowship" of sorts in the Gnostic camp, but it is not like "*our* fellowship."   "Our fellowship" is something special compared to theirs.   Christians in fellowship with the Father[42] have the same feelings, aims, and purposes that God has.   They have attachment to the same truths.   They love the same principles.   They are involved in the same good work in the world.   None of these can be said of the Gnostics.   Embracing the Gnostic message destroys any possibility of fellowship with the Father.

And with His Son Jesus Christ – The repeated *meta* ("with") distinguishes the personalities of the Father and the Son.   The full title brings out both aspects of the Lord's person,

---

[39] A church life whose principle of cohesion is a superficial social comradery instead of a spiritual fellowship with the Father and with His Son, is not what the church is to be.

[40] Glen Barker, "1,2,3 John" in *Expositor's Bible Commentary* (Grand Rapids: Eerdmans, 1981), Vol. 12, p.307.   The Greek word *koinōnia* means to "have [something] in common," "to do something together." It is used of Peter, James, and John who as partners in a fishing business (Luke 5:10) had something in common.   Paul and Titus shared a common faith (Titus 1:4).   Christians share in the grace of God (Philippians 1:7).   In the early church there was a mutual sharing of material goods, as for example when the churches of Macedonia and Achaia "raised a common fund" for the poor saints at Jerusalem (Romans 15:26; 2 Corinthians 9:13).   There was a mutual sharing in the benefits of the gospel (1 Corinthians 9:23). The term here in 1 John should be understood in light of John 15:1-8.   It refers to the life believers share with Christ and with one another.

[41] "That the words 'fellowship with us' precede in the text the words 'fellowship is with the Father and with His Son, Jesus Christ' may be significant.   Westcott (*in loc.*) sees here a reminder that there can be no fellowship with the Father or with the Son that is not based on apostolic witness." (Barker, *op. cit.*, p.307).

[42] See notes on verse 2 where "Father" was explained.

both His deity and humanity. We call Him "Son" because of the incarnation. At the same time "His Son" has overtones of deity. "Jesus" has reference to His historical life and human nature.[43] "Christ" speaks of His divine commission as God's promised Messiah. John's readers cannot (with meaning) give our Lord His full title and at the same time embrace Gnostic ideas about Him, whether they be Docetic or Cerinthian. Since it is true that if men do not honor the Son, they do not honor the Father (1 John 2:23; John 5:23), it follows that if a man wishes to have a relationship ("fellowship") with the Father, he had better be in relationship with the Son Jesus Christ.[44] Christian fellowship is possible only on the basis of a common belief in Jesus. Those religious groups which treat Jesus as a created being, or once an archangel, or a good teacher (but not God in the flesh) have no basis for claiming fellowship with the apostles, or the Father, or the Son, because their beliefs do not match what the New Testament teaches about Jesus the Christ, the Son of God.

1:4 -- *And these things we write, so that our joy may be made complete.*

And these things we write – "We" (*hēmeis*) is emphatic. There is no "to you" in the better manuscripts after "we write."[45] Thus John is claiming that other apostles ("we [who] have seen and heard") in addition to himself have written "these things" about Jesus. There is no real need to limit "these things"[46] to what John has witnessed to and proclaimed in the first 3 verses. It may well apply to what he writes in the whole epistle. Perhaps what he is most anxious about is that their fellowship may continue.

So that our joy may be made complete – Verse 3 had a *hina* clause in it, expressing why the apostles continually proclaimed the Word of Life: fellowship depended on it. This *hina* clause expresses a reason why the apostles write as they do: continuing joy depends upon it. "Joy" or gladness is a term often found in John's writings. Delight and satisfac-

---

[43] Our Lord is called Jesus in 1 John 1:7, 4:3,15, 5:1,5. He is called Jesus Christ in 1:3, 3:23, 4:2, 5:20. When there is reference, direct or indirect, to heretics who denied the Incarnation, the name Jesus is specially used as appropriate to the human nature. (Alexander, *op. cit.*, p.305)

[44] "In some way the heretics were claiming it was possible to have life and a relationship with God without Jesus playing any significant part in it" (Marshall, *op. cit.*, p.106). A religion without Christ is not Christianity! Eternal life is found only in Jesus (John 6:68). There is no other name under heaven, given among men, whereby we must be saved (Acts 4:12). Readers of 1 John who wish to have an intimate relation with Jesus Christ will have to embrace the message about Him the apostles proclaimed. Embracing the Gnostic doctrine about Jesus (v. the Christ) will destroy any possibility of fellowship with Jesus Christ.

[45] In this context "we" must mean "we who have seen and heard." It is the last time the plural "we write" occurs in the Johannine epistles. In 2:1ff John gets very personal by using the verb "I write." Thereafter, he uses the first person singular throughout the remainder of the letter.

[46] This is the first use of the demonstrative adjective *houtos* ("this" [singular], "these things" [plural]) in 1 John. It occurs frequently in the letter, and in nearly every case we are uncertain whether *houtos* points backwards to what has just been written, or forward to what is about to be written. In classical Greek, the demonstrative *houtos* points back to something already said, while the demonstrative *hode* points forward to what follows. However, this distinction is not always followed in Koine Greek.

tion are involved.   It is difficult to decide between the two readings found here in the manuscripts, "your joy" (*humin*) and "our joy" (*hēmōn*).   Both are well supported, and Westcott declared that "a positive decision on the reading here is impossible."[47]   If we read "our joy," the reference may be to those apostles who, like John, found joy in the faithfulness and continuing fellowship of their converts.   The writer's joy is dependent on converts continuing to do well.   "May be made complete" (*hē peplērōmenē*) is a periphrastic perfect participial construction.   It may be translated, "Our joy, having been filled completely in past times, may persist in that state of fulness through the present time."[48]   The word is *peplērōmenē*, not *teleioō*.   It is "full, complete" joy, not "perfect" joy.   The idea expressed is that "the joy will lack nothing.   Their hearts will be filled to the brim.   They will be as glad as they possibly can be."[49]   That's what the readers remaining in the fellowship ultimately means to the apostles!

I. FELLOWSHIP'S CONDITIONS.   1:5 - 2:11[1]

Summary: If John's readers are to continue to enjoy fellowship (as verse 3 looks forward to), they will have to understand what makes such fellowship possible. Most of the paragraphs are directed against Gnostic ideas, which if embraced would make continuing fellowship with the apostles, the Father, and the Son impossible.

A. Conformity to a Standard.   1:5-7

Summary: The basic truth that God is light becomes the touchstone by which anyone's teaching and behavior can be measured.   Since God is light, fellowship with Him is conditioned on walking in the light.   This section is directly contradictory to the Gnostic doctrine that moral conduct is a matter of indifference to an enlightened one.

1:5 -- *And this is the message we have heard from Him and announce to you, that God is light, and in Him there is no darkness at all.*

---

[47] B.F. Westcott, *The Epistles of St. John* (Grand Rapids: Eerdmans, 1952 reprint), p.13.

[48] K. Wuest, *In These Last Days* (Grand Rapids: Eerdmans, 1954), p. 98.

[49] Haas, *op. cit.*, p.29.   "Complete" recalls such verses as John 15:11 and 16:24 both of which speak of joy being "completed."   Jesus spoke to His disciples just before He went away, telling them what would make Him serenely happy (John 15:11).   So now John expresses what makes the apostles happy.   In both cases it is the faithfulness of their disciples.   It would be helpful here in 1 John if the word were translated exactly as it is in the Fourth Gospel.   It would help us to see the relationship between 1 John 1:3,4 and John 17:13-21.

[1] Most students of 1 John begin the first major division of the outline at this place.   But there is little agreement on where in chapter 2 this division ends.   Some think verse 28, some think verse 29.   We opt to close the first division with verse 11 of chapter 2.

And this is the message we have heard from Him – In comments on verse 2, it was observed that John characteristically uses the simple conjunction to begin many of his sentences. In most of these instances, there is no need to search for some "connection" to what he has just written previously. If we must find such a link here, perhaps it is to be found in the topic of fellowship. If we are to have fellowship with God and with the brethren, we must know what God is and what we are. We must submit to the conditions which make continuing fellowship possible. In form the opening of this letter is closely parallel to the opening of the Fourth Gospel. This verse corresponds to John 1:19, and it is introduced in exactly the same way ("this is the witness"). "Is," which stands first in most Greek papyri and uncial manuscripts, is emphatic. It marks the permanence and absoluteness of the message. "This IS the message!" "This" (*hautē*) here likely refers to what follows.[2] "Message" (*aggelia*)[3] here and in 3:11 basically means "lesson" or "communication" of some important truth contained in the gospel. The specific content of this "message" is indicated later in the verse by the *hoti* clause. Unlike the self-invented lessons taught by the Gnostics, the apostles' message was not invented by man; they heard it from Jesus Himself.[4] The verb "heard" is in the perfect tense, indicating past completed action with present continuing results. The message is still vivid in their minds, so they can announce it without any error or mistake. "It is unlikely that John is quoting any specific saying of Jesus, for no such saying as 'God is light' has survived. Rather, John is summarizing the Lord's teaching in a way similar to how He presented it in his Gospel."[5]

And [we] announce to you – The verb is present tense. 'We apostles continually preach this message,' is the idea. The Greek verb here (*anaggellomen*) is not the same verb that was translated "proclaim" in verses 2 and 3.[6]   The preposition *ana* prefixed to the verb

---

[2] See notes on the demonstrative pronoun ("these things") at verse 4.

[3] There is a manuscript variation at this place. Some Greek texts have *epaggelia*, a "promise" or a "pledge." Codex Sinaiticus stands alone in reading here, "This, then, is the *love of the* message."

[4] The pronoun used (*autos*) is not the one (*ekeinos*) commonly used to refer to Christ in this epistle. Nevertheless, here the context decides. "Him" refers back to "His Son Jesus Christ" of verse 3. John did not write 'respecting Him,' or 'about Him,' but "from Him." This is key. Redaction critics explain the "we" as being the redactor and the orthodox members of the Johannine community who were committed to the preservation and propagation of the message as they interpreted it. But how can they ever demonstrate that all those folks, two generations separated from the apostles, heard the message from Jesus Himself, like John here claims for the apostles?

[5] Stott, *op. cit.*, p.70. Of Jesus' ministry in Galilee, we are told "the people who were sitting in darkness saw a great light" (Matthew 4:16). Jesus was the light of the world (John 8:12). "A light of revelation to the Gentiles and the glory of Thy people Israel" (Luke 2:32). "In Him was life, and the life was the light of men" (John 1:4). John the Baptist bore witness to the light (John 1:6-8), about the time the true light was coming into the world (John 1:9). "Light has come into the world" (John 3:19). "Christ proclaimed light both to the Jewish people and the Gentiles" (Acts 26:23).

[6] *Apaggellein* (used in verses 2 and 3) means to announce with a distinct reference to the source or place from which the message comes. *Kataggellein* means to proclaim with authority, as commissioned to spread the tidings throughout those who hear them. Both are distinct from the form used here.

carries the idea of "again" – we preach it again. Could there be a slight rebuke of the readers in that the apostles find they must continually repeat the message for their readers? The audience to whom ("to you") 1 John is addressed is the churches of Asia Minor.[7]

That God is light – God, the one who has revealed Himself in the Bible and in creation and in the incarnation, is not "*the* light" nor "*a* light;" He *is* "light." That is His nature, His essential being.[8] The statement is absolute and anarthrous to express quality. This simple statement, easily remembered, is a basic and fundamental truth of God's revelation of Himself. As we read on in 1 John we become aware John is not talking about physical light; he is using symbolic language[9] to talk about moral, ethical, and spiritual light. Plato said, "It is difficult to open up sufficiently any of the highest and most transcendent subjects without using symbols." What ideas are conveyed by the symbol "light"? To answer, think about how light works in our physical world, and then give each idea a spiritual turn.

- Brilliant light is hard to look at. God, who dwells in unapproachable light, is awesome!
- When light is present in the world of nature, life and action become possible. It a greenhouse, for example, light stimulates plants to grow. God makes both physical and spiritual life and action possible.
- Light helps men to see. As light enables them to know where and how to walk, God likewise illumines the pathway He expects men to walk. As light helps men see imperfections in the things they have made with their hands, God's light helps men see imperfections in their lives.

Light suggests God's excellence: His perfect moral purity, without limit and without taint, His unutterable majesty, His goodness and righteousness. This is an anti-Gnostic thrust, for in early Gnostic thought, God was the great unknowable. When John says, on the basis of revelation from Jesus Christ, that "God is light," he thereby is saying that "God is not the *arrētos sigē* (i.e., unspoken silence) nor *buthos* (i.e., depth) of the more developed Gnostic systems, nor the 'unknowable' God of the Gnostic thought which preceded those systems."[12] "That God can be 'known,' and known by those to whom this letter is written,

---

[7] See "Destination" in the Introductory Studies, p.lv.

[8] What John writes here in verse 5 is similar to "God is love" (1 John 4:8,16) and "God is spirit" (John 4:24) and "our God is consuming fire" (Hebrews 12:29). These statements all express the essence, the essential Being, of God.

[9] On the use of symbolic or metaphorical language to express religious truths – a feature common to all religions, not just the revealed religion of the Bible – see "Additional Note" on such symbolism in Stott, *op. cit.*, p.70ff. Greeks, Bible writers, and the Qumran literature used "light" and "darkness" in a metaphorical sense, so John's readers would have been familiar with the ideas being expressed. See Stephen S. Smalley, *1,2,3 John* in Word Biblical Commentary (Waco, TX: Word Books, 1984), Vol.51, p.19-20, for references.

[12] Brooke, *op. cit.*, p.12.

is one of the leading ideas on which John lays stress."[11]

And in Him there is no darkness at all – There is a double negative in the Greek, *ouk oudemia*, making the negation emphatic. *Oudemia* means 'no, not even one speck.' There is absolutely no exception to the statement that God is light. "Darkness" is another expressive symbolic term. John frequently uses this word to denote error and sin (e.g., 1 John 2:8,9, 11; John 8:12). "Darkness exists, physical, intellectual, moral, and spiritual; there is abundance of obscurity, error, depravity, sin, and its consequence, death. But not a shade of these is 'in Him'."[13] The combination of "light" and "darkness" (one claimed for God, and the other emphatically denied) is very likely a refutation of the heretic's dualistic views, drawn from Eastern religions. From Zoroastrianism Gnosticism embraced the speculations about two opposing spiritual powers, a "god of light" and a "god of darkness." Soon, Gnostics had invented a "Supreme Being" who is good, as contrasted in their system of thought to the lesser God of the Old Testament whom Gnostics tried to say was devious, ignorant, sneaky, and corrupt. If there is no darkness in God, then again it can be said that He reveals Himself to men. Complete knowledge of God is not possible to finite humans, but because of His self-revelation, because He is light and no darkness at all is in Him, more can be known of Him than the Gnostics were wont to admit. The Gnostics could never have laid claim to a private, esoteric knowledge into which they alone had been initiated, if their conception of God had been of One who manifests Himself freely, and in whom there is no secrecy at all. In the next seven verses John unfolds certain every-day theological, ethical, and practical implications that are based on the simple, fundamental truth that "God is light, and in Him is no darkness at all." He is directing his readers to test the teachings of the Gnostics against this simple, fundamental standard. Remember it, use it to guide your thinking, reject what does not harmonize with it, and you will not be adversely affected by Gnostic teachings. If this rejection of Gnostic ideas and practice is realized, their "fellowship" with the apostles and with the Father and His Son (verse 3) will continue uninterrupted.

1:6 -- If we say that we have fellowship with Him and yet walk in the darkness, we lie and do not practice the truth.

If we say – Three "if we say" clauses occur in quick succession (verses 6,8,10). Each, apparently, reflects a doctrine or practice of the Gnostic-like heretics. Each "if we say" clause is followed by a consequential statement showing there is something wrong with the doctrine or practice because it is out of harmony with the basic truth (stated in verse 5) that "God is light." Once the incorrect doctrine or practice has been refuted, there follows

---

[11] *Ibid.*

[13] A. Plummer, *Exposition of the Epistles of St. John* in the Pulpit Commentary (Grand Rapids: Eerdmans, 1962 reprint), Vol.22, p.4. (Note: Whenever reference is made to Plummer's comments in Pulpit Commentary, the footnotes will read "Pulpit Commentary." All other citations from Plummer come from the Cambridge Bible.)

a contrasting "if" clause stating what is the correct idea or practice if one would continue in fellowship with God who is light.[14]   The parallel presentation of these three heretical claims and their refutations raises again the matter of the outline of the epistle.   We have chosen to treat the three claims as two different subpoints, but many students of Scripture treat all three together as one subpoint.   John writes "we" again just as he has in the first five verses, but the identity of the "we" seems to have changed, as is evident from the context.[15]   Perhaps in these "if" clauses he uses the first person plural as a way of stating a general principle which is applicable to all men equally, apostles, church members, or false teachers.[16]   Anyone who lives and preaches like the "if" clauses picture, even if he were an apostle, would be in error!

That we have fellowship with Him – "We have fellowship with Him [God]"[17] is apparently a reflection, if not a quotation, of a claim actually made by the heretics.[18]   Other expressions reflecting other heretical claims follow in 1:8,10; 2:4,6,9; and 4:20.   Each time John identifies one of the doctrines or practices of the false teachers, he immediately brands it as an error, and gives certain simple tests by which his readers may judge the truth or error of any who profess to teach Christian doctrine.

And *yet* walk in the darkness – We doubt that the heretics went around claiming "We walk in darkness!"   Our NASB translators have added "yet" to show that "walking in darkness" is not part of the claim made by the heretics, but is rather John's estimate of their lifestyle.   When used figuratively, "walk" means "to live habitually."[19]   Jesus used the same metaphor (John 8:12, 9:9,10), so that it became part of the natural religious language of Christians.   "Darkness" (the same word as used in verse 5) means to live without paying

---

[14] God's self-revelation has made it clear that "God is light." It follows that to have fellowship with Him, men must demonstrate a similar "light" in their own thinking and behavior. If God is light, then men are expected to walk in the light (1 John 1:7). If God is spirit, then men are expected to worship in spirit (John 4:24). If God is love, then men are expected to manifest loving actions towards their brothers (1 John 4:7,8,16).

[15] To make "we" in verse 6ff a reference to the apostles gets us into trouble. John is certainly not saying that he or any of the apostles ever said any of the maxims he is about to quote. The apostles never did teach any of the errors he is rebutting.

[16] "With great gentleness John puts the case hypothetically, and with great delicacy he includes himself in the hypothesis." Plummer, *op. cit.*, p.80.

[17] "Fellowship" has been explained in notes on verse 3. "We have fellowship" is a simple assertion of the enjoyment of the privilege.   "With Him" = "with God" – given the nearest antecedent in verse 5.

[18] Some commentators think John is quoting the actual slogans or maxims used by the heretical teachers. Others are not so sure these are actual quotations, but they certainly represent and summarize the pernicious teaching of the heretics.

[19] "Walk" as a metaphor for how one lives is a term familiar from the Old Testament. Compare also the Hebrew term *halakah* ("rule," literally, "how to walk"). The Greek verb is present tense, denoting continuous walking. It expresses not merely action, but habitual action.

any attention to God's beneficial revelation of the right way to think and live.[20] Apparently the heretics about whom John writes were habitually claiming fellowship with God while habitually living in sin. Not only did their actions result from darkness, but so did their thoughts, because they attempted to justify their wrong behavior. Some later Gnostics insisted behavior was unimportant since a man's spirit could not be contaminated by deeds of the body.[21] Perhaps some of the heretics claimed a spiritual man could grow beyond the possibility of any sin or defilement; that is, they could be righteous without necessarily doing righteousness (cp. 1 John 3:7). Both of these attempts to justify their wrong behavior are wrong-headed! Habitual sin is totally incompatible with the character of God, Who is light.

We lie – The claim of enjoying fellowship with God is a lie. Darkness and light cannot co-exist in the same place. If God is light, then people living in darkness are not in fellowship with God. Folk who think they are going to heaven when they die, but who have lived lives of habitual sin with no thought of any need for repentance, are lying to themselves about their real condition.[22] "A life in moral darkness can no more have communion with God, than a life in a coal pit can have communion with the sun. For 'what communion [*koinōnia*] has light with darkness?' "[23]

And do not practice the truth – Just as "we lie" matches "if we say," so "do not practice the truth" matches "walk in darkness."[24] It asserts that all such walking in darkness is a not-doing of the truth. This is the first appearance in 1 John of the word "truth," a word which will occur 20 times in the Johannine letters. God's "truth," the truth revealed by Jesus (verse 5), is the standard to which men are to conform, both in thought and action. God's revelation of Himself and His will for men requires corresponding action or response from men.[25] "Truth" is something that men can and are expected to "do." The verb *poi-*

---

[20] Thayer (*Lexicon*, p.580) has explained "darkness" as being "ignorance respecting divine things and known duties, and the accompanying ungodliness and immorality, with the resultant misery."

[21] See the quotation from Irenaeus in a footnote on p.xlviii in the Introductory Study of "Gnosticism."

[22] It is just as impossible today to claim fellowship with God while at the same time seeing no necessity either first to go to the cross of Christ for cleansing and forgiveness, or thereafter seeing no necessity to lead a consistently holy life. "We are right to be suspicious of those who claim a mystical intimacy with God and yet 'walk in darkness' of error and sin, paying no regard to the self-revelation of an all-holy God." If God is light, such claims are empty and hollow, and a long way from the truth. Unforgiven sin is always a barrier to fellowship with God (Psalm 5:4, 66:18; Isaiah 59:1,2). (Paraphrased from Stott, *op. cit.*, p.74)

[23] Plummer, *ibid.*

[24] These two phrases are another case of antithetic parallelism of which John is so fond of using.

[25] According to John 3:19-21, "practicing the truth" is opposed to "practicing evil." "The one who practices evil does not even come to the light, lest his deeds be exposed. But the one who practices the truth comes to the light, that his deeds may be manifested as having been wrought in God." Ephesians 4 and 5 also unfold the idea that there is a close correspondence between "light" and "truth." In 1 Corinthians 13:6, Paul shows that "truth" and "unrighteousness [iniquity]" are opposites.

oumen is present tense in the Greek, indicating continuous action.[26]   Our translators have rendered the word "practice" in an attempt to show English readers the word is not a one-time doing, but a continual doing.   If we wish to remain in fellowship with God, we will regularly and habitually do what God has commanded in the "truth" He has given us.

1:7 -- *But if we walk in the light as He Himself is in the light, we have fellowship with one another, and the blood of Jesus His Son cleanses us from all sin.*

But if we walk in the light – Here begins John's statement of correct Christian teaching and behavior in opposition to the Gnostic claims and behavior.   "But" (*de*) underlines the contrast.   We interpret "walk" and "light" in harmony with the symbolic meanings of "light" and "walk" already introduced in verses 5 and 6.   "Walk[ing] in the light" is consistently to avoid sinning ("walk[ing] in the darkness").   The present tense speaks of habitual walking in the light (not sinless perfection).   It involves an attitude of mind and corresponding action, just as "walking in darkness" did.   It denotes a "conscious and sustained endeavour to live a life in conformity with the revelation of God"[27]   Ephesians 5:8ff unfolds some of the ethical details involved in walking in the light.   As the following verses show, walking in the light excludes asceticism (fellowship with one another is not asceticism) and antinomianism (confession of and forgiveness of sin would exclude this).

As He Himself is in the light – We suppose that John's imagery is flexible.   God can Himself be light (verse 5), and be in the light (verse 7), at the same time.[28]   "The light" is the element in which God lives (1 Timothy 6:16).   "As" indicates similitude, not equality.   "This phrase indicates the degree to which we should walk in the light, as completely and fully as we can."[29]

We have fellowship with one another – This begins John's conclusion to the "if" clause of verse 7.   In his conclusion John states two positive results of living in the light God has made available in Jesus.   The first thing that happens is that "we have fellowship with one

---

[26] The verb "do" followed by an abstract noun (sin, lawlessness, truth, righteousness, will of God) is a Hebrew idiom. (We are familiar with French, Spanish, or German words in English speakers' mouths. So Hebrew expressions occur in the Greek New Testament, especially when the writer grew up in the "old country.")

[27] Brooke, *op. cit.*, p.15.

[28] Because God has been described as being "light," some suppose Jesus ("He") is the reference when John writes "He Himself is in the light." Since His resurrection and ascension, Jesus has been enthroned within that sphere of light that surrounds God. Thus, fellowship with Jesus demands walking in the light, just as fellowship with the Father requires walking in the light.

[29] Alexander, *op. cit.*, p.307.

another." Notice the slight change from "fellowship with Him" that we had in verse 6.[30] By varying his wording slightly, John carries the idea of verse 7's contrast a step further, and states that walking in the light contributes to fellowship among the brethren too! "One another" includes the whole company of God's people.[31] "We have" is a present tense. We continue to have fellowship. "Just as men at war with God are at war with one another, so men reconciled to God are reconciled to one another."[32]

And the blood of Jesus His Son cleanses us from all sin – "And" shows this is a second result of walking in the light.   "The blood of Jesus ... cleanses (continues to cleanse) us

---

[30] Some manuscripts, here at verse 7, have been altered (to *autou* or to *cum Deo*) to match the wording of verse 6. Textual critics have made a believable case for each reading. See the arguments discussed in Smalley, *op. cit.*, p.17. We accept the reading "with one another."

[31] "This certainly refers to the mutual fellowship of Christians among themselves, as is clear from 3:23, 4:7,12, 2 John 5. It does *not* refer to fellowship *between God and man* ... John would scarcely express the relation between God and man by such a phrase as 'we have fellowship with one another' (*met' allēlōn*)." Plummer, *op. cit.*, p.82 (emphasis per the original).

[32] Clint Gill, *Hereby We Know: A Study of the Epistles of John* in the Bible Study Textbook Series (Joplin, MO: College Press, 1966), p.30. He goes on to illustrate in this fashion: "Suppose a group of people are confined in a strange room which is cast in pitch darkness. They do not know the shape of the room. They do not know where the furnishings are or what their purpose is. As these people begin to grope about in the darkness they stumble over the furniture. They hurt themselves against what they cannot see. In their frustration and discomfort they bump into one another. They strike out at one another in anger and animosity.
    Suppose now that someone turns on the light. Each occupant of the room sees the others not as strange beings contributing to his discomfort, but as human beings, pretty much like himself. He sees the shape of the room as it was designed for human tenancy. He sees the furnishings not as obstacles over which to stumble, but as items created for his own use. So he sits down and begins to share with his fellows the blessings which the light has brought to all.
    So it is with the fellowship of the redeemed. When we were outside of Christ we did not understand the moral laws of the world in which we lived. We banged ourselves against the spiritual realities which were created for our benefit, and in our bafflement we struck out at each other. But in Christ, when we walk in the light as He brings it, we realize that the world in which we live was ordered for our occupancy to the glory to God. We understand that the moral laws of God are not designed to make us miserable and filled with guilt complexes, but are rather for our spiritual benefit. By the light of Christ we see that all men are created in the image of God, that all are lost in and victims of the same darkness, that aside from God's light there is no hope for any, but that in it there is hope for all (see 2 Corinthians 5:14-21). In these realizations we become reconciled to one another and begin to share the blessings which Christ has revealed.
    The person who walks in darkness, and especially one who leaves the light and returns to the darkness, cannot have fellowship with those who remain in the light (2 Corinthians 6:14-16)."
    Plummer, *op. cit.*, p.82, has an illustration from Scripture. "In that 'thick darkness' which prevailed 'in all the land of Egypt for three days, *they saw not one another, neither rose any from his place* for three days' (Exodus 11:22,23). I.e., there was an absolute cessation of fellowship. Society could not continue in the dark. But when the light returned, society was restored. So also in the spiritual world: when the light comes, individuals have that communion one with another which in darkness is impossible."

from all sin."[33]   "*All* sin" speaks of all sinful deeds, sin in all its manifestations and forms.[34]   "The blood of Jesus His Son" is a designation that may have been chosen deliberately by John, for such a Christology would be a direct refutation of the views of the heretics.   Jesus was genuinely human; He could shed blood.   He therefore was able to be a sacrifice for human sin.   To place together "the blood of Jesus His Son" contradicts the Cerinthian heresy.   "Jesus" and "the Son" weren't two people.   "Blood" in Jesus' case was literal blood, flowing through his veins.   However, "blood" is also a vivid and moving image that puts before the reader's mind the whole atoning sacrifice Jesus made on Calvary.[35]   Not only was He human, but being God's own "Son" He was deity (see comments at 1:3).   And John reminds his readers that in Him, God (in whom there is no darkness) is acting.   God does more than forgive; He erases the stain of sin.[36]   "Cleanses us" is a present tense verb in the Greek.   Cleansing is something that continues to happen.   It is not so much the cleansing that takes place at baptism, but everyday cleansing when the conditions of forgiveness and cleansing are met.   John will go on to mention some of these conditions in the following verses.[37]   "Sin" here is *harmartia*, to miss the mark.   It is a failure to measure up to God's standards and expectations.[38]   What sin needs to be cleansed if we are "walking in the light"?   The answer to that question is this: habitual walking in the light does not equal being "sinless perfect."   After a believer is initially justified (sins forgiven), there are still occasions when Christians sin (verse 9).   These are the sins that are forgiven (cleansed) as a result of "walking in the light."   The "light" tells

---

[33] Redaction critics who regard this whole clause as an addition to the original text by a pedantic redactor have certainly erred.   Rather than being an unnecessary addition, it is this very clause that gives John's readers a simple test by which to assess the claims of the heretics.

[34] Brooke, *op. cit.*, p.16.

[35] In ordinary language, an abridged description, when the part selected is vivid, picturesque, pregnant, gives force and color to "the poetry of common speech."   Thus we speak of "souls" for persons, or "sails" for ships.   Such is the word "blood" in Christian theology.   It is dogma with pathos.   It is picturesque while drawing out our sympathy.   It implies the reality of the human body of Jesus, the reality of His sufferings, the reality of His sacrifice, and the indispensable value of His present ministry in heaven.   It is a one-word salvo in the heart of the Gnostic camp.   (Paraphrased from Alexander, *op. cit.*, p.307)

[36] Jesus spoke of the blessing of being purified in heart (Matthew 5:8).   Sin contaminates and soils and renders a person spiritually unclean.   Christ's blood "cleanses" (removes) the soil.   We probably are not talking just of removing the guilt of sin.   There seems to be more to the "stain" than that.   The blood of Christ cleanses the conscience for service to Him who is the Living God (Hebrews 9:13ff, 22ff).   Jesus gave Himself for us, to cleanse for Himself a peculiar people (Titus 2:14).   And Jesus cleanses the church to present it to Himself in glory (Ephesians 5:26ff).   "Cleansing" (ritual cleansing in the Old Testament) is connected in Scripture with suitable preparation for divine service and divine fellowship.

[37] Unforgiven sin separates a man from God.   What is the believer who sins to do to insure the fellowship is not broken?   Avail himself or herself of the blood of Jesus.   Doing this, the believer is "practicing the truth" (something the heretic, as verse 6 indicates, did not do).

[38] *Hamartia* ("sin") can refer to the violation of the standards set by God (1 John 3:14).   *Hamartia* (leaving the road, missing the mark) also calls attention to the personal responsibility each person has for the sins he or she commits.

sinners what to do to be forgiven and cleansed. Even the best of Christians need cleansing (cp. what Jesus said, John 13:10).[39] "When 'all sins' are cleansed, men are like God in Whom is no darkness."[40]

In summary, John's first condition on which fellowship depends is conformity to a standard. That standard is found in the basic truth that "God is light" (verse 5). The condition of fellowship is habitually walking in the light.[41]

B. Consciousness of and Confession of Sin. 1:8-2:2

> *Summary*: We are in the first major portion of John's letter, a section we have titled "Fellowship's Conditions." Contrary to what the Gnostics taught, sin is real in our lives and must be confessed (verses 8-9). Christ has made possible the forgiveness of confessed sins (1:10-2:2).

1:8 -- *If we say that we have no sin, we are deceiving ourselves, and the truth is not in us.*

If we say that we have no sin – On the meaning of "if we say," see notes at verse 6. "We have no sin" is another claim, albeit a false one, made by the heretics about whom John is

---

[39] Several theological issues are raised by this present tense verb, "continues to cleanse." (1) The doctrine of some, that forgiveness of sins occurs just once in a man's life (namely at his baptism, Acts 2:38, 22:16) is evidently shown to be wrong. It is the sins committed before baptism that are remitted when one is immersed. Those individual sins committed after baptism are cleansed each time the conditions for forgiveness (Acts 8:27, 1 John 1:9) are met. (2) The Novatians, who denied pardon for any sin committed after baptism, should have paid attention to what John has here written. (3) The Scriptures have much to say about Jesus' continuing ministry in heaven on behalf of the saints. As the Jewish high priest took the sacrificial blood into the Holy of Holies and sprinkled it on the cover of the Ark of the Covenant, so Jesus is pictured as having offered His blood in heaven (Hebrews 9:11ff). "He ever lives to make intercession" (Hebrews 7:25). "We are saved by His living" (Romans 5:10). When we obey we are sprinkled by the blood (1 Peter 1:2). "How much more shall the blood of Christ ... cleanse your conscience" (Hebrews 9:14). "These are they who are coming out of the great tribulation, and they have washed their robes and made them white in the blood of the Lamb" (Revelation 7:14). "Blessed are those who are continually washing their garments ... (Revelation 22:14). (4) It was in connection with this verse, and with particular reference to Leviticus 17:11, that Westcott (*op. cit.*, p.34-37) developed his thesis that the blood of Jesus in the New Testament, rather than pointing in particular to His *death*, "always includes the thought of His *life* preserved and active beyond death." Stott, *op. cit.*, p.76, and Marshall, *op. cit.*, p.112 footnote, both object to Westcott's presentation.

[40] Westcott, *op. cit.*, p.22

[41] Scripture elsewhere teaches that God looks at the tenor of a man's life: was he habitually doing what is right, or was he habitually doing what is wrong. See Romans 2:6-10 (where the verbs are present tense, indicating continuous action) and Matthew 7:24ff (where the "builders" are pictured either as habitually "acting" on Jesus' sayings, or as not habitually "acting" on Jesus' sayings).

warning his readers.[42]   Now exactly what the proto-Gnostics were claiming about "sin" is not so simple to determine.[43]   In the light of John's corrective in the next verse (where "forgive" and "cleanse" are used), it seems the claim the heretics made is that there is nothing in their thoughts and behavior that needs to be forgiven, nothing that needs to be cleansed.   "Cleanses" implies that sin contaminates a person.   Perhaps the Gnostics were saying their actions did not contaminate them.[44]   "Forgive (removal)" implies that sin controls or enslaves.   Perhaps the Gnostics were saying they weren't enslaved as a result of any of their actions.   We have noted the tendency of the Gnostics to excuse whatever the body did, as though bodily actions had no real affect on the spirit.   Their dualism said that matter could not affect their enlightened spirits; "Sin doesn't affect me!" they argued.   Such a doctrine John repudiates vehemently.[45]

The word "sin" in this verse is singular.   Great care must be exercised when explaining the possible meaning of the singular "sin" that John has written.   Since Augustine's time, when the doctrine of inherited total depravity as part of the penalty to the race for Adam's sin became a church dogma, a rather common explanation of "sin" (singular) in this verse is that the Gnostics denied "original sin" or an "inherited sinful nature."   Then when John uses the plural "sins" he is speaking of individual acts of sin, something the Gnostics also denied for themselves.   This explanation is unlikely.[46]   There seems to be no great distinction between John's use of "sin" (singular) when he words the false claim of the heretics, and when in the next verse he uses "sins" (plural) as he gives

---

[42] Perhaps this claim is a response to John's picture of the Gnostics "walking in darkness." Far from walking in darkness, as John accuses them, the heretics are pictured as saying, "We are without sin," and "We do not need cleansing from sin, so your appeal to the blood of Jesus is irrelevant." (The verb is present tense, indicating continuing action in the present. Advocates of sinless perfectionism like to translate it, "If we say we have not sinned in the past (before we became a Christian)." But such a translation is inconsistent with the present tense verb John uses in this verse

[43] "To have sin" is exclusively a Johannine expression; it is used in the New Testament only in the Gospel of John (9:41; 15:22-24; 19:11) and in this epistle. As expositors have examined John's use of this phrase, they have arrived at a general agreement that the phrase "denotes the guiltiness of sin," as though the heretics were saying "I'm not guilty of committing any sin." R. Law, *The Tests of Life: A Study of the First Epistle of John* (Edinburgh: T & T Clark, 1914), p.130. The RSV translates the expression "you would have no guilt" at John 9:41. Moffatt translates 1 John 1:8, "If we say 'we are not guilty' ...."

[44] In other words, the Gnostics were denying there was any such thing as being "dead in trespasses and sins" (i.e., the spirit is affected by one's own sins), as Ephesians 2:1ff affirms does happen. Westcott (*op. cit.*, p.14) writes about "the unreality of sinfulness as a permanent consequence of wrong action."

[45] In this passage John is reflecting on what the Gnostics falsely claim. Later on (1 John 3:6,9; 5:18) John will argue that the Christian does not, and cannot sin habitually. On the surface it might appear that John contradicts himself. The resolution of this apparent contradiction will be stated in the course of the comments on those passages.

[46] See the special studies on "The Doctrine of Sin" and "Original Sin" in the author's *Commentary on Romans* (Moberly, MO: Scripture Exposition Books, 1987), p.190ff. (The pagination varies in the later printings of this book.) The thrust of the comments on Romans 5:12-21 and the thrust of the special study on "Original Sin" is that these doctrines are not taught in the Bible, but entered the church after Greek philosophy (spirit is good, but matter is evil) began to influence the church fathers.

the correct Christian doctrine about this matter ("no sin" and "confess our sins" are opposite sides of the same coin).

We are deceiving ourselves – Whatever the heretic's claim, John repudiates it with two forceful statements. The first is, 'Whoever makes such a claim is self-deceived' (rather than being a deliberate liar). The reflexive form *heautous planōmen* (rather than a simple passive form with no pronoun) is used here, showing that the persons concerned are held responsible. The deceiving is something we have done to ourselves. "The evidence was there; only wilful blindness refuses to accept it."[47] A person who deceives himself, or wanders (*planaō*) from the right path, will find he is in poor company.[48] "The heretics fatal error is not only a fact, but is a fact of which they are the responsible authors."[49]

And the truth is not in us – This is the second forceful statement of repudiation of the Gnostic's claim, "We have no sin." Not only do the heretics fail to do the truth (see comments on "truth" at verse 6[50]), they are void of it. They may claim to have the "truth" inside of them, but that claim is hollow. "To be in" is a phrase John uses to "express close and intimate relationship. ... 'To live in,' 'to belong to,' 'to abide in,' 'to be in our heart' are ways of expressing this relationship."[51] The present tense verb "is" has a continuous or durative force. The truth is not in us now, and it will continue not to be in us as long as we make the claim the heretics are making.

1:9 -- If we confess our sins, He is faithful and righteous to forgive us our sins and to cleanse us from all unrighteousness.

If we confess our sins – As he did in verse 7, though there is no "but" introducing this verse, John here presents in positive contrasting language the true Christian doctrine. "We" as explained at verse 6 includes John as well as his readers. Walking in darkness involves an insensitivity or indifference to acts of personal sin, a denial of any personal responsibility in bad acts, and a failure to confess such sins. Walking in the light involves

---

[47] Brooke, *op. cit.*, p.18.

[48] Cognate forms of the word ('wander' or 'deceive') are used of false messiahs (Matthew 24:5) and false prophets (Matthew 24:11), of Satan (Revelation 20:10), of Babylon (Revelation 18:23), and of Balaam (Jude 11).

[49] Westcott, *op. cit.*, p.23.

[50] We explain "truth" in verses 6 and 8 as meaning the same thing. Some commentators treat "truth" in verse 6 as objective truth (the gospel), and "truth" in verse 8 as subjective truth (a truthful disposition).

(In later Gnosticism, "truth" was the name of one of the aeons. Valentinian, in the 2nd century, speculated that the Godhead was made up of 30 aeons. These were regarded as male and female pairs, and among them Intellect and Truth produced Word and Life, who in turn produced man and the Church. [Smalley, *op. cit.*, p.30]. It is doubtful that John is reflecting this Gnostic idea when he writes "the truth is not in [them].")

[51] Haas, *op. cit.*, p.37.

confession of personal sins.   "The more a man knows the meaning of 'God is light,' i.e., the more he realizes the absolute purity and holiness of God, the more conscious he will become of his own impurity and sinfulness."[52]   "Confess" our sins means to say the same thing about our sins that God says about them.[53]   "If we acknowledge our sins" is how Smalley would translate it.[54]   The verb tense here is present tense, continuous action.[55] Jesus taught His followers to regularly acknowledge their sins (Luke 11:3,4).   It is not a confession of sins in general ("forgive us our sins") but a confession of particular and individual and specific acts of sin; as we deliberately call to mind the evil deeds we are actually doing, we confess and forsake them.[56]   Confession involves not only acknowledgment of our sins, but it implies repentance has occurred also.[57]   Some writers have insisted that public admission of sins before men, as well as God, is what John writes about.   Gnostic teachers would never make such a public acknowledgment before men; in fact, their public claim was "we have no sin."   Indeed, there are appropriate occasions when confession before men of our sins is called for (cp. James 5:16).   However, we suppose John here speaks of private and individual confession to God (as the TEV reads) since the following clause speaks of what God ("He") will do when we confess.[58]

He is faithful and righteous – "He" refers to God the Father, not to Christ.   "Faithful" tells us that God is true to His nature and character; He is reliable, He does what He has promised He will do.[59]   He has promised that on certain conditions He will forgive sins.

---

[52] Plummer, *op. cit.*, p.83. Plummer calls attention to Job 9:2, 14:4, 15:14, 25:4; Proverbs 20:9; Eccles. 7:20 to illustrate the point he has made.   We might also call attention to Isaiah (Isaiah 6:1-5) and Peter (Luke 5:8).

[53] The Scriptures also speak of a confession of our faith in Jesus as something to be done before men.   Luther calls attention to three kinds of confession of sin: 1) Before God;   2) Towards our neighbor; 3) The false confession that the Pope orders men to make secretly in the ears of the priest.

[54] *Op. cit.*, p.30.

[55] It is this section of 1 John (1:8-10) that the Church of England uses as a proof text for having confessional morning and evening every day throughout the year, as well as at the celebration of the Lord's Supper.   (Plummer, *Pulpit Commentary*, p.5, tells of the practice and gives his approval to it.)

[56] See Psalm 32:1-15 and Proverbs 28:13.

[57] Repentance is 'a change of mind and a change of action resulting from Godly sorrow for sin, and including restitution where possible.'   Alexander (*op. cit.*, p.419) speaks of "inward contrition."

[58] "Obviously confession to Him who is 'faithful and righteous,' and to those 'selves' whom we should otherwise 'lead astray' (verse 8), is all that is meant."   Plummer, *op. cit.*, p.83.

[59] The faithfulness of God in Scripture is constantly associated with His covenant promises (e.g., Psalm 89:1-4, Hebrews 10:23).   He is true to His word and faithful to His covenant when He forgives sins through the blood of Christ.   The classic New Covenant prophecy has God promising, "I will forgive their iniquity, and I will remember their sin no more" (Jeremiah 31:34).   God is faithful to what He promised He would do.   He keeps His word.

This is precisely what He does! John wrote "He *is* faithful." God does not *become* such by forgiving; He *is* such. "Righteous" (*dikaios*) tells us God is "upright, equitable, acting properly in the circumstances of the case, giving to each his due."[60] Without the blood (sacrifice) of Christ as a perfect sin offering, God could not forgive sin and still be "right." It is a crooked judge who acquits the guilty. Romans 3:26 speaks of God being "just" while at the same time being One who "justifies" those who have faith in Jesus. His being faithful and just does not *depend* on our confessing our sins. God has these attributes before, and will ever continue to have them, whether we confess or not.[61] But the way both divine qualities are called into action is by open confession of our sins.[62]

To forgive us our sins – This *hina* clause expresses result. John identifies two results of our confession of sins combined with God's attributes of "faithful and righteous." The first is forgiveness. "Sins" is *hamartia*, a word we've already commented upon in verses 7 and 8. The word John uses for "forgive" (*aphiēmi*) is a forensic word meaning to release from a debt (cf. Luke 7:43), or to dismiss the charges. The aorist tense (one act) indicates that each time we confess, God forgives the act of sin confessed.[63] Sin does bind a man. Does "release" include removal of what is called (in Romans 6) slavery to sin?

And to cleanse us from all unrighteousness – This is the second result of confessing our sins to a faithful and righteous God. "Unrighteousness is failure to maintain right relations with other men or with God."[64] Did John choose "unrighteousness" (*adikia*) to contrast with the "righteousness" (*dikaios*) of God? For "all unrighteousness" compare notes on "all sin" in verse 7; it denotes unrighteousness in whatever form it may manifest itself, including "injustice, unrighteousness by which others are deceived, a deed violating law and justice" (Thayer). "Cleanse" here has the same connotation it did in verse 7. It is not the initial cleansing when a man is first justified; it is the cleansing of a Christian who has sinned. It might be said to be one facet of the process of sanctification. Sin contaminates

---

[60] Some writers treat "righteous" as though it means no more than "gentle" or "benign" or "good." However, the use of "unrighteousness" at the close of the verse tends to rule out this watered-down meaning.

[61] Paraphrased from Alexander, *op. cit.*, p. 429.

[62] If God visits upon the sinner his sin and "will by no means leave the guilty unpunished" (Exodus 34:7), how can He forgive sins? This is a problem fit for God. The Judge of all the earth cannot lightly remit sin. The cross is, in fact, the only moral ground on which He can forgive sin at all, for there the blood of Jesus His Son was shed that He might be "the propitiation" for our sins (cf. 2:2, and Romans 3:25). Perhaps, with the blood of Jesus in the equation, it would be wrong of God to withhold forgiveness to the penitent.

[63] Some English versions translate the subjunctive as a future tense. Whenever we confess (now or in the future), He does, or He will, forgive.

[64] Brooke, *op. cit.*, p.21. "The distinction which refers 'faithful' to mortal sins and 'righteous' to venial ones is frivolous." Plummer, *op. cit.*, p.84.

a man; God removes the contamination.[65]   When our sins have been forgiven and cleansed, fellowship with a "faithful and righteous" God continues unbroken.[66]

1:10 -- *If we say that we have not sinned, we make Him a liar, and His word is not in us.*

If we say – On "if we say," see verses 6 and 8.   This is the third false claim made by the heretics that John repudiates as being contrary to the simple gospel truth (as proclaimed in apostolic doctrine) that God is light.   This claim is far more blatant and defiant than the claim voiced in verse 8.

That we have not sinned – The proto-Gnostics are pictured as affirming "We have not sinned!"   How are we to explain this change of verb tense, from the present tense of verse 8 to the perfect tense here in verse 10?   What was this new claim the heretics were making?[67]   Did they claim that their experience of superior enlightenment (*gnosis*) rendered them incapable of sinning?   Were they claiming sinless perfectionism since the time of their enlightenment, such as "Whatever may be true about other people sinning, we as Gnostic believers have transcended it all"?   Is this what the heretics would say in response to the call to confession of sins in verse 9?   The claim "we have not sinned" has a double consequence as the rest of the verse goes on to state: we make God a liar, and His word is not in us.

We make Him a liar – To claim sinless perfection since our conversion/enlightenment is not just to tell a deliberate lie (verse 6), or to deceive ourselves (verse 8).   It is worse.   It is tantamount to accusing God of lying to us since His Word frequently declares that sin is universal.[68]   The Gospel, which calls all men everywhere to repent, assumes the universal nature of sin.   God sent His Son into the world to be a sin offering because He knows that men do sin and need such an offering.   Even Christians sin (Romans 6:12, 13).   The idea

---

[65] Romans 6:19 speaks of people presenting their members as slaves to impurity and lawlessness. 'Impurity' says that sin defiles a man.   Does cleansing include removing those 'desires of sin' that have been excited and stirred up by the devil's temptations?   Does cleansing include the removal of the guilt that resulted from the sins?

[66] God, who is light (and has revealed how He does things), has said that forgiveness and cleansing, issuing from the faithfulness and justice of God, are conditional on confession of our sins.   Hear it!   This is one of many warnings in Scripture concerning the deadly danger of hiding or ignoring of sins, or treating them lightly.

[67] Believers in the doctrine of total hereditary depravity appeal to that doctrine to explain the change of verb tenses.   They would have verse 8 be a denial of an indwelling sinful nature, and verse 10 to be a denial of specific acts of sin.   (See Wuest, *op. cit.*, p.106; and A.T. Robertson, *The First Epistle of John* in Word Pictures in the New Testament [Nashville, TN: Broadman Press, 1933], Vol.6, p.208.)   See footnote #45 on verse 8, for further notes on total hereditary depravity.

[68] 1 Kings 8:46; Psalm 14:3; Ecclesiastes 7:20; Isaiah 53:6, 54:6; Romans 3:23.   In passing, even if we believed in the doctrine of an inherited sinful nature, it is hard to reconcile the Catholic doctrine of the immaculate conception of Mary with what John here writes.

of making[69] God a liar challenges the imagination. All of God's dealings with creation since Adam's fall have been done on the basis of the fact that sin is in the world. For the creature to dispute the Creator's knowledge of reality to the extent that he must argue that God has been acting according to that which is not real staggers the faculties of perception! Yet this, says John, is precisely what one does when he claims to know God and at the same time claim he has not sinned.[70]

And His word is not in us – The construction here is parallel to the one in verse 8: "His word (*ho logos*) is not in us" here in verse 10 matches "the truth (*hē alētheia*) is not in us" of verse 8. The "word of God" here is tantamount to the "truth" that verse 8 spoke of, the "message of the gospel."[71] If anyone claims "we have not sinned," he is a stranger to the preaching of the apostles. Is "His word is in us" another slogan of the heretics? Does John here allude to that slogan, showing it is just as false as some of the other ones he has attacked in this paragraph? "The expressions 'to be in' and 'to abide in,' which express intimate relationship, are characteristic of John."[72]

2:1 -- My little children, I am writing these things to you that you may not sin. And if anyone sins, we have an Advocate with the Father, Jesus Christ the righteous.

My little children – Three false claims made by the heretics have been introduced in 1:6,8, 10. Previously when replying to the false claims, John began his presentation of correct Christian practice with an "if" clause (1:7,9). This time (2:1,2), before he writes the "if" clause, he inserts some very personal language as he presents the correct Christian thought and practice in direct opposition to how the heretics behaved ("we have not sinned," 1:10). To address his readers as "my little children" suggests the writer is advanced in years and is speaking to a younger generation.[73] It also suggests, metaphorically, that he has a special, spiritual relationship towards them.[74] While some readers may owe their conver-

---

[69] The use of the verb "make" in the sense of "assert that one is" is frequent in John's writings. See John 19:7,12, 5:18, 8:53, 10:33.

[70] Man's proper attitude is "Let God be found true, and every man a liar," Romans 3:3. If anyone is telling a lie, it is not God.

[71] Compare John 17:17 where Jesus declares that God's "word" is "truth."

[72] Plummer, *op. cit.*, p.85.

[73] The diminutive form (*teknia*) should not be taken literally, as though John were addressing "babies" or preteen children. The final warning against idols, literal or metaphorical, that comes later in the Epistle (5:21) could hardly be addressed to children as opposed to grown-up members of the church. For this reason we treat John's "little children" as a metaphorical expression.

[74] Sometimes he writes *paidia* (children) as in 2:13,18, and sometimes *teknia* (little children) as here and in 2:12,22. Here alone he adds the possessive adjective "my." *Pais* gives prominence to age, denoting a child as one who is young. Sometimes the word is used of a servant. *Teknon* gives prominence to descent, and often beautifully describes those who are God's children (as at 3:1), having been born again. John could have learned the use of both words from Jesus Himself – *teknia* in John 13:33 and *paidia* in John 21:5.

sion to Christianity to John's ministry, all of them, he feels, are his responsibility to watch over like a loving, concerned parent watches over the younger ones in the home.[75]

I am writing these things to you that you may not sin – With these words John explains the purpose of what he is writing at this point in this epistle. In this verse and in many of the following verses,[76] John uses the first person singular ("I") in order to give his exhortation a personal touch. As in 1:2,3,5, John addresses his readers as "you." "These things" likely is intended to refer to what he has written about "sin" since 1:7.[77] John has written about the cleansing blood of Jesus (1:7) and how God forgives those who confess their sins (1:9). But these precious promises are not intended to lead the readers to think lightly of the gravity of sin. Just the opposite. John is holding out the high ideal that Christians ought to have it as their aim not to sin at all.[78] God's plan of redemption includes the means by which such an aim may be more and more realized in the lives of Christians. Paul worded it this way, "[Stop letting] sin reign in your mortal bodies ... and do not go on presenting the members of your body to sin as instruments of unrighteousness, but present yourselves to God as those alive from the dead, and your members as instruments of righteousness to God" (Romans 6:12,13). In diametric contradiction to what the Gnostic lived and taught, continuing fellowship with God requires self-control and steadfast resistance to temptations to sin. Only in the recognition of sin and of the exceeding sinfulness of it is there any hope of gradually eliminating sin from one's life. If we will recognize that there is such a thing as acting contrary to God's will, and that when we do so act we are personally guilty and held accountable for the act by God, we will have begun to view sin as God views it. There are moral absolutes. God has revealed what is right, and the opposite of right is wrong! If we will recognize what it cost Christ on Calvary to make forgiveness possible for us, we may begin to see the tremendous serious-

---

[75] John's concept of the Church is that of a family, in which all are children of God and brethren one of another, but in which also some who are elders (older in years and in the faith) stand in a parental relation to the younger ones. Thus there are families within the family, each with its own father. And who had a better right to consider himself a father than the last surviving apostle? (Adapted from Plummer, *op. cit.*, p.86.)

[76] See 2:7,8,21,26; 5:13,16. John's use of "I" stands in bold contrast to his use of "we" (1:1-4), which called attention to himself as one of the eyewitnesses of Jesus' ministry, and thus one of the guardians of the apostolic faith which he had been commissioned to transmit.

[77] In a footnote on 1:4 the difficulty of explaining demonstrative pronouns in 1 John was introduced. That difficulty is easily recognized when one compares the comments offered at this place (e.g., "these things refers to the contents of the whole epistle," or "to that which follows," or "to the preceding chapter").

[78] The aorist tense, *hina mē hamartēte*, shows John has in mind individual acts of sin rather than habitual actions. No encouragement is given to those who continue to habitually sin in the present, or to those who with no compunction contemplate future sin. On several occasions Jesus commanded one who would be His follower to "Sin no more!" (e.g., John 5:14, 8:11). "Stop sinning!" Christians, too, are to live by this command from their Lord.

ness of sin. To know that the blood of God's only Son is required each day to cleanse us from the normal guilt of 'well adjusted' lives, is to realize the phenomenal deadliness of sin. Such recognition will go far toward changing the pattern of our behavior, and sinful acts will become less and less frequent.

And if anyone sins – "Anyone" (any individual Christian) may find himself or herself committing acts of sin, because none is sinless perfect. The verb tense here (aorist) refers to individual acts of sin, just as did the previous phrase.[79] Individual acts of sin are to become less and less frequent, but Christians do not, in this life, reach the point of perfection where they do not need the blood.[80] To commit a sin is a serious matter, but the Christian should not ever think his act is unforgivable. Instead of deceiving themselves about the gravity of their acts of sin, or lying about their actions, or ceasing to walk in the light, they should recognize that the actions of the Advocate in heaven, Jesus Christ the righteous, are required for and are capable of providing forgiveness.

We have an Advocate with the Father – Just as we Christians always have sin (1:8), so we always have (*echomen*[81]) One who is ready to speak to the Father on our behalf.[82] John wrote "we," including himself in the group who has need of an Advocate with the Father. For the third time (see 1:7,9) John comes to the question of forgiveness, and in so doing replies once more to the heretical claim to be free from sin. In fact, the heretical claim involves a denial of one of Jesus' great services on behalf of the children of God, that He is our Advocate. For the person trying to sin less ("not sin"), Jesus serves as "advocate." He is not an advocate for the person who carelessly continues to sin or who denies he has any sin. What is an "advocate" (*paraklētos*), and what does an advocate do? An "advocate" or "paraclete"[83] is one who is called to someone's side, one who comes to help

---

[79] At 1 John 3:9 and 5:18 we will have a present tense verb, indicating continuous or habitual action. But the verb here is aorist, pointing to single acts of sin into which a believer may lapse as against the true tenor of his life.

[80] The "if" clause does not imply a doubt that there ever will be occasional acts of sin, as some defenders of sinless perfectionism have asserted. The very opposite is true: a present general condition (such as we have here) implies that the condition in the protasis can be expected to occur with some regularity.

[81] "We have" is present tense, indicating what is a fact now and will continue to be so till the end of the age, since Jesus has been designated the believer's advocate.

[82] Perhaps attention should be directed to 1 Timothy 2:5 which tells us there is "one mediator between God and men, the man Christ Jesus." This rules out the popular notion that there are many roads to God. It rules out the idea that others (e.g., the saints or the virgin Mary) can intercede for us and serve as our Advocate. No human can take the place of Jesus. If we do not have Jesus as our Advocate, we do not have an advocate with the Father.

[83] The word in both its Latin and Greek equivalents (*advocatus* and *paraklētos*) was used in the law courts of a barrister, whose responsibility it was, as counsel for the defense, to plead the cause of the person on trial. Commentators have written long on the question of whether the word should be translated "comforter" as was often done in the KJV at John 14:16,26, 15:26, 16:7. A good summary and defense of using "advocate" in all instances can be found in Plummer, *op. cit.*, p.86-87.

a person, a go-between who acts to establish or restore friendly relations.[84]   Unconfessed sin is a barrier to fellowship with God.   But when Christians confess their sins, the Advocate is allowed to go to work, to make sure the fellowship continues.[85]   What John is probably picturing in the words "advocate with the Father"[86] is that the very Jesus, who for a while was incarnate on earth and who is now ascended and enthroned alongside the Father, is the One who addresses Himself to the Father on behalf of His followers.   He asks the Father for the penitent's forgiveness when any one sins and comes confessing and asking forgiveness.[87]   From this picture of Jesus' intercession, we should not infer the idea that God is an unwilling judge, from whom forgiveness has to be wrested by our Advocate. 1 John 1:9 has already pictured God as faithful and just to forgive our sins, so He is not "unwilling."   This verse pictures Him as a "loving Father" with whom Jesus has to plead.

Jesus Christ the righteous – This clause serves to explain who the Advocate is, and why He is qualified to perform the function of advocate.   The composite expression indicates

---

[84] Jesus promised the apostles (John 14:16) that He would pray to the Father, and the Father would send "another paraclete" (*allon paraklēton*), implying that while the Spirit functions here on earth as paraclete, Jesus will be functioning in heaven as paraclete.   In fact, before Jesus went back to the Father, He already had been functioning as "advocate" while here on earth (Luke 22:31,32).   This same idea of Jesus functioning as an "advocate" is expressed in Romans 8:34 ("Christ ... at the right hand of God, who also intercedes for us"), in Hebrews 9:24 ("Christ ... [entered] into heaven itself, now to appear in the presence of God for us"), and in Hebrews 7:25 ("He always lives to make intercession for them").

[85] Christians do need continuing justification, a pronouncement of acquittal from God the Judge. Romans 4:5 ("justifies [present tense, continuous action] the ungodly") pictures justification as something that happens over and over during a Christian's lifetime on earth.

[86] The preposition "with" (already explained at 1:2) refers to the place where the Advocate is, "near to, before, at the side of" the Father.   He is intimately close to the Father, face-to-face with the Father.   As indicated in comments at 1:2, "Father" is a reference to the first member of the Godhead.   We pray in the name of Christ.   And as we pray in this way, we each time acknowledge that Christ is making intercession for us.   "Father" (rather than "God") at this place brings out the idea that the Advocate is none other than His Son, and that through Him we believers are made sons.

[87] God only can forgive sin.   Though we have no claim on the Father, yet there is One who can plead our cause and on whom we can rely to manage our interests there in the courts of heaven.   It is just here that the real meaning of Jesus' incarnation experience begins to be seen in the life of the Christian.   To the person who has committed his life to God, who constantly accepts not only the fact of his own sin but also its guilt, there is blessed comfort of knowing that an understanding Friend intercedes for him before God.   There is no need to make excuses.   There is no need to deny or explain away sin.   One who knows Jesus as a personal Friend can confidently confess his sins and ask for forgiveness, confident that Jesus will intercede with the Father on his behalf.

His human nature (Jesus), His Messianic office (Christ),[88] and His righteous character.[89] As true man, Jesus can state the case for men with absolute knowledge and real sympathy; after all, He was tempted in all points like as we (Hebrews 2:17,18; 4:15). As Messiah, He is God's messenger to men and the divinely sent sacrifice for sins; He is a reason to be heard by Him before whom He pleads. Because He is "righteous," because Jesus always does what is right before God,[90] He can enter the Presence from Whom all sin excludes. "This makes Him a most effective advocate with God. His requests are not hindered by sin and, therefore, will certainly be heard by God (cp. John 9:31; James 5:16)."[91] "It is as being righteous Himself that He can so well plead with the 'righteous Father' (John 17:25; 1 John 1:9) for those who are not righteous."[92] Hebrews 7:25,26 is a good commentary on the relationship between Christ's sinlessness and His living to make intercession for the saints.[93] Jesus' advocacy and His propitiatory sacrifice (next verse) are the remedy when Christians do sin.

2:2 -- *And He Himself is the propitiation for our sins; and not for ours only, but also for those of the whole world.*

And He Himself is the propitiation for our sins – "He Himself" is emphatic: "He Himself and no one else is the propitiation" is the idea. "Is" is present tense; He continues

---

[88] Although John at this point is dealing with the problem of sin as raised by the heretics, for him to write this double name is certainly a glance at the low Christology typical of the Gnostic. Later he will specifically insist that "Jesus IS the Christ" (2:22).

[89] *Dikaios* is a predicate adjective, 'Jesus Christ who is righteous.' See comments on "righteous" at 1:9. The word has no article here in 2:1, so the word is not a title but emphasizes quality. Jesus was styled "the Righteous One" in apostolic preaching (e.g., Acts 3:14, 7:52). Peter spoke of Jesus as the righteous One who died on behalf of the unrighteous, so that He might bring them to God (1 Peter 3:18). It is the same thought which John is expressing here. It is hardly possible to translate the Greek without using the English word "the." If we pause and emphasize "righteous" as we read the passage, we will draw attention to who and what Jesus is, just as the Greek does. (To think of Jesus as a only a sage who taught beautiful ideas to a school is to miss what John here says of Him. He is "the righteous [One].")

[90] In this description of Jesus, note the contrast to chapter 1 where men are all said to be sinners. The reference to Christ being *righteous* parallels the description of God in 1:9 as being "righteous." The adjective *dikaios* is used in both verses for this attribute of deity. Whereas men are sinners, "the righteousness, purity and sinlessness of Christ's character are mentioned several times, directly or indirectly, in this epistle (2:6,29; 3:3,5,7). It is self-evident that only through a *righteous* Savior could we be cleansed from 'all unrighteousness' (1:9). Cp. 2 Corinthians 5:21 and 1 Peter 3:18." (Stott, *op. cit.*, p.81.)

[91] Haas, *op. cit.*, p.41.

[92] Plummer, *op. cit.*, p.87.

[93] In Hebrews, Christ intercedes as our "priest." In 1 John He intercedes as our "advocate."

to be this every day! Translators struggle to find an English equivalent for *hilasmos*:[94] "propitiation," "expiation," and "remedy" have been suggested.[95] So have "sin offering" and "atoning sacrifice."[96] Our Advocate, Jesus, does not maintain that we are innocent. Instead, He confesses our guilt and then reminds our Father that His blood makes it possible to forgive us our sins. We can use the English word "propitiation" if we give it a different definition than the word normally carries. God's wrath is not *appeased* by sacrifices of human origin. Rather, it is *conciliated* because of the shed blood of Christ, a sacrifice which God Himself has provided (1 John 4:10). Our sins are *atoned*, and that which might have occasioned alienation is covered (1 John 1:7). Our Advocate reminds the Father of this when we confess our sins. All this is foreign to what the heretics taught. Gnostics taught that the death of Jesus had nothing to do with the forgiveness of sins.[97] John, in contrast, shows that the death of Christ is the thing that makes forgiveness possible.

And not for ours only, but also for *those of* the whole world – This seems to be saying that Christ's sacrifice is sufficient for all, and it is necessary for all.[98] Jesus' sacrifice is not limited to one particular group of readers, not even John's immediate readers. Hebrews 2:9 tells us that Christ tasted death "for every one." The Gnostic fancied himself

---

[94] A noun with a *-mos* ending denotes action; a noun with a *-ma* ending indicates the result of that action. Jesus is here pictured as "acting" as men's covering.

[95] Modern readers' vocabularies often do not include these theological terms from earlier times. So modern translators have tried to find modern equivalents. Some paraphrase to express the idea in the Greek word.

[96] Paul uses a cognate form of the word "propitiation" (*hilastērion*) at Romans 3:25. What is said in this commentator's book on Romans at that place is true of the word used here in 1 John. In Greek literature, *hilaskomai* carries the idea of an offering made by a guilty person in order to placate or appease someone (a god) who has been offended. It is such an idea that the English word "propitiate" conveys. Since Westcott's time (*op. cit.*, p.85), some scholars have argued that the Greek word does not so much mean placate, but rather alludes to the altering of the character of that which, from without, occasions a necessary alienation, and interposes an inevitable obstacle to fellowship. Scholars who are convinced by Westcott's arguments prefer the English word "expiate" as a suitable translation. In comments at Romans we have discussed the fact that *hilastērion* is the word used in the LXX for the "covering" or "mercy seat" on the Ark of the Covenant. In Old Covenant times, blood sprinkled on that "covering" shielded the sinner from the wrath of God. (To get an idea about how this word was used in the Greek, we might compare the Hebrew of Numbers 5:8, "the ram of atonement," with the LXX, "the ram of the *hilasmos*"; the emphasis is propitiation. Compare also the Hebrew at Psalm 130:4, "there is forgiveness with Thee," with the LXX, "before Thee is the *hilasmos*"; propitiation is again the idea.) In New Covenant times, the blood of Christ is the "covering" that shields penitent sinners from the wrath of God.

[97] Redemption for the Gnostic involved a release from ignorance, not from sin.

[98] "World" here seems limited to the "people" who live on this globe. *Kosmos* has a number of meanings in the Bible. (1) It can mean "ornament" (1 Peter 3:3). (2) It can refer to the whole ordered universe (Romans 1:20). (3) It can refer to this terrestrial ball on which we live (John 1:9). (4) It can refer to the human inhabitants on this earth (John 3:16). (5) It can refer to all that is alienated from God (1 John 2:1-17, 5:19; John 12:31, 14:30). Each time we come to the word, we must decide the meaning intended.

to be part of an exclusive few in whom God took special interest. Not so, says John! Jesus is not the means whereby an elite few are brought into special relationship with God: His sacrifice avails for all – not just a few.[99] Christians ("ours") need the covering Christ's blood provides, and so do lost and wicked men ("the whole world"[100]) in all ages of the world's history.[101]

---

[99] This language ought not to be construed as supporting universalism, the doctrine that all men are automatically saved by Christ's death and that, therefore, none will be lost. The tests or conditions being presented by John are evidence that those who do not meet the tests do not have life, much less fellowship with God. The dogma of "limited atonement" (wherein Jesus dies just for the "elect") also hardly harmonizes with what John here writes. Christ's death was offered for the whole world, without limitation. All who will may profit by it. It remains to be seen who will (of their own free choice) avail themselves of the opportunity (1 John 4:9,14; John 1:29, 3:16, 5:24).

[100] This statement "whole world" relates not to every creature God has made, for then the fallen angels also would share in Christ's redemption, and such a wholesale sharing is not what Scripture holds out for fallen angels (Matthew 25:41, Hebrews 2:16,17). John uses the adjective *holos* (whole) instead of *pas* (all, every) to communicate the idea of universality. The word *holos* has "an indefinite meaning which *pas* does not have" (Kistemaker, *op. cit.*, p.255).

[101] Christ's blood covered the sins of faithful men in Old Testament times, as well as the sins of faithful men in New Testament times (Romans 3:25,26; Hebrews 9:15). Jesus' forerunner introduced Him as "the Lamb of God who takes away the sin of the world" (John 1:29). The Samaritans acclaimed Jesus as "the Savior of the world" (John 4:42).

C. Copying the Example of Christ. 2:3-6

> *Summary*: John has emphasized two conditions of fellowship with God in 1:5-2:2. Now he presents a third condition of fellowship with God. All of the conditions are simply an unfolding of the major thesis that "God is light" (1:5).[1] When copying the example of Christ, we have both the word of Christ (verses 3-5) and the walk of Christ (verse 6) to be copied.

2:3 --*And by this we know that we have come to know Him, if we keep His commandments.*

And by this we know – The plural "we" (expressing Christian assurance) in this verse is contrasted with "the one who says" (expressing the spurious claim of the Gnostics) in the next verse. "By this we know," by this we can be sure, is a characteristic expression found in 1 John nine times.[2] The verb is present tense; we know from time to time, from day to day, whenever our hearts need assurance. Perhaps John is picking up the language of the heretics, whose claims (verse 4) to know God were spurious. He counteracts their claims by giving the correct Christian means of assurance. Perhaps we should understand that the teachings and claims of the heretics had caused the Christians to begin to doubt their standing with God and/or their relationship to Christ. To counteract such a deleterious effect, John gives certain tests by which a man can know by experience (*ginōskō*)[3] what his relationship is and where he stands.[4] John challenges the Gnostic claim of *special* knowledge by an appeal to *experimental* knowledge.

That we have come to know Him – We have chosen to treat the pronoun "Him" in this paragraph as being a reference to Jesus.[5] We may suppose that John foresees a question

---

[1] At this point we are plunged into the difficulties of outlining this epistle. Some argue that since verse 3 begins with "and" it precludes beginning a new section here. Yet the same writers began a new section at 1:5 which also begins with "and." Those who begin a new section with verse 3 cannot agree on its extent. Some think the paragraph extends to verse 11. Some extend it to verse 13. We are following the paragraphing of the NASB when we end the paragraph at verse 6.

[2] 1 John 2:3,5; 3:16,19,24; 4:2,6,13; 5:2.

[3] Twenty-five times in this epistle, John uses the verb *ginōskō*, to know by experience. Thirteen times in this epistle, he uses *oida*, to know by instruction.

[4] "By this" (*en toutō*) evidently points to what follows and serves to call attention to it. Following each of the "by this we know" statements, John gives various means of testing what it is a Christian may be assured of: to "know Him," "that we are in Him," "to know love," "to know we are in the truth," "to know that He abides in us," "to know the Spirit of God" or "the Spirit of error," "that we are the children of God," and "that we are abiding in Him." Sometimes "we know" is followed by a *hina* clause, sometimes by *ean* or *hotan*.

[5] "Jesus Christ the righteous" (2:1) is the nearest antecedent. Nevertheless, commentators are about evenly divided in their opinions whether "Him" here in verse 3 is Jesus or God the Father. The older commentators opted for Christ's commands. But some modern expositors have tried to show that when the pronoun *autos* ("Him") is used (as here in verse 3) the reference is to God the Father, and when *ekeinos*

being raised in his reader's minds: "How can I be assured that Christ is all this to *me* – that He is *my* propitiation, *my* advocate?   And how can I be assured that *my* interest in Him is genuine?"   John answers by calling attention to two conditions: keeping His commandments, and walking as He walked.   This verb translated "have come to know" is a perfect tense in the Greek: "we gained this knowledge in the past and we still do know Him."   The Christian way to knowing Christ differs greatly from the Gnostic way.   The Gnostics claimed, "I have come to know Him" (verse 4).   Were the heretics in John's day like the 2nd century Gnostics[6] whose "knowledge" of deity came through mystical insights or by direct visions?   Were they inducing an altered state of consciousness, having an experience, and then claiming to have had a personal experience of/with God/Jesus?   If so, John may well be counteracting the Gnostic approach to knowledge through an altered state of consciousness.   The way to know Christ, John flatly says, is by keeping His commandments, not by inducing a vision.   Christians don't have to sit on the sidelines when some heretic says "I know Him" (because I have had an ecstatic experience), and wonder if they have missed something.   There is a genuine, tangible experience any Christian may point to as evidence he knows Christ.

If we keep His commandments – *Tereō* ("keep") means "to attend carefully, to guard [something precious], to observe" (Thayer).   Involved is not merely the act of obeying His commands, but also a solicitous desire to obey them.[7]   The present tense speaks of continuous action: do we habitually obey His commandments?   It is habitual, moment by moment guarding of the Word by the saint, lest at any moment he violate one of its precepts.   It is the habitual keeping, the tenor of a man's life, that counts.   We reveal what kind of people we are by what we do.   "Commandments" translates *entolē* (not *nomos*).   If it were *nomos*, we might think of the commands recorded in the Mosaic Law, for John uses *nomos* 15 times in his Gospel in this connection.[8]   *Entolē* is almost a technical term

---

is used, the reference generally is to Jesus. As we read the commentaries on verses 3-6, we find a great difference in the identification of "Him." We will have to make a decision each time we come to the pronoun.

[6] *Corpus Hermetica* 10.5-6 is an example: "Not yet are we able to open the eyes of the mind and to behold the beauty, the imperishable, inconceivable beauty, of the Good. For you will see it when you cannot say anything about it. For the knowledge of it is divine silence and annihilation of all senses ... Irradiating the whole mind, it shines upon the soul and draws it up from the body, and changes it into divine essence."

[7] As opposed to *phulassein* (*custodire*, Lat), *terein* (*observare*, Lat.) denotes sympathetic obedience to the spirit of a command, rather than the rigid carrying out of its letter (Brooke, *op. cit.*, p.30). We may compare the rich young ruler's statement, "All these things have I kept (*ephulaxamēn*) from my youth" (Mark 10:20 KJV). He had obeyed the letter, but not the spirit, so Jesus set about to correct that deficiency.

[8] While Christians are not under the Law of Moses, they are under law to Christ (1 Corinthians 9:21).

for a "divinely-given order."   For the commands of the gospel, John uses *entolai*, or *logos theou* [or *christou*].[9]   Indeed, since Jesus is God, the commands He spoke and those written by His apostles as they spoke on His behalf are "divinely-given orders."   Keeping Christ's commands is both a condition of coming to know Him, and of continuing to know Him.[10]   Safely, we may assume that John's test includes the willingness and the effort to obey "all things, whatsoever I have commanded you" (Matthew 28:20).

2:4 -- *The one who says, "I have come to know Him," and does not keep His commandments, is a liar, and the truth is not in him;*

The one who says – This wording is closely parallel to 1:6,8,10, and likely reflects something the heretics habitually were saying.[11]   There is a striking parallel between the beginning of this paragraph and the beginning of the previous one.   In both there is a statement of a theme: to have fellowship is to walk in the light (1:5) and to know Him is to keep His commandments (2:3).   Next there is a statement of and a rejection of the claims or assertions the false teachers regularly made.   Then the implication of the false claim is contrasted to the blessing one has who holds the truth.

"I have come to know Him" – This is a quotation of one of the claims the heretics voiced.[12]   It has been suggested in the notes on verse 3 that by such language the heretics were calling attention to an ecstatic visionary experience (seen during a self-induced altered state of consciousness).   As there, so here, we would make "Him" a reference to Christ, rather than to God the Father.   "I ... know Him" was perhaps tantamount to saying, 'Because of the experience, I am saved, I am a Christian, I have a special relationship with Him.'

And does not keep His commandments – It is the same person who "says" and who "does not keep."[13]   The tense of the participles in this verse indicate that the "saying" and the "not keeping" are contemporaneous events.   As in verse 3, the "does not keep" is present tense, continuous action.   It speaks of a day-by-day failure to obey what Christ has com-

---

[9] "Commandments" (here introduced in the epistle for the first time, but see 3:22-24, 4:21, 5:2,3) answers to such other expressions as "the message" (1:5), "His word" (2:5), "the truth" (2:21) and "what you heard from the beginning" (2:24).   These are all general expressions to denote the teachings of Jesus.

[10] If it is objected that in this case no one knows Christ because no one is perfectly obedient, we may reply the Greek does not imply perfect obedience.   The verb "obey" is present tense, continual action.

[11] "The one who" is probably not an attack on one particular Gnostic teacher.   It rather expresses something that any Gnostic was likely to affirm.

[12] In indirect discourse such as this verse is, *hoti* is Greek for "quotation marks."

[13] The participle "keep" is dependent on the introductory "the one who" just as is the participle "says." Sharp's rule of grammar shows this connection.

manded.   Apparently we are to gather from this that the heretics were indifferent to the commands of Christ.[14]

Is a liar – The saying of words, where there is no keeping of the commands, is a lie.[15]   His conduct contradicts his profession and proves it to be false.   John's denunciatory language has become stronger.   In 1:8 he spoke of the heretics being deceived.   John no longer speaks of deception.   Their claim is just an out-and-out lie!

And the truth is not in him – Except for the last two words, this statement is identical to that in 1:8.   The emphasis falls on "in him," meaning in such a one as habitually disobeys (sins).[16]   The truth of the gospel is what is absent.[17]   If the readers will listen to the apostle John, the heretical claims will no longer be enticing to them.   The heretics are obviously not presenting God's truth; they are telling lies.   Who, in their right minds, would want to buy into that?

2:5 -- *But whoever keeps His word, in him the love of God has truly been perfected.   By this we know that we are in Him:*

But whoever keeps His word – "Whoever" destroys the religious exclusiveness of the Gnostics.[18]   "Keeps" was explained in verse 3.   It is a present subjunctive speaking of habitual, continual action: "Whoever keeps (keeps on keeping) His word."   John's style is to make use of contrasts as he makes his point.[19]   Here he states the opposite of what he just wrote in verse 4.   Another characteristic of his style is to use various terms (like "truth" and "word" and "commandment") to express the same thought, though each term may introduce a new element into the argument.   "His word" is a wider expression than "His commandments."   Perhaps John intends by this change of term to cover the sum total of

---

[14] If a man today were to say, "I know that Jesus commanded repentance and immersion, but I don't believe immersion is necessary today," and at the same time claims to be saved, we could say with John, "that is a lie, and the truth is not in you."   The man who is ignorant of Christ's commands is in a different class than the man who is willful in his disobedience.

[15] Colwell's rule of grammar shows this definite predicate nominative should be rendered "the liar."

[16] The Greek also could be translated "in that," i.e., in that behavior.

[17] The word translated "truth" (*alētheia*) has the connotation of "genuineness," something which the heretics cannot claim for their teaching and practice.   See John 8:31.   The truth respecting Christianity, the truth respecting duties to God, the truth respecting duties to man – all these are missing.

[18] The relative pronoun ("whoever") and the Greek particle *an* or *ean* followed by a verb in the subjunctive can serve as the introduction to the protasis in a conditional sentence.   That is what we have here.

[19] For example, he contrasts truth and lie, light and darkness, love and hatred, keeps and does not keep.

the revelation of God's will that has been delivered through His Son in these last days (Hebrews 1:1-2).[20]

In him the love of God has truly been perfected – *En toutō* can be masculine ("in him") or neuter ("in this"). If we take it as neuter, it speaks of obeying the commands (verse 3) and keeping God's word (verse 5). If we take it as masculine, it speaks of the person whose life is right. "The love of God" reminds us of John 3:16. It was the love of God for men which brought Jesus into the world (1 John 4:9,10).[21] The long years of preparation recorded in the Old Testament were overtures of this divine love. One cannot read the Gospel accounts of the crucifixion without being moved by the demonstration of God's love for a world which was deserving of anything but love. The insults, the shame, the humiliation, the pain of the cross, bespeak a love beyond human comprehension. God first loved us (1 John 4:10), then we love Him and express that love by keeping Christ's commandments. "Perfected"[22] tells us that the purpose for which God loved men has been accomplished, that God's love has reached its goal, in the person who habitually keeps His word. God wanted a family who would love Him, and whom He could love. That is why He created. That is why He provided redemption for fallen man. The person who habitually obeys the Word is the person who has become a Christian (1 John 4:7), been adopted into the family of God, and demonstrates his "sonship" by living as His Father wills His children to live. All the plan of God decided upon before He began to create, all the call to service, all of the covenants, all the ages of preparation, all the agony of the cross, are meaningless until they produce in the individual heart the "obedience of faith"

---

[20] On the use and meaning of "word" see notes at 1:1 and 1:10.

[21] We are treating this genitive expression as meaning "God's love for man" rather than "man's love for God." Expositors are not in agreement how to treat this genitive. Some treat it as a subjective genitive ("God's love for man"); some treat it as objective ("our love for God"); some treat it as a descriptive or qualitative genitive ("God's kind of love"). Supportive arguments have been advanced for each of the possible interpretations. For the reader who wishes to pursue this, Westcott and Kistemaker argue for the subjective meaning ("God's love" [verse 5] compares to "God's truth" [verse 4]; Brooke, Marshall, and Stott call attention to the parallel expressions in 2:15 and 5:3 to support the objective interpretation ("our love for God"); and Schnackenburg defends the descriptive idea. Alford (*op. cit.,* p.434) observes that "some [Protestant commentators] have shied away from the subjective view in order to avoid any possible thought of the Romish folly of supererogation." Taking it as objective ("our love for God"), it was this and other references in this Epistle (4:12,17f) which led John Wesley to his doctrine of "perfect love" as the characteristic of the mature Christian. To Wesley, perfect love for God would issue in perfect obedience. (John Wesley, *A Plain Account of Christian Perfection*, London, 1952 ed.) These views were expressed in song by Charles Wesley, "Love divine, all loves excelling ... take away our love of sinning ... Thee we would be always blessing, serve Thee as Thy hosts above ... Pray, and praise Thee without ceasing ...."

[22] *Teleioō* ("perfected, completed, finished, reached its goal") is a favorite word with John (see John 4:34, 5:36, 17:4, 19:28,30). The verb here is perfect tense, indicating past completed action with present continuing results.

(Romans 16:26). So John writes, "... whoever goes on keeping His word, truly in that one the love of God has reached its intended end."[23]

By this we know that we are in Him – The NASB punctuates the last part of verse 5 and verse 6 so that the phrase "by this ..." introduces what is said in verse 6.[24] "Walking as He walked" is how we can know. This expression ("by this we know") is the same expression of assurance we had in verse 3. "The whole context, and especially verse 6, suggests that the phrase 'in Him' again refers to Christ. To be 'in Christ' is Paul's characteristic description of the Christian. But John uses it too."[25] "We are" (*esmen*, present tense) means we continue to be in Him. How do we come to be "in Him" in the first place? We are baptized into Christ (Romans 6:3, Galatians 3:27). This is the first time in 1 John that the idea of being "in Christ" occurs.[26] What does the expression to be "in Him" involve? John seems to use this language to describe a genuine spiritual experience as contrasted with the counterfeit experience claimed by the heretics and for which they used the Biblical language "abide in Him" (verse 6).[27]

*2:6 -- **The one who says he abides in Him ought himself to walk in the same manner as He walked.***

The one who says – This formula introduced a false claim in verse 4. Perhaps the same is true of verse 6. The heretics claimed to "abide in Christ" but the claim was a lie, just like the claim in verse 4 was a lie.

He abides in Him – This expression, habitually repeated, is another way the heretics described their relationship with Christ. Exactly what they were claiming by this language we do not know. Perhaps as a result of their mystical experiences or visions of light they

---

[23] Those who insist this verse speaks of man's love for God urge that the verse means that love for the Savior would be defective without keeping of His commands. Some even appeal to Jesus' own statement, "He who has My commandments and keeps them, he it is who loves Me" (John 14:21).

[24] All that was said in comments on "by this" at verse 3 apply here. Just as there, so here, commentators cannot decide whether the phrase points backward to what has gone before, or whether it points forward to what will be said in verse 6.

[25] Stott, *op. cit.*, p.91

[26] We are more familiar with the idea of "being in Christ" from Paul (Philippians 1:1; Romans 8:1, 3:24). After 1:6,7, John does not use the term "fellowship" but instead seems to substitute the expressions "be in Christ," "to know him," or "abide in him." Robertson, *op. cit.*, p.43,44.

[27] Jesus spoke about "abiding in Him" (John 15:4-10). Is that where the heretics picked up their "biblical language" to describe the "spiritual experience" (an altered state of consciousness) they had learned to induce? Does John deliberately pick up their claims in order to show how untrue they are?

were claiming a permanent relationship with Jesus.[28]   Or perhaps they were making a claim of total commitment to Christ without any corresponding lifestyle.[29]

Ought himself to walk in the same manner as He walked – The first "walk" is present tense, continuous or repeated action; the Christian is to habitually so live, to keep on walking.   The second "walk" is aorist tense; Jesus' "walk" on earth has been completed at the time 1 John is written.   Not only does the Christian keep Christ's word (verse 5), he has a "moral obligation ("ought," *opheilō*[30]) to walk ..." as Jesus walked.[31]   John here makes one of the rare allusions in his epistles to the earthly life of our Lord.[32]   The way in which John refers, almost elliptically, to the historical earthly life of Jesus, presupposes that his readers had some factual information on which to base their imitation of Christ which is being advocated.   What was the source of this historical information for the readers?   Was the source of information the preaching that led to their conversion in the first place?   Was the source of this information the Fourth Gospel, with the further implication that that Gospel was written before this epistle, and that it contains factual, historical, and authentic information about Jesus?   One of the stanzas of the song "Trust and Obey" conveys eloquently what John here teaching:

> When we walk with the Lord in the light of His Word,
> What a glory He sheds on our way!
> While we do His good will, He abides with us still,
> And with all who will trust and obey.

It is implied that the heretics did not walk as Jesus walked.   Thus John's readers can sort out the fact that the heretics' claims to "abide in Him" are specious, hollow, and false.   At

---

[28] "Abides" is present tense (continuous action), so perhaps they were claiming a permanent, lasting relationship which was unconditional.   ('Once saved, always saved,' the Gnostics seemed to be saying.)

[29] In comments on the Gospel of John, where the expression "abide in Him" occurs (John 15:4-7), we have offered the explanation that this is John's expression for "total commitment to Christ."

[30] John does not write "must" (*dei*, "must"), a necessity arising out of the nature of things, but rather *opheilō*, which indicates a personal obligation, a moral obligation, something one is bound by duty to do.

[31] On "walk" used metaphorically of a lifestyle, see notes at 1:6.

[32] The reference to Christ as an example is frequently found in some form (*kathōs ekeinos*) in our epistle.   See 2:29, 3:3,7, 4:17; cp. also John 13:15, 15:10; and 1 Peter 2:21.   Alford (*op. cit.*, p.435) calls attention to Luther's apposite remark, that it is not Christ's walking on the sea, but His ordinary walk, that we are called on here to imitate.

the same time, his readers can grasp that in which their own duty consists.[33]   One specific example to be imitated about how Jesus walked will be given in the following verses.

D. Compassion for our Brothers.   2:7-11

> *Summary*:   The fourth condition of fellowship with God (1:6ff) is love for our brothers.   John has just spoken (verse 3-6) of keeping Christ's commandments, and "walking as He walked."   Now (verses 7-11) he specifies a specific example of the kind of behavior he has in mind.

2:7 -- Beloved, I am not writing a new commandment to you, but an old commandment which you have had from the beginning; the old commandment is the word which you have heard.

Beloved – The KJV reads "brethren" (*adelphoi*), but manuscript evidence suggests that John wrote "beloved" (*agapētoi*).[1]   As he is about to write concerning brotherly love,[2] he appropriately addresses them as his "beloved."[3]

I am not writing a new commandment to you, but an old commandment – John has been writing about the Christian obligation to keep Christ's commands (verses 3,4,5). Now he singles out one of them, a command which in one sense is "old" (verse 7),[4] and in

---

[33] Not simply "as" (*hōs*) but "even as" (*kathōs*):   the imitation must be exact (Plummer, *op. cit.*, p.91.) John is not claiming that the walk of Jesus can be perfectly imitated by the Christian, but John does speak of a "consistent walk, a habitual walk" (present tense verb).   There is a personal, moral obligation, which must be taken seriously, for believers to live consistently in harmony with the way Jesus lived.

[1] This is the first occurrence of the writer's favorite form of address in these epistles.   Cf. 3:2,21; 4:1,7,11; 3 John 1,2,5,11.   (Brooke, *op. cit.*, p.34)

[2] For reasons to be given below, this is the interpretation of this passage that we have decided to follow.

[3] Sometimes the emphasis on the verbal adjective *agapētoi* is that the ones so addressed are "divinely loved."   Here, we think, John expresses his own love for his readers.   Perhaps this word also shows John's attitude as he writes.   1 John is written as a warning.   It contains much criticism and harsh language concerning the Gnostics, those who were denying the faith.   But John had learned the lesson that many present-day preachers and teachers have not learned.   While he detested the false teaching and called the false teachers "antichrists" (1 John 2:18ff), he loved those who were in danger of being misled by it and them.   While his denunciation of error is pointed and at times scathing and blunt, there is no, "You're wrong and you're lost and I'm glad!"

[4] There are two Greek words that are translated "old."   One is *archaios*, "ancient, that which has been from the beginning," and *palaios* (the word used here), "old, that which has been in existence for a long time."   Something that is *archaios* is older than that which is *palaios*.   *Palaios* also has a secondary meaning of that which is old and worn out, having suffered more or less from the injuries and ravages of time.

another sense is "new" (verse 8).[5] "The order of the Greek is worth keeping: *not a new commandment do I write*. What commandment is meant? To imitate Christ (verse 6)? Or to practice brotherly love (verses 9-11)? Practically it makes little matter which answer we give, for at bottom these are one and the same."[6] We opt for the command to practice brotherly love. That commandment is not "new;" John's readers have been aware of it for a good while. Yet John goes on to say that when it comes to practicing this command, it is something that is, one might say, almost eternally new.

Which you have had from the beginning – The context speaks of "you have had" and "you have heard," so "from the beginning" seems to point to the beginning of the readers' Christian experience.[7] The Gnostics were teaching new (*neos*) things; John was doing something exactly opposite. John's instructions were as old as the gospel itself. He was reminding them of truths that had regularly been part of the Christian message. John affirms there never was a 'gospel' that did not have this command at its heart. If the Gnostics leave it out of their doctrine and lifestyle, their doctrine and lifestyle differs markedly from what the apostles taught, and that makes their doctrine to be in error!

The old commandment is the word which you have heard – "Word" here is the "doctrine" or "gospel message" which was taught by those who first evangelized John's readers.[8] So basic was this instruction about loving the brethren that John is confident it was part of the message the readers were familiar with since they first became Christians. "Heard" says that the readers learned the gospel by oral instruction. John has changed verbs from "had" to "heard." "Hearing" is how they came to "have" it. They have heard this commandment from the beginning of their instruction in Christian doctrine and lifestyle.

---

[5] There are two words in Greek that are translated "new." One is *neos*, meaning "new in point of time, new, never existing before. The other (the one used here) is *kainos*, which expresses quality, new, or fresh, as opposed to worn out and obsolete.

[6] Plummer, *op. cit.*, p.92. "I am writing" has reference to what he is writing at this place (cp. notes at 2:1). On "commandment" (*entolē*), see notes at verse 3. Much difference of opinion has been expressed as to what "commandment" in particular John is speaking. Those scholars who think John is looking back at walking as Christ walked (verse 6) struggle to explain "old" and "new." One offers the doubtful suggestion that "old" refers to the Old Testament prophecies of Christ, and "new" to their New Testament fulfillment.

[7] There are those who say "from the beginning" takes us back to Old Testament times, where in Leviticus 19:18 God called on men to love their neighbors. Others insist that the "old commandment" to love one's brother was implicit in the story of Cain and Abel (cf. 1 John 3:11,12). Still others take us back to the beginning of the teaching of Christ. In the upper room, Jesus called on his apostles to love one another (John 13:34).

[8] This does not seem to be saying that the readers once lived in Palestine and there they were familiar with the teaching of the Lord Himself (as the KJV, which reads "which ye have heard from the beginning," might lead one to believe). The second occurrence of "from the beginning" included in this verse in the Textus Receptus and KJV does not enjoy integrity, being omitted by the majority of better and older manuscripts.

2:8 -- *On the other hand, I am writing a new commandment to you, which is true in Him and in you, because the darkness is passing away, and the true light is already shining.*

On the other hand – *Palin* is often translated "again," so some suggest a new point is begun at this place.[9]   But *palin* occasionally has an adversative sense (as in 2 Corinthians 10:7).   If so treated here, verse 8 introduces another description of the same commandment talked about in verse 7.   "I am not writing a new commandment ... *yet* I am writing a new commandment."   There is a sense in which it can be referred to as "new."

I am writing a new commandment to you – What in one sense was not fresh, in another sense is fresh and new.   The commandment was old not only because John's readers had been aware of it since the beginning of their Christian lives, but also because it had been taught even in the Patriarchal and Mosaic ages.   Yet John will go on to explain that it was also new – in the way Jesus taught it, and in its point of realization and fulfillment in the lives of the readers.   Again, the word "new" is *kainos*.   Loving the brother is a refreshing way to live!   It is an old commandment, to love – but never had love been seen in practice before Jesus came and walked in love.   The Jews, who had love as a commandment in the Old Testament, spoke of the Samaritans as dogs and considered the Gentiles as unfit for social relationships.   The Christian, whose life is controlled by love, knows "no man according to the flesh" (2 Corinthians 5:16).

Which is true in Him and in you – "Which" is a neuter relative pronoun.   Both "commandment" and "new" in the previous clause are feminine, so the relative "which" has no definite antecedent.   This has led to several different translations.   Some make the "commandment" to be true in both Christ and the readers.   Some make the "new[ness]" to be true both in Christ and the readers.   Some read, "a new command I write unto you, a thing which is true ...."   We should also note the double preposition which implies "that it is true in the case of Christ in a different sense from that in which it is true in the case of Christians.   He reissued the commandment and was the living embodiment and example of it; they accepted it and endeavored to follow it: both illustrated its truth and soundness."[10]   "In Him" leads us to recall that the law of love was illustrated in Christ.   It was manifested by Him in His dealings with His disciples, who were often so slow to learn; in His dealings with the publicans and sinners, because they found in Him someone who understood them and cared for them; and even in His dealings with His enemies, the Pharisees and Sadducees.   "In you" leads us to understand that John was aware that his readers were putting brotherly love into practice.   The love which Jesus commanded becomes new in John's readers as daily they put it into practice.

---

[9] In almost every phrase of this verse, the divergences of interpretation are almost endless.   We have had to choose from these options so that there is a train of thought that results.

[10] Plummer, *op. cit.*, p.93.

Because the darkness is passing away – "Because"[11] introduces a reason why John can call the commandment about brotherly love "new" and "true." "Darkness" in this verse is contrasted to the "true light," so stands for the Patriarchal and Mosaic ages which preceded the greater light of the Christian age. In those earlier ages, men had no help (like the indwelling Holy Spirit helps Christians[12]) to put into practice what God had commanded. Even though God gave the command to love one's neighbor, men found it difficult to practice. They found themselves walking in darkness (as chapter 1:5 spoke about). "Is passing away" is a present tense verb; the action is going on at the very time John was writing, as far as those who accept the gospel are concerned.[13] It wasn't completely gone, but it was in the process of giving way to the light. The thing John writes is "new" because Christians are living in a new age, the age when darkness is already passing, so a new kind of love can be expected and exemplified.

And the true light is already shining – It is possible for John's readers to love like Jesus commanded and exemplified "because" the new age had dawned. Jesus ushered in the new age ("the age to come," Matthew 12:32) which had long been anticipated by the Jews. "True light" here stands for the Christian message.[14] Christians have been delivered out of the present evil age (Galatians 1:4) and have already begun to taste the powers of the age to come (Hebrews 6:5; 1 Corinthians 10:11). Paul expressed a similar thought in Romans 13:12, "The night is almost gone, and the day is at hand." The more the true light shines, the more the darkness disappears.[15] The light is "true" (*alēthinos*) not in the sense in which a statement is true as opposed to false (*alēthes*, the word used at the beginning of this verse), but in the sense in which the real differs from the unreal, the genuine from the spurious, the substance from the shadow, and the prototype from the type. Perhaps John alludes to the fact that the Old Testament (which they had for a long time) was the shadow

---

[11] It seems better to translate *hoti* as "because" rather than "that." Even though some have attempted to make the words "in Him and in you" modify "darkness is passing" or "light is shining," this is to completely ignore the Greek word order. Therefore, we doubt that the phrase which follows (about the darkness passing, etc.) gives the content of the thing "which is true."

[12] Romans 8:4 shows that the indwelling Spirit can aid the Christian to fulfill the Law's demands in a way the old Jew with no indwelling Spirit never could.

[13] Bengel, (*Gnomon* 5:117) argued that *paragetai* is passive, not active. Thus the literal meaning is something like "the darkness is being caused to pass." God was understood to be the implied agent. Others have supposed the form is a middle voice, with an intransitive meaning. The Greek present tense was translated by the perfect tense in the Vulgate. Some commentators (including Luther and Calvin), following the lead of the Vulgate, treated it as meaning "the darkness is past." In this commentator's opinion, Luther's & Calvin's approach misses the point of what John is saying.

[14] Though in passages like John 1:9 Jesus Himself is the "true light," the term *phōs* here in 1 John means the light brought by Jesus, as the contrast with "the darkness" shows. "True light" here characterizes the revelation brought about by the coming of Jesus Christ, the Savior (cp. John 8:12; Ephesians 5:8-14; 1 Thessalonians 5:4-8).

[15] The present tense verbs ("is passing" and "is shining") correspond with each other. The moment is described in which the darkness is retreating before the light, and which therefore neither has the darkness already completely disappeared, nor is the light completely dominant.

of which the gospel is the substance. Perhaps John's statement about "true" light is an anti-Gnostic thrust. The gospel is "real" and "genuine," not make-believe and counterfeit like the Gnostic teachings. Christ and Christianity is the real, the perfect light, compared to those "wandering stars, for whom the blackness of darkness has been reserved forever" (Jude 13 NASB margin).

2:9 -- *The one who says he is in the light and* yet *hates his brother is in the darkness until now.*

The one who says – This verse introduces another false claim made repeatedly by the heretics (see the present tense participle), and John denies this claim (as he did the other false claims introduced in 1:6,8,10 and 2:4,6). As he denies the false claim, John spells out the meaning of the "new commandment" to which he has just called attention.

He is in the light – The heretic who claimed "I am in the light" may well have been claiming to be living by the light of the gospel.[16] That claim, John will show, was false. Of course, the Gnostic would have to claim to be following the gospel. Had the Gnostics said, "We are opposed to the gospel," no Christian would have paid attention to them.[17]

And *yet* hates his brother – "Hate" here is the direct opposite of "to love."[18] John does not focus simply on feelings of aversion (as in 3:13), but on lack of deeds of helpfulness and compassion (3:7).[19] Here he notes the attitude (note the present participle *misōn*, literally "hating" or "detesting"), i.e., indifference towards the brother and his needs. The early Christian writer Ignatius has documented how the Gnostics of his time had no concern for brotherly love.[20] Perhaps John has such people in mind in the many passages in this

---

[16] The same contrast between light and darkness found in verse 7 is repeated here in verse 8. That is why we interpret "light" in this verse just as we interpreted it in verse 7.

[17] Occultists still try to find Biblical justification for their odd and demonic behavior by twisting Scriptures and then claiming they are simply doing what one can read in the Bible.

[18] Love unexpressed is not love at all. When love is absent, hate is present. There is no neutral ground. Jesus said, "He who is not with Me is against Me" (Luke 11:23). Instead of letting John's words guide our thoughts, we try to express a neutral attitude. In so doing, we say, "We do not love them," rather than "We hate them." After all, there are numerous people in the world with whom our contacts are slight. We don't hate them, we don't love them; we aren't acquainted with them enough to love or hate, we tell ourselves. But it is not folk with whom we have only a nodding acquaintance that John is talking about. It is our "brother" – our brother in Christ, a member of the congregation where everyone knows everyone else. If we are not actively doing what is spiritually best for them, we "hate" them.

[19] Jesus spoke about religious people who disregard the plight of the robbed and afflicted (Luke 10:30-37). He spoke about withholding a cup of cold water from the thirsty, and about making no effort to welcome the stranger, or clothe the naked, or help the sick (Matthew 25:42,43).

[20] Ignatius, a Christian writer around AD 110, in his letter to Smyrna, wrote against the false teachers who denied the incarnation of Jesus. In that epistle (6.2) he quoted the new commandment and said, "Mark those who have strange opinions concerning the grace of Jesus Christ which has come to us, and see how contrary they are to the mind of God. For love they have no care, none for the distressed, none for the afflicted, none for the prisoner, or for him released from prison, none for the hungry and thirsty."

epistle which mention love and hate. One cannot be living in the light of the new age while at the same time ignoring Jesus' new commandment to love His brethren. There is a running debate among expositors whether "brother" in this paragraph refers to "fellow-Christian" or to "fellow-man."[21] Who "brother" is in these verses likely depends on who it is who is hating or loving. The Gnostics were not Christians (2:9,11,19), so to say that they were failing to love their "brothers in Christ" is probably not right. They were self-centered and indifferent to the needs of any of their fellow men (brothers in Adam).

Is in the darkness until now -- Right up to the present moment (*heōs arti*), the one who does not love his fellow men *remains* (present tense) in darkness (the same "darkness" verse 8 spoke of). He was never out of it, for 2 Peter 1:5ff indicates that "brotherly love" is developed after one becomes a Christian.[22] In spite of the fact that the increasing light of the gospel is shining in the world, if a man hates his brother, he is living in darkness still.[23] "For those living in darkness, John tactfully leaves the door open so that they may

---

[21] Haas (*op. cit.*, p.51) calls attention to the fact that the word "brother" was sometimes used by Jews and non-Jews in a limited sense to indicate a member of one's own religious group. If our Bible books follow this pattern, when Christians are speaking, "brother" would mean "fellow Christian," whereas "neighbor" (as used, for example, in Luke 10:27,36) would be the term to identify one's "fellow man." In the Johannine writings, "brother" (when it does not speak of an actual physical relationship) is a living metaphor. Christians are each other's brothers because they are all "children of God" (5:2), have the same characteristics (3:9ff), follow Christ's commandments (2:7; 2 John 5), and are called "my brothers" by Jesus Himself (John 20:17). Elsewhere in 1 John, "brother" seems to be limited in meaning to "fellow-Christian" (see 5:16; also 3:10,14-17, 4:20,21). This fact does not mean that "brother" must always be limited to one meaning. Elsewhere in the New Testament there perhaps are a few passages where "brother" has a wider signification than "fellow believer" (e.g., Acts 9:17), but they are not many. What "brother" signifies in passages such as Matthew 5:22, Luke 6:41, and James 4:11 is disputed. "As we have opportunity, let us do good to all men, but especially those of the household of faith," is how Paul words it (Galatians 6:10). The thrust of the majority of "brotherly love" passages in the New Testament speaks of our relationship with our brothers in Christ. This passage in 1 John, which depicts the behavior of the heretics, may suggest "brother" in this place is "fellow man."

Marshall (*op. cit.*, p.51) has called attention to the fact that John has been criticized by some expositors (after they have interpreted "brother" in this passage to mean "fellow Christian") for saying nothing about loving our brother in Adam. That's unfair criticism. John is castigating the heretics for not loving their brothers; John is not in this passage dealing with whom real Christians love. The teachings in the Sermon on the Mount (about loving one's enemies) and in the Parable of the Good Samaritan are in no way contradicted by the statements of this epistle.

[22] 1 John 2:19 will say plainly that the heretics were never genuine converts to the Christian religion.

[23] The command to love one another was one of the most solemn and earnest which Jesus ever spoke (John 15:17). He made it the peculiar badge of discipleship, and by it His followers were to be known everywhere (John 13:35). Therefore, it is impossible to be walking in the light while at the same time failing to love as Jesus commanded his followers to love. See also what Paul wrote about the absence of brother love at 1 Corinthians 13:2.

repent and come to the light. John writes that they are 'still' in darkness. They need not stay there. They are welcome to come to a knowledge of the truth, lead a godly life, love the members of the church, and live in the light of the gospel."[24]

2:10 -- *The one who loves his brother abides in the light and there is no cause for stumbling in him.*

The one who loves his brother abides in the light – "Brother" in this verse would have the same connotation as it did in the previous verse. "Loves" (present tense, "continues to love") is the opposite of what John pictures the heretics as doing (verse 9). "Abides in the light" indicates that not only has the person entered the light when he became a Christian, but he is staying in the light, as if he has made it his home.[25] He continues to embrace and exemplify the "true light" (verse 8) which Jesus taught and practiced. It should be impressed on our consciousness that John did not write, "Whoever *says* that he loves his brother lives in the light." John wrote, "Whoever *loves* his brother." Genuine Christians don't just talk and boast; they act! They love![26]

And there is no cause for stumbling in him – The root idea in *skandalon* ("cause for stumbling" or "occasion of stumbling") is either something a person stumbles over or something that acts like a snare trap. Used metaphorically the word denotes something that leads to or results in sin. The translation of the Greek pronoun and the antecedent of the Greek pronoun are both uncertain,[27] so we are not sure whether the thought is that the man himself does not stumble into sin, or whether he does not cause other people to stumble

---

[24] Kistemaker, *op. cit.*, p.263.

[25] Perhaps we may say that "abiding in the light" and "having fellowship with Him" are vitally related to each other. There can be no continuing fellowship unless one walks in the light, and in this case, specifically, unless he loves his brother.

    Some have treated "abides in the light" as another of the slogans of the heretics that John has picked up and refutes. (Others were "I have come to know Him" [verse 4] and "I am in the light [verse 9].") It is currently said in higher critical circles that the early Gnostics loved John's Gospel (even though its thrust from the first was anti-Gnostic) and drew some of their language from it in an attempt to give an "apostolic veneer" to their aberrant claims, thus making it easier to dupe potential converts. If the critics are right, then it might be possible to trace the heretic's mottos to verses in the Gospel. Perhaps the idea of "knowing [Him]" came from Jesus' words in John 17:3. Perhaps the idea of "abiding in Him" came from Jesus' words in John 15:4. Perhaps the idea of being "in the light" came from John 12:46.

[26] As we have offered comments on the preceding verses we have given several concrete examples of how "love" (*agapē*) expresses itself. It meets the physical and spiritual needs of others. It sacrifices and endures discomfort for the other's sake. If need be, it corrects sin, and upbraids folk for their unbelief and hardness of heart. It bears the weaknesses of the weak brothers.

[27] *En autō* can either be masculine, "in him" (the man who loves), or neuter, "in it" (the light).

and be trapped. While a good case can be made for either interpretation,[28] in view of the author's aim in this epistle, it seems probable to this commentator that John is saying that the one who loves his brother and abides in the light will never cause the kinds of offense the heretics are causing.[29]

2:11 -- *But the one who hates his brother is in the darkness and walks in the darkness, and does not know where he is going because the darkness has blinded his eyes.*

But the one who hates his brother is in the darkness – See this language explained in comments on the last part of verse 9, where it described the behavior and spiritual state of the heretics against whom John writes.

And walks in the darkness – This expression about habitually walking in darkness is a stronger expression than simply being in the darkness. "Walks" is John's word for how one lives. In one of the Suffering Servant poems in Isaiah, God challenges men, "Who is among you ... that walks in darkness and has no light? Let him trust in the name of the Lord and rely on his God." God then speaks to those who refuse to take advantage of the Light of the world, "Behold all you who kindle a fire and encircle yourselves with fire brands," and then God calls them to "Walk in the light of your fire and ... brands you have set ablaze." The word picture is that sparks made by flint and steel and used to kindle a fire do not give much light to see by. Men still could not see where to go. God then warns them what will happen to them, "This you will have from My hand: and you shall lie down in torment" (Isaiah 50:10,11).

And does not know where he is going – "It is good advice to mountaineers lost in a mist without a compass to stay where they are until the mist clears or help comes, rather than to wander around without any sense of direction."[30] John affirms the Gnostics have no sense of direction. They do not know which way to go, or what to do,[31] or how to find their way

---

[28] Consider first the idea that darkness causes one to stumble. What could be more true? Who is not familiar with the sight of a blind man tapping his way along the walk with his red-tipped cane to avoid stumbling? A blind man lives in perpetual darkness. So also does the one who is walking in spiritual darkness. He is in constant danger of stumbling. That over which such a person most frequently stumbles is human relations (e.g., lack of love for the brother). And how frequent are the stumbles!

But the other interpretation is equally true. The man who fails to love not only sins himself, but he regularly causes his brother to stumble. He who walks in the light of God's truth has as his first concern the spiritual welfare of others (for that's what love for the brother is). Such a person does not have in his life that over which his brother may stumble.

[29] Romans 14-15 would be a parallel passage, for they too speak to the matter of loving the brother and not putting a stumbling block in the path of the weak brother.

[30] Marshall, *op. cit.*, p.133.

[31] Since "going" refers to behavior, a possible explanation for this clause is "he does not realize what he ought to do" (i.e., that he ought to be loving his brother).

to salvation.   They never know whether they are closer to or farther from their destination. Perhaps this is a direct quotation from John 12:35 ("he who walks in the darkness does not know where he goes").   He doesn't realize the enormity of his sin and where it will lead him.   He certainly is not a suitable guide for others.

Because the darkness has blinded his eyes – Someone has said that sin cuts the optic nerve of the soul.   The verb tense is aorist, referring to an act that occurred in the past. He lived in darkness so long that his eyes no longer see.[32]   "Having chosen to live in the darkness, he now finds that his eyes can no longer see the light."[33]   Paul wrote in 2 Corinthians 4:4 that the god of this world (the devil) "blinds the minds of the unbelieving, so that they cannot see the light of the gospel of the glory of Christ, who is the image of God."   Perhaps John also alludes to the judicial penalty God imposes on those who refuse to see (Isaiah 6:10, 29:10; Romans 11:8).

II. CAUTIONS ABOUT DANGERS THAT CAN RUIN FELLOWSHIP.   2:12-27

> *Summary*: In the epistle thus far (1:5-2:11), John has refuted six claims made by the false teachers, while at the same time driving home the correct Christian doctrine and behavior.   In this new section,[1] John assures his readers of their standing with God and Christ (verses 12-14), and then issues two warnings lest that standing be lost: one against worldliness (verses 15-17), and one against antichrists (verses 18-27).

A. John's Threefold Statement of Assurance About Their Standing with God and Christ.   2:12-14

> *Summary*: Before issuing certain pointed warnings about two serious dangers that can destroy fellowship with God, John assures his readers of their present standing with God and Christ.

---

[32] Plummer (*op. cit.*, p.96) calls attention to the ponies once used in the coal mines of England.   They were kept underground, in the dark.   In time they became blind, because their eyes were not used.

[33] Marshall, *op. cit.*, p.133.

[1] It is not easy to decide upon how to outline the epistle at this place.   Some treat the rest of chapter 2 as a conclusion of the major division which was begun at 1:5.   We have chosen to treat these verses as an independent part of the outline.   Plummer (*op. cit.*, p.97) offers several reasons for so treating these verses: (1) The idea of *light* which runs through the whole of the division just concluded (1:5-2:11), and which is mentioned six times in it, now disappears altogether.   (2) The epistle now takes a distinctively hortatory turn.   (3) The apostle seems to make a fresh start.   Verses 12-14 read like a new introduction.

2:12 -- *I am writing to you, little children, because your sins are forgiven you for His name's sake.*

I am writing to you – As it did in 1:4 and 2:1,7, the present tense verbs "we write" or "I am writing" certainly refers to this very epistle which John is in the midst of composing. Four general problems face interpreters of verses 12-14. (1) The two sets of three parallel statements generally say the same thing. What is the explanation of the apparent repetition? (2) What is the reason for the change of verb tenses from "I write" (present tense) to "I have written" (past tense)?[2] (3) How shall we translate the Greek word *hoti*? In each case, the word can be translated either "because" or "that." Is John explaining "why" he is writing to his readers, or stating "what" he has to say to them? (4) How shall we understand the terms by which he addresses his readers (children [verse 13c], fathers [verse 14a], young men [verse 14b]) – literally or metaphorically?

Little children – *Teknia* ("little children") is John's favorite term to designate his readers as a whole (cf. 2:1,28; 3:7,18; 4:4; 5:21).

Because your sins are forgiven you – "Are forgiven" (*apheōntai*, a perfect passive form[3]) means they were forgiven in the past and remain forgiven.[4] John is now thinking of the conversion of his readers, whereas in 1:9 (with its present tense verb) his thought was more of the continual forgiveness for which the Christian prays daily. The implied agent is God, who is the only One who can forgive sins (Luke 5:21). The forgiveness of sins at conversion is the start of the Christian life; therefore, it is put first in this list of assurances to the readers.[5] All John's readers, the "little children,"[6] have been forgiven. That is an experience every Christian can consciously recall and recount. It is no elite, esoteric experience available only to a favored few, like "gnosis" was.

For His name's sake – Because the "name" calls attention to who Jesus Christ is, what He

---

[2] The NIV does not indicate there is any distinction between verb tenses.

[3] See comments at 1:9 on the meaning of the word "forgiven."

[4] It makes little difference to our understanding of this verse whether we use "because" or "that" to translate *hoti*. Since the later and somewhat parallel statements (in this verse and the next and verse 21) make better sense if we use "because" to translate them, we choose to use "because" in this instance also. We suppose John is giving the reason for his writing, not the substance of what he has to say.

[5] Kistemaker (*op. cit.*, p.266) writes that if there is good news from Jesus Christ, it is the announce-ment that our sins have been forgiven (cp. Luke 24:47; Acts 13:38). The paralytic carried by four of his friends to the house where Jesus stayed heard Him say, "My son, your sins are forgiven" (Mark 2:5). The sinful woman who entered the home of Simon the Pharisee and anointed Jesus' feet heard these words, "Your sins have been forgiven" (Luke 7:48). What reassuring words John speaks when he tells his readers they are indeed forgiven.

[6] Since we have concluded John is using the term "little children" metaphorically, this verse cannot be used to justify the baptism of infants, for the "children" are also said to have come to know the Father (verse 13).

has done on Calvary, and as our Advocate (1:7, 2:1,2), we could explain these words as meaning "because of what Jesus did."[7]   Forgiveness of sins has been made possible because of the person and ministry of Jesus Christ.   This is a direct affirmation of a truth that the Gnostics denied.   They treated Calvary as having nothing to do with redemption and forgiveness.   This language also prepares us for what will be written in 3:23 and 5:13, that belief in His name is mandatory if one would be saved.[8]

2:13 -- *I am writing to you, fathers, because you know Him who has been from the beginning. I am writing to you, young men, because you have overcome the evil one.   I have written to you, children, because you know the Father.*

I am writing to you – John refers to this very letter, just as "I am writing" did at the beginning of verse 12.

Fathers – If it is correct that the designation "little children" in verse 12 included all of John's readers,[9] then the "fathers" and "young men" of this verse in some way refer to smaller groups that make up parts of the whole.[10]   Under this view, it is still argued whether the difference between "fathers" and "young men" refers to age as men or age as Christians.   Having treated "little children" metaphorically, it suggests we should treat "fathers" and "young men" metaphorically, also.   What meaning might John have had in mind as he wrote to "fathers"?   It is an unusual form of address for any church member; in fact, the use of "fathers" to describe a group of Christians is unparalleled in the New Testament.   Sometimes, in the Jewish world, "fathers" were leaders of the past (the patriarchs).   Sometimes, it is a title of respect given to the current generation of leaders (Acts 7:2; 22:1).   In light of Jewish practices, some have supposed John is addressing those who served as elders of the congregations to which the readers belonged.   Others, rightly in this commentator's opinion, have supposed John is speaking of those long-time members of the church, those who knew the history and doctrine of the congregation from

---

[7] In Jewish thought, one's "name" is not merely appellative.   This expression is not a periphrasis for "Jesus Christ."   Names in Scripture are constantly given as marks of character possessed or of functions to be performed.   The New Testament predicates salvation upon the name of Jesus Christ (Acts 2:38, 4:12).

[8] It is by believing on His name that men receive Him and are given the right to become children of God (John 1:12).

[9] A few expositors have rejected the idea that "little children" (verse 12) embraces the whole of John's readership, and instead have affirmed that John is addressing three separate groups.   Some opt for the view that John is using the terms literally as he addresses three different age groups, though some have expressed hesitancy because the order is slightly odd.   (We might have expected children, young men, fathers.)   Some ancient Latin commentators favored the view that John uses the terms metaphorically or spiritually, having in mind three different stages of the Christian's spiritual pilgrimage.   The little children are the newly baptized.   The young men and fathers represent progressively advanced states of spiritual maturity.

[10] The early Greek fathers regularly explained "little children" as a reference to all the readers who were subsequently divided into two groups, "fathers" and "young men."

its very beginning.   They were the "charter members," having been personally involved in the original planting of the congregations and the winning of the first new converts.[11]

Because you know Him who has been from the beginning – "Him who has been from the beginning" recalls what was written about the deity, eternality, and incarnation of Jesus the Christ at 1 John 1:1ff and John 1:1ff.   "Know" is a perfect tense verb, implying past completed action with present continuing results.[12]   The "fathers" have known who Jesus is[13] from the time of their conversion.   With the passing of time, who He is has not changed in their estimation.   That is commendable!   That truth should be taken into account by those who have been tempted to listen to the different presentation of Jesus made by the heretics.   John has thus assured his readers that their long-standing knowledge of who Jesus is was correct.

I am writing to you young men – If we have properly explained the metaphor involved in "fathers," then "young men" would be their converts, a generation of believers younger than the ones involved in planting the churches in which the readers were now members.[14]

Because you have overcome the evil one – The "evil one" is one of the Biblical names for the devil.[15]   "Have overcome" is a perfect tense verb.[16]   These "young men" won a

---

[11] While Jesus spoke against the spirit of pride and ambition which covets and abuses such titles as "father" (Matthew 23:9), "father" is an acceptable term for those who were involved in winning others to Christ (1 Corinthians 4:15).

[12] John's language here should not be interpreted to mean that the "fathers" had once lived in the Holy Land and thus had personally witnessed Jesus' earthly ministry.   Very few of John's readers would have had that privilege.   On the contrary, the knowledge of "Him who has been from the beginning" was not limited to a select few, as the Gnostics claimed.   All the "fathers," indeed all the "little children," were privy to this knowledge of who Jesus was and is.

[13] "There is no doubt that *ap' archēs* here must refer to the beginning of time and not to the beginning of the Christian era or the readers' Christian experience" (Marshall, *op. cit.*, p.139).   The Greek text reads simply "the (One) from the beginning."   We thus must supply the verb.   Perhaps John wrote it this way to refute the heretics' doctrine which refused to believe the pre-existent Logos had become truly incarnate in Jesus of Nazareth. (Brooke, *op. cit.*, p.45).   The phrase "Him who was from the beginning" could refer equally to either the Father or the Son, for both existed from eternity past.   No one doubted that the Father was from the beginning, so that is why we conclude that John is significantly stressing the pre-existence and eternality of Jesus.

[14] Of course, those who believe that "fathers" were leaders who held the function of elders will affirm that the "young men" likewise designate those church leaders who served as "deacons."

[15] For this name for Satan, see 1 John 3:12; 5:18,19; and Matthew 6:13, 13:19.   Greek has two words for "evil": *kakos* (wicked, bad in itself) and *ponēros* (pernicious, evil in opposition to the good).   The *kakos* person is content to do evil by himself and perish in his own corruption.   The *ponēros* person seeks to drag everyone else with him in his downfall.   He tries to get others to be bad also.

[16] Throughout both the Gospel and Epistle of John, "eternal life" is a present possession of the believer (John 3:36; 5:24; 6:47,54; 17:3).   The contest involved in "overcome" is not to gain eternal life, but to retain it. (Plummer, *op. cit.*, p. 100).

signal victory over the devil when they became Christians.[17] John represents the "evil one" as controlling the world of darkness rather than light (5:18-19; 2:14; 3:12). He is the one behind what the heretics are trying to do. John's implication seems to be, 'Are you now going to let the evil one capture you back?' That is exactly what is involved if you join the heretics in their religion. There is a certain appropriateness to the thrust of John's argument against the heretics in each of the qualities attributed to the different groups of readers. At the same time, all of the qualities were equally true of each believer. Taken together, these qualities give a special emphasis to what will be lost if the readers give up their present position in Christ. By addressing the different groups John certainly would have produced a feeling of solidarity among the readers as they see all that is involved in the issues being discussed.

I have written to you[18] – Most editions of the Greek New Testament begin verse 14 at this point, and a few English versions begin verse 14 with this clause, following the versification in modern editions of the Greek text. The change from the present tense "I am writing" (used earlier in verses 12 and 13) to the aorist tense "I have written" (here and in verse 14) seems to have been deliberate. Noting this change of tense, the first impression one would get is the impression that most ancient commentators embraced: John is telling his readers that this is not the first time he has written this to them, and that the assurance he is giving them now as Christians is precisely the same assurance he gave in his earlier writing. The simplest explanation of the change of tense is that this epistle was written after the Gospel.[19] "I am writing" refers to the epistle; "I wrote" would refer

---

[17] The believer's initial victory over the evil one (i.e., their conversion) is possible because in the past Jesus Christ has conquered the devil (4:4, 5:4f).

[18] The Textus Receptus (and KJV) reads present tense (*graphō*) here, "I am writing." The better attested reading is aorist tense (*egrapha*), "I have written."

[19] Plummer, who accepted the view that "I have written" (in verses 13,14) alludes to the Fourth Gospel, admits that "I have written" at 2:21 cannot easily be referred to the Fourth Gospel. So some search elsewhere to find the writing alluded to in the past tense, "I have written." Since the arrangement of the books of the New Testament in our Bibles is according to length, rather than date of writing, some have opted for the view that what we call 2 John or 3 John might be the previous writing. Perhaps a case could be made for 2 John being the previous writing (see Wendt, ZNW 21 [1922], p.144-146). However, detractors from this opinion insist that neither of those letters seems to fit what John here says "I have written." Others have postulated there was a letter written by John – one written before the one we call 1 John – which is now lost. This raises the whole question of whether or not there were inspired, apostolic letters to churches that have been lost, and so are not included in our New Testament Canon. It raises the parallel issue of whether our Canon has preserved only a selection of the writings produced, say, only the ones later deemed to be orthodox. Without taking time to discuss all the pros and cons of these questions, let us say that while we believe it is *possible* inspired letters to churches have been lost, we do not think it is *probable*. And let us say that the making and accepting of the books of the Canon occurred while spiritual gifts (including the discerning of spirits) were still operative. That would involve the Holy Spirit in the choice of what books were recognized and collected, not just men in powerful places. If we grant that John's "I have written" has reference to the Gospel, all this conjecture becomes needless.

to the Gospel which had been written earlier for the benefit of the same readers.[20]   John does tell us that he wrote his Gospel so that his readers might continue to believe that Jesus is the Christ, and that believing they might have life in His name (John 20:30,31).   That sounds like the very kind of assurance that 1 John 2:12-14 offers.

Children – John uses *paidia* in this verse, where he used *teknia* in verse 12.   *Teknia* is related to *tiktō* ("to give birth to") and emphasizes the idea of descent from parent to child. *Paidia* is related to *paideuō* ("to train children") and emphasizes the need for discipline and guidance.   Perhaps it implies that at the earlier time when the Gospel was written, John's readers were in need of training and guidance.   Now they simply need to be reminded of who they are and where they stand.

---

[20] Rejecting out of hand the idea that when John uses the aorist "I have written" he refers to an earlier writing, expositors in the past hundred years or so have offered a bewildering number of attempts to explain the change of verb tense and the apparent repetition in verses 12-14.   (1) Some have proposed that an error has crept into the text when some scribe accidentally copied a portion of the verses over.   On this view, what should be done is omit a portion of these verses in order to avoid any repetition.   However, there is no manuscript authority for omitting any portion of these three verses.   (2) A variation of this view is the theory of displacement to account for the repetition.   Oke (*Exp.Tim.* 51 [1939/40], p.349-0) proposed that 2:12-13b originally followed 1:10, and 2:13c-17 originally provided the conclusion to 1 John (after 5:21). His explanation was that the papyrus sheets on which the letter was written became brittle, broke up in places, and a later copyist put the pieces together in the wrong order.   Again, there is no manuscript evidence for this hypothesis.   Even the earliest papyrus copies still in existence have the verses in the place where we are accustomed to find them.   (3) Another offers the suggestion that John repeated himself as an attention getter or for emphasis.   But if this were the case, we might expect the verbs to be "I write, and I write it again."   (4) A third proposal makes "I write" refer to what follows, and "I have written" to what precedes.   Then the preceding and following verses are combed for indications which were addressed to little children, which to fathers, and which to young men.   This is all very arbitrary.   (5) A variation of this view is that "I write" refers to the whole letter, and "I have written" refers to what precedes. But this makes the verse ridiculous.   What would induce John to tell each class that he writes the whole epistle to them, and then to tell them that he wrote the first part to them?   (6) Not a few opt for the view that "I have written" is an epistolary aorist.   Under this hypothesis, John projects himself forward to the time when the readers hear the letter read out loud.   At that time the event of John's writing would be past. For all intents and purposes, then, there is no difference in meaning between "I am writing" and "I have written."   Both expressions embrace the whole letter.   Perhaps this view influenced the translators of the NIV to allow the change of verb tenses to go unnoticed in their translation.   Even if we admit that there are places in this letter where John does employ the epistolary aorist, no satisfactory explanation has resulted from the idea that the verbs in verses 13 and 14 are to be treated as epistolary aorists.   (7) It has even been suggested that John's dictation of the letter was interrupted after the first part of verse 13.   The next time he began to dictate, he began his dictation by repeating the same words.   But repetition with slight changes not insignificant is a regular feature of John's style.   No one has supposed interruptions at those other repetitive places.   (8) A variation of this view has the letter being read out loud in the public assembly. It was so arranged that it could be read in two parts -- first 1:1 to 2:13b, then 2:13c to the end.   The words with which verse 13c and 14 begin would serve to remind the hearers what had been read at the last meeting.   But is this epistle so long that readers in the 1st century would have felt a need to divide it up into two "lectionaries"?   (9) Redaction critics, who think 2nd and 3rd generation editors used the material in a way different from how it occurred in their sources, blame a clumsy editor for the embarrassing repetition at this place.   Such a view about how our Bible books came to their present form surely does not inspire us to want to read on in John's epistle, or any other book, for that matter.   In this commentator's judgment, it is better to treat "I have written" as an allusion to the Fourth Gospel.

Because you know the Father – When compared with verse 12, this gives a second assurance to John's readers. In addition to the awareness of forgiven sin (verse 12), there is also the awareness of their "sonship." To the person who has become a Christian, this is an overpowering realization. The Almighty Creator and Sustainer of all is my Father! I'm a child of the King! One reason assigned for the writing of the Gospel to them is that John's readers had personally become acquainted with God as Father.[21] The implication of this is that John wants them to continue to show themselves dutiful and faithful children of their Father in heaven. They will do that by repudiating the temptation to join the heretics in their folly.

2:14 -- I have written to you, fathers, because you know Him who has been from the beginning. I have written to you, young men, because you are strong, and the word of God abides in you, and you have overcome the evil one.

I have written to you, fathers, because you know Him who has been from the beginning – This is verbatim as before (see verse 13). For many years, even before the Fourth Gospel was written, they have been acquainted with what Christianity says about who Jesus is. This fact would tend to urge them to continue to contend for the faith once for all delivered to the saints.

I have written to you, young men – The "young men" here are the same group so designated in verse 13b. The first and last lines written to the young men repeat verse 13b, with the addition of two further points of explanation in between.

Because you are strong, and the word of God abides in you – These two phrases seem to give a hint as to the reason for the young men's victory over the evil one. The reference in "strong" is not, of course, to physical strength. It is speaking of character and spirit, to be courageous or steadfast. Their strength comes from the word of God which abides in them.[22] They have grasped the elements of the Christian revelation and are seeking to conform their lives to its ethical demands. It lives in their hearts/thoughts. Any Christian in living contact with the source of life may be spiritually strong.[23] John's words suggest to his readers that they need to allow that Word to continue to have a lasting influence on them. That will insulate them from the errors of the heretics.

---

[21] "Know" is another perfect tense, referring to something that happened in the past and has present continuing results. For "Father" see notes at 1:2. The Holy Spirit indwelling within the Christian makes him aware of his sonship and causes him to cry "Abba! Father!" (Romans 8:15,16; Galatians 4:6).

[22] For the "Word of God," see notes on "His word" at 1:10. Expositors also point to verses like Luke 11:21, Matthew 12:29, and Ephesians 6:10 to help explain the sense in which the young men are "strong."

[23] Some have been reminded of John 15:7, where Jesus speaks about His words abiding in His disciples, and of John 8:31, "If you abide in My word, then you are truly disciples of mine." Others have recalled Psalm. 119:9, "How can a young man keep his way pure? By keeping it according to Thy word."

And you have overcome the evil one – This assurance is repeated just as it was in verse 13.[24] Marshall comments that "it is good for Christians to be reminded and assured of their spiritual standing. Christians are 'special people' in God's sight, and such an awareness is a great help to continuing to hold on to the truths we have embraced. With confidence of who we are, the evil one has much less opportunity to tempt us to head off in some other direction."[25] John uses this assured position as Christians as the ground of his appeal to them in the following paragraphs, as he warns them to be cautious about the dangers that can spoil their fellowship with God and with one another.

B. Warning Against Worldliness.   2:15-17

> *Summary*:   On the basis of their Christian standing (verses 12-14), John appeals to his readers to avoid the love of the world, lest they forfeit their standing.   Such a forfeiting would result in the delightful experiences of the gospel becoming, for them, a thing of the past.   He gives two reasons for not loving the world: (1) such love precludes any love for God, and (2) the world is passing away; any investment in it will prove to be only temporary at best.

2:15 -- *Do not love the world, nor the things in the world.   If any one loves the world, the love of the Father is not in him.*

Do not love the world – This prohibition is written with a present imperative in the Greek, so it forbids the continuance of something already going on.   "Stop loving the world!" John writes.   "Love," the same word (*agapaō*) used at 2:10 ("loves his brother"), is an emotion (some say a "desire") that drives a person's behavior.   *Agapē* is a "love" that can be willed, and is the only one of the "loves"[26] that can be commanded; indeed, it is the only one that is commanded in the Bible.   "Love" is the same word used at John 3:16 ("God so

---

[24] In comments on verse 13 we spoke of the victory over the devil at the time of their conversion. Some expositors have wondered whether there might be a reference to a more recent crisis, say a significant victory won over the antichrists (whose false teaching was diabolical). It is even suggested that younger Christians were specifically targeted by the heretics as they tried to lure believers into their camp (cp. 2 Peter 2:18).

[25] Marshall, *op. cit.*, p.141 (paraphrased).

[26] Other words for "love" include *eros*, *storgē*, and *phileō*.   *Eros* (love, lust) is the root for our word "erotic," and speaks of a selfish desire interested only in what pleasure it can get from someone else. *Storgē* ("love, family affection") speaks of the warm affection between members of the same family, say parents "love" for their children.   *Phileō* ("love, romance") speaks of the desire for someone aroused by the attractiveness or other desirable qualities in the object of the love.   *Agapē* behaves the way it does because it decides to do so whether it be out of selfish or altruistic motives (if altruistic, it does so regardless of what it may or may not get in return).   *Agapē* is the word used at 1 Corinthians 13, and the word used at 1 John 4:8 where we are told that "God is love."

loved the world"). Obviously, one or both words, "love" and "world," are used in a different sense here than in John 3:16. No one would say that what God did when He "so loved the world" was wrong, but John's prohibition to stop loving the world indicates that what the readers of this epistle were doing was wrong. We have had *kosmos* ("world") at 2:2, but in this paragraph (verses 15-17) where it occurs six times, it seems to be used with a negative connotation, for there is something about the "world" that it triggers lusts and pride; there is something about it that is the exact opposite of "does the will of God" (verse 17); there is something about it that is "passing away" (verse 17) and is "not from the Father" (verse 16); and there is something about "love for the world" that is diametrically opposed to "love for the Father" (verse 15). The "world" here is that from which James says the truly religious man keeps himself "unspotted" (James 1:27 KJV). Now John is certainly not countenancing the cosmological dualism taught by the heretics (that all matter is evil, but only spirit is good),[27] nor is he teaching asceticism. Instead, perhaps John's prohibition to stop loving the world reflects the very thing Jesus taught in His Sermon on the Mount, when He said,

> Do not lay up for yourselves treasures upon earth, where moth and rust destroy, and where thieves break in and steal. But lay up for yourselves treasures in heaven, where neither moth nor rust destroys, and where thieves do not break in or steal; for where your treasure is, there will your heart be also. The lamp of the body is the eye; if therefore your eye is clear, your whole body will be full of light. But if your eye is bad, your whole body will be full of darkness! If therefore the light that is in you is darkness, how great is the darkness. No man can serve two masters; for either he will hate the one and love the other, or he will hold to one and despise the other. You cannot serve God and Mammon. [He went on to speak about not being anxious about what to eat or drink or wear. Instead, He counsels His followers to ...] Seek first the kingdom of God and His righteousness, and all these things shall be added to you [i.e., they will find that all these "earthly" things will be taken care of by God]. (Matthew 6:19-33)

Perhaps this paragraph is John's way of saying the same thing Paul did in his letter to the Colossians: "If then you have been raised up with Christ, keep seeking the things above, where Christ is, seated at the right hand of God. Set your mind on the things above, not on the things that are on earth. For you have died and your life is hidden with Christ in

---

[27] God created this world and everything in it, and behold it was very good! But something has happened to this world so that now there is a side to it which is not good. The devil is identified as the "god of this age" (2 Corinthians 4:4), and a great part of the world is under the control of Satan (1 John 5:19; John 12:31, 14:30). Having been cast down to the earth, and knowing he has only a short time, the devil is doing all in his power to ruin God's creation (Revelation 12:9,12). Because of the devil's influence, human beings have become rebellious and Godless, and have tainted much that they touch. An order of spiritual beings, evil in nature and led by Satan, exists in the world. Satan has also persuaded men to align themselves with him and his forces, rather than with God. Such men end up loving the darkness rather than the light. Such men turn the created world, its materials, and their own bodies into instruments of evil. This world and the things in it are a creation of God. But when men center their affections on the creation rather than on the Creator, that is idolatry (Romans 1:25). This is the "loving" the readers are exhorted to stop. It is the attractions of this present earthly life that are in opposition to the will and commandments of God that the Christian has been called out of and which he is not to love.

God" (Colossians 3:1-3).   Since God is love (1 John 4:8) and man is made in the image of God, man cannot but love something.   Man must choose carefully the object or person to whom he commits himself, exercising special care to "stop loving this world"; there are things about this present world that can turn a man's heart away from the Lord, especially if the man doesn't carefully control his affections.[28]

Nor the things in the world – Examples of the "things in the world" that John particularly has in mind will be specified in verse 16.

If any one loves the world, the love of the Father is not in him – This is one reason John gives why his readers should stop loving the world.   "If any one keeps on loving the world" is how the present tense could be translated.[29]   The man who "loves the world" places a higher value on the world than he does on the Father who is in heaven; he places a higher value on darkness than he does on light (John 3:19).   Since the contrast with "love of the Father" is love for the world, it prompts us to treat the genitive as objective, "Love for the Father."[30]   "A man cannot love the Father and love the world at the same time" (Phillips). James 4:4 has a similar statement, "to be the world's friend means to be God's enemy" (TEV).   The two loves are mutually exclusive.   If a man is so enamored with the outlook and pursuits of this world that he rejects Christ, it is evident that he has no love for the Father.   Now we can identify specifically what is meant by "worldliness" as used in the title of this paragraph.   "Worldliness" means focusing on the transitory pleasures of this world, rather than having eternity's values in view.   "Worldliness" means "disobedience to God's rule of life," and its presence can be discerned (not by making a human list of taboos, but) when a man regularly fails to ask "What is God's will?" and habitually shows little or no interest in putting the kingdom of God first in his life.

2:16 -- For all that is in the world, the lust of the flesh and the lust of the eyes and the boastful pride of life, is not from the Father, but is from the world.

For all that is in the world – "For" shows that verse 16 can be a reason for something just said, or a further explanation.   Perhaps John is explaining what he meant by "world" and "things of the world."   "All" is neuter singular here, whereas "things" (verse 15) was neuter plural.   John thus guarantees that the heretics cannot use what he says to corroborate their

---

[28] Demas is said to have loved (same word for "love") this present world (2 Timothy 4:10).   He found it desirable and precious and thus gave himself to it.   But he had to forsake the ministry to do it.

[29] The same drive that leads one to be compassionate to people (1 John 2:10) can also lead one to seek the pleasure which can be derived from material things.

[30] See notes at 2:5 about objective and subjective genitives.

doctrine of matter being evil.[31]   Perhaps John is giving a reason for what was said about the love for the world and love for God being mutually exclusive.   The "desires" he is about to enumerate are examples of love for the wrong objects or persons that John calls on his readers to stop.[32]   The "desires for" and "pride in" merely physical and temporal things are the essential characteristics of how a man lives who has little interest in things spiritual and eternal.   He has set his affections on the wrong things.

The lust of the flesh – This genitive, as well as the two following, are all subjective.   John is referring to the desires which the flesh beget.[33]   Twice in this verse *epithumia* is rendered "lust" in many of our English translations; this may be unfortunate, for the word "lust" has come to have the rather limited connotation of excessive and unrestrained sexual gratification that *epithumia* does not have.   The Greek word has a broader meaning, describing all the God-given drives and appetites that are common to man.   That includes sex, but it also includes the appetites for food, for sleep, for drink, or for pleasure.   Such drives or desires may be good or bad,[34] depending on the context.   Marshall[35] calls attention to the fact that such fleshly appetites[36] have been created by God, and they need to be satisfied, and the satisfying of them produces pleasure.   When we are hungry, we need food.   We want a meal, and the eating of the food produces pleasure that is perfectly proper.   In fact, when the body needs food or drink, it would soon be fatal to deprive it of what it needs.   But there are times when eating may not be right.   It would be clearly sinful to enjoy a good meal all by myself,   when I could share my resources with a poor,

---

[31] "All that is in the world" cannot refer to the material and physical elements that make up the world, for to say these did not originate with God (later in this verse, John says "is not from the Father") would be to contradict what John himself says in the Gospel (John 1:3,10).   He would then agree with the Gnostics, who taught that everything material was radically evil and was created, not by God, but by the evil one, or at least by an inferior deity (aeon).

[32] The "things of the world" which John lists are probably intended to be illustrations or examples, and not a complete description.   Hence, Plummer (in an appendix to his commentary) is probably in error to regard these three things as "a summary of all the various kinds of temptation and sin."

[33] If the genitives were treated as objective, they would speak of "desire for the flesh" or "desire for the eyes," and that would make little sense.   The genitives after the word "desire" are generally subjective in the New Testament (e.g., Romans 1:24; Galatians 5:16; Ephesians 2:3).

[34] *Epithumia* (lust, desire) is a morally neutral word.   For the good sense of the word see Matthew 13:17; Philippians 1:23; 1 Thessalonians 2:17; for the more common bad sense see Mark 4:19; Romans 1:24; Galatians 5:16; Ephesians 2:3; 1 Peter 2:11.

[35] Marshall, *op. cit.*, p.143.

[36] We have been very careful to avoid any comment at this place that might lend support to the idea that "flesh" is "our old sinful nature."   In this commentator's book on Romans we have shown that the dogma of an inherited sinful nature (total depravity) is Greek philosophy rather than Biblical truth.   In fact, would not the idea that "flesh" is innately evil have played right into the doctrine of the heretics which John is refuting?   If men become slaves to sin, slaves to their appetites, it is not because they were born that way.   It is because of their own sins that they become dead in trespasses and sins, and become slaves to sin (Ephesians 2:1; Romans 7:14 [sold into bondage, not born that way]).

starving brother (Luke 16:19ff).   It would be wrong to suppose I could enjoy a meal in the idol's temple (1 Corinthians 10:20,21).   Eating amounts of food that could be called gluttony is quite the opposite of the self-control the Scriptures call for.

And the lust of the eyes – This speaks of the desires that are triggered or stimulated by what the human eye sees.   When applied, as John applies it in verse 16, to "the desires of the eyes," the word *epithumia* shifts in emphasis from the appetites and drives associated with the physical body to the externals of which we are aware by the use of our perceptive senses.   "The basic thought here is of greed and desire for things aroused by seeing them."[37]   The eyes, by themselves, are neutral.   There is nothing inherently bad about eyesight.   One can desire the good they see, or they can develop a desire for the bad.   Many of man's desires for wrong things are aroused by what he sees with his eyes.   Eve's view of the forbidden tree as 'a delight to the eyes' (Genesis 3:6), Achan's covetous sight among the spoil of a 'goodly Babylonish garment' (Joshua 7:21), and David's lustful looking after Bathsheba as she bathed (2 Samuel 11:2) are obvious examples where forbidden desires were stimulated by eye-sight.[38]

And the boastful pride of life – Pride stimulated by earthly possessions is the general idea.   Translators struggle to find an equivalent English expression for the two Greek words involved.   "Life" (*bios*) occurs again at 1 John 3:17 in the expression translated "the world's goods."[39]   *Bios* denotes the means of supporting and sustaining our earthly existence: what is on the table, the size or location of one's house, the furniture in the house, one's income, one's lifestyle.[40]   Ostentatious pride stimulated by the earthly goods one possesses is the idea in *aladzoneia*.[41]   The *aladzōn* was a braggart, a pretender, who sought to impress everyone he met with his own non-existent importance.[42]   To folk who don't know him, he may even claim to own houses and lands, boats and investments, and drop names of famous people as though he were moving in their circles, all in order to inflate his status in their opinion.   If we are not careful, such "boastful pride" can begin to

[37] Marshall, *op. cit.*, p.145.

[38] Stott, *op. cit.*, p.100

[39] Two Greek words are translated "life" in the New Testament.   *Zōē*, the other one, denotes "life in its essential principle."   It is used for both spiritual life and immortal life.

[40] Vance Packard's book, *The Status Seekers*, was an indictment of a people who all their lives claw and scratch after the baubles which will set them (at least in their own sight) just one notch above their neighbors.

[41] The word occurs one other place in the New Testament, at James 4:16, though cognate forms are found at Romans 1:20 and 2 Timothy 3:2.   Some Latin versions use "secular ambition" to translate the word.

[42] John has listed three examples of "all that is in the world."   Westcott drew a parallel with the three temptations of Jesus in the wilderness, and with the three chief vices of medieval ethics – *voluptas* (sensual pleasure), *avaritia* (covetousness), and *superbia* (haughty spirit).   But there is not a very obvious correspondence with either.   See Brooke, *op. cit.*, p.47ff, for criticism of Westcott's attempted parallels.

control all our behavior. Clearly, all people need a certain amount of "earthly goods," food, shelter, and clothing. It cannot be wrong to want and take pleasure in what God has provided for our needs. But there is much wrong with "boastful pride," where one begins to think that our life does consist in the abundance of the things we possess, where we begin to make the acquisition of more earthly goods our main ambition, and hold in contempt those who do not possess as much in the way of this world's goods as we do. If my reputation, my status, my public image, matters more to me than the glory of God or the well-being of my fellow believers in Christ, then I am guilty of loving this world more than I love God. Christians are to have a more meaningful and eternal set of values!

Is not from the Father – This phrase picks up the sentence begun in 16a, "for all that is in the world ... is not from the Father." It does not derive its origin from (*ek*) Him and does not meet His approval.[43] Worldly desires stimulated by flesh and eye, and "boastful pride" stimulated by this world's goods, have their origin not in God, but in the devil. Compare Jesus' words, "You are of (*ek*) your father the devil, and you want to do the desires of your father" (John 8:44).

But is from the world – It is unspiritual in its source. It may call attention to the transitory nature of the things that are the objects of such ungodly desires. If so, the next verse would carry on the thought. Or it may call attention to the devil's involvement. The devil takes something perfectly good (something God has created) and uses it to cause men to turn bad. That is so devilish! Human desires, human existence, and material possessions are not sinful in themselves, but the devil uses them to turn men's affections away from their heavenly Father. Worldliness is tantamount to idolatry!

2:17 -- And the world is passing away, and also its lusts; but the one who does the will of God abides forever.

And the world is passing away – This is a second reason for the command to "stop loving the world" (verse 15). The first reason was that love of the Father and love of the world are mutually exclusive (verses 15-16). As in verse 8, *paragetai* ("passing away") is present tense and pictures the process as now going on. It is not only part of Biblical revelation that the world and all that is in it were created by the word of God. "In the beginning God created the heavens and the earth" (Genesis 1:1). It is also specifically stated in that same Biblical revelation that "the [outward] form of this world is passing away" (1 Corinthians 7:31, same verb as here) and one day the renovation will be completed (2 Peter 3:10; Revelation 21:1-4). Before that, for numerous generations, there is death, and shrouds have no pockets in them. You cannot take this world's goods with you. Those whose lives are absorbed with accumulating the *bios* of the world (this world's

---

[43] "To be from/of" (that is how the Greek reads) is a characteristic expression used by John. See 2:16; 3:8,12,19; 4:1ff, etc. As Westcott (*op. cit.*, p.66) points out, the use of the formula "to be from" expresses both derivation from and dependence upon.

goods, 1 John 3:17) will find them gone!   Things that are not permanent are really of little ultimate value.

And *also* its lusts – We supply the verb "is passing" from the previous clause.   When earth's shades are riven and time is no more, the day will have dawned when desires such as those triggered by the flesh and the eye will no longer be a concern.   In the world to come there will be no desires for anyone or anything but God!   People who have lived for the moment will find their priorities were sadly misplaced.   Men are spiritually blind if they do not realize what is going on before their very eyes, that the world and its lusts are passing away.[44]

But the one who does the will of God abides forever – Only one class of people will remain when this present world has given way to the next, those who habitually do the will of God.[45]   Jesus spoke about a wise builder, who habitually does all He taught men to do (Matthew 7:24).   He also said that "whosoever habitually does the will of God" was His "brother, and sister, and mother" (Mark 3:35).   "The will of God" seems to be the exact opposite of "all that is in the world" (about which verse 16 spoke).   Doing the will of God is how one behaves who loves God.   True love involves obedience.   One becomes more and more like that whom he loves.   If he loves the world, he takes on more and more the nature of the world.   If he loves God, he more and more exhibits in his life the things God wills a man to do.   And the consequences of both "loves" are eternal.   The world is passing away, and the things of it.   The one who loves the world will pass away with it.   In direct contrast to this, the one who becomes more and more like God will remain into eternity, the age to come.[46]   Those who live as Jesus lived (1 John 2:6) will remain as Christ Himself remains (John 12:34, "the Christ remains forever").   The "son remains forever" (John 8:35).   How important it is for Christians to keep their priorities right.   "He who loves his life will lose it; he who loses his life will keep it to life eternal," said Jesus on more than one occasion.   John here has repeats that important lesson as he warns his "children" about the dangers of worldliness.

---

[44] One of the most misplaced phrases in modern language is that which says some person has "passed away."   It is apt at the death of one who has loved the things of this world, but it fundamentally misses the point when used at the funeral of one who has directed his love toward the Father in heaven.

[45] The present participle ("does") pictures continued action: "The one who keeps doing the will of God" or "The one who habitually does the will of God."   "To do the will of" is a Hebraistic expression, meaning "to act according to God's will," "to do what God tells one to do."   John is writing about the thing which God wills for men to do, not His action of willing.   For comparable Hebraisms in John's writings, see notes at 1:6 on "do not practice."

[46] "Abides forever" is literally, "he abides unto the age," i.e., unto the age to come.   The idea of eternal existence is expressed by another phrase in the Greek, "unto the ages of the ages" (see Ephesians 3:21 in the Greek).   The word translated "forever" here in 2:17 is the same root word translated "eternal" at 1 John 1:2.   When the expression is "unto the age," the context defines the age (Luke 20:34,35 NIV).   In this context, "abides forever" is another way of describing fellowship with God, now and hereafter (1 John 2:25, 3:15).   Not only are God and His ways permanent, but so are those who do His will.

C. Warning Against Antichrists. 2:18-27

> *Summary*: This major portion of the epistle began with John assuring his readers of their Christian standing (verses 12-14), but he issues two warnings lest that status be lost. The first one against worldliness was in 2:15-17. Now (verses 18-27) he comes to a second warning, to avoid the teachings of the antichrists. He indicates that the arrival of such false teachers was not unexpected (verse 18), draws a clear distinction between the heretical teachers and genuine Christians (verses 19-21), then defines the content and effect of their heretical teaching (verses 22,23), and finally reminds them of two safeguards against such heretical teaching (verses 24-27).

2:18 -- *Children, it is the last hour; and just as you heard that antichrist is coming, even now many antichrists have arisen; from this we know that it is the last hour.*

Children – The beginning of this new subpoint is signaled by a fresh address to his readers as "children" (the same term used at 2:13). All his readers are addressed, irrespective of age,[1] but who, like "children," are in need of understanding and instruction.

It is the last hour – Twice in this verse John wrote *eschatē hōra* with no article either time.[2] Perhaps the absence of the article (there is no "the" in the Greek) calls attention to the character or quality of the period.[3] The Christian dispensation is the last of the ages

---

[1] The term is to be taken metaphorically, for there is little in this section suited to children of pre-teen age. Indeed, this teaching is for believers old enough to understand and profit by heeding such instructions.

[2] In the New Testament, the expression "last hour" is found only here in 1 John. The Greek has several synonyms for "time." *Chronos* is time in reference to duration, or chronological succession. *Kairos* is time in reference to events, or historical adaptation. *Hōra* is time, generally brief, in reference to a fixed period, a chronologically assigned limit of human or divine purpose. The noun *hōra* can refer either to a short or long period of time (John 4:23, 16:2).

[3] If we observed the absence of the article in our English translations, they would read "a last hour." However, before we insist on omitting the article in English, we should observe that Colwell's rule of grammar may come into play here. That rule says that when a predicate nominative precedes the linking verb, it is definite. Such a construction at John 1:1c throws emphasis on the quality ascribed to Jesus, "and GOD was the Word" (Greek word order). Here in 2:18 the predicate nominative throws emphasis on "last hour."

Hidden beneath the surface of the comments offered on this verse is the thorny issue of whether or not the early New Testament writers were mistaken about the date of the Second Coming. Some have treated "last hour" as though John thought the Parousia of Jesus was only a little while in the future. This (allegedly) mistaken notion is then used to impinge on the idea of the inspiration and inerrancy of apostolic writings. Only if "last hour" is first interpreted to mean "the end of time, when Jesus returns and the dead are raised," can we then accuse John of being mistaken about the time of the Parousia. If "last hour" can cover the whole Christian dispensation, there is no reason to charge John with a mistake. Did John believe there were just a few more days till Christ would return? Had John himself lived to see all the perilous changes and developments which 2 Thessalonians 2 indicates must occur before Christ's Second Advent? If not, why present John as thinking the Second Advent was any nearer in time than Paul did?

or dispensations in God's management of earth's history.[4] This "last hour," thus described, calls attention to the fact that it is an "hour" of crisis (cp. John 2:4; 4:21,23; 5:25,28), the final and decisive period in the history of the world.[5]

And just as you heard that antichrist is coming – The present tense "is coming" suggests it is going to happen. God has told us so. One of the prophetic events still to be fulfilled when John wrote was the appearance of antichrist.[6] That event formed a regular topic of

---

(Romans 11:25,26 and Luke 21:24-26, both written about AD 57 or 60, also indicate that the Parousia is not soon.) Contemporary scholars, who first impose their interpretations on the verses and then assure us the apostles were mistaken, and then assure us that we cannot share the eschatological hopes of the New Testament writers, are just plain wrong.

[4] Slightly different expressions are found elsewhere. "The last day" (*hē eschatē hēmera*, singular) has reference to the end of the world; this phrase occurs in the Fourth Gospel seven times (John 6:39,40,44,54; 11:24; 12:48) and never without the article. There is also "the last days" (*ai eschatai hēmerai*, plural) in Acts 2:17 and 2 Timothy 3:1 (without the article); and "in the last time" (*en kairō exchatō*, at 1 Peter 1:5 but *en eschatō chronō* at Jude 18). In the Old Testament times, the future appearance of the promised Messiah was prophesied to occur "in the last days" (Isaiah 2:2; Hosea 3:5; Micah 4:1 LXX). Hence arose among the Jews the distinction of the two eras, "this age" and "the age to come," the former the time up to the appearance of the Messiah, the latter embracing the whole era after the Messiah came. In New Testament writings, "the last days" covers the whole age from the first to the second coming of Christ (Acts 2:17; 2 Timothy 3:1; Hebrews 1:2; 1 Peter 1:20; 2 Peter 3:3). While the phrase "the last time" refers more specifically to the final point in world history (the day of the coming of Christ and the Final Judgment), the "last hour" has a sense more like that of "the last days."

Some later heretics taught that the gospel dispensation which had begun was not the last in the history of God's dealings with man. The Montanists taught that a dispensation of the Spirit, distinct from the dispensation of the Son, was to follow and supersede the gospel, as the gospel had superseded Judaism (the age of the Father). Did John write "last hour" to correct a heretical belief that another, better "hour" of world history was yet to follow the Gospel dispensation, and that they were heralds of that coming age?

[5] We are treating "last hour" as an idiom meaning "this is a very critical time to be alive." It is critical because how men respond to Jesus the Christ during this closing dispensation in the world's history has eternal consequences. (It certainly will be a very critical time when antichrist himself does appear on the scene of history, and deceives many. In the meantime, it is certainly very critical when anyone encourages unbelief in Jesus the Christ.) John does not say that the end of the world would soon occur, nor does he intimate how long this dispensation would be. The period might continue many centuries, and still be the last dispensation – the age in which the affairs of the world would be finally closed.

[6] The word "antichrist" occurs in the Bible only in the Epistles of John (1 John 2:18,22, 4:3; 2 John 7). In His discourses that have been handed down to us, Jesus did not speak of this event, for the "false prophets" and "false christs" whose appearance Jesus does foretell (Matthew 24:24) appeared in connection with the AD 70 destruction of Jerusalem. Some have appealed to Daniel's 70 Weeks prophecy (Daniel 9:24-27) as being a prediction of antichrist, but we doubt it, for Jesus said that prophecy was fulfilled in the AD 70 destruction of Jerusalem (Matthew 24:15; Mark 13:14; Luke 21:20,21). Others have interpreted Daniel 11:31ff and 12:11 to be a reference to the future antichrist, but we understand those passages to be a prediction of Antiochus Epiphanes who desecrated the temple in Jerusalem in 168 BC. Scripture passages where "antichrist" is predicted may include Daniel's "little horn" (Daniel 7:8ff), Paul's "man of lawlessness" (2 Thessalonians 2), and the "8th beast" of Revelation 17:11. (We do not suppose Revelation was written before 1 John, but we do suppose that John has preached about the "beast" all during his apostolic ministry.)

apostolic teaching and preaching (2 Thessalonians 2:3-5).[7] "Antichrist" is a transliteration of the Greek *antichristos*.   The preposition *anti* can mean against (hostility, antagonism, opposition to) as well as instead of (substitution, in the place of).   Both these possible ideas have been called into action as attempts are made to explain who antichrist is and what he will do.[8] If we have understood the prophetic passages that tell of his coming, then we expect Antichrist to be a government ruler who appears at the close of the church age, perhaps presiding over a coalition of nations, offering himself as a savior for the troubled world he lives in, and acting as he is empowered by the devil.   He is a usurper who under false pretenses assumes a position which does not belong to him, and from that position opposes the rightful Ruler of the world.[9] Antichrist will be slain simply by a spoken word as Jesus first becomes visible on the day of His Parousia (2 Thessalonians 2:8).

Even now many antichrists have arisen – In the preceding clause, "antichrist" (in the singular) referred to a figure who will come at the end of time. In the present clause the same term is used in the plural with reference to the false teachers whom John and his readers were encountering every day.[10] John does not deny the future coming of the antichrist; he is just more concerned with the present fact of the heretics who are a danger to the Christians.[11]   The "many antichrists" are identified as human teachers in verse 19.

---

[7] See on the word "heard" at 1 John 2:7.   The aorist tense refers "to a definite point in their instruction in the faith." Plummer, *op. cit.*, p.107.

[8] Since examples of both "against" and "instead of" may be found in Greek, it is clear we cannot solve this question about 'antichrist' by philology alone. Alford, *op. cit.*, p.447.

[9] Read 2 Thessalonians 2:1-12 and Revelation 17:8-17. We strongly question the standard Protestant identification of the Pope (or all of the Popes together) as being Paul's "man of lawlessness," Daniel's "little horn," and the 8th beast of Revelation. Of course, the Roman church replied in kind, identifying the reformers (Luther, etc.) as being antichrist. For more details see the chapter titled "The Man of Lawlessness" in the author's pamphlet *Let's Study Prophecy* (Moberly, MO : Scripture Exposition Books, 1970, revised 1982).

[10] The verb *gegonasin*, translated "have arisen," comes from *ginomai*, and means have come, have appeared, are present, are at work.

[11] Some contemporary commentators (Dodd, p.49-50, and Bultmann, p.36) have proposed that John's language "many antichrists have arisen" indicates he no longer looks for the appearance of a future antichrist coinciding with the final states of history. They have John here deliberately demythologizing the "antichrist myth" (as they call it) that some 1st century folk superstitiously held. They interpret him to say that any one who in any way denies Jesus is antichrist. But John does not say that the antichrists who are present in the churches at the time he writes 1 John completely fulfill the prophecy of the coming of THE antichrist. Alford (*op. cit.*, p.448) long ago pointed us in the proper direction. "'Christ' (*ho christos*) and 'antichrist' (*ho antichristos*) stand over against one another, an analogy that requires that if one be personal, the other should be also. 'Antichrist' to come is not just an aggregate of all the antichrists who have bothered the church and world." Alford also reminds us that John says more about "antichrist" than what we have here in 2:18. He also wrote 4:3, and there "we are not told that all there is to Antichrist is 'the spirit of *antichristou*.' Instead the personal reference is still kept as John writes *tou antichristou*."

The heretics against whom John warns demonstrate the same spirit or attitude or doctrine the final antichrist will. Later in this letter, John tells us that the "spirit of the antichrist, of which you have heard it is coming" is already at work in the world (1 John 4:3). Teaching a similar idea, Paul said the "mystery of lawlessness was already at work" when he wrote 2 Thessalonians 2:7. What did these antichrists teach? They denied the Father and the Son (verse 22). They denied that Jesus is the Christ (verse 22). They did not confess that Jesus Christ is come in the flesh (4:3). By designating the heretics as "*anti-christs*" – that is, "opponents of Christ" – John is helping his readers decide whom they shall follow. Clearly, if they choose to side with the heretics, it is obvious they have chosen against the real Christ.

From this we know that it is the last hour – "From this" (*othen*, from which) is one of the writer's favorite methods of exposition. First he makes a statement and then gives the facts by which his readers can assure themselves of its truth. "We know" means we can be sure or we can conclude (see at 2:3). The presence of the heretics (many antichrists) proves John's time has all the characteristics of "a last hour." The "we" is a preacher's "we." It includes John and his readers. It would have been difficult to have an "antichrist" arise (come to be) until first the real Christ had been here. Until the long promised Messiah actually appeared on the scene of history, as Jesus the Christ did beginning with His incarnation and birth in Bethlehem, it was not yet the "last hour." The only way "antichrists" can be present is if Christ has already been here. If Christ has been here, the period of world history called the "last hour" has begun. John's day differs little from the last day when it comes to the evil influences Christians will face from the one who pretends to be Christ and opposes Christ.

2:19 -- *They went out from us, but they were not really of us; for if they had been of us, they would have remained with us; but they went out, in order that it might be shown that they all are not of us.*

They went out from us – With absolute precision, John here identifies the "antichrists" about whom he is warning his readers. They formed a large group ("many," verse 18) who have recently withdrawn from the congregation where John worships. The verb "they went out from" is an aorist tense, indicating a definite event in the past. They were not excommunicated. For some reason[12] they deemed it best to end their attempts at assembling with the Christians where John was. 1 John 4:1 indicates some of them have traveled abroad as Gnostic missionaries. Before they went a separate way, although they

---

[12] Some have suggested that before the heretics withdrew, John's Gospel had been published and had made an impact on the home congregation. It had become obvious that where John's apostolic teaching was welcomed and embraced the heretics would have little influence. Before the Gospel circulated, as they tried to recruit followers, they found it to their advantage to associate with the Christians. Now they found whatever advantage association had afforded had ended, so they quit pretending to be Christians.

were not genuine converts to Christianity,[13] for a while they associated with the Christians. Was this to try to recruit Christians, or to give the world the idea they were Christians, too?

But they were not *really* of us – John flatly says the heretics were not Christians. "Of us" may be a genitive of source, or a partitive genitive. If the former, John is saying that the heretics did not have their origin in Christianity.[14] If the latter, the genitive denotes the whole, of which a part is mentioned. Before they withdrew, the heretics did not really belong to the church, they just had their names on the local church roll.[15] As Gill puts it, "We would have said, 'None of them are of us.' Neither the Gnostic in the church nor the

---

[13] John distinguishes sharply between *they* who have left and *us* who remain. Five times in this verse John (writing as a Christian) uses the word "us" to identify the faithful believers who are still in fellowship with John the apostle and with the Father and the Son.

[14] Behind John's statement may be the fact that the Gnostic heresy was first a Jewish heresy before it began to infiltrate the church and became a problem among Christians. Or perhaps John may have in mind that the ultimate origin of heresy is the devil.

[15] The antichrists had been members only in the outward appearance of things, not in the full sense of the word. Today, such folk might be called "nominal Christians." Because of their association with church members, for a while, to outsider observers, the heretics appeared to be church members. Perhaps even in their own minds, for a while, the heretics regarded themselves as "legitimate Christians." But John did not! What John here writes is one of the clearest statements in the New Testament that we must be careful to distinguish between those who have their names on a local church roll and those whose names are written in the Lamb's book of life (Revelation 13:8).

How these people got into the congregations in the first place is not clear. Did they make a "confession of Christ" and mean by "Christ" something vastly different from its Biblical meaning? How did 1st century folk indicate an interest in being part of a local congregation, and by what criteria did local congregations accept or reject applicants? Did the Gnostics sneak in, pretending to be Christians all along? The Judaizers who troubled churches at an earlier time did precisely that, i.e., they sneaked in. Paul characterized them as "false brethren who had sneaked in to spy out our liberty" (Galatians 2:4). The "Judaizers" were Pharisees who pretended to become Christians; they associated with the Christians, and even assumed teaching positions, but they were never Christians themselves (Acts 15:1,5). John later (1 John 4:1) labels these Gnostic heretics as "false prophets" who "have gone out into the world."

We must be careful as we attempt to characterize the life of the congregations to whom John writes. In our postmodern era, when all speech (it is alleged) is deliberately used by folk in power to control the society over which they domineer, and when a plurality of beliefs are accepted (even if they are mutually exclusive), it has become fashionable to assert that in the early days of the church life was just as it is now. It is claimed that there were several "faiths" which in the early decades vied for acceptance, and the one which won is the one that left us our New Testament – which is really nothing more than a "propaganda piece" for the winning party. All the other religious books which were treasured by the losing groups were suppressed. (If we moderns would be well-rounded, we would not narrow-mindedly limit ourselves simply to the winning propaganda! We would find truth in the other religious books, too!) We do agree that at Corinth, for a while at least, there was some doctrinal disagreement between the members of the congregation (e.g., whether or not there will be resurrection of dead bodies, 1 Corinthians 15). At Rome there was disagreement over diet (vegetarian v. flesh eater), whether or not to observe special days, and over what was "clean" or "unclean" (Romans 14,15). But there was no fellowship between belief and unbelief (2 Corinthians 6:14-16). So when we read of the heretics "going out," we should not characterize it as "Christians" dividing into separate groups over doctrinal issues. It would be more nearly correct to say that heterodoxy and orthodoxy were going separate ways. "The existence of such divisive sects in the New Testament, with the clear-cut way in which they are denounced, implies a discriminating form of doctrine and fellowship in the primitive church. Even with the desire for unity, the early church did not lose sight of the value of holding fast to what had been taught from the beginning." (Roberts, *op. cit.*, p.64.)

Gnostic outside the church is really of us. The physical presence of a false teacher in the assembly does not make him a Christian."[16] The imperfect *ēsan*, "were," embraces the whole previous period during which the antichristians were connected with the believers, and does not merely refer to the time immediately preceding their separation.

For if they had been of us, they would have remained with us – "If they had been of us ..." is a contrary-to-fact condition in the Greek. The heretics were not Christians, not part of the body of Christ. "They would have remained" is a translation of the verb *menein*, "to abide," which in this epistle (see 2:6) is one of the distinctive terms for fellowship or communion. The verb form here is pluperfect (without an augment) with *an*.[17] The pluperfect expresses a past completed act with continuing results up to some time in the past, in this case, the time when the heretics "went out." If they really were Christians, they would have remained with us instead of seceding, but they were not.[18] John wrote "with us" (*meth' hēmōn*), not "among us" (*en hēmin*), which brings out more clearly the idea of outward fellowship as distinguished from inward communion.

But *they went out*, in order that it might be shown that they all are not of us – The sentence is elliptical: we must supply the verb from the previous clause. "In order that" (a *hina* clause) can express either purpose or result, and the verse has been treated both ways. Folk who are strongly predestinarian in their theology discern a divine purpose being served in the departure of the heretics.[19] The separation was willed by God so that

---

[16] Gill, *op. cit.*, p.62. It is not surprising to read in Scripture of the possibility of nominal members. Good and evil grew together till the harvest in the Parable of the Tares (Matthew 13:24-30). Among the guests at the banquet was one who did not have on wedding garments (Matthew 22:11).

[17] Several English versions (e.g. KJV) read "they would no doubt have continued with us." The "no doubt" represents the *utique* of the Vulgate, which was the result of a mistaken endeavor to translate the Greek particle *an*.

[18] Some writers, anxious to defend the doctrine of the absolute indefectibility (perseverance) of the saints, have pressed this passage into service in an attempt to provide Biblical proof that those who fall away were never saved in the first place. It is not quite right to say that the heretics whom John says "went out (away)" were once saved. Nor is it quite right to say "went out (away)" is synonymous with fell away. Elsewhere, John shows that it is possible to once be a Christian and to fall away (John 15:1-6; 1 John 2:24; 2 John 8). While none of us can be certain a true believer won't fall away (neither John nor we expect folk to become false), that is not the topic John is dealing with. Other writers, anxious to defend certain theories of predestination, make use of this passage to confirm their doctrine. That is pressing "they would have remained" too far.

[19] Augustine (who says men are elected to grace, and that salvation is infallibly secured to the elect [*De Dono Perseverantiae*, 8,9], and that a certain fixed number of individuals is predestined [*De Correptione et Gratis*, 99]), followed by Calvin, Beza, etc. "find in these words a confirmation of their doctrine of predestination, but only by inserting into them ideas which are foreign to them, since the subject here is neither a *donum perseverantiae* nor a distinction of the *vocati* ("called") and *electi* ("elect")" (Huther, *op. cit.*, p.533).

the elect would not be led astray by the false prophets.[20]   We think treating the *hina* clause as expressing result gives a good sense here.   John sees a good result coming from their departure.   Their departure was their unmasking as being pretenders or play actors.   No longer can they pretend that their doctrine and lifestyles were "Christian."   Any one, whether John's readers or outsiders, should be able to see that the heretics were not legitimate Christians; their leaving the fellowship of the assembly of believers makes that obvious![21]

2:20 -- *But you have an anointing from the Holy One, and you all know.*

But you – "You" is emphatic in the Greek, "you" as contrasted with others is the idea. The contrast is with the heretics.   Christians truly have what the heretics falsely claimed to have.   "But" is not the common way we translate *kai*.[22]   However, adversative ideas can be connected by a simple *kai*, and there is a contrast here between the "antichrists" who separated themselves from the Christians and John's Christian readers whom John identifies as "you."   Instead of being adversative, it is also possible that the *kai* connects this verse with verse 19 in such a way as to indicate a second evidence why the Christian readers can know the heretics are not really Christian brethren.   One line of evidence was their "going out."   Another strong evidence is the "anointing" John here calls attention to.

Have an anointing from the Holy One – No agreement is found in the commentaries concerning the identity of "the Holy One."   The evidence is far from decisive.   Some believe John has reference to the Holy Spirit.   Others believe "the Holy One" is Christ ("the Holy One of God," Mark 1:24; John 6:69).   Still others affirm "the Holy One" is God ("the Holy One of Israel," Psalm 71:22; Isaiah 1:4; Habakkuk 3:3).   Nor is there any agreement in the commentaries concerning what the "anointing" is.   The Greek word is *chrisma*.[23]   Greek words ending in *-ma* emphasize the result of the action denoted by the root of the word.   If that is true here, John is calling attention to the result of an "anointing" of some kind.   That "result" is what proves the heretics to be wrong.

---

[20] Believers in such predestination insist that parallel constructions at John 1:8, 9:2, 13:18, and 15:25, all have the connotation of something that is ordained by God.

[21] In "all are not of us" (*ouk eisin pantes ex hēmōn*), it is the verb that is negated.   Still interpretation of the phrase is difficult.   Does it refer to "all the heretics" who have left?   (I.e., don't equate Gnosticism with Christianity!)   Or does it refer to "all the remaining people" in the congregations to which John writes?   It has already been shown that some in the past were nominal members at best.   It is likely (John implies) some still attending the assembly are but nominal members.   In our comments we opt for the former view.

[22] The Vulgate translators apparently took *kai* as adversative for it reads *sed* ("but").   So do numerous English translations.

[23] Occasionally in the LXX (e.g., Exodus 29:7; Deuteronomy 30:25), the word *chrisma* is used for the unguent or anointing oil itself rather than the completed act of anointing.

The two most popular explanations of what is meant by "anointing" are (1) the 'indwelling of Holy Spirit' (received when folk become Christians)[24] and (2) the 'written Word of God' (the result of the Holy Spirit, received at Pentecost, guiding the Bible writers).[25] Both these suggestions take account of the fact that oil or anointing in both the Old and New Testaments is used figuratively for the Holy Spirit (Psalm 45:6,7, 10:15; Isaiah 61:1; Acts 10:38; Hebrews 1:9; 2 Corinthians 1:21). Let us briefly explore the two popular options.

(1) To interpret "anointing" as referring to the indwelling gift of the Holy Spirit has some things that can be said in its favor. It is a measure of the Spirit that every Christian receives when they are immersed into Christ. This could be harmonized with the "you all" later in this verse. One of the things the indwelling Spirit does is illumine the Word; that is, He helps folk to understand the "truth" (Word of God) given by revelation and spoken by inspiration (1 Corinthians 2:12-15). This might satisfy the context here in 1 John where what we need is some kind of test by which to judge Gnostic doctrine. The indwelling Spirit view also has some things not in its favor. It takes no account of the emphasis of the -ma ending on "anointing." Most telling is the fact that an appeal to the indwelling Spirit easily declines into an appeal to one's individual experience. In other words, this explanation of "anointing" is open to the danger of subjectivism. "The antichrists could claim spiritual illumination: how, then, could John's readers know for sure that their spiritual experience was of superior quality? If it is simply a matter of comparing claims to spiritual illumination, one person's claim may be as good as another."[26]

(2) Several arguments point rather to "anointing" being a reference to the written Word of God. It permits us to call attention to the result the -ma ending emphasizes. What is it the readers possess that is the result of an anointing by the Holy Spirit? Might this be a reference to the Gospel of John? The inspiration that helped in the writing of that document would be the result of an "anointing" by the Holy Spirit, i.e., the baptism of the Holy Spirit received by the apostles to empower them for their mission (Acts 1:8, 2:1ff; 2 Peter 1:3). This interpretation results in this test for truth being objective. If the readers consult the Gospel (the Word of God), they will have an objective standard of truth by which they will be able to discern the error of the antichrists. In harmony with this view, the "Holy One" is Christ (Mark 1:24; John 6:69; Acts 3:14; Revelation 3:7; Psalm 20:10),

---

[24] Some versions paraphrase, "You have had the Holy Spirit poured out on you" (TEV), or "you have had the Holy Spirit poured out on you by Christ" (GNB), or "the Holy Spirit has come upon you" (LNT).

[25] Other views: (1) Some writers have found evidence of a confirmation service following baptism in this "anointing." (2) Some writers have found evidence that each of John's readers had received a spiritual gift subsequent to their baptism (along with the indwelling Spirit). (3) Others interpret the language to mean that the readers had been set apart to some sacred task which Christ ("the Holy One") had in mind for them. One problem shared by each of these suggestions is that it is not easy to trace a connection to the point being made, how such an "anointing" helps the readers ascertain the truth or error of the Gnostics.

[26] Marshall, op. cit., p.154-155.

who promised the apostles He would send the Holy Spirit on them (John 14:26, 15:26, 17:7,14).[27] Just like Jesus promised, the preposition "from" (in "anointing from the Holy One") identifies the "Holy One" as the source from which the anointing comes. The Holy Spirit guided the apostles into all truth (John 16:13).[28] This explanation of "anointing which you received" (verse 27) would compare with "which you [have] heard from the beginning [i.e., the gospel]" (verse 2:24). Furthermore, John speaks of the "anointing" remaining with the readers the same way he spoke of the Word of God or the truth remaining with them (1 John 2:14; 2 John 2). The expression "abides in you" at verse 27 would be explained the same way we explain the same language at verse 24 (where "which you heard from the beginning" refers to apostolic preaching, a message in total harmony with the later written records we call the Gospels and epistles). When we compare "have" (verse 20) with "received" (verse 27), it becomes apparent that possession depends upon a reception. John's Christian readers are thus able to detect the doctrinal error of the heretics, not only by observing the fact of their separation from the congregation, but also by drawing upon the *chrisma* ("anointing," the Word of God) which they had received.

And you all know – This clause apparently is intended to express a result of the "anointing" upon John's readers, but exactly what result is indicated is not easy to determine given the variation in readings within the ancient sources for our text. We must choose between four different readings. (1) Some read *kai oidate panta* ("and you know all things").[29] (2) Some read *kai oidate pantes* ("and you all know [it]").[30] (3) Some read *oidate pantes*

---

[27] The description of Jesus as "holy" is comparatively rare in the New Testament. Because unclean spirits recognized Jesus as "the Holy One of God" (Luke 4:34; Mark 1:24), some have suggested that John deliberately drew a contrast between the "anointing" the Christians have and the one the Gnostics have. If the Christian one comes from the "Holy One" (Christ), then it is implied that what the Gnostics have came from one who is not holy (i.e., the devil).   Others suggest that John intended to express the idea that Jesus shares the Father's divine holiness (1 Peter 1:15ff; John 10:36), another direct refutation of Gnostic claims about the God of the Bible.

[28] Everyday Christians do not have revelations or inspiration like the apostles had.

[29] So read the uncials A,C,K,L, and the Vulg., Syr.H, Copt., Aeth., and Arm. versions. It is the text followed by the KJV and ASV.

[30] So read the uncials Sinaiticus and Vaticanus, P, and a few others (though Vaticanus and the Sahidic omit the *kai*). It is the reading given in the Nestle text, and reflected in the RSV, NEB, TEV, NASB.

("you all know") with no *kai*.[31]   (4) One ancient version[32] reflects a Greek text that read *oidate pantas* ("you know all [those people]", i.e., the antichrists).   Choosing #1, the verse says "you Christians (i.e., John's readers) know all things relative to salvation," no matter what the Gnostics may claim about superior knowledge.[33]   Choosing #2, we must supply an object for the verb "know."   We might supply "the truth" from verse 21, or "all things" from verse 27.   We might supply "about the result of the anointing" from this very verse.   Either way, Christians are in possession of true knowledge, and all they need to do to see the error of the Gnostics is to compare the true knowledge with what the Gnostics say and do.   The lack of correspondence or consistency with "the truth" shows the error of the Gnostics.[34]

2:21 -- *I have not written to you because you do not know the truth, but because you do know it, and because no lie is of the truth.*

I have not written to you because you do not know the truth – Whatever may have been true in verses 13,14 concerning the verb "I have written," what we have here is very likely an epistolary aorist.   It makes little difference in meaning whether we suppose it refers to the whole letter thus far written, or just to the present section about the antichrists (as seems clear from verse 26).   There is certainly some relationship between "the result of the anointing" (verse 20) and "knowing the truth" (verse 21).   We recall that Jesus had said that if people know the truth, they will be made free (John 8:31,32).   The "truth" to which Jesus refers is His own revelation of the will of God ("My Word" is how He identified it in John 8:31).   If John's readers have the results of the anointing (e.g., the Gospel of John), and they "know all the truth" (John 16:13), why is John writing this letter, they might wonder.   He anticipates their possible question and goes on to explain.

But because you do know it – John's response to their "Why are you writing?" basically is this: "I am not writing something new to you, something you don't already know.   I am simply calling attention to what you do know, in order that by referring to it you may be safeguarded against the dangers presented by the heretics."   "It," which is particularly

---

[31] When we encounter "you all know" (with no *kai*), it is usually understood to be the beginning of a new sentence or verse, rather than the conclusion of the previous one.   However, to treat "you all know" as the beginning of verse 21 makes the middle part of that verse redundant.

[32] Syr.P.   The Phillips translation reflects this reading.

[33] It would not be saying that Christians are omniscient, but that in the "results of the anointing" the Christians have a basis of all that is needed for salvation.   By the influence of the Holy Spirit on the apostles (since Jesus promised they would be led into "all truth") the readers have been made thoroughly acquainted with the truths and duties of Christianity.

[34] "Many passages emphasize this confidence that even the average Christian who had learned the gospel well enough to obey it could recognize a deviation from the tradition learned from Christ (1 Thessalonians 4:9; Romans 15:14,15)."   Roberts, *op. cit.*, p.66.   Systematic consistency with the Word of God is the Christian's test for truth.

John's point, is the "truth" about Jesus the Christ, as the following verses will make clear.[35]

And because no lie is of the truth – The particular "lie"[36] John has in mind is also explained in the next verses. The Greek conjunction *hoti*, found three times in this verse, is translated "because" the first two times in most English versions.[37] Some scholars think it should be translated "because" this third time. It makes John say that he is aware the readers know that "truth" does not contain a mixture of what is true and what is false. Truth is self-consistent.[38] Others argue the third occurrence of *hoti* in this clause should be translated "that," making what is here affirmed to be part of what the readers "know." They know "it" (the truth), and they know that every lie is not of the truth (the negative particle negates the verb in Greek). Any religious teaching out of harmony with the New Covenant Scriptures is false![39] There is a sharp contrast between truth and error. Folk who know the truth are in a position to detect falsehood at once and mount the proper opposition to it.[40]

2:22 -- Who is the liar but the one who denies that Jesus is the Christ? This is the antichrist, the one who denies the Father and the Son.

Who is the liar – The Greek reads *tis estin ho pseustēs* and translators have debated whether or not to translate the article "the." "We must beware of exaggerating the article in *interpretation*, although it is right to *translate* it."[41] When the English reads "who is a liar?" we interpret it to mean there are no liars if the one who denies that Jesus the Christ is not one. When the English reads, "who is the liar?" we interpret it to mean there is no

---

[35] The most unlettered Christian need not shrink before the self-proclaimed scholarship of anyone who denies the incarnation or deity of Jesus, or that Jesus is the Christ. The knowledge of truth that can be gained by a simple reading of the New Testament books in such a case is more reliable than that gained by the unbeliever's philosophical deductions.

[36] The word John used is "lie." It is not merely an error or mistake, but a "lie" – the absolute antithesis of "truth."

[37] Of course, the explanation offered for each of the phrases will vary depending on which word ("because" or "that") is chosen to translate the conjunction. Comparing English versions, Bible readers will find "because ... because ... that"; or "because" in all three clauses; or "that" in all three clauses.

[38] John here presents the correspondence theory of truth, where systematic consistency is the test for truth.

[39] "Of the truth" is exactly analogous to "of the Father" and "of the world" (verse 16 KJV) and to "of us" (verse 19). Every lie is in origin utterly removed from the truth; the truth springs from God; lying from the devil, for he is a liar and the father of lies (John 8;44). Plummer, *op. cit.*, p.112

[40] It may be noted that John's sternly severe view of truth makes it certain that he would have shrunk with horror from the modern suggestion that discourses were manufactured and dramatically put into the mouth of our Lord, or from any false or highly-colored representation of His work. (Adapted from Alexander, *op. cit.*, p.321).

[41] Plummer, *op. cit.*, p.112.

greater lie than the denial of Jesus the Christ. The one making such a claim is "the liar *par excellence.*"[42] Some have questioned this implication, asking whether or not a denial of the existence of God might not be a bigger lie. The article before "liar" perhaps is the article of previous reference, pointing back to "lie" in verse 21. When John says, "Who is the liar ...?" he has not stooped to name calling.[43] The question is more profound than that.[44] With this rhetorical question,[45] John calls attention to the method used by the heretics (lies) and their message (a denial that Jesus is the Christ). Verses 22-23 specify what John had in mind when he said that "every lie is not of the truth." The particular lie John had in mind had to do with what the heretics taught about the person of Jesus Christ.

But the one who denies that Jesus is the Christ? – This is one of the false doctrines taught by those who left the churches. The clause following "that" is indirect discourse, and contains the actual words publicly spoken by the heretics, *Iēsous ouk estin ho Christos,* "Jesus is not the Christ." This denial could have been used to express either a docetic or adoptionist view of Christ.[46] The negative particle *ouk* in the Greek negates the verb *estin.* Maybe one could say he 'became' the Christ, or the Christ came upon the human Jesus, but the heretics claimed you cannot say He "is" the Christ. The heretics accepted Jesus in some sense (e.g., He might have been the Messiah[47] for a short time during His life), but they denied that the divine Son was permanently incarnate in Jesus the Messiah.[48] Gnostics

[42] R.C. Foster in a class on 1 John commented at this place, "Who is the biggest liar in the world, if not this man who denies Jesus is the Christ?"

[43] Not only were the heretics not Christians (verse 19), they were liars. It is not name calling when one points out the facts of the case.

[44] "John's black and white contrasts are healthily clear-sighted. Opposing views are not to him 'complementary insights' but 'truth and error' (verses 21,27). If we claim to enjoy fellowship with God while we walk in darkness, 'we lie' (1:6). He who says he knows God but disobeys His commandments 'is a liar' (2:4, *pseustēs*). But what is to be said of him who denies that Jesus is the Christ? We must pronounce him 'the' liar (*ho pseustēs*), the liar *par excellence.*" Stott, *op. cit.*, p.111.

[45] "The interrogative form, with which John addresses his readers who know the truth, is explained by the vividness of the feeling with which the apostle is writing. Comp. 5:8." Huther, *op. cit.*, p.536

[46] There was no one heretical view in the Mediterranean world of the first two centuries AD. Instead there was a multitude of differing and conflicting views entertained and promulgated by those who embraced the dualistic philosophy popular at the time.

[47] Some Jewish folk denied that Jesus was the Christ; that is, they denied He was the long-promised Messiah (cp. John 4:29, 7:26-31,42-43; Acts 5:42, 9:22, 17:3, 18:28). A study of these epistles (especially 2 John 7 and 1 John 4:3) makes it plain that the denial voiced by the Gnostic heretics was not simply a denial like the unbelieving Jews voiced.

[48] To later Gnostics, the "Christ" was a higher being or "aeon" who descended on Jesus at His baptism and left Him before the crucifixion. In repudiating the full reality of the incarnation, the heretics were flatly contradicting what John 1:14 says ("the Word became flesh"). (See documentation for later Gnostic views in the Introductory Studies.) In the latter part of verse 22 and in 23, John speaks of denying Jesus was the "Son." In 1 John 4:2,3 and 2 John 7 the heresy John combats is defined as a denial that "Jesus Christ has come in the flesh" (or that "Jesus is the Christ come in the flesh").

made Jesus a mere man invested for a brief period with special powers. "For John, the identity of Jesus as the Christ was the main and crucial point of the Christian faith. Everyone who denied it could not be but a liar in his eyes."[49]   Numerous modern theologians separate the so-called historical Jesus from the Christ of faith.   Is there any real difference between what the theologians of today teach and what the Gnostics of old taught?   Both presentations can be castigated as "lies"!   Both strike at the heart of Christianity.[50]

This is the antichrist – *Houtos* points to the "liar" just described.   It is possible to translate the Greek, "The antichrist is this."[51]   In other words, the Gnostics of John's day and the future antichrist are in perfect agreement when it comes to their denial of who Jesus is.[52]   Implied also would be the idea that the heretic's theology is not just defective; it is as diabolical as will be antichrist's opposition to Jesus.

The one who denies the Father and the Son – This clause is an expansion of what John wrote before about "denying that Jesus is the Christ."   Now he says "denies the Father and the Son."   As a consequence of their false Christology ('Jesus is not the Christ,' they said) the heretics have automatically denied what Scriptures say about God being the Father of Jesus Christ, and about Jesus Christ being the Son of God.[53]   Those are serious and damning departures from the faith once for all delivered to the saints!   To deny that "Jesus is the Christ" is to strike at the very heart of the incarnation.   If we deny that Jesus is God's Son, then we deny that God is the Father also.   "If there is no Son, there is no Father."[54] Correct views of the Father cannot be held without first holding correct views of the Son.

2:23 -- *Whoever denies the Son does not have the Father; the one who confesses the Son has the Father also.*

---

[49] Haas, *op. cit.*, p.68.

[50] "The fundamental doctrinal test of the professing Christian concerns his view of the person of Jesus. If he is a Unitarian or a member of a sect denying the deity of Jesus, he is not a Christian.   Many strange cults which have a popular appeal today can be easily judged and quickly repudiated by this test."   Stott, *op. cit.*, p.111-112.

[51] "This," as in 1:5 and 2:25, may be the predicate.   If we read the Greek as the NASB does, the definite article "the" before "antichrist" does not mean that the one personal antichrist predicted for the end of time is to be identified with one of these Gnostic false teachers.   This is the article of previous reference. Thus A.T. Robertson (*op. cit.*, p.217) does not seem to be correct when he identifies Cerinthus himself as being "the one" whom John singles out as antichrist.

[52] Teachers who taught what the heretics were teaching were certainly opposed to God's Son, Jesus Christ, whom we meet in the pages of the New Testament.

[53] For "the Father" see on 1:2.   For "the Son" see on 1:3 and 3:8.

[54] Kistemaker, *op. cit.*, p. 282.

Whoever denies the Son does not have the Father – "Whoever" means 'everyone who' – there is no exception.   What John has asserted at the close of verse 22 is now carefully unfolded and explained.   A man cannot teach about Jesus what the heretics did and still have any valid claim to knowing God the Father.   *Oude* means "not even"; everyone who denies the Son does not even have the Father.   The person who rejects the view that Jesus is the Christ, the Son of God, thereby also loses all claim to knowing God, and of having a relationship with Him.[55]   Jesus Himself (John 5:19ff) said that anyone who denies His deity denies the Father also.   If a man does not honor the Son, he does not honor the Father! (John 5:23).   On the other hand, "To as many as received Him – i.e., believed on His name – [Jesus] gave them the power to become Sons of God" (John 1:12, personal translation).   Jesus declared that no man could come to the father but by Him (John 14:6).

The one who confesses the Son has the Father also[56] – "Confess" (*homologeō*) means "to say the same thing."[57]   Here it is the same thing God says, or the apostles say, about "Jesus is the Christ."[58]   John has in mind more than a privately held belief or disbelief. How, then, would one go about confessing the Son?   It might be done audibly before an audience (Matthew 10:32; Romans 10:10; 1 Timothy 6:13).   It might then also be done in one's lifestyle.   There are only two options – denial or confession.[59]   John's favorite method of emphasizing a great truth is to state it both positively and negatively.[60]   In the first part of this verse we have the negative statement.   In this latter part, we have the positive.   The statement John here makes, that one must confess the Son to have the Father, has broader application than just the Gnostics.[61]   To "have the Father" might speak

---

[55] The history of philosophy verifies this statement.   Deism has ever had a tendency to end in pantheism or atheism.

[56] This phrase does not appear in most editions of the KJV; it is not part of the Byzantine text and therefore is not found in the Textus Receptus.   Actually it is included in the best manuscripts (Sinaiticus, Vaticanus, Alexandrinus, Ephraemi) and is certainly genuine.   Some scribe likely omitted it accidentally since both halves of the verse end with the same three words (*ton patera echei*).   That copy then became the exemplar for the Byzantine manuscripts that likewise omit it.   Though some manuscripts connect the last half of the verse to the first with the conjunction "but," in the Greek there is an impressive absence of conjunctions in verses 22,23,24.   "The sentences fall on the reader's soul like the notes of a trumpet. Without cement, and therefore all the more ruggedly clasping each other, they are like a Cyclopean wall" (Haupt).

[57] *Homologeō* is the same verb used at 1:9, 4:2,3,15; 2 John 7.

[58] Compare 1 John 4:2, 5:5,6; Matthew 16:16; Mark 8:29; Romans 10:9,10.

[59] For the stress laid on "denial" and "confession" see John 1:20; 9:22; 12:42.

[60] Compare 1 John 1:5,8; 2:4,27; 3:6; 4:2,3,6,7,8; 5:12.

[61] Anyone who claims to know or have a relationship with the Father, while at the same time excluding the Son, is sadly mistaken about having a relationship with the Father.   Modern Rationalism, Deism, Judaism, and Islam all are indicted by this plain statement from the apostle John.   These systems, expounded with touching eloquence and consummate ability, desire to give up the historical Christ, and yet to cling to the idea of the Father.   It needs to be observed that these systems, rejecting the worship of Christ, professedly out of reverence for the Father, are constantly sliding into atheism or pantheism. Adapted from Alexander, *op. cit.*, p.322.

of having correct beliefs about the Father. It might speak of having God's approval. It might speak of having any fellowship or relationship at all with the Father.[62]

2:24 -- *As for you, let that abide in you which you heard from the beginning. If what you heard from the beginning abides in you, you also will abide in the Son and in the Father.*

As for you – Verses 24 to 27 are an exhortation to the readers to abide in the truth of God and to confess the Son.[63] The "you" stands first in the Greek: "you" as distinct from the antichrists. At this point, John's writing becomes very personal. He uses the plural "you" numerous times in these three verses. He speaks directly to his readers and says in effect, "You, I want your attention!"[64]

Let that abide in you which you heard from the beginning – "Let it abide (remain)" (*menetō*) is a present imperative; it is a command.[65] He appeals to their will. Addressing his readers directly he appeals to them to decide to continue to embrace what they have always been taught (namely, that Jesus is the Christ) and to determine they will soundly reject the false teachings he has denounced in the preceding verses. Adhere to the old fashioned gospel steadfastly. Let God's eternal truth have a permanent place in your heart and life. It is implied that there is nothing automatic about continuing to believe what one was first taught. Instead, a conscious effort must be made to remain *conservative* in one's

---

[62] The verb "has" (*echei*) is the same in both parts of the verse. See 5:12 and 2 John 9. We cannot possess, i.e., have fellowship with, the Father if we do not confess the Son. Only the Son can reveal the Father to men (Matthew 11:27; John 1:18, 12:44,45, 14:9). Our only approach to the Father is by the Son, and only He can represent and reconcile men to the Father (1 John 2:1,2; John 14:6; cf. 1 Timothy 2:5). Adapted from Stott, *op. cit.*, p.112

[63] Because of its missing clause (see footnote #56 above), the correct point of this verse ("you therefore") is missed by the Textus Receptus. This same Byzantine text mistakenly inserted a "therefore" at the beginning of verse 24, likely because the copyist realized something was missing in the reading of the truncated exemplar he was copying.

[64] Adapted from Kistemaker, *op. cit.*, p.283. This advice (i.e., to stick with the old-time gospel) is suggested pointedly to John's readers by use of the emphatic personal pronoun. The point of the contrast is this: others may deny the Son, but *you,* you cannot do that if you hold fast the teaching given you when you first learned the gospel.

[65] Third singular imperative forms (such as this) have to be translated with a helper, "Let (it) ...." John purposely stresses the concept *remain* (abide), for he weaves it into this passage (verses 24-28) six times." Kistemaker, *op. cit.*, p.283. The KJV renders John's favorite verb "abide" by three different English words in this one verse, "abide," "remain," and "continue." If we are not careful, we will miss John's emphasis.

theology.[66] The power of the gospel in a person's life depends on the freedom permitted it. "Which (what) you heard" simply means the basic teaching of the gospel, especially about Jesus. "Heard" is an aorist tense and points to the definite period when they were first instructed in the Christian faith. "From the beginning" probably refers to the beginning of their life as Christians (see on 2:7). The separation of "Jesus" and the Christ" as the heretics were doing was a new doctrine. John entreats them to go back to what they believed before the rise of the false teachers. That will help settle any confusion which has been caused by the lies the heretics have told.

If what you heard from the beginning abides in you – This is a vivid future condition in the Greek, implying that John believes they will abide in the old fashioned teaching, rather than embracing the innovations of the false prophets.[67] The word order "from the beginning" is slightly changed in this phrase as compared with the previous one. That change may lay stress on the fact that from the first day they preached, even before the readers of this epistle became Christians, the apostles were preaching the same Christian message. The repetition of the language gives all this a ring of authority and importance.[68] The present tense "abides" emphasizes again the fact that "the word of the Gospel must not only be heard but it must be given a vital place in one's life."[69]

You also will abide in the Son and in the Father – "You" again is emphatic. You as contrasted to the false teachers and their followers who do not have either the Father or the Son. "In the Son" is put first, perhaps to emphasize the fact that "access to the Father becomes possible only through the Son (John 10:10, 17:2, 20:31). This is why denial of the Son has such fearful consequences."[70] Apostolic testimony was concerned essentially with the Son. That is why if they remain true to it, they will remain true to Him and to His Father.[71]

---

[66] "Christian theology is anchored not only to certain historical events, culminating in the saving career of Jesus, but to the authoritative apostolic witness to these events. The Christian can never weigh anchor and launch out into the deep of speculative thought. Nor can he forsake the primitive teaching of the apostles for the subsequent traditions of men." Stott, *op. cit.*, p.113.

[67] For an explanation of the various words and phrases, see the explanations offered for the previous clause, where we had the same language.

[68] This thought is common in other Christian documents of the same period (1 Timothy 6:3; 2 Timothy 1:13, 4:3ff; Titus 1:9; 2 Peter 3:2; Jude 3,17,20). Written after the Gnostic heresy began to trouble the churches, they all counsel holding fast to the teaching given in the past which constitutes what Paul calls "sound doctrine" and what Jude calls "the faith that God has once for all delivered to the saints."

[69] Barker, *op. cit.*, p.326.

[70] *Ibid.*, p.327.

[71] It is obvious that to the writer *menein* means something more than 'standing still.' It is the 'abiding' (living) of the son who grows up in the house. On the term "abide," see notes at 2:6,10,29, 3:24.

2:25 -- And this is the promise which He Himself made to us: eternal life.

And this is the promise which He Himself made to us – "This" is probably the predicate, and points to what follows as being the thing promised.[72]   "And" indicates there is a connection between what was said in verse 24 and what is about to be written in verse 25. For those who let God's Word remain in them there is an appropriate reward promised. The thing promised or pledged "is" (*estin*, present tense) continually present.   "He Himself" is Jesus,[73] and the word "He" is emphatic: Jesus, and no one else.   Here is a promise that Jesus Himself has made to us, says John: it is eternal life.   *Hēmin* ("to us") is the better attested reading, rather than *humin* ("to you").

Eternal life – If "this" points forward, then "eternal life" is a new thought John adds to the picture as he writes.[74]   What John would have us feel is that there can be no promise to compare with this, that we should share the eternal life, the life of God (see at 1:2).   "We read the promise Jesus made about eternal life in many passages of the Fourth Gospel; e.g., John 3:15,16, 4:14, 6:40,47,57, 11:25,26, 17:2,3."[75]   John 17:3 records Jesus as saying "this is eternal life," to know the Father and the Son.   "Eternal life" has both a present and a future connotation.   The Christian already has eternal life abiding in him (John 3:16,36, 6:40,47).   In addition to the "eternal life" available here and now, there is a future aspect to "eternal life," a quality of life that only the redeemed participate in.[76]   Verse 25 seems to promise a reward additional to that which was given in verse 24.   "Some writers argue for the future meaning of eternal life on the grounds that John is giving his readers a motive for perseverance and remaining in fellowship with God."[77]   In addition, the future dimension was already introduced at 2:17.   In verses 15 and 16, John gave two reasons for shunning the world: (1) because the world is passing away, and (2) because the world is alien to the Father.   So here, John gives two reasons for holding fast to the truth originally delivered to them: (1) because the truth leads to fellowship with the Son and with the Father, and (2) because the truth of God leads to eternal life.

---

[72] "This" (*hautē*) is feminine singular, just as is the following word "promise" (*epaggelia*) of eternal life, and so likely points forward.

[73] Is "He" Jesus, or is "He" the "Father," the nearest antecedent?   Because the whole paragraph has centered around "Jesus is the Christ," "He" is most likely "Jesus."   Comp. 3:2,3, and other passages.

[74] If "this" points backward, then the idea is that the "abide in the Son (remaining in Him)" (verse 24) means the same thing as does the expression "eternal life" (verse 25).

[75] Alford, *op. cit.*, p.455.

[76] See 1 Timothy 4:8; 2 Timothy 1:1; Titus 2:1; James 1:12.   See further on "eternal life" in the comments on 1 John 3:15.

[77] Marshall, *op. cit.*, p.161.

2:26 -- These things I have written to you concerning those who are trying to deceive you.

These things I have written to you – Verses 26 and 27 conclude this section of warning about the antichrists.[78] "I have written" is an epistolary aorist, referring back to verses 18-25, to what has been said about the false teachers and how the danger they pose can be detected and met.[79]

Concerning those who are trying to deceive you – This is a new element in the summary[80] as John calls attention to another activity of the heretics, namely, they "are trying to deceive you (lead you astray)."[81] Compare 2 John 7 where John speaks of "many deceivers." The target audience from which the heretics hoped to win converts consisted of church members. The present participle indicates the continual attempt of the false teachers to seduce or lead the Christians astray. The use of the present tense does not determine the extent to which the heretic's attempts had met with success (cp. Revelation 12:9). Though the heretics "went out from (among) us" (2:19), they have not stopped trying to get converts from among the Christians. They were trying to seduce faithful Christians away from church, away from Christ, and away from God. Christians should not underestimate the danger, for it is real,[82] and perhaps by the time 3 John and Revelation were written some Christians had defected.

2:27 -- And as for you, the anointing which you received from Him abides in you, and you have no need for anyone to teach you; but as His anointing teaches you about all things, and is true and is not a lie, and just as it has taught you, you abide in Him.

And as for you – The same expression opened verse 24. As before, the emphatic "you" makes a contrast between John's readers and the antichrists. While Christians enjoy the results of an "anointing," the antichrists do not! John makes one final exhortation to his Christian readers to oppose what the heretics were trying to do. His exhortation is based on what he had said earlier, for he repeats some of the ideas found in verses 20 and 24.

The anointing which you received from Him abides in you – Whatever decision was made on "anointing" at verse 20 should be reflected here.   We opted for the result of the

---

[78] "These things" (*tauta*) probably means the warnings about the antichrists, though Bengel (*Gnomon*, V.5, p.124) connects the *tauta* of verse 26 with verse 21 (note the repeat of "I have written to you"), and regards verse 27 as continuing the thought of verse 20 (note the reference to *chrisma*, "anointing" in both verses).

[79] There is no need to detect a reference to a former epistle in this aorist tense verb.

[80] Previously they were described as opponents of Christ and as purveyors of falsehood.

[81] We had the same root word used at 1:8.   Notes there explain the meaning of "deceive."

[82] Christians can be deceived by others (3:7); they can also deceive themselves (1:8).   Such deception ultimately is traced to the devil, who is the arch-deceiver (John 8:44).   John is silent at this place about what happens to those who end up being deceived.

anointing, and pointed to the gospel as delivered by the apostles of Jesus.[83] "Received" (aorist tense) points back to the same time as "you have heard" in verse 24. "Abides in you" would have the same meaning here in verse 27 that it did in verse 24. All the way through these next phrases "you" is plural (*humeis, humin, humas*); John is addressing numerous genuine believers. "Abides" (present tense) is how John assures his readers of their standing with the Father and the Son. They have not defected because they still hold the old-fashioned gospel.

And you have no need for anyone to teach you – The faith has already been delivered once for all to the saints (Jude 3). John has already depicted his readers as believers whose faith is based on consistent and continuing apostolic teaching such as was preached and heard from the beginning. No johnny-come-lately Gnostic can come along and attempt to woo an audience by claiming to have something new and/or better to offer than what the "anointing" gave them.[84] So complete is the spiritual instruction which the true believers had already received, they had no need for any new teachers (like the Gnostics[85]) to constantly instruct[86] them on truths supposedly missed or omitted in that earlier instruction.

But as His anointing teaches you about all things – The last part of verse 27 seems to summarize reasons why John's readers need "no one to teach them."[87]   "Anointing" has

---

[83] "From Him" points to Jesus Christ. The Holy Spirit is called the "Spirit of Jesus" in Acts 16:7 and the "Spirit of Christ" in Romans 8:9.

[84] The Greek word translated "for" is *hina*. It could be translated "that" since it introduces a declarative statement after "you have (no) need." It could be translated "in order that," but attempts to make it a purpose clause have produced rather forced interpretations.

[85] The identification of the "someone (anyone)" is disputed in the commentaries. Some think it means apostolic teachers are no longer continually needed in the church. Some think it means no one teacher is the only and ultimate source of instruction for the saints. Those who treat the "anointing" as something every Christian receives at baptism urge that the Holy Spirit is the Christian's only needed teacher. What is being rejected is, in fact, the teaching given by the heretics. It is not a statement that no human teacher was or is ever needed. John's readers certainly have had human teachers in the past (verse 24) from whom they heard. They have John the apostle who writes this very letter to them, and it is certainly didactic. Care must be taken lest the affirmation "you have no need for anyone to teach you" be treated in an incautious or exaggerated fashion as though no Christian ever needed any human teacher! "Other passages of the New Testament refer not only to the general ministry of teaching in the church (e.g., Acts 4:18, 5:28,42, 13:1; 2 Timothy 2:24), but also to specially gifted 'teachers' (1 Corinthians 12:29; Ephesians 4:11). We need to balance these verses with what John has here written." Stott, *op. cit.*, p.114.

[86] The verb "teach" is present subjunctive, continued action.

[87] The number of reasons depends on how we punctuate the remainder of the verse, a matter that is debated by the scholars because the second half of this verse is cumbersome in its Greek expression. We do have a conditional construction (conditional sentences have an "if-clause" [protasis] and a "conclusion" [apodosis] clause), but even then there are at least two options. We may treat the rest of verse 27 as one long sentence with all the words after "as" being the "if-clause," and the closing words "abide in him" being the "conclusion" clause. Or we may treat the rest of the verse as two sentences. The first "if" clause begins with "as," and the words "it is true, and is not a lie ..." would be the first "conclusion" clause. Then a second protasis begins with "even as it taught you," followed by a second apodosis, "abide in it!"

been explained in verses 20 and 27. The language of this verse echoes something Jesus said in His Farewell Discourse (John 14-17), especially about the Spirit of truth who would guide the apostles into "all truth" (16:13) and "teach them all things" (14:26). This is one reason why John's readers don't need to hear the teaching of the Gnostics. Those false prophets have nothing they can add to the "all things" the apostles have already taught. "Teaches" is present tense, expressing continuing activity. As believers keep studying the Word (the result of the "anointing"), the teaching is an ongoing process.

And is true and is not a lie – This is a reason John's readers can have confidence in the "anointing" (the apostles' words). "True" represents the Greek adjective *alēthes* (genuine),[88] while "lie" represents the noun *pseudos* (counterfeit).[89] Both of the positive qualities found in the Word of the apostles are obviously lacking in the heretic's doctrine. The whole thing the false teachers are offering is a lie; they are trying to pass off counterfeit religion as the real thing! If our God is the *true* God (e.g., 2 Chronicles 15:3; Jeremiah 10:10; John 17:3; 1 Thessalonians 1:9; cf. 1 John 5:20), and if Jesus Christ is "the *truth*" (John 14:6), and if the Holy Spirit is "*true*" (I John 5:7; John 15:26, 16:13), then anything that originates with them (think of the "result of the anointing") has to be true and not a lie.

And just as it has taught you – "Just as" (*kathos*) means 'in accordance with' or 'in proportion as.' The pronoun "it" (from the third-singular verb ending) refers to "the anointing." The teaching the readers have received from the "anointing" has been going on "from the beginning" (verse 24). Earlier in this verse John has used a present tense verb as he wrote, "His anointing *teaches* you about all things." This verb "taught" is aorist tense. This change brings out the thought that what they have been taught first and completely in the past is essentially the same as the now ongoing teaching. This is the reason why no new teaching, like the Gnostics were trying to palm off on the believers, should even be considered!

You abide in Him – The Greek reads, *menete en autō*.[90] It makes better sense[91] to translate *menete* as imperative and treat *autō* as neuter.[92] This results in, "Abide in it!" In this

---

[88] On "true" see notes at 2:8.

[89] On "lie" see notes on verse 21.

[90] There is a manuscript variation here, some texts reading *meneite* (future indicative) and some reading *menete* (a form that can be either present indicative or present imperative). Modern critical texts rather unanimously adopt the second reading here. Translators who treat the latter as indicative may be influenced by the indicative from the previous verse. Those who choose to treat it as imperative may be influenced by the imperative form that certainly occurs in the following verse.

[91] If we treat the verb as indicative, it makes John say that the readers are remaining in the Christian state (or will remain, if we opt for the future indicative). Instead of John saying they are faithful, in this commentator's judgment, the imperative is better for it makes John to be encouraging them to be faithful.

[92] Those translators who opt for "remain in Him!" mean "remain in Christ" instead of following the Gnostics, who never were genuine converts, and now have separated themselves from the churches.

climax of the whole paragraph about the danger posed by the antichrists and their heresy, John is calling for his readers to remain in the old-fashioned gospel teaching! *Menete* is a present imperative, "Continue to stay with it!" Stay with what you learned from the "anointing"! It recalls Jesus' ringing words, "If you hold to my teaching, if you remain in my word, you are really my disciples" (John 8:31, personal translation).[93]

III. FELLOWSHIP'S DISTINCTIVE REWARDS AND BLESSINGS. 2:28-3:24a

> *Summary*: Having warned about dangers from worldliness and antichrists that could ruin continuing fellowship with the Father, John now begins to list some rewards and blessings that result from Christian fellowship, and which make continuing fellowship with the Father, the Son, and the Christian brethren a most desirable thing. There seem to be four such blessings: hope for the future (2:28-3:3), righteousness increases (3:4-10), brotherly love and benevolence are encouraged (3:11-18), prayers are answered (3:19-24a).

A. Hope For the Future. 2:28-3:3

> *Summary*: When a person has his hope set on Jesus Christ, the future (with the second coming, and a glorified body, and its awesome judgment) becomes a motive for righteous and holy living.

2:28 -- *And now, little children, abide in Him, so that when He appears, we may have confidence and not shrink away from Him in shame at His coming.*

And now, little children – It seems to this commentator that this is John's way of beginning a new section of his letter.[1] "Little children" is one of John's frequent and familiar ways of addressing all his readers (the word is *teknia* as at 2:1,12).

---

[93] "So again the antidote to falling into false ideas of the Christian faith is to be found in holding fast to the initial statement of Christian truth as given by the apostolic witness ... It cannot be otherwise with a religion based on a historical, once-for-all revelation. Any new doctrine not in harmony with the Apostolic Word is self-condemned." Marshall, *op. cit.*, p.164.

[1] Anyone who has read the commentaries on 1 John knows there is little agreement concerning where to make paragraph breaks. Most writers opt for some kind of division as we come to the close of chapter 2. Some include verse 28 (and some even include verse 29) as the closing part of the previous section. Some treat verses 28 and 29 as a transitional bridge between chapters 2 and 3. Marshall (*op. cit.*, p.22-26) has a useful survey of scholarly opinion on the structure/outline of the letter at this point. "Now" with which the verse begins, can be either logical or temporal. If we treat it as logical, then verse 28 is the close of the preceding paragraph. If we treat it as temporal, then verse 28 is the beginning of a new point in the discussion. With this latter interpretation we agree, as do many English Bible translators who begin a new paragraph with this verse.

Abide in Him – These are the very same Greek words with which verse 27 closed. *Menete* is certainly to be taken as a present imperative, and John is thus calling for their continuing fellowship.   Though we opted to treat *autō* as neuter in verse 27, here we are influenced by the words immediately following to take it as masculine, referring to Jesus. The heretics are not and never were abiding in Christ.   But John's readers are, and he strongly urges them to let that relationship continue.[2]   The imperative "abide" (addressed to a person's will) indicates that such abiding is something that can be willed or rejected by each individual believer.   Whether or not they abide in Christ depends on whether or not they abide in His word (2:24-27).

So that when He appears – *Hina* is the word translated "so that."   This seems to be a result clause, with the thought completed by the next phrase.   This clause expresses one of the results that will come true for John's readers when Jesus comes back, *if* the readers remain faithful to Him.   Two different Greek words are used in this verse to describe Jesus' second coming to earth: *phanerōsis* (here) and *parousia* (at the close of the verse).[3] *Phanerōsis* means "to become visible (to human eyes)" and was used at 1 John 1:2 of Jesus' first coming to earth.[4]   Like he was visible to human eyes during His earthly ministry, so He will become visible again!   There can be no mistaking this reference to our Lord's second coming, and there is no doubt expressed about whether or not such an event is still on God's calendar.[5]   Several times the root word for "appear" occurs in this present paragraph because it is the theme of the paragraph.

We may have confidence and not shrink away from Him in shame at His coming – John writes "we may have" (*schōmen*, subjunctive),   including himself with his readers.

---

[2] John's exhortation to them to be constantly abiding in Christ is because of the uncertainty of the time of His return.   Whether it be sooner or later, if they are in fellowship with Him, all will be well when He does appear.

[3] The words do not describe two different future "comings" of Jesus, but are two attempts to describe what His Second Coming will be like.   The *phanerōsis* of Christ is His *Parousia*, and it occurs at the end of the *eschatē hora*.   Compare Colossians 3:4.

[4] "Appear" in the Greek is actually the passive form of the verb "to reveal".   Though the agent who causes the appearance to happen is not named, it conveys the thought that Jesus is made to become visible.   It is not just something spontaneously popping up in men's imaginations.   "The first coming of Jesus was the revelation of the previously hidden Word of God in human form, so that those with eyes to see could confess, 'We have seen his glory, the glory of the one and only Son, who came from the Father, full of grace and truth' (John 1:14).   Now (since His ascension), He is again hidden from view ... but one day He will again be revealed from heaven."   Marshall, *op. cit.*, p.165.

[5] There is a manuscript variation here.   The TR reads *otan*, "whenever," while the better texts have *ean*, "if [He should appear]."   The use of *ean* does not place the fact of the coming in doubt, but merely its time.

He needs boldness, just as do his readers, when Jesus returns and the judgment occurs. We regularly use the expression "second coming"[6] to talk about this "coming" to which John alludes. "Coming" is *parousia*, a word often transliterated into English as Parousia. This is the only place in John's writings where he uses the word *parousia*.[7] Evidence from ancient literature shows that *parousia* was used to describe the festivities that accompanied the visit of a king or emperor to a city of the realm.[8] Christians picture the return of Jesus as just such a joyous and majestic visit to our earth. *Parousia* means literally "presence," and the two words together ["His parousia"] imply that our Lord's return will involve the personal presence of One now absent, the visible appearing of One not now seen.[9] Depending on whether or not they have remained in Christ, John and his readers will react to Christ's second coming in one of two ways. Some will "have confidence," while others will "shrink away from Him in shame" (*aischunthōmen ap' autou*). "Confidence" or "boldness" (*parrēsia*)[10] is a lack of any feeling of misgiving, an assurance, a confidence with which a person may enter into the Royal presence and speak with the King without any fear. The word speaks of a heart attitude of the saint who lives so close to the Lord Jesus that there is nothing between him and his Lord when He comes. It is a fearless trust with which the faithful soul meets its Creator. *Aischunthōmen* can be either middle voice (to feel ashamed) or passive voice (to be put to shame, to be disgraced). This passage may speak of "hiding in shame from Him" (TEV), being too embarrassed to face Him. They will shrink back and withdraw from Him in shame as they realize their horrible sin and their ineligibility to come into His holy presence. Elsewhere, Scripture speaks of the wicked crying for the rocks and mountains to cover them from the presence of God and the wrath of the Lamb (Revelation 6:12ff). They try to run away in shame from His presence.

---

[6] We perhaps get the expression "second" coming from Hebrews 9:28. The actual expression "second coming" (of Jesus) is postbiblical and appears first in Justin (*Apology* 1.52.3).

[7] It is familiar to us from its use in Paul's Epistles, James, and 2 Peter (e.g., 1 Corinthians 15:23; 1 Thessalonians 2:19; James 5:7,8; 2 Peter 1:16; etc.). John uses this word (just as he did "the Word" and "the evil one") confident his readers are well instructed and will understand what he means.

[8] "Even today, although we have become accustomed to seeing the face of the monarch or president on TV, people will still turn out in great numbers on state occasions to see and cheer the ruler; how much more must this have been the case in the ancient world where to see the emperor was possibly the event of a lifetime. It is this kind of atmosphere which is conveyed by this word." Marshall, *ibid*. The Latin word *Adventus* was used in the same way, as is evident from the coins struck to commemorate Nero's visit to Corinth, on which was the inscription, *Adventus Aug.Cor.*

[9] To abandon John's eschatology as being "mythical" (as many contemporary scholars are accustomed to do) or to treat these eschatological statements in John's writings as the work of a third-generation redactor (as Bultmann did), robs this whole paragraph of any promised reward or blessing.

[10] *Parrēsia* originally indicated the democratic right of citizens to express opinions in a public forum. It was used of confidence to speak in God's presence in Job 27:10 (LXX). It is used of the confidence with which the Christian may draw near to God in prayer (1 John 3:21, 5:14; Hebrews 4:16, 10:18).

The passage may speak of being disgraced by Jesus.[11]   The opponents of Jesus such as the "antichrists" and those who have not remained faithful to Him, will be openly disgraced, for the coming of Jesus means judgment and rejection for them.   It will be a great disgrace to hear the words "depart from Me, accursed ones!" (Matthew 25:41).   From the word of God we learn that we are living in the last age in God's dispensation of history.   That same word tells us this age will be closed by Christ's visible coming on the clouds of heaven.[12] "Abide in Christ" is not only the important antidote to false belief and unchristian behavior in the present, but it is the only way to be ready for the future appearance in glory of our great God and Savior, Jesus Christ.   There will be a consummation of history, and a final judgment after the one personal antichrist is revealed at the end of time.   Jesus will come again, and receive His own unto Himself.   But what about those who are not His own?   In flaming fire He will take vengeance on those who know not God and who have not obeyed the Gospel of Jesus Christ (2 Thessalonians 1:8 KJV).   Luke 21:28 instructs faithful Christians to "lift up your heads" at the second coming of Christ.   That can be done by the person who has remained in Christ.   There will be no greater shame at His coming than to be denied by Him before the Father in heaven.   There will be no greater joy than that experienced by the faithful at His coming.

2:29 -- *If you know that He is righteous, you know that everyone also who practices righteousness is born of Him.*

If you know that He is righteous – John has just spoken of children who have confidence.   Who are these children?   How did they come to have confidence (i.e., to so live as to avoid being ashamed)?   Verse 29 goes on to answer this question.   As the rest of this verse and the one following imply,   "He" seems to refer to God the Father rather than

---

[11] The two possibilities arise because *apo* can mean "from" (its usual meaning) or may be equivalent to *hupo*, "by" (Luke 6:18, 8:43).   In the latter case we would make "shrink" to be passive and "by Him" to be the agent, and the thought is of judgment by Christ, rather than of psychological feelings in His presence.

[12] Acts 1:9-11; Matthew 26:64; Revelation 1:7.   Some recent commentators on the New Testament have suggested that the vivid expectation of the Parousia in the earlier writings of Paul and the other apostles was rewritten or reinterpreted when it became obvious the expectation of a soon return was going to be disappointed.   Instead of Christ's personal return, it has been replaced, allegedly in John's writings, by the coming of the Spirit; instead of a resurrection body, theologians began talking about "rising to walk in newness of life."   Such a theory ignores the teaching on the Second Coming which occurs here in 1 John.   In fact, the doctrine of the Lord's return was part of the primitive apostolic faith.   However, because of the uncertainty of when it would occur, at times it is spoken of as being near; at times it is spoken of as being far off.   No man knew the time, neither the angels, nor the Son, but the Father only (Matthew 24:36).   This uncertainty about "when" should not be twisted into a false affirmation that Jesus and early writers were mistaken (wrong) in what they said about Christ's return.   James M. Boice remarks concerning the return of Christ: "It is mentioned 318 times in the 260 chapters of the New Testament.   It is mentioned in every one of the New Testament books, with the exception of Galatians ... and the very short books of 2 and 3 John and Philemon." (*Epistles of John* [Grand Rapids: Zondervan, 1979], p.96).

to Jesus.[13]   "Since you know" is perhaps a better way to translate the Greek "if" clause than "if you know."[14]   *Oida* is the Greek synonym for "know" that often pictures a knowledge gained by reflection, by inference, or acquired information gained by study, by reading the word of God, or by observing how God has acted in and toward His creation. In 1:9 John has already called attention to God's character as being "righteous" (see also John 17:25).   The present form *esti* ("is") pictures a continuing/abiding/constant characteristic.   John is calling attention to a well-known truth.   Everyone who has any knowledge of God must have the fullest conviction that He is a righteous being.

You know – *Ginōskete* can be either indicative or imperative.[15]   A number of ancient writers took it as imperative, which (put together with the words following) expresses this idea: "Don't ever forget that 'practicing righteousness' is the only behavior that harmonizes with being born of God!"[16]   If taken as an indicative, then John is saying, "Then you will know by experience (*ginōskein*) that only those who practice righteousness are ones born of God."[17]

---

[13] In light of the previous verse which speaks of the Second Coming of Christ, some Bible scholars have tried to make a case for "He" being Christ.   For example, David Smith who comments on "The Epistles of John" in *Expositor's Greek Testament* [Grand Rapids: Eerdmans, 1967], p.182, has this note: "In view of the preceding verse, *dikaios* must refer to Christ (cf. 2:1), and it is equally certain that *ex autou* refers to the Father, since 'begotten of Christ' ... is not a Scriptural idea.   The abrupt transition evinces John's sense of the oneness of the Father and the Son (cf. verse 24, John 10:30)."   That "He, Him, His" in verse 28 refers to Christ, while "He, Him" in verse 29 refers to the Father has been used by some as confirmation of the view that a new section of the letter should begin with verse 29.   We have opted not to do so, but if we were to do this, then just as 1:5 stated the main subject of the verses in the first main division which follows, so 2:29 would be treated as the main subject of the verses following in this division. If this new division deals with righteousness, since that topic can be traced as far as 3:12, it probably requires us to find a new point of the outline beginning at that place.

[14] The "if" clause expresses no doubt about *God* being righteous.   If any doubt is expressed, it is whether or not the *readers* know the facts.

[15] *Ginōskō* is the Greek synonym for "know" that often means to know by experience.   If someone tells you a hot stove will burn, you have *oida* of what burn means.   If you touch the hot stove, you have *ginōskō* of what burn is.   It is not clear whether John is using *oida* and *ginōskō* as interchangeable terms, or whether the old distinction between the meaning of the synonyms is part of John's argument.   A century ago commentators pressed the distinction; today many do not.

[16] Smith (*ibid.*) argues that "it enfeebles the sentence to take the verb as indicative."   Perhaps John is offering a response to a heretical claim (made by folk who did not practice righteousness) to have been born again, and is saying it is obviously a false claim.   Children have the characteristics of their parents.

[17] Gill (*ibid.*) thinks that the two words for "know" in this verse are a direct denial of Gnostic teaching. "The Gnostic's major premise was a neatly packaged and absolute dualism which placed an irreconcilable gulf between what they considered 'spiritual' and what they saw as 'material.'   According to the Gnostic, all spirit was good, all matter was evil.   Since 'God is spirit' (John 4:24), they arrived by deduction at the knowledge that God also was righteous.   (Note the first word for know in this verse is *oida*, to know by deduction.)   John's challenge is, in effect, 'If God is righteous, and you are begotten of Him, then you know by experience (note the second word for know is *ginōskō*), even in this world of matter, that the sons of God are also righteous.'   This strikes at the heart of the Gnostic's conclusion that the physical behavior of the individual was unrelated to his spiritual relationship with God."

That everyone also who practices righteousness is born of Him – When it introduces indirect discourse, "That" is almost "Greek for quotation marks." John's direct statement is "everyone also who practices righteousness is born of Him." "Also" (*kai*) emphasizes an intended correspondence between this "that" clause and what was affirmed in the preceding one ("[God] is righteous"). "Everyone" includes those who practice righteousness and no one else. In *poiōn tēn dikaisunēn* ("does/practices[18] the righteousness"[19]), "practices" is put first for emphasis. This should not be overlooked. The article before "righteousness" marks this out as a particular righteousness; it is doing what is right, doing the "righteousness" everyone knows is required by God's will.[20] "Righteousness" must be shown in conduct, not merely in a desire to do right; otherwise, it is not "practice."[21] John completes this conditional sentence in an unexpected way. We might have expected "everyone who practices righteousness will not be ashamed at His coming." Instead, John speaks of being "born of Him" (NASB) or "begotten of Him" (ASV) or, more popularly, "born again."[22] The synonymous phrase "born of God" occurs five times in this epistle (3:9, 4:7, 5:1,4,18) and calls to mind Jesus' conversation with Nicodemus (John 3:1-15) as well as what John wrote in the prologue to his Gospel (John 1:12,13). Not only does the new birth figure prominently from here on, so does the idea of our relationships as children in God's family. We Christians are 'little born ones'. The verb form here ("is born") is

---

[18] *Poiōn* is a present participle.   Habitually doing the right which God wills, is what John underlines.

[19] "Practices righteousness" is a Jewish type of expression (Psalm 99:4, 106:3, 119:121), similar to "practices the truth" (cf. 1 John 1:6). It speaks of measuring up to the divine standard of right.

[20] Sometimes "righteousness" speaks of giving God what is due to Him.   Sometimes "righteousness" speaks of right relationships with our fellow man (i.e., giving our fellow men what God says is due to them). See notes at 1 John 2:1 and 3:7. Care must be taken to keep our thinking correct at this place. When John says "everyone who practices righteousness is born of God," this does not mean that every morally upright person is a child of God, even though he has no fellowship with the Father or the Son, any more than when John says that "everyone who loves is born of God" (4:8) means that atheists who love are really Christians.

[21] Gill (*op. cit.*, p.69-70) calls attention to how verse 29 is not only an attack on Gnostic doctrine and behavior, it is also fatal to the New Morality (a system of ethics made popular late in the 20th century). The "new morality" of our day does not accept the idea that there are any moral absolutes established by God. "The contrast between the divine standard of morality and the subjective existentialism of the new morality is seen in the contrast of two Greek synonyms for moral goodness: *dikaios*, righteousness measured by divine standard, and *agathos*, righteousness regarded as perfect in its own kind, so as to produce pleasure and satisfaction for the [selfish] advantage of the person coming into contact with it. This 'new morality' is not new at all. It is the 'walk of the Gentiles' (Ephesians 2:2) determined by what is popular."

[22] The question of the origin of John's terminology (born, begotten) is an important one, but cannot be pursued here in detail. The idea of a spiritual birth is absent from the Old Testament, and there is little that is relevant in Judaism. If we take John 3:1-15 at face value, and we do, then we can affirm John learned the idea of being born again from Jesus. However, not every contemporary scholar is willing to do that. Some suppose John has appropriated the language of rebirth from the mystery religions or Gnosticism. Many modern scholars (Dodd, Bultmann, etc.) suppose that here a Hellenistic idea has been imported into Christianity. (Adapted from Marshall, *op. cit.*, p.168.)

perfect tense.[23]   For the person who practices righteousness, the new birth occurred in the past and has present continuing results.   Scholars have not come to a consensus concerning why John introduced this unexpected expression "born of Him."

(1) Perhaps John is reflecting and refuting a heretical claim that they had experienced a "new birth." A later Gnostic group called their initiation into "knowledge" (*gnōsis*) a 'regeneration' or a 'religious rebirth.'[24]   The heretics apparently claimed a rebirth, but there was no noticeable improvement in lifestyle; there was no habitual practice of righteousness. If John here is correcting such a Gnostic claim about the new birth, he is doing so in a context which reminds his readers that a genuine new birth results in changed personal and ethical behavior. It is more than simply possessing, intellectually, the right knowledge. John says in effect to his readers, if you use your brains you can easily recognize that the claims of the Gnostics are false. Their lives do not match the righteous life of the One they claim as their Father.

(2) Perhaps there is no reflection of Gnosticism at this place. Instead, "in this instance the expression gives a reason for the righteous conduct John is emphasizing."[25]   Without a new birth, such consistent living ("practices righteousness") is not possible. Since we have earlier seen the Gnostics never were converts to Christianity, no wonder their lifestyle was in error. They were slaves of sin! In any case, the point being made by John is that habitual practice of righteousness will result in confidence (and anticipation) when the Lord appears in all His glory.[26]

---

[23] The Greek word *gennaō* was used for both what we call "conception" and "birth." Every time we come across the word in the Greek, we must decide which it is. Some of the older English translations use the word "begotten" when conception is in view, and use "born" when the birth is in view. The ASV uses "begotten" every time the perfect tense form of *gennaō* occurs in the Greek of 1 John. In this writer's commentaries elsewhere (at John 3:1-5; at Acts 2 on the work of the Holy Spirit; at Matthew 19:28 on "regeneration"; at 1 Corinthians 4:15; and at Titus 3:5) are detailed studies on the new birth. A brief summary of what is there taught is as follows: Scriptures seem to teach man is made up of body, soul, and spirit. When a man commits his first sin, his spirit dies (ceases to function), so he is described as "dead in trespasses and sins" (Ephesians 2:1), and he becomes a slave to sin and lives in a body of sin (Romans 6:6). What is needed for his spirit is a "new birth" (John 3:6). When the man hears the gospel and believes it, he has been conceived (1 John 5:1, ASV). When he repents and is immersed (is obedient to the truth) the process of the new birth is completed. His spirit is again alive (Romans 6:1ff, 8:10) and he can walk in newness of life because the old slavery to sin has been broken. He has been redeemed! By the help of the indwelling Holy Spirit, he now can control the body he lives in, and this self-control results in "practicing righteousness" that John here writes about.

[24] In the 3rd century *Corpus Hermeticum* is a treatise entitled *Peri Paliggenesias* ("Of Regeneration") describing the "new birth" of a spiritual initiate into Gnosticism.

[25] Kistemaker, *op. cit.*, p.288.

[26] In thought this verse is closely connected with the preceding. One can "abide in Him" by "keeping His commandments" or "practicing righteousness." What John here writes (in light of the final judgment when Christ's Parousia occurs, verse 28) matches exactly what Paul wrote in Romans. Romans 2:6-10 tells us that when the final judgment occurs, the judgment will be on the basis of deeds. He who habitually does evil will be condemned. He who habitually does right will receive glory and honor and immortality. Carefully pay attention to the present tense verbs Jesus used when He described how the judgment will be (Matthew 7:24-27). The difference between the wise and foolish builders is how they habitually obeyed or did not obey what Jesus taught.

3:1 -- *See how great a love the Father has bestowed upon us, that we should be called children of God; and* **such** *we are. For this reason the world does not know us, because it did not know Him.*

See how great a love the Father has bestowed upon us – John begins this sentence with a second person plural imperative, "See!" or "Behold!" He wants all his readers to take notice of, or to contemplate, the wonder of God's love. The qualitative interrogative[27] word translated "how great" (*potapos*, literally, "of what country?") expresses astonishment or great admiration.[28] "It is as if the Father's love is so unearthly, so foreign to this world, that he wonders from what country it may come."[29] God's love, which invites us to become His children, is so amazing and wonderful as to defy comparison with anything in this world. It has been noticed that the train of thought here in 1 John is similar to what is found in John 3. There, Christ's conversation with Nicodemus about the new birth is "followed by the magnificent declaration of God's love which sent His only Son that we might have eternal life."[30] Perhaps John deliberately chose the title "the Father" for God, and "children" for believers (verse 2) in order to emphasize the special "Father-child" relationship that exists between Christians and their heavenly Father. "Bestowed" translates the perfect tense verb *dedōken*; it could also be translated "the Father *has lavished* His love on us." God's lavish gift determines the believer's present condition. By using "us" John has included himself among those who are recipients of God's love.

That we should be called children of God – In 2:29 John introduced the concept of being "born of Him." Now those born ones are designated as being "children of God." Some of the older English versions have "sons of God," though the Greek word here is *tekna* rather than *huioi*.[31] Under Roman law, sons who were such by adoption were absolutely equivalent to children who were such by birth. In this letter, all the occurrences of "children of God" follow a passage where the believers are said to be born of God. "Should be

---

[27] Robertson, *op. cit.*, p.220. The word expresses quality rather than size.

[28] The disciples used the same word when looking in awe at the massive stones used in the building of Herod's temple at Jerusalem, Mark 13:1.

[29] Smalley, *op. cit.*, p.118. On God being called "Father" see notes at 1:2 and 2:1. Concerning His love for man, see notes at 2:5 and 2:15. "Love" is a key word from 2:28 on. In some form (noun or verb or adjective) the word occurs 46 times in the remainder of this letter.

[30] Marshall, *op. cit.*, p.170.

[31] The difference between the two words is that one calls attention to "lineage" (the birth process), while the other calls attention to the legal relationship. John regularly uses *tekna* ("children") for Christians (saving "Son of God" as a term to use of Jesus), viewing them as God's children by birth (the new birth). Paul, on the other hand, uses both *tekna* ("children," Romans 8:16) and *huioi* ("sons," Romans 8:16) of Christians, the latter term viewing them as God's children by adoption (Romans 8:15). Perhaps, here at 1 John 3:1, the older English versions were influenced by the Latin Vulgate which reads *filii Dei*.

called"[32] is passive, and the implied agent is the Father. Contemplate God looking lovingly at us and saying, "My children!" The term "child" is "used here metaphorically to describe the intimate relationship which God has made possible between Himself and the believers."[33] Perhaps the main idea John is unfolding is that children are to be like their Father (see 2:29).

And *such* **we are** – Manuscript evidence shows this clause (*kai esmen*) was part of what John wrote,[34] though on the basis of several late manuscripts the words are omitted from the Textus Receptus and the KJV. Such a parenthetical reflection (if we might call it such) is typical of John. "Looking back on some sixty years as a child of God, John is still astounded at the privilege."[35] "Children of God" is no mere title. It is really true; we Christians are His children! Whatever the world may think, this is the believer's standing in God's sight here and now. "To be a child of God one must receive Jesus (John 1:12). This is precisely what the Gnostic could not do. His prejudice concerning the incompatibility of spirit and matter made it impossible for him to believe that 'the Word became flesh and dwelt among us' (John 1:14)."[36]

For this reason the world does not know us – "For this reason" (*dia touto*) probably points forward,[37] with the *hoti* phrase explaining the reason why Christians are not recognized by the world; "the world did not know [our Father]," either. For "world," meaning

---

[32]"Should be called" does not refer to some future time (e.g., the day of Final Judgment). That we are "children of God" is something that is true now, as the next phrase will specifically affirm.

[33] Stott, *op. cit.*, p.77.

[34] They are included in P[74], Sinaiticus, Alexandrinus, Vaticanus, Ephraemi, etc.

[35] Gill, *op. cit.*, p.72. Gill wrote further, "The amazement on the part of the apostle stands out in vivid contrast to the self-asserting assumption of many of our day that all men are the children of God. In the presence of such pious platitudes as the "fatherhood of God and the brotherhood of man," it is well to remind ourselves that brotherhood is the result of a common fatherhood, rather than an easy-going tolerance. The eternal Word of God left the golden-decked streets of heaven where His praises are sung continually for the stinking disease-ridden streets of a fifth-rate planet. Here He was mocked and betrayed and denied and spit upon by those whose best are not worthy to stoop down and untie His sandals! And He did that in order that we might be called and indeed become the children of His father. It sounds lofty today to talk about God's love to all men, and to assume that all men are therefore His sons. However, to remain outside the pale of this love, as it is focused upon our need of redemption in the incarnation, is to fall into the same trap as the Gnostic, and hence, fail to ever become a child of God!"

[36] Gill, *ibid.*, p.73.

[37] The KJV has one long sentence, with a period at the end of verse 1, which requires us to understand that "for this reason" points backward to something said earlier in the verse. And if we omit "such we are," it might be supposed that "for this reason" points backward to the fact that we are called God's children (as the reason the world does not recognize us). Against the attempt to have "for this reason" pointing backwards is this: it is not easy to explain the *hoti* phrase which follows. Some attempt to translate *hoti* as "that," supposing it serves as an additional explanation of the main clause. The ASV/ NASB instead begin a new sentence with the words "For this reason," showing the translator's opinion that the "reason" follows.

godless people, or people who are not much concerned about spiritual things, see notes at 2:15. Perhaps John even has the Gnostics in mind. Christians (he argues in these verses) are concerned to practice self-control, and so they sin less and less as they purify themselves. That's an idea the "world" hasn't yet grasped. "Know" (see notes at 2:3 on *ginōskō*) is present tense, with durative force. From their experience, unsaved people have never had such a relationship with and knowledge of God the Father. Thus, the people of the world, while recognizing us as Christians, do not come to an understanding and appreciation of the nature of the persons we are, that we are in fact children of God!

Because it did not know Him – "Him" may refer either to God the Father or to Jesus the Son. Precisely the same argument is found in John 15:18ff, which leads us to believe that "Him" is a reference to Jesus the Christ, as in verse 6. So also does the fact that the verb "did know" is an historical aorist tense. During His earthly ministry, men saw the human Jesus but did not recognize Him as the Son of God. "As His glory was veiled in flesh, so our 'life is hid with Christ in God' (Colossians 3:3). Our sonship, though real, is not yet apparent (Romans 8:19)."[38] The world had no right views of the real character of the Lord while He was on earth. His contemporary countrymen rejected Him because they could not accept a Galilean carpenter's son as being also the Son of God. On the fact that the world did not know Him, see 1 Corinthians 2:8, Acts 3:19, John 17:25. On the fact that Christians may expect to be treated as was Christ, see John 15:18-20, 16:3, Matthew 10:24,25.

3:2 -- *Beloved, now we are children of God, and it has not appeared as yet what we shall be. We know that, when He appears, we shall be like Him, because we shall see Him just as He is.*

Beloved – In this context, where John has just spoken of God's love for us, this verbal adjective speaks of Divinely loved ones,[39] as John continues to stress the special relationship we have with God.

Now we are children of God – "Now," placed first for emphasis, contrasts with "not yet" in the next clause. Our present and future condition as God's children are placed side by side. "Our privileges and position in this world are certain; our glories in the world to come still continue to be veiled."[40] After emphatically reiterating what verse 1 affirmed, that we are "children of God" whether the world recognizes it or not, in this verse John calls attention to what the future holds for those who are children of God. In our inner nature we already are children of God. The time is coming when the children of God will have a new body, too!

---

[38] Stott, *op. cit.*, p.118.

[39] In 2:7 where the same verbal adjective was used, it emphasized that John loves the readers, too. In the rest of this epistle, this becomes a common form of address (3:21; 4:1,7,11).

[40] Plummer, *op. cit.*, p.121.

And it has not appeared as yet what we shall be – The neuter interrogative pronoun "what" (*ti*, not *tines*, "who"), which anticipates "what we shall be," asks about identity or quality. Children grow up, and just what will Christian "children of God" grow up to be? Not all the details about the future life have been revealed, though since the next verse speaks of purity, we might assume there will be "no lapses into sin" in the world to come. "John here confesses that the exact state and condition of the redeemed in heaven has not been revealed to him."[41] "Not ... yet" looks at things as they stand at the moment John is writing this letter. "What we shall be" was not fully manifested[42] to John or the apostles on any occasion.

We know that, when He appears, we shall be like Him – In the KJV, there is a "but" at the beginning of this clause, but on overwhelming manuscript evidence it is omitted in the ASV/NASB. "What we shall be" has not been disclosed, but this much we do know, "we shall be like Him."[43] "We know" (*oidamen*) this by revelation. Though we do not know all that is involved in the change ("what we shall be"), we do know when the change takes place. It takes place when Jesus returns in all His glory. *Ean phanerōthē* ("when He appears"[44]) probably should be taken personally,[45] and should be understood to allude to Christ's second coming. "Like" indicates similarity, not identity.[46] "We shall be like Him" does not mean we are going to be deity as He is, but we are going to have glorified bodies just like the glorified body Jesus now has.[47]

---

[41] Stott, *op. cit.*, p.119. As was true of the Old Testament prophets (Deuteronomy 3:24), the apostles only knew what was revealed to them (1 Corinthians 2:10-13). Not even the earlier statement that the "anointing teaches you about all things" (2:27) is to be pressed literally. John here tells us that not all the details about the future life had been revealed to the apostles.

[42] The same verb ("appear") was used at 2:28. Here it is an aorist tense, pointing to a completed act in the past time.

[43] Commentators differ as to whether "Him" refers to the Father or to Christ. Part of our decision hinges on whether we translate the Greek as "He shall appear" or "it shall be manifested." 2:28 favors "He," as does 3:5. On the other hand, children are found to be like their Father. So not a few commentators prefer "it shall be manifested."

[44] Here there is no difference of reading (as there was at 2:28). The Greek here is "if." The "when" found in our English versions probably reflects the influence of the Vulgate (*cum apparuerit*). If any doubt is expressed by the preposition "if," the doubt concerns not the fact of His coming, but its time. There is no doubt about the results that accompany that appearance. (Compare, "*If* I be lifted up from the earth," and "*If* I go and prepare a place for you" (John 12:32, 14:3). Plummer, *op. cit.*, p.121

[45] See footnote #43 above. Since no subject is stated, we must supply either "he" or "it" from the third-person singular verb. Thus, our translation could be either, "If it is disclosed" (meaning "what we shall be hereafter"), or "if He is manifested (appears)." Either makes sense; probably "He" is better in this clause.

[46] John wrote *homoioi* ("like") not *isoi* ("equal").

[47] Romans 8:29; Philippians 3:21; Colossians 3:4; 1 Corinthians 15:48,49. This passage in 1 John makes us think of 1 Corinthians 15:35ff, "With what kind of body do they come?" As he compares the present mortal body with our coming glorified body, Paul goes on to speak of dissolution but continuity, of diversity but identity. Our physical bodies, "now limited by corruption and dishonor and weakness, shall

Because we shall see Him as He is – This *hoti* clause probably gives the reason why John affirms "we shall be like Him."[48] "As He is" says that Jesus even now has His glorified body.   It is no illusion, nor is it unreal, nor is it merely a replica.   It is true to His essential character.   He has had His glorified body ever since His bodily resurrection from the dead.   Jesus prayed that His followers would be able to see Him in His glory (John 17:1,5,24).   Christians have the hope of sharing in that glory (Romans 8:17-19).   The process of glorification (first inwardly, then outwardly) already begun here and now in the lives of believers (2 Corinthians 3:18) will reach its completion when Jesus returns.[49]   On that occasion the dead in Christ will be raised incorruptible, and the living will be changed in a moment, in the twinkling of an eye.[50]

3:3 -- *And everyone who has this hope* **fixed** *on Him purifies himself, just as He is pure.*

And everyone who has this hope *fixed* **on Him** – "Everyone who" in 1 John often has a polemical thrust, aimed at discrediting the Gnostics.[51]   "This hope" is the hope of being

---

be raised in incorruption and glory and power. As we have borne the image of Adam, so shall we bear the image of the risen Christ." Gill, *op. cit.*, p.74.

[48] The Bible says much about the possibility of the faithful "seeing God."   The Old Testament Psalms make such a promise (Psalm 11:7; 17:15; 42:1-5).   The New Testament Scriptures likewise hold out the hope of "seeing" God or Christ in heaven (see Matthew 5:8; John 17:24; 2 Corinthians 5:7; Hebrews 12:14; 1 Peter 1:8; Revelation 1:7; 22:4).   If God can only be seen by those who are like Him, and the Bible holds out the promise of seeing God or Christ, then we can deduce that we shall be like Him.

[49] When a man sins, he is "ruined" inside and out.   Adam's sin left his whole race with a dying physical body.   Our own sin leaves us "spiritually dead" (Ephesians 2:1).   Redemption goes to work to restore what was "broken."   The inside gets fixed in this life – conversion, followed by holiness.   So that we might be "conformed to the image of his Son" (Romans 8:29), the indwelling Holy Spirit has been transforming us "into His likeness from one degree of glory to another" (2 Corinthians 3:18; 1 John 2:6).   In this later passage the transformation is said to be due to the fact that we are "with unveiled face beholding ... the glory of the Lord"; so it is understandable that when we see Him as He is, and not our face only but His too is unveiled, we shall be finally and completely like Him, including our bodies (Philippians 3:21; 1 Corinthians 15:49).   From the time of our physical death, our souls shall be with Christ (2 Corinthians 5:8; Philippians 1:23; 1 Thessalonians 4:17; Luke 23:43; John 14:3, 17:24).   When Christ returns on the clouds of heaven, the souls of the redeemed accompany Him (1 Thessalonians 4:14).   Resurrection bodies are put on, and the living are transformed without seeing death.   2 Peter 3:13 and Revelation 21-22 picture the redeemed living in a renovated universe, and coming up to the Holy City from time to time.   We inherit what Jesus inherited when He received His glorified body.

[50] The idea that "We shall see God" in all His fullness, as He really is, may be a Johannine response to the Gnostic concept about the means (intellectual knowledge or an altered state of consciousness) by which a vision of God may be attained.   Gnostics taught that such a vision was something that could be attained in this life.   Contrary to such Gnostic dogma, John affirms that it is not something that occurs in this life.   It awaits Christ's return.   And it is not accomplished by intellectual knowledge.

[51] See notes at 2:23,29;   3:4,5,9,10,15;   4:7;   5:1,4,18; and 2 John 9.

like Christ hereafter, as was described in verse 2.[52]   "On Him" means "on Christ," not "on himself."[53]   As shown by the Greek preposition *epi*,[54] the hope is grounded on Christ. "Has" equals has and holds on to.[55]

Purifies himself – The hope of being like Christ in the future glory will become a reality if Christians live this present life as they have been instructed to do.   One of the things the future glory is contingent upon is "purifying" one's self.   In fact, hope for the future is an incentive for careful living in the present.   "Purifies" is a present tense verb, and signifies continuous activity; the Christian keeps on purifying himself.[56]   *Agnidzein* ("purify") was used of ceremonial purification (John 11:55; Acts 21:24,26 as in Exodus 19:10), and then came to refer to ethical and moral purity, the cleansing of the heart (James 4:8) and the soul (1 Peter 1:22).   Old Testament ceremonial cleansing was intended to teach the worshippers a spiritual lesson about moral purity.   It is this moral purity, not just ceremonial, that John refers to.   "Purifies himself" strongly suggests freedom of the will to choose how he will live.   The believer constantly pursues holiness, without which no man shall see God (Hebrews 12:14).   A line from a familiar old song (Christ Receiveth Sinful Men) says, "Purged from every spot and stain, heaven with Him I'll enter in."   Did not Jesus teach that it is the "pure in heart" who shall see God (Matthew 5:8)?   As our eternal lives begin here and now, so does our reflection of the image of Christ.

Just as He is pure – "He" is Christ; throughout 1 John the pronoun *ekeinos* refers to Jesus

---

[52] Barker, *op. cit.*, p.333, calls attention to a helpful analysis of "hope" as found in the *Translator's Handbook* and elsewhere.   "There are to be distinguished four main semantic components which combine in various ways to represent the concept of 'hope'.   These are (1) time, for hope always looks to the future; (2) anticipation, for there is always some goal to the time span;   (3) confidence, namely, that the goal hoped for will occur;   and (4) desire, since the goal of hoping is represented as a valued object or experience."   If the confidence is missing, it is just "wishing," not "hope."   John uses the word "hope" in two other places (2 John 12, 3 John 14), but it is common in the writings of Paul and Peter.

[53] The NEB which reads "everyone who has this hope before him" makes "him" to be the believer, and the hope is something that is a goal he has in view.   It is better, in this commentator's opinion, to understand the pronoun "Him" to refer to Christ, or perhaps to God, or to God in Christ (Westcott), than to have it refer back to the believer.

[54] "For the construction 'to have hope on' a person, cp. 'On Him shall the Gentiles hope' (Romans 15:12; cp. 1 Timothy 4:10, 6:17)."   Plummer, *op. cit.*, p.122.

[55] To see how the verb "has (to have)" is used in 1 John, see notes at 1:8.   In this place, the verb involves the idea that hope is a continuous source of influence on how the Christian lives.   See 2 Peter 1:3 for how hope influences how men live.

[56] John does not write a wish ("may he purify himself") or a possibility ("he may purify himself") or a command ("he ought to purify himself").   He rather states what a Christian does.   (Kistemaker, *op. cit.*, p.296.)   "In 1 John 1:7 it is 'the blood of Jesus' which 'cleanses us from all sin:' here the Christian 'purifieth himself.'   Both are true, and neither cleansing will avail to salvation without the other.   Christ cannot save us if we withhold our efforts: we cannot save ourselves without His merits and grace." (Plummer, *op. cit.*, p.122,123.)

(cf. notes at 2:6). Christ has set us an example.[57] He was and is the perfect realization of conformity to God's standard of purity. "This verb is present tense because purity is an essential characteristic not only of the earthly but also of the heavenly Christ."[58] "He is pure" and "in Him there is no sin" are synonymous expressions.[59] Our destiny is "to be conformed to the image of His Son" (Romans 8:29 KJV), and that conforming is something that is to begin in this life. The Gnostic indifference to sin is in diametric opposition to the purity expected of God's children.

B. The Practice of Righteousness Increases. 3:4-9

Summary: John links the increasing practice of righteousness with Christ's first appearing on earth. He came the first time to remove sins and destroy the works of the devil. This makes possible another of fellowship's distinctive rewards and blessings: righteousness increases with practice.

3:4 -- *Everyone who practices sin also practices lawlessness; and sin is lawlessness.*

Everyone who practices sin also practices lawlessness – As in verse 3 and throughout this epistle, "everyone who" introduces a polemic against the Gnostics. John does not give the simple opposite "everyone who does not purify himself," but rather expanded the idea by saying "everyone who practices sin." Gnostics "practiced sin" and many of them defended their behavior by stating they could live a life of debauchery in order to demonstrate that the spirit was not touched or affected by physical behavior. John affirms that such "continuing in sin"[1] (as the Gnostics did, or advocated) is completely opposed to God's laws and to the whole redemptive purpose of Christ's incarnation and ministry. Habitual sin and habitual lawlessness are one and the same thing.[2] "Lawlessness" (*ano-*

---

[57] *Kathōs* ("just as") might signify that Christ is the pattern for Christian believers to follow. Or it might point to the *motivation* for such imitation ("just as [because] He is pure"). At 1 John 2:6 we have already had Christ held up as an example to believers.

[58] Haas, *op. cit.*, p.80.

[59] There is a slight difference in meaning between *hagios* ("holy") and *agnos* ("pure," i.e., sinless), the word used here of Christ.

[1] For the meaning of the word "sin" (*hamartia*) see notes at 1:7. The word "sin" was last used in 2:12, but now we have a succession of five verses in which it is repeatedly used. John hammers the point home by repetition ("sin, sin, sin...") that sin is bad, wrong, damning. John emphasizes that sin is a serious matter – a stark contrast to the indifference towards sin which characterized the heretics. The same verb ("doing," *poieō*) that was used in 2:29 is used here. In both passages the present tense expresses a durative or continuous idea. To "practice sin" is the antithesis of to "practice righteousness" (2:29), and is the opposite of "purifies himself" (3:3). "Sin[ning]" (verse 4) and "purity" (verse 3) are incompatible.

[2] Both nouns have the article in the Greek. It is "the sin" and "the lawlessness."

mia) means to break God's laws.[3]   God is the One who identifies those acts and thoughts He calls sin.   "Lawlessness" is to act as if there is no God-given law by which men are expected to live; it is wanton disregard for His revealed rules by which He expects men to live.   The heretics, whatever their position, were treating God's laws with disdain or indifference.

And sin is lawlessness – This is one definition of sin.[4]   Sin is transgression of the law; it acts out an attitude of rebellion against God (verse 8).   "Is" (*estin*) amounts to "is equivalent to."   Both nouns have an article.[5]   "'Sin [*hē hamartia*] is lawlessness [*hē anomia*]' identifies the two as to render them interchangeable terms.   Wherever one is read, it is possible to substitute the other."[6]   John's treatment of sin is in bold contrast, not only to the Gnostics of his day, but to the present world which tends to treat sin as something not really serious.[7]   We would be better served in our efforts to purify ourselves (verse 3) if we memorized John's definition and kept it constantly in our minds.

3:5 -- *And you know that He appeared in order to take away sins; and in Him there is no sin.*

And you know that He appeared in order to take away sins[8] – As John described the nature of sin in verse 4, his intention was not just to define its character, but also to encourage his readers to stop sinning.   "And" shows there is a connection between verse 5 and

---

[3] John used two words for sin: *hamartia* and *anomia*.   In the LXX the terms *hamartia* ("sin," missing the mark) and *anomia* ("lawlessness," "lawbreaking," literally "no law") are used as if they are synonymous (cf. Psalm 31[32]:1-2, quoted in Romans 4:7-8; Psalm 50[51]:2,4).   [*Note:*   "32" and "51" in brackets remind us that the Psalms are numbered differently in the LXX than they are in our English versions.]   In the New Testament, too, "lawlessness" is often synonymous with "sin."   See Romans 4:7 ("blessed are those whose wrongs [lawlessnesses] God has forgiven") and Hebrews 10:17 ("I will remember their sins and wicked deeds [lawlessnesses] no longer").

[4] There are other definitions or descriptions of sin in the New Testament.   E.g., Romans 14:23; James 4:17; 1 John 5:17.   "Sin" cannot be limited in this passage to one kind of sin, whether it be mortal sin as distinguished from venial (as say the Roman Catholic expositors), or notorious and unrepented sins, or sins against brotherly love (as Luther and others).   Every sin whatever is transgression of God's law.

[5] The first article may be the article of previous reference: "the sin" I just spoke about when I wrote "practices sin."   "If either of the words were anarthrous, it would become predicative of quality: 'is of the nature of', as in *theos hēn ho logos*.   Since *both* have the article, both are distributed logically, and the one is asserted to be co-extensive and convertible with the other."   Alford, *op. cit.*, p.464.

[6] Stott, *op. cit.*, p.122.   "In other passages (e.g., Matthew 24:1-13, 7:22f; 2 Corinthians 6:14-16; 2 Thessalonians 2:1-12), 'lawlessness' seems to serve as a technical term for the Satan-inspired rejection of God and His law."   Haas, *op. cit.*, p.81.

[7] The world has its own definition of sin.   For some, sin is a naughty deed, about which they chuckle and laugh as they tell about it.   Others think of it as a weakness or imperfection resulting from some psychological defect.   Still others talk in terms of a "mistake" that any human being can and does make. (Paraphrased from Kistemaker, *op. cit.*, p.300.)

[8] The KJV reads "our sins," but the "our" probably does not enjoy integrity.   It is omitted in Alexandrinus and Vaticanus, though it is found in Sinaiticus and Ephraemi.   If it is retained, it includes both the apostle and his readers.

what precedes.   'Not only is sin lawlessness, but if you continue to commit sins, you are in opposition to the very purpose why Jesus Christ came into the world, for, as you know, He came to take away sins.'   "You know" (*oidate*, a knowledge derived from revelation) is an appeal to common Christian knowledge, likely imparted to potential and new converts by oral instruction.   "He" (*ekeinos*) refers to Jesus Christ (see 2:6).   John has already used the verb "appeared/manifested" of Jesus' incarnation (1:2 and at John 21:1).[9]   It refers to the incarnation here, too, rather than to the Second Coming (as at 2:28), for the verb tense here is aorist, which shows that the reference is to Jesus' appearance in history, something that is already past when 1 John is written.   "Sins" includes all sins, not merely certain sins (see on 1:9).   "Take away" (*airō*) suggests that Jesus intended to remove sins from men's lives.[10]   That is what John the Baptist exclaimed when he recognized the Lamb of God.   "Look!   There is the Lamb of God who takes away (*arē*) the sin of the world!" (John 1:29, personal translation).[11]   Jesus wanted men to be people who sin no more, people who abolish sinful acts from their lives.

And in Him there is no sin – "And" serves to coordinate this clause with the preceding one.   Perhaps John is appealing to a second thing the readers "knew" by what they had heard preached and taught about Jesus.[12]   Perhaps this is another way of saying "He is pure" (verse 4).[13]   "Is" translates *estin* and says that the sinlessness of Christ is limited neither to His pre-existence, nor to the days of His flesh, nor to His present heavenly condition (life with the Father).   It is something that was and is true all the time.   Chris-

---

[9] "Manifested" implies a previous existence before He came to earth, but one in which He was not visible to human eyes.   John may be countering the Gnostic ideas that it was the man Jesus (not the incarnate Son of God) who died on Calvary, and that this man Jesus' death had no salvific value.

[10] The verb here means "to take away" sins, rather than "to atone for" sins.   In the Hebrew, *nasha* meant both "take away" (remove or forgive) and "to bear" (in the sense of an atoning sacrifice).   However the LXX when translating *nasha* consistently uses *airō* for "take away, remove" and *pherō* for "bear" or "atone."   Of course, Jesus bore our sins in His own body on the tree (1 Peter 2:24; Hebrews 9:28; Isaiah 53:11,12), but John seems to have more than His atoning sacrifice in view here in verse 5.

[11] Dogmatic disputes have arisen as to the exact meaning of the verb rendered "take away," and these are reflected in the long "explanation" offered at this place in many of the commentaries.   What is at issue is whether the stress is on the "taking away" of sin that occurs in expiation/propitiation, or whether it is the "taking away" that occurs by way of sanctification.   While the context is dealing with how Christians purify themselves, the word is general enough to speak both of deliverance from sin in general in Christ's sacrifice, as well as removal of sins the Christian has committed (2:2).   The point John is making is not how Jesus takes away sins, but rather that Jesus stands in opposition to sin – something shown both by what He came to do, and how He himself lived (sinless).

[12] "In Him" likely refers to Christ.   Some suppose it refers to Christians, whose lives are to become more and more sinless.   We think that is what verse 6 speaks about, rather than this clause in verse 5.

[13] "In Him" here has the same meaning which "in Him (there is no darkness)" had in 1:5.

tians are to attempt to imitate Jesus in whom there was no sin.[14]   This is another reason they should renounce sin and stop sinning.

3:6 -- *No one who abides in Him sins; no one who sins has seen Him or knows Him.*

No one who abides in Him sins – The NASB hides the fact that the Greek is "everyone who," the same anti-Gnostic polemic we've had at 2:29, 3:3,4.   Verse 6 contains a logical deduction from what has been said about sin in verse 4 and about Jesus in verse 5. Sometimes in 1 John, "abiding *in Him*" refers to God (3:24, 4:13,15,16), and sometimes it refers to Christ (2:6,28).   It could be either here, but what was just written in verse 5 leads us to make it a reference to Christ.[15]   "Abides" is a present tense verb, "keeps on abiding." "Sins not" is also a present tense verb, likewise indicating continuing action.   Whoever continues to abide in Him does not habitually sin is what John affirms; the Christian who keeps on abiding does not keep on sinning.[16]   If a Christian sins habitually, there comes a time when he no longer abides in Christ (Romans 6:23).   Since Christ and sin have nothing in common, an intimate and ongoing relationship with Christ ("abides in Him") rules out any habitual practice of sin.

No one who sins has seen Him or knows Him – Again John wrote "everyone who ..." and his statement is a direct attack on the Gnostics.   "Who sins" is a present tense verb, describing a life characterized by habitual sin.[17]   No doubt John deliberately employed the verbs "has seen" and "knows" to refute the false teachers, who used to boast of having true vision and knowledge of Christ.   Just what the Gnostics meant when they claimed to have "seen Him" is not certain.[18]   Perhaps they used the word "seen" metaphorically, to

---

[14] The Greek word order is "sin in Him does not exist."   "Sin" is in the singular and without an article – not even one instance of sin of any kind was found in Jesus.   Jesus Himself claimed sinlessness (John 7:18, 8:46) for Himself, and so do the New Testament writers (2 Corinthians 5:21; Hebrews 4:15, 7:26, 9:13; 1 Peter 1:19, 2:22).

[15] For "abide" see 1 John 2:6,27,28 and John 15:4-10.

[16] "Sins not" has been used by some theologians as a proof-text for a second work of grace, which (it is alleged) makes a man so that he does not sin any more at all.   There is even a familiar song (There Is A Fountain) that has the phrase in it, "till all the ransomed church of God be saved to sin no more," which speaks of this supposed second work of grace.   To make 1 John 3:6-9 speak of sinless perfection creates a contradiction with 1:8-10, and ignores the verb tenses in each place (cf. 2:1).   See the NASB's translation of the verb tenses in these places.   It helps clear up the problem even for the English reader.   See further comments below at verse 9 on the apparent contradiction between 1 John 1:7-10 and 1 John 3:6ff on the matter of the Christian sinning or not sinning.   He may sin now and then, but he does not go around habitually sinning.

[17] John is not saying this (about not "seeing Him" or "knowing Him") of any Christian who commits a single sin, but rather of the habitual sinner (present tense).

[18] Some proponents of unconditional eternal security treat "seen Him" as being equal to "conversion." They then affirm that the perfect tense ("have not seen") is proof that those who habitually sin were never converted in the first place.   To impose such an interpretation on this passage makes it contradict other plain passages that folk once saved can again lose their salvation if their lifestyle remains bad (Hebrews 6:4-6; Romans 6:12ff; John 15:6).

see with the eye of faith.[19]   Perhaps it speaks of the kind of "vision" the heretics would "see" in an altered state of consciousness.   They saw someone or something, though it wasn't Jesus the Messiah.   On "knows Him," see notes at 2:3.   It speaks of being on intimate terms with Him.   Both verbs "has seen" and "knows" are perfect tense.   In the Greek perfect tense (which depicts past completed act with present continuing results), the present predominates (whereas in the English perfect tense, the past predominates).   John is saying, "The Jesus you claim to see now and to be intimate with now is not the Jesus I am personally acquainted with."   John had seen Jesus (1 John 1:1-3), and is able to appeal to experiential knowledge.   The Gnostics also claimed to see and know Jesus, but their position in regards to sin was so contrary to what John knew about Jesus from personal experience that he can brand the Gnostic claims as bogus.

3:7 -- *Little children, let no one deceive you; the one who practices righteousness is righteous, just as He is righteous;*

Little children – See on 2:1 for this expression.   Many of the readers were John's converts, and others were students he had personally taught.   Because the readers were in grave danger on account of the heretics among them, John addresses them with the tenderness of a loving father who is trying to counsel his beloved children.

Let no one deceive you – The Greek forbids the continuance of an action already going on.   "Stop letting anyone lead you astray!"   "Break the spell of any Gnostic charmer!"[20] When they said that to the spiritual man all conduct is alike, and that the practice of sin brings no danger to enlightened ones, the heretics were contradicting the gospel John preached.   The ones who were trying to deceive John's readers, both theologically (2:26) and morally (3:7), were antichrists (2:18)!

The one who practices righteousness is righteous – Here is a rule of thumb which will save the readers from being deceived by the false teachers.   "The heretics appear to have indulged in the subtly perverse reasoning that somehow you could 'be' righteous without necessarily bothering to 'practice' righteousness."[21]   John flatly denies this reasoning by saying, "He who keeps on doing (present participle) righteousness is righteous."   Actions do matter, whatever the heretics might claim.   "There is a difference between the two ideas 'to practice righteousness' and 'is righteous.'   The first signifies the action, the second

---

[19] The same verb, *horaō*, is used by John with a literal meaning at John 1:18 and 20:19. However, it is very doubtful that the Gnostics to whom John alludes could claim to have personally seen Jesus during His earthly ministry, like John claims to have seen Him. The verb here is more likely used as it is in 3 John 11.

[20] Robertson, *op. cit.*, p.222.

[21] Stott, *op. cit.*, p.124.

the state.[22]   The reality of the latter is proved by the former.   He who does not do righteousness shows thereby that he is not righteous."[23]   Character and practice cannot be separated.

Just as He is righteous – "He" is again emphatic, is again *ekeinos*, and again refers to Christ (see 2:6).   But for the adjective this clause is identical with the similar "as"-clause in verse 3.   "Just as" (*kathōs*) does not mean that the Christian is identical or equal to Christ in every respect, but it does highlight the fact that the Christian is to imitate Christ in his behavior.   The standard by which one measures what is right conduct is Christ's righteousness.[24]

3:8 -- The one who practices sin is of the devil; for the devil has sinned from the beginning. The Son of God appeared for this purpose, that He might destroy the works of the devil.

The one who practices sin is of the devil – Verse 8 begins almost the same way verse 4 did.   Not only does the habitual sinner break the law of God (verse 4), but such a person is in fact linked with the devil (verse 8).   As the repetition of "the one who practices ... the one who practices" shows, verse 8 also is a direct contrast with what was written in verse 7b.   The man who practices right lives according to God's norms (verse 7); the man who habitually sins lives according to the norms of the devil (verse 8), and like the Devil is God's adversary.   "Practices sin" (a present participle in Greek) expresses continuous action, habitual sinning.   "Is of (*ek*) the devil" means "originates from, and has the quality of the devil."   3:10 makes this meaning clear, for there the sinners are called a "children of the devil."25   (For this same use of *ek*, see "is of the Father" in 2:16.)   It is the behavior of the sinner that emanates from the devil, not the physical life and existence of the person doing the sin.[26]   John is speaking of spiritual parentage, just as Jesus did when he spoke to the Pharisees about their spiritual parentage (John 8:44, "you are of your father the devil").   "Devil" is *ho diabolos*,"the slanderer, the defamer."   The words function as the

---

[22] In some places in the Scripture, "righteous" is used with a forensic sense (God declares men "saved" or "righteous").   Perhaps here John is saying the habitual practice of righteousness by a Christian results in God's continual justification of that man.   In other places, "righteous" speaks of "right relationships with men and God."   Perhaps here John is saying that habitual practice of righteousness results in such right relationships with both man and God.

[23] Huther, *op. cit.*, p.559.

[24] "Righteous" in verse 7 seems to be synonymous with "in Him there is no sin" (verse 5).

[25] We have here another of John's reasons why Christians are to avoid sin.   Sin is missing the mark. Sin is disregard for God's law.   Sin is a denial of the redemptive work of Christ.   Sin is a wandering from the path of right (deceive, lead you astray).   Now the real seriousness of sin is shown by disclosing the spiritual parentage of the one who habitually sins.   "He who practices sin is of the devil."

[26] A number of writers have quoted Augustine at this place, who wrote, "The devil made no man, begat no man, created no man."   He went on to compare the Biblical expression "child of Abraham" (which means that one imitates the faith of Abraham) with "child of the devil" (which also means one imitates the actions of the devil).

proper name of the supreme ruler of the forces of evil.[27]   As John writes about the devil, he notes with precision the existence of the devil,[28] the personality of the devil, his relation to sin, sinners, and to God's efforts at redemption from sin.

For the devil has sinned from the beginning – The verb translated "has sinned" (*hamartanei*) is present tense, indicating continuing, habitual, repeated action.   The devil was sinning when the world began, and has continued uninterruptedly to do so ever since.   Men who habitually sin are acting just like the devil.   "From the beginning" stands first in the Greek sentence for emphasis, but exactly what is intended has caused commentators no little problem.[29]   It can hardly mean "from the beginning of the devil's existence,"[30] for that would deny the Biblical idea that the devil is a fallen, rebellious creature.   It might mean "from the beginning of human history," with an obvious allusion to the Genesis account of the first sin committed by man, and the devil's instigation of it.   It might mean "from the beginning of the devil's career," with an allusion to the rebellion in heaven that led to the devil and his helpers being cast out of heaven.[31]   Some Gnostics (having embraced dualism) taught the devil was the good character, while the Jehovah of the Bible was the bad character.   That is not how John presents it!

The Son of God appeared for this purpose – Having usurped a position for himself, the devil has functioned as "prince of this world" (John 12:32) or "god of this world" (2 Corinthians 4:4).   This very fact necessitated the appearance (incarnation) of Christ, who came to break the devil's power.[32]   It was *God's* Son who acted against the Devil, and from this the attitude of God the Father towards the devil can be deduced.[33]   "For this

---

[27] Haas, *op. cit.*, p.83. Who is the devil? Stott (*op. cit.*, p.136ff) offers an additional note on John's teaching about the devil (his origin, activity, power, and overthrow). Stott notes that the devil and his helpers and his followers eventually will be cast into the lake of fire (Revelation 20:10ff).

[28] The language must not be rationalized away, as is done by those who deny the personal existence of the devil. It is the distinct opposite of "is of God" (verse 10). If one doesn't exist, then by parity of reasoning neither does the other. (Adapted from Alford, *op. cit.*, p.467)

[29] It is not likely the expression "from the beginning" here has the same meaning it did in 1 John 1:1.

[30] That the devil sinned from the beginning of his existence was a Manichaean dogma.

[31] Revelation 12:7-9; see also Luke 10:18; 2 Peter 2:4; Jude 6. How long the devil remained in his pristine angelic state before he rebelled, we do not know. The time came when he rebelled and was thrown out of heaven, and he has been sinning ever since.

[32] "Appeared," "manifested" is *aphanerōthē* again, as in verse 5. His incarnation and earthly ministry are in view. He was God in the flesh, and He was that from His incarnation (not His baptism, as some heretics were wont to suggest). The incarnation was not an illusion (as some other heretics were wont to affirm).

[33] On Jesus being God's "Son," see notes at 1 John 1:3.

purpose" points to what follows, and is completed by "[in order] that."[34]

That He might destroy the works of the devil – The "works of the devil" include the sins (verse 5) that he tempts men to commit, all his plans of wickedness, all his control over the hearts of men.   Not only sins, but the consequences of sin (pain, sorrow, death), were the target of Christ's mission into the world.   Fellowship with God had been destroyed by the devil, but Christ came to make renewed fellowship with God possible for all.   The verb *luō* can be translated "loose, break, or destroy."   Jesus came to undo, to do away with, to put an end to, all the diabolical works insinuated into God's creation by the devil.[35] Readers of John's Gospel (John 12:31) would need no proof that Jesus came to defeat the devil.   "If, then, the whole purpose of Christ's first appearing was to remove sins and to undo the works of the devil, Christians must not compromise with either sin or the devil, or they will find themselves fighting against Christ."[36]   Instead of continuing to sin, the child of God will "purify himself" (verse 3).[37]

3:9 -- *No one who is born of God practices sin, because His seed abides in him; and he cannot sin, because he is born of God.*

No one who is born of God practices sin – As has been true each time John has used this language, the construction of this sentence (beginning with "everyone who ...") reflects negatively on the heretics (see verse 4 notes).   Their habitual behavior ("practices sin"[38])

---

[34] The Greek reads, "the reason the Son of God appeared was to destroy the works of the devil."   In other words, "for this purpose" points forward to the next phrase in the verse; it does not refer to what precedes, as though it was only because the devil has sinned from the beginning that Christ became incarnate.

[35] Satan's works were not "destroyed" in the absolute sense that he can work no more (as the efforts of the antichrists proved).   The devil's power has been broken by the atoning work of Christ, and the Christian who utilizes Christ's victorious power can negate, limit and, through Christ's pardon, eradicate the evil of sin from his life (Romans 6:6, 8:1-3, 8:13; 2 Timothy 1:10; Hebrews 2:14).   (Adapted from Roberts, *op. cit.*, p.84)

[36] Stott, *op. cit.*, p.125.

[37] If we may let what John has written guide us, we might say that the first step towards holiness is to recognize the sinfulness of sin, both in its essence as lawlessness and in its diabolical origin.   The second step is to see its absolute incompatibility with Christ in His sinless Person and saving work.   The more clearly we grasp these facts, the more determined we shall be to be rid of sin and to become holy. (Adapted from Stott, *ibid.*)

[38] The verb is a present tense in the Greek, and both NIV and NASB render the verb to show its nature as a present tense, indicating continuous action.   Those who have been born of God do not have sin as a manner of life, a habit of life.   They do not habitually sin.   It does not say that one who is born of God is sinless perfect, never committing any sinful act.   Rather, it emphasizes that such a person will not persist in sin.

belies their claim to have been "born of God."[39]   That is the only logical conclusion that can be drawn from what has been written in verse 8.   The devil's children (and that includes the Gnostics) sin just as their spiritual parent does.   God's children, on the other hand, reflect their spiritual Parent's values and behavior.   The absence of sinning is not automatic.   Christians, by the Spirit, must put to death the deeds of the flesh (Romans 8:13, 6:12ff).

Because His seed abides in him – This phrase gives the reason why one who has been born of God cannot habitually sin.   But it has been hard for the commentators to determine exactly what the reason is.[40]   Perhaps some decision about John's meaning can be reached as we work backwards through the phrase.

(1) Who is the "him" in whom the seed is said to abide?   Some would encourage us to capitalize it ("Him"), and then the verse says that the one born of God remains in God, and that is the reason he or she does not sin habitually.   Others opt for small "h" ("him"), and then the verse says that the seed remains in the one who has been born again, and that is the reason he or she does not sin habitually.   The NASB translators, in this commentator's opinion, have rendered it correctly.

(2) What is meant by "His seed"?   (a) Some think it speaks of the influences of the Holy Spirit.   Just as the Holy Spirit works through the Word to bring about belief in Jesus (and consequently the new birth), so the Holy Spirit is given to Christians to help them live the Christian life.   While all that has been said about the Spirit's work to help a person become a Christian and then to live the Christian life is true,[41] against treating "seed" as a reference to the Holy Spirit is the fact that no parallel example can be found where "seed" is used to mean the Holy Spirit.   (b) The RSV paraphrases "for God's nature abides in him."   Behind this is the hypothesis that when a man is born again a whole new spiritual nature (God's nature) is implanted in him, which (as it were) pro-

---

[39] See notes at 2:29 and 5:1 concerning "born of Him" or "born of God." The idea of the new birth is very frequent in 1 John (see 2:29; 3:9; 4:7; 5:1,4,18). *Gennaō* can be translated "to be conceived (begotten)" or "to be born." Both things happen when a person is "born again." Which is in John's mind here cannot be decided for certain. He is about to speak of "seed," which might indicate that it is the conception he has in mind. On the other hand, he also speaks of "children of God," which might indicate that the birth has taken place. The Greek verb is a perfect tense – the "begetting" or "birth" is a past completed action with present continuing results. "Everyone who has been born [begotten] again and remains a child of God" is the idea. It is the "spirit" which is reborn (John 3:6), and the perfect tense indicates that new-born spirit is still alive. (It is implied that folk can be once regenerate and die spiritually again. Of this latter person, John is not speaking, when he says "no one born of God practices sin.")

[40] Perhaps we should listen to the suggestion that John deliberately alluded to Gnostic language in order to refute their views. "We know from the statements of early Church writers that the Gnostics taught that once the Gnostic had been reborn [or enlightened], the divine nature or seed remained in him and became a power in him making him spiritual by nature (Irenaeus, *Against Heresies* I.1.11; Hippolytus, *Refutation of All Heresies* V.8.112f; Clement of Alexandria, *Excerpts from Theodotus* 1,2,38,40,49,53) ... Over against the Gnostic claim of rebirth with its effect, John is setting the Christian concept of the new birth." Roberts, *op. cit.*, p.86.

[41] John teaches that as Christians we have been given the Holy Spirit (1 John 4:13). This Spirit, which Paul refers to as the "indwelling Spirit" (Romans 8:9-11), is a means by which we put to death the deeds of the flesh (Romans 8:13). When the deeds of the flesh are mortified, the Christian finds himself or herself sinning less and less (or as John words it, "no one born of God practices sin").

grams his whole life in a different direction so that he doesn't sin habitually.   In this commentator's opinion, neither Titus 3:5 ("renewing by the Holy Spirit") nor 2 Peter 1.4 ("became partakers of the divine nature") teach such an implanting as this hypothesis suggests.[42]   (c) The RSV margin reads "the offspring of God abide in Him."   This takes "seed" metaphorically as a collective noun for the children of God (as in "the seed of Abraham," Galatians 3:29).   "Him" is taken to refer to "God," and the phrase then means that such an "offspring" (cp. John 8:33,37) of God remains in (fellowship with) God, and this precludes habitual sinning.[43]   (d) Many commentators think "seed" is a metaphor for the word of God, and not a few point to John 5:38 ("you do not have His word abiding in you") as holding the key to this interpretation.   1 John 2:24 is also pointed out as a parallel concept.[44]   The Bible does point out a close relationship between the word of God and victory over temptation to sin, e.g., "Thy Word have I hid in mine heart that I might not sin against thee" (Psalm 119:11 KJV).[45]

And he cannot sin – There is little difference between this affirmation and "no one born of God practices sin" earlier in verse 9.   What does John mean by this?   Note that John does not say "cannot commit a [single] sin" (*ou dunatai hamartein*, aorist tense, even one act) but "is not able to sin continually" (*ou dunatai hamartanein*, present tense).[46]   Habitual sin is not an option for the Christian.   Instead, every effort must be made to put to death the deeds of the flesh since those desires are planted there by the devil.   Every effort must be made to stop letting sin reign in our mortal bodies (Romans 6:12).   Instead of being indifferent toward temptation and sin (as were the Gnostics),   the Christian is to

---

[42] In the author's commentary on Romans the whole matter of "infused" versus "imputed" righteousness has been carefully studied, and the conclusion is there reached that "infused" is not a Biblical doctrine.

[43] Those who teach "once saved, always saved" tend to treat this verse as a promise of unconditional eternal security.   Those who really are God's offspring do not fall away (cannot sin); they abide in Him.

[44] In the Parable of the Sower, the "seed" is the word of God (Matthew 13:3-9,18-23 and Luke 8:11). Elsewhere, the New Testament notes a close association between the word of God and the new birth. For example, in 1 Peter 1:23 we are told, "You have been born again, not of seed which is perishable but imperishable, that is, through the living and abiding word of God."   See also James 1:18 (though the Greek word there, "brought forth," is slightly different).

[45] This explanation of "seed" would also be in accord with descriptions elsewhere in the New Testament of purification from sin as the result of the Word (cf. John 15:2-4).   Or we might appeal to the example of Jesus who discomfited the Tempter by quoting Scripture (Matthew 4:1ff).   Christians can resist temptations by the same method.   Such an interpretation harmonizes with John's allusion to *chrisma* ("result of anointing") which indwells the believer (2:20,27), since in our view that term also refers to the word of God.

[46] "Cannot sin (is not able to sin)" does not mean that one who is born again has no physical ability to do wrong, for every moral agent has that ability.   Nor can it mean that no one who is a true Christian never does wrong even once in thought, word or deed; no one could seriously maintain this.

practice self-control and master those desires that would lead to sin.[47]   The Christian just cannot go on sinning!   In fact, one of the blessings of fellowship with God that His children enjoy is that as they purify themselves they see less and less sin in their lives. They habitually practice righteousness rather than habitually practicing lawlessness.

Because he is born of God – "Born of God" is a perfect tense verb.   The new birth took place in the past; since then the person has been a Christian.   What John says, in effect, is that habitual sin is not acceptable behavior for the Christian, for one who has been "born of God".[48]   Paul teaches precisely the same thing about "continuing in sin" in Romans 6:1 ("Shall we continue in sin?" is a present linear subjunctive), when he emphatically says, "May it never be!"   While the folk Paul was refuting were not Gnostics, they were putting

---

[47] The thoughtful reader will have observed how we have proposed to harmonize or reconcile the teaching of 1 John 1:5-10 and 3:4-9.   We have opted to pay careful attention to John's grammar.   John uses present tense verbs throughout chapter 3.   To represent what John wrote, many translators carefully render the present tenses of the verbs "sins" (verse 6) and "practices sin" (verses 8,9) in order to show habitual action ("does not go on sinning," "cannot continually live in sin";   TEV, "not continue to sin";   or NIV, "he does not keep on sinning"; or NASB, "does not practice sin").   This makes John's statements much less rigid than they seem to be when read in an English version that does not carefully translate the verb tenses.   Careful attention to the verb tenses also eliminates the places that chapters 1 and 3 have been alleged to be contradictory.   The very words (including present and perfect and aorist tense verbs) that the writers used were the subject of inspiration (1 Corinthians 2:10ff), and were something that a Greek reader or listener would catch and understand.   The believer makes every attempt to purify himself, every attempt to overcome temptation to sin (1 John 3).   The believer may sin occasionally (1 John 1:5-10), but whenever he sins, he repents, confesses it, is forgiven by his heavenly Father, and then he continues to persevere with his self-purification.

We acknowledge that other attempts to harmonize the two allegedly opposite paragraphs have been offered.   (1) The Neo-orthodox (with their Hegelian philosophical roots of thesis, antithesis and synthesis) simply embrace the idea that there is a contradiction in what John has written about sin and the Christian.   That "no other New Testament author contradicts himself so sharply within such a short span of writing" is no great problem to those who allege that "truth" is to be found somewhere between the two opposite sides of a paradox.   Since the whole Neo-orthodox methodology has fallen into disrepute, we are very hesitant to appeal to it here.   (2) Stott (*op. cit.*, p. 126) offers what has been called the "situational" explanation.   Stott proposes that in each of the two different paragraphs John is opposing a different error. Gnosticism led its adherents to different conclusions concerning acceptable lifestyles.   Some supposed that their possession of gnosis had made them perfect; others maintained that sin did not matter because it could not harm those who had been enlightened.   According to Stott, John attacks one view in the first paragraph, the other view in the second.   When all that John has written is combined, we see that both positions are to be rejected.   (3) Some in the Roman Catholic Church have embraced what has been called the "theological" explanation.   First, an appeal is made to 1 John 5:16-17, which speaks of a sin unto death (i.e., a mortal sin) and a sin not unto death (i.e., a venial sin).   Then it is affirmed that when John speaks of "not sinning" and "cannot sin" (interpreted to be one act), he has one particular type of sin (the sin unto death) in mind.   And when he speaks of the occasional sins a Christian commits, he has one of the "sins not unto death" in view.   (4) Redaction critics blame a clumsy redactor who was editing earlier sources, and did it poorly.   In this way, they account for the alleged diverse teachings about sin in 1 John. Redaction critical attempts to identify the work of redactors run counter to the unity and integrity which is everywhere evident in the letter (and indeed all the manuscripts of the letter).

Having studied these options, we return to the one which treats the verb tenses John wrote as being the important key to understanding what he is saying.

[48] The expression "born of God" has been explained in comments on verses 2:29 and 3:9.

a malicious twist to Paul's doctrine of grace. They alleged that such a doctrine gave men a license to sin continually. Paul replied to this twist to his doctrine by setting forth his great exposition that Christians must stop giving the members of our bodies over to sin and lawlessness, and instead present them to righteousness. After all, habitual sin will result in slavery to sin (Romans 6:16), and habitual sin has its wages – death (Romans 6:23). Whether the writer be John or Paul, the doctrine is the same.

C. Brotherly Love and Benevolence.   3:10-18

> *Summary*:   John continues his presentation of the distinctive rewards and blessings that enrich the life of a man who is in fellowship with God. He presents these two points, brotherly love and benevolence, by contrasting how the Gnostics are without these blessings, and then by calling on his readers to imitate (not the example of Cain, but) the pattern of Jesus who laid down His life for others.

3:10 -- *By this the children of God and the children of the devil are obvious; any one who does not practice righteousness is not of God, nor the one who does not love his brother.*

By this the children of God and the children of the devil are obvious – "By this" is best understood as pointing forward to what is said in the last part of verse 10.[1] If it points forward, a new paragraph begins at this place. The Gnostics claimed to be "children of God" and their claims may have raised questions in the minds of John's readers. So John is about to give another rule of thumb by which his readers can plainly distinguish between who are God's children, and who are not.[2] Jesus had counseled, "By their fruits ye shall know them" (Matthew 7:20 KJV). The children of God practice righteousness and love their brethren. The children of the devil do not practice righteousness and are selfish. It may not yet be obvious[3] what we shall be in our final state (3:2), but already in this life it

---

[1] If it points backwards, then verse 10 is the conclusion of the previous paragraph. Some Bible students in fact argue that verse 10a concludes the development of the thought begun in verse 7 with the sharp antithesis between "the children of God" and "the children of the devil." But such students are left with the problem of where to begin a new paragraph. Some attempt to begin a new paragraph at verse 10b. The NASB starts the new paragraph with verse 13.

[2] The people of the world are divided into two groups, the saved and the lost. There are not three, nor is there only one. "A creature endowed with free will can choose his own spiritual parent ... The Father offers him the 'right to become a child of God' (John 1:12); but he can refuse this and become a child of the devil instead." (Plummer, *op. cit.*, p.128). On "children of God," see notes at 3:1,2. On "children of the devil," see notes at 3:8. John includes the Gnostics among the "children of the devil." It is an error to label them as heretical Christians, or as Christians whose beliefs do not quite harmonize with the beliefs of other Christians.

[3] The word translated "obvious" in verse 10 is the same Greek root that is translated "appeared" in verse 2.

is obvious whether people are children of God or children of the devil.

Any one who does not practice righteousness is not of God – As has been true at 3:3,4, 6,9, "any (every) one who ..." is a polemic against the Gnostics.   John here flatly asserts they were not habitually practicing righteousness[4] and therefore it is obvious they were not children of God.[5]

Nor the one who does not love his brother – The NASB translates *kai* as "nor," though literally it is "and."[6]   The word order in this clause is the same as the word order in the previous clause, save for the words "is not of God."   Greek readers noting this parallel word order would naturally supply the missing words, and the sentence would read, "And every one who does not love his brother is not of God."   John here accuses the Gnostics of being selfish rather than demonstrating brotherly love.[7]   This behavior, too, makes it obvious they are not children of God.

3:11 -- For this is the message which you have heard from the beginning, that we should love one another;

For – With *hoti* John introduces the basis of the statement he made in verse 10b about loving one's brother.   Verse 11 is proof that absence of love excludes one from God's family.[8]

This is the message which you have heard from the beginning – "This" points forward to the following "that-clause" which gives the contents of the message.   "This is the message" (*aggelia*[9]) is a repetition of the phrase with which the body of this epistle began (1:5).   A "message" was something delivered by word of mouth.   "Heard" was something

---

[4] On the meaning of "practice righteousness," see notes at 2:29 and 3:7. The meaning is the same here as in those passages. John uses a present tense participle, so he is talking about a habit of not doing right. (Cf. Matthew 7:24,26 on "doing" and "not doing.")

[5] On "is not of God," see notes at 2:16 on "is not of the Father." As it was at 3:8, spiritual parentage is in view (at 3:8 it was "of the devil"), so "is not of God" equals "is not a child of God."

[6] Alford (*op. cit.*, p.471) argues that the *kai* which binds this clause to the previous one serves, as in verse 5, to co-ordinate that clause with the foregoing. We cannot treat verse 10b as a completely new topic, thus making a new paragraph begin here.

[7] On what is involved in "loving the brother," see notes at 2:9 and also 3:14-18. The participle ("love") here in verse 10 is present tense, picturing continuing, active, repeated demonstrations of love. R. Bultmann (*The Johannine Epistles*, in the Hermeneia Series. Philadelphia: Fortress Press, 1973, p.41) has noted that in Gnostic literature "there is no mention of brotherly love."

[8] The connector *hoti* keeps verse 11 linked to verse 10 (rather than beginning a new section with verse 11, as some commentators try to do).

[9] *Aggelia* ("message") is the better attested reading here, though a few manuscripts have *epaggelia* ("promise, announcement, commandment") at this place.

done publicly and openly, not in secret as the heretics' message was.   "From the beginning" refers to the beginning of the preaching of the Gospel.[10]   "John's appeal here, as in 1:5, is to a primitive authority which was also public knowledge in contrast to the private and secret enlightenment which the false teachers claimed."[11]   When in 2:24 John wrote "Let that abide in you which you heard from the beginning," it was doctrinal matters which were highlighted as being permanent.   Now John deals with ethical matters as being permanent.   "The Gospel message does not change.   The truth about the Person of Christ and about Christian conduct is unalterable."[12]   When the heretics brought forth new and esoteric doctrines about faith and morals, their very newness refuted them.

That we should love one another – This is the first time the words "love one another" occur in 1 John (cp. 3:23; 4:7,11,12; see also 2 John 5), but the expression is not essentially different from "love the brother" in 2:10 and 3:10.   In comments at 2:10 it was observed that the command to love one's brother goes back to the teaching of Jesus Himself (John 13:34, 15:12), and hence belongs to the foundation of Christian teaching.[13]   The verb "love" is present tense, expressing continuous, repeated, or customary action.

3:12 -- Not as Cain, who was of the evil one, and slew his brother.   And for what reason did he slay him?   Because his deeds were evil, and his brother's were righteous.

Not as Cain, *who* was of the evil one – John calls attention to what the Bible says about the absence of brotherly love, so that his readers can have no excuse for not understanding how people behave when brotherly love is absent.   The Greek construction is irregular, elliptic, or some say awkward.   To smooth it out, many translations add some words (such as, Do not be as ...), but nothing need be supplied for the sense is clear.   In fact the elliptic construction better expresses the unexpected horror of how a devil's child behaves.   Perhaps John chose Cain as a representative example of what happens when people do not

---

[10] Compare notes at 2:7 for the meaning of "from the beginning." Contemporary Redaction critics, who hypothesize that there were competing Christian doctrines during the first two centuries AD, until one (what we have in our New Testaments) finally won out over all the others, need to listen to John's "from the beginning" statements (2:7,24; 3:11). The Gnostics he combatted were not Christians (they were children of the devil), and their doctrine and life were absolutely out of touch with genuine Christianity. It was not a competing form of Christian doctrine. There were not "faiths" delivered to the saints, but one "[the] faith" (Jude 3). Genuine Christian doctrine – as first propounded by Jesus, as delivered by His apostles, as God guaranteed the message by miracle (Hebrews 2:2-4) – has been one unified message "heard from the beginning."

[11] Stott, *op. cit.*, p.139.

[12] Stott, *ibid*.

[13] This commandment to love one another was also part of the original kerygma, the message preached by those who planted the church. Paul reminded Timothy that the goal of our ministry is that believers "love" one another (1 Timothy 1:5).

love their brothers precisely because some Gnostics idolized Cain.[14] The reference to Cain (see Genesis 4:1-16 for the account of Cain and Abel) is the only explicit reference to any Old Testament character in John's letters.[15] The "evil one" is the devil,[16] and to be "*of* the evil one" resumes (from verse 8) "to be of the devil."[17] When it comes to who one's spiritual father is, Cain and the Gnostics have the same father.

And slew his brother – The Greek verb rendered "slew" (*sphazō*) is a rather strong one, and means literally to cut the throat.[18] John is the only New Testament writer who uses the verb; see also his use of this verb at Revelation 5:6,9,12. We cannot tell if he uses it literally or generically (of any form of murdering a man, whether by hand, stone, or club). Cain's behavior was the enactment of a violent passion, but we cannot beyond any doubt deduce the manner of Cain's murder of Abel from the use of this verb.[19] "His brother" reminds us that Abel who was slaughtered was Cain's younger brother.

And for what reason did he slay him? – What[20] caused Cain to behave the way he did?

---

[14] We have documented in the Introductory Studies to 1 John that we do not know how developed the incipient Gnostic systems which John is counteracting were. One later group of Gnostics were inclined to be vegetarians, and used Cain (who "was a tiller of the ground" whereas Abel "was a keeper of flocks" [Genesis 4:2]) as one of their Biblical examples of such a position (Epiphanius, *Haer.* 30.13,22, alluding to the Gnostic writing known as "The Gospel of the Ebionites"). Another Gnostic sect which existed somewhat later, the Ophites (a.k.a. Naasenes), worshiped the serpent (Irenaeus, *Against Heresies* I.31). Their motivation was this: in their dualistic belief of the origin of the world, they held that the God (Jehovah) of the Old Testament was evil. He was a tyrant who would have kept man in ignorance. Hence, the serpent (the devil), who in their system was the good god, attempted to bring man enlightenment. Adam and Eve, and Cain later, they taught, were justified in their rebellion against Jehovah. John's presentation here shows that the Gnostic system was a complete inversion of the moral principles taught in the Old Testament as well as the New.

[15] There are allusions to Old Testament events and teachings. See, for example, 1 John 2:7 ("old commandment"), and the allusion to Genesis 3 in 1 John 3:*8*.

[16] For "evil one" (*ponēros*) see on 2:13. *Tou ponērou* is not neuter but masculine. *Ho ponēros* ("the evil one") = *ho diabolos* ("the devil"), cp. Matthew 13:38.

[17] We also had "to be of" at 2:16 and 3:8. It speaks of spiritual paternity. The passage should not be read to mean that the devil was the physical father of Cain, whereas Adam was the physical father of Abel. John's language precludes any idea of physical dualism.

[18] *Sphazo* was used in classical Greek of slaughtering animals for sacrifice by cutting the throat. It was used in the LXX for the slaying of Levitical sacrifices. The Latin version reads, *jugulare*, to cut the throat.

[19] Wuest, *op. cit.*, p.151, reminds us that "the inspired writer [John] goes out of his way to use a specialized word to describe the murder of Abel by Cain ... God said to Cain, 'What have you done? The voice of your brother's blood cries unto Me from the ground' (Genesis 4:10). The cutting of the jugular vein would fit that description."

[20] The Greek here is *kai charin tinos esphaxen auton*. "For what reason" translates *charin tinos*. This construction is unusual (using *charin* in the accusative case as a preposition followed by *tinos* in the genitive), and occurs only here in John's writings.

John will go on to say that it was a part of his consistent lifestyle. Folk who do not practice righteousness and don't love their brothers will go to great lengths to quiet those who do.

Because his deeds were evil, and his brother's were righteous – Cain's deeds were evil before he slaughtered his brother. "His deeds were evil" is much the same as saying "he was of his father the evil one." "Evil" (*ponēros*) is the synonym for "evil" that implies not just bad, but trying also to get others to be bad. Such behavior is learned from the devil himself, who has been characterized at 2:13,14, 3:12, and 5:18,19, as "the evil (*ponēros*) one." "The sequence of thought in this section of 1 John is probably significant. It is not that Cain by murdering his brother became a child of the devil; but, being a child of the devil, his actions were [habitually] evil and culminated in the murder of his brother."[21] Some have supposed that the record in Genesis 4:1-8 of Cain and Abel does not tell us explicitly why Abel's sacrifice was acceptable and Cain's was not. God did speak to Cain about "do[ing] well" and "not do[ing] well" (Genesis 4:7); this language, we suppose, is reflected in John's "his deeds were evil." God's words to Cain, "if you do well," imply that Abel was doing right. The other Biblical records agree with this assessment. Jude 11 suggests to us that Cain was guilty of deliberate disobedience. Hebrews 11:4 tells us, "[Abel] had witness borne to him that he was righteous," and also tells us why Abel's sacrifice was better: it was because Abel was determined to be faithful to God that he offered the sacrifice he did. "Faith" is doing what God says,[22] or as John words it, "[Abel's deeds] were righteous." When Abel offered his sacrifice, he was doing things like God revealed they were to be done. Cain was not, and when he could not get Abel to change, he killed him.[23] "Righteousness draws hatred from the devil and hatred from the children of the devil. Darkness cannot tolerate light; immorality cannot tolerate morality; hatred cannot tolerate love; greed cannot tolerate loving sacrifice."[24]

3:13 -- *Do not marvel, brethren, if the world hates you.*

---

[21] Barker, *op. cit.*, p.335.

[22] That Abel acted by faith implies that God had made an unrecorded (in our Genesis' record) revelation concerning acceptable sacrifice, and that this revelation was known to both brothers.

[23] In a sermon on this passage, John Leinbaugh (who taught at that time at Central Christian College of the Bible in Moberly, Mo.) listed the chain of events in Cain's life, and the lessons to be learned. **Events**: (1) *Disobedience*: Cain's sacrifice was wrong because he disobeyed God's instructions. (2) *Sin*: heart trouble (Hebrews 11:4). (3) *Rejection by God* (Genesis 4:5-7). (4) *Dejection of Cain* (Genesis 4:5). (5) *Jealousy* that resents the fact that another, whose acts were righteous, should have God's approval (1 John 3:12). (6) *Hatred* (1 John 3:12-15). (7) *Murder*. **Lessons**: A lack of brotherly love is a deadly evil. When a man's behavior is consistently wrong, it is because there is no repentance. People in the wrong often try to get others to do wrong with them. People in the wrong often take their sin (hatred) out on the righteous.

[24] Adapted from Barker, *ibid*. This is the last mention of either "righteous" or "righteousness" in 1 John. Because the word has been used numerous times between 2:29 and 3:12, some have treated those verses as one major section as they have tried to outline 1 John.

Do not marvel, brethren – "Cease being surprised!"   The Greek forbids the continuance of an action already going on.   Here is one lesson John draws from his illustration of Cain and Abel.   The attitudes and actions of those first two brothers are archetypes of the two families of this world – the children of God and the children of the devil.   And from the history of these two families, men should learn that if they are righteous, they can expect the world's hatred.   Earlier, John has addressed his readers as "beloved" (3:2) and as "little children" (3:7).   Here he uses a word ("brethren") that includes himself together with them as brothers in Christ.   He, too, has felt the hatred of the world about which he speaks.

If the world hates you[25] – When one recalls what Cain did to Abel, it should come as no surprise if Christians are hated by the world.   Jesus warned us that it would be so (e.g., John 15:18, where the very construction used here came from Jesus' lips, "If the world hates you, you know that it has hated Me before it hated you."   See also John 15:19,25; 16:1ff; 17:14).   "Hates" is present tense, continuing action.   Who are the individuals who make up the "world"[26] who are hating John's readers?   Gnostics?   In this context, they are the ones who do not love the brothers.   Unconverted townspeople?   John does not say that everyone in the world will always hate everyone who practices Christian love. Indeed, many instances may be cited from the Scriptures to show otherwise.   However, since hate is the natural reaction of unrighteousness towards righteousness, the Christian ought not be surprised with it happens.

3:14 -- *We know that we have passed out of death into life, because we love the brethren. He who does not love abides in death.*

We know that we have passed out of death into life – Here is another lesson John draws from the illustration of Cain and Abel.   "We" is emphatic; the contrast is between John and his brethren (verse 13) on the one hand, and the Gnostics on the other.   "Know" is *oidamen*, a knowledge that comes by divine revelation.[27]   "We know" implies there was a common awareness of God's revelation concerning these matters among John's readers. "Passed out" or "crossed over" translates the perfect tense verb *metabebēkamen*.[28]   When

---

[25] "If" (*ei*) is a common construction after verbs of emotion like *thaumazo* ("marvel").   There is no doubt expressed by the "if."   The same construction is sometimes translated "that."   (Cf. NEB at Mark 15:44, Pilate "was surprised to hear *that* Jesus was already dead").

[26] See notes on 2:15 on "world."   It is a wicked and disobedient people, Cain's spiritual posterity, a people who are "dead" spiritually (3:14).

[27] We must not forget that Cain's slaying of Abel is still in the background of what John here writes. So is language about the new birth (2:29, 3:9) to which John alludes again in the verb "passed over." Bultmann's characterization (*op. cit.*, p.55) of "we know" as being "arrogant" might be true if there were no Word from God on the subject.

[28] It is likely that John learned this language from Jesus, who on one occasion said, "Truly, truly, I say unto you, he who hears My word, and believes Him who sent Me, has eternal life, and does not come into judgment, but has passed out of death into life" (John 5:24).   The metaphor "crossed over" (the compound Greek verb means "they have stepped over out of") also brings to mind the crossing through the Red Sea (Exodus 15:16), or the crossing over of the Jordan River as the children of Israel entered the Promised Land.

they were immersed into Christ is when they rose to walk in newness of life (Romans 6:4-6). It was part of the new birth experience. That past act of commitment to Christ has enduring effects for the person who continues to practice righteousness,[29] "Out of death into life" says that the readers were once dead spiritually,[30] but no longer.[31] There has been a new birth. They have started over religiously. When they were in death they were not children of God. Now that they have been born again, they are "in[to] life"[32] and are "children of God."

Because we love the brethren – "Because we love" is given as evidence[33] that the readers have passed from death to life. It should be emphasized that spiritual life does not result from loving the brother. Rather, loving the brother results from spiritual life. Galatians 5:22, which speaks of the fruit of the spirit,[34] gives "love" as one of the fruit. So if we love (consistently, habitually, a present tense verb), it is an indication that our spirit is alive and is able to direct our behavior to acts of love. The plural "brothers" is used here in verse 14 and again in verse 16 to show that the reference is to individual persons, and to call attention to the fact that each believer may have multiple opportunities to express his love, first to this individual, then to that, then to another. The Christian loves the very people whom the world hates (verse 13).

He who does not love abides in death[35] – The absence of love (a present participle, denoting continuing, repeated, customary action) is given as evidence a person has never risen

---

[29] It is improper to appeal to the perfect tense verb (with its present continuing results) as being proof of once in grace, always in grace. It is possible to pass back to death again. Revelation 3:5, "I will not blot his name out" (KJV) indicates it was there before being blotted out. Romans 6:16,23 threatens death to the Christian who continues to sin.

[30] Paul spoke of those who were "dead through your trespasses and sins wherein you once walked" (Ephesians 2:1ff ASV). When a man commits his first sin, his spirit dies. It is no longer able to guide and direct the man's behavior.

[31] "He who believes in the Son already has eternal life abiding in him" (John 3:36).

[32] Paul speaks of a similar thing when he writes in Romans 8:10 about a man's "spirit [being] alive because of righteousness (God's way of saving man)."

[33] It is not the cause of "have passed out of death into life." "Love of the brother" is not one of the steps of initial salvation (crossing over).

[34] Notice we have deliberately opted for small "s" at Galatians 5:22, on the studied belief the passage deals with man's spirit from verse 16 to 25a, and (with a possible exception at verse 18) not untill verse 25b is there a reference to the Holy Spirit's direction and guidance of the human spirit.

[35] The KJV reads "he that loveth not his brother," but on the basis of manuscript evidence we should omit "the brother." The gloss may contain the correct idea, being understood from the context, but it evidently was not part of what John originally wrote.

to walk in newness of life.[36]   He is living "in darkness till now" (2:9,11).   Because he died spiritually, his spirit does not function as God intended the spirit of man to function, so fruit such as "love" is conspicuously absent.   The "death" John refers to is spiritual death.   The present tense "abides" emphasizes the idea of a continuing reality.   Ever since he committed his first sin, his spirit has been dead (Romans 7:9-11).[37]   There has been no "crossing over" in this person's case.   "Abides (remains) in death" is a sharp contrast to abiding in God.   The Gnostics who do not love (see verse 10) have not been born again; they do not have spiritual life.[38]

3:15 -- *Every one who hates his brother is a murderer; and you know that no murderer has eternal life abiding in him.*

Every one who hates his brother is a murderer – John is saying that there is not much difference between Cain and the Gnostics.   The expression "every one who ..." has focused attention on the Gnostics each time it has been used since 3:3.   *Miseō*, here translated "hate," may mean simply indifference.[39]   It is the absence of the self-giving concern called love.   It is habitual failure ("hates" is present tense in the Greek) to become involved meeting the needs of our brothers.   The Greek word *anthrōpoktonos* translated "murderer, man-killer" is an old compound, combining *anthrōpos* (man) and *kteinō* (to kill).   It is used in the New Testament only here and at John 8:44 (where it refers to the devil).   It is not the same verb used in verse 12 ("slew").   In meaning, this term is the more generic of the two in that it does not suggest violent passion.   It is not the murder of the needy brother's soul that is intended.   It speaks of snuffing out physical life, just as Cain snuffed out physical life when he killed his brother.   Needs are not met; they pile up one on another, until they overwhelm the needy person and he dies from lack of love on the part of the one who might have helped meet the needs.[40]   Lack of love led to the needy man's death, just as surely as would an act of violent passion.

And you know that no murderer has eternal life abiding in him – "You know" translates *oidate*, a knowledge that comes by revelation from God.   It is common know-

---

[36] "The absence of love is not the reason why he remains in death; it is the sign of his so remaining." Alford, *op. cit.*, p.474.

[37] Spiritually dead is not something men are by nature.   The resulting slavery to sin is something into which men are "sold," not born (Romans 7:14).

[38] The words "abides in death" do not have a reference to how it must be ever in the future.   The "dead" person John refers to could become a convert and follower of Christ and thus cross over into life.

[39] See notes on "hate" at 2:9.

[40] Rather than indifference eventually resulting in the needy person's death, some commentators take "hate" literally and are reminded of Matthew 5:22-30 where Jesus taught that "hate equals murder."   In their hearts, the motives of the hater and the murderer are the same.   If the hate were acted out, it would lead him to commit murder, as it did in the case of Cain.

ledge among John's readers.[41]   John has already used the ideas of "abiding" and "eternal life" a number of times.   "Eternal life" is qualitative and describes the new life which is manifested in Jesus Christ and in which the believer participates now.[42]   The participial phrase "abiding in him" is present tense and has a durative force.[43]

3:16 -- *We know love by this, that He laid down His life for us; and we ought to lay down our lives for the brethren.*

We know love by this – "By this" points forward to what is about to be said in the following "that-clause."[44]   The word "love" (*tēn agapēn*) has a variety of meanings in our language and culture, so John makes sure his readers understand how he is using the term.[45] He does so by calling attention to a wonderful illustration of what love looks like (Christ). "Love" (*agapē*) is doing what is spiritually best for the other person.[46]   "We know" (*ginōskō*) is knowledge that comes by experience.   The verb is a perfect tense, and says "we have come to know in the past and we still know;" that is, we "realize what it is like and what its practical implications are."[47]

That He laid down His life for us – "He" (*eikeinos*, "that One") refers to Christ,[48] and likewise the pronoun "His" refers to Christ.   John's readers had no need to be told Who it was Who laid down His life.   Some of the older English versions translate *hoti* as "because," making this verse say we become aware of what love is, especially "because" Christ died for us.   The newer English versions read "that," making this verse say that what Jesus did is the best example of the kind of "love" John has been talking about.   When

---

[41] Revelation 21:8, likely written after 1 John, lists "murderers" among those who are excluded from heaven. We should not deduce from this passage that "murder" automatically causes the killer to be lost eternally. John is not denying the possibility of repentance and of forgiveness to a murderer; remember, Jesus prayed that his murderers might be forgiven. But "eternal life" is possible only if "everyone who hates (does not love) his brother" repents and turns to Christ. They need to "cross over" from death to life.

[42] For "eternal life," see comments on 1:2, 2:25, and on "life" at 3:14. A man is either saved or lost right now. He is either spiritually alive or spiritually dead. He either does or does not have eternal life abiding in him right now (John 3:36).

[43] "Abiding" is one of John's favorite words to express fellowship or close association. See notes at 2:6 and John 15:4-10.

[44] See notes at 2:3 for "by this (hereby, KJV)."

[45] The KJV reads "the love of God" but in the better manuscripts there is no "of God" at this place.

[46] See notes at 2:9 on "love." Stott (*op. cit.*, p.143) quotes C.S. Dodd as saying that love is "the willingness to surrender that which has value for our own life, to enrich the life of another."

[47] Haas, *op. cit.*, p.91.

[48] See 2:6 and 3:3,5.

we contemplate what Jesus did, we understand that genuine love is active, seeking the other's person's good, and involves a willingness even to sacrifice one's life for one's brother.   The expression "laid down His life" (*tithenai tēn psuchēn autou*) is found nowhere else in the classics or the New Testament, save in John's writings.   John's readers would at once recall the Gospel picture[49] of the Good Shepherd who "lays down His life" for the sheep (John 10:11), and "for this reason the Father loves Me, because I lay down My life ... I lay it down of My own initiative" (John 10:17,18).   John records Jesus as speaking the same words on other occasions (John 13:37,38; 15:13).   The aorist tense "laid down" used here shows that the reference is to a specific event in history, namely, to Jesus' death.[50]   The preposition "for" (*huper*) indicates that there was more to Jesus' death than simply an example of "love."   It was a substitutionary atonement.[51]   The contrast with Cain gives this passage its special point.   Cain's hate took the life of his brother.   Jesus' love cost Him His own life so that others might be helped.   That is what "love" looks like and how "love" acts!

And we ought to lay down our lives for the brethren – Jesus laying down His life for us is an example of real love.[52]   Once we have seen what real "love" is, we are expected to demonstrate it in our lives.   Obviously, our lives cannot be given as the means of atonement for others; only Jesus could do that.   But we can follow His example of loving, if the occasion calls for it.   In fact, "ought" (*opheilō*) speaks of a moral obligation[53] to act as Jesus did.   The pronoun "we" is emphatic; it contrasts with "every one who" in the previous verse.   "We" on our part, as followers of Christ, are contrasted with the behavior of the heretics.   By writing the plurals "we" and "our lives," John makes it perfectly clear this is something expected of each and every one of us.   "Lay down" is an aorist infinitive.   If it were present tense, it might speak of the habit of mind being ever ready to die; the aor-

---

[49] We treat the Fourth Gospel as having been written earlier than the epistle.   See this matter discussed in the Introductory Studies.

[50] Technical works have been written on the meaning of *tithenai*, "to lay down."   Some suppose it means "to lay aside" as one would lay clothing aside; the verb is so used in John 13:4 where Jesus laid aside his garments.   Others have offered "to expose to danger or to risk one's life."   Some writers in an earlier century argued the word represents Christ's sacrificial death as a ransom paid, since in classical Greek Demosthenes used the verb for paying interest, tribute, taxes.   In fact, this is the view expressed by C. Maurer, TDNT 8 (1972) 155-156.   Maurer argues that "to lay down his life" is the Johannine version of Mark 10:45b = Matthew 20:28 (using *dounai tēn psuchēn autou*, the Son of man came "to give his life" as a ransom for many), and that it derives directly from the Hebrew text of Isaiah 53:10 ("makes his life" a guilt offering).   Still others prefer "to give up," and that is how it has been treated in our comments on this passage.

[51] *Huper* has long been acknowledged as having a substitutional meaning.   The affirmation of Jesus' voluntary death in behalf of all is repeated in other language in many passages, e.g., Mark 10:45; Galatians 1:4; Titus 2:14; Hebrews 10:8-10; 1 Peter 3:18.

[52] John is not talking about the giving of our surplus to meet the needs of others.   That is not love.   It is not even giving.   Jesus did not give a spare life.   He gave the only one He had.

[53] For "ought," see notes at 2:6.   The present tense of the Greek verb indicates duration of the obligation.

ist infinitive looks at the once-for-all occasion when such is called for.   John's argument seems to show that though "brothers" specially refers to believers, yet unbelievers are not excluded.   After all, Christ laid down His life not for Christians only, but also for the whole world (2:2).   "Christians must imitate Him in this: their love must be (1) practical, (2) absolutely self-sacrificing, (3) all embracing.   'God commends His own love toward us, in that *while we were yet sinners*, Christ died for us' (Romans 5:8)."[54]

3:17 -- *But whoever has the world's goods, and beholds his brother in need and closes his heart against him, how does the love of God abide in him?*

But whoever has the world's goods – "But" is full of meaning.   Not many of us are called to lay down our lives in some deed of heroism, but we constantly have opportunities for smaller sacrifices as we share our possessions with those in need (cf. James 2:15,16).   "The world's goods" (*bios*, as explained at 2:16) refers to the ordinary things whereby physical life is sustained – food, clothing, wealth, possessions, medicine.

And beholds his brother in need – What the brother needs is food, or clothing, or a job, or a place to stay.[55]   That's what we who have these things to share[56] must share with those who have not.   No sharing, no love.   Two factors lead to an obligation (an inescapable responsibility) to demonstrate our love – (1) we have the means to help, and (2) we see the need.   "Beholds" (*theōreō*, a present tense, continuous action) is more than a casual glance.   It involves the mind as well as the eyes, and it is "contemplation" long enough to appreciate and understand the circumstances of the case.

And closes his heart against him – "Closes" is *kleiō* in the aorist tense and could picture the slamming of a door, or the snapping of a lock.[57]   The NASB has a marginal note on "heart" (*splagchna*) which reads "inward parts," i.e., the intestines.[58]   The unloving person is pictured as deliberately squelching any sympathy or desire or feelings he might have had when he first observed the need.   He just deliberately quits thinking about it.

---

[54] Plummer, *op. cit.*, p.132.

[55] "Having need" (present participle) recalls the vivid picture like James 2:15ff describes.

[56] Someone has said, "Everyone who can afford to buy this book comes into the category of 'those who have the world's goods'."   Commentators who treat the expression as meaning "excessive wealth" have missed John's point.

[57] A similar word was used at Matthew 16:18, "I will give you the keys (*kleis*) of the kingdom."   There is a fellow out in the cold who says, "I'll freeze if you don't let me in," and you just shut the door, turn the key in the lock, and walk away.   "Against him" is literally "away from him," and pictures moving away and turning one's back on the needy brother.

[58] Many languages have a similar figure of speech – though they may speak of liver, stomach, spleen, gall, abdomen, etc.   "I've got a gut-feeling ..." is a familiar way of expressing the same idea.

How does the love of God abide in him? – The genitive "of God" may be objective, describing our love for God (2:5,15, 4:20); or it may be definitive or qualitative, describing a love like God's love; or it may be subjective, referring to love for us that comes from God (as at 3:1). The latter one suggests that even God has difficulty loving a stingy man! The second one fits the context that has been describing what real love is and how it acts. Since God's love is self-giving, sacrificing for the good of the other, if we are hard-hearted and grasping, we don't love like God loves. If we take it as objective (and in light of 1 John 4:20, many opt for this view), the idea is that if we don't love our brother whom we have seen, what evidence can we give that we love God like we claim we do?

*3:18 -- **Little children, let us not love with word or with tongue, but in deed and truth.***

Little children – John's parting admonition on this point with respect to brotherly love and benevolence is a fatherly one. The word "children" may again be intended to call attention to the theme of divine sonship (3:1ff).[59]

Let us not love with word or with tongue, but in deed and truth – John is not condemning kind words which are comforting and cheering on those occasions when words are all that are called for. What John is saying here about loving in deed and truth (not just words) remind us of what is said about works in James 2:14-16. When there are needs that require actions to alleviate those needs, words are not enough. If our love is to be like Christ's love, or like God's love, it will have to be genuine ("in truth," i.e., our loving actions should match God's divine revelation about love) and it will have to be active ("in deed"). Another of fellowship's distinctive rewards and blessings is that because their spirits are alive, Christians are able to love the brethren and be lavishly benevolent.

D. Answered Prayer.   3:19-24a

> *Summary*: Verse 19a seems to conclude the previous paragraph. Then at verse 19b, we have come to the fourth of fellowship's distinctive rewards and blessings: constantly receiving from Him what we ask. This blessing is conditioned on "confidence" before God so that that we may approach Him in prayer (verses 19b-21), and is also conditioned on obedience (verses 22-24a).

*3:19 -- **We shall know by this that we are of the truth, and shall assure our heart before Him,***

We shall know by this – Here is another of John's characteristic "by this we know" statements (see notes at 1 John 2:3), though this differs slightly from the others in that,

---

[59] Some older English versions read "My little children," but there is no "my" in the better manuscripts here at 3:18 like there was at 2:1.

in this instance only, the verb "know" is future tense.[1]   Perhaps the future tense anticipates any moment in the future when such knowledge is needed; perhaps such knowledge comes every time we love in deed and truth.[2]   To what does "by this" point?[3]   When the various issues have been studied, one of two possible options is most likely.   Either:

(1) Verse 19a begins a new paragraph, with the result that "by this" points forward to "for God is greater than our heart."[4]   Or

(2) Verse 19a is a complete sentence and is the conclusion of the previous paragraph, with the result that "by this" in verse 19a points back to "love in deed and truth" in verse 18.[5]   Then another sentence and the new paragraph is begun at verse 19b.[6]

The CEV's wording, "When we love others, we know that we belong to the truth" reflects

---

[1] There is a manuscript variation at this place.   The Textus Receptus and the Majority Text reflect manuscripts that have the verb "we know" in the present tense.

[2] Future tense can refer to one act in the future, or continuous action in the future.   Thus this knowledge could be continual in the future, or it could point to a coming time of crisis when knowledge will be needed.

[3] Before we can, with any confidence, affirm to what "by this" here in verse 19 points, attention must be called to the fact that John's intended meaning in verses 19 and 20 is difficult to determine due to textual differences and to questions about the meaning of certain key words.   The numerous variant readings found in these two verses betray the felt difficulty of sorting out the grammar and intended meaning even in the early days of the church.   The problems have been summarized thus: (1) Does verse 19 begin with *kai*, thus connecting this paragraph to what precedes?   (2) Does "by this" point backward or forward?   (3) How shall we punctuate these verses?   (4) How shall we interpret *kardia* ("heart")?   (5) What is the meaning of the verb (*peisomen*) translated "assure" (or "persuade," NASB margin)?   (6) How shall we translate the two clauses in verse 20 which begin with *hoti* (or perhaps the first one begins with *ho ti*)?   (7) What characteristic of God is being emphasized when John tells us that God is "greater than our heart" (verse 20)?   When we come to the appropriate place in each of the verses, we shall attempt to answer each of these questions.

[4] The chief objection against this view is the difficulty of explaining how a knowledge of God's greatness serves as evidence we are of the truth.

[5] A few commentaries have called attention to 1 John 4:6 as evidence that "by this" may indeed look back.   Caution must be exercised when making this argument because 4:6, where the Greek is *ek toutou* ("from this"), is the lone place (save for a poorly attested variant reading here at 3:19 which also has *ek toutou*) where the Greek for "by this" is not *en toutō*.   Perhaps that change at 4:6 was intentional because in that place the reason by which we know is to be found in what precedes.

[6] The chief thing against this view is that it requires us to treat "by this" in a manner not consistent with how it is used elsewhere in 1 John.   John has written "by this (we know)" numerous times in this letter.   In other passages, when he identifies what the reason is by which we know [something], he worded it in several different ways.   At times, he simply made a statement (as at 4:2 and 5:2).   At other times, he introduced the reason by writing "if" [such and such is so] (as at 2:3), or "because" (as at 4:13), or "by" (as at 3:24).   We would expect to find a similar construction here to which "by this" points.   In those verses where the Greek behind "by this" is *en toutō*, the reason or way "we know" follows the phrase "by this we know."   So, in this place, our first impulse would be to look for something that follows "by this" which would explain or give the reason for "by this we know."   Our only option is "because God is greater than our heart, and knows all things" at the close of verse 20.   In view of the objection to this view given above in footnote #4, perhaps we should treat "by this" here in verse 19 differently than in the other places it occurs.   Remember the verb tense here (future tense) is different than we have become accustomed to when we read "by this we know."

the second option, and several things may be said in its favor.   "We shall know" (*ginōskō*, to know by experience) might be easier explained if we look back to "loving in deed and truth" as the evidence, rather than forward to "God is greater than our heart and knows all things."   There is some evidence that verse 19 once began with *kai* ("and").   There is no "and" in the NASB because Nestle's 23 edition of the critical Greek text does not have *kai*, but the fourth edition of the UBS text does carry the *kai* in square brackets.[7]   If verse 19a actually begins with *kai*, we would have a further reason for believing "by this" points backward, for the "and" at the beginning of verse 19 would tie verse 19a to verses 10-18.

That we are of the truth – The expression "(to be) of the truth" was used at 2:21,[8] where "truth" referred to the teachings of Jesus Himself, as now reflected in the apostolic writings of the New Covenant Scriptures.   At that place we called attention to what is recorded in John 8:31,32 to help us understand how "truth" is used in John's writings.   In 1 John 2:4 Christ's commandments are equated with "truth."   In addition we recall that the children of God have been brought forth "by the word of truth" (James 1:18).   John has been driving home the point that God's truth is ascertained by appealing to what Jesus and His apostles taught, not by appealing to what the Gnostics were teaching.   To be "of the truth" (verse 19) is a different matter than to tell the truth, or to speak truthfully about our love (verse 18).   Loving in deed and truth (verse 18), something Jesus taught, may well be the evidence we belong to the truth.   Doing what God's revealed truth requires would be a sign we belong to that realm.   The interpretation that puts a period after "truth," making verse 19a a complete sentence, relies partly on the fact there were no punctuation marks in the older manuscript copies of 1 John, either papyrus or uncial.   Men add the punctuation marks to both the Greek text and our English versions in an attempt to make what was written more understandable to the reader.[9]

---

[7] Neither the uncials Vaticanus and Alexandrinus, nor the Vulgate or Coptic versions, nor Clement carry the "and." Sinaiticus, Ephraemi, the Old Latin and Syr.H., the Byzantine family of manuscripts, and numerous church fathers do have the "and." The brackets around *kai* indicate the dubious validity of the reading, while the apparatus at the bottom of the page gives it a C rating. That is, there is a considerable degree of doubt whether the text [with *kai*] or the apparatus [without *kai*] contains the superior reading. Of course, if there was no "and" in what John wrote, then a case can more easily be made that "by this" could point forward to something said later in verses 19 or 20.

[8] The word "truth" also was used at 1 John 1:6,8 and 2:4.

[9] A brief history of punctuation marks is given by Robert Milligan, *Commentary on Hebrews* (St. Louis, MO: Christian Board of Publication, 1875), p.127. Punctuation marks were invented by men and began to be used in secular Greek writings about the 3rd century AD. They began to be used by Christian writers about the middle of the 5th century, and not till the 10th century AD did the custom become universal. Here in 1 John, our English versions punctuate in such a manner as to reflect the decisions of the translators concerning the answers to all the other questions (see footnote #3 above). One option is to put a period at the end of verse 19a (which requires "by this" to be taken as looking back). Verse 19b then begins a new sentence which runs through verse 20, "And we shall set our hearts at rest in His presence whenever our hearts condemn us, for God is greater than our hearts, and He knows everything" (author's translation). Other options can be found by studying the various English versions. The KJV, by putting a period after "Him" at the end of verse 19, makes two sentences out of verses 19 and 20. The NASB and RSV read verses 19 and 20 as one long sentence, with a semicolon after "us" in the middle of verse 20, thus dividing the verses into two ideas. The NEB offers three alternatives (two in the margin). Two of the alternatives

And [we] shall assure our heart before Him – The preferred punctuation of the passage starts a new sentence and the new paragraph with this clause.   "And we shall assure our heart before him in whatever ...."   "And" serves to connect the new idea with what has just been written.   We have derived the subject "we" from the first-person plural personal ending on the verb *peisomen*.   "Heart" in the Greek is singular because the Greek idiom so requires.[10]   "Our" is plural and the Greek says each person has a "heart" that may from time to time need persuading.   What is the "heart"?[11]   The Biblical "heart" (*kardia*) often refers to what we call the "mind."   It is the place where thoughts are formed and put into action.[12]   It is not uncommon to find "conscience"[13] offered as a translation for "heart" in our modern English versions, but we should be slow to talk about the conscience when offering an explanation for this passage, even though that is the conclusion of many commentators.[14]   What does *peisomen* (future tense of *peithō*, and translated "assure" in the NASB) mean?   This is one of the major problem terms within this section, for on it

---

attempt to make the phrase "because God is greater than our hearts" (verse 20b) to be the explanation of "by this we know" (verse 19a).   The NIV puts a period after "us" in the middle of verse 20, thus making two separate sentences out of verses 19 and 20 (but not quite the same two ideas as suggested by the KJV's two sentences).   What all this means is that we are free to change the punctuation if it will help us develop a train of thought that fits the text and the context.

[10] The KJV has "hearts" plural.   The Greek manuscripts are much divided between singular (Vaticanus, Peshitta Syriac) and plural (Sinaiticus, Ephraemi, and the Textus Receptus).   Good English would have the plural ("hearts") because the subject is in the plural.

[11] This is the fourth issue raised in footnote #3 above.   Though the NASB has "heart" both in verse 17 as well as in verses 19-21, the Greek word is different in verse 17.   Nevertheless, there may be an underlying thought connecting what verse 17 says with what verses 19-21 say.   When the heart condemns any attempt at meeting the needs of the needy, the heart needs to be reasoned with!

[12] See John 13:2, where the devil put it into the "heart" of Judas to betray Jesus.   See 1 John 5:1, where with the "heart" man believes.   See Acts 7:23, where something "entered his mind" (*kardia* in the Greek).   See James 4:8, "purify your hearts."

[13] "Conscience" is an innate faculty that prompts us to do what our mind thinks is right, and criticizes us when we do what our mind thinks is wrong.   See this teaching at Romans 2:15.

[14] Thayer (*op. cit.*, p.326) lists 1 John 3:20 as one of but three or four Biblical instances where "heart" might mean "conscience."   It should be remembered that Augustine influenced Western Christianity for over 1000 years.   He treated "heart" as being the "conscience," and he treated "God is greater than our heart" as meaning that God is more rigorous in His judgment of our sins than our own conscience is.   Many churchmen since Augustine's time (including Calvin) have simply repeated his conclusions.   The punctuation of these verses in the KJV tends to treat "heart" as being synonymous with "conscience," and many of the older commentaries were based on the KJV.   Some have modified Augustine's views, so that while conscience is still a suitable equivalent for "heart," "assure/quiet" is chosen as an acceptable rendering for *peisomai*, and "God is greater than our heart" is an expression of mercy rather than rigor.

Defenders of "conscience" as the meaning of *kardia* also appeal to the fact that the Hebrew language had no word for "conscience" and so used both "heart" (*kardia*) and "spirit" (*pneuma*) to designate what we call "conscience" (Proverbs 4:23, 28:14; Ecclesiastes 7:22).   Greek thought came up with the word (*suneidēsis*) to designate "conscience" and Paul and Peter both use it, and perhaps so also does John (John 8:9 in the TR/KJV, "convicted by conscience").   That John follows Hebrew usage, using "heart" for "conscience" here in 3:19, is the point to be proven, not just assumed.

much of the meaning of the whole passage turns.[15]   The regular meaning of *peithō* is to "convince" someone that something is true (so that he agrees with us), or to "persuade" (appeal to) someone to do something (so that he thinks or acts as we wish).[16]   When the "heart" condemns, we convince the "heart" it is wrong.   "We" shall persuade our hearts, John wrote.   "We" are distinct from our "heart," and have control over what goes on in our "heart."[17]   Of what are we convincing our heart?   When the verb "persuade" occurs, it is usually followed by a clause which defines the truth of which the person is to be convinced.   We think that is exactly what verse 20 does.   "At those times when our heart condemns, we shall convince our heart that God is greater than our heart and knows all things."   We persuade our heart that its condemnation (verse 20) is in error,[18] and we do this persuasion "before Him," that is with the awareness that God is watching what we do.[19]

3:20 -- *In whatever our heart condemns us; for God is greater than our heart, and knows all things.*

In whatever our heart condemns us – Originally Greek was written in all capital letters with no breaks between words.   It is therefore not possible to be certain about the first three Greek letters of this verse -- whether they are one word (*hoti*) or two (*ho ti*).   Thus when the words are divided it might read, *hoti ean kataginōskē hēmōn hē kardia*, or it might be read, *ho ti ean kataginōskē hēmōn hē kardia*.[20]   If we treat *hoti* as one word, it is a con-

---

[15] This is the fifth issue raised in footnote #3 above.

[16] *Apeithō*, a negative form of the verb used here and often translated "disobedience," literally speaks of a stubborn refusal to be persuaded.   Whether or not the word here even means to assure, or to conciliate, or to pacify, or to set at rest, is debated by the grammarians.   Some appeal to Matthew 28:14 as one place where it likely means "to pacify" or "to assure."   Others appeal to Acts 12:20; 2 Corinthians 5:11; and Galatians 1:10.   After studying all these passages Alford concludes "[This verb] does not mean 'quiet' or 'assure,' except insofar as its ordinary import, 'persuade,' takes this tinge from the context" (Alford, *op. cit.*, p.478).   "The substitution of 'assure' for 'persuade' appears to be somewhat violent, for it is a meaning which the verb (*peithein*) does not in itself possess" (Plummer, *op. cit.*, p.135).   At best, if the word has the meaning "pacify," that usage is rarely found in our literature.   Every effort then, it seems, should be made to explain John's words as though he wrote "persuade" or "convince."

[17] Compare "bringing every thought captive to the obedience of Christ," 2 Corinthians 10:5 (ASV).

[18] If we treat verse 20 as the truth of which our heart needs convincing, there is no need to supply "that we are of the truth" after "persuade" as some propose.

[19] "Before Him" stands first in the clause, so it has an emphasis on it.   The future tense "we shall persuade" (how we translate the verb) does not refer to the final judgment, but refers to how we stand before His all-seeing eye during the coming days of our present life.

[20] This is the sixth issue raised in footnote #3 above.

junction and would be translated either "because [for]"[21] or "that."[22]   If we treat the three letters as two words, we have *ho ti*, the neuter form of the relative pronoun *ostis* ("who/which").[23]   This is the solution reflected by the NASB's "in whatever," the RSV's "whenever," and is the choice adopted by most modern commentators.   The NASB has two pronouns, "our" (our heart) and "us" (condemns us); however the Greek has the first person personal pronoun only once.   It may be taken with the verb, "the heart condemns us," or with the noun "our heart condemns."   We opt for the latter.   That makes the new sentence that began in the middle of verse 19 say this: "Whenever our heart condemns (helping the needy [cp. verse 17]), we shall persuade our heart that God knows better (and He has required helping the needy)."   *Kataginōskein* occurs in the New Testament only here (verses 20, 21) and at Galatians 2:11.   It is basically a legal term which means "to judge against, to give sentence against, to condemn."   What seems to be pictured is our mind giving sentence against helping the needy.   That is the time Christians need to "persuade" their hearts concerning what is Godly behavior.[24]

For God is greater than our heart – Though the Textus Receptus and KJV do not have the word at the beginning of this clause, on overwhelming manuscript evidence we insert a *hoti* at the beginning of this clause.   As before, we have two choices of translation for the conjunction, either "because" or "that."   If we translate it "that," this phrase explains the truth of which we convince our hearts.[25]   Who has the greater authority, our own heart (mind), or the sovereign God?   When it comes to how we shall behave, whose directions shall we give priority?[26]

---

[21] This is how the KJV translators understood the passage should read.

[22] Some have tried to make the verse read "we reassure our heart that if it condemns us, God is greater than our heart ...."   However, treating these first three letters as the conjunction *hoti* (meaning either "because" or "that") makes it difficult to discern what might have been John's train of thought in verses 19 and 20.

[23] See Galatians 5:10 and Acts 3:23 for New Testament examples of the relative pronoun *ostis* followed by *ean*.

[24] This is the seventh issue raised in footnote #3 above.   Those who approach this seventh issue differently than we have will have different explanations for "our heart condemns us."   One supposes that "condemns us" refers to "doubts" or "questions" about our standing with God (are we "of the truth"?)   Another supposes that "condemn" pictures the conscience pronouncing a verdict of guilty against the erring Christian.   Stott (*op. cit.*, p.145) is typical of this last suggestion: "If the RSV/NIV are correct in translating this first phrase of verse 20 'whenever our hearts condemn us' – the suggestion seems to be that it may not be either an unusual or an infrequent experience for the Christian's serene assurance to be disturbed."

[25] If we translate this conjunction as "because," then this phrase becomes the truth by which we pacify or assure our hearts.   See the discussion above on *peisomen* ("assure" or "persuade").

[26] We are now into the issues involved in what we have called issue seven in footnote #3.   Those who think John is writing about "our conscience condemning us" debate whether "God is greater than our heart" means He is more rigorous in His judgment than our hearts are, or whether He is more merciful in His judgment than our hearts are.   If we translate *peisomen* as "persuade" we would opt for rigorous.   If we translate it "assure," we would opt for merciful.   None of this debate is necessary if we take the Greek words "heart" and "persuade" in their primary meaning, as we have advocated above in our notes.

And knows all things – This clause seems intended to explain in what sense God is greater than our hearts. Our hearts are by no means infallible. The condemnation the heart sometime offers, that this or that helpful act to benefit the needy is really not necessary, is hardly the right behavior in God's sight. He is the One who is omniscient and infallible. We are to persuade our hearts that God's rules should be followed, rather than our negative thoughts.

Let's sum up what verses 19 and 20 seem to say. Verse 19a finishes the previous paragraph and treats brotherly love and benevolence as evidences that let us know we are of the truth. Verse 19b begins a new sentence and a new paragraph. John tells his readers of the need to persuade their hearts (whenever our hearts condemn the idea of doing some helpful act to benefit the needy) that God knows better than their hearts what is the right thing to do.

3:21 -- *Beloved, if our heart does not condemn us, we have confidence before God.*

Beloved – John is speaking to those who are loved by God (see 3:1,2), who have forgiveness and have been born into God's family.

If our heart does not condemn us – Literally, "if the heart does not condemn." Whereas in verse 20 there was but one personal pronoun in the phrase like this one, in this phrase there is no personal pronoun in the Greek (though "the" modifying "heart" could be translated as the pronoun "our").[27] In the present tense verb "condemn," the heart is pictured as not habitually condemning, i.e., it is not habitually telling us "You don't need to help the needy!"[28] It does not habitually condemn because we have persuaded our heart (verse 19) that such benevolence is exactly what their heavenly Father expects.[29]

We have confidence before God – As we learned at 2:28, "confidence" (*parrēsia*) means courage, confidence, assurance, lack of fear, even boldness, especially in the presence of persons of higher rank.[30] It is because of this phrase, taken in the light of what follows and what precedes, that in our summary of this point in the outline of 1 John we speak of

---

[27] It likely is not saying "our conscience condemns us" because of the sin in our lives, as the English translation might on first sight suggest.

[28] We should treat "heart" and "condemn" in this verse the same way we explained the same words in verses 19 and 20.

[29] Several writers have said that the force of *ean ... mē* ("if not") *kataginōskē* is "if (our heart) *no longer* condemns us." In other words, a resolution of the tension outlined in verse 19b-20 is presupposed.

[30] "The word rendered confidence stood in ancient Greece for the most valued right of a citizen in a free state, the right to 'speak his mind' ... unhampered by fear or shame." (Dodd, *op. cit.*, p.93.) Hebrews 4:16 encourages the believer to approach the throne of grace with confidence. Such confidence is something that we will need to have at the Parousia (2:28), but it is something that we also want now so that we can pray to God.

"confidence" as being one of the conditions of answered prayer.[31]   "Before God"[32] pictures the Christian as standing face to face with God in prayer.   We have fearless confidence that we are His beloved children, and that He will welcome and hear our requests.[33]

3:22 -- *And whatever we ask we receive from Him, because we keep His commandments and do the things that are pleasing in His sight.*

And whatever we ask we receive from Him – *Kai* ("and") closely connects this verse with the preceding.[34]   It is because of the way this verse begins that we talked about prayer in the previous verse ("confidence before God").   Both the verbs ("ask" and "receive") are present tense describing the Christian's habitual experience: it is continual asking and continual receiving.[35]   *Aiteō* ("ask") is a request being addressed to a superior.   While "whatever we ask" seems to be unlimited, the context might lead us to think the Christian is asking for wisdom to know what is best as he sets about to help the needy person he has observed (verse 17).

Because we keep His commandments – This is the *first of two reasons* why we regularly receive the answer to our prayers.[36]   It speaks of habitual obedience to God's commands.[37]   God does not hear sinners (John 9:31),[38]   but He does hear those who habitually obey His

---

[31] The following verses will give obedience as another condition.

[32] The Greek preposition translated "before" here is different from the one used in verse 19.   *Pros* (used here) serves here to express direction, a friendly relationship toward.   "We do not fear to talk to God."   It has been called the "face-to-face" preposition.   Compare "the Word was with [*pros*] God" at John 1:1.

[33] Those who interpreted *peisomen* as "assure" rather than "persuade" (verse 19b), "heart" as "conscience," and "condemn" as a "guilty conscience" (verse 20), have a slightly different explanation for this verse.   It often goes like this: If we are guilt-ridden and conscience-stricken because we have not "assured" our hearts of God's mercy and compassion, then rather than enjoying His presence, we will flee from His presence.   We don't pray; we won't ask anything from Him; and He has no opportunity to answer any prayer, because none has been offered.

[34] "This verse is so closely connected with the preceding one, that not more than a comma or semicolon should be placed between them."   Plummer, *op. cit.*, p.137.

[35] John's words remind us of our Lord's promise, where the same two verbs occur: "Ask, and it shall be given to you ... for every one who asks receives" (Matthew 7:7,8).

[36] The second reason is stated in the following clause.

[37] On "keep His commandments," see notes at 2:3.

[38] "The Lord is far from the wicked, but He hears the prayer of the righteous" (Proverbs 15:29).   See also Psalm 34:16 (quoted at 1 Peter 3:12), 61:18,19; Job 27:8,9; Isaiah 1:11-15.

commands.[39]   The next verse will specify the kind of commands John has in mind which we must guard and carefully keep.   There are conditions that must be met before God hears and answers prayers.[40]

And do the things that are pleasing in His sight – This is the *second of the two reasons* why Christians regularly receive answers to prayers.   If the previous phrase spoke of the "commandments" of God, what "things" are left to be covered by this phrase?   Perhaps this phrase refers to those areas of life where there is no "thus saith the Lord."[41]   In such cases, the Christian's habitual course of action must be motivated by the desire to be well-pleasing to God.[42]   "In His sight" translates a compound word (*enōpion*) made up of "to see" and "in" – thus "a penetrating gaze."[43]   It reminds us that God watches what people on earth are doing.   Do love!   Do be obedient!   Do act so as to please Him!   Do pray!   All these exhortations lie just beneath the surface of this paragraph.

3:23 -- And this is His commandment, that we believe in the name of His Son Jesus Christ, and love one another, just as He commanded us.

And this is His commandment – This is what God commands.   The demonstrative pronoun "this" points forward to and is explained by the "that" clause which immediately follows.   In verse 22, John wrote of "commandments" (plural), which God's children must obey if they would receive what they ask of Him.   Now he writes "commandment" (singu-

---

[39] Children who live confidently in communion with their parents are not hesitant to make requests of their father.   (May I have the car?   May I have an advance on my allowance?   Etc.)   Children who have shown by their past behavior they respect the rules and guidelines laid down by their parents are often granted exceptions/permissions when they ask for something unusual.   The parents know they can trust their children, so say "yes."   How like our heavenly Father!

[40] Of course, James takes it for granted that other conditions of answered prayer have been met. This very passage in 1 John identifies two such conditions.   To learn about other conditions, the clear teaching of Jesus on this subject can be studied with profit.   See Mark 11:24; Luke 11:9, 18:1-8; John 14:12ff, 15:7, 16:23, and Jesus' own example (Mark 14:36 and parallel).   The same combination of "confidence (boldness)" and answered prayer is found in 1 John 5:14,15.

[41] Most Protestant commentaries on this verse have a statement like this: Obedience is the condition of answered prayer, not the meritorious cause.   That statement is a short repudiation of Roman Catholic theology which, at this place, distinguishes between keeping the commandments of God (which they identify as being the moral law in the Decalogue) and doing what is well-pleasing in his sight (which is interpreted as a reference to the counsels of the Gospel which are extra and therefore [in their system] meritorious).   Such an identification of the commandments of God, which treats the Law of Moses as still a binding statute upon Christians, is certainly contradicted by Hebrews 7:12-10:9, a passage that plainly shows that the covenant given at Mt. Sinai has been replaced by the New Covenant validated by Jesus' blood shed on Calvary.

[42] "Pleasing in His sight" says there is human behavior that delights God.   He is pleased or deeply satisfied to see it.   He is the most important audience before whom men perform their moral actions.

[43] "In His sight" is common vernacular found in the papyri and LXX, meaning "in God's eye," as in Hebrews 13:21. (Robertson, *op. cit.*, p.227.)

lar), and then names two.   Perhaps all His commands are summed up into one short, memorable statement.

That we believe in the name of His Son Jesus Christ – Repeatedly in 1 John we are reminded that the child of God must habitually "keep His commandments."   It is not surprising, then, to find that the verb "believe" is a present tense in a number of ancient manuscripts.[44]   Continuing belief in "Jesus the Christ, the Son of the Living God" is imperative in the face of the claims the Gnostics were making as they tried to lead the Christians astray.[45]   This is the first use of the verb *pisteuō* ("to believe)" in 1 John, but it occurs several times from this point onward.[46]   The verb *pisteuō* is followed by different constructions in the Greek, and each has a slightly different nuance.   Sometimes it is followed by a direct object (4:16); sometimes it is followed by a simple dative (here and 4:1);[47] sometimes it is followed by a prepositional phrase (5:10,13);[48] sometimes it is followed by a "that" clause (5:1,5).   In the Bible, "name" frequently stands for the character and authority and all that a person himself is and does.   To believe the "name" of someone means to believe all that his name stands for.   "In respect to Jesus it means the revelation about Him, His claims for His person and work: His deity, sonship, incarnation, lordship, Christhood, his saviorhood."[49]   A Jesus who is not the Son of God

---

[44] Since the time of Westcott and Hort until recently, a heavy reliance was placed on Vaticanus. A reading found in Vaticanus was often accepted as being original, even if other important manuscripts agreed on a variant reading. Since Vaticanus has an aorist subjunctive here (*pisteusōmen*) it is not surprising to read in many commentaries "the aorist subjunctive probably represents the original reading of the Greek text." However, since Sinaiticus, Alexandrinus, and Ephraemi all support the present tense, and a present tense verb would make excellent sense in this context, we would not be surprised if the present tense was what John wrote. The somewhat parallel text, John 6:29, uses a present tense "believe."

[45] Those who adopt the aorist reading for the verb "believe" usually point back to the time the readers were converted. Since the verb tense in moods other than the indicative refers only to the *kind* of action (not to the *time*), to talk about the past will not do for a subjunctive mood verb. All subjunctives picture an action in the future, the difference being this – a present tense subjunctive speaks of continuous action in the future, whereas the aorist tense subjunctive points to a single act in the future. A proper explanation of the aorist subjunctive would be this: when the Gnostic comes to you in the future attempting to lead you astray, don't listen! Instead, on that future occasion, "Believe in the name of His Son Jesus Christ."

[46] See "believe" in 4:1ff; 4:16; 5:1,5,10 [thrice],13, and "faith" in 5:4. Some have called attention to the emphasis on belief from hereon in the letter as they have tried to discover what John's outline was. On the basis of the emphasis on belief, some have begun a new major point of the outline at this place and have treated belief in His name as the dominant theme of the rest of the letter.

[47] "Believe" followed by a simple dative (personal) means to give credence to a person and accept him as speaking the truth.

[48] "Believe" followed by a prepositional phrase is an "obedient faith." See, for example, John 3:16, "whosoever believes in Him ...."

[49] Roberts, *op. cit.*, p.99. For "Son," see notes at 1:3. For "Christ," see notes at 2:1,22. "Jesus" calls attention to the historic person, the incarnate son of God, the one born at Bethlehem, the very One who died on the tree. The choice of all these terms to identify the one John is talking about was no doubt deliberate, countering the heretical positions concerning Jesus.

and the Messiah would not be able to save the readers from their sins or to bring them into fellowship with God.

And love one another, just as He commanded us – Jesus gave this commandment to love one another while He was in the upper room (John 13:34, 15:12,17), the evening before His crucifixion.   The verb "love" is present tense; it is something the follower of Jesus is to do regularly, exactly like He commanded.[50]   For a number of verses John has worded it "love the brother."   Now he words it "love one another."

> The second command confronting the child of God in the Gnostic crisis is that we love one another.   To understand the vital necessity of obedience to this command, we must keep in mind the prayer of Christ (John 17), and the insistence of the apostles (e.g., Ephesians 4:1-6) that the church must be united if it is ever to do the will of God or be worthy of the call of the Gospel.   The controversy brought about by the introduction of Gnosticism was furious, and a century after John wrote, threatened to tear the church permanently asunder ... In the Gnostic crisis facing John's readers, the commands which the Father sets before His children are "belief" and "love." Obedience to the first is necessary if the Christian Gospel is to survive at all. Obedience to the second is necessary if the family of God is to remain united rather than torn asunder by the quarrel over the Gnostic heresy.[51]

3:24 -- *And the one who keeps His commandments abides in Him, and He in him.   And we know by this that He abides in us, by the Spirit whom He has given us.*

And the one who keeps His commandments abides in Him – In the outline we are suggesting for 1 John, the first part of verse 24 concludes the previous paragraph.   It is the one who habitually keeps God's commandments, like the ones just highlighted in verse 23, who continues to have fellowship with God (i.e., abides in Him[52]).   Both here and in John 15:10 the condition of continual communion with God (i.e., abiding in Him) is obedience.   Abiding in Christ is not some mystical experience such as the Gnostics advocated.   No one may dare to claim that he abides in Christ, or Christ abides in Him, unless he is habitually obedient to the fundamental commandments which John has been repeating and repeating: belief in Christ, love for the brethren, and steadfast efforts to overcome sin in the everyday life.

And He in him – The Christian remains in communion with deity, and deity remains in communion with the Christian.   The concept of a mutual abiding, mentioned here in this epistle for the first time, we in Him and He in us, is derived ultimately from our Lord's alle-

---

[50] For *kathōs* ("just as"), see notes at 3:3.

[51] Gill, *op. cit.*, p.91,92.

[52] For "abides in Him," one of the great keynotes of the epistle, see notes at 2:6 and 2:28.   Actually in this place there is some question concerning to whom the personal pronoun "His" refers, since the antecedent is found in the previous verse, but that verse speaks of both God and Christ.

gory of the vine and the branches (John 15:1ff), where it is Christ who dwells in His own, and they in Him. In what sense God (or Christ)[53] abides in the Christian John will go on to explain in the next paragraph. In the case of the apostles, He inspires their words as they deliver God's message (3:24b). In the case of the individual Christian, the indwelling Holy Spirit (4:4) is alluded to.

IV. FELLOWSHIP'S ENCOURAGEMENTS. 3:24b-5:17

Summary: Each of the paragraphs following serves as an encouragement to continue the fellowship with God and one another the readers already share. Each paragraph gives a reason why they should continue in the fellowship.
- First is the Holy Spirit's inspiration of the the apostles' message (3:24b-4:6).
- There is God's love to believers, resulting in their love toward their brethren (4:7-12).
- There is the apostles' eye-witness testimony concerning Jesus (4:13-16a).
- There is a loss of fear of punishment resulting from perfect love (4:16b-21).
- There is encouragement through victory won by faithfulness (5:1-4)
- There is God's testimony concerning eternal life (5:5-12)

A. The Inspiration Of The Holy Spirit   3:24b-4:6

Summary: This is the beginning of a new paragraph and a new section of 1 John, entitled "Fellowship's Encouragments." One reason to remain in the fellowship is because of the source of the message that produces that fellowship. The apostles are Holy Spirit inspired, and those who know God listen to what the apostles say. The world listens to the false prophets (4:4). Children of God listen to apostolic declarations.

3:24b -- **And we know by this that He abides in us** – "By this" points to what follows, and focuses attention on what is about to be said. In contrast to the spirit who animates and speaks through the Gnostic false prophets, the Holy Spirit who prompts the apostles' preaching and writing offers a true statement about Jesus. "We" and "us" in both this and the next phrase likely refers to the apostles of Jesus,[1] such as John who is writing this let-

---

[53] While we may struggle to identify which member of the Godhead is indicated by the personal pronouns, it is very likely that the difference between God and Christ would have been unimportant to John, for in John 17:21 Jesus prays that "they may be in *us*" and in John 14:23, Jesus said to His apostles, "If any one loves Me, he will keep My word, and My Father will love him, and *we* will come to him, and make Our abode with him."

[1] A number of commentators have chosen to treat the "Spirit whom He has given to us" in this passage as a reference to the indwelling Spirit, a gift given to all believers (Acts 2:38). And apparently 4:4 speaks of a measure of the Spirit that all of John's readers have, by which they have overcome the allurements of the false prophets.   *(Continued on the next page)*

ter. "Know" (*ginōskō*) is a knowledge that comes by experience. The apostles, empowered by the Holy Spirit (Acts 1:8), at times being inspired to speak in foreign languages as they evangelized people of different nationalities (as on the day of Pentecost in Acts 2:4,11), and more often being inspired to speak by inspiration in a language known both to them and their audience, thus, certainly had a personal "knowledge" of the Holy Spirit's presence and work in their lives and ministry. "Abides in us" reminds us of Jesus' promise to the apostles that the Holy Spirit would abide in them (John 14:17).

By the Spirit whom He has given us – "Spirit" is a reference to the Holy Spirit. Though John does not call Him "Holy" Spirit in 1 John, the NASB rightly capitalized the word.[2] This is the first time in this epistle He has been called "Spirit"; earlier, He was alluded to as the "Holy One" (2:20). The aorist tense "given" points to a certain time, a definite act, in the past. If indeed "us" refers to the apostles, then the time the Spirit was given to them was when they were baptized with the Holy Spirit on Pentecost (Acts 2:1ff; 2 Peter 1:3).[3] It was the baptism with the Holy Spirit that empowered them for their apostolic mission.[4]

However, a strong argument can be made that the Holy Spirit *in the apostles* is what John is writing about in the beginning of this paragraph. (1) He speaks about the Spirit "abiding in them" and that reminds us of Jesus' promise to the apostles (John 14:16,17). (2) In John 14:26, 15:26, 16:7b, it is the apostles who were promised the Spirit who would inspire them and be the source of the truth they were to teach. (3) It was the apostles who spoke as the result of the "anointing" in 1 John 2:20,27, the result of which gift was available to John's readers. If our present paragraph speaks of the Spirit in the apostles, it strongly parallels what John wrote in 2:20,27. (4) John's language at this place presupposes his readers have knowledge about the Spirit and His work about which John writes. If we are limited to the Fourth Gospel for the source of such knowledge, it is likely the apostles whom John refers to as "us" in verse 24b since the Fourth Gospel says little about the indwelling Spirit (John 7:37-39 and perhaps 20:22). (5) The contrast between the spirit of truth and spirit of error (4:6) seems to point to some activity like "inspiration." Inspiration would fit the apostles, but not all Christians. (6) Is the witness of the Spirit in 5:7 the same as the witness here in chapter 3:24b? Doesn't that point to the apostles? (7) If this paragraph (3:24b-4:6) deals with the reason why the apostles' message can be trusted, it displays the same connection of ideas found in 4:12,13, where the eyewitness testimony which the apostles can give is alluded to. Through the years since the Reformation, some Protestant commentators have opposed the idea that this paragraph is limited to the apostles because Roman Catholic writers took that position.

[2] Socinus, who was not a trinitarian, treated *pneuma* ("spirit") here as synonymous with an attitude or disposition (similar to love) which is given by the Father to His children.

[3] The apostle Paul, not one of the original Twelve, also affirms that he had been "empowered" to be an apostle (1 Timothy 1:12, where the word translated "strengthened" in the NASB is the same root word translated "power" at Acts 1:8).

[4] Commentators have to be careful at this place, especially those who think the indwelling gift all Christians receive is the topic. The Gnostics emphasized subjective criteria to prove their claims. What John writes here (these commentators insist) must not be thought of as introducing a subjective criterion by which his readers may "know" their standing. Comments such as "The Spirit manifests Himself objectively in the lives of the Christian as He helps them confess Christ, overcome the Gnostics, and listen to the apostles," are offered lest we substitute one subjective experience for another.

"By" translates *ek*,"out of" or "from."[5]   The Spirit's presence and work is the source from which the knowledge that "He abides in us (apostles)" flows.   In John's writings, the Father and the Son are both regarded as the source of the Spirit (John 15:26, 14:26, 16:7b), so "He" may be a reference to either.   The verses numbered as chapter 4:1-6 in 1 John continue the topic here introduced.

4:1 -- *Beloved, do not believe every spirit, but test the spirits to see whether they are from God: because many false prophets have gone out into the world.*

Beloved – The encouragement to remain in the fellowship with God and the apostles, begun in 3:24b, continues.   This and the following verses are an amplification of the sentence with which 3:24 ends.   This vocative ("beloved") has the effect of reminding the readers they are the objects of God's love and of John's love, too.[6]   Three times in chapter 4 (verses 1,7,11) John uses this address.   He writes these encouragements out of love.

Do not believe every spirit – The Greek construction forbids the continuation of an action already going on: "Stop believing every spirit!"[7]   Do not confide implicitly in every one who professes to be under the influence of the Holy Spirit.   There are unholy spirits who can inspire men, and some deceivers, in order to dupe their listeners, will claim their evil-spirit inspiration is actually the Holy Spirit at work.[8]   John reminds his readers there are two spiritual spheres in this world.   One is either with God, or against God.   One is either in fellowship with God, or in fellowship with the devil.   If they continue to listen to the false teachers, they will forfeit their fellowship with God.

---

[5] It would be possible to translate the Greek "by the Spirit of which He has given us," a partitive genitive, meaning "some of which." (Plummer, *op. cit.*, p.139.) Our translators have treated the genitive "whom" as being genitive by attraction, rather than partitive.   Plummer argued that John regularly inserted the preposition *ek* when he was treating a genitive as partitive, and there is none before "whom."

[6] Compare 2:7 and 3:2,21.

[7] *Mē panti pneumatic pisteuete*.   The negative *mē* negates the adjective "every," not the verb.   Greek word order has the negative particle immediately preceding the word it negates.   For the verb "believe" see notes at 3:23.   *Pisteuein* followed by the dative always means to accept as true the statement someone makes.   Cp. John 8:31.

[8] "Spirit" is a word that has a number of different meanings.   Thayer (*op. cit.*, p. 522) says that the word "spirit" as used here refers to "one in whom a spirit is manifest or embodied, hence one actuated by a spirit, whether divine or demonical."   Paul found the source of false doctrine in demons who actuated or inspired the false teachers who propounded heresy (1 Timothy 4:1, "doctrines of demons").   We suppose John has reference to demonic spirits when he warns about the false teachers whom they inspire.   At Corinth, where prophets functioned, Paul commands the listeners to "pass judgment" on the messages the prophets spoke (1 Corinthians 14:29).   The reality of demonic spirits is everywhere assumed, whether it be in the Gospels, Acts, or in the New Testament epistles.   "Christians need to be reminded that demonic activity can penetrate their congregations" (Marshall, *op. cit.*, p.204).   "Still today there are many voices clamouring for our attention, and many cults gaining widespread popular support.   Some of them claim some special revelation or inspiration to authenticate their particular doctrine.   There is an urgent need for discernment among Christians.   We are often too gullible, and exhibit a naive readiness to credit messages and teachings which purport to come from the spirit-world" (Stott, *op. cit.*, p.153).

But test the spirits to see whether they are from God – The plural "spirits" probably reflects the fact there were numerous "teachers" claiming divine inspiration for their Gnostic message.[9] "Test" is a present imperative. "Continually (or regularly) put the spirits to the test!" is a positive command.[10] This test is to come before "belief" is granted to what the teachers say. In the next verse John gives the "acid test," the criterion or standard by which such spirits should be tested.   What is implicit in John's argument is that the Holy Spirit would not contradict in later prophets the revelation He had already given "from the beginning" (2:24) through the apostles. Their teachings and revelations were to be the standard of comparison.[11] "Test(ing) the spirits" is not the responsibility only of church leaders (as the Roman Catholic Church teaches), but is the responsibility of each individual Christian, leader or not.[12] "Whether" introduces an indirect question: This spirit, is it from God or not? There are at least two "spirits" in the world – the Holy Spirit (aka. the "Spirit of God," verse 2), and the spirit of the antichrist (4:3).

Because many false prophets have gone out into the world – Here is why critical assessment of religious teachers is absolutely imperative.[13] The danger is not imaginary, or potential; it already exists. The "false prophets" of this verse are the same people identified as "many antichrists" in 2:18. A "prophet" is one who speaks by inspiration.[14]

---

[9] It is doubtful that the plural "spirits" means that each individual teacher was "host" to numerous spirits. There are many "evil spirits" (demons), but that is not likely the point in this context where John uses the singular "spirit of error" (4:6) and "the *spirit* of antichrist" (4:3).

[10] "Test ... to see" comes from one Greek verb, which refers to examination and evaluation, like a metallurgist uses an acid test to determine if his metals are genuine or fake. For example if a metal coin stands the test, it is acceptable (*dokimos*, 2 Corinthians 10:18), otherwise it is rejected (*adokimos*, 1 Corinthians 9:27, 2 Corinthians 13:5-7). Every Athenian was subjected to an examination (*dokimasia*) as to his origin and character before he could hold office.

[11] When someone claims to be a prophet, his message should be tested by comparing it with the word of God (cp. 1 Thessalonians 2:4; 5:20,21). The same verb *dokimazō* is used at 1 Corinthians 12:10, "distintuishing (discerning, testing) of spirits," where such an ability was one of the miraculous "spiritual gifts." See also 1 Corinthians 14:29. Paul describes one of the spiritual gifts which only a few believers had, whereas John refers to an ability to "pass judgment (discern)" which any Christian could exercise, whether or not he had the "gift of distinguishing of spirits."

[12] Both the verbs "believe [not]" and "test" have second plural personal endings. "You" (plural), the individual readers, are to test the spirits.

[13] Those who claim to be inspired must be "tested." One gets the idea that an inspired teacher was not a regularly experienced event in the congregations to which John writes. Not every Christian had the genuine gift of prophecy (1 Corinthians 12:29). John's language implies that from time to time, "prophets" (some "true" and some "false") would appear on the scene and seek opportunity to speak at the public assembly of the Christians. But when they spoke, their message could deceive and lead the Christians astray (2:26).

[14] A prophet could be a prophet of God, inspired by the Holy Spirit. One could be a "false prophet," inspired by some other spirit. True prophets spoke, as we read in 2 Peter 1:21, as they were "moved (borne along) by the Holy Spirit." One of the miraculous spiritual gifts which resulted from the Holy Spirit's influence was the gift of prophecy (see 1 Corinthians 12:10). That John is thinking of those who exercise the gift of prophecy when he speaks about "spirits from God" is clear from the next statement about "false prophets" who also have gone out into the world.

Roberts reminds us "the gift of prophecy" (one of "spiritual gifts" given by the Holy Spirit, 1 Corinthians 12:8-10) played an important part in the spread of the gospel in the early church (1 Corinthians 14:24ff; Acts 11:27, 13:1, 21:9,10; Revelation 10:7, 16:6, 22:9).[15] In diametric contrast to a true prophet who was Holy Spirit inspired, a "false prophet" could be one who was inspired by some other spirit, and who claimed falsely to be God's prophet,[16] or one whose message is not in harmony with what God says because it is inspired by the "spirit of error" (4:6).[17]   "Into the world" suggests these Gnostic teachers,[18] like missionaries (cp. 2 John 7), have spread all over the Roman world, endeavoring to win converts to their cause.   The perfect tense verb *exelēluthasin* ("have gone out") indicates that they went out in the past, they are still abroad going up and down the land, and the results of their preaching and teaching tours are being felt at the time John writes.

4:2 -- By this you know the Spirit of God: every spirit that confesses that Jesus Christ has come in the flesh is from God;

By this you know the Spirit of God – As has been the customary use of *en toutō*, "by this" refers to what follows, and gives the criterion by which the readers can test the spirits. "Hereby *you* know" is slightly different from "Hereby *we* know" with which we are familiar from 1 John.   The verb "know" (*ginōskete*) could be a present imperative (know this!) or a present indicative (you may know this).[19]   John has already written two imperatives in verse 1 (Do not believe! and Test!) so perhaps he is here issuing another command, this one identifying the precise test the readers are to employ in this situation.   "Spirit of God" means that He is the Spirit who is present and inspiring the speaker to speak (cp. verse 1).

Every spirit that confesses that ... is from God – "Confess" (*homologeō*) means "to say the same thing."   A teacher or prophet who is inspired of God ("is from God") says the

---

[15] Roberts, *op. cit.*, p.104.

[16] Even more dangerous than those false teachers, who had never been Christians at all, are those who profess to be members of the church.

[17] "Enthusiasm [an old word used to describe an altered state of consciousness] is no guarantee of truth" (Law, *Tests*, p.265).   Have the Gnostic teachers fallen into trances, "prophesied" [against Jesus], and claimed the message was from God?

[18] John does *not* say the Gnostic missionaries were Christians who "have gone out of the church." 2:19 does say that non-Christian heretics had separated themselves from the public assembly of the Christians.

[19] Since every other occurrence in the epistle (2:3,5, 3:16,19,24, 4:13, 5:2) of the phrase "by this we know" is followed by an indicative verb, many expositors prefer to take this as indicative also, even though in this place the verb is second person ("you"), whereas in all the other occurrences it is first person ("we").

same thing about Jesus that God says, and says it openly and boldly.[20]   The words "Jesus Christ has come in the flesh" is the fact or truth being confessed.[21]

Jesus Christ has come in the flesh – It is probable that this phrase should be translated "confesses that Jesus is the Christ come in the flesh," thus treating it as a double accusative.[22]   In this way both His Messiahship and the reality of the incarnation of Jesus are emphasized.   It is not that the Christ came "into" the flesh of Jesus, but Jesus came "in the flesh."   He "became flesh, and dwelt among us" (John 1:14).   When He came, Jesus was the Christ from the first, and not as adoptionism taught (that the Christ came upon the human Jesus at His baptism, and left before the human Jesus was hung on the cross).   The clause "Jesus ... has come" implies the pre-existence of the Son whom the Father sent into the world.   "In the flesh" (*en sarki*) means "in human form."   Jesus came in the flesh (His actual humanity), not in a phantom body as the Docetic Gnostics taught.   "Has come" translates a perfect tense Greek participle *elēluthota*,[23] which implies that Christ Jesus' coming in the past still influences the present.   The flesh assumed by the Son of God in the incarnation has become His permanent possession.   He had no human body before He came.   He had a body just like other human bodies during His stay on earth.   Because of His resurrection, He now has a glorified human body.   Three elements are included in this test by which to discern true inspiration: (1) that the pre-existent One named "*Jesus*" was involved, (2) that from the moment He came, He was the *Christ*, and (3) that from the moment He came He was fully incarnate in the *flesh*.   Anyone who claims inspiration for his message while denying any of these three elements does not have the Holy Spirit as the

---

[20] Though the demons (evil spirits) recognized the deity of Jesus during His ministry (e.g., Mark 1:24, 3:11, 5:7,8; cf. Acts 19:15), they did not acknowledge or "confess" Him, save on occasion when terrified. What a contrast when the Holy Spirit inspires men such as the apostles to speak.   He leads them to honor the Son in what they say about Him.   Jesus taught His apostles that it would be the Holy Spirit's particular ministry to them both to testify to and to glorify Him (John 15:26, 16:13-15; cf. also 1 Corinthians 12:3).   It is understandable that the same Spirit, through whom the miraculous conception of Jesus took place (Matthew 1:20; Luke 1:35), should bear faithful witness to it as He prompted the apostles to tell about Jesus' coming in the flesh.

[21] Sometimes the verb "confess" is used absolutely (John 12:42).   Usually, the verb "confesses" is followed by the object which gives the substance of the thing confessed.   Sometimes this object is introduced by the particle "that" (*hoti*) beginning a noun clause (1 John 4:15).   At other times the confession may be expressed by an infinitive (Titus 1:16) or by a supplementary participle following the name of the person confessed (2 John 7 and here at 1 John 4:2).   Sometimes a single accusative follows the verb (1 John 1:9, 2:23).   In other cases the person confessed and the thing confessed about him are both expressed by an accusative case (a double accusative as in Romans 10:9 and John 9:22).

[22] For a similar formula, but using a present tense verb for "come," and in the negative, see 2 John 7. Stott (*op. cit.*, p.156) argued against the translation that has "Jesus Christ" as the one coming in the flesh: "John does employ the combined name 'Jesus Christ' (1:3; 2:1; 3:23; 5:20) but to speak of 'Jesus Christ' as having 'come in the flesh' would be a strange 'theological anachronism' (Findlay) since it was not until after the incarnation that He is called 'Jesus'."

[23] The correct text (attested in Sinaiticus, A,C,K,L) is a perfect active participle, not the infinitive (*elēluthēnai*) found in B and the Vulgate.

cause of his inspiration.   Such a false presentation of Jesus should be swiftly and certainly repudiated!   There are variantly worded confessions found in the pages of Scripture. Each of them is important.   But in an anti-Gnostic context, this test is absolutely vital.[24]

4:3 -- *And every spirit that does not confess Jesus is not from God; and this is the spirit of the antichrist, of which you have heard that it is coming, and now it is already in the world.*

And every spirit that does not confess Jesus is not from God – As in verse 2, "every spirit" refers to teachers who are inspired (or who claim inspiration).   In this case, the false teachers are referred to and John flatly affirms they are not God's mouthpieces.   The spirit who prompts the false teachers is not the Holy Spirit whom God sent to His genuine messengers.   For "does not confess Jesus" the KJV reads "confesseth not that Jesus Christ is come in the flesh."   The simple accusative *ton Iēsoun* is undoubtedly the true text.[25] The article before Jesus ("the Jesus") in the Greek must not be overlooked, for it may well be the article of previous reference.   "The Jesus" whom the false teachers did not confess is the very "Jesus" which the previous verse identified.   Or sometimes when the name "Jesus" is used, it puts emphasis on His historical earthly ministry.   John may here be contradicting the doctrine of the Gnostics, for those "false teachers did not confess Jesus when they ascribed the work of healing, not to Jesus, but to the aeon Christ."[26]   "Does not confess" is a translation of *ho mē homologei*.   It is unusual to find the negative adverb *mē* in a relative clause with an indicative mood verb.[27]   "The adverb *mē* indicates the *contradiction* of the true confession, whilst *ou* would only express the simple negation."[28]

There is a variant reading for "confess" that requires separate discussion.   Instead of *mē homologei* ("does not confess"), a few ancient sources have *ho luei* ("loose, break, destroy") with no negative particle.   The text thus reads "every spirit that *looses* (or separ-

---

[24] This is the third criteria by which genuine faith can be distinguished from Gnostic aberrations.   The first two given by John were "the practice of righteousness" (2:29, 3:10), and "love the brethren" (3:14, 4:8). The truth known and received "from the beginning" (2:24), which teaches all these things, is the touchstone.

[25] The words "Christ is come in the flesh" are omitted in A,B, Vg. Copt.   The variants found in some manuscripts, *Iēsoun Christon, kurion, elēluthota en sarki*, are scribal attempts to expand what must have seemed an abrupt phrase.   When two phrases or clauses have the same word order (as is true of verses 2 and 3, save for an article before *Iēsoun* in the second), it is permissible to include words from the first where they are missing in the second.   That is what most scribes who added words in verse 3 have apparently done.

[26] Joh. Ed. Huther, *Critical and Exegetical Handbook on the General Epistles of James, Peter, John, and Jude* (Winona Lake, IN: Alpha Publications, 1980 reprint), p.581.

[27] Other examples of *mē* with an indicative mood verb are found at 2 Peter 1:9 and Titus 1:11.   *Ou* is the regular adverb for use with the indicative.

[28] Huther, *ibid.*

ates) Jesus."[29]   Somewhere about the time of Irenaeus (AD 180) who quotes this whole passage, the verb *luein* became a technical word for the Gnostic heresy which "separated" Jesus from the Christ.   Perhaps the scribal change was made in the heat of the 2nd century controversy against Gnosticism.

And this is the *spirit* of the antichrist – The Greek reads *touto estin to tou antichristou*. The demonstrative "this" (*touto*) refers back to the spirit that does not confess Jesus.   After the neuter gender definite article "the" (*to*) we must supply a neuter noun.   The word often supplied in such constructions is *pragma* (thing, matter, a thing done), the "neuter of essence or character."[30]   Our translators have suggested "spirit" which is a neuter word found in the immediate context.   The "spirit [from Satan]" who will animate/inspire/ prompt antichrist is the same spirit who has been inspiring the Gnostics (false prophets) whom John is combating.[31]   In Paul's writings, false doctrines were "doctrines of demons"

---

[29] The materials textual critics must sift and evaluate include these facts.   No Greek manuscript (save for a marginal note in one Greek manuscript dating from the 10th century) and not one version besides the Old Latin and the Vulgate supports *luein*.   The Latin form of *ho luei* (*qui solvit*) is found in the Old Latin version, in the Vulgate, in the Latin translations of Irenaeus (*Haer.* III.16.8) and Origen (on Matthew 25:14), Tertullian (*Adv. Marcion* V.xvi), in Clement of Alexandria, and in one quotation by Augustine.   Socrates the historian (AD 440) charged the Nestorians with tampering with the text and ignoring the reading "who severs Jesus."   However, several church fathers, even Latins, quote the passage as it stands in the Greek Texts (see the critical apparatus in the UBS *Greek New Testament*, p.820.)   One can also study the quotation of pertinent paragraphs from the fathers both in Latin and Greek in Alford, *op. cit.*, p.485-486. From about AD 140-150, Polycarp's epistle (*Phil.* VII), alluding to this passage from 1 John, has "confess." Metzger (*Textual Commentary on the Greek New Testament* [New York: United Bible Society, 1975], p.713) accepts the reading *luei* "because of overwhelming external support."   Few other textual critics have followed his lead, nor has this commentator found the support "overwhelming;" in fact. it is just the opposite.

[30] Alexander, *op. cit.*, p.333.

[31] A denial of Jesus as incarnate Lord is an activity of antichrist.   Contemporary scholars who ridicule and deny the deity of Jesus are displaying the precise same attitude that the coming antichrist will display as he opposes Jesus Christ.   Kistemaker (*op. cit.*, p.326) has a provocative application of John's test for a true teacher.   "Without exception, liberal theologians refuse to accept the biblical doctrine that Jesus Christ always has been, is, and will be the Son of God, that He came from heaven to redeem His people, that He took upon Himself our humanity yet remained truly divine, that He rose bodily from the dead and ascended in His glorified body to heaven, and that He will return at God's appointed day in the same body in which He ascended.   If you compare the teaching of these theologians with God's Word, you will notice that their opinions are based on human philosophy and not on Scripture.   Ask them what they think of the Christ, then go to your Bible and study the teachings of Scripture (Matthew 16:15).

Then there are members of sects.   In pairs they canvass the neighborhood, ring your doorbell, and announce that they are missionaries – even though they do not carry Bibles.   When you listen to them, you soon learn that they do not bring the teaching of Christ.   The apostle John advises, "If anyone comes to you and does not bring this teaching (of Christ), do not receive him into your house and do not give him a greeting" (2 John 10).

What does John mean?   He means that you may receive members of the sect into your home only when you intend to teach them about Jesus Christ.   Tell them that you are happy in the Lord, because He is your Savior; and that you are pleased to introduce them to Jesus Christ.   Then you will be a missionary for the Lord and you are in control of the situation.   But if you do not intend to teach these visitors about the Lord, receive them not into your home!"

(1 Timothy 4:1). So also we picture John claiming the same source for the doctrines taught by the Gnostics.

Of which you have heard that it is coming – No doubt many of the readers have heard this from John himself when he previously preached and taught among them.[32]   In one of the earliest letters of the New Testament to be written, the coming of antichrist was already an integral part of Christian teaching (cf. 2 Thessalonians 2:5).[33]   The coming of antichrist into the world is as real and historical as the coming of the true Christ into the world.[34] "The present tense 'is coming' indicates antichrist's appearance is a thing fixed and determined, without any reference to time."[35]

And now it is already in the world – While the real/final antichrist was still future when John wrote this epistle, the "spirit of antichrist"[36] had already come and was active in the world.   That spirit was the one prompting the message taught by the Gnostic false prophets.

4:4 -- *You are from   God, little children, and have overcome them; because greater is He who is in you than he who is in the world.*

You are from God, little children – "You" (emphatic *humeis*), "you" in contradistinction to the anti-Christian false prophets.[37]   By the phrase "are from God" (*einai ek*) John seems to denote more than merely belonging to.[38]   It suggests primarily spiritual origin.   This language reminds the readers they have been "born again" into God's family, they are children (*teknia*, little born ones) of God.

---

[32] Less likely is the suggestion John is referring to the previous passage about antichrist in this letter (2:18ff).   "Heard" is perfect tense, not aorist as in 2:7.   They heard it in the past, and it is still in their mind.

[33] Antichrist's appearance and activities are also described in Revelation 17-18, but we doubt that the writing of Revelation preceded the writing of 1 John.

[34] The verb *erchetai* ("is coming") is used of the Second Coming of Christ.   Here it is used for the future coming of antichrist.

[35] Alford, *op. cit.*, p.486.

[36] John wrote "now" (*nun*) and "already" (*ēdē*) in this passage, i.e., "even now."   "Already" hints that something more may be expected to follow.   John does not say antichrist himself is already in the world. When Paul wrote to the Thessalonians, "the man of lawlessness" was still to be revealed in the future, yet "the mystery of lawlessness" was already at work, albeit under restraint (2 Thessalonians 2:3-8).   Similarly, antichrist's appearance is future, but the "spirit of antichrist" is already at work when John writes.   With similar meaning, John has said there are already many antichrists abroad (1 John 2:18,22).

[37] As in 2:20, John passes abruptly from the false teachers to his true children by using an emphatic pronoun.   In the Greek text, each of these three verses (4,5,6) begins with an emphatic personal pronoun: "you" (verse 4, *humeis*), referring to his Christian readers in general; "they" (verse 5, *autoi*), referring to the false teachers; and "we" (verse 6, *hēmeis*), referring to himself as representative of the authoritative apostles (Stott, *op. cit.*, p.157).

[38] For "are from (to be of)" see on 2:16 (page 43, footnote #61).

And have overcome them – The reference in "them" (masculine in the Greek) is to the false prophets (4:1) who have been overcome. "Overcome" is a perfect tense verb.[39] The overcoming was an event that happened in the past, with present continuing results. Other people may have been led astray by the false prophets who denied 'Jesus as the Christ come in the flesh,' but not John's "children." By using the perfect tense verb John is expressing calm confidence of continuing and final victory.[40] When the false teachers came to their town preaching their message, John's readers "overcame" them by remaining true to the Christianity which they had been taught from the beginning.[41]

Because greater is He who is in you than he who is in the world – "He who is in you" is likely to be the "Spirit of God" (verse 2).[42] Just as the Holy Spirit was at work in the apostles (3:24b), so the indwelling gift of the Holy Spirit was at work in the lives of individual believers. The victory was not won just by their own strength; the Holy Spirit gave them help to overcome. "So the early Christians were taught: 'He may grant you to be strengthened with might through his Spirit in the inner man, and that Christ may dwell in your hearts through faith' (Ephesians 3:16,17). See also 2 Timothy 1:7."[43] The Spirit often works through the word as He strengthens Christians in their faith.[44] "He who is in the world" is probably the spirit of antichrist (verse 3), the spirit of error (verse 6), rather than being a reference to the devil who has not been specifically named in this context.[45]

---

[39] Elsewhere *nikaō* is used of overcoming Satan and the hostile world (John 16:33; Revelation 2:7, 5:5, 12:11, 17:14, 21:7).

[40] "John constantly teaches that the Christian's work in this state of probation is to conquer 'the world.' It is, in other words, to fight successfully against that view of life which ignores God, against that complex system of attractive moral evil and specious intellectual falsehood which is organized and marshalled by the great enemy of God, and which permeates and inspires non-Christianized society" (Liddon). Quoted by Plummer, *op. cit.*, p.144,

[41] Is this why the false teachers have felt obliged to depart, as 2:19 declares? "Overcome" probably does not mean that the false teachers were physically driven out of the church; rather, their effort to change the beliefs of the Christians has failed. Folk who try to change a church (to another belief system) will leave when it becomes obvious to them they have failed in what they were trying to accomplish.

[42] "He" is masculine in the Greek. Because God (or Christ? See notes at 3:24) was said to abide in them "by the Spirit whom He has given us," some commentaries affirm the pronoun "He" probably refers to God.

[43] Roberts, *op. cit.*, p.108-9.

[44] See "anointing" in 2:20,27. See Revelation 2:1,7, etc., where the Spirit speaks to all the churches through each letter. See also Hebrews 3:7, 9:8, 10:15, where the Spirit speaks to the Hebrew readers through words of Scripture.

[45] Though the devil is the ruler of this world (John 14:30), the god of this world (2 Corinthians 4:4), and also the father of these lying teachers (3:10), the reference here is probably not to the devil personally, but rather to one of his tools. Not many verses suggest the devil himself invades men, but rather one of his demonic helpers. (There was an occasion when "Satan entered into Judas" [Luke 22:3, John 13:27], but we do not know for certain whether this means tempted him, possessed him, or what.)

"World" refers to our globe/universe, the sphere of operation for Satan and his demonic helpers. By saying "in the world" instead of "in them," John indicates the false prophets belong to the world (a fact he makes clear in the next verse). "Greater" likely refers to relative power (power v. more powerful), and the "power" of the spirit of antichrist is assumed when we are told that the Holy Spirit is "greater." Stott remarks that "we may thank God ... that the Holy Spirit is 'greater,' and that by His [help] we may overcome all false teaching."[46]

4:5 -- *They are from the world; therefore they speak* as *from the world, and the world listens to them.*

They are from the world – The pronoun "they," referring again to the false prophets, is in emphatic position, and contrasts with "you are from God" in verse 4, and with "we" in verse 6a. In verses 5 and 6, John contrasts not only the false prophets and the true apostles ("they" and "we"), but also the different audiences who are listening either to the false prophets or the true apostles. One audience is "from the world"; the other is made up of "children of God." As noted earlier, "world" has several nuances of meaning. Here it is used with a different meaning than it had in 4:1,3 where it had the broad connotation of a place of human life. Here it means a world of people and spirits who are hostile to God (see 3:1,13). "The false prophets derive their principles, zeal, goals, and existence from the world of hostility in which Satan rules as prince (John 12:31)."[47] How different the false prophets are from Jesus and His disciples who are "not of the world" (John 17:14ff).

Therefore they speak *as* **from the world** – "Their teaching is derived from its wisdom,[48] not from the revelation which God has given in His Son."[49] What they say is "from the world." They speak as the world speaks; their teaching belongs to this world; they speak the language of the world; they talk about worldly things. They do not acknowledge Jesus, the Christ (verses 2,3).

And the world listens to them – This statement implies some success by the Gnostics in raising a following, and explains the reason for their popularity. The people of this world recognize their own kind of people and love to listen[50] to a message that affirms their own

---

[46] Stott, *ibid*.

[47] Kistemaker, *op. cit.*, p.328.

[48] John does not say the false prophets speak "concerning the world." To "speak ... of" (*lalein ek*, the Greek used here) is not the same as "to speak concerning" (*legein peri*).

[49] Brooke, *op. cit.*, p.114.

[50] The verb *akouō* ("to hear," "to listen to," "to give attention to" [Thayer]) signifies intentional, attentive hearing, and may imply that the agent agrees to or obeys what is said, as is the case here.

worldly outlook.[51]   "The false teachers are successful 'in the world' because their thinking, their theology, is accommodated to the world's beliefs.   Their teaching is philosophically congenial to the prevailing currents of the day."[52]

4:6 -- *We are from God; he who knows God listens to us; he who is not from God does not listen to us.   By this we know the spirit of truth and the spirit of error.*

We are from God – "We" (emphatic) is contrasted with "you" in verse 4, or "they" in verse 5.   If "you" referred to all John's readers, and if the "they" means the false teachers, the "we" must be true teachers, namely the New Testament apostles and prophets.   "You are from God" in verse 4 declares the divine origin of his Christian readers.   Here John claims that the true teachers such as he draw their inspiration from God.[53]

He who knows God listens to us – The present tense of *ho ginōskōn* ("he who knows") suggests that "such knowledge is recognized as progressive and not complete."[54]   "John has already spoken of those who 'know God' (2:3,13, 3:1,6), defining this knowledge in terms of recognizing His commandments, observing them, and avoiding sin."[55]   Now he further defines what it means to "know God" by affirming such people "listen to us."[56]   For "listens" (*akouei*), see comments on the same verb at verse 5; for the identity of "us" (the apostles of Jesus), see comments on "we" at the beginning of verse 5.   In other words, to know God intimately is always linked with hearing and obeying what Jesus' original apostles have taught from the beginning.   They were the ones whom He promised that the Spirit would guide into all truth.   "The fact is that he is not speaking in his own name, nor even in the name of the Church, but as one of the apostles, who were conscious of the spe-

---

[51] "These words remind us of Jesus' statements in passages like John 15:19, where He speaks of the world loving its own and hating the disciples who have been chosen out of the world."   (Roberts, *op. cit.*, p.109.)   A professed Christian may determine much about his Christian life by asking himself what kind of persons desire his friendship and wish him for a companion.

[52] Barker, *op. cit.*, p.341.

[53] "Here again we hear the magisterial tone of Apostolic authority which is so conspicuous in the Prologue (1:1-4)."   (Plummer, *op. cit.*, p.145.)   One of the reasons for believing in the inspiration of New Testament writings is that the writers, such as John does here, claim Holy Spirit inspiration for themselves.

[54] M.R. Vincent, *Word Studies in the New Testament* (Wilmington, Del: Associated Publishers and Authors, 1972 reprint), p.540.

[55] Roberts, *op. cit.*, p.110.

[56] John here echoes the words of Jesus: "He who belongs to God hears what God says" (John 8:37 NIV) and "My sheep listen to my voice ... and they follow Me" (John 10:27 NIV), and again, "everyone on the side of truth listens to Me" (John 18:37 NIV).   Just as Jesus came from above and spoke from above (John 3:31), so did His apostles speak.

cial authority bestowed upon them by Jesus Christ."[57]   While John's readers were not to believe "every spirit" (4:1), John has now identified the "spirit" they can trust, and to whom they should listen. We must remember that John is giving a test to distinguish, not the children of God from those who are not children of God, but the spirit of truth from the spirit of error.   Here John is extending the rule of verse 3 by which false teachers may be recognized.   The test of a prophet of God is not only that he "confesses Jesus as the Christ come in the flesh," but that his teaching is in total harmony with the essentials of faith and practice as taught by all the apostles.

He who is not from God does not listen to us – "From God" has alluded to the source of inspiration behind the message (4:1). "He who is not from God" is one of the false prophets (4:3).   John here observes that the false prophets do not pay much attention to the apostles of Jesus, or to the message they delivered.   In this language there is an implicit appeal to his readers to resist the message of the heretics, or they, too, will end up being not from God.

By this we know the spirit of truth and the spirit of error – "We" is the translation of the first person plural personal ending found on *ginōskomen*, "we know."   This unemphatic form includes John's readers, all of God's children (verse 4).   Some have translated the present tense *ginōskomen* as 'we get to know.'   It takes a little longer process of intelligent study to hear the apostles' message (than it does to listen to any teacher's "confession").   "By this" is not the usual *en toutō*, but *ek toutou*, "out of" or "from this," indicating a source.   Perhaps this subtle change of prepositions tells us that the pronoun in this place points backward to what has been said in this whole paragraph.   "By this" draws a deduction from what has been written.   The way to detect God's inspiration (the Spirit of truth[58]) versus the inspiration by unholy spirits (the spirit of error[59]) is by applying the tests just given.   What they say about Jesus (verse 3) and their attitude toward the body

---

[57] Stott, *op. cit.*, p.158. Such a claim as John here makes would sound like the height of arrogance if it were spoken by individual Christians.   But they are genuinely true when it came to the apostles.   "The phrase 'he ... heareth us' cannot be referred to the traditions of the church (or to the Papacy) without doing violence to John's insistence in this Epistle upon primitive apostolic doctrine, quite apart from the historical question whether the consensus of Christian opinion has been a reliable criterion of truth." Stott, *ibid.*, p.159

[58] Most translators parallel the two instances of "spirit" in this verse, and treat "spirit" as meaning the same thing here in verse 6 that it did in verse 1.   However, some capitalize the first use of "spirit" making "Spirit of truth" another name for the Holy Spirit.   For the title "Spirit of truth" as applied to the Holy Spirit, see John 14:17, 15:26, 16:13. All these passages from the Fourth Gospel were Jesus' words to the apostles; therefore, we suppose they have the same import here in 1 John.   John is speaking of the Spirit who has inspired the preaching of Jesus' apostles.   Compare the apostle Paul's similar claim found in 1 Corinthians 2:12.   For "truth" see notes at 1:8 (page 23) and 2:4 (page 37).

[59] The root of the Greek term for "error" (*planē*) is the same as the verb translated "to deceive" in 1:8. The word conveys a sense that is the direct opposite of "truth."   The "spirit of error" and the "false prophets" (verse 1) are linked as cause and effect.   Since John issues warnings to his readers against being taken in by the false teachers (2:24-26, 4:1-6; 2 John 7-11), he appears to be warning of the possibility of true believers going astray.

of apostolic truth (verse 6) are prime indicators of which spirit is speaking through them.[60]

B. Encouragement to Love One Another Because of God's Love. 4:7-12

> *Summary*:   For the third time in this letter (see 2:7-11 and 3:11-18) John takes up the topic of love for one another.   This time, the reason we children of God should love is based on the nature of God our Father.   The refrain "love one another" occurs three times in this paragraph, first as an exhortation (verse 7), then as a statement of duty (verse 11), and finally as a hypothesis (verse 12).

4:7 -- *Beloved, let us love one another, for love is from God; and every one who loves is born of God and knows God.*

Beloved – The term "beloved" may refer to their having been loved by God (as in 1 John 3:1,2), or it may refer to John's own care for them.   Before John asks for love, he reminds them God loves them, and that he loves them.   If it seems like an abrupt change of topics as John turns from his discussion of true and false spirits to present his readers with a further appeal to love one another, one might recall what John wrote at 3:23.   There he announced the topics of faith and love, and the verses following take up each of those topics.   "Faith comes from hearing ... the word of Christ"; so 3:24b-4:6 take up the apostolic preaching on which faith in Christ is based, as well as one of the major elements of that faith ("Jesus [as the] Christ has come in the flesh").   Now in 4:7-12 he turns to the second commandment alluded to in 3:23.

Let us love one another – It is a present tense subjunctive,[1] an exhortation to continuous action: Let us continually be loving one another!   or, Let us go on loving one another!   "Love one another" is a reciprocal love: you love me, I love you, we love each other.   As in 3:11, "'Love one another' applies primarily to the mutual love of Christians.   The love of Christians to unbelievers is not expressly excluded, but it is not definitely before the Apostle's mind."[2]   As explained earlier, "love" (*agapē*) is doing what is spiritually best for

---

[60] How different are the tests John gives to detect the source of inspiration from what many people today claim.   People today who claim to have direct guidance base their teaching on "how they feel" – i.e., their personal experience.   John calls us back to the Word and to the Testimony!

[1] The word should be treated as a hortatory subjunctive (rather than a present active indicative, which is identical in form).   (Kistemaker, *op. cit.*, p.331.)

[2] Plummer, *op. cit.*, p.146.   "Of course, Jesus' directions had included this attitude toward even our enemies.   It is not that John is exclusive and would be narrower than Jesus.   Rather, his concern is for the present condition existing in the church caused by the attitude of the false teachers." (Roberts, *op. cit.*, p.111.)

the other person.[3]   In the face of the Gnostic threat, believers need to be committed to and supportive of one another lest they accept the heresy and lose faith and drop out along the way. Instead of becoming committed to the false teachers, John appeals for love to one's Christian brethren.

For love is from God – The Greek reads, *hoti hē agapē ek tou theou estin*. The article before *agapē* is likely the article of previous reference. Such love as John exhorts his readers to exhibit has its source in the nature and being of God, and reflects His nature and attitude.[4] Since "we are from God" (verse 6) and "you are from God" (verse 4), and since "love is from God," there should be a family bond of love between us. To love the false teachers rather than their brethren would be at odds with what love should be.

And every one who loves is born of God and knows God – This clause is an inference drawn from what immediately precedes. If love has its source in God, then men who live in love must have gotten that love from God. Even though the clause has no object for the verb, the initial exhortation "Let us love one another" leads us to believe that "every one who loves" means love of one another. "Loves" is a present participle indicating habitual love. "It is generally recognized that love is here presented, not as the cause of the new birth from God or of the knowledge of God, but as their effect."[5] Care must be exercised here, for the English translation is open to misunderstanding. One might conclude that anybody (whether heathen or Christian) who shows love is a child of God and knows God, regardless of whether he actually believes in Jesus Christ as the Son of God. A study of Greek synonyms for "love" helps us appreciate what John is saying. "It should never be forgotten that *agapē* is a word born within the bosom of revealed religion; it occurs in the LXX, but there is no example of its use in any heathen writer whatever."[6] Heathen folk are not likely to show *agapē* (doing what is *spiritually* best for the other person), though they may show *philos* (friendship) or *eros* (lust) or *storgē* (family affection). It is possible that John's emphasis on both the new birth and the knowledge of God are anti-Gnostic polemic. Against the Gnostics who may have been claiming secret regeneration through the divine "seed" (see comments at 3:9), and initiation into esoteric spiritual knowledge (cf. 2:20), John makes it clear that birth from God and the knowledge of Him are already manifest characteristics of "*every*" loving Christian believer. One need not join the Gnostics to be born again or to have knowledge.

---

[3] "We know from 3:18 that John is concerned with love in action, rather than with "love" in the abstract. It is likely, therefore, that when he speaks about every one who is 'loving' (*agapōn*), he means not only an *attitude* of love but also the *practice* of love." Smalley, *op. cit.*, p.237.

[4] The whole of the Biblical revelation of God emphasizes the fact that man is made in the image of God, not God in the image of man. Thus, if we love, we must learn it from Him. Whatever is good in man is a reflection of what God is like. (Adapted from Brooke, *op. cit.*, p.117)

[5] Brooke, *op. cit.*, p.118. For "born (or begotten) of Him" see 2:29, 5:1. For "knows (*ginōskei* is experiential knowledge) God," see 2:3ff, 13ff, 3:1,6. See 4:6 for what is implied by the present tense verb.

[6] R.C. Trench, *Synonyms of the New Testament* (Grand Rapids: Eerdmans, 1953 reprint), p.42. Trench has five beautiful pages describing the difference between the Greek synonyms for "love."

*4:8 -- **The one who does not love does not know God, for God is love.***

The one who does not love does not know God – As he has done frequently throughout this letter, John here emphasizes the point he made in verse 7 by stating its opposite, while at the same time adding a new thought as he changes tenses for the verb "know." "Know" in this verse is an aorist tense, and the idea is the one who does not habitually love "*never* knew God." "The one who does not love" is a present tense participle, keeps on not loving. Since John has earlier shown that it is the Gnostics who demonstrate a lack of such love, this affirmation is certainly a strong anti-Gnostic thrust.

For God is love – Marshall has called "this little clause ... one of the high peaks of divine revelation in this Epistle ... [In] the pages of Scripture there is no comparable picture of God."[7] The Greek reads *hoti ho theos agapē estin*. The same construction is found in 1 John 1:5 ("God is light"), in John 4:24 ("God is spirit"), and in Hebrews 12:29 ("God is a consuming fire"). Of these great truths about God's very nature, this one is chief. The others are incomplete without it. Here, as in the other cases, the predicate ("love") has no article, so it expresses a quality which makes up the very essence of God.[8] With the predicate being anarthrous, we cannot turn it around and say "love is God."[9] The absence of the article emphasizes nature, essence, character. Love is not a quality He possesses; it is what He is.[10] We must beware of watering down "God is love" into God is loving or even God of all beings is the most loving. It does not mean that loving is only one of God's many activities. Love is not a mere attribute of God; it is His very nature. It is His nature to do for others what is best spiritually. It was the compulsion of His loving nature that led to the creation described in the early chapters of Genesis. When He rules, or judges, or sends His only begotten Son into the world, it is an expression of His nature which is to "love" (to do what is spiritually best for man). The following verses focus on some of the ways God's love has expressed itself.

*4:9 -- **By this the love of God was manifested in us, that God has sent His only begotten Son into the world so that we might live through Him.***

By this the love of God was manifested in us – "By this" points forward to the following "that" clause. God is love (verse 8), but how does anyone know that? We wouldn't, un-

---

[7] Marshall, *op. cit.*, p.212, 213.

[8] "God is spirit" describes His metaphysical nature, while "God is light" and "God is love" deal with His character, especially as He has revealed Himself to men (Marshall, *op. cit.*, p.212). Plummer (*Pulpit Commentary*, p.103) wrote, "As 'God is light' sums up the being of God intellectually considered, so 'God is love' sums up the same on the moral side."

[9] The Greek construction (i.e., the word "God" has an article while the world "love" does not) indicates that the two words are not interchangeable or synonymous.

[10] There may be anti-Gnostic polemic in this presentation of God's nature. Some Gnostics taught that the devil was the "good god" while the God of the Old Testament was an evil person, cruel, terrible, wrathful, exhibiting ill-will. Not so, says John!

less He revealed Himself to us. At 3:16, John has already told us how we know what love is, and has "thereby safeguarded his readers from the danger of confusing God's love with human substitutes of inferior quality."[11] "Was manifested" speaks of something becoming visible to human eyes.[12] *Ephanerōthē* expresses the objective fact, not the subjective knowledge. The aorist tense here points to a definite moment in the past when God's love became visible in time and space. It points to the incarnation of Jesus, as John goes on to show. "In us" (*en hēmin*), which is likely connected with the verb "manifest" rather than with "the love of God," may mean among us.[13] While it may not be true of the world in general, we Christians certainly have seen that God is love.

That God has sent His only begotten Son into the world – "Sent" is a perfect active indicative form of *apostellō*, which means to send on a mission, or send with a commission.[14] The perfect tense implies that the mission of the Son was over when John wrote, but it has a permanent, continuing effect (spelled out in the next clause). It should be noted that the concept of God sending His son (verses 9,10,14) "involves the doctrine of Christ's pre-existence and divinity" (Ebrard).[15] "His Son, the only begotten" translates *ton huion autou ton monogenē*. The repetition of the definite article emphasizes the noun *huion* (Son)[16] and the adjective *monogenē* (unique). *Monogenēs* is a compound word formed by the components only/alone (*monos*) and race/stock/class/kind (*genos*).[17] It means "the only one of its class/kind."[18] Used in connection with "son" or "child," the

---

[11] Marshall, *op. cit.*, p.213.

[12] See on 1:2 for this verb (pages 6,7).

[13] Westcott (*op. cit.*, p.149) held that *en hēmin* meant that God's love is revealed "in us" believers as the medium through which it becomes known to the world. "Toward us" is not an adequate translation, for with the preposition the phrase is more than a simple dative. Brooke (*op. cit.*, p.119) argues that if John had wished to write "to us" he could easily have written *eis hēmas*. Other examples of *en hēmin* that may help us grasp the meaning of the preposition "in" are Acts 4:12 and 2 Corinthians 8:1.

[14] Note that John does not use the verb *pempō* (send). We are so used to the language "God *gave* His Son," that "sent" His Son causes us to pause and contemplate.

[15] Quoted by Stott, *op. cit.*, p.161. "Rationalists have tried to escape from this assertion of Christ's pre-existence by giving peculiar meanings to the words John here wrote. Such commentators may well be expected to give an answer to the question, how a Christ so understood could be our life (verse 9), our atonement (verse 10), or our salvation (verse 14)." (Alford, *op. cit.*, p.489-490.)

[16] For "Son" see on 1:3 (page 11). The concept has overtones of deity.

[17] The *-genēs* part of the compound is concerned with derivation or kind (*genos*) rather than with birth (*gennaō*). The Greek word for "only begotten" would be *monogenētos* (using a form of *gennaō*), and is common in the LXX in this sense (e.g., Judges 11:34; Psalm 21:21, 25:16). See Moulton and Milligan, *Vocabulary of the Greek New Testament* (London: Hodder & Stoughton, 1930, 1963 printing), p.416-17.

[18] (1) The use of the term *monogenēs* in Scripture. (a) In the Old Testament the Hebrew word *yachid*, "single, only" is sometimes rendered into Greek by *agapētos*, "beloved" (Genesis 22:2,12,16; Jeremiah 6:26; Amos 8:10; Zechariah 12:10 LXX), and sometimes by *monogenēs* (Judges 11:34 LXX, cf. the later Greek versions of Genesis 22:2,12; Jeremiah 6:26; Proverbs 4:3; Jos. Ant. 1.222, 5:264). This has sug-

word says God has no other sons or children like this One.[19]   John's designation of Jesus as "only Son" is likely an anti-Gnostic polemic for Gnostics saw Jesus only as one of many aeons.   In addition, the title which John chooses here for our Lord indicates and enhances the extent and preciousness of the Father's gift when His Son became incarnate and lived on our earth.

So that we might live through Him – This clause is where the emphasis in verse 9 rests. When God manifested His love in sending His Son, it was for this purpose: that we might

---

gested that *monogenēs* may contain the nuance "beloved," especially since an only child is particularly loved by his parents. (b) In the New Testament Scriptures, the word *monogenēs* is sometimes used to denote one who is the only child of his parents (Luke 7:12, 8:42, 9:38; Hebrews 11:17), and it is applied to God's Son in John 1:14,18; 3:16,18, as the only Son of God, "besides whom His father has none." (c) In Hebrews 11:17, Isaac is called Abraham's *monogenēs* (NASB, "only begotten son"), even though Abraham had already fathered Ishmael. In Isaac's case, the word *monogenēs* means there was something "special," something "unique," about Isaac. Of all Abraham's sons, he was the one thru whom the "Seed" was to come.

(2) *Monogenēs* has proven to be a controversial term over the years. (a) We who have grown up reading the KJV are so accustomed to *monogenēs* being translated as "only begotten" (John 3:16 is especially familiar) that any other wording sounds strange, if not entirely wrong. When we hear "only begotten," we usually think of the Incarnation (and Jesus' miraculous conception). But Jesus' miraculous conception may not at all be what the writers had in mind who used *monogenēs* to describe Jesus. (b) The idea that *monogenēs* might be translated as "only begotten" began with Jerome, who used the Latin word *unigenitus* (only begotten) in his Vulgate version instead of the word *unicus* (only) which the Old Latin translators had used to translate *monogenēs*. The 4th century saw a major Trinitarian controversy, Arianism. The basic tenet of Arius was a denial of the deity of Jesus. The Father alone is true God whose essential attribute was *agennesia* (unbegotten). God, Arius argued, is by necessity not only uncreated, but unbegotten and unoriginate. Jesus, Arius argued, who is described in Scripture as the "first-born of creation" (Colossians 1:15, cp. Revelation 3:14) cannot be true deity, for that implies He (unlike the Father) was "begotten." The Nicean Creed (an attempt to settle the controversy) has the phrase about Jesus, "true God from true God, begotten not made [created]." But the debate about Jesus continued till the end of the century. Late in that century is when Jerome began work on the Latin Vulgate version. Whenever Jerome entered theological frays, he had but one rule to guide him in matters of doctrine and discipline: the practice of Rome and the West. Having discovered what the Western practice was, he set his tongue and pen to spreading that view. In the context of the continuing debate about Jesus' deity, Jerome's choice of *unigenitus* (only begotten) in such passages as John 1:14 and 3:16 may be viewed, in harmony with the views in the West, as a deliberate attempt to refute the Arians and to strengthen the argument that Jesus is deity. [Jerome used *unicus* to translate *yachid* or *monogenēs* in passages (such as Psalm 35:17; Luke 7:12, 8:42, 9:38) where someone was an only son, and where there was no reference to Jesus.] (c) Jerome's word passed into the English translations of Wycliffe and others (though Tyndale did not use this expression in his 1534 edition), and then into the KJV. (d) In the 20th century, some who have wanted to deny the virgin birth of Jesus have deliberately excluded the word "begotten" from their 20th century versions of Scripture. "The charge is then made by some defenders of Jesus' virgin birth that any translation besides 'only begotten' robs Christ of His deity and makes Him only another of the many sons of God. The flaw in this argument is the assumption that 'begotten' is used of the Son to refer to the virgin birth. As a matter of fact, the term 'begotten' (verb root *gennaō*) is never used by John of the birth of Jesus" (Roberts, *op. cit.*, p.114,115).

(3) Jesus is God (Hebrews 1:1-3,8; John 1:1-18; Romans 9:5), and co-eternal with the father (John 17:5). We certainly are not defending the idea that Jesus is not deity/God when we call attention to the meaning of *monogenēs*.

[19] God has many "sons" in other senses. Angels are called "sons of God" (Job 38:7). Those who become Christians are adopted "sons" in God's family (Romans 8:14, 9:26).

live.[20] As we come to "live" we have come to one of the two emphatic words in this sentence which are *monogenē* and *zēsomen*. *"Such* a Son was sent that we might *live."*[21] "Live" includes spiritual life now and a resurrection body when Jesus returns.[22] Westcott points out that the term *zēsomen* ("that we might live") stresses the *activity* which is demanded of the believer, and not just a passive reception of "life."[23] "Through Him" (*di' autou*) refers to "the only begotten Son." God (or His love expressing itself) is the ultimate cause or initiator of the process. Jesus is the intermediate agent (*dia*) involved in "living" being made available to men.[24]

4:10 -- *In this is love, not that we loved God, but that He loved us and sent His Son* to be *the propitiation for our sins.*

In this is love – From telling how God's love was made manifest so everyone could see it (verse 9), John now shows that God's love has become the source of love which Christians may have for God. The definite article before "love" indicates that not any kind of love is intended, but the particular love (*agapē*) that inheres in God's nature. The demonstrative "in this" points to what follows and is explained both by a negative and a positive "that-clause."

Not that we loved God – God's love for man came first, not the other way around. In verse 7, John has said that love "is from God." Now he emphasizes the fact that genuine love originates, not in man's love to God, but in God's love to man. "We" and "He" in this clause and the next are emphatically contrasted with each other. The perfect tense verb (*ēgapēkamen*),[25] "loved," says not only that we loved God in the past, but we still do.

But that He loved us and sent His Son *to be* **the propitiation for our sins** – "He" is an emphatic nominative, signifying God. "Loved" (*ēgapēsen*) in this clause is an aorist tense and looks at the historical moment when God sent Jesus into our world. "Loved" does not

---

[20] It seems best to treat *hina* as a purpose clause.

[21] Alford, *op. cit.*, p.490.

[22] On "live" see notes at 1:1 on "life". See also on John 5:25; 6:51,57ff; 11:25; 14:19. The expression is virtually identical with "have eternal life."

[23] Westcott, *op. cit.*, p. 149. The verb "might live" is an aorist subjunctive in the Greek. Marshall and Smalley call it an "ingressive aorist," indicating the beginning of an ongoing process.

[24] What is said in verse 9 must be kept in mind when attempts are made to explain the doctrine of the atonement. The atonement did not placate an angry God and get Him to love us. It was not in consequence of the atonement that we became objects of God's love. Rather, the sending of the Son was an evidence of a love which already existed.

[25] The UBS text, on the basis of B,1739, prints the perfect tense, though most later texts have an aorist tense form *ēgapēsamen* (cp. the Textus Receptus). The aorist, referring to a single act in time past, would imply that no act of love of ours to God done at any time furnishes the initial example of love. Rather, it was an act of His toward us.

mean that God approves the actions of sinners, but that He desires their welfare, and selflessly gets involved to meet their needs. What men needed desperately was a covering for their sins.[26] That is precisely what Jesus came to do. He came to die for the sins of the world. There is a pattern in verses 9,10,14.

(1) Each says that God sent His Son.[27]
(2) The Son was sent to die for us.
(3) The greatness of God's love can be seen by looking at the beneficiaries (sinners).

God did not love us because we were lovable and loving: "God demonstrates His own love toward us, in that while we were yet sinners, Christ died for us" (Romans 5:8). Perhaps there was an anti-Gnostic reason for this repeated pattern. The false teachers may have claimed to "love God"; however, their love was not *agapē* love, but rather their definition of love was understood in terms of Greek philosophy. "Love in the Hellenistic world had become a metaphysical principle, so that man's craving for union with the Infinite, the Absolute, the Eternal" was called "love for God."[28] Two things resulted from this misguided understanding of love. First, love for God as it was expressed by the false teachers becomes primarily an exercise in self-gratification. How different from God's unselfish, lavish giving to others. Second, one can never attribute love to God and say, for example, that "God loves us," for God as the Absolute is always passionless.[29]

4:11 -- *Beloved, if God so loved us, we also ought to love one another.*

Beloved – The readers are here addressed as being those whom God loves. This is the last time in the epistle John addresses his readers as "beloved" and there is no other salutation until 5:21. Verse 11 is a conclusion drawn from verses 9 and 10, and gives the motive for the exhortation with which this paragraph began (verse 7).

If God so loved us – To insure this clause leaves no doubt about God's love, we would translate it "Since God so loved us."[30] "So" (*houtōs*) calls attention to the extent of God's self-sacrificial love detailed in verse 10. The past tense of "loved" (as in verse 10) points to the historical event of Jesus' ministry and death, the supreme manifestation of love.

We also ought to love one another – "Also" modifies "we"; we as well as God is the idea.

---

[26] Earlier in this letter (2:2), John wrote the same words, "propitiation for our sins." For "sins," see notes at 1:7 and 1:9 (in "confess our sins"). The plural shows that the reference is to specific sinful deeds.

[27] No more costly gift is conceivable. God had nothing greater to give as He expressed His love. This was God's "indescribable gift" (2 Corinthians 9:15).

[28] Dodd, *op. cit.*, p.111. Compare the New Age advocates' desire to become one with the impersonal God whose nature and existence has been conjured up.

[29] Adapted from Barker, *op. cit.*, p.343.

[30] *Ei* with the indicative in the "if" clause of a fifth class condition is the supposition of a fact. In such a condition, nothing is implied about whether or not the conclusion will happen or not.

"Ought" (*opheilomen*) expresses obligation,[31] and the obligation rests on the fact that God loves us and gave His Son for us. Our obligation as God's children is to "keep on loving" one another.[32] Instead of saying we should love God in return, John speaks of our obligation to one another.[33] If God loves my brother in Christ, surely I, too, must love the one whom God loves. Perhaps "John is reacting to false teaching that would say one could love God without any corresponding obligation to love his brethren."[34] John continues to drive home the truth that the nature of true love is unselfish and sacrificial.

4:12 -- *No one has beheld God at any time; if we love one another, God abides in us, and His love is perfected in us.*

No one has beheld God at any time – The word "God" is in the emphatic position, coming first in the Greek sentence. "God no one ever yet has seen."[35] What is the connection of this sudden, startling statement with the context? In verse 11 we had an unexpected substitution, "We also ought to love (not God, but) one another." Why so? Verse 12 helps guide us to the proper answer. Likely there is a refutation of the Gnostics who claimed "visions" of God, and because of such self-induced visions were certain of their personal relationship with Him. With the words, "No one has beheld God at any time,"[36] John offers a flat rejection of such a claim.[37] Then he immediately goes on to assure his readers that there is a way to be certain of a personal relationship with God.

---

[31] For "ought" see 2:6. It is the "must" of an inward constraint, not the "must" of external compulsion.

[32] "If the children of God must be holy because He is holy (Leviticus 11:44ff; 1 Peter 1:15ff), and merciful because He is merciful (Luke 6:36), so they must be loving because He is loving." F.F. Bruce, *The Epistles of John* (Grand Rapids: Eerdmans, 1979), p.109.

[33] For the present tense verb "keep on loving," see notes at 3:11. For the duty of Christian self-sacrifice for the spiritual benefit of others, see on 3:16

[34] Roberts, *op. cit.*, p. 116.

[35] "God" has no article. The absence of the article throws the emphasis on the nature and character of God. As He is in His true nature He cannot be made visible to the eyes of men, so that they can grasp the meaning of what they see. 1 Timothy 6:16 says of God, "whom no man has seen, or can see," and 1 Timothy 1:17 describes Him as "invisible." "The question how this statement is to be reconciled with Matthew 5:8; 1 John 3:2; and with the sight of Deity attributed in the Old Testament to Abraham, Isaac, Jacob, Job, Moses, Micaiah, Isaiah (Genesis 18:1; 26:2; 32:30; Job 38:1; Exodus 33:11; 1 Kings 22:19; Isaiah 6.1), is discussed at length by Augustine in his epistle *De Invisib. Dei*" (Alexander, *op. cit.*, p.335).

[36] Here in verse 12, John uses *theaomai* ("beheld"), a verb that emphasizes "contemplation." John is saying that no amount of contemplation (like the false teachers were doing and advocating) ever yet enabled anyone to detect God's presence, or to get any idea of His nature and character. Compare John 1:18 ("No man has seen God at any time: the only begotten God, who is in the bosom of the Father, He has explained Him.") where the synonym *eōraken* is used. *Eōraken* denotes simple sight.

[37] It is doubtful John intends to say that it is impossible to love an invisible Being. The idea that we cannot return God's love because He is invisible is alien to John's thought. Rather, it is not so much "love for God" that John now highlights, but the means to confidence of a personal relationship with Him. For John's rejection of visions of God in moments of ecstasy, see not only John 1:18, but 5:37 and 6:46.

If we love one another – We may not become acquainted with God by visions such as the false teachers claimed, but we may know Him by love if indeed we keep on loving. John has thus rejected the idea that a mystical experience is the high point of a man's religion. Instead of retreat from the world of men into the privacy of a vision of God, John advocates involvement with men, love of a very practical kind (cp. 3:17ff).

God abides in us – If we continue to love one another, we may know that God abides in us and that we are in fellowship with Him. As we exhibit love (*agapē*) we have experiential proof of the presence of the invisible God.[38]

And His love is perfected in us – When God initiated a manifestation of His love toward man, He had a goal[39] in mind. He wanted men to be "lovers," too. When the saints love one another habitually, that shows that this love which God is in His nature (verses 7,8) and which was manifested in His Son (verses 9,10), has accomplished its purpose in their lives.[40] His love has reached its intended goal when His children are loving and self-sacrificial in character. It is when God's love is reproduced in our lives that His love is perfected.

C. Encouragement Because of the Apostles' Testimony. 4:13-16a

> *Summary*: This is the third paragraph in the series of encouragements that began at 3:24b. This encouragement deals with testimony any apostle could give. The readers would be encouraged as they recalled the source of the apostolic message (verse 13), the content of that message (verse 14), and the continuing fellowship they had with God as a result of their continuing confession that Jesus is the Son of God (verses 15,16a).

4:13 -- *By this we know that we abide in Him and He in us, because He has given us of His Spirit.*

By this we know that we abide in Him and He in us – This new paragraph is introduced by the familiar formula, "hereby we know (KJV)." John goes on in the following words

---

[38] On God "abiding in us," see on 3:24 (p.130).

[39] *Teleioō* means "to bring to completion, to accomplish, to finish" (see on "perfected" at 2:5). The form here, *teteleiōmenē estin*, is a periphrastic perfect passive indicative. In 2:5, "obedience" from man was what God's love had in mind. When we obey, God's love has accomplished its intended purpose. In this passage, "mutual love" for man was what God's love had in mind. When we do it, God's love has accomplished its intended purpose.

[40] The Greek reads "the love of Him" and here we have the same problem of interpretation we faced in 2:5 and 3:17. Is it God's love for us, our love for God, or God's kind of love? In this paragraph which has been explaining "God is love," we take it as being God's love for us.

to give the reason why they know. The words of this verse are parallel with what John wrote in 3:24b, and we treat both as the Holy Spirit at work in the apostles, rather than the indwelling Spirit at work in individual Christians.[1] Both the verbs "we know" and "abide" are present tense, suggesting continuous experience of the Spirit's presence.[2]

Because He has given us of His Spirit – This *hoti* clause is likely causal, "we can be sure ... because ...." "He" is God (verse 12). "Has given" is a perfect tense here. In the apostles' case, the gift given when they were baptized with the Spirit continues to empower them.[3] *Ek tou pneumatos* is a partitive genitive; He has given us a share of His spirit.[4] Verse 6 has required the readers to listen to the apostles if they want the truth. Verses 13-14 claim inspiration from the Holy Spirit for the apostles' message. John's testimony is that the Spirit's work in their lives is evidence of their continuing fellowship with God.

4:14 -- *And we have beheld and bear witness that the Father has sent the Son* **to be** *the Savior of the world.*

And we have beheld and bear witness – The emphatic personal pronoun "we" (*hemeis*) has reference to the apostolic circle, the actual eyewitnesses of the life of Jesus on earth. The verb "have beheld" is in the perfect tense, showing that the seeing was a past completed action[5] but the results have left a lasting impression. "Bear witness" is a present tense verb, expressing continual action. The testimony now from the apostles is the same testimony as given from the beginning. The thought included in this phrase is parallel to

---

[1] The plural pronouns ("we" and "us") of this paragraph are not as broad (the whole fellowship of John and his readers) as in verses 10-12. Verse 14 suggests that the first-person plural pronouns are limited to the apostles who had seen Jesus personally. Commentators who attempt to make this paragraph speak of the indwelling Spirit, whom all Christians receive, soon express dissatisfaction with their attempts to find the train of thought as they move from verse 13 to 14. Such dissatisfaction is eliminated if we recognize that John uses "we" and "us" differently in verses 13-16a (apostles) than he does in verses 10-12 and verses 16b-21 (all Christians).

[2] "Know" (*ginōskō*) is the verb that speaks of knowledge that comes from experience. For an explanation of the verb "abide" see at 2:6 and on "mutual abiding," see notes at 3:24. In His Farewell Discourse, Jesus had promised the Spirit would be with them and in them and that He and the Father would thus abide in them (John 14:17,23). This theme of fellowship with the Father and with each other was also sounded forth at 1 John 1:3.

[3] Just as John here claims continuing empowerment and inspiration from the Holy Spirit for himself, so Peter (2 Peter 1:3) claimed that he too had received the "divine power" which Jesus had promised to the apostles (Acts 1:8).

[4] Christ alone had the Spirit "without measure" (John 3:34).

[5] The act of viewing or contemplating what they were seeing as they examined Jesus was not a momentary thing. It consisted of a process, which process (at the time John writes) was now a completed one.

1:1-2, and speaks of the apostolic eyewitnesses and their testimony concerning Jesus.[6] Putting verses 13 and 14 together, John says it is the Holy Spirit who enables the apostles to testify that "the Father has sent the Son to be the Savior of the world."[7]

That the Father has sent the Son – What the message was to which the apostles bore witness is specified in this *hoti*-clause ("that"). "Those who saw Jesus alive testified concerning such things as His miracles, His life, His teaching, His resurrection, and His ascension. The extraordinary nature of His life proved that He was more than simply a man."[8] "Father" was explained at 1:2 and 2:22-24. What readers are reminded of is that there exists an intimate relation between the Father and the Son. "Sent [on a mission]" (*apestalken*) was used at verse 10. This perfect tense verb indicates Jesus' ministry was concluded, but that there were present, continuing results of that ministry that could still be experienced and appropriated.

***To be* the Savior of the world** – "For God sent not His Son into the world to condemn the world, but that the world through Him might be saved" (John 3:17 KJV). "This is a most profound statement: God the Father commissioned His Son to assume the task of saving the world. And God initiated this mission of the Son because of His love for the sinful world."[9] What is said here about the purpose of Jesus' entrance into the world is similar to what was said in verse 10. "Son" and "Savior" are key words here.[10] It is through His atoning sacrifice for sins that Jesus can be "Savior of the world." What John writes here reminds us of John 3:16 and of what the Samaritans recognized, that Jesus "is indeed the Savior of the world" (John 4:42).[11] Jesus' own claim that He came to give His life as a ransom for sinners was verified by the testimony of those who saw Him "doing and teaching" (Acts 1:1). In Acts we read how the apostles preached that Jesus is Savior. They said, "God exalted Him to His own right hand as Prince and Savior that He might give repentance and forgiveness of sins to Israel" (Acts 5:31, personal translation; see also 13:23). "World" (explained at 2:2) is important. It says Jesus is the Savior not of Jews only, nor of "enlightened" Gnostics only. He died for all men. But there is more. Jesus'

---

[6] "Beheld" (*tetheametha*, contemplation of the incarnate Son of God; the same word as used in verse 12) and "bear witness" (*marturoumen*, public declaration of what was seen) are differing ideas.

[7] This is precisely what Jesus promised the apostles the Holy Spirit would do for them (John 15:26,27). Jesus promised them the Holy Spirit would come upon them, and then they were to "testify" (bear witness) concerning what they had seen and heard as they travelled with Jesus during His earthly ministry. It was the apostolic body whom Christ appointed His witnesses (Acts 1:8).

[8] Roberts, *op. cit.*, p.118.

[9] Kistemaker, *op. cit.*, p.336.

[10] "Savior" is a predicate accusative, like *hilasmon* ("propitiation") was at verse 10.

[11] The term "Savior" is less common than might be expected in the New Testament. Sometimes it is used with reference to Jesus, and sometimes with reference to God the Father. The word means "to preserve," "to rescue from danger," "to cause to get well," "to deliver from the power and penalty of sin."

death not only helps men who were ruined by sin, but it makes possible the renovation of the physical world that was blighted and blasted by sin (Romans 8:19-22).

4:15 -- *Whoever confesses that Jesus is the Son of God, God abides in him, and he in God.*

Whoever confesses that Jesus is the Son of God – Who are the people of the world who benefit from Jesus' mission to save?   Those who confess Jesus as the divine Son of God.[12] "Whoever" means "anyone."   Unlike the conditions as taught by the Gnostics which made fellowship with them available only to a favored few, this condition for fellowship with God broadly includes "whoever confesses" this great truth, "I believe Jesus is the Son of God!"[13]   "Confesses" (*homologēsē*) is an aorist tense subjunctive.   John is referring to a single and decisive public confession, at any time in the future.   The next time the Gnostics come teaching, let John's readers acknowledge their faith in Jesus.[14]   That is something that their continuing fellowship with God would encourage them to do.

God abides in him, and he in God – Confession of the divine sonship of Jesus leads to the mutual indwelling of God and His people.   Whoever confesses Jesus is the Son of God, that is the person who has fellowship with God.   The fact that the false teachers do not confess Jesus as the Son of God is proof that they do not have any fellowship with the Father or the Son.   This fellowship is the closest relationship one can conceive.   Even apostles, who have beheld and borne witness, can have no more than this divine fellowship, which is open to every believer.

4:16 -- *And we have come to know and have believed the love which God has for us.   God is love, and the one who abides in love abides in God, and God abides in him.*

And we have come to know and have believed the love which God has for us – The emphatic "we" here in verse 16 has the same meaning as in verse 14.   It refers especially to the apostles whose testimony is here given to encourage the readers.   Both verbs John uses are in the perfect tense.   "We have come to know" in the past and we still do know

---

[12] For "whoever" see on 2:5.   For "confess" see 2:23 and 4:2ff.   For "Son of God" see 1:3.   For "abide" see 3:24.

[13] The truth confessed is variously worded (cf. 4:2; 2 John 7; Philippians 2:11, etc.), but whichever way it is stated, the essential point seems to be the acknowledgement of identity of Jesus.   The confession that "Jesus is the Son of God" embraces an awesome theological truth.   The word "Jesus" embodies the entire history of Jesus from His birth to His ascension and coronation at the right hand of God.   The term "Son of God" has its roots in Old Testament prophecies (e.g., Psalm 2:7; 2 Samuel 7:14; Hebrews 1:5) and speaks of Jesus' essential deity (cp. Hebrews 1:2-3).   Thus, the confession "Jesus is the Son of God" gives voice to a conviction concerning His humanity and deity.

[14] The confession must be from the heart.   The man who merely says these words, without any proper understanding of the truth they embody, will not meet the condition of fellowship with God.

that God loves us. "We ... have believed" in the past and we still do.[15] The apostles came to believe during Jesus' earthly ministry (a time in the past), and they still hold to that belief (in the present).[16] "The love" reminds us of all that has been written about God's essential nature and how it was manifested to the world (4:8ff). The verb "has" in "the love which God has for us" is present tense, expressing duration/continuation. The unusual Greek phrase *en hēmin* translated "for us" was explained at 4:9. Alexander[17] reminds us that it is impossible to understand the epistle here without a reference to the Gospel, John 17:26 for example, where Jesus says concerning the apostles, "I have made Thy name known to them, and will make it known [to them]; that the love wherewith Thou didst love Me may be in them, and I in them."

D. Encouragement Because of Loss of Fear.   4:16b-21

> *Summary*:   Now John is no longer talking only about the apostles' experience of God's love.[1]   In this fourth paragraph in a series of encouragements, John talks about the readers' living in the sphere of God's love and the encouragement that lifestyle brings.   An awareness of God's love can give full assurance and cast out fear.

4:16b -- **God is love** – For "God is love" see at verses 8-10.

And the one who abides in love abides in God, and God abides in him – In the previous paragraph, we have seen how the "love of God" affected the apostles. In this paragraph, we see how the love of God affects John's readers, too. "Abides in love" is a way of saying that the believer lives in a sphere of love.[2] He keeps himself (*menei*, present tense, he continues to remain) in a place where God can continue to love him. Living in the sphere of God's love is presented as a condition of fellowship with God ("abides in Him"). It is

---

[15] The use of *pisteuō* (believe) followed by a direct object is unusual (John 11:26; 1 Corinthians 13:7). Perhaps the accusative was called for because of the previous verb, "come to know."

[16] John has knowledge before belief. Plummer (*op. cit.*, p.151) calls this "the natural order; progressive knowledge leads up to faith. But sometimes faith precedes knowledge (John 6:69). In either case each completes the other. Sound faith is intelligent; sound knowledge is believing."

[17] Alexander, *op. cit.*, p.336.

[1] There is some uncertainty whether 4:16b concludes the previous paragraph or is the beginning of the next paragraph. The Nestle text and several modern versions (including GNT, NAB, NEB, NIV) treat 16b as the beginning of a new paragraph. It is easier to find a train of thought if we begin a new paragraph here.

[2] Commentators are uncertain whether John is referring to our living in God's love for us, or our living in love for Him and our brothers. In light of the way this paragraph begins, and in light of the following verse, this commentator is rather inclined to opt for the view that living in the sphere of God's love for us is what is intended.

possible by belief or lifestyle to depart from the sphere where we are the objects or recipients of God's great love. John is warning against such a departure, and such a departure is precisely what happens when one joins the Gnostics.

4:17 -- *By this, love is perfected with us, that we may have confidence in the day of judgment; because as He is, so also are we in this world.*

By this, love is perfected with us – "By this" (*en toutō*) points to the *hina*-clause ("that") which follows this clause.[3] "Love" here seems to be God's love,[4] the sphere of love in which the Christian remains (verse 16b). As in 2:5 and 4:12, "perfected" means to complete [an intended purpose], to reach its intended goal. One goal God had in mind when he manifested His love was that men should love one another (4:12). Now we learn another goal God had in mind, namely, that we might have confidence when we stand before the judgment seat of Christ. The phrase translated "with us" (*meth' hēmon*) is unusual.[5] Perhaps it means "in our case" or "in our community. " Westcott, calling attention to Acts 15:4, held that this phrase was used to show that in perfecting His love, God works along with men.[6] As verse 16b stated, men must "abide (remain)" in His love. Unless they do, it will not be "perfected" and our confidence will be gone.

That we may have confidence in the day of judgment – "Boldness" or "confidence" (*parrēsia*) is a characteristic word of this epistle.[7] "The day of judgment" (or the day when all men are judged) follows the Lord's return.[8] That day will be one of shame and terror for the wicked, but not for the redeemed people of God. In the next verse, John will ex-

---

[3] It is the general usage of John that "by this" refers to what follows whenever the sentence contains a clause which allows such a reference (Brooke, *op. cit.*, p.123). The careful reader will observe that commentators debate at length whether "by this" points forwards or backwards, or both. One point often made to support the argument that "by this" points back to verse 16b is that, unless John 15:8 is an example, there is no certain instance of the construction *en toutō* being followed by a *hina*-clause.

[4] "Love" is literally "the love," the love of God talked about earlier (the article of previous reference). Wesleyan "perfect love," (as in "Love divine, all loves excelling ...") treats this as being man's love for God being perfected. So interpreted, this passage became one Scripture verse on which a "second work of grace" was posited.

[5] Sinaiticus reads *en hēmin*.

[6] Westcott, *op. cit.*, p.157. The phrase goes not with "love" but with the verb "perfected."

[7] John has already written of unshrinking confidence before Christ at His Second Coming if we continue to abide in Him (2:28), and of our confidence before God in prayer (3:21,22).

[8] The full phrase used here, "the day of the judgment" (Greek), occurs nowhere else; however, the phrase "day of judgment" is a technical term found both in the Old and New Testaments (e.g., Matthew 10:15, 12:36; 2 Peter 2:9, 3:7). Allusions to the event are also found in John 5:22,27 and 1 John 2:28ff, where we are told it is Christ who judges in the name of God. Expressions such as this tend to lead this commentator to believe in one general judgment at the close of the church age. (Cf. Romans 2:15,16.)

plain how believers come to have confidence in the day of judgment. Remaining in the sphere of God's love is what leads to the conviction we shall not be condemned when the day of judgment comes.

Because as He is, so also are we in this world – "Because" (*hoti*) gives the reason for the confidence. "He" ("as He is," *kathōs ekeinos estin*) is probably Jesus.[9] "So also" (*kathōs ... kai*) brings out a similarity between Jesus and believers.[10] "So also are we in this world" says we live in the sphere of God's love just as Jesus lives in that love.[11] "In this world" goes with "are we," and reminds us there will come a time when we shall be like Jesus now is, but for the moment we are still "in this world"[12] but not "of the world."

4:18 -- *There is no fear in love; but perfect love casts out fear, because fear involves punishment, and the one who fears is not perfected in love.*

There is no fear in love – Verse 18 serves to explain the preceding thought, that where love is perfected there is confidence in the day of judgment. If God loves us, we do not fear. God's love for His children and fear (in their hearts) about their future at His hands are mutually exclusive ideas. A person who stands in the sphere of God's love can look forward to the future day of judgment without fear or apprehension.[13]

---

[9] *Ekeinos* in this epistle is regularly a reference to Jesus Christ (2:6, 3:3,5,7,16).

[10] Compare 3:3 for *kathōs*.

[11] Note it says "He is," not "He was." Jesus abides in God's love now, just as He did while on earth. A clue to John's thinking at this point, and a resolution of the apparent complexities in this text, may be provided by the Farewell Discourse in the Gospel, which we have discovered elsewhere to underlie the teaching in 1 John ... Between God and Jesus, according to the Fourth Gospel, exist perfect love, obedience and fellowship. So John 15:9-10 ("As the Father has loved Me, so have I loved you. Now remain in My love. If you obey My commands, you will remain in My love, just as I have obeyed My Father's commands and remain in His love." NIV). Note also John 14:10-11,20, 17:21-21,26. Smalley, *op. cit.*, p.259.

[12] Some scholars have seen a difficulty here in that we are not in fact like Jesus, and shall only become like Him when we see Him at the second coming (3:2). That felt difficulty is reflected in the various readings introduced by some scribes at this place. The real difficulty arises from scholarly decisions concerning the point of comparison. Some talk about Christ's righteousness (as in 2:29). Some talk about Christ's purity (as in 3:3). Some suppose the similarity lies in the fact we are not of this world. Rather than attempting to rewrite the text, or concluding that John is inconsistent, why not abandon the decision about the point of comparison that led to the supposed difficulty? The actual point of comparison is God's love for Jesus and us believers.

[13] The term *phobos* ("fear") has two meanings. (1) It can signify "reverence, respect" for God (Romans 3:18; 2 Corinthians 7:1; Acts 9:31). Christians do live their days on earth in "reverent fear" (like obedience to a father, as in 1 Peter 1:17), and clearly Christians must serve God "with fear and trembling" (2 Corinthians 7:15; Ephesians 6:5; Philippians 2:2). (2) *Phobos* also can mean "alarm, fright" or "terror, dread" (like a bond slave towards an implacable master, as in Romans 8:15; John 19:38, 20:19). Here it means the latter. This verse does not contradict Psalm 19:9 which says "The fear of the Lord is clean, enduring forever." The fear that John talks about is terror, servile fear, afraid of punishment for unforgiven

But perfect love casts out fear – "Perfect love" is God's love that has reached its goal in us (as explained in comments on verse 17a). "Casts out" (*exō ballei*) means to chase away, to get rid of, to banish. It expresses a forceful removal.[14] "Fear," as the next phrase shows, refers to man's fear of the judgment, or that the sentence passed is likely to be adverse. "Love" speaks of attraction; "fear" speaks of repulsion.

Because fear involves punishment – This gives the reason why fear and love cannot coexist. The reason people "fear" is because of the threat of punishment. It is guilt that makes a man fear what is to come. He who has his sins pardoned need not dread the great day of the Lord. "Punishment" (*kolasis*) is torment, suffering.[15] There will be no "punishment" for God's beloved children, so there is no need for them to fear.[16]

And the one who fears is not perfected in love – The one who continues to be afraid of the Judgment is the one in whom (because of false views about Jesus, or because of failure to love one another, or because of lack of obedience to Christ's commands) God's love has not yet reached its intended goal.[17]

4:19 -- *We love, because He first loved us.*

---

sin. "The fear spoken of here is not to be confused with reverence for God. Reverence will only deepen through the experience of God's love" (Barker, *op. cit.*, p.348).

[14] See *ballō exō* in John 6:37, 9:34ff, 12:31, 15:6, where the term means "to turn out-of-doors," which expresses a powerful word picture (Robertson, *op. cit.*, p.235).

[15] The noun *kolasis* occurs elsewhere in the New Testament only at Matthew 25:46, though the related verb is used at 2 Peter 2:9. Each time the word occurs, it occurs in passages which speak of the Last Judgment. The suffix *-sis* on the ending of the word denotes "process." (Sometimes in classical Greek the word included the idea of discipline rather than retribution. Commentators who opt for this meaning talk of "fear" being a painful experience in this life. Bultmann [*op. cit.*, p.73] even argued that John has abandoned the idea of Hell by reworking the meaning of *kolasis*. Indeed!) "Torment" in the intermediate state, as distinct from final "punishment," is expressed by a different word, *basanos*, which occurs at Matthew 4:24 and Luke 16:23,28.

[16] Kistemaker (*op. cit.*, p.341) offers an apt illustration. Television viewers are able to witness courtroom sessions almost on a daily basis. We have become accustomed to the judge, jury, defendant, plaintiff, and lawyers. We hear the verdict and see the innocent acquitted and the guilty sentenced. Often we witness the expressions of emotions that no longer can be controlled. At times, these emotions depict anxiety and fear; at other times joy and happiness.

Every human being will have to appear before the judgment throne of Christ. Feelings of guilt and remorse will fill the hearts of all those who have refused to obey God's commands, to believe His Word, and to accept Christ as Savior. Their hearts will be filled with fear (Revelation 6:15-17), for they realize that the Judge will sentence them because of their sin.

They who have lived in fellowship with the Father and the Son have nothing to fear. Their hearts are filled with joy and love. And they will hear the word *acquitted* from Jesus.

[17] Since each of us believers sins occasionally, we will find that fear of the judgment is not entirely banished. But the closer we remain in fellowship with God, the more our occasional fears diminish.

We love – "We" (emphatic *hēmeis*) means "we Christians," as in verse 17. Perhaps the contrast is with God's love for us which has been the topic of previous verses.[18] "As for us, we love, because He loved us first." "Love" (*agapōmen*) can be either an indicative ("We love") or a subjunctive form ("Let us love"). The choice may rest on the perceived connection of verses 19-20 with the previous line of thought (i.e., God's love for us in verses 16b-18).[19] We opt to treat it as an exhortation, "Let us love!"[20] Because of what is said in the following verses we suppose John intends love for one another.[21]

Because He first loved us – In this clause, John repeats the truth he has asserted in verse 10. "He" (*autos*) has a variant reading, *ho theos*, which is probably the true explanation. Perhaps the aorist tense verb *ēgapēsen* ("He loved") points back to the historical action in which God's love (in Jesus) was supremely manifest. These words of reminder offer a powerful incentive to exercise the love to which the readers are exhorted. God is love. Because He loved and sent His Son, we can enter into His fellowship. As His love reaches its intended goal in our lives, we lose our fear of judgment. We love Him in return, and as a result we love our brother.

4:20 -- *If some one says, "I love God," and hates his brother, he is a liar; for the one who does not love his brother whom he has seen, cannot love God whom he has not seen.*

If some one says, "I love God"[22] – Earlier in the letter (see 1:6,8, 2:4,9), when John wrote, "If anyone says," he was expressing the claims made by the false teachers. If that is the idea here, then the rest of the verse is John's refutation of the claim and the blame he lays on their behavior.[23] "Love" is present tense: I am constantly loving God, I love Him all the time!

---

[18] Others suppose the contrast is with "he" in the next verse.

[19] In 5:1a the discussion of another theme seems to start. However, many treat 4:19 as the beginning of this new paragraph, rather than waiting till 5:1 to make a paragraph break. Another perceived way of following the train of thought is to treat verse 19 as being one means by which we "abide in His love" (verse 16).

[20] In the better manuscripts (A,B,424^mg vg^w), there is no object for the verb "we love." In some later MSS, an object (*auton* or *ton theon*) has been added by scribes, and the KJV, which reads "we love Him," reflects this addition. Those who choose to treat *agapōmen* as indicative do so because they are convinced the emphatic "we" fits the indicative better than the subjunctive.

[21] Some commentators argue it is both love for God and love for man, since verse 20 reads both "I love God" and "love his brother."

[22] It is probably a mistake to start a new section here, as some commentators do. Verses 20 and 21 are closely connected with what precedes. They show what kind of love was in view in verse 19.

[23] It is unusual to find John using the verb *agapan* ("to love") to speak of man's "love for God." He does not use *agapan* of love for God in the Fourth Gospel, though at John 21:15,16 Peter uses it to speak of his love for Jesus. *Agapan* is the kind of "love" that can be willed. However, outside of John's writings, this verb usage is common in other New Testament books. "While men are continually bidden *agapan t. theon* (Matthew 22:37; Luke 10:27; 1 Corinthians 8:13) and good men are declared to do so (Romans 8:28; 1 Peter 1:8; 1 John 4:21), the *philein t. theon* is commanded to them never" (Trench, *op. cit.*, p.40).

And hates his brother – "Hates" is present tense, depicting an ongoing situation.[24]   Since "hate" is a subjunctive mood, this clause ("and hates his brother") is a continuation of the protasis of the conditional sentence begun earlier in this verse ("if any one says ...").

He is a liar – This is the conclusion of the conditional sentence begun with "if some one says ..." "Liar" is blunt and to the point. *Pseustēs* points to real falseness of character, not just that he is speaking what is false.[25]

For the one who does not love his brother whom he has seen – "The one who does not love" is a present active negative articular participle which means "the one who does not keep on loving." "Has seen" is *heōraken*, a perfect tense verb. Not only was the brother seen in the past; the beholder continues to feel the influence of that sight. It is implied there has been ample opportunity to serve that brother in love. "Love must express itself in action. He who refuses to make use of the obvious opportunities, which his position in the world affords him, cannot entertain the highest love."[26]

Cannot love God whom he has not seen – "Is not able to go on loving."[27] (Compare 2:9, "is not able to go on sinning.") "Cannot" does not express "man's incapacity to love God, but rather the proof that he does not."[28]   The last verb ("seen") is perfect tense, indicating that he saw (not) and still sees (not). "John argues that one who does not do the easier thing (i.e., loving one's visible brother) will surely not be able to do the more difficult thing, loving the invisible God."[29]

4:21 -- And this commandment we have from Him, that the one who loves God should love his brother also.

And this commandment we have from Him – In addition to the argument from common sense (verse 20) about brotherly love, John adds another powerful one, namely, a commandment from the Lord.[30] "We" refers to all the followers of Jesus. If we wish to continue in fellowship with God, then we obey the commandments of Christ.

---

[24] For "to hate" and "brother" see on 2:9.

[25] For "liar" see on 1:6,10 and 2:4.

[26] Brooke, *op. cit.*, p.126.

[27] Some manuscripts (A,K,L) at this place have a question (*pōs dunatai*, "how can he?") rather than an assertion (*ou dunatai*," "he is not able"). John loves such absolute statements as *ou dunatai*.

[28] Stott, *op. cit.*, p.171.

[29] Haas, *op. cit.*, p.114.

[30] It is difficult to decide whether we are to understand "Christ" or "God" as being signified by "from Him." John usually uses "that one" (see notes at verse 17) when he refers to Christ, but not always. Jesus Himself commanded His followers to love one another (John 13:34, 15:12,17; Mark 12:30,31).

That the one who loves God should love his brother also – "That" simply introduces the content of the commandment. John here continues this encouragement with a reminder of the command about loving one another. The folly of the liar's position is seen not only in its inherent inconsistency, but in the fact that he is being disobedient to what children of God have been commanded to do.[31] He who continues loving God is the idea in the present participle. The verb "should love his brother" is also present tense, indicating that the obligation to love is constant and continuing.[32]

---

[31] In 2:7-11 and 3:10-23, John has already stated the need to love one another.

[32] See the discussion in 2:9 of "brother" (p.46, footnote #21).

E. Encouragement Because of the Victory Won Through Faithfulness. 5:1-4

Summary: Chapter 4 closed with a requirement that we love God and love our brothers.   Who is a brother?   We need an objective test by which we may know whether someone else is a child of God and is our brother.   We also need an objective test by which we can know we love.   John here provides both tests.[1]

5:1 -- *Whoever believes that Jesus is the Christ is born of God; and whoever loves the Father loves the* child *born of Him.*

Whoever believes that Jesus is the Christ – The Greek construction "whoever believes" ("everyone who" followed by a present participle) is identical to what we have read in 2:29; 3:3,4; 4:2,3,7.   The present participle *pisteuōn* ("believes") shows that this is a continuous faith.   Continuing to believe that Jesus is the Christ[2] is virtually synonymous with the "confession" or acknowledgment demanded of the true believer according to 2:22-23 and 4:2, 15.   Such a faith is diametrically opposite to the beliefs being taught by the Gnostics, and against which John has been cautioning throughout this whole letter.   To believe that "Jesus is the Christ" is to believe that the One who was known as the man Jesus is also the Messiah.   The whole incarnation is in view.   Messiah and Jesus are not two different persons as some Gnostics maintained.

Is born of God – For "is born of God" (*ek tou theou gegennētai*) see 2:29, 3:9, and 4:7. The marginal note in the NASB offers "begotten" as a possible translation for *gegennētai*. *Gegennētai* is a perfect tense form of the verb *gennaō*.   It is a word not easy to translate since it can refer either to conception or birth, and thus may be rendered "begotten" (conceived) or "born" according to the emphasis of the context.   Abbott-Smith's Greek Lexicon tells us that *gennaō* is to be translated "beget" when referring to a *father's* contribution to new life.   In reference to a *mother's*, the same word is translated "born" or "to bring forth."[3]   This being true, the marginal reading "begotten" is to be preferred.

---

[1] We have opted to treat 5:1-4 as a separate reason why the readers should be encouraged.   A good case could be made that these verses actually conclude the paragraph begun at 4:16b.

[2] *Pisteuein hoti* expresses belief in the truth of a statement or thesis.   For the meaning of the various constructions found with the verb "believe" see comments at 3:23.   1 John 5:1 does not say "believes *in*," which would be connected to an obedient faith.   Rather, John writes "believes *that*," signifying that an acceptance of testimony concerning Jesus is what is involved in being begotten (spiritual conception).

[3] The problem of translation (and thus of the meaning conveyed) is complicated by the diversity of renderings of *gennaō* in popular English versions.   In the KJV, "born" is used at John 1:13, 3:3,5 and 1 John 5:1a, but "begotten" occurs at 1 John 5:1b.   The NASB and NIV have "born" at John 1:13, 3:3,5 and at 1 John 5:1a, but have "child" at 1 John 5:1b.   Neither the "born of God" nor the "is a child of God" is a very satisfactory translation of *ek tou theou gegennētai*.   The ASV did a better job of translating.   It has "born" at John 1:13, 3:3,5; but uses "begotten" every time *gegennētai* occurs in 1 John.   (In 1 John, the ASV follows the guidelines for translation offered in Abbott-Smith, rightly so in this commentator's judgment.)

A major consequence of this whole discussion is its impact on the doctrine of the new birth. In John 1:12,13 and 1 John 5:1, is John saying that everyone who believes has been "born" from God, or has been "begotten"? If "born" is intended, then being a child of God depends entirely on "believing in the fact that Jesus is the Christ."[4] If "begotten" is John's intention, then belief marks only the beginning of the process by which one becomes a child of God. In harmony with the fact that *gennaō* means "beget" when it is the Father's activity in view, and in harmony with the way the ASV translates this verse, we do teach that the person who believes has been begotten. Faith comes by hearing the word of God (Romans 10:17). When faith results from hearing (i.e., we believe that Jesus is the Christ), the new birth has begun; at this stage, conception has taken place. "Conception" is synonymous with believing what God says about Jesus (John 1:12,13; 1 John 5:1 ASV). It is man's "spirit" that is born again (John 3:6). Man's "spirit" becomes "dead" through trespasses and sins. A conception and birth are needed for the "spirit" to become alive again. That this conception or begetting is "of God" (i.e., caused by God) does not teach what is called a first work of grace.[5] The doctrine of first work of grace and the Biblical statement that "faith comes by hearing the Word of God" are two diametrically opposed ideas. In the Parable of the Sower we learn that the "seed" is the word. The conception is "of God" in that God provides the seed (via inspired preaching, inspired scriptures) by which we become believers. He also sends the preachers who broadcast the seed. He doesn't overwhelm our freedom of choice to cause us to believe or to be conceived. When we are immersed, He causes our spirits to be alive again. Divine power has been exercised to enable us to start over religiously.

And whoever loves the Father loves the *child* born of Him – As the NASB margin shows, there is no word for "Father" in the Greek. All John wrote is "everyone who loves him who begat" (*pas ho agapōn ton gennēsanta*). The aorist participle *gennēsanta* points back to the time of conversion, and according to the first part of this verse, the one who did the "begetting" is God. "Loves the child born of him" is *agapa ton gegennēmenon ex autou*, which translates literally as "loves the one who has been begotten of Him." "Him that is begotten" is any believer.[6] The ASV translation retains more obviously the truth that it is the "begetting" and the experience of being "begotten" which establish a relationship between Christians. God is the one who "begat" them; therefore, they are brothers,

---

[4] Observe carefully that in John 1:12,13 it says that the one who believes has been "conceived" and has the power to become a son/child (but he isn't one yet).

[5] "First work of grace" is the doctrine that because a man inherits total depravity, he cannot even want to do good (i.e., believe) until God first operates on his heart to make it possible for him to believe. In harmony with this doctrine, Calvinistic writers rather consistently affirm that the combination of verb tenses here in verse 1 (present tense "believes," and perfect tense "has been born/begotten") shows clearly that believing is the result of a previous experience of the new birth. Concomitant with this is the view that God gives faith to the elect; when He does give faith, that faith is evidence or proof that we are one of God's children.

[6] Augustine suggested that "him who has been begotten" is really a reference to Jesus, and that John is calling for his readers to continue to love Jesus (as He has been presented to them from the beginning). However, it would not be in harmony with John's normal usage to make the perfect tense participle *ton gegennēmenon* a reference to Jesus. John consistently uses the perfect participle of Christians.

the children of a common Father.   The verb form *agapa* ("loves") can be either indicative or a hortatory subjunctive.   The idea seems to be this: Everyone who loves his father should love also his father's children because they are his own brothers and sisters. "Loves" (*agapaō*) always means to deliberately do what is spiritually best for the other person (see at 2:15, including footnote #26 at that place).

5:2 -- *By this we know that we love the children of God, when we love God and observe His commandments.*

By this we know – Does *en toutō* ("by this") point backward to what was said in verse 1[7] or forward to what is said in the next clause?[8]   Taking it as pointing forward, we have an answer to the question, Just how is it that we know we love (or should love)?   It is part and parcel of loving God to keep His commandments.   So interpreted, the truth taught here is similar to the truth insisted on in 4:20,21.   In chapter 4, love and obedience to God was shown to involve love for His children; here love for God's children is said to result from our love and obedience to God.

That we love the children of God – *Agapōmen* ("love") can be either an indicative or subjunctive form, just as was true in the close of verse 1.   If we take it as a subjunctive form it would be understood as meaning we *ought* to love.   The ones who are the objects of our love are called "children of God;" that is, believers in Jesus who have become "children of God" as a result of the process that began with their "begetting."[9]

When we love God – This *hotan* clause has caused problems for interpreters.[10]   *Hotan* with a present tense subjunctive usually indicates repeated action; so the meaning would be "whenever, as often as, every time that, in every case where."   Whenever a man loves God, he also has an attendant obligation to love God's children; as John has already made clear at 3:17, 4:20, love for God involves love for His children since they are our brethren.

And observe His commandments – Another way to know we ought to love the children of God is this: when we love we are simply carrying out His orders.   The verb "observe"

---

[7] If "by this" is taken as pointing back to the two "whoever" clauses given in verse 1, then verse 2 is a conclusion drawn from those clauses.

[8] With but one or two exceptions (e.g., 3:19), it is clearly the established usage of *en toutō* in the epistle that it points forward.   What causes commentators to pause is that the following clause is introduced by *hotan* instead of the usual constructions (i.e., *ean*, *hoti*, or a disconnected sentence).

[9] For "children of God" see on 3:1.   The use of the phrase "children of God" instead of "brethren" is significant.   Every one who has been born of God ("children" is *tekna*) ought to love all those who have been similarly ennobled.

[10] As indicated in footnote #7 above, some treat the "by this" with which this verse begins as pointing backwards to verse 1.   One of the reasons for so interpreting is an attempt to give an explanation to this *hotan* clause.

here (*poiōmen*) means do, act according to, carry out; it suggests active obedience.[11] *Entolē* ("commandments") speaks of divine orders. As we keep God's commands, we treat our brothers differently than we would were we not keeping God's commands.

5:3 -- *For this is the love of God, that we keep His commandments; and His commandments are not burdensome.*

For this is the love of God – "For" shows that this verse is developing an idea introduced in verse 2. This is what is involved in "when we love God." As the following "that" clause explains, there is no such thing as true love of God which does not also involve obedience.

That we keep His commandments – In essence, love for God is expressed, not so much by spoken words, or by beautiful thoughts, or by an emotion of the heart, as it is by habitual obedience to His commands.[12]

> John is the New Testament writer who provides a number of pithy definitions. For example, in his Gospel he defines eternal life (17:3) and in his first epistle he repeatedly explains spiritual truths (consult 2:5-6; 3:4; 3:10,23,24; 4:2,10; 5:14). Here he states what love for God means: "to obey His commands." Love for God does not consist of spoken words, even if they are well intentioned, but of determined action that demonstrates obedience to God's commands.[13]

Indeed, whether the object of one's love is God or man, *agapē* ("love") is practical and active. John has told us (3:17,18) that love for the brethren expresses itself "in deed and in truth," in sacrificial service; now he reminds us (cp. 2:4ff) that love for God expresses itself in keeping His commandments. Jesus taught the same thing about how one expresses love to Him (John 14:15,21). What commandments in particular does John have in mind? 4:21 has spoken of loving God and loving the brother. These are the commands that are not burdensome. It just takes faithfulness, day in and day out.

And His commandments are not burdensome – *Bareiai* can be rendered grievous, severe, unsparing, irksome, oppressive.[14] God's commands are not oppressive, so as to

---

[11] The usual phrase in 1 John is *tas entolas aoutou tērein* ("to keep His commandments"); see 2:3, 3:22, and 5:3. Indeed, there is a manuscript variation at this place. *Poiōmen* is read by Vaticanus and other uncial manuscripts, the Vulgate, and the Syriac; "the variant *tērōmen* is an assimilation of an unusual phrase (found only here in the New Testament) to the more usual form found in the next verse" (Metzger, *op. cit.*, p. 715).

[12] "Keep" is *tērōmen*. (Compare *poiōmen* of verse 2.)

[13] Kistemaker, *op. cit.*, p.349.

[14] The adjective *bareiai* (burdensome, heavy) is used in Matthew 23:4 of the "heavy loads" (hundreds of man-made rules) imposed upon the people by the Pharisees; of "wolves" in Acts 20:29; of Paul's letters in 2 Corinthians 10:10; and of the charges against Paul in Acts 25:7. (Robertson, *op. cit.*, p.238). Many commentators call attention to the words of Jesus where He said "My yoke is easy and My burden is light" (Matthew 11:30, KJV). However, it should be noted that "light" at Matthew 11:30 is *elaphrai eisin*, not the *bareiai ouk eisin* that John here writes.

crush the freedom and spontaneity of love.   It is not John's intention to make light of God's commandments.   God's commands are exacting and demanding, but the Christian finds them a delight to do.   The heavenly Father has commanded only what is beneficial to His children.   Instead of unreasonably restricting one's behavior, God's commands allow God's children the freedom and liberty they so ardently long for.   The present tense verb ("are") serves to characterize this description of God's commands as something that is true all the time.   The next verse gives further reason why God's commands are not burdensome.

5:4 -- *For whatever is born of God overcomes the world; and this is the victory that has overcome the world -- our faith.*

For whatever is born of God overcomes the world -- "For" suggests this verse is intended to introduce a reason why God's commandments are not burdensome.   Obedience to them enables the child of God to overcome the world.   That is a cause for joy, not grief! "Whatever" shows that the Greek construction is neuter, all that is born of God.   Alford calls it a "comprehensive categorical neuter"[15] and Plummer supposes John wrote the neuter to emphasize not "the victorious *person*" but "the victorious *power*."[16]   All over the world, those begotten[17] of God continually overcome the world by their faithfulness. "Overcomes"[18] is present tense, expressing continuation; the Christian keeps on conquering the world.   "To go down to defeat is the exception, not the rule."[19]   "The world"[20] in this context certainly includes a hesitation or refusal to obey God's commands.   The clause serves to say that in the continuing effort to overcome the temptations to evil, the Christian doesn't have to struggle under his own power.   It is rather difficult (yea, impossible) to live the Christian life without first becoming a Christian.   But, what a change is wrought by the new birth!   As a result of the new birth, our "spirit" is alive (Romans 8:10) and can prompt our behavior (Romans 8:5ff).   The old slavery to sin is gone (Romans 6:7).   The child of God has been delivered from the dominion of darkness and transferred into the kingdom of God's dear Son (Colossians 1:13).   The Christian has the help of the indwelling Holy Spirit to live the Christian life.   As a result, when one has become a Christian, faithfulness to God is the norm.   That's why, for the Christian, God's commands are not impossible.

---

[15] Alford, *op. cit.*, p.498.

[16] Plummer, *op. cit.*, p.157.

[17] On "born (begotten) of God" see 2:29 and 5:1.   On the perfect tense for "born of God" see on 3:9.

[18] For the verb "to overcome" see on 2:13.

[19] Wuest, *op. cit.*, p.174.

[20] For "the world" see notes at 2:15.

And this is the victory that has overcome the world -- our faith – There is a play on words in the Greek (*autē estin hē nikē hē nikēsasa*) that is difficult to convey in English.[21] Attempts to reproduce the paronomasia include, "this is the conquest that has conquered the world" and "the overcoming/defeating that overcomes/defeats." If "the world" that is overcome includes a disinclination to obey God's commands, then perhaps Kistemaker is correct when he affirms that the aorist participle translated "has overcome" is "a timeless aorist, expressing a fact that is always true."[22] "This" points forward to "faith," so John writes that "faith is the victory that has overcome the world."[23] Depending on the context, the noun "faith" can refer to behavior, or to assent to the facts (cp. 5:1).[24] The word often can rightly be translated "faithfulness" (e.g., Matthew 23:23 NASB), a word that depicts a lifestyle of doing what God says. "Faithfulness" is the victory.[25] Doing God's commands, day in and day out, is how victory is won and the world overcome, and God's commands are proven to not be burdensome. Each of us probably has a favorite Bible hero. Hebrews 11 points to numerous people who were faithful and are heroes of the faith. They were not superhuman, just faithful. Their determination to be faithful to God is what made them great! Anyone who is a child of God can claim a similar victory by imitating their faithfulness.[26]

---

[21] In the NASB, "victory" translates *nikē* and "overcome" translates *nikēsasa*.

[22] Kistemaker, *op. cit.*, p.351. Some think the aorist participle points back to the time of the readers' conversion. Others think it points back to the readers' decisive rejection of the Gnostic false teaching (4:4) which resulted in the withdrawal of the false teachers from the church (2:19). While both of those were victories, they hardly satisfy what this context seems to call for, which is a reason why God's commands are not burdensome.

[23] "Victory" (*hē nikē*) and "faith" (*hē pistis*) stand in apposition. This is the only place the noun *pistis* ("faith") occurs in the letters and Gospel of John. "Faith" (*pistis*) and "believes" (*pisteuō*, verse 1) come from the same root. In English, "believes" is the verb form of "belief," but neither English nor Latin has a verb that corresponds to the noun "faith." Both substitute another verb when translating *pisteuō*.

[24] When we compare verses 3 and 4 (one speaks of obedience, "keep[ing] God's commandments," and the other of "faith") might this not be another place where "obedience" and "faith" are interchangeable terms? On the other hand, when we compare verses 4 and 5 (one speaks of "faith" and the other of "believing that Jesus is God's Son"), perhaps "faith" here is assent to facts. If so, as Stott (*op. cit.*, p.175) suggests, "the unshakable conviction that the Jesus of history is 'the Christ' (5:1), in the sense in which the false teachers denied it (2:22), the pre-existent 'Son of God' (5:5,6), who came to bring us salvation and life (4:9,14), is the victory that enables us to triumph over the world."

[25] Arndt-Gingrich, s.v., show that it was customary to speak of the emperor's *nikē* as the power that granted him victory. By parity of reasoning, faithfulness is the power that gains victory for the Christian.

[26] The songwriter John H. Yates has captured the encouragement this passage affords.

> Encamped along the hills of light, Ye Christian soldiers, rise,
> And press the battle ere the night Shall veil the glowing skies.   *(Continued next page)*
> Against the foe in vales below Let all our strength be hurled;
> Faith is the victory, we know, That overcomes the world.

F. Encouragement Because of God's Testimony Concerning Eternal Life. 5:5-12.

Summary: Faith (belief that Jesus is the Christ) is based on testimony. Verses 6-8 call attention to three witnesses to Jesus. Verses 9-12 call attention to the results of negative and positive response to that testimony.

5:5 -- *And who is the one who overcomes the world, but he who believes that Jesus is the Son of God?*

And who is the one who overcomes the world – "Who is" (*tis estin*; cf. 2:22) suggests "What other person can do it (overcome the world)?" The implied answer is "no one!" "The world" has the same negative connotation it did in verse 4. Or perhaps, in this new paragraph, there is an attack on the Gnostics under the rubric "world," for Gnosticism is antagonistic to the spiritual life and all that God has tried to do in the sending of His Son to redeem the world. The present participle (*nikōn*) describes continuing activity: "the one who keeps on conquering the world."[1]

But he who believes that Jesus is the Son of God? – "He who believes" is present tense, expressing continual action: "The one who continues to believe."[2] Every individual believer, every one who keeps believing that Jesus is the Son of God, is the one who keeps on conquering the world. Compared with 5:1, there has been a slight shift in terminology. In verse 1 the thing to be believed was "Jesus is the Christ," whereas here the thing to be believed is that "Jesus is the Son of God." Both ways of wording the "fact" to be believed are likely intended to resist Gnostic teaching. The human Jesus "is" (continuous action,

---

On every hand the foe we find Drawn up in dread array;
Let tents of ease be left behind, And onward to the fray.
Salvation's helmet on each head, With truth all girt about,
The earth shall tremble 'neath our tread, and echo with our shout.

To him that overcomes the foe, White raiment shall be given;
Before the angels he shall know his name confessed in heaven.
Then onward from the hills of light, Our hearts with love aflame;
We'll vanquish all the hosts of night, in Jesus' conqu'ring name.

Faith is the victory! Faith is the victory!
O glorious victory, That overcomes the world.

[1] See 1 Corinthians 15:57 for the same note of victory (*nikōs*) through Christ. John uses *nikaō* ("overcomes") numerous times in Revelation (2:7,11,17,26, 3:5,12,21) in a way that is nearly synonymous with keeping the faith.

[2] For "the one who believes" see on verse 5:1.

all the time) both Messiah and Son of God (deity).[3]   To believe anything less about Jesus is to believe in somebody who does not have the ability to give us the victory over the godless world.

> A faith which did not really believe that the Son of God was incarnate in Jesus would not be a faith that would overcome.   It would lack the blood of Jesus by which cleansing from sins comes (1:7); it would lack the intercession of Jesus as advocate for sins and failures (2:1ff); and it would rob the love of God of the depth which the knowledge that God was in Christ Jesus reconciling the world unto Himself gives to it.[4]

5:6 -- *This is the one who came by water and blood, Jesus Christ; not with water only, but with the water and with the blood.*

This is the one who came by water and blood, Jesus Christ – Few passages of Scripture have produced such a mass of widely divergent interpretations as have been offered for verses 6-8.   The general idea in these verses is rather agreed on by all.   *Houtos* ("this [one]") is Jesus, who is both Christ and Son of God.   5:1 and 5:5 have called attention to the imperative of believing who Jesus is.   Now belief or faith depends on testimony since faith comes by hearing.   Verses 6-8 call attention to three witnesses on whose testimony the reasonableness of believing in Jesus as the Christ and as the Son of God is grounded. The disagreement concerns exactly to what water, blood, and Spirit refer.

Before we offer a brief survey of interpretations, we must call attention to some guidelines the passage offers to us to help choose between the options.

(1) We presume, in harmony with the thrust of the whole epistle, that John's presentation here has an anti-Gnostic thrust.
(2) "Is" (present tense, continuous action) has the same meaning here it did in 5:1.   Jesus was and is and always will be the Messiah.   It is not something He became at some point after His incarnation.
(3) "Came" translates an aorist participle *ho elthōn*.   If it were the present participle *ho erchomenos* ("the One who is coming") then the emphasis would be on the Messiahship.   The aorist *elthōn* points to an historic event.[5]   The pre-existent person to whom John alludes (Jesus the Christ, the Son of God) "came" into the world (an historical event).   He who came (from heaven, that is) is the same as He who passed through water and blood.
(4) In the clause *di' hudatos kai haimatos* ("by water and blood") John uses the preposition *dia* to express something through which Jesus who was already the Christ passed.

---

[3] Note how many times reference is made to "Son of God" in this epistle.   See 1:3,7; 2:1,22,23; 3:23; 4:2,3,15; 5:1,5.   If "our faith" in verse 4 and "he who believes" in verse 5 go together, then we are told that "the faith that conquers is no mere vague belief in the existence of God, but embraces a definite belief in the Incarnation" (Plummer, *op. cit.*, p.157).

[4] Roberts, *op. cit.*, p.129.

[5] We have already met the word "come" in the wording of the confession in 1 John 4:2, where it refers to the coming of Jesus into the world as the incarnate Son of God.

Jesus the Christ passed *through* water and *through* blood.[6]   Water and blood must point to some historical facts in the earthly life of our Lord.[7]

(5) There is some sense in which the witnesses continue to "bear witness" (verses 7-8) long after the earthly ministry of Jesus has been completed.   Whatever explanation we give to the witnesses must take this fact into account.

There have been four principal options as men have attempted to identify these two witnesses, "water" and "blood."[8]   *Two interpretations take the words as figurative or symbolic.*   They likely were adopted in an effort to give due consideration to the continual witness to which verses 7 and 8 refer.   (A) Water refers to justification and blood to sanctification.   Some have posited a connection between "water and blood" and what are called the first and second works of grace (justification and sanctification).   The popular song "Rock of Ages" reflects such theology in the words, "Let the water and the blood from thy riven side which flowed be of sin the double cure.   Save from wrath and make me pure." "Water" is thus a reference to baptism/justification; "blood" is a reference to the second work of grace (sanctification) that erases the old inherited sinful nature.   One serious problem with this view (besides the faulty idea of an inherited sinful nature) is that it violates guideline #3 above.   It is not logical to say that Jesus "came" through these first and second works.   They might bear witness (as verse 8 may say) to His coming, but He can hardly be said to have come through them.   (B) Water and blood refer to the ordinances of Christ, baptism and the Lord's Supper.   Several objections to this interpretation have been voiced.   Blood is one of the things symbolized in the elements of the Lord's Supper, but "blood" is not found elsewhere in the New Testament as a designation for the Lord's Supper.   It is doubtful that John is here alluding to the Lord's Supper as somehow being an anti-Gnostic testimony to who Jesus is.   Although it might be possible to describe Jesus as "coming" through the ordinances, it is difficult to see how it could be said that He "came" (aorist tense) through them.   To have John making reference to baptism and the Lord's Supper would imply that the false teachers had dissenting opinions about those ordinances, but nothing in this epistle or in extra-Biblical references to the Gnostics supports such an assumption.

Two interpretations take the words literally, and both result in an anti-Gnostic polemic.   (C) John alludes to the blood and water which flowed from Jesus' pierced side (John 19:34,35) when the Roman soldier thrust a spear into his body while it hung on the cross.   So interpreted, John would be arguing against the Docetists here in 1 John, just as he was in the Gospel.   Contrary to Docetism, Jesus' body was not make-believe.   When you pierced it, it bled, just like any human body does.   Commenting on what he personally

---

[6] In this clause, neither word has the definite article.   However, in the following prepositional phrase beginning with *en* (with, in"), both nouns do have the definite article.

[7] The terms likely should not be interpreted symbolically or figuratively, for to do so would detract from the powerful and abiding testimony the two are intended to convey.

[8] Attempts to identify the third witness, "spirit" or "Spirit" will be dealt with in comments on verses 7 and 8.   As will be seen, some of those attempts will affect how "water and blood" are explained.

observed at Calvary, John wrote, "He who has seen has borne witness, and his witness is true; and he knows that he is telling the truth, so that you also may [continue to] believe." (John 19:35).   This incident gives a definite fact which would justify the use of the aorist "came" (*ho elthōn*).   Objections to this interpretation have been voiced.   The fact that no real explanation for the difference in word order (*exēlthen haima kai hudōr* [John 19:34] v. *hudatos kai haimatos* [1 John 5:6]) has proven to be a difficulty to some.   A bigger difficulty is to see how what happened when Jesus' side was pierced can explain the following words "not by water only, but by water and blood" here in 1 John 5:6 (KJV). No one has ever shown that the Gnostics put an undue emphasis on "water" while downplaying "blood" in the case of the human Jesus.   Stott has argued that it would be forced to say that in this incident Jesus "came *through* water and blood," when in fact they came *out* of Him.[9]   (D) Water refers to Jesus' baptism in the Jordan River, and blood refers to Jesus' death on the cross.   This interpretation nicely refutes certain Gnostic tendencies against which John is warning.   Against the teaching of Cerinthus, John's statement makes good sense and is quite pointed.   The Christ as incarnate in Jesus came "not with water only" when He was baptized in the Jordan River at the beginning of His public ministry,[10] but "with the blood" also at His death.   It was the Holy Spirit who came on Jesus at His baptism, not the divine aeon Christ as the Gnostics taught.   Christ Jesus was still in the body when He was crucified; the divine Christ had not left the human Jesus to suffer alone. This second literal explanation is the one that has come to be rather commonly accepted by the commentators.[11]   We, too, adopt it, since it explains the emphatic addition, "not with water only, but with the water and with the blood."   Jesus was the Christ before and when He was baptized.   He was the Christ when and after He died on Calvary.

Not with water only, but with the water and with the blood – Why has John added this sentence?   Evidently he felt that further precision was necessary in order to make his meaning clear and unmistakable.   The article before "water" and "blood" is the article of previous reference.   John also changes the preposition from *dia* ("through") to *en* ("with" or "in"), a preposition that Kistemaker says "denotes accompanying circumstance."[12] These added words stress the fact that the "by blood" (verse 6a) was as important as "by

---

[9] Stott, *op. cit.*, p.177.

[10] If "water" in 1 John 5:6 refers to Jesus' baptism, then denominational writers have little reason to object to "water" in John 3:5 being a reference to baptism as a part of the process of being born again.

[11] Many commentators who do not opt for this second literal explanation choose instead a combination of two or more of these options.   Some find a reference to Jesus' baptism and death in verse 6a (through water and blood) and a reference to the ordinances in verse 6b (in the water and in the blood). Some find a reference to Jesus' baptism and death in verse 6, and then a reference to the ordinances in the continuing witness about which verse 8 speaks.   Some (e.g., Westcott, p.181) combine the literal interpretations.

[12] Kistemaker, *op. cit.*, p.355.

water." This added sentence certainly was intended to be a refutation of the doctrine held by the false teachers.[13]

*5:7 -- **And it is the Spirit who bears witness, because the Spirit is the truth.***

And – The words that are numbered as verse 7 in the NASB are included as part of verse 6 in the KJV. Then the KJV/NKJV include a whole sentence that is not found either in the text or the margin of the NASB. That sentence reads as follows: "For there are three that bear record in heaven, the Father, the Son, and the Holy Ghost: and these three are one."[14] It is a matter of record that this added verse appears first, not in any Greek Manuscripts of the New Testament,[15] nor in any of the ancient versions,[16] but in a fourth-century Latin sermon.[17] It is improbable that such a weakly attested reading was an original part of the text of 1 John.

An interesting circumstance led to the introduction of this so-called "Comma Johanneum" (i.e., the Johannine [interpolated] clause) into our English Bibles. After the invention of printing, the first person to publish an edition of the printed Greek text was Erasmus. His first edition came out in the year 1516. Neither it nor his second edition included this additional verse. A mild controversy was stirred up because the verse was indisputably in the contemporary Latin versions. Erasmus insisted that his text was right,

---

[13] Cerinthus and his followers are dead. There are not many adherents today to their beliefs. But those who deny the incarnation (God became in the flesh) make no trivial error. Such a belief undermines the foundation of the Christian faith and robs us of the salvation in Christ (Stott, *op. cit.*, p.179). "As soon as we reduce the death of Jesus to that of a mere man, so soon do we lose the cardinal point of the New Testament doctrine of the atonement, that God was in Christ reconciling the world to Himself. So-called theologies, which reduce talk of the incarnation to the status of myth, may be attractive to modern men, but they take away our assurance that God's character is sin-bearing love." Marshall, *op. cit.*, p.233.

[14] The translators of the NKJV, however, state in a footnote that the Greek New Testaments (Nestle-Aland, UBS, and Majority Text) omit the words from "in heaven" (verse 7) through "on earth" (verse 8). The added words cause a break in the sense. In their controversy with the Gnostics, John's readers did not need a group of witnesses in heaven (as the KJV reads).

[15] The words do not occur in any Greek manuscripts, version or quotation before the 15th century. They do occur in the minuscules numbered 61 [16th century], 88mg, 429mg, 629, 636mg, 918 (so the UBS apparatus notes). As far as modern printed Greek texts are concerned, the words in Greek were first inserted into the Complutensian edition of 1514.

[16] None of the ancient versions of the New Testament contains the words, except the Latin version, and even there the evidence is ambiguous. The words appear, with considerable variation (including inversion of the order of the two sets of witnesses), in some Old Latin and Vulgate manuscripts, but not in the earliest form of the Old Latin or in Jerome's edition of the Vulgate. The Old Latin manuscripts that have the verses date from the 8th century. The Vulgate manuscripts [Amiatinus and Harleianus] which have the verses date from after the 6th century.

[17] Priscillian, a Spanish heretic who died about AD 385, is the earliest Latin writer to show acquaintance with the added verse (he does so in a Latin sermon included in his *Liber Apologeticus*). Roberts believes Priscillian was the one who first made up these words, and then from Priscillian's sermon the verse was added to a Latin manuscript of Pseudo-Vergilius, and then came to work its way into later Latin texts. Roberts, *op. cit.*, p.131.

and was so sure of himself that he rashly promised to include the verse in his next Greek text if one single Greek manuscript could be found in support of it. At length a copy turned up (there is some evidence that the manuscript shown to Erasmus, MS 61 [Codex Britannicus probably written in 1520], was translated from the Latin to the Greek and deliberately produced just to provide a "Greek manuscript" such as Erasmus demanded), and true to his word, Erasmus put this verse in his third edition (1522) of his Greek New Testament, though not without forcible protest. He did not include it in subsequent editions of his Greek text. William Tyndale was the first man to translate the New Testament into English based on a Greek text (instead of Latin), and it was Erasmus' third edition which he employed in making his translation. It was Erasmus' third edition that was used by the scholars who eventually produced the text that came to be called "the Textus Receptus" from which the King James Version was translated. That's how the "Comma Johanneum" became part of our English Bibles.[18] It is proper to confine our comments to the three witnesses concerning whom John did write, namely, the Spirit, the water, and the blood.

It is the Spirit who bears witness – When John writes, "And the Spirit is the one who bears witness," he is saying there is another testimony to the incarnation besides the water and the blood. "Spirit" undoubtedly means the Holy Spirit (as in 4:2).[19] "To bear witness" (*to marturoun*) expresses the characteristic office of "the Spirit," just as "the one who came" (*ho elthōn*) is characteristic of "Jesus Christ."[20] When John says the Spirit "is bearing witness" (present tense, continuous action in the present), it is likely that John is claiming inspiration for himself as he writes the words of this letter.[21] Behind his letter is the "testimony" of the Holy Spirit, precisely as Jesus promised His apostles they would have such power when the Holy Spirit came upon them.

> The reference is probably to the entire revelation of the Holy Spirit in the experience
> of the church,   first of all in the apostolic proclamation of the gospel by the inspired

---

[18] Neil R. Lightfoot, *How We Got The Bible* (Austin, TX.: R.B.Sweet, 1962), p.37.

[19] Numerous other attempts at explaining *pneuma* have proven unsatisfactory. Included are these: (1) The "spirit" which Jesus, when dying, commended to the Lord. (2) Like water and blood were sacraments, "spirit" is another sacrament, absolution. (3) The power by which Christ worked His miracles. (4) The transformation the Spirit works in the lives of Christians. (5) The "spiritual man," i.e., John the Baptist whose testimony is recorded in John 1:19ff and 3:22ff.

[20] In Jesus' Farewell Discourse we learn it is the special ministry of the Spirit (Helper/Comforter/Paraclete) to testify about Jesus. Jesus said, "When the Helper comes, whom I will send to you from the Father, that is the Spirit of truth, who proceeds from the Father, He will bear witness of Me" (John 15:26). See also John 14:26, and 16:7-11,13-14.

[21] John has already written twice how the Spirit works to inspire the apostles' message (3:24, 4:13). He has also alluded to the *chrisma* (anointing) of the Spirit (2:20,27). Scholars have called attention to other occasions when the Spirit bore witness. The Spirit inspired the Old Testament prophets who looked forward to the coming of the Messiah (1 Peter 1:10-12; 2 Peter 1:19-21; cf. John 5:39). The same Spirit descended on Jesus at His baptism (Matthew 3:16; Luke 3:22) to empower Him (Acts 10:38). But these testimonies in the past do not quite satisfy the present tense verb "bears witness" which John here writes. While the New Testament apostles and prophets were alive and functioning, the Spirit continued to testify to God's truth with reference to the person and work of Jesus.

apostle, prophets, and preachers who preached the gospel "through the Holy Spirit sent from heaven" (1 Peter 1:12).   Secondly the Spirit's testimony was shown in the signs He gave confirming this word (Acts 14:1,2, Hebrews 2:1-4).   Then eventually this led to the Christian Scriptures, and so there remains the testimony of the Spirit within the church even for us.   That testimony, as represented by the four Gospels, the preaching imbedded in the Acts of the Apostles, and in the epistles of Paul, Peter, etc., confirms the doctrine of the divine incarnation of Christ Jesus (cf. 1 Timothy 3:16; John 1:1,14,18, 6:51; Colossians 1:22; Hebrews 2:14, 5:7; 1 Peter 4:1).[22]

The next verse will specify what the testimony was when the Spirit bore witness,.   It has to do with who Jesus was (Christ and Son of God) all through his earthly ministry from Bethlehem to His post-resurrection ascension to the right hand of the Father.

Because the Spirit is the truth – *Hoti* is likely causal.   If so, this phrase explains why the Spirit can give only absolutely reliable testimony.   The very nature of the Spirit is truth.[23]   With such a nature, the only thing the Spirit can do is tell the truth.   He cannot lie or deceive.   The Spirit shares with other members of the Godhead the character of not being able to lie (Titus 1:2; Hebrews 6:18).   This is what makes His witness so weighty.

5:8 -- *For there are three that bear witness, the Spirit and the water and the blood; and the three are in agreement.*

For there are three that bear witness – "For" shows this verse serves to introduce an explanation of something just said.   In verse 6, John called attention to "by water *and* blood" then opened verse 7 with these words, "and the Spirit bears witness."   Just in case we missed the "and" which shows that water and blood were witnesses just like the Spirit is, John now brings the three together and declares that they all "bear witness."   How can water and blood testify along with the Spirit?   Perhaps we should look at the text from a Semitic point of view, wherein impersonal objects can be said to testify.   For example, the heap of stones Jacob and Laban put together was called a witness (Gen. 31:48).   Perhaps the water and blood are what we would call circumstantial evidence.   "Three" reflects the practice of the ancient world of requiring a plurality of witnesses to establish a case.   According to the Mosaic law (Deuteronomy 19:15, author's translation), "One witness is not enough ... A matter must be established by the testimony of two or three witnesses."   (See also Deuteronomy 17:6 and Matthew 18:16.)   2 Corinthians 13:1 seems

---

[22] Roberts, *op. cit.*, p.132.   "The attack of modern rationalism against the deity of Jesus began with an attack on the written testimony of the Spirit.   The claim that Jesus was a deceiver rather than a deliverer depends upon the destruction of Scriptural evidence to the contrary.   No honest scholar can deny that the writings of the Scripture claim for Jesus exactly what the rationalist (as well as the Gnostic) cannot accept: that He is God as man.   Since this is obviously the claim of these writings, it becomes necessary to disprove the reliability of the writings themselves.   To do so is to deny the inspiration, or to use John's term, the testimony, of the Spirit in the Bible, and especially the New Testament."   Gill, *op. cit.*, p.130-31.

[23] One of the titles Jesus used for the Holy Spirit was "the Spirit of truth" (John 14:26, 16:13, cf. 1 John 4:6).

to show that the requirement of such multiple evidentiary witness was more wide-spread than simply in the Jewish world. The Greek sentence is grammatically incongruous. Although Spirit, water, and blood are all neuter nouns in Greek, they are referred to here by a clause written in the masculine plural: *treis eisin hoi marturountes*. The verb "are" and the participle "bear witness" are present tense, suggesting a continuous testimony to Jesus that takes place at the present time. The Spirit, water, and blood, "are not merely witnesses who might be called, or who have once been called, but witnesses who are perpetually delivering their testimony."[24]

The Spirit and the water and the blood – Here we have the same three witnesses of verses 6 and 7 repeated with the Spirit first. This leads us to believe that the same interpretation must be given to "Spirit," "water," and "blood" in this verse as in the preceding verses, especially since John gives no indication of a change in meaning.[25] Taking "Spirit" in verse 8 in the same way we explained it in verse 7, what John is doing in verse 8 is affirming that what the Spirit prompts him to say/write about Jesus is no different from what was shown to be true at Jesus' baptism and crucifixion.

And the three are in agreement – The Greek *eis to en eisin* literally means "are into the one. " All three witnesses say the same thing; they are united in their testimony, all witnessing to the truth that Jesus is the Christ, the Son of God. This threefold, legally valid testimony is in flat opposition to the Gnostic doctrine that the divine Christ came upon Jesus at His baptism and abandoned Jesus before He was nailed to the cross. "The implication of this last remark is that their witness stands or falls together: a person cannot claim that he is accepting the witness of the Spirit if he rejects the witness of the water and the blood to the true character of Jesus."[26]

5:9 -- If we receive the witness of men, the witness of God is greater; for the witness of God is this, that He has borne witness concerning His Son.

If we receive the witness of men – The importance of this verse is that it declares explicit-

---

[24] Plummer, *op. cit.*, p.161.

[25] A surprising number of commentators treat "Spirit, water and blood" differently in verse 8 than they did in verses 6 and 7. First, attention is called to the fact that the present tenses ("is" and "bears witness," verse 7) contrast with the aorist which the Greek uses in "the one who came by water and blood" (verse 6). Consequently, it is supposed the reference in verse 8 is no longer to events that happened at a specific moment in the past, but to something that takes place in the present. What is it that takes place in the present? Not a few have supposed John has changed topics from what happened to Jesus during His earthly ministry to what happens when the ordinances (baptism, Lord's Supper) are observed. In reply, we ask this: Rather than highlight a supposed contrast just two verses apart, why not observe that the present tense "bear witness" in verse 8 precisely matches the present tense "bears witness" in verse 7? In addition, why cannot past events continue to bear witness, in the same way as the Old Testament Scriptures can still bear witness to Jesus; or in the same way that Abel, though long dead, still speaks of the value of faithfulness (Hebrews 11:4)?

[26] Marshall, *op. cit.*, p.237.

ly what has so far only been hinted.   It contains an argument from the lesser to the greater. The testimony of three *human* witnesses in legal matters is enough to settle a matter.   If the testimony of three human witnesses establishes the facts in a case, then certainly three *divine* witnesses should provide unimpeachable and irrefutable testimony to the facts concerning Jesus being the Son of God.   The present tense verb "receive" indicates something that habitually occurs.[27]   The word "if" expresses not a doubt, but a fact: "we [men in general] do accept human testimony."   "Witness" here means "what is said by a witness."   Since "men" is plural, it is probably an error to attempt (as some have done) to limit this to the testimony to Jesus given by one man, John the Baptist.

The witness of God is greater – "Greater" means "more worthy of acceptance."   For one reason or another, men don't always tell the truth.   God, however, can speak nothing but pure holy truth.   As explained in the following clauses, the "witness of God" is His testimony concerning His Son Jesus Christ.   Because God was involved in all three,[28] the three witnesses in fact give a harmonious, consistent, divine testimony concerning Jesus.

For the witness of God is this, that He has borne witness concerning His Son – "For" has an explanatory force, identifying what it is to which God has testified.   "This" (*hautē*) should be taken as pointing forward to the *hoti*-clause.[29]   The "that" clause says God's testimony concerned His Son, a subject on which God the Father is fully competent to speak.   Jesus Himself said, "No one knows the Son, except the Father" (Matthew 11:27). John again uses a perfect tense ("has borne witness") because he thinks of God's testimony as having permanent validity.   That being true, men (especially John's readers, if not his opponents) would be well advised to listen when God speaks!

5:10 -- *The one who believes in the Son of God has the witness in himself; the one who does not believe God has made Him a liar, because he has not believed in the witness that God has borne concerning His Son.*

The one who believes in the Son of God has the witness in himself – Having carefully reported exactly what the threefold divine witness testified concerning the Son, John now proceeds to show how men are affected by the testimony.   He does so both positively and

---

[27] For "receive" in the sense of "accept as valid," see John 3:11,32,33.

[28] When one looks for specific examples of God's witness to Jesus, it is natural to think of the declarations made by God at the baptism of Jesus (Matthew 3:17) and at the transfiguration (Matthew 17:5), and the time when God spoke in answer to Jesus' prayer (John 12:28).   In this latter case, as soon as God promised Jesus that in His death and resurrection God would glorify His (the Father's) name, Jesus went on to explain the world-changing ramifications of His death on Calvary (John 12:30-36).

[29] There is a manuscript variation at this place.   The reading *hoti* (in *hoti memartureken*) is undoubtedly right.   Should the inferior reading *en* ("which") of the Textus Receptus be adopted, the *hautē* must refer back to the witness already described, i.e., that borne by the three witnesses, the Spirit, the water, and the blood, and the remaining clauses of this verse must be given a different explanation than the one we shall offer.

negatively. First he states what is involved when one accepts God's testimony. The purpose of God's testimony to Christ is to lead the hearers of that testimony to faith in Christ (e.g., John 1:7, 20:31). Faith comes by hearing the word of Christ (Romans 10:17). There is a cause and effect relationship between "receive ... the witness of God" (verse 9) and "believes in the Son of God" (verse 10). For the first time in 1 John we have the phrase "believes in" (*pisteuōn eis*) which occurs so many times in the Fourth Gospel. This is the construction that expresses an obedient faith.[30] Here in verse 10a, since *pisteuōn* is present tense, this obedient faith ("believes in") is continuing action, a continuing lifestyle.[31] What John meant when he wrote "has ... in himself"[32] has been vigorously debated. It is not so much what the verb "has"[33] means as what "in ... himself" is intended to convey. As we have seen, John's practice is to write things nearly opposite. "Has ... in himself" in this clause is the opposite of "made Him (God) a liar" in the next. The contrast is between accepting what God has said and rejecting it. Since it is "with the heart [that] man believes" (Romans 10:10)," perhaps we can even talk about the "heart" as we explain "in himself."[34] The person who holds God's testimony in himself is one who accepts it and holds on to it in his mind, meditates on it, and carries it out.

The one who does not believe God has made Him a liar – John, as he does so frequently, having given what is involved in a positive response to God's testimony concerning Jesus, proceeds to put his proposition in the strongest light by highlighting what is involved in a

---

[30] In comments at 3:23 and 5:1,5, it was explained that whereas *pisteuō* followed by the dative means no more than to believe what someone says, *pisteuō* followed by a prepositional phrase is a faith that is expressed by corresponding and appropriate actions. "Believes" is used 3 times here in verse 10, with different constructions following. In verse 10a it is *pisteuō eis* ("believes in"); that signifies an obedient faith (as indicated by the prepositional phrase after *pisteuō*). In verse 10b, *pisteuō* is followed by the dative to refer to a lack of trust in [what] God [says], in the sense of not accepting His testimony. The third use of *pisteuō* in verse 10c, "he has not believed in (*pisteuō eis*) the witness (testimony)" is unique in the New Testament. A simple dative would have sufficed if simple assent to the facts was intended. The prepositional phrase suggests that God expects a personal response to the testimony He has borne to His Son Jesus.

[31] "Belief" is not a one-time thing, after which a man is forever saved. The security of the believer is conditioned on faithfulness.

[32] The manuscripts vary between a reflexive pronoun *eautō* (Sinaiticus Y 049 88 1739) and a personal pronoun *autō* (B K 81 TR). Both are grammatically possible and convey the same meaning.

[33] The sense of *echein* ("have, hold") is the same as the having or holding to the testimony of Jesus in Revelation 6:9, 12:17, 19:10, cf. 20:4), where the witnesses or martyrs hold that testimony fast and bear it whenever the opportunity comes (see Revelation 1:2). Roberts, *op. cit.*, p.134.

[34] We must be careful here when we speak about the heart, lest we be thought to be saying something we reject. Some commentators (reading verse 7 and verse 10 together) suppose John is speaking of the inner witness of the Spirit in the heart of the believer when they read "has this witness (testimony) in himself." This explanation is a corollary to the idea that "faith" is something miraculously produced by God in men's hearts. The very presence of belief is then taken as proof (an inner witness) that God's testimony is true. This whole idea of an inner witness is based on the flawed idea that faith is purely a gift of God, when the Bible shows clearly that faith comes by hearing the word of Christ (Romans 10:17).

negative response to that testimony. "The one who does not believe God"[35] places emphasis on the testimony which God has given about His Son (verse 9). Not to believe in the Son of God is equivalent to saying that God was not telling the truth when on numerous occasions He bore witness to His Son. The perfect tense "has made" (*pepoiēken*) suggests a definite choice made in the past, whose effects abide. The rejection has been made, and its effects are continuing. The charge of making God to be a "liar"[36] is directed against any who refuses to "believe in the Son of God" (i.e., become Jesus' obedient followers), whether they be the false teachers or those who choose to be followers of the false teachers. "It is inconsistent to profess belief in God, as John's opponents did, and yet to disbelieve what God has said."[37] "There is no room for ignorance or misconception. To reject the witness is to deny the truthfulness of God. He has spoken and acted deliberately, and with absolute clearness ... The witness must therefore either be accepted or rejected. It cannot be ignored or explained away."[38]

Because he has not believed in the witness that God has borne concerning His Son – The phrases of verse 9 ("that [God] has borne" and "concerning His Son") are repeated for emphasis. Both perfect tense verbs in this clause ("has not believed" and "has borne [witness]") express past completed action with present continuing results. As noted earlier, this unusual prepositional phrase ("[not] believed in the witness") suggests that God expects a personal response to the testimony He has borne to His Son Jesus.

5:11 -- And the witness is this, that God has given us eternal life, and this life is in the Son.

And the witness is this – "The witness is this (this is the witness)" is the same expression we had in verse 9, and has the same meaning here it did previously.[39] "And" shows that John is calling attention to additional items included in the testimony God has given.[40] God's testimony concerned His Son (verse 9), but also there are two further truths to which God has borne testimony: that God has given us eternal life and that life is in the Son.

That God has given us eternal life – "That" (*hoti*) is most likely declarative, telling in what the "testimony" consists. "Eternal life" is emphatic in the sentence. "The anarthrous

---

[35] There is a great diversity of readings in the manuscripts at this place: "God," "the Son," "the Son of God," "His Son," "Jesus Christ." Of these, "God" (Sinaiticus B K L P) is certainly the best attested.

[36] Another example of "making God a liar" was found in 1:10, where the false teachers who made claims to be without sin are said to be "make Him a liar".

[37] Marshall, *op. cit.*, p.241.

[38] Brooke, *op. cit.*, p.139.

[39] The demonstrative points forward to the "that" clause.

[40] For "witness/testimony" see comments on verses 9 and 10.

phrase emphasizes character or quality.   The gift was something which is best described as 'spiritual life'."[41]   When we read "us," in the light of passages like John 3:16 we must mentally supply "who believe."   (It would not do to affirm that "unbelievers" have been granted the "eternal life" of which this passage speaks.)   He does not say that eternal life will be given (future tense) but that God gave it (aorist tense) to us.   It is not the hope of eternal life that God has given, but "eternal life" itself.   "Has given" (in the aorist tense) refers to something that happened once in the past, but to what event does John refer?   "Some commentators refer it to the historical career of Jesus (cf. 1:2 and John 10:10,28, 17:2) and some to our conversion, at which we personally appropriated, or were given, the life that is in Christ (cf. 3:14)."[42]   If we were to look for examples of God's testimony concerning "eternal life," we might appeal to passages like John 10:10, "I am come that they might have life, and that they might it more abundantly" (KJV).   This was the characteristic emphasis God had in mind when He sent His Son on a mission to this world.

And this life is in His Son – This is the third item in this context included in God's testimony.[43]   First was the testimony concerning His Son (verse 9), and second was the testimony concerning the gift of eternal life (verse 11a).   Now, third, God's testimony is that such life is in His Son.   "Is" is present tense, suggesting is and always will be.   "In His Son" is the only place where eternal life is constantly available, a point which verses 12-13 directly affirm.   If we were to look for an example of God's testimony concerning life in the Son, John 3:15ff would be a good beginning place.   Another verse would be John 3:36, "He who believes in the Son has eternal life, but he who does not obey the Son shall not see life, but the wrath of God abides on him."   The preposition "in" ("in His Son") serves to show that what God's testimony says includes the fact that the only way to obtain eternal life is by being in the Son.   In this context, obedient faith ("believes in the Son," verse 10) is the way one comes to be "in His Son" (verse 11).   Compare 3:24, "The one who keeps His commandments abides in Him."

5:12 -- *He who has the Son has the life; he who does not have the Son of God does not have the life.*

He who has the Son has the life – In this verse, John expresses his thought first positively, then negatively, as he succinctly summarizes the encouragement based on God's testimony concerning eternal life.   "Has the Son" means being in close association or fellowship with Him.[44]   Continuing to be a believer in Jesus is the way to possess the Son and the life

---

[41] Brooke, *op. cit.*, p.140. See the notes on "eternal life" in comments on other passages where the expression occurs in this epistle (1:2, 2:25, 3:15, 5:13,20).

[42] Stott, *op. cit.*, p.183.

[43] We treat this clause as being governed by "that" earlier in the verse.

[44] For the verb *echein* ("to have"), here in the form *ho echōn* ("the one who possesses"), see the comment on 2:23 ("the one who confesses the Son has [possesses] the Father also"). Compare the similar idiom "having" a friend (Luke 11:50), "had" one as an assistant (Acts 13:5), "have" a master (1 Timothy 6:2).

He brings.   "Has" in both cases is present tense, showing that having the Son and having life are contemporaneous.   As long as one has the Son, he continues to have life.[45]   If one no longer has the Son, he forfeits eternal life.

He who does not have the Son of God does not have the life – Here is John's statement of the negative side of this summary.   Of course this converse is true.   If one does not have the Son of God,[46] he does not have life, for there is "no other name under heaven that has been given among men, by which we must be saved" (Acts 4:12).   There is no other sacrifice for sins that avails, save the death of Christ (Hebrews 9:11ff).   Eternal life is not granted to the whole world.   It is given to individuals, soul by soul, according as each does or does not believe in the Son of God.   That John should close on this negative note agrees with the fact that the verse, like most else in this letter, is polemic.   The false teachers may have claimed to know Christ (2:3ff) and to be in fellowship with God (1:6), but those claims were false.   Likewise, false is their claim to have "life" when they have repudiated the Son of God in whom alone is eternal life.[47]

G. Encouragement Because of Opportunities to Pray for the Erring. 5:13-17

> *Summary*:   John tells us that one of his purposes for writing this letter has been to assure the believer that he has eternal life (verse 13).   Such assurance of salvation leads to boldness in prayer (verses 14,15).   Believers should pray for brethren who are sinning, but not for folk who are sinning "a sin unto death" (verses 16,17).

5:13 -- These things I have written to you who believe in the name of the Son of God, in order that you may know that you have eternal life.

---

[45] The article (article of previous reference, i.e., eternal life," verse 11) should be translated "has THE life." We have already learned that "eternal life" is something the believer already participates in even while continuing to live this earthly life. Cp. John 3:16,36, both of which affirm "eternal life" is the present possession of the believer.

[46] In the first part of the verse, John simply said "Son." Now he says "Son of God," perhaps thereby intending to indicate once again the enormity of the offense, and the impossibility of having God as Father without accepting His Son.

[47] It must be remarked that the question as to whether eternal salvation is altogether confined to those who in the fullest sense "have" the Son (to the exclusion, e.g., of those who have never heard of Him) does not belong here, but must be entertained on other grounds. John here is confining his saying to those to whom the divine testimony has come. To them, according as they receive or do not receive it (and thus they have or do not have the Son of God), the gospel is an aroma of life unto life or of death unto death (2 Corinthians 2:16). (Adapted from Alford, *op. cit.*, p.508.)

These things I have written – Most commentators and many of our English and Greek Bibles start a new paragraph with verse 13. About the only difference concerns the perceived thrust of these verses. For some, this is the beginning of the conclusion of the epistle.[1] For others, the conclusion does not begin until verse 18. Our comments and outline reflect this latter opinion. *Tauta* ("these things") likely refers back to the epistle as a whole, rather than being limited to the section immediately preceding (5:1-12). *Egrapha* ("I have written") is an epistolary aorist, referring to this very letter we call 1 John.[2] When the readers receive this letter, John's activity of writing will be a past event ("I have written").[3]

To you who believe in the name of the Son of God – By these words John shows he has addressed this letter to Christians (i.e., those who believe in the name of the Son of God). In the Greek, this clause is placed at the end of the sentence, making it deliberately emphatic.[4] John says that it is "believers" and not the heretics who have eternal life! "Who believe" is a present participle, expressing continuation, "You who continue to believe ...." John has not written this letter to lead the readers to initial belief. The readers are already believers. For "believe in the name of the Son of God" see comments on 1 John 3:23, where one of God's commands was that we "believe in the name of His Son, Jesus Christ".[5] For "Son of God" see on 1:3.

In order that you may know that you have eternal life – In the same way that John sum-

---

[1] Some compare verse 13 to John 20:30,31, which they tend to call "the original conclusion" of the Gospel. The language, "original conclusion," presumes that chapter 21 was added to the Fourth Gospel at a later time than the writing of the first 20 chapters. They offer the comment that the remainder of this epistle (5:14-21) is a postscript or an appendix (added possibly by another hand), analogous to how they suppose chapter 21 was added to the Gospel. Some go so far as to conjecture that the same person added both chapter 21 to the Gospel and the last 9 verses to the epistle, and did so after the apostle John died. External evidence is certainly against such views. No manuscript or version seems to exist in which these closing verses are missing. As early as the 2nd century, various of these verses in 5:14-21 are quoted by Tertullian and Clement of Alexandria, with both writers naming John as the author of the words. (See Plummer, *op. cit.*, p.164, for documentation.)

[2] Interpreted as an historical aorist, "I have written" would point to a previous letter. In an English translation, the idea behind an epistolary aorist is better represented as "I have written" or "I am writing" rather than by the literal translation of the aorist, "I did write" or "I wrote."

[3] "I" (the subject of the verb) is the apostle John. See the matter of authorship discussed in the Introductory Studies.

[4] In the Greek, the clause "that you may know that you have eternal life" follows directly after "I have written [this] to you." The order of this and the next clauses is transposed in the NASB from what the Greek reads in order to make a smoother English sentence.

[5] At 3:23 "believe in the name" of God's Son is mentioned, but the construction is in the dative (*hina pisteusōmen tō onomati*, "that we [should] believe in the name"). The use of *eis* ("in," literally, "into") in the present context may indicate total devotion to Jesus, as a person who possesses the active qualities denoted by the name "Son of God," whereas the dative in 3:23 may be understood in terms of a merely intellectual assent to the true confession about Christ. (Smalley, *op. cit.*, p.291.)

marizes his purpose for writing his Gospel (John 20:30,31), here in verse 13 he summa-rizes his purpose for writing this epistle.[6]   In the Gospel he says he wants his readers to continue to believe so that they may continue to have life.   In the epistle he says "that you may *know* that you (continue to) have eternal life."[7]   The verb translated "know" (*oida*) means to know through reflection, study, and mental deduction.   *Oida* can also be translated to be sure, to be assured, to have no doubt.   The form here is aorist active and suggests that the readers may be assured once and for all that, from what John has written, in God's Son Jesus Christ they already have eternal life.[8]   "You have" is present tense, indicating that to have eternal life is not a future but a present and ongoing reality for the obedient believer.   The unsettling statements to the contrary by the false teachers should not shake their confidence!   Time and again John has written "by this we know."   He is saying, The tests I have shared in this letter assure you that you have eternal life.   "Eternal life" is a quality of life, a kind of life, an abundant life both now and hereafter.   The old life (after the flesh) is changed for something new and glorious (after the spirit).   The difference in quality can be seen when we compare descriptions of the old and new ways of living.   Whereas the old life was characterized by "immorality, impurity, sensuality, idolatry, sorcery, enmities, strife, jealousy, outbursts of anger, disputes, dissensions, factions, envyings, drunkenness, carousings, and things like these" (Galatians 5:19-21), the new life is characterized by "love, joy, peace, patience, kindness, goodness, faithfulness, gentleness, self-control" (Galatians 5:22-23).   The next verse will identify another characteristic of the new life we have in Christ.

5:14 -- *And this is the confidence which we have before Him, that, if we ask anything according to His will, He hears us.*

And this is the confidence which we have before Him – One of the blessings of being in possession of eternal life is the "confidence" that results.   This is the fourth time John has alluded to the Christian's "confidence" or "boldness" (*parrēsia*, absolute freedom of speech):   twice in connection with the day of judgment (2:28, 4:17), twice (3:21,22, and

---

[6] We say "purpose" (singular) because the additional sentence found in the Textus Receptus, Majority Text, KJV and NKJV ("and that ye may believe on the name of the Son of God") is rightly omitted.   The shorter form of the text is found in Sinaiticus, Vaticanus, Alexandrinus, Codex Amiatinus, and in the old Coptic word for word.   According to the longer reading, the purpose for writing 1 John was twofold: (1) That those who continue to believe may know they have eternal life; and (2) that they should continue to believe on the name of Jesus Christ.

[7] In 1 John 1:4, John told us he was writing "so that our joy may be made complete."   The context there shows what constitutes this joy.   It is the consciousness of writer and readers together in fellowship with God and His Son and His saints; in other words it is the conscious possession of eternal life (John 17:3).   Thus the opening and closing of this letter, in effect, say the same thing.

[8] In the Greek the adjective "eternal" is separated from its noun "life" by the verb, and so is emphatic by position: You have life – yes, eternal life.   See also on 3:15 and 5:11,12.   In this verse eternal life is conditioned on faithfulness (see the two present tense verb forms "you who believe" and "you have").   The New Testament teaches the security of the "believer" (the security of the one who continues to believe).

here) in connection with approaching God in prayer.[9]   In each place where John speaks of "confidence," it is the Christian's connection with Christ and the Father which provides the grounds for great boldness or confidence toward them.   In this verse, the pronoun "Him" probably refers to God.[10]   The preposition *pros* ("before") may point to an active approach to God as we come to Him in prayer, or it may reflect the face-to-face fellowship with Him, which are expressions of the eternal life about which John has been writing (verses 11-13).

That, if we ask anything according to His will, He hears us – This *hoti* ("that") clause (with its verbs "ask" and "hear") points to that to which the Christian's confidence is directed.   It is a confidence about God hearing and answering prayer.   The middle voice in Greek indicates the subject of the verb is pictured as acting for its own benefit.   Thus, John's use of the middle voice verb "ask" may indicate that the answer to the prayer in some way has a personal or subjective significance:[11]   "we keep on asking for ourselves." The promise of answered prayer here in verses 14 and 15 repeats what John wrote earlier about answered prayer: "We have confidence before God, and whatever we ask we receive from Him" (3:21-22).   There, the request may have had something to do with helping one's needy brother.   Here, one issue being prayed about is the brother who is seen committing a sin.   The consistent use of the first person plural ("we") through the closing verses of this chapter implies that John is thinking of those readers who are Christians.   The equally consistent use of present tense verbs ("we have," "we ask," "He hears") suggests that a continuing truth is being set forth.   "According to His will" (*kata to thelēma autou*) is a qualification concerning the prayers to which God listens.[12]   Subject

---

[9] "This" (*hautē*) points forward to the "that" clause.   The pronoun "we" is true of any who "believe ... in the Son of God" (5:13), and so share in the eternal life that God grants.

[10] However, the reference to God's Son in verse 13 may mean that an allusion to Jesus as mediator cannot be entirely excluded from consideration.

[11] Westcott, *op. cit.*, p.189-90.   The verb translated "ask" is *aiteō*, an inferior asking something of a superior.

[12] For God's "will (the thing He wills)" see on 2:17.   Behind many of the comments offered at this place is the doctrine of absolute predestination.   According to this view, God can't and doesn't do anything (in answer to prayer) other than what was foreknown by Him and predestined to occur.   If everything is so predestined, then it can hardly be said that "prayer changes things."   While the Bible does speak of God's plan and purpose for the world, we must not think in deterministic terms as if God programmed, down to the minutest detail, everything that is going to happen, including the fact that we are going to pray in a particular way and at a particular time.   Such absolute determinism is inconsistent with the freedom of will which the Bible assigns to God's children, and it is inconsistent with the cases where God altered what He said He would do in response to men's prayers.   In answer to Abraham's prayer, did He not alter the number of righteous men on whose presence the fate of Sodom and Gomorrah rested?   In Elijah's time, when it would not have otherwise rained, did not God send rain in answer to that righteous man's prayer? While His ultimate plan will be carried out, is it not so that intermediate steps can be altered in answer to the prayers of the saints?   (We have thus been introduced to the contemporary debate called "Open Theism."   A useful introduction is "Does God Know Your Next Move?" a two-part article in *Christianity Today*, beginning on page 38 of the May 21, 2001, issue.   For an in-depth presentation, see Greg Boyd,

to this condition, His hearing is assured, whatever the petition may be.[13]   He "hears us" must mean to hear favorably; God has promised to listen to the prayers of His children! Elsewhere we are told that God's ears are unto the prayers of the righteous (1 Peter 3:12). We have entitled this paragraph "encouragement because of opportunities to pray for the erring."   It is not "any" prayer that He listens to, nor is it just "anybody" to whom He listens.   It is God's children (including John's readers), those who share eternal life, whose prayers He delights to hear.   What an encouragement!

5:15 -- *And if we know that He hears us in whatever we ask, we know that we have the requests which we have asked from Him.*

And if we know that He hears us in whatever we ask – The word John has used for "if" is *ean* followed by an indicative, a colloquial usage, the only instance of *ean* with the present indicative found in the New Testament.   John is not expressing any doubt that God listens to His children's prayers.[14]   Some modern English translations substitute "because" for "if," lest the reader think the sentence expresses doubt.   Here for the first time in the closing verses of chapter 5, the key word *oidamen* ("we know") occurs.   It will be repeated several times, each time setting forth something the Christian is assured of. The remainder of this "if" clause expresses the same idea found in verse 14 ("He hears us in whatever we ask"), but with *ho* ("whatever") instead of *ti* ("anything," verse 14),[15] and with the qualification "according to His will" (verse 14) missing but implied.   For "whatever," see on 3:22.   Again "we ask" is a middle voice verb, indicating that we keep on asking for ourselves.

We know that we have the requests which we have asked from Him – Again John writes *oidamen* ("we know"), we are confident!   Verse 15 is not just a simple repetition of what he wrote in verse 14.   A new thought is added.   Not only are we confident that God loves to hear our prayers, but we are confident that He answers them, too.   The Greek

---

God of the Possible: A Biblical Introduction to the Open View of God [Grand Rapids: Baker, 2000].)

Still there is something to be said about our attitude towards prayer.   God is not a celestial vending machine out of which goodies may be distributed simply by punching the right prayer button.   Prayer is not a convenient device for imposing our will upon God, or bending His will to ours.   The petition of the Model Prayer, "May Your will be done on earth as it is done in heaven" (Matthew 6:10, personal translation) not only is a call for others to submit to God's will, but also requires that the petitioner freely yield his or her will to God, so that He is able to accomplish His will through us and our prayers.   "It is by prayer that we seek God's will, embrace it and align ourselves with it" (Stott, *op. cit.*, p.185).   Jesus Himself (Matthew 26:39) is a model for us, "My Father ... not as I will, but as thou wilt."

[13] As noted earlier, Scripture calls attention to other conditions for answered prayer.   For example, in 3:22 the condition of answered prayer is whether we obey God's commandments and "do the things that are pleasing in His sight."

[14] For "he hears us," see comments on verse 14.

[15] Whereas in the previous verse the petitions in mind were specific ("whenever we ask anything"), the allusion now is general ("whatever we ask").   Westcott, *op. cit.*, p.190.

words translated "requests" and "asked" are both formed off the same root. *Aiteō* ("asked") was explained in verse 14. "We have" (*echomen*) means we possess, we hold [in our hands]" the very thing for which we have been praying. *Echomen* is not a future tense ("we will have"), but the present tense, "we (already) have." God doesn't put off answering to some remote time in the future. When prayers are offered to God that are in harmony with His will, He answers speedily, as soon He hears the prayer.[16] "From Him" (*ap' autou*) can be taken with "we have" or with "whatever we ask."[17] The point John is emphasizing is "God answers prayer!"[18] John reminds his readers of this wonderful boon in order to encourage them to continue to be faithful to Jesus.

5:16 -- *If any one sees his brother committing a sin not* leading *to death, he shall ask and God will for him give life to those who commit sin not* leading *to death. There is a sin* leading *to death; I do not say that he should make request for this.*

If any one sees his brother committing a sin not *leading* to death – In the confidence that God listens to prayer, and immediately answers, the Christian may offer intercession on behalf of others whose sins are observed. It is very possible that this topic of intercession for sinning brethren is the topic to which he has deliberately been leading. "If" does not express doubt, but what actually does occur from time to time. The aorist subjunctive verb "sees" denotes a specific occasion when a brother is actually caught in the act of "committing a sin."[19] When John writes "brother" in this epistle, he means a fellow believer, a fellow Christian.

What "death" is talked about? "Death" is used three ways in the New Testament. Physical death (Acts 2:24, John 11:4), the death of a man's spirit (John 5:24, Ephesians 2:1), and the second death (hell, Revelation 20:14). Which of the three is intended here? Obviously, "death" and the "eternal life" in this passage must correspond. If so, "death" is the loss of the "eternal life" which is the possession of those who have the Son (5:12). Concerning "a sin not leading to death," in notes offered later in this verse we shall discuss in detail how it takes continual sin to kill the Christian's spirit and so cause him to forfeit

---

[16] Many have tried to reduce prayer to a mere psychological exercise, a sort of mental gymnastic in which we talk to our own best selves. What John has written here about prayer cannot be harmonized with such an idea. What John says is that we are talking freely to God. And God listens to us. He answers immediately. He grants our requests.

[17] John apparently wrote *ap' autou* (found in Sinaiticus and Vaticanus) but as the years passed this was altered into the commoner *par' autou* found in the Textus Receptus.

[18] Some of God's answers to His children's prayers are recognized immediately, others later, and some are not recognized in our lifetime. But this is not John's point. The point he is emphasizing is that God answers prayer! The confidence that He answers, and does so as soon as He hears the prayer, is not dependent solely upon whether or not we have personally observed the answer.

[19] The phrase "committing a sin" (literally, "to sin a sin") occurs nowhere else in the New Testament. The present participle is not merely predicative, but graphic, as describing the "brother" actually caught in the act of sinning. (Alford, *Greek Testament for English Readers*, p.1754.) "Sin" is anarthrous in the Greek. Most English versions insert the indefinite article "a" before sin. Some omit the article in verse 17 after inserting it here in verse 16, as though the reference there were more general than in verse 16.

eternal life.   We shall also explain how there is a sin that is immediately fatal.   "To (unto) death" (*pros thanaton*) probably means a sin that is fatal to one's spiritual life, just as sickness "unto death" in John 11:4 means a sickness from which there is no hope of recovery.

He shall ask – The verb is a future indicative form.   Some suppose the future indicative is equivalent to a gentle imperative, suggesting what should be done.   If so, then this passage lays an obligation on Christians to intercede in prayer for their brothers whom they see committing sin.[20]   Others explain that the future tense "he shall ask" expresses not the writer's command but the Christian's inevitable and spontaneous reaction.[21]   When a Christian observes his brother committing a sin, he will go to God in prayer for the sinning brother.[22]   And for what does he ask?   At the least that the sinner will be given the opportunity to repent and to confess his wrong.   And perhaps for wisdom to know how to do some fraternal intervention and rebuking in the sinner's life in order to encourage such repentance.[23]

And *God* will for him give life to those who commit sin not *leading* to death – "And" introduces what the result of this prayer will be.[24]   The NASB adds "God" in italics because the Greek is ambiguous.   Since there is no word in the nominative case, we must get the subject from the third person singular personal ending, "he", "she," or "it."   "He" (in the verb) may mean either God or the person who is praying.[25]   "Him," the pronoun, is likewise ambiguous, and may mean either the person interceding or the sinner for whom he intercedes.[26]   Perhaps the correct choice here is that it is the sinner, not the intercessor, who is given life.   "Life" here is the "eternal life" that 5:11,12 emphasized.   "Those who commit sin" is plural in Greek, yet stands in apposition to "him."   The plural serves to gen-

---

[20] For exhortations to intercession elsewhere in the New Testament, see 1 Thessalonians 5:25; Hebrews 13:18,19; James 5:14-20; and cp. Philippians 1:4.

[21] Stott, *op. cit.*, p.186.   Could it be said that an absence of intercessory prayer when we see a brother sinning is as much a betrayal of our love for the brother as if we withheld material aid from him when he is hungry or thirsty (3:17)?

[22] It is likely John has personal and private prayers, rather than public and congregational prayers, in view.   He is speaking about what one Christian does when he sees another in need of prayer.   Our private prayers are the place to intercede specifically for those who fall into sin.

[23] Certainly, we should not read this verse to say that the sinner will be forgiven without any repentance or confession.   That would contradict 1:9.   Nor should we understand John to say that simply because a Christian has prayed, God automatically and unconditionally infuses "life" into the heart of the one whose sins are slowly killing his spirit.

[24] Haas, *op. cit.*, p.127.

[25] The Greek verbs *aitēsei kai dōsei* ("he will ask and he will give") are closely connected.   To some commentators, it seems rather surprising to give them two different subjects as our NASB does.   Yet the context is speaking of God hearing and answering prayer, so perhaps the NASB translator's choice is defensible.

[26] A similar issue (whose sins are covered?) is raised at James 5:15,20 and 1 Peter 4:8.

eralize the preceding proposition, collecting all such cases into a class; this offer applies to all those whose sin is not a sin leading to death.   Sins which do not lead to spiritual death are possible for believers.   God will continue to give (*dōsei* is future tense) life to them.[27] The sinner already has life because he is a Christian.   The life he already has will continue, John promises.[28]

There is a sin *leading* to death – The qualification "not leading unto death" (verse 16a) implied the existence of such a sin.   What was implied is now clearly and explicitly stated by John.   There is a sin that results in "spiritual death."[29]

The exegesis of verses 16-17 is governed by the interpretation given to the expressions "sin unto death" and "sin not unto death," so perhaps an attempt should be made now rather than later to identify those "sins."

First, we must call attention to some *guidelines* that should inform our conclusions. (1) "Death" and the "life" in the passage must correspond.   The former cannot be bodily death, while the latter is eternal and spiritual death.   The terms must either be both physical or both spiritual.[30]   (2) Since "sin leading to death" is not further explained at this place, it must be presumed as meant to be understood by what John has elsewhere laid down concerning the possession of eternal life and death.   Recall what 5:12 said, "He who has the Son has the life.   He who does not have the Son of God does not have life."   "We may safely say that the words 'to death' here are to be understood as 'involving the loss of *this life* which men have only by union with the Son of God'."[31]   (3) "Sees his brother committing a sin" (i.e., caught in the act) indicates it is a definite act or kind of sin, not a habit of sinning.   The words "a sin" in "there is a sin leading to death" point in the same direction (i.e., a definite act).   (4) The sin unto death is something that those who embrace Gnostic doctrines are doing.   The context has spoken of the false teachers' denial that Jesus Christ is the Son of God.

Next, *a brief listing of the major views* may provide helpful information for making an informed decision.   Among the proposed explanations are these:

---

[27] Future tense verbs speak either of one act or continuing action in the future.   "God will continue to give life to the one whose sin does not lead to death" seems to be the idea.

[28] The Christian has "passed out of death into life" (3:14; John 5:24).   Spiritual death is a thing of the past; he has risen to walk in newness of life (Romans 6:4). He "has life" as a present and abiding possession (5:12).   When he stumbles into sin, which he may (2:1), he has a heavenly Advocate (2:1). He needs to be forgiven and cleansed (1:9), and when he is, John says that the "new life" he already has will continue.   The converse is also true.   Habitual, continual, unrepented sin of any kind will lead to spiritual death (Romans 6:12ff and 6:23).

[29] "To (unto) death" (*pros thanaton*) denotes the same thing here it did earlier in the verse, the opposite of "eternal life" (verse 13).

[30] Alford, *op. cit.*, p.1755.

[31] Alford, *Alford's Greek Testament*, p.511.

(1) A crime for which civil authorities may exact the death penalty. Typical of such crimes would be those which the Mosaic law listed as capital offenses, punishable by death (e.g., Leviticus 20:1-27; Numbers 18:22).

(2) Sin punished by divine visitation with death or sickness. God did inflict physical death on the sinners Ananias and Sapphira (Acts 5). Either physical or spiritual death resulted from improper participation in the Lord's Supper (1 Corinthians 11:30).

(3) A sin which the church would punish by excommunication. Clement of Alexandria and Origen both accepted the idea that a line could be drawn between forgivable and unforgivable sins, but declined to classify them. Tertullian went a step further and listed the grosser sins (including murder, adultery, blasphemy, and idolatry) as beyond pardon, while all other sins, being minor offenses, could be forgiven. This later developed into the familiar, casuistical differentiation between "mortal" and "venial" sins and the specification of the "seven deadly sins."[32]

(4) Any single sin (such as those named in Galatians 5:18-21) which is not repented of, thus causing the sinner to be lost. Guy N. Woods indicates that the "sin unto death" is any sin that a man will not confess (cp. 1 John 1:9).[33]

(5) Blasphemy of the Holy Spirit. "This sin, committed by the Pharisees, was a deliberate, open-eyed rejection of known truth. They ascribed the mighty works of Jesus, evidently done 'by the Spirit of God' (Matthew 12:28), to the agency of Beelzebub. Such sin, Jesus said, would never be forgiven either in this age or in the age to come. He who commits it 'is guilty of an eternal sin' (Mark 3:29, Matthew 12:22-32)."[34]

(6) Apostasy (a Christian falls away from the faith). Christians can quit believing. It is possible to read 1 John 5 as though it is a Christian brother who commits the sin unto death, just as it is a Christian brother who is committing the sin not unto death.

(7) A deliberate sin (sin with a high hand); namely, repudiation of Jesus (as the Gnostics were doing). In the Old Testament, generally, a distinction was drawn between sins of ignorance, committed unintentionally, which were forgivable and for which therefore sacrifice could be offered, and presumptuous sins, committed defiantly (with

---

[32] Explanatory notes are adapted from Stott, *op. cit.*, p.188.

[33] Woods' argument is this: There is much about sin and its forgiveness in 1 John. The fact of sin in the lives of all Christians is affirmed, 1:8-10. Its origin is indicated, 3:8. The means by which it may be avoided is revealed, 3:9. In the event of sin in one's life, we have an Advocate with the Father, Jesus Christ the righteous, 2:1. And we have the promise that if we confess our sins, He will forgive us and cleanse us from all unrighteousness, 1:9. The apostle's teaching may be thus summarized: The Lord will forgive every sin that a brother confesses, 1:9. There is, however, a sin which the Lord will not forgive, 5:16. The sin which the Lord will not forgive, is simply a sin, any sin, all sin which the brother will not confess. Guy N. Woods, "Peter, John, and Jude" in *New Testament Commentaries* [Nashville, TN.: Gospel Advocate, 1957], p.321-22.

[34] Stott, *op. cit.*, p.188,

a high hand), for which there was no forgiveness (Numbers 15:27-31; Deuteronomy 17:12; Psalm 19:13), nor for which was any sacrifice to be offered. Hebrews 6:4ff and 10:26-29 explains that this "defiant (deliberate)" sin, for which there is no possibility of repentance and forgiveness, is repudiation of Jesus. (In Hebrews the repudiation was accompanied by an intention of reverting to Judaism.) By parity of reasoning, the "sin leading to death" in 1 John is a repudiation of Jesus Christ as the Son of God (as revealed by God) to convert to Gnosticism. Folk who so repudiated Jesus were warned they would face God's denial of them (2:22-23; 3:10-15). Like the false teachers of 2 Peter 2:1ff, the false teachers about whom John writes were "denying the Master who bought them." That was the "sin unto death."

A *further brief discussion* and an evaluation of these major views offered to explain what the "sin leading to death" may be, *should help solidify our convictions*:

- (1) and (2) make "death" to be physical death, which violates Guidelines #1 and #2. If it is physical death meted out by the civil government, "What are we to think of making the prayer of a Christian dependent on the penal decrees of civil law?"[35]
- (3) has history against it. There is no New Testament warrant for such an arbitrary classification of sins into mortal and venial, and certainly "it would be an anachronism to try to apply it here" (Dodd). To suppose this passage affords any support for the dogma that some sins that will be forgiven *after* death and some that will not be forgiven *after* death is difficult to accept. It is likewise difficult to justify the translation "mortal sin" that some English versions use at this place.
- (4) seems to be flawed since it is not a single unconfessed sin, but habitual sin, that kills the Christian's spirit (Romans 6:12ff). Furthermore, at the time a Christian sees an individual sin being committed, how would he know whether or not the sinner will/ might repent?
- For (5), some have tried to equate the Pharisees' repudiation of Jesus with the Gnostic repudiation of Jesus (i.e., Gnosticism's repudiation came in spite of the Spirit's testimony to Jesus), so that both might be called blasphemy of the Holy Spirit. Is "continual rejection of the gospel in this age of the Holy Spirit" the same thing as Jesus was speaking about when He spoke of the sin against the Holy Spirit?
- The possibility that apostasy is involved in view (6) is strongly rejected by Calvinistic interpreters as being incompatible with the doctrine of unconditional eternal security. Some have tried to show that John does not specifically identify the person who is seen committing a "sin leading to death" as being a brother (i.e., a Christian). Others attempt to give brother a broad definition, including all of Adam's descendants (but not the seed of Abraham). However, as pointed out above, "a sin leading to death" implies that the person committing it is spiritually alive when the sin is committed. It is the Christian who has eternal life, and who can forfeit it. It seems it is a "brother" who sins unto death, not just the Gnostic false teachers who never were converted.
- (7), the denial that Jesus Christ is the Son of God, such as the Gnostics were teaching, fits all the guidelines. Who commits this sin that leads to death? The person who rejects Jesus as the Christ come in the flesh. We suppose the one whom a Christian

[35] Huther, *op. cit.*, p.616.

"sees committing a sin leading to death" is a brother who, influenced by the Gnostics, has defected from Christianity to Gnosticism.   Because he no longer believes in the Son, he has forfeited eternal life.

> This alone of all the proposed solutions seems to satisfy all the canons above laid down.   For in it, the life cast away and the death incurred strictly correspond: it strictly corresponds to what John has elsewhere said concerning life and death, and derives its explanation from those other passages, especially from the foregoing verse 12:   and it is an appreciable act of sin, one against which the readers have been before repeatedly cautioned (2:18ff, 4:1ff, 5:5,11,12).[36]

By becoming a Gnostic convert – which involves becoming an unbeliever in Jesus the Son of God, failing to keep the commands of God, and a lack of love for the brethren that reflects a Cain-like hatred – Christians actually reverse the blessed transition "from death unto life" (1 John 3:14), and pass from "life back to death," i.e., into a state of spiritual death.   Such spiritual death will one day become eternal death.

I do not say that he should make request for this – John has just written that the child of God has assurance that God listens to and answers the prayers of those who continue to believe in the Son of God.   John now says there is an exception to this.   That exception concerns prayers for the person who is committing "a sin unto death."   What is a Christian to do when he sees a brother committing a "sin unto death"?   John's answer, careful but resolute, is given in what follows: he does not explicitly forbid intercessory prayer, but he does not encourage it, for he clearly doubts that God either hears or answers such a prayer.[37]   The Greek word translated "make request" is *erōtaō* (see verse 14, an equal asking of an equal).   John's use of *erōtaō* may imply that such a prayer for one sinning unto death is presumptuous.   It presumes to tell God what to do from an "equal" standpoint, as if the one doing the praying knew as much as God when it comes to how He should inflict and withhold His righteous judgments.   God does hear and answer prayer, but if we do pray for one who is sinning a "sin unto death," we should not be surprised when "nothing happens."   After all, not every sinner can be given life in answer to prayer because there is, after all, "a sin unto death."   Prayer for those who have turned away from Jesus, the world's only Savior, is a pointless exercise.[38]

---

[36] Alford, *Greek Testament for English Readers*, p.1756.

[37] "For this" means concerning such a brother who is seen sinning a sin unto death.   The Greek negative *ou* precedes *peri ekeinēs legō* and so likely modifies "I ... say" rather than "make request."   If it immediately preceded and so modified "request" then this would be a prohibition of such prayers.   However, "make request" is in the subjunctive; if that word were negated, we would expect the form to be *mē* rather than *ou*.   Against all this, Alford (*op. cit.*, p.1755) argues that just as the previous language expressed a command to pray for the one sinning not unto death, so this language implies a prohibition against praying for the one seen sinning unto death.   There are Biblical examples where God has forbidden prayers.   He forbade Jeremiah to pray for the people of Judah (Jeremiah 7:16, 11:14, 14:11; cf. 1 Samuel 2:25).

[38] Once more we return to the topic of God hearing and answering prayer.   Not only is God's hearing and answering conditioned on the one praying (i.e., he must ask according to God's will), but answers can also be limited by the will of others.   If the person for whom we might pray wills to commit a sin unto death, God will not overrule that, or coerce him to do otherwise.   Though we are confident God hears and answers

5:17 -- *All unrighteousness is sin, and there is a sin not* **leading** *to death.*

All unrighteousness is sin – John here guards against his readers drawing a wrong inference from his distinction between a sin unto death and a sin not unto death. No one should be misled by the distinction into thinking that some sins are not serious. John has already characterized sin as unrighteousness (1:9),[39] and lawlessness (3:4). By either definition, sin is violation of God's standard.[40] Whether it is a "sin leading to death" or a "sin not leading to death," it is "unrighteousness" and that is "sin" (*harmartia*, to miss the mark). Perhaps "the statement also serves as a farewell declaration against the Gnostic doctrine that to the enlightened Christian declensions from righteousness involve no sin."[41]

And there is a sin not *leading* **to death** – This verse is apparently intended to be a statement of the wide scope which exists for the exercise of Christian intercession. Although all wrongdoing is sin, the distinction between a sin unto death and a sin not unto death remains valid. Many evil deeds, although undoubtedly sin, do not lead to death, and can be forgiven (cp. 1:7-9; 2:1ff; 4:10).[42] Intercessory prayer in these cases of "sin not unto death" is proper and will help the one in danger.

V. FELLOWSHIP'S CONFIDENCES.   5:18-20

Summary: In verses 18-20, John summarizes three solid facts of which he and his readers are fully assured.   Not only is confidence expressed by, but fellowship with one another is included in, the threefold "we know" with which these verses begin.   The Christian is confident he has been born of God, and that he need not sin habitually because he is kept by the Son of God who limits what the devil can do (verse 18).   He is confident of his lofty position, since he belongs to God and not to the world (verse 19).   And he is confident that the Son of God has come to help men know God, and that fellowship with Him and eternal life through Jesus are available (verse 20).

---

we should not expect God's answers to our prayers to impinge on the sinner's freedom of will. The sinner's deliberate and obstinate will can and does make it impossible for God to act like the intercessor might like.

[39] "Unrighteousness" is *adikia*, a synonym for sin that means to wrong someone else, to act wickedly towards him, a deed that violates law and justice, depriving someone of what is rightfully his. Specifically it denotes unrighteousness by which others are deceived. (Thayer, *op. cit.*, p.12)

[40] "Unrighteousness" means actions which do not conform to the objective moral "standard of right set by the revelation of God's will" (Roberts, *op. cit.*, p.142).

[41] Plummer, *op. cit.*, p.168.

[42] Had Bible students listened to John, the Montanist and Novatian contention that one sin committed after baptism would result in damnation might not have flourished.

A. The Christian is Confident of the Lord's Protection.   5:18

Summary: The Christian is confident that righteousness is the normal course of life for the child of God.   Such right living is possible because of the Lord's help, and because of the limitations He puts on the devil.

5:18 -- *We know that no one who is born of God sins; but He who was born of God keeps him and the evil one does not touch him.*

We know that no one who is born of God sins – Whenever John wants to mark the contrast between the confident certitude of the Christian faith (which is based upon divine revelation in Christ) and the spurious knowledge of the Gnostic (which is based upon human speculation), he uses this verb "we know" (*oida*).[1]   "We know" (*oidamen*) at the beginning of each of verses 18, 19, and 20 is the link which holds them together.[2]   What is affirmed in this first clause of verse 18 is virtually identical to 3:6, 9.   The Christian is again described as one who, literally, has been begotten (*gegennēmenos*; cf. 5:1,4) of God. The perfect tense describes past action with present continuing results.   That begetting results in a new life and new behavior.   "Sins" is a present tense; the Christian is not to be habitually sinning.   John has just admitted that Christians sin – sins of "unrighteousness," and "sins not leading to death."   But he repeats what he emphasized in 3:6-10, that Christians do not habitually sin.   A Christian is not a person who never sins; he is a person who resists temptations to sin, precisely because continuing to sin is contrary to what is expected of a child of God.[3]   John is aware of the difficulties involved in living the new life and of the quality of the opposition from the evil one.   Still, John is adamant in his confidence that the evil one need not prevail.   Christians do not have to continue in sin, nor should they.

But He who was born of God keeps him – John now gives the reason for his assurance that the Christian does not habitually sin.   He introduces it with a strong adversative "but." "Keeps" (*tēreō*) means to keep safe, to guard, to protect, to watch over carefully, to defend.

---

[1] We have had "we know" earlier in the letter (3:2,14; 5:15 [twice]), and "you know" (2:20,21; 3:5,15; 5:13).   As noted earlier John regularly avoids the favorite word of the Gnostics, *gnōsis*.

[2] In comments on verse 13 we introduced the problem some scholars have with chapter 21 of the Gospel, urging that it was added to the other 20 chapters later, and perhaps by a different hand.   Plummer replies, "The triple 'we know' at the close of this Epistle confirms the view that John 21:24 is by the Apostle's own hand, and not added by the Ephesian elders."   Plummer, *op. cit.*, p.167.

[3] The Christian does not have the notion that when he is sanctified he will not commit another single sin.   Rather, the Christian's constant attitude toward sin is to avoid it.   (Gill, *op. cit.*, p.145)

The one being kept (i.e., "Him") is the believer.   But who is the one doing the keeping?[4] Our answer to this question depends partly on which Greek text we are following and partly on how we explain the aorist participle "was born (begotten)."   A look at a Greek apparatus shows us there is a manuscript variation here.

- A number of manuscripts (Sinaiticus, A^c K P ψ 33 81 1739) have the reflexive pronoun *heauton* ("himself").   This is the way the text behind the KJV reads, i.e., "he that is begotten of God keepeth himself."[5]
- The reading *auton* ("him," referring to the believer being kept by someone else) is to be preferred, and is supported by A* B 3309, 614, Old Latin, and the Vulgate.
- The one doing the keeping is described as "the one who was born (begotten, *ho gennētheis*, aorist tense participle)," an attention-getting change from the perfect tense participles used to describe Christians (*ho gegennēmenos*, who have been begotten).   There must be some reason for the abrupt change to the *aorist* participle here, which John uses nowhere else.

John's use elsewhere of the perfect tense *ho gegennēmenos* (never the aorist *ho gennētheis*) for the believer (cp. 3:9; 5:1,3; John 3:6,8) probably means that the aorist here is a reference to Christ.   Thus the NASB has capitalized "He."   The one who keeps/guards/watches over the Christian ("him") is Jesus Christ.   There seems to be a reference to the incarnation in the words "was born."[6]   It is a reference to the incarnate Eternal Son of God preserving the frail children of the Father from the common foe, the devil.   The truth taught in this clause (as the NASB translates it) is not that the Christian keeps himself but that Christ keeps him.

---

[4] A survey of English translations will quickly show the options.   The KJV makes it to be the believer who keeps himself.   The ERV's "It keeps him" (i.e., the divine birth keeps him) is a poor translation of the masculine article and participle.   The NIV renders the article *ho* as an indefinite pronoun, "the one who."   The NEB supplies the subject "he" while the RSV/NASB capitalize "He" to make clear that in the opinion of those translators the reference is to Christ.

[5] For the concept of "keeping oneself," see 1 Timothy 5:22; James 1:27; Jude 21; and also 1 John 3:3.   The believer practices self-control when tempted, and thus does not habitually sin.   Compare 5:21 where the readers are encouraged to keep themselves from idols.

[6] The aorist passive participle "was begotten" points to a specific event in the past.   Jesus' incarnation fits this allusion nicely.   *Ho gennētheis* as a description of Jesus is unique, occurring nowhere else in the New Testament, "unless the Western variant in John 1:13, *hos ... ek theou egennēthē*, for which there is interesting Patristic evidence in the second century, is to be regarded as original" (Brooke, *op. cit.*, p.149).   The expression in the Nicene Creed, "begotten of the Father" (*ton ek tou Patros gennēthenta*) uses the same form of expression as that used here for begotten of God (*ho gennētheis tou theou*).   Moreover this interpretation produces another harmony between the Gospel and the epistle.   Christ both directly by His power and indirectly by His intercession keeps the children of God: "I kept them by Thy name" (John 17:12 KJV).   "I do not ask Thee to take them out of the world, but to keep them from the evil one" (John 17:15). (Plummer, *op. cit.*, p.170.)   John may have used the aorist participle "begotten of God" for Jesus as he has used the perfect participle for believers to emphasize the relation between the two somewhat after the pattern of the epistle to the Hebrews (Barker, *op. cit.*, p.356).   The thought of Jesus keeping His disciples is also found in Revelation 3:10.

And the evil one does not touch him – "And" introduces the result of Christ's protection. The "evil one" is the devil.[7] "Touch" may not be the best English word to translate *haptetai*. *Haptomai* means to lay hold of or to grasp (cp. the word used of Mary Magdalene, John 20:17, who tried to hold on to Jesus so He couldn't get away). Greek has other synonyms for this word: *thigganō* which means a light or superficial touch, and *psēlaphaō* which means to feel or feel after. The devil may tempt and harass the Christian, but he cannot capture him, or lay hold on him to harm him.[8] As Jesus "keeps" the Christian, He puts limits on what the devil can do. The Model Prayer has this petition, "Do not permit us to be tempted, but deliver us from the evil one" (personal translation). With such limitations on the devil's activities, the Christian faces fewer temptations. With fewer temptations, there are fewer opportunities to habitually sin. "The present tenses throughout verse 18 ('does not continue to sin,' 'protects,' 'does not harm') suggests a spiritual state and covenant relationship which is on-going."[9]

B. The Christian is Confident He Belongs to God.   5:19

> *Summary*: The second great fact concerning which believers have confidence is that while mankind is divided into two camps (those who belong to God and those who belong to the evil one), believers are in the former group.

5:19 -- *We know that we are of God, and the whole world lies in* **the power of** *the evil one.*

We know that we are of God – As he writes "We know that we," the apostle associates himself with his readers and thus with all Christian people. "We know" again is *oidamen*, a knowledge that comes by divine revelation which results in unshakable confidence.[10] John supposes that true Christians have such clear evidence on the subject as to leave no doubt in their minds that they belong to God. Whereas verse 18 spoke of Christians as "having been begotten of God," this verse reads simply, "are of God." "Of God"[11] is emphatic by position. Not only is God the source of the believer's spiritual life and being, but believers belong to Him. What is said in verse 19 is a combination of the substance of 1:6; 2:8,15; 3:1-3, and 3:10,13.

---

[7] See 2:13ff, 3:12, for *ho poneros*, "the evil one." The use of *poneros* to characterize Satan pictures him as not being content simply to perish in his own corruption, but as seeking to drag everyone else down with himself to his final doom (Wuest, *op. cit.*, p.183).

[8] For *haptomai* meaning "to lay hold of somebody in order to harm them" see 1 Chronicles 16:22; Job 2:5; Psalm 105:15; Jeremiah 4:10; Zechariah 2:8, 2:12.

[9] Smalley, *op. cit.*, p.303.

[10] On "we know" see notes at verse 18. This is the second verse in a row to begin with *oidamen*.

[11] For the meaning of the idiom "to be of God" see 2:16, 3:10, and 4:6.

Throughout the epistle John has sought to establish the status of the true disciple and to reassure him against the false claims of the Gnostics. He can truly know God: know that he is in Him (2:5), know that he knows Him (2:3), know that he has been born of Him (2:29), know he is His child (3:1ff), know that he is of the truth (3:19), and know that he is abiding in Him (4:13). We know such things by keeping His commands (2:3) and His word (2:5), walking in light (2:6), doing right (2:29, 3:10), loving the brethren (3:10), the Spirit's witness (3:24, 4:13), listening to God's teachers (4:6), our confession of faith (4:15), our loving God (5:2).[12]

And the whole world lies in *the power of* the evil one – In dreadful contrast to how it is with the children of God, "the whole world lies in the power of the evil one." After reading the first part of this verse, the exact antithesis one might expect is that others are "of the devil," but as he writes the contrast, as is his custom, John's wording adds a thought to what precedes. "World" includes all the rest of mankind, who are not sons of God. While *en tō ponērō* may be either masculine (in the evil one, i.e., the Devil) or neuter (in wickedness [KJV]), it is best to treat it as masculine, just as in the previous verse and in 2:13,14 and 3:12. The reference to "the evil one" is in the Greek emphatic by position. It contrasts with the reference to God in verse 19a. *Keimai*, "lies (in the power of)," is a common idiom and means to be the servant of some chief. The evil one cannot get a hold on the child of God (verse 18), but he does have hold over the world. He has it in his embrace.[13] John does not say the world is "of" the evil one, but "in" him, since he is thinking now not so much of the godless world's origin as of its present sad and perilous condition.[14] Verse 19 summarizes what has been written in 2:15-17, 3:1ff,8, 4:5, and 5:4,5. John wastes no words and blurs no issue. There are only two options: everyone is therefore either "of God" or "in the evil one." There is no third category. Fellowship with God and His Son and each other makes the Christian conscious that he belongs to God. "Christians are conscious, immediately and by revelation, of the difference between the power which dominates their life and that which controls absolutely the life, intellectual and moral, of the world, i.e., of the world of men so far as they remain estranged from God."[15]

C. The Christian is Confident that the Son of God Has Come. 5:20

---

[12] Roberts, *op. cit.*, p.144.

[13] For the devil's sway over the world, see his title "the ruler of this world" in John 12:31, 14:30, 16:11 and in Paul's teaching in Ephesians 2:2 and 6:12.

[14] Stott, *op. cit.*, p.193. The "world" has not passed over from death into life like the Christians have. Being excluded from the kingdom of the Son of God's love, they are still under the dominion of the devil.

[15] Brooke, *op. cit.*, p.150.

> *Summary*:   Here is the third great fact of which believers have confidence. God's Son – none other than Jesus Christ – has come into the world.   He has brought us understanding of the truth so that we may know the One who is true.

5:20 -- *And we know that the Son of God has come, and has given us understanding, in order that we might know Him who is true, and we are in Him who is true, in His Son Jesus Christ. This is the true God and eternal life.*

And we know that the Son of God has come – "And" renders a Greek particle (*de*) which sometimes indicates a contrast, but here likely marks continuation ("Moreover").   What is said in verse 20 sums up the teaching of previous sections, especially 3:8, 4:9ff, and 5:6-12, about God's sending the Son and the Son's reason for becoming incarnate.   Following the affirmations in verses 18 and 19, this third affirmation is the most important of the three, for it undermines the whole structure of the heretics' theology.   For "we know" (*oidamen*), see notes at 5:15 and 5:18.   In contrast to whatever the Gnostics might invent, or what the world and its philosophy chooses to assert, because their confidence is based on the inspired testimony given by God and the apostles of Jesus, Christians know that the Son of God has come in the flesh.   The Christian's certainty is not fanaticism or superstition or credulity; the Christian is ready to give the reason for his hope to anyone who asks.   For "Son of God" see on 3:8.   "Has come" (*hēkei*) has reference to the incarnation of Jesus,[16] and corresponds to the manifestation of Jesus described in 1:2 and 3:5,8.   We know that the Son of God has come by the evidence John has referred to in this epistle (1:1-4, 5:6-8), and in his Gospel.   The message of the apostles was consistent "from the beginning" (2:7,13,14,24).

And has given us understanding – The perfect tense verb "has given" shows that the past event of His coming still has continuing results in the present.   *Dianoia* ("understanding") is the "power or capacity of knowing" (Ebrard), or the "faculty to understand or perceive" (Haas).   It is not the wisdom or understanding itself, but the tools or means to make a person capable of attaining such understanding.[17]   Just as Jesus opened the minds of the two on the way to Emmaus that "they might understand the scriptures" (Luke 24:44ff), so His coming has provided men with the tools needed to know the true God.   We are reminded of Jesus' claims, "If you had known Me, you would have known My Father also"

---

[16] The present tense verb can be translated come, arrive, to be present.   Compared with *erchomai*, which speaks only of the act of coming, *hēkō* includes both the idea of coming and also of continuing personal presence.   See *exēlthon kai hēkō* in John 8:42.   There has been emphasis in 1 John both on Jesus' incarnation and on His continuing ministry in the world.

[17] Possibly because of their potential misuse by heretics, John (both in the Gospel and letters) is reluctant to use nouns such as *gnōsis* ("knowledge") and *nous* ("mind") which express intellectual powers. *Gnōsis* is absent from the Johannine writings, and *nous* occurs only twice (Revelation 13:18, 17:9)

(John 14:7) and "He who has seen Me has seen the Father" (John 14:9).[18]   The Gnostic claim to superior knowledge about God, while at the same time repudiating the "understanding" available in Jesus, obviously proves the Gnostic claim to be spurious!

In order that we might know Him who is true – *Hina* may express purpose.[19]   God sent His Son "so that (in order that) we may know Him who is true," or literally, "that we may continue to recognize, as we do now."   It is a knowledge that has to be appropriated.[20] Hence "recognize" may be a good choice of words to translate *ginōskō*.   "Him" likely means God, since this verse, as it continues, makes a distinction between "Him" and "His Son."   God is not described as "true" or truthful (*alēthēs*),[21] but as real or genuine (*alēthinon*).[22]   He is genuine and real as opposed to the counterfeit God invented by the fertile imaginations of the heretics and/or the false or nonexistent gods of verse 21.   The world wonders if there is a God; the philosophers have speculated as to what God is like; and the modern fool has decided "God is dead!" (cf. Psalm 14:1).   But taking advantage of the "understanding" available in Jesus, Christians know the genuine God.[23]

And we are in Him who is true, in His Son Jesus Christ – Perhaps we should treat the rest of verse 20 as a fresh sentence, not dependent on either preceding "that."   Thus it explains how we are "in Him who is true" – by being "in His Son Jesus Christ."   "Him who is true" is God.[24]   Several positive contrasts are suggested.   We not only "know Him" (verse 20b), we are also "in Him."[25]   Unlike the world who are "in ... the evil one" (verse

---

[18] Christianity is a religion based on revelation.   It is this important element which is expressed here. Of himself man cannot find the way to God and eternal life; he needs a revelation from God Himself.   So God has sent His Son to reveal the truth, and those who accept the revelation come to know the true God. (Marshall, *op. cit.*, p.254.)

[19] *Hina* and the subjunctive express purpose, and some manuscripts (K and those represented by the Textus Receptus) do have the subjunctive form *ginōskōmen*.   However, a number of important manuscripts (Sinaiticus, A B L P) have the indicative form *ginōskomen*.   For *hina* followed by a future indicative, see Mark 15:20, Luke 14:10, etc.   For its use with a present indicative (as here), the evidence is less clear (a variant reading at John 5:20 being one example).   And whether or not the indicative construction expresses purpose is less clear.

[20] "Know" is a present tense verb expressing continuation.   For the connotation of the word *ginōskō*, see comments at 2:3-4.

[21] See on 2:8 where we had the word *alēthēs* ("true").

[22] This is a favorite Johannine adjective.   Jesus called Himself the "genuine" bread and the "genuine" vine (John 6:32; 15:1).   He was claiming to be the substance of which baker's bread and the farmer's vine were but shadows.   The God whom Jesus has revealed is the "genuine" God.   In these words in 1 John 5:20, we have another parallel to Christ's high priestly prayer, "that they may know You the only true God" (John 17:3, personal translation).

[23] Adapted from Gill, *op. cit.*, p.147.

[24] On God being "true" (genuine), see the previous phrase in this verse.

[25] On being "in Him," cp. 2:5,24,27.

19), we Christians are in God, enjoying fellowship with Him.[26]   Thus, the epistle closes as it began, speaking about fellowship.   It was to promote fellowship with the apostles of Jesus, a fellowship which is also "with the Father and with his Son Jesus Christ," that John began his letter (1:3).   Now he ends it with the confident assurance that he and the readers are united to Him, belong to Him, and are His friends.   It is likely that the clause "in His Son Jesus Christ" is intended to explain how it is that we are in the Father.[27]   It is by being "in His Son Jesus Christ" that we are "in Him [God] who is true."   In the beginning of this letter (1:3) John used Jesus' full title.   Now here at the ending of the letter, he uses it again. "Jesus" (the man) is "Christ" (the promised Messiah) and He is deity (God's "Son").   If these truths are kept in view, the readers will have the criteria by which to judge and refute the Gnostic teachings.

This is the true God and eternal life – "True God" means what it did before: genuine, not counterfeit.   "And" introduces a second predicate to "this is," and as such it is syntactically parallel with "true God."   The clause probably means "He causes people to live eternally" or "He gives eternal life."[28]

The most controversial issue in this final sentence of verse 20 is to whom does *houtos* ("This") refer: to the Father or to the Son?   It is possible to interpret the language of verse 20 in more than one way: (1) Take all the clauses as referring to the Father.[29]   (2) Take all the clauses as referring to Jesus Christ.   (3) The early clauses refer to the Father, and the closing ones to Jesus.   It is the conclusion of this commentator that #3 is correct, and that John is ascribing deity to Jesus.[30]   Several factors point to this conclusion.   (a) The nearest antecedent to "this" is "Jesus Christ."   Normally we choose the nearest antecedent unless such a choice would produce a contradiction or theological error.   (b) The champions of orthodoxy so interpreted the passage in their controversy against Arius.[31]

---

[26] John uses the phrases "fellowship with Him" and "abiding in Him" and being "in Him" with something like that same meaning (1:3; 2:6,24,27,28; 3:6,24; 4:13).

[27] Tyndale so understood the passage and boldly turned the second "in" to "through."   His translation thus reads, "We are in Him that is true, through his Sonne Jesu Christ."

[28] For "eternal life" see 1:2ff and 5:13.

[29] It is the opinion of several commentators that John is not attempting to ascribe deity to Jesus.   They treat *houtos* ("this") as referring to the principal subject of the sentence rather than the nearest antecedent. On dogmatic grounds, Arians and anti-trinitarians and German Rationalists argue that the reference is to God the Father.   Then it is claimed that the language of John 5:26, "the Father has life in Himself," justifies the interpretation that the expression "eternal life" here refers to God.

[30] It does not mean to say that Christ and God are one and the same being, but that Jesus is deity as much as the Father is deity.   Elsewhere in the New Testament, Jesus is called God: John 1:1,18; 5:18ff; 20:28; Romans 9:5; Titus 2:13; Hebrews 1:1-3,8-10.

[31] Athanasius three times in his *Orations Against the Arians* interpreted the passage as referring to the deity of Jesus (III.24.4; 25.16; IV.9.1).

(c) It is Jesus who is the source of eternal life (1:2).[32]   (d) The main truth emphasized in this letter is that Jesus Christ is God's Son.   He is the true God and eternal life.   It is fitting that in this final statement of Christian confidence, John should hammer home the point that "He – Jesus – is the true God and eternal life."   If we interpret "this" as Christ, the conclusion of the letter is brought into striking harmony with the opening of the letter, in which Christ is spoken of as "eternal life" who was with the Father, and was manifested to us (1:2).   This is precisely the concluding note we would expect in a letter directed against a Gnostic heresy which treated Jesus as something far less than deity.   (e) The thrust of this verse as a whole is that the Son has given us an understanding to know the one True God.   There can be no more certain way of knowing the True God than to have a Teacher who is True God.

CONCLUSION: FINAL PLEA.   5:21

> *Summary*:   With one final, pointed warning, John urges his readers to avoid being led astray into false religion.

5:21 -- *Little children, guard yourselves from idols.*

Little children – One last time, John uses his favorite form of address to introduce this final appeal.   This tender and affectionate address, "little children," which has not occurred since 4:4, serves to remind John's readers of his genuine commitment to them and their spiritual welfare.

Guard yourselves from idols[1] – The verb here translated "guard" is not *tēreō* (as in verse 18) but *phulassō*, which pictures standing watch at a gate or on a bulwark, to guard against an assault from without.[2]   The Gnostics were the ones who were attacking from without the church.   John did not write a present tense form of the verb "guard," as commanding a habitual guarding.   He wrote an aorist imperative, which marks a crisis.   The Gnostic heresy was "a desperate assault demanding a decisive repulse" (Smith).   "Once for all be on your guard and have nothing to do with."   The use of the reflexive pronoun *heauta*

---

[32] It is not accidental that in the Gospel it is only of Christ that it is said that He is life (11:25; 14:6).

[1] The KJV closes verse 21 with an "Amen."   Plummer (*op. cit.*, p.174) explains it on this fashion: "Here, as at the end of the Gospel and the Second Epistle, 'Amen' is the addition of a copyist.   Sinaiticus A B and most Versions omit it.   Such conclusions, borrowed from liturgies, have been freely added throughout the New Testament.   Perhaps that in Galatians 6:18 is the only 'Amen' that is genuine; but that in 2 Peter 3:8 is well supported."

[2] *Tēreō*, the other word often translated "keep" (see notes on "observe" at 5:2) pictures an inward principle of watchful observation.   Thayer, *op. cit.*, p.622.   David Smith points out that *phulassō* is used of guarding a flock (Luke 2:8), of guarding a deposit or trust (1 Timothy 6:20; 2 Timothy 1:12,14), and of guarding a prisoner (Acts 12:4).

("yourselves") with *phulaxate* instead of the middle voice is significant and can be regarded as "emphasizing the duty of personal effort" on the part of each of John's readers.[3]   What are the *eidōlōn* ("idols")[4] to which John is referring"?   Two possibilities for interpretation arise.   (1) One possibility is that we take the word literally.   The Greek reads "the idols," i.e., those which abounded in the 1st century world.[5]   Usage of the word elsewhere in the New Testament might suggest it be taken literally here.[6]   (2) The other possibility is that we take the word "idols" figuratively.   In 1 Thessalonians 1:9, where *theos zōn kai alēthinos* ("living and true God") is opposed to *eidōla*, we might have a similar figurative use of "idols."   Nowhere in this letter has John spoken of the danger of worship of the material images, but John has referred to false conceptions of God and Jesus taught by the Gnostics.   Having emphasized in verse 20 that God the Father is "true" and that Jesus is the "true God," we picture John's final warning to his readers as calling attention to the danger of being misled into the worship of any other alleged manifestation or representation of God.   And John is blunt.   The false teachers propose not the worship of the true God, made known in His Son Jesus, but a false god – an "idol" they have invented.

Plummer calls attention to the fact that verse 21 gives the last of the contrasts of which the epistle is so full.   We have had light and darkness (1:5-7), truth and falsehood (1:8-10), doing righteousness and doing sin (3:10), the children of God and the children of the devil (3:10), the spirit of truth and the spirit of error (4:6), the believer untouched by the evil one and the world lying in the evil one (5:18), and now at the close (5:20) we have what was the real difference between apostolic Christianity and Gnosticism – the contrast between the true God and the heretics' false ideas of God.

---

[3] Westcott, *op. cit.*, p.197.   John frequently uses this reflexive pronoun construction: at 1 John 1:8, 3:3; at John 7:4, 11:33,35, 13:4, 21:1; and at Revelation 6:15, 8:6, 19:7.

[4] A study of Greek synonyms yields this distinction: *eidōlōn* is used of a figure (image, representation) of an imaginary deity, while a *homoiōma* (likeness, similitude) is that of some real person or thing made into an object of worship (Alford, *Alford's Greek Testament*, p.515).

[5] Barclay (*The Letters of John an Jude* in the Daily Study Bible Series [Philadelphia: Westminster, 1960], p.146-148) and Plummer (*op. cit.*, p.173) give exhaustive descriptions of the "idolatry" faced by 1st century folk living in Asia Minor.

[6] References in the New Testament where the word is used literally include Acts 7:41,15:20; Romans 2:22; 1 Corinthians 8:4,7, 10:19, 12:2; 2 Corinthians 6:16; and Revelation 9:20.

SELECTED BIBLIOGRAPHY FOR 1,2,3 JOHN

Akin, Daniel L., *1, 2, 3 John*, in the New American Commentary series, Nashville: Broadman, 2001.
> Akin states that the two purposes of 1 John are "to combat the propaganda of the false teachers" and "to reassure believers" (p.29-30). The epistle "provides not so much 'tests of life' ... as 'tests for assurance'" (p.30). Akin takes the view that 1 John 1:9 refers to confession of sin in relation to salvation, not in relation to the believer's walk with the Lord. On 3:6, "No one who abides in Him sins," Akin says this means that "a genuine believer will not live in continual sin" (p.143). The water and blood in 5:6 refer to the terminal points in Jesus' earthly ministry, namely, his baptism (water) and His crucifixion (blood). He believes the "lady" in 2 John is a figurative reference to a local church and its members. Akin draws attention to chiastic structures in all three epistles. According to the editors, "all NAC authors affirm the divine inspiration, inerrancy, complete truthfulness, and full authority of the Bible." A brief review of recent approaches to the study of the Johannine literature is included in the introduction. There are homiletical outlines offered for all three epistles.

Alexander, Neil, *The Epistles of John: Introduction and Commentary*. New York: Macmillan, 1962.
> The author repudiates the Johannine authorship, attributing the letter to "John the Elder." Alexander openly denies the authority of the Scriptures.

Alexander, William, *The First Epistle General of John. The Second Epistle of John. The Third Epistle of John,* in the Bible Commentary series, edited by F.C. Cook. New York: Scribners, 1904. Vol. 4 of the New Testament. p.271-382.
> Introductory studies deal with the apostle John's life; the polemical element in the epistles of John; the close and pervading connection of the Fourth Gospel to 1 John which, Alexander holds, is inconsistent with the theory that the writer of the epistle forged it (writing with the Gospel before him so he could mimic John's style); the external testimony to the epistle; and finally an analysis of the epistle. Alexander has the second epistle addressed to a Christian woman named Kyria, and opts for the conclusion that the third epistle is addressed to Gaius of Corinth. (This commentator has consistently found the comments in the Bible Commentary to be a good place to search when beginning the study of any Bible book. The series was produced by writers affiliated with the Anglican church.)

Alford, Henry, *1 John, 2 & 3 John*, in Alford's Greek Testament: An Exegetical and Critical Commentary. London: Rivingtons, 1871. Vol.4. Prolegomena, p.154-187, comments p.421-528.
> Greek text. Variant readings cited by manuscript or ancient church father or ancient versions. Introductory studies. Verse-by-verse explanations.

Arndt, William F., and F. Wilbur Gingrich. *A Greek-English Lexicon of the New Testament and other Early Christian Literature*. 2nd ed. Chicago: University of Chicago Press, 1979.
> This work (based on Walter Bauer's German Lexicon) is now in its third edition (AD 2000), and is recognized as the standard in this field. Definitions of Greek words are concise, yet complete. Each entry contains a wealth of bibliographic data.

Ashton, J., *Understanding the Fourth Gospel*. Oxford: Clarendon, 1991.
> Perhaps the most comprehensive technical survey of Johannine scholarship to date. Written for the scholar.

Barclay, William, *The Letters of John,* in the Daily Study Bible series.   Philadelphia: Westminster: 1976.
> While Barclay is found in almost every parish library, he often takes up one view on an issue and fails to let readers know what options are available.   Always interesting, but best supplemented with other writers because his theology tends to be neo-liberal.

Barker, Glen W., *1 John, 2 John, 3 John*, in the Expositor's Bible Commentary series, edited by Frank E. Gaebelein. Vol. 12.   Grand Rapids: Zondervan, 1981.
> A spiritually penetrating study of John's letters by a beloved provost at Fuller Seminary, well known for pastoral wisdom.

Barnes, Albert, *Notes on the New Testament, Explanatory and Practical – James, Peter, John, and Jude*, edited by Robert Frew.   Grand Rapids: Baker, 1953 reprint.
> This Presbyterian preacher regularly arose daily between 4 and 5 o'clock in the morning so he could spend several hours in study and writing of his own commentary on Scripture as part of his preparation to preach through the books once he completed his commentary.   The phrase-by-phrase coverage gives an explanation of each verse.   Greek lexicons are cited to help explain the meaning of Greek terms.   Each chapter ends with practical applications of the teachings of Scripture to everyday life.

Bengel, John Albert, *Gnomon of the New Testament*.   Vol. 5.   Edinburgh: T & T Clark, 1860.
> Greek word studies.   An old classic.

Berry, George Ricker, *New Testament Synonyms*.   Chicago: Wilcox & Follett, 1948.
> A knowledge of the connotation of synonyms is helpful to understanding the Greek text.   Much material has been drawn from R.C. Trench, *Synonyms of the New Testament*, as well as from the New Testament lexicons of Thayer and Cremer, as well as from the small ones by Green and Hickie.

Blaiklock, Edward M., *Faith is the Victory: Studies in the First Epistle of John*.   Grand Rapids: Eerdmans, 1959.
> Brief devotional comments.   Prints the author's own translation.   Not a commentary in the ordinary sense, but rather studies the outstanding themes of the epistle.   Archaeological data is used for illustrative purposes, as are allusions to persons and customs of the ancient world.

Boice, James M., *The Epistles of John: An Expositional Commentary*.   Grand Rapids: Zondervan, 1980.
> A series of messages preached at a large Presbyterian church in Philadelphia   They deal with ethical and spiritual concerns of a Christian's everyday life.

Braune, Karl, *The Epistles General of John*, in Lange's Commentary on the Holy Scripture, translated from the German by J. Isidor Mombert.   Reprint, Grand Rapids: Zondervan, 1952.
> An abundance of doctrinal, ethical, and homiletical material is included.

Brooke, Alan E., *A Critical and Exegetical Commentary on the Johannine Epistles*, in the International Critical Commentary series.   Edinburgh: T & T Clark, 1912.
> This classic study of the Greek text is useful particularly for critical textual issues such as the extended treatment of the passage about the "heavenly witnesses."   This work is theologically unreliable and

must be read with discrimination. Brooke deprecates the deity of Jesus, minimizes the value of Christ's death on the cross, and rejects as "legend" the teaching regarding antichrist.

Brown, Raymond E., *The Community of the Beloved Disciple. The Life, Loves, and Hates of an Individual Church in New Testament Times.* New York: Paulist, 1979.
> A redactional critical attempt to reconstruct the history of the imaginary Johannine community, using the Fourth Gospel and John's letters as windows into community life.

Brown, Raymond E., *The Epistles of John*, in the Anchor Bible series. Vol. 30. New York: Doubleday, 1982.
> Written by one of the most famous Johannine scholars, Brown's commentary covers every detail with encyclopedic depth in 812 large pages. In light of his Roman Catholic background, at times issues of importance to Catholics surface in the comments. Brown's attempt at reconstructing the historical situation reflected in the epistles is an original one and may almost be said to constitute a new chapter in the history of the early days of the church. Brown maintains that John's epistles, studied in relation to the Fourth Gospel, begin to yield an important and intelligible picture of those formative years. The writer of 1 John, not to be identified with the writer of the Gospel, he says, is a second-generation Christian, possibly a disciple of the beloved disciple, and one of the transmitters of the tradition represented by the Fourth Gospel. In Brown's view, both the writer and his opponents have the Fourth Gospel in hand and are interpreting it. The false teachers are interpreting the Fourth Gospel in a Gnostic sense; the writer (redactor) is interpreting the Gospel in a non-Gnostic sense. 1 John was addressed to a Johannine community "from which a major secession has taken place, and where the faith of those who remained was endangered by the propaganda of the secessionists" (p.88). The second and third epistles (which are real letters while the first is not, he says) were sent to other places. The writer of those two short epistles had no constitutional authority. Indeed, all he can do is express outrage at the conduct of Diotrephes and commend the conduct of Gaius. Brown sees no likelihood that 2 John is the previous letter referred to in 3 John 9. In Brown's view, the type of interpretation given to the Fourth Gospel in 1 John "accomplished the purpose for which it was written – it saved the Johannine Gospel, no longer for the elect of the Johannine Community but for the Great Church and for the main body of Christians ever since" (p.115). Brown dated the Gospel about AD 90 and 1 John about AD 100 ("after an interval long enough for debate to have arisen about the implications of" the Gospel [p.110]), and then 3 John is written between AD 100 and 110.

Bruce, F.F., *The Epistles of John.* Grand Rapids: Eerdmans, 1970.
> An easy-to-read commentary by one of the leading conservative scholars of New Testament studies in the 20th century. Textual, linguistic, and critical problems are but lightly touched on. Emphasizes the need for Christians to guard against the temptation to make the gospel conform to current trends of thought and modes of theology.

Bultmann, R., *The Johannine Epistles*, in the Hermeneia series, edited by Robert Funk. Philadelphia: Fortress, 1973.
> A brief study in the Hermeneia series, Bultmann's work shows his mastery of the religious currents in the Hellenistic world. Bultmann's theology is neo-liberal, so evangelicals will find the work less useful for preaching and exposition.

Burdick, Donald W., *The Epistles of John,* in the Everyman's Bible Commentary series.. Chicago: Moody, 1970.
> Perhaps intended for Bible study classes. Presents a spiral outline similar to Law's, in which each of three cycles takes the argument to an ascending stage of spiral development. Burdick sees John's purpose in writing to refute Gnosticism by presenting two basic tests, a correct view of Jesus Christ, which then should result in an ethical life of love and righteousness.

Burge, Gary M., "John, Letters of" in the *Dictionary of the Later New Testament & Its Development*, edited by Ralph P. Martin and Peter H. Davids. Downers Grove, IL: Inter-Varsity, 1997. p.587-599.

> A good source to get an introduction to current scholarly concerns and conclusions concerning the letters of John. Burge covers the attempt at recovering the history of John's church, the theological struggle, John's secondary concerns, authorship and dating, and epistolary structure.

-----, *The Letters of John*, in the NIV Application Commentary series. Grand Rapids: Zondervan, 1996.

> Two approaches are found in this volume: the original meaning is explained, and then the contemporary significance of the passage is given. Burge regards all three epistles as written by John, the same apostle who wrote the Fourth Gospel (though Burge thinks the final version of the Gospel as it appears in our Bibles was the result of editing of an earlier draft by John's followers after his death). He supposes the epistles were written ca. AD 70-90 in the general vicinity of Ephesus. "First John is the author's full broadside against his opponents, while 2 and 3 John are personal notes that either accompanied 1 John or were sent separately to another destination" (p.41).

Candlish, Robert, *The First Epistle of John*. Grand Rapids: Zondervan, nd.

> A series of 46 expository messages first published in 1866, this volume, a product of the times, vigorously attacks Roman Catholicism as it warns against apostasy. Zondervan republished it as one of their Classic Commentary Series.

Connor, Walter T., *The Epistles of John*. Nashville: Broadman, 1957.

> A reprint of a 1929 volume, these expository messages defend the Johannine authorship, attack liberal theological tendencies, and warn against false teachers.

Cullman, O,. *The Johannine Circle: Its Place in Judaism, Among the Disciples of Jesus, and in Early Christianity*. Translated by J. Bowden. London: SCM, 1976.

> A redaction critical attempt to place the (imaginary) community of John in the wider framework of the New Testament.

Culpepper, R.A., *The Johannine School: An Evaluation of the Johannine-School Hypothesis Based on an Investigation of the Nature of Ancient Schools*. Missoula, MT: Scholars, 1975.

> An important technical study of "schools" or academic/religious "communities" in antiquity and how this relates to the "Johannine community."

de Jonge, M., "An Analysis of 1 John 1:1-4." *The Bible Translator* 10 (1978). p.322-330.

> An appeal for the use of discourse analysis (as used by Eugene Nida and his colleagues) to help understand this difficult passage. He insists it is needful to "clarify semantic units" and to employ discourse analysis ("the study of linguistic patterns, structure, or systems beyond the sentence") since "meaning" is relatively independent of the surface structure of language.

Dodd, C.H., *The Johannine Epistles*, in the Moffatt New Testament Commentary series. New York: Harper & Row, 1946.

> The Biblical text printed is Moffatt's. Occasionally eccentric and theologically radical, Dodd's commentary takes issue with John for his crude view of sin, and advances some of Dodd's own views concerning "realized eschatology" rather than what he chooses to call John's "crude mythology." A work scholars often quote, but it has limited application to the contemporary church.

Findlay, G.G., *Fellowship in the Life Eternal*. London: 1909. Reprinted, Grand Rapids: Eerdmans, 1955.
Students who have used this work have found it to be a first-rate work of exposition.

Gill, Clinton R., *Hereby We Know: A Study of the Epistles of John*, in the Bible Study Textbook Series. Joplin, MO: College Press, 1966.
J.B. Rotherham's paraphrase. Reproduces Owen Crouch's lessons on 1 John.

Guthrie, Donald, *New Testament Introduction: Hebrews to Revelation*. Chicago: Inter-Varsity, 1966.
A readable conservative introduction to the books of the New Testament. A good beginning study to acquaint the Bible student with the issues and problems involved.

Haas, C. and M. de Jonge, *A Translator's Handbook on the Letters of John*, in the Helps for Translators series. London: United Bible Societies, 1972.
Introductions for all three letters. Exegetical notes to help readers understand the original text. Where different interpretations are possible, the majority scholarly opinion is presented, though the authors freely present their own view if it differs. Translations are offered which help us to choose a word in the receptor language that expresses best the idea in the text.

Hill, Charles E., *The Johannine Corpus in the Early Church*. Oxford: Oxford University Press, 2004.
Hill challenges current scholarly consensus at each of the three planks on which that consensus is built: (1) The alleged swift and enthusiastic acceptance of John's writings among heterodox groups, while acceptance by the orthodox groups came only after they vetted John's writings during a long and mighty struggle; (2) The alleged silence of early orthodox sources about John's writings, supposedly indicative of the failure of those sources to make use of John's texts; and (3) A perceived Gnostic preference for John's Gospel, which led in turn to orthodox hesitancy to accept John's writings.

Hodges, Zane, *The Epistles of John: Walking in the Light of God's Love*. Irving, TX: Grace Evangelical Society, 1999.
Many commentaries on 1 John suppose its purpose is to help readers determine if they have eternal life. Is this the purpose of John? Hodges says no. He insists that the purpose is clearly stated in 1 John 1:3, "that you also may have fellowship with us; and indeed our fellowship is with the Father, and with His Son Jesus Christ." Hodges' conclusions on some of the problem verses in 1 John include: (1) The challenge to confess one's sins (1:9) is addressed to believers as a condition for maintaining fellowship with God. It is not addressed to the unsaved (p.63). (2) Does 1 John 2:3 ("by this we know that we know Him, if we keep His commandments") mean that keeping God's commands is a way of knowing whether a person is saved? No, says Hodges, for whom faith is the only condition for salvation. (3) The "little children," "fathers," and "young men" (2:12-14) do not distinguish different levels of spiritual development, nor do these verses address unbelievers. All three terms, Hodges insists, "refer to the entire readership [believers] from various points of view" (p.94). Not everyone will agree with Hodges' view that the Johannine epistles were written in the AD 60s, nor with his presentation of the idea that faith that saves is a faith devoid of obedience to what God says. As for 2 John, Hodges holds that the "chosen lady" is the local church to which he was writing, that her "children" were the church members (p.251), and that her sister (verse 13) refers to members of the church (perhaps in Jerusalem, p.268) from which John was writing his three epistles.

Howard, W.F., "The Common Authorship of the Johannine Gospel and Epistles." *Journal of Theological Studies* 48 (1947). p.12-25.

Huther, Joh. Ed., *Critical and Exegetical Handbook to the General Epistles of James, Peter, John, and Jude*, in Meyer's Commentary on the New Testament.   Vol. 10. Edinburgh: T&T Clark, 1883.   Reprinted, Winona Lake, IN: Alpha Publications, 1979.
Commentary on the Greek text.

Kelly, William, *An Exposition of the Epistles of John the Apostle.*   London: T. Weston, 1905.
Twenty wordy lectures by a Plymouth Brethren scholar defend the deity of Jesus, uphold the divine inspiration of the Scriptures, and attack Pelagianism and liberalism in the churches. The Biblical text used is the author's own translation.

Kistemaker, Simon J., *Exposition of the Epistle of James and the Epistles of John,* in the New Testament Commentary series. Grand Rapids: Baker, 1986.
Written from a Reformed conservative position. He presents the evidence to show the author of all three Johannine letters is the apostle John, the son of Zebedee. He tends to treat 2 John as written to a local church (under the figurative name of the "chosen lady"). He identifies the false teachers as Gnostics. He dates the epistles from AD 90-95. From time to time Kistemaker pauses in his comments to offer "practical considerations" in which he makes application of John's writings to the present situation faced by the church.

Kruse, Colin G., *The Letters of John*, in the Pillar New Testament Commentary series. Grand Rapids: Eerdmans, 2000.
Kruse's conclusions on introductory matters are fairly conservative (e.g., the apostle John, the son of Zebedee, is the author of all three letters). This is not because he is unaware of modern hypotheses to the contrary, for he interacts with many of these in his footnotes. He simply was unpersuaded by them. In the introductory discussion there are helpful compilations of patristic references to John (p.11-14) and to the false teachers against whom John may have been reacting (p.20-26). In some nearly two dozen special studies he does a good job of boiling down much technical discussion (e.g., "A Note on Sinless Perfectionism"). His own solution to the alleged tension between 1 John 2:1 and 3:6-9 is to say that there may be no solution at hand.

Law, R., *The Tests of Life: A Study of the First Epistle of St. John*. Edinburgh: T&T Clark, 1914. Reprint, Baker, 1968.
This famous early study of the letters weds scholarly insight with pastoral wisdom, arranging the contents of the letters topically. He covers theological and Christological themes plus the doctrine of sin, propitiation, and the tests of righteousness, love, and belief.

Lenski, R.C.H., *The Interpretation of the Epistles of St. Peter, St. John and St. Jude.* Columbus, OH: Wartburg, 1945. Reprint, Minneapolis: Augsburg, 1996.
A conservative Lutheran exposition based on the Greek text. Tends to be wordy at times, but the student who will take time to read it will grow in his appreciation of these letters.

Lightner, Robert, *The Epistles of John and Jude.* Chattanooga: AMG Publishers, 2003.
Following are Lightner's views on some of the problem passages. 1 John 1:9 refers to believers and their need to confess their sins in order to maintain fellowship with God. "Little children," "fathers," and "young men" indicate levels of spiritual maturity (p.30). The "elder" of 2 John 1 is the apostle John, the "chosen lady" is an assembly of believers, not an individual in a local church (pp.90-91). God's seed (3:9) "refers most likely to the new nature imparted to the believing sinner at the time of salvation" (p.51). 2 John 9 speaks of people who had professed Christ but were not saved, as seen in the fact that they do not abide in the teaching of Christ. Several appendixes are included which cover antichrist, Gnosticism, John's use of *kosmos*, and the doctrine of confession.

Marshall, I. Howard, *The Epistles of John*, in the New International Commentary on the New Testament series. Grand Rapids: Eerdmans, 1978.
> An evangelical scholar at Aberdeen University, Scotland, Marshall brings a wealth of pastoral experience to careful exegetical work. An outstanding volume that richly repays careful study. Many would view this commentary as the standard evangelical commentary on John's epistles.

McDowell, Edward A., *1-2-3 John*, in the Broadman Bible Commentary series. Vol. 12. Nashville: Broadman, 1972.
> Conservative conclusions are defended on introductory matters. On authorship, having noted the ancient church held that the apostle John, the son of Zebedee, wrote the Gospel and epistles, whereas there is no agreement among modern writers concerning authorship of either the Gospel or the epistles, it is "reasonable to accept the testimony of the early church fathers." Accepting the apostle John as the author, he dates the epistles in the last quarter of the first century. The purpose of 1 John was to warn against false teachers whom McDowell identifies as "pre-Gnostics." The purpose of 2 John is to warn against extending hospitality to traveling missionaries who carried heresy. The purpose of 3 John was to encourage hospitality to traveling missionaries who carried the true gospel.

Moody, Dale, *The Letters of John*. Waco, TX: Word, 1970.
> Moody sees John's letter as a polemic against Gnostic Judaism. The comments reflect interaction with contemporary theological theories.

Morris, Leon, *1 John, 2 John, 3 John*, in the New Bible Commentary: Revised. Grand Rapids: Eerdmans, 1970, p.1259-1273.
> Brief introductory notes are conservative in tone: the apostle John is the author of all three letters; the false teaching warned against was of a Gnostic type; the first epistle was written to give assurance to believers of the possession of life-giving faith; the second epistle seems to be addressed to a church; the third epistle is a purely private letter to Gaius; the epistles were written toward the end of the first century. The comments (often not longer than a single sentence) are given for key phrases in each paragraph.

Painter, J., *The Quest for the Messiah: The History, Literature and Theology of the Johannine Community*. Edinburgh: T&T Clark, 1993.
> This thorough scholarly treatment surveys the current research on the literature of the Johannine community and provides outstanding academic background to the study of the Fourth Gospel and the letters of John.

Perkins, Pheme, *Gnosticism and the New Testament*. Minneapolis: Fortress, 1993.
> It was inevitable after the discoveries at Nag Hammadi that new surveys on the theme of Gnosticism and the New Testament would be provided. This book is a good place to start for an overview. Analysis of treatises from Nag Hammadi have led to a kind of consensus: forms of gnosticism (especially "Sethian" Gnosticism) with roots in late Jewish exegesis and thought existed apart from Christianity and provided the groundwork for more refined versions of the Gnostic myth in later Christian circles. In this Perkins seems to be on solid ground. Perhaps, too, in her presentation of the view that the world of Paul (toward the end of his ministry) can be illuminated by a better knowledge of the history of incipient Gnosticism, the kind of heresy that John faced a quarter of century later. Other major conclusions by Perkins are disappointing: (1) that the Gospel of Thomas occupies an important place alongside the canonical synoptic Gospels and can be used fruitfully to help sift the traditions about Jesus in those writings; (2) Paul's Christology is rooted in a mixture of speculation on Wisdom and Adam like that found in Gnosticism.

Plummer, Alfred, *The Epistles of S. John*, in the Cambridge Bible for Schools and Colleges series. Cambridge: Cambridge University Press, 1883. Reprinted 1938.
This volume is intended for the English student.

-----, *The Epistles of S. John*, in the Cambridge Greek Testament series. Cambridge: At the University Press, 1894. Reprint, 1938.
This volume is intended for the student who can read Greek.

-----, *The Epistles of S. John*, in the Pulpit Commentary series, edited by H.D.M. Spence and Joseph S. Exell. Grand Rapids: Eerdmans, 1962. Vol.22.
The exegetical notes in this volume supplement what can be read in his brief commentaries in *The Cambridge Bible* and *Cambridge Greek Testament* volumes alluded to above.

Price, Robert M., "The *Sitz-im-Leben* of Third John: A New Reconstruction," *Evangelical Quarterly* 61:2 (1989), p.109-119.
Redaction criticism is anxious to reconstruct the historical background of the second or third generation communities or schools which (in redaction criticism's view) were responsible for constructing the books of the New Testament as we have them. Price briefly reviews the history of this research during the 20th century (Wm. Alexander, Adolf Harnack, Walter Bauer, Ernst Kasemann, and John C. Meagher), and then offers his own attempt, since the others have failed to capture widespread acceptance. Price first posits the epistles were written in the reverse order in which they are printed in our Bible, and then offers his own reconstructed sequence of events that led to their writing.

Roberts, J.W., *The Letters of John,* in the Living Word Commentary Series, edited by Everett Ferguson. Vol.18. Austin, TX: Sweet, 1969.
Succinct notes which open up the thread of thought in John's epistles.

Robertson, A.T., *The First Epistle of John, Second John, Third John*, in Word Pictures in the New Testament series. Nashville, TN: Broadman, 1933. Vol.6, p.197-266.
Surprisingly, Robertson opts for the view that the first epistle was written before the Fourth Gospel, and treats the two as being written by the same author (the apostle John, the son of Zebedee). He sees 1 John as a polemic against Gnosticism. "The [first] epistle was clearly sent to those familiar with John's message, possibly to the churches in the [Roman] province of Asia" (p.201). Since Dom Chapman (*John the Presbyter and the Fourth Gospel* [1911]) has disproved the very existence of a "presbyter John" as distinct from the Apostle John, Robertson opts for the apostolic authorship of both 2 and 3 John. "The obvious way of taking 'chosen lady' is [to take it as referring] to a woman of distinction in one of the churches ..." (p.249). "It is possible that in 3 John 9 there is an allusion to 2 John and, if so, then both letters went to individuals in the same church (one a loyal woman, the other a loyal man)" (p.259). Robertson transliterates the Greek words and explains the nuances of Greek verb tenses for the English reader.

Ross, Alexander, *Commentary on the Epistles of James and John*, in the New International Commentary on the New Testament series. Grand Rapids: Eerdmans, 1954.
Follows in the reformed tradition, including eschatology. Written by a conservative Scottish scholar.

Rudolph, Kurt, *Gnosis. The Nature and History of an Ancient Religion*. Edinburgh: T&T Clark, 1983.
This volume has been recognized as an authoritative survey of the history and doctrines of a wide variety of Gnostic groups. Rudolph makes it clear that he intends to treat the patristic heresiological

evidence with some reserve (the Christians in his view, of course, are giving a biased account). He includes extensive quotations from the Nag Hammadi Gnostic texts (and does not exhibit any reserve about these). He notes there was a diversity of Gnostic teaching (within the limits of a dualistic cosmology, and a theology of redemption that involved deliverance from slavery to the natural order). He documents that not all Gnostics were docetic. The discussion of "Community, Cult and Social Practice" (p.204-272) is a helpful introduction to gnostic worship. Rudolph discounts many of the familiar allegations of antinomianism among the Gnostics. The discussion of the origins and development of gnosticism (in the book's third section) advances the idea that "Jewish skepticism" is an important seedbed for Gnostic ideas. There are portions of the book that invite challenge. For example, it is assumed throughout that the Bultmann-Kasemann understanding of *gnosis* in the New Testament, and especially in the Johannine literature, is beyond dispute, even though it leaves the character of pre-Gnostic or non-Gnostic Christianity very obscure indeed. Others will take issue with one of the basic premises of Rudolph's book, that *Gnosis* was a *religion*.

Ryrie, Charles C., *1, 2, and 3 John* in The Wycliffe Bible Commentary, edited by Charles F. Pfeiffer and Everett F. Harrison. Chicago: Moody, 1962.
> Both the introductory studies and the comments are given more paragraphs of explanation than was true of the other one-volume commentary in this bibliography (that by Leon Morris). Having briefly summarized the arguments for and against the apostle John being the author of the epistles that bear his name in their titles, Ryrie opts for the apostle as the author of the Fourth Gospel as well as the Johannine epistles. He does a similar summary of arguments for a late date (between AD 110 and 165) and, having given evidence to the contrary, opts for a date in the early AD 90s for the epistles. Comments are offered on most verses, with significant phrases in each being explained. He treats the "chosen lady" of 2 John as being figurative either for the whole church, or at least some particular congregation.

Sinclair, W.M., *The Epistles of St. John*, in Ellicott's Commentary on the Whole Bible, edited by Charles John Ellicott. Vol. 8. Grand Rapids: Zondervan, 1981 reprint.
> Originally printed in 1903, this set of commentaries has proven its value over time. This verse-by-verse commentary is always a good place to search for information on difficult verses.

Smalley, S.S., *1, 2, 3 John*, in the Word Biblical Commentary series. Vol. 51. Waco, TX: Word, 1984.
> Stephen Smalley is a famous Johannine scholar and here culls the best insights from massive scholarly literature. An essential volume for serious exegetes since each paragraph of Scripture is provided with a bibliography, the commentator's own translation, notes which list and assess textual variants, a discussion of form, structure, and setting, followed by a detailed commentary on the Greek text. Smalley disputes the traditional view that the apostle John wrote all three epistles. He dates the writing of the epistles about 10 years after the writing of the Fourth Gospel. He regards 1 John as a "paper" explaining, for the benefit of heterodox members, how the Gospel should properly be interpreted. His long discussion of 1 John 2:22 declines to identify the Christological heresy which John is refuting.

Smalley, S.S., *John: Evangelist and Interpreter*. Exeter: Paternoster, 1978. Reissued, 1983.
> A good introduction for those beginning a critical study of the Johannine literature.

Smith, David, *The Epistles of John*, in the Expositor's Greek Testament series, edited by W. Robertson Nicoll. Vol.5. Grand Rapids: Eerdmans, 1967.
> Based on the Greek text, Smith defends the Johannine authorship. Comments are essentially conservative.

Smith, D. Moody, *First, Second, and Third John*, in the Interpretation series.   Louisville: John Knox, 1991.

> This series of expository commentaries is based on the RSV, but contributions written since the appearance of the NRSV (Smith's work, for one) incorporate and comment on significant changes made in the newer version.   In introductory matters, Smith assumes the priority of the Gospel of John over the letters.   He believes the letters were written by a single author, but not the author of the Fourth Gospel.   Nevertheless, he sees a strong Johannine influence in the epistles (whoever wrote them was strongly influenced by the apostle himself, or by the community of believers schooled in Johannine theology).   The overall purpose of the three letters was "to lay down the true doctrine and defend it against proponents of the false."   From time to time Smith compares and contrasts the Johannine letters with the Pauline.   When he finds affinities he attributes the similarity to the influence of a common tradition that the writers (redactors) shared.   At the end of each section of notes, Smith includes a brief summary, capsulizing each unit with a teaching and/or preaching synopsis, and reiterating the major theme(s) with a context of practical Christian living in mind.

Staton, Knofel, *Thirteen Lessons on First, Second, and Third John*.   Joplin, MO: College Press, 1980.

> "A student book for thirteen weeks of study."   He arranges the chapters of these three letters under these titles: "Life because of the Son," "Life in the light," "Life in the walk," "Life in the family of God," "Life in the Spirit," "Life in assurance," "II John and III John."   Each chapter ends with questions for discussion.

Stott, John R.W., *The Epistles of John*, in the Tyndale New Testament Commentaries series.   Grand Rapids: Eerdmans, 1964.

> Combines exegesis with a knowledge of the local church situation that lies behind these epistles. Anglican in perspective.

Strecker, Georg, *The Johannine Letters*, in the Hermenia series..   Philadelphia: Fortress, 1995.

> Strecker was once a student of Rudolf Bultmann.   This is a new volume in the Hermenia series, designed to supplement, if not replace, Bultmann's earlier work.   This is a critical commentary in the strict sense.   As is usual for volumes in the Hermenia series, knowledge of Greek is required to make sense of the discussion.   Strecker seeks "critical readers who are open-minded enough to question traditional positions" (p.xiii).   This warning is an understatement since "traditional positions" are not only questioned but are consistently put to flight with no mercy and few exceptions.   In Strecker's view, the apostle John wrote none of the canonical documents bearing his name.   Instead a "Johannine school" produced them (though Strecker departs from Bultmann in his depiction of the development of this school).   He has 2 and 3 John written first (ca. AD 100 and possibly as late as AD 130), and 1 John coming later, and the Fourth Gospel still later.   What about P[52] (a fragment of John's Gospel) usually dated AD 125?   The early date for this manuscript "should be relegated to the realm of the creation of pious legends" (p.xli, n.78).   Strecker's redaction-critical approach to these letters is less difficult to follow than Raymond Brown's complicated and shifting theory of a burgeoning, often warring Johannine community.   Strecker is reluctant to embrace a pre-Christian Gnosticism as an important component of the milieu of the Johannine literature.   He argues that 2 John 7 (unlike 1 John 4:2) refers to Jesus' future coming, His *parousia*, not His incarnation.   (If Strecker is wrong in his interpretation of the present participle ["coming"] at 2 John 7 as having a future meaning, then his whole attempted reconstruction of the growth of the hypothetical "Johannine school" is wrong!)   This volume is one of the most comprehensive of all the historical-critical commentaries on John's epistles.

Strecker, Georg, *John: Witness and Theologian*.   London: SPCK, 1975.

> A helpful and readable introduction to Johannine studies by students just breaking into the field.

Stott, J.R.W., *The Epistles of John: Introduction and Commentary*. Grand Rapids: Eerdmans, 1964.

> Perhaps one of the best popular commentators, Stott writes passionately about these letters' message for the church today. Always creative, always penetrating.

Thayer, Joseph H., *A Greek-English Lexicon of the New Testament*. Chicago: American Book Company, 1889.

> A translation of Grimm's *Clavis Novi Testamenti*, it was the standard lexicon of a previous generation. The work is still valuable for Thayer's comments, his discussion of synonyms, and word distinctions.

Thomas, John Christopher, *The Pentecostal Commentary on 1 John, 2 John, 3 John*. Cleveland: Pilgrim, 2004.

> Thomas is both the editor of this new series and the author of this commentary within it. The purpose of the series, he writes, "is to provide reasonably priced commentaries written from distinctively Pentecostal perspective primarily for pastors, lay persons, and Bible students." Thomas holds that the author of these letters is probably the same author as the fourth evangelist, but not the apostle John. Thomas opts for John the Elder. There is no attempt in this volume to relate the Christological denials that John confronts with Gnostic or other movements of about the same period. The introduction ends with a short section on "The Holy Spirit in 1 John" (the "anointing" language of chapter 2 reflects the work of the Spirit; the Spirit assures believers of their relationship with God [3:24, 4:13]; the Spirit helps believers distinguish between the Spirit of truth and the spirit of error [4:1-6]; and the Spirit confirms (through the prophetic ministry of human spokespersons) the significance of blood and water [5:6-8]). The commentary itself works first through 3 John, then 2 John, and then 1 John (since that, in Thomas' opinion, is the order in which they were written). Thomas takes 3 John to be a genuine private letter. The "chosen lady" of 2 John is a local congregation, and her "children" are her members. Thomas does not think that 1 John is a letter at all. Rather, following Raymond Brown's lead, it is a commentary on the Christological and other issues raised by the Fourth Gospel that have been misunderstood.

Thompson, Mirianne Meye, *1-3 John*, in the Inter-Varsity Press New Testament Commentary series. Downer's Grove, IL: Inter-Varsity, 1992.

> A professor at Fuller Seminary, Meye Thompson's study gives lively, outstanding illustrations for preaching, based on a wealth of scholarly research.

Trench, Richard, *Synonyms of the New Testament*. Grand Rapids: Eerdmans, 1953.

> Though newer linguistic theories stress what are called semantic domains which affirm there are no such things as synonyms in the Greek of New Testament times, this author still finds rich illustrations in the meanings of Greek words that apparently were synonyms.

Van Ryn, August, *The Epistles of John*. New York: Loizeaux, 1948.

> Exposition is based on the American Standard Version (1901). Devotional in thrust.

Vine, William E., *The Epistles of John*. Grand Rapids: Zondervan, reprint.

> Defends the traditional view that John wrote to defend Christianity against the false teachings of the Ebionites, Docetists, and Cerinthians. Vine's work is thoroughly conservative and is based on a thorough knowledge of the Greek text. The author's eschatological viewpoint is premillennial.

Watson, D.F., "Rhetoric, Rhetorical Criticism, " *Dictionary of the Later New Testament & Its Development*, edited by Ralph P. Martin and Peter H. Davids. Downers Grove, IL: Inter-Varsity, 1997. p.1041-1051.

Westcott, B.F., *The Epistles of St. John*. London: Macmillan, 1883. Reprint, Grand Rapids: Eerdmans, 1952.
> The Greek text with notes and addenda. Long recognized as the classic commentary on the Johannine epistles. Readers will need fluency in Greek to appreciate his comments.

White, Reginald E.O., *An Open Letter to Evangelicals: A Devotional and Homiletic Commentary on the First Epistle of John*. Grand Rapids: Eerdmans, 1964.
> A volume that disappoints evangelicals since it advocates many of the errors propounded by C.H. Dodd. The comments are weak theologically, following the neo-orthodox view that authority for Christians is not found in the words of Scripture, but in Christ.

Woods, Guy N., *A Commentary on the New Testament Epistles of Peter, John, and Jude*. Nashville, TN: Gospel Advocate, 1954.
> A commentary intended to aid Sunday School teachers in their preparation to present these Bible books to their classes. Where there are alternative interpretations that might be alluded to, the work tends to give just one position, and seldom gives reasons for the choice. A helpful tool for an introduction to the basic teaching of the letters.

Wright, D.F., "Docetism," *Dictionary of the Later New Testament & Its Development*, edited by Ralph P. Martin and Peter H. Davids. Downers Grove, IL: Inter-Varsity, 1997, p.306-309.

Wuest, Kenneth S., *In these Last Days: II Peter, I, II, III John, and Jude in the Greek New Testament for the English Reader*. Grand Rapids: Eerdmans, 1954.
> Wuest's works were written for students who do not have access to the Greek text but who would like to know something about what the Greek beneath the surface of the English translation says. Included are Greek word studies, explanations of nuances of grammar, and quotations from the works of scholars fluent in the Greek.

Yamauchi, E. M., *Pre-Christian Gnosticism: A Survey of the Proposed Evidences*. Grand Rapids: Eerdmans, 1973.
> Yamauchi's volume is an attempt to refute Bultmann's idea that Christianity copied Gnostic sources. He tried to show there was no pre-Christian Gnosticism. While he was correct in his assumption (namely, that Christianity is a divinely revealed religion, not one copied from pagan sources), he was evidently in error when he attempted to show that there was no such thing as pre-Christian Gnosticism.

2 JOHN

INTRODUCTORY STUDIES

HISTORICAL ALLUSIONS

The place to begin a study of any New Testament book is to read it through, looking for any intimations that will help us identify the author, the date, the destination, and the purpose for which the book or letter was written.

The first thing that catches our attention as we read any of the New Testament books is the title at the top of the page. The information to be learned from the title on this and other letters known as "The First Epistle of John," "The Second Epistle of John," and "The Third Epistle of John" has already been commented upon in the Introductory Studies on 1 John. Concerning authorship, the titles reflect the conclusion of those who first collected the letters for use in the churches. Their conclusion was that "John" was the writer.

Verse 1 – Instead of giving his name, the writer uses a title ("the elder") as his signature.

This descriptive title, we may be sure, was sufficient to identify the writer to the letter's intended audience. If not, the messenger who carried the letter could have personally filled in the needed identification. Our problem is that we are so many years separated from when this letter was written that the best we can do is to draw some educated conclusions, even though these conclusions will not offer absolute certainty.

The writer does write with a certain air of authority (see verses 3,8,9,10), and at the same time he has a loving personal interest in the welfare of the recipients of the letter (see verses 5,8,12).

Verse 1 – The letter is addressed to "the chosen (elect, KJV) lady and her children."

Kuria (the feminine form of "Lord, master," and here translated "lady" in the NASB) can be a personal name or it can be an official title used to address a woman who holds a leadership position. ("Head of a household church," says Albertz; "a lady 'elected' to the position," say Ross and Guthrie).

The word can also be taken in a metaphorical sense. The church is called the bride of Christ (Revelation 19:7; cp. Ephesians 5:22ff), so perhaps "chosen lady" (or "elect lady" KJV) is another expression referring to Christ's bride, or to a portion thereof.

- In support of this view that "lady" is metaphorical for a congregation of believers, it can be pointed out that the letter does go on to treat certain problems that could be matters of concern in the life of a Christian congregation (see verses 5,7,10).

- "Chosen" or "elect" can likewise be harmonized with the view that "lady" should be taken metaphorically. Christians who make up the churches are now God's "chosen people" (2 Thessalonians 2:13; 1 Peter 1:1, 2:9). So the members of the congregation addressed are "chosen/elect" (verse 1). Likewise, the members of a congregation in the vicinity where the writer is working also includes "chosen people" (verse 13, "chosen sister").

How are we to explain the "children" included in the letter's address? Are the "children" physical children or spiritual children? If the letter is addressed to a Christian woman, "her children" is easily understood. If the letter is addressed to a congregation of believers, who are "her children"?

Verse 1 – Having signed and addressed his letter, the writer emphasizes the bond of love which unites him with the addressee. Those who know the truth also have a similar warm place in their hearts for the addressee. Is "the truth" a reference to Christ, or to the gospel?

Verse 2 – What has the writer written in verse 1 that can now be said to be "for the sake of the truth"? Is it the writer's love for the addressees, or is it other people's love for the addressees?

Does the writer say that all who know the truth love the elect lady *because* they love the truth?

"Truth which abides in us, and will be with us forever." Is there an implied contrast with some doctrine (i.e., Gnostic doctrine) that will not be as permanent as the truth?

Does this say that "the truth" is believed and practiced by the elder and his beloved readers, and not by some other group (say, the Gnostics)?

Verse 3 – The salutation is an affirmation that "grace, mercy, and peace" will be with us (not with the deceivers who are specifically introduced in verses 7ff).

"From God the Father, and Jesus Christ, the Son of the Father." Salutations often introduce some of the key ideas later to be unfolded in the body of the letter. Is that the case here?

"Truth ... truth ... truth ... truth." Four times the word is used in the first four verses; the word rings like a bell. Something is not the truth. What is it?

Verses 4-9 are an admonition to walk in truth and love, and a warning against deceivers who are traveling up and down the land, who do not confess Jesus Christ as having come in the flesh, and whose teachings "go too far" (verse 9) rather than abiding in the simple apostolic doctrine now held.

Verse 4 seems to allude to the occasion or impetus which led to the writing of this letter. Some of the "lady's" children are walking in the truth, just as it was received from the Father.

- Does the word "some" imply that there other children who are not walking in the old-time truth, but rather have embraced something newer and therefore not really the truth? If "some" of the lady's children departed from the faith, does this help us date this second epistle after 1 John?

- Or does "some" say that John, having encountered a few of the lady's children, has found her children to be faithful to Jesus Christ, and that's great! (This interpretation would give little help deciding the order of writing for the Johannine literature).

Verse 5 calls attention to "a ... commandment ... we have had from the beginning," that "we love one another."

The Fourth Gospel records Jesus' command to "love one another" (John 13:34,35, 15:12,17). One of the earliest books of the New Testament to be written also repeats this solemn injunction (1 Thessalonians 3:12, 4:9).

We are reminded of what we read in greater detail in 1 John, where we found the false teachers were not walking in love as Jesus commanded His followers to do.

Verse 6 – In "the commandment ... you have heard from the beginning," "you" is plural.

This, too, is reminiscent of language encountered in 1 John: the message that is to be embraced is not some new doctrine, but is the one heard from the beginning of gospel preaching, just as it was declared by Jesus and His apostles.

In 1 John such language was an aside directed towards the Gnostic ideas that are not as old as the gospel. Likely the same reason for rejecting those new Gnostic ideas is emphasized here, too.

Verse 7 – "Many deceivers have gone out into the world." Do we know them by any other name?

These deceivers "do not acknowledge (confess) [that] Jesus Christ as coming in the flesh." Does "coming" speak of His incarnation?

Such a false doctrine is the same as will be taught by antichrist.

- The use of "antichrist" in verse 7 rather suggests that the false teachers being warned about are the same as introduced in 1 John 2:18ff.

- 1 John 2:19 indicates the false teachers had gone out before that letter was written. Does the aorist tense of verse 7 look back on that occasion?

Verse 8 – The plural "watch yourselves" must be taken into account as we identify the addressees to whom this letter is addressed. Verse 1 may well explain the plural "yourselves" as referring to "the chosen lady and her children."

Verse 8 – "That you might not lose what we have accomplished, but that you may receive a full reward" is how the NASB reads. The KJV has "that we lose not those things which we have wrought, but that we receive a full reward."

- Who is intended by the plural "we" in "what *we* have accomplished"?

- Are we sure of what the elder actually wrote? And what does it mean?

- Can the readers abandon what "we" accomplished?

- Whose reward is in view, that of the readers, or that of the "we" who have worked with the readers to win them to Christ in the first place?

Verse 9 – "Goes too far (or goes beyond) and does not abide in the teaching of Christ."

Does this word reflect claims made by the deceivers? Were the deceivers claiming to take their converts beyond the simple teachings of the apostles to something deeper and more advanced?

Verses 10-11 are a prohibition of listening to or supporting those deceptive missionaries, lest they have the finances to journey elsewhere with their evil doctrine and deeds. This certainly is the key point of this whole letter.

- False teachers are traveling among the churches, taking advantage of the hospitality of Christian people, it is implied.

- The plural "you" in verse 10 must be taken into account as we attempt to identify to whom this letter is addressed. (Remember, it is "the chosen lady and her children." That would account for the plural.)

- The elder expressly instructs, "Do not receive him into your house (do not extend hospitality to such)" and "do not give him a greeting (do not provide him with financial support so he may continue his journey at your expense)."

Verse 11 gives the reason for the prohibition against hospitality or financial support. To extend such would involve the chosen lady and her children personally in the evil deeds the deceivers are doing.

Verse 12 – The epistle closes with an expressed hope on the writer's part that he may soon visit with the readers personally. Notice that "you" is plural. The elder is not writing to one individual person, but to a plurality of readers.

Verse 13 – The "children of your chosen (elect) sister" also send their greetings to the addressee.

"You" is singular in this verse. What effect does this have on our conclusion concerning the identity of the "chosen lady"?

We might wish the historical allusions gave more specific information so we could with confidence speak of the author, date, destination, and purpose of the letter. Let us see what Bible scholars have done with the information we do have.

AUTHORSHIP

Before redaction criticism became for some an accepted method of Bible study, nearly all Bible scholars allowed that the Fourth Gospel and the First Epistle were written by the same author. In the same fashion, it was generally admitted that the letters commonly known as the Second and Third Epistle of John were written by one hand.[1]

---

[1] In the Introductory Studies on 1 John, we have briefly outlined the ideas proposed by redaction critics. They propose that it was a Johannine circle which produced the Johannine literature found in our New Testaments. Bultmann (*The Johannine Epistles* [Philadelphia: Fortress Press, 1973], p.1) first observed that 3 John follows the regular form of a 1st century personal letter, and that 2 John follows the same general pattern. Then Bultmann alleged that 2 John is more formal and artificial in style, and hence is not really a letter, but a literary fiction based on the pattern of 3 John. C.H. Dodd (*The Johannine Epistles* [London: Hodder and Stoughton, 1946], p.lxiv-lxv) admits the possibility that 2 John is an imitation letter, composed on the basis of 1 and 3 John in order to claim the elder's authority for boycotting heretics. But Dodd also goes on to point out that if an imitator was at work he did his work with "rare skill." His vocabulary is entirely Johannine, and when he echoes the Fourth Gospel he seems to be doing so unconsciously rather than deliberately. Moreover, the (slight) external evidence suggests that 2 John received earlier canonical recognition than 3 John, and this argues against the view that 2 John was a fictitious imitation. "We therefore do not accept that 2 John was either an earlier draft of 1 John or an imitation of 3 John." (Adapted from Smalley, "1,2,3 John" in *Word Biblical Commentary* [Waco, TX: Word Books, 1984], p.316)

What was debated is whether *all four* writings were by the same person; that is, whether "the elder" who signed the two short Epistles is one and the same person known as the apostle John, the beloved disciple of the Gospel, and the author of the First Epistle.[2] The evidence on which such a question can be decided is of two kinds – external and internal.

External Evidence for Authorship

The voice of antiquity is strongly in favor of the first and simplest hypothesis: that all four writings are the work of the apostle John.[3]

(1) The Eastern Church (Egypt, Palestine, Syria)

Polycarp (AD 115)

It is possible that Polycarp (*Ad Phil.* VII.1) contains an allusion to 2 John 7.[4]

Clement of Alexandria (AD 190)

In harmony with the whole Alexandrian school, Clement testifies to the belief that 2 John was by the apostle John. He quotes 1 John 5:16 with the introductory words, "John, in his longer Epistle (*en tē meizoni epistolē*) seems to teach ..." (*Strom.* II.15), which shows that he knows of at least one other and shorter Epistle by the same John.

In a fragment of a Latin translation of one of Clement's works we read, "The second Epistle of John, which is written to virgins, is very simple: it is written indeed to a certain Babylonian lady, Electa by name; but it signifies the election of the holy Church." A few lines later in the same fragment he quotes verse 10

---

[2] A. Plummer (*The Epistles of St. John* [Grand Rapids: Baker, 1980 reprint], p.lxxii-lxxiv) has a chart showing similarities between the four writings (Gospel, First, Second, Third Epistles) to enable readers to judge for themselves whether or not the simplest explanation for the similarities is to accept the primitive church's tradition (though not universal) that all four proceeded from one and the same author.

[3] The evidence for 2 and 3 John is not so full or so indisputably unanimous as for the apostolicity of the First Epistle. But when we take into account the brevity and personal nature of these two letters, the amount is considerable.

[4] Allusions show a cited work was already in existence, but does not identify who wrote it. (In the case of this citation, it is also possible that the allusion is to 1 John 4:2,3, which some argue furnishes a better parallel than 2 John 7.)

of John and comments upon it. (*Adumbrations on 2nd John*. ANF, V.2, p.576,77.)[5]

Origen (AD 210)

Origen knew of second and third John, but says that "not all admit that these are genuine [i.e., written by John]. Both of these together, however, contain only a hundred lines." (*apud.* Eus. H.E. VI.25.10).

Dionysius of Alexandria (AD 200-265)

In a statement where he is arguing against the apostolic authorship of Revelation, Dionysius cites the epistles as examples of the style of writing used by John the apostle, especially his custom of not signing his letters. It reads on this fashion:

> Nor yet in the second and third epistles ascribed to John, though they are but short epistles, is the name of John prefixed: for without any name is he called the elder. (*apud.* Eus. H.E. VII.25)

So far from thinking "the elder" an unlikely title to be taken by the apostle John, Dionysius rather affirms that John's not naming himself in the epistles or in his Gospel (compared with how the writer of Revelation several times calls himself "John") is in fact most like the apostle's usual manner.

Alexander, bishop of Alexandria (c.273-326)

He quotes the second epistle, ascribing it to John the apostle. "For it becometh us Christians ... not to say to such, God speed, lest we be partakers of their sins, as the blessed John directs." (*apud.* Socrat. H.E. lib.i, chap. 6)

Athanasius (c.297-373), the author of the *Synopsis Sacrae Scripturae*, and Didymus (c.309-394), received the second Epistle as canonical. They would hardly have done so if they had any doubts about the apostolic authorship of the letters.

(2) The Syrian Church

Syriac versions of the New Testament have gone through several recensions. There was an Old Syriac version (c.AD 190-200), extant manuscripts of which contain only the Gospels. Yet Ephraem the Syrian (c. 308-373) quotes 2 John 9 after an introduction which

---

[5] D. Guthrie (*New Testament Introduction: Hebrews to Revelation* [Chicago: InterVarsity Press, 1964], p.207) suggests the statement about it being written "to virgins" may possibly have originated with the Latin translator.

reads, "The word of John the divine."[6]   Ephraem was not acquainted with Greek, so it is clear that he must have read the epistles in a translation, and it would seem most probable that it was a Syriac version.   (At this early date, it would have been the Old Syriac version that would have been available to him.)

About AD 425 a revision of the Old Syriac was made, now called the Peshitta (i.e., Simple) Syriac version.   The Peshitta contained all the New Testament books except 2 Peter, 2 and 3 John, Jude and Revelation.   These were omitted because they were not recognized as canonical by the Syrian church at the time the Peshitta revision was made.[7]

In AD 508, as we know from the colophon appended to the Gospels in the manuscripts of this version, a fresh translation of the New Testament was prepared for Philoxenus, Jacobite bishop of Mabug (or Hierapolis) in Eastern Syria, by one Polycarp. Little is known of the Philoxenian version, for the manuscripts that have come down to us contain only the books not in the Peshitta, viz., 2 Peter, 2 and 3 John, Jude, and Revelation. Two other Syriac versions are known: the Palestinian Syriac (c. AD 550), and the Harkleian Syriac (AD 616).   (In modern printed Syriac texts, the four omitted Catholic Epistles have been supplied from the Philoxenian Syriac, and Revelation from the Harkleian Syriac.)

On the whole, the voice of the Syrian church is unfavorable towards the apostolic authorship, and therefore the canonicity, of 2 John.

Eusebius of Caesarea (AD 325)

As he writes his history, he calls attention to the beliefs of church people concerning the various New Testament books.

"But of the writings of John, not only his Gospel, but also the former of his epistles, has been accepted without dispute both now and in ancient times.   But the other two are disputed.   In regard to the Apocalypse, the opinions of most men are still divided."   (HE. III.24.17,18)

In the next chapter Eusebius classifies the writings known to the churches as "accepted" (i.e., canonical), "disputed" (i.e., some people in some places had doubts about their canonicity), and "spurious" (i.e., everyone agrees they do not

---

[6] *De Amore Pauperum*, vol.3, p.52.

[7] Theodore of Mopsuestia, Leontius of Byzantium, and Chrysostom, held that 2 John (and 3 John) were not canonical.

belong in the canon). He records the fact that 2 and 3 John were treated as "disputed" because of a question about authorship, whether they were written by the apostle John or by someone who had the same name.

> "Among the *disputed* (*antilegomena*) books, which are nevertheless recognized by many, are the epistle circulated under the name of James, and that of Jude, also the second epistle of Peter, and those that are called the second and third of John, whether they belong to the evangelist or to another person of the same name." (Eus. H.E. III.25.3).

Elsewhere Eusebius himself speaks in a way which leaves one less in doubt as to his own opinion (*Dem. Evan.* III.3), which appears to be favorable to the Apostolic authorship. He speaks of them without qualification as being by the apostle John. Speaking of the apostle John, he writes, "In his epistles, he either makes no mention of himself or calls himself only elder, no where apostle or evangelist."

Jerome (c.347-c.420)

Jerome wrote that while the First Epistle of John is approved by all Churches and scholars, the two others are ascribed to John the presbyter, whose tomb was still shown at Ephesus as well as that of the Apostle. (*Vir. Illus.* IX)[8]

(3) The Western Church (Italy, Gaul, North Africa)

2 John was known and received in the Western Church in the 2nd and 3rd centuries.

The Muratorian Canon (c.AD 170, from Rome)

This work was quoted in our Introduction to 1 John, noting that the writer quotes the First Epistle in his account of the Fourth Gospel, and later on speaks of "two Epistles of the John who has been mentioned before."

While the author of the two epistles is identified as the same one who wrote the Fourth Gospel and the work we call 1 John, it is by no means clear how the words "two epistles" are to be explained. Perhaps the reference is to 2 and 3 John, since the author had earlier alluded to 1 John. Perhaps the reference is to 1 and 2 John, with 3 John being omitted.[9] Perhaps 2 and 3 John (being short) were treated as one letter in the Muratorian Canon.

---

[8] The question of "Two Johns at Ephesus" is discussed in the Introduction to 1 John.

[9] Was there a time when 3 John was not included in the canon, so there were but two epistles by John included in the Muratorian canon? As evidence that this may have indeed been the case, it is observed that Eusebius twice speaks of the First Epistle as "the *former* Epistle of John" (H.E. III.25.2; III.39.16), just as Clement speaks of "the *longer* Epistle," as if in some arrangements there were only two Epistles.

Irenaeus (AD 180, in Gaul)

This most important witness was born in Smyrna, and lived not long after the time when the apostle John was alive.   He was a disciple of Polycarp, who was personally acquainted with the apostle John.   Since he spent his early life in Asia Minor, he must, in the circumstances in which he was placed, have been familiar with the writings of John, and have known well what writings were attributed to him.

He quotes the second epistle (verses 10 and 11) with express reference to the apostle John as the author.

> John, the disciple of the Lord, intensified their condemnation by desiring that not even a 'God-speed' should be bid to them by us: For, says he, he that biddeth him, God speed, partaketh in his evil works.   (*Adv. Haer.* II.16.3)

A little further on, having quoted 1 John 2:18 as being by "John the disciple of the Lord" (*Adv. Haer.* III.16.5), and still alluding to what the apostle John wrote, Irenaeus wrote:

> These are they against whom the Lord warned us beforehand; and His disciple, in his Epistle already mentioned [2 John], commands us to avoid [the heretics] when he says: Many deceivers are gone forth into this world, who confess not that Jesus Christ is come in the flesh [a quotation of 2 John 7].   This is the deceiver and the Antichrist.   Look to them, that ye lose not that which ye have wrought [a quotation of 2 John 8].   (*Adv. Haer.* III.16.8)[10]

Cyprian (AD 256)

In his account of the Council at Carthage, AD 256, Cyprian gives what we may fairly consider to be evidence as to the belief of the North African Church.   He says that Aurelius of Chullabi, giving his opinion on the question of baptizing heretics, quotes the verse 10 of the Second Epistle, as the words of "John the Apostle."

> John the apostle laid it down in his epistle, saying: 'If any one come unto you, and have not the doctrine of Christ, receive him not into your house, and say not to him, Hail.   For he that saith to him, Hail, partakes with his evil deeds.'   How can such be rashly admitted into God's house   who are prohibited from being admitted into

---

[10] In one or two respects, it will be observed, Irenaeus must have had a text slightly different from ours.   But these quotations still show that he was well acquainted with the Second Epistle and believed it to be by the beloved disciple.   Whether "the epistle already mentioned" is 1 John or 2 John, this only shows all the more plainly how remote from Irenaeus' mind was the idea that the one Epistle might be by the apostle John and the other not.

our private dwelling?   (Cyp. *Conc. Baptism of Heretics* [ANF, v.5, p.572])[11]

Cyprian took part in this council.   It may therefore be inferred that he received the Epistle to be John's, and so did the other council members.[12]

Church Councils

> The councils of the church held in the West (e.g., the council of Laodicea, AD 325, the council at Hippo, AD 393, and the council of Carthage, AD 397) recognized 2 John as canonical.   Implied in this recognition is that the letter was understood to be the work of the apostle John.

Summarizing the external evidence: (1) It is apparent that precisely those witnesses who are nearest to the apostle John in time are favorable to the apostolic authorship of 2 John, and seem to know no other view.   (2) A. Plummer (*The Epistles of St. John* [Grand Rapids: Baker, 1980 reprint], Appendix E) argues that "it is doubtful whether any such person as John the elder, as distinct from the apostle and evangelist John, ever existed." So, those writers who attribute the two shorter letters to John the elder, whether they know it or not, are really attributing them to the apostle John.

Internal Evidence for Authorship

The author designates himself as "the elder," so it is clearly necessary to discuss the significance of this title.   The title "elder" is used in several different senses in the Scriptures.[13]

(1) Men selected to be leaders in the local congregations were called "elders."   (Acts 14:23; Philippians 1:1; Titus 1:5).   Each congregation had a plurality of such elders. If 2 John 1 read "an elder" rather than "the elder," we might suppose the letter were written by some elder in a local congregation.   But to style himself "*the* elder" if he were but one of many such leaders is totally out of place.

---

[11] This quotation exhibits no less than ten differences from the Vulgate of Jerome (*Cod. Am.*) and proves the existence of an early African text of this Epistle.

[12] There is no reason for concluding that Tertullian and Cyprian were opposed to the authenticity or genuineness of these two epistles merely because they do not quote them in their extant works.

[13] *Prebuteros* ("elder") was used of members of the Jewish Sanhedrin (Matthew 16:21).   It denoted the dignity and office held by these men.   We also read of the twenty four elders sitting around God's throne in heaven (Revelation 4:4,10).   To this commentator's knowledge, no one has proposed that 2 and 3 John's "the elder" is used with either of these meanings.

(2) Apostles of Jesus were sometimes designated as "elders." Papias' well-known reference to John the elder[14] includes within it references to seven apostles of Jesus whom Papias called "elders" just as he calls the apostle John "the elder John." Quite apart from the dispute whether Papias intended to make a distinction between John the apostle and John the elder, it would seem that he saw no incongruity in calling apostles "elders," and it would, therefore, be wrong to conclude *ipso facto* that the "elder" of second and third John could not be John the apostle.[15]

The last surviving apostle might well be called, and call himself, with simple dignity, "the elder," a descriptive title indicative both of the age (*presbuteros* is the comparative of *presbus*, "old," and so thus signifies old man, senior citizen, seniority) and the authority of the writer.

A second topic related to the internal evidence is what some have called "the severe and harsh remarks made in the epistle in regard to heretics." Some object to the genuineness of these epistles because 2 John 10 and 3 John 10 are supposedly not in the spirit of the mild and amiable "disciple whom [Jesus] loved." They suppose such language breathes a temper of uncharitableness and severity which could not have existed in the apostle John, and especially when, as an older man, he is said to have preached nothing but "love one another."

But viewed correctly, such direct and pointed language is actually an evidence of the genuineness of this letter. (1) These expressions accord with what we *know* to have been the character of John at least prior to Pentecost. They are in character to one who was named by the Master Himself, "Boanerges ... Son(s) of Thunder" (Mark 3:17). They are in character to one who was disposed to call down fire from heaven on the Samaritan who would not receive the Lord Jesus (Luke 9:54). They are in character to one who, when he saw another casting out devils in the name of Jesus, took upon himself the authority to forbid him (Mark 9:38). (2) These expressions accord with what we can read in the Fourth Gospel, which was written by John post-Pentecost. John states that unbelief in Jesus as the Son of God (i.e., His deity and equality with the Father) immediately brands a man as not honoring God. In making this statement, John is simply reflecting what Jesus Himself taught (John 5:18ff, especially verse 23). See also John 3:18-21 for some strong words about who is and who is not judged.

---

[14] Eus. H.E. III.39.4; III.39.7.

[15] Adapted from Guthrie, *op. cit.*, p.209. "Elder" is a humbler title than "apostle." That the writer of 2 John styles himself "the elder" is an evidence the letter is not the work of a forger. This humbler title would not be likely to be assumed by one who wished to pass himself off as an apostle; and less so, because no apostolic writing in the New Testament begins with this appellation, except the epistles in question. Therefore, these epistles are not like the work of a forger imitating the apostle John in order to be taken for the apostle John.

The truth is, that there was a remarkable mixture of both *gentleness* and *severity* in the character of John, and both of these characteristics are reflected in his writings. Further, if such expressions as these 'severe and harsh remarks' were so obviously uncharacteristic of John, their use would have been studiously avoided by one who was attempting to forge an epistle in the name of John.

A third topic related to the internal evidence are the numerous expressions in the letter that are perfectly natural for an apostle to speak, but would be out of place for a non-apostle to speak.

- An apostle could say "the truth which abides in us and will be with us forever" (verse 2).
- An apostle, speaking by inspiration, could confidently affirm "grace and mercy and peace will be with us ..." (verse 3). Such words on the lips of a non-apostle would be arrogant.
- An apostle could speak of a "commandment" which "*we* have had from the beginning" (verse 5) far better than a second-generation Christian could.
- "Jesus Christ as coming in the flesh" (verse 7) reminds us of the emphasis on this very important truth found both in the Fourth Gospel and in 1 John.

Much internal evidence causes us to think of what the apostle John has written elsewhere.

In sum, the internal evidence agrees with the external, and both point to John the apostle as the author of 2 John.

DESTINATION

The NASB translates the Greek words which identify the recipients of the letter in this manner: "to the chosen lady and her children." Again in verse 5, we have the addressee called "lady."

Any decision concerning the intended recipient(s) will depend to a very great deal upon the translation of the opening words *eklektē kuria*,[16] which may mean: (1) to the elect lady; (2) to an elect lady; (3) to the elect Kyria; (4) to the lady Electa; (5) to Electa Kyria.

Another decision interpreters must make is whether to take the terms "lady" and "children" literally or figuratively. This difficulty was felt even by early Christian writers, where two distinct views found support. Some held that the title "lady" describes an indi-

---

[16] *Eklektē* may be treated as an adjective translated "chosen," "elect," "select," or it may be treated as a proper name. *Kuria*, the feminine form of "lord", may be translated "lady" or "mistress" (the manager of a house), or it, too, may be treated as a proper name.

vidual person; others held that it describes a community (i.e., a congregation or church). When it comes to explaining "children," proponents for both a literal meaning and a figurative meaning (spiritual children) can easily be located in the commentaries.

We may not be able to propose a solution that will prove entirely satisfactory, but we can weigh the evidence others have put forward as they have defended or criticized the hypotheses concerning the destination of 2 John and thus reach a tentative conclusion about "the chosen lady and her children."

Was this letter addressed to a church?

This view takes "lady" as figurative based upon "chosen/elect" being a common description of Christians (cf. Romans 8:33; 1 Peter 1:1).[17]   Multiple conjectures have then been offered regarding which specific church John was writing to:

(1) *The church in Babylon.*   This conjecture is supported by making an appeal to 1 Peter 5:13 ("she who is in Babylon ...").[18]

(2) *Some local church*, whose location cannot now be determined.   Attempts to identify which particular church was addressed have not been highly successful.   Guesses about the identity of the church include Pergamum,[19] Philadelphia, Jerusalem, Ephesus, Rome,[20] Thyatira,[21] and Corinth.[22]   "The fact is that nobody knows, although

---

[17] "Chosen" or "elect" are both possible translations of *eklektos*.   In Old Testament times, Israel was God's chosen people.   In New Testament times, the church (spiritual Israel) is now God's chosen people. "Applied to Christians it denotes that it was God who called them to be His people; the word always signifies those who have responded to this call and thus actually become the people of God (Matthew 22:14)."   (I.H. Marshall, "The Epistles of John," in *The New International Commentary on the New Testament* [Grand Rapids: Eerdmans, 1978], p.61)   For more details, see the explanation in the commentary on verse 1.

[18] The only similarity between 2 John and 1 Peter is the fact that the Greek is feminine in both places. Though the KJV reads "the church in Babylon," there is no word for "church" in the Greek manuscripts of 1 Peter.   Even the Greek word translated "elect" is different.

[19] G.G. Findlay (*Fellowship in the Life Eternal* [Grand Rapids: Eerdmans, 1955 reprint], p.31) suggested Pergamum as being the church to which 2 John was sent on the grounds that the church there was troubled by false teachers, very likely of the same type as mentioned in this epistle (verse 7, cf. Revelation 2:12ff).

[20] Dom Chapman (*JTS*, V, 1904, p.357ff, 517ff) suggested Rome, basing his argument on 1 Peter 5:13 being a figurative designation for the same church.

[21] J.V. Bartlet (*JTS*, VI, 1905, p.240ff) disagreed with Chapman and tentatively suggested Thyatira. (Cited by Donald Guthrie, New Testament Introduction: Hebrews to Revelation, p.215).

[22] If the Gaius of 3 John is Gaius of Corinth, and if 3 John 9 refers to 2 John, then 2 John would be addressed to Corinth, too.

somewhere in Asia is highly probable," says Guthrie.[23]

(3) *The church universal.* Clement of Alexandria[24] and Jerome[25] thought "elect lady" signified the whole church, thus making this letter a general letter, addressed to the church universal.[26]

Proponents of the view that "chosen (elect) lady" is to be taken as figurative language referring to a congregation offer a number of arguments in an attempt to convince others this view is correct.

a) The language of verse 1 ("whom I love in truth, and not only I, but also all who know the truth") is more natural if addressed to a church.[27]

b) The predominance of the second person plural ("you," verses 8,10,12) suggests a congregational destination for the letter.[28] In the Third Epistle, which is addressed to an individual called Gaius, the second person singular is employed consistently throughout.[29]

c) The mutual love that is enjoined (verse 5), it is alleged, is easier to explain if it is a congregation addressed.

---

[23] *Ibid.* Asia Minor was most likely the area where John would have traveled among the churches as he exercised apostolic supervision.

[24] See how Clement worded it in the allusions quoted above.

[25] Jerome (*Ep. Ad Ageruchian* cxxiii.12) applied "chosen lady" to the one church which is the bride of Christ. (NPNF, Series II, vol. 6, p.234)

[26] Several variations of this theme can be found in more recent writings. Hammond had the curious idea that *kuria* = the Latin *curia* (church), and Michaelis thought "chosen lady" designated the church assembled on the Lord's Day. Bultmann (p.107f) thought the letter is a "catholic" epistle to be taken to a number of churches. But to justify this view he has to argue that the details in the letter which suggest one particular destination are fictitious. (Cited by Marshall, *op. cit.,* p.60).

[27] "He uses the Greek word *agapaō*, which often functions in the Greek Old Testament and in the New Testament to express the particular kind of love shown by God to men, and which must be shown by men to God and to one another. The use of this word, rare in secular writing, shows how a new word was needed to bring out the special elements in Christian love. It contains such thoughts as caring for other people, showing loyalty to them and seeking their good, in contrast with other words [for love] which are more expressive of seeking one's own enjoyment in the object of love or of mutual attractiveness and affection" (Marshall, *op. cit.*, p.61).

[28] In this commentator's opinion, there is within this very letter an explanation for the use of the plural "you." The fact is that the letter is addressed to "the chosen lady and her children."

[29] John R.W. Stott, *The Epistles of John,* in the Tyndale New Testament Commentary Series (Grand Rapids: Eerdmans, 1964), p.201.

d) "Bringing of doctrine" (verse 10 KJV) is mentioned, which sounds very much like a congregational setting.

e) The "new commandment" of the Lord, referred to in verse 5, has more point if applied to a congregation rather than to the narrower limits of a family circle.[30]

f) Verse 13 is supposed to favor a local church. A sister church might naturally salute another. "The greeting in verse 13 is more natural if sent from one church to another, than from a group of people to their aunt by means of a third party."[31]

g) There are no obviously personal references in the Second Epistle as there are in the Third Epistle, viz., to Gaius, Diotrephes and Demetrius (verses 1,9,12). This seems to point to Second John being addressed to a local church, rather than a lady who is head of a rather large household.[32]

h) The subject matter, with its warnings against false teachers, is probably more suitable for a community than an individual.[33]

i) The personification of the church in a feminine form is in harmony with other New Testament usage. Paul speaks of the church as the bride of Christ (Ephesians 5:29ff; 2 Corinthians 11:2ff); Peter uses a feminine expression to describe the church "in Babylon" (1 Peter 5:13).

j) If 3 John 9 is a reference to 2 John, then 2 John is addressed to a local church, and both letters deal with hospitality.

As appealing as this hypothesis may be, it is not free from certain difficulties. (1) One of those difficulties is how to explain who the "children" are. If the "lady" is already the church, and the church is made up of people, how can we explain that the "children" are members of the church? How can you differentiate between the church and the individuals who make up the church?[34] (2) It is unlikely that John would use allegorical

---

[30] Guthrie, *op. cit.*, p.214.

[31] Guthrie, *ibid.*

[32] Stott, *ibid.*

[33] Would not such a warning be equally necessary for a private person who was at the same time an influential person in the church, or who used his or her home as a meeting place for the local church?

[34] Attempts to get around this difficulty include: (a) The "children" are no longer in the community where the home church is. (b) The "children" are nearby mission churches started by the mother church. (c) The "children" are orphans, at an earlier time taken in by congregation, but who have now grown and some moved away. (d) The expression "the lady and her children" is similar to Isaiah 54,55 and Baruch 4,5, where the city of Jerusalem and her inhabitants are addressed under the image of a woman and her children. In reply to this last suggestion, John's language is not quite the same as "Jerusalem and her children," for the city can be the physical buildings, and children the inhabitants. The church, in Scripture, is not a building, but people. (e) The expression "chosen lady and her children" is not a parallel to the language found in Galatians 4:26 ("the Jerusalem above ... she is our mother"), for the "Jerusalem above" is not a church/congregation here on earth, as the "chosen lady" is supposed to be.

language in so short an epistle without any hint that he was using such.[35]   (3) If "the elect lady" is the church universal, as Jerome suggests, what possible meaning is to be found for the elect lady's *sister* (verse 13)?   Are we to suppose that John contemplates a visit to all the churches in the Empire (verse 12)?   Rather, were we to take "chosen lady" figuratively, it must refer to a single local congregation.   It appears that those who think 2 John was originally an encyclical are mistaken.

The arguments for the figurative interpretation are not absolutely convincing, nor are they so strong that the literal view can be excluded or ignored.

Was this letter addressed to an individual?

This view takes "chosen lady" literally, though there is hardly unanimity of opinion about who that real woman was.   Conjectures concerning her identity include:

(1) She was *a lady named Electa* (making *eklektē* a proper name).   We do not know why Clement of Alexandria speaks of her as being a "Babylonian lady" but he does say her name was "Electa."   Oecumenius and Theophylact also supposed the proper name of the lady referred to was Electa, and that the epistle is addressed to "lady Electa."[36]

- Hiebert has objected to all this, stating, "the term 'elect (chosen)' is an adjective, rather than a proper name, [as] is suggested by its position without the article in the Greek."[37]
- That "Electa" might be a person's name is possible (for Electus occurs as a man's name, e.g., the chamberlain of Commodus), but a feminine form has not been found in any ancient inscription or literature.
- There is another difficulty facing us if we try to treat *eklektē* as the proper name, "Electa":   verse 13 would then indicate that she has a sister with the same name (*eklektē*).

On the whole, it is incredible that there would be *two sisters* (verse 1 and verse 13) each bearing the same name ("Electa"), and a name so unusual name that it is nowhere else attested.[38]

---

[35] Is a sustained allegory of this kind likely in the case of so brief a letter?   Is not the form of the First Epistle against it?   Is there any parallel case in the literature of the first three centuries?

[36] H. Alford, *Greek Testament* (London: Rivingtons, 1871), v.4, p.186.   Law opts for this view [ISBE, V.2, 925].)

[37] D.E. Hiebert, *An Introduction to the Non-Pauline Epistles* (Chicago: Moody, 1962) p.233.

[38] J. Rendel Harris (*Expositor*, Mar. 1901), "The Problem of the Address to the Second Epistle of John," argued from papyri examples that *kuria* is a term of endearment ("my dear" or "my lady").   He pictured 2 John as a love letter written to a certain Electa.   This view supports an individual destination. He suggests the word was used by relatives when addressing female relatives, and is equal to "my dear." Findlay (p.26) replied that the word "elect" "lifts us into the region of Christian calling and dignity" (i.e., 2 John is not a love letter.)

(2) She was *a lady named Kyria* (making *kuria* a proper name).   The Peshitta Syriac version regarded *kuria* as a proper name, for it transliterated the Greek word into Syriac ("to the elect Koureea").   Athanasius seems to have adopted this interpretation.   It is offered as an alternate translation in the margin of the ASV (1901).   Such a personal name is found in a few places in ancient literature (cf. Lucke, p.444n, who cites an inscription which reads *phenippos kai hē gune autou kuria*, "Phenippos and his wife Kyria").[39]   Not a few Greek scholars have urged that in 2 John 1 the grammar is against the idea that *kuria* should be understood to be a proper name.[40]   Even if we grant that *kuria* is a female name (since there is some evidence it was so used in ancient times), what have we gained in our understanding of the destination of this letter?   We know of no lady by such a name from elsewhere in Christian writings.

(3) She was *a lady named Electa Kyria*. This hypothesis treats both words as forming the lady's compound name ("to Electa Kyria").   This view removes the difficulty of the construction, but the resulting combination is somewhat strange.   It also is doubtful that her sister (verse 13) also had the unusual proper name "Electa."

(4) Though unnamed,[41] she was *an influential Christian lady.*   The Latin Vulgate has the letter addressed "to an elect lady (*electa domina*)."   "An elect lady" is the most natural rendering of the Greek text, says Westcott.[42]   Perhaps "chosen" says she was a Christian, as would the references to "the truth" (verses 1-4).   Perhaps "chosen" says she was an "excellent" or "precious" or "beautiful" example of what a Christian lady

---

[39] Cited by A.E. Brooke, *A Critical and Exegetical Commentary on the Johannine Epistles* (Edinburgh: T&T Clark, 1912), p.168.

[40] B.F. Westcott, *The Epistles of St. John* (Grand Rapids: Eerdmans, 1952 reprint), p. 224, argues that "it is in the highest degree unlikely that John would have written *eklektē Kuria* and not *Kuria tē eklektē*" if *kuria* were to be taken as a proper name.   Other places in the New Testament when we have a proper name modified by an adjective, we regularly find an article in the Greek.   See *Gaiō tō agapētō* ("the beloved Gaius") at 3 John 1; or *adelphēs sou tēs eklektēs* ("your chosen sister") in this very letter at verse 13; or *Rouphon ton eklekton* ("Rufus the chosen man") at Romans 16:13; or *Apphia tē adelphē kai archippō tō sustratiōtē hēmōn* ("Apphia our sister, and to Archippus our fellow-soldier") at Philemon 2.   See also Romans 16:5,8,9,10,12.   Grammatically, the words *eklektē kuria* at 2 John 1 present a perfect analogy to 1 Peter 1:1, *eklektois parepidēmois* ("to the elect sojourners [ASV]," where *parepidēmois* cannot be a proper noun.   By parity of reasoning, therefore, *kuria* cannot well be taken as a proper name.

[41] "Unnamed" because neither *eklektē* nor *kuria* is treated as a proper name.   Certain attempts to identify this unnamed lady have not met with success.   Bengel proposed the lady was Martha of Bethany, because the Greek word *kuria* answers to the Hebrew "Martha."   "Kuria" means "mistress," and "Martha" means "mistress."   Several Catholic commentators have endeavored to show that this letter was addressed to the Virgin Mary, who is supposed to have resided in Galilee.   The view did not gain acceptance, partly because the Catholics had difficulty with the words "and her children" in the address.   They also have trouble with the early tradition that Mary accompanied John to Asia Minor.   If it is addressed to Mary, she likely was living in Asia Minor, not Galilee.   If the mother of our Lord is the one addressed, assuming that the 2 John was written about AD 85 or 90, Mary would have been of exceedingly old age, since she gave birth to Jesus about 4 BC.   And had some of her children fallen away (as might be implied in verse 4)?

[42] Westcott, *ibid.*   The term "lady" might be illustrated by the German *Frau* (mistress, married lady), and by the German *Herrin* (mistress, lady of the house).

should be. Writers use the word "influential" to help catch the nuance intended by the word "lady." It describes, perhaps, a woman in whose house a congregation of Christians met (implied in verse 10), or a woman like Priscilla (Acts 18:2ff,26; Romans 16:3), Lydia (Acts 16:14,15), or Phoebe (Romans 16:1,2), who played an important part in the life of the early church.[43] In Romans 16, Paul sends his greetings to a number of Christian women. It would not be beyond the realm of the believable were John to write a letter to some leading Christian lady. Haas instructs potential translators of "lady" with these words, "The word should be rendered by the term the receptor language employs when respectfully referring to, or addressing, a woman of certain position or authority."[44]

Proponents of the view that "chosen lady" is to be taken literally, referring to an actual woman living toward the close of the 1st century, offer a number of arguments in an attempt to convince others this view is correct.

a) It is a principle of interpretation to take words literally if such a literal meaning makes good sense. There is no need to suppose that "lady" is simply a polite or courteous form of address. Think of the one being addressed as a well-esteemed woman, a church member, the lady of the house.

b) The reference to the lady's children is quite intelligible if these were by now grown-up. Some of them are still living at home (verse 1).[45] In his travels, the writer meets other of her children (verse 4), who were no longer living with her, but who were ordering their behavior in the sphere of the truth. He also has met some of her sister's children (perhaps in the town from which he writes this letter), and sends greetings to the elect lady from her sister's children.

c) The greeting from the lady's nephews in verse 13 is quite possible if taken literally. The salutation from nephews and nieces to their aunt via the writer may be regarded as perfectly normal, in view of what often happens in correspondence, when relatives may say, "Give them our greetings when you write."[46]

d) The reference to the elect lady's house (verse 10) makes sense if we take the words of

---

[43] The cognate verb *eklegō* is used of choosing men for office (Acts 6:5), and of choosing men to discharge some special task (Acts 15:22,25). Perhaps the idea should be considered that the "lady" to whom this letter is addressed has been "chosen" for some special task by her home congregation. It should not be inferred that she was chosen to be an elder or a deacon since only the "husband of one wife" was qualified for those tasks (1 Timothy 3:2; Titus 1:6). The task this "chosen lady" might have been selected to do could be similar to Phoebe, who is designated as a "servant of the church" at Cenchrea (Romans 16:1).

[44] C. Haas, *A Translator's Handbook on the Letters of John* (London: United Bible Societies, 1972), p.138.

[45] Why the lady's husband is not mentioned has been the subject of conjecture. Perhaps he is deceased, leaving her a widow living with her grown-up children. Perhaps her husband has never become a Christian is another suggestion.

[46] Guthrie, *op. cit.*, p.214.

the address literally. Such a warning as given in verse 10 would certainly be appropriate if addressed to a private person who at the same time was influential in the life of the local church.

e) The adoption of the literal meaning might help to account for the reluctance of some in the early church to include the epistle in the canon. A private letter written to a lady would not seem of sufficient importance to receive canonical status.[47]

f) No one doubts that 2 John's twin epistle (3 John) is addressed to an individual. The formula of address in both epistles is exactly the same. The similarity may be seen by setting them out side-by-side:

> "The elder unto the elect lady and her children whom I love in truth"
> "The elder unto Gaius the beloved whom I love in truth"

In letters so similar it is scarcely probable that in one case the person addressed is to be taken literally while in the other the language of address is to be taken as the allegorical representation of a church.

> It seems more reasonable to suppose that in both Epistles, as in the Epistle to Philemon, we have precious specimens of the private correspondence of an Apostle. We are allowed to see how the beloved Disciple at the close of his life could write to a Christian lady and to a Christian gentleman respecting their personal conduct.[48]

g) When John says that she was loved by "all who know the truth," he makes it plain that her name was at least well-known in the Asiatic Churches, and that she was a person of real and high excellence. A Christian who was particularly generous in hospitality could have been known throughout a wide circle of churches. The "all" of verse 1 seems to mean that all true Christians who knew the lady loved and respected her as much as the writer himself did.

h) If we examine the whole contents of 2 John, we can hardly escape the conclusion that while the letter is addressed to individuals ("the chosen lady and her children"), it was also intended for the church's hearing. The lady would see that it was read at church. The collective plural exhortations (verses 8,10,12) would fit the wider audience as the letter was read out loud to those Christians assembled in the lady's home.

As appealing as the literal translation may be, it is not free from difficulties. (1) The possibility of a lady being "chosen" to a position of influence (or assigned responsibility for some special task) in the church has proven, for some, an idea difficult to accept. We are not quite ready to affirm that "chosen lady" or "elect lady" is a possible title for a leadership position in the congregation, as some groups have made it. Yet, for some reason, John describes the lady as "chosen." The only other place in the New Testament

---

[47] Guthrie, *ibid.*, p.215. If the letter is addressed to an unnamed individual, it is no more surprising that 2 John should have found its way into the canon than it was for 3 John to be included or Paul's epistle to Philemon (all of which were addressed to individuals rather than to churches).

[48] Plummer, *op. cit.*, p.lxxvi.

where "chosen" (i.e., the best of its kind or class) is applied to an individual is Romans 16:13, where Rufus is described as "a chosen man in the Lord." Thayer says the expression in Romans means "eminent as a Christian."[49] By parity of reasoning there was something "prominent" or "excellent" or "eminent" in the "lady" to whom this letter is addressed. (2) In the commentary on 3 John 9 the question of whether or not 2 John is the letter there referred to is carefully studied. It will be documented that whether or not 2 John is the letter 3 John 9 alludes to is a matter of vigorous debate.[50] If 2 John is the letter John wrote "to the church," then we must either accept that 2 John was intended for a wider audience than "the chosen lady and her children" or that "chosen lady" should be taken in a figurative sense. Without yet making a decision concerning 3 John 9, we have opted for the view that indeed the addressees ("the chosen lady and her children") would see to it that the congregation which met in the house in which they lived would hear the letter from the apostle. (3) If 2 John is the letter John wrote "to the church" (3 John 9), then we have raised the question of who might have been members of that congregation. Did Gaius (to whom 3 John is addressed) and Diotrephes (who was hostile to John and to Christian missionaries in general, and who maneuvered to run or boss the congregation he was a part of) belong to the same congregation? Were the "chosen lady and her children" also members of the same congregation to which Gaius belonged? Or may we suppose there were several congregations (house churches) in the town where Gaius and Diotrephes and the "chosen lady" lived? We will address these questions as we comment on 3 John.

Conclusions concerning the destination of 2 John

In this commentator's judgment, the reference to "her children" creates insurmountable difficulties to accepting the view that "chosen lady" is figurative language for a local church.

Of the possible literal translations of *eklektē kuria*, the first option seems preferable ("to *the* elect lady" KJV, or "to *the* chosen lady" NASB). The person who carried the letter would know to whom to hand this letter. It was not to just "any" lady (as "*a* chosen lady" might be interpreted) but to one particular lady. The carrier would also know who "the elder" was who sent the letter.

Suggestions have even been offered why the lady's name was suppressed. Dodd suggests the possibility that, during a time of persecution for the church, the names of the

---

[49] Jos. H. Thayer, *Greek-English Lexicon of the New Testament* (New York: American Book Co., 1889), p.197.

[50] There are many issues raised. Did the letter alluded to in 3 John deal with hospitality, or was it a letter of commendation? Do any of the canonical Johannine works deal with either topic? If not, are we ready to accept the idea that a letter written by an apostle to a church has been lost (perhaps because it was deliberately destroyed)? If one letter has been lost, what is the possibility others, too, have perished?

addressees were omitted out of caution.[51]   A better suggestion, in our judgment, is that of Farrar who wrote, "The delicate suppression of the individual name in a letter which might probably be read aloud in the Christian assembly is perfectly explicable."[52]

PURPOSE & OCCASION

Purpose

These are the things that may be inferred from the historical allusions in 2 John.   (1) Verse 5 reminds the chosen lady about the teaching of the Lord, that His followers are to "love one another."   One way to express such love in concrete terms is to extend hospitality to Christian brethren, which is what the lady and her children have been doing and are encouraged to continue to do.   (2) 2 John is directed against Gnostics similar to those who were combated in 1 John.   2 John 7-10 implies that Gnostic teachers were traveling from town to town, just like missionaries of the gospel journeyed from place to place.   In the same way missionaries of the gospel often relied on the hospitality of Christians found along the way as they journeyed, so the false teachers were taking advantage of Christian hospitality to provide (to some extent) for their livelihood, and to give them an introduction to the Christian community for two purposes: (a) to get an opportunity to spread their erroneous doctrines, and (b) to get finances to continue their mission to other towns.   John makes quite clear that the doctrine these missionaries teach is not the doctrine of Christ and that these people are not of God (verse 9).   They are, in fact, opposed to Christ since their doctrine about Jesus Christ is the same as that which the coming "antichrist" will teach (verse 9).   They are deceivers!   The readers are challenged to actively hinder the false teachers, lest what the gospel preachers have accomplished in their midst be lost.   Not only that, if they accept the false teachers' doctrine, or help them on their way to ruin the faith of some other church, the lady and her children will lose the full reward they otherwise might have had.   (3) Verses 10 and 11 are a directive that "love one another" is not a blanket rule, but rather that love is discerning.   Extend hospitality to traveling Christian missionaries, yes, but stop extending it to those who would destroy the Christian faith.

The New Testament makes it clear that Christians have a responsibility to offer hospitality to their brethren (Romans 12:13; Hebrews 13:2; 1 Peter 4:9).   John R.W. Stott (*op. cit.*, p.198-99) has several delightful paragraphs helping us to understand how things were in the first century world, and especially the need for hospitality.

---

[51] Dodd, *op. cit.*, p.145. Such an allusion to persecution might be directly tied to the question of the date of writing. We know about a Neronic (AD 65-68) and a Domitianic persecution (c.AD 90-96) that affected Christians all over the empire. Nero's time, we judge, is too early for the writing of 2 John. But maybe not Domitian's. Then, again, a local persecution also would make it wise to shield the identity of Christians from the authorities. Since there were sporadic local persecutions, such an allusion would ultimately give us little help for a possible date for the writing of 2 John.

[52] Plummer, *op. cit.*, p.lxxvi.

The establishment and consolidation of the Roman Empire made travel throughout the inhabited world much easier and safer than it had ever been before. It was facilitated by the great roads which the Romans built and the *pax Romana* which their legions maintained, as well as by a commonly understood language. The rapid spread of the gospel in the first century AD owed much to these advantages.

But where should traveling Christians stay when they came to some city on a business journey or, more important still, on a missionary journey? "The comforts of the modern hotel, or even of the village inn, were then unknown" (Findlay). Besides, according to W.M. Ramsay (article "Roads and Travel [New Testament]" in *Hastings' Dictionary of the Bible*), "the ancient inns ... were little removed from houses of ill-fame ... The profession of inn-keeper was dishonourable, and their infamous character is often noted in Roman laws." "Inns were notoriously dirty and flea-infested, while innkeepers were notoriously rapacious" (Barclay). As a result, it was natural that Christian people on their travels should be given hospitality by members of local churches. There are many traces in the New Testament of this custom. For example, Paul was entertained by Lydia in Philippi, Jason in Thessalonica, Gaius in Corinth, Philip the evangelist in Caesarea, and the Cypriot Mnason in Jerusalem (Acts xvi.15, xvii.7; Rom. xvi.23; Acts xxi.8,16).

Such hospitality was open to easy abuse, however. There was the false teacher, on the one hand, who yet posed as a Christian: should hospitality be extended to him? And there was the more obvious mountebank, the false prophet with false credentials, who was dominated less by the creed he had to offer than by the material profit and free board and lodging he hoped to gain. It is against this background that we must read the Second and Third Epistles of John, for in them the Elder issues instructions concerning whom to welcome and whom to refuse, and why. Genuine Christian missionaries, he writes, may be recognized both by the message they bring and by the motive which inspires them. If they faithfully proclaim the doctrine of Christ (cf. 2 Jn. 7), and if they have set out not for filthy lucre but for the sake of His Name (3 Jn. 7), then they should be both received and helped forward on their journey "as befits God's service" (3 Jn. 6, RSV).

It is against such a background that John writes to the chosen lady and her children with this apparent purpose: to correct their too-generous practice of hospitality. "Stop receiving those who go too far (i.e., Gnostic missionaries) into your home, " he instructs them. Refusal of hospitality to these dangerous teachers would be one effective way to stop the spread of their false message. So, alongside a clear responsibility to extend hospitality to genuine Christians, "there is an equal responsibility to use discernment in refusing hospitality to the opponents of truth."[53] To do otherwise than exercise discernment and refuse hospitality to false teachers was tantamount to actively participating with them in the spread of error.

The elder commands the readers to enter into no kind of relationship with such people. Upon what authority "the elder" can give such an instruction is not specifically stated, but if he were an apostle of Jesus, such an authoritative statement is at once understandable.

---

[53] Guthrie, *op. cit.*, p.215.

Occasion

Verse 4 likely reflects a chance meeting between John and some of the chosen lady's children. John found them still faithful to Christ, and is delighted to say so. Perhaps from them he learns about the rest of the family extending hospitality to traveling missionaries, including some they should not be welcoming into their home.

Since many deceivers have become missionaries trying to spread their erroneous views about the incarnation of Jesus (verse 7), John writes this brief note to the chosen lady and her children, in an effort to make sure they cease giving aid and comfort to the enemy.

DATE & PLACE

There are no historical references in the letter, so we know nothing certain about the time this epistle was composed. Nor do we have any solid information concerning the place of writing. In broad outline, this is what we see. (1) The apostle John, toward the close of his life (for this letter presupposes both the Gospel and first epistle) is engaged in the supervision and direction of the churches, for the task of an apostle included care of all the churches (2 Corinthians 11:28). 2 John 12 and 3 John 10,14 both suggest a possible journey by John in the near future to visit personally with the readers of both these epistles. Such a journey, too, could well be part of his usual work of supervision and direction of the churches. (2) The false teaching about which the readers are warned in 2 John is of the same kind refuted in 1 John. That leads us to suppose the two letters were issued during the same general time frame. (3) Just before he writes, John has met two separate groups of people related to the "chosen lady," (a) some of her children, and (b) some of her nephews and/or nieces. (But where their mother [the sister of the chosen lady] is, whether she is dead, or is living elsewhere, we have no way to ascertain.) The sister's children send their greeting in this letter, and thus show they share John's loving anxiety respecting the chosen lady's household. (4) One final thing needs to be drawn to our attention. The arrangement of these three letters in our Bibles is not indicative of the order in which they were written. The books are arranged, not in the chronological order in which it was assumed they were written, but according to length, longest to shortest. Thus "1 John" is first because it is longest, "2 John" is second because it is second longest, and "3 John" is third because it is the shortest of the three letters. The names we have on them (i.e., 1,2,3 John) should not be taken as determinative of the order of their composition.

Using the scant data gained from the historical allusions, several conjectures concerning time and place of writing have been proposed, some of which are flatly contradictory of others.

Was 2 John written before or after 1 John?

Scholars have offered conflicting answers to this question.

1) Since early Christian literature pictures John as very feeble in the closing days of his life, some have tried to date 2 John from early in John's ministry at Ephesus because it indicates he is vigorous enough to propose a journey among the churches (2 John 12; see also 3 John 10,14). A slight variation of this idea says 2 John must have been written before 1 John because 2 John is more vigorous than 1 John. But who shall say that there is an older tone and style in 1 John than in 2 John, or that the intended journey was one requiring a certain degree of strength which could only be found at a certain age, and not after? Most of the considerations about the feebleness of John's old age as having something to do with the time of the writing of this letter are fruitless.

2) The similarities between 2 John and 1 John have led some scholars to regard the former as a shorter form of the latter (perhaps a first draft), and written before 1 John was written. Clues that some think might suggest 2 John was written earlier have been gleaned from 1 John 2:19 and 2:26. Marshall is one who appeals to 2:19. He has 1 John being "a full-scale expression of the kind of things that John wanted to say in 2 John."[54] Later he concludes, "2 John appears to have been written to the same Christian community as 1 John but at an earlier date (since the false teachers evidently still had access to the church in 2 John, but had seceded from it in 1 Jn 2:19) ...."[55] What about 1 John 2:26? When John writes, "I have written," is he employing a historical aorist tense verb, and thus pointing in the direction of the priority of 2 John? If the aorist tense verb in 1 John 2:26 could be shown to be a historical reference, and if that reference can be shown to be to 2 John, then 2 John was written before 1 John. However, as comments at 1 John 2:26 show, this identification is doubtful. Even if the aorist verb in 1 John 2:26 is taken as an historical aorist (rather than epistolary), it is more likely a reference to the Fourth Gospel than it is a reference to 2 John.

3) In this commentator's judgment, it is probable that the writing of 2 John *followed* the writing of 1 John since the fuller notices of the false teachers given in the first epistle are presupposed in 2 John. (For example, compare 2 John 7 with 1 John 2:18ff.) This view also presupposes the idea that the chosen lady and her children were acquainted with the letter we call 1 John. Such a presupposition fits nicely with the idea that 1 John was a circular letter, intended for all the churches.

Was John in Ephesus, or elsewhere, at the time of writing?

Scholars have given conflicting answers to this question, too.

1) According to early Christian literature, Ephesus (Asia Minor) served as John's head-quarters. Some scholars, thinking John was on a journey when he met some of the chosen lady's children and some of her nephews, also propose that he waited till he finished the journey and had returned to his Ephesus headquarters before writing this letter to the chosen lady.

---

[54] See Marshall, *op. cit.*, p.4.

[55] Marshall, *ibid*, p.10.

2) Other scholars, who also suppose John was in the midst of a journey, think it more likely that as soon as he became aware of the situation through a chance meeting with some of the lady's children, he paused during the journey in order to write this letter immediately to the chosen lady and her children. In this scenario, the place from which the letter was written was elsewhere than Ephesus.

3) Still other scholars think John was not on a journey at all when he met some of the chosen lady's children. The meeting took place in Ephesus, the lady's children having come to the town where John was living. Perhaps their meeting took place on the streets of Ephesus, or perhaps the children visited the Sunday assembly at Ephesus, and that is where John met them.

Our tentative conclusions are in harmony with the traditional views: It is our judgment that 2 John was written after both the Fourth Gospel and 1 John had been written and dispatched to the churches. It is this studied conclusion that has led to the traditional dates of c.AD 85-90 being assigned to the letter. The place where the letter was written may have been Ephesus where early Christian literature places the bulk of John's later ministry.[56]

OUTLINE

Signature, Address, and Greeting. verses 1-3
    A. The Writer. 1a
    B. The Address. 1b-2
    C. Greeting and Assurance. 3

I. The Message of the Epistle. verses 4-11
    A. The Occasion. 4
    B. An Appeal for Love & Obedience. 5-6a
    C. Warning Against False Teachers. 6b-9
    D. Prohibition Against Aiding the False Teachers. 10-11

II. The Conclusion. verses 12,13
    A. The Explanation About the Brevity of the Letter. 12
    B. The Greeting From the Children of Her Sister. 13

---

[56] See "The Life of John, the Son of Zebedee" in the Introductory Studies to 1 John.

2 John[1]

SIGNATURE, ADDRESS, AND GREETING. Verses 1-3

A. The Writer. Verse 1a

Verse 1 -- *The elder to the chosen lady and her children, whom I love in truth; and not only I, but also all who know the truth,*

The elder – The usual beginning found in ancient letters, and observable at Acts 15:23, 23:26, and James 1:1, was "A (says) to B, greetings." "A" was the name of the writer, and "B" the name of the person to whom the letter or note was addressed. In this case we do not have the writer's name, but rather a title. It is evident that the writer was well known by this title to his readers. However, among scholars today, there is a long-running debate about the meaning of the title "the elder." In the Introductory Studies on 2 John, we opted for the long-held view that the "elder" is none other than the apostle John, and that John uses this title to indicate age, office, and dignity. Calling attention to his age would immediately recall in the readers' minds his long-standing connection with the original heritage of the church as contrasted with some newer doctrines that were being promulgated by the Gnostics concerning Jesus Christ. Shortly after John's time it was the custom in the Asian churches to use the title "elder" to represent the original apostles of Jesus,[2] thus recognizing their position in point of time and their fatherly relation to the churches.

B. The Address. Verse 1b-2

To the chosen lady – Scholars have long argued about the meaning of the words *eklektē kuria* ("chosen lady"). *Eklektē* can be translated "chosen" or "elect."[3] "Chosen" may say

---

[1] The title of this writing, like the titles of 1 John and the Gospel of John, exists in various forms (the older it is, the shorter it is), and likely was not on the autograph copy. Sinaiticus and Vaticanus read "of John B." Several later codices add the word "epistle" (epistle of John B), and one adds "catholic" (catholic epistle of John B), with catholic meaning canonical. We do not know what the title was in Alexandrinus for it has been torn off. One uncial reads *tou hagiou apostolou Iōannou tou theologou epistolē deutera* ("the second epistle of the holy apostle John who taught the deity of the Word").

[2] See the apostles styled as "elders" in Papias as quoted by Eusebius, H.E. III.39, and disciples of the apostles so called in Irenaeus, *Adv. Haer.* V.33.3, and 36:2. We presume the early church writers learned to use "elder" to designate a particular group of leaders from John (2 and 3 John) and from Peter (1 Peter 5:1). For the history of the title "elder" see Lightfoot's *Philippians*, p.226-230. "Elder" was used in Asia Minor to denote those who were apostles or had been personally taught by apostles, and were therefore in a position to bear trustworthy witness to Christianity.

[3] This "elect" or "chosen [people]" term was applied to the Jewish people in Old Testament times (Deuteronomy 4:37; Isaiah 45:4) to designate them as those whom God chose from among men and drew into a covenant relationship with Himself. This term is applied to Christians in the New Testament Scriptures (1 Peter 1:1; 2 Timothy 2:10). It refers to the fact that from the totality of mankind God has chosen those who are in Christ not only to be His special family but also to be His chosen instruments to evangelize others.

the "lady" is chosen of God, included among God's chosen people, i.e., a Christian (since in this post resurrection era it is Christians who are God's chosen people). Being a Christian, but not being a Gnostic, the "lady" would not have been considered as being among God's "elect" by the Gnostics. John's apostolic word here would be very reassuring. "You are one of God's special people!" he says, in essence. Alternately, "chosen" may simply be a commendation of the "lady," much as Rufus is commended as being "a choice (eminent, quality) man in the Lord" (Romans 16:13).[4] A suitable English expression to catch this idea here would be "excellent lady" or "noble lady." As was explained in the Introductory Studies to this epistle, from ancient times opinion has been divided as to whether this letter was addressed to an anonymous noble lady or whether it is addressed to a congregation of Christians, figuratively identified as a "chosen lady." In the comments to be offered on this letter, we are proposing the view that the "lady" is an anonymous lady, and yet the letter is intended for a wider audience than just the lady and her children. We rather like the suggestion that a house-church meets in her home, and that John's instructions are intended as much for the congregation in general as they are for the lady in particular.

And her children – Not only is the letter addressed to "the chosen lady," it is also addressed to "her children." The main part of the letter is addressed to more readers than one.[5] *Tekna* ("children") may be understood either literally (as in 1 Timothy 5:14) or spiritually (as in Galatians 4:19,25, 1 Timothy 1:2, and likely as it is used in 1 John 2:1,12). Our choice between these two options will be determined by several factors.

- One is our conclusion concerning the destination. If a literal "lady" is addressed, then the word "children" is taken literally, indicating that her biological children are intended. If "lady" is taken figuratively referring to a church, then the term "children" is likewise to be taken figuratively, indicating children after the spirit are intended.

- This raises a second factor. The church is made up of people. If the "lady" is already a reference to the "church," who are the "children"? We can't very well say "members of the congregation," since they have already been included under the figurative term "lady."

- A third factor to be taken into consideration is the greeting included in verse 13, "The children of your chosen sister greet you." This greeting is much easier to explain on the hypothesis that the "chosen lady" (verse 1) and the "chosen sister" (verse 13) are literal women, and that the "children" are the physical offspring of the two ladies, rather than trying to give some figurative meaning to all these expressions.

---

[4] Thayer, *Lexicon*, p.197, offers "the best of its kind or class" to explain the meaning of *eklektos*. When used of person, he suggests "excellent, prominent," and when "in the Lord" is added, the idea is the person is eminent as a Christian.

[5] "You" in verses 6, 10, and 12 are all in the plural.

Whom I love in truth – The usual signature and salutation ("A" to "B") are here and in the next verse amplified as the circumstances of the case lead the author to amplify them.[6] *Hous* ("whom") is masculine plural, and might refer to the nearest antecedent "children," but the masculine plural probably includes both the "lady" and her "children."[7]   "I" (*egō*) is emphatic in the Greek.   (Compare 3 John 1 where the identical phrase occurs.)   There is an implied contrast with others who do not love the lady and her children in truth.   We suppose the Gnostics are in the background, and the emphatic "I" says this: however others may treat the lady and her children, they may be assured of the writer's genuine affection.[8]   Bible expositors are divided whether or not to translate *en alētheia* as "in truth" (NASB) or "in the truth" (KJV, RSV).   It is true there is no article ("the") in the Greek,[9] and therefore the expression could be treated as having adverbial force, which might be expressed as "truly" or "really," i.e., John's love is genuine and springs from the heart.   However, prepositions tend to make nouns definite, and in light of the fact that the two following references to "the truth" in the immediate context do carry the article, John may well be saying that the relationship between himself and the readers is one determined by their mutually holding to the truth of the gospel, the truth about Christ.   It is the truth about Christ which bound John in love to this "lady," especially the truth about Christ in opposition to the "lie" of the Gnostic false teachers (1 John 2:21-23).   John loves in a way that is consistent with the Christian revelation that has been received by him and his readers.   The love he has for the readers is the "love" revealed in the Christian message (e.g. 1 John 3:11) as being what God expects of men redeemed by the blood of Christ.

And not only I, but also all who know the truth – John claims that he is not "alone" in the "love" which he has for the "lady and her children."   Many other Christians ("all who know the truth") share this love.   "All" Christians who had opportunity to know the addressee loved the "chosen lady and her children" just as John did.   It would seem from verse 10 that the addressee had generously extended the hospitality of her home as she entertained traveling Christian missionaries.   Not only her faith, but her hospitality, has helped to make the "lady" known to the brotherhood.   Here the Greek has an article; it reads "the truth," – denoting the truth of the gospel.   *Tēn alētheian* ("the truth") is John's term for the revelation of God in Christ, and he learned it from Jesus Himself (John 14:7).   The "truth" is identical with Christ's message (John 1:17) and with Christ's person (John

---

[6] A similar amplification can be seen in Romans 1:1-7 and in Galatians 1:1-5.

[7] *Hous* is masculine accusative plural, while *teknois* ("children") is neuter plural dative. So the construction is according to sense, rather than according to strict grammatical gender. Such constructions according to sense often occur in the Greek New Testament. Cp. Matthew 28:19 where "the nations" (feminine) is followed by a masculine "them" ("baptizing them"), where the masculine surely includes both men and women. It is very precarious to attempt to base any argument about whether the letter is addressed to a literal lady or to a church on the use of the masculine relative pronoun "whom."

[8] "Love" (*agapaō*) is a Christian love, not a sexual love, as was explained in comments on "love" at 1 John 2:5,10. It speaks of doing what is spiritually best for the other person.

[9] Compare the similar wording found at 3 John 1; John 17:19, 4:23, and 1 John 3:18. John appears to use the phrase with or without the article, without any obvious difference in meaning.

14:7).[10]   We think there is an allusion to the fact that the false teachers were preaching a doctrine concerning Christ's person and work that was not "truth."   The author is speaking in clear contrast to the heretics.   They do not have the truth nor do they know what it means to love the brethren.   The word *egnōkotes* ("know") is in the perfect tense in the Greek.   A perfect tense indicates past completed action with present continuing results.   The Christians' knowledge of the truth had its origin in the past, and it has effects which continue in the present.   A long-time knowledge of the truth "makes the family the object of the apostle's love and of all believers, [and also] implies the reason of this Epistle and its importance."[11]

Verse 2 -- *For the sake of the truth which abides in us and will be with us forever;*

For the sake of the truth which abides in us – "For" (*dia*) means on account of.   Verse 2 gives a reason why Christians love the lady and her children.   All who have known the truth (Christ or the Christian way) love the chosen lady and her children precisely *because* they have a mutual interest in the truth.[12]   One of the things involved in "love" (i.e., doing what is spiritually best for the other person) of the brotherhood is a concern for their beliefs, that those beliefs be orthodox.   The repetition of "truth" is quite like John's style.   Four times in these three opening verses John writes about "truth," God's truth as revealed in His Son.[13]   "In us" includes all the people alluded to in verse 1:   the apostle, his readers, and those who loved the chosen lady and her children.   The apostles of Jesus were God's chosen channels of Christian truth.   The verb "abides" (*menō*) is often used in the Gospels of one living as a guest in the home of another.[14]   Thus the truth is a welcome guest in the heart of the Christian.   Truth is not said to abide "in you" or "in them," but "in us."   The Christian society, not the Gnostics, is where one finds the truth believed and practiced.   The apostle at once identifies himself with the whole society of the faithful.   "The situation revealed by both the first and second epistles is that the fellowship of the church is endangered by deceivers who do not continue to hold to the truth as it was proclaimed from the first (1 John 2:18ff; 2 John 8-11)."[15]

---

[10] Compare notes on "the truth" at 1 John 1:6,8.

[11] John Peter Lange, *The Second and Third Epistles General of John*, in Commentary on the Holy Scriptures (Grand Rapids: Zondervan, 1950 reprint), p.187.

[12] In the Greek, verses 1 and 2 are one sentence.

[13] See 1 John 2:4.

[14] The verb "abide" is one of John's favorite words.   His concern in this epistle, as in 1 John, is that Christians abide in the doctrine, or word (i.e., that the truth which they had received from the beginning), and that they let this truth abide in them (1 John 2:6,14,24,27).

[15] J.W. Roberts, *The Letters of John*, in The Living Word Commentary (Austin, TX: Sweet, 1968), p.154.

And will be with us forever – Since "abides" was a participle, we might have expected a participle in this clause, too. Instead we have a future tense finite verb. The change of construction (i.e., a lack of exact grammatical sequence) gives prominence to this additional thought. The future tense "will be" is not a wish but a confident assertion of a fact. "Truth is not going to change![16] What we apostles teach is truth,[17] and no Gnostic can ever change it or add to it!" The *meth' hēmōn* ("with us") is emphatic. "With us" it shall be, whatever the false teachers claim! "Forever" (*eis ton aiōna*) means to the end of the age.[18] Gospel truth is not a temporary message, like the revelation to Moses was. Contrary to any Gnostic assertion about their doctrine, no new revelation will replace the truth the apostles taught.[19]

C. Greeting and Assurance.   Verse 3

Verse 3 -- *Grace, mercy and peace will be with us, from God the Father and from Jesus Christ, the Son of the Father, in truth and love.*

Grace, mercy *and* peace will be with us – The one-word greeting *chairein* was common in letters in the ancient world. Christian writers often replaced *chairein* ("greetings") with *charis* ("grace") and added additional words to the greeting that anticipated the heart of the letter. Here in 2 John, we note four additions to the customary formula of greeting. First, greetings were usually worded as a prayer or a wish ("may[20] grace be with you"). John here makes a flat declaration as he asserts that grace, mercy, and peace "will be" with us. Just as "truth ... will be with us" (verse 2), so "grace, mercy and peace" will be with us.[21] We suppose there is a deliberate contrast with the Gnostics. Grace and mercy and

---

[16] In the contemporary movement towards church unity we must beware of compromising the very truth on which alone true love and unity depend. What is going on in the "emerging church" is a cause for grave concern. See D.A. Carson, *Becoming Conversant with the Emerging Church* (Grand Rapids: Zondervan, 2005).

[17] Some commentators have seen here an echo of Christ's farewell discourse spoken to the apostles: "He will give you another Helper, that He may be with you forever, that is the Spirit of truth" (John 14:16, 17). What is said in John's Gospel about the Spirit of truth, that He will dwell in the apostles of Jesus (John 14:15-17), is referred to here as the truth itself. Perhaps this allusion to Jesus' promise to His apostles is evidence that the "elder" who writes this letter is one of the original apostles (as would be the case if it is John).

[18] On "forever" see the comment on "eternal" life at 1 John 1:2. The same Greek word is used in both places.

[19] The apostles of Jesus were led into all truth (John 14:26, 16:13). That truth was once for all delivered to the saints (Jude 3) by the time Jude wrote his letter, c. AD 75.

[20] The verb was written in the optative mood.

[21] The Textus Receptus and the KJV read "be with you" and the "you" is singular. Older manuscripts such as Vaticanus and Sinaiticus read "us" (plural). Just as the plural "us" in verse 2 was explained as including all Christians (John, the chosen lady and her children, and those who loved her in the truth), so the "us" here in verse 3 embraces the same group.

peace will not be their lot!   A second difference is the addition of "mercy" between "grace" and "peace."[22]   "Grace" is God's unmerited favor towards sinners resulting in actions to rescue them from their sin.[23]   God vividly expressed His favor at Calvary where His Son became a sin offering and a substitutionary atoning sacrifice for sinners.   God's grace is in action when He sends preachers to lost people to explain to them the way to be saved.   God continues to demonstrate His grace daily as the Holy Spirit ministers to the spiritual needs of the saint.   "Mercy" is God's compassion, kindness, and goodness toward the miserable and afflicted, joined with a desire to relieve them.   Whereas grace is extended to the guilty, God's mercy is extended to the miserable.[24]   "Peace" is "a conception distinctly peculiar to Christianity, the tranquil state of the soul assured of its salvation through Jesus Christ, and so fearing nothing from God and content with its earthly lot, whatever sort that is."[25]   "Peace" is the result when the guilt and misery of sin are removed.   In his inimitable manner, J.A. Bengel summarizes the meaning of the phrase "grace, mercy and peace" in these words: "Grace removes guilt; mercy removes misery; peace expresses a continuance in grace and mercy."[26]

From God the Father and from Jesus Christ – The greeting goes on to specify the source of the blessings.   The blessings will continue to come from God the Father and from Jesus Christ;[27] *para* means from the presence of or from the hand of.   As John does say "God Father" but "God the Father," he evidently is emphasizing the Father's relationship to Jesus,

---

[22] A quick survey of Paul's and Peter's letters find two words in the greeting, *charis humin kai eirēnē* ("grace and peace to you"), though in 1 and 2 Timothy the same three words occur that we find here in 2 John.   Jude has three words of greeting, *eleos humin kai eirēnē kai agapē* ("mercy and peace and love ... to you").

[23] "Grace" embraces two ideas, both attitude and action.   In another place we have offered this definition for "grace":   "All that God thinks and does to save man."

[24] R.C. Trench, *Synonyms of the New Testament* (Grand Rapids: Eerdmans, 1966 reprint), p.225.   "Here it refers to God's unfailing concern for His people, His consciousness of their needs and His readiness to help them.   In the Greek version of the Old Testament it usually translates the Hebrew *chesed* 'stedfast love' (RSV, replacing AV's 'loving-kindness')."   C. Haas, *A Translator's Handbook on the Letters of John* (London: United Bible Society, 1972) Vol.12, p.140

[25] J.H. Thayer, *A Greek English Lexicon of the New Testament* (New York: American Book Company, 1889), p.182.

[26] J.A. Bengel, *Gnomon of the New Testament* (Edinburgh: T. & T. Clark, 1860), vol.5, p. 156.

[27] The KJV reads "from the Lord Jesus Christ," but the better manuscripts omit "Lord."   "It may be noted that the title 'Lord' [before "Jesus Christ"] which is added by some early authorities, is not found in the epistles of John, though it occurs in every other book of the NT except the Epistle to Titus." B.F. Westcott, *The Epistles of St. John* (Grand Rapids: Eerdmans, 1952), p.226.
    Since the Holy Spirit, the third member of the Godhead, is not named by John as a source of the three blessings, O. Cullmann, *The Earliest Christian Confessions* (London: Lutterworth, 1949) tried to make a case for the view that John is here making use of a "binitarian" formula which came down from the early church, and which placed the Father and Son on the same level of reality.   Critics go to great lengths in an attempt to show that not only the deity of Jesus, but that also of the Holy Spirit was not an original doctrine of Jesus and the apostles, but was a belief that gradually grew by evolutionary increments as the decades of Christianity passed.   If we accept the traditional dating of the New Testament writings (and we

in refutation of Gnostic beliefs.[28] "Father" lays special stress on the revelation of God in this absolute character, and what a different presentation this is than that made by the Gnostics.   The repetition of the preposition *para* before "Jesus Christ" not only calls attention to the personality and independence of the Son by the side of the Father, but also denotes the equality of the Divine nature and character of Jesus Christ, who, along with the Father, are the sources of these blessings of grace, mercy, and peace.

The Son of the Father – In his third addition to the customary form of greeting in ancient letters, John adds "Son of the Father" as he describes the source from which grace, mercy, and peace come.   This additional phrase is, perhaps, a deliberate repudiation of the errors of the Gnostics, which are condemned in this letter (verses 7,10), in 1 John, and in the Fourth Gospel.   Rather than being an aeon emanating from the Father, Jesus is the "Son of the Father."   "As John insists elsewhere, it is through the revelation of his Son that God is known as the Father, not merely of the Son but also of all believers; it follows that rejection of the Son means rejection of the way in which God has revealed Himself to be the Father.   To say 'no' to God's way of revealing Himself is to say 'no' to God Himself, for He will not let himself be known by men except on His own terms."[29]   Treat Jesus as the Gnostics treated Him, and the blessings of grace, mercy, and peace available from His hand dry up.

In truth and love – This is John's fourth additional statement to the usual greeting in ancient letters.   This phrase is not to be connected with the expression "the Son of the Father," as if it meant that He was God's Son "in truth and love."   The phrase is rather to be connected with "will be with us."   That is, receiving God's blessings of grace, mercy, and peace will continue with us *if* we continue in the truth and love.   These two keynotes will make up much of the rest of this brief letter.   As these two keynotes are unfolded, we shall see that "truth" is the truth of the Gospel, and "love" is love of the brethren.[30]   Grace, mercy, and peace flourish in an environment where truth and love prevail.   Both of these channels were blocked and repudiated by the false teachers.

---

do), and if we accept their record as an accurate presentation of what Jesus said and did (and we do), then the idea of three members in the Godhead, a "trinitarian" view, is not something whose source is hidden in ancient superstition and whose truth is therefore doubtful.

[28] Lest his readers miss this nuance, John specifically goes on in the next clause to emphasize the truth that Jesus was "the Son of the Father."   On the meaning of "the Father," see notes at 1 John 1:2.

[29] I. Howard Marshall, *The Epistles of John* (Grand Rapids: Eerdmans, 1978), p.64.

[30] John R.W. Stott, *The Epistles of John*, in The Tyndale New Testament Commentaries (Grand Rapids: Eerdmans, 1971), p.204-205, noted some of the proper conclusions to be drawn when we consider that verse 3 introduces some of the key ideas following.   "Truth should make our love discriminating. John sees nothing inconsistent in adding to his command to love one another (5) a clear instruction about the refusal of fellowship to false teachers, who are deceivers and antichrists (7-11).   Our love for others is not to undermine our loyalty to the truth.   On the other hand, we must never champion the truth in a harsh or bitter spirit.   Those who are 'walking in truth' (4) need to be exhorted to 'love one another' (5).   So the Christian fellowship should be marked equally by love and truth, and we are to avoid the dangerous tendency to extremism, pursuing either at the expense of the other.   Our love grows soft if it is not strengthened by truth, and our truth grows hard if it is not softened by love.   We need to live according to Scripture which commands us both to love each other in the truth and to hold the truth in love."

I. THE MESSAGE OF THE EPISTLE.   Verses 4-11

A. The Occasion.   Verse 4

> *Summary*:   John has met with some of the chosen lady's children, probably somewhere in Asia Minor.   Their Christian lives delighted him and apparently prompted him to write this letter.

Verse 4 -- *I was very glad to find* some *of your children walking in truth, just as we have received commandment* to do *from the Father.*

I was very glad to find *some* **of your children walking in truth** – Ancient letters, like their modern counterparts, often followed the address and greeting with an expression of joy or thanksgiving on the part of the writer for good news concerning his readers. We probably should treat *echaran lian* ("I was very glad" or "I rejoiced greatly" KJV) as an historical aorist pointing to some moment in the past before he composed this letter. *Hoti heurēka* ("to find") could just as well be translated "because I have found ..." (ASV).[31] We need not suppose that John has gone seeking or looking for the lady's children, nor that John has conducted a formal investigation as to their beliefs or conduct. Actually, John does not say how he learned this, whether he had personally met them, or had been told by others. It is generally supposed these "children"[32] came to Ephesus, and there their path and John's intersected. The words appear to refer to an experience of the writer in some other place than that in which the "chosen lady" lived.   "Some of your children" is an effort to express the idea in the partitive genitive expression *ek tōn tektōn sou*. John commonly elides the indefinite pronoun "some" when he writes this expression, but it seems that if John had meant to say that he had recently found all of her children walking in truth he would not have used *ek*.[33] We suppose some of the chosen lady's children are still at home with her (verses 1, 8, 10, 12), while "some" have recently visited with John.

---

[31] The perfect tense verb indicates that what John found to be true in the past is still true in the present as he writes this letter.

[32] We are treating "children" in this verse as the lady's biological children, just as we did in verse 1. See this whole issue discussed in detail in the Introductory Studies on 2 John.

[33] We doubt that "some" has a negative connotation, as though John is sadly aware that some of the lady's children are not faithful. It rather means no more than recently he has seen only some of her children. Those he encountered proved to be faithful.

It is these latter ones who have brought John joy.[34] "Truth" is the same truth which verses 1 and 3 alluded to, the truth of the gospel as delivered by Jesus and His apostles.[35] If we translate *en alētheia* as "in truth," it pictures truth as the sphere in which one lives.[36] We might also translate it 'by the truth,' in which case it means to live in accordance with God's revelation in the gospel and the standards contained in it.[37] Or perhaps truth is here "likened to a path along which we walk, by which we keep course, and from which we should not deviate."[38] "Walking" (*peripatountas*, a present participle in agreement with *tinas*, "some") is a Greek metaphor for how one lives daily; it is translated "following the truth" in the RSV and "living by the truth" in the NEB. It speaks of a life committed to God's truth as revealed in Jesus, and expressed in obedience to His commands. The present tense indicates that these "children" who have given John joy are constantly living in the light, rather than in the darkness. They have not embraced the false doctrines or the poor ethics of the Gnostics.

Just as we have received commandment *to do* from the Father – "Just as" means 'in harmony with' or 'in accordance with' the commandment received from the Father. Those who are "walking in truth" are fulfilling something the Father has commanded His children to do. "We" likely includes John the writer, the lady, her children, and all Christians in general. "Commandment" (*entolē*) is John's way of making clear that what he is saying is a direct expression of God's will.[39] Though it is not easy to find a commandment with these exact words elsewhere in the New Testament writings, this last phrase in verse 4 seems to treat "walking in truth" as being the commandment from God that John has par-

---

[34] Perhaps these "children," as they were on a journey away from home and having visited with John, are now, as they return home, the ones who carried this letter to the chosen lady.

[35] On "walking in truth" as denoting not only the Christian state, but true, vital Christianity, see 1 John 1:6,7, 2:6; 3 John 3,4; and John 8:12.

[36] The sphere in which one walks (lives, Greek metaphor) is usually designated (as here) by the preposition *en* followed by a noun. For example, "in good deeds" (Ephesians 2:10), or "in sins" (Colossians 3:7).

[37] "Although the definite article is missing here in 2 John, the parallel at 3 John 4 (where the article is present) shows that John is speaking here of Christian truth as such, the content of which has been explained more fully in 1 John itself." Stephen S. Smalley, *1,2,3 John*, in Word Biblical Commentary (Waco, TX: Word Books, 1984), Vol.51, p.323.

[38] Stott, *ibid*.

[39] Glen W. Barker, *1,2 and 3 John*, in The Expositor's Bible Commentary series (Grand Rapids: Zondervan, 1981), V.12, p.363. Some treat "commandment" as the third keynote word in this epistle, since it occurs four times.

ticularly in view.[40]   On "from the Father" see the comments in verse 3 regarding "from the hand of the Father" (*para*).   "The Divine command has come direct from the Giver.   'All things that I heard from My Father I have made known unto you (John 15:15)," said Jesus, and that includes the Father's commands."[41]   The fact that the commandment is ascribed to the Father rather than to Jesus indicates that the Father is thought of as the ultimate source of the message declared by Jesus (John 7:16ff) and by His apostles (1 John 1:5).   We are reminded of Hebrews 1:1,2 where we are told that "God ... has spoken ... in His Son." "God has not revealed His truth in such a way as to leave us free at our pleasure to believe or disbelieve it, to obey or disobey it.   Revelation carries with it responsibility, and the clearer the revelation, the greater the responsibility to believe and obey it (cf. Amos 3:2)."[42]

B. An Appeal for Love and Obedience.   Verses 5,6a

Verse 5 -- *And now I ask you, lady, not as writing to you a new commandment, but the one which we have had from the beginning, that we love one another.*

And now I ask you, lady – The words "I ask you" are "a common formula in letter writing, used when the writer comes to the subject matter of his letter."[43]   "And now" (*nun*) is probably logical rather than temporal.[44]   Past faithfulness is made the foundation of the appeal John is about to write.   When John words his appeal using *erōtō se* ("I ask you"), he is using the same verb he used in making request about the "sin leading to death" (1 John 5:16).   *Erōtaō* is the verb used when persons of equal dignity make direct personal

---

[40] Not only did Jesus say "If you abide in My word ... you shall know the truth" (John 8:31,32), but we recall that when He was finishing His Sermon on the Mount, He spoke about folk who habitually do the will of His Father who is in heaven (Matthew 7:21), and then immediately went on to speak of a wise builder who "hears these words of Mine, and acts upon them" (Matthew 7:24).   Surely it is not difficult to picture John's words about "walking in truth" as being a succinct summary of what Jesus was saying on occasions like those just cited.   Some appeal to 1 John 3:23 as being similar in thrust: "This is His commandment, that we believe in the name of His Son Jesus Christ, and love one another, just as he commanded us." Others call attention to John 6:29, "This is the work of God, that you believe in Him whom He has sent." Still others have expressed the opinion that the command referred to here must be the new commandment to love as Christ loved (cf. 1 John 4:21), which it is argued suits the context (verse 5) best.   The problem with this last view is that verse 5 seems to speak of mutual love as something other than the command of verse 4.

[41] Alfred Plummer, *The Epistles of St. John* (Grand Rapids: Baker, 1980 reprint) p.135.

[42] Stott, *ibid.*

[43] Haas, *op. cit.*, p.143.

[44] If we make the connection temporal, the contrast is between "now" and the past moment when he was filled with joy at meeting some of the lady's children.

appeal to each other.[45]   "The Elder who has the right to command merely grounds a personal request, as between equals, on the old command laid on both alike by the Master."[46]   That old commandment, that "we love one another" will be spelled out as this verse concludes.   "Lady" in the Greek is in the vocative case which underlines the personal nature of the appeal being made, and only in this verse and in verse 13 does John use the singular "you."[47]

Not as writing to you a new commandment, but the one which we have had from the beginning – When John emphasizes that, as he writes[48] this letter, he has no new teaching to give the lady, it very well may be an aside directed against the false teachers who were visiting and troubling the churches.[49]   The false teachers were promulgating new teaching which had not been a part of the Christian doctrine taught from the beginning of gospel preaching.[50]   John does not write "you have had" but "we have had."   He regularly identifies himself with those to whom he is writing, Christian with Christian.   Both he and they have an obligation to live by the command they both have received.

That we love one another – This *hina* clause could be an example of indirect discourse continuing the sentence begun with "I ask," or this clause can clarify the specific content of the commandment which they have had from the beginning and to which John is calling attention.   "Love" (*agapōmen*) is a present tense verb, signifying we are to continue to love one another.[51]   If someone should object that "love" is not something that can be commanded, this objection is answered by observing what *agapē* is deliberately choosing

---

[45] *Aiteō* is the verb for "ask" that is used when an inferior asks something of a superior.

[46] A.E. Brooke, *A Critical and Exegetical Commentary on the Johannine Epistles,* in The International Critical Commentary (Edinburgh: T&T Clark, 1912), p.173.

[47] Since the plural form of "you" is used in verses 6,8,10, and 12, scholars debate the possible implications of the change. What is the meaning of the change if the letter is addressed to a church? What is the meaning of this change if the letter is addressed to a lady and her biological children? We have treated the singular "you" (spoken to a lady who is still mistress of her house) as a means of making the appeal personal.

[48] The manuscripts show several variations at this place. The location of the word "new" in the sentence varies, and so does the verb form translated "writing," with some manuscripts having the indicative *graphō* and some having the present tense participle *graphōn*. It is the latter which is represented in the NASB translation and our notes.

[49] Except for a few minor differences, this phrase repeats what was written in 1 John 2:7.

[50] "Have had" translates an imperfect tense verb form (*eichomen*) which implies continuous action in the past. For "from the beginning" see notes at 1 John 2:7. While the context often determines the first point of time indicated in the word "beginning" (see 1 John 1:1, 2:24, 3:8; Hebrews 1:10; Acts 11:15), in this case John evidently is saying from the time when the gospel was first made known to us. We may reasonably suppose that John is here reminding the lady of the contents of his First Epistle. There are at least eight such parallels to his First Epistle in these 13 verses of 2 John.

[51] On "love one another" see comments at 1 John 3:11.

to do, and to continue doing, what is spiritually best for the other person.[52]   As this letter will go on to make clear, Christian love (*agapē*) is discriminating.   For example, it does not show hospitality to those who deliberately come to teach error.   To show hospitality to teachers of error would not be what is spiritually best for them or those who would hear them.   The next verse will explain this discrimination even more.

Verse 6 -- *And this is love, that we walk according to His commandments.   This is the commandment, just as you have heard from the beginning, that you should walk in it.*

And this is love – There is a definite article with "love" here in the Greek, the article of previous reference.   The "love" about which I speak, says John, is consistent with walking according to His commandments.   As we Christians express our love to one another, we do so without disobeying God's commandments.   "The apostle has no sympathy with a religion of pious emotions: there must be a persevering walk according to God's commands."[53]

That we walk according to His commandments – "Walk" is a present tense verb, meaning 'keep on walking' or 'continue to walk.'   "According to" is *kata* ("down").   It says we are to order our behavior and conduct ourselves as governed by the commands of God.   In verse 4, John spoke about "walking in truth, just as we have received commandment" and in this verse he calls attention to the commandment to "love one another," "which we have had from the beginning."   "John is saying, in his characteristic way of repeating phrases which are virtually equivalent, that to love one another is to be taken in the context of God's commandments and truth.   He is not therefore merely telling his readers that they are to 'love everybody' indiscriminately."[54]   Alongside our love for our brother, there must be an active and unremitting obedience to all that God has commanded.[55]   We cannot substitute "love for man" for active obedience to God, and still be acceptable in God's sight.

C. Warning Against False Teachers.   Verses 6b-9

This is the commandment – As we read through these verses, several features cause us to

---

[52] It is when love is defined as an emotion that it becomes something that cannot be commanded. *Agapē* belongs to the sphere of the will and action, rather than to the sphere of emotion.

[53] Plummer, *op. cit.*, p.136.

[54] Roberts, *op. cit.*, p.159.

[55] The Christian life is here viewed from the standpoint of commandments -- keeping God's commandments, only one of which is "love the brother."   Christian liberty is not inconsistent with "law" (commandments), any more than love is.   The Christian is not under the Law (for the Law of Moses was temporary, and was nailed to the cross), but the Christian is under law to Christ (1 Corinthians 9:21).   The freedom with which Christ has made us free is not freedom to break His law, but freedom to keep it.   The relevance of John's point is obvious in the modern situation where we are sometimes told: All you need is love.   Such advice is meaningless if the nature of love is not defined and unfolded.   Love must follow divine guidelines as it expresses itself, if it is to be a love that God approves.

propose beginning a new paragraph here in the middle of verse 6. There is a notable variation between singular (commandment, verse 6b) and plural (commandments, verse6a) nouns.[56] *Ḥautē* ("this") is the demonstrative pronoun that usually points *backward* to something aforesaid. Somewhere in an earlier verse this topic was already introduced. Verse 7 begins with "for," and it will hardly do to attempt to begin a paragraph at that place. So perhaps the easiest solution is to begin a new paragraph here in the last part of verse 6. The last part of verse 6 then becomes the doctrinal criterion on which the following warning is based. That criterion would be found in the commandment alluded to in verse 4 about "walking in the truth."[57]

Just as you have heard from the beginning – Not only was the commandment to "love one another" something they had heard from the beginning (verse 5), so is, John would be saying here, the commandment to "walk in the truth." It, too, is part and parcel of the gospel as it has been preached by Jesus and His apostles.[58]

That you should walk in it – "In it" (*en autē*) is a feminine form of the pronoun, and so we must look for some word in the feminine gender to be its antecedent. Three words in the context are feminine: "truth" in verse 4, "love" in verses 5 and 6,[59] and "commandment" in verses 4 and 6.[60] Having chosen to begin a new paragraph with this second part of verse 6, we understand that the "truth" is what Christians are habitually to live by. Christians are to abide in what they have always known, the truth taught by Jesus, and let it regulate their whole conduct and life.

Verse 7 -- *For many deceivers have gone out into the world, those who do not acknowledge Jesus Christ* **as** *coming in the flesh.* *This is the deceiver and the antichrist.*

For many deceivers have gone out into the world – We would normally expect the Greek word translated "for" (*hoti*, "because") to give a reason for something just said before this verse. It is as if John were saying, "I am recalling our obligations to mutual love and to obedience to the Divine command to walk in the truth, because there are men with whom

---

[56] A similar transition from plural to singular ("commandments" to "commandment") in 1 John 3:22-24 has also proven a difficult thing for the expositors to explain.

[57] The one command that sums up all the commandments is "walk in truth."

[58] Our explanation has followed the text found in Vaticanus, the Byzantine text, and the Syriac that has no *hina* before *kathōs*. If the reading *hina kathōs* found in Sinaiticus, Alexandrinus, 33,69 and the Vulgate is correct, then the *hina* which precedes *en autē* in the next clause must be resumptive.

[59] If we were to opt for "love" being the antecedent, then the command to love in a way consistent with all the commands of God would be the way to decide how one will behave towards false teachers.

[60] The Latin Vulgate treats "commandment" as being the antecedent. This puts emphasis on "walking" and "as you have heard."

you and yours come in contact, whose teaching strikes at the root of these obligations."[61]
Planoi ("deceivers") could also be rendered seducers;[62] that is, one who causes others to
go astray.   John wrote in his First Epistle that "many false prophets" were abroad (4:1).
Here he calls them "deceivers," just as he described them (using a cognate form of *planoi*)
at 1 John 2:26 as "those who are trying to deceive you."   He is referring to the Gnostic
deceivers.[63]   "Deceivers" is a strong word, and this shows how dangerous John views the
teaching and influence of the false teachers to be.   Already they have gone out like
missionaries to spread their falsehoods.[64]   "Gone out" pictures the false teachers going on
evangelistic tours just like missionaries for Christ went on tours (cp. 3 John 7 of orthodox
missionaries going on a journey).   "Into the world" pictures these itinerant false prophets
as traveling along the highways and the byways, going from town to town, seeking to gain
an entrance into homes and churches, where they hoped to find an audience for their
teachings.

Those who do not acknowledge Jesus Christ *as* coming in the flesh – This phrase is in
apposition to "deceivers."   When missionaries are visiting their town, how are Christians
to know whether or not they and the missionaries share the same faith?   This is a matter
that must be determined if the Christian is to fulfill his God-given obligation to "love"
(verse 5) while at the same time continuing to "walk in truth" (verse 4).   Here John not
only indicates that his readers have an obligation to "test the spirits," but he proposes a
clear test by which the lady and her children, to whom he is writing, may test the orthodoxy
of any visiting preacher, teacher, or missionary.   At the same time, John warns his readers
that such people ("false teachers") may indeed attempt to visit them.   While it is not the
only test for orthodoxy which one finds in the New Testament scriptures, the one that would
serve in John's time to distinguish between true believers and the Gnostic false teachers
was the one concerning Jesus' incarnation.   Where the NASB has "do not acknowledge"
for *mē homologountes*, the ASV has "that confess not."   The word translated confession

---

[61] Adapted from Plummer, *op. cit.*, p.136,137.

[62] The lexicons give a number of possible ways to translate the word: wandering, roving, misleading, leading into error, a vagabond, a tramp, an imposter, a corrupter, a deceiver; thus a false teacher who leads others into heresies.   See Thayer, *op. cit.*, p. 515.

[63] Jesus' warning about the rise of "false Christs and false prophets" in His Olivet Discourse (Mark 13:22,23), who would appear on the scene before the fall of Jerusalem in AD 70, likely refers to a different group of deceivers than John has in view.

[64] We are reminded of 1 John 4:1 ("many false prophets are gone out into the world").   The language is also reminiscent of 1 John 2:19.   This is the passage that Irenaeus (*Haer.* III.16.8), by a slip of memory, quotes as from the First Epistle.   If they are the same persons, that slip of memory is more understandable. We must carefully observe that neither here nor at 1 John 2:19 (see our comments *in loc* on "went out from us, but were not of us") does John say that the false teachers were once Christians, but have since defected from the church.   Redaction critics, trying to reconstruct the *sitz im leben* behind 2 John, are wont to say this verb ("gone out") reflects a crisis in the congregation of which John was a part, a crisis which resulted in the congregation being broken up, with many (perhaps the majority) leaving because they have decided to side with the Gnostics.   This is reading more into the verb than the word requires.

means "to say the same thing [that God says about Jesus]."[65]   If instead of the negative *mē* we had *ouch*, the words "do not acknowledge (confess not)" might be equivalent to deny.   What *me* implies, however, is not a simple, open, categorical denial of what God says about Jesus, but refers "to a contradicting, which by various turnings and twistings evades and endangers the definite confession."[66]   The Greek is a little difficult to translate so that we catch what John was saying,[67] so the addition of "as" in italics by the NASB is helpful.   We might have expected it to read 'Jesus Christ came in the flesh,' since when John wrote the incarnation was a thing of the past (cp. 1 John 5:6).[68]   "Coming" is a present participle, and it gets its time from the tense of the main verb (which, in this case, is "do not acknowledge").   Ask the visiting missionary about the incarnation.   At the moment he or she answers you, if the incarnation ("Jesus Christ as coming in the flesh"[69]) is not clearly confessed, you have pegged that person as not teaching the truth.

This is the deceiver and the antichrist – "This" (singular) points back to the "those who (plural) do not acknowledge" and treats them as a class.   "The deceiver" has reference to what they do to their fellow men; "the antichrist" has reference to what they do in opposition to Christ our Redeemer.[70]   Since the devil is called the "deceiver" (Revelation

---

[65] See notes on "confession" at 1 John 2:23.

[66] Lange, *op. cit.*, p.191.

[67] C.H. Dodd has put forward the idea that the present tense used here is poor grammar, and is used because "our author is not skilled in the niceties of the Greek idiom" (*The Johannine Epistles* [London: Hodder and Stoughton, 1949], p.149).   It would be more to the point, however, to assume that the writer did know the difference between a present participle and a perfect tense, and that his intention was to say something here (by using the present participle) beyond what he was saying in 1 John 4:2 (where he used the perfect tense).

[68] Barker (*op. cit.*, p.364) would explain John's words as being a refutation of both Adoptionism and Docetism.   He tries to treat the present participles as timeless, implying that Jesus did not become the Christ or the Son at His baptism, or cease to be the Christ or the Son before His death.   He argues that "the union between Messiah's humanity and deity was true from His conception in Mary's womb, through His childhood and ministry and suffering, through the resurrection and ascension, and remains true of Him as He sits at the right hand of the Father.   The union is permanent and abiding, though the body He now has is a glorified human body." (For information about Adoptionism and Docetism, see what is written about Cerinthianism and Basilides in the Introductory Studies to 1 John, and in comments on 1 John 2:22ff, 4:1,15, and 5:6ff.)

[69] "Note that Jesus Christ is never said to come *into* the flesh; but either, as here and 1 John 4:21, to come *in* the flesh; or, to *become* flesh (John 1:14).   To say that Christ came *into* the flesh would leave room for saying (as Adoptionism teaches) that the Divine Son was united with Jesus after He was born of Mary; which would be no true Incarnation." Adapted from Plummer, *op. cit.*, p.137.

[70] "This completes the series of condemnatory names which John uses in speaking of these false teachers: liars (1 John 2:22), seducers (1 John 2:26), false prophets (1 John 4:1), deceivers (2 John 7), antichrists (1 John 2:18,22, 4:3; 2 John 7)." Plummer, *op. cit.*, p.138.   Perhaps a word of caution is needed. We must be careful whom we label as false teachers and deceivers and antichrists.   John seems to reserve these terms for those who attack the central citadel of Christian belief, namely the person and work of Jesus, the Son of God.   It is being harsh and unloving to call those who differ on matters of Christian liberty (such as vegetarianism v. meat eating, Romans 14:1ff) "false teachers" or "deceivers."

12:9 ASV), perhaps John is saying that folk who speak of Jesus as the false teachers do are speaking just as the devil wants them to. They use words their listeners can put any meaning on they want to, while at the same time the words hide and camouflage and conceal the real beliefs held by the false teachers. Without using such deceptive words the false teachers would get no audience or converts at all. The word "antichrist" is found only here and in 1 John 2:18,22 and 4:3.[71] Whatever it means elsewhere (and in one passage it speaks of a supremely evil antagonist of Christ in the last days,[72] one who opposes Christ and attempts to mimic His powers), here it is used to "characterize people who are radically opposed to the true doctrine about Christ and are supremely His opponents, even if they protest that they hold the truth about Him and are Christians."[73]

Verse 8 -- *Watch yourselves, that you might not lose what we have accomplished, but that you may receive a full reward.*

Watch yourselves – On the factual situation that many deceivers are going up and down the land, John bases a double warning to his readers: first, not to be deceived themselves lest they lose their full reward (verses 8,9); and secondly, not to give any encouragement to the deceivers (verses 10,11). The use of the reflexive pronoun *heautous* ("yourselves") with an active voice verb emphasizes the need for personal effort in vigilance. Deceivers are so subtle and insidious, and the consequences of being deceived so serious, that believers must constantly beware.   It is also true that many false teachers do not attempt to evangelize the unchurched.   Instead they become sheep stealers and robbers, preying on those who are already Christians and seeking to divert them from the Way.   So John cautions, 'Ever keep a watchful eye upon yourselves' or 'Think carefully about what you hear and believe.' They would do this by weighing any teaching which comes into their midst with what they have heard from the beginning (1 John 4:1-6), lest they, too, be deceived.   When error abounds in the world, our first duty is not to attack it and make war upon it; it is to look to the citadel of our own souls, and see that all is well guarded there. When all is secure at home, then the error may be attacked.

That you might not lose what we have accomplished – John highlights the dangers to believers if they succumb to the wiles of the deceivers.   The work of the apostles will be neutralized, and there is a reward to be lost.   "Lose" translates *apollumi* ("ruin, destroy"). Were the believers to embrace the teachings of the Gnostics, John's readers would destroy all that had gone in to their becoming Christians in the first place.

---

[71] "This clause gives a similar view on the relationship between the false teachers and the antichrist as found in 1 John 4:3, but it is phrased differently." Haas, *op. cit.*, p.145.

[72] This note assumes that John's "antichrist" and Paul's "man of lawlessness" (2 Thessalonians 2:1-12) and Revelation's "eighth beast" (Revelation 17:11ff) all are predictions of the same evil person at the end of time.

[73] Marshall, *op. cit.*, p.71.

The manuscripts contain three different readings for this verse:

(1) "that *we* do not lose the things *we* have worked for, but that *we* receive a full reward"[74];
(2) "that *you* do not lose all *you* have worked for, but that *you* may be rewarded fully"[75];
(3) "that *you* do not lose all that *we* have worked for, but receive *your* reward in full."[76]

The texts and versions that read "you" in the first and last instances are almost certainly right.   The manuscript evidence for the middle verb, at present, is about evenly divided between "we" and "you."[77]   The criterion of the more difficult reading tips the scales in favor of "we."   So John is understood to be expressing a fear that his and his colleagues' missionary work will end up in failure if his converts turn aside from the truth which they had committed to them.   John's feelings coincide with similar feelings expressed by Paul in his letter to the Galatians: "I fear for you, that somehow I have wasted my efforts on you" (4:11, NIV).   "As one in charge of the message that was 'from the beginning,' all the apostle John's labors were directed to the maintenance of the truth of Jesus Christ as one come in the flesh.   If anyone failed to continue this message, then in a real sense John's apostolic mission had failed."[78]   "What we accomplished," written by an apostle, is "a bold self-testimony concerning their labors and preaching (cp. 1 John 1:3, 4:6).   The 'we' does not require us to understand that the Apostle must have converted the lady and her children – he only includes himself in the number of those genuine witnesses of Christ."[79]

But that you may receive a full reward – As noted earlier, the KJV reads "*We* receive a full reward."   If we take it "we receive," it is a reference to the saints being the apostle's reward in the judgment.   The idea is similar to Paul's expression in 1 Thessalonians 2:19,20 where the Thessalonian Christians in the presence of Jesus at His coming will be Paul's "joy or crown of exultation."   However, the better attested text reads "you (plural) may receive a full reward."   The Christian life leads in the end to a reward, and failure to persevere in the truth and in right conduct can lead to loss of what God has promised to His people.   The word translated "reward" is *misthon* ("pay," the wages paid to a workman for his labor; see also Matthew 20:8; James 5:4).   John uses similar language at John 4:36,

---

[74] The KJV reflects the Byzantine text here using "we" throughout.

[75] The NIV, RSV, and NASB mg. read "what you have worked for," the reading found in Sinaiticus and Alexandrinus.   If this reading is adopted, perhaps the idea is similar to John 6:27,28 ("work ... for the food which endures to eternal life") or Philippians 2:12 ("work out your salvation with fear and trembling").

[76] The ERV, ASV, NEB, JB, NASB read "you" for the first and third verbs, and "we" for the second. Lachmann, Tischendorf, Tregelles, Nestle, and UBS choose this reading, though it is preserved only in Vaticanus and the Thebaic version.   In 1 John 2:14,20 there may be other instances of Vaticanus and the Thebaic preserving what may have been the original reading.

[77] Roman Catholic commentators have used "you accomplished" as one of their proof texts for merit of human works.

[78] Barker, *op. cit.*, p.364.

[79] Lange, *op. cit.*, p.191.

"Already he who reaps is receiving wages, and is gathering fruit for life eternal." But what does "full reward" mean? Perhaps Plummer is right when he suggests that "full reward" compares heaven to the incomplete rewards Christians enjoy in this life – grace, mercy, peace, joy, and the like.[80] Perhaps Jesus' words recorded in Mark 10:29,30 convey the same idea: "Truly I say to you, there is no one who has left house or brothers or sisters or mother or father or children or farms, for my sake and for the gospel's sake, but that he shall receive a hundred times as much now in the present age, houses and brothers and sisters and mothers and children and farms, along with persecutions; and in the age to come, eternal life." Or, perhaps, "full reward" reflects the Biblical teaching that there are degrees of reward ("great is your reward in heaven," Matthew 5:12 KJV) some of which can be lost without salvation being forfeited (1 Corinthians 3:14,15, "If any man's work which he has built upon it remains, he shall receive a reward. If any man's work is burned up, he shall suffer loss; but he himself shall be saved, yet so as through fire"). According to this view, John envisions two possibilities in verses 8 and 9. Verse 8 speaks of the situation where one of John's readers is partially deceived and so loses some of his reward for faithfulness and perseverance. Verse 9 then pictures the same believer but a more radical departure from the faith. The situation in verse 9 is one where the person ceases to "abide in the teaching of Christ" and so forfeits the relationship he once had with God. He not only loses rewards, but also forfeits eternal life (such as was promised in 1 John 2:25).

Verse 9 -- *Any one who goes too far and does not abide in the teaching of Christ, does not have God; the one who abides in the teaching, he has both the Father and the Son.*

Any one who goes too far – John's warning to his readers about the danger of the false teaching is not exaggerated. What is at stake is no less than one's relationship with the Father and with the Son. In 1 John 3:3ff, *pas ho* ("everyone who" or "anyone who") referred to the Gnostic false teachers. Here in 2 John the same expression may refer either to the teachers or to any of John's readers who fail to "watch" (verse 8) and as a result are deceived and converted to the Gnostic way of thinking. The Greek text which reads *proagōn* ("goes too far") is better attested than the text which reads *parabainōn* ("transgresses").[81] Stott suggested[82] that when John uses *proagōn* (goes onward, goes ahead, advances), he is almost certainly borrowing from the vocabulary of the heretics. They claimed to have "go-ahead" views, a superior *gnōsis* ("knowledge"), which had en-

---

[80] Plummer, *op. cit.*, p.138.

[81] Perhaps the "transgresses" of the Textus Receptus was a change because the copyists did not understand what John wrote, and so attempted to correct it into an intelligible commonplace. If we interpret the KJV's "transgresses" to mean it is sin to accept the teachings of the Gnostics, it might be a right idea. But if we were to interpret "transgresses" in the KJV to mean that any single violation of some law or commandment means the Christian no longer abides in Christ, that would be an erroneous idea.

[82] Stott, *op. cit.*, p.211.

abled them to advance beyond the simple facts and simple moral teaching of the gospel in which the common herd were content to "abide."[83]

And does not abide in the teaching of Christ – "Goes too far" (*proagōn*) and "does not abide" (*mē menōn*) describe the same persons, positively and negatively.[84] The non-repetition of the article before *mē menōn* is significant. All "progress" is not condemned. Of course, John is not against growth in understanding of Christian doctrine, nor is he depreciating growth in the grace and knowledge of Christ (2 Peter 3:18). What he warns against is a progress that causes a person to no longer abide in the teaching of Christ. Roberts tells us that "abide" sometimes has the idea of "holding on to, and not leaving a realm, sphere, or custom to which one had previously adhered. So John had spoken of abiding in the light (1 John 2:10), of abiding in what was heard from the beginning (1 John 2:24), and now of abiding in the doctrine."[85]

Didachē (which is translated both "teaching" and "doctrine" in our English versions) speaks of a body of doctrine which was the ultimate type and norm in the church.[86] The Greek genitive ("of Christ") may be subjective (i.e., the doctrine which Christ taught) or objective (i.e., the doctrine about Christ). It is not an easy choice to make. Either meaning can be fitted into what John is writing.

- If we opt for the subjective genitive, John is speaking about the "teaching" (body of doctrine) which Christ Himself delivered during His earthly ministry. The context of 2 John would cause us to refer to Jesus' teachings about His own Christology: who Jesus said the Christ is, His deity, eternality, incarnation, and exaltation. Such Christology is specifically a contradiction either of Gnostic presentations of Jesus or their presentations of the Christ. That doctrine came from God Himself. Jesus Himself said to the Jews, "My teaching is not Mine, but His who sent Me ..." (John 7:16,17). And when Jesus' ministry on earth was complete, He sent the Holy Spirit on the apostles and caused that same doctrine to continue to be propagated (John 14:26,

---

[83] It is possible that *pas ho proagōn* means no more than 'everyone who takes the lead' or who 'sets himself up as a teacher' – i.e., chooses a line for himself, which in matters of doctrine means creating a heresy, and then attempts to spread it. The difficulty with this view is that it limits the ones who are in danger to the teachers, and not the potential hearers whom John is warning.

[84] There is an article before *proagōn*; there is no article before *mē menōn*. Sharp's rule of grammar says, "When two nouns in the same case are connected by the Greek word 'and,' and the first noun is preceded by the article 'the,' and the second noun is not preceded by the article, the second noun refers to the same person or thing to which the first noun refers, and is a further description of it." H.E. Dana and Julius R. Mantey, *A Manual Grammar of the Greek New Testament* (New York: Macmillan, 1927), p.147.

[85] Roberts, *op. cit.*, p.163. It is not possible to abide in something in which a person has never been. What John writes causes great difficulty for those who would hold the Calvinistic view that no saved person can ever apostatize.

[86] Titus 1:9; Romans 6:17, Romans 16:17; and cp. Matthew 16:12; Acts 5:28, 17:19; Hebrews 13:2. A cognate form of the word, *didaskalia*, is the one which speaks of the act of teaching, since it is closely related to *didaskalos* (teacher) and *didaskein* (to teach). This nice distinction in the Greek is an idea that is no longer observed in the use of the English word "teaching."

16:13; and Acts 1:8).[87]   One had to abandon the "doctrine (teaching) of Christ" to embrace Gnostic doctrine.   That's a poor trade.

- If we opt for the objective genitive,[88] John is saying that the person who refuses to confess or acknowledge Jesus as coming in the flesh, and who in deception tries to lead others into this denial, can only do so after first abandoning orthodox doctrine about Christ.   Since John himself had been one of the apostles instrumental in sharing orthodox doctrine, he may be implying that in denying the incarnation of Jesus the false teachers were not conforming their doctrine to the apostolic doctrine about Christ handed down by inspiration.   To abandon the orthodox doctrine about Christ has fatal consequences.

Does not have God – To "have God" means to have a saving spiritual relationship with Him (cp. 1 John 2:23, 5:12).   People who reject the teaching of Christ no longer "have God."   Plummer is probably correct in his comments here, "This must not be watered down to mean 'does not know God.'   It means that He has Him not as his God; does not possess Him in his heart as a Being to adore, and trust, and love."[89]   The Gnostics may claim they have God, but that claim is false, for without a proper understanding of Jesus Christ, a person cannot have a true relationship with God.   A man "who does not honor the Son does not honor the Father," either (John 5:23).   Putting the previous clause together with this one, we learn that "any one who goes too far" means to go beyond the "teaching of Christ."   They profess their teaching is something more profound than the revealed truth of the gospel.   They may claim to have go-ahead views, a superior knowledge, an advanced teaching.   John sarcastically uses their own claim to say they had indeed gone ahead.   They have gone beyond the boundaries of true Christian belief. They had advanced so far they had left God behind!   They had departed from the truth![90]

The one who abides in the teaching, he has both the Father and the Son – John's warning about the "many deceivers" (verse 7) and what happens to those who do not abide in the teaching of Christ   culminates in a positive promise of   spiritual blessing for those

---

[87] John did not regard Paul or any other apostle as the inventor of what was characteristic of the Christian faith as he knew it.   Genuine Christianity is the "doctrine (teaching) of Christ"!

[88] Some have argued that it must be an objective genitive since John does not use "Christ" by itself as a name for the earthly Jesus.

[89] Plummer, *op. cit.*, p.139.

[90] "The warning is still valid for us.   Any teaching which goes beyond the plain message of Scripture should at once put us on the alert lest it actually contradicts the truth revealed in Scripture.   When the teaching of the Bible needs to be supplemented by some 'key' to the Bible or by some new revelation, it is a sure sign that 'advanced' doctrine is being put forward."   Marshall, *op. cit.*, p.73.

who do continue to abide in the teaching of Christ.[91]   Abiding in the doctrine of Christ is critical.   On that condition depends a man's relationship with both the Father and the Son. As earlier in this verse "have" (Father and Son) means to have a saving spiritual relationship with those members of the Godhead.[92]   Notice that the Son is placed on the same level as the Father.

> In both passages (here and 1 John 2:23), "the Christ" and "the Son" are equivalent expressions.   No man can have the Father without confessing the Son.   The Son is the revelation of the Father (e.g., John 1:18; 14:7,9; 1 John 5:20; cf. Matthew 11:27) and the way to the Father (John 14:6; cf. 1 Timothy 2:5), combining the functions of prophet and priest.   Therefore to confess the Son is to possess the Father; to deny the Son is to forfeit the Father.   This is as true today of all non-Christian religions as it was of Cerinthian Gnosticism in the 1st century.   Many today want God without Jesus Christ.   They say they believe in God, but see no necessity for Jesus.   Or they want to bring non-Christian religions on to a level with Christianity, as alternative roads to God.   Such errors must be strenuously resisted.   In this the Christian is conservative, not progressive, seeking to "abide" in the doctrine of Christ, not to "advance" beyond it.[93]

Whether it be the Gnostic who denies Christ while claiming a superior knowledge of the Father, or whether it be the Jewish opponents who repudiated Jesus as Messiah while claiming belief in the God of Israel – they are both here flatly shown to be mistaken.[94]

D. Prohibition Against Aiding the False Teachers. Verses 10,11

Verse 10 -- *If any one comes to you and does not bring this teaching, do not receive him into* your *house, and do not give him a greeting.*

If any one comes to you – "Comes to you" indicates that the deceivers, who are going from town to town, can be expected to arrive at the doorstep of the chosen lady's home.[95] John instructs the chosen lady and her children (the "you" is plural) how to treat the many deceivers who, having "gone out into the world" (verse 7), now come to her house.   How

---

[91] The KJV reads "doctrine of Christ."   However, the better manuscripts do not carry the words "of Christ."   The fact that this phrase corresponds to the previous one ("teaching of Christ") leads us to understand that this is what John means even if he didn't repeat the whole phrase as he wrote.

[92] See 1 John 2:23 where the same language is used and explained in our notes.   For "Father" and "Son" see 1 John 1:3 and 2:22.

[93] Stott, *op. cit.*, p.211.

[94] Adapted from Brooke, *op. cit.*, p.178.

[95] The way the "if" clause is written in Greek is *ei tis erchetai*.   *Ei* with the indicative, not *ean* and the subjunctive, implies that such people do come.

shall we understand the indefinite pronoun "any one"?[96]   Are the anticipated visitors simply travelers who need lodging for the night, or are they traveling teachers looking for an opportunity to spread their lies?   In all likelihood, we should picture the visitors as coming in an official capacity as teachers.[97]   The situation pictured was rather common in the 1st century.   In Titus there is allusion to traveling preachers of the gospel, whom Titus is to see are hospitably entertained and then sent on their way to their next destination (Titus 3:14,15).   Lydia opened her home to the missionaries who brought the gospel to Philippi (Acts 16:15).   Paul expected the church at Rome to help support him on his planned evangelistic tour to Spain (Romans 15:24).   What we have in these passages is a picture of preachers/teachers (whose message was orthodox) who went from town to town preaching the gospel as they went, and who depended on the generosity of fellow believers and of already established congregations for their housing and keep.   It appears the "deceivers" tried to take advantage of the hospitality Christians were regularly ready to extend to traveling missionaries.   All the deceivers had to do to find an open door was pretend they were Christians on a mission for the Lord.

And does not bring this teaching – "This teaching" or doctrine which the visitors were not bringing is what John has just called "the teaching of Christ" (verse 9).   To "bring" a teaching is an expression that occurs nowhere else in the New Testament.   A similar use of "bring" is found in John 18:29 ("what accusation do you bring against this Man?").   We also speak of a merchant bringing his wares for sale.   There is a difference, apparently, between *believing* a doctrine, and *bringing* a doctrine.   It is the person bringing the teaching that John has in view.   How would the chosen lady and her children identify the wrong teaching?   John has already provided the means to "test the spirits (or prophets) to see whether they are from God" (1 John 4:1ff).   The visitors were to be given a chance of acknowledging or confessing "Jesus Christ as coming in the flesh" (verse 7).   This key point of doctrine would be sufficient for purposes of identification.   Those who confess Jesus may be shown hospitality.   Those who do not confess Jesus need not and should not be shown hospitality.[98]

---

[96] The identification of the visitors is vitally important to us as we attempt to make application of John's prohibition against aiding certain visitors.   Does John have in mind *teachers* who seek an opportunity to teach, or simply casual *visitors* who claim to be Christians (but whose beliefs show they in fact are not)?   See Ketcherside's "Receive Him Not" in *The Twisted Scriptures*, reprinted herein as a Special Study at close of these notes on 2 John.

[97] There are times in Scripture when "comes" (*erchetai*) means more than a mere visit; it implies coming on a mission as a teacher (see 3 John 10; John 1:7,30,31, 3:2, 4:5, 5:43; 1 Corinthians 2:1, 4:18,19,21, 11:34).   The next phrase does speak of "bringing this teaching" which tells us they came to communicate something to the people who extended hospitality to them.   They were looking for opportunity to teach.

[98] John is referring to teachers of false doctrine about the incarnation, and not to someone who may hold different views, say, on matters of Christian liberty.   The apostle John is not contradicting what another apostle (Paul) wrote about welcoming folk who hold different views about vegetarianism, special days, clean and unclean meats, and other differences of opinion (Romans 14:1-15:13).   The false teacher whom John will not have entertained by the chosen lady and her children is both "the deceiver" and "the antichrist" (verse 7).

Do not receive him into *your* house – The way the prohibition is written in the Greek (a present imperative with *mē*) forbids the continuance of an action already going on: "Stop welcoming him into your house! Stop inviting him to be a guest in your house!" John requires them to refuse to offer to the "deceivers" the hospitality which as a matter of course the lady and her children were extending to faithful Christians. The Bible may teach Christians to extend hospitality to those is need (Hebrews 13:2, Romans 12:13; 1 Peter 4:9), but the exhortation does not include showing hospitality to Gnostic false teachers. "Into [your] house" (*eis oikian*) might be the dwelling where the lady lives, or it might speak of a "house church" that meets in her home.[99] Perhaps it is private hospitality which John is prohibiting. If so, John is saying that every Christian house was to be closed to the deceivers/teachers/false prophets. The commandment to love does not require Christians to be hospitable to those who would destroy the faith. Doing what is spiritually best for the false teacher is to refuse to encourage him and aid him. Perhaps John is prohibiting giving the deceivers an official welcome into the assembly of believers, which would afford the false teacher an opportunity to spread his errors. If the reference is to a house church, then what John is forbidding is an official welcome into the congregation, and perhaps also an invitation to be today's Bible "teacher." Paul told Titus that false teachers' "mouths must be stopped" (Titus 1:10). One way of stopping their mouths would be to deny them an opportunity to address the assembled Christians. Perhaps John's language is general enough that it prohibits both private hospitality and an official welcome to such teachers as he has been describing. At the same time, a refusal of hospitality, by offering a place to stay overnight, does not exclude inviting someone to enter your home when your purpose is to seek to bring such a person to a better understanding of God's revelation. While the situations envisioned are not quite parallel (in that Apollos' beliefs were not as wrong Christologically as were the Gnostic views John warns about, nor is Apollos called a "deceiver" or a "false teacher") we find the example of Aquila and Priscilla taking Apollos "aside" and explaining "to him the way of God more accurately" (Acts 18:24-26).

John's prohibition has been perceived as being harsh; so harsh, in fact, that it has proven unacceptable to many contemporary scholars. They ask, Is it not a contradiction of the idea that Christians are "given to hospitality"? Is it not incompatible with Jesus' teaching that His followers are to "love their neighbor"? Both Barclay and Dodd hesitate to make John's words of prohibition a guide for modern Christian conduct.[100] In reply, are we to suppose John is contradicting himself? In verse 5, John called attention "to the commandment … we have had from the beginning, that we love one another." Is he here breaking that commandment? Is there not a difference between showing love to a person,

[99] For such congregational meetings in private houses, see Romans 16:5; 1 Corinthians 16:19; Colossians 4:15; Philemon 2.

[100] C.H. Dodd (*The Johannine Epistles*) has suggested these are "emergency regulations" relating to "a situation of extreme danger to the church." He affirms that John's words of prohibition are "offensive" and are not "a sufficient guide to Christian conduct" (p.152). William Barclay (*The Letters of John and Jude*, in The Daily Study Bible [Philadelphia: Westminster, 1960], p.168-69), saying that the situation John writes about "has no parallel in western civilization," also hesitates to make John's prohibition a guide for modern Christian conduct.

and aiding and encouraging them in their anti-Christian propaganda?   Is there not a difference between being loving toward a person, and giving them a base from which to work and even supporting their work financially?   If John's instruction, intended to curtail the influence of teachers who would destroy men's souls and rob Jesus Christ of His glory, still seems harsh, is it perhaps because his concern for the glory of the Son and the good of men's souls is greater than ours, and because the tolerance on which we pride ourselves is in reality an indifference to truth?

It is also true that not all Christians have done well trying to practice John's ethical injunctions – both to walk in truth and love, and to refuse hospitality.   Some have emphasized one and ignored the other.   One result has been an extreme called separatism, which withdraws from everybody who differs on any matter of doctrine.   Another result has been compromise, which stems either from indifference to the truth or a lack of any doctrinal convictions concerning the central affirmations of the gospel, and therefore refuses to withdraw from anyone.   In the light of such past failures, the greatest care will be necessary before we can venture to act upon the injunction given by John to the chosen lady.   Not everyone who holds religious views different from those we hold should be categorized as a "deceiver" or an "antichrist" as these Gnostics were by John.   In an earlier note we have already called attention to verses where there are legitimate differences of opinion that we must not allow to drive a wedge between us.   We must always be ready to ask, "Are the cases really parallel?   Are we quite sure that the teacher from whom we propose to withhold hospitality and aid is indeed an opponent of Christ to the degree the Gnostics were?"

While John's prohibition is strong, "we today can only be grateful that the infant church took heresy regarding the person of Christ seriously.   Christianity stands or falls with its Christology.   From the human point of view, if John and other apostolic leaders had tolerated the 'antichrists' who denied the basic truth of the Incarnation, the church might never have survived.   We today are the beneficiaries of the spiritual discernment and moral courage of John and others like him."[101]   Will our beneficiaries benefit from a matching spiritual discernment and moral courage on our part?

And do not give him a greeting – The Greek construction shows this prohibition, like the one at the beginning of the verse, prohibits the continuance of an action already going on. The word "greeting" (*chairen*) can be the hearty welcome ('how glad we are to see you') at first meeting (Acts 15:23, 23:26; James 1:1) or the farewell when the visitor departs (2 Corinthians 13:11).   The word carried the idea of wishing one success, health, prosperity,

---

[101] Barker, *op. cit.*, p.366.

and goodspeed.[102]   Christians do not wish such for false teachers!   In 3 John 6, Gaius is praised for his support of loyal teachers and for sending them on their way with provisions so that they may reach their next destination.   Such support through lodging and provisions was a definite factor in the early spread of the gospel.   This kind of help was the very thing the chosen lady and her children were to withhold from those teachers who refused to acknowledge Jesus as coming in the flesh.   The prohibition against aiding the false teachers is clear and definite.   Do not welcome the known false teacher when you first meet, whether by spoken words, or an embrace, or a kiss on the cheek, and do not offer him a farewell or give him any greeting or help him on his way when he leaves.   If all the church members adopted such measures, it obviously would curb the influence of the false teachers.

        With whom do we fellowship is always a pressing question.   We recall that according to John, Christian fellowship with each other and with the Father and with the Son is based on the reception of the message of the incarnate Lord (1 John 1:1-4).   Anyone who does not acknowledge Jesus Christ as coming in the flesh has destroyed any basis for Christian fellowship.   When a person embraces the Gnostic error, whether or not he goes out to teach it, he has done something that leads to loss of fellowship with God (verse 9, "does not have God"), and also the loss of fellowship with other Christians.   The faithful demonstrate that they recognize the fellowship is broken by refusing hospitality and by refusing to aid them in their travels.

Verse 11 -- *For the one who gives him a greeting participates in his evil deeds.*

For the one who gives him a greeting – "For" with which this verse begins shows it is intended to give a reason for the stringent prohibitions against extending hospitality and greetings voiced in the previous verse.   "Him" is the Gnostic false teacher about whom the previous verses warn.   "Gives him a greeting" can either mean welcoming the false teacher into your home when he first arrives in town so that he has a headquarters from which to spread his false teaching, or it may mean to provide funds so when he leaves your town he has the means to make his way on to the next town.   John is concerned with the consequences to the chosen lady and her children (and perhaps to the church members who meet in their home) to whom he is writing, who may decide to align themselves with the false teachers.   That is a course of behavior that can have eternally bad consequences.

Participates in his evil deeds – The word order in Greek puts emphasis on "evil."   What the Gnostic missionaries are doing is "evil," wicked!   "Evil" (*ponēros*) is the same word used of "the evil one" at 1 John 2;13,14, 3:12, 5:18,19.   The teachers are not just bad themselves; the word to use in that case would be *kakos*.   *Ponēros* indicates they are trying to get others to be bad.   Translators have struggled to find a suitable English word to trans-

---

[102] KJV has "Do not bid him God speed!" This helps us to see that the injunction covers any act which might seem to give sanction to the false doctrine or show sympathy with the movement represented by the false teacher.

late *ergois*, for they want a word that will cover both the words (i.e., spreading false ideas about Christ) spoken by the false teachers and the ethics they taught (e.g., denying the importance of love for the brother) by word and deed.   Some versions (KJV, NASB) prefer "deeds" and some (ASV) prefer "works."   "Participates" (*koinōnein*, fellowship, participation in a common cause) indicates an active involvement.   Providing a place to stay and providing traveling expenses is not passive sharing.   It is active involvement and it makes the supporter of the false teacher an accomplice in his evil deeds.   "It is to be borne in mind that the churches often met in private homes, and if these travelling deceivers were allowed to spread their doctrines in these homes and then sent on with endorsement as Apollos was from Ephesus and Corinth (Acts 18:27), there was no way of escaping responsibility for the harm wrought by these propagandists of evil."[103]   To give countenance and sanction to false doctrine is to share in the responsibility for all the harm which such false doctrine does.[104]   John's point needs reiterating and reemphasizing in an age when the church has become much more tolerant of deviation and heresy.

II. THE CONCLUSION.   Verses 12,13

A. The Explanation about the Brevity of the Letter.   Verse 12

Verse 12 -- Having many things to write to you, I do not want to do so *with paper and ink; but I hope to come to you and speak face to face, that your joy may be made full.*

Having many things to write to you – The position of *humin* ("to you," plural) is emphatic, and means 'especially to you,' namely, to the chosen lady and her children.   This language ("many things") is such as would be used by one who was hurried, or who hoped to soon see the person written to.[105]   "Write" is a verb that speaks of any manner of communication; for example, we could translate it as 'I have much to tell you.'[106]

---

[103] A.T. Robertson, *The General Epistles and the Revelation of John*, in Word Pictures in the New Testament (Nashville: Broadman, 1933), Vol.6, p.255.   Just as people can participate in someone's good acts (Paul thanked God for the Philippians' fellowship in the furtherance of the gospel [Philippians 1:5], so we can participate in another person's evil acts.   Compare sharing with demons (1 Corinthians 10:20), sharing in the sin of others (1 Timothy 5:22).

[104] This may seem to us to be strong language that John uses.   But if we think it "unloving" or "unchristian," there is a strong likelihood that we do not understand how God views those who try to hinder what He wants done in the world.

[105] This remark is almost conclusive against the supposition that 2 John was sent as a companion letter with 1 John.

[106] Haas, *op. cit.*, p.147.

I do not want to *do so* with paper and ink – "Apparently John wrote this letter with his own hand."[107]   "Want" (*boulomai*) is a desire which comes from one's reason.   John had considered the matter carefully and had come to the conclusion that it would be wiser to wait till he saw this "lady" again to talk things over with her, rather than include them in this letter.[108]   Papyrus[109] and ink[110] were the normal writing materials for 1st century letters.

But I hope to come to you – "Hope" (*elpizō*) is a complex emotion made up of both a desire for something and a confident expectation that it will happen.   If either the desire or the expectation is missing, it is not "hope"; it is just wishing.   "To come to you" (*genesthai pros humas*) means 'to appear before you,' 'to come into your presence,' 'to pay a visit to you.'[111]   "You" (*humas*, plural) in this verse includes both the chosen lady and the children mentioned in verse 1.   John apparently traveled around among the towns and congregations in the area, or perhaps he is planning a special trip just to visit the lady and her children.   John provides no information about where they lived or how far he has to travel to reach them.   He simply says he plans to make the journey and see them personally.   His coming to them as their true teacher will be very different from the coming of the false teachers.   He assumes they will welcome him.   We can only speculate why John felt it necessary to send this brief letter if he hoped to visit with the readers soon.   It would certainly be natural for him to wish to prevent possible dangers to his readers; if he waits to say anything till he arrives personally, it may be too late.   With no postal service as we know it, the only way to get a letter delivered was to find someone going to its destination and entrust it to them.   If John had such visitors from the town where the lady and her children lived, it would be natural to take advantage of the opportunity.

---

[107] Robertson, *ibid*.

[108] Actually the verb "want" (*eboulēthēn*) is an aorist tense in the Greek. It is likely an example of what is called the epistolary aorist: the writer puts himself in the temporal position of his readers, for whom his act of writing took place in the past. So the verb is translated as a present tense in our NASB.

[109] *Chartēs* is Egyptian papyrus, not paper. It was made of a tall, smooth reed, which had a triangular stalk. This stalk contained the pith from which the sheets of papyrus were made. The sheet was made by arranging strips of pith side by side, then laying other strips crosswise, uniting these two layers with paste, and putting all under heavy pressure till the paste dried. It was a comparatively cheap form of writing material; a sheet sold for about a day's wages for a working man. In great measure, it superseded the earlier materials for writing – plates of lead, clay tablets, stones, skins of animals. It was the usual material for correspondence and for the cheaper kinds of books. Contrast this with the mode of writing noted in 2 Timothy 4:13, "parchments" (*membranas*, which were animal skins). The very perishable nature of papyrus on which many of the New Testament books probably were originally written may account for the early loss of the apostolic autographs.

[110] "Ink" (*melan*, literally, "that which is black") is mentioned again in 3 John 13; elsewhere in the New Testament it is only at 2 Corinthians 3:3; cp. LXX of Jeremiah 36:18. Various combinations of ingredients were used to make "ink." Some was made of lampblack and [nut] gall-juice; some was made soot and water; a very durable ink was made of egg white and soot; red iron oxide with gum arabic was another mixture that made a lasting ink. (In comments on 3 John 13 we will detail how pens were made.)

[111] *Genesthai* is used frequently of visiting ("came," in John 10:25; Acts 10:13; 1 Corinthians 2:3, 16:10).

And speak face to face – Literally, "mouth (*stoma*) to mouth," as in Numbers 12:8 and Jeremiah 32:4.[112]   The phrase is a common one, denoting conversation with anyone. "Face to face" is contrasted with "to write" and "to do so with paper and ink."   "Talking face to face ... is a more satisfactory method of communication between persons than writing.   Spoken words are less easily misunderstood than written words, because it is not only by language that the speaker conveys his meanings, but also by the tone of his voice and the expression on his face."[113]   The communication which the coming visit will make possible is emphasized rather than the "coming."

That your joy may be made full – The marginal note tells us that some ancient manuscripts read "our joy" rather than "your joy."   If John wrote "our joy" (and manuscript evidence for this is late), he is expressing his hope that both he and the readers will find pleasure from such "face to face" conversation.   John wrote (3 John 4) of the joy he felt when he learned his children were walking in truth.   If John wrote "your joy," then he is anticipating his readers will continue to walk in truth, and to experience the joy (both in this life and the life to come) that such a walk imparts.   He talks about the joy being made full or made complete.   "Fulfilled joy is the result of fellowship.   The New Testament knows nothing of 'perfect joy' outside fellowship with each other through fellowship with the Father and the Son (cf. 1 John 1:3,4)."[114]

B. The Greeting From the Children of Her Sister.   Verse 13

Verse 13 -- *The children of your chosen sister greet you.*

The children of your chosen sister – It was the practice of the time to close a letter with a word of greeting.   John adds such a greeting here.   The greeting comes from the "children," not from the sister herself.[115]   Commentators have speculated as to the reason the sister herself sends no greetings.   Some suppose she is dead.   Some suppose she lives in a different town than her children live and from where John writes.   Perhaps it was from these nephews or nieces of the "chosen lady" that John had knowledge of the state of things in the chosen lady's house.

---

[112] In 1 Corinthians 13:12, it does read "face (*prosōpon*) to face."   Cp. Genesis 32:30.

[113] Stott, *op. cit.*, p.215.

[114] Stott, *ibid.*

[115] In the Introductory Studies on 2 John, we have written in detail concerning the use of this verse by some to prove (1) that the "chosen lady" was a church, or (2) that she was an individual person.   Likewise the appeal to "the children" has been pressed into the argument, being used by the commentators to substantiate both views.   "Chosen" (*eklektēs*) has the same meaning here that it had in verse 1. "Children" has the same meaning here that it had in verse 1.

Greet you – "You" is singular, so this greeting is being addressed to the "chosen lady" of verse 1.   The sending of this greeting to the chosen lady from her sister's children is, perhaps, intended as a delicate intimation that they know why the elder is writing, and join in his anxiety for her and in his affectionate warning against the deceiving missionaries.

[Amen] – The KJV closes with an "Amen."   The NASB omits it, and it should be omitted because it is not found in the better manuscripts (*Aleph*, A B P ψ 33).   Such concluding "amens" were frequent liturgical additions, intended to elicit an "amen" from the listeners when the letter was read out loud as part of the church worship services.

Special Study

RECEIVE HIM NOT

by W. Carl Ketcherside[116]

"If there come any unto you, and bring not this doctrine, receive him not into your house, neither bid him God speed;

For he that biddeth him God speed is partaker of his evil deeds" (2 John 10,11).

This is one of the more prominent "twisted scriptures." It has become the handle for every factional tool used to pry apart the living stones in the temple of God. It is the murderous knife employed to dismember the body of the Lord. It was written by the apostle of love to protect the flock of God from the prowling wolves who sought to seduce them through denial of the foundational fact that Jesus came in the flesh. It is now used to convert the sheep into snarling dogs, snapping at each other over every stray scrap of doctrine. It has substituted the law of the pack for the love of the flock.

No other passage so well illustrates the danger of ignoring the context. That the leaders of religious thought in some sects should have been betrayed into adopting an interpretation which makes unity impossible and renders ridiculous their vaunted claim to respect for the authority of the word of God, is one of the amazing developments in the Restoration Movement of which we are heirs. Any use of the written word which makes impossible the fulfillment and realization of the prayer and purpose of the Living Word is abuse and misuse. We can never regain our integrity as scholars until we repudiate the partisan explanation which makes every vagary of thought and dissent an occasion to destroy the fraternal relationship created by the blood of Jesus, and stab love dead at our feet.

What is "the doctrine" which is so transcendent that one who does not attest to it must not be allowed to enter the house, nor be given a greeting on the street or in the marketplace? Or, looking at it from the opposite position, what is it that, when advocated is so heinous and so poison to the fellowship, that to merely salute its opponent is to make one a participant in his vicious works? To this question a medley of things is contributed by factional voices. Every trivial idea which has been magnified out of all proportion to its value and worth is exalted to the status of the doctrine which is to preclude hospitality and make all greeting a violation of the Word

---

[116] Chapter 9 in The *Twisted Scriptures* (St. Louis, MO: Mission Messenger, nd), p.134-155.

of God. So ludicrous are some of these that it serves no good purpose to even mention them.

The depth of one's love for the family of God can be determined by the relative value of those things which will cause one to sacrifice it or to break up the relationship. The triviality of those views elevated to a higher station than the family ties created by the blood of the cross is indicative of the shallowness and superficiality of thought eating like a pernicious cancer at the heart of a wonderful fellowship created by God and inaugurated by the indwelling Spirit.

Who can believe that the apostle who wrote more about brotherly love than any other man, would recommend that we refuse entrance to our homes to those saints who disagree with us over some of the things about which we debate? What sane reasoner can actually conclude that to greet a brother who disagrees with us about these matters is to become a participant in some "evil deed"? The very absurdity of such a conclusion renders obnoxious the common usage of the passage by expositors who should know better.

I do not hesitate to say that so long as men maintain such an unrealistic attitude toward the sacred scriptures they can never make an impact upon the thinking world. They will only be purveyors of prejudice, agents of animosity, and disseminators of distrust. Such explanations are exercises in eisegetics, not exegetics. They inject a meaning into the holy oracles rather than extracting one from them. And while there was a time when dogmatism held men and women in line because the masses could neither read nor write, that day is over. We face another "Great Awakening" in the religious realm. Enlightened people are growing less satisfied with the dry husks thrown out to them by factional debaters.

To what did John refer by "this doctrine"? Who were the wandering teachers who were to be refused entrance when they applied for hospitality? What condition existed at the time which made it imperative that the "elect lady and her children" refrain from giving a greeting to certain teachers? Who were those who "went beyond" and did not remain in the doctrine of Christ? Surely what they denied must have been related to the very fundamental and essential facts upon which the faith was predicated to require such drastic measures to preserve it inviolate.

General Observations

Every reputable scholar known to us believes that John was writing to counteract the pernicious effects of Gnosticism. Upon no other ground can we account for the approach of his gospel record and first two epistles. Who were the Gnostics? What did they teach? Why were they so dangerous to the Christian concept? How did John become involved in the controversy? It is not our purpose here to analyze this synthetic philosophy, interesting though it might be. We shall be content with supplying our readers with sufficient background material to enable them to see the purpose and intent of John and to recognize how modern "interpreters" among us have warped and wrested what the apostle wrote. For your own convenience and to aid the reviewers of what I write I will number the various observations.

(1). The word "gnostic" is from **gnōsis**, knowledge. The Gnostics were "the knowing ones." It was believed by the Gnostics that all matter was inherently evil and only spirit was good. Since the spirit was imprisoned in the body, and the body composed of matter, the chief aim was to free or liberate the spirit. Taking their cue from the Greek mystery religions they taught that only by probing the depths and ascending the heights of knowledge, could that which was real be delivered from the material. This required an elaborate secret ritual coupled with painful, arduous and disciplined investigation and research into the mystical infinite wisdom of God. All men were not equipped to do this, either from lack of time, inclination or ability, and the majority of these would continue on a more animal plane. The Gnostics were in a class by themselves. They were the initiated. They could "go beyond."

(2). This idea of a spiritual aristocracy made up of specially endowed thinkers who were on "the inside" would wreak havoc upon the idea of fellowship. For this reason John emphasizes over and over that all saints have access to knowledge. They all possess it. The word "know" appears in various forms eleven times in chapter two of the first epistle. "Ye have an unction from the Holy One, and **ye know** all things" (2:20). "I have not written unto you because ye know not the truth but because **ye know it**" (2:21). The one who doesn't know where he is going is the one who hates his brother (2:11). In chapter three "know" is found 8 times, in chapter four 7 times, and in chapter five 7 times. In every instance the disciples are comforted with the thought that knowledge is not the special privilege of the few. Note the recurrence of "we know" and "ye know."

(3). The Gnostics held that matter was evil. On this basis they speculated that God could not have created the earth because it was material. By the same token the idea of the incarnation was unthinkable. One group held that Jesus was simply an ethereal person, a mere phantom. They insisted he never had a real flesh and blood body, that he was pure spirit. These were called Docetics, from **dokeō**, to appear, to seem. John attacked this speculation by affirming that the apostles had heard, seen, scrutinized, and handled Jesus with their hands.

(4). Cerinthus was the first Gnostic leader whose name has come down to us. He lived in Ephesus where John apparently wrote his epistles. According to Eusebius, the father of church historians, John knew Cerinthus for what he really was. Cerinthus made a distinction between Jesus and the Christ, or Logos. He taught that Jesus was human, the son of Joseph and Mary. But Jesus increased in wisdom and favor with God (see Luke 2:52), which He could not have done if He had been God, according to Cerinthus. When Jesus was thirty years of age, He had lived in such a state of purity that God adopted Him, publicly announcing that Jesus was His Son in whom He was well pleased. Upon this occasion the Christ (anointing) descended upon Him in the shape of a dove. Cerinthus reasoned that Jesus could not have been God prior to this as He did not have the Spirit of God until it descended upon Him. The Christ came upon him at John's baptism.

Cerinthus further contended that the Christ (Spirit) could not be killed or made to suffer pain. The human Jesus was nailed to the cross and endured agony but the Christ had withdrawn as He came, and was beyond the reach of men. It is for this reason John insists that, "This is he that came by water and blood, even Jesus Christ; not by water only, but by water and blood" (1 John 5:6). It was not just Jesus who came to be baptized but Jesus Christ; it was not just Jesus who was crucified but Jesus Christ. He did not come by water (baptism) only, but by water and blood (crucifixion).

(5). The crux of the whole matter as it affected Christian faith lay simply in the fact that a Gnostic could not believe in the incarnation. It was impossible for such a person to admit that the pre-existent Logos was made flesh. This provided a real test. If one, upon being asked, "Do you believe that Jesus Christ is come in the flesh?" answered in the affirmative, you could be sure he was motivated by the Spirit of God. If he denied or hedged, as the record says, "Every spirit that confesseth not that Jesus Christ is come in the flesh is not of God; and this is that spirit of antichrist" (1 John 4:1-3).

Specific Observations

Having given this meager outline of Gnostic philosophy we turn to consideration of the cult of Gnostics against whom John sought to protect the saints. Let us list some of the things about them which we can learn from John's writings.

(1). We know that these men pretended to have access to a source of knowledge which made them superior in wisdom to the average member of the body. It was their aim to make the Way intellectually acceptable to the philosophic schools by expressing their concepts of Christ is the language of Oriental mysticism. They belonged to an arrogant group of Philosophic aristocrats who claimed to have the ability to **go beyond** and penetrate the veil of true learning. The idea that Jesus had come in the flesh was spiritual pap for infantile mentalities, but could not be countenanced by the advanced reasoner. John declared that the true *gnōsis* was the apostolic testimony and the test of **knowledge** of God was willingness to receive that testimony. "We are of God; he that **knoweth** God heareth us: he that is not of God heareth not us. Hereby **know** we the spirit of truth and the spirit of error" (1 John 4:6).

(2). We know the Gnostics were respected and received by many and that they were numerous. They were regarded as possessing visionary insight and revelatory power because they were accepted as prophets. For this reason the apostle cautioned the saints to test the spirits "because many false prophets have gone out into the world" (1 John 4:1). John labels them antichrists, and says, "Even now there are many antichrists."

(3). We know these men were traveling from place to place as did many of the philosophers and teachers in the Greek world, and they no doubt depended upon the homes they contacted in each community to extend them hospitality. Any such home would then be used as a base for their efforts. It is significant that John says, "Many false prophets are **gone out into the world.**" The false prophets were doing what Jesus commissioned the apostles to do.

(4). We know that the Gnostics were separatists and schismatics and that they abandoned the body of saints to create a sect of their own. The unity of the body is based upon acknowledgoment of the great fact that Jesus is the Christ. When men no longer are willing to accept this foundation upon which the community of heaven was planted they become antichrists. "They went out from us, but they were not of us; for if they had been of us, they would no doubt have continued with us" (1 John 2:19). It is interesting that, in this context, John shows the one creed which can bind us together, repudiation of which will fragment us. "Who is a liar but he that denieth that Jesus is the Christ? He is antichrist that denieth the Father and the Son" (2:22). So long as one accepts fully the fact that Jesus is the Christ, the Son of God, he remains upon the foundation upon which Jesus said he would construct his community. When he forsakes that foundation he forsakes all that is Christian.

(5). We know that even though the Gnostics withdrew they still sought to influence those Christians who allowed what had been heard from the beginning to remain in them, and were continuing in the Son and in the Father (2:24). The false apostles were proselytizers. Under the guise of teaching advanced truth, they wormed themselves into any home which would receive them, and led those who dwelt there to deny that Jesus was the Christ. It was to warn against such teachers that John wrote, "These things have I written to you concerning them that seduce you" (2:26).

The reply of those who were solicited by these "advanced thinkers" was to be simply that they did not need any man to teach them, but having been anointed by the Holy Spirit they had access to all truth, and that truth was always consistent. The additional truth must be measured by what they had formerly been taught by the apostles. "But the anointing which ye have received of him abideth in you, and ye need not that any man teach you: but as the same anointing teacheth you all things, and is truth, and is no lie, and even as it hath taught you, ye shall abide in him" (3:27). Those who were taught by the Spirit would abide in Christ, that is, in what they had been taught by the anointing. The Gnostics "went beyond and abode not in the doctrine of Christ" (2 John 9).

All history bears out the truth that during the lifetime of John, and in the very area where he resided and wrote, this synthetic philosophy was presented with ruthless disregard for the unity of the congregations. False prophets insinuated themselves into every company of the saints and promulgated their unhallowed speculations. It became necessary to issue blunt warnings to the saints against extending a welcome to such teachers, or allowing their homes to be used as bases from which to launch war on the elemental fact of the incarnation. This brings us to an analysis of the short epistle known as Second John. It contains the passage with which we are concerned in this article, a passage which has been twisted so that it can be used to stifle thought and stamp out all honest dissent with the partisan status quo.

The Second Epistle

We shall not enter into the controversy as to identity of the addressee of this letter. It is my personal opinion that it was written to a Christian sister and her family. It is altogether possible, and appears even probable,   that the congregation of saints met in her home. It will be observed how John speaks of truth and love in the same connection. He does not regard truth as being composed merely of facts which have been verified. Truth is a relationship which transcends human relationships. John loves the elect lady and her children in the truth (verse 1). All others who have known the truth exhibit the same love. The truth dwells in God's children and is age-lasting (verse 2). The trinity of divine blessings – grace, mercy and peace – these are shared in truth and love (3). We walk in truth as required by God (4).

John approaches the primary purpose of his letter of admonition and warning with familiar language. Certain phrases are at once associated with certain writers. One of these phrases used by John is "a new commandment." Every such phrase should be considered in the light of its other appearances. That which John wrote to the elect lady will be correctly understood only in conjunction with what he wrote elsewhere upon the same topic. We must never forget the gospel record and first epistle of John are **general.** They were written to meet a condition faced by the community of saints at large. The second epistle is **specific.** It deals with the same condition on a local basis and provides a specific approach to it. But the specific must always be understood in the light of the general. One is not qualified to diagnose and treat a specific cancer until he knows the nature of cancer in general.

(1). John filled his gospel record and first two epistles with a dissertation on love (*agapē*) but these were not written primarily to be treatises on love at all. They were produced to offset a dangerous philosophy which threatened dissolution of the community by destroying the foundation upon which it was built. Love is the antidote to such a condition because it cements and holds the hearts of the saints together in times of greatest stress. One who reads the writings of John about love will derive much pleasure from the observations of the apostle but he will never understand why John injected the teaching as he did until he remembers that love was a prescription for the body at a time when certain errors were becoming epidemic.

(2). John besought the elect lady to remember that he wrote no new commandment. He simply reminded her of the commandment heard from the beginning. He identifies that commandment – **that we love one another** (5). Only if we recall constantly the nature of this commandment which was had from the beginning can we ever understand John properly. In 1 John 2:7, the brethren are told that John will write no new commandment unto them, but an old commandment which they had from the beginning. They are told that the old commandment is **the word** which they heard from the beginning.

The word is not the new covenant scriptures. They did not have this from the beginning. The new covenant scriptures grew out of needs created by later circumstances. Philemon was a letter of commendation for a runaway slave, Onesimus, who was returning to his master. Philippians was a letter of thanks for assistance to Paul when he was in prison. First Corinthians was written to deal with a demoralizing state of affairs disclosed by the visiting family of Chloe, and to answer queries in a letter brought by Stephanas, Fortunatus and Achaicus. All this came later. The word which was heard from the beginning was "Love one another."

From the beginning Jesus said, "This is my commandment, that ye love one another, as I have loved you" (John 15:12). Again, "These things I command you, that ye love one another" (15:17). John wrote to the elect lady, "This is love, that ye walk after his commandments" (2 John 6). Those who regard the Way as being a legalistic system lay great stress upon this, but they fail to grasp the significance of the following statement "This is his commandment, that, as ye have heard from the beginning, ye should walk in it." The previous verse tells us that what we heard from the beginning was to love one another. This is the commandment of Christ. What John is here saying is, "This is love, that we walk after his commandments, and his commandment is that we love one another, and walk in love." But why does John use "commandments" (plural) and "commandment" (singular) in the same sense? The answer is found in Romans 13:9 where we are told that all the commandments are summed up in one word, "Thou shalt love thy neighbor as thyself." This lifts the commandments of Christ above the level of law to the plane of love. This is the word we had from the beginning.

(3). The reason for the admonition to the lady and her children to walk in love is that, "Many deceivers are entered into the world, who confess not that Jesus Christ is come in the flesh. This is a deceiver and an antichrist" (7). Here John pointedly identifies the kind of traveling false teachers against whom he warns the recipients of this epistle. This letter was written to counter the efforts of the Gnostics. "The many deceivers who have entered into the world" are "the many false prophets who are gone into the world" (1 John 4:1). The deceivers of whom he now writes are the seducers of whom he has written. "These things have I written unto you concerning them that seduce you" (1 John 2:26). The things written identify the personages as anti-christs (1 John 2:18). This first century apostolic letter was a pertinent and poignant warning against those who deny the teaching that Jesus was the incarnate Son of God.

The Fundamental Doctrine

(4). The elect lady and her children are cautioned, "Look to yourselves, that you may not lose what you (or we) have worked for, but may win a full reward" (verse 8). The purpose of the apostolic message was to build men in love, or the Christhood of Jesus, so that the eternal life they possessed by having the Son might eventually terminate in fullness of joy in His presence. Those who face up to the fact of His divine Sonship in the flesh will be rewarded with fellowship face to face in the future. If we abide in Him here we will abide in His presence over there. But if antichrists seduce us to forfeit our faith in the greatest fact in the universe we will lose all. So fundamental is this fact of faith that rejection of it is the elemental falsehood of this age. "Who is a liar but he that denieth that Jesus is the Christ?" (1 John 2:22). There is one foundation of salvation and one foundation of damnation. Both are directly con-cerned with the same fact. "He that believeth ... shall be saved; he that believeth not shall be damned." (I trust that no carping critic will conclude that I have intentionally devalued baptism in making this point.)

(5). "Whosoever transgresseth and abideth not in the doctrine of Christ, hath not God. He that abideth in the doctrine of Christ, he hath both the Father and the Son."

To whom does the apostle relate the expression, "Whosoever transgresseth and abideth not in the doctrine of Christ?" What is "the doctrine of Christ?" In order to have a better perspective let us notice some of the other translations.

> "Anyone who goes ahead and does not abide in the doctrine of Christ does not have God" (Revised Standard Version).

> "No one who has God goes too far and fails to stay by the teaching of Christ" (Charles B. Williams).

> "Whoever goes beyond, and does not remain within Christ's teaching, will not possess God" (Authentic Version).

> "Anyone who runs ahead too far, and does not stand by the doctrine of Christ, is without God" (New English Version).

> "Anyone who is 'advanced' and will not remain by the doctrine of Christ, does not possess God" (Moffatt).

> "The man who is so 'advanced' that he is not content with what Christ taught, has in fact no God" (J. B. Phillips).

It will be noted that these substitute for "transgresseth" (King James Version) such expressions as: goes ahead, goes too far, goes beyond, runs ahead too far, and advanced. Both Moffatt and Phillips indicate by a usage of quotation marks that the term "advanced" is used in a special sense. Those who are under consideration are not really advanced thinkers; they just flatter themselves that they are. These later versions are more nearly correct than the King James Version. The word "transgress" is a translation of *parabainō,* and it is true that this is found in a few manuscripts. But all of the rest have *proagōn,* which means to go ahead, to advance beyond.

This was the very claim of the Gnostics. They looked with disdain and contempt upon "the common herd" who thought of Jesus as being the Word (Logos) made flesh. They regarded him as an incorporeal emanation from the Creator who led them into advanced thought which made them "the knowing ones." In their intellectual arrogance they had advanced to the place where they could see that Jesus was not the Christ. Jesus was human. The Christ was spirit. These two were not the same. They did not deny that Jesus existed. They did not deny that the Christ existed. They did not deny that for a period the two had been invested in the same person. But they did deny that Jesus was the Christ or that the Christ was Jesus. Jesus was not the Word (Logos) and had no prior existence to the incarnation, as they viewed it. Therefore there was no incarnation; Jesus Christ did not **come** in the flesh.

The apostolic declaration was that Jesus Christ had come in the flesh. This was basic, elemental and fundamental. The spirit which confessed this was of God; the spirit that did not confess it was not of God, but was antichrist. This was the test proposed by which to "try the spirits whether they are of God" (1 John 4:1-3). This was the foundation. One who was on that foundation might be mistaken about many things and all of them were, but there could be no mistake about the foundation. It is noteworthy that one was built upon this foundation by a positive action — confession that Jesus Christ is come in the flesh (1 John 4:2).   The opposite is not denial, which is also a positive action, but simply "not confessing."   "Every spirit that confesseth not that Jesus is come in the flesh is not of God."   This eliminates not only positive denial, but also neutrality.   One cannot occupy a neutral position as to the identity of Christ and be built upon the foundation.   The foundational fact must be confessed – **as a fact!**   One cannot be either a gnostic or an agnostic.

(6). We can determine what the "doctrine of Christ" is in this sense by the effect of "going beyond" or "abiding in it."   One who **advances** has not God; one who "abides in it" has both the Father and the Son.   The doctrine of Christ, in this case, does not consist of **the things** Jesus taught, but of **the thing** taught about Jesus.   The ethical and moral values of Jesus are very important.   Nothing we say here must be understood as minimizing their value.   One must "keep the commandments of Jesus" (John 15:10), and if he loves Jesus he will keep them, naturally, automatically and spontaneously, for this is the only possible reaction of love.   Only one who does not love Jesus will not keep His sayings (John 14:24).   Yet we must all, without exception, place some qualification upon living up to the requirements of Jesus.   "As far as we are able," "to the extent we understand them," "as we learn what he wishes," – these are all our own qualifications and limitations to explain how we can have God, and how He can have us, while we fail to live up to His perfect example.   We often transgress and often disobey.   If we did not the Father would not need to administer chastisement.   Yet we are told that all of us are partakers of such chastisement, and without this we would but demonstrate that we are bastards, and not sons.

But "the doctrine of Christ" about which John wrote cannot be qualified.   It cannot be governed by mitigating circumstances.   One who does not abide in it has not God.   It is just that plain.   It is just that positive.   What is the doctrine one absolutely must have in order to have God?   Whatever it is, it was possessed by all who had God while the apostles were still alive.   It was possessed by "the lady and her children" and by "all others who are in the truth."   It could not have been a copy of the new covenant scriptures, for no person on earth possessed that, not even the apostle John.   It could not have included the Second Epistle of John for those to whom it was written were already "walking in truth" before John wrote it.   This epistle could not have been a part of "the doctrine of Christ" under consideration, for there were those who had already gone beyond that doctrine when this epistle was written.

Fortunately John identifies the doctrine essential to having the Father and the Son.   "Who is a liar but he who denies that Jesus is the Christ ... No one who denies the Son has the Father.   He who confesses the Son has the Father also" (1 John 2:23).   **Jesus is the Christ!**   This is the foundation of the community of saints, the colony of heaven on earth.   **Jesus is the Christ!**   This is the only confession we may scripturally require of any penitent seeking admission to the fellowship of the redeemed.   **Jesus is the Christ!**   Every spirit which confesses this is of God.   **Jesus is the Christ!**   This is the only creed essential to overcoming the world. **Jesus is the Christ!**   The one who believes this has the witness in himself.

But what of the advanced thinker who denies this great fact, and who poses his syncretism as special knowledge for the initiated?   How was the Gnostic teacher to be treated?   How was one who did not abide in this doctrine to be regarded by those who did abide in it?

(7). "If there come any unto you, and bring not this doctrine, receive him not into your house, neither bid him God speed; for he that biddeth him God speed is partaker of his evil deeds" (10,11).

> "Do not receive him into the house or give him any greeting, for he who greets him shares his wicked work" (Revised Standard Version).

> "If any one who comes to you does not bring this teaching, do not receive him under your roof nor greet him; for he who greets him is a sharer of his evil deeds" (Weymouth).

> "If anyone comes to you and does not bring this doctrine, do not welcome him into your house or give him a greeting; for anyone who gives him a greeting is an accomplice in his wicked deeds" (New English Version).

> "If anyone comes to you and does not bring this teaching, do not receive him into your homes, do not even bid him welcome; for he who bids him welcome shares in his evil deeds" (Authentic Version).

In the face of what has already been said I would not presume upon the intelligence of the reader to further identify "the doctrine." Only those who ignore background, setting, contemporary issues and context, could ever mistake it. The application to other matters could only be made by those with a party axe to grind – those who would fasten upon the phrase "receive him not," to deny their relationship with the very brethren whom Jesus taught us to love. The warping and wresting of this scripture by factional defenders should serve as a warning to us of what happens to those whose hearts are filled with the acid of the party spirit and who search the scriptures for a means to separate and segregate themselves from other brethren in the Lord.

I have already once quoted at length from the pen of Frederic W. Farrar in his book "The Early Days of Christianity." When he produced this noteworthy volume in 1882, he was Canon of Westminster and Chaplain in Ordinary to the queen of England. Perhaps I should be reluctant to burden you with further material from his book, but that volume contains almost a whole chapter dealing with the matter we are now considering. I must omit most of it, as difficult as I find it to do so, and quote for you from his closing paragraphs.

> I know nothing so profoundly irreligious as the narrow intolerance of an ignorant dogmatism. Had there been anything in this passage which sanctioned so odious a spirit, I could not have believed that it emanated from St. John. A good tree does not bring forth corrupt fruit. The sweet fountain of Christianity cannot send forth the salt and bitter water of fierceness and hate. The Apostle of love would have belied all that is best in his own teaching if he had consciously given an absolution, nay, an incentive, to furious intolerance. The last words of Christian revelation could never have meant that these words have been interpreted to mean – namely, "Hate, exclude, anathematize, persecute, treat as enemies and opponents to be crushed and

insulted, those who differ from you in religious opinions." Those who have pretended a Scriptural sanction for such Cain-like religionism have generally put their theories into practice against men who have been infinitely more in the right, and transcendently nearer God, than those who, in killing or injuring them, ignorantly thought that they were doing God service.

Meanwhile this incidental expression of St. John's brief letter will not lend itself to these gross perversions. What St. John **really says,** and **really means,** is something wholly different. False teachers were rife who ... robbed the nature of Christ of all which gave its efficacy to the Atonement, and its significance to the Incarnation. These teachers, like other Christian missionaries, traveled from city to city, and in the absence of public inns, were received into the houses of Christian converts. The Christian lady to whom John writes is warned that, if she offers her hospitality to these dangerous emissaries who were subverting the central truth of Christianity, she is expressing a public sanction of them; and by doing this and offering them her best wishes she is taking a direct share in the harm they do. This is common sense; nor is there anything uncharitable in it. No one is bound to help forward the dissemination of teaching what he regards as erroneous respecting the most essential doctrines of his own faith. Still less would it have been right to do this in the days when Christian communities were so small and weak. But to interpret this as it has in all ages been practically interpreted – to pervert it into a sort of command to exaggerate the minor variations between religious opinions, and to persecute those whose views differ from our own – to make our own opinions the exclusive test of heresy, and to say, with Cornelius a Lapide, that this verse reprobates 'all conversation, all intercourse, all dealings with heretics' – is to interpret Scripture by the glare of partisanship and spiritual self-satisfaction, not to read it under the light of holy love.

Alas! churchmen and theologians have found it a far more easy and agreeable matter to obey their distortion of this supposed command, and even to push its stringency to the very farthest limits, than to obey the command that we should love one another! From the Tree of delusive knowledge they pluck the poisonous and inflating fruits of pride and hatred, while they suffer the fruits of love and meekness to fall neglected from the Tree of Life. The popularity which these verses still enjoy, and the exaggerated misinterpretation still attached to them, are due to the fact that they are so acceptable to the arrogance and selfishness, the dishonesty and tyranny, the sloth and obstinacy, of that bitter spirit of religious discord which has been the disgrace of the Church and the scandal of the world.

Inconsistency of Orthodoxy

If I may be allowed the indulgence of using a specific example to illustrate the unwarranted application of this passage, let me state that I have heard the expression "this doctrine" applied to every item of controversy among the various factions denominating themselves "The Church of Christ." Depending upon the particular party whose champion quoted it, the expression has been related to individual cups in the observation of the Lord's Supper, to Bible classes, colleges, orphan homes, the premillennial viewpoint, instrumental music, missionary societies, and a diversified host of motley issues which have made "the robe of righteousness" a Joseph's coat which puts the rainbow spectrum to shame.

In every instance these partisan exponents have shown themselves to be utterly inconsistent. They have slashed themselves with one side of the knife which they have sharpened in eager anticipation of stabbing others. But their very inconsistency proves that each is better than his unwritten creed. These brethren dare not apply practically what they claim to believe. Take for example the preacher who quotes 2 John 10,11 in condemnation of one who cannot see that instrumental music as an aid in corporate worship is a sin. Does not the one who deplores the use of the instrument receive the other into his house – either the public meetinghouse or his private dwelling?

The fact is that all of the non-instrumental Church of Christ groups I know, not only receive into their houses those who disagree with them, but go to great lengths to try and get them into their houses. When they hold a meeting they spend money on radio and television programs, as well as newspaper advertising, all beamed at the very ones whom they condemn as "bringing not this doctrine." They go from door to door, greeting and saluting all and sundry, and when they find someone who does not agree with their position they **urge** him to come. They meet him at the door, welcome him warmly and give him a "chief seat in the synagogue."

If 2 John 10,11 applies to "a Christian Church preacher" as my factional brethren so childishly designate those who use instrumental music, I charge that to even allow him to enter the house (much less invite him to come) makes them "accomplices in his evil deeds." It is such absurd, ridiculous, and puerile reasoning which will keep thinking people from seeing the real force and beauty of a plea which began as "a project to unite the Christians in all of the sects." The very essence of sectarianism is exclusiveness, and if anyone is more exclusive than those who twist this scripture to justify their own sectarian prejudices, I have yet to meet him. Our brethren should be ashamed to live and afraid to die!

Every party among us, even the most reactionary, will greet any person who attends their meetings – after they get over their surprise. Because of a traditional posture they would not call upon him to pray to the Father who is in all, over all and through all, but the ushers will go halfway across the house to provide him with a songbook already turned to the right page, so he can praise God with the congregation. He cannot pray out loud by himself, but he can pray as loud as he wants with others, if the prayer is set to a tune. I am thankful that literally hundreds of brethren are becoming embarrassed by the imbecility and senselessness of the preposterous position in which they find themselves. The party spirit has driven them so far down a blind alley that at least some are trying to scale the fence at the other end and escape back to Main Street again. This is good and I intend to give them a hand when I can.

I propose to regard all of God's children as my brothers. I intend to treat them as brothers. I have resolved to make nothing a test of fellowship which God has not made a condition of salvation. I shall accuse no one of being an antichrist who is built upon the one foundation simply because he differs with me about such things as instrumental music or the millennium. I will not allow our divergent views upon such matters to keep me from associating with any of my brothers, or helping all of them.

I shall go visit any group to share what I have learned, and to share in what they have learned. I shall go with none of them in partisan alliance, for my allegiance is to Jesus Christ. I am joined to Him and through Him to all others who are joined unto Him. Never again will I be a champion of any party, faction or clique. I refuse to be affiliated with any clan in which my love for **these** precludes my love for **those.** He is my all!

Under no circumstances will I apply to those who believe that Jesus is the Christ, those passages written to condemn those who do not confess this fact. My brethren are not Gnostics. They have not gone out from us even though we differ about many issues which disturbed our tranquility. When brethren come to where I am speaking, I shall not seek to determine where they stand on all of the troublesome issues before I call upon them to pray. These are matters between them and our Lord. If they can explain their position to His satisfaction, they need not try to satisfy me with their explanation. I am not so much interested in where they stand as in the direction they are facing. I shall recognize their right to pray because they are in Him and not because they are in some party. I have no party and no party has me! This last is more important than the first. I know a lot of brethren who claim to have no faction, but a faction has a claim upon them. They stand in jeopardy every hour!

Upon the one foundation living stones are builded together. These stones are not all the same size, shape, texture, or variety. A stone house must be built with the stones available in the area. Since stones vary from one area to another, a house in one location may not look like that in another. The house of God is not made of stones that are uniform in knowledge, perception, ability, or aptitude. It is composed of those who are joined together by mutual faith in Jesus and cemented by love. The foundation for all is the eternal abiding principle in confessional form, that "Jesus is the Christ, the Son of God." What a majestic truth! What a glorious fact! "If any man come and bring not this doctrine receive him not into your house, and give him no greeting!"

3 JOHN

INTRODUCTORY STUDIES

HISTORICAL ALLUSIONS

Verse 1 – This letter is signed "the elder" in the same way 2 John was.

Who could write "the elder" and expect his readers to know who was writing? The same person who authored 2 John, namely, John the apostle.[1]

Verse 1 – The letter is addressed to a man with a rather common 1st century name (transliterated both as Gaius and Caius).

Should this Gaius be identified with any other person of the same name found in the New Testament writings?

Several persons of this name are mentioned in the New Testament, such as Gaius of Macedonia (Acts 19:29); Gaius of Derbe (Acts 20:4); and Gaius of Corinth (1 Corinthians 1:14; Romans 16:23).

Verse 1 – "Whom I love in truth." The "elder" loves Gaius because he has a firm embrace of gospel truth, because he is a Christian. See also verse 3 where the "elder" affirms that Gaius is "walking in truth."

Verse 2 is a prayer that Gaius may prosper – both financially and physically, just as his soul prospers.

Why might such prosperity be needed? Would such prosperity enable Gaius to continue to be a generous supporter to itinerant Christian missionaries?

Verse 3 – "Brethren came and bore witness to your truth"

Brethren "keep coming;" the Greek verb pictures continuous action. On more than one occasion such reports have been given, and verse 6 indicates the report was given in the public assembly (i.e., in church).

The verse seems to say that traveling missionaries who recently enjoyed Gaius' hospitality have come to the town where "the elder" lives and have reported to the church there, warmly praising Gaius for his open home and generous support.

---

[1] See Introductory Studies on 2 John for a detailed discussion concerning the identity of the author who identified himself simply as "the elder."

"*Your* truth" is emphatic, with a contrast implied. Is the contrast with Diotrephes who was not "walking in the truth"?

Verse 4 – "To hear of my children"

Are these spiritual children, converts, folk for whom the writer felt a keen responsibility?

Was Gaius one of "the elder's" converts? (If so, and the elder is John the apostle, the Gaius to whom this letter is addressed can hardly be Gaius of Corinth.)

Were all Christians the spiritual family and the spiritual responsibility of the last living apostle? (Apostles had a care or concern for all the churches, 2 Corinthians 11:28)

Verses 5-8 – Gaius is commended for extending hospitality and financial aid to traveling Christian missionaries, and is encouraged to continue to do so in the future.

"Strangers" tells us that Gaius extended hospitality to those Christians with whom he was not previously personally acquainted.

Verse 6 is the only place in all of John's writings where he uses the word "church," the public assembly of the brethren.

Verse 6 – "You will do well to send them on their way."

Is the "elder" anticipating Gaius will have future opportunities to extend hospitality and financial assistance so the missionaries will have the means to reach their next stopping place?

Verse 7 gives the reason why Christians need to support the missionaries. The Christian missionaries made it their practice to expect nothing in the way of financial support from the "gentiles" (i.e., the unconverted whom they were trying to evangelize). Why the Christian missionaries resolved to refrain from asking their potential converts for money is not stated.

Verse 8 affirms that Christians have an obligation to support Christian missionaries. It is a way to be vitally involved, to be fellow workers, with the spread of the Gospel.

Verse 9 – "I wrote something to the church." What letter is referred to?

- Was it a letter of commendation? Have the brethren of verse 3 gone on a missionary journey from the "elder" with a letter of commendation to the churches (verse 9)? Had they been rejected by the church (at Corinth?) because of the influence of Diotrephes? Had they then been hospitably entertained by Gaius, and again returned to the "elder," reporting favorably concerning Gaius as verse 3 indicates? (Remember, verse 3 indicates they "keep coming," a continuous action. The reports have been made on more than one occasion.)

- Did the letter of commendation deal with hospitality, in particular to whom to, and to whom not to, extend Christian hospitality?

- Was it a letter we now have in our New Testament canon?

- Is the letter, written by John (if he is the "elder"), now lost?

Verse 9 – "Diotrephes"

This is the only place in New Testament this man's name appears. We know nothing more about him than what is here specified. He is evidently a person of influence in the congregation where he lived (verse 10).

"Loves to be first." – "The elder" tells us what Diotrephes' motivation was: he was power-hungry; he wanted to be church boss.

- Was he assuming authority to which he was not entitled by virtue of an office he held in the church?

- Was he abrogating rights which he did not have? Was he trying to take over the church?

- Was he a Christian believer? Or is it more likely that he was a Gnostic? (Remember the contrast implied in "your truth," verse 3).

"Does not accept what we say." (An alternate reading give "does not accept us".) "Does not accept" means "to close doors against."

- Perhaps it means Diotrephes does not receive hospitably Christian missionaries who stop in his town.

- If the "elder" is John the apostle, does this say that Diotrephes opposes John's apostolic authority? Does it say he refused to recognize John's apostolic right to direct the affairs of the church(es)? Should we be surprised to find that people rejected/shut out/opposed "apostles" of Christ?

- Does it say he opposes the gospel preachers who preach the same gospel that the "elder" did? (Who is the "us" whom Diotrephes refuses to accept?)

Verse 10 – "If I come" – Compare verse 14. The writer is expecting to soon make a visit to the town where Gaius lives and to the church where Diotrephes is trying to run things.

"I will call attention to his deeds." The "elder" is saying he would see to it that Diotrephes' arrogance and presumption would be properly dealt with in a congregational meeting.

"Accusing us with wicked words." Diotrephes has been bad-mouthing John and those missionaries who preached the gospel as the "elder" did. Diotrephes spoke against Christian preachers as he attempted to destroy the "elder's" influence in the church while, at the same time, most likely trying to convert the brethren to Gnosticism.

"Neither does he himself receive the brethren." The same word ("neither does he ... receive" = closes the doors against) is used here as was used in verse 9, "does not accept." He does not treat the missionaries as Christian missionaries should be treated. He refuses to extend hospitality to them. Note that "receive," "forbids," and "puts ... out" are all present tense verbs, which indicates the continued conduct of Diotrephes. Time and again he so acts.

"He forbids those who desire to do so." There were those in the church who would have been hospitable to the itinerant Christian teachers had it not been for the influence of this one man, Diotrephes. Like the Pharisees about whom we read in the Gospels (Luke 11:52), Diotrephes not only refused to walk in the right path himself, but he even tried to hinder those who were entering upon it.

"(He) puts them out of church." Who is intended by "them"?

- Does it refer to the traveling evangelists who had stopped looking for a place to stay?
- Does it refer to the members of the congregation who dared defy Diotrephes and extend hospitality to the missionaries?

"(He) puts them out of church." What does "put them out of the church" mean?

- Does it mean they are not welcome at the house church where Diotrephes was influential?
- Does it mean excommunicated? Can one man wield such power in the church?

Verse 11 – Gaius is urged to repudiate such an example in the words "do not imitate what is evil."

"Beloved" refers to Gaius, as it did in verses 1 and 5.

"Do not imitate."   The Greek seems to forbid the continuance of an action already going on.   Has Gaius begun to be swayed by Diotrephes bad influence?

> Were Gaius and Diotrephes members of the same congregation?   Several verses, like this one, seem to imply that this was so.   On the other hand, some verses make us wonder.

> An argument advanced that they were not members of the same congregation is this: Wouldn't Gaius know about the letter referred to in verse 9 if he and Diotrephes were members of the same congregation?   Perhaps, but not necessarily.   Diotrephes may have intercepted the letter from John before anyone else in town or the church knew of it.

"He that does evil" likely is a reference to Diotrephes.   He "has not seen God" at least says he is not a Christian.

Verse 12 – "Demetrius"

Who is "Demetrius"?

- Is he a member of the same congregation, a good example for Gaius to follow, rather than being influenced by Diotrephes' bad example?   Has he at some point opposed Diotrephes, just as Gaius is encouraged to do?

- Is he a Christian missionary, perhaps the bearer of this letter to Gaius, and is here commended to Gaius' hospitality?

- Is he the silversmith of Artemis (Acts 19:24), who was now preaching the faith which he once attempted to make havoc?

"Has received a good testimony from everyone."[2]

> Does this imply Demetrius is just being introduced to Gaius?   If they were from the same congregation, Gaius would already know about Demetrius' character.

---

[2] Clarence McCartney has a book of sermons entitled *Bible Epitaphs*. He calls attention to several one-line statements found in the Bible about various men, statements which sum up their lives. "He went away sorrowful" could have been the Rich Young Ruler's epitaph. "The disciple whom Jesus loved" could have been on John's tombstone. "He is not here: He is risen!" could have been carved on the tomb where Jesus lay. Though it is not one of McCartney's sermons, we would suggest that "He received a good testimony from everyone" would have been a delightful inscription to put on Demetrius' tombstone.

"And from the truth itself." How has "the truth" testified to Demetrius' good character?

- Is "the truth" a shortened form for "the Spirit of truth" (John 14:17, 15:26, 16:13; 1 John 5:7) who speaks in the apostles?

- Is "the truth" synonymous with the facts of the case? Demetrius' reputation was not founded on mere appearances, but on truth and reality.

"And we also bear witness." The "elder" himself, and perhaps the friends with him, (verse 14), adds personal testimony in vouching for Demetrius' character.

> Compare John 19:35, 21:24, where similar language was used by the writer of the Fourth Gospel. This similarity is one of the indications that 3 John and the Fourth Gospel are by the same author.

"And you know that our witness is true." In the better manuscripts, "you" is singular.[3] Gaius is the one who knows about the truthfulness of the writer's words.

Verses 13,14 – "I had many things to write" closely parallels 2 John 12,13. This is one of the key evidences that the two were written about the same time.

"Pen and ink" – "Pen" is *kalamos*, a reed pen rather than quill or stylus.

"I hope to see you shortly." "You" is again singular. John looks forward to seeing Gaius. Observe that in a similar promise of a coming visit made to the elect lady noted in 2 John 12, the "elder" did not say "shortly." If the same journey is in view, then 3 John is written at a later time than 2 John.

"The friends greet you." Some Christians, known to both the "elder" and to Gaius, are aware the "elder" is writing this letter. Their greeting is given, to contrast the hostility of Diotrephes.

"Greet the friends by name." In the town where Gaius lives are some Christian brethren who are friendly toward the "elder." They stand in marked contrast with Diotrephes. Gaius is to greet each of them individually. As he gives these greetings, will Gaius find encouragement to continue to extend hospitality to the Christian missionaries, in spite of the opposition he may get from Diotrephes and his comrades?

---

[3] Perhaps the plural "you" found in some later manuscripts grew out of the belief that the epistle was a circular letter, rather than a private letter.

Now, it is time to draw upon these brief historical allusions to see if they tell us who the author was, the person addressed, the purpose, the place and date of writing, and for what purpose the letter was written.

AUTHORSHIP AND ATTESTATION

External Evidence

The external evidence is not as extensive as that for many books included in our New Testaments. There are no allusions or quotations from 3 John till nearly a century after it was written.

The Eastern Church (Egypt, Syria, Palestine)

A. *The Alexandrian Church* is favorable to the apostolic authorship of 3 John.

Dionysius of Alexandria (AD 200-265), a disciple of Origen

He admitted 3 John as an authentic production of the apostle John, as appears from his use of 3 John in arguing against the Johannine authorship of Revelation. (*Ap.* Eus. H.E. VI.25)

"Nor yet in the second and third epistles ascribed to John, though they are but short epistles, is the name of John prefixed: for without any name he is called the elder." (*Ap.* Socrat. H.E. i.6)

Athanasius (AD 298-373)

In his *Synopsis of Sacred Scripture,* he received 3 John as canonical, which tends to imply acceptance of apostolic authorship.

Didymus (c.AD 309-394) also received 3 John as canonical.

B. *The Syrian Church*

What was written about the attitude of the Syrian church concerning the authorship of 2 John (see Introductory Studies on 2 John) could be written about 3 John. We do not know what books were included in the Old Syriac version since the extant manuscripts of this version contain only the Gospels.   At the time when the only Syriac version available was the Old Syriac, Ephraem, the Syrian (c.308-373) quotes 3 John 4, introducing it with "the Scripture says" (*Ad Imitat. Proverb.* vol.i, p.76).

Like 2 John, 3 John was not included in the Peshitta Syriac version.   At the time this revision was made, the Syrian church did not recognize these epistles as canonical, which they likely would have had they thought an apostle wrote the letters.

In AD 508 the Philoxenian Syriac version was made, and it did include 2 and 3 John, as well as some other books omitted in the older Peshitta.

As a result of this slight but mixed evidence, it is usually summarized by saying that the voice of the Syrian church, which for some time did not receive it as canonical, is unfavorable towards the apostolic authorship of 3 John.

C.   *The Palestinian Church*

Eusebius (AD 325)

> He placed 3 John in the *Antilegomena* (H.E. III.24,17,18)

> Eusebius himself seems to have accepted all the *antilegomena* as canonical, though he admits that some people in some places speak against those books so classified.   Speaking of the apostle John, he wrote "in his epistles, he either makes no mention of himself or calls himself only elder, nowhere apostle or evangelist."   (*Demonstratio Evangelica* III.5)

Cyril of Jerusalem (AD 349)

> Cyril accepted all the catholic epistles as belonging in the canon.   (*Catech. Lectures* iv.36.)

Jerome (AD 385)

> Jerome held that while 1 John was by the apostle John, 2 and 3 John were by "John the presbyter."   (*Vir. Illus.* IX[4])

---

[4] The question of "Two Johns at Ephesus" was discussed in the Introductory Studies for 1 John.

The Western Church (Italy, Gaul, North Africa)

The wording found in the Muratorian Canon (c.AD 170), which may or may not include a reference to 3 John, has been given on page 10 of the Introductory Studies on 2 John.

Other than this possible reference to 3 John, there is no statement either for or against the canonicity or apostolic authorship to be found in any of the Western Church Fathers.

Summarizing the external evidence: (1) There is considerable evidence for the acceptance of *two* Johannine Epistles, i.e., 1 and 2 John, before all three were generally recognized.[5] "The private character of the smaller Epistles, as well as their relative unimportance, are quite enough to account for the more gradual acceptance, even if they were written by the author of the First."[6] (2) After AD 300, 3 John was generally received as genuine. 3 John was recognized by the Council of Laodicea, the Council of Hippo, and the third Council of Carthage as canonical and therefore genuine.

Internal Evidence

The internal evidence for 3 John is of the same kind as the internal evidence for 2 John.[7] This tends to point to the same author for both letters.[8] The author designates himself as "the elder." As noted in Authorship studies for 2 John, this lack of a personal signature is in the style of John, who in only one of his letters signs his name. In early Christian literature (e.g. Papias), the title "the elder" seems to have been used for those who had personally witnessed the earthly ministry of Jesus and had been His followers. This fits the apostle John who, as the 1st century drew to a close, grew to be an elderly man in Ephesus.[9]

The key to the authorship decision lies in the Fourth Gospel. It is agreed by nearly everyone that the writer of the Fourth Gospel is the writer of 3 John. Just as there were

---

[5] See the quotation from Clement of Alexandria and footnote #18 in the study about "Authorship" in the Introductory Studies to 1 John.

[6] Brooke, *op. cit.*, p.lxxvi.

[7] "... [I]t must be pointed out that, if the Second Epistle did not exist, the claims of the Third to be apostolic would be more disputable" (Plummer, *op. cit.*, p.lxxiii).

[8] "... [I]t is impossible to separate these two letters, and assign them to different authors" (Plummer, *op. cit.,* p.lxxix).

[9] See documentation for this in "The Life of John" included in the Introductory Studies for 1 John.

expressions in 2 John which are very similar to the Fourth Gospel (see 2 John 6,9,12), so there are expressions in 3 John which are similar to the Fourth Gospel. "Is of God" and "seen God" (3 John 11) are examples. Just as a resemblance to the Fourth Gospel is found in 3 John, so are strong resemblances to 1 John, and this helps confirm the Johannine authorship of 3 John, since both the Fourth Gospel and 1 John are by the same author. 3 John 11 is one verse which fits Brooke's comment, "A knowledge of 1 John seems almost necessarily presupposed in some passages of the smaller epistles."[10]

For some, the conduct of Diotrephes is hardly explicable if the author of 3 John were an apostle. They characterize Diotrephes as a "prominent Christian presbyter," and believe such a person would not repudiate the authority of an apostle, or refuse to recognize traveling missionaries sent an apostle, or try to influence others to be negative toward an apostle. Therefore, in their view, it is very difficult to accept the idea that "the elder" is the apostle John. The flaw in this presentation is calling Diotrephes a "Christian." While he is involved in the life of a church, he is also Gnostically inclined rather than being inclined toward "the truth." We would expect Gnostics to repudiate the apostles and their message that goes back to the beginning. Furthermore, even while the apostles were still living, reverence for apostolic authority was not universal. This is especially true for unbelievers. Believers sometimes chaffed at apostolic authority (cp. 2 Corinthians) while unbelievers tended even more so to repudiate their authority and teaching (cp. the Judaizers of Acts 15/Galatians 2). 3 John seems to imply that Diotrephes is not a true believer.

Conclusions concerning authorship

In spite of the century-long rejection by the Syrian Church, we see no reason to doubt the other rather uniform testimony from the Eastern and Western church that 3 John was written by the apostle John.

The manner in which the "elder" addresses Gaius harmonizes well with apostolic authority. It is as we would expect if the apostle John is the author, just as early writers identified him to be. There must have been convincing reasons for the folk who collected the books to attach the title "3 John" to this letter.

It must be acknowledged that neither the internal nor external evidence for 3 John is as strong as that for 2 John. It is neither quoted nor mentioned as early or as frequently as 2 John. Nor does 3 John have as many resemblances to the Fourth Gospel and 1 John as does 2 John. However, although the evidence is not as strong for 3 John as it is for 2 John, still it is strong enough that when spurious books were being rejected and refused inclusion in the canon, 3 John won its way in.[11]

---

[10] Brooke, *op. cit.*, p.lxxv.

[11] It must not be forgotten that when decisions were being made about canonical status in the 3rd and 4th centuries, it was not the first time the books were accepted as canonical. Books addressed to churches were first accepted or rejected the moment they were received by the addressees. The decisions of the later councils were simply guarding and re-affirming what the churches had already decided.

3 John is the shortest epistle in the New Testament, shorter in Greek than 2 John by 1 line.[12]   3 John is also personal in nature, being private correspondence addressed to an individual rather than being addressed to a church.   These likely contributed much to 3 John's lack of use in the churches, the absence of allusions or quotations in early Christian literature, and to its apparent slow acceptance into the canon.

DESTINATION

This epistle is addressed to Gaius.   We must assume that a more precise identification of the recipient was given to the messenger who carried the letter.   But we are at a loss to know what town, or which Gaius, was addressed.   Gaius, which is the same as the Latin Caius, was a common name in the 1st century, one of the most common names in the empire.   It was so common that in Roman law books "Caius" was similar to our "John Doe" or "John Q. Citizen."   The Gaius to whom 3 John is addressed was a Christian contemporary of John ("the elder"), for John says of him "whom I love in truth," and John planned to make a personal visit to Gaius in the very near future after this letter was delivered to him (verse 14).   This Gaius was a Christian who was well known for the hospitality he extended to Christians, whether friends or strangers (verses 5ff).

Three persons named Gaius are mentioned in the New Testament.   (1) Gaius of Macedonia (Acts 19:29).[13]   This man, mentioned together with Aristarchus as being a traveling companion of Paul, spent some time with Paul at Ephesus where he was seized by the mob incited by Demetrius, the silversmith.   The date for that riot at Ephesus is about AD 57.   We have no information about what happened to this Gaius after the riot. Perhaps he was still alive and "walking in the truth" a quarter of a century later, and somehow has become a friend of the apostle John during that time.   (2) Gaius of Derbe (Acts 20:4).[14]   When we first meet this Gaius, he, too, was a traveling companion of Paul, one of the messengers of the churches who was helping take an offering to the poor at Jerusalem, about AD 58.   We have no information about this man's later life after his brief introduction in connection with the offering for Jerusalem.   Of course, it is in the realm of possibility that this man has settled in some community besides Derbe, has made his home a welcome stopping place for Christians, with John, perhaps, even being welcomed into his home.   Such hospitality would be just like what is implied of the Gaius to whom

---

[12] "Counting the letters, and allowing 36 letters for the ancient line, gives for 2 John 32 lines, and for 3 John not quite 31 lines" (T. Zahn, *Introduction to the New Testament* [Chicago: Kregel, 1953], V.3, p. 382.   "The length of 2 and 3 John may have been determined in each instance by the amount of material which could be placed on a single sheet of papyrus."   (J. W. Roberts, "The Letters of John," in *The Living Word Commentary* [Waco, TX: Sweet, 1968],   p.170)

[13] This is probably not the Gaius named "Gaius of Corinth", for the designation of Macedonia as being his place of origin seems different from the one who lived in Corinth.

[14] This Gaius is clearly distinguished from the Macedonian Gaius by the epithet *Derbaios*, "of Derbe."

3 John is addressed.[15]   According to the 4th century so-called *Apostolical Constitutions* (VII.46.9), it was Gaius of Derbe to whom 3 John was sent, after John appointed him the first bishop of Pergamum.[16]   (3) Gaius of Corinth (1 Corinthians 1:14, Romans 16:23). The Gaius of Corinth named in 1 Corinthians 1:14 ("Crispus and Gaius"), whom Paul baptized, is probably to be identified with the one named in Romans 16:23.   In Romans 16:23, Paul mentions a Gaius who lived at Corinth, whom he calls his "host" and "host of the whole church."[17]

There would seem to be something to say for the opinion of those who identify the Gaius of 3 John with the Corinthian Gaius, though we must keep in mind that it is not at all certain that any such identification should be made.   (1) The trait of character indicated (3 John 5-8, hospitality) is, as far as it goes, exactly the same generous character indicated in Romans 16:23.   The house of Gaius the Corinthian was a place of worship, and a center of hospitality for missionaries.   (2) John mentions certain troubles which disturbed the church where Gaius worshiped or ministered.[18]   Diotrephes has arisen in unholy rebellion against the authority of an apostle.   He had tried to cut off from the Church's fellowship those whose only offence was that they did not do as he wanted them to do and would not yield to his high-handed methods of lording it over the church.   So, because of Diotrephes, the church was troubled and disturbed and divided.   This fits with what we know of Corinth.   There certainly were people in Corinth who were not averse to opposing apostles.   See 1 Corinthians (1:12ff, 4:5ff, 9:1ff, 14:37) and 2 Corinthians (2:1-9, 3:1ff, 5:11ff, 7:2, and chapters 10-13), where Paul's authority was ignored and scorned by some at Corinth.   As we shall see below, 3 John was most probably written toward the close of the 1st century.   It was toward the close of the 1st century (AD 96) that Clement of Rome wrote his epistle to the Corinthians.   The painful picture drawn by Clement of the feuds in the Corinthian Church might match with the expressions of 3 John 9,10. Perhaps 3 John pictures continuing opposition from such as Diotrephes.[19]   (3) Athanasias

---

[15] Davidson feels that if any of the men named Gaius in the New Testament is to be identified with the Gaius of 3 John, it would be Gaius of Derbe.

[16] Stott, *op. cit.*, p.217.   Did apostles appoint "bishops"?   The document is late and there is no earlier support for the statement it contains.

[17] Origen (*Comm. in Ro.* 10:41) says that Gaius of Corinth eventually became bishop of Thessalonica. (Cited by Plummer, *op. cit.*, p.lxxx)

[18] Whether Gaius was an elder, or whether he held any position in the church, we do not know for certain.   Certainly no such conclusion can be inferred from 3 John 8.

[19] Restoration Movement proponents are sometimes chided that it is not possible to find a perfect church in the Scriptures to restore.   It has been asked, "Which one would you restore?   The one at Corinth?   The ones in Galatia?   The one at Antioch of Syria?"   It is true that an ideal primitive church, bright in the unbroken possession of truth and holiness, is difficult to identify.   For example, of the seven churches of Revelation, only two had no words of condemnation from the glorified Christ.   The other five had things that needed to be corrected.   Yet, from the pages of the New Testament, one can get a rather complete outline of how the Lord intended things to be in his church.   When one looks at the things that are commended, he gets some idea of how things should be in the church.   When one looks at the corrections given, one gets some idea of how things ought not to be in the church.   Just the opposite of

(AD 298-373) likely had use of materials to which we have no access. In his *Synopsis of Sacred Scripture*, Athanasias not only identifies the Gaius of 3 John with the Corinthian Gaius of whom Paul speaks, but connects him with John, with Ephesus, and with the publication of John's Gospel.

Appealing as this suggested identification of the Gaius of 3 John with the Gaius of Corinth might be, there are some important cautions that prevent us from making an unqualified statement about this identification. (1) Since "Gaius" was perhaps the most common of all names in the Roman Empire, and since we know so little about this person from the historical allusions in 3 John, perhaps it would be safer to resist any attempt to identify the Gaius addressed in this epistle. (2) The Gaius mentioned in 3 John is identified as one of John's "children" (verse 4). According to some, this seems to intimate that the Gaius to whom 3 John is addressed was converted by the apostle John.[20] That hardly fits Gaius of Corinth since according to 1 Corinthians 1:14 that Gaius was one of Paul's converts. (3) The idea that Gaius (addressed in 3 John) lived in Corinth, and that 2 John was sent to the same place (see 3 John 9), has been supposed by some to raise a problem about John's age and ability to travel. John does, in both 2 and 3 John, speak of visiting the readers. It is alleged that a trip from Ephesus to Corinth would have been a formidable journey for an old man. If John went by land, he must traverse the western end of Asia, go through Thrace, Macedonia, Thessaly, and down to Corinth in Achaia. That would be a long and difficult journey on foot. If he went by sea, it was a journey across the Aegean Sea, through the Cyclades Islands. While always a dangerous voyage, this was a voyage regularly made. A round trip from Ephesus to Corinth could be accomplished in a week, and so was not beyond the stamina of an older man.[21] Just like these letters promise the readers that such a journey was being planned by the writer, we could see John making a trip from Ephesus to Corinth by ship, even at an advanced age.

If we were to pick any of the men named Gaius in the New Testament as being the one to whom 3 John was sent, we would be inclined to choose Gaius of Corinth, and thus have this letter sent to Corinth. 3 John has less reason than 2 John to be styled "catholic" or "general," for beyond all reasonable doubt 3 John is addressed to an individual.[22]

---

what is condemned should prevail. Putting these together, we do have guidelines on how we can pattern our church after the model God intended for the church. There is validity to the ideal of restoration of the apostolic order of things.

[20] It may be more than we know to say that "my children" speaks of John's converts. John uses "children" for his readers in 1 John, and we doubt that all of them were his personal converts. Perhaps we should not push "my children" here to mean John has personally baptized Gaius.

[21] Clarke, *op. cit.*, p.491, thinks even the voyage by sea too long and dangerous for a man of John's advanced age to think of taking.

[22] Of course, just as we have proposed that the "chosen lady" of 2 John might see the letter was read to the congregation, perhaps there is some evidence that the elder may have had in his mind the congregation of which Gaius was a member (note 3 John 3-4, 8-9, and 14), anticipating that Gaius would see to it the church was aware of the contents of this letter from John.

PLACE AND DATE OF WRITING

There are no historical allusions in 3 John that would help us fix precisely either the place or the date of writing.   Therefore all is conjecture concerning the time and place of writing.

Place

We are told in early Christian literature that John spent most of his later years in and around Ephesus.   Suggesting that John may have written this letter from Ephesus would be as good a guess as any.

Date

Our conjecture for the dating of 3 John is based on the following: (1) We treat 2 John as being written after 1 John since various expressions in 2 John presume an acquaintance with 1 John.   (2) We believe that 3 John was written after 2 John.[23]   This belief is based on two suppositions.   (a) Both letters anticipate the same pending journey. (b) At 2 John 12, John writes, "I hope to come to you."   At 3 John 14 he writes, "I hope to see you *shortly*."   3 John implies the journey is closer to being a reality than when 2 John was written.   (3) In 3 John there is no intimation of persecution such as resulted in John's being exiled to Patmos about AD 96.   So it is a good guess to suppose 3 John was written before that persecution began.

Taking into account all these bits of information, the date we assign to the writing of 3 John is AD 85-90.

OCCASION AND PURPOSE OF WRITING

The intimations from 3 John as to the occasion and purpose are these.   It would seem that John was aware that certain Christians had been on a missionary-preaching tour, in the midst of which they came to the town where Gaius lived.   But when these missionaries arrived, Diotrephes – who loved to wield considerable power in the local church – had spoken against the apostle John, had refused to recognize the messengers of the gospel, and had made life miserable for those who opened their homes to Christian missionaries.   Diotrephes intended to "put ... out of the church" any members who should

---

[23] This belief is not based on the titles currently attached to these writings. The titles "Second John" and "Third John" were not on the original letters, but were added later as men began collecting the letters for use in the churches. As explained in a footnote in 2 John, the numbers "2" and "3" refer to length, not the chronological order in which they were written.

receive the messengers from John. In spite of this, Gaius welcomed them with the affection which became a true Christian, and when they were ready to depart, he helped them on their way. When these itinerant preachers arrived in the town where John was, they witnessed to the church there of the goodness of Gaius (verse 6). This proved to be the stimulus that prompted John to write this letter to Gaius.

John wrote this brief letter to commend Gaius for his hospitality, to urge him to show it again whenever occasion presented itself, and also to commend Demetrius to him. John further announces his intention of a personal visit to deal with the trouble-maker Diotrephes.[24]

CRITICAL MATTERS

Does 3 John 9 ("I wrote something to the church") allude to a letter now lost?

Only books deemed to have been Holy Spirit inspired (i.e., written by an apostle, or a close associate of an apostle) were included in the canon. The question arises about the possibility of whether there were some inspired books that were left out of the canon.

Is there the possibility that an inspired writing might have been lost? This commentator thinks we shall have to admit the possibility. We do know that some inspired but spoken words were not preserved. For example, very little of Jesus' ministry is preserved. And many of the sermons in Acts are condensed; we are given only bare outlines. There is no passage in the Bible that says that every inspired word was to be preserved; in fact, John 21:25 says many things in the ministry of Jesus have not been recorded. Only that was preserved which is necessary for our salvation.

So, admitting the possibility that some inspired writing *might* be lost, is there any evidence that such has happened?

(1) *From early Christian literature, are there any specified letters of apostles alluded to that we do not have?* It is striking that we do not have quotations of the apostles from sources unknown to us. When the early Christian writers quote the apostles, we can find the quoted words in the canonical writings that we have. For example, when Clement of Rome says that Paul said "such and such" in an epistle to Corinth, we can find that quotation in one of the letters we have. There are simply no quotations in early Christian writings from letters now supposedly lost.

---

[24] The above presentation of the occasion and purpose for 3 John is the traditional, conservative view. This conservative view has been all but abandoned by contemporary scholars, some of whose attempts at the reconstruction of the historical situation reflected in the letter will be outlined in the following section of these Introductory Studies.

(2) *Does the New Testament itself allude to any "lost inspired writings"?*

    (a) In Colossians 4:16, mention is made of "the epistle from Laodicea." Some say, "We have no letter named 'Laodiceans' in our Bibles. Here is evidence that an inspired writing has been lost." *Reply*: New Testament Introductory Studies indicate that we do very likely have in our New Testament canon the letter alluded to in Colossians 4:16. We have it under the name "Ephesians." Ephesians gives every appearance of being a circular letter that started in Laodicea and ended up in Ephesus.

    (b) 2 Peter 3:1 is alleged to be another reference in a New Testament book of an inspired letter that has now been lost. *Reply*: It is indeed a matter of study and personal conviction as to whether 2 Peter refers to a lost letter, or to the letter we know as 1 Peter. It is this commentator's contention that 1 Peter is the epistle referred to; and if this is true, there is no evidence of a lost letter at 2 Peter 3:1.

    (c) 1 Corinthians 5:9 is a passage regularly appealed to in order to prove that there are lost inspired writings by apostles. *Reply*: "I wrote in my epistle" may be either what is called a historical aorist (referring to a previous letter) or an epistolary aorist (referring to a previous portion of the very letter in which the verb appears). Even were we to admit that the reference is to a previous letter (which we doubt), it would not prove there are lost *inspired* writings. It would need to first be shown that the alleged previous letter was inspired. Remember, not every word and deed of an apostle was inspired.

    (d) 3 John 9 is quoted as evidence of lost inspired writings. *Reply*: 3 John 9 could well be a reference to the epistle we call 2 John. Or it might merely be a reference to a letter of commendation (i.e., a letter of introduction to a church) which was uninspired. In either case, it is far from being proof of a lost inspired writing.

We have been unable to discover any indisputable evidence, either in early Christian literature or in the New Testament itself, that any inspired writing has been lost. Whether or not a writing was inspired[25] was likely the dividing point as to whether or not the writings were collected and preserved. It is this commentator's conviction that God brought together His word, keeping it brief[26] but all-sufficient to make a man wise unto salvation.

Having found no evidence that any inspired writing was lost, we conclude that it is improbable that any inspired writing is lost. While admitting the possibility (but not the probability) of an inspired letter to an *individual* being lost, we doubt that any church would let an apostolic letter to the *church* just pass into oblivion. Paul wrote both to churches and to individuals. It is possible that we do not have all his letters to individuals. But

---

[25] It is not likely that the only letters John wrote to individuals during his 60+ years of ministry were one to a chosen lady and another to Gaius. But perhaps those two were the only *inspired* letters he wrote to individuals.

[26] Brevity means there is no redundant material, little overlap or repetition. There are cases where repetition is necessary, viz., the Gospel accounts. Yet even in the Gospels, new material is given in the parallel accounts.

the letters to churches are another matter. Would a church be so negligent as to lose the writings of an apostle? We find this hard to accept. In times of persecution, books of Scripture were sometimes destroyed. But always someone had a copy that was safely preserved from the destruction. Unless the autographed writing was destroyed before any copies could be made, it is difficult to envision inspired letters being lost. (If letters to individuals were not shared with the local church – and so read regularly in the public assembly – then they might have become lost to us.) Theoretically, it is possible that some letters were lost, but practically, it is highly improbable. If any has been lost, it has been by the choice of the Holy Spirit.

We conclude that there is little reason to think that some letters God originally intended to be in our New Testaments have been lost. In fact, when it is worded in this way, it tends to sway our thinking to the other side. We would word it that all the inspired letters God intended us to have in his written Word, He has seen to it that they have been preserved and transmitted down through the generations and centuries to this day.

Attempts at a reconstruction of the *Sitz-im-Leben* for 3 John.[27]

Any attempt to reconstruct the historical situation which is addressed in 3 John must take into account three basic details. First, who are the characters – the elder, Gaius, Diotrephes, and Demetrius – and what is their relationship to one another? Second, what has led to Diotrephes' negative behavior toward the elder? Third, how is 3 John related to either or both 1 John and 2 John? The letters all say something about hospitality, with 1 and 3 John encouraging it, while 2 John condemns it. Over the past century, a number of hypotheses, each conflicting with the others, have been presented as scholars have attempted to reconstruct the historical situation.

1. William Alexander[28]

His view, which can be called the traditional view, included these explanations of the basic details: (a) The elder who writes this letter is the apostle John, the same one who wrote the Fourth Gospel. (b) Gaius, to whom the letter is addressed, is Gaius of Corinth,[29] who on an earlier occasion extended hospitality to Paul (Romans16:23) when he

---

[27] In the Introductory Studies to 1 John we have already called attention to Raymond Brown's attempt at reconstructing the social and theological history of the hypothetical Johannine community. In the following presentation we are following the lead of Robert M. Price (The *Sitz-im-Leben* of Third John: A New Reconstruction in *Evangelical Quarterly* 61:2 [1989] p.109-119) who surveys five major attempts at reconstructing the historical situation reflected in John's epistles before he offers his own reconstruction.

[28] "The Epistles of John" in *An Exposition of the Bible* (Hartford, CT: S.S. Scranton, 1910), p.825ff.

[29] Not all traditional scholars made this identification. Plummer for example hesitated to identify the Gaius of 3 John with any of the men named Gaius found elsewhere in the New Testament. J.A. Bengel (*Gnomon of the New Testament* [Edinburgh: T&T Clark, 1860], Vol. 5, p.159), commented, "Caius of Corinth, who is mentioned Rom. xvi.23, either closely resembled this Caius, the friend of John, in his hospi-

was in that city. Two key points led Alexander to this conclusion: (i) 3 John 5 and Romans 16:23 both take note of Gaius and his hospitality; (ii) the statement found in the *Synopsis of Sacred Scripture* written by Athanasius, which links the apostle John to Paul's host Gaius, and makes this Gaius the publisher of the Fourth Gospel. (c) Diotrephes' exclusion of the itinerant missionaries, whose message is in harmony with the elder's, is a strategy to consolidate his control of the church in Corinth. (d) Finally, Demetrius is perhaps the Ephesian silversmith of Acts 19, who Alexander conjectures was converted and became a close associate of John in Ephesus. He is now a missionary who is being commended to Gaius.

Opponents of Alexander's view set forth these arguments: (a) They vigorously question the identification of "the elder" with the apostle John. (b) The name "Gaius" was so common in the ancient world that it would be the greatest coincidence were 3 John's Gaius and Paul's Gaius the same person. (c) The characterization of Diotrephes as an ambitious church politician (and thus the bad guy) is also disputed.

2. Adolf Harnack[30]

Harnack's explanation of the basic details include: (a) A denial that the elder who writes this letter is the apostle John. (b) Diotrephes is identified as "the first monarchical bishop we know," a precursor to Ignatius of Antioch. (c) Having posited the idea that Diotrephes was a bishop over an area, the elder must be identified as a local church officer who should have been subordinate to the bishop. However, the elder apparently defied the bishop's authority by taking it upon himself to send out a group of itinerant missionaries. (d) In Harnack's view, the decision of Diotrephes not to accept John and at the same time to ban these missionaries must be understood as being a part of the spirit of the age – for at the close of the 1st century and the beginning of the 2nd, there was a wide-spread tendency by the ecclesiastical establishment to quench the Spirit of prophecy.

Opponents of Harnack's view raise these issues: (a) Harnack offers no satisfactory motive to explain the action of Diotrephes. They question both the implied motives in Harnack's reconstruction (namely, a church polity that would elevate a man to be a monarchical bishop) and the idea that Diotrephes simply reflects the spirit of the times.[31]

---

tality, or he is the same person: if he were the same person, he either migrated from Achaia into Asia, or John sent this letter to Corinth." J. Chapman, "The Historical Setting of the 2 and 3 Epistles of St. John," *Journal of Theol. Studies*, 1904, p.357ff, identifies Gaius of 3 John with Gaius of Corinth.

[30] "Uber den dritten Johannesbrief," *Texte und Untersuchungen zur Geschichte der altchristlichen Literatur* 15:#3b [Leipzig, 1897], p.3-27.

[31] Raymond Brown (*The Community of the Beloved Disciple* [NY: Paulist Press, 1979], p.160-161) tried to supply the allegedly missing motive. Rival missionaries were calling on churches and teaching radically different doctrines. Diotrephes found himself without adequate criteria to tell the wolves from the sheep, so he closed the door of his church to both. Brown's reconstruction supplies the specific motive lacking in Harnack's theory, but it has a weakness of its own. 3 John 10 seems to make it clear that Diotrephes' actions stemmed from some animosity toward the elder, not simply panic at a confusing situation. Rather than banishing all missionaries, it seems Diotrephes wanted to hear no more from the elder or his representatives.

(b) In the Harnack reconstruction, there was no allusion to any relationship between 3 John and the other two epistles.   In other words, Harnack's model does not account for all the phenomena, and is therefore to be faulted.

3. Walter Bauer[32]

Bauer's attempt to fit the basic details into a pattern include these explanations: (a) The motive behind the elder's warning against Diotrephes stems from the fact that Diotrephes is a heretic who holds the very views condemned by the elder in 1 and 2 John. (b) The elder expelled and debarred those who embraced the heretical doctrine in 1 John 4:3 and 2 John 7, so now Diotrephes has simply returned the favor, slamming the door in the faces of the missionaries who taught the same message as did the elder.   (c) On the instructions about extending hospitality (3 John 5-8) and withholding hospitality (2 John 10,11), the letters merely reflect the two sides of the conflict between orthodoxy and Gnosticism.   Christians are to be welcomed; heretics are not.

Opponents of Bauer's reconstruction raise these issues: (a) If the elder's complaint against Diotrephes were heresy, surely he would not have neglected to mention it in 3 John.[33]   (b) It is a flaw in Bauer's reconstruction that he must assume that Gaius has read 1 and 2 John, for Bauer uses them as a key to interpreting what "truth" means in 3 John.[34]

4. Ernst Kasemann[35]

Kasemann's explanation of the basic details include: (a) The elder who wrote the letter is "a simple presbyter of the third Christian generation" (p.311), who should have been submissive to the district bishop, as elders were expected to be in the 2nd century AD.

---

[32] *Orthodoxy and Heresy in Earliest Christianity* (Philadelphia: Fortress Press, 1971).

[33] It seems to this commentator that Bauer anticipated this objection.   He wrote, "To be sure, 3 John does not contain an explicit warning against false teachers.   Nevertheless, its close connection with 2 John is a sufficient indication of its thrust.   And the assurance repeated no less than five times in this brief writing that the brethren who support the elder possess the 'truth' – that entity which in 2 John and also in 1 John distinguishes the orthodox believer from the heretic – renders it very unlikely, to my way of thinking, that we are dealing merely with personal frictions between the elder and Diotrephes" (*op. cit.*, p.93.) Scholars who have objected to Bauer's view that the issue was heresy often propose the idea that the antipathy was simply personal friction.   Can any better case be made for the view that the elder's trouble with Diotrephes is a "personal friction," or a clash of personalities, rather than a heresy?

[34] How is it possible to suppose that "truth" means one thing in 1 and 2 John, and something else in 3 John?   We should be very slow to adopt a view that 1 and 2 John cannot be a key to understanding what "truth" is in 3 John.

[35] "Ketzer und Zeuge: Zim johanneischen Verfasser-problem," *Zeitschrift fur Theologie und Kirche*, 48 [1951], p.292-311)

(b) Kasemann made Diotrephes the hero of the story and the writer of the letter the heretic. In Kasemann's view (as in Harnack's), Diotrephes is an early example of a monarchical bishop, and he based this hypothesis mainly on the ground that Diotrephes had the power to excommunicate (so Kasemann understands verse 10).   (c) The elder had been serving in Diotrephes' diocese but has been excommunicated by Diotrephes because of his Gnosticising (naive docetic) treatment of Jesus Christ.[36]   (d) The elder writes the letter known to us as 3 John, therefore, to justify his actions and to re-establish himself before the church from which he has been excommunicated (so Kasemann infers from verse 10).

Opponents of Kasemann's reconstruction[37] raise these issues: (a) Any idea of apostolic authorship for 3 John must be abandoned if Kasemann's theory is correct.[38]   3 John's right to be included in the canon as "Scripture" is greatly diminished, if not altogether abandoned.   (b) Wilhelm Michaelis (*Einleitung in das Neue Testament* [Berne: Berchtold Holden Verlat, 1961], p.299) insisted Diotrephes' power as pictured in verse 10 is not that of excommunication, but is a refusal to grant hospitality.   (c) Is there any mention of the excommunication of the elder?   If this had really happened, the author would hardly have restricted himself to accusing Diotrephes merely of speaking slanderously of him.   And how would he have been able to anticipate the possibility of confronting Diotrephes when he came on a visit?[39]   (d) Elders in local churches exercised authority only in the local church.   "*The* elder" shows the writer did not picture himself as one of a plurality of local elders.   The "elder" who wrote 2 and 3 John claims an authority that extends to congregations in places other than where he lives.   This indicates the title "the elder" cannot be intended in the sense of an office-bearer in a local church.

5.   *John C. Meagher*[40]

Meagher's reconstruction treats the basic details in this fashion: (a) The crucial clue to any reconstruction of the historical circumstances is to be found in the commands about

---

[36] According to Kasemann (*The Testament of Jesus* [Philadelphia: Fortress Press. 1978], p.26) John's alleged Docetic view of Jesus is found in the Fourth Gospel.   This is certainly a misreading of John's Gospel, which, if anything, is anti-Gnostic (whether Docetic Gnosticism, or Cerinthian Gnosticism) in its presentation of the incarnation of the Son of God, Jesus Christ.

[37] Kasemann's proposal has been carefully examined and strongly disagreed with by G. Bornkamm in his article '*Presbuteros*,' in Kittel's *Theological Dictionary of the New Testament* (Grand Rapids: Eerdmans, 1968), VI, p.671.

[38] "An even more serious difficulty for Kasemann's view [that the apostle John is not the author] is the Johannine colouring of the letter, which Kasemann explains as a working in of traces of Johannine theology.   But the skill required to do this vitiates the whole theory, for it is highly improbable that a simple presbyter would have been capable of giving such a presentation of Johannine flavouring that the original purpose of the letter became entirely forgotten" (Guthrie, *op. cit.*, p.220).

[39] "The writer does not write as a pleading excommunicant, for verse 10 does not suggest that he expects any difficulty in gaining a hearing when he comes to the church" (Guthrie, *op. cit.*, p.220).

[40] *Five Gospels, An Account of How the Good News Came to Be* (Minneapolis: Winston Press), 1982.

offering and excluding hospitality which we read in 2 John and 3 John. Because one letter advocates hospitality whereas the other bans it, 3 John must be by a different author than 2 John, and in Meagher's view 3 John was written to refute what 2 John taught. (b) Both 2 John and 3 John as pseudepigraphic writings.[41] (c) Meagher says 3 John is a "fossil remain of an alien gospel" which omitted the mediation of Jesus Christ[42] and offered its adherents an immediate vision of God.[43] (d) The very weak external attestation to 3 John, and the fact that some writers knew of 1 and 2 John but not 3 John, suggests to Meagher that early Christians understood 3 John to be heretical and to have been written by a different author than the other two letters.

Opponents of Meagher's reconstruction raise these issues: (a) The idea that pseudepigraphic writing was an accepted practice among the churches is suspect. (b) Meagher's reconstruction of the elder's theology hangs from entirely too thin a thread. The extreme brevity of the letter may account for the lack of Jesus' name in it (though it is surely "the Name" of Jesus that is referred to in verse 7). (c) The style and jargon of 2 John and 3 John suggest the same author produced both writings. (d) As for the early church's neglect of 3 John, the traditional explanation seems entirely adequate: the letter was so brief and so personal that many churches had never seen it.

6. Stephen S. Smalley[44]

Smalley sees 3 John as giving evidence that the Johannine community was beginning to disintegrate. 1 John set out the doctrinal and ethical teaching which was designed to keep the community together. But the disintegration had already begun (1 John 2:18-19). 2 and 3 John depict a hardening of the heretical lines (cf. 2 John 7) together with increasing division expressed by a denial of friendship, as well as by secession (2 John 10-11, 3 John 9-10).

Conservative scholars want to know where the evidence is for the hypothetical Johannine community. They want to know why it is taken as axiomatic by Redaction

---

[41] Meagher thinks 2 John may be the work of the elder but is more likely a pseudepigraph seeking to appropriate the elder's authority to exclude heretics. 3 John, he reasons, is certainly a pseudepigraph subsequently invoking the elder's authority against those, including Diotrephes, who engineered or implemented 2 John's exclusionary policy.

[42] Meagher noted that Jesus Christ is not mentioned in 3 John, and from this extrapolated the idea its author omitted the mediatorial work of Christ from his "alien gospel."

[43] Meagher sees in the phrase "the one who does evil has not seen God" (3 John 11b) an implication that one who does good can in this life see God in some mystical sense. Such mysticism is alien to the Gospel, since both the Fourth Gospel and 1 John teach that no one can see God (John 1:18, 6:46, 1 John 4:12,20) at least until the second coming of Christ (1 John 3:2).

[44] "1,2,3 John" in *Word Biblical Commentary* [Waco, TX: Word Books, 1984.

Critics that there are three levels of material in our New Testament writings as we now have them. They want to see solid proof there were competing "faiths" even among the apostles of Jesus, with the survival of the fittest resulting in Christianity as we know it.

7. Robert M. Price[45]

Price makes these proposals as he attempts his reconstruction: (a) Take the strong points from each of the earlier proposals. (b) The letters were written in the reverse order they appear in the New Testament canon. (This is theoretically possible since books are arranged and numbered in our Bibles according to length). (c) The Elder is not the apostle John, but a leader in the [hypothetical] Johannine community that is supposed to have grown up after the apostle's death. (d) The Elder has sent out itinerant, circuit-riding missionaries, all of whom were prophets who spoke by inspiration.[46] (e) The Elder and this Johannine community are pictured as guiding and supervising a network of satellite churches, apparently small house churches, over a wide area. They kept in touch with those satellites by means of these traveling brethren who lived by the charity of their hosts in each town, while also directing the satellites by presiding in the weekly worship service where they would prophesy, teach, read encyclicals from the elder, or all three. Here is how, in such a context, in his own words Price proposes the 3 epistles came to be written:

1) One day among the brethren in the home Johannine community, one prophet receives a revelation containing a radical new Christological development, one of a docetic character, either that Jesus Christ only seemed to have a body of flesh (as in the *Acts of John*, supposedly the work of Leucius, a purported disciple of John [so says Epiphanius, *Panarion* 51.6.9]) or that the Christ-Spirit only temporarily rested on the human Jesus (as Cerinthus, the traditional opponent of John, thought). The first idea seems to be reflected in 1 Jn 4:2-3; 2 Jn 7; the second in 1 Jn 2:22. The origin of this doctrine in a revelation is reflected in 1 Jn 4:1. Its supposed character as an advanced teaching is mentioned in 2 Jn 9.

2) This docetic revelation was vouchsafed in a small prophetic circle, not the larger community meeting. After discussion among themselves the (apparently few) "enlightened ones" correctly surmise that their fellows would not appreciate their revelation, so rather than risk casting their pearls before swine, they decide to teach the new Christology in their travels to receptive listeners in the satellite congregations. This condescension toward the "unenlightened" is reflected in 1 Jn 2:9, etc. Should they risk submitting their revelation to be weighed by the others (cf. 1 Cor 14:29; 12:2-3), they knew that they might be expelled, and if that happened their welcome in Johannine circles would be withdrawn. So here was another reason to teach their new doctrine "on the road" without the knowledge or

---

[45] "The *Sitz-im-Leben* of Third John: A New Reconstruction" *Evangelical Quarterly* 61:2 (1989), p.109-119.

[46] Price arrives at his conclusions about the inspired speaking of the missionaries on the basis of internal evidence, analogy with the Gospel of Matthew (7:15-20, 10:5-15,40-42, 25:31-36), and the *Didache* (ch.11).

permission of the Elder. They would claim to represent him in order to gain a hearing and then the new Truth would commend itself.

3) The docetic teachers pursue this course of action as soon as it is their turn to set out on a mission. They preach docetism without obstacle or event, apparently making a goodly number of converts, since by the time 2 and 1 John are written, many seem to adhere to the new doctrine; only "some" of the members of one church still embrace orthodox doctrine (2 Jn. 4). Those in the churches who accept the new Christology believe it to be new teaching from the Elder since it was claimed (by his well-known representatives) to have his authorization.

4) All goes reasonably well for the docetic teachers until they reach the church of which Diotrephes is the local head. At first he welcomes them, but is immediately shocked and disturbed by what he hears. He knows genuine, traditional Johannine doctrine ("what was from the beginning" – 1 Jn 1:1) too well to believe that this new "prophecy" could be genuine. Yet it does not occur to him to doubt that the docetic teachers really do have the Elder's authorization. Most likely he has entertained and honored those very teachers in the past and knows them as the Elder's emissaries. So Diotrephes concludes that the Elder is responsible and thus must have become a heretic if not a madman. He loses no time in announcing this to his congregation and in ejecting the docetic teachers. Since he believes docetism is the new Johannine "orthodoxy," Diotrephes severs connections with the Johannine community, forbidding his members to have anything to do with the mad Elder and his false teachers.

5) Rudely expelled from Diotrephes' congregation, the docetic teachers continue on their way and meet with no further incident. We may imagine them shaking the dust from their feet as they left the community of Diotrephes (Mk 6:11). Upon their return to the home base (cf. Acts 14:26,27), they do not tell of the trouble with Diotrephes, because of course that would expose their secret either immediately or as soon as messengers were sent to find out why Diotrephes expelled them. Naturally the docetic teachers want to keep their secret as long as possible so as to keep their Johannine credentials and assure themselves a wide hearing for as long as possible.

6) Eventually another team goes on their rounds. They, too, make most of their journey without incident. Since there is no reason to imagine that Christology, orthodox or not, was the topic every time a Johannine team came into town, the subject may not have come up, and no conflict was apparent between this team and the previous, docetic, one.

7) The new team reaches Diotrephes' church and meet with a rude surprise. All church members with whom they are accustomed to stay either suspiciously or regretfully turn them away, having been ordered not even to speak to any Johannine emissaries (the same policy as 2 Jn 10 – see No.11 below). They find shelter with Gaius, who is a local friend and colleague of the Elder, apparently not a member of Diotrephes' congregation (see below). They complete their circuit without further incident.

8) The teachers return to the home community, where they share their unpleasant experience and what little they understand about it. All they have been able to glean is that Diotrephes has condemned the Elder and warned his congregants to have nothing to do with his representatives. The Elder, still unaware of the surreptitious preaching of docetism in his name, has no idea of the real motives of Diotrephes. All he can conclude is that Diotrephes has gone power-mad and is maligning him as an excuse for repudiating the Elder's supervision. Through all this the docetic teachers are keeping mum.

9) The Elder fires off a letter to Diotrephes' church, sending it perhaps with the next group of missioners, or perhaps by special direct messenger. In either case, he is not given a hearing. (Of course Diotrephes, zealot for "that old time religion," will not countenance the reading of an epistle full, as he thinks, of heresy.) This letter is that mentioned in 3 Jn 9.

10) Eventually the Elder sends out another missioner. The Elder knows Demetrius can expect no hospitality from Diotrephes' congregation, so he sends him to lodge with nearby Gaius instead. 3 John is the letter of recommendation for Demetrius, presented to Gaius on Demetrius' arrival. Presumably Demetrius was a relatively new recruit and Gaius had never met him before. Gaius is not actually a member of Diotrephes' church or he would not need to be informed of Diotrephes' actions. Gaius seems not to be a member of another local church either, though, because if he were, 3 John would not refer to Diotrephes' congregation as "*the* church." At any rate, the Elder thanks him for his recent support of the brethren rejected by Diotrephes and urges him not to adopt Diotrephes' policy. He seems to be apologizing for imposing on Gaius' hospitality, explaining that the local church of Diotrephes will not fulfill what should be its responsibility. He promises to come personally to set matters in order, but until he does, he appreciates Gaius' kind generosity.

11) The Elder finally makes his way to Diotrephes' church and confronts him. What does he mean by slandering the Elder and breaking off all ties to him? Does his egotism know no bounds? Diotrephes heatedly replies that he is only doing his best to safeguard the true doctrine once learned from the Elder before the latter had begun listening to the doctrines of demons. Diotrephes explains that of course he means the docetism taught in the Elder's name by his travelling brethren. John is shocked! He angrily repudiates any such mad teaching. Then he pauses. The light dawns. He begins to realize what has really happened. Diotrephes is made to understand the true situation as well, and the two shake hands, agreeing to fight side-by-side to preserve the orthodoxy as taught by the Johannine community. The Elder now agrees with Diotrephes' strategy of non-cooperation with docetists and decides to adopt it himself and to advise all his churches to do the same.

12) The Elder returns home and expels those docetic teachers whose names have been supplied by Diotrephes. The Elder cannot be sure either that these heretics may not continue misrepresenting themselves as his agents, or that there may be other docetists in the fold (more of the original prophetic coterie who however did not embark on the mission with the others, or converts recruited by the original doce-

tists) who may continue the deceptive practice. So he begins to write a series of letters to his various churches. 2 John is one of these. In them he supplies a doctrinal shibboleth rather than a blacklist of names, since he cannot be sure who the hypothetical secret docetists might be, at least not without finding out the hard way as he did in the case of Diotrephes' church.

13) The Elder is generally disinclined to write letters anyway (2 Jn 12; 3 Jn 13), so he soon decides that instead of writing individual letters to all his churches he will compose a longer and more detailed encyclical (1 John) to all the churches explaining the danger of the docetic imposters, how they teach a doctrine inspired by the antichrist (4:3), how the fact of their past membership in the Johannine organization counts for nothing now that they teach heresy (2:18-19), etc.

Opponents of Price's reconstruction raise these issues: (a) The Johannine authorship of the letters is too quickly rejected. (b) The Johannine community is created and exists only in the fertile imagination of the Redaction Critics. (c) False revelations are accepted by Price as commonplace, and he implies that 1 John has contradictory statements contained within its short scope. Furthermore, Price's reconstruction is based on a careless picture of the place of "prophecy" in the early church. The itinerant missionaries, who are supposedly leaders in the early church, are pictured as working their claims via lies and deception. The Elder is pictured as evidently not having the ability to discern spirits (1 Corinthians 12:10 ASV) so that he could evaluate the truthfulness of what the itinerants were saying. And in the congregations to which the itinerant preachers came to speak, there was no gift of discerning of spirits. The congregations simply accepted that the Elder would endorse docetism, that Christians should call the docetists and Cerinthians "brethren," and that the speakers of false doctrine were delivering a prophecy from God! (d) Price's reconstruction has different "faiths" contending for supremacy in those early post-apostolic years, till one finally won out. (e) Price's idea that the Elder writes in a letter some ill-founded, if not absolutely wrong, suspicions about Diotrephes (charging him with being power-mad, which is actually an untruth, says Price) impinges badly on the doctrine of Holy Spirit inspiration. (f) Price's point #11 leaves us with the impression that the apostles' doctrine evolved and changed as a result of their education in the school of hard knocks. (g) Price's point #13 certainly gives a peculiar twist to 1 John 2:18-19.

After all the failed attempts shared above, scholars are becoming skeptical that the *sitz-im-leben* can be reconstructed. Judith Lieu (*The Second and Third Epistles of John*, Edinburgh: T&T Clark, 1986) has concluded, "Ultimately any attempt at a confident reconstruction must founder on the silences of the letter ... and on our ignorance about the constitution and self-identity of the first Christian groups." What a mess we are led into by redaction criticism! How much more satisfying is the traditional view of the historical situation reflected in 3 John.

OUTLINE

Signature, Address and Prayer.   verses 1,2

I.   The Occasion for this Letter.   verses 3,4
II.   Gaius is Praised for His Hospitality.   verses 5-8
II.   Diotrephes' Arrogance is Denounced.   verses 9-11
IV. Demetrius is Commended to Gaius.   Verse 12

The Conclusion and Greeting.   verses 13,14

3 John[1]

SIGNATURE, ADDRESS, AND PRAYER.   Verses 1,2

A. The Writer.   Verse 1a

Verse 1 -- *The elder to the beloved Gaius, whom I love in truth.*

The elder – Instead of signing his name, the author identifies himself by a title.   Gaius, to whom this letter is addressed, would recognize immediately who the author is.   The writer of the letter we call "Third John" is the same writer who penned the one we call "Second John."   In the Introductory Studies on 2 John we opted for the apostle John, the son of Zebedee, as being the one using this title.   That certainly was the view of the ancient church as the "title" ("of John") added to the letter by scribes in later generations shows. Plummer draws two conclusions from the use of the title "elder" in both 2 and 3 John: (1) It is a title that John regularly used for himself.   (2) The letters were written at nearly the same time, and at a time in his life when the writer was using this title for himself.[2]

B. The Address.   Verse 1b

To the beloved Gaius – The one to whom this letter is addressed was named "Gaius," a common Roman name meaning rejoicing.   In the Introductory Studies on 3 John, in the topic on "Destination," we tentatively opted for the view that Gaius of Corinth is the person who received this letter from John.   Whether or not that identification is correct, the thrust of what John writes is this: trouble has arisen in the church (or town) where Gaius lived. Traveling preachers or missionaries, perhaps sent by John, had stopped to visit the church. But Diotrephes, apparently an influential person in the community, had spoken against the apostle John, had refused to recognize the visiting preachers of the gospel, and had opposed any who had welcomed them.   Nevertheless, Gaius opened his home to the visitors. John writes this letter to commend Gaius for his hospitality.   "Beloved" is an epithet used

---

[1] The title of this writing, like the titles of 1 and 2 John and the Gospel of John, exists in various forms (the older it is, the shorter it is), and likely was not on the autograph copy. Codex Sinaiticus reads "of John." Vaticanus reads "of John G." Codex Ephraemi reads "Epistle of John G." (The "G" is the Greek number "3.") Codex Angelicus reads "Third Epistle of the apostle John." In Codex Alexandrinus, the title is missing for this letter just as it was for 2 John.   Some later manuscripts insert the word *katholikē*, which for this letter must mean "canonical" since beyond doubt the letter is addressed to an individual rather than being an "encyclical" intended for a catholic or general audience.

[2] Alfred Plummer, *The Epistles of St. John*, in The Cambridge Bible for Schools and Colleges (Cambridge: University Press, 1884), p.144. See the notes at 2 John 1 on the title "elder" being used to designate the apostles and those who were personally taught by the apostles.

repeatedly in 1 John,[3] where it frequently had the connotation divinely loved or loved by God.   Perhaps John is saying to Gaius, who has been spurned by Diotrephes, "God loves you!"   Or, perhaps John is saying that Gaius' fellow saints love him.

Whom I love in truth – "I" is emphatic in the Greek, a construction that implies a contrast.[4] In this case the contrast is between John who loves Gaius and some gainsayer who is hostile toward Gaius.   Perhaps it was Diotrephes who was hostile to Gaius.   Perhaps there is an aside at the Gnostics who are opposed to John and all those who love the truth.[5]   "Truth" (versus what the Gnostics teach) has been a prominent emphasis in John's epistles.[6] Perhaps "truth" is a reference to Christ.   "I love you because you are my Christian brother," says John.   Perhaps truth means true to the gospel.   If so, John is saying, "I love you because you are true to the gospel."   (Verse 3 will say Gaius is "walking in truth.")

C. The Prayer.   Verse 2

Verse 2 – *Beloved, I pray that in all respects you may prosper and be in good health, just as your soul prospers.*

Beloved, I pray that in all respects you may prosper – This letter has no customary greeting such as we find in 1st century letters.   The prayer expressed here in verse 2 takes its place.   The word *euchomai* is translated "pray" in the NASB; it was translated "wish" in the KJV.   If this were an entirely secular letter, the translation "wish" might be acceptable since *euchomai* was used in a nonreligious sense to mean "wish" or "hope."   In the Scriptures, however, *euchomai* is regularly translated "pray."[7]   The Greek word order catches our attention, for *peri pantōn* ("in all respects" NASB; "above all things" KJV) stands first in the sentence for emphasis.   The KJV reads "I wish above all things ..." and

---

[3] See 1 John 2:7; 3:2,21; 4:1,7,11.

[4] Compare notes on the emphatic personal pronoun at 2 John 1.

[5] See comments on similar language at 2 John 1.   Here in 3 John, it is difficult to decide whether John is using the prepositional phrase "in truth" adverbially.   There is no article in Greek here as there is at the close of 2 John 1, "the truth".   If it is used adverbially, it simply means "whom I truly love."   If it is not used adverbially (and it would be quite common to omit the definite article after the preposition in Greek), then John is saying that "the truth" is the area or sphere where his love for Gaius exists.   That is, "I love him because we have a common bond in the gospel of Jesus Christ."   Either way, this clause is not just a repetition of the idea already expressed in "beloved."   That spoke of God's sentiment respecting Gaius; "I love" is John's own feeling toward Gaius.

[6] There are six different references to "truth" in 3 John (verse 1,3,4,8,12, and note "true" in verse 12). See also 1 John 2:21, 4:7-21; 2 John 1,2,3,4.

[7] See 2 Corinthians 13:7,9; Acts 26:29, 27:29.

this may be misleading.[8]   "All respects" ("all things" KJV) evidently goes with "prosper" rather than "I pray," so that "all respects" refers not to John's wishes (he wishes this above all) but to Gaius' prosperity ("in all respects").   John prays for the prosperity of Gaius in all respects.   "Prosper" translates *eudousthai*, a compound word made up of *hodos*, "road," and *eu*, "good," and means, literally, a good road, a prosperous journey.   In this place it should be taken metaphorically in the sense of getting along well, to prosper, to succeed.   We do not know what Gaius' occupation was by which he earned his livelihood. Whatever it was, John may well have been praying for Gaius' prosperity therein, precisely because of the expenditures that he would be called on to make as a Christian in extending hospitality to traveling brethren.[9]   John prays that God will prosper Gaius so that Gaius can continue to generously extend Christian hospitality.[10]

And be in good health – The present tense infinitive *hugiainein* likely means continue to be in good health.[11]   The context likely leads us to think of physical health rather than spiritual health.[12]   Ill health would hinder Gaius' attempts to extend hospitality.   Since there is no doubt that this verse is a prayer for physical blessings as well as spiritual prosperity, we have here a good Biblical example of praying for temporal blessings for our friends in Christ.

Just as your soul prospers – The implication is that Gaius is doing well in spiritual matters.   John's prayer is that Gaius' physical prosperity and health may equal the prosperity of his soul.   "Undoubtedly John is implying that the emphasis here is the proper one: How one's soul is doing ought to be the rule by which he judges prosperity in wealth and health, not the other way around."[13]   "Soul" is a word that has various shades of meaning in the Bible writings.

---

[8] To translate the phrase "above all things" is to fall back on how the language was used in Homer. The meaning in Koine Greek is not necessarily the same as it was in classical Greek.

[9] In Titus 3:13,14 Paul expressed a similar interest.   He wanted Titus to diligently help traveling preachers on their way, and to teach the church members to engage in similar good deeds to meet pressing needs.

[10] It may be a needful reminder that Scripture teaches Christians first how to give – and to then trust God to provide the means to continue to give.   See Philippians 4:15-19, 2 Corinthians 9:6-11.

[11] We should not conclude from John's prayer that Gaius had been ailing in health or fortune. Deissmann (*Light from the Ancient East*) shows that the words of this whole verse are found frequently in letters of that day.   Deissmann appends this note: "Many commentators on the third Epistle of John, misunderstanding this formula, have assumed that Gaius, the addressee, had been ill immediately before."

[12] In the Pastoral Epistles *hugiainein* is always used figuratively of being sound or healthy in faith and doctrine.   Luke the physician uses the term of physical health (Luke 5:31, 7:10, 15:27).   It seems quite clear from the phrase that concludes this verse that "prosper and be in health" do not refer to Gaius' spiritual condition.

[13] J.W. Roberts, *The Letters of John*, in The Living Word Commentary Series (Austin, TX: R.B. Sweet Co., 1968) p.172.

(1) "Soul" sometimes stands for the whole man.   (Genesis 12:5, 17:14; Ezekiel 18:4; Acts 2:43 (where "everyone" in the Greek is "every soul"), 3:23, 27:37, Romans 13:1)

(2) Soul sometimes stands for the animating principle that causes a physical body to be what we call "alive."   See Acts 20:10 where a body was alive if its soul was in it. See Acts 5:5,10, 12:23 where the soul departed as physical death occurred.   See 1 John 3:16 where it says that Jesus laid down his life [*psuchē*, soul] for us.   And see Psalm 16:10 (quoted at Acts 2:27) where following Jesus' physical death, though His body was in the tomb, His "soul" would not be abandoned in Hades.

(3) Soul sometimes stands for the whole personality, the entire spiritual entity that lives in a physical body, and continues to exist even after the soul is separated from the body (Matthew 10:28; James 5:20; Revelation 6:9, 20:4). Soul stands for the whole inner man (Matthew 16:25,26; Hebrews 6:19, 10:39, 13:17; 1 Peter 2:11, 4:19).   As such, the "soul" may be "saved" or "lost" (Mark 8:36; Hebrews 10:39; James 1:21; 1 Peter 1:9).   As such, the "soul" may experience punishment after the final judgment ("tribulation ... upon every soul who does evil," Romans 2:9 ASV).

When John comments about how Gaius' soul is prospering, it is in this latter sense, referring to Gaius' spiritual life and growth, that the word "soul" is used.[14]   How John knows about the prosperity of Gaius' soul we learn in the next verse.

I. THE OCCASION FOR THIS LETTER.   Verses 3,4

Summary: The hospitality extended to traveling missionaries was gratefully acknowledged by them in a church assembly where John was present.   John writes to Gaius to express his joy over what he heard about Gaius.

Verse 3 -- *For I was very glad when brethren came and bore witness to your truth, that is, how you are walking in truth.*

For I was glad when brethren came – "For" likely gives the reason for John's expression of praise concerning Gaius' soul prospering.   It means "I know your soul prospers (you are making spiritual progress), *for* I have it on good authority."[15]   The evidence to which

---

[14] "The spiritual dimension of a Christian's being is normally described in the New Testament by the use of *pneuma* ('spirit').   E.g., Romans 8:16; James 2:26; 1 Peter 3:4; see also 1 John 4:2" (Stephen S. Smalley, *1,2,3 John,* in Word Biblical Commentary [Waco, TX: Word Books, 1984], p.346).   We also find "inner man" used to describe man's spiritual nature (Romans 7:22; 2 Corinthians 4:16; Ephesians 3:16).

[15] Plummer, *op. cit.*, p.145.   A few manuscripts omit the "for."   Though the latest critical texts carry it, the NIV leaves it untranslated.

John can appeal is this: brethren were constantly coming and telling[16] him about Gaius' spiritual welfare.   The "brethren" are likely the same "brethren" of whom he speaks in verse 5 and following, who appear to have been traveling evangelists or missionaries who were working to evangelize the Gentiles (verse 7).   If this identification is correct, then we may understand (verse 6) they have enjoyed Gaius' hospitality when they paused during their travels in his town.   Now the reports John hears gladden his heart.[17]

And bore witness to your truth – Two things are included in the report of the brethren that allow John to know about Gaius' spiritual prosperity: the truth that is in him (verse 3) and his love (verse 6).   The verb "bore witness" ("testified," KJV) means they spoke of what they had personally seen, heard, and experienced when they were with Gaius.[18] "Your truth" may refer to soundness of Gaius' faith; it may say that Gaius is living a lovely Christian life in harmony with the truth of the Christian gospel.

That is, **how you are walking in truth** – This clause begins with "how" (*kathōs*, "according as, even as") and may be part of what the brethren reported,[19] or this clause may express John's convictions about Gaius, based on his own knowledge of Gaius.   Either way, "walking in truth" evidently is intended to explain what he meant by "your truth." Gaius is walking, he is living,[20] in harmony with the standard of the Christian revelation ("in [the] truth").[21]   1 John has defined "the truth" as being the apostolic gospel, the doctrine taught about Jesus "from the beginning" (1:1).   We see John's commendation of Gaius as being a follower of the old-time gospel, rather than the new *gnosis* that was beginning to capture men's imaginations.   "You" is emphatic, so Gaius is contrasted with others who are not walking in truth.   Is Diotrephes (verse 9ff) in John's mind, or are Gnostics in general being contrasted with Gaius?   In the face of heresy, Gaius was being faithful to the truth as it had been taught by the apostles.

Verse 4 -- *I have no greater joy than this, to hear of my children walking in the truth.*

I have no greater joy than this – In the Greek, "greater" is put first for emphasis; "Greater

---

[16] Both participles ("came" and "bore witness") are present tense in the Greek, indicating continuing or repeated action.

[17] For "I was very glad" (*echaran*) see notes on 2 John 4 for a similar expression of joy by John, and for the same reason.

[18] Testimony can only be borne to what has been seen. (See notes on 1 John 1:2.)

[19] On this view, *kathōs* is used to introduce indirect discourse and is equivalent to *pōs* or *hōs*.

[20] On the figurative expression "walking" see notes on 1 John 1:6.

[21] For the expression "living/walking in (the) truth" see 1 John 1:6, 2:6,11, 5:4; 2 John 4,6; and Romans 6:4.

joy have I none than this." This verse further develops "I was very glad" of verse 3.[22] "Than this" (*toutōn*) is plural in the Greek, so literally "than these" – i.e., the frequent reports of the brethren. It is difficult to express in English the force of the double comparative *meizoteran* ("greater").[23] "John might have been glad to hear many things about his children in such reports, but he could, with his attitude, have no greater joy than the news which he had heard."[24]

To hear of my children walking in the truth – "Children" (*tekna*, from *tiktō*, to be born, brought forth) is used figuratively here, referring to Christians who having been born again have become "children of God" (Romans 8:16,17). As he wrote "my children" John used a possessive pronoun (*ta ema tekna*) rather than a simple personal pronoun in the genitive case (which is how he wrote 1 John 2:1). This construction of the possessive puts the emphasis on "my." Is he referring to those believers who were his personal converts? "A preacher delights to know that those whom he has converted and has helped to mature in Christ are being faithful to what has been taught."[25] Or is he referring to those believers whom he thought of as being his personal responsibility? Adherents of the old-time gospel (such as John had preached from the beginning) were his special responsibility since he is by now the last living apostle of Jesus. "Walking" is figurative for living, indicating habitual activity, and it is a present tense participle.[26] The "children" who thrill John's soul are those who were continuing to walk in the truth; compare the nearly duplicate expression of joy John offers for the chosen lady in 2 John 4. The use of the article in the phrase "the truth" (where "the" is an article of previous reference) makes "the truth" refer back to the previously mentioned truth of Gaius (verse 3). Not only that, it also probably helps define the former reference as the objective truth, the word of God, or the gospel rev-

---

[22] Westcott-Hort adopt the reading *charin*, "grace" (with Vaticanus and Memphitic and Vulgate), rather than *charan*, "joy" (supported by A B C K P ψ 81 614 1739 and various versions). If we read it "grace," it means that John considers the constant reports he hears as being a favor from God. John R.W. Stott (*The Epistles of John*, in Tyndale New Testament Commentary [Grand Rapids: Eerdmans, 1971], p.220) judges that "grace" in Vaticanus is most certainly a copyist's error.

[23] Greek adjectives have three degrees, positive, comparative, and superlative (as does English, "great, greater, greatest"). *Meizon* is already the comparative form. The suffix *-teros* is an additional comparative ending. The two comparatives say "greater + er" and perhaps "doubly great" is as close as we can come to catching the idea. Perhaps John is inferring that the good reports concerning Gaius are a greater joy to the apostle than the evil report of Diotrephes is a sorrow to him.

[24] Roberts, *op. cit.*, p.173.

[25] Roberts, *ibid.* If "my children" are those personally taught and led to Christ by John, it would cause us to rethink our tentative conclusion about where Gaius lived. Verses 3 and 4 together would cause us to understand that the Gaius being addressed in 3 John is one of those believers whom John calls "my children." It is very doubtful that Gaius of Corinth was one of John's converts. It is usually conjectured as being most probable that the Corinthian Gaius was converted by Paul years before John was ever in this part of the Mediterranean world.

[26] We have observed that "walking" is one of John's favorite expressions: "walking in darkness" (1 John 1:6, 2:11); walking in the light" (1 John 1:7); "walking in love" (2 John 6).

elation which was being followed.[27]   With the Gnostics beginning to make inroads into the churches, and with disciples wavering and abandoning the apostolic gospel for the Gnostic fables, John keeps looking for evidence that his "children" are not defecting.

II. GAIUS IS PRAISED FOR HIS HOSPITALITY. Verses 5-8

Summary: Christian missionaries did not expect the unconverted audiences to whom they preached to provide financial support.   So the kind of hospitality Gaius extended is exactly what Christians have an obligation to do.   Therefore, John expresses his hope that Gaius will continue to so treat visiting missionaries.

Verse 5 -- *Beloved, you are acting faithfully in whatever you accomplish for the brethren, and especially* **when they are** *strangers;*

Beloved – This affectionate address marks the beginning of a new section (cp. verses 2 and 11).   "Verses 5-8 are an exhortation to Gaius to continue giving help and hospitality to the traveling preachers, and not to do as Diotrephes is doing (see v.9ff)."[28]   Like 2 John, this letter also is about hospitality, with this difference: 2 John speaks of not extending hospitality to false teachers like the Gnostics, whereas 3 John encourages extending hospitality to true teachers of the gospel.

You are acting faithfully in whatever you accomplish for the brethren – Translators have found it hard to translate this clause satisfactorily.   Two difficulties must be faced:

(1) To determine the meaning of *piston poieis* ("acting faithfully" in NASB).   *Piston* is an adjective,[29] for which we must supply a noun.   The ASV did it well, "thou doest a faithful work."   Or it could be a faithful act, or a faithful thing.   To act faithfully possibly means to do what is worthy of a faithful man or of a believer.   The man's actions correspond to the Christian faith he has embraced.

(2) To bring out the meaning of the verb *egrasē* ("accomplish" in NASB).   The aorist subjunctive verb *egrasē* occurs in a conditional clause, so the doing or the accomplish-

---

[27] "To John the truth (gospel) mattered.   He did not regard theological issues as unimportant trivialities.   It was from truth, believed and obeyed by his children, that he derived his greatest joy."   Stott, *op. cit.*, p.220.

[28] Simon J. Kistemaker, *Exposition of the Epistles of John* in New Testament Commentary series (Grand Rapids: Baker, 1986), p.151.

[29] The NASB translation ("faithfully") treats the adjective as though it were an adverb.   Some conjecture that *piston* is put here for *pistin*, and that the phrase signifies "to keep" or "preserve the faith" or "to be bound by the faith" or "to keep one's engagements."   (Adam Clarke, *The Third Epistle of John* in Clarke's Commentary (New York: Methodist Book Concern, 1832), Vol. 6, p.491.)   Codex 80 has the singular reading *misthon poiein* ("you do a rewarding work") for *piston poieis*.

ing is thought of as being in the future.[30]   John anticipates that Gaius will continue to show hospitality to "the brethren"[31] in the future just as he has in the past.   (In verse 8 John will state his expectations more forcefully.)

The hospitality Gaius is pictured as extending was not merely a kind, generous act.   John reminds Gaius that his hospitality was a work for the Lord Jesus; it was a Christian service.   Such hospitality is simply what was expected of a believer in the light of his Master's teaching (Matthew 25:35).   Gaius can continue to demonstrate his loyalty to the truth of the gospel as he extends loving service to the messengers of that gospel.

And especially *when they are* strangers – "Strangers" were Christians (e.g., missionaries on their way to or from the field, or helpers like John Mark was, Acts 13:5) who were unknown to Gaius personally when they arrived at his doorstep looking for lodging.   As he looks into the future, John sees Gaius welcoming under his roof every Christian traveler.   He sees Gaius continuing to generously open his home to Christian travelers, not picking and choosing by showing hospitality to those he knew and liked, while neglecting the rest.   "It was a signal feature of Gaius' hospitality that he was prepared to extend it to people who were otherwise unknown to him and had no claims on him except that they formed part of the company of those who like him had come to know the truth (cf. 2 John 1)."[32]

Verse 6 -- *And they bear witness to your love before the church; and you will do well to send them on their way in a manner worthy of God.*

And they bear witness to your love before the church – How does John know that Gaius is in the habit of welcoming brethren who are strangers into his home?   Because he has heard some of the traveling Christian workers tell about being welcomed into Gaius' home even though they were strangers.   The aorist tense verb "bear witness"[33] would point to some definite occasion in the past.   It is natural to interpret this verse as referring to one of the occasions mentioned in verse 3.   "The church" is the congregation of believers who meet in the town wherever John was when he wrote the letter.[34]   Perhaps we are to under-

---

[30] The subjunctive mood pictures the action of the verb as being in the future.   The aorist tense seems to mean that each instance of hospitality (and John hopes there will be many such instances) extended to visiting missionaries is an act of faith.   "The use of *ho ean* with the subjunctive is indefinite and implies an unspecified number of ways or occasions of helping the brothers."   I. Howard Marshall, *The Epistles of John*, in the New International Commentary on the New Testament (Grand Rapids: Eerdmans, 1978), p.85.

[31] "The brethren" are identified in verses 6 and 7 as being travelling missionaries who are taking the gospel to the Gentiles.   "There is not a word here, about the "pilgrims" or "penitential journeys" which the [Roman Catholic commentators] contrive to bring out of this text."   Clarke, *ibid*.

[32] Marshall, *ibid*.

[33] For the meaning of the verb "bear witness," see comments on verse 3.

[34] "'The church' is originally a term for any kind of assembly; the Greek version of the Old Testament used it of the Israelites when assembled for religious purposes.   In the New Testament the term can refer to the universal Church,   or to the congregation in a particular city or house which forms a representative

stand that the missionaries have returned to the home church which sent them on their journey in the first place, and that they were reporting to the home church all that had happened on their missionary tour.[35]   One of the highlights of the tour was how they were treated so hospitably by Gaius.   "So impressed had the brothers been by Gaius' kindness that they made special mention of it when they had told their story at a meeting of the church attended by the Elder."[36]   Gaius' "love"[37] (doing what is spiritually best for the other person) had been tangibly demonstrated by his generous hospitality and perhaps also by providing the means for the missionaries to continue on their journey to the next town.

And you will do well to send them on their way in a manner worthy of God – Basing his appeal on Gaius' past behavior as reported in the assembly, John anticipates future occasions when such fellowship with traveling missionaries will again be needed, and he gently urges Gaius to continue doing such good work.   It appears that the pronoun "them" refers back to the same missionaries (verses 5 and 6a) who before had found help from Gaius, and now were going to need it again for the special work they were going to do. "You will do well" might be an idiom that means 'please,' as though John were expressing a polite request, 'Please send them on their way ....'   The word *propempō* ("to send on their way") refers to aid rendered to someone on their journey.   It means "to help on one's journey with food, money, by arranging for companions, means of travel, etc."[38]   It means to take care of their anticipated needs on the journey they are about to begin.[39]   A "manner

---

part of the universal Church. In the present verse it is used in the latter meaning" (Kistemaker, *op. cit.*, p.151). We do not know exactly which church this was, but it is usually considered to be Ephesus, where John spent his later years of ministry and life. Only in Revelation and in 3 John does the apostle use the word *ekklēsia*, a called out body of people, an assembly. John heard the missionaries' report in a meeting of the congregation with which he worshipped.

[35] Just as Paul, after each missionary journey, returned and reported to the church at Antioch, so these evangelists would give their home church an account of their missionary journey.

[36] Marshall, *ibid.*

[37] "Charity" in the KJV was a good word 400 years ago. Now it has a narrow connotation of almsgiving to the poor. It would be a serious misunderstanding of this passage were it to be supposed that "alms" were what the visiting strangers were receiving.

[38] Wm. Arndt and F.W. Gingrich, *A Greek-English Lexicon of the New Testament* (Cambridge: At the University Press, 1952), p.716.

[39] "Here we have laid out for us one of the ways in which the early church carried on mission work. Men were selected and ordained to a mission and sent out by congregations (Acts 13:1ff), with that congregation supplying the means for the early part of the trip. The expectation was that the churches already established along the way would receive such men, take care of their needs among them, and send them on with provisions for their forward trip ... The teachers sent out from Ephesus thus seem to work on this rule: they were sent out by one church, expected other churches or individual Christians along the way to take care of their needs, and practiced the principle of making known to the [Gentiles] the gospel without taking anything for the work from them." (Roberts, *op. cit.*, p.175.)
     (Note this sentence in light of the Herald of Truth controversy among the churches of Christ. Some churches of Christ argued it was an "innovation" for the Highland Church of Christ in Abilene, Texas, to sponsor the "Herald of Truth" radio and television programs, yet asked other congregations and individuals to help pay for it.)

worthy of God" may mean in a manner such as He can approve, or it may mean to be as generous to the messengers who are serving God as you would be to God Himself. Jesus had so taught, "He who receives you, receives Me, and he who receives Me receives Him who sent Me" (Matthew 10:40).[40]

Verse 7 -- *For they went out for the sake of the Name, accepting nothing from the Gentiles.*

For – This verse, which begins with "for," furnishes a reason why Gaius should continue to practice his wonderful hospitality. If Christians don't help the traveling missionaries, who will help them?

They went out for the sake of the Name – The visitors whom Gaius would host will have undertaken their journey, not on their own account, but for the sake of preaching the gospel of the grace of God, and making known Jesus to the unconverted. "Went out" (*exēlthan*) is used in the same absolute way in Acts 15:40 to speak of a missionary journey from some Christian center.[41] To do something "for the sake of the Name" is to do something for that person. Here "the Name" of course means the Name of Jesus Christ.[42] This is the nearest John comes to actually naming Jesus in this letter.

Accepting nothing from the Gentiles – "Gentiles" (*ethnikon*, all who were not Jews) likely means the unconverted Gentiles whom these missionaries were trying to evangelize.[43] Since they accepted nothing (no money, no food, no other help) from the unconverted Gentiles among whom they were preaching and teaching, the missionaries would be in great difficulties if Christians did not come forward with needed financial support. The present tense verb ("accepting nothing") indicates that this was the habitual custom or practice of the itinerant evangelists, not merely that they did so on one occasion. "The negative (*mēden* rather than *ouden*) seems to imply that it was their *determination* not

---

[40] When a preacher or evangelist comes to minister among us, or is just traveling to his new place of service, do we send them forth in a manner worthy of God? Do we make reasonable provision for the journey which they are obliged to take?

[41] The same verb was used of false teachers (1 John 2:19, 4:1; 2 John 7) who also were traveling salesmen for their inimical product. It depicts a deliberate setting out on a mission.

[42] Compare Acts 5:41 ("rejoicing that they had been considered worthy to suffer shame for His name," i.e., the name of Christ), Matthew 18:20; Romans 1:5; Colossians 3:17; 2 Timothy 2:19; Revelation 2:13, 3:8. A "name" is that by which a person, place or thing is marked and known. Bible names were often descriptive of the person or his position, and often denoted the character and work of the person. "You shall call His name Jesus, for it is He who will save His people from their sins" (Matthew 1:21). Just as to the Jew "the Name" meant "Jehovah" (Leviticus 19:12; John 17:11), so to the Christian "the Name" means Jesus Christ.

[43] Compare Matthew 5:47, 6:7, 18:17, the only other places where the word occurs. It hardly means Gentile converts, for what possible objection could there be to receiving help from them?

to accept anything, not merely that as a matter of *fact* they received nothing."[44]   There were good reasons why the Christian missionaries did not ask the unconverted for help.[45] To have done so would open them up to the slander they were just preaching for the money. To have done so would have left the impression that Christians back home did not think the mission important enough to back it financially.   If Christians didn't think it important, why should potential converts think it important enough to listen?   To have done so would have made the Christian missionaries look just like the wandering devotees of various pagan religions[46] who traveled up and down the roads, extolling the virtues of the deity of their choice, and collecting money from their chance listeners.   If His messengers acted just like any other contemporary peddlers of religion, instead of being a unique being, Jesus would thus be thought of as just another deity in the pantheon of the 1st century world.

Verse 8 – *Therefore we ought to support such men, that we may be fellow workers with the truth.*

Therefore we ought to support such men – "Therefore" catches up all that has just been said, namely, because as a matter of principle itinerant Christian evangelists did not ask the heathen for financial support.   If the first reason for supporting "such men," i.e., the traveling missionaries, is that they are brethren whom we should honor for setting out for the sake of the Name (verse 7), the second reason is the practical one that they have no other means of support.   "We" is in emphatic contrast to the Gentiles just mentioned. "*We* Christians must do for the missionaries what they will not ask the Gentiles to do."[47] John softens the injunction by including himself in the obligation to support[48] the missionaries.   "Ought" (*opheilō*) says that Christians have a moral obligation to support

---

[44] Plummer, *op. cit.*, p.147.

[45] Stott, *op. cit.*, p.222,223 has these thoughtful comments.   "The phrase 'taking nothing' need not be pressed into meaning that these Christian missionaries would refuse to accept gifts voluntarily offered to them by the unconverted ... Jesus Himself asked for and accepted a glass of water from a Samaritan woman ... We must remember, however, that the doctrine is everywhere taught in the Bible that it is the *duty* of those Christians to whom the gospel is preached to contribute to the support of those who preach it.   'The laborer is worthy of his hire' is what Jesus taught.   Jesus' followers heed their Lord's behest.   Cf. 1 Corinthians 9:13,14,15 ... A Christian congregation supporting its minister is one thing; missionaries taking money from the heathen is another."   "It is more blessed to give ... and those congregations of Christians who prize the Gospel most, and who bear all expenses incident to it, profit by it most.   And vice-versa."   Clarke, *op. cit.*, p.491.

[46] A. Deissmann (*Light From the Ancient East* [Grand Rapids: Baker, 1965], p. 108ff) has noted an inscription where one such servant of a Syrian Goddess traveled in the service of his "Lady," and "at each journey brought back seventy bags [of gold for her]."

[47] Stott, *op. cit.*, p.223.

[48] The KJV reads "we ought to receive such" because of a manuscript variation.   The Textus Receptus has *apolambanein* ("to receive") instead of the reading found in most ancient manuscripts, *hupolambanein* ("to take up, to catch hold from underneath and lift up") or in our language "to underwrite" or "to assume the responsibilities and expenses of someone else."

the preachers of the gospel.[49]   Earlier, John had implied what he expected faithful Gaius to do; John now states that expectation in a more forceful way.

That we may be fellow workers with the truth – "That we may be" (*hina ginōmetha*) means "that we may prove to be" rather than "that we may become."   Compare John 15:8. "Fellow workers"[50] says that the supporters of the missionaries are working together with the missionaries.[51]   For the meaning of "truth" see the comments on verses 3 and 4 above. "The itinerant evangelists were not 'deceivers' (2 John 7), bringing with them the lie that Jesus is not the Christ, the Son of God.   On the contrary, they [teach] 'the truth'."[52]   The two words in the dative case (*tē alētheia*, translated "with the truth" NASB) have given commentators some trouble.[53]   The prepositional helpers 'to' or 'for' or 'in' or 'with' are all possible choices to translate the dative, and each gives a slightly different thrust to this verse.   Perhaps John means that supporters and preachers and the truth all work together to win the unconverted to Christ.   That seems to be the idea the NASB is attempting to express by rendering the dative as "*with* the truth."   "Faith comes by hearing ... the word of Christ" (Romans 10:17, KJV) and the gospel "is the power of God unto salvation ..." (Romans 1:16, ASV) would be parallel passages for this rendering.   Perhaps John means that the supporters and missionaries are working together to win men "*to* the truth." Translating the dative "*to* the truth" would make "truth" the object to which the work of the missionaries and their supporters is devoted.

---

[49] What John here has written is a good guiding principle in Christian giving.   When it comes time to receive the offering, some congregations have begun to explain to the people assembled that visitors are not required to give.   They may, if they wish, but this time of sharing and fellowship is something expected only of the believers.

[50] "The word used here ('fellow-workers') is one of Paul's favorite words to define those who accompanied him and worked with him on his journeys of preaching (Romans 16:3,9,21; Philippians 2:25; 4:3; Philemon 24).   But as this verse indicates, the term is applicable not only to those who cooperate in preaching, but to those as well who, as members of the churches, supply the preachers with the means to go forth and preach.   In the same way, Paul told the church at Philippi [which on more than one occasion had sent him a missionary offering] that they had fellowship with him in preaching the Gospel from the day when he set foot among them (Philippians 1:5)."   Roberts, *op. cit.*, p.176.

[51] John warned the chosen lady that to welcome and support false teachers was to partake of their evil works (2 John 11).   Now he encourages Gaius and his friends with the thought that to welcome and support teachers of the truth is to partake of their good works.   Jesus taught the same thing: "He who receives a prophet in the name of a prophet shall receive a prophet's reward" (Matthew 10:41).

[52] Stott, *op. cit.*, p.224.

[53] The Greek grammar used at this place is puzzling.   In classical Greek the word translated "fellow workers" would have been followed by a dative case (as here) to designate those with whom the fellow worker works.   However, in New Testament Greek we are more accustomed to find the genitive case used to designate those with whom the fellow worker works (see Romans 16:3,9, 21; 1 Corinthians 3:9; 2 Corinthians 1:24; Philippians 2:25, 4:3; Philemon 24).   We even have a few examples of "fellow worker" followed by the accusative with a preposition (Colossians 4:11; cp. 2 Corinthians 8:23).   So how shall we explain John's dative?

III. DIOTREPHES' ARROGANCE IS DENOUNCED.
Verses 9-11

> *Summary*:   In vivid contrast to the generous hospitality to Christian missionaries shown by Gaius is the opposition shown by Diotrephes to John and the missionaries who preach the same message as John does.   Gaius is exhorted to stop imitating what is evil, and instead to imitate what is good.

Verse 9 -- *I wrote something to the church; but Diotrephes, who loves to be first among them, does not accept what we say.*

I wrote something to the church – The point of this verse seems to be that John knows Gaius will have opposition to face should he extend the requested hospitality to the visiting brethren.   Nevertheless, John encourages him to go right ahead with his usual expression of Christian love, rather than be deterred by Diotrephes' opposition.

At first sight, the language of this verse seems plain enough, but there are many issues hidden beneath its surface.

(1) There are several manuscript variations within this verse.

(a) Instead of "I wrote" some have "I would have written."   These few manuscripts (Sinaiticus 33 81 Vg) supply *an* after *egrapsa*,[54] with the resultant meaning "I would have written to the church to receive these men kindly, but I knew Diotrephes would interfere with my wishes.   So, Gaius, I have written to you, rather than the church."   The better attested reading, "I wrote" (*egrapsa*, aorist tense, with no *an*), means that on some former occasion John had written "something" to the church, and that Diotrephes had opposed John's wishes.

(b) Not all manuscripts carry the word "something."   The KJV does not have "something" or "somewhat" because the Textus Receptus did not carry this word.[55]   What the letter was is not clear.   Plummer (*ibid.*) suggests a short letter of commendation (*epistolē sustatikē*) written in behalf of certain "strangers" (visiting missionaries).   Roberts (*op. cit.*, p.177) thinks it was a short letter concerning hospitality, or the support of visiting missionaries.[56]

---

[54] Plummer (*op. cit.*, p.149) and Brooke (*op. cit.*, p. 187) think this addition is an obvious corruption to avoid the unwelcome conclusion that an official letter from John has been lost.   The "would have" (*an*) must have been added at a time when a supposed reference to 2 John was unknown, or at any rate not accepted.   (Brooke, *op. cit.*, p.187.)

[55] The best manuscripts (Sinaiticus* A (B) 048 1241 1739) read *egrapsa ti*, but these were not available to the KJV translators, so there is no "something" or "somewhat" in that version.   (C K L P ψ and most minuscules, the manuscripts behind the TR, simply read *egrapsa* with no *ti*.)

[56] Both Plummer and Roberts speak of a "short letter" likely because the indefinite pronoun *ti* indicates neither something great nor something insignificant.   Perhaps we should agree that the letter concerned extending hospitality to visiting missionaries.   Brooke (*op. cit.*, p.188) argues that 3 John 9 must be read

(2) I wrote "to the church," says John. How would one write to 'the assembly' (*tē ekklēsia*)? In some cases, such a note or letter would have to be sent to an individual, who then would be responsible to see it was read in the assembly.[57] In other cases, a messenger would have been entrusted with delivering the letter and seeing that it was read out loud in the assembly to which it was addressed.[58]

(3) What town? In the Introductory Studies on 3 John, we have called attention to the possible options: some town in Asia (Thyatira, Pergamos), some town in Macedonia, or Corinth. The control Diotrephes exerts might be related to the continuing strife at Corinth to which Clement alludes in his AD 96 letter to Corinth (*1 Clement* xlvii).

(4) Can we infer anything about "the church"?

  (a) It evidently was a congregation the missionaries were likely to visit during the course of their travels.

  (b) If verse 9 is a reference to 2 John, then we would also understand that the "chosen lady" to whom that letter was sent is also a member of the same congregation.

  (c) Were both Gaius and Diotrephes members of the same congregation?

      i. Perhaps Gaius is *not* a member of the congregation in which Diotrephes is influential. Several arguments have been offered to support this conjecture.

          ▪ John says Diotrephes lords it over *them*, which could be understood to refer to a congregation (house church) other than the one Gaius attended.
          ▪ Murray asks (*op. cit.*, p.88) "Would Gaius need to be told about Diotrephes' opposition if he were a member of the same congregation?"[59]
          ▪ John does not suggest that Gaius should attempt to intervene in order to deal with Diotrephes. John will do that when he comes.

      ii. Perhaps both men *are* members of the same congregation.

          ▪ "I wrote to the church" would speak of a previous letter (prior to this one to Gaius) written to the congregation of which Diotrephes was an influential member (a fact implied in verses 9 and 10).
          ▪ 'Diotrephes does not receive us' would say he is not in agreement with the apostle John or the missionaries who preach the old-time gospel that John

---

as it stands, between verses 8 and 10.   The reception of, or the refusal to receive, the missionary brethren is the subject of both those verses. The letter to which reference is made in the intermediate verse, and which the writer fears that Diotrephes suppressed or persuaded his church members to neglect, must have contained some reference to the question of the hospitable reception of these brethren.

[57] An example of such a delivery system would be 1 Timothy.   1 Timothy was intended as much for the church to which Timothy was preaching (the "you" at 1 Timothy 6:21 is plural) as it was for Timothy whose name appears in the address (1 Timothy 1:2). Timothy would have been expected to see that the letter was read in the congregation's hearing.

[58] Tychicus apparently had such a responsibility with reference to the letters we know as Ephesians (Ephesians 6:21,22) and Colossians (Colossians 4:7-9).

[59] This may be a misapprehension of the reason John calls attention to Diotrephes' opposition.

has preached from the beginning.   Because of his opposition to the gospel, Diotrephes has sought to stop any hospitality or support being given to those missionaries.

- How is Gaius to respond to Diotrephes' attempts at intimidation and control?   John flatly says, Do not be influenced to do evil by Diotrephes' example (verse 11).   The failure of the congregation to welcome the missionaries because they have been intimidated by Diotrephes' opposition meant the burden fell on Gaius.

- Did John hope his friend Gaius would share this letter with the whole congregation, thus circumventing Demetrius' opposition?   Is that part of the reason why John lets Gaius know he was cognizant of the situation and proposed to deal with Demetrius when he comes?   This would encourage the brethren in the congregation to join Gaius in extending aid to the missionaries, knowing Demetrius' opposition would soon be ended.

   iii. Whether they were members of the same congregation, it appears from verse 10 that both men lived in the same town.   This much is certainly to be inferred from John's announced intent of visiting Gaius and of dealing with Diotrephes as part of the same visit.

(5) What letter is referred to in the words "I wrote"?

  (a) One view is that whatever letter John wrote to the church is now lost.   Some have proposed that John's language "does not accept what we say" suggests the letter was destroyed by Diotrephes.   This raises the difficult question, Are there inspired letters from apostles or prophets that have been lost, and are therefore not in our collection of New Testament Scriptures?   1 Corinthians 5:9 and Colossians 4:16, as well as 3 John 9, are sometimes urged as proof such has happened.[60]   Lewis Foster used to teach that it is *possible* letters to individuals might be lost, but that it is not *probable* that letters to churches were allowed to become lost.   Letters from apostles and prophets were treated as Scripture the moment they were received.   The churches kept them, treasured them, and regularly read them out loud in the weekly public assemblies.   Early Christian literature quotes from New Testament writings, and all the quotes can be found in our canonical books.   This evidence, as far as it goes, tends to confirm the idea that no letters to churches have been lost.   If Foster was correct, then it is highly improbable that the letter John wrote "to the church" (3 John 9) has somehow perished, unless we are willing to admit that Diotrephes was so arrogant that he destroyed an apostolic letter.

  (b) The other view is that we still have the letter that John wrote to the church.

    i. *Perhaps it is 1 John.*   At 1b above, we have alluded to some of the scholarly conjectures concerning the contents of the letter John wrote to the church.   1

---

[60] This commentator is not convinced that either 1 Corinthians 5:9 or Colossians 4:16 will bear such an interpretation.   "I wrote" in 1 Corinthians 5:9 very likely is an epistolary aorist, referring back to what has already been written earlier in the letter we call 1 Corinthians.   Colossians 4:16 ("my letter that is coming from Laodicea") is likely the circular letter we know by the title of "Ephesians."   If these conclusions are correct, then there is no evidence in either of these passages of lost inspired letters.

John can easily be harmonized with these conjectures. The ones commended in 1 John are those who remain in fellowship with the message taught by the original apostles of Jesus. The Gnostic false teachers who have gone abroad on missionary tours are not commended. 1 John speaks of "love of the brethren" several times, just as 3 John uses "love" (verse 6) as synonymous with hospitality. On the other hand, we have presented 1 John as an encyclical letter, which doesn't fit well with the words of verse 9, "I wrote ... to the church."

ii. *Perhaps it is 2 John.* This is the explanation long held by this commentator. While attractive, this explanation has some difficulties:

- 2 John seems to have been addressed to an individual (i.e., "chosen lady"). If so, that does not seem to fit the description here in 3 John 9, that John wrote "to the church." If we wish to identify 2 John as being the letter John wrote "to the church," what we must assume is that John intended the chosen lady to share it with the congregation.

- Does 2 John say anything about the support of missionaries (i.e., the most likely conjecture concerning the content of the letter alluded to in 3 John 9)? 2 John 10 indicates hospitality is to be denied to false teachers. The language implies that the readers of 2 John were accustomed to extending hospitality. When it comes to whom they entertain, John is directing them to be more discriminating in the future than they had been in the past.

- If we accept the identification of 2 John as the letter alluded to in 3 John 9, it would follow that Diotrephes objected to the elder's denunciation of the false teachers (2 John 7-11) and retaliated by refusing to accept preachers associated with the elder. Is there any indication that Diotrephes was Gnostically inclined, and that this sympathy led him to reject the teaching of 2 John 7-11 about refusing hospitality to the Gnostic false prophets? Marshall and Smalley object, saying there is nothing in 3 John to suggest that Diotrephes was sympathetic to *gnosis* (false teaching). However, we would ask, What about all the references to "truth" we have in 3 John?

But Diotrephes, who loves to be first among them – "Diotrephes" (meaning 'nourished by Zeus') is a Gentile name as rare in the ancient world as "Gaius" was common. Of Diotrephes nothing more is known than is here specified. He was unholy ambitious; that is known from John's characterization of him (he "loves to be first").[61] Findlay has suggested that since the name "Diotrephes" is found only in "ancient and noble families," there is the possibility that Diotrephes was used to his family being recognized as leaders in the community. Just as his family had always held a prominent social position in the community, he now wanted the same position in the church. Diotrephes had not heeded the Jesus' warnings against unholy ambition and the desire to rule (e.g., Mark 10:42-45; cp. 1 Pet 5:3), so the root of his behavior was a sin problem. That ambition (that love of being

---

[61] The Greek verb *philoprōteuō* ("loves to be first") appears here for the first time in Greek literature (it occurs in later Patristic writings, likely being derived from this passage), though the noun *philoprōtos* is well attested. Arndt and Gingrich, *Lexicon*, p.868. The idea in the word is very close to an attitude Jesus warned about, "whoever wishes to be first among you" (Matthew 20:27). *Philoprōteuō* "expresses ambition, the desire to have first place in everything." (A.E. Brooke, *A Critical and Exegetical* Commentary *on the Johannine Epistles*, ICC [Edinburgh: T&T Clark, 1912], p.189).

first) is one reason assigned to Diotrephes' repudiation of what John wrote. "Them" refers to members of the congregation to whom John had written.[62]   Diotrephes wanted the church members to know that he was in charge. What he wanted was what the church was going to do! Perhaps Diotrephes was an elder or deacon or preacher; or perhaps he was a member of the church who held no official leadership position. Whatever his position, he loved being the boss. He behaved haughtily as he let folk know his authority!

Does not accept what we say – Literally, the Greek reads (as the marginal note shows), "Does not accept (welcome) us."[63] "Us" seems to include more than just the writer of this letter. The plural likely includes not only John but also the Christian missionaries for whom John is seeking hospitality and support. These words seem to describe Diotrephes' response toward John and the Christian missionaries who preached a message similar to John's. Diotrephes has said there is to be no hospitality, no sending them on their way with their needs supplied! He said, You are to close the doors of your home and heart against them![64]

Verse 10 -- *For this reason, if I come, I will call attention to his deeds which he does, unjustly accusing us with wicked words; and not satisfied with this, neither does he himself receive the brethren, and he forbids those who desire* **to do so,** *and puts* **them** *out of the church.*

For this reason – Namely, his refusal to accept and welcome us.

If I come – John was evidently intending soon to make a visit to the area where Gaius lives. ("I hope to see you shortly," verse 14.   Compare also 2 John 12).   "The conditional sentence does not necessarily place in doubt the likelihood of the proposed visit."[65]   "When I come" is how Smalley would render it.[66]

I will call attention to his deeds which he does – John promises that he will deal with the ambitious Diotrephes when he visits.   "Call attention" translates *hupomimnēskō* (which is literally "to remind").   "The sense here is similar to that in Wisdom of Solomon 12:2, 'For

---

[62] "Them" *autōn* (plural) after the singular "church" (*ekklēsia*) earlier in the sentence is a pronominal agreement according to the sense.

[63] The Greek word translated "accept" is *epidechomai*. Thayer (*A Greek-English Lexicon to the New Testament* [New York: American Book Co., 1889], p.181) explains that Greek has two words translated "receive" or "accept." One is *lambanō*, which puts emphasis on the thing received. The other is *dechomai*, which puts emphasis on the attitude with which the gift is received. A word often used to translate *dechomai* is "welcome."

[64] This commentator has difficulty seeing where some writers get the idea (if this phrase is all we have) that the letter John wrote to the church has been destroyed by Diotrephes. Its directives have been challenged, yes. But it may be reading into the text to say that Diotrephes destroyed that letter.

[65] B.F. Westcott, *The Epistles of St. John* (Grand Rapids: Eerdmans, 1952), p.240.   On the conditional "if I come" compare the conditional sentence ("if He should be manifested," ASV) at 1 John 2:28.

[66] Smalley, *op. cit.*, p.357.

this cause thou doest correct offenders little by little, admonishing them and reminding them of their sins, in order that they may leave their evil ways'."[67]   John promises that he will direct public attention[68] to Diotrephes' whole conduct and show it in its true light. The phrase "which he does" uses a present tense verb, denoting continuous action.   In the remainder of this verse, John specifies four "deeds" in which Diotrephes has been consistently at fault: he speaks wicked (evil) words; he refuses to be hospitable; he hinders those who wish to be hospitable; he expels his adversaries from the congregation.

Unjustly accusing us with wicked words – Since "wicked words" translates *logois ponērois*, the connection with "the evil one" (*ho poneros*, e.g., Matthew 13:19) should not be missed either here or in 2 John 11.   See also 1 John 3:12.   "Unjustly accusing" is how the NASB translates the verb *phluarōn*; the word means to bubble up, to boil over.[69]   The KJV has "prating (against)," an English word that conveys the idea of talking much but saying nothing of value, to talk nonsense.[70]   "Apparently before the congregation, Diotrephes had not only disavowed the advice of the elder about the messengers, but had also attacked him [and the messengers] with false charges."[71]

And not satisfied with this – As bad as the false charges were, Diotrephes was not satisfied[72] to leave his opposition to that.   He openly took measures to attempt to stop the spread of the apostolic gospel.

Neither does he himself receive the brethren – *Epidechetai*, here translated "receive," is the same word used at the end of verse 9 ("accept").   It means that Diotrephes refuses to extend hospitality to the brethren; he closes his doors to the traveling messengers who stopped in Diotrephes' town as they were on their way to or from the mission field.   The present tense verb shows it was Diotrephes' constant practice to refuse hospitality.   "Presumably a lack of hospitality in the home, rather than in the church, is being described."[73]

---

[67] Marshall, *op. cit.*, p.91.

[68] It is not necessary to supply "him" or "church" after "I will call attention to."   (The accusative of the person is added in John 14:26 and Titus 3:1, but is absent from 2 Timothy 2:14 where the verb is used of instruction to the congregation by a church leader.)   There is a parallel use of the word in 1 Clement 62:3.

[69] Arndt-Gingrich (*op. cit.*, p.870) suggest the word means to "bring up unjustified charges" against someone.

[70] The cognate noun form *phluaroi* is translated "gossips" or "tattlers" (KJV) at 1 Timothy 5:13.

[71] Roberts, *op. cit.*, p.178.

[72] "*Arkoumenos epi toutois*.   The *epi* is unusual.   Both in the New Testament and in classical Greek, *arkeisthai* usually has the dative without a preposition: Luke 3:14; 1 Timothy 6:8; Hebrews 13:5." Plummer, *op. cit.*, p.150.

[73] Murray, *op. cit.*, p.91.

And he forbids those who desire *to do so* – The present tense verb "forbid" (*koluō*, to hinder, prevent, forbid) indicates that on more than one occasion Diotrephes forbade or tried to stop the Christians who were inclined to help the "brethren." It is clear that there were those in the church who were inclined to receive these messengers in a proper manner. The church, as such, would have been inclined to do so, if it had not been for the influence of this one man.

And puts *them* out of the church – Constantly (present tense, *ekballō*) Diotrephes "puts out" (or 'tries to put out') those who don't agree with him. "The language describes a policy or practice rather than a single incident."[74] The exact meaning of *ek tēs ekklēsias ekballei* ("puts out of the church") is uncertain, as we have not sufficient knowledge of the circumstances. Who is "put out of the church"? The NASB adds "them" in italics, evidently understanding that the Greek indicates that it is the members of the church who wish to practice hospitality to the visiting brethren who are put out of the church; that is, it is not the messengers themselves who are put out. But what does "put out" mean? A similar expression is found in John 9:34,35 of the action of the Jewish religious leaders toward the man born blind. "They put him out," it reads, which apparently means they excommunicated him. Was Diotrephes in a position that he could unilaterally excommunicate those who tended to oppose him?[75] Is the "church" from which they were excluded the one that met in Diotrephes' home? If congregational meetings were held in Diotrephes' home, then he could refuse admittance to those who were opposed to him. This "puts them out" would not be excommunication, but simply ostracism.

Perhaps we should revisit the question "Just what was the cause of the hostility of Diotrephes toward John and the missionaries to whom Diotrephes refused hospitality?"[76]

---

[74] Brooke, *op. cit.*, p.190. Note that "receive," "forbids," and "put out" are all present tense, which indicates the continued conduct of Diotrephes. Time and again he so acts.

[75] Some commentators wish to regard *kōluei* ("forbids") and *ekballō* ("puts out") merely as conative in force (Westcott, *op. cit.*, p.241; cp. John 10:31; 13:6). It was something he attempted to do. If he were unilaterally exercising "discipline," he was assuming authority more than an apostle would do. (See 1 Corinthians 5, where Paul expected the congregation to discipline the sinning member, rather than doing it himself. The cases of Ananias and Sapphira in Acts 5:1-11, Hymenaeus and Alexander in 1 Timothy 1:20, and Elymas in Acts 13:8-11 are not quite parallel.) To take it upon one's self to discipline and put out of the church is really "loving to be first." It is a long way removed from the way Jesus taught his followers to discipline erring members (Matthew 18:15-18).

[76] We do so because not a few modern writers, as they are marshaling any evidence they can find to reject the apostolic authorship of 3 John, call attention to this "astounding behavior toward the last surviving apostle" (Plummer). If the "elder" were not an apostle, the argument goes, then perhaps the opposition depicted in 3 John would not be so hard to believe. But on the contrary, apostles were not exempt from opposition and persecution (John 15:20; Mark 10:30). Just because a man was an apostle did not guarantee immediate acceptance. According to 2 Corinthians, there were folk at Corinth who opposed Paul's authority. Alexander the coppersmith opposed Paul's teaching (2 Timothy 2:14,15). "Those who accept [as I do, GLR] as historical the initial unbelief of Christ's brothers, the treachery of Judas, the flight of all the Disciples, the denial of Peter, the quarrels of apostles both before and after their Lord's departure, and the flagrant abuses in the church of Corinth, will not be disposed to think it incredible that Diotrephes acted in the manner described here towards the apostle John" (Plummer, *op. cit.*, p.148).

(1) John specifically identifies the cause as being Diotrephes' unholy ambition.   It was a matter of being boss, of being in control.   As an apostle of Jesus, John rightly exercised authority over all the local congregations.   (Jesus had promised the apostles would "judge" or rule over spiritual Israel, Matthew 19:28.   Compare 2 Thessalonians 3 for apostolic commands requiring obedience.)   Now Diotrephes wanted to be "first."   But if he has to submit to John's directives, who doesn't even live in the same town that Diotrephes does, then Diotrephes is no longer "first."[77]   John writes as one who expected his instructions to be obeyed.   That rankled Diotrephes.   If he is going to be "first," he cannot accept John's control and he certainly doesn't want the interference of wandering missionaries.[78]

(2) Was there doctrine involved as well as unholy ambition?   We've already alluded to Diotrephes' possible Gnostic inclinations in notes above.   It is certainly within the realm of possibility that Diotrephes may have opposed the reception of the traveling missionaries for doctrinal reasons, because he leaned to the position of the false teachers (1 John 2:18ff; 4:1ff) rather than to that of the apostle John.   That would explain the several references to "the truth" in this short letter.   There is some kind of error that is in the background!   In the last quarter of the 1st century (i.e., the likely time frame when this letter was written), the most prominent error was *gnosis*.   It is much easier to picture Diotrephes as a spokesman for heresy than a spokesman for orthodoxy.[79]   Under this scenario, it is even possible that Diotrephes was one of the Gnostic missionaries referred to in 1 John 2:18,19 and warned about in 2 John 7-11.   He came to the church (the one addressed in 2 John through the "chosen lady") as a missionary, and won enough of its members over to his heretical views that he is accepted as the local leader.   Gnostics did refuse to recognize the authority or message of the apostles of Jesus.   In harmony with Gnostic antipathy to

---

[77] C.H. Dodd, who concluded "the elder" was not the apostle John, but a sub-apostle with even lesser authority than an apostle, thinks Diotrephes resents this "subordinate" telling him what to do.

[78] As scholars have attempted to reconstruct the historical background, there have been several other suggestions proposed to explain Diotrephes' ambition.   One has Diotrephes trying to make his congregation independent and autonomous rather than being under the authority of John who lived miles away in Ephesus.   Diotrephes' problem was a mistaken view of what local autonomy involves.   Even independent, or locally-autonomous churches, are not free of apostolic oversight!   Even in our time, apostles still exercise oversight of the autonomous local congregations through their written Word.   Another view has Diotrephes hankering to be a bishop with as much or more power in the churches than apostles exercised.   It is true that the pattern of church polity was changing as the 1st century drew to a close and the 2nd century began.   By AD 115, when Ignatius wrote letters to the churches of Asia Minor, a new form of government (the monarchical episcopate, in which a single bishop had authority over a group of elders) had become the accepted way.   In the closing years of the 1st century, when John is the last surviving apostle, there is a period of transition and tension.   Is Diotrephes already maneuvering to make himself as such a bishop?

[79] Ernst Kasemann (ZTK 48 [1951] p.292-311) has pictured Diotrephes as a spokesman for orthodoxy.   Under his attempted reconstruction of conflicting beliefs in the early years of Christianity, it is the elder (who in Kasemann's view was not the apostle John) who was an incipient Gnostic heretic, and Diotrephes (an orthodox Christian leader) opposes him and the missionaries who preach the same message.   Such a handling of the material in 3 John seems to fly against what is said in verse 11.   It is Diotrephes who is the "evil" one, not the writer of the letter.

the ancient gospel, Diotrephes' unjust accusations with wicked words (verse 10) would be Gnostic polemics against orthodox Christianity.

Verse 11 -- *Beloved, do not imitate what is evil, but what is good.   The one who does good is of God; the one who does evil has not seen God.*

Beloved – The reference is to Gaius, because "beloved" is singular.   Diotrephes will offer some formidable opposition, but John appeals to Gaius to do what is right, rather than be influenced negatively by Diotrephes.

Do not imitate what is evil, but what is good – It may be that in this exhortation, John had Diotrephes particularly in view.   If so, this is an exhortation to Gaius not to follow Diotrephes' example because what he is doing is "evil."   In the Greek, the prohibition is written with a present imperative, a construction which prohibits the continuance of an action already going on.   "Stop imitating ...!" would catch the idea.   It seems that Gaius has been influenced enough by Diotrephes that John must call on him to stop his bad behavior.[80]   For "imitate" (*mimou* from *mimeomai*), compare 2 Thessalonians 3:7,9 and Hebrews 13:7.   There is no verb in the second clause.   When we supply the present tense imperative verb from the first clause, the second then reads "Be in the habit of imitating what is good!"   "Good" in this case means continue to do acts of liberal and generous hospitality to the brethren.   "Everyone is an imitator.   It is natural for us to look up to other people as our model and copy them.   This is all right, the elder seems to be saying, if you choose your model carefully – one who models the good."[81]   Even though folk recognize what is good and evil, there are times that a word of encouragement will reinforce people's choices of the good.

The one who does good is of God – John seems to be giving Gaius a reason for imitating the good.   "It is not just because of the effect our behavior has on others, but because of the evidence our behavior supplies of our spiritual condition."[82]   "Is of God" here in 3 John is reminiscent of 1 John 3:10.[83]   Doing "good" is how a child of God behaves, for he in this way resembles his Father.   The word "does good" suggests "the demonstration of love which will not suffer any restriction."[84]

---

[80] The word for "evil" here is not the one (*ponēros*) used in the previous verse.   In verse 11, John uses *kakos*, the most common word in Greek to express the idea of bad or evil.

[81] Adapted from Stott, *op. cit.*, p.228.

[82] Stott, *ibid.*

[83] See also 1 John 2:16,29, 4:4,6,7, 5:19.   Those who found three tests of life in 1 John (truth, love, and goodness) find those same three tests here in 3 John (truth in verses 3,4; love in verse 6; and goodness in verse 11).

[84] Roberts, *op. cit.*, p.179.

The one who does evil has not seen God – Diotrephes, habitually doing evil, is not of God, is one implication.   Another implication is that if Gaius habitually chooses to do evil, that, too, will be indicative of his spiritual condition.[85]   As in 1 John 3:6 and John 14:9, to "see God" may mean to be in intimate relationship with God.   If that is the meaning here, then just as the Gnostics of 1 John 2:19 were not part of the church, perhaps John is here saying that Diotrephes is not part of the church of Jesus Christ – even though he wields considerable influence in a congregation of believers.   He who is rebellious to the apostles of Jesus and to the message they carry has no proper knowledge of that God.   Alternately, "has not seen God" may refer back to Gnostic doctrine.   Gnostics claimed a special vision of God (cp. 1 John 4:12).   John may be saying, From the way he acts, it is obvious that Diotrephes has not "seen God"!

IV. DEMETRIUS IS COMMENDED TO GAIUS.   Verse 12

Verse 12 -- *Demetrius has received a* **good** *testimony from everyone, and from the truth itself; and we also bear witness, and you know that our witness is true.*

Demetrius has received a *good* **testimony from everyone** – Literally, 'Witness has been borne to Demetrius by all men and by the truth itself.'   The verb is perfect tense, and the force of the perfect tense is that what was testified in the past is still true.   The 'all men' ("everyone") are orthodox Christians who have known Demetrius over a period of time.   Who was Demetrius?   All that we know of Demetrius, as of Diotrephes, is just what is told us here and no more.   For some reason, John seems to be commending Demetrius to Gaius.   Is Demetrius unknown to Gaius?   Has Demetrius had derogatory words spoken against him by Diotrephes, thus raising doubts in Gaius' mind?   In this case, John contradicts the evil words of Diotrephes and sets the record straight.   Is Demetrius a traveling missionary, perhaps the bearer of this letter to Gaius?   In this case, the commendation would be intended to secure Gaius' hospitality for Demetrius.   Is Demetrius the new preacher being sent by John to work in the town where Gaius and Demetrius live?[86]   Is this something else to which Diotrephes strongly objected?   In this case, John's commendation is intended to enlist Gaius' support for the new preacher.   Is this "Demetrius" to be identified with any other New Testament person of the same name? (1) Is Demetrius of 3 John none other than the silversmith of Ephesus who once made silver shrines for Artemis (Acts 19:24), but is now a Christian missionary?   (2) Is Demetrius of 3 John the same man known as Demas from Paul's epistles (Colossians 4:14; Philemon 24; 2 Timothy 4:10), since Demas is a shortened form of "Demetrius."   Paul's last words about Demas (2 Timothy 4:10) were that "he has deserted me, having loved this present world."

---

[85] A Christian who belongs to God's family must not habitually act as though he belonged to the other group.   Such actions will endanger continuing fellowship with God (Romans 6:16-23).

[86] It appears that apostles did sometimes send men to be preachers of established congregations (Titus 3:12; 2 Timothy 4:12).   According to the *Apostolic Constitutions* (a 4th century document which may not be historically reliable), John later appointed Demetrius as bishop of Philadelphia.

But if we have dated the writing of 3 John correctly, that faulty behavior on the part of Demas occurred some 20 or 25 years earlier.   Chapman's suggestion is that Demas, in the meantime, has repented and become a missionary whom the churches can once again trust. Whoever Demetrius was, John's brief note contains a threefold recommendation: 1) the testimony of all men; 2) testimony from the truth itself; and 3) John's own testimony. (Compare also 1 John 5:8 and Deuteronomy 19:15.)

And from the truth itself – A great deal has been written about this clause because it is a puzzling statement.   (1) Perhaps "the truth" is equal to 'the facts of the case.'   The meaning would be that Demetrius' reputation was not founded on mere appearances, but on truth and reality.   In this interpretation, "truth" is personified.   If the truth could speak, it would testify that Demetrius' life and teachings are in accord with its own standards. (2) Perhaps "the truth" refers to the Holy Spirit (cp. 1 John 5:7, "the Spirit is the truth"). The Holy Spirit has given Demetrius a personal commendation through prophetic utterance (as in Acts 13:2).   (3) "The truth" is a reference to the gospel of Christ.   "John's normal use of the term 'truth' suggests a deeper significance is intended here."[87]   "Truth" in John's writings is a metaphor for the orthodox Christian tradition.   Just as all Christian men testify positively about Demetrius, the Christian gospel ("truth") also testifies to Demetrius' character.   In this view, the gospel stands against the "wicked words" spoken by Diotrephes.

And we also bear witness – "We" probably refers to John and his "friends" (verse 14) who are personally acquainted with Demetrius.[88]   John and his friends here vouch for Demetrius' reputation and trustworthiness.   This is a third and independent testimony about Demetrius.   "We" is emphatic, implying a contrast with someone (Diotrephes?) who has impugned Demetrius.   By use of the emphatic "we," this testimony is highlighted as of weighty importance.   The verb here is *marturoumen*, a present tense signifying continuing testimony.

And you know that our witness is true – In the better attested text "you" is singular.[89] John appeals to Gaius' own personal knowledge of John and his friends.   This is the manner of John, who always spoke of himself as having such a character for truth that no

---

[87] Smalley, *op. cit.*, p.361.

[88] The meaning of "we" (*hēmeis*) in the epistles of John is often difficult to determine.   This matter was studied at 1 John 1:1-4, where "we" seemed to include personal eyewitnesses of Jesus' earthly ministry.   There may be times when the first person plural is the plural of authority.   It is the judgment of this commentator that we cannot assign a single, common meaning to the use of "we" across all of John's writings.

[89] The evidence for the singular *oidas* (Sinaiticus A B C and most versions), versus the plural, *oidate* (KL), and the two or three 11th or 12th century manuscripts which read *oidamen* ("we know"), is quite decisive.

one who knew him would call it into question.[90]   John's friends, too, have always been transparently truthful in their testimony.   "In this commendation we see something of the way the early church protected itself from false teachers.   Apostles and leaders sent representatives and teachers bearing letters of commendation from their hand to congregations known to them.   See Acts 18:27; 2 Corinthians 3:1; Romans 16:1; Colossians 4:10."[91]

THE CONCLUSION AND GREETING.   Verses 13-14

Verse 13 -- *I had many things to write to you, but I am not willing to write them to you with pen and ink;*

I had many things to write to you – The change from "we" in the previous verses to "I" in the conclusion may suggest John picked up the pen and wrote these words by his own hand.   We tend to use stereotyped "closing sentences" in our letters.   Perhaps John did likewise, for there is a marked similarity to the conclusion of 2 John.   Others suggest that the similarity is strong evidence that the two letters were written about the same time.   "I had" is an imperfect tense (*polla eichon*); at the time he began to write this letter there were many things which John intended to communicate to Gaius.   "The imperfect verb may be an example of the imperfect [tense] being used to express an unfulfilled obligation or duty."[92]   His pending visit (verse 14), when he can share all the many things with Gaius, relieves John of the obligation he earlier felt to write all of them.   "To you" (*soi*, singular) is found in Aleph, A B C, and is therefore included in ASV/NASB (but not found in KJV).

But I am not willing to write *them* **to you with pen and ink** – John writes *ou thelō* ("I am not willing"); by contrast, he wrote *ouk eboulēthēn* ("I do not want to") at 2 John 14.   *Thelō* is perhaps the stronger word.   It denotes active resolution, the person's will urging him on to action.[93]   "You" again is singular, with Gaius as the person intended.   In 2 John

---

[90] Our Introductory Studies on 3 John noted that this passage bears on the authorship of 3 John. We indicated that the authorship of the Gospel of John was the key to deciding the authorship of 3 John. Two passages in the Gospel speak directly to the point.   John 19:35 reads "he who has seen has borne witness, and his witness is true ...."   John 21:24 reads "This is the disciple who bears witness of these things ... and we know that his witness is true."   This language about "testimony" or "bearing witness" is a strong indication that both writings are by the same author.   (In those same Introductory Studies we addressed the problem raised by some that John 21 is an appendix added to the Fourth Gospel at a later date, and therefore should not be appealed to as we are doing when we compare its language to 3 John.)

[91] Roberts, *op. cit.*, p.181.

[92] F. Blass and A. Debrunner, *A Greek Grammar of the New Testament* (trans. by R.W. Funk) (Chicago: Cambridge, 1961), p.358.

[93] Berry, (*Synonyms*, p.128,129) cites Thayer, Grimm, and Cremer, giving three distinct choices for the meaning of these synonyms.   Behind the comments offered for these words by some is the theological topic of the absolute sovereignty of God.   Those who teach absolute sovereignty insist that when God "wills" (*boulomai*) something, it has to happen; if He only "wishes" (*thelō*), then it is not set in stone.   This commentator is not convinced that this presentation of the meaning of these synonyms is valid.

12 it was "paper and ink."   Here it is "pen and ink."   "Pen" translates *kalamos*, a reed pen, as distinguished from a sharper stylus (which was used for writing on waxed tablets) or quill (which was not used until the 5th century or later for writing on parchment).[94]   Some things, especially delicate matters, are best discussed personally.   Body language and tone of voice can convey meanings that are impossible to convey on paper.   If this letter encouraged Gaius to receive the messengers in continuation of his hospitality, if the reasons for Diotrephes' opposition were made clear, and if the elder's recommendation of Demetrius was accepted, other things could wait.[95]

Verse 14 -- *But I hope to see you shortly, and we shall speak face to face.   Peace be to you.   The friends greet you.   Greet the friends by name.*

But I hope to see you shortly – Beginning with the word *de* ("but"), this verse continues the thought begun in verse 13.   Having the hope of seeing Gaius shortly, John will wait to speak these things face to face, rather than putting them in this letter.   John had already announced his intention of coming to the town where Gaius lives (verse 10).   Now he says "I am hoping to see you shortly."   "Shortly" translates *eutheōs*, 'immediately, very soon, straightway.'   "Shortly" or "very soon" is an idea lacking in the parallel passage 2 John 12.   Its presence here may suggest that the intended journey is nearer than when 2 John was written.   "We suppose John made periodic visits to the churches which looked to him for leadership, and it was near the time for such a visit.   Or perhaps the distressing circumstances of the church had made him resolve to visit it."[96]

And we shall speak face to face – Literally 'mouth to mouth,' just as in 2 John 12.[97] Speaking "face to face" is a way of saying that he wanted to have a personal or private talk with Gaius.

Peace *be* to you – This phrase and the remaining words in this letter are numbered "verse 15" in some English versions including the updated NASB (1995).   The letter closes with three greetings being conveyed.   First, John conveys his own greetings to Gaius.   Second, friends send greetings to Gaius.   Finally, John asks that his greetings be conveyed to his friends who are living nearby and acquainted with Gaius.   Instead of the usual 'farewell' of 1st century letters, we have a Christian blessing, full of spiritual meaning.   The NASB supplies the verb "be," thus making this a prayer.   John's prayer for Gaius is "peace."   Perhaps it is peace instead of warfare (i.e., the struggles and strife triggered by Diotrephes).   Perhaps it is the peace of God, a peace that provides every requisite good,

---

[94] In LXX of Ps.44:1 (45:1 NASB), *kalamos* is used of "the pen of a ready writer."

[95] Adapted from Roberts, *op. cit.*, p.181.

[96] *Ibid*, p.182.

[97] For "mouth to mouth," see notes at 2 John 12.

both of a spiritual and temporal kind.[98]   Perhaps it is "the tranquil state of a soul assured of its salvation through Christ, and so fearing nothing from God and content with its earthly lot, of whatever sort that is."[99]

The friends greet you – Christians ("friends"[100]) in the place where John lived and wrote knew the letter was being sent.   They wish to be affectionately remembered to Gaius ("you" is singular).   They "greet" (*aspazontai*, "embrace") you.   Perhaps this is given to contrast the hostility of Diotrephes and his followers.   Here is the salutation of friends, rather than the prating of enemies.   By including their greetings to Gaius, the friends associate themselves with John's sentiments and back up his requests with what influence their friendship might wield.

Greet the friends by name – John closes by asking Gaius to convey John's warm personal greeting (*aspazou*) to all of John's Christian friends who live nearby to Gaius.   Rather than the greeting being delivered in a general way, John wants Gaius to deliver his greeting to each individual separately (*kat' onoma*, "by name").[101]   Perhaps Gaius could deliver the greeting whenever he met one of the friends.   Perhaps Gaius will have to make a special trip to visit each one's home.   In any case, when he delivers this greeting, the friends would have opportunity to encourage Gaius.

A few manuscripts add the common liturgical "Amen" after "by name."   A few of the ancient manuscripts and versions carry a subscription.   The Philoxenian Syriac and the Complutensian Polyglot (both Latin and Greek texts) have "the third epistle of St. John the apostle is ended."   Alexandrinus and Vaticanus have "the third of John."   Codex Angelicus has "The third epistle of the holy apostle John."

---

[98] The Hebrew greeting *shalom* ("peace") was invested with new meaning by Jesus after His resurrection.   John's greeting here may well reflect the greeting of the Lord after His resurrection (John 20:19,21,26).

[99] Thayer, *op. cit.*, p.182.

[100] Instead of *philoi* and *philous* ("friends"), Codex Alexandrinus and several others read *adelphoi* and *adelphous* ("brethren").   "Friends" as an appellation of Christian brethren is unusual, perhaps found elsewhere in Scripture only in Jesus' farewell discourse ("You are my friends," John 15:13,14) and in Acts 27:3 ("Julius treated Paul with consideration and allowed him to go to his friends and receive care").   The Greek reads simply "the friends."   There is no reason the KJV should read "Our friends salute thee" either as translation or interpretation.   While there are times the definite article may be translated as a pronoun, if any is chosen here, it should be "your," since the friends alluded to are likely friends of Gaius.

[101] Arndt and Gingrich, *op. cit.*, p.574.

INDEX TO 1 JOHN

Roman numerals indicate pages in the introductory studies. Arabic numbers indicate pages in the commentary section. An "n" following indicates a footnote on that page.

Genitive case --
    Objective or subjective? -- 38n,58
    Partitive -- 130n,151
Genre Criticism -- *lviii*
Georgius Hamartolus -- *xiv*
Gethsemane -- *x*
Glorified body -- 93,94
Glory -- 84n
Gnosis, Gnostic, Gnosticism -- *ii, vii, viii, xxxiv-xl,* 14,15,46,89,128
    Characteristic ideas -- *xliv-xlviii*
    Christian opponents of -- *xxxviii*
    Cosmogony -- *xxxiv, xlv*
    Gnostic writings -- *xxxix, xlii-xliv*
    Jesus and Christ two separate beings – *xix, xxxiv,* 20,74
    Morality –*xl,* 12,17
    No love for the brother -- *xxxviii(n),* 45,46
    Not a Christian heresy -- *xxxvi,* 107n, 133n
    Possible New Testament references to -- *vii-viii, xxxvii-xxxviii*
    Teachings inconsistent -- *xliv(n)*
    Use of John's writings (?) -- *xxxii, lii(n),* 39n,47n
    See also: Adoptionism; Docetism; Pleroma; Pneumatic; Demiurge; Aeons; False teachers
God -- 14
    Answers prayer -- 184
    Can be "known" -- 14
    Faithful and Righteous -- 24,25
    First loved us -- 158
    Him who is true -- 194,197
    Is a consuming fire -- 14n,144
    Is greater than our heart -- 123
    Is light --*xvii, xxvi, lxiii(n), lxiv,* 12, 14,16n,144
    Is love -- *lxiv,* 14n,16n,58,143,144, 154
    Is righteous -- *lxiii(n),* 86,87
    Is spirit -- 14n,16n,144
    Knows all things -- 123
    Not seen -- 159
    "Unbegotten" -- 146n
    v. 'Supreme Being' of Gnosticism – *xl, xli, xlv, xlviii(n),* 8n,15, 109n, 144n
    See also: Father, God as
Godhead -- 30n

Good Shepherd -- 115
Gospel (apostolic preaching) - *viii, xviii, xx, lxviii,*9,42,72n,77n,78,82,100,109
Gospel of John -- *i, xii, xx, xxi, xxx, xxxi, xxxii, l, lii, liii(n),* 9n,40,53,70,103,180n
Gospel of Judas -- *xliii, lxix*
Gospel of Mary (Magdalene) -- *xlii(n)*
Gospel of Philip -- *vi(n)*
Gospel of Thomas -- *xliii, lxix,* 4
Gospel of Truth -- *xli, xliii*
Grace -- 106
Grammatical-Historical Method – *i(n), xxxiv, lviii,* 105n
Great Exposition -- *xxxix*
Greater is He Who is in You -- 138
Greek Philosophy -- See: Philosophy, Greek
Greek Syntax, broken -- 2
Greek Text of 1 John -- See: John, Epistle of -- Greek Text
Greek Verbs, Mood --
    Indicative or imperative -- 82,87
    Indicative or subjunctive -- 127n,142n,158,163
Greek Verbs, Tense --
    Aorist -- 4,7,25,29,40,53,93n,144
        Epistolary -- *liv(n),* 54n,72,79,180
        Historical -- *liv*
    Future -- 118,122n,185,186n
    Perfect -- 4,13,38n,52,99,103n,106, 137,145,151,159,177
    Pluperfect -- 68
    Present -- 9,13,16n,20,29n,34,35,40, 44,61,62n,95,101,103n,105n, 117,165,167
Greek Word Formation -- 31n,69,157n
Greeting -- *i, xvi, lix(n)*
Guard yourselves from idols – 198

Hadrian, Emperor -- *v, xl*
Hands handled -- 5
Hate -- *xxxv(n),* 45,48,111,114,158,159
Have (verb used with nouns) -- 9n,77n,176
Heard, hearing -- 42,65n,77,108,136,139n
Heart -- 117,118,120,121,176
    Condemns us -- 122,124
    God is greater than – 122

Kingdom of Light -- *xlvii*
Know, knowledge -- *viii, lxx*, 87,97
    All things -- 71-72
    Different Greeks words for -- 34n, 87,181
    Gnostic, based on special revelations – *xliv*, 34
    God -- 99,143

Last Hour -- See: Hour, Last.
Latin Versions -- *lxi*
    Old Latin -- See: Old Latin Version
    Vulgate -- *lxii*,44n,69n,119n,134n, 135n,146n,158n,171n,191
Law, legalism -- 35n
    Greek words for -- 35
    Of Moses, disdained by Gnostics – *xxxix*
    Of Moses, temporary -- 126n
Lawlessness -- 66,96,97
Letter to Rheginus -- *xli*
Letter writing -- 54n
Leucius, Leucian Fragments -- *xi*
    On John's Burial -- *xv*
Liar, liars, lie, lying -- *xxxv, lxvi*, 17,26,37, 72,73,82,159,176
Libellus -- *lix*
Libertinism -- *xxxix*
    See also: Antinomianism
Life -- 6,178
    Greek synonyms for -- 6n,60n
    Lay down one's -- *lxviii*, 115,116
    New (characteristics of) -- 181
    Old (characteristics of) -- 181
    Passed from death to -- 112
    Pride of -- 60
    Spiritual -- 14,113,114n,185
    See also: Eternal life
Light -- *xvii, lxvii, lxviii(n)*, 12,13n,14,44
    Abides in -- 47
    True, is already shining -- 44
    Walk in -- 18
Like, Greek Synonyms for -- 93n
Limited atonement -- 33n
Listens --
    He who knows God, to us -- 140
    World, to them -- 139
Literary Criticism -- *xxxiii, lix*

Live, living -- *xvii, lxvii*, 146
    See also: Walking
Logos (Word) -- *xli(n)*, 5n,6
Lord's Supper -- *x, xxxviii(n), xli*, 24n,169, 174n, 187
Love -- 56,115,154
    Bestowed by the Father -- 89,90
    Greek synonyms for -- 56n,143
    In deed and truth -- 118
    Is from God -- 142
    One another -- 127,141,142,148
    Perfected -- 150,155,157
Love for God -- 58,160,163
Love for the Brothers -- *xix, lvi, lxv, lxviii*, 41,43,106,108n,113,141,142,160
Love of God -- 38,89,90,117,144,147,150n, 164
Luke -- 5
Lust -- 62
    Of the eyes -- 60
    Of the flesh -- 59
Lycus River -- *ii, iii(n)*
Lydia (kingdom) – *iv*
Lying -- See: Liar
Lysimachus -- *iv*

Magic -- *xxxvi(n), xxxix(n), xli, xlvi*
Mandaism -- 37
Manichaeism -- 102n
Manifestation -- See: Jesus Christ – Manifestation
Manifesto -- *lix*
Manual of Doctrine -- *lix*
Manuscript Variations -- See: Variant Readings
Marcion -- *xxix(n), xli*
Marcosians – *xlvii*
Martyrdom -- *ix, xiv*
Marvel, do not -- 111
Menander -- *xxxix*
Message -- 13,108
Messiah -- See: Christ
Miletus -- *ii*
Ministry of Jesus -- See: Jesus Christ – Earthly Ministry
Missionaries -- *viii*, 133
Mithridates -- *vii(n)*
Montanus, Montanism -- *xii*, 64n,190n

Treatise – *lix*
Trinity -- *xix,* 88n
True -- 195,196
Truth -- xviii, xxiv, 17,23,27,36n,37,72,
73n,75n,82,120,141
   No lie is of the -- 72
   Practice of the -- 17
   Tests for -- See: Tests -- Of Truth
   We are of the -- 119,120
Truth, Gospel of -- See: Gospel of Truth

Unbegotten -- See: Jesus Christ – "Unbe-
gotten"
Unbelief -- 67n
Unconditional eternal security – 99n,104n,
188
Understanding, given by the Son -- 194,195
Universalism -- 33n
Unknown God -- *xl, xlv,* 14
Unrighteousness -- 25,189
Upper Country – *iii*

Valentinus, Valentinianism -- *vii, xxiv,*
xxxvi(n), xli
Variant readings–*xviii, xix, l(n), lxi,lxii, lxix,*
9n,12,13n,19n,41,42n,53n,71n,76
n,82n,84n,91n,97n,108n,115n,
118n,123,126n,134n,135,147n,
155n,158,159n,164n,171,175n,
176n,181n,184n
Vegetarianism -- 109n
Victory -- *lxv,* 137,166
Visions, vision of God -- *xlvi, xlviii(n),lxix,*
35,36,94n,99,149
Vulgate -- See: Latin Versions

Walk, Walking -- 16,39,40
   In darkness -- 16,22n,48
   In the light -- *lxvii,* 18,21
   See also: Live, living

Water, not with, only -- 170
Water and blood -- *xx, lxii,* 168-170,174
Western Church -- *xxvii, lvi*
Will of God -- *xvii, lxii,* 68,182
Witness -- See: Bear Witness; Testimony
Word (of God, of life) -- *liv,* 5,6,27,37,42,
55,70,104,132n
   See also: Logos
Word Order, Greek -- See: Order of Greek
Words
Works of the Devil -- 102
World -- *xxxv,* 32,56,57,58,61,139,152,165
   Did not know Him -- 92
   Does not know us -- 91
   False prophets are from the -- 138, 139
   Hates you -- 111
   He who is in the -- 138
   In the power of the evil one -- 193
   Listens to false prophets -- 139
   Passing away -- *xxiv,* 61
Worldliness -- *lxv,* 49,56,58
World's goods -- 116
Worldview -- *xxxvii, xliv37,44*
Worship, Gnostic -- *xlvii*

Xerxes -- *iv*

Young men -- 52,55

Zodiac -- *xxxvi(n)*
Zoroastrianism -- 15

INDEX TO 2 JOHN

INDEX TO 3 JOHN

Roman numerals indicate pages in the introductory studies. Arabic numbers indicate pages in the commentary section. An "n" following indicates a footnote on that page.

www.ingramcontent.com/pod-product-compliance
Lightning Source LLC
Chambersburg PA
CBHW050637150426
42811CB00053B/966